The Sport Psychologist's Handbook
A Guide for Sport-Specific Performance Enhancement

Edited by

Joaquín Dosil

John Wiley & Sons, Ltd

Other Wiley Editorial Offices

John Wiley & Sons Inc., 111 River Street, Hoboken, NJ 07030, USA

Jossey-Bass, 989 Market Street, San Francisco, CA 94103-1741, USA

Wiley-VCH Verlag GmbH, Boschstr. 12, D-69469 Weinheim, Germany

John Wiley & Sons Australia Ltd, 42 McDougall Street, Milton, Queensland 4064, Australia

John Wiley & Sons (Asia) Pte Ltd, 2 Clementi Loop #02-01, Jin Xing Distripark, Singapore 129809

John Wiley & Sons Canada Ltd, 22 Worcester Road, Etobicoke, Ontario, Canada M9W 1L1

Wiley also publishes its books in a variety of electronic formats. Some content that appears
in print may not be available in electronic books.

Library of Congress Cataloging-in-Publication Data

The sport psychologist's handbook : a guide for sport-specific
performance enhancement / edited by Joaquín Dosil.
       p.   cm.
    Includes bibliographical references and index.
    ISBN-13: 978-0-470-86355-8 (cloth : alk. paper)
    ISBN-10: 0-470-86355-2 (cloth : alk. paper)
    ISBN-13: 978-0-470-86356-5 (pbk. : alk. paper)
    ISBN-10: 0-470-86356-0 (pbk. : alk. paper)
    1. Sports—Psychological aspects—Handbooks, manuals, etc.   I. Dosil, Joaquín.
GV706.4.S675   2005
796.01—dc22   2005015432

British Library Cataloguing in Publication Data

A catalogue record for this book is available from the British Library

ISBN-13   978-0-470-86355-8 (H/B)   978-0-470-86356-5 (P/B)

Typeset in 10/12pt Times by TechBooks, New Delhi, India
Printed and bound in Great Britain by CPI Antony Rowe, Chippenham, Wiltshire

Contents

About the Editor

Dr Joaquín Dosil is a professor at the University of Vigo in Northwest Spain and head of the doctoral course: "Current Perspectives of Physical Activity and Sport Psychology". His areas of research interest include peak performance in different sports, eating disorders in sport, cyberpsychology of sport, and referees' sport psychology. He is a foundation member and the current President of the Ibero-American Society of Sport Psychology (SIPD), as well as a member of the International Society of Sport Psychology. He is on the editorial board for the two most important sport psychology journals in Spain, along with various sport science reviews. Dr Dosil is the Director of a sport psychology unit in Santiago de Compostela, where he attends athletes and sport teams from various modalities and levels. In particular he works with many Olympic athletes, golfers, world-leading motorcyclists and tennis players, while directing psychological programmes with various professional football and basketball teams. He has published 11 sport psychology books—most notably, the leading text in the Hispanic world: *Psicología de la Actividad Física y del Deporte (Psychology of Physical Activity and Sport)*, published by McGraw-Hill—and has produced over 70 articles and chapters. Professor Dosil frequently participates as a lecturer in international and national congresses, master's and doctoral degree programmes. He is an avid runner, specialising in distance events, particularly the half-marathon. In his free time, he enjoys spending time with his wife (Olaia), family and friends, as well as practicing surfing, beach volley, football, basketball and tennis.

Contributors

Bruce Abernethy is the Chair and Director of the Institute of Human Performance at the University of Hong Kong. Dr Abernethy is an international fellow of various scientific organisations such as the American Academy of Kinesiology and Physical Education. He is an editorial advisory board member of the *Journal of Sports Sciences*, past editor of the *Australian Journal of Science and Medicine in Sport*, and an editorial board member of several other sport psychology journals. Dr Abernethy has published extensively on the topic of movement expertise and skill learning focusing on perceptual aspects of skilled performance. Furthermore, he has experience in playing cricket to first-class (provincial) level.

Dorothee Anders is a postgraduate student at the University of Hamburg (Germany) and completed her master's degree in psychology in April 2005. Since 2003 she has been involved in the psychological consultation of the German Under 23 and Junior National Rowing Team as a trainee at the faculty of sports science at the University of Bochum and the Olimpiastutzpunkt Westfalen. Currently, she is working on "Stress, Recovery and Action Control in Rowing" for her thesis and to complete her work to become a certified sport psychologist.

Mark B. Andersen is a registered psychologist and Associate Professor at Victoria University in Melbourne (Australia). He teaches in the School of Human Movement and co-ordinates the master's and doctor of applied psychology degrees (sport and exercise psychology emphasis) in the School of Psychology. His areas of research interest include: the psychology of injury and rehabilitation; the role of exercise in mental health, wellbeing and quality of life; the training and supervision of graduate students; and the practice of sport psychology service delivery. He has published more than 100 refereed journal articles and book chapters and has made over 90 national and international conference presentations. His edited book *Doing Sport Psychology* is used around the world in graduate applied sport psychology programmes.

Mark H. Anshel is a professor at Middle Tennessee State University (USA). He has authored several books including *Sport Psychology: From Theory to Practice*. His numerous book chapters and research articles cover topics such as coping with stress, perfectionism, and drug use in sport, and strategies to promote exercise adherence. Dr Anshel is a member of various scientific societies such as the American Psychological Association and the Association for the Advancement of Applied Sport Psychology.

Mark Bawden is a sport psychologist who has been working in elite sport for 10 years. Mark was the Head Quarters Sport Psychologist for Great Britain at the Paralympics Games in Sydney (2002). He has worked with a range of paralympic sports including shooting, table tennis and fencing. Mark also works with the English Cricket Board, the Great British Speed Skating Squad, the English Table Tennis Association, the English Amateur Boxing Association and the England Netball Association.

Cal Botterill has been a professor at the University of Winnipeg (Canada) since 1980. He is a member of many professional organizations including the International Society of Sport Psychology, the Association for the Advancement of Applied Sport Psychology (Certified Consultant) and the Canadian Mental Training Registry (Accredited). In his specialized field of ice hockey he has had experience working as a consultant at 7 different Olympic Games, with 10 different World Championship teams/athletes and with 5 different NHL Hockey Teams, to mention but a few. He has participated in over 200 international, national and regional conferences as a keynote speaker in sport, psychology, medicine, education and business. Author or co-author in over 120 publications, his current areas of scholarly interest include "perspectives in sport and life", "peak performance skills and attributes in sport and life" and "human potential and possibilities".

Don Bridgeman is a PhD candidate in the Department of Psychology at the University of Southern Queensland (Australia) where he is furthering previous equine studies including an associate diploma of applied science (horse husbandry), postgraduate diploma in applied science, and a research master's of applied science (animal studies). Don's research has included horse behaviour during abrupt weaning, isolation and transportation. He has since combined the psychological and physiological aspects of equine and human performance to study the relationship between the horse and rider during dressage and cross-country training and competition. The motivation for his academic study and research is 40 years of working with horses, having started over 500 under saddle for stock work and recreational riding. He has been a recreational rider in polo, various western disciplines and dressage.

Linda K. Bunker is the William Parrish Professor of Education at the University of Virginia (USA) and a professor of human services. She was awarded the Luther Halsey Gulick Medal from the American Alliance for Health, Physical Education, Recreation and Dance (AAHPERD) in 2004. Dr Bunker was the 2001–2002 AAHPERD Alliance Scholar, a fellow in the American Academy of Kinesiology and has received the NASPE Hall of Fame award, the NAGWS Honor Award, the R. Tait McKenzie Award, and in 1994 received the President's Award from the Women's Sports Foundation. Dr Bunker's activities include being a tireless advocate for girls and women in sport. Linda Bunker has written 14 books and over 100 articles and presentations related to enhancing human performance. As Director of the Motor Learning Laboratory, Linda Bunker is involved in research related to optimizing the acquisition of motor skills. Her particular interest areas include cognitive strategies for performance enhancement, especially understanding the mechanisms and uses of imagery and self-talk.

Kevin L. Burke is Professor and Chair of the Department of Physical Education, Exercise and Sport Sciences at East Tennessee State University (USA). Dr Burke is a licensed professional counsellor with a private practice. A fellow, charter member, current member of the performance enhancement/intervention committee, and past Secretary-Treasurer of the Association for the Advancement of Applied Sport Psychology (AAASP), Dr Burke also served on AAASP's original executive board as the first student representative. He has co-authored two books entitled, *Sport Psychology Library Series: Basketball* and *Tennis*.

He has also served as co-editor of seven editions of the *Directory of Graduate Programs in Applied Sport Psychology*. Dr Burke is currently an associate editor for the *Journal of Applied Sport Psychology*. He has been an intercollegiate basketball official and is a past member of the International Association of Approved Basketball Officials, completing 23 seasons as an interscholastic basketball official.

Gaby BuBmann works freelance as a sport psychologist in Germany. She wrote her dissertation on the problem of dropout in sport. For many years she has worked together with the Westphalia Olympic Training Centre. She looks after and supports world-class athletes in the field of psychology. In addition to her work at the Olympic Training Centre in Westphalia, Gaby Bussmann cooperates closely with the German events riders and the German national rowing team, along with Michael Kellmann. She also works with the German track and field association. Gaby Bussmann has been a world-class athlete in the past (track and field: 400 metres and 800 metres). She won a bronze medal at the Olympic Games in Los Angeles in 1984 with the 4×400 metres relay.

Karen D. Cogan is a licensed psychologist and holds a joint appointment at the University of North Texas (USA) Counseling Center and Psychology Department. She is on the faculty of the UNT Center for Sport Psychology and Performance Excellence and has a private practice. She is a certified consultant and currently consults with a variety of individual athletes and teams including the US Freestyle Mogul Ski team and the University of North Texas Athletic Department. In 2000, she published the book: *Sport Psychology Library: Gymnastics*. She is a member of the Association for the Advancement of Applied Sport Psychology and the American Psychological Association.

Deborah L. Feltz is a professor and chairperson in Kinesiology at Michigan State University (USA). She has research interests in the interrelationships among self-efficacy, anxiety, and motivation in sport and physical activity among youth, women and teams. She has published over 100 articles on these topics and received numerous awards for her work in these areas. In addition, Professor Feltz has served on several professional editorial boards, including the *Journal of Sport and Exercise Psychology, Research Quarterly for Exercise and Sport* (section editor), *Measurement in Physical Education and Exercise Science*, and *Quest*. She also served on the United States National Research Council's Committee on Techniques for the Enhancement of Human Performance and the sport psychology advisory committees to the United States Olympic Committee. Dr Feltz served as President of the American Academy of Kinesiology and Physical Education from 2000 to 2003 and is a fellow in the American Psychological Association.

Enrique Garcés de Los Fayos is a professor of sport psychology at the University of Murcia (Spain). He is Director of the journal *Cuadernos de Psicología del Deporte* and Director of the Sport Psychology Unit at the aforementioned university. Together with Joaquín Dosil, he is the author of two publications on applied psychology of motor sports, and applied psychological strategies for improved performance in motorcycling. He has also been a co-ordinator in general sport psychology texts such as *Manual de Psicología del Deporte: Concepto y Aplicaciones, Manual de Psicología del Deporte,* and *Áreas de Aplicación en Psicología del Deporte*. Moreover, he is a sport psychology member of the Official College of Psychologists in Murcia, as well as being a member of the State Co-ordinating Council of Sport Psychology, within the same organisation. Likewise, over recent years he has worked directly with motorcyclists competing in Spanish and European motorcycling championships.

Diane L. Gill is a professor and graduate director in the Department of Exercise and Sport Science at the University of North Carolina at Greensboro (USA). Her research interests focus on physical activity and wellbeing across the lifespan, with an emphasis on social psychology, gender and cultural diversity. At UNCG she has served as Associate Dean of the School of Health and Human Performance, Head of the Department of Exercise and Sport Science, and as the founding Director of the Center for Women's Health and Wellness. She has over 100 publications including the text, *Psychological Dynamics of Sport and Exercise*, several book chapters, and many articles in research journals. She has presented over 100 research papers and invited addresses at national and international conferences, and received several awards for her research and professional work. She is a past-president of Division 47 (Exercise and Sport Psychology) of the American Psychological Association, a former president of the North American Society for the Psychology of Sport and Physical Activity and of the Research Consortium of AAHPERD, and former editor of the *Journal of Sport and Exercise Psychology*.

Wayne Halliwell is a professor in the Department of Kinesiology at the University of Montreal (Canada). He is a past-president of the Canadian Society of Psychomotor Learning and Sport Psychology and is also a fellow member of the Association for the Advancement of Applied Sport Psychology. For the past 20 years he has been the team sport psychology consultant with many of Hockey Canada's highly successful ice hockey teams at World Championships and Winter Olympic Games. He has also attended a number of Summer Olympic Games and the America's Cup as a consultant to the Canadian National Sailing Team. As the lead author of a recent book entitled *Consultant's Guide to Excellence*, Dr Halliwell and his colleagues provide insight into the art of delivering sport psychology consulting services to athletes, coaches and teams.

Tom Hanson is the founder of www.FocusedBaseball.com, a mental toughness resource for players, coaches and parents (2002). He has also been the full-time Performance Enhancement Director for the New York Yankees (2001), the Performance Enhancement Consultant for the Texas Rangers (1999, 2000), as well as providing performance enhancement services for Anaheim Angels and Minnesota Twins. Hanson has been the head baseball coach and tenured professor at Skidmore College (NY) (1990–1997). Moreover, he is the co-author of *Heads-Up Baseball: Playing the Game One Pitch at a Time* and has conducted interviews with Hank Aaron, Rod Carew, Pete Rose, Tony Oliva, Carl Yastrzemski, Stan Musial, Kirby Puckett, Billy Williams and others for research on the mental aspects of hitting. He has also interviewed pitching greats Nolan Ryan, Tommy John, Ferguson Jenkins, Bert Blyleven and many current major league players.

Kathleen M. Haywood, FAAKPE is a full-time lecturer at the University of Missouri (USA). She began archery as a teenager and as a result of both that experience and her preparation as a physical education teacher, taught archery at three different universities. She also completed a US National Archery Association instructor certification course and competed in archery at many levels, winning eight state titles and finishing in the top three at several regional and national championships of the US National Field Archery Association, all with a compound bow. Professor Haywood also competed for a short time with the Professional Archers Association, taking second place in one tournament. Now retired from active competition, she combines her competitive archery experience with her professional expertise in the psychological aspects of motor performance to author *Archery: Steps to Success*, with a third edition now in preparation, *Teaching Archery*, and two chapters related to teaching archery in secondary schools.

Ken Hodge is an associate professor in sport psychology at the School of Physical Education, University of Otago (New Zealand). His research focuses primarily on the psychosocial effects of participation in sport. Dr Hodge serves on editorial boards for the *Journal of Applied Sport Psychology* and the *Psychology of Sport and Exercise* journal. He currently works for the NZ Rugby Union (as a staff coach), and has worked for Netball NZ, NZ Swimming, and NZ Golf providing psychological skills training for a number of different teams and individuals. In 1992 he worked as Team Psychologist for the NZ Olympic Team at the Barcelona Games. Dr Hodge has written several books and has co-authored two rugby publications entitled *Thinking Rugby: Training Your Mind for Peak Performance,* and *Smart Training for Rugby: The Complete Rugby Training Guide*. He is a former president of the NZ Sport Psychology Association and also served as Deputy-Chairman of the NZ Federation of Sports Medicine from 1993 to 1995. Dr Hodge has 27 years' rugby playing experience and has 16 years' rugby coaching experience, as well as 15 years' experience teaching psychology skills to rugby players and coaches.

Michael Kellmann is an assistant professor of sport psychology in the Faculty of Sport Science at the Ruhr University of Bochum (Germany). He is a member of the Association for the Advancement of Applied Sport Psychology and German Psychological Association. He serves on the executive board of the German Association of Sport Psychology and the editorial board for *The Sport Psychologist,* the *German Journal of Sport Psychology,* and the *German Journal of Sport Medicine*. Dr Kellmann's works have appeared in more than 50 publications; he is co-author of *Recovery-Stress Questionnaire for Athletes: User Manual* and he edited the book *Enhancing Recovery: Preventing Underperformance in Athletes*. He has consulted with and conducted research for the National Sport Centre Calgary in Canada, the Olympic Training Centre Westphalia (Dortmund/Bochum), and the German national rowing team.

Jeff Kress earned both a master's of science degree and a doctor of philosophy degree in sport psychology and has done sport psychology consultation work with numerous teams and athletes. He is currently an assistant professor at California State University, Long Beach (USA). Dr Kress raced bicycles competitively for 15 years from the age of 15. During two of those years, he competed for the United States National Road Cycling Team, racing in such international stage races as the Tour of Belgium and the Vuelta de Chile.

Chris Lonsdale holds an MA and is a PhD candidate in sport psychology at the University of Otago (New Zealand). His areas of expertise include motivation, athlete burnout and psychological engagement in sport. Over the past seven years Chris has consulted with athletes in a variety of sports, including volleyball, ice hockey, athletics, tennis, golf, lawn bowling and equestrian. A former rugby player himself, Chris has also provided mental skills training for rugby union players at club, Super 12 and international levels. He is currently a mental skills consultant for Rugby Canada.

Michael Martin is Head of the Performance Psychology Department at the Australian Institute of Sport (Australia). He earned his PhD in sport psychology from the University of Wollongong. His main professional interests include exceeding client expectations, service delivery structures and mental skills. He has written over 50 articles for various journals, and on many occasions has written for the *Australian Surf Lifesaver.*

Ian Maynard took up the position of "Professor of Sport Psychology" at Sheffield Hallam University's Centre for Sport and Exercise Science (United Kingdom) in April 1999. He attended the Barcelona and Athens Olympics, the Victoria and Manchester Commonwealth Games and has been a consultant at World Championships in eight different sports. Dr Maynard is also the director of the RYA World Class Performance and World Class Potential Sport Science Support Programmes and has acted as consultant to various sports associations such as the All England Women's Lacrosse Association and the English Women's Bowling Association. He served as the Executive Secretary of the British Association of Sport and Exercise Science (BASES) and chaired the BASES Sport Science Special Committee. Moreover, he is currently the Editor of *The Sport Psychologist* and an associate editor (performance enhancement) for the *Journal of Applied Sport Psychology*, and Director of the Centre for Sport and Exercise Science at Sheffield Hallam University.

Alex McKenzie currently works for the Hurricanes Super Rugby Team in New Zealand as the "Professional Development Manager"—a role that includes mental skills training for players. From 2001 to 2004, Dr McKenzie worked in the same role for the Highlanders Super Rugby Team in New Zealand. Prior to his work in professional rugby he was a senior lecturer in sport and exercise psychology at the School of Physical Education, University of Otago (New Zealand). He is the co-author of a "rugby" sport psychology book entitled *Thinking Rugby: Training Your Mind for Peak Performance*; and co-author of a book on "rugby" training entitled *Smart Training for Rugby: The Complete Rugby Training Guide*. Dr McKenzie has 25 years' rugby playing experience, including 3 years' representative rugby experience. In addition, he has 13 years' rugby coaching experience, and 11 years' experience teaching psychology skills to rugby players and coaches.

Eva A. Monsma is an assistant professor in the Department of Physical Education at the University of South Carolina (USA). Her experience with figure skating includes four years as Head Coach of the University of Guelph Gryphons varsity figure skating team, as well as two years of professional and six of amateur coaching in Ontario. She was also a sport psychology consultant to several adolescent female figure skaters. Her dissertation, titled "The Psychobiological Profile of Competitive Female Figure Skaters", led to five publications involving psychological and physical factors of maturational status and timing as well as developmental correlates of self-concept and disordered eating risk.

Sean Müller is currently completing his doctoral studies at The University of Queensland (Australia) in the School of Human Movement Studies. Sean's PhD has investigated *when* and from *where* world-class cricket batsmen pick up visual cues to anticipate bowlers' deliveries, using a combination of video-based and field-based assessment tools. His research interests include the performance and learning of sport skills, with particular focus on perceptual skill in expert sport performance. Sean has lectured courses on skill performance and learning at university level, as well as presented his research at scientific conferences. In addition, he has given invited presentations to professional organisations including Cricket Australia and high performance coaches on topics relating to perceptual mechanisms of expert sport performance and skill learning. Furthermore, Sean has coached cricketers in Australia and the United Kingdom and played cricket at club level.

David Pargman has recently retired as Professor in the Department of Educational Research, Florida State University (USA), where he completed 31 years of service. While at FSU he served as Programme Co-ordinator for Educational Psychology and Co-ordinator of Sport Psychology. Dr Pargman has authored or co-authored more than 80 articles, book chapters, refereed abstracts, etc. and has delivered approximately 200 regional, national and international lectures at various professional forums. He is currently working on his sixth book, which focuses on the relationships between psychology and physical activity. Dr Pargman has served on the executive board of the Association for the Advancement of Applied Sport Psychology, was a chairman of its health psychology Section, and is a past chairman of the Sport Psychology Academy of the American Alliance for Health, Physical Education, Recreation and Dance. He is a member of the USOC Sport Psychology Registry and a certified consultant of the AAASP. Dr Pargman is also a member of the International Association of Applied Sport Psychology, the International Society of Sport Psychology, and the North American Association for Sport Psychology and Physical Activity.

John M. Payne (DA 1995, Human Performance, MTSU, USA) is an ex-professional kick boxer and martial arts instructor who was promoted to sixth degree black belt in 2004. He has instructed over 10,000 students in martial arts and has given numerous demonstrations and seminars in martial arts and self-defence. Dr Payne has given many speeches and conducted seminars on troubled youths, stress, and various areas of sport psychology.

Grace Pretty is an associate professor in the Department of Psychology at the University of Southern Queensland (Australia) where she contributes to the Sport and Exercise Psychology Programme. For 20 years Dr Pretty has worked with athletes in her practice as a clinical health psychologist. She has been schooled in the equestrian disciplines of dressage and showjumping, currently competes as a recreational rider in dressage, and is an EFA accredited dressage judge. Combining the ethology of horses with the psychology of human behaviour and relationships, Dr Pretty researches mental and behavioural connections between horse and rider. She presents rider and trainer workshops across various equestrian disciplines. These are based on her research findings, as well as the experiences of her clients and her own time in the saddle. She has published her work in academic form as well as in the equestrian popular press, and has presented at sport psychology conferences.

Brent S. Rushall is Professor of Exercise and Nutritional Sciences at San Diego State University (USA). He has published 46 books and over 400 articles, book chapters and psychology tests. His academic recognitions have included the designation of being the founding scholar in behavioural sport psychology and a world authority in coaching science. Dr Rushall has been an Olympic Team psychologist for Canada, in the sports of swimming, freestyle wrestling, ski-jumping, and cross-country skiing. He has represented Canada at Commonwealth Games, World Championships and World Cup events in a number of sports. As a participant, Dr Rushall played international rugby football and was a member of the first all-American rugby team. He has received national coaching appointments in the sports of swimming, rugby football, and rowing. His innovative psychology practice over the Internet (Sports Science Associates) has facilitated the provision of services to exceptional athletes and teams as they follow competitive and training schedules around the world. Brent Rushall was first involved with freestyle wrestling in Canada in the 1970s. During that time, he was psychologist to many top performers as well as being on the staffs of Olympic, Commonwealth Games and World Cup teams.

David N. Sacks earned his PhD in sport psychology at Florida State University (USA). He is currently an associate in research for the Learning Systems Institute at FSU, as well as an adjunct professor at FSU and Flagler College. Prior to assuming his present positions, he worked with children, athletes and families in a variety of capacities. He spent several years as a high school teacher and coach before serving as a counselor for ungovernable children and their families. He has also coached youth sport clubs at the local, national and international level, both in the United States and New Zealand. For the past 11 years, he has been a high school sports referee.

Sebastian Schulte is an extremely accomplished rower in the eights. In 2004 he was placed fourth in the Olympic Games, was vice-world champion in 2002 and won the World Championships Bronze Medal in 2001. He was also Under 23 World Champion in the eights in 2000 and has won a total of nine German national champion titles. Moreover, he is a member of the competitive sports committee of the German Rowing Federation (DRV), a member of the directors' board of the DRV and is the Athletes' Representative in the DRV.

John M. Silva is a professor of sport psychology in the University of North Carolina at Chapel Hill (USA). Dr Silva has published over 50 research-based articles, which have appeared in noted academic journals. He has served as a sport psychology consultant for athletes and teams competing at national and international level for over 25 years. Dr Silva was elected to the USA Team Handball Board of Directors in 2000 and has served on their Sports Medicine Committee since 1987. He is co-editor of two sport psychology textbooks including the widely used *Psychological Foundations of Sport*. Dr Silva has served as president of the Association for the Advancement of Applied Sport Psychology. He was the inaugural editor of the *Journal of Applied Sport Psychology*. He is a fellow in AAASP, a certified AAASP consultant, a member of the USOC Sport Psychology Registry, a Research Consortium fellow and a member of the American Psychological Association. Dr Silva has coached numerous USA Team Handball National Team players including two members of the 1996 USA Team Handball Olympic Team. He coached the Women's South Team in the 1993 Olympic Festival, and the Men's South Team, which won the Gold Medal in the 1995 Olympic Festival. In March 2004 he coached the Carolina THC to the USA Team Handball Collegiate National Championship. As a participant, Dr Silva played on the Carolina Team Handball Club Team that won a Bronze Medal at the US National Championships in 1991.

Robert N. Singer After receiving his PhD from Ohio State University, Dr Singer was on the faculty at different universities, most notably Florida State University, for 17 years and then at the University of Florida for 16 years. He served as a chair of the Department of Exercise and Sport Sciences at that university, and is presently professor emeritus in the Departments of Applied Physiology and Kinesiology. His research in general has dealt with cognitive processes and learner/performance strategies involved in skill acquisition and high levels of skill. His publications include over 200 research, scientific and professional articles, and 25 chapters in books. His last book publication is the *Handbook of Sport Psychology*. Dr Singer has served as Head of the Sport Psychology Division of the first Sports Medicine Committee of the United Stated Olympic Committee. He has been elected President of the Division 47 of the APA as well as President of the American Academy of Kinesiology and Physical Education. As Past-President of the International Society of Sport

Psychology for eight years, he remains actively involved in international developments and the advancement of sport psychology. His career has been awarded with various prizes including the Distinguished Contributions to the Science of Exercise of Sport and Exercise Psychology award in 1999 by the Division 47 of the APA.

Dave Smith is Senior Lecturer in Sport and Exercise Psychology at University of Chester in the United Kingdom. Dr Smith has worked with numerous body builders, both as a coach and consultant, and has had several recent papers published in scientific journals on psychological aspects of body-building. He is a member of the Advisory Boards of both the International Association of Resistance Trainers and the Fitness Standards Council, and is a life member of the English Federation of Body Builders.

Ronald Smith is Professor of Psychology and Director of the Clinical Psychology Training Programme at the University of Washington (USA). Dr Smith's major research interests are in: personality; the study of anxiety, stress and coping; and in performance enhancement research and interventions. A recent grant to Dr Smith and Smoll will fund the development, evaluation and national dissemination of new coach and parent intervention programmes and the training of sport psychologists to deliver them. For 12 years, he directed a psychological skills training programme for the Houston Astros professional baseball organisation and has served as a team counsellor for the Seattle Mariners. He has also served as a training consultant to the Oakland Athletics Baseball Club and to Major League Soccer. Dr Smith is a fellow of the American Psychological Association and a past-president of the Association for the Advancement of Applied Sport Psychology. He has published more than 150 scientific articles and book chapters in his areas of interest. He also has authored or co-authored 23 books, including *Children and Youth in sport: A Biopsychosocial Perspective*, *Psychology: The Science of Mind and Behavior* and *Personality: Toward an Integration*.

Frank Smoll is a professor of psychology at the University of Washington (USA). He is Codirector (with Ronald Smith) of the Sport Psychology Graduate Programme. Dr Smoll's research focuses on coaching behaviours in youth sports and on the psychological effects of competition on children and adolescents. He has authored more than 100 scientific articles and book chapters, and he has co-authored/edited 15 books and manuals on children's athletics. Professor Smoll is a fellow of the American Psychological Association, the American Academy of Kinesiology and Physical Education, and the Association for the Advancement of Applied Sport Psychology (AAASP). Dr Smoll is a certified sport consultant and was the recipient of AAASP's Distinguished Professional Practice Award. In the area of applied sport psychology, Dr Smoll has extensive experience in conducting psychologically oriented coaching clinics and workshops for parents of young athletes.

Jim Taylor has been a consultant for the United States and Japanese Ski Teams, the United States Tennis Association, and USA Triathlon, and has worked with professional and Olympic athletes in tennis, skiing, triathlon, football, baseball, cycling, golf and many other sports. A former alpine ski racer who held a top-20 national ranking and competed internationally, Dr Taylor is a certified tennis coach, a second degree black belt in karate, a marathon runner and an Ironman triathlete. Dr Taylor is also the author of the *Prime Sport* book series, *Psychological Approaches to Sports Injury Rehabilitation*, *Comprehensive Sports Injury Management*, *Psychology of Dance* and *Positive Pushing: How to Raise a Successful and Happy Child*. He has published over 400 articles in popular and professional publications and has given more than 500 workshops and presentations throughout North America and Europe.

Gershon Tenenbaum is currently Professor of Sport and Exercise Psychology at Florida State University (USA). He served as the President of the International Society of Sport Psychology between the years 1997 and 2001 and, since 1996 to the present, as the Editor of the *International Journal of Sport and Exercise Psychology*. He is a member of numerous scientific societies in the fields of sport and exercise psychology and statistics, and a member of the editorial boards, and reviewer for 16 journals. Dr Tenenbaum has published more than 150 articles in peer-refereed journals. He published 40 book chapters, and edited two English books (*The Practice of Sport Psychology* and *Brain and Body in Sport and Exercise–Biofeedback Applications in Performance Enhancement* with Blumenstein and Bar-Eli), and six books in the Hebrew language. Dr Tenenbaum has received several scientific honorary and meritorious awards for contributions to science and practice, including the 1987 Award for Meritorious Contribution to Educational Practice through Research (*Journal of Educational Research*) and the ISSP Honor Award (1997).

Robert Weinberg is a professor at Miami University in Ohio (USA). Before coming to Miami University, Weinberg was a professor in the Department of Kinesiology at the University of North Texas from 1978 to 1992 including being Regents Professor from 1988 to 1992. He was also voted one of the top 10 sport psychology specialists in North America by his peers. Dr Weinberg has published approximately 135 journal articles, contributed 20 book chapters, and published 7 books, as well as presenting more than 300 refereed and invited papers at sport and exercise psychology conferences. He has served as president of both the North American Society for the Psychology of Sport and Physical Activity and the Association for the Advancement of Applied Sport Psychology. He is the former Editor of the *Journal of Applied Sport Psychology* and has served on a variety of editorial boards of major journals in the field. He is a certified consultant, member of the United States Olympic Committee Sport Psychology Registry, and a fellow in the American Academy for Kinesiology and Physical Education.

Len Zaichkowsky is a professor of education, Professor of Psychiatry and Graduate Medical Sciences and Head of Graduate Training in Sport and Exercise Psychology in "Mental Health and Behavioral Medicine" at the Boston University School of Medicine (USA). He holds a joint appointment in the School of Education and School of Medicine and is Director of the Sport Psychology Clinic in the BU Department of Athletics. He has authored or edited seven books, with the most recent being *Medical and Psychological Aspects of Sport and Exercise,* and has published over 80 papers on sport psychology, research design and related topics in scholarly journals or books, plus numerous magazine and newspaper columns on applied aspects of sport psychology. Dr Zaichkowsky played, coached and refereed hockey before going into academia. Actively involved with USA hockey and the development of young hockey players, for 20 years he has served as the consulting sport psychologist for the Boston University Terriers team, and for 3 years served as the consulting psychologist for Harvard University Women's hockey team. He has also consulted for the National Hockey League Player's Association, and the Calgary Flames (2002–2003).

Foreword

Jaume Cruz Feliu

Professor of Sport Psychology, Universitat Autónoma de Barcelona, Spain

Psychological training and counselling with athletes, coaches, referees and others involved in the sports environment should promote a series of psychological strategies to cope with practices and competitions with greater guarantees of success. With this in mind, *The Sport Psychologist's Handbook* offers a series of intervention programmes, specific to each sport, which highlight the need for a greater specialisation in Sport Psychology according to the psychological demands of the different sporting disciplines.

The focus of this text is novel, since the majority of sport psychology manuals published in recent years present standardised programmes of psychological training which fail to analyse the psychological characteristics and demands of each individual sport. Nevertheless, an important text preceding this publication is that of Vanek and Cratty (1970), *Psychology and the Superior Athlete*, which, following the ideas of one of the Soviet forefathers of sport psychology, Peter Roudik, considers that psychological training should be conducted according to: (a) the psychological demands of each sporting situation; and (b) the specific needs of each athlete.

The message sent by *The Sport Psychologist's Handbook* and another publication by Dosil (2002)—*El psicólogo del deporte: asesoramiento e intervención*, written in Spanish— is as clear as it is imperative: applied sport psychologists should know and analyse the diverse situations produced during the competition, season or Olympic cycle of the sport in which they are to carry out psychological training, and they must evaluate the needs and psychological resources of the sportsmen and women and technical team with whom they are to collaborate, in order to optimise the performance and wellbeing of the athletes.

Throughout the various chapters of this book, it is demonstrated that the wellbeing of athletes, and not only their performance, will become a significant aspect in the psychological interventions carried out with sportsmen and -women of the future. Therefore, the relationship established between athletes and sport psychologists becomes very important, as indicated by Mark Andersen in Chapter 30. Hence, it is not only necessary to show sport psychologists *which* techniques to apply in their psychological interventions, but also *how* they should carry out such psychological interventions. Along these lines, in the introduction to *Doing Sport Psychology*, Andersen (2000) stresses that sport psychologists must respond to the following questions prior to embarking on any intervention:

(a) *Which* aspects of an athlete are they to improve on?
(b) *Where* will they conduct the intervention?

(c) *When* is the most appropriate moment to carry out the intervention?
(d) *Why* use certain techniques and intervention programmes instead of other alternatives?
(e) *Who* will receive the interventions and *who* will carry them out? and
(f) *How* are these interventions to be conducted?

To respond adequately to these questions, sport psychologists must have sufficient knowledge of psychology, applied sport sciences and the sport itself. Moreover, when working with elite athletes, psychologists must take into consideration the values and identity of these athletes when carrying out interventions, since "sport psychology interventions must fit within the value system of the athlete and be congruent with the meaning that activity has for that individual", as indicated by Balagué (1999, p. 91).

The aforementioned reflections allow us to state, as suggested by Smoll and Smith in Chapter 2 of this book, that: "The sport environment is an important milieu for psychosocial development and adaptation. An increasing number of sport psychologists have thus focused on the impact of competition on athletes' personal development." Taking this into account, I believe it is not all about athletes' performance in applied sport psychology. In fact, there is something previous—such as athletes' personal and psychosocial development, shaped by their relationships with others around them (parents, coaches, peers, officials and umpires) within the youth sports environment—meaning sport psychologists must bear in mind three goals, as previously outlined (Cruz, 1992):

(1) The psychological training of coaches of young and elite athletes;
(2) The elaboration of programmes for young athletes with an educational focus; and
(3) The elaboration of specific psychological preparation programmes for each sport.

Consequently, to begin with, sport psychologists should carry out an indirect intervention with athletes, counselling parents within the sporting facility, and coaches, in those psychological aspects which may be incorporated into the atheletes' daily training. Second, sport psychologists must elaborate educative psychological training programmes for young athletes, with the aim of them developing the necessary skills for peak performance sport. This preparation will avoid some drop-outs, given that competition eliminates not only those athletes with less developed physical or sporting skills, but also those who have not known how to cope with the ever increasing demands of high performance. Third, sport psychologists must elaborate and apply specific psychological training programmes for each sport, which are sufficiently flexible to be adapted to the diverse requirements of each individual athlete, as suggested in the various and intriguing chapters of *The Sport Psychologist's Handbook*.

Finally, it must be highlighted that if psychological training programmes are elaborated with an educative focus, respect the values of athletes and are introduced at an early stage in youth sport to complement physical training, not only will the majority of psychological risks of peak performance sport be avoided, but also such psychological preparation will prove useful to athletes in successfully coping with competitive situations in other aspects of their professional or academic life. In reading *The Sport Psychologist's Handbook*, I believe that applied sport psychologists will find interesting ideas and suggestions for carrying out their work in accordance with these principles.

REFERENCES

Andersen, M. (2000) Introduction. In M. Andersen (ed.), *Doing Sport Psychology* (pp. XIII–XVII). Champaign, II.: Human Kinetics.

Balagué, G. (1999). Understanding identity, value and meaning when working with elite athletes. *Sport Psychologist, 13*, 89–98.

Cruz, J. (1992). El asesoramiento y la intervención psicológica en deportistas olímpicos. (Psychological counselling and intervention with Olympic athletes). *Revista de Psicología del Deporte, 2*, 41–46.

Dosil, J. (2002). *El psicólogo del deporte: asesoramiento e intervención.* (The sport psychologist: counseling and intervention). Madrid: Síntesis.

Vanek, M. & Cratty, B. (1970). *Psychology and the Superior Athlete.* London: Collier.

Preface

Over the last few decades sport psychology has undergone sustained development. Various elements may be used to analyse the evolution of this area of knowledge: from an academic perspective, an ever increasing number of training courses, master's and doctoral programmes related to sport psychology are being offered; the research field has been consolidated and various scientific journals have emerged in this area of study; sport psychology congresses and publications are a frequent occurrence year after year; and sport psychology associations have spread throughout the world, with international and national organisations, etc. Nevertheless, as time goes on, one subject remains unsettled: the applied field.

The value of psychological aspects to those within the sporting context (coaches, athletes, managers, referees, etc.) is undeniable, and yet few support the integration of the sport psychology figure within teams and clubs. This distance between sport psychology professionals and their subjects within the sporting environment is the result of certain attributes, still attached to our profession (limiting activity to a clinical focus and theoretical aspects, associations with laboratory experiments, etc.) and, principally, an ignorance of what sport psychologists can really provide in each sporting discipline (both for improved performance and increased wellbeing).

Many texts have been published in an attempt to solve this "problem". The majority of these publications focus on how sport psychologists should work, how to use psychological techniques and the description of case studies illustrating the most effective procedures. Currently, we are able to contemplate a base of knowledge between sport psychologists which allows them to guarantee a service in accordance with the most common requirements demanded of them. However, this has not been sufficient to achieve the inclusion and total acceptance of sport psychology. The challenge we have faced over the years is knowing how to transfer theoretical knowledge to the specific field of sport and, more specifically, to each sporting discipline. Many sport psychologists have failed to effectively market their product, believing that "simply" being a good professional is enough to work in the applied field. Conducting quality marketing may prove one of the keys to the sport psychologist being more widely accepted in the future, as just another member of the technical staff of teams and athletes. To achieve this, it becomes fundamental to follow a double strategy: having a good product and knowing how to sell it. Having a good product refers to sport psychologists being highly qualified specialists in the applied field. Therefore, it is necessary to know how to apply psychology, be familiar with sport sciences and, principally, delve deeper into the uniqueness of the sporting discipline in which one is to work. Selling this product is a much simpler step if the training has been adequate, given that if sport psychologists combine the three aforementioned conditions in their training, they will find it much easier to explain exactly what they can offer to a sports team or athlete, and how they will go about it. In this respect, it is important to raise awareness of the need to open up our profession, proposing action guidelines and not remaining static, waiting for others to offer us work. In other words, we refer to knowing how to "move ourselves" throughout the world of supply and demand.

These are some of the ideas which have driven us to publish this text. From our point of view, a change of strategy in the training and promotion of sport psychology is called for. This book presents the key elements which sport psychologists should take into consideration if they want to become qualified in the applied field, under the premise that the greater their specialisation in a sporting discipline, the better the service they can offer. Hence, perhaps in the future we will speak of "sport psychology specialists in different sporting disciplines", as previously defended in other publications. The justification of this denomination is valued on a day-to-day basis in the applied field, where various professional colleagues have achieved success in specific sports for being considered the best in each discipline. This proposal is not aimed to be rigid and, as such, does not limit sport psychologists to certain sporting disciplines. It defends the principle of having a sufficient background in sport psychology, which allows professionals who wish to work with athletes or teams to gain the capacity to optimise their professional performance through studying the sporting event with which they are to work. This book aims to fill the current void in sport psychology training, proposing action guidelines used by some of the most important professionals in the world, and offering what is unique in each sport, with the idea of achieving sport psychology peak performance. The result is this consultant's handbook, recommended to any sport psychologist hoping to work in the applied field.

The structure adopted in *The Sport Psychologist's Handbook* is very simple. It commences with a general "introduction to working with athletes", in which five chapters deal with the basics that sport psychologists should take into consideration before working in the applied field: educational training, coach–athlete relationships, the athlete's family and interventions in the sport, through assessment, evaluation and counselling. From this generic approach, we then enter the sections offering specific psychological work with 26 sporting disciplines—basketball, football (soccer), baseball, rugby, handball, cricket, athletics, tennis, golf, cycling, martial arts, wrestling, ice hockey, figure skating, sailing and windsurfing, rowing, surfing, motorcycling, archery, dressage, showjumping, polo, fitness activities, bodybuilding, gymnastics—and athletes with disabilities. In each of these chapters we have tried to adhere to a certain structure: a description of the sport and the psychological aspects implied, general aspects of psychological evaluation, psychological work in training and psychological work with competitions. The wealth of this focus lies in the fact that readers have the opportunity to study specific psychological strategies used in each sporting discipline. In this way, they are able to form personal consulting systems which may be adapted to diverse contexts. Finally, the Afterword tries to answer some questions about athlete–sport psychologist relationships.

From our point of view, the contents of this book and its adaptation to specific cases will contribute to a greater specialisation within the sport psychology profession, thus definitively promoting applied sport psychology. Coaches, directors and athletes alike will find psychologists trained in their specific sport. That is to say, they may turn to authentic sport psychology experts in each sporting discipline.

Definitively, this work will mark a before and after in applied sport psychology literature.

Acknowledgements

The adventure of editing a book is similar to training a sports team. At the beginning of the season (when the book is still just a project), a proposal is made to a sponsor (the publishers) with the objectives we aim to achieve. Once they accept the initial ideas, it becomes fundamental to form a good team (contributors). From this moment on, the regular league matches begin (the process of creating the work), in which each member of the team has a function, and depending on how they carry it out, we achieve one outcome or another. In our case, we have had the opportunity to "train" a great team, who have performed extraordinarily throughout our particular season. For this reason, I direct my words of thanks to the 43 contributors who have made this text possible. They have been the authentic stars in this "sport" of writing. Secondly, I would like to mention the support given to me from the beginning of this project by Manuel Vazquez. He has played the role of second coach, evaluating everything concerned with this publication with precision. Thirdly, I give thanks to my assistant Suzanne Hasler, since without her help it would have been impossible to write the chapters I took on. I would also like to express my satisfaction at working with Gillian Lesley, the editor at Wiley, whose kind words have helped me to remain motivated at every moment; as well as Deborah Egleton and Claire Ruston, who have always been ready to collaborate. And I couldn't forget the person who has lived with me through the different production phases of this work, my wife Olaia. She, along with my family, are always there when I need them and are the basic support of all my work.

Finally, as any good coach would do at the end of a season, it's necessary to carry out a final balance. Without a doubt, we will find aspects to improve on in the next edition, but needless to say, we can conclude by saying that this team has been an authentic "dream team". Thank you so much to all of you.

PART I

Introduction to Working with Athletes

CHAPTER 1

Applied Sport Psychology: A New Perspective

Joaquín Dosil
University of Vigo, Spain

INTRODUCTION

Traditionally, coaches and athletes have focused their efforts on physical training. Over time, however, the technical, tactical and psychological aspects have gained a more important role. Despite psychology being perceived as one of the key factors to peak performance and wellbeing in sport, few systematically train this facet.

Since applied sport psychology has yet to achieve the same development as in those areas dedicated to education and research, new approaches are required to get closer to the needs of athletes and people in sport, definitively opening the doors to the incorporation of the sport psychology figure in clubs and teams. The current situation in peak performance sport reflects an increasing equality between the physical, technical and tactical domains, with psychology excelling on many occasions. Along these lines, and as already defended in other texts (Dosil, 2002), a greater specialization is required in the applied field, in which psychologists are able to confront any situation presented to them within the sport they work in. To achieve this, in the coming years there should be an emergence of authentic sport psychology specialists in football, basketball, tennis, golf, etc. with perfect knowledge of their sport and a greater ability to adapt their skills to it. This idea constitutes the driving force behind this publication, which endeavours to serve as a handbook for psychologists, bringing within their reach the essential elements to commence work in different sports.

This chapter is developed on these assumptions, gathering the basic characteristics of mental training, going through an athlete's psychological preparation and reflecting on one of the future trends in the applied field: mental peak performance. The final part of the chapter presents two applied sport psychology training programmes: the field and clinical applied learning programmes, which stand out for the success they are having incorporating new psychologists into the sports world.

The Sport Psychologist's Handbook: A Guide for Sport-Specific Performance Enhancement.
Edited by Joaquín Dosil. © 2006 John Wiley & Sons, Ltd.

AN OVERVIEW OF MENTAL TRAINING

Mental training involves providing athletes with a series of psychological strategies for improving their ability to confront training and competition with greater guarantees of success. Therefore, it is a specific task aimed at increasing the performance and wellbeing of athletes or anyone involved in the sports context. The principal idea of mental training, as with physical preparation, is that a determined number of hours are needed to acquire psychological strategies, for which a weekly practice session may be suitable. In the majority of cases, such dedication to maximum mental development is impractical given the structure of sport and the current situation of applied sport psychology, which limits the training possibilities. In reality, if the aim is for athletes to become mental control specialists (just as they are physical control specialists), it becomes necessary to perform psychological training on a daily basis, on the premise that the greater the dedication, the greater the improvement will be. However, in the event that athletes do decide to become involved with psychological training in a similar way to their physical preparation (e.g. two hours daily), would sport psychologists be prepared to offer such an intensive service?

Mental training entails a series of difficulties experienced by both those who direct it, psychologists, and those who receive it, athletes, and others involved in sport. Psychologists require an extensive experience-based training in the applied field, which is still not widespread (in the second part of the chapter we will see two possible training programmes), as well as an in-depth knowledge of psychology, other sport sciences and, of course, the sport in which they work. On the other hand, mainly due to an ignorance of what mental training consists of and how it is carried out, members of the sporting "community" remain unaware of its potential, impeding its integration into daily training. The few who do appreciate its importance usually regard it as "something" suitable for use on isolated occasions when problems arise.

These circumstances force psychologists to adapt mental training to the conditions they find themselves working in. Various texts have described possible programmes which sport psychologists may use as a guide for their assessment and intervention work with clubs and athletes (e.g. Tenenbaum, 2001; Weinberg & Williams, 2001). However, they should consider every circumstance as unique, requiring them to adapt to the context and individuals with whom they are working. The objectives professional sport psychologists should set will vary according to these conditions, becoming more or less ambitious depending on the possibilities (for example, the service should be adapted to the financial capacity of athletes, clubs or teams, offering a quality assessment which corresponds to the contract or earned remuneration). Baillie & Ogilvie (2002) offer some reflections on this issue.

Mental training can be carried out both in a clinical environment (office) or in the field (stadium or sports centre). Nonetheless, one context or the other will become more suitable depending on the service required (e.g. if an athlete wishes to solve a personal problem, the privacy of an office may be more appropriate; whereas if the aim is to evaluate a specific aspect of the athlete's speciality, the field becomes the more favourable option, increasing the reality of the situation and allowing them to practice in the usual place). In recent years, a new form of mental training for athletes has been developed: "therapy on-line" (related to cyber sport psychology). The general characteristics of these three types of psychological training are as follows (Dosil, 2004):

- *Clinical intervention* The classic option in sport psychology. It stems from clinical psychology and involves carrying out psychological training in the office or consultancy. Although the clinic can be used to assess and treat athletes, important contextual information is easily lost. Any myths surrounding clinical psychological work should be dispelled, especially when many athletes still struggle with the idea of going to a sport psychology clinic to improve performance rather than solve problems, which continues to be the most frequent reason for their visits (e.g. lack of motivation to train, lack of consistency, being overly negative, becoming nervous, etc.). In the office, while priority should be given to athletes' problems, it remains an exceptional opportunity to inform them of how psychological training can increase performance and well being.
- *Field intervention* involves going into the athletics environment to perform psychological assessments of coaches and athletes. The principal objective of this form of psychological training is to integrate psychologists into the teams with which they are collaborating, operating in their natural setting and providing them with strategies which adapt to their day-to-day situations. It is advisable for use in those sports where successful clinical assessment is more difficult. On occasions, problems may arise when sport psychologists have no suitable place to meet with athletes (i.e. an office) and, to some extent, lose the confidentiality this setting would provide. This has certain repercussions in the training of some strategies which require time to be learned and an adequate location in which to work on them correctly (e.g. relaxation or visualization).
- *On-line intervention* is one of the lesser developed methods in psychology and is scarcely employed in sport psychology. Nevertheless, various studies have shown its use to be just as effective as the more traditional forms of guidance, if not more so (Zizzi and Perna, 2002). As demonstrated in other studies (Dosil and García-Prieto, 2004), it may become one of the professional possibilities of the future since it offers certain advantages over the aforementioned approaches (e.g. confidentiality, anonymity for those athletes who wish to remain unknown, speed of response/treatment, etc.). However, this form of guidance is limited in the requests and athletes it can respond to. On some occasions psychologists need to consult with athletes in person or refer cases to another professional. Nevertheless, to guide coaches (by way of "psychological advice"), give simple action guidelines to some athletes, work using records, etc. it is extremely effective, making it a tool of undoubted value in present-day sport psychology.

The success of these three types of intervention lies in the skills of sport psychologists to adapt the most suitable method to the needs of teams or athletes. Ideally, all three approaches should be employed to achieve maximum performance in psychological assessments, since the multitude of situations experienced in sport will demand one method or another. For example, as can be seen in Chapter 7 on football, what is known as the "mixed model" (Dosil, 2004) may be employed, which encompasses characteristics of all three techniques. Initially, resources provided by email are used to gather information about teams and coaches, followed up with direct observation and field interviews where individual and group assessments may be carried out. Subsequently, clinical or "on-line" intervention may be appropriate for some athletes or coaches.

PSYCHOLOGICAL INTERVENTION LEVELS AND THE ATHLETE'S PSYCHOLOGICAL LEVEL

The use of the three aforementioned intervention systems depends on the depth of psychological training required. Currently, two "levels" of sport psychology intervention are usually employed: problem solving (level 1) and mental training (level 2). At the first level, many studies have focused on identifying the most effective methods of solving problems common to athletes; while mental training, yet to become "standardized" in the current sports climate, involves dedicating a specific amount of time to learning strategies and improving psychological skills throughout the season. This level of assessment and intervention is frequently found in training schedules developed in high performance centres, where athletes are able to dedicate time on a weekly basis to psychological training programmes, or when national teams spend time "focused" in holding camps prior to representing their country in international championships. Nevertheless, while agreeing on the need for the two "classic" levels of psychological intervention, this text proposes a third level, superior to the previous two, which may be termed "mental peak performance". This level of guidance is still underdeveloped and few sport psychologists approach it, either for lack of knowledge or for its infeasibility in the current circumstances. Table 1.1 describes the differences between the three techniques.

Levels 1 and 2 have been well documented in sport psychology scientific literature (e.g. for clinical treatment, see Andersen, 2002; or for the planning of psychological training, see Weinberg & Williams, 2001). The majority of applied studies refer to these levels, assuming that athletes turn to sport psychologists to solve personal or sport-based problems, or to train skills which allow them to improve their performance. The limitation of these levels lies in the fact that only a certain improvement is achieved, with psychologists acting as a

Table 1.1 Psychological intervention levels

Level	Objective	Consequences
Level 1	Solution of athletes' problems	Faced with a problem, sport psychologists provide one or more techniques which allow athletes to find solutions to their problems (e.g. problems sleeping prior to competition: they are shown an effective relaxation technique which enables them to resolve their predicament).
Level 2	Basic mental skills training	This is used to avoid rather than solve problems, giving athletes a series of psychological strategies to employ in different situations, depending on the requirements (e.g. to sleep well prior to a competition: control their arousal levels, perform visualization, maintain concentration, etc.).
Level 3	Mental peak performance	Athletes achieve maximum mental control, producing optimum performance in any circumstance. They have internalized the techniques and apply them consciously or unconsciously in the face of adverse situations (e.g. capacity to sleep in any situation: despite having a companion who snores, noise from the street, little time, etc.).

complementary element to athletes' physical preparation. However, level 3 has a different focus, proposing that athletes who wish to reach the elite require special psychological conditions that can only be achieved through *psychological peak performance training*. With this approach, psychological training becomes a necessity rather that just a complementary factor, distinguishing one athlete from another.

The term "mental peak performance" is perceived as the perfection of strategies and skills acquired by athletes at level 2, adapting them automatically to any situation and arming them with a psychological capacity superior to that of the average population, which enables athletes to confront specific situations in their sport (both in training and competition). As may be understood, this method calls for daily training, with planning running parallel to the physical preparation, and total integration between the two aspects (physical + mental). The main purpose is to accomplish a perfect balance between the physical and psychological control of the body (something unthinkable for some athletes, and nevertheless a characteristic of the elite few). An example of this is an athlete who is capable of running the 1500 metres in 3 minutes 30 seconds, and has the capacity to mentally respond at this level. That is to say, an athlete who has the ability to process information quickly, concentrate, make decisions, control thoughts, control suffering and their body's limits, etc. whilst physically "on the edge". Likewise, in mental peak performance, training is carried out to enable the psychological techniques to be employed in the extreme conditions athletes face in competition (e.g. a Formula One driver must have the ability to remain alert after having completed a large part of the race, a tennis player needs to maintain concentration even when the results are negative or when the public criticize an action, etc.). In conclusion, the objective is to endow sportspeople with a mental control that matches their superior physical condition.

One way to understand mental peak performance compared to the other two forms of training is to subject three hypothetical athletes to a scenario which often affects them in real life (Table 1.2). The three levels of the psychological guidance and intervention previously described can be used to define an athlete's psychological "level". At level 0, athletes will

Table 1.2 Examples of athletes at psychological levels 1, 2 and 3

Situation	Sleeping in a hotel with noise from people on the street
Level 1	These athletes will perhaps not manage to get to sleep because of the "extra" noise to which they are not accustomed. They attended a psychologist to solve their anxiety problem prior to competitions and seem to have gained some improvement. However, this particular situation overcomes them and they are invaded by negative thoughts. They feel unable to control their arousal levels, and are therefore unable to sleep with the noise.
Level 2	Despite normally being able to sleep before competitions and having worked on relaxation and arousal control, in these circumstances they find it difficult to sleep. These athletes face the situation in a positive manner, appreciating that the most important thing to help them sleep is to stay relaxed. The noises will surely disappear (they won't last all night).
Level 3	Their *mental peak performance* training allows them to sleep in any situation . . . These athletes have the ability to sleep with the light on, in a hard bed, with a companion who snores, etc. They have the skills to block out any surrounding sounds and, although they may wake at some point, are quickly able to fall back to sleep.

Source: Dosil, J. (2004). *Psicologia de la actividad física y del deporte*. Madrid: McGraw-Hill.

not have received any form of psychological training, or had any contact with a psychologist. Level 1 athletes will have solved some problems related to their sporting activities through attending a sport psychologist. At level 2, athletes will have carried out a mental training programme and acquired the basic psychological strategies to confront training and competition. Finally, level 3 embodies those sportspeople who have assimilated the psychological strategies and adapt them to any training or competition situation, strengthening their performance. In a situation such as that described in Table 1.2, training at level 3 would be based on progressive work with athletes: having evaluated their ability to get to sleep and studied their habits and routines, they would move to the strategy learning phase to be taught thought control and relaxation (e.g. through visualization). Once they have mastered this, they would begin applying these techniques in varying situations, gradually increasing with difficulty (e.g. (1) sleeping with a light on outside the bedroom, (2) sleeping with the bedside lamp switched on, (3) sleeping with the bedroom light on . . .).

The psychological "level" athletes can reach will vary according to the psychological preparation they receive. Nevertheless, some will display similar psychological strengths to those who have been working with sport psychologists over time, without ever having had any form of guidance. This can be considered normal, similar to what occurs in the physical domain. Just as some athletes require more training than others to develop their physical skills, some need more preparation than others to develop their psychological abilities.

As suggested in the introduction, one of the characteristics common to all top sportspeople is their excellent physical condition. Although this is achieved through years of hard training, they are often blessed with certain natural abilities and a physique suited to their event. Likewise, before beginning any form of mental training, athletes will already possess certain psychological skills, usually dependent on key experiences in their life. The explanation for athletes who display psychological qualities to confront training and competition without ever having been to a psychologist is usually related to key experiences or sporting moments in which their capacity to confront situations was strengthened (e.g. a basketball player who learned to "forget" his family problems in his childhood by doing sport will perhaps have a greater ability to focus on the task). By contrast, other athletes will have had damaging experiences which have limited their psychological growth (through not having learned to confront situations). This first group of athletes are frequently described as "tough athletes", while the latter are often called "soft athletes", referring to their mental strength. The role of the sport psychologist is to strengthen the "toughness" of the tough-minded and "toughen up" the soft-minded. Between one extreme and another fall the "other athletes", and in these cases the sport psychologist can develop a *subjective scale of mental "toughness"*, measuring (e.g. 1–10) the psychological level (mental "toughness") of athletes and obtaining the preliminary information to commence work with them. This scale can be complemented with the athletes' and coaches' perceptions of mental "toughness".

Employing this method, it becomes necessary to follow a personalized plan of psychological training (in group as well as individual sports), with the aim of adapting as much as possible to the circumstances of each athlete. The first step to creating the outline of this psychological work is carrying out a detailed study of the sport, its context and its components.

The typical outline of mental training is established from a *Psychological Guidance and Intervention Programme* (PGIP) consisting of four stages (Table 1.3): evaluation, planning, psychological preparation of training sessions and psychological preparation of competitions (seen in more detail in Chapter 5).

Table 1.3 The typical stages of a *Psychological Guidance and Intervention Programme*

PGIP stages	Basic objectives
Evaluation	The collection of important information for problem solving or psychological training.
Planning	The detection and prevention of problems that may emerge throughout the season and the structuring of psychological work to be carried out.
Training preparation	Psychological guidance and treatment to increase performance and wellbeing in training.
Competition preparation	Optimizing performance in competitions.

Applied sports psychology training is required to work at any of these three levels—an area generally neglected in the academic field, which tends to focus more on theory and research. This may be partly explained by a lack of sport psychologists working full time in the applied field, the majority having other jobs and dedicating only a proportion of their time to this area to complement their usual occupation (mostly university professionals). Therefore, there is a call to create training systems in the applied field. In the following section, two applied learning programmes based at assessment levels 1 and 2 as described in the previous section are presented. Once these have been mastered, the sport psychologist is more likely to go on to work at level 3.

APPLIED LEARNING PROGRAMMES

Applied learning programmes (ALPs) have been created with the objective of preparing future sport psychologists in the applied field. The need for this style of training programme becomes evident in the current climate, where specialized and experienced psychological treatment is a principal requirement of teams, clubs and athletes. The ALP models aim to incorporate the psychology figure into the "professional world" of sport through providing suitable training for this setting. Experience in developing these programmes shows that participants are prepared to commence working with guarantees in the applied sports field in less time than with any other form of training. The versions being followed for field and clinical training are detailed below (Dosil, 2004).

The Field Applied Learning Programme (Field ALP)

The Field ALP was designed in the hope of increasing the flagging supply of sports psychologists dedicated to the applied area and to compensate for the impossibility of conducting work experience (learning through observation) within the sports industry itself. This programme speeds up the learning process, combining the training and professional stages, and assists the incorporation of the sport psychology figure in the physical activity and sport environment. The programme is backed by a specialist figure and a group of collaborators (trainee sport psychologists) who supervise and guarantee the work undertaken (Figure 1.1).

The trainee sport psychologist maintains a direct relationship with the team's technical staff or those responsible for the athlete's preparation, and is well integrated within the unit

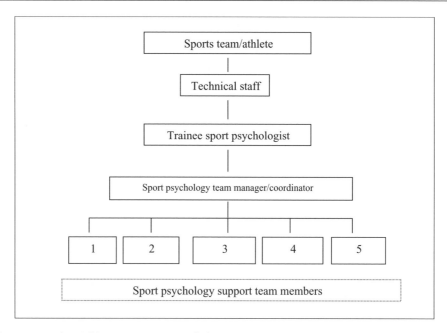

Figure 1.1   The Field ALP organizational chart

or acts as a member who independently guides the athlete. The trainee support psychologists form the link between the team/athlete and the sport psychology support unit. The
director/coordinator (the sport psychology expert) performs the function of trainee sport
psychologist evaluator, organizing meetings with the team members and directly supervis-
ing activity. The support team is formed by three to five members, who in turn usually work
with other clubs/athletes. Regular meetings are held, directed towards sharing experiences,
evaluating the development of the work conducted and discussing future forms of intervention. The organization of these meetings allows everyone to participate and exchange
information/knowledge.

The work model used by support team members (the trainee sports psychologists) involves
several steps:

Step 1: The process begins when the sport psychology unit receives a request from a club,
athlete or team. The director/coordinator, together with the sport psychologist assigned to the case, designs an action plan and collects relevant information (either in
the field or by email, fax, mail or telephone). There are usually two marked planning
stages: evaluation and intervention (see Chapter 5). The team director/coordinator
sets out the objectives of the initial field sessions (evaluation stage). There will be
more or less participants in the Field ALP according to the demand for sport psychologists. Likewise, the support team will vary in size depending on the training
requirements and the existing possibilities. In this sense, as many combinations
as desired can be established: two groups of three trainee sport psychologists, one
group of two psychologists working with teams and a student working without a
team, etc. The aim is for sufficient learning to be acquired at Step 3.

Step 2: Each trainee sport psychologist goes into the field to work with the team or athlete who has requested the services of the sport psychology unit, gathering the necessary information to perform suitable interventions (following the planning established by the director): carrying out video sessions, specific treatments, player assessments, interviews with coaches, and game observation. During this period the trainee sport psychologist counts on the support of the director/coordinator who guides them according to the various requirements as and when they emerge.

Step 3: A meeting is held between the trainee sport psychologists working with the various teams/clubs and the director/coordinator (these psychologists form the support team). A presentation is given on the field work conducted, in order to evaluate the development of the interventions and set out action plans for the future. This situation brings security to the psychologists, who are supported by a group of colleagues, assisting them resolve doubts and offering new ideas. Moreover, by participating in this activity all the support team members contribute to enriching each other's experiences.

Step 4: Preparation of individual sessions. Each trainee sport psychologist structures the information obtained from the meeting and transfers it to their specific environment: creating self-reports, preparing new materials, tables, etc. Likewise, depending on how the meeting with the support team has gone, the director/coordinator may choose to hold assessment interviews prior to them going back into the field.

Step 5: Competition interventions. The trainee sport psychologist follows the procedure established in steps 3 and 4. Once the process has been completed, they return to step 3 and hold a new meeting with the support team, and so forth.

The meetings described in Step 3 form the base on which the Field ALP supports itself, offering participants an individual/group work system which strengthens their interventions and enhances the learning process. The structure of these reunions varies according to the number of trainee sport psychologists working in the sports field. However, the most frequently used model is a round of presentations, given by each team member:

(1) Brief presentations of each case, limited in time (around ten minutes).
(2) The support team members ask questions about any aspects not made clear in the presentation (around five minutes).
(3) The presenter responds to these questions and explains any doubts/problems which arose during their work experience (around five minutes).
(4) Comments from group members regarding any doubts as well as any aspect they consider beneficial to the future activities of the *trainee sport psychologists* (around 10 minutes). Once this process is complete, the agreed intervention is begun . . .

The value of these sessions goes beyond the specific field of sport psychology. Obviously, members of the Field ALP see and participate in various cases at the same time, providing a unique learning opportunity and an extraordinary wealth of knowledge to confront the professional environment with confidence. However, the following non-psychology related improvements were noted by participants in these group sessions:

• Improved capacity to summarize, through having to present the fundamental aspects of interventions in a limited space of time (on occasions, a large quantity of information in little time).

- Advanced capacity to structure information, highlighting the main ideas and stressing the really important problems in an orderly manner.
- Learning to listen, accept criticism, share experiences, respect the opinions of others and pay attention when it is another person's turn to speak.
- Learning to appreciate the work of others and that of the actual trainee sport psychologist.
- Increased ability to speak fluently in public.
- Learning to be critical with oneself, providing security and confidence in the work carried out.
- Promoting creativity in presentations and sports interventions.
- Increased group cohesion, consolidating a professional support relationship.
- Reduced "maturity" time to becoming a sport psychologist.
- An "escape valve" on occasions when there is a certain lack of understanding in the sports environment and the trainee sport psychologist requires empathy from other professionals who understand their work.
- Etc.

Sessions may be lengthened or shortened depending on the difficulty of the case, the problems which arise with the team or athlete, the experience of the trainee sport psychologist, and the degree of dedication to their club, etc. Likewise, the director/coordinator will be required to spend more or less time with each case/group according to the capability shown by its members.

Meetings are usually arranged once a month, although their frequency will depend on the number of trainee sport psychologists and the number of days they dedicate to their case (e.g. if three people work every day with a club, then fortnightly meetings are recommended).

The Clinical Applied Learning Programme (Clinical ALP)

The Clinical ALP trains sport psychologists in the traditional treatment environment. Since Martens' article ('About smocks and jocks') was published in 1979, highlighting the need to focus more on the applied setting, many authors have defended field intervention, overlooking the fact that clinical intervention continues to play an important role in sport, with some treatments becoming more effective when conducted in this setting. It has not only educated many athletes in the possibilities of sport psychology, but has also allowed an important number of specialists in this area to maintain their profession alongside other clinical cases when the demand from athletes is low. Moreover, clinical training is important to gain the necessary experience to exercise the functions of a sport psychologist with guarantees (Hays & Smith, 2002). The Clinical ALP proposes a learning system which assists the progressive incorporation of a recently qualified sport psychologist. It is structured in three stages.

Stage 1: Experience with Fictitious Cases (Role Playing)

The objective of this first stage is to gain experience with fictitious cases. The aim here is for the student to learn to confront the clinical consultation situation. With this goal in mind, a form of intervention similar to that of a clinical setting is created through role playing. One student acts as the sport psychologist and another as the athlete, coach, manager . . . ensuring the situation is as realistic as possible. Depending on the available resources, various learning methods may be employed; some of the most common being:

(a) Video recordings: the intervention is recorded on video and once the session is over, the recording is shown and commented upon.
(b) Presentation/debate in reduced groups: in the same room as the intervention was carried out in, or behind a two-way mirror, a group of observers (four or five) record the different moments of the treatment. At the end or at regular intervals, the therapist and students comment on how the intervention is being conducted, highlighting the important elements to consider (the athlete's entrance in the office, their opening words, the initial interview, their reason for attending, etc.).

Stage 2: Experience with Real Cases

Learning at this stage depends on the experience of the psychology specialist and their form of working. Therefore, the style and direction of the therapy (behavioral, cognitive, cognitive-behavioral, systematic, psychoanalytical, etc.) plays a crucial role in a student's learning process (trainee sport psychologist).

The process followed at this stage of the Clinical ALP allows students to gradually acquire a more significant role in sessions. From an observer, they become a co-therapist and later, a therapist. The flexibility of this experience permits the process to be lengthened or shortened according to a student's level (qualifications, previous experience, personal characteristics, etc.). Likewise, it is important to highlight that the role of the therapist's companion (trainee sport psychologist) should be made clear to athletes (the patients) from the beginning of a session. In some cases, according to the criteria of sport psychology specialists, trainee sport psychologists should leave the sessions (e.g. if an athlete becomes anxious through the student's presence), or not participate at all (e.g. if an athlete has an intimate problem they do not wish to share with anyone but their therapist). Below, the three substages of this phase are described, each with their corresponding sessions:

(a) Substage 1: Student observer–co-therapist:
    In this substage, the aim is for students to gradually take a more active part in athlete assessments and interventions. Nevertheless, it should be made clear from the beginning that the role of therapist will be occupied at all times by the sport psychology specialist (teacher).
    (i) Session 1: Student observer
        In the first session, the student acts as an observer and intervenes at some points if they feel capable of doing so and always with the prior agreement of the therapist (this depends on the degree of skill shown at level 1). If the student considers themself sufficiently qualified to participate, it is advisable for them to agree on the most propitious moment to do so, assisting the athlete (patient) appreciate a coordination between the psychologists and not interference on behalf of the student (which may be interpreted as the therapist's lack of authority).
    (ii) Session 2: Student observer–co-therapist
        This second session (in accordance with the results of the first session) gives the students certain prominence, participating at previously established moments or when the therapist specifies that they may do so. The athlete should perceive the

student as having passed the observer stage and achieved participant status. For example, at the end of a session they may be asked to present the conclusions.

(iii) Session 3: Student co-therapist
The student now begins to exercise the role of co-therapist, with the teacher or "role model" maintaining the position of therapist. In this situation, although it is the teacher who directs the session, the student may participate in certain moments, subject to prior agreement. This participation should not imply a change of focus; rather reinforce the direction of the session.

(b) Substage 2: Student therapist under supervision
Only in exceptional cases may the role of co-therapist become that of therapist. The athlete will consider the student as "their psychologist" from the beginning of the session.

(iv) Session 4: Student therapist–co-therapist
The student now occupies the role of therapist, directing the sessions with the teacher/model as co-therapist. The teacher may intervene at any point, but tries to ensure it is the student who leads the session from the beginning. They will only lose the position of therapist if, after some time, the teacher considers the session is not being directed correctly. On all accounts, this change of roles should be subtle, avoiding any form of negative influence on the session.

(v) Session 5: Student therapist
In the final stage, the student faces the session alone, occupying the role of therapist, planning the session according to objectives previously established and discussed with the teacher.

Stage 3: Supervision of Cases

The supervision of clinical cases is conducted with a similar outline to that of the Field ALP. A student–teacher meeting or a student–work group meeting (similar to the support groups in the Field ALP) is the most commonly used procedure. In the first instance, students present their development to the teacher and explain their future strategies. In the latter, following a brief presentation of the case and explaining how intervention is being carried out, time is given for comments and suggestions from the work group; the teacher then ends the session with their closing comments.

A summary of the Clinical ALP work model is represented in Figure 1.2. As with the Field ALP, a series of implicit learning processes are described:

- Therapeutic skills acquired in a short period of time.
- Increased motivation through active participation in the entire process.
- Self-confidence gained through a progressive learning process.

CONCLUDING REMARKS: FUTURE PROSPECTS

The future of applied sport psychology will depend fundamentally on the specific training received in different sports and the marketing employed to promote the services available.

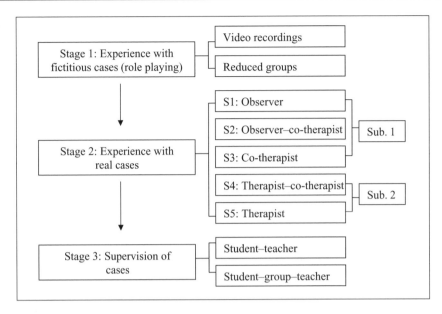

Figure 1.2 The Clinical ALP work model

Although the training possibilities have increased in recent years (Sachs, Burke & Schrader, 2001), there remain few institutions where applied sport psychology can be studied. Opportunities are restricted to cases where higher education professionals voluntarily choose to collaborate with teams and athletes. In contrast, sport demands professionals with a wealth of knowledge in the applied sport psychology of their discipline; that is to say, authentic specialists in their sport. Over time, sport psychologists have not known how to make their way into the applied field, failing to use suitable strategies to adapt to the reality of each sport. More often than not, it is ignorance rather than a lack of training which prevents sport psychologists from accessing the professional world. The most suitable way to bring about change is through training psychologists in the very sport setting they wish to work in, which is the aim of the previously described training programmes (in Chapter 4, some resources which may be used to complement this training are described).

Marketing is considered the second key element for launching sport psychologists into the applied field. Another study (Dosil, 2003) suggests that marketing has been one of the most neglected resources throughout the history of sport psychology, proving detrimental to the incorporation of the psychological figure in teams and clubs. In many cases, the participation of psychologists in the sports world has been held back by ignorance of the work they can perform. This has been true for a long time and the solution may lie in the suitable use of marketing. On this matter, it should be considered that the keys to effective marketing are the following factors: having a good product and knowing how to sell it.

Regarding "having" a good product, sport psychology training is gradually increasing in quality and quantity, allowing guaranteed professional performance. Nevertheless, certain "insecurity" can still be seen in the process of incorporating sport psychologists into teams and clubs. Both potential clients as well as the "pioneering psychologists" err on the side of caution, demanding only experienced psychologists, or insisting they work under supervision. On many occasions, this has been an obstacle for recently qualified psychologists who fail to comply with the difficult requirement of having professional experience. Likewise, the required criteria to obtain qualifications are not unified between countries, creating an international debate over who has the right to be called a sport psychologist, and who can practice as such (see Anshel, 1992, 1993; Silva, 2001; Singer & Burke, 2002; Zaichkowsky & Perna, 1992; Zizzi, Zaichkowsky & Perna, 2002).

Once a good "product" is achieved (adequately trained sport psychologists), the "only" thing left to do is take that next step, perhaps the most problematic: "selling" the product to teams, federations, clubs, gyms, and athletes, etc. (the professional "market"). Another study offers (Dosil, 2003) basic indications of how to achieve this mission, stating that the first stage is to carry out a suitable market survey, appreciating that every situation is unique and requires a different form of intervention strategy. For example, in institutions where no knowledge exists of sport psychology, giving a simple and brief presentation is recommended, explaining how it can be of benefit to them (today many institutions have a web page, giving information to help prepare a presentation beforehand). The second stage involves studying the potential of each sport psychologist and clarifying what they can offer to an institution (depending on economic resources). At the third stage, having obtained a realistic vision of the market and studied the product on offer, meetings with the various institutions should be set up to explain what the sport psychology service involves. More often than not, if the organization is interested in the presentation and is able to do so, they will arrive at some form of agreement to incorporate some if not all of the services offered.

Along these lines, it is recommended to come to collective agreements with sports federations, given that they represent all the clubs and teams in each sport. From there on, meeting with teams and clubs in the nearest areas will allow them to gradually increase the scope of intervention.

In conclusion, throughout the entire process, it is the sport psychologist who provides the services. Without their input it would be impossible to meet the psychological needs of today's athletes. Perhaps one of the errors committed in the past was waiting for these services to be demanded when the sports world was unaware they existed.

REFERENCES

Andersen, M.A. (ed.) (2002). *Doing Sport Psychology.* Champaign, IL.: Human Kinetics.
Anshel, M.H. (1992). The case against the certification of sport psychologist: in search of the phantom expert. *The Sport Psychologist, 6*, 256–286.
Anshel, M.H. (1993). Against the certification of sport psychology consultants: a response to Zaichkowsky and Perna. *The Sport Psychologist, 7*, 344–353.
Baillie, P.G.F. & Ogilvie, B.C. (2002). Working with elite athletes. In J.L. Van Raalte & B.W. Brewer (eds), *Exploring Sport and Exercise Psychology* (2nd edn; pp. 395–416). Washington, DC: American Psychological Association.
Dosil, J. (ed.) (2002). *El psicólogo del deporte: asesoramiento e intervención.* Madrid: Síntesis.
Dosil, J. (2003). 20 claves para afrontar el futuro de la Psicología de la Actividad Física y del Deporte en España. *Revista de Psicología General y Aplicada, 56*, 519–529.
Dosil, J. (2004). *Psicología de la actividad física y del deporte.* Madrid: McGraw-Hill.
Dosil, J. & García-Prieto, D. (2004). Asesoramiento on-line en psicología del deporte. *Cuadernos de Psicología del Deporte, 4*, 19–28.
Hays, K.F. & Smith, R.J. (2002). Incorporating sport and exercise psychology into clinical practice. In J.L. Van Raalte & B.W. Brewer (eds), *Exploring Sport and Exercise Psychology* (2nd edn; pp. 479–502). Washington, DC: American Psychological Association.

Martens, R. (1979). About smocks and jocks. *Journal of Sport Psychology, 1*, 94–99.

Sachs, M.L., Burke, K.L. & Schrader, D. (2001). *Directory of Graduate Programs in Applied Sport Psychology.* Morgantown, WV: FIT.

Silva, J.M. (2001). Current trends and future directions on sport psychology. In R. Singer, H.A. Hausenblas & C.M. Janelle (eds.), *Handbook of Sport Psychology.* New York: John Wiley & Sons.

Singer, R.N. & Burke, K. (2002). Sport and exercise psychology: a positive force in the new Millennium. In J.L. Van Raalte & B.W. Brewer (eds), *Exploring Sport and Exercise Psychology* (2nd edn; pp. 525–540). Washington, DC: American Psychological Association.

Tenenbaum, G. (ed.) (2001). *The Practice of Sport Psychology.* Morgantown, WV: FIT.

Weinberg, R.S. & Williams, J.M. (2001). Integrating and implementing a psychological skills training program. In J.M. Williams (ed.), *Applied Sport Psychology: Personal Growth to Peak Performance* (4th edn; pp. 284–311). Mountain View, CA: Mayfield.

Zaichkowsky, L.D. & Perna, F.M. (1992). Certification of consultants in sport psychology: a rebuttal to Anshel. *The Sport Psychologist, 6*, 287–296.

Zizzi, S.J. & Perna, F.M. (2002). Integrating web pages and e-mail into sport psychology consultations. *The Sport Psychologist, 16*, 416–431.

Zizzi, S., Zaichkowsky, L.D. & Perna, F.M. (2002). Certification in sport and exercise psychology. In J.L. Van Raalte & B.W. Brewer (eds), *Exploring Sport and Exercise Psychology* (2nd edn; pp. 459–478). Washington, DC: American Psychological Association.

CHAPTER 2

Enhancing Coach–Athlete Relationships: Cognitive-Behavioral Principles and Procedures

Frank L. Smoll and Ronald E. Smith
University of Washington, USA

INTRODUCTION

Sport is a complex psychosocial system in which many topics of interest to behavioral scientists can be studied. The athletic environment is an inviting research setting for several reasons. Specifically, it is a naturalistic setting in which people occupying a variety of roles (e.g. athletes, coaches, parents, officials, administrators) are often strongly engaged, and sport-related psychological processes and variables can be operationalized with high ecological validity. Beyond that, the sport environment is an important milieu for psychosocial development and adaptation. An increasing number of sport psychologists have thus focused on the impact of competition on athletes' personal development (see Brustad, Babkes & Smith, 2001; Malina & Clark, 2003; Smoll & Smith, 2002a; Weiss, 2004). Their research consistently has shown that the type of leadership provided by coaches is a major determinant of the quality of sport participation. This is understandable, for coaches occupy a central and influential leadership role within the athletic environment, and their influence often extends beyond the sport domain into other areas of athletes' lives.

As research has accumulated on coach–athlete interactions, it has become clear that coaches can have either a positive or a negative impact on the lives of athletes at all levels of competition. A positive coach–athlete relationship can enhance athletes' psychological and social well-being, foster the development of self-efficacy, positive values and coping skills, and promote continued involvement in healthy physical activity. In contrast, negative coach–athlete relationships create distress, foster the development of dysfunctional attitudes toward achievement and competition, create needless interpersonal stress, and contribute to sport competition attrition (e.g. Côté, 2002; Ewing, Seefeldt & Brown, 1997; Martens, 1997; Smith & Smoll, 2002). Given the influential role that coaches play in athletes'

The Sport Psychologist's Handbook: A Guide for Sport-Specific Performance Enhancement.
Edited by Joaquín Dosil. © 2006 John Wiley & Sons, Ltd.

psychosocial development and well-being, sport psychologists can have a notable positive impact by researching the consequences of particular coaching styles and behaviors on athletes who play for them. Such information, applied in conjunction with behavior change methods of proven efficacy, can result in training programs that enhance the instructional and interpersonal competencies of coaches, thereby contributing to a more positive athletic environment that promotes skill development and salutary psychosocial outcomes. The past two decades have seen the development and evaluation of such programs.

This chapter begins with an overview of coach training programs that contain sport psychology components. We then describe the theoretical and empirical foundation for an intervention designed to assist coaches in creating a healthy psychological environment for athletes. Next, we present a series of scientifically validated behavioral guidelines for enhancing coach–athlete relationships. The chapter concludes with a discussion of achievement goal theory and its implications for coach–athlete interactions. Although the focus throughout is on young athletes, the basic principles promoted by coach training programs apply not only at the youth sport level, but also at higher competitive levels, including professional sports. In fact, the cognitive-behavioral principles presented below have been applied in professional baseball to train managers and coaches in how to create a more positive learning and performance environment for their athletes (Smith & Johnson, 1990).

NATIONAL COACH TRAINING PROGRAMS

National coaching associations of many countries have developed educational programs with specific teaching modules designed to enhance the competencies of coaches (cf. Australia [Oldenhove, 1996]; Canada [Wankel & Mummery, 1996]; Finland [Laakso, Telama & Yang, 1996]; Japan [Yamaguchi, 1996]; Portugal [Goncalves, 1996]; Scotland [Hendry & Love, 1996]; and the Netherlands [Buisman & Lucassen, 1996]). In reviewing the structure and content of programs offered around the world, Campbell (1993) observed that "a national coach education strategy is largely determined by the culture, politics, and traditions of the nation concerned. As a result, there is no single system that can be considered an ideal model for others to copy" (p. 62). There are, however, certain commonalities among the programs that can be identified. Specifically, most programs provide training centered around two key areas: (a) sport-specific knowledge related to skills, techniques and strategies, and (b) performance-related knowledge in sport sciences, such as biomechanics, exercise physiology, growth and development, nutrition, sports medicine and sport psychology. Information pertaining to sport pedagogy, program planning and risk management is commonly included as well. Many countries operate four- or five-level certification programs, the lower levels delivered outside of academia and the top levels presented as a university-level course. Additionally, certification courses typically place emphasis on practical coaching experience, the amount required to move to a higher level varying considerably from one country to another.

As one might expect, the balance of the various training program components and the relative importance placed on each reflects the particular needs of the sport and the level at which the coach functions. Whatever their focus, however, it is important to know what effects training programs have on coaches and athletes and how well they achieve their objectives. Unfortunately, relatively little formal evaluative research has been done on national programs, causing some to question their effectiveness (e.g. Douge & Hastie, 1993;

Gilbert & Trudel, 1999; Woodman, 1993). Given that coach training has become a large-scale enterprise, it is surprising that national certification programs have not received more empirical attention. Perhaps understandably, developers of such programs have focused primarily on development and dissemination, rather than evaluation. In any event, the scant evaluation research that has been conducted on national coach training programs is reviewed elsewhere (see Smith & Smoll, 2005).

Unlike other countries, the United States does not have a national coaching association that provides a unified system for training and certification of coaches. Rather, four currently available training programs include curricular components designed to influence the manner in which coaches interact with athletes—the American Coaching Effectiveness Program (ACEP; American Sport Education Program, 2003), Coach Effectiveness Training (CET; Smoll & Smith, in press), the National Youth Sports Coaches Association (NYSCA; National Alliance for Youth Sports, 2003), and the Program for Athletic Coaches' Education (PACE; Seefeldt, Clark & Brown, 2001). ACEP, NYSCA and PACE are relatively lengthy (8- to 16-hour) programs. They offer broad-spectrum workshops that cover an array of topics, including those subsumed under the rubric of sport psychology (e.g. goal setting, motivation, stress management). Critical analysis reveals that these three programs share two shortcomings. First, they lack a core theoretical and/or empirical foundation upon which their sport psychology components are based. Rather, the eclectic nature of their content is generally derived by borrowing principles from educational and psychological literature. Second, there is an absence of systematic research to validate the efficacy of these programs. Consequently, very little is known about their impact on coaches or the athletes who play for them. In essence, ACEP, NYSCA, and PACE "have provided coaching workshops to thousands of individuals involved in community-based and school-sponsored sports, but evaluation research is essential to determine the effectiveness of these training programs on increasing sport science knowledge and applications" (Weiss & Hayashi, 1996, p. 53).

The Positive Coaching Alliance (2003), established in 1998, is a recent entry into the psychologically oriented coach-intervention domain. The Positive Coaching program appears promising but, to this point, it has not been evaluated in terms of its ability to change coaching behaviors or affect athletes' sport outcomes. Unfortunately, of the four programs cited above, CET is the only one that has been subjected to systematic evaluation to determine its influence on coaches' behaviors and the effects of such behaviors on athletes' psychosocial development (Brown & Butterfield, 1992). We now present CET as an illustration of the data-based development and evaluation of a psychosocial coach intervention program.

THEORETICAL AND EMPIRICAL FOUNDATION OF CET

A crucial first step in developing a training program is to determine *what* is to be presented. In this regard, our work was guided by a fundamental assumption that a training program should be based on scientific evidence rather than on intuition or what we "know" on the basis of informal observation. An empirical foundation for coaching guidelines not only enhances the validity and potential value of the program, but it also increases its credibility in the eyes of consumers. CET is based on nearly 25 years of basic and applied research in the youth sport environment. The empirical work has focused on coach–athlete relationships and the development and assessment of an intervention designed to assist coaches in creating a sport environment that fosters athletes' personal, social and athletic development.

Theoretical Underpinnings

Our research program has focused on coaching behaviors, their determinants and their effects on athletes. The work has been guided by a social-cognitive framework that emphasizes interactions between situational and individual difference factors that relate to important cognitive-affective processes (Bandura, 1986, 1997; Mischel, 1973; Mischel & Shoda, 1995). This cognitive-behavioral framework has strongly influenced the choice of constructs, measurement approaches, and intervention techniques.

Recognition of the potential impact of coaches on athletes' psychological welfare prompted us to develop a cognitive-mediational model of coach–athlete interactions (Smoll, Smith, Curtis & Hunt, 1978). The basic elements of the model are represented as follows:

Coach behaviors → Athletes' perception and recall → Athletes' evaluative reactions

This model stipulates that the ultimate effects of coaching behaviors are mediated by the meaning that athletes attribute to them. In other words, what athletes remember about their coaches' behaviors and how they interpret these actions affects the way that athletes evaluate their sport experiences. Furthermore, a complex of cognitive and affective processes are involved at this mediational level. The athletes' perceptions and reactions are likely to be affected not only by the coaches' behaviors, but also by other factors, such as the athlete's age, what they expect of coaches (normative beliefs and expectations), and certain personality variables, such as self-esteem and anxiety. In recognition of this, the basic three-element model has been expanded to reflect these factors (Smoll & Smith, 1989). The expanded model specifies a number of situational factors as well as coach and athlete characteristics that could influence coach behaviors and the perceptions and reactions of athletes to them. Using this model as a starting point, we have sought to determine how observed coaching behaviors, athletes' perception and recall of the coaches' behaviors, and athlete attitudes are related to one another. We have also explored the manner in which athlete and coach characteristics might serve to affect these relations. An overview of our basic and applied research is presented below. A more detailed account appears elsewhere (Smoll & Smith, 2002b).

Empirical Underpinnings

Several questions served as an impetus for our preliminary work. For example, what do coaches do, and how frequently do they engage in such behaviors as encouragement, punishment, instruction and organization? What are the psychological dimensions that underlie such behaviors? And, finally, how are observable coaching behaviors related to athletes' reactions to their organized sport experiences? Answers to such questions not only help describe the behavioral ecology of one aspect of the youth sport setting, but they also provide an empirical basis for the development of psychologically oriented intervention programs. In accordance with our model, we have sought to determine how observed coaching behaviors, athletes' perception and recall of the coaches' behaviors, and athlete attitudes are interrelated. We have also explored the manner in which athlete and coach individual difference variables might serve as moderator variables and influence the basic behavior–attitude relations.

The Coaching Behavior Assessment System (CBAS; Smith, Smoll & Hunt, 1977) was developed to permit the direct observation and coding of coaches' actions during practices and games. Following development of the CBAS, field studies were conducted to assess relations between coaching behaviors and athletes' reactions to their sport experiences (Curtis, Smith & Smoll, 1979; Smith & Smoll, 1990; Smith, Smoll & Curtis, 1978; Smith, Zane, Smoll & Coppel, 1983; Smoll et al., 1978). We found that the typical baseball or basketball coach engages in more than 200 coded actions during an average game. By collecting observational data on four or five occasions, we were thus able to generate behavioral profiles of up to several thousand responses for each coach over the course of a season. In large-scale observational studies, we coded more than 85,000 behaviors of some 80 male baseball and basketball coaches, then interviewed and administered questionnaires to nearly 1,000 of their athletes after the season to measure their recall of their coaches' behaviors and their evaluative reactions to the coach, their sport experience and themselves (e.g. Curtis et al., 1979; Smith et al., 1983).

At the level of overt behavior, three independent behavioral dimensions were identified through factor analysis—supportiveness (comprised of reinforcement and mistake-contingent encouragement), instructiveness (general technical instruction and mistake-contingent technical instruction versus general communication and general encouragement), and punitiveness (punishment and punitive technical instruction versus organizational behaviors). Relations between coaches' scores on these behavioral dimensions and player measures provided clear evidence for the crucial role of the coach. The most positive outcomes occurred when children played for coaches who were high on the supportiveness and instructiveness dimensions—coaches who engaged in high levels of reinforcement (for both desirable performance and effort) and who responded to mistakes with encouragement and technical instruction. Not only did the children who had such coaches like their coaches more and have more fun, but they also liked their teammates more. Although only about 3 per cent of the coded behaviors were punitive and critical in nature, they correlated more strongly (and negatively) than any other behavior with children's attitudes.

"Winning isn't everything. It's the only thing." Or is it? In the case of attitudes toward the coach, is it indeed true that everyone loves a winner? A notable finding was that the teams' won–lost records were essentially unrelated to how well the athletes liked the coach and how much they wanted to play for the coach in the future. On the other hand, athletes on winning teams felt that their parents liked the coach more and that the coach liked them more than did youngsters on losing teams. Apparently, winning made little difference to the children, but they surmised that it was important to the adults. It is worth noting, however, that winning assumed greater importance beyond age 12, although it continued to be a less important attitudinal determinant than coach behaviors.

Another important issue concerned the degree of accuracy with which coaches perceive their own behaviors. Correlations between CBAS observed behaviors and coaches' ratings of how frequently they performed the behaviors were generally low and nonsignificant. The only actions on their self-report measure that correlated significantly (around .50) with the observational measures were the punitive behaviors. Overall we found that children's ratings on the same CBAS Perceived Behaviors Scale correlated much more highly with CBAS measures than did the coaches' own reports. It thus appears that coaches were, for the most part, blissfully unaware of how they behaved and that athletes were more accurate perceivers of actual coach behaviors. Because behavior change requires awareness of how one is currently behaving, this finding clearly indicated the need to increase coaches' self-awareness when developing an intervention program.

Assessing the Psychosocial Outcomes of CET

Sweeping conclusions are often drawn about the efficacy of intervention programs in the absence of anything approximating acceptable scientific evidence. We therefore felt it was important not only to develop an empirical foundation for a coach training program, but also to measure its effects on coaches and the athletes who play for them. Five important outcome questions have been the focus of CET program evaluation studies. First, does the CET program affect the behaviors of trained coaches in a manner consistent with the behavioral guidelines? Second, how does it affect athletes' reactions to their sport experience? Third, does exposure to a positive interpersonal environment created by trained coaches result in an increase in general self-esteem, particularly among low self-esteem children? Fourth, does CET training help reduce athletes' performance anxiety? And, finally, do positive changes in the first four outcomes increase the likelihood that athletes will choose to return to the sport program?

All five of these desirable outcomes have been demonstrated in a series of outcome studies in which experimental groups of youth coaches exposed to the CET program were compared with untrained or attention-placebo control groups. Coaches exposed to CET differed from controls in observed (CBAS) and athlete-perceived behaviors in a manner consistent with the behavioral guidelines. Trained coaches were more reinforcing, more encouraging, gave more technical instruction, and were less punitive and controlling than were control group coaches. In turn, the athletes who played for the trained coaches indicated that they enjoyed their experience more and liked their coach and teammates more. Such children also demonstrated significant increases in general self-esteem and significant decreases in performance anxiety over the course of the season (Smith, Smoll & Curtis, 1979; Smith, Smoll & Barnett, 1995; Smoll, Smith, Barnett & Everett, 1993). We also found that athletes who are low in self-esteem are the ones who react most positively to trained coaches, indicating that the program has a salutary impact on the children who are most in need of a positive sport experience. Finally, a study of attrition showed a dropout rate of 26 per cent among athletes who played for control group coaches, a figure that is quite consistent with previous reports of 30 to 40 per cent annual attrition rates in youth sport programs (Gould, 1987). In contrast, only 5 per cent of the children who had played for CET-trained coaches failed to return to the program the next season (Barnett, Smoll & Smith, 1992). These positive psychosocial outcomes are all the more noteworthy in light of the fact that experimental and control groups have not differed in average won–lost percentages in any of the studies. We attribute the consistently positive results derived from our relatively brief intervention to the fact that our basic research helped to identify a set of core principles that are relatively easy for coaches to learn and that have a strong impact on young athletes.

COACHING PRINCIPLES AND PROCEDURES

Data from our basic research indicated clear relations between coaching behaviors and the reactions of youngsters to their athletic experience. These relations provided a foundation for developing a set of behavioral guidelines (i.e. coaching *dos* and *don'ts*) that constitute the core of the CET program (Smith & Smoll, 2002). In a CET workshop, which lasts approximately 2.5 hours, coaching principles are presented verbally with the aid of PowerPoint slides and cartoons illustrating important points. Additionally, coaches are given a printed manual (Smoll & Smith, 2005), which supplements the guidelines with concrete suggestions for communicating effectively with athletes, gaining their respect and relating effectively to their parents. The importance of sensitivity and being responsive to individual differences among athletes is also stressed. The manual eliminates the need for coaches to take notes; it facilitates their understanding of the information; and it gives coaches a tangible resource to refer to in the future. In essence, five key principles are emphasized in CET, and behavioral guidelines are presented for implementing each principle. The core principles and coaching guidelines are summarized below.

1. *"Winning" is defined not in terms of won–lost records, but in terms of giving maximum effort and making improvement. The explicit and primary focus is on the objectives of having fun, deriving satisfaction from being on the team, learning sport skills and developing increased self-esteem.*

   The conventional notion of success in sports involves achieving a victorious outcome. But when winning games becomes the sole or primary goal, athletes can be deprived of important opportunities to develop their skills, enjoy participation and to grow as people. We have therefore developed a four-part philosophy of winning that is taught in CET (Smith & Smoll, 2002, pp. 16–18):

   - *Winning isn't everything, nor is it the only thing.* Athletes cannot get the most out of sports if they think that the only objective is to beat their opponents. Although winning is an important goal, it is *not* the most important objective.
   - *Failure is not the same thing as losing.* It is important that athletes do not view losing as a sign of failure or as a threat to their personal value.
   - *Success is not equivalent to winning.* Neither success nor failure need depend on the outcome of a contest or on a won–lost record. Winning and losing pertain to the outcome of a contest, whereas success and failure do not.
   - *Athletes should be taught that success is found in striving for victory (i.e. success is related to commitment and effort).* Athletes should be taught that they are never "losers" if they give maximum effort.

   This philosophy is designed to maximize athletes' enjoyment of sport and their chances of deriving the benefits of participation, partly as a result of reducing competitive anxiety (Smith, Smoll & Passer, 2002). Although seeking victory is encouraged, the ultimate importance of winning is reduced relative to other participation motives. Specifically, in recognition of the inverse relation between enjoyment and competitive anxiety, *fun* is highlighted as the paramount objective (Scanlan & Lewthwaite, 1984; Scanlan & Passer, 1978, 1979). The philosophy also promotes separation of the athlete's feelings of self-worth from performance and game outcomes, which serves to help overcome fear of failure.

2. *Coach–athlete interactions are based on a positive approach that emphasizes the use of positive reinforcement, encouragement and sound technical instruction that help create high levels of interpersonal attraction between coaches and athletes. Punitive behaviors are strongly discouraged.*

CET guidelines are based primarily on social influence techniques that involve principles of positive control rather than aversive control. Positive and aversive control underlie what we have labeled the *positive approach* and the *negative approach* to coaching (Smith & Smoll, 2002). The positive approach is designed to strengthen desired behaviors by motivating athletes to perform them and by reinforcing the athletes when they do. This "relationship style" complements the philosophy of winning presented above. Conversely, the negative approach involves attempts to eliminate unwanted behaviors through punishment and criticism. The motivating factor in this "command style" is fear.

- *Use of reinforcement after a behavior increases the likelihood that the behavior will occur in the future.* As noted in our second principle, the cornerstone of the positive approach is the skilled use of reinforcement to increase athletic motivation and to strengthen desired behaviors. Examples of positive reinforcement include both verbal and nonverbal forms of communication, such as a pat on the back, a smile, applause and a friendly nod. To derive maximum benefits from their "reinforcement power", we emphasize to coaches that reinforcement should not be restricted to the learning and performance of sport skills. Rather, it should also be liberally applied to strengthen desirable psychosocial behaviors (e.g. teamwork, leadership, sportsmanship). Coaches should look for desired behaviors and increase their future likelihood by reinforcing them.

  Skillful use of reinforcement involves having realistic expectations and consistently reinforcing achievement. In CET, coaches are instructed to gear their expectations to individual ability levels. For some athletes, merely running up and down the field or court without tripping is a significant accomplishment deserving of praise. For more advanced performers, expectations should be set at appropriately higher levels. The guideline concerning consistency of reinforcement is particularly true during the early phase of the learning process. When skills are being taught, continuous reinforcement (i.e. reinforcement after each desired response) should be given. More specifically, during the initial stages of learning, continuous reinforcement should be given for any sign of improvement or progress toward the ultimate objective. However, research has shown that once skills are well-learned, a partial reinforcement schedule is more effective in maintaining motivation and producing higher resistance to extinction. The selective administration of reinforcement thus requires thorough knowledge of sport skills teaching–learning progressions, sensitivity to individual differences in athletes' levels of abilities and learning rates, and use of good judgment in applying reinforcement.

  Perhaps the most important coaching guideline is to reinforce effort as much as results. This guideline has direct relevance to developing a healthy philosophy of winning and a reduction in performance anxiety. To put this philosophy into practice, coaches should tell athletes that their efforts are valued and appreciated, and support the verbalization with action (i.e. reinforcement). Simply stated, athletes' efforts should not be ignored or taken for granted. Coaches should keep in mind that athletes have complete control over how much effort they make, but they have only limited control over the outcome of their efforts. By looking for and reinforcing athletes' effort, coaches can thereby encourage athletes to continue or increase their output.

- *Use of encouragement helps athletes to develop a positive motivation to achieve.* The second supportive behavior that is emphasized in CET is encouragement, particularly that given in response to mistakes. Like positive reinforcement, encouragement helps to promote an enjoyable interpersonal climate. Coaches can generally assume that athletes are already motivated to develop their skills and play well. By appropriate use of encouragement, a coach can help to increase their natural enthusiasm. If, however, athletes are encouraged to strive for unrealistic standards of achievement, they may feel like failures when they do not reach the goals. Therefore, coaches should base encouragement on reasonable expectations. Again, emphasizing effort rather than outcome can help avoid problems.

- *High-quality technical instruction is essential for realization of athletic potential.* Athletes expect their coaches to help them satisfy their desire to become as skilled as possible. Coaches must therefore establish their teaching role as early as possible. In doing this, they should emphasize the fun and learning part of sport, and let their athletes know that a primary coaching goal is to help them develop their athletic potential. CET thus includes several guidelines pertaining to the appropriate use of technical instruction. For example, when giving instruction, we encourage coaches to emphasize the good things that will happen if athletes execute correctly rather than focusing on the negative things that will occur if they do not. This approach motivates athletes to make desirable things happen (i.e. to develop a positive achievement orientation) rather than building the fear of making mistakes.

    When giving instructions, coaches should be clear and concise. Some athletes may have a short attention span, while others may not be able to comprehend the technical aspects of performance in great detail. Coaches should therefore provide simple yet accurate teaching cues, using as little verbal explanation as possible. Moreover, they should demonstrate or model skills being taught. If coaches cannot perform the skill correctly, they can use accomplished athletes for demonstration purposes. A proper teaching sequence to follow includes (a) introducing a skill via demonstration, (b) providing an accurate, but brief verbal explanation, and (c) having the athlete actively practice the skill.

    In line with the positive approach, athletes' mistakes can be excellent opportunities to provide corrective instruction. Athletes know when they have made a poor play and often feel embarrassed about it. This is the time they are in most need of support from their coach. In fact, if an athlete knows how to correct a mistake, encouragement alone is sufficient. Telling athletes what they already know may be more irritating than helpful, and coaches should not overload athletes with unnecessary input. If a coach is not sure if an athlete knows how to correct a mistake, they should ask the athlete for verification (e.g. "What's the correct thing to do in that situation?").

    When it is appropriate to give corrective instruction after a mistake, we recommend that coaches always do so in an encouraging and positive way. Three keys to giving mistake-contingent technical instruction include knowing (a) *what* to do—the technical aspects of correcting performance, (b) *how* to do it—the teaching–learning approach, and (c) *when* to do it—timing. Most athletes respond best to immediate correction, and instruction is particularly meaningful at that time. However, some athletes respond much better to instruction if the coach waits for some time after the mistake when the athlete can respond in a more objective fashion.

    When correcting mistakes, a three-part teaching approach is recommended: (a) Start with a *compliment* ("Way to hustle. You really ran a good pattern!"). This is intended to reinforce a desirable behavior and create an open attitude on the part of the athlete. (b) Give the *future-oriented instruction* ("If you follow the ball all the way into your hands, you'll catch those just like a pro does."). Emphasize the desired future outcome rather than the negative one that just occurred. (c) End with another *positive statement* ("Hang in there. You're going to get even better if you work at it."). This "sandwich approach" (two positive communications wrapped around the instruction) is designed to make the athlete positively self-motivated to perform correctly rather than negatively motivated to avoid failure and disapproval.

It should also be noted that we discourage coaches from giving instruction in a sarcastic or degrading manner. Even if a coach does not intend the sarcasm to be harmful, some athletes do not understand the meaning of this type of communication. They may think the coach is amusing others at their expense, resulting in irritation or frustration or both.

- *Use of punishment suppresses/weakens behavior.* Coaching tactics oriented toward eliminating mistakes often involve punishing and criticizing athletes who make them. Punishment is the most damaging feature of the negative approach, and CET guidelines strongly discourage the use of aversive control. Punishment is not just yelling at athletes; it can be any form of disapproval, tone of voice, or action. Indeed, frequent use of verbal and nonverbal forms of punishment leads to resentment of the coach and is a factor contributing to decisions to drop out of sport programs. We therefore admonish coaches to avoid giving corrective instruction in a hostile, demeaning, or harsh way. Although a coach may have good intentions in giving negatively toned instruction, this kind of communication is more likely to increase frustration and create resentment than to improve performance.

  Does this mean coaches should avoid all criticism and punishment of their athletes? Not at all. Sometimes these behaviors are necessary for instructional or disciplinary purposes, but they should be used sparingly. When using punishment as a last resort, it should not be directed at the athlete. Rather, it should be clearly communicated that the coach dislikes the undesirable behavior, not the person.

  Although abusive coaches may enjoy success and may even be admired by some of their athletes, they run the risk of losing other athletes who could contribute to the team's success and who could profit personally from an athletic experience. Those who succeed through the use of aversive control usually do so because (a) they are also able to communicate caring for their athletes as people, so that the abuse is not "taken personally", (b) they have very talented athletes, and/or (c) they are such skilled teachers and strategists that these abilities overshadow their negative approach. In other words, such coaches win *in spite of*, not because of, the negative approach.

3. *Norms are established that emphasize athletes' mutual obligations to help and support one another so as to increase social support and attraction among teammates and thereby to enhance cohesion and commitment to the team.*

   One of the most important CET guidelines is for coaches to encourage athletes to be supportive of each other, and to reinforce them when they do so (e.g. "Way to go, Chris! That's the way good teammates support each other!"). Our third principle is based on the premise that mutual encouragement can become contagious and contribute to building team cohesion. This is most likely to occur when coaches (a) model supportive behaviors, and (b) reinforce athlete behaviors that promote team unity.

   We also instruct coaches in how to develop a "we're in this together" group norm. Coaches should stress that every member of the team is important and can contribute to success of the team. For example, coaches should emphasize that during a contest, all members of the team, even those on the bench, are part of the action and are expected to support one another. This norm can play an important role in building team cohesion and mutual support among teammates, particularly if the coach frequently reinforces relevant bench behaviors (e.g. "Way to stay in the game, guys. Be ready for when your time comes to go in."). Likewise, during practice, every member of the team, including the less skilled athletes, should receive attention, encouragement and instruction. Some coaches have found it useful to have the more skilled athletes help the less skilled (the "buddy" system), but the coach must ensure that this is done in a supportive fashion that helps the bonding process.

4. *Compliance with team roles and responsibilities is promoted by involving athletes in decisions regarding team rules and reinforcing compliance with them rather than by using punitive measures to punish noncompliance.*

Our fourth principle is designed to create a willingness on the part of athletes to follow team rules, and several of the CET guidelines address issues of establishing team rules, as well as encouraging and reinforcing compliance with them. Coaches should recognize that athletes want clearly defined limits and structure. They do not like unpredictability and inconsistency, nor do they like it when a coach continuously has to play the role of a policeman or enforcer. Thus, an important objective in building a productive team culture is to structure the situation in a way that the coach can teach discipline without having to constantly work to keep things under control. We therefore encourage a cooperative approach to team rules in that athletes are given a share of the responsibility for determining their own governance. The rationale for this approach is that people are more willing to live by rules (a) when they have a hand in forming them, and (b) when they have made a public commitment to abide by them.

Team rules should be developed early in the season. In helping athletes to share responsibility for forming rules, the coach should (a) explain why team rules are necessary (they keep things organized and efficient, thereby increasing the chances of achieving individual and team objectives), (b) explain why the team rules should be something that they can agree on as a group (they will be their rules, and it will be their responsibility to follow them), (c) solicit suggestions and ideas, and listen to what athletes say to show that their ideas and feelings are valued, (d) incorporate athletes' input into a reasonable set of rules (they should provide structure and yet not be too rigid), and (e) discuss the kinds of penalties that will be used when team rules are broken (here again, athletes should participate in determining the consequences that will follow rule violations). The advantage of this approach is that it places the responsibility where it belongs—on the athletes themselves. In this way, team discipline can help develop self-discipline. Thus, when someone breaks a team rule, it is not the individual versus the coach's rules, but the breaking of their own rules. Moreover, this approach encourages athletes to police themselves and share responsibility for ensuring rule compliance.

The positive approach also applies to promoting compliance with team rules. One of the most effective ways of eliminating negative behaviors (and avoiding the negative side effects of punishment) is to strengthen incompatible positive behaviors. Thus, coaches are encouraged not to take rule compliance for granted, but to acknowledge instances of compliance with the rules. By using positive reinforcement to strengthen desirable behaviors, coaches can often avoid having to deal with misbehaviors on the part of athletes.

5. *Coaches obtain behavioral feedback and engage in self-monitoring to increase aware-*
ness of their own behaviors and to encourage compliance with the positive approach
guidelines.

One notable finding from our basic research was that coaches had very limited awareness of how often they behaved, as indicated by low correlations between observed and
coach-rated behaviors (Smith et al., 1978). Similar findings occurred in another observational study of coaches (Burton & Tannehill, 1987). Thus, an important goal of CET
is to increase coaches' awareness of what they are doing, for no change is likely to occur
without it. CET coaches are taught the use of two proven behavioral-change techniques,
namely, behavioral feedback (Edelstein & Eisler, 1976; Huberman & O'Brien, 1999)
and self-monitoring (Kanfer & Gaelick-Buys, 1991; McFall, 1977). To obtain feedback,
coaches are encouraged to work with their assistants as a team and share descriptions
of each others' behaviors. Another feedback procedure involves coaches soliciting input
directly from their athletes.

Self-monitoring (observing and recording one's own behavior) is another behavioral
change technique that has the potential for increasing coaches' awareness of their own
behavioral patterns and encouraging their compliance with the guidelines. Because of the
impracticality of having coaches monitor and record their own behavior during practices
or games, CET coaches are given a brief form that they are instructed to complete immediately after practices and games (see Smoll & Smith, 2005, p. 21). On the form, they
indicate approximately what percentage of the time they engaged in the recommended
behaviors in relevant situations. For example, coaches are asked, "Approximately what
percentage of the times they occurred did you respond to mistakes/errors with encouragement?" Coaches are encouraged to engage in self-monitoring on a regular basis in
order to achieve optimal results.

ACHIEVEMENT GOAL THEORY AND COACHING

Because the sport environment is inherently a competence and achievement context, motivational factors play an important role in the ultimate effects of participation on psychosocial development. A potentially useful formulation for understanding variations in young
people's interpretations of and responses to the youth sport setting is the achievement goal
framework (Ames, 1992b; Dweck, 1999; McArdle & Duda, 2002). Achievement goal theory
focuses on understanding the function and the meaning of goal-directed actions, based on
how participants define success and how they judge whether or not they have demonstrated
competence. The two central constructs in the theory are individual *goal orientations* that
guide achievement perceptions and behavior, and the *motivational climate* created within
adult-controlled achievement settings.

Goal Orientations

Nicholls (1984, 1989) identified two different ways of defining success and construing
one's level of competence, labeling them *task involvement* and *ego involvement*. When
people are *task-involved*, subjective success and perceived competence are processed in

a *self-referenced* manner. Task-involved people feel successful and competent when they have learned something new, witnessed skill improvement, mastered the task at hand and/or given their best effort. Importantly, even if people perceive themselves as possessing lower ability than others, they can still feel competent and successful if focused on task-involved criteria (Nicholls, 1989). On the other hand, when individuals are in a state of *ego involvement*, their definitions of personal success and demonstrated competence are *other-referenced*. The goal here is to show that one is superior to relevant others (approach ego orientation), or to avoid appearing inferior to others (avoidance ego orientation; Elliott & Church, 1997). As a result of their experiences in achievement contexts, particularly exposure to the conceptions of success emphasized by significant adults such as teachers, coaches and parents, children come to develop relatively stable task and ego goal orientations that represent "interpretive lenses" through which they process and respond to achievement situations (Dweck & Leggett, 1988; Nicholls, 1989). As a result, children differ in the conception of ability they emphasize and in their personal criteria for "successful" achievement.

Motivational Climate

Whether a person is task- and/or ego-involved at a given time is influenced by individual differences in goal orientations and by situational factors that make definitions of success more salient (Treasure et al., 2001). Moreover, the degree to which task- and/or ego-involving goals are emphasized by significant others has a direct effect on the social context or *motivational climate* in which achievement occurs (Ames, 1992b; Maehr, 1983). Like the classroom setting, sport is an environment in which evaluation, recognition and organizational practices of adult figures and athletes' motivation for learning and participation are often intertwined. Thus, researchers in the sport domain have highlighted the relevance of considering the role of adult significant others (such as coaches and parents) when explaining the achievement behaviors of young participants (Brustad, 1992; Duda, 1987).

Research in the educational domain indicates that children are more likely to invest in learning and adopt adaptive achievement strategies in task-involving environments, where the emphasis is on learning, personal improvement and developing new skills rather than on interpersonal evaluation and social comparison (Ames & Archer, 1988). On the other hand, maladaptive achievement strategies and motivational problems tend to occur in predominantly performance-oriented or ego-involving climates, where mistakes are punished, children with greater ability receive more encouragement and rewards, and social comparison is emphasized (Ames, 1992a; Midgley et al., 1998).

Relations between task and ego-involving motivational climate and such variables as students' perceived causes of success and failure, perceptions of ability, reasons for participation and indicators of the quality of experience have received considerable attention in educational settings (e.g. Ames & Archer, 1988; Nicholls, Cheung, Lauer & Patashnick, 1989). Research in sport has replicated and extended the findings from many of these classroom-based studies. Sport studies have shown an association between athletes' goal orientations and the situational goal structure created by coaches and parents (e.g. Duda & Hom, 1993; Ebbeck & Becker, 1994; Fry & Newton, 2003; Papaioannou, 1994).

Altering the Motivational Climate

In the academic realm, Ames (1992a), Dweck (1986), and Epstein (1988, 1989) have described specific methods that can be used to create a motivational climate that supports a task-orientation (also termed a mastery or learning orientation). These principles are designed to foster an orientation toward developing new skills, intrinsic motivation for learning, a focus on effort rather than social comparison, reduced fear of failure, and improved competence based on self-referenced standards. Among the most important principles are the following:

- Design learning tasks that are novel, diverse, challenging and engaging. Help students establish short-term, self-referenced mastery goals. Focus on the meaningful aspects of learning the activity, and support the development and use of effective learning strategies.
- Allow children to participate in decision making regarding aims and regulations that affect their actions and encourage them to take shared ownership of the learning process. Support the development and use of self-management and self-monitoring skills.
- Focus on individual improvement, progress and mastery. Tailor the rate of personal instruction to the individual student where possible. Recognize effort exerted, performance improvement in relation to individual goals and learning from mistakes. Encourage a view of mistakes as a natural and necessary part of the learning/mastery process rather than as something to be feared.
- Involve the student in the evaluation process. Minimize social comparison and ability distinctions in favor of individual progress.

Consistent with the above, Epstein (1988, 1989) coined the acronym *TARGET* to describe structures of the learning environment that are relevant to understanding and influencing motivational processes. The dimensions include *T*ask design, use of *A*uthority, learner *R*ecognition, implementation of *G*roup structure, *E*valuation procedures and performance *T*imetable. Ames (1992a) translated the TARGET principles into specific classroom strategies/practices and tested their influence on children who were motivationally and academically at risk. Students in a task- or mastery-oriented TARGET intervention condition were compared with control classrooms on measures of intrinsic motivation, academic attitudes and self-perceived competence. By the end of the semester, the children in the mastery condition were higher in intrinsic motivation and had more favorable attitudes toward learning than did the children in the control classrooms.

Ames (1992b) argued that the principles of achievement goal theory developed in the academic learning environment are readily applicable to the sport environment as well. Both environments are characterized by adult-defined authority and reward structures, and both are based on ability grouping, normative and social comparisons, and public individual performance. Accordingly, several researchers have applied the principles to physical activity settings (e.g. Harwood & Swain, 2002; Papaioannou & Kouli; 1999). Considered as a whole, the current literature on motivational climate in both academic and sport domains strongly supports the hypothesis that a task-orientated climate is associated with a wide range of salutary motivational, self-evaluative, affective and behavioral outcomes (see McArdle & Duda, 2002).

Though derived independently and from different theoretical systems, striking similarities exist in the goals and behavioral guidelines derived from CET and achievement goal theory. Both are designed to create a task- or mastery-oriented motivational climate that focuses on the learning process rather than on outcome. Sport is viewed as a personal development arena, and the emphasis is on becoming "your best" rather than "the best". CET guidelines explicitly define "winning" as exerting maximum effort and commitment to learning the skills of the sport, a position that is highly consistent with a mastery-based motivational climate. Likewise, mistakes are conceived as stepping stones to achievement that provide the feedback needed to improve performance. That is, mistakes are viewed as an important part of the learning process, rather than something to be feared. CET guidelines emphasize that to the extent that athletes are appropriately instructed in technical skills, focused on effort and preparation, and freed from unnecessary performance anxiety, winning as an outcome will take care of itself within the limits of their abilities. These goals are facilitated by a mastery-oriented motivational climate created by the coach and, ideally, supported by parents. CET and achievement goal theory thus share the goal of creating a positive interpersonal and athletic environment that fosters intrinsic enjoyment of the activity.

CONCLUSION

In concluding this chapter, it is appropriate to state our firm belief that extended efforts to improve the quality and value of coach training programs are best achieved via well-conceived and properly conducted evaluation research. Several multifaceted programs, such as ACEP, NYSCA and PACE, have achieved wide circulation, but have undergone little formal evaluation. The content of these programs seems intuitively valid, yet we know little about their influence on either coaching behaviors or their impact on the athletes who play for trained coaches. In multifaceted programs of this type, each component (e.g. pedagogy, sport psychology) or module should be subjected to empirical evaluation, using appropriate outcome measures tailored to each domain. There are welcome signs of increased attention to evaluation methods for such programs (e.g. Abraham & Collins, 1998; Gilbert & Trudel, 1999), and new qualitative approaches have appeared as well that could be applied to program development and evaluation (e.g. Côté, Salmela, Trudel, Baria & Russell, 1995). Hopefully, these new models and methodological advances will help stimulate an increase in evaluative research.

Although CET has undergone more extensive evaluation than other coach training programs, additional research is needed. All of the outcome studies have been done in the sport of baseball, and all have involved male coaches and athletes. In part, this is due to the fact that baseball is especially suitable for the use of the CBAS behavioral assessment instrument because coach behaviors occur in a relatively discrete fashion. However, the CBAS can be used in other sports as well (e.g. Smith et al., 1983), so that coach training program evaluations in other sports can also make use of this instrument. As suggested by the mediational model underlying our research program (Smoll & Smith, 1989), however, perceived behaviors are assumed to be the proximal cause of athlete attitudes. A recent unpublished analysis of data from our original study on observed and perceived coaching behaviors (Smith et al., 1978), using modern structural equation methods to assess mediational effects, provided evidence that athletes' perceptions of supportive and punitive behaviors partially mediated relations between the corresponding observed behaviors and attitudes toward the coach. Therefore, even in the absence of observed behavioral measures, the CBAS Perceived Behaviors Scale constitutes an acceptable outcome measure.

At this point, nothing is known about the effects of CET in girls' sports. However, given the importance of social relationships for girls (Eagly, 1987; Maccoby, 1999), we might expect a program that increases the supportive behaviors of coaches to have an equal if not greater effect on the attitudes of female athletes. This remains an untested hypothesis at the present time, however. Likewise, no research has been done on female coaches and on the effects of training on their behavior and on athlete outcomes. We are hopeful that future research will address the myriad of interesting questions that remain about coach training, the processes that determine program effectiveness, and the effects of training in various athletic systems and athlete populations.

AUTHOR NOTE

Preparation of this chapter was supported by Grant 2297 to Ronald E. Smith and Frank L. Smoll from the William T. Grant Foundation.

REFERENCES

Abraham, A. & Collins, D. (1998). Examining and extending research in coach development. *Quest, 50*, 59–79.

American Sport Education Program (2003). *Coaches*. Retrieved from http://www.asep.com

Ames, C. (1992a). Classrooms: goals, structures, and student motivation. *Journal of Educational Psychology, 84*, 261–271.

Ames, C. (1992b). Achievement goals and adaptive motivational patterns: the role of the environment. In G.C. Roberts (ed.), *Motivation in Sport and Exercise* (pp. 161–176). Champaign, IL: Human Kinetics.

Ames, C. & Archer, J. (1988). Achievement goals in the classroom: students' learning strategies and motivation processes. *Journal of Educational Psychology, 80*, 260–267.

Bandura, A. (1986). *Social Foundations of Thought and Action: A Social Cognitive Theory*. Englewood Cliffs, NJ: Prentice-Hall.

Bandura, A. (1997). *Self-efficacy: The Exercise of Control*. New York: Freeman.

Barnett, N.P., Smoll, F.L. & Smith, R.E. (1992). Effects of enhancing coach–athlete relationships on youth sport attrition. *The Sport Psychologist, 6*, 111–127.

Brown, B.R. & Butterfield, S.A. (1992). Coaches: a missing link in the health care system. *American Journal of Diseases in Childhood, 146*, 211–217.

Brustad, R.J. (1992). Integrating socialization influences into the study of children's motivation in sport. *Journal of Sport and Exercise Psychology, 14*, 59–77.

Brustad, R.J., Babkes, M.L. & Smith, A.L. (2001). Youth in sport: psychosocial considerations. In R.N. Singer, H.A. Hausenblas & C.M. Janelle (eds), *Handbook of Sport Psychology* (2nd edn, pp. 604–635). New York: John Wiley & Sons.

Buisman, A. & Lucassen, J.M.H. (1996). The Netherlands. In P. De Knop, L-M. Engstrom, B. Skirstad & M.R. Weiss (eds), *Worldwide Trends in Youth Sport* (pp. 152–169). Champaign, IL: Human Kinetics.

Burton, D. & Tannehill, D. (1987, April). Developing better youth sport coaches: an evaluation of the American Coaching Effectiveness Program (ACEP) Level 1 training. Paper presented at the meeting of the American Alliance of Health, Physical Education, Recreation and Dance, Las Vegas, NV.

Campbell, S. (1993). Coaching education around the world. *Sport Science Review, 2*, 62–74.

Côté, J. (2002). Coach and peer influence on children's development through sport. In J.M. Silva III & D.E. Stevens (eds), *Psychological Foundations of Sport* (pp. 520–540). Boston: Allyn & Bacon.

Côté, J., Salmela, J., Trudel, P., Baria, A. & Russell, S. (1995). The coaching model: a grounded assessment of expert gymnastic coaches' knowledge. *Journal of Sport and Exercise Psychology, 17*, 1–17.

Curtis, B., Smith, R.E. & Smoll, F.L. (1979). Scrutinizing the skipper: a study of leadership behaviors in the dugout. *Journal of Applied Psychology, 64*, 391–400.

Douge, B. & Hastie, P. (1993). Coach effectiveness. *Sport Science Review, 2*, 14–29.

Duda, J.L. (1987). Toward a developmental theory of children's motivation in sport. *Journal of Sport Psychology, 9*, 130–145.

Duda, J.L. & Hom, H.L. (1993). The interrelationships between children's and parent's goal orientations in sport. *Pediatric Exercise Science, 5*, 234–241.

Dweck, C.S. (1986). Motivational processes affecting learning. *American Psychologist, 41*, 1040–1048.

Dweck, C.S. (1999). *Self-theories and Goals: Their Role in Motivation, Personality, and Development.* Philadelphia: Taylor & Francis.

Dweck, C.S. & Leggett, E.L. (1988). A social-cognitive approach to motivation. *Psychological Review, 95*, 256–273.

Eagly, A.H. (1987). *Sex Differences in Social Behavior: A Social-role Interpretation.* Hillsdale, NJ: Erlbaum.

Ebbeck, V. & Becker, S.L. (1994). Psychosocial predictors of goal orientations in youth soccer. *Research Quarterly for Exercise and Sport, 65*, 335–362.

Edelstein, B.A. & Eisler, R.M. (1976). Effects of modeling and modeling with instructions and feedback on the behavioral components of social skills. *Behavior Therapy, 7*, 382–389.

Elliott, A.J. & Church, M.A. (1997). A hierarchical model of approach and avoidance achievement motivation. *Journal of Educational Psychology, 72*, 218–232.

Epstein, J. (1988). Effective schools or effective students? Dealing with diversity. In R. Haskins & B. MacRae (eds), *Policies for America's Schools* (pp. 89–126). Norwood, NJ: Ablex.

Epstein, J. (1989). Family structures and students motivation: a developmental perspective. In C. Ames & R. Ames (eds), *Research on Motivation in Education: Vol. 3. Goals and Cognitions* (pp. 259–295). New York: Academic Press.

Ewing, M.E., Seefeldt, V.D. & Brown, T.P. (1997). Role of organized sport in the education and health of American children and youth. In A. Poinsett (ed.), *The Role of Sports in Youth Development* (pp. 1–157). New York: Carnegie Corporation.

Fry, M.D. & Newton, M. (2003). Application of achievement goal theory in an urban youth tennis setting. *Journal of Applied Sport Psychology, 15*, 50–66.

Gilbert, W. & Trudel, P. (1999). An evaluation strategy for coach education programs. *Journal of Sport Behavior, 22*, 234–250.

Goncalves, C. (1996). Portugal. In P. De Knop, L-M. Engstrom, B. Skirstad & M.R. Weiss (eds), *Worldwide Trends in Youth Sport* (pp. 193–203). Champaign, IL: Human Kinetics.

Gould, D. (1987). Understanding attrition in children's sport. In D. Gould & M.R. Weiss (eds), *Advances in Pediatric Sport Sciences* (pp. 61–85). Champaign, IL: Human Kinetics.

Harwood, C. & Swain, A. (2002). The development and activation of achievement goals within tennis: II. A player, parent, and coach intervention. *Sport Psychologist, 16*, 111–137.

Hendry, L.B. & Love, J.G. (1996). Scotland. In P. De Knop, L-M. Engstrom, B. Skirstad & M.R. Weiss (eds), *Worldwide Trends in Youth Sport* (pp. 204–221). Champaign, IL: Human Kinetics.

Huberman, W.L. & O'Brien, R.M. (1999). Improving therapist and patient performance in chronic psychiatric group homes through goal-setting, feedback, and positive reinforcement. *Journal of Organizational Behavior Management, 19*, 13–36.

Kanfer, F.H. & Gaelick-Buys, L. (1991). Self-management methods. In F.H. Kanfer & A.P. Goldstein (eds), *Helping People Change: A Textbook of Methods* (4th edn, pp. 305–360). New York: Pergamon.

Laakso, A., Telama, R. & Yang, X. (1996). Finland. In P. De Knop, L-M. Engstrom, B. Skirstad & M.R. Weiss (eds), *Worldwide Trends in Youth Sport* (pp. 126–138). Champaign, IL: Human Kinetics.

Maccoby, E.E. (1999). *The Two Sexes: Growing Up Apart, Coming Together*. Cambridge, MA: Harvard University Press.

Maehr, M.L. (1983). On doing well in science. Why Johnny no longer excels; why Sarah never did. In S.G. Paris, G.M. Olson & H.W. Stevenson (eds), *Learning and Motivation in the Classroom*. Hillsdale, NJ: Erlbaum.

Malina, R.M. & Clark, M.A. (eds) (2003). *Youth Sports: Perspectives for a New Century*. Monterey, CA: Coaches Choice.

Martens, R. (1997). *Successful Coaching* (2nd edn). Champaign, IL: Human Kinetics.

McArdle, S. & Duda, J.L. (2002). Implications of the motivational climate in youth sports. In F.L. Smoll & R.E. Smith (eds), *Children and Youth in Sport: A Biopsychosocial Perspective* (2nd edn, pp. 409–434). Dubuque, IA: Kendall/Hunt.

McFall, R.M. (1977). Parameters of self-monitoring. In R.B. Stuart (ed.), *Behavioral Self-management: Strategies, Techniques and Outcomes* (pp. 196–214). New York: Brunner/Mazel.

Midgley, C., Kaplan, A., Middleton, M., Maehr, M.M., Urdan, T., Anderman, L.H. & Roeser, R. (1998). The development and validation of scales assessing students' achievement goal orientations. *Contemporary Educational Psychology, 23*, 113–131.

Mischel, W. (1973). Toward a cognitive social learning reconceptualization of personality. *Psychological Review, 80*, 252–282.

Mischel, W. & Shoda, Y. (1995). A cognitive-affective system theory of personality: reconceptualizing situations, dispositions, dynamics, and invariance in personality structure. *Psychological Review, 102*, 246–268.

National Alliance for Youth Sports (2003). *National Youth Sports Coaches Association*. Retrieved from http://www.nays.org

Nicholls, J.G. (1984). Achievement motivation: Conception of ability, subjective experience, mastery choice, and performance. *Psychological Review, 91*, 328–346.

Nicholls, J.G. (1989). *The competitive ethos and democratic education*. Cambridge, MA: Harvard University Press.

Nicholls, J.G., Cheung, P.C., Lauer, J. & Patashnick, M. (1989). Individual differences in academic motivation: perceived ability, goals, beliefs and values. *Learning and Individual Differences, 1*, 63–84.

Oldenhove, H. (1996). Australia. In P. De Knop, L-M. Engstrom, B. Skirstad & M.R. Weiss (eds), *Worldwide Trends in Youth Sport* (pp. 245–259). Champaign, IL: Human Kinetics.

Papaioannou, A. (1994). The development of a questionnaire to measure achievement orientations in physical education. *Research Quarterly for Exercise and Sport, 65*, 11–20.

Papaioannou, A. & Kouli, O. (1999). The effect of task structure, perceived motivational climate and goal orientations on students' task involvement and anxiety. *Journal of Applied Sport Psychology, 11*, 51–71.

Positive Coaching Alliance. (2003). *PCA Coaches*. Retrieved from http://www.positivecoach.org

Scanlan, T.K. & Lewthwaite, R. (1984). Social psychological aspects of competition for male youth sport participants: I. Predictors of competitive stress. *Journal of Sport Psychology, 6*, 208–226.

Scanlan, T.K. & Passer, M.W. (1978). Factors related to competitive stress among male youth sports participants. *Medicine and Science in Sports, 10*, 103–108.

Scanlan, T.K. & Passer, M.W. (1979). Sources of competitive stress in young female athletes. *Journal of Sport Psychology, 1*, 151–159.

Seefeldt, V., Clark, M.A. & Brown, E.W. (eds). (2001). *Program for Athletic Coaches' Education* (3rd edn). Traverse City, MI: Cooper.

Smith, R.E. & Johnson, J. (1990). An organizational empowerment approach to consultation in professional baseball. *The Sport Psychologist, 4*, 347–357.

Smith, R.E. & Smoll, F.L. (1990). Self-esteem and children's reactions to youth sport coaching behaviors: a field study of self-enhancement processes. *Developmental Psychology, 26*, 987–993.

Smith, R.E. & Smoll, F.L. (2002). *Way to Go, Coach! A Scientifically-proven Approach to Coaching Effectiveness* (2nd edn). Portola Valley, CA: Warde.

Smith, R.E. & Smoll, F.L. (2005). Assessing psychosocial outcomes in coach training programs. In D. Hackfort, J.L. Duda & R. Lidor (eds), *Handbook of Research in Applied Sport Psychology*, 295–318. Morgantown, WV: Fitness Information Technology.

Smith, R.E., Smoll, F.L. & Barnett, N.P. (1995). Reduction of children's sport performance anxiety through social support and stress-reduction training for coaches. *Journal of Applied Developmental Psychology, 16*, 125–142.

Smith, R.E., Smoll, F.L. & Curtis, B. (1978). Coaching behaviors in Little League Baseball. In F.L. Smoll & R.E. Smith (eds), *Psychological Perspectives in Youth Sports* (pp. 173–201). Washington, DC: Hemisphere.

Smith, R.E., Smoll, F.L. & Curtis, B. (1979). Coach effectiveness training: a cognitive-behavioral approach to enhancing relationship skills in youth sport coaches. *Journal of Sport Psychology, 1*, 59–75.

Smith, R.E., Smoll, F.L. & Hunt, E.B. (1977). A system for the behavioral assessment of athletic coaches. *Research Quarterly, 48*, 401–407.

Smith, R.E., Smoll, F.L. & Passer, M.P. (2002). Sport performance anxiety in young athletes. In F.L. Smoll & R.E. Smith (eds), *Children and Youth in Sport: A Biopsychosocial Perspective* (2nd edn, pp. 501–536). Dubuque, IA: Kendall/Hunt.

Smith, R.E., Zane, N.W.S., Smoll, F.L. & Coppel, D.B. (1983). Behavioral assessment in youth sports: coaching behaviors and children's attitudes. *Medicine and Science in Sports and Exercise, 15*, 208–214.

Smoll, F.L. & Smith, R.E. (1989). Leadership behaviors in sport: a theoretical model and research paradigm. *Journal of Applied Social Psychology, 19*, 1522–1551.

Smoll, F.L. & Smith, R.E. (eds) (2002a). *Children and Youth in Sport: A Biopsychosocial Perspective* (2nd edn). Dubuque, IA: Kendall/Hunt.

Smoll, F.L. & Smith, R.E. (2002b). Coaching behavior research and intervention in youth sports. In F.L. Smoll & R.E. Smith (eds), *Children and Youth in Sport: A Biopsychosocial Perspective* (2nd edn, pp. 211–231). Dubuque, IA: Kendall/Hunt.

Smoll, F.L. & Smith, R.E. (2005). *Coaches Who Never Lose: Making Sure Athletes Win, No Matter What the Score* (2nd edn). Palo Alto, CA: Warde.

Smoll, F.L. & Smith, R.E. (in press). Development and implementation of coach-training programs: cognitive-behavioral principles and techniques. In J.M. Williams (ed.), *Applied Sport Psychology: Personal Growth to Peak Performance* (5th edn). Boston: McGraw-Hill.

Smoll, F.L., Smith, R.E., Barnett, N.P. & Everett, J.J. (1993). Enhancement of children's self-esteem through social support training for youth sport coaches. *Journal of Applied Psychology, 78*, 602–610.

Smoll, F.L., Smith, R.E, Curtis, B. & Hunt, E. (1978). Toward a mediational model of coach-player relationships. *Research Quarterly, 49*, 528–541.

Treasure, D.C., Duda, J.L., Hall, H.K., Roberts, G.C., Ames, C. & Maehr, M.L. (2001). Clarifying misconceptions and misrepresentations in achievement goal research in sport: a response to Harwood, Hardy, and Swain. *Journal of Sport and Exercise Psychology, 23*, 317–329.

Wankel, L.M. & Mummery, W.K. (1996). Canada. In P. De Knop, L-M. Engstrom, B. Skirstad & M.R. Weiss (eds), *Worldwide Trends in Youth Sport* (pp. 27–42). Champaign, IL: Human Kinetics.

Weiss, M. (ed.) (2004). *Developmental Sport and Exercise Psychology: A Lifespan Perspective*. Morgantown, WV: Fitness Information Technology.

Weiss, M.R. & Hayashi, C.T. (1996). The United States. In P. De Knop, L-M. Engstrom, B. Skirstad & M.R. Weiss (eds), *Worldwide Trends in Youth Sport* (pp. 43–57). Champaign, IL: Human Kinetics.

Woodman, L. (1993). Coaching: a science, an art, an emerging profession. *Sport Science Review, 2*, 1–13.

Yamaguchi, Y. (1996). Japan. In P. De Knop, L-M. Engstrom, B. Skirstad & M.R. Weiss (eds), *Worldwide Trends in Youth Sport* (pp. 67–75). Champaign, IL: Human Kinetics.

CHAPTER 3

Providing Sport Psychology Services to Families

David N. Sacks, Gershon Tenenbaum and David Pargman

Florida State University, USA

INTRODUCTION

The majority of interventions designed and implemented by sport psychology consultants are aimed at assisting individual athletes or athletic teams. Despite this emphasis, few athletes enter the sport arena alone. Most do so with a certain level of family involvement, and many coaches recognize the importance of working with parents and other family members (Côté & Hay, 2002; Côté & Salmela, 1996; Hellstedt, 1987). Even if one's primary objective is to help individual athletes enhance their performances, family issues are apt to emerge, especially if one works with younger athletes. Most sport psychology consultants can expect to address family-related topics on a regular basis. Interventions may take the form of discussing family matters with individual clients, interacting with parents and other relatives, or both. In all cases, an understanding of and sensitivity to family processes is vital. Therefore, the purpose of this chapter is to provide a set of guiding principles to assist practitioners in their work with sport-involved families.

We begin by offering a synopsis of the major research findings regarding family influences on athletes, with an emphasis on how these findings translate into interventions with athletes and their families. Next, we summarize the major tenets of the family systems approach and provide a rationale for adopting a systemic view when working with athletic families. We then present a number of case studies representing some of the diverse family systems that sport psychologists may encounter. For each case study, we offer background information for the athlete and family, describe presenting problems and discuss possible interventions. The chapter concludes with a discussion of several additional, pertinent issues relating to work with families, including difficulties involved in conducting valid family assessments, qualitative differences between an "athletic family" and a "family with an athlete," and ethical considerations.

The Sport Psychologist's Handbook: A Guide for Sport-Specific Performance Enhancement.
Edited by Joaquín Dosil. © 2006 John Wiley & Sons, Ltd.

Knowledge about Athletes' Families and How to Apply It

Not surprisingly, most of the published research concerning familial influence on athletes' sport experiences involves youth sport. Certainly, young participants are not the only athletes involved in a family system, but the effects of familial involvement are most conspicuous in youth sport settings. Thus, this section is heavily weighted towards influences on young athletes and, in turn, on interventions aimed at their family members, especially parents.

Before proceeding, however, a few interrelated caveats are in order. First, no single intervention is appropriate for every family. Second, our suggestions are based upon a careful review of the research evidence, our own formal and informal research, and our experiences as sport psychology practitioners and as participants in sports from a variety of perspectives (coach, athlete, parent and referee). Nonetheless, when describing sport psychology base interventions with families, it would be unwise for any group of authors to claim such authority as to suggest specific pieces of advice that guarantee successful outcomes in all cases, or even to guarantee that families will always listen. Finally, given that all families, including those that are sport-involved, are both unique and complex, the practitioner who works with an athlete's family faces a considerable challenge in assessing the family system and deciding upon a course of action, based upon their own training and available resources. Each suggestion offered below and in later sections is not provided as the single correct intervention, but rather as an idea that may well increase the probability of a positive outcome. With these stipulations in mind, we turn now to some general findings regarding family influences in sport, along with their implications for coaches and sport psychology practitioners.

THE BENEFITS OF PROVIDING SUPPORT

Sport psychologists have for some time reported the benefits of family members' support on young athletes' sport participation. Research has consistently revealed that children of parents who provide high levels of support are more likely to enjoy participating in sports and are less likely to drop out than are their less supported peers (Babkes & Weiss, 1999; Brustad, 1996; Fredricks & Eccles, 2004; Martens, 1978; Martens & Seefeldt, 1979; Power & Woolger, 1994; Smoll, 2001). These findings tend to encourage parental support for children's athletic pursuits. Such a suggestion is generally appropriate for family members of athletes of all ages and competitive levels. Sport is simply more enjoyable and appealing for the participant with family encouragement and support.

As straightforward as this advice appears, in practice determining the types of parental behaviors that a young athlete considers supportive may be problematic. The difficulty stems largely from the fact that, even among families with strong parent–child relationships, children do not always perceive their parents' actions as they are intended. For example, a parent may purchase a pitching machine in order for a son or daughter to take batting practice while at home. The parent's intention may very well be to support the child's increasing interest and proficiency in baseball or softball and, for many children, the parent's investment will be perceived as a sign of support. Other children, however, might view this action as parental pressure to practice even when away from the field. Much depends on the unique circumstances of the family. As a general rule of thumb, a parent is more likely to be perceived as supportive if she follows her child's lead (e.g. supports the child's request to attend a skills clinic), as opposed to making unilateral decisions for the young athlete (e.g. signing the child up for a clinic without his knowledge).

Another type of overtly "supportive" behavior addressed in the literature is parents' offering advice to their children, in the form of coaching, during the game or event. When a parent is not formally fulfilling a coaching role, offering advice or suggestions during the contest tends to be detrimental (Kidman, McKenzie & McKenzie, 1999; Smoll, 2001). Parents often attempt to coach their children from their spectator seats, and most do so with the intention of being supportive. Despite such intentions, however, confusion for the young athlete may be the consequence. The child may feel obliged to listen and respond either to the coach or parent, particularly if advice from each source is in conflict with that of the other. Thus, as a rule, parents should be advised to refrain from coaching their children during a contest and encouraged to offer supportive but less technical comments (e.g. "Way to go" or "Great effort").

Some parents and other family members attempt to support the young athlete by offering gifts or monetary rewards as reinforcement for successful performances. Though to our knowledge this practice has not been the subject of scientific research, parents are often known to pay their children previously determined amounts of money for specified competitive achievements (e.g. each goal or run scored). Our own work with families has included parents who rewarded their successful young athletes with expensive gifts, such as vacations or a new boat, which were "earned" by a child for winning a particular competition.

Again, the intentions of most parents are laudable. Many see the practice of rewarding outstanding performances as a healthy source of motivation or as a reward for the child's hard work. The child may also see it this way, but offering gifts based on observable outcomes may also be detrimental to the parent–child relationship, since it conveys the message to a child that his parents are most proud of him or love him most when he plays well. Monetary or other gifts based on athletic performance can also convey the message that the child is competing not for her own benefit and satisfaction, but rather for her parents, who feel obligated to compensate her for performing well, not unlike an employer offering increased compensation to high-performing workers.

It is our view that family members should generally avoid rewarding young athletes' achievement by offering money or gifts. However, if parents feel strongly that providing these types of rewards are in the child's best interests, and if the family dynamics allow the child to recognize their parents' laudable purpose for doing so, then gifts should be tied to the child's efforts rather than to competitive outcomes. Better to reward a child for perseverance and fortitude than for scoring goals (Roberts, Treasure & Hall, 1994).

Despite the preceding examples, which tend to imply that each family's idiosyncrasies solely determine whether a parent's actions qualify as supportive, some efforts are widely viewed as beneficial and should be encouraged in virtually any situation. Regardless of the sport or age of the individual, family members can support an athlete by voicing encouragement during competitions, by being sensitive to the child's emotional shifts, and by emphasizing the value they see in the child's participation. Moreover, supportive family members express equal levels of pride regardless of the particular competitive outcome. However, even this seemingly straightforward suggestion can be difficult to implement. As Rosen (1978) points out, a talented baseball player who suffers a poor performance does not want a father to say, "You did just fine, son", for the child is unhappy about his own play (p. 323). The parent should thus avoid belittling the child's disappointments, even while communicating support.

In summary, an athlete certainly derives the most benefit when family members offer support. Support comes in many forms, however, and actions intended to support an athlete are not always perceived as such. It is, therefore, difficult and perhaps ill-advised for a sport psychology consultant to provide a specific list of "dos and don'ts" to parents of athletes. Rather, the consultant can provide the greatest benefit to a family by first considering the perspectives offered by the parents, child and other family members before recommending the most supportive course of action.

THE PITFALLS OF PARENTAL PRESSURE

The previous section described certain behaviors that, despite a parent's good intentions, can actually induce pressure rather than support. Children who experience high levels of pressure tend to derive less enjoyment from sports, experience higher levels of anxiety and are more likely to drop out than are their less-pressured counterparts (Babkes & Weiss, 1999; Brustad, 1996; Coakley, 1992; Fredricks & Eccles, 2004; Martens & Seefeldt, 1979; McPherson & Brown, 1988). However, while it is a relatively simple matter to advise parents to "avoid pressuring" their young athletes, it is quite another to delineate exactly what constitutes parental pressure. Again, much depends on the parent–child relationships and the overall family dynamics.

Wuerth, Lee and Alfermann (2004) found that active involvement by parents, as well as praise and understanding, were not associated with pressure. Increased directive behavior, by contrast, was correlated with young athletes' perceived pressure from their parents. The authors acknowledge that providing support without pressure is a difficult balance to strike, stating, "In order to encourage without pressuring, parents need to refrain from becoming so involved with the child's sport that they take on responsibility for, or interfere with, the training of the young athlete" (p. 31). They do acknowledge that some athletes are successfully coached by their parents but that, for most families, the child should be given the freedom to work with other coaches. This would allow the coach to provide specific, directive behavior, with the parents' involvement reflecting a more supportive and encouraging role. Recent research has provided additional evidence that when a parent acts in a directive manner by attempting to coach a young athlete, especially after a poor performance, the result tends to be an increase in perceived pressure.

Many readers have likely witnessed some conspicuously pressure-inducing behaviors, which may include statements such as, "We didn't drive all the way down here for you to lose", or "Don't go out there and embarrass me", that parents have made to their children. Others may have experienced parents actually berating or even assaulting their children after a disappointing performance, as reported by DeFrancesco and Johnson (1997). Many families pressure young athletes in less conspicuous ways.

It is often the more subtle forms of family pressure that are most difficult to combat, since they may be embedded in a background devoid of concrete or specific events. One example is the family that structures its home to promote the child's particular athletic activity, to the extent that not participating on a daily basis is no longer an option. This might take the form of a young wrestler's basement being converted to a wrestling room, with a weight room in the garage. Another example of subtle pressure would be a parent's continual reference to a scholarship that the child will some day earn to an elite university, or to the lucrative financial contract to be signed when the child becomes a professional. In any of these cases, there may be no single pressure-inducing event, but high expectations are communicated to the child quite effectively, which can become a burden to fulfill.

It should be noted, however, that not all children would perceive such situations as pressure-inducing. If an athlete is committed to a high level of performance, then she may indeed welcome any additional opportunities to train and would view her parents' high expectations as both motivating and supportive. Determining whether an athlete perceives the family environment as pressure-filled is often a challenge for the sport psychology consultant. However, as a general rule, if the athlete appears to lack a sense of control over his sport participation, then the family is likely to be providing excessive pressure (see Coakley, 1992; Deci & Ryan, 1985).

Whereas determining if the family is providing insufficient support and/or too much pressure is difficult, deciding upon an appropriate intervention is often an even more substantial challenge. Selecting interventions becomes less complicated if one can identify the underlying cause of the problem. If, for example, the parent is acting with purely praiseworthy intentions, then simply pointing out the unintended consequences of his actions may be sufficient. On other occasions, merely increasing the lines of communication between the athlete and her family members will go a long way towards solving the problem. On the other hand, if a parent appears to have her own agenda, such as increased fame or financial gain through a child's sport-related success, interventions designed to educate her about the potentially harmful consequences of her approach are unlikely to be effective. An equally difficult challenge occurs when a family's high levels of sport-related pressure are indicative of problems with the members' general methods of interacting. In such situations, interventions aimed at affecting the overall family dynamics may be in order. Deciding at what level to intervene is an ongoing challenge when working with families. We address the issue in further detail in a later section of this chapter.

INAPPROPRIATE FAMILY BEHAVIOR IN THE SPORT SETTING

Instances of parental behaviors that are detrimental to the youth sport experience are not uncommon in many organizations. The literature includes a variety of examples. Smith (1988) describes the occurrence of verbal arguments, fights among parents, and insults directed towards opponents in youth hockey leagues. DeFrancesco and Johnson (1997) found that several elite tennis players reported being physically assaulted by a parent following an unsatisfactory performance. Ferguson (1999) proposes that the pushy, screaming parent at a youth sporting event has become an American archetype. Such detrimental behaviors are not restricted to America's borders, however. Kidman et al. (1999) examined the verbal comments of parents at youth sporting events in New Zealand, finding that 34.2 per cent of the comments were of a negative nature. Others (Grisogono, 1985; Wood & Abernathy, 1991) provide an inventory of frequently exhibited detrimental behaviors that parents are advised against. Clearly, there is room for improvement in the behavior of sportsparents.

Recently, parental behaviors have become so extreme and violent that the resulting injuries and deaths have captured the attention of print (Nack & Munson, 2000; Swift & Munson, 1999) and broadcast media (Greenburg & Bernstein, 2000; O'Connor & Bury, 2002). Unfortunately, such violent behaviors among the families of youth sport participants are not rare.

Such deleterious effects of parental involvement lead some to question whether parents should be permitted to be involved in their children's sports competitions at all. Rosen

(1978) relates the suggestion of some little league baseball critics to post a "Keep Out" sign for parents. Indeed, Smith (1988) reports some efforts to prohibit parent attendance at youth hockey events. Most experts disagree with such a sentiment, however, citing the need for parents to contribute to a supportive atmosphere conducive to a child's participation in sport (FEPSAC, 1996; Martens & Seefeldt, 1979; NAYS, 2000). The challenge is not to restrict the family's involvement, but rather to provide an environment that will improve the experience for the child.

Perhaps the most common suggestion offered in the literature for positively affecting parental involvement in youth sports is providing educational and training programs for parents (DeFrancesco & Johnson, 1997; Hellstedt, 1987, 1990; Martens, 1978; Wood & Abernathy, 1991). However, the various recommendations for such interventions appear to be a function of their authors' intuition, rather than a consequence of empirical research. While educating sportsparents to alter their behavior makes intuitive sense, no published data-based studies are available that support the effectiveness of educational interventions.

Notwithstanding this limitation, most of the research in the area of parental involvement in youth sports supports the notion that parents can exert positive influences on their children's sport experiences. This process does not occur spontaneously, however, and education may be needed if parents are to create the proper environment and support their children's athletic endeavors without generating undesired consequences.

Smoll (2001) provides a useful guideline for planning and conducting an effective coach–parent meeting, one purpose of which is to enhance parents' understanding of youth sports. He also provides suggestions for communicating with parents who engage in inappropriate behavior. Addressing these parents has the potential to lead to conflict, and Smith offers specific advice for interacting in a manner that is likely to produce a desirable result. For example, rather than directly confronting a parent who screams inappropriately from the spectator area during a contest, one potential strategy is to offer the individual a task, such as scouting opponents, that will help the team in a more desirable way.

To promote increased awareness of appropriate behavior, several agencies have begun to provide sportsparents' training curricula (NAYS, 2000; Wilson, 2001) that have been adopted by various youth sports organizations. Though published studies on the effects of these educational programs are not yet available, initial indications suggest that leagues with mandated training for parents are witnessing improved behavior and a decrease in the number of problematic incidents (Greenburg & Bernstein, 2000).

Such developments are highly encouraging and represent an important step towards improving the sport experience for children. It should be noted, however, that educating parents regarding proper ways to behave in sport environments is not equivalent to addressing the dynamics of a family system. Clearly, the pervasiveness of problematic behaviors on the part of many parents warrants action, and any improvements in this regard are laudable. Nevertheless, one must recognize the inherent limitations of programs that focus primarily on specific behaviors that emerge in the sport environment. Problematic behaviors may serve as indicators of underlying causes associated with family processes, as these processes require attention as well.

DEVELOP MENTALLY APPROPRIATE SPORTS-PARENTING

The previous passage alluded to the undesirable consequences that can occur when parents place greater importance on winning in sports than do their children. Unfortunately, such a scenario occurs frequently enough to warrant its own descriptor. The "adultification" of youth sport refers to the adult-like characteristics that often dominate activities that are, after all, overtly designed for the benefit of children. In its position statement on children in sport, the European Federation of Sport Psychology (FEPSAC) (1996) advises, "Those involved in children's sports should understand that children are not mini-adults" (p. 225). Other European and North American writers have been offering similar cautions for some time (Byrne, 1993; Martens, 1978; McPherson & Brown, 1988). Nevertheless, reports from the field reveal that many parents, as well as coaches, continue to find it difficult to restrain their own desire for success and fail to adhere to the premise that youth sports are designed for the benefit of children (Greenburg & Bernstein, 2000; NAYS, 2000). In addition to conspicuous problems, such as violent behavior, that result from these deficiencies, Coakley (1992) suggests that the perception among young athletes that control of their very own sport activities has been usurped by their parents may lead to burnout.

Interventions addressed at families exhibiting behaviors that are developmentally inappropriate will be most effective for practitioners who have at least a working knowledge of developmental psychology. Research in this discipline provides evidence that children are not only less mature than adults, but also exhibit qualitative differences in terms of their ways of thinking (Piaget, 1959), moral reasoning (Kohlberg, 1968) and psychosocial processes (Erikson, 1963). For example, if a parent admonishes a child for a poor performance, the child may lack the cognitive ability to distinguish this behavior from general parental disapproval. In addition, advising a young athlete to circumvent the rules of a contest may send a message that it is also permissible to violate rules elsewhere, since the child's level of moral development may not permit him to consider that "different moral principles" apply in sport and non-sport contexts, as an adult might believe (Bredemeier & Shields, 1986; Conroy, Silva, Newcomer, Walker & Johnson, 2001). In short, adult family members should be sensitive to the fact that a young athlete is not simply a smaller version of an adult. Sport psychologists can provide valuable service to athletes and families by educating family members on these developmental processes and stages, as well as suggesting age-appropriate practices.

When led appropriately, the sport experience certainly has the potential to enhance a child's healthy development. If a child is angry at a teammate for making an error during competition, the parent can use this as an opportunity to help the child distinguish their frustration regarding the game from general disapproval of the peer. Similarly, parents can help their children learn to cooperate with individuals on a team, even if they are not social companions (see Carron, Brawley & Widmeyer, 1998, for a discussion of task and social cohesion). Likewise, the common practice of shaking hands with opponents can help children distinguish competition from personal conflict. Certainly, sport has the potential to enhance young athletes' development, and the family plays an important role in aiding this process.

Intensity of Family Involvement

One means of characterizing the appropriateness of family behaviors is to determine whether parents are under- or over-involved with their children's sport participation. Experts in this area advise that parents provide the greatest benefit when they adopt a moderate level of involvement (Byrne, 1993; Hellstedt, 1990). Several scenarios of

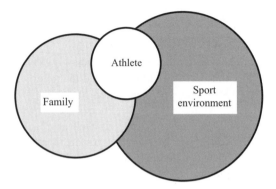

Figure 3.1 A family with a moderate level of involvement in the child's sport participation

the possible interactions among athlete, family, and sport environment are depicted in Figures 3.1–3.3.

Figure 3.1 represents a family that is moderately involved with the child's sport environment. As the overlapping circles indicate, some of the family's activities revolve around the sport, but the major portion of the family system's identity is independent of this environment. In addition, the athlete's identity includes membership in the family and sport environment, as well as outside activities. In this scenario of moderate involvement, a parent is presumed to provide encouragement and support for the young athlete without inducing undue pressure to win or overemphasizing the importance of the child's sport participation (Byrne, 1993; Hellstedt, 1990).

The family depicted in Figure 3.2 is over-involved in the child's sport. Nearly all of the family's activities are enmeshed with the sport environment. For the athlete, this means that being a part of the family requires participation in the sport. Thus, the child may perceive that in order to develop her own identity, she must seek non-sport activities, which may also involve the risk of disappointing her parents. Such a situation may cause the child to drop out of sport (Coakley, 1992).

Figure 3.3 portrays a family that is under-involved with the child, as well as with his sport. In this scenario, the athlete is likely to experience a lack of connectedness with his

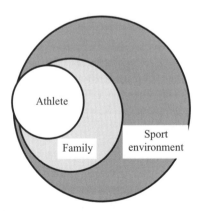

Figure 3.2 A depiction of a family that is over-involved with the child's sport participation

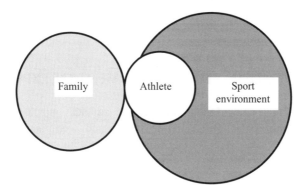

Figure 3.3 A depiction of a family that is under-involved with both the athlete and the sport environment

family, and participating in sport may allow him to enter an environment wherein he can become an integral component of a system. Thus, sport allows him to fulfill a need for belongingness that is not met via his family of origin (Maslow, 1968).

Obvious problems exist with parents who are over-involved or under-involved with their children's sports; thus the published sport-related literature suggesting that a moderate level of involvement is ideal (Byrne, 1993; Hellstedt, 1990). The implication here is that once the intensity of the family's involvement with the sport is assessed, parents can be counseled to increase or decrease their involvement accordingly. While such a notion is relatively straightforward and appealing, it assumes that the intensity of parental involvement is a sport-specific phenomenon, rather than a reflection of family system dynamics. Thus, while a coach or sport psychologist might wish to caution parents to tone down their intense involvement with a young athlete's sport participation, such advice may impact only upon the surface of an ongoing parenting style. As indicated in Figures 3.1–3.3, the relationship between athlete and family, represented roughly by the proportion of the overlapping circular areas, is assumed to supercede and influence the child's participation in sport.

Support for this perspective is found in several lines of evidence. First, when describing their work with young athletes and their families, practitioners reveal that, oftentimes, the presenting sport-related problem is merely an indicator of an underlying family issue (Hellstedt, 1995, 2000; Stainback & LaMarche, 1998). Second, as Stein, Raedke and Glenn (1999) have demonstrated, more critical than the *amount* of parental involvement on sport-related variables such as anxiety and enjoyment is the child's perception regarding the *appropriateness* of involvement levels. The child's perception of parental behaviors may, indeed, more adequately reveal the nature of the interaction among family members, as some children perceive moderate levels of involvement as "too much", while others view relatively high levels as "too little". In addition, the limited published research on children coached by their parents (who are thus, by definition, heavily involved with the children's sports) shows that these athletes experience levels of motivation and competitive anxiety similar to that of their peers (Barber, Sukhi & White, 1999). Finally, qualitative studies examining the family's role in the development of expertise reveal that certain family patterns, common across a variety of sport and non-sport domains, exist prior to the eventual expert's experience with the chosen activity (Bloom, 1985; Côté, 1999; Durand-Bush & Salmela, 2002; Sloane, 1985;

Stevenson, 1990). These patterns include parental involvement in their children's activities that may be considered quite intense. Findings from this line of research are discussed next.

THE FAMILY'S ROLE IN THE DEVELOPMENT OF EXPERTISE

Several researchers have studied the family's role in athletes' pursuit and achievement of expertise in a variety of sports. The family has been found to be a necessary component in the development of expertise and, for all of the family systems studied, a gradual process of change occurred as the children developed into expert performers (Bloom, 1985; Côté, 1999; Côté & Hay, 2002; Sloane, 1985; Stevenson, 1990). Bloom (1985) characterized this process as consisting of the early, middle and later years. More recently, Côté, Delter and Hay (2002) described the development of expertise in terms of the sampling years (when the child samples a variety of sport and non-sport activities), the specializing years (when the child demonstrates aptitude in a specific domain and elects to pursue it exclusively), and the investment years (when the child and family commit to the pursuit of elite status). Côté, Baker and Abernathy (2003) describe a progression from playful engagement in sport to more serious forms of commitment, with an athlete transitioning from free play to deliberate play to structured practice to deliberate practice. This gradual process in the development of athletic expertise has been supported by recently published studies of world and Olympic champions (Durand-Busch & Salmela, 2002; Gould, Diffenbach & Moffet, 2002).

The family dynamics involved in this developmental process contrast sharply with images presented by the mass media portraying sportsparents who decide that their children, still at a young age, are destined for elite levels of play (Ferguson, 1999; Greenburg & Bernstein, 2000). This disparity suggests that a great number of parents, by emphasizing the importance of performance and winning to their young athletes at too early an age, are ironically undermining their children's chances for success in sport (Coakley, 1992; Roberts et al., 1994). It should be noted, however, that performers in certain sports (e.g. gymnastics) tend to reach expert levels at relatively young ages. These notable exceptions are addressed in the relevant chapters of this volume.

Given the tremendous amount of time and effort an individual must commit in order to achieve expertise in a performance domain (Ericsson & Charness, 1994), it is not surprising that the families of expert performers tend to contribute intensively to this process. For many sport activities, a child simply does not possess the resources, monetary or otherwise, that are generally required to achieve elite status. Certainly, exceptions exist, especially in particular sports that do not entail a great deal of cost, and exceptional individuals with little or no family support may still achieve success (such a scenario is reflected in Figure 3.3). Notwithstanding such possibilities, results from studies on talent development suggest that a total family commitment is required to take advantage of the ideal coaching, training and competitive opportunities available. Thus, the families of experts appear to be heavily involved, perhaps even over-involved, with their children's athletic pursuits (Bloom, 1985; Côté, 1999; Sloane, 1985; Stevenson, 1990). Such intensity of family involvement appears a reasonable, if not necessary, component in the development of talent, yet it contradicts the suggestions of sport psychology practitioners and researchers who encourage moderate levels of parental involvement (Byrne, 1993; Hellstedt, 1990).

Several explanations may resolve this apparent contradiction. The first has to do with the possibly improper use of the term "involvement" (and the associated terms of "moderate", "over-", and "under-involvement"), which has been utilized to describe a rather complex series of interactions among parents, children and the sport environment. Parents who pressure their children to win or who interfere with a coach's attempt to discharge his responsibilities may be characterized as "over-involved". Likewise, a parent who conveys little concern for the child's experiences is said to be "under-involved". Such usage of these terms, however, implies that parental involvement is a uni-dimensional, linear variable that is present in low to high amounts. It may be more appropriate to consider involvement as a multi-dimensional construct that includes "healthy" and "unhealthy" interactions among family members and the sport environment. Thus, the parent who behaves inappropriately at a child's sporting event might appear to be over-involved, but a more accurate description would characterize this family member as being involved in an unhealthy manner. The deciding factor, therefore, is not how heavily the parent is involved, but whether this involvement reflects healthy forms of interactions (Stein et al., 1999; Wuerth et al, 2004; Wylleman, 2000). We turn now to a brief overview of a family systems perspective, which favors examining an individual's actions in light of the inter-relationships among family members.

The Sport-Involved Family as a System

Of those practitioners who regularly address family-related issues in their work, such as family therapists and social workers, the vast majority operate from a systems perspective. A detailed description of family or general system theories is beyond the scope of this chapter, and only a brief overview will be provided. For readers seeking more thorough explanations, a number of sources are available (see, for example, Becvar & Becvar, 1996; Bertalanffy 1968). In a family systems approach, the behaviors, thoughts and feelings of an individual are viewed in light of that person's role in the family. Since members of a family share a variety of complex interactions, it is virtually impossible to understand an individual's situation without also having explored general family processes.

The notion that the whole does not equal the sum of its parts is a central tenet of general system theory, of which family systems theory is one application. As Bertalanffy (1968), states:

> It is necessary to study not only parts and processes in isolation, but also to solve the decisive problems found in the organization and order unifying them, resulting from dynamic interaction of parts, and making the behavior of parts different when studied in isolation or within the whole. (p. 31)

Systemic thinking can be beneficial whenever one is working with "sets of elements standing in interaction", which is a straightforward definition of a system offered by Bertalanffy (p. 38). Examples include business organizations, athletic teams and, of course, families. While individuals often appear to act independently in each of these examples, a system member's actions influence and are influenced by other members. Thus, instead of asking *why* something happened when an event occurs, the systems theorist asks *what is going on* in attempting to describe the patterns of interactions (Becvar & Becvar, 1996).

A visual depiction of a system is provided in Figure 3.4. In this depiction, the large arrow on the left represents input the system receives from the environment. If we use this figure to represent a six-member sport-involved family, then the input could be feedback from the sport environment regarding the athlete's performance. When this input is received, the

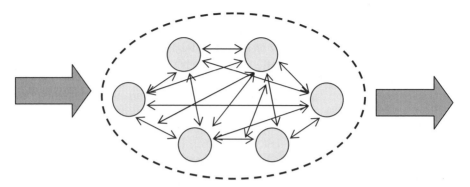

Figure 3.4   A visual depiction of a system operating in its environment

system components interact with each other. This interaction occurs not only wherein one component acts upon another, but also with multiple components interacting in concert, such as an athlete's father and older sibling, who might collaborate in advancing a training routine to address a perceived weakness in the athlete's play (note that the figure depicts a limited number of possible interactions). As a result of these continual interactions, the system acts on its environment to produce output, represented by the large arrow on the right. For the family operating in the sport environment, output usually takes the form of the athlete's actions. In this regard, the athlete serves as the family system's point of entry into the sport environment, not unlike the manner in which a salesperson represents a business organization. To the casual observer, the athlete appears to act independently, but a family systems approach suggests that all family members are operating to some extent behind the scenes.

Applying a Systems Approach: Deciding How and Where to Intervene

Sport psychologists have been criticized by systems-trained practitioners for failing to employ a system perspective. Specifically, in the American Journal of Family Therapy, Zimmerman and Protinsky (1993) stated, "Although sport psychology is a valuable and important part of athletic training, it subscribes to a linear, individualistic, cause-effect epistemology" (p. 16). It is our belief that by thinking in a systemic manner about athletes and their families, sport psychology practitioners can serve their clients more effectively. However, this is not to imply that interventions should always address family dynamics that may underlie a presenting problem. Rather, it is to recommend that a practitioner employ a systems perspective when assessing the situation but, before intervening, to consider the extent to which the dynamics of a particular family are able to be altered, as well as the likelihood of family-based interventions being well received. A number of other considerations must be made as well, not the least of which is the practitioner's own qualifications to intervene at the family level.

Consider, for example, a case in which a parent contacts a sport psychologist for assistance with a young athlete's failure to perform up to her potential in important competitions. An initial interview with the parent, child or both may yield some useful information about the athlete's interactions with family members, with the sport psychologist hypothesizing that the child's performance decrements result largely from pressure imposed on her by the family. At this point, it would be necessary to decide whether to intervene at the family level, in the hope of reducing the pressure or, instead, to work with the athlete individually to cope with the stressors more effectively. Decisions such as these must be made on a case-by-case basis, in light of the considerations listed above. In the next section we provide several case studies, in order both to illustrate the types of family-related issues one may encounter and to demonstrate the type of thought process one may undergo in deciding at what level to intervene.

CASE STUDIES: EXAMPLES OF FAMILY-RELATED PRACTICE IN SPORT PSYCHOLOGY

The Case of "Danielle"

Background Information

"Danielle" is a 14-year-old who has been raised to be a professional tennis player. Both of her parents were somewhat successful players themselves, and they have committed much of the family's time and income to providing the best training and instruction for their daughter. Her two older, adult brothers tried tennis briefly, but quit the sport to pursue other interests. Both have since moved away from the home. Danielle became successful in the sport at a young age, but when she moved to a higher age group, her small size became a weak point in her game. Recognizing this, Danielle's parents hired a nutritionist for her and started Danielle on a strength and conditioning program. These efforts have had a positive impact upon Danielle's performance, and now her family is considering relocating to an area of the country where they will have easier access to the best coaching and tennis facilities. The degree of this family's sport involvement is most closely represented by Figure 3.2.

Figure 3.2 reveals a family system that is almost entirely consumed by the sport environment. While this, in itself, is not detrimental, the schematic illustrates that the family engages in an extremely small proportion of interactions with the environment outside of the sport system. The athlete, Danielle, also has relatively few opportunities to interact with the environment outside of her family system and outside of her sport. Additionally, virtually all of her sport experiences are subsumed within her family system. In effect, she does not operate so much as an individual playing a sport, but rather as a visible representative of her tennis-involved family.

Presenting Problem

A sport psychologist is contacted by Danielle's father for help regarding what the father describes as "motivational problems" and "lack of effort". It seems that since the family began discussing a possible relocation, Danielle has exhibited reduced levels of effort, both in practice and competition. The father is quick to point out that Danielle still wins most tournaments she enters, but is not playing to her capabilities. He is at a loss to explain why, since she seems so excited when the family talks about moving so she can attend one of the country's elite tennis academies.

The sport psychologist arranges to meet with Danielle, and she and her father arrive at the office. Tension is apparent between them. During introductions, the father says to Danielle, "This man is going to help you get motivated again." Danielle responds by mumbling, "If you say so." After gathering some family history, with particular attention to the role of sports for Danielle, her brothers and her parents, as well as an individual discussion with Danielle, the sport psychologist begins to realize that this young person feels pressured by her family to achieve success as a professional tennis player. She has not enjoyed the sport for some time and, if she thought it possible, would consider quitting. Her parents have invested too much time and money into her tennis career, though, for this to be a viable option, she explains. In addition, despite her father's belief to the contrary, she does not want to move away from her friends, though she agrees that attending the elite tennis academy would benefit her as an athlete. She expressed hopefulness that her parents, especially her father, would tone down their involvement once she began working with better coaches.

Possible Interventions

A practitioner working with Danielle and her family has a number of intervention options available. Though she was referred by her father for individual issues, it is clear that family dynamics play a central role in her on-court performance and demeanor. This being the case, intervening at the family level would be an appropriate option, if the practitioner has the training and ability to work with the family. Individual meetings with Danielle, her parents and possibly her siblings, as well as session with the whole family, would be in order. One particular issue likely to emerge would be the communication patterns among the family members. The sport psychologist would attempt to address the processes by which Danielle's father had been able to misconstrue or ignore his daughter's true thoughts and feelings regarding a major decision such as relocating. Alternatively, it might be discovered that Danielle has failed to express herself in a meaningful fashion. Family-based interventions would aim to uncover the underlying communication patterns. Does Danielle keep silent to avoid upsetting her parents? Do they discount her thoughts if they differ from what the parents wish to hear? The answers to these types of questions bear heavily on both the athlete's and the family's sport-related experiences and can guide the practitioner in facilitating healthier patterns of familial interactions.

Another possible objective would be to assist Danielle in gaining a greater sense of control over her athletic pursuits. At present, she appears to be quietly rebelling against her parents' forcing her to participate in elite-level sport. This parental pressure may, in fact, be extreme, or it may only be Danielle's perception. One might expect an individual in early adolescence to strive for independence (Erikson, 1963), and this process may be playing out through sport. If this was the case, and Danielle were encouraged to quit tennis, she might regret the decision. Perhaps other options are available to her for gaining a greater sense of control.

Clearly, these issues are complicated and require the practitioner's careful attention and sensitivity to family processes. Another option would be to focus not on the family, but rather on the presenting problem articulated by the father, namely Danielle's lack of effort. Especially if other family members refuse to be involved in the process, then working one on one with the individual (on family and non-family-related issues) may be the only available course of action. However, given that Danielle's family is on the verge of a major decision, engaging the entire system would be more desirable.

The Case of "Elliot"

Background Information

"Elliot" grew up with a single mother after his father was killed in a car accident when Elliot was six years old. His mother, struggling to hold down a job, meet monthly expenses and satisfy accumulated debts while raising her children, encountered difficulty preserving the family system's stability. Elliot began to spend less time at home and engaged in a variety of ungovernable behaviors. When Elliot became involved in a youth soccer league, however, he began what would become a dramatic turnaround. He referred to his coaches and teammates as "my family". Throughout his sport participation, Elliot's mother has not interfered with his efforts (she somewhat begrudgingly has paid for equipment and various fees), though she has not provided a good deal of support either. When asked about Elliot's sport involvement, his mother has been known to say that as long as it keeps him out of trouble, it is fine with her. Figure 3.3 most closely represents his experience, in terms of family involvement in the sport setting.

Presenting Problem

Now a sophomore in high school, Elliot plays for a highly successful varsity soccer team, which has regularly participated in seminars provided by a sport psychology consultant. After a presentation to the team, Elliot approaches the consultant to ask questions about fitting in with his teammates. It appears that, although he had embraced members of earlier teams as extended family members, Elliot is now beginning to feel somewhat isolated. After speaking for a few moments with Elliot and later with his coach, the sport psychologist learns that the majority of the team members' parents are highly supportive of the soccer program. Most assist in fundraisers, staffing the concession stand and the like. The parents, coaches and players regularly meet together for meals after games. Elliot, in contrast, does not attend social gatherings with his teammates or their families. He expresses feeling like an "abandoned kid" during these types of events.

Possible Interventions

Though Elliot at first described his difficulty as one of fitting in with his teammates, it quickly became apparent that family-related issues were a major source of his discomfort. As his mother appears to be under-involved with his athletic activities and unlikely to participate willingly, one might discount potential interventions at the family system-level as unrealistic. Instead, the practitioner may opt to address Elliot's family concerns via an individual setting. A major focus here would be on helping Elliot cope with his unique family situation. Nevertheless, it is quite possible that Elliot's mother would welcome interventions. One may find that she would actually prefer to be more involved with his sport, but fears being viewed as an outsider by other parents and finds the prospect of attending Elliot's athletic events intimidating. Certainly, one cannot ascertain the potential efficacy of family-based interventions without making the attempt. A likely course of action would be to begin work with Elliot on an individual level, inquiring about the extent to which he has addressed family-related issues with his mother. Eventually, she might be invited to participate in the process.

The Case of "Jessica"

Background Information

"Jessica" is a 28-year-old cyclist training to qualify for her country's Olympic team. She is married and is the mother of two children, ages 4 and 2. Jessica had been one of her country's top cyclists before taking leave from the sport to start a family. Her 30-year-old husband had been an athlete while a university student, but retired from competitive sports at age 22 to pursue a business career. At present, he works an average of 50 to 60 hours per week. Shortly after giving birth to her second child, Jessica began riding again. More recently, after first discussing the matter with her husband, she committed to regaining her elite status and attempting to qualify for the Olympic Games. Jessica's mother-in-law lives in the local area, and she agreed to help care for the children in order to provide time for Jessica to train.

Presenting Problem

Jessica contacted the cycling union's sport psychology consultant following a particularly troubling week of training. During an initial meeting, she explained that she was still committed to making the national Olympic team, but was beginning to have her doubts. Her required daily training hours were increasing, and this would necessarily take more time away from her family. Making the team was not a certainty, and she dreaded the possibility of asking her family members to make sacrifices in order for her to pursue a dream that might remain unfulfilled. Her mother-in-law had not complained to Jessica directly about caring for her grandchildren during this time, but Jessica's husband had been hinting that his mother was grumbling to him about, "Your wife out there riding her bicycle while I raise your children." Complicating matters further, Jessica is finding herself too tired in the evenings to enjoy her time with her family. She reports that her husband has been supportive throughout and insists that Jessica pursue her goals. However, she questions his sincerity. She is also fearful that if she desists in her training, she will somehow resent her children for preventing her from achieving her goals.

Possible Interventions

As in the previous two cases, a practitioner working with Jessica is charged with deciding the level at which to address family-related issues. Operating at the individual level, the consultant may assist Jessica with her decision making and time management, help her achieve a balance among her multiple roles (as an athlete, mother, wife and daughter-in-law), and advise her in the process of expressing her concerns to family members. Here again, intervening at the level of the family system offers the potential for benefiting all family members, but also is ripe with challenges. An effective family-based intervention is likely to raise significant issues relating to parental roles and differences in values, among other concerns. An ongoing objective would be to prioritize Jessica's athletic goals in light of the goals and needs of the family system.

To our knowledge, very little published research exists regarding family issues affecting adult athletes such as Jessica. However, in the field of vocational counseling, researchers have devoted more attention to family influences on adults' careers (Naidoo & Reyhana, 2003; Whiston & Keller, 2004). These studies suggest that family dynamics continue to affect one's activities into adulthood and that successful individuals often perceive conflict between their career and family roles.

ADDITIONAL CONSIDERATIONS FROM A SYSTEMS PERSPECTIVE

Challenges to Assessing Family System Dynamics

Measurement Issues

A major challenge facing researchers and practitioners who wish to address family dynamics is assessing "family functioning" in a valid manner. Measuring this construct is especially problematic because it is defined in various ways by different parties (Halvorsen, 1991; Sawin, Harrigan & Woog, 1995). According to Halvorsen, "Some professionals define family functioning in terms of structure, others in terms of the family's interactional nature, others in terms of transactional processes, and still others in terms of the psychological characteristics of family members" (p. 50). Notwithstanding this impediment, a number of systems-based, self-report instruments have been validated for the purpose of measuring family functioning, and are currently in use by mental health practitioners working with families (Grotevant & Carlson, 1989; Halvorsen, 1991; Sawin, Harrigan & Woog, 1995). Some of the more prevalent measures include the Family Assessment Device (Epstein, Baldwin & Bishop, 1983), the Family Environment Scale (Moos & Moos, 1986), and the Family Assessment Measure (Skinner, Steinhauer & Santa-Barbara, 1995). These instruments can be quite useful for measuring specific aspects of family dynamics in order to compare a family to a norming sample.

There are, however, drawbacks involved in using quantitative measures to assess a family system. As Deacon and Piercy (2001) note, these instruments actually assess an individual family member's perceptions of the family, rather than the actual functioning of the system. While perceptions of family functioning can be useful in themselves, and while discrepancies among various members' perceptions can be used to infer the presence of dysfunction, it should be recognized that a self-report instrument has limitations in this regard.

Several writers (Deacon & Piercy, 2001; Sawin et al., 1995) also point out that quantitative instruments tend to reduce holistic systems to specific variables measured on a linear continuum and, in the process, fail to capture important nuances within a family. These authors suggest that qualitative forms of assessment provide a useful complement to quantitative measures. Some of the qualitative techniques employed by family therapists and researchers include observational methods, genograms, family networks, eco-maps, art assessments, want-ads, family sculptures and re-enactments of an important event or typical day, to name a few (Deacon & Piercy, 2001; Sciarra, 2001; Widmer & La Farga, 2000).

These and other qualitative methods of assessing families have their limitations as well. Only a trained therapist is qualified to implement these strategies and interpret the results that they generate. Often, a good deal of trust must be established between a family member and therapist before these assessments can occur, as engaging in activities that reveal private family matters is, in itself, part of a therapeutic process. Thus, to conduct this type of assessment, one must be sensitive to the welfare of the athlete and his family members, as well as to one's own qualifications to gather these types of data.

Becoming a Fly on the Wall

In addition to employing available instruments, a practitioner can gain a clearer understanding of the dynamics operating within a family system through careful observation. Events with the potential to yield useful information include family members' behavior at sport events, changes in an athlete's behavior during the presence versus the absence of family members, and family interactions during formal and informal meetings with the sport psychologist. Nevertheless, even with careful scrutiny, gaining an accurate assessment of family dynamics is an elusive goal, as a majority of interactions are not available for observation. For example, recent work (Sacks, 2003) revealed that dysfunctional family interaction patterns are kept from public view, but often emerge in a private setting, such as the car ride home from a competition.

One strategy that allows a practitioner to generate some inferences about family dynamics is to interview family members individually and as a group. For example, one might conduct an interview with the child and parents separately before beginning a family session. Often, both subtle and conspicuous differences can be observed between a family member's behavior in individual and group sessions. For example, a young athlete might readily express his frustrations in an individual session with the practitioner but remain largely silent when his parents are present. Such differences in behavior provide useful data for assessing the family dynamics. In summary, a guideline for practitioners is to use all means at their disposal to assess family dynamics, while maintaining a healthy skepticism regarding the accuracy of the assessment.

A "FAMILY WITH AN ATHLETE" VERSUS AN "ATHLETIC FAMILY"

The systemic approach offered above proposes that the family itself be considered the unit of interest. Thus, associated research methods and intervention techniques would address the "athletic family", as opposed to a "family with an athlete". As employed here, these terms are adapted from a common practice among family counselors and therapists to distinguish, for example, an "alcoholic family" from a "family with an alcoholic". In the former, the family adapts to the alcoholic member, and the remaining members interact in such a way (e.g. by taking on added responsibilities) to allow the system to maintain its unhealthy method of operation. In the latter, the health of the family as a whole emerges as the greater concern, which tends to encourage the identified patient to change, or at least to operate independently as an alcoholic.

In the present analogy, a family with an athlete could be any family with a member who happens to participate in sport. The fact that an individual engages in this particular activity does not necessarily alter the goals or dynamics of the family system. For this type of system, the family may nurture the sportsperson and retain a certain level of influence on this activity, but the athlete acts more or less as an independent agent. The case of "Elliot" represents this type of system.

An athletic family, by contrast, may be characterized as a system that is arranged according to one or more members' athletic endeavors, as illustrated in the case of "Danielle" (with "Jessica's" family on the cusp of this description). For a family characterized as this type, sport-related goals serve as the system's organizing principles. That is, sport becomes the family's identity, and the interactions among members of the system are geared towards these goals. Here, the concept of family influence is subsumed by a reality in which the athlete is the center of the system, and her goals become the system's goals. Indeed, as reported earlier, it is not unusual for an entire family to alter its lifestyle and relocate in order to take advantage of elite training and coaching opportunities (Sloane, 1985).

It may be tempting to propose that an athletic family provides increased facilitative effects on sport-related outcomes, compared to a family with an athlete, though this is not necessarily the case for a variety of reasons, including added pressure on the sport participant. It is fair, however, to assume that for an athletic family, the stakes are higher in the sport environment. With the potential for increased stress levels for the athlete, a high degree of family health becomes especially valuable for these systems.

ETHICAL CONSIDERATIONS

Of course, any practitioner working with athletes must be sensitive to ethical concerns. Work with families raises additional considerations. Maintaining confidentiality, for example, becomes a more complicated matter. Certainly, information regarding the family itself should be kept in strict confidence. The extent to which each family member can be assured confidence *within the family* is less obvious. Especially if a practitioner meets individually with family members and as a group, it is not always clear what information is to be shared and withheld from one's relatives. Errors that result in a perceived violation of confidence can quickly undermine one's efforts. On the other hand, being overly restrictive about sharing information can raise suspicions about the process, wherein the practitioner appears to be keeping secrets from certain family members. A guideline for good practice is to encourage family members to share information with one another, when deemed appropriate, rather than to reveal something that may have been expressed in confidence. When in doubt, it is also good practice to ask an individual whether a piece of information offered in an individual meeting can be shared with relatives.

In addition to concerns about confidentiality, the sport psychologist working with family-related issues must be careful to work within one's qualifications and areas of competence (see Moore, 2003, and Whelan, Meyers and Elkins, 2002, for discussion). Just as training or certification in sport psychology does not permit one to operate as a psychologist, most sport psychology consultants are not qualified to conduct family therapy. This is not to imply that one should avoid conducting family meetings, but instead to be sensitive to situations in which the focus veers away from sport-related concerns to more therapeutic issues. When this occurs, the more ethically sound course of action might be to refer a family for treatment.

CONCLUDING REMARKS

In this chapter, we have attempted to present some of the research findings regarding family-related issues in sports, while extrapolating guidelines for applying these findings to sport psychology practice. Family involvement is most conspicuous for children in sport. Therefore, much of the research in this area, and in turn much of our attention, has focused on families of younger athletes.

Since a family constitutes a system comprised of separate but interactive components, a systemic approach can enhance one's effectiveness when working with athletic families. Even if one does not attempt to alter the functioning of the family itself, adopting a systemic manner of thinking can help the practitioner to assess family dynamics more efficaciously and, thus, offer more appropriate interventions to the athlete coping with relevant issues.

In order to illustrate the types of issues that emerge among families of athletes, as well as potential intervention strategies, we provided three case studies. Certainly, each family is unique, and these examples highlight only a small proportion of possible presenting problems. As stated in the opening paragraph of this chapter, athletes do not exist in a vacuum; they bring to the sport environment a varied and unique family history. Attending to family-related issues is an essential component of effective practice in sport psychology.

REFERENCES

Babkes, M.L. & Weiss, M.R. (1999). Parental influence on children's cognitive and affective responses to competitive soccer participation. *Pediatric Exercise Science, 11*, 44–62.

Barber, H., Sukhi, H. & White, S. (1999). The influence of parent-coaches on participant motivation and competitive anxiety in youth sport participants. *Journal of Sport Behavior, 22*, 162–180.

Becvar, D.S. & Becvar, R.J. (1996). *Family Therapy: A Systemic Integration* (3rd edn). Boston: Allyn & Bacon.

Bertalanffy, L.V. (1968). *General System Theory: Foundations, Development, Applications*. New York: George Braziller.

Bloom, B.S. (1985). Generalizations about talent development. In B.S. Bloom (ed.), *Developing Talent in Young People* (pp. 507–549). New York: Ballantine Books.

Bredemeier, B.J. & Shields, D.L. (1986). Game reasoning and interactional morality. *Journal of Genetic Psychology, 147*, 257–275.

Brustad, R.J. (1996). Parental and peer influence on children's psychological development through sport. In F.L. Smoll & R.E. Smith (eds), *Children and Youth in Sport: A Biopsychosocial Perspective* (pp. 112–124). Dubuque, IA: Brown & Benchmark.

Byrne, T. (1993). Sport: it's a family affair. In M. Lee (ed.), *Coaching Children in Sport* (pp. 39–47). London: E. & F.N. Spon.

Carron, A.V., Brawley, L.R. & Widmeyer, W.N. (1998). Measurement of cohesion in sport and exercise. In J. Duda (ed.), *Measurement in Sport and Exercise* (pp. 213–226). Morgantown, WV: Fitness Information Technology.

Coakley, J. (1992). Burnout among adolescent athletes: a personal failure or social problem. *Sociology of Sport Journal, 9*, 271–285.

Conroy, D.E., Silva, J.M., Newcomer, R.R., Walker, B.W. & Johnson, M.S. (2001). Personal and participatory socializers of the perceived legitimacy of aggressive behavior in sport. *Aggressive Behavior, 27*, 405–418.

Côté, J. (1999). The influence of the family in the development of talent in sport. *The Sport Psychologist, 13*, 395–417.

Côté, J., Baker, J. & Abernathy, B. (2003) From play to practice: a developmental framework for the acquisition of expertise in team sports. In J.L. Starkes & K.A. Ericsson (eds). *Expert Performance in Sports: Advances in Research on Sport Expertise.* (pp. 89–113) Champaign, IL: Human Kinetics.

Côté, J. & Hay, J. (2002). Children's involvement in sport: a developmental perspective. In J.M. Silva & D. Stevens (eds), *Psychological Foundations of Sport* (2nd edn, pp. 484–502). Boston: Merrill.

Côté, J. & Salmela, J.H. (1996). The organizational tasks of high performance gymnastic coaches. *The Sport Psychologist, 10*, 247–260.

Deacon, S.A. & Piercy, F.P. (2001). Qualitative methods in family evaluation: creative assessment techniques. *American Journal of Family Therapy, 29*, 355–373.

Deci, E.L. & Ryan, R.M. (1985). *Intrinsic Motivation and Self-determination in Human Behavior.* New York: Plenum.

DeFrancesco, C. & Johnson, P. (1997). Athlete and parent perceptions in junior tennis. *Journal of Sport Behavior, 20*, 29–36.

Durand-Bush, N. & Salmela, J.H. (2002). The development and maintenance of expert athletic performance: perceptions of world and Olympic champions. *Journal of Applied Sport Psychology, 14*, 154–171.

Epstein, N.B., Baldwin, L.M. & Bishop, D.S. (1983). The McMaster Family Assessment Device. *Journal of Marital and Family Therapy, 9*(2), 171–180.

Ericsson, A.K. & Charness, N. (1994). Expert performance: its structure and acquisition. *American Psychologist, 49*, 725–747.

Erikson, E.H. (1963). *Children and society* (2nd edn). New York: Norton.

European Federation of Sport Psychology (FEPSAC) (1996). Position statement of the European Federation of Sport Psychology (FEPSAC): II. Children in sport. *The Sport Psychologist, 10*, 224–226.

Ferguson, A. (1999, 12 July). Inside the crazy culture of kids sports. *Time, 154*, 52–60.

Fredricks, J.A. & Eccles, J.S. (2004). Parental influences on youth involvement in sports. In M.R. Weiss (ed.), *Developmental Sport Psychology: A Lifespan Perspective* (pp. 145–164). Morgantown, WV: Fitness Information Technology.

Gould, D., Dieffenbach, K. & Moffett, A. (2002). Psychological characteristics and their development in Olympic champions. *Journal of Applied Sport Psychology, 14*, 172–204.

Greenburg, R. & Bernstein, R. (executive producers) (2000, October). *Real Sports with Bryant Gumbel* [Television broadcast]. New York: Home Box Office.

Grisogono, V. (1985). Children at risk: danger awaits on the touchline for young sportspeople with over-keen coaches or parents. *Sport and Leisure 25*(6), 30.

Grotevant, H.D. & Carlson, C.I. (1989) *Family Assessment: A Guide to Methods and Measures.* New York: Guilford Press.

Halvorsen, J.G. (1991). Self-report family assessment instruments: an evaluative review. *Family Practice Research Journal, 11*, 21–55.

Hellstedt, J.C. (1987). The coach-parent-athlete relationship. *The Sport Psychologist, 1*, 151–160.

Hellstedt, J.C. (1990). Early adolescent perceptions of parental pressure in the sport environment. *Journal of Sport Behavior, 13*, 135–144.

Hellstedt, J.C. (1995). Invisible players: A family systems model. In S.M. Murphy (ed.), *Sport Psychology Interventions* (pp. 117–147). Champaign, IL: Human Kinetics.

Hellstedt, J.C. (2000). Family systems-based treatment of the athlete family. In D. Begel & R.W. Burton (eds), *Sport Psychiatry: Theory and Practice* (pp. 206–228). New York: W.W. Norton & Company.

Kidman, L., McKenzie, A. & McKenzie, B. (1999). The nature and target of parents' comments during youth sport competitions. *Journal of Sport Behavior, 22*, 54–68.

Kohlberg, L. (1968). The child as a moral philosopher. *Psychology Today, 2*(4), 25–30.

Martens, R. (ed.). (1978). *Joy and Sadness in Children's Sports*. Champaign, IL: Human Kinetics.

Martens, R. & Seefeldt, V. (eds.) (1979). *Guidelines for Children's Sports*. Reston, VA: American Alliance for Health, Physical Education, Recreation, and Dance.

Maslow, A. (1968). *Toward a Psychology of Being* (2nd edn). New York: Van Nostrand.

McPherson, B.D. & Brown, B.A. (1988). The structure, processes, and consequences of sport for children. In F. Smoll, R. Magill & M.J. Ash (eds), *Children in Sport* (3rd edn; pp. 265–286). Champaign, IL: Human Kinetics.

Moore, Z.E. (2003). Ethical dilemmas in sport psychology: discussion and recommendations for practice. *Professional Psychology: Research and Practice, 34*, 601–610.

Moos, R.H. & Moos, B.S. (1986). *Family Environment Scale Manual* (2nd edn). Palo Alto, CA: Consulting Psychologists Press.

Nack, W. & Munson, L. (2000, 24 July). Out of control. *Sports Illustrated, 93*, 86–95.

Naidoo, A.V. & Reyhana, J. (2003). Role conflict of South African women in dual-career families. *Psychological Reports, 93*, 683–686.

National Alliance for Youth Sport (2000). *Promoting Positive and Safe Sports for Youth* [on-line]. Available: http://www.nays.org

O'Connor, J. & Bury, C. (producers). (2002, 9 January). *Nightline* [television broadcast]. New York: American Broadcast Company.

Piaget, J. (1959). *The Language and Thought of the child* (3rd edn; M. Gabain, trans.). London: Routledge & Kegan Paul.

Power, T.G. & Woolger, C. (1994). Parenting practices and age-group swimming: A correlational study. *Research Quarterly for Exercise and Sport, 65*, 59–66.

Roberts, G.C., Treasure, D.C. & Hall, H.K. (1994). Parental goal orientations and beliefs about the competitive sport experience of their child. *Journal of Applied Social Psychology, 24*, 634–645.

Rosen, A. (1978). Advice for fathers. In R. Martens (ed.), *Joy and Sadness in Children's Sports.* (pp. 320–326). Champaign, IL: Human Kinetics.

Sacks, D.N. (2003). *Family influences and the athlete's sport experience: a systemic view.* Unpublished doctoral dissertation, Florida State University.

Sawin, K.J. Harrigan, M.P. & Woog, P. (eds.) (1995). *Measures of Family Functioning for Research and Practice*. New York: Springer.

Sciarra, D.T. (2001). Assessment of diverse family systems. In L.A. Suzuki, J.G. Ponterotto, & P.J. Meller (eds), *Handbook of Multicultural Assessment: Clinical, Psychological, and Educational Applications* (2nd edn; pp. 135–168). Josey-Bass; San Francisco, CA.

Skinner, H.A., Steinhauer, P.D. & Santa-Barbara, J. (1995). *Family Assessment Measure Version III Technical Manual.* North Tonawanda, NY: Multi-Health Systems.

Sloane, K.D. (1985). Home influences on talent development. In B.S. Bloom (ed.), *Developing Talent in Young People* (pp. 439–476). New York: Ballantine Books.

Smith, M.D. (1988). Interpersonal sources of violence in hockey: the influence of parents, coaches, and teammates. In F. Smoll, R. Magill & M.J. Ash (eds), *Children in Sport* (3rd edn; pp. 301–313). Champaign, IL: Human Kinetics.

Smoll, F.L. (2001). Coach-parent relationships in youth sports: increasing harmony and minimizing hassle. In J.M. Williams (ed.), *Applied Sport Psychology: Personal Growth to Peak Performance* (4th edn; pp. 150–161). Mountain View, CA: Mayfield.

Stainback, R.D. & LaMarche, J.A. (1998). Family systems issues affecting athletic performance in youth. In K.F. Hays & E.M. Stern (eds.), *Integrating Exercise, Sports, Movement, and Mind: Therapeutic Unity* (pp. 5–20). New York: Haworth Press.

Stein, G.L., Raedke, T.D. & Glenn, S.D. (1999). Children's perception of parent sport involvement: it's not how much, but to what degree that's important. *Journal of Sport Behavior, 22*, 591–601.

Stevenson, C.L. (1990). The early careers of international athletes. *Sociology of Sport Journal, 7*, 238–253.

Swift, E.M. & Munson, L. (1999, 20 December). Paralyzing hit. *Sports Illustrated, 91*, 34–35.

Whelan, J.P., Meyers, A.W. & Elkins, T.D. (2002). Ethics in sport and exercise psychology. In J.L. Van Raalte & B.W. Brewer (eds.), *Exploring Sport and Exercise Psychology* (2nd edn; pp. 503–523). Washington, DC: American Psychological Association.

Whiston, S.C. & Keller, B.K. (2004). The influences of the family of origin on career development: a review and analysis. *Counseling Psychologist, 32,* 493–568.

Widmer, E.D. & La Farga, L-A. (2000). Family networks: a sociometric method to study relationships in families. *Field Methods, 12,* 108–128.

Wilson, K.A. (2001). Performance parenting: a model for better youth sports through education [on-line]. Available: http://momsteam.com/

Wood, K. & Abernathy, B. (1991) Competitive swimmers' perceptions of parental behaviors: guidelines for parents. *Sports Coach, 4,* 19–23.

Wuerth, S., Lee, M.J. & Alfermann, D. (2004). Parental involvement and athletes' career in youth sport. *Psychology of Sport and Exercise, 5,* 21–33.

Wylleman, P. (2000). Interpersonal relationship in sport: uncharted territory in sport psychology research. *International Journal of Sport Psychology, 31,* 555–572.

Zimmerman, T.S. & Protinsky, H. (1993). Uncommon sports psychology: consultation using family therapy and techniques. *American Journal of Family Therapy, 21,* 161–174.

CHAPTER 4

An Overview of Interventions in Sport

Robert N. Singer
University of Florida, USA
and
Mark H. Anshel
Middle Tennessee State University, USA

INTRODUCTION

The sport psychologist has been viewed in different ways in the world of sport, possibly as a performance enhancer, a mental skills trainer, a counsellor, a therapist, a mediator, a motivator or a healer, or some combination of these roles. This is due to various interpretations as well as potential functions and delivery models. Sport psychologists may perceive themselves primarily as educators, clinicians or researchers. From an applied perspective, the sport psychologist may be expected to educate, diagnose, remedy and prepare athletes for competitive success as well as to prevent or overcome psychological obstacles detrimental to performance.

Furthermore, perspectives may be provided for the well-being of athletes, considering developmental, social and psychological factors. Sport psychologists may consult with coaches, teams and family members. Many of the roles of sport psychologists involve situations in which guidance is provided to an athlete, coach, team or family member in order to assist the athlete to achieve and to have positive experiences in and through sport. The process by which such outcomes may occur is called an "intervention". When collaborating with coaches, insights about athletes could be provided that might be advantageous in refining an athlete's mental and psychological skills as well as promoting satisfying experiences. Team cohesion might be improved. Meaningful analyses of a young athlete's reactions to intense training and serious competition in their sport may be helpful to family members. Many of the roles of sport psychologists involve situations in which assistance is provided to an athlete, coach, team or family member in order to assist the athlete to achieve and have positive experiences. The process by which sport psychologists attempt to influence the thoughts, emotions or performance quality of sports competitors and teams is called an "intervention".

The Sport Psychologist's Handbook: A Guide for Sport-Specific Performance Enhancement.
Edited by Joaquín Dosil. © 2006 John Wiley & Sons, Ltd.

DEFINING INTERVENTIONS

In the title of this chapter, the word "intervention" broadly represents the nature of the types of involvement sport psychologists usually have with an athlete, but on occasion with a coach, team or significant family. Intervention implies different meanings, and the dictionary does not clarify the term as we use it here and how is it is popularly used elsewhere in education and psychology. In fact, the dictionary states that the literal meaning of "to intervene" is to come between. Primarily, negative interpretations are provided, that it may be hindrance that alters conditions between two parties. An intervener could be a third party in a legal proceeding. The thesaurus associates an intervention with an intrusion, interposition, an insertion, intermeddling, or mediation. A mediator is described as an intervener, an intermediate agent, a go-between, a middleman, and a moderator. Most interpretations do not accurately portray what the sport psychologist does and attempts to accomplish. One could say, however, that sport psychology consultants "intervene" by positioning themselves between the athlete and the competitive environment by suggesting how athletes might use cognitive, behavioral or performance strategies, whichever may seem to be most advantageous for the situation.

In this way, we believe in a positive interpretation of the meaning of the word "intervention", as adopted by sport psychologists. The sport psychologist is frequently the third party, an outsider, who comes between athletes and the environment in which they compete to enhance their level of satisfaction and performance quality. Proper diagnostics and assessment will lead to the use of appropriate interventions, such as building mental and psychological skills, which, in turn, will help athletes reach their performance potential. Perhaps personal issues and problems will be identified and resolved. The sport psychologist could also collaborate with coaches, full teams or small groups of team members, and even the athlete's family as the primary parties. Furthermore, such experiences may relate to addressing everyday occurrences not connected to sport. These include coping with stress and learning achievement-oriented skills that may carry over to numerous situations in life. Many sport psychologists explain and strengthen the relationship between experiences in sports and the other aspects of the athlete's life in order to contribute to overall personal development.

PURPOSES OF INTERVENTIONS

Interventions can take a variety of forms and serve various purposes, as described in Murphy's (1995) edited book. The book contains a comprehensive coverage of a great variety of intervention possibilities with athletes, and we advocate a broad interpretation of the concept of interventions. For the most part, interventions provide performance enhancement techniques benefiting individual athletes to be more successful at higher levels of competition. In this role, the sport psychologist is considered to be a mental skills and/or psychological skills trainer. Another role is that of a learning specialist. Examples of issues addressed in this role include the designing of efficient and effective practice conditions and explaining the information-processing demands imposed on athletes in particular sports or within certain competitive situations. A different role is one of counsellor, in which certain personal problems of the athletes are addressed. Personal issues that are directly sport-related or indirectly sport-related may need to be resolved in order for the athlete to be a successful performer and, at the same time, satisfied and fulfilled. Pathological issues such as eating disorders, chronic anxiety or addictions may require referral to a clinical psychologist or psychiatrist who has special training and licensure in psychopathology. A variety of services provided to US Olympic athletes in different sports has been described by Roberts and Gould (1989) in a special issue of *The Sport Psychologist*.

As indicated earlier, interventions may be oriented to a team or a sub-group of that team, potentially leading to better cohesion and morale among the athletes. With team building, productivity should increase. There are occasions for interventions to be directed at coaches, with the intention of assisting them to be more effective in how they interact and communicate with athletes, as well as to guide athletes in developing relevant mental and psychological skills. This possibility depends on the relationship between the sport psychologist and the coach, and the receptivity of the coach for such feedback. Sport psychologists may also educate family members in better understanding and motivating their children, helping young athletes to reach their potential for ultimate success. Meaningful analyses of a young athlete's reactions to intense training and serious competition in sport may be insightful and helpful to family members. Also, the appropriate roles for family members might be determined through parent education programs.

At this point, we need to explain how we have described and will continue to address the person considered to be an athlete. In general terms, the athlete is a person with a high level of skill in a sport, or the potential to realize it, and who is engaged in formal, serious and structured competition. This interpretation allows us to be to be more focused in the chapter as we offer possible interventions. It is impossible here to explain the many ways approaches to interventions may vary depending on who the athlete is, and any special considerations about the athlete or who might be called an athlete. Our assumption is that the selection and delivery of an intervention will wisely match any special characteristics of "the athlete", and how a person is defined as an athlete.

Examples of special considerations include (a) young versus mature athletes, (b) the elite versus the good athlete versus the serious recreational person versus the beginner, and possibly (c) male versus female athletes. Special populations (e.g. the handicapped and disabled) require special intervention delivery considerations. Obviously, individual versus team sports impose somewhat different demands on athletes. Such is the case from sport to sport. Sports like golf, bowling, billiards, gymnastics and archery demand consistent control and self-regulation associated with an effective immediate pre-performance routine. Ideally, this would lead to a narrow focus of attention and what appears to be a state of flow and unconsciousness during execution. Such sports as boxing and wrestling, and for the most part hockey and soccer, require continual on-line adjustments depending on swift and accurate situational awareness, anticipation and decision-making. Other sports, like basketball, tennis and volleyball, possess characteristics of both situations considering when the ball is in play versus certain circumstances (e.g. shooting a penalty shot in basketball and executing the serve in volleyball and tennis). Athletes need to acquire the unique "mentality" for a particular sport as well as events in a sport (Singer, 2000). In spite of the many unique considerations for interventions in situations, many of them have commonality in purpose and effectiveness across sports and individuals. Some examples are interventions that address competitive sport stress-management, confidence-building, concentration refinement and mental preparation for competition.

In summary, interventions may be:

- athlete-centered
- team-centered
- coach or family-centered.

Interventions may involve providing:

- performance enhancement skills
- learning improvement skills
- life adjustment skills
- team-building skills.

Usually associated with interventions are attempts "to fix" something that is not working well. Perhaps the athlete has lost confidence in performing according to expectations. Maybe the stress of significant competition is perceived by the athlete to be threatening instead of challenging. Then again, practice may not simulate real competitive conditions meaningful enough in helping athletes in acquiring information-processing and self-regulation skills, especially relevant for success in competition. Possibly the athlete does not know how best mentally to prepare for competition immediately before an event. Other example situations involve psychologically overcoming severe injuries and pain; sustaining motivation to train hard to compete well over time; generating an appropriate attributional style when performance is less than desirable; and working effectively with team-mates and the coach (in team settings). There are many examples besides the ones just described that might be resolved with appropriate guidance. The sport psychologist is frequently involved in remedying problems and enhancing achievement potential with relevant intervention techniques. Ideally, the athlete learns how to be resourceful and to self-regulate behaviours so that they are appropriate in different situations (Carver & Scheier, 1998).

The most advantageous interventions would be guidance provided by the sport psychologist to the athlete (or team and/or coach) *before* problems arise and the athlete is faltering. For instance, presentations, clinics, discussions and other communication mediums can educate athletes about mental and psychological skills appropriate for mastering a particular sport and in demonstrating a degree of excellence. This may not technically be considered as traditional intervention activity. However, we think that it is pertinent to recognize the value of educating athletes about the best ways to become successful competitors as well as satisfied in their experiences, thereby minimizing the need for corrective intervention sessions at some later point. Therefore, we also view pre-problem situations, where athletes are informed about mental and psychological strategies and techniques that should benefit subsequent learning, performance and general well-being, as interventions. This approach enables the athlete to adopt appropriate strategies that blend in with the overall training program. The intent is to maximize achievement potential quickly by minimizing the occurrence of inappropriate and ineffective mental and psychological habits in the future.

ASSESSMENT AND PLANNING

Many interventions are provided as remediation. After a performance issue is identified by the coach, athlete or both parties, the sport psychologist is expected to understand and analyze the dilemma, and then offer a particular technique or strategy that might resolve the issue. Here is where appropriate assessment enters: how to determine the nature of the problem. Simply put, three possible separate or coordinated approaches can be used:

- problem identified by the athlete or the coach
- problem determined by the sport psychologist through interview and discussion with the athlete
- problem determined by the sport psychologist through the use of a standardized psychological test.

Such matters will be covered in more depth in the Assessment and Diagnosis section of this chapter, especially the nature of psychological tests, test selection, testing and the use of the data. It is crucial to be able to identify the problem area, the cause and the potential solution. The analogy is similar to someone wanting to go to a physician for a cure of severe migraine headaches. How will the physician determine what is causing the pain? Through discussion? Through instrumentation, such as brain scan testing? Measurement of the presence of unusual biochemical patterns in the blood stream? Does the physician have a solution? Medication? A stress reduction technique? Life-style changes?

The *sport psychology consultant* may face the same circumstance with regard to factors perceived by the athlete as undermining performance. How should the problem be clarified? Some sport psychologists are well-trained in administering valid and reliable tests (if available), and interpreting the data for counselling purposes. Other sport psychologists may favor approaches that emphasize discussion, exploration and mutual problem-solving. Of course, a particular problem area may suggest which direction to go. Tests that measure such psychological attributes as sport motivation, competitive sport anxiety, sport performance confidence, various self-perceptions and general personality profiles are associated with one model of intervention (Beckmann & Kellmann, 2003). However, there are mental attributes related to specific sports, from a narrow focus of attention (concentration) to attentional switching and adaptability, and the ability to make rapid and good decisions in quickly changing circumstances, that are difficult if not impossible to test directly with any available instruments. The ability to self-regulate, control and direct thoughts and emotions effectively in sport situations is also challenging to capture with any evaluation instrument. In such cases, a discussion format with the athlete and the coach may lead to a better understanding of what needs to be addressed. In addition, observing the athlete in competition may provide insights as to the presence or absence of certain behaviors.

Following assessment, what should be done next? For example, if the athlete is too anxious with overwhelming fear of doing badly and losing immediately prior to competition, performance failure will likely occur. What should the sport psychologist prescribe? Determine the potential cause, and propose a certain self-regulation skills program to combat these negative feelings? Suggest alternative stress management techniques? A relaxation program? A pre-performance routine? Many options are available, and a decision needs to be made as to what might work out best for the athlete, and how the athlete can learn to deal effectively with negative thoughts. Intervention decisions depend on what the sport psychologist identifies as the source of the problem through appropriate assessment techniques. Then, one or more remedial strategies would be selected to help the athlete help himself or herself in controlling thoughts, emotions and behaviors, and in constructing a positive approach to performance. In subsequent sections of the chapter, various interventions for different situations will be described.

After the assessment process is completed, and an intervention is determined, careful planning for implementation is crucial. Of consideration is how to deliver an intervention to make the greatest impact. Of concern to the sport psychologist is to develop the athlete's trust and confidence when providing service. A plan needs to be prepared by the sport psychologist, preferably in writing, indicating what the athlete should do and when in order to obtain maximum benefits from the intervention. What will have to be determined is how effective the athlete will be in applying the intervention strategy in practice and in competition. To be considered in the planning process is how the sport psychologist and the athlete will collaborate to ensure appropriate strategy use.

Telephone discussions and subsequent direct meetings are typical for feedback and guidance. Furthermore, for whatever reason, a particular intervention may turn out not to be beneficial for that athlete, and need to be replaced with another type of strategy. The planning process includes how to attain problem resolution, how to assess the effectiveness of the intervention, and when to determine the possibility of an alternate strategy. Finally, the sport psychologist should realize if he or she cannot assist the athlete at the onset or any more, and if a differently trained sport psychologist (or psychiatrist or clinical psychologist in the case of suddenly recognized deeper personal issues, such as severe maladaptive tendencies) should be recommended to the athlete. Various potential intervention models exist, and the perfect match of model with a particular performance issue and person is ideal.

INTERVENTION MODELS AND CONSIDERATIONS

Models serve as the basis for determining appropriate interventions. A variety of models that emphasize different purposes and have different frameworks is presented by Murphy (1995). Authors of chapters in this book describe the nature of a life development model, an educational model, a multi-systematic model, a family systems model, an integrated organizational model, a developmental psychology model and a marital therapy model. Each model has uniqueness in theme and approach to interventions for attaining certain goals. These models indicate different perspectives, with unique emphases and purposes. Each one provides a framework that may suit a particular sport psychologist.

There is no single intervention model that serves all athletes for all purposes or all competitive situations. The professional background, knowledge, competencies and experiences of the sport psychologist and, of course, the problem to be resolved and characteristics of the athlete as well as the competitive environment, will influence favored approaches. Being educated in a counselling or clinical psychology program should lead to understanding personal problems and crises, maladaptive behaviors, and interventions to overcome them. Eating disorders, drug and alcohol abuse, uncontrollable frustrations and anger, excessive aggression tendencies and severe depression are examples of major concern. Certain clinical and counselling psychologists as well as psychiatrists may be specifically trained for dealing with such disorders.

Being educated and prepared in a sports science department contributes to understanding the mental demands of a sport, and effective learning and performance enhancement strategies. Examples are how to: mentally rehearse performing away from the sport environment (a form of homework); develop an effective pre-performance routine; allocate attention properly (narrow concentration vs. attentional switching, depending on the demands of the event); and formulate a meaningful goal-setting program. And so, the approach to intervention may be more skill acquisition/performance enhancement-based as applied by the sport scientist or more clinically/therapeutically-based as preferred by the psychologist. Of consideration as to which approach is more desirable is the relationship to what needs to be addressed.

An intervention model may be one that focuses on one or a few concerns, or may be much more global. In the first case, an isolated problem, such as the inability to sustain motivation over time and remain engaged and dedicated to improve, may need to be addressed and overcome. Such involvements may be considered as brief contact interventions. In the second case, many traditional areas in sport psychology would be covered as part of the educational process of the athlete. So, perhaps an eight-week mental/psychological skills training program would be designed for and provided to an athlete or a team (most likely the latter). Topics might include goal-setting, time management and self-assessment of progress; sustaining motivation over time; understanding stress and how to manage it; confidence-building; generating ideal self-perceptions; training the mind and emotions to function favorably (self-regulation); optimizing one's preparatory state before and during performance; and sport-specific information-processing and control concerns.

A medium of communication favored by the sport psychologist with the athlete might depend on what issues are being addressed and conditions available to deliver an intervention. Performance enhancement techniques are best explained and applied during actual practice on occasion. An example would be the sport psychologist playing a practice round of golf with the golfer. Discussions could be held before the golfer is ready to address a shot and following it as to attaining the optimal state for execution each time. Reminders and feedback connected with actual performance creates an active medium to train mental skills on-line.

Of course, in the majority of cases and with most sports, this is not a practical avenue of interaction between the athlete and the sport psychologist. Meetings with the sport psychologist and athlete typically occur in an office or some comfortable, isolated setting. Deep-seated issues and maladaptive behaviours would definitely be addressed in an office with a licensed psychologist. On the other hand, team cohesion and productivity concerns could be discussed in a large enough room to handle a group. The sport psychologist might carefully orchestrate the agenda to arrive at consensus and meaningful goals through discussion and interaction.

As we can see, intervention models favoured by a sport psychologist vary depending on expertise, goals to be accomplished and available opportunities. Similar to physicians and their specializations, sport psychologists do not possess expertise in all kinds of situations. It is important to realize what one knows and therefore has capabilities to be effective, and when and where expertise may reside with someone else. This comment leads us to the next section, which deals with uses and abuses of interventions.

USES AND MISUSES OF INTERVENTIONS

As is the case with dramatic and varied claims about different nutritional aids to benefit health, weight loss or life expectancy, and fitness programs to provide instant benefits, sport psychology has suffered from those who would falsify their credentials and abilities to transform an athlete's performance status to a higher level. Abuses of interventions or claims of beneficial interventions are primarily attributed to those individuals without credentials and formal educational training. Unfortunately, there are many opportunistic entrepreneurs who exaggerate their competencies. They proclaim how they can benefit athletes and coaches seeking mental and psychological advantage over opponents. The average coach or athlete does not know what to believe. Hope and expectations are high.

Presently, there are no clear safeguard measures against those who would attempt to fabricate their credentials and portfolios, and who make extravagant and exaggerated claims about their competencies. Coaches and athletes need good judgment. The same is true with the public in general in regard to claims made by self-proclaimed experts about their ability to produce instant weight reduction, health, fitness and energy in clients. Elevating standards and identifying competencies for those who wish to be considered as sport psychologists have been seen as complex issues for some time in many countries, such as the USA, Canada, Great Britain and Australia. Many professional articles have been written on the topic with various points of view (e.g. Silva, 1989). Professional societies have attempted to define standards, qualifications, accountability and acceptability of being recognized as a sport psychology consultant. In the USA, the Association for the Advancement of Applied Sport Psychology has developed criteria for certification.

As to psychologists and sport scientists with formal experiences in and knowledge about sport psychology, they have to realize their capabilities and limitations in providing services. Those recognized professionally as psychologists in their country, through formal education and licensure, have the ability to provide clinical and counselling services. These services, of course, are restricted to education expertise. On the other hand, sport scientists are not technically recognized as psychologists in many countries, and may more likely provide services as performance enhancement and mental training specialists.

To summarize what has been covered in this chapter so far, qualified sport psychology intervention specialists may provide services that are:

- clinical/therapeutic or educational/instructional
- preventive or remedial
- brief contact or extended duration
- focused on one issue or topic or a combination of issues, topics, themes (a program)
- provided in an office, a conference or class room, or in a sport setting.

Sport psychologists generally serve as consultants to individual athletes, or to teams, or to coaches, or to significant family members. And, in such capacity, their roles are relatively restricted. In other cases, sport psychologists may be considered and designated as an official part of a team and organization. They would have the ability to continually function in a support service capacity, and be involved in a variety of ways. In whatever capacity, it is important to be continually familiar with the sport psychology and psychology literature. Latest research findings and scholarly information as well as material on practical applications should suggest the kinds of interventions a sport psychologist might use to be most effective in particular situations.

USE OF THE SPORT PSYCHOLOGY AND GENERAL PSYCHOLOGY LITERATURES

The practice of sport psychology, through the application of intervention techniques, is ideally based on well-founded knowledge. Knowledge (and the resulting use of it) is best defended when reflecting empirical evidence. Another basis is the experience of acknowledged leaders in the field, as reported by them. However, scientific documentation for any intervention is most desirable. Unfortunately, in many cases the evidence may only be strongly suggestive of what conditions and processes should contribute to achieving, without any prescriptive details for application. Cookbook recipes are lacking. Thus, the sport psychologist will have to learn through experience how to best implement a number of intervention protocols that seem to be defensible and useful.

A similar situation exists in a number of fields with strong clinical and scientific programs of research, such as clinical psychology. Serious debates indicate cleavages and alternative perspectives from the different professional interests and occupational emphases in the same field. Sometimes tensions are apparent between researchers and practitioners. At the extreme, opinionated scientists believe that therapies, interventions, treatments and services should not be endorsed and provided without empirical support. Optimistic practitioners, on the other hand, think that although research is not adequately developed to serve as the sole basis for services rendered, they can use personal experiences and intuition to their advantage. In the middle ground, researchers do realize the need for more relevant research. Practitioners are becoming more aware of how existing research can benefit the services they might offer. Attempts at resolution benefit the scientist and the practitioner in many cases, including those associated with sport psychology.

The dedicated sport psychologist who is continually motivated to pursue the best possible intervention techniques would try to keep up with the last relevant reputable psychology and sport psychology/motor learning publications. The psychology literature contains an abundance of books, scholarly articles and studies dealing with themes applicable to sport settings. These include, as examples, stress management and techniques to self-regulate; circumstances that contribute to intrinsic versus extrinsic motivation, persistence, achievement and fulfillment; and strategies to elevate self-confidence and other self-perceptions in order to promote accomplishments. Publications are available to address many issues and circumstances.

Many sport psychology and motor learning books, professional articles and research journals provide information specifically useful for the more dedicated scholar and applied sport psychologist. Refereed sport psychology scholarly journals in which experts determine the creditability of articles for publication are increasing in number and quality in many parts of the world. For example, three North American journals, *The Sport Psychologist*, the *Journal of Applied Sport Psychology*, and the *Journal of Sport and Exercise Psychology* contain useful articles. So does the *Psychology of Sport and Exercise*, published in Europe. The International Society of Sport Psychology has been responsible for producing the *International Journal of Sport Psychology* since 1971. This was the first journal exclusively to publish sport psychology research and professional practice articles. In addition, many books, ranging from the very practical to the highly academic, have been published in recent years indicating interest in and the popularity of the field by students, athletes, coaches and serious sport recreationists.

Some books may be classified as very general, written in an entertaining manner, with information presented loosely and more intuitively with little scientific documentation. Sometimes the ideas seem to be very creative and potentially useful. Most books are middle ground, balancing practical examples with scientific findings. Such is the case with Williams' (2001) book that contains many useful chapters contributed by experts in their fields. Addressed is research into application considerations, with an emphasis on techniques for developing and refining psychological skills to enhance performance and personal growth. Anshel (2003) has produced a meaningful sport psychology textbook that blends research findings (without confusing jargon and statistics) and case studies with useful practical material for sport psychologists, athletes and coaches.

Moran (2004) has done a remarkable job in his text primarily covering skill acquisition to expertise considerations. The same is true with Murphy's (1995) ground-breaking book that deals with sport psychology interventions of all kinds for a variety of target populations and situations. Yet other books are meant to be very academic and to serve as texts or resource books at the graduate level of study. *The Handbook of Sport Psychology* (2001) edited by Singer, Hausanblas and Janelle is a significant contribution that falls into that category and contains implications for intervention possibilities.

Finally, it helps if the sport psychologist is familiar (directly or indirectly) with the sport in which they provide intervention services. Effective consultation requires sensitivity to and understanding of what an athlete goes through in order to attain a high level of achievement. Furthermore, it contributes to gaining the confidence and receptivity of an athlete for intervention possibilities. The consultant becomes more credible, not unlike a coach whose credibility and respect is enhanced if they are a former athlete of the sport for which they are coaching.

SKILL ACQUISITION AND PERFORMANCE ENHANCEMENT INTERVENTIONS

The continual refinement of skill and therefore improvement in a sport, as well as the ability to perform well consistently under demanding competitive situations, are the aspirations and goals of any serious athlete. Some athletes learn quickly and intuitively what they need to do for attaining success. Many others never learn enough. In this section, we describe many types of intervention possibilities for advancing the acquisition and development of skill, as well as considerations for enhancing performance capabilities. Individual and later team situations will be examined.

The nature of skill acquisition through expertise performance is usually associated with the motor learning, cognitive psychology (information-processing models) and ecological psychology (systems dynamics, perception-action models) body of knowledge. Comprehensive academic resources for cognitive motor learning are the textbooks written by Schmidt and Lee (1999) and Schmidt and Wrisberg (2004), and one for perception-action systems in sport is the book produced by Williams, Davids and Williams (1999). Implications can be drawn for improving the function of learning processes and practice conditions. Major topics of interest are intentions, attention, perception-action relationships, mental strategies, the processing of situational information leading to movement skill, and experiences contributing to improved skill. On the other hand, traditional sport psychology publications are usually associated with goal-setting, motivation, confidence-building, stress management, arousal control and direction, the flow state (optimal performance zone) and attribution training. Mental preparation for competition and related topics are provided in various textbooks (see, for example, LeUnes & Nation, 2002; Weinberg & Gould, 2003; and Williams, 2001). The main focus in performance enhancement is the learning of self-regulation behaviors and the belief in reasonable personal control over self and destiny. One general issue is what the athlete can do to unlock performance potential and therefore to achieve on a regular basis at a high level.

In a number of ways, it is convenient but not necessarily accurate to separate performance enhancement intervention techniques from skill development techniques. On occasion, a technique or intervention or strategy could be considered as belonging in either category. However, the motor learning/perception-action body of knowledge is reported somewhat distinct from the traditional sport psychology/psychological intervention literature. The foci in each tend to be different. In our chapter, we will separate the two for convenience in presenting material. Liberties are taken to broaden the dialog about the nature of potential interventions in order to provide the most comprehensive perspectives about the analysis of sports and athletes, and what it take to realize proficiency. We now turn to discussing the importance of understanding the nature of learning processes and conditions, with implications for skill development and ideas for interventions.

Skill Development and Interventions

Many factors potentially contribute to the development of skill, the transition to higher levels of accomplishing, and possibly a level of excellence and expertise. Of course, the optimal performance state (flow, the zone, peak performance) cannot be demonstrated without exceptional learning of what needs to be done, and how, in the particular sport and in challenging competitive situations. The learning and expertise knowledge base contains certain implications for the design of favorable instructional and practice conditions facilitative of effective learning and performance.

Before describing intervention possibilities, a brief overview of major research directions in this area is provided here as a frame of reference. These include the study of:

1. Beginners and those with an intermediate level of skill, determining what kinds of practice conditions (e.g. how practice should be organized and proceed for efficient and productive experiences, how instruction is provided, what is emphasized, how feedback is given) is favorable to elevate skill.
2. Experts as compared with the lesser skilled or novices, ascertaining ways in which they differ in extent of deliberate practice over a long period of time.
3. Perceptions, attention, cognitions and brain activity immediately prior to and during execution; strategies; and action planning in a specific sport.
4. "Mental attributes" most beneficial to use immediately prior to and during performance, considering:
   a. Individual alone performance in target-aiming, self-paced acts under self-control with time to prepare for execution, and requiring optimal immediate preparation and self-regulation skills.
   b. Continuous interactive situations with others, under rapidly changing and unpredictable conditions requiring fast and accurate situation awareness, anticipation of what is going to happen, and decision-making as to what initiatives to take or how to respond.

From these and related themes of interest, interventions can be offered that cut across many sports and those that are sport-specific or event-in-sport-specific. They can be included in presentations to individual athletes or to teams or to coaches, or to individuals to remedy a

lack of progress. As to general interventions with regard to the nature of practice considerations, attention should be given to the objective of acquiring skill, developing skill, or
attaining a level of expertise. Stages of skill learning were described by Fitts and Posner
(1967), and this early general reference is useful in understanding transitions.

Acquiring Skill

In order to begin to make progress, the athlete needs to:

1. Practice seriously with the intent to improve, understand how and what to improve,
   and use time in practice efficiently and productively instead of merely "being there" or
   finding excuses to avoid practicing and working hard.
2. Establish high, specific, measurable and attainable short- and long-term personal achievement goals and time-management skills.
3. Understand the danger of over-practice, under-practice or practicing inefficiently; recognize the process of correcting bad performance execution habits (making the correct
   response dominant), and comprehend how to be strategic.
4. Understand the importance of observational learning and other means of gaining skill,
   of how to receive and use feedback about performance, and how to stay attentive and
   motivated throughout practice sessions.
5. Understand the nature of implicit versus explicit learning situations, that structured,
   directed, and conscious conditions as well as problem-solving, discovery and non-
   awareness conditions can be mutually beneficial for developing skill.

For those athletes fortunate to have good coaching, such information and guidance would
be provided to them. However, many athletes may not have sufficient help at the early stages
of learning skills, and therefore could benefit from assistance from a sport psychologist who
understands learning processes and effective practice conditions. Unfortunately, space here
does not permit elaboration on how to create interventions about maximizing the benefits of
practice. Hopefully, the ideas presented can be transformed into meaningful interventions
by the resourceful reader.

Developing skill requires much dedicated and refined practice. Practice offers opportunities to rehearse actions repetitively so that they become habitual, to be performed as
if automatically, like driving a car or riding a bicycle. In a number of sports, adaptive,
improvisational and even creative behaviors are necessary personal resources. These behaviors become possible when basic movement patterns for a sport become automatic, like
dribbling a basketball. A general rule to remember is that practice by itself does not make
perfect. Rather, good (meaningful) practice increases the probability of attaining a level
of proficiency. With practice and understanding, knowing what to do (declarative knowledge) leads to knowing how to do it (procedural knowledge). And with even more sufficient
practice, the athletes learn how to do it better than their competitors.

Developing Skill

To proceed to a higher level, special considerations must be made for more sophisticated
practice conditions, considering the nature and demands of the sport, or type of events in a

sport. For *self-paced* (closed) acts, an appropriate pre-performance routine facilitates learning and performance. An inability to be effective—in shooting penalty shots in basketball, serving in tennis or volleyball, hitting a golf ball, shooting in archery—and in many other sports, may be due to a lack of a good pre-performance routine or readiness procedure. Without it, too many thoughts, especially negative, may creep in during execution. Too much attention may be allocated to distracters. Confidence and therefore performance expectations become reduced. The best athletes are as good as they are because they have mastered not only skilled movement acts but also control over their thoughts and emotions when it counts. These are related to the focus of attention immediately prior to and during the act.

What follows is an example pre-performance routine, called the Five-step Strategy, and how it might be implemented as an intervention. It has been developed by Singer and researched in a variety of ways by Singer and his colleagues. Scientific explanations are offered elsewhere (Singer, 2000). In addition, Lidor and Singer (2003) have authored a chapter with good practical advice. Many other similar routines are available in the literature, and sometimes they are referred to as a strategy, a pre-shot routine, a protocol, a plan, a procedure and even a ritual.

An Example Intervention for a Pre-Performance Routine

The example here will be shooting the penalty (foul) shot in basketball, and basically all the comments can be applied to various target-aiming events where there is time to prepare, preview the situation and control the act. The athlete should know that the goal while executing is to generate the ideal harmony of mind, emotions and action. Great shooters appear to be automatic in their preliminary and shooting behaviors. From the stance to how many breaths are taken, how the ball is held, how many times the ball is bounced, the focus of attention, the movement rhythm and the ultimate release of the ball, everything is synchronized—and consistent. The pattern is remarkably consistent.

This outcome does not come naturally. Every player has to work hard to refine the mechanics of the shooting pattern, as well as how to direct and control thought and emotional processes. The Five-step Strategy may be considered as the psychology of effective foul shooting. It should aid in the learning of the skill and correcting faulty shooting as well as when performing in contests. Like the shooting movement itself, it should be practiced until it occurs as if automatically. The strategy intervention, or something like it, is recommended for all skill-level players. It has been formulated on the basis of interviews with many athletes and personal experience in working with them, research conducted on selected aspects of the overall strategy, as well as on the strategy itself.

The steps in the strategy are: readying, imaging, focusing attention, executing with a quiet mind, and evaluating. This routine should be used each time when practicing the foul shot as well as when shooting in a contest. The key ingredients are as follows:

- *Readying* This includes positioning of the body at the foul line at the same place each time; getting in an optimal emotional state; having positive expectations of a confidence in making the shot; and developing a comfortable breathing and ball-bouncing routine.
- *Imaging* The player should briefly picture in their mind the rim and how large the basket is, the shot going in, the arc of the ball, and the feeling of the release, from the result of

the act to the initiation of the movement. This process should aid in confidence-building and in pre-cueing the nervous system and the muscle patterns to be used in the act.

- *Focusing attention* The next crucial process is concentrating hard on a cue or a thought. Typically this allocation of attention is to the front of the rim, with the intention of blocking out any irrelevant and performance-damaging thoughts. Intense concentration should eliminate the possibility of thinking too much about what is involved in the act, any potential distracters and concerns about missing the shot.
- *Executing with a quiet mind* When everything feels just right, the ball should be released with no attempt to think about anything. This is the "just do it" approach. It involves self-trust, that the shot does not need to be deliberately and consciously controlled.
- *Evaluating* If time permits, as in practice or in the first of two shots in a game, the player should quickly determine if everything went well. If the shot was missed, was it due to bad mechanics or a failure in one or more of the steps in the strategy? If needed, adjustments should be made in the next attempt.
- As a final point, the pre-performance procedure (although the Five-step Strategy also involves during-execution considerations) should be rehearsed repeatedly in practice with each foul shot. In time, it will become very routine in practice as well as in games, and especially in crucial games when much potential stress is present. Each player needs to develop a routine that is comfortable and yields confidence to perform well. Consistency in routine is crucial.

For *externally paced* situations, timely initiatives as well as quick and accurate reactions to what others are doing and where objects (like a ball) are contribute to success. In a basketball game, the player needs to activate appropriate actions adaptively in response to changing circumstances. With better awareness and anticipation of what might occur, there is more time for judgment, decisions and relevant actions. Attending to the most important and yet minimal predictive sources of information or cues in the situation is essential. Research indicates that experts compared to non-experts have more elaborate sport-specific knowledge; make more meaning of available information; are more efficient in processing information; visually detect and locate objects and patterns in their visual field faster and more accurately; use situation probability information better; and make more rapid and appropriate decisions (Singer, 2000). Therefore, the challenge is to explore means to assist athletes in the way that they function in regard to these behaviors.

Better competitors tend to become quickly aware of an opponent's capabilities, preferences and tendencies; what most opponents might attempt to do under the particular circumstances; and any meaningful sources of information revealed from the opponent's intentions and actions (see Singer, 1998, for many examples of these considerations and other ones in racket sports). In major theories of attention in psychology as to tasks involving thought and action, one concept is that three psychological components are involved (Hunt & Ellis, 2004). The first is perceptual analysis in which the appropriate stimulus or cue (or whatever term is used to describe what should be reacted to), is identified. The second is response decision; what to do. The final one is response production; how to execute. Especially in complex sport situations in which events occur rapidly, overload in attention can cause breakdowns in performance. Ineffective performances may be due to not being continuously situationally aware, not taking in the best sources of immediate information, not anticipating the opponent's intentions very well, not making good decisions as to what to do, and/or not executing according to personal intentions. Therefore, not being successful could be due to various mental/perceptual functions and/or performance mechanics ineptitude.

An Example Intervention for Situational Awareness in Reactive Sport Situations

For an athlete being judged as lacking in performance in time-demanding reactive situations, an assessment needs to be made as to contributing factors. Discussion with the athlete, observations made by the coach and observations in competition made by the sport psychologist may provide insights as to causative agents. If the mechanics of the movements are ruled out as a problem, then other issues arise. The ability to sustain concentration throughout a contest is of paramount importance and, if this is a problem, then an intervention dealing with sustained attention is a requirement. Moran (1996) has dedicated an entire book to explaining the nature of attention and concentration, and techniques for improving concentration in sport. If that is not the major issue, then assessment (typically through discussion) needs to be made as to where there are deficits in processing information leading to actions. The areas of possible deficits are:

- *Visual distributed attention and being situationally aware* Relevant situational and opponent cues need to be perceived and updated continuously. Taking in the right information at the right time, being situationally smart, is the beginning mental operation.
- *Anticipation* The next critical step is judging what the opponent's intentions are, what his or her actions would lead to, on a subjective probability basis. Understanding what might happen, as quickly as possible, leads to more time to make decisions about what to do.
- *Decision-making* A decision of where to go on the court and what to do, and planning and selecting the action, is the subsequent consideration. This process requires adaptability and possibly creativity.
- *Movement initiation* Considering the situation and temporal and spatial factors, when and how to activate the movement plan is the next step. Acceptable movement completion depends on the previous processes as well as the ability to execute effectively

Anyone can improve strategically with the right understanding of what needs to be corrected and how to correct it. A failure of ideal functioning of any of the previously identified processes can be remedied with "mental conditioning" programs that can occur off-court, during practice and immediately prior to and during competitive matches.

Example interventions are described by Singer (1998) for racket sports and are very briefly indicated here. Off-court preparation includes mental rehearsal, where the athlete visualizes playing and attending to the processes and behaviors to be implemented on the court. The purpose in this form of mental homework is to be prepared to think intelligently on the court, to cue oneself, and be aware of in what ways to improve. Most mental rehearsal research and practice deals with thinking about the movement skills to be performed, and their execution. However, here the emphasis is on player strategy, thinking about how to think and what to think about on the court. The obvious ultimate goal is for court behaviors to become automatic, whereby conscious thinking is replaced by what appears to be automatically produced correct behaviors.

Another off-court approach is using video of self in previous competitions to study court position in different situations, the appropriateness of playing strategies and the effectiveness of decisions and actions. Video of future opponents leads to knowing what playing style and tendencies to expect. Mannerisms and techniques may lead to tipping off intentions. Videos of playing situations, with the player responding as to what to do as in a computer game, can be helpful.

On-court practice can include special drills that emphasize using and improving the mental processes of interest here (see Steinberg, Chaffin & Singer, 1998, for examples in tennis). In many practice situations, players respond too mechanically and indifferently without attempting to train their mental processes to be more aware, adaptive and creative. As to pre-competition, the player may need self-reminders of intentions of how to play and to what to attend. Training movement skills and mental skills requires a degree of conscious awareness and purpose at first. With training, both can be produced as if automatically. Automatic behaviors are effortless, involve fast information-processing and appropriate perception and action coupling, and are produced efficiently. They represent a characteristic of expertise.

Gaining a Level of Excellence and Expertise

Many of the areas already discussed could also be considered here in helping making better athletes even better. In addition, the study of expertise in academic areas, chess playing, music and sport is somewhat consistent in findings. Extensive deliberate practice is a prerequisite for success. Intentions to succeed, persistence to achieve, and meaningfulness of training and practice conditions as dedicated over many years make a huge difference in the potential to realize proficiency. Based on the work of others and his own research, Ericsson (1996) has proposed that a minimum of 10 years of deliberate and effortful practice is a necessary foundation for expertise. Understanding the nature of sport expertise has become a popular area of research in recent times, and implications about attaining excellence can be made for those who wish to be reach that status. Indeed, Starkes and Ericsson's edited book (2003) provides many perspectives about research on sport expertise.

Some interventions, for those athletes in need, may cover:

1. The necessity to recognize the importance of practice on many occasions to simulate real competitive events. The playing conditions, as well as the psychological and mental approach to practice competitions, should simulate what is intended in real competition. An athlete does not suddenly play with competitive intensity and remain focused throughout the duration of a contest, as well as cope with stress and frustrating moments, unless there are adequate experiences in practice and competitions to refine these personal characteristics.
2. The desirability of variable practice conditions with many different types of opponents and conditions for those events that require adaptive interactions with others. The transference of knowledge and skills from circumstance to circumstance is more likely to occur from a variety of practice and competitive experiences.
3. The necessity of a good pre-performance routine for attaining a state of automaticity and flow in self-paced events (Singer, 2002). Execution in brief acts are more likely to be demonstrated well repeatedly when a good pre-performance routine is used to facilitate performance.

4. The ability to control conscious attention during performance so that it does not deteriorate because of too much attention to control processes (what is involved in the execution of the act) or to distracters. A quiet mind is a desired state so that choking (performance in a contest in a very meaningful situation that is below proven capability) does not occur.
5. The awareness and use of the latest technology related to the sport of dedication. Computer graphics to assist learning and performance, computer data about self and opponents in competitive situations, video use, virtual reality possibilities, and more, suggest the potential contributions of technology for enhancing performance and elevating proficiency.
6. We can see that interventions having to do with acquiring, developing and realizing high levels of skill are very much dependent on understanding favorable practice conditions as well as improving the way internal processes (cognitive and attentional) function. We now turn to the nature of performance enhancement interventions.

However, before that, a section is presented on what is known about psychological and mental attributes associated with superior performance. This information is suggestive about which areas interventions may be generally needed and helpful for all kinds of athletes in many sports.

Psychological and Mental Characteristics of Excellence

There is significance in identifying what world-class athletes determine are the greatest contributors to their potential and actual achievement. Athletes aspiring for success can then appreciate what these factors are, and therefore in what areas they might try to improve. Research in which superior athletes are of interest indicates how they perceive the relative importance of various psychological and mental factors associated with preparing to compete as well as actual performance during competition. On occasion, coaches have been asked their opinions. Factors generally connected with proficiency with any sport have been reported, as well as those specific to particular sports. Interventions provided by sport psychologists can be instructional and guiding, as in describing what these personal attributes are and how to develop them, or for remedying problems that undermine chances for realizing achievement potential.

Perspectives about what it takes psychologically and mentally to accomplish in sport have been determined by comparing more versus less successful athletes with data derived from various tests of profiles, questionnaires and other self-report instruments, as well as interviews. A number of reports have influenced research and practice in sport psychology, too many to include here. Some of the more influential will be described briefly in chronological order. Overlap and uniqueness are apparent in the characteristics identified.

Based upon personal experiences and observations, Loehr (1986) suggested seven factors associated with success in sport with use of the Psychological Performance Inventory (PPI): self-confidence, negative energy, positive energy, attention control, visual and imagery control, motivational level, and attitude control. The Psychological Skills Inventory for Sport (PSIS) was created by Mahoney, Gabriel and Perkins (1987), and has been referred to frequently in research dealing with the assessment of psychological skills. Measures included anxiety control, concentration, confidence, mental preparation, motivation and team emphasis. In subsequent years, other instruments have been developed due to concern over the psychometric properties of such inventories.

One such instrument is the Athletic Coping Skills Inventory (ACSI) produced by Smith, Schutz, Smoll and Ptacek (1995). Factors labeled are coping with adversity, peaking under pressure, goal-setting/mental preparation, concentration, freedom from worry, confidence and achievement motivation, and coachability. A more recent inventory, the Test of Performance Strategies (TOPS), was designed by Thomas, Murphey and Hardy (1999) as a general measure of psychological skills for use for assessment as well as to monitor the effects of psychological skills training programs on skill development. Data for practice and competition yielded eight factors: goal-setting, relaxation, activation, imagery, self-talk, attentional control, emotional control, and automaticity. The authors suggest that the test, based on preliminary data, is well suited for assessing the effectiveness of interventions.

Using an interview technique with US Olympic champions, Gould and Dieffenbach (2002) determined that the athletes characterized themselves as possessing the ability to cope with and control anxiety, confidence, mental toughness/resiliency, sport intelligence, the ability to focus and block out distractions, competitiveness, a hard-work ethic, the ability to set and achieve goals, coachability, high levels of dispositional hope, optimism, and adaptive perfectionism. Finally, after summarizing various sources of data in an attempt to determine the existence of a certain psychological profile that might be linked to high-level performance, Williams and Krane (2001) offered the following characteristics: self-regulation of arousal (energized yet relaxed, no fear), high self-confidence, better concentration (being appropriately focused), in control but not forcing it, positive preoccupation with sport (imagery and thoughts), and determination and commitment

A review of these sources, although on occasion identifying different characteristics (a possible reflection of scholars' interpretation of research along with personal experiences, research methodology and instruments used, and subjects selected), nevertheless paints a picture of the typical ones related to performance excellence. They are the foundation for success in many sports. As such, potential interventions for improving upon the functioning of strategies and processes related to them should be understood by the sport psychologist. Ideally, also recognized would be additional issues that might emerge unique from sport to sport, athlete to athlete, and situation to situation, with possible interventions. We now turn to the nature of performance enhancement techniques, what they are, and how they are typically prescribed in sport psychology settings.

PERFORMANCE ENHANCEMENT AND INTERVENTIONS

The ability to develop, refine and generate personal resources contributing to expertise differentiates the success athletes are likely to experience, and to experience frequently. They learn to maximize their performance capabilities, to enhance them. Unfortunately, people are not machines. Fluctuations occur in one's ability to consistently deploy optimal personal resources in practice and from contest to contest. The attainment of high levels of skill and the continued capability to demonstrate excellence in meaningful competitions over a long period of time reflect the development of ideal psychological and mental characteristics. The athlete who is knowledgeable about self-management and self-regulation skills, and able to use them when it counts, is at a decided advantage over competitors.

In sport psychology, many non-scientific or popular ("pop") books, textbooks, scientific academic books, studies in research journals and professional articles have presented and discussed various ideal personal characteristics as well as techniques to improve upon their development. The sport psychologist can locate much material about the nature of the characteristics of exceptional performers, as identified in the previous section, as well as potential interventions. With regard to educational and interventional possibilities, some areas are fairly well established; others may be more speculative. For example, the stress management literature suggests a variety of alternatives that might be helpful for the athlete who is challenged in dealing with competitive stress. The same is true with goal-setting procedures for athletes who have difficulty in staying on target to make progress over a long period of time. Likewise, mental rehearsal and imaging techniques for preparation for competition have been described in many publications. Other topics, like developing concentration and mental toughness, are more vague.

It is beyond the scope of this chapter to describe all the intervention possibilities for enhancing performance. Specific chapters in this book will include descriptions of sport-specific interventions. Also, as was mentioned earlier in the chapter, programs of psychological skills education and training have been proposed elsewhere, as have interventions for specific needs. General sport psychology textbooks (e.g. Anshel, 2003; Weinberg & Gould, 2003; Williams, 2001) include ample descriptions of the nature of the most frequently identified psychological processes as well as potential interventions in many cases. *The Sport Psychologist* and the *Journal of Applied Sport Psychology*, among other journals, contain many research and professional articles on these topics. As Conroy and Benjamin (2001) point out, however, sport psychology consultations often focus only on teaching psychological skills and neglect explaining insights to athletes about their performances and themselves, and underlying issues. They recommend a psychodynamics approach to enhance consultation, an important point to consider.

Such observations are very relevant for remedial interventions. For the presentation of information about mental strategies and psychological skills as part of the education of the athlete prior to the need for remedy, information can be more general. Examples of general approaches in certain areas will be provided next: goal-setting, imagery and mental rehearsal, confidence building, and formulating a contest-readiness plan.

AN EXAMPLE INTERVENTION FOR GOAL-SETTING

Many athletes have dreams and hopes of attaining excellence. The challenge is to extend such thinking to planning in an organized way about how to train and sustain motivation for high expectations to potentially materialize. Goal-setting is a powerful motivational technique. It is especially helpful for those athletes who are weak in organization and planning skills, time management, objective self-appraisal, and understanding what needs to be done and achieved by a particular date in order to progress according to some time schedule.

Achievement goals commonly take one of three different forms. They might be what the athlete hopes to attain, will be satisfied in attaining or expects to attain. The last goal is most desirable, as it exhibits commitment. The other types are more vague, as more useful goals are not merely wishful thinking or comprised of minimal expectations. The athlete needs to consider present status, motivational level, time available and effort planned to put forth. What level of performance might be expected in a certain time frame, such as in six months? What conditioning and fitness considerations, nutritional and life-style changes, performance skills and strategies, and mental and psychological skills need to be improved? How might this be done? Goals should be expressed not only for performance outcome itself, but also for all those factors that might contribute to performance excellence.

Goals are most meaningful if they are stated in precise terms, are high, and attainable. It is advisable to set short-term (perhaps weekly) and longer-term goals (perhaps in six months). Short-term goals, assessed subjectively or objectively, determine if the athlete is on target to reach the longer-term goals. The process of goal-setting makes the athlete commit to accomplishing something in a specified period of time. In other words, it is a time-management procedure to achieve what is possible and desired personally. Establishing short-term and long-term goals can help to maintain motivation and perseverance. It is a self-improvement technique as one is not being compared to others. A diary or record book might be maintained. It would include weekly and longer-term goals, and the degree of accomplishment along the way in the areas specified as related to improvement. Depending on degree of fulfilment, goals may be elevated or lowered, and practice/training/daily life routines may be changed.

Furthermore, a personally established goal-setting protocol makes the athlete more accountable to himself or herself. Many athletes dream of being Olympians or professional, but in order to fulfil the dream, energy and time must be dedicated for purposeful activity. A goal-setting plan is especially useful for the athlete when the motivation to persist is fading, the level of achievement is considerably lower than potential and poor time and training management skills are present. As to the setting of goals, the athlete alone, or with the help of the coach, should determine what is possible, how, and in what time frame. The coach is the specialist who is experienced in determining present capabilities and possible future achievements. Even with assistance, the athlete needs to make the commitment and feel the ultimate responsibility for the goals stated and the degree to which they are realized. They are personal statements of expected progress.

AN EXAMPLE INTERVENTION FOR IMAGERY AND MENTAL REHEARSAL

Many athletes do not realize that they can do mental homework away from the sport environment in preparation for practice and competition. Imaging, also called visualizing, personally intended actions and strategies can help to enrich actual performance. Likewise, opponents can be pictured, how they compete, and how the athlete will respond. Imagery refers to forming a mental picture of a desirable performance in a forthcoming context, be it in practice or real competition. Mental rehearsal is repeated practice of an act or a sequence of events in the mind.

Such dedicated time is useful for the athlete faltering in certain aspects of their performance, and can serve as a reminder of how to perform. In addition, it can pre-cue what to expect and what needs to be done in a subsequent performance situation. An athlete can also image an attitude, playing intensity, being under control, and other behaviors that might be deemed appropriate. The athlete should designate mental rehearsal sessions about when, how long and where they should occur. A possible approach is to allocate late afternoons or early evenings, when alone and relaxed. Perhaps 15 minutes a session, maybe 3 times a week, could be attempted. There is no documentation as to session frequency and length of time, so the athlete will have to determine what works best as to holding interest and clarity of images. Also, it is recognized that some individuals are much better at visualizing than are others. Programs have been proposed to improve concentration and visualization skills.

The ability to internally create images related to effective performance, and using specially designed mental rehearsal sessions, can make a contribution in a number of ways that have been speculated about. Thoughts can trigger neural and muscle pattern activity in the corresponding parts of the body. As a part of a body is thought about in action, neural activity increases at that location. Perhaps in some way neural pathways appropriate for skilled movement execution are strengthened. Also, by imaging what we want to do and expect to do, we cue ourselves. The process is a reminder, in detail, as to performance expectations. A mental rehearsal session may be a source of motivation, of inspiring the athlete to be focused and ready to perform the next day. Finally, it could be a confidence-builder; as such experiences are associated with thinking good (performance-relevant) thoughts. Confidence level may be raised because positive images are created in preparation for competition.

AN EXAMPLE INTERVENTION FOR CONFIDENCE FOR IMPROVED SELF-CONTROL

Performing under self-control implies the ability to feel capable and confident in competing at one's best. Feelings of inadequacy and of not being able to compete well correspond to becoming overwhelmed, not meeting expectations and perceiving a lack of personal control over what happens. Of course, much depends on a realistic self-appraisal of capability, especially as compared to opponents. Furthermore, degree of success against opponents and standards contributes to confidence. A better judgment of self is continual improvement in performance rather than winning as a sole criterion of success and satisfaction. An athlete cannot dictate winning as an outcome, but effort in practice and training, preparing to compete well, and trust in performing at one's level of competency are important ingredients for the motivation to persist and to improve. Determination of the quality and effort in preparation and in performance can provide a person with a degree of satisfaction, even if winning does not occur.

Virtually every athlete who has committed to experiencing excellence has felt doubt on occasion and has had to deal with losing, bad performances, adversities and problems. Losing confidence is inevitable. Overcoming obstacles is related to self-perceptions, what we think of our chances to cause circumstances to favor us. The belief in reasonable personal control over destiny is the foundation of confidence in changing circumstances for the better. Confidence is related to looking forward to competing, looking forward to performing up to capabilities instead of dwelling on what will go wrong. Success, as defined here as competing at a high level of personal potential, contributes to the probability of winning.

Coping style is important. For instance, an athlete with a mastery-orientation may reason that personal failure is a result of not enough effort in training or in not preparing well enough. The result is not a loss of confidence but rather trying harder and preparing better in the future, and determining what needs to be done through objective analyses. An individual with a helpless-coping orientation thinks of failure as due to a lack of ability or being unfortunate. The perception is that it is not worth trying harder because it will not make a difference. Confidence diminishes. Too much emphasis is on winning and on factors perceived to be beyond personal control.

Confidence consists of believing that one is capable of performing well in situations. Hard work, dedication and intelligent preparation are perceived to lead to favourable results, and that there are alternative solutions to difficulties. With this kind of mind-set, optimism and perseverance will be demonstrated. Too little or too much confidence may be detrimental to performance. Self-perceptions are under the control of the athlete and, when appropriate, lead to favorable outcomes over a duration of time.

A SAMPLE INTERVENTION FOR FORMULATING A CONTEST-READINESS PLAN

A great competitor develops as consistent a routine as possible before each competition. It includes what to adhere to the day before, the evening before, the day of, and immediately before an event. Of course, many factors will not allow for this plan to be followed without modification. However, every attempt is made to be as consistent as possible. In turn, it is likely that actual performance will be at a consistently high level. A plan for readying for competition could be outlined so that the athlete has something concrete to follow. This type of plan may be especially helpful for athletes who are inconsistent in their performances.

The routine covers everything the athlete does, including sleeping and eating patterns, as well as the rest of the daily and evening activities. It should be made on an individual basis, considering what the athlete favors and believes will work best. To start with, it is ideal if a practice session a day before the competition could be held at the same location at the same time. Familiarization with facilities reduces uncertainty. The day and evening before competition should include considerations of what is eaten and when, and what situations seem to be favorable for relaxation/motivation. Some athletes like to listen to music or watch a movie or television; others may want to be with friends and to socialize. Some athletes may want to be alone and to focus on what they intend to do the next day during competition, while others may want to be involved with activities that divert their attention away from the competition. An ideal time to try to go to sleep is desirable.

For the day of competition, a typical pattern of "comfortable" behaviors is advocated from wake-up time, what to think about (hopefully, positive thoughts about the day and the competition), and what and when to eat. Immediately prior to competition, the athlete needs to follow a routine that enables them to feel ready to compete, to do well. There is no one way to prepare. Readiness procedures are personal expressions, and it is important for each athlete to adopt a consistent plan, one that is believed in and should lead to desired outcomes.

The very nature of events and when and where they are scheduled make it almost impossible to follow the same preparatory regimen. However, the contest plan indicates the attempt to be as routine as possible before each event. The athlete could indicate in writing those behaviors and activities from the day before until the actual event that they would like to be consistent if that can possibly be controlled. Thinking about previous best performances and what was done prior to them can aid in creating the plan. The plan should be modified as necessary. Keeping a diary of each competitive event, the outcome and evaluation of personal performance, along with the 24-hour pre-contest list of behaviors and activities, will indicate the relationship of variables to best accomplishments. The athlete should determine if a pattern unfolds whereby best performances are consistently associated with certain pre-contest activities. The ultimate goal is to create a plan that can guide the athlete toward performance consistency. It cannot be too rigid, but it does suggest a routine to follow.

The examples just offered can be used for presentations to athletes or to help remedy problems they are experiencing. Many other examples are available, as are explanations and interventions for a wide range of psychological and mental processes connected to attaining a degree of excellence. Most of them are individual athlete-centered. We now discuss considerations for team success, which are typically directed to improving cohesion and morale, individual productivity for the good of group effectiveness, and ideal leadership qualities.

Teams and Groups

Many sports are team in nature, requiring members to work together to reach common goals—like winning. Members interact with each other and influence each other, creating a situation of interdependence. Also, a number of athletes may be engaged in individual sports, such as tennis, golf or bowling, where they are a part of a team. The coach's role is not only in teaching athletes performance skills and tactics, and what each one has to improve in to be more proficient, but also how members can make contributions for the good of the team. It is frequently observed that successful teams in many sports seem to have player chemistry. Each has a role and believes in that role making a significant contribution to team effectiveness. Some players invariably evolve as leaders. Yet, the coach is the ultimate leader, the maestro, with responsibilities of coordinating everyone and everything by creating unity, designating player roles, having players' support in their approach to leadership, and producing a winning team Preferred leadership style, perception of style and athlete satisfaction have been discussed by Riemer and Chelladurai (1995) and in many other sources.

Consequently, it is generally realized that team success on a consistent basis will depend on many factors. These include individual player abilities, especially for the responsibilities unique to each position; the coach's leadership style in teaching, communicating, motivating and delegating roles to players; and team cohesion, morale and spirit. Of course, there have been examples of teams in which players did not get along well, but personal ambitions, talent and task motivation were able to overcome a low level of cohesion. However, for the most part, cohesion and morale are considered to be desirable commodities. Cohesion generally refers to players sticking together, almost like a family. Morale has to do with optimism, enthusiasm and positive attitude of the members. A fun, collegial and bonding atmosphere is what many athletes look forward to, especially considering the intensity, time and rigor of training regimens and practice sessions, and the pressure of competition itself.

With regard to these perspectives, the sport psychologist may be invited to make presentations to a team and coach about the nature of cohesion and morale, what they might contribute to, and how they might be improved. Furthermore, there may be a discussion on accepting player roles, be they starters or substitutes, and the importance of all members contributing to the good of the team. A coach may want to meet privately with the sport psychologist to discuss leadership behaviors and coaching philosophy related to the team in the context of the psychology of communication, principles from social psychology and organizational psychology, and the nature of group dynamics. Another type of meeting might deal with a particular problem athlete, with advice given to the coach. Possibly the sport psychologist will be asked to work with that person who may not be fitting in, is not a team player, is disgruntled, and is making fewer contributions than expected to the team. The various authors contributing chapters in the book edited by Lidor and Henschen (2003) include many scenarios in team settings and how to deal with them. A general intervention having to do with improving the positive dynamics and cohesiveness of a team is called "team-building" (see Hardy and Crace, 1997, for example techniques), which can occur directly or indirectly.

Team-building Interventions

Procedures and processes to be incorporated in promoting the way a team functions, considering effectiveness, satisfaction and cohesion, are generally termed "team-building". Ideas generally include ways to communicate better and how to establish a sense of unity. Also considered are how to understand each other more, how to set individual and collective goals, as well as to commit to them, how to be more effective and how to establish pride. The process is certainly much more than a pep talk or a motivational speech. Intervention possibilities may be direct; that is, having discussions directly with team members (e.g. Yukelson, 1997), or indirect; that is, working solely with the coaching staff. Each situation is different as to whether the sport psychologist will be allowed or encouraged to meet directly with the team on one or more occasions, or whether the coach will prefer to discuss matters solely with the sport psychologist.

In direct team-building, separate discussions with the coaching staff and team members, as well as observations during practice and competition, are helpful to set the stage for the sport psychologist to have a feeling for the situation. Then, sessions are planned by the sport psychologist to fit in and be accepted by the group. Through an interactive environment, team members are educated about an ideal group situation. They are encouraged to contribute to the process of evolving to establish favorable conditions. Problem areas are identified and resolved to reasonable satisfaction. Expectations are mentioned and common goals established, and ways in which all can contribute to the good of the team are determined. With periodic sessions, evaluation of progress can be made, new ideas discussed, and opportunities for problem-resolution presented.

A different situation is indirect team-building, where the sport psychologist advises the coach about preferential ways to enhance team-building. The coach in turn uses those ideas that are most convincing. Many coaches appear to be sceptical or nervous about the notion of an outsider to the team, in the case of the sport psychologist, delving into the chemistry of the team and possibly uncovering issues that might be threatening to the coach. They tend to believe that they know how to guide teams psychologically. And a number of them do an excellent job. However, in those situations where the sport psychologist gains the confidence of the coach, receptivity leads to motivation to learn about ways for developing team cohesion and team-building. The coach needs to feel comfortable in accepting a particular role for establishing favorable communication channels. Then they have to learn how best to use strategies that will foster team togetherness and identity, clarify individual and team expectations, and contribute to pride and cohesion. Excellent suggestions are made by Moran (2004).

CONCLUDING COMMENTS

To summarize this chapter, it is apparent that much needs to be understood about what it takes mentally and psychologically to achieve at a high level of competency in sport. A remarkable array of interventions is available for improving the way learning processes function and for enhancing performance capabilities in competition. Presentations and discussions can be educational while special sessions for assessment can lead to specifically designed remedy programs for those in need. Finally, team-building strategies serve to potentially improve individual contributions to the group, morale, cohesion and success. Whereas this chapter dealt with interventions that might be useful for the athlete free of maladaptive behaviors and serious disorders, Chapter 5 discusses such issues and the counselling process.

REFERENCES

Anshel, M.H. (2003). *Sport Psychology: From Theory to Practice* (4th edn). San Francisco: Benjamin-Cummings.

Beckmann, J. & Kellmann, M. (2003). Procedures and principles of sport psychological assessment. *The Sport Psychologist, 17*, 338–350.

Carver, C.S. & Scheier, M.F. (1998). *On the Self-Regulation of Behavior.* Cambridge, UK: Cambridge University Press.

Conroy, D.E. & Benjamin, L.S. (2001). Psychodynamics in sport psychology consultation: application of interpersonal theory. *The Sport Psychologist, 15*, 103–117.

Ericsson, K.A. (ed.) (1996). *The Road to Excellence: The Acquisition of Expert Performance in the Arts and Sciences, Sports and Games.* Mahwah, NJ: Erlbaum.

Fitts, P.M. & Posner, M. (1967). *Human Performance.* Belmont, CA: Brooks/Cole.

Gould, D. & Dieffenbach, K. (2002). Psychological characteristics and their development in Olympic champions. *Journal of Applied Sport Psychology, 14*, 172–204.

Hardy, C.J. & Crace, R.K. (1997). Foundations of team building: introduction to the team building primer. *Journal of Applied Sport Psychology, 9*, 1–10.

Hunt, R.R. & Ellis, H.C. (2004). *Fundamentals of Cognitive Psychology.* New York: McGraw-Hill.

LeUnes, A. & Nation, J.R. (2002). *Sport Psychology: From Research to Practice.* Pacific Grove, CA: Wadsworth.

Lidor, R. & Henschen, K.P. (eds). (2003). *The Psychology of Team Sports.* Morgantown, WV: Fitness Information Technology.

Lidor, R. & Singer, R.N. (2003). Preperformance Routines in Self-Paced Tasks: Developmental and Educational Considerations. In R. Lidor & K.P. Henschen (eds). *The Psychology of Team Sports.* Morgantown, WV: Fitness Information Technology.

Loehr, J.E. (1986). *Mental Toughness Training for Sports: Achieving Athletic Excellence.* Lexington, MA: Stephen Greene Press.

Mahoney, M.J., Gabriel, T.J. & Perkins, T.S. (1987). Psychological skills and exceptional athletic performance. *The Sport Psychologist, 1*, 181–199.

Moran, A.P. (1996). *The Psychology of Concentration in Sport Performers: A Cognitive Analysis.* East Sussex, UK: Psychology Press.

Moran, A.P. (2004). *Sport and Exercise Psychology: A Critical Introduction.* East Sussex, UK: Routledge.

Murphy, S.M. (ed.) (1995). *Sport Psychology Interventions.* Champaign, IL: Human Kinetics.

Riemer, H.A. & Chelladurai, P. (1995). Leadership and satisfaction in athletes. *Journal of Sport and Exercise Psychology, 17*, 276–293.

Roberts, G.C. & Gould, D. (eds). (1989). Special issue on psychological services to Olympic teams. *The Sport Psychologist, 3*, 299–385.

Schmidt, R.A. & Lee, T.D. (1999). *Motor Control and Learning.* Champaign, IL: Human Kinetics.

Schmidt, R.A. & Wrisberg, C.A. (2004). *Motor Learning and Performance.* Champaign, IL: Human Kinetics.

Silva, J.M. (1989). Toward the professionalization of sport psychology. *The Sport Psychologist, 3,* 265–273.

Singer, R.N. (1998). From the laboratory to the courts: understanding and training anticipation and decision-making. In A. Lees, I. Maynard, M. Hughes & T. Reilly (eds), *Science and Racket Sports* (pp. 109–120). London: E. & F.N. Spon.

Singer, R.N. (2000). Performance and human factors: considerations about cognition and attention for self-paced and externally-paced events. *Ergonomics, 43,* 1661–1680.

Singer, R.N. (2002). Preperformance state, routines, and automaticity: what does it take realize expertise in self-paced events? *Journal of Sport and Exercise Psychology, 24,* 359–375.

Singer, R.N., Hausanblas, H.A. & Janelle, C.M. (eds). (2001). *Handbook of Sport Psychology.* New York: Wiley.

Smith, R.E., Schutz, R.W., Smoll, F.L. & Ptacek, J.T. (1995). Development and validation of a multidimensional measure of sport-specific psychological skills. *Journal of Sport and Exercise Psychology, 17,* 379–398.

Starkes, J.L. & Ericsson, K.A. (eds). (2003). *Expert Performance in Sports: Advances in Research on Sport Expertise.* Champaign, IL: Human Kinetics.

Steinberg, G.M., Chaffin, W.M. & Singer, R.N. (1998). Mental quickness training: drills that emphasize the development of anticipation skills in fast-paced sports. *Journal of Physical Education, Recreation, and Dance, 69,* 37–41.

Thomas, P.R., Murphey, S.M. & Hardy, L. (1999). Test of performance strategies: development and preliminary validation of a comprehensive measure of athletes' psychological skills. *Journal of Sport Sciences, 17,* 697–711.

Weinberg, R.S. & Gould, D. (2003). *Foundations of sport and exercise psychology.* Champaign, IL: Human Kinetics.

Williams, A.M., Davids, K. & Williams, J.G. (1999). *Visual Perception and Action in Sport.* Routledge, UK: E. & F.N. Spon.

Williams, J.M. (ed.) (2001). *Applied Sport Psychology: Personal Growth to Peak Performance* (4th edn). Mountain View, CA: Mayfield.

Williams, J.M. & Krane, V. (2001). Psychological characteristics of peak performance. In J.M. Williams (ed.), *Applied Sport Psychology: Personal Growth to Peak Performance* (4th edn; pp. 162–178). Mountain View, CA: Mayfield.

Yukelson, D. (1997). Principles of effective team building in sport: a direct services approach at Penn State University. *Journal of Applied Sport Psychology, 9,* 73–96.

CHAPTER 5

Assessment, Evaluation and Counseling in Sport

Robert N. Singer
University of Florida, USA
and
Mark H. Anshel
Middle Tennessee State University, USA

INTRODUCTION

This chapter will focus on issues and suggestions concerning interventions that might be useful in a variety of sport settings and for various sports and athletes. Potential purposes of interventions involve performance enhancement and counseling, and potential targets include individual athletes, teams, coaches or family. Determining which interventions could be used and for what purpose, their scientific credibility, and how they should be delivered, are the themes of this chapter.

This chapter is divided into two major sections. The first covers many topics related to assessment and evaluation, and factors that contribute to obtaining the most pertinent and valuable information. Ideally, reliable and valid measures would be used, and used by those sport psychologists who have the expertise requisites for administering a particular test or a protocol that might involve interviews and discussion. Many acceptable approaches are presented, suggestive of possible interventions as well as assessing their effectiveness. The second section is directed towards counseling issues, which ones are most common, and how personal problems might be dealt with and overcome. As well, ways to improve the counseling process are described. We now present the first section that deals with assessment and diagnosis.

INTERVENTION ASSESSMENT AND DIAGNOSIS

Interventions define the work of sport psychology practitioners, particularly if they engage in psychological skills training as opposed to psychotherapy and counseling methods. The different cognitive and behavioral strategies and programs intended to alter an athlete's

The Sport Psychologist's Handbook: A Guide for Sport-Specific Performance Enhancement.
Edited by Joaquín Dosil. © 2006 John Wiley & Sons, Ltd.

thought patterns, emotions and performance have been ubiquitous and well entrenched in the sport psychology literature. And so have the different instruments that deliver them. Far less is known, however, about the appropriateness of using particular strategies for certain athletes in specific situations. It is important to be aware of the array of personal and situational factors that surround every intervention attempt. The concerns in this section include addressing the ways of measuring intervention effectiveness, and ensuring that instruments are reliable and valid. A brief overview of the different ways of delivering services will be provided.

Measurement Issues for Determining Intervention Effectiveness

This section will address the factors that should be taken into consideration prior to and during the delivery of any sport psychology service. Optimal intervention effectiveness is best assured when five conditions are compatible: (1) the athlete's personal needs are ascertained, (2) situational factors and environmental conditions are considered, (3) the tools used to measure individual needs, limitations and psychological constructs are reliable and valid, (4) the style used to deliver services is compatible with the athlete's needs and with the environment in which service is provided, and (5) personal characteristics and communication style of the service provider are compatible with the athlete's expectations.

Awareness of Athletes' Needs

Two issues must be addressed first in the sport psychology consulting process: the need to be aware of each athlete's needs and preferences, and the athlete's needs and perceptions of sport psychology consulting. The first item brings one particular past experience to mind. During an in-service training seminar for sport psychologist' in Australia, one group participant—a licensed psychologist—complained to the group of his frustrations that certain athletes were unable to engage in relaxation training. It had never occurred to him that individual differences exist in using strategies to overcome emotional limitations and performance barriers. The particular athlete to whom he was referring preferred taking a light jog than to lie down and "relax". Jogging was the athlete's form of relaxing.

The second item reflects the athlete's responses to sport psychology consulting. As Ravizza (1990) asserts, many athletes are not seeking a "psychologist" who administers "counseling" in the formal sense. Instead, athletes are often searching for strategies to gain a mental edge over their opponents. More recently, however, Holt and Strean (2001) and Anderson, Knowles, and Gilbourne (2004) contend that the successful practitioner is less focused on problem-centered issues and more on humanistic athlete-centered approaches based more on counseling than on mental skills. To Anderson et al., "the personality of the practitioners and their ability to develop a working alliance with athletes has been consistently identified as a major influence on practice" (p. 188).

Unquestionably, an athlete's comfort level in working with a sport psychology consultant is partially a function of the sport or the sport environment. For example, sport psychologists were found to be more involved with professional tennis players (Loehr, 1990), but far less common in professional baseball in the USA (Ravizza, 1990). However, in more recent years, it seems as if more and more sport psychologists are collaborating with an increased number of athletes in different sports. Olympic athletes, for instance, now accept sport psychologists as an integral part of their training staff (Vealey & Garner-Holman, 1998). Thus, it is imperative that consultants determine the athlete's history, familiarity and expectations of the consulting experience—if, that is, the consultant will be accepted. There are also situational factors and environmental conditions that influence the client–provider relationship.

Situational Factors and Environmental Conditions

In his ground-breaking article on gaining entry with athletic personnel in sport psychology consulting, Ravizza (1988) acknowledged three primary barriers in sport psychology consulting: (a) the negative connotations of the "sport psychologist as shrink" image; (b) the consultant's lack of sport-specific knowledge, and (c) the lack of knowledge of and experience with the politics of each sport environment. The political issues, often erroneously ignored by many consultants, concern awareness of the power structure of each organization, the need for consultants to maintain a low, "behind the scenes" profile, and for consultants never to take credit for an athlete's (or coach's) performance success. Ravizza calls for compatibility between athletes' needs, the provider's delivery style and environmental requirements. Athletes are far more comfortable with mental skills training than being asked to disclose highly personal information on written tests—unless the athlete's needs require a clinical intervention and involve psychopathology (e.g. addictions, disorders and dysfunction).

Personal Characteristics and Communication Style of Service Provider

Without question, effective sport psychology consulting requires knowledge of the applied literature and relevant information about the particular sport's demands and skills. However, formal qualifications, credentials and knowledge are not enough. Establishing trusting relationships with team members and gaining entry in the consulting process also requires personal skills.

Rotella and Connelly (1984) urge sport psychologists to take the necessary time to develop a warm chemistry with client members of the team and organization. Nurturing relationships with clients takes effort and a long-term commitment to detecting then overcoming performance barriers. Athletes know if consultants are sincere in helping them improve their performance. Other pitfalls that should be avoided include engaging in short-term consulting, which communicates to the athlete that the consultant lacks the time and commitment to perform the job properly, as well as making false promises of rapid performance improvement. Bombarding the athlete with tests can also be a problem, especially early in the relationship, and if the assessment test does not take the specific problem into consideration (Beckmann & Kellmann, 2003).

Maniar, Curry, Sommers-Flanagan and Walsh (2001) list several plausible reasons for an athlete's or coach's discomfort in seeking sport psychology services. These include the consultant's professional title, jargon used to describe treatments, previous experiences to treatment, and social factors such as the athlete's cultural background, gender, or type of sport. For example, the authors contend that using the term "psychologist" may yield particular negative perceptions, since this term is often associated with "psychological problems".

Testing

Beckmann and Kellmann (2003) capture one dilemma of sport psychology assessment in three words: "Athletes hate paperwork" (p. 338). Most consultants can identify with this sentiment when working with sports teams. Reasons could include a distain for revealing personal information and discomfort with self-disclosure, not trusting how the data will be used or to whom it will be revealed, perhaps not perceiving the value of inventory responses as improving future performance, or perhaps possessing poor reading skills which the athlete can find embarrassing. It is clear, then, that many consultants choose to refrain from using assessment tools with the possible exception of observation checklists or structured personal interviews. Nevertheless, for many sport psychology consultants, measurement remains an inherent feature of the consultation process, especially for licensed psychologists and therapists whose education includes extensive training in the selection, administration and interpretation of psychological tests.

Self-report Tests for Evaluation

The primary function of assessment in sport psychology consultation is to obtain information from athletes about themselves. However, the nature of this information differs from test to test. Each test is constructed with a different objective. Tests that are intended to measure a client's personality traits will differ from others that measure the person's thought processes, dispositions or behavioral tendencies. Herein lies the dilemma in the field of sport psychology. Often, tests are used inappropriately; there is a gap between the psychologist's objectives in using a given test as opposed to the original intentions of the researcher who constructed it. Here we examine the purposes, values and limitations of using psychological inventories in applied sport psychology, and provide guidelines for their proper use.

Valid and Reliable Tools

The use—and *misuse*—of self-report inventories is a widespread and integral part of sport psychology consulting. Tests differ in the ways in which they are planned, constructed, interpreted and used in sport psychology settings. Some inventories are intended for research purposes only, while others have diagnostic properties. It is imperative to realize that not every inventory is meant to serve diagnostic purposes (e.g. detecting the athlete's current barriers, psychological characteristics or thought patterns) commonly used by trained licensed psychologists. An additional problem, as noted by Marsh (1998), is that many of the inventories appearing in journal articles have not received the level of psychometric analyses that ensure validity (the inventories measure what they are purported to measure). Another concern is reliability of the data. Reliability refers to consistency among responses from the same person to items within a particular inventory, as well as to consistency of scores if the same inventory is administered twice. Thus, it is important that assessment in sport psychology interventions be conducted with tools that provide valid and reliable results, and that tests were constructed and intended for use with sports participants.

Developing Psychometric Tests

Although a full description of the process for developing reliable and valid diagnostic tests in sport psychology consulting goes beyond the scope of this chapter, it is important that sport psychologists know the purposes, intended audience and proper use of tests. Some tests were constructed for research purposes, for example, to detect group differences due to a treatment, while other tests serve diagnostic purposes. Each category of test may have been constructed to meet its specific purpose and has received different types of validation for that purpose. The American Psychological Association (APA) has published standards for educational and psychological testing. Part I of this publication consists of "Technical Standards for Test Construction and Evaluation."

General Recommendations for Test Use

Here are a few specific recommendations from *The Standards for Educational and Psychological Testing* (APA, 1999) that have particular relevance to sport psychology practitioners:

1. *Evidence of test validity* A test should include evidence of validity of the relevant types of inferences for which its use is recommended. Therefore, if the primary purpose of a test is to determine cognitive and somatic forms of state anxiety, *evidence* that supports these measures, the intended *interpretations* and, if relevant, the *applications* of test scores should also be provided (our italics).
2. *Lack of validity* If validity for the meaning of tests scores has not been examined, that fact should be made clear. This point is particularly relevant considering the vast number of inventories published in research articles and used exclusively for research, not practical diagnostic, purposes. In other words, many inventories are constructed for data collection in a particular study, such as a trait measure (e.g. trait confidence, trait anxiety, trait anger). These tests were not intended and, therefore, should not be used to ascertain the athlete's propensity to exhibit these feelings, emotions or actions in sport settings. This is one concern about a valuable sport psychology publication called *The Directory of Psychological Tests in the Sport and Exercise Sciences* (2nd edn, Ostrow, 1996), discussed in the next section. The directory does not clarify the intended purposes of each test.
3. *Interpreting scores* Any evidence that justifies the interpretation of subscores, composite scores, score differences or profiles should be made explicit. For example, the instrument to measure perfectionism, the Multiple Perfectionism Scale (Frost, Marten, Laharat & Rosenblate, 1990), includes a total score and five subscores (e.g. personal standards, parental criticism, doubts about actions) defined by different dimensions that each possess unique characteristics and indicators that reflect this construct. Therefore, providing individuals with an overall (total) test score would be far less informative than communicating each subscore and the meaning of those scores.
4. *Describing the validation sample* Early literature in contemporary sport psychology is replete with studies in which tests that were generated for non-athlete populations were used to evaluate athletes. The APA suggests, therefore, "the composition of the validation sample should be described in as much detail as is practicable" (p. 14).

5. *Psychometric scrutiny* What is the primary purpose of the test? Is it strictly for research purposes or is there an attempt to diagnose and treat an individual? Diagnostic tests can be misused, which is why all licensed psychologists in many countries are required to complete graduate courses on administering and interpreting diagnostic tests. The APA recommends, " A report of a criterion-related validation study should provide a description of the sample and the statistical analysis used to determine the degree of predictive accuracy" (p. 16).

Test Use in Counseling

The APA makes it clear that test use for counseling purposes differs from other test uses "in that the test-taker is viewed as the primary user of test results" (p. 55). Here are a few primary recommendations for using tests in counseling settings, including athletes.

1. *Reviewing test scores* It is of paramount importance that counselors review the interpretive materials that they provide to clients to ensure accuracy, clarity and usefulness. Test manuals or computer-based interpretations should be evaluated for validity. It is strongly suggested that counselors do not merely distribute written scores and interpretations without the counselor's personal involvement. Written interpretations of scores require professional training that test-takers have not received. In addition, test manuals, printouts, and other written forms of test interpretation lack the sensitivity and insights that a live counselor can provide. This is often needed in counseling settings.
2. *Interpreting caution from test results* In support of the previous point, "counselors should review the test materials that are provided to the test-takers to be sure that such materials properly caution the test-taker not to rely on the test scores solely when making life-planning decisions" (p. 57). Along these lines, the counselor is encouraged to work with the client to consider other information, produced directly from the client, that might lend credence to or refute the authenticity of the results of the test in real world settings. Thus, a counselor might: (a) discuss the test and then ask the client if they agree with the interpretation of the data; (b) ask the client to provide examples of incidences that reflect score accuracies or inaccuracies, and (c) work jointly with the client to find solutions to overcome problems, concerns or limitations, or to acknowledge areas of strength that should be maintained.

Use and Misuse of Self-report Inventories

In the early days of contemporary sport psychology, researchers and clinical psychologists were adopting psychological tests for athletes that were constructed for very different populations. For example, the 550-item Minnesota Multiphasic Personality Inventory (MMPI) was developed to detect clinical depression, yet was once used as a technique to detect psychological limitations in athletes (Butt, 1987). In addition, other personality measures generated for non-athlete populations (e.g. Sixteen Personality Factor Questionnaire, Eysenck Personality Inventory) were used predict future success in competitive sport. Tests and testing procedures have advanced considerably since those days. One example of the development and maturation of sport psychology is the increased use of validated sport-specific tests that address particular needs of the athlete.

Another example of the dilemma facing consultants in knowing which inventories to use or not use for consulting (as opposed to research) purposes is the vast array of inventories. *The Directory of Psychological Tests in the Sport and Exercise Sciences* (2nd edn), edited by Ostrow (1996), contains 314 tests. Some of these have received extensive psychometric scrutiny and are used for diagnostic purposes, whereas others were developed strictly for research purposes or are undergoing further development and validation. In his review of the first edition of this directory, Marsh (1998) found that "only 1/3 of these assessments had items based on a conceptual framework, less than 1/4 reported factor analyses, and less than 10% showed evidence of extensive reference support" (p. xv). Thus, too often, sport psychology consultants attempt to diagnose an athlete's thought processes, emotional status or behavioral disposition with instruments that have not received proper validation procedures.

As indicated earlier, the APA has published *The Standards for Educational and Psychological Testing* (1999) that provides guidelines for proper instrument validation. While data are lacking in sport psychology as to sport-specific tests, articles in applied journals and conference presentations are replete with examples in which sport psychologists are using tests that have not received an appropriate level of scrutiny, or else are administering them and interpreting the results ineffectively.

Here is a list of questions consultants should ask before using a self-report psychological inventory as part of the counseling process (Anshel, 2003a).

- Do I need to administer a test to obtain the information I want? Would conducting an interview be sufficient for my purposes?
- Would the client-athlete's self-disclosure of personal information be more forthcoming with a personal interview, or would a test be more revealing? While the test answers will remain confidential, it cannot be anonymous; the athlete must be identified.
- Is there a test available for my purposes that has been validated and has received proper psychometric scrutiny?
- About the test I plan to use: Will this test tell me what I could learn from a personal interview? What are the advantages of using it? Do I have experience administering and interpreting the results?
- Was the test developed and validated for the specific sport population with whom I will consult? Do the items reflect the unique demands and qualities of this particular sport?
- Is this the proper test given my goals for using it? For example, is it a trait or state measure? Will this measure provide me with the appropriate information?
- Will the athlete feel comfortable answering all of the items? In fact, is my relationship with the athlete sufficiently trusting in which I can anticipate full, candid disclosure?
- Will using this test be perceived by the athlete as advantageous to their performance or have some other personal benefit?
- Does the test include items that lack sensitivity to cultural or gender differences? Are there any items that seem inappropriate, particularly if the athlete is from a foreign country?
- Can I be certain that the athlete's responses will be kept strictly confidential and their coach will not have access to it?
- What will the test score indicate? How can I use the score in future consultation with this athlete?

- Finally, did I obtain the athlete's permission: (a) to administer the test, (b) to fully disclose how the score would be to used, and (c) to give the athlete the option of either not answering *selected* items or to discontinue participation at any time—at which time the test would be destroyed—without any negative ramifications?

If the sport psychologist answers "no" to any of these questions, there should be considerable reflection about the test's usefulness. Two final questions, therefore, should be posed: What are the benefits and (perhaps more important) the psychological and emotional costs of using this test? And, second, are the costs acceptable? If the costs include harming the future relationship with that athlete, or that the test results will be ignored, shared with the coach, or in any way used against the athlete, the costs are clearly unacceptable and the test should be not administered. If, however, the test information has implications toward learning more about the athlete that an interview will not provide, and that one benefit of the test is to enhance the consultation experience, then the benefits may warrant administering the test.

Types of Outcome Measures

As noted earlier, there are two schools of thought about the value of test-taking in sport psychology consulting. One approach is to rely on relationship-building as the main vehicle for establishing trust and rapport, resulting in optimal consultation benefits (e.g. Orlick & Partington, 1987; Ravizza, 1988, 1990). Individuals who have worked directly with elite athletes and whose published studies have addressed the characteristics of effective and ineffective consultants support this approach based on the perceptions of athletes and coaches. They support the need for prioritizing the consultant's personal qualities (e.g. rapport, integrity, knowledge of the sport and of the mental skills literature) over clinical techniques. Examples of these techniques include greater reliance on reviewing the athlete's past history, which is often unrelated to sport. Then, focusing would occur on the present sport setting, use of test scores to obtain information, and lack of knowledge about the athlete's sport in using the sport psychology literature. Other experts, however, assert that test data, if used prudently, can provide very valuable information about the athlete that is often lacking from interviews (e.g. Beckmann & Kellmann, 2003; Butt, 1987). It is apparent that each situation calls for its own unique approaches for establishing the optimal benefits of "doing" sport psychology. Another related consideration is the training and preference of the sport psychologist.

The literature is replete with attempts to validate and to use instruments that measure constructs that have relevance for sport competitors and coaches (see Ostrow, 1996). Measures that provide valuable insights into the characteristics, strengths and limitations/barriers of athletes will build credibility and promote effectiveness among sport psychology consultants in sports settings and throughout the field of psychology. Providing a list of instruments that have been used for consultation purposes and possess the proper psychometric properties goes beyond the scope of this chapter. Readers interested in the topic are referred to Anshel (1987), Ostrow (1996), and to the following website for references of valid and reliable diagnostic tools to measure psychological constructs relevant in sport psychology: www.emt.org/userfiles/youthLit_Final.pdf Here is a brief review of the purposes of using selected types of tests for identifying various types of thoughts, emotions, and behavioral tendencies common in competitive sport.

Cognitive and Affective Measures

A basic tenet of sport psychology is that athletic performance is often affected by the athlete's thoughts, referred to as "cognitions", and emotions, also called "affect". A vast array of tests describes processes that are used primarily to detect, monitor and perhaps modify the athlete's thoughts or emotions if they are believed to be counterproductive to performance. Other times, consultants (or researchers) want to ascertain the athlete's attitude, perhaps prior to, during or immediately after a competitive event or to determine the possible factors that contribute to successful or unsuccessful performance outcomes.

One inherent limitation in using these instruments should be noted: they are based on self-report. This means that athletes can respond in ways they perceive as expected of them or to obtain the consultant's approval, a concept called "social desirability". Or, they can be deceitful due to the discomfort associated with self-disclosure. This is why it is important to establish trust and rapport with athletes before they complete self-reporting tests.

- *Selected cognitive measures* Cognitive measures may include: (a) attentional style (i.e. an athlete's tendency to use certain types of concentration skills to meet performance demands, typically measured on two dimensions, broad–narrow and internal–external), (b) attitudes (e.g. attitudes toward physical activity, attitudes toward one's coach/toward playing one's sport), (c) commitment, (d) use of coping strategies, (e) sources of stress such as fear of failure, (f) ratings of perceived effort, (g) confidence, (h) perceived competence, (i) group cohesion, (j) perceptions of leadership, (k) explaining the causes of performance outcomes (called causal attributions), (l) locus of control, (m) flow, (n) exercise dependence/addiction, (o) cognitive style (i.e. an individual's preferences for processing information through visual, verbal, or tactual process), and (p) sport motivation.
- *Selected emotion measures* Measures of affect, some of which were developed for competitive athletes, while others were constructed for non-sport populations, have traditionally focused on somatic and cognitive anxiety, somatic and cognitive arousal, trait and state anxiety, perceived stress intensity, trait and state anger, hostility, affect recovery, mood (profile of mood states; POMS), and feeling.

Behavioral Measures

In comparison to cognitive and emotional measures, assessing athlete or coach behaviors has received relatively scant attention by researchers. In some situations and for particular individuals, it may be easier—even more valid—to assess and interpret actions rather than self-reported thoughts and emotions of the competitor. Intervention strategies may also be more effective. Behavioral assessment is concerned with "helping clients to overcome behavioral deficits (too little behavior of a particular type) and decrease behavioral excesses (too much behavior of a particular type)" (Tkachuk, Leslie-Toogood & Martin, 2003, p. 104). The behavior to be changed is called the "target behavior". The sport psychologist's role is to identify and describe target behaviors, determine the causes of these behaviors, select appropriate treatments to stop or alter the behaviors, and to evaluate intervention outcomes (Smith, Smoll & Christensen, 1996).

Behavioral assessment techniques consist of six stages: (1) gathering initial information, (2) choosing and prioritizing target behaviors, (3) devising ways to monitor target behaviors,

(4) assessing problem behavior, (5) selecting an appropriate intervention, and (6) evaluating intervention effectiveness. While a full description of this program goes beyond the scope of this chapter, here is a brief overview.

Tkachuk et al. (2003) list behavioral interviewing, across-sport behavioral inventories, within-sport behavioral checklists and performance profiling as typical techniques for initial information gathering. *Behavioral interviewing*, for example, consists of identifying the primary problem areas, determining specific behavioral deficits or excesses, detecting the factors that control the problem behavior and determining specific behavioral objectives for the treatment. Often, the athlete must first unlearn current, ineffective responses before new responses can be learned.

For example, the second author of this chapter (Anshel) worked with a university female soccer player who was a self-described perfectionist. She engaged in negative self-evaluation throughout her participation in the match, even if the event was beyond her control. In addition, she would not make positive self-evaluations despite many apparent performance successes. She identified the problem area because the tendency to be self-critical reduced her confidence and enjoyment as a team member. The behavioral deficit was chronic self-criticism, and a controlling factor of this habit was failing to recognize her competencies. Three specific behavioral objectives were determined; to complete her negative self-evaluation within a period of five *seconds* after it had occurred; second, to focus externally on the next task at hand (thereby ignoring her internal dialogue); and third, to use positive (confidence-building) self-talk after performance success.

A checklist was generated consisting of reminders about executing specific strategies before and during the match. These included making positive self-statements before the soccer match, using challenge appraisals in response to undesirable events (e.g. "Come on, stay with it; I can do this"), recognizing her competent performances, and expressing appreciation to her teammates and coaches after receiving a compliment. Athlete self-monitoring is an effective way to track the behavior of interest.

A *functional assessment of the problem behavior* consists of attempting to understand the antecedents and factors that control the athlete's actions. What precipitates the behavior? Failure to meet performance expectations? A competitive environment, as opposed to practice situations? A clinical psychologist might suggest attempting to understand the genesis of problem behaviors; for example, trying to gain approval from a critical parent or coach, or fearing failure and humiliation in the presence of others. At times, a person's recognition of the factors that underlie the problem behavior is comforting because it explains a habit that has plagued the person for years.

Selecting a treatment plan concerns developing a strategy to change the athlete's targeted behavior. For instance, athletes who failed to adhere to their injury rehabilitation program may lament the early (6 a.m.) time they are required to appear in the training room. When the coach agrees that the afternoon is an option for rehabilitation, the athletes' rate of adherence may improve dramatically.

Evaluating treatment effects consists of recording behaviors during three phases: baseline, treatment and follow-up. It is important to collect performance data during each phase in order to detect change and intervention effectiveness.

In summary, behavioral assessment is a very promising and effective intervention technique in competitive sport. In addition to providing salient, observable and desirable changes in behavior, it is an approach that is often consistent with the athlete's needs and wishes. For athletes who are uncomfortable with completing inventories or engaging in self-disclosure, and have a dim, albeit inaccurate, perception of sport psychology, behavioral assessment is relatively non-threatening. Of course, the athlete's thoughts and emotions may also play an integral role in producing or maintaining the problem behavior, and these factors cannot be ignored. However, the primary goal of athletes and coaches is to find ways for improving performance. Behavioral assessment and interventions meet those expectations. Other behavioral assessment techniques include self-monitoring checklists and behaviorally anchored rating scales.

Self-monitoring checklists (SMCs) consist of within-sport items that provide guidelines for the proper use of cognitive and behavioral strategies to optimize performance success. Checklists are "reminders" to the athlete about engaging in thoughts and actions; they are not diagnostic tools and, therefore, do not warrant psychometric scrutiny as do most inventories that measure constructs such as anxiety, coping style and competitiveness. One particular value of SMCs is their credibility and perceived value by athletes. Because consultants generate them with input from the athletes and coaches who use them (Orlick, 1990), they have great meaning to competitors. Checklist format may consist of "yes–no" responses (e.g. "I am focused on the ball prior to my golf swing") or a Likert-type scale, ranging from 1 (*not at all*) to 5 (*very much*) in which athletes indicate the extent to which they think or act in a certain manner (e.g. "I am feeling confident in my preparation during the warm-up period"). Checklists have been used for years by sport psychology consultants (e.g. Kirschenbaum & Bale, 1980; Orlick, 1990).

Behaviorally-anchored rating scales (BARS), developed originally to determine performance competence in non-sport settings (Anshel, 1995), consists of defining valid and reliable job criteria; that is, competencies that reflect desirable sport performance, and to assess sport performance as derived from the behavioral evidence, called "behavioral indicators" that are identifiable and measurable. A minimum of two expert panels reach a consensus on the set of competencies that define desirable performance of the targeted group, and the behavioral indicators that manifest each competency. BARS have been generated for football coaches (Anshel, Housner & Cyrs, 1987) and basketball referees (Anshel, 1995).

Trait and State Tests

Sport psychology researchers and practitioners are interested in measuring both stable (long-term) and changeable (short-term) factors that influence performance. Tests are constructed to measure one of these, but not both. For example, a practitioner or researcher who wants to determine an athlete's level of anxiety just prior to an important competition must use a test that was constructed to measure what is called "state anxiety", not trait anxiety, a construct suggesting stable scores over time and across situations (Schutz, 1998). In other words, trait measures may be used inappropriately instead of state measures.

A *trait* is defined as "the relatively stable behavior of a certain kind over an ecologically representative sample of situation occasions" (Epstein, 1990, p. 99). Attributes such as self-esteem, extraversion, neuroticism, trait anxiety, trait anger and intelligence fit the criteria of stability over time and, therefore, fit the criteria of personality traits. Others (e.g. Caspi & Bem, 1990), however, differentiate traits from dispositions/styles/orientations, which are not entrenched predispositions. Instead, Caspi and Bem recognize the existence of an array of thought processes and behavioral tendencies that reflect situational demands and environmental conditions. Examples include competitive orientation, goal orientation, coping style, decision-making style, state anxiety, mental toughness, and attribution style. Thus, an athlete may exhibit certain personal characteristics during competitive events, while displaying the opposite set of characteristics when not engaged in sport competition. Traits, then, are not amenable to change through typical sport psychology interventions (with the exception of long-term counseling), while dispositions/styles/orientations are. Understanding the difference is very important in selecting the appropriate intervention techniques, and evaluating their effectiveness.

Personal dispositions differ from personality traits. Traits are fixed, stable and unique attributes that shape a person's behavior. They are usually determined in early childhood. Clinical psychologists claim personality traits can be altered only through extensive psychotherapy (Greenson, 1967). Thus, it would take years of counseling to alter a personality trait. The individual is expected to possess the same set of personality traits in different situations. While traits are, by definition, inherent and always present within the person, situational factors will provide a stimulus for selected traits to surface, and influence behavior. For example, in sport, competitive trait anxiety lies dormant until athletes experience a situation perceived as threatening. High trait anxious athletes will more likely feel situational (state) anxiety than their low trait anxious peers. Thus, while personality traits are often manifested by certain environmental conditions, the same set of traits is always present (Vanden Auweele, De Cuyper, Van Mele & Rzewnicki, 1993).

Dispositions, on the other hand, are a person's tendencies to possess certain thought patterns that influence emotion and behavior. Dispositions, also called orientations or styles (Anshel, 2003b), are not fixed, are strongly influenced by situational characteristics and, thus, are highly susceptible to mental skills training and counseling. Researchers have found that dispositions can predict an athlete's emotional response and level of performance quality in competitive events (Gauvin & Russell, 1993). For example, several studies have shown that determining an athlete's dispositional coping style following a certain type of stressful event is an accurate predictor of the type of coping strategy or set of strategies the athlete will use following the same stressor (see Anshel, Kim, Kim, Chang & Eom, 2001, for a review). Knowing the difference between personality traits and dispositions is important in determining the source of an athlete's thoughts, emotions and barriers that affect sport performance. Traits cannot be changed, but they can be controlled through mental skills and various types of cognitive-behavioral interventions. However, it is possible to change athletes' dispositions, which might be the source of maladaptive thought patterns, emotions and performance outcomes. This is important in determining the best strategies and intervention for improving performance.

Characteristics of the competitive event, or *situational factors*, also help predict the extent to which the athlete's dispositions will influence thoughts, emotions and performance quality. For example, Vealey (2002) correctly contends that certain dispositions are likely to influence the athlete as a function of the type of event (e.g. closed versus open skills, high versus low skill complexity, perceived skill level of team versus opponent), or selected event characteristics (e.g. start versus end of game, type of stressful event, perceived control of the situation). Thus, if an athlete possesses high trait anxiety, then high-pressure situations are more likely to stimulate thoughts of worry and threat than competing in a more relaxed environment.

Dispositions often predispose an athlete's tendency to respond to competitive situations with certain thoughts and emotions, which, in turn, affect performance quality. Examples of thoughts considered undesirable are negative self-talk, the anticipation of failure—a condition called self-handicapping—and poor concentration. Undesirable emotions include state anxiety, over- or under-arousal, anger, unhappiness/sadness, frustration and fear. Certain situations will produce manifestations of these thoughts and emotions. Understanding the personal and situational factors that cause or accompany undesirable thoughts or emotions will allow sport psychologists to provide athletes with interventions that provide optimal effectiveness.

For example, the second author of this chapter (Anshel) consulted with a very talented starting baseball outfielder attending an NCAA Division I university. He stated his problem this way: "A million things go through my mind as I step into the batter's box, and I'm in a terrible slump." He listed the various problems and sources of worry that were plaguing him at the time, including the pending birth of his child, school exams and many others. While his *trait* anxiety level was not tested, he was obviously experiencing extensive *state* anxiety about a vast array of issues about which he had little or no control. Similar to the pre-shot routines prior to a golf shot, a tennis serve, or a basketball free throw, we worked on ways to "filter out" extraneous thoughts seconds before stepping into the batter's box. Once he was standing in the batter's box, he would attend externally—"focus like a laser" on the pitcher, more specifically, on the ball sitting in the pitcher's hand or glove. He built a "mental wall" around the batter's box, so that no other thoughts could enter. Soon, his concentration on the task at hand improved dramatically, and so did his batting average.

In summary, tests should be used cautiously. While instruments used in sport psychology for research and consultation purposes may differ in their construction, each should receive psychometric scrutiny so that the data on which these tests are based have proven validity and reliability. This is not always the case. Readers are advised to examine the construction and proper use of any inventory on which they plan to gather information from athletes. With the exception of checklists, which do not serve diagnostic and analytical purposes, only tests with reported psychometric data, indicating proper validity and reliability, and preferably published in a scientific refereed journal should be considered.

THE COUNSELING PROCESS

Gaining entry, acceptance and reputability for providing service for others—in this case, sport participants (e.g. athletes, coaches, contest officials)—is a challenging task. This is because clients are being asked to break away from tradition and comfortable routines, and to move into areas that are unfamiliar and possibly threatening. This is especially true with coaches, a profession highly regulated by tradition. Bringing in one additional person as part of the group of experts to assist the team can be uncomfortable and awkward for everyone. While the team's athletic trainers, physicians and assistant coaches are well entrenched as necessary contributors to team services, sport psychologists do not enjoy the same perception. Thus, forming relationships and building trust with athletes, coaches and other members of the sport organization is the foundation of successful sport psychology counseling.

Psycho-behavioral Interventions

Perhaps at the heart of the counseling process in applied sport psychology is the use of psycho-behavioral interventions. They are often prescribed, either in isolation or in combination, to alter the athlete's thoughts and emotions to optimize performance outcomes. A growing list of techniques and programs has emerged in the literature, many of which have received research scrutiny to determine their effectiveness. The effectiveness of these interventions, however, must reflect the athlete's needs and the conditions under which the intervention can be used.

In another example of determining intervention effectiveness is the frequently cited use of positive self-talk (PST) in sport psychology. PST is a mental skill intended to provide rational thoughts for various purposes, depending on the situation and desired outcome. Building or maintaining confidence, coping with stressful events, or enduring physical effort are examples of situations in which PST has been effective (Zinsser, Bunker & Williams, 2001). The content of PST, then, is dependent on situational demands and the athlete's needs. In fact, for some athletes and under highly selected conditions, negative self-talk (NST) might be more useful than PST. For example, Martin and Anshel (1995) found that using NST resulted in more accurate performance than PST when performing easy motor tasks, whereas PST was more effective under difficult task conditions. Thus, intervention effectiveness is often dependent on the athlete's personal needs, the proper environmental conditions and with situational demands. Here are a few guidelines that should be considered in selecting and applying interventions in sport psychology for each of these areas.

Guidelines for Effective Interventions

As previously noted, there is a vast array of barriers to providing psychological counseling services to sports participants, including athletes (individual and team), coaches, organizations and sports officials. Sadly, an extensive body of psychological techniques and interventions is "sitting on bookshelves" in computer files in the form of applied books, journal articles and useful programs. In this section, we take you through the primary issues that guide intervention effectiveness.

Establishing Relationships and Trust

Usually, a field of professional practice such as psychology attracts individuals whose personality is very non-threatening to others. These individuals thrive on helping others. They manifest warmth, sensitivity, empathy and genuine care toward their clients. One goal of exhibiting these characteristics is to promote the client's trust and openness toward the therapist or consultant. It is surprising, therefore, that many athletes do not easily trust others and take considerable time to reveal personal feelings or reject the counseling process out of hand.

A related concept that describes the importance of building trust in sport settings is *rapport*. In their chapter on the role of sports medicine professionals in counseling athletes, Ray, Terrell and Hough (1999) contend that "counseling is what happens when rapport is established and clear and effective communication is maintained between the sports medicine professional and the athlete" (p. 5). Heil, Bowman and Bean (1993) define rapport as a feeling of being comfortable or in harmony with another person. The consultant builds rapport through active listening, empathy, and by providing assistance that the athlete perceives as helpful and effective. At times, closeness between the parties develops if the consultant has a history of previous involvement in competitive sport, particularly at the elite level (Butt, 1987). In addition to the consultant's personal skills, other factors that may promote trust and rapport between client and consultant is training in the sport sciences and demonstrating mastery of the sport psychology literature—as opposed to strict use of psychotherapeutic approaches, in which the clinician focuses primarily on the athlete's personal history without reference to the sport environment (Danish, Petitpas & Hale, 1993).

The Athlete's Personal Needs

Athletes differ in their personality, thought patterns, emotional tendencies, and in their limitations that require interventions. Each athlete arrives at the sport venue with his or her own set of beliefs, expectations, strengths and limitations. Many of these thoughts are dispositional; that is, an integral part of the competitor's personal characteristics. At other times, however, thought patterns are manifested by situational events. For example, some athletes are more susceptible than others to sport situations they consider threatening—a condition called "trait anxiety" (discussed earlier). While their anxiety is controlled and at relatively low levels prior to the contest, the actual competitive experience automatically heightens what is called "state anxiety" due to the individual's propensity to feel threatened or worried. Other personal dispositions that may alter an athlete's thought patterns just prior to or during the competitive event include self-efficacy, need achievement, competitiveness, win orientation, appraisal style, coping style, risk-taking, hardiness, learned resourcefulness, attentional style, cognitive/learning style, and many others.

One problem often associated with providing athletes with interventions is information overload (Singer, 1980). While athletes tend to process information quickly and respond automatically and skillfully to an array of environmental demands, they can be distracted by attempting to apply mental skills that may have been recently learned, yet not integrated automatically into their performance sequence. The result is "over thinking", in which the competitor is more concerned with incorporating the mental skill than in attending to the task at hand and executing the skill automatically. Thus, it is imperative that sport psychologists: (a) teach athletes only one mental skill at a time, and (b) ensure that the mental skill has been mastered and applied with minimal thought. Subsequently, additional mental skills can then be taught and mastered.

One approach to reducing the amount of information-processing in learning and applying mental skills is to formulate *programs* that consist of two or more components consisting of mental or behavioral strategies. Often, these programs are conducted in a specified sequence, for example, Anshel's (1990) COPE Model, Orlick's (1986) Mental Plan, or Smith's (1980) Stress Management Training (SMT). Taken together, the athlete's personal needs should be ascertained, preferably through personal interviews, an approach perceived by many athletes to be less threatening and intrusive than administering selected inventories (Weinberg & Williams, 2001).

Environmental Conditions

Some interventions are intended for use under certain conditions; for example, with certain sport types or goals of the sport environment. Certain strategies are more compatible for closed skill sports, in which the environment is stable and the performer initiates skill execution, while other strategies are intended for open skill sports, in which the environment is unstable and the performer responds to externally paced cues (Singer, 1980). Examples of closed skill interventions include imagery, pre-shot routines, positive/instructional self-talk, planning, approach coping and attentional focusing. Open skill interventions, on the other hand, might involve situational awareness, distraction of attention, distribution of attention, sustained attention, anticipation, decision-making, developing a flow state, and integrative team skills (if a team sport).

Conducting Player Interviews and Sessions

The athlete interview is the primary means by which sport psychologists build trust and rapport with their athletes, and obtain information about the athlete's needs. Sport psychologists generally agree that asking athletes to complete inventories as a first step in the consultation process is inappropriate and ineffective until trust and rapport between consultant and athlete have been established. In fact, completing inventories is not the preferred consulting style for many sport psychologists. Instead, the interview may serve as the most reliable and effective means of obtaining and responding to initial information the athlete provides. There are several pre-interview issues that should be addressed (Butt, 1987).

Finally, on the other end of the spectrum, a initial interview might reveal issues that do not require a professional intervention. Butt (1987) suggests the consultant could guide the athlete away from treatment "when the individual is capable of solving his or her own problems or developing his or her own psychology training program or does not need psychological services at all" (p. 206).

Guidelines for a Professional Interview

There are fundamental rules that will enhance the interview process and make it more productive, according to Butt (1987) and Smith (1999).

- *Facilities* A warm, clean, relaxing and quiet atmosphere facilitates communication and allows the client to feel increasingly comfortable to disclose personal feelings. The surroundings should not be distracting, such as "loud" colors or artwork. Seats should be comfortable.
- *Phone calls and other intrusions* Incoming calls should be rerouted to voice mail and phones should be in the "off" position. A client should also be asked to turn off their cell phone, if one is present. A sign on the door should indicate a session is in progress and that there should not be any disturbance.
- *Physical barriers* There should be no desk or other barrier between consultant and client. The counseling literature generally recommends a distance of 4 to 7 feet (1.22 to 2.13

meters) between the parties. Physical barriers may be accompanied by distancing in communication and less openness and disclosure.

- *Punctuality* The consultant should be prepared to begin on time. Clients may perceive lack of punctuality as disrespectful, leading to resentment and lack of trust, in some cases.
- *Contact information* Consultants and clients should have each other's contact phone numbers (office and mobile phones), and perhaps e-mail addresses. This is to ensure that an appointment can be quickly cancelled or if either party is running late.
- *Ending the interview* The interview should be ended at the planned time. Another client may be waiting. In addition, all sessions should have end points that allow an opportunity to conclude and summarize the session.
- *Summarizing the interview* Within five minutes of ending the interview the consultant should summarize interview content, and add to other relevant points. A summary allows the consultant to highlight and reinforce important points, which promotes retention of this information. In addition, a summary allows the client to detect areas of change, growth and achievement from the session.
- *Determining a revisit* Continuation of the program of treatment is the client's—not the consultant's—decision. The consultant, however, can recommend future directions to the client. Options include returning soon for another visit to address specific areas that need rapid attention (perhaps agreeing to a specific number of subsequent interviews to resolve the issues under discussion), allowing considerable time to pass before a return visit, referring the client to another specialist, or suggesting that treatment should end given the client's progress and ability to carry out the treatment.
- *Follow-up written summary* Providing a written summary of the session to clients within a week of the session is rare because it is time-consuming. However, some consultants have found it enormously popular and effective among their client-athletes. Athletes will report rereading the consultant's written summary repeatedly, even taping it to their wall or reading it daily. Because this task occurs outside of the client's consultation time, it's a free service, and some consultants do not have the additional time.

Brief Interventions

At times, interventions are needed on a very short-term basis to deal with a specific issue or problem. These are referred to as "brief interventions".

Sample Brief Interventions

Anshel (1990) developed an approach for coping with sudden stress, called the COPE model. It can be taught relatively quickly, and takes under 30 seconds—sometimes less, depending on the type of stressor. The model consists of executing a sequence of four strategies following certain types of stressful events. COPE is an acronym that reflects each strategy. The sequence is: **C**ontrol emotions, **O**rganize information, **P**lan a response and **E**xecute. The genesis of COPE was to assist football players in being able to manage stress and anxiety after being reprimanded by their coach, or to handle any form of unpleasant verbal input. Thus, COPE did not serve the purpose of coping with chronic (long-term) forms of stress, nor in response to other forms of acute stress.

The COPE model, as a brief intervention tool, is intended to assist the athlete to respond productively and efficiently to stressful events, acute (not chronic) stress. The model, developed by the second author, consists of four cognitive and behavioral strategies performed consecutively almost immediately upon experiencing the stressor. For example, in response to a coach's verbal reprimand, the athlete, in sequence, would: (1) control emotions (C) by taking a deep breath, using calming self-talk ("Relax; stay in control"), while remaining receptive to the input. After all, a coach who is upset may also be providing valuable instruction that should not be ignored. (2) Organize information into meaningful and non-meaningful categories (O). The content of incoming information can be meaningless and destructive, while other input can provide information that will help the athlete's subsequent performance. The emotions of an emotional coach, teammate or opponent should not deter the player from obtaining any information that might prove helpful. Therefore, while the athlete should perceive all input—positive and negative, helpful and meaningless—this stage in the COPE model consists of sorting out the difference, then moving forward. (3) Moving forward means planning (P) the next task at hand. The game is continuing and there may be little time to reflect, evaluate and become stagnant. This phase occurs in seconds, in which the athlete quickly decides upon and plans future action. Finally, the plan is executed (E) with relatively little cognition.

Case Study Example of Short-Term Intervention in Baseball—the COPE Model

A member of a NCAA Division I university men's baseball team indicated he was struggling with his hitting. There were numerous issues in his life that were distracting him from fully concentrating on the task at hand, which was hitting the ball effectively. He described his thought patterns while waiting for his turn at bat, and again, when he entered the batter's box. We listed the array of personal problems and distractions (all unrelated to baseball), and the content and timing of his thoughts prior to and during his turn at bat. Not surprisingly, he was thinking about his personal life during this time, and not concentrating on the situation at hand. He was also distracted by his father's high performance expectations. He focused his attention internally, which produced even greater anxiety. He felt muscles tightening. Both cognitive and somatic forms of anxiety were apparent and his hitting performance suffered.

We worked out a mental plan based on a set of routines that preceded his turn at bat, and another set of routines between each pitch that incorporated the COPE Model. Specifically, the first stage consisted of "locking up" all distracting thoughts upon leaving the dugout to wait for his turn at bat. If he had an argument with someone that day, or thought about any other issue that would impede his concentration, he left it in the dugout. He was "not allowed" to bring that thought with him to the "on deck circle" and then to the plate. Instead, he focused externally on the pitcher's habits and tendencies. If a personal, distracting thought entered his mind, he would say to himself, "Focus", and keep his attention on the type of pitches the opposing pitcher was throwing to the hitter. At the same time, he made occasional positive self-statements, such as "I'm ready" and "I can hit this guy." When his turn to bat approached, he moved quickly to the plate, feeling confident and enthusiastic.

We developed a second set of routines immediately before entering the batter's box. He looked at the third base coach for signals, scanned the field to detect fielders' positions, and then planned his hitting strategy. Upon entering the batter's box, he took a deep breath and said to himself, "Focus." This was his cue to immediately filter out any external stimuli (e.g. comments or actions of others, extraneous noise) and to prevent thoughts unrelated to preparing for the pitch. His eyes were focused on the ball in the pitcher's hand. Between pitches, he left the batter's box and started the same preparation sequence, this time using the COPE intervention. He took control of his emotions (C), organized meaningful information (e.g. coach feedback) from non-meaningful input (e.g. crowd noise, opponent's remarks), planned his strategy (P), and then entered the batting box to execute the next attempt (E). If he felt tension between pitches, he said to himself, "Think practice", as if he was in batting practice where he felt relaxed and hit the ball well. This player's batting success improved immediately, he reported.

Issues that Warrant Psychotherapy in Sport Psychology

Counseling is a skill that requires training by a university graduate program, usually certified by some recognized agency, such as the APA in the USA. Counseling involves a trained professional assisting a "client" in identifying and defining social and emotional problems, developing goals for addressing and overcoming these problems and, finally, implementing strategies, or action plans, that solve these problems (Ivey & Authier, 1978).

Briefly, psychotherapy concerns dealing with an individual's personal problems or "issues" in isolation from the influence of society or the environment in which those problems existed (Heyman, 1987). Frank (1984) contends that, at least among the non-athlete population, the majority of psychotherapy patients are demoralized; encouragement is the primary non-specific therapeutic effect of treatment. Psychotherapy requires the expertise of a specialist who is a licensed psychologist or psychiatrist.

Methods of conducting psychotherapy include hypnosis, dream analysis, biofeedback and psychological testing. Issues in psychotherapy that would be relevant for competitive athletes would include eating disorders, chronic anxiety and depression, helplessness and hopelessness, sleep disorders, low self-esteem, negative (neurotic) perfectionism, frequent injury, sources of chronic self-defeating thought patterns, mental barriers to injury recovery, personality disorders, use of maladaptive coping strategies, and addictions (Brewer & Petrie, 2002).

Giges (2000), a psychiatrist who has incorporated sport psychology in his practice, offers interesting insights into the difference between practicing traditional psychotherapy and sport psychology consulting. To Giges, "the greatest challenge in working in sport psychology was the shift from the clinical perspective to the educational one" (p. 18). When consulting with competitive athletes, in contrast to the clinical population, Giges found "concentrating on the present became more important than the past and opened new possibilities for effective interventions . . . present functioning and here-and-now experience are the starting points of intervention" (p. 18). A licensed clinician can adapt to a new population by using a different intervention style. Consultants, however, are not licensed as psychologists and are not trained to diagnose nor treat certain conditions. Consequently, they are restricted about the types of issues and interventions they can employ when counseling athletes. In addition, the unlicensed consultant is ethically bound to refer the athlete to a professional with the proper training and credentials, which is called the "referral process".

In summary, the type of intervention path taken, performance enhancement or therapy, often depends on the type of issue that needs to be addressed. For example, an athlete's propensity to "choke", that is, not performing well in high pressure, as opposed to low-pressure (practice) situations, is often a performance enhancement issue. The use of mental rehearsal in reflecting the problem, and an array of anxiety management techniques (e.g. positive self-talk, attentional focusing) that build confidence and reassurance is taught to athletes. However, if the athlete is burdened by self-doubt, thought patterns that reflect low self-esteem and thoughts of quitting, perhaps psychotherapy is needed to understand the antecedents and personal factors that may be causing what may be called irrational thinking or some other related problem. It is imperative that sport psychologists know when to engage in mental skills training/education, learn counseling skills and know when a particular problem or issue requires professional counseling, and when to refer an athlete to a clinical psychologist for psychotherapy. It is particularly important that consultants become aware of the issues and signals that go beyond their own training, and require the expertise, training and credentials of a licensed psychologist.

The counselor's skills, background and training are another factor that contributes to which type of intervention is warranted. For example, only individuals who are licensed in their state (in the USA) as a psychologist and are allowed to use that title to describe the type of service rendered may engage in psychotherapy. Another factor that dictates application of psychotherapy versus counseling is the expectations of coaches and athletes. There is a stigma associated with having mental problems and seeking professional help to resolve them. Many athletes may be willing to engage in mental skills training but are loath to reveal their personal history and hidden thoughts, while being "analyzed" by a virtual stranger. On the other hand, athletes whose thoughts or behaviors are self-destructive may suffer from psychopathology, requiring psychotherapy to determine the antecedents and underlying causes of these thoughts or actions. Individuals who lack the expertise, experience or credentials in addressing a particular problem are ethically bound to refer the athlete to another provider. This is called the "referral process".

The Referral Process

The referral process is complicated and delicate. As Brewer, Van Raalte and Petitpas (1999) point out, "Referrals can be complicated by the stigma associated with mental problems and the derogation of those who seek help from mental health practitioners" (p. 164). Writing about psychological services in sports injury rehabilitation, the authors suggest developing a referral network. Individuals in the network should "have knowledge of sport and experience working with athletes. At the least, they should be interested in learning about sport and exercise and open to working with an athletic population" (pp. 164–165).

The conditions under which a sport psychology consultant would refer a client/athlete to a psychotherapist, or vice versa, in which a licensed psychologist refers a client to someone with more training and experience in the mental skills area are less than clear. There are no strict criteria for referral. When, for instance, would sport psychology consultants—persons having completed a master's or doctoral degree in the area of sport and exercise science—detect an issue that warrants referral to a licensed psychologist? Under what conditions would a licensed psychologist conclude that the athlete requires extensive mental skills training, not psychotherapy, that goes beyond the psychologist's training? There are no clear answers to these questions. As Andersen (2001) points out in his review of this literature, athletes, and often their coaches, may not wish to engage in psychotherapy and, instead, ask for advice about overcoming a specific problem. As Andersen notes, "An athlete coming to a coach or sport psychologist may be uncomfortable if an interview probes personal areas" (p. 402). In addition,

> If trust and rapport have been built between the sport psychologist and the athlete, sending the athlete away to someone else when material comes up that the sport psychologist does not feel competent to handle may not be the optimal choice. (p. 404)

Instead of "referring out" to another therapist or consultant, "referring in" may be the better choice. Andersen describes referring in as "bringing in a qualified professional and having all three parties sit down and discuss a plan" (p. 404). This approach is less threatening to the athlete in promoting the therapeutic process. See Van Raalte and Andersen (2002) for more insights on the referral process unique to sport psychology.

In summary, then, the two important issues in offering psychological interventions are, first, to be able to separate issues requiring performance enhancement techniques as opposed to a clinical or counseling intervention and, second, to know when to refer the athlete to a specialist who possesses a different set of skills that will meet the athlete's particular needs. Individuals whose education and experience have been primarily in applied sport psychology or in clinical psychology each possess a unique set of skills that will provide athletes with needed interventions and address specific needs. More challenging, however, is the consultant's willingness to acknowledge their own limitations in training and expertise in dealing with particular issues the athlete presents, and to refer that athlete to a consultant or clinician whose skills and credentials are more likely to result in successful outcomes. For example, a sport psychology consultant might be able to help the athlete overcome negative thinking before or during the contest, perhaps suggesting a change in self-talk or learning an anxiety management program. However, addressing the athlete's tendency to perform poorly under pressure conditions or to become physically ill before each contest might require a clinical intervention. To address intimate issues, consultants need to develop a relationship with the athlete based on trust, openness, mutual respect and sensitivity.

A Model Depicting the Intervention Process

The intervention process, represented as a flow chart in Figure 5.1, illustrates stages and options by which sport psychology consultation is usually practiced. The process begins by acknowledging the athlete's performance barriers, problems or issues that need attention. The goal, here, is to focus on specific areas that may impede reaching optimal performance and to focus on the athlete's specific needs. The consultant then identifies personal and situational factors that play an important role in addressing the athlete's concerns, short-comings or limitations. Personal factors would include the athlete's dispositions and behavioral tendencies, usually under his or her control, that create or contribute to the problem. Drug-taking, unhealthy habits, boredom, lack of self-motivation or emotional immaturity that lead to lack of commitment or of taking responsibility are examples. Sample situational factors that contribute to the athlete's limitations include lack of playing opportunity, poor relationship with the coach, lack of support from significant others and lack of financial resources.

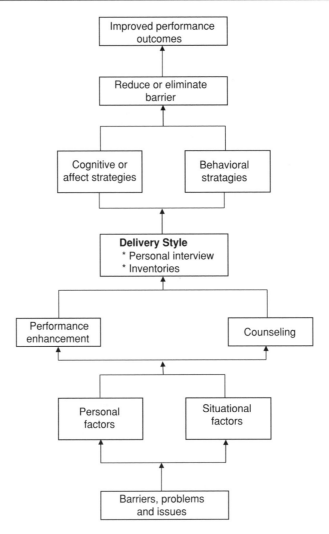

Figure 5.1 Flow chart of the counseling process in sport

After the personal and situational factors have been identified, a consultant must determine the type of intervention that is needed—performance enhancement/mental skills training or counseling. The athlete is then referred to the caregiver who possesses the appropriate credentials and skills. While many consultants have the experience and skills to perform both functions, most often professionals differ in their primary areas of expertise. Licensed psychologists and sport psychology (performance enhancement/mental skills) consultants have different training and usually bring different sets of skills to the counseling relationship. For example, it is the rare licensed psychologist who has completed graduate courses in sport psychology and is highly familiar with this literature. Thus, psychologists would not be expected to have the same level of mastery of the performance enhancement literature as professionals. Understanding the antecedents and sources of some issues, however, warrants psychotherapy, the purpose of which is to address and, ostensibly, resolve the underlying factors that are causing the problem. An athlete's addictive behaviors, for instance, cannot be resolved by positive self-talk or simply by acknowledging that they must take greater responsibility for their actions. Instead, addictions require far deeper understanding and treatment by a trained clinician.

At the next stage of the model, in the consulting process, is the style by which the counseling service will be delivered. Many sport psychologists shun the use of inventories; there is considerable debate about their usefulness and the extent to which they impede rather than promote building trust between the athlete and consultant (see Maniar et al., 2001, for an updated review of this issue). Not surprisingly, licensed psychologists who are trained to deliver and interpret test data will lend greater support for including test results as an inherent component of the consulting process (Gardner & Moore, 2004). It is plausible to suggest that reliance on both delivery styles is appropriate in response to the athlete's needs and the types of issues that must be resolved. Brewer and Petrie (2002) list several types of psychopathological conditions that would warrant test use to confirm a diagnosis. These include addictions and other substance abuse disorders, eating disorders, bipolar disorder, clinical depression, obsessive compulsive disorder, panic disorder, cognitive impairments, attention deficit hyperactive disorder (ADHD) and chronic anxiety, among others. Thus, while psychological interventions, which do not require testing, remain the primary thrust of sport psychology consulting, trained and licensed therapists must also address clinical issues that strongly relate to impaired athletic performance.

At the next stage of the model, the sport psychologist determines the types of strategies required to address the athlete's needs. These strategies are usually categorized as psychological (cognitive or affective) and behavioral.

Cognitive strategies are concerned with conscious thoughts that are intended to change some aspect of the ways in which incoming stimuli are processed (Singer, 1980). For example, a strategy called "pre-cueing" might alert the athlete to relevant cues in the environment prior to skill execution. Pre-cueing is intended to enhance the athlete's ability to anticipate the stimulus. Pre-cueing in football consists of the player visually scanning the formation of his opponents prior to the ball being snapped in anticipation of the kind of play that is forthcoming. Elite athletes of racquet sports tend to detect movement characteristics of their opponent before the shot (e.g. bending of the knee, direction of visual focusing) in anticipation of the next shot's type, speed or direction. Examples of other cognitive strategies include mental imagery, positive self-talk, attentional focusing, anticipation and thought-stopping.

Imagery can be used for skill mastery, coping with stressful events, error detection and correction, muscular or emotional relaxation, or anxiety management (Cornelius, 2002). Self-talk can be used prior to performance, perhaps as part of a pre-performance routine when there is the time and opportunity for thinking and planning. However, the demands of certain situations require that performers execute skills with relatively little thinking, a concept called "automaticity". Thus, use of cognitive strategies may be enacted both before (e.g. planning, pre-cueing, anticipation) and during skill execution (e.g. self-talk, psyching up, association, attentional focusing).

Results of a recent study among 13-year-old female competitive soccer players indicated that instructional self-talk—combining the words "down" and "lock" in rapid succession ("downlock") that reflected the proper technique of the low drive shot—significantly improved soccer shooting performance (Johnson, Hrycaiko, Johnson & Halas, 2004). In a study of basketball free throw shooting, Wrisberg and Anshel (1989) found that 10 to 12-year-old boys who trained to use mental imagery were significantly superior to a no-treatment control group on shooting accuracy. The researchers also reported that participants in the imagery group "appeared extremely receptive and enthusiastic about gaining a mental edge that they thought might enhance their skill performance" (p. 102). It is apparent, then, that younger athletes, similar to their older, better skilled counterparts, are both willing and capable of learning and properly executing sport psychology interventions. Weiss (1995) suggests that while children in sport should be able to master psychological skills (e.g. coping with competitive stress, positive self-perceptions, positive affect), the real focus with children should be to build competence (i.e. skill learning), affiliation (i.e. making friends), team identification (i.e. feeling part of a group), health and fitness (i.e. getting in shape), competition (i.e. demonstrating skills), and fun. As sport skills are mastered, child athletes will be more receptive and capable of demonstrating psychological interventions.

Behavioral strategies are consciously pre-planned actions that are intended to favorably affect the athlete's performance (Anshel, 2003b). Behavioral strategies include goal-setting, light exercise (a strategy that reduces state anxiety), record-keeping, self-regulation, self-monitoring (if executed in written rather than mental form), and social support. For example, the most commonly used behavioral strategy, goal-setting, has received extensive support in the extant literature for use by both elite athletes (Weinberg, Burton, Yukelson & Weigand, 2000) and for coaches (Weinberg, Butt & Knight, 2001). In a study of self-regulation strategies as a function of skill level among volleyball players, Kitsantas and Zimmerman (2002) reported more frequent use of planning, self-monitoring, self-evaluation, making causal attributions and adapting to error than their less skilled counterparts. Thus, behavioral intervention techniques are useful in enhancing sport performance and other desirable cognitive and affective outcomes.

In the model's final stages, ostensibly the athlete's perceived barrier should be reduced or eliminated resulting in improved performance outcomes. This final stage is an important reason for using assessment tools to detect change. For example, Grove, Norton, Van Raalte and Brewer (1999) extol the virtues of systematic evaluation of mental skills. They propose several approaches for assessing the use and effectiveness of using mental skills, primarily with pretest–posttest factorial designs. Other forms of assessment include action research (Gilbourne, 2000), which requires the researcher/consultant to examine intervention efficacy using intact groups (e.g. teams or segments of teams) as a function of a treatment, a technique that does not include a control group, and qualitative assessment (Culver, Gilbert & Trudel, 2003), in which athletes may be interviewed about changes in pre-determined variables (e.g. emotion, performance, communication effectiveness, the nature of relationships).

Ethical Issues

Maintaining proper ethical procedures in the counseling process is inherent in providing psychological services. Yet, there has been increased concern in recent years about ethical considerations in the practice of counseling psychology. Not surprisingly, ethical issues in sport psychology counseling have also been reported. Examples include use of interventions that are untested, making false promises to athletes about intervention outcomes that are difficult or impossible to support, addressing issues for which the professional is not qualified (e.g. unlicensed persons addressing issues requiring licensure such as addictions and disorders), and engaging in personal conduct with clients that is outside the bounds of the provider–client relationship. In the context of this chapter, ethics involves protecting participants/clients in the practice of sport psychology counseling. Suggested references for examining ethical issues in sport psychology include Mahoney (1986), Singer (1993), Sachs (1993), and Whelan, Meyers and Elkins (2002).

While a full review of ethics goes beyond the scope of this chapter, there are several important issues that should be acknowledged in providing sport psychology counseling. According to the National Institutes of Health (NIH, 2002), there are three fundamental ethical principles that guide the ethical conduct in research that have implications for sport psychologists when working with athletes of all ages and skill levels: (1) respect for persons, (2) beneficence and (3) justice. *Respect for others* includes treating individuals as autonomous agents; that is, a person "capable of deliberation about personal goals and of acting under such deliberation" (p. 13). Thus, an athlete should be under no pressure to enter into a relationship with a sport psychologist and to seek intervention services voluntarily and with adequate information. What is the nature of involvement with the sport psychologist, and what is involved in time, availability, the content of interventions, meeting location, confidentiality and cost? Should consulting occur if the coach mandates it? Should athletes be obligated to complete inventories or to provide any personal information unwillingly because the team has hired a sport psychologist?

Beneficence obligates the sport psychologist to "maximize possible benefits and minimize possible harm" (p. 14). Athletes are treated in a respectful and ethical manner by respecting their decision not to participate, and protecting them from harm and by making efforts to secure their well-being. Thus, sport psychologists who provide clients with test results without interpreting test scores, or who make judgments and draw conclusions about the athlete's needs or limitations, then prescribe interventions based on test results without confirming these scores with the client, are acting contrary to beneficence. Coercion of team members by the team's coach to engage in sport psychology consulting without the athlete's approval is another example.

Justice requires sport psychologists to help all participants of sport psychology interventions and other services (e.g., athletes, coaches, athletic trainers, administrators) to use well-established techniques that are within the provider's skills and training, to avoid placing the client at risk of their mental health, to avoid embarrassment or humiliation, and to avoid excluding any team member who wishes to participate. It would be unethical, for example, to begin a counseling relationship with an athlete at no cost (e.g. volunteering to consult with a team), and then require payment. Justice also means to represent credentials or the lack of credentials openly and accurately.

There are numerous issues that might give rise to ethical concerns. For example, is the sport psychologist certified by the Association for the Advancement of Applied Sport Psychology, or do they have previous skills, experience and knowledge in prescribing sport psychology techniques? Is the provider familiar with the sport psychology literature? If the provider is not a licensed psychologist, are they addressing issues for which they are not trained or licensed to provide? Does the provider have previous experience working with this particular sport or level of competition? Is the athlete being subjected to psychotherapy techniques rather then addressing performance enhancement skills? Is the athlete required to complete tests that address issues associated with disorders rather than with specific sport-related needs because the provider is a licensed psychologist or psychiatrist who is transferring their skills and knowledge from the non-athlete population to the unique needs of athletes?

   With respect to providing interventions in sport psychology, the following ethical procedures appear warranted.

- *Accurate representation of skills* It is imperative that sport psychologists acknowledge the
  boundaries of their expertise, and know when to refer clients to other professionals who
  are better able to meet the client's particular needs. Each athlete, situation and problem
  requires different approaches and knowledge by providers of psychological services. As
  indicated earlier, licensed psychologists are trained to provide assistance in resolving
  certain types of issues (e.g. addictions, dysfunctional behavior, various disorders) that
  performance enhancement consultants are simply not trained, educated or licensed to
  handle. However, additional training and expertise is needed to attempt to enhance the
  athlete's mental skills. On the other hand, professionals with performance enhancement
  expertise and not licensed as psychologists are required to refer their athlete-client to a
  licensed psychologist when "clinical" issues arise.
- *Making false promises* While the field of sport psychology has made great strides in
  developing mental skills and psycho-behavioral interventions that have been shown to
  enhance athletic performance, making hyperbolic promises about the expected outcomes
  from these techniques lacks proper ethics. It is well known that "one size does not fit all".
  That is, one technique may result in successful outcomes for one athlete or in particular
  situations, while proving to be ineffective for other athletes or in different situations. New
  mental skills and interventions are best learned and applied in practice settings before
  they are used in competition.

Betrayal of Trust and Confidentiality

On-site participation As Mahoney (1986) suggests, "Be prepared to leave your office and
enter the locker room or playing field" (p. 67). OK, so some consultants are quite satisfied
providing psychological services strictly within the confines of their office, and choose
not to observe nor interact with the athlete in the sport competition environment. Does the
counselor's behavior reflect poor ethics or is this a matter of being less effective? Perhaps
the answer depends on the extent to which the counselor is committed to and invested in
helping the athlete, and how much the athlete is depending on the sport psychologist to help
overcome their personal limitations. Consciously avoiding a procedure, such as attending a
practice session or contest, that the counselor knows will enhance intervention effectiveness
might be considered unethical. In this case, as addressed earlier in this chapter, a referral to
another professional who is able to make on-site visits to the athletic venue is warranted.

CONCLUDING REMARKS

This chapter addressed issues in assessment and diagnosis, with many recommendations as
how to evaluate (what procedures to follow) and how to use information gathered. Various
self-report inventories were explained as were the nature of interview/discussion sessions
that could be used to measure personal cognitive processes and behaviors associated with
successful performance. Implications were drawn for intervention possibilities, as well as
for determining their effectiveness.

The second section included ideas about counseling athletes for coping with in-sport and out-of-sport personal problems. Sample issues were identified. Approaches that sport psychologists might adopt in counseling sessions were explored, as well as considerations for improving the counseling process.

In this chapter, we have attempted to describe various approaches to and considerations about interventions that should be applicable to a variety of sports and sport participants with different levels of skill. The remaining chapters are oriented to those interventions related to specific sports.

REFERENCES

American Psychological Association (1999). *The Standards for Educational and Psychological Testing*. Washington, DC: American Psychological Association.

Andersen, M.B. (2001). When to refer athletes for counseling or psychotherapy. In J.M. Williams (ed.), *Applied Sport Psychology: Personal Growth to Peak Performance* (4th edn; pp. 401–415). Mountain View, CA: Mayfield.

Anderson, A.G., Knowles, Z. & Gilbourne, D. (2004). Reflective practice for sport psychologists: concepts, models, practical implications, and thoughts on dissemination. *The Sport Psychologist, 18*, 188–203.

Anshel, M.H. (1987). Psychological inventories used in sport psychology research. *The Sport Psychologist, 1*, 331–349.

Anshel, M.H. (1990). Toward validation of the COPE model: strategies for acute stress inoculation in sport. *International Journal of Sport Psychology, 21*, 24–39.

Anshel, M.H. (1995). Development of a rating scale for determining competence in basketball referees: implications for sport psychology. *The Sport Psychologist, 9*, 4–28.

Anshel, M.H. (2003a, August). Correct and incorrect use of psychological inventories in sport psychology consultation. A paper presented at the American Psychological Association Convention, Toronto, Ontario, Canada.

Anshel, M.H. (2003b). *Sport Psychology: From Theory to Practice* (4th edn). San Francisco: Benjamin-Cummings.

Anshel, M.H., Housner, L. & Cyrs, T. (1987). Defining competence for effective coaching in high school football. *Journal of Applied Research in Coaching and Athletics, 2*, 79–95.

Anshel, M.H., Kim, K.W., Kim, B.H., Chang, K.J. & Eom, H.J. (2001). A model for coping with stressful events in sport: theory, application, and future directions. *International Journal of Sport Psychology, 32*, 43–76.

Beckmann, J. & Kellmann, M. (2003). Procedures and principles of sport psychological assessment. *The Sport Psychologist, 17*, 338–350.

Brewer, B.W. & Petrie, T.A. (2002). Psychopathology in sport and exercise. In J.L. Van Raalte & B.W. Brewer (eds), *Exploring Sport and Exercise Psychology* (2nd edn; pp. 307–323). Washington, DC: American Psychological Association.

Brewer, B.W., Van Raalte, J.L. & Petitpas, A.J. (1999). Patient-practitioner interactions in sport injury rehabilitation. In D. Pargman (ed.), *Psychological Bases of Sport Injuries* (2nd edn; pp. 157–174). Morgantown, WV: Fitness Information Technology.

Butt, D.S. (1987). *Psychology of Sport: The Behavior, Motivation, Personality and Performance of Athletes* (2nd edn). New York: Van Nostrand.

Caspi, A. & Bem, D.J. (1990). Personality continuity and change across the life course. In L.A. Pervin (ed.), *Handbook of Personality: Theory and Research* (pp. 549–575). New York: Guilford.

Cornelius, A. (2002). Intervention techniques in sport psychology. In J.M. Silva & D. Stevens (eds), *Psychological Foundations of Sport* (pp. 197–223). San Francisco: Benjamin-Cummings.

Culver, D.M., Gilbert, W.D. & Trudel, P. (2003). A decade of qualitative research in sport psychology journals: 1990–1999. *The Sport Psychologist, 17*, 1–15.

Danish, S.J., Petitpas, A.J. & Hale, B.D. (1993). Life development intervention for athletes: life skills through sports. *Counseling Psychologist, 21*, 352–385.

Epstein, S. (1990). Comment on the effects of aggregation across and within occasions on consistency, specificity, and reliability. *Methodika, 4*, 95–100.

Frank, J.D. (1984). Therapeutic components of all psychotherapies. In J.M. Myers (ed.), *Cures by Psychotherapy: What Affects Change?* (pp. 15–27). New York: Praeger.

Frost, R.O., Marten, P., Laharat, C. & Rosenblate, R. (1990). The dimensions of perfectionism. *Cognitive Therapy and Research, 14*, 449–468.

Gardner, F.L. & Moore, Z.E. (2004). The multi-level classification system for sport psychology (MCS-SP). *The Sport Psychologist, 18*, 89–109.

Gauvin, L. & Russell, S.J. (1993). Sport-specific and culturally adapted measures in sport and exercise psychology research: issues and strategies. In R.N. Singer, M. Murphey & L.K. Tennant (eds), *Handbook of Research on Sport Psychology* (pp. 891–900). New York: Macmillan.

Giges, B. (2000). Removing psychological barriers: clearing the way. In M.B. Andersen (ed.), *Doing Sport Psychology* (pp. 17–31). Champaign, IL: Human Kinetics.

Gilbourne, D. (2000). Searching for the nature of action research: a response to Evans, Hardy, and Fleming. *The Sport Psychologist, 14*, 207–214.

Greenson, R.R. (1967). *Technique and Practice of Psychoanalysis*. New York: International Universities Press.

Grove, J.R., Norton, P.J., Van Raalte, J.L. & Brewer, B.W. (1999). Stages of change as an outcome measure in the evaluation of mental skills training programs. *The Sport Psychologist, 13*, 107–116.

Heil, J., Bowman, J.J. & Bean, B. (1993). Patient management and the sports medicine team. In J. Heil (ed.), *Psychology of Sport Injury* (pp. 237–249). Champaign, IL: Human Kinetics.

Heyman, S.R. (1987). Counseling and psychotherapy with athletes: special considerations. In J.R. May & M.J. Asken (eds), *Sport Psychology: The Psychological Health of the Athlete* (pp. 135–156). New York: PMA Publishing Company.

Holt, N.L. & Strean, W.B. (2001). Reflecting on initiating sport psychology consultation: a self-narrative of neophyte practice. *The Sport Psychologist, 15*, 188–204.

Ivey, A.E. & Authier, J. (1978). *Microcounseling*. Springfield, IL: Charles C. Thomas.

Johnson, J., Hrycaiko, D.W., Johnson, G.V. & Halas, J.M. (2004). Self-talk and female youth soccer performance. *The Sport Psychologist, 18*, 44–59.

Kirschenbaum, D. & Bale, R.M. (1980). Cognitive-behavioral skills in gold: brain power gold. In R.M. Suinn (ed.), *Psychology in Sports: Methods and Applications* (pp. 334–343). Minneapolis, MN: Burgess.

Kitsantas A., & Zimmerman, B.J. (2002). Comparing self-regulatory processes among novice, non-expert, and expert volleyball players: a microanalytic study. *Journal of Applied Sport Psychology, 14*, 91–105.

Loehr, J.E. (1990). *The Mental Plan: Winning at Pressure Tennis*. New York: Penguin.

Mahoney, J.M. (1986). Clinical sport psychology. *Clinical Psychologist, 39*, 64–68.

Maniar, S.D., Curry, L.A., Sommers-Flanagan, J. & Walsh, J.A. (2001). Student-athlete preferences in seeking help when confronted with sport performance problems. *The Sport Psychologist, 15*, 205–223.

Marsh, H.W. (1998). Forward. In J.L. Duda (ed.), *Advances in Sport and Exercise Psychology Measurement* (pp. xv–xix). Morgantown, WV: Fitness Information Technology.

Martin, M.B. & Anshel, M.H. (1995). Effect of self-monitoring strategies and task complexity on motor performance and affect. *Journal of Sport and Exercise Psychology, 17*, 153–170.

National Institutes of Health (2002). *Human Participant Protections Education for Research Teams*. Washington, DC: US Department of Health and Human Services.

Orlick, T. (1986). *Psyching for Sport: Mental Training for Athletes*. Champaign, IL: Human Kinetics.

Orlick, T. (1990). *In Pursuit of Excellence* (2nd edn). Champaign, IL: Human Kinetics.

Orlick, T. & Partington, J. (1987). The sport psychology consultant: analysis of critical components as viewed by Canadian Olympic athletes. *The Sport Psychologist, 1*, 4–17.

Ostrow, A.C. (1996). *The Directory of Psychological Tests in the Sport and Exercise Sciences* (2nd edn). Morgantown, WV: Fitness Information Technology.

Peterson, C. (2000). The future of optimism. *American Psychologist, 55*, 44–55.

Ravizza, K. (1988). Gaining entry with athletic personnel for season-long consulting. *The Sport Psychologist*, 2, 243–254.

Ravizza, K. (1990). SportPsych consultation issues in professional baseball. *The Sport Psychologist*, 4, 330–340.

Ray, R., Terrell, T. & Hough, D. (1999). The role of the sports medicine professional in counseling athletes. In R. Ray & D.M. Wiese-Bjornstal (eds), *Counseling in Sports Medicine* (pp. 3–20). Champaign, IL: Human Kinetics.

Rotella, R. & Connelly, D. (1984). Individual ethics in the application of cognitive sport psychology. In W.F. Straub & J.M. Williams (eds), *Cognitive Sport Psychology*. Lansing, NY: Sport Sciences Associates.

Sachs, M.L. (1993). Professional ethics in sport psychology. In R.N. Singer, M. Murphey & L.K. Tennant (eds), *Handbook of Research on Sport Psychology* (pp. 921–932). New York: Macmillan.

Schutz, R.W. (1998). Assessing the stability of psychological traits and measures. In J.L. Duda (ed.), *Advances in Sport and Exercise Psychology Measurement* (pp. 393–408). Morgantown, WV: Fitness Information Technology.

Singer, R.N. (1980). *Motor learning and human performance* (3rd edn). New York: Macmillan.

Singer, R.N. (1993). Ethical issues in clinical services. *Quest, 45*, 88–105.

Smith, A.M. (1999). Assessing athletes through individual interview. In R. Ray & D.M. Weise-Bjornstal (eds), *Counseling in Sports Medicine* (pp. 75–91). Champaign, IL: Human Kinetics.

Smith, R.E. (1980). A cognitive-affective approach to stress management training for athletes. In C.H. Nadeau, W.R. Halliwell, K.M. Newell & G.C. Roberts (eds), *Psychology of Motor Behavior and Sport—1980* (pp. 54–72). Champaign: IL: Human Kinetics.

Smith, R.E., Smoll, F.L. & Christensen, D.S. (1996). Behavioral assessments and interventions in youth sports. *Behavior Modification, 20*, 3–44.

Tkachuk, G., Leslie-Toogood, A. & Martin, G.L. (2003). Behavioral assessment in sport psychology. *The Sport Psychologist, 17*, 104–117.

Vanden Auweele, Y., De Cuyper, B., Van Mele, V. & Rzewnicki, R. (1993). Elite performance and personality: from description and prediction to diagnosis and intervention. In R.N. Singer, M. Murphey & L.K. Tennant (eds), *Handbook of Research on Sport Psychology* (pp. 257–289). New York: Macmillan.

Van Raalte, J.L. & Andersen, M.B. (2002). Referral processes in sport psychology. In J.L. Van Raalte & B.W. Brewer (eds), *Exploring Sport and Exercise Psychology* (2nd edn; pp. 325–337). Washington, DC: American Psychological Association.

Vealey, R.S. (2002). Personality and sport behavior. In T. Horn (ed.), *Advances in Sport Psychology* (2nd edn; pp. 43–82). Champaign, IL: Human Kinetics.

Vealey, R.S. & Garner-Holman, M. (1998). Applied sport psychology: measurement issues. In J.L. Duda (ed.), *Advances in Sport and Exercise Psychology Measurement* (pp. 433–446). Morgantown, WV: Fitness Information Technology.

Weinberg, R.S., Burton, D. Yukelson, D. & Weigand, D. (2000). Perceived goal setting practices of Olympic athletes: an exploratory investigation. *The Sport Psychologist, 14*, 280–296.

Weinberg, R.S., Butt, J. & Knight, B. (2001). High school coaches' perceptions of the process of goal setting. *The Sport Psychologist, 15*, 20–47.

Weinberg, R.S. & Williams, J.M. (2001). Integrating and implementing a psychological skills training program. In J.M. Williams (ed.), *Applied Sport Psychology: Personal Growth to Peak Performance* (4th edn; pp. 347–377). Mountain View, CA: Mayfield.

Weiss, M.R. (1995). Children in sport: an educational model. In S.M. Murphy (ed.), *Sport Psychology Interventions* (pp. 39–69). Champaign, IL: Human Kinetics.

Whelan, J.P., Meyers, A.W. & Elkins, T.D. (2002). Ethics in sport and exercise psychology. In J.L. Van Raalte & B.W. Brewer (eds), *Exploring Sport and Exercise Psychology* (2nd edn, pp. 503–523). Washington, DC: American Psychological Association.

Wrisberg, C.A. & Anshel, M.H. (1989). The effect of cognitive strategies on the free throw shooting performance of young athletes. *The Sport Psychologist, 3*, 95–104.

Zinsser, N., Bunker, L. & Williams, J.M. (2001). Cognitive techniques for building confidence and enhancing performance. In J.M. Williams (ed.), *Applied Sport Psychology: Personal Growth to Peak Performance* (4th edn; pp. 284–311). Mountain View, CA: Mayfield.

PART II

Team Sports

CHAPTER 6

Using Sport Psychology to Improve Basketball Performance

Kevin L. Burke

East Tennessee State University, USA

INTRODUCTORY COMMENTS

The purpose of this chapter is to discuss the roles sport psychologists may play in consulting with coaches, players and other related team members of basketball teams. The sport of basketball provides numerous opportunities for sport psychology professionals to assist individuals and groups (and subgroups) in an exciting, interactive environment that may claim to offer the world's most popular sport for both genders! While sport psychology consulting in basketball situations can be stimulating for all participants, the challenges may be overwhelming and demanding, like a "full-court press". This chapter's goal is to provide sport psychology consultants with ideas, suggestions and techniques that may assist in successfully meeting those challenges and "breaking the press".

INTRICACIES OF BASKETBALL

It would be interesting to know what Dr James Naismith's thoughts would be on how the game he invented in 1891 (Naismith, 1941) is being played today. Little did he know that his physical education innovation would be arguably the most popular participant and spectator sport in the world! From a simple game with peach baskets of yesteryear, the playing, coaching and officiating of basketball has developed into a sport science all its own. Many basketball enthusiasts make a career of being involved with basketball by playing, coaching, administrating, officiating and analyzing this fast-paced game. College and universities offer courses and programs of study that allow interested persons to increase their knowledge of various aspects of basketball (and the realm of sports in general) in areas such as sports medicine, sports management, sport sociology, coaching and sport psychology. Numerous books, videos and websites are available on many aspects of playing and

The Sport Psychologist's Handbook: A Guide for Sport-Specific Performance Enhancement.
Edited by Joaquín Dosil. © 2006 John Wiley & Sons, Ltd.

coaching basketball. Recommendations for learning more basketball coaching aspects are books by Hall of Fame Coach Dean Smith (1999; his *Basketball: Multiple Offense and Defense* is considered a "must-read" by serious coaches), and *Coaching Basketball Successfully* by Morgan Wootten (2003). To learn more about the psychological side (mental aspects) of playing and coaching basketball, *Sport Psychology Library Series: Basketball* (Burke & Brown, 2003) is available. One helpful website for players and coaches is "Basketball's Best" available at the following web address: http://www.basketballsbest.com (for a list of other basketball related websites, please see the end of this chapter). Due to the increased emphasis on sport in most societies, athletes are beginning to "specialize" and, therefore, participate in basketball at very young ages. (Several years ago, a coach in the United States was accused of offering basketball shoes and clothing to 10- and 11-year-old kids so as to "recruit" future high school players for his team!) Also, while basketball does have a season like other sports, many basketball aficionados choose to participate almost all year long. The National Basketball Association's season is nine months long; the college season is six months in length, while the high school season lasts approximately four months. Almost all levels of play encourage their participants to continue to play in the "off-season" in various leagues and/or summer camps. Because of these aforementioned circumstances, the psychological aspects of basketball have taken on increased importance.

Although basketball is a team sport, it is played by individuals. Therefore, the influences and interactions of the team on the individual and the individual on the team can make for complex and interesting situations. Various different subgroups can, and usually do, form among this group of usually 12 to 15 players, coaches, managers, trainers and administrators. "Cliques" when monitored closely (and sometimes encouraged) can be helpful to a team. Yet negative cliques can be a major disruption to the team's cohesion (Henschen & Cook, 2003). The coordination of day-to-day basketball activities is a monumental task. Notwithstanding, the "meshing" of the various personalities while performing these activities is just as important to the success of the team.

While many in the sport psychology field state that extensive knowledge by a sport psychologist of a particular sport is unnecessary to help those involved with that sport, knowing the intricacies of playing and coaching basketball certainly provides great advantages to consulting with basketball participants. While it is not imperative that a sport psychologist knows how to operate a 3–2 zone defense, run the "shuffle" offense, or design an in-bounds play (Smith, 1999), the sport psychologist's knowledge of basketball terminology and mental and physical performance demands will assist in intervention planning. Some sport psychologists have initially either played or officiated a scrimmage game with a team that they will consult with. This allows the players and coaches to see "firsthand" that the sport psychologist has an understanding of the sport of basketball. Although initial "down in the trenches" participation with the team may be considered a luxury not always available, coaches and athletes will usually be impressed with the sport psychologist who attends games or practices, and can "talk the talk"—speak in basketball terminology. The potential influence of these previously mentioned actions on building rapport with the athletes and coaches is immeasurable.

For most basketball teams, sport psychology interventions may be placed into two classifications. Interventions may be utilized for (1) individuals or (2) the team, and the consequences of the interventions may be influential on and off of the basketball court. Some examples of individual situations include a lack of confidence in free throw shooting, field goal shooting slumps, excessive performance anxiety, lack of showing good sporting behavior (sportsmanship or sportpersonship), unable to "let go" of a poor performance, and worries about the coach–player relationship. Team situations may include inappropriate team performance expectations, low morale, communication problems (Burke, 2005), proper coordination and cooperation of the teammates (i.e. team cohesion issues). Some sport psychologists suggest that team psychological skill acquisition meetings (i.e. concentration or imagery sessions) are not as effective as individual practice of these skills, and that team "meetings" are best to explore team issues such as team goal setting or cohesion (Henschen & Cook, 2003). While this suggestion is true in many basketball situations, the sport psychologist must be able to adapt to the particular team environment and provide mental skills training in the manner most likely to be helpful and acceptable.

It is also important to realize that, particularly among the younger age groups, sport psychology techniques are not readily utilized. Many basketball players first come in contact with sport psychology training techniques in college or the professional leagues. This means on many occasions when the sport psychologist is requested to consult with a team there is a good possibility that this may be the initial experience for the players and coaches. Also, on a team of 15 players, a sport psychologist may expect five players to be highly interested in mental skills training, five with a moderate interest, and five who are uninterested. The sport psychologist should have the goal that if one player may be helped by sport psychology techniques, then the experience is worthwhile. In many situations when the other basketball players see improvements in a teammate who is applying sport psychology techniques, they will become more interested.

FUNDAMENTAL INDIVIDUAL PSYCHOLOGICAL BASKETBALL SKILLS

In many cases, sport psychologists will be asked to assist teams but only given a brief amount of time to accomplish their tasks. Also, while it is usually most conducive to work with basketball participants during the off-season or preseason (Weinberg & Gould, 2003), most players and teams will seek assistance during the competitive season. Therefore, it is imperative that sport psychologists plan for effective, informative and efficient consultations that coaches and players may implement during the busiest times of their participation. In other words, many of the interventions with basketball teams will be "brief or solution-focused interventions" (Kottler, 2000; Thompson & Rudolph, 2000) which require immediate applications in a short amount of time. Brief interventions have become more popular in mental health care situations due to professionals seeking more time efficient strategies, client to therapist ratios, and managed care organizations (Thompson & Rudolph, 2000). According to Kottler (2000), this problem-solving focused intervention usually is based upon the following assumptions:

1. If the interventions are specific and focused, change may quickly occur.
2. Emphasize the present instead of focusing on the past.
3. Precise objectives are defined and to be attained within a set time limit.

4. Sport psychologists are directive, active and innovative to help athletes establish new productive behavior patterns.
5. Various flexible and practical approaches are used to solve problems.
6. Initial small changes may lead to more dramatic changes later.
7. Attention is directed to what is wrong *and* what works well.

Due to the usually limited interactions available, brief or solution-focused approaches can be very effective when working with basketball teams, players and/or coaches.

While there are numerous ways to psychologically practice basketball, basketball players usually are most receptive to three fundamental individual basketball performance "boosters"—imagery, concentration and self-talk (Burke & Brown, 2003). Helping players (and coaches) succinctly acquire and improve these three important skills may produce numerous playing benefits and personal satisfaction for all involved. On many occasions sport psychology consultations may involve a combination of imagery, concentration and/or self-talk. The value of these psychological skills in aiding learning and performance has been established by research (Burke, 1990; 1992; Carboni, Burke, Joyner, Hardy & Blom, 2002; Hatzigeorgiadis, Theodorakis & Zourbanos, 2004; Landin & Herbert, 1999; Mamassis & Doganis, 2004; Murphy & Martin, 2002; Theodorakis, Weinberg, Natsis, Douma & Kazakas, 2000).

As mentioned earlier, the sport psychologist must devote a considerable amount of time developing relationships and building rapport with the players, coaches, athletic trainers (sports medicine specialists) and team managers. Because of proximity (at the very least), often players will first tell the athletic trainers (Kolt, 2000) (or team managers) of their need for assistance. The athletic trainers and managers may then serve as an avenue of referral to the sport psychologist. The old adage, "They don't care what you know, until they know that you care" applies to basketball teams. How quickly an effective working relationship is developed depends on many factors (number and quality of interactions, receptivity of the team, presentation style, etc.). Henschen and Cook (2003) suggest that relationship building may take as long as two years! No matter the time frame needed to build the "working alliance" (Andersen, 2000), sport psychologists must not overlook this essential aspect of building the consulting relationship.

UNDERSTANDING THE SPORT PSYCHOLOGIST'S ROLE WITH THE TEAM

Another area that must be dealt with immediately with players and coaches is clarifying the sport psychologist's role in relation to the team. Sport psychologists should be sure the coaches and players understand confidentiality, and the limitations therein. Players should feel they can meet with the sport psychologist, without the sport psychologist reporting the meeting, or its contents, to the coaching staff. Even if coaches send or require their players to meet with the sport psychologist, the sport psychologist should get permission from the players *before* informing the coach that the meeting took place. Also, it is important that sport psychologists explain these working principles to the coaching staff. Good communication of the working principles with the coaches early in the relationship can prevent later misunderstandings. If the sport psychologist has experience in coaching and playing basketball, it is a good idea to inform the coaching staff that the sport psychologist will not attempt to directly coach physical skills. In some cases where coaches are concerned that the consultant will attempt to "play coach", reassuring the coaches this will not occur is a very good idea.

Potential Performance-related Sport Psychology Basketball Scenarios

While it is impossible to list in one book chapter all of the potential situations in which sport psychologists may be engaged with individual players or entire basketball teams, the following briefly discusses some of the most likely scenarios to be encountered by sport psychologists.

Practice Performance vs. Game Performance (Dealing with Pressure)

One of the most often encountered problems experienced by basketball players is playing well in practice, but not performing well during games. Many times these players are simply told to "pretend" that games are practices—which is usually impossible to do. Wearing the team uniform, playing in front of spectators and cheerleaders with the team's won/loss record 'on the line' is a much different climate than most isolated, spectator-free practice sessions where the atmosphere is usually more relaxed. While there may be many reasons for the "practice player" to choke during games, the most common reason for this problem is the basketball player begins to focus more on outcomes during the games, while usually focusing on performance during practices. This outcome-oriented thinking may lead to perceptions of pressure and the inability to deal effectively with it. Sport psychologists should encourage "practice stars" to utilize self-talk "practice" statements during the games. If the player has difficulty doing this, then basketball players should be encouraged to use appropriate "game" statements during practice to allow the player more experience using these self-statements for actual competitions. With the latter strategy, the player gets more "game simulations" in practice that may allow the athlete to get more accustomed to dealing with "prime time" effectively.

Dealing with and Overcoming Slumps (Loss of Confidence)

Many basketball players will helplessly wait until a slump (poor performance over an extended time period) ends by happenstance. Sport psychologists can help athletes to actively attempt to get out of a slump. Basketball players get caught in the vicious negative self-talk cycle of "I don't have confidence, therefore I won't play well. And, because I am not playing well, I don't have any confidence." Imagery may be utilized to help players see and feel what they need to do to be successful. Utilizing successful imagery, along with physical practice, can help a player to think confident thoughts and see positive images.

Concentration can also be a significant problem for players when in the midst of a performance slump. Often players will notice they are inappropriately distracting themselves with thoughts irrelevant to the task at hand. The use of appropriate self-talk cue words or phrases can be helpful to build confidence and maintain appropriate concentration in these situations.

"Pine Time" or Sitting on the Bench

Basketball players rarely set the goal of playing on a basketball team and then plan to sit on the bench. However, at any moment in a game 8 to 10 players may be sitting down while their teammates participate. One of the most difficult challenges for sport psychologists (and coaches) is keeping the "bench" players motivated, focused and satisfied. One idea for working with this challenging situation is to have the players focus on what is under their direct control. While the coaching staff determines (controls) the amount of playing time players receive, basketball players control their reactions to these decisions. Therefore, sport psychologists may encourage basketball players to spend the time wisely on the bench that may increase their chances of earning playing time later. One suggestion is to have the players actively cheer their teammates during the games. To help bench players appreciate how much their vocal support means to their playing teammates, remind the bench players how meaningful it is when their teammates (and coaches) support them in this manner. Another recommendation is to suggest potential substitutes closely watch the teammates on the court for whom they are most likely to substitute. This benefits the observer by being able to notice what is working and not working for the team. Actively observing teammates can also help bench players give their playing teammates advice that may help the team. Bench players can have the goal of attempting to learn more about basketball or the team during every game. Encouraging the bench players to "cheer" and/or "observe" keeps the athletes actively focused on the game and allows them to be involved with each competition, rather than brooding over a lack of playing time.

While sitting on the bench, self-talk is critical in determining players' attitudes toward the team and their enjoyment of being on a basketball team. If players anticipate limited playing time, they may focus on self-improvement during practices, becoming a team player, and staying positive. Self-talk can easily become negative when players receive limited playing time. One way to break the habit of negative self-talk statements is to interrupt and replace them with realistic, positive self-talk. Table 6.1 gives examples of negative self-talk changed into positive self-talk statements:

Table 6.1 Changing negative statements to positive self-talk

Negative	Positive
I never get to play.	My time will come.
I'm not a valuable teammate.	I will help the team in any way I can.
People think I can't play.	There are many people who would be proud to be on this team.
They don't need me.	I am an important part of this team. My role is important.
I'm not any good.	I'm getting better.
The coach doesn't like me.	I have to show coach more in practice.

Source: From Burke, K.L. & Brown, D. (2003). *Sport Psychology Library Series: Basketball.* Morgantown, WV: Fitness Information Technology, Inc.

Getting along with Teammates and Coaches

No matter how enjoyable the sport of basketball, there will be some players and coaches who will present challenges to have positive relationships with. One way sport psychologists can help athletes confront these situations is through appropriate self-talk that promotes making the best of the situation and stresses the "team first" philosophy. If an athlete does not have a fond relationship with one of the coaches, remind the player the coach is usually trying to help that person and the team improve. If the relationship difficulty is teammate-related, sport psychologists may encourage athletes to discuss the situation openly with the teammate the player is having difficulty with. Sometimes simply allowing basketball players an opportunity to "vent" or express their feelings (to the sport psychologist and/or teammate) helps them feel better about the situation. In rare cases, players may need to take the mentality that they will enjoy their basketball experiences "despite" the offending coach or player!

Controlling Temper and Emotional Outbursts

Emotional expression makes playing and coaching basketball fun and exciting. If basketball players lose control of their emotions, a variety of basketball performance problems may result such as inferior performance, fouls, fighting, ejection from one or more games and/or injuries. Therefore, it is important that sport psychologists help players and coaches develop positive "thought habits" to help maintain control of their emotions. Self-talk and imagery can be an effective "double-team" to learn emotional control. Sport psychologists may take a cognitive approach to this challenge by helping basketball players understand the following realization: emotions are caused by thoughts; thoughts are controlled by the player; therefore, the player is in control of his or her own emotions. Once players and coaches understand that emotions are not "automatic happenings", appropriate self-talk words and phrases such as "Calm", and "Cool", or positive self-statements like "That's all right" and "I'll do better" can help the participant remain focused on the task at hand (Burke & Brown, 2003). Also, imagery sessions may be tailored to rehearse game situations not going as desired with mentally practicing staying in emotional control. For example, a player may image committing a turnover. Then, instead of getting upset, image staying calm and focused. Another strategy to quickly deal with emotions properly is named the "three-seconds rule" (Burke & Brown, 2003). This strategy is based upon the assumption that clients can control emotions and not experience serious "out-of-control" outbursts by avoiding an emotional "build-up". Some coaches and players will attempt to hold in their emotions, but eventually will "blow up", often leading to embarrassing actions or negatively affecting performance. The premise of the "three-seconds rule" is that rather than holding emotions in only to explode later, players and coaches have *just three seconds* to say or think positive or negative thoughts. The thoughts may be critical (negative), instructive or positive. However, these thoughts are limited to what may be said or thought in a three-second time period. (Much can be said/thought in this brief time period!) After the three-second time limit is over, the participants must begin to focus on what their next tasks are. This technique allows "letting off steam" and then getting focused for the next basketball situation. The three-seconds strategy helps prevent the major explosion that occurs from trying to hold emotions in. By adhering to the time limit, coaches and players can also get quickly refocused on the appropriate game or practice tasks.

Dealing with Basketball Burnout

An extreme loss of motivation to play or coach basketball may result in burnout. Burnout occurs when participants no longer feel rewarded by playing or coaching basketball. Burnout has become a common problem for many participants because of the lack of a "true" off-season for many basketball players and coaches. Even when their actual playing season is over, many are required to continue (or it is strongly suggested that they continue) involvement throughout the year. Burnout occurs because participants are not receiving meaningful rewards, and they may need mental and physical time away from basketball. Sport psychologists may help players and coaches deal with burnout through "preventive medicine"—attempt to keep burnout from occurring. Although difficult for some players and coaches, the sport psychologist should encourage an "off-season" with another sport and promote time away from basketball. Sport psychologists should help basketball participants realize that a mental and physical hiatus from basketball for a significant time after each season may make basketball even more enjoyable. Even during the season, basketball should not consume the participants' lives. Attention must be given to the other areas of life for players and coaches (and sport psychologists) to maintain a balanced existence. Through time management and self-talk techniques, basketball participants can keep their sport in proper perspective. To help focus on the rewards of coaching and playing, sport psychologists may help participants devise a list (written or typed) and think about the rewarding aspects of playing or coaching the game. Helping basketball participants remember and refocus on their original reasons for involvement in the game can be a refreshing exercise in this time of need.

If a player or coach gets to the point of total burnout, taking an extended break from basketball may be all that can be done. Continuing to "muddle through" while totally burned out runs the risk of making playing basketball a extremely miserable experience. However, in many cases it is simply unrealistic to "take a break" if burnout occurs during the season. In these circumstances, sport psychologists may assist by helping the coach or player to emphasize and focus on the aspects of basketball enjoyed most (i.e. seek rewards for participation) and providing opportunities for the clients to discuss their feelings.

Dealing with Injury

One of the most mentally and physically challenging situations encountered in basketball is injury, rehabilitation and recovery. Overcoming injury requires both mental and physical rehabilitation. Attitudes toward the injury and rehabilitation process will have a significant impact on the recovery and rehabilitation experiences. For example, studies have shown that having an optimistic attitude enhances physical recovery and well-being in a variety of settings (Czech, Burke, Joyner & Hardy, 2002; Scheier & Carver, 1992). One of the best strategies is to help athletes view (through self-talk) the injury and recovery process as another challenge to be faced in basketball. Have the athletes treat the recovery from injury as another opponent to be dealt with. Also, imagery can be a valuable technique during times of injury. Imagery can be used for two important purposes. First, during the time when athletes are not allowed to physically practice basketball, imagery allows mental practice of the skills and strategies. At the very least, imagery can help injured athletes stay involved with the basketball team. For instance, if a coach introduces a new defense while players are recovering, then imagery may be utilized to help learn the new defense. Also, using imagery to see and feel playing basketball again can be very motivational during rehabilitation. The following is a partial imagery script a basketball player may use to remain motivated while recovering from a knee injury. The player may utilize the following example script while at home, traveling or any place that is comfortable. The script that follows is only an brief and partial example. Imagery scripts should be altered to fit the specific needs of the person.

Imagery Rehabilitation Script

> I see myself practicing in the gym alone. The gym is quiet, but feels comfortable to me. I slowly begin dribbling the basketball from one sideline of the court to the other. The basket is on my left and empty bleachers on my right. I feel the ball touch my hand on each dribble. I can hear the squeaking of my shoes on the wood floor and the ball hitting the floor on each dribble. My knee feels secure. I dribble to one sideline with the right hand, then back to the other sideline with the left hand. I then begin to pick up speed, working in some behind-the-back, through-the-legs, and crossover dribbles. My knee feels strong and flexible. Then as I approach the top of the key, I make a quick drive toward the left side of the basket. I plant my right foot on the ground near the goal, jump up with the ball in my left hand while aiming for a specific spot on the backboard, and bank the ball into the goal. I feel confident that my mental and physical rehabilitation has been successful. My knee feels great! Next, I begin working on my defensive movements. I get into my defensive stance and begin moving...(Burke & Brown, 2003)

Another way that imagery may help during the rehabilitation process is by giving the basketball player a stronger sense of personal control over the recovery process. Some athletes have reported better recovery using imagery to visualize their performance and healing (Ievleva & Orlick, 1991). Sport psychologists may encourage basketball players with an injured muscle to image the muscle healing, as well as playing basketball again. Healing imagery could be performed every day before or after (or even during) physical rehabilitation. At the very least, using "healing" imagery may help players to have more of a feeling of control over their situation. Healing imagery gives basketball players another way to meet the challenge of recovery and rehabilitation.

CONSULTING EXAMPLES IN BASKETBALL

To provide complete services to basketball teams, sport psychology specialists must be ready to provide both team and individual interventions. The following section provides specific examples of two types of consultations that many "basketball psychologists" may be presented with.

Individual Consultation

Free Throw Shooting

Free throw shooting has always been challenging for some basketball players and overall free throw shooting percentages seemed to have gotten poorer over the last decade. Basketball players usually develop a physical routine so each free throw, no matter the situation, seems familiar and comfortable. This encourages using the correct and successful techniques. Although most players use the same physical routine, there can be much inconsistency in the mental routine used in free throw shooting. A free throw is the only shot in basketball that is exactly the same every time. Only the situations in which the free throws are taken provide any variety to the challenge. Some players are better free throw shooters during the early part of a game, but their percentages go down in the final, critical seconds of a close game. Other players focus better when more is "on the line" such as in the last few minutes of a close game, but have trouble during the first half when the free throws are seen as less crucial. To get basketball players to focus properly at any time during a game, sport psychologists should encourage one consistent mental routine to use for all situations. The following routine uses all three psychological skills (imagery, concentration & self-talk) to assist with free throw shooting.

While the player is properly positioned and waiting to receive the basketball from the referee, imagery may be used to see the ball leaving the hands and entering the basket. This "quick imagery" serves as a confidence booster. Next, focus on the rim or ring and use focusing self-talk words such as "ring" or "hole" repeatedly. Repeating the assist word helps the player to focus for the upcoming shot. Then the player may think calming self-talk words like "ready" or "calm" to remain composed. After receiving the ball, the athletes may perform and count a number of dribbles before each free throw, using the same number of dribbles before each attempt. The dribble counting again serves as a concentration technique, but more importantly can help to prevent self-distraction from negative cognitions (e.g. "I hope I don't miss this one"). Then as the player stares at the rim, and a deep breath may be taken while again using calming self-talk words such as "calm" or "relax". Next, the free throw shooter may focus on the rim and think the word "rim" or "ring" while shooting the free throw. Also, other players may wish to further concentrate on their follow-through, and therefore could think "form" or "through" after releasing the ball. Table 6.2 is an example of a free-throw mental and physical routine that sport psychologists may use with basketball players.

Paring an appropriate mental routine with the proper physical routine at the free throw line keeps basketball players in the proper mind set for free throw shooting. Rather than focusing on making or missing the attempt, basketball players become focused on the process of shooting free throws, which research shows is usually helpful to performance (Filby, Maynard & Graydon, 1999: Kingston & Hardy, 1997).

Table 6.2 Mental and physical free-throw shooting routine

Physical step	Mental step
1. Get positioned at line.	1. Use quick imagery and/or think "rim" or "hole".
2. Wait for ball.	2. Think "relax" or "calm".
3. Receive ball and dribble.	3. Count each dribble.
4. Take a deep breath.	4. Think "relax" or "calm".
5. Stare at the rim and shoot.	5. Think "rim" or "hole".
6. Maintain follow-through.	6. Think "through" or "form".

Source: From Burke, K. and Brown, D. (2003). *Sport Psychology Library Series: Basketball.* Mergantown, WV: Fitness Information Technology, Inc.

Team Consultation

Team Building through the Bull in the Ring Exercise

The "bull in the ring" technique (Burke, 2005) can be used with players when the team is experiencing tension due to an unsuccessful season or almost any team disruption. When handled properly, this method/intervention usually gets the players involved and can be quite an "eye-opening" group and self-awareness session. The "bull in the ring" session (BITR) may be held in two parts. First the players are asked to sit in a circle where a chair is placed in the center of that circle. For the first part of the session an item is placed in a center chair that represents the team. The item could be a media guide, team jersey (without a player's name or number showing), basketball, or simply a card that has the team's name, mascot or logo on it. The basketball players are told to adhere to four basic rules:

1. Speak freely, honestly and forthrightly.
2. Do not explain the brief statements. (Discussion may occur later.)
3. Do not openly react to the statements.
4. Keep an open mind.

Proceeding clockwise around the circle, each basketball player is asked to make a constructive, negative statement about the team while looking at the symbol in the center chair. (For each "round", it is usually a good idea to grant the first person a 30-second pause to give an adequate amount of time for a thoughtful response.) For this part of the BITR session, the players are not allowed to make statements about any individual, but to make relevant statements about the basketball team. After hearing all of the negative statements and following the same guidelines, each player is required to make a positive statement about the basketball team. After hearing all of the positive statements, each player is then allowed to make *one* comment or ask *one* question of any teammate related to the positive or negative comments made in this part of the session. The second part of the BITR session follows the same format as the first part, but each basketball player is required to sit in the center chair to hear comments directed at him or her. This means that players will hear one positive and one negative statement about themselves from teammates. Each team member is given the opportunity to select whether to hear the positive or negative statements first. Teammates making the comments may pass (only once) if not ready to respond and must look the center player ("the bull") directly in the eyes while making all comments. Each time a new "round" of comments begins, the participant next in the circle after the person who last began the previous round of comments, begins the next round of comments.

Obviously this activity can be a sensitive encounter for a basketball team. The sport psychologist's role, however, is to enforce the rules, keep the team on task, and help the process flow as smoothly as possible. After all of the basketball players complete their turns in the center chair, then each team member is given a chance to ask *one* question of any *one* of the teammates about the positive or negative comments made at him or her. (Most "bulls" tend to ask a question regarding a negative statement from one of their teammates.) The sport psychologist should keep these "mini-discussions" brief. These questions may bring about short discussions and interactions from teammates who do not interact often. Also, issues not normally discussed among the teammates who do interact often may be discussed.

Then, depending if the climate is facilitative after the second part of this exercise, allow any teammate *who volunteers* to make one comment, or ask one question of any other teammate, as long as the comment/question *does not relate* to the statements made during the BITR session. After the conclusion of the "bull in the ring" session, the sport psychologist may wish to have the group discuss the process just encountered.

The "bull in the ring" session can be an excellent method for reducing uncertainty within a basketball team. Through these sessions teammates learn what each other is thinking about the team, and how they are perceived by teammates. By learning how one is perceived by one's teammates, the "bull in the ring" session helps promote self-awareness through seeing oneself through others' eyes. Another purpose of BITR is to "clear the air" about issues that are hurting the team chemistry, and to help promote better communication. Many times the BITR session will promote a "bonding" experience for the team members.

Three Goals of the Bull in the Ring Session

1. Cohesion.
2. Communication.
3. Clear the air.

Online Counseling

With the popularity of the Internet it is not surprising that electronic mail (email), "chat sessions" and online communication are being utilized in a therapeutic manner. In recent years several books, such as *Online Counseling: A Handbook for Mental Health Professionals* (Kraus, Zack & Stricker, 2004), *Technology in Counselling and Psychotherapy* (Goss & Anthony, 2003) and *e-Therapy: Case Studies, Guiding Principles, and the Clinical Potential of the Internet* (Hsiung, 2002), have become available to assist counselors (and sport psychologists) in becoming effective with this modality. Also, in 1997 a non-profit professional organization known as the International Society for Mental Health Online (ISMHO) was developed to promote the appropriate use of online counseling. The ISMHO has released a set of guidelines known as "Suggested Principles for the Online Provision of Mental Health Services" to guide practitioners and clients in online counseling activities. The Code of Ethics of the American Mental Health Counselors Association already provides ethical guidelines for Internet counseling. Also, the Association for the Advancement of Applied Sport Psychology has proposed updated ethical standards for Internet (and telephone) services (Watson, 2004). However, one of the most important signs of the acceptance of online counseling is that on 1 January 2004, the American Medical Association published a Current Procedural Terminology (CPT) code (0074T) that will allow licensed practitioners to be reimbursed by insurance companies for online consultations! This online CPT code was implemented on July 1, 2004, but is not necessarily recognized by all insurance companies. (In a related vein, the American Medical Association has listed other codes related to "in-person" services that licensed sport psychologists may be reimbursed for by insurance companies. The Health and Behavior Assessment Intervention [HBAI] codes allow licensed practitioners to bill insurance companies for treatment of clients for "psychological, behavioral, emotional, cognitive, and social factors important to the prevention, treatment, or management of physical health problems" (American Medical Association, 2003, p. 292) without having to label athletes (or non-athletes) as having a "mental disorder". These HBAI codes are being used on a trial basis and are scheduled to be re-evaluated no later than 2005.)

It would behoove sport psychologists to become familiar and acquainted with Internet counseling services and the various parameters associated with this newer intervention (logistics, maintaining records, confidentiality, etc.). Many basketball players and coaches (and other sports clients) are comfortable using the Internet (i.e. instant messaging) to contact and discuss issues with the sport psychologist. Research investigating comparisons between online (and other computer-mediated interventions such as videoconferencing) with face-to-face (f2f) counseling has shown online counseling to be promising for clients and clinicians (Cohen & Kerr, 1998; Ghosh & Marks, 1987; Mallen & Vogel's study as cited in Mallen, 2004; Selmi, Klein, Greist et al., 1990). For athletes and coaches, online counseling affords many advantages such as the potential for even more privacy, allows getting assistance without having to go to a counseling office, and can present a more comfortable atmosphere for athletes to receive assistance. This latter advantage may assist in establishing the working alliance (Kraus et al., 2004) without having to depend upon f2f cues. At least one warning should be heeded with online counseling. If sport psychologists establish a working alliance with basketball players f2f, then a *sudden* switch to the online mode may hinder therapeutic results. Basketball players (and other clients) should be made aware in advance of the change from f2f to online counseling (Kraus et al., 2004). In the immediate future many sport psychologists will probably remain uncomfortable with utilizing (exclusively or supplementally) online counseling with basketball participants. Yet, practitioners should have this "tool in their arsenal" to support interventions and maintain communication with basketball players, especially while the athletes are traveling or it is inconvenient to visit personally with the sport psychologist.

SUGGESTIONS FOR FUTURE SPORT PSYCHOLOGY INTERVENTIONS

Past research has shown that having a positive outlook on life, or being optimistic, has many health benefits (Burke, Joyner, Czech & Wilson, 2000; Lewis, Dember, Schefft & Radenhausen, 1995; Taylor, Kemeny, Reed, Bower & Gruenewald, 2000). In a related vein, having and using a sense of humor has been shown to have several psychological and physiological benefits (Burke, Peterson & Nix, 1995; Grisaffe, Blom & Burke, 2003; Lehman, Burke, Martin, Sultan & Czech, 2001; Weaver & Cotrell, 1988). As is suggested in this next section, more emphasis on positive (exercise and) sport psychology (Singer & Burke, 2002) may help sport psychologists provide more effective interventions for those they work with. Sport psychology professionals should strive to develop their own "optimistic attitudes" and "senses of humor" to model these behaviors for their clients.

Explanatory Style—Optimism

Recently professionals have suggested that sport psychology, and the entire field of psychology, should focus more on the positive aspects of life (Seligman & Csikszentmihalyi,

2000; Singer & Burke, 2002). Since Peterson (2000) suggested that research investigating optimism would be an good way to add knowledge to the area of positive psychology, a few studies have in sport psychology investigated this variable (Burke et al., 2000; Czech et al., 2002). As suggested by Wilson, Hawkins, Joyner, McCullick and Lomax (2004) and Schinke and Peterson (2002), coaches and other support staff influence the level of optimism experienced by the athletes. Therefore, optimistic attitudes can be learned, and may have "state" and "trait" components (Burke et al., 2000). The reasons athletes and coaches give for their behaviors is an important coping mechanism. With this in mind, sport psychologists should assist coaches, team personnel and players in learning optimistic attitudes toward participating in basketball. Numerous studies outside of sport have indicated the positive benefits of optimistic attitudes on achievement and productivity (Schulman, 1995), physical health (Buchanan, 1995; Peterson, 1988), and other areas. An earlier study with a basketball team found that players who used optimistic explanations for losing games were more likely to win the next game (Rettew & Reivich, 1995)! Through the appropriate use of positive self-talk, sport psychologists can help basketball teams develop an optimistic explanatory style that may help the team climate and performance.

Humor

Another avenue to promote a more positive sport psychology is to encourage coaches and athletes to utilize and develop the sense of humor. Like optimism, use of humor research indicates many positive benefits. Studies have investigated both the psychological and physiological effects of humor (Lehman et al., 2001). Research results have indicated that humor has positive effects on relationship building (Weaver & Cotrell, 1988), student outcomes and teaching evaluations. (Burke et al., 1995; Neuliep, 1991). In one study of coaches' use of humor (Burke et al., 1995), significant positive correlations were found between the coaches' uses of humor and the players' evaluations of those coaches. Therefore, sport psychologists should encourage coaches to use and share a sense of humor with the team. Also, players should be persuaded to use their sense of humor as a coping mechanism and to help improve relationships among the team. Helping players and coaches to focus on the humorous side of their duties may help to prevent burnout and stimulate a more satisfying atmosphere and team experiences.

CONCLUDING COMMENTS

Sport psychologists can be a valuable asset and provide much needed resources for basketball participants. To increase the likelihood that basketball players and coaches will be more receptive to sport psychology services, sport psychologists should explain the advantages of psychological skills training for basketball, and the transfer of these psychological skills to "real life" (and often more important) situations. Finally, sport psychologists should also emphasize that while playing and coaching is very important to the basketball participants and spectators involved, "Naismith's invention" should be kept in proper perspective. By helping basketball participants keep this sport in an appropriate frame of reference for life, sport psychologists may provide their most important service to their clients.

APPENDIX

Basketball-related Websites

International Basketball Federation	http://www.fiba.com/fs_main.asp
National Collegiate Athletic Association	http://www.ncaabasketball.net
Continental Basketball Association	http://www.cbahoops.com
Basketball Hall of Fame	http://www.hoophall.com/index.cfm
National Junior College Atheletic Association	http://www.njcaa.org
Women's Basketball Coaches Association	http://www.wbca.org
National Federation of State High School Associations	http//:www.nfhs.org/index.htm
National Basketball Association	http://www.nba.com
National Wheelchair Basketball Association	http://www.nwba.org/index2.html
United State Basketball League	http://www.usbl.com
Women's National Basketball Association	http://www.wnba.com
Women's Basketball Hall of Fame	http://www.wbhof.com
American Atheletic Association of the Deaf, Inc.	http://www.usadb.org
National Association of Intercollegiate Athletics	http://www.naia.org
National Association of Basketball Coaches	http://www.nabc.com
Amateur Athletic Union	http://www.aausports.org/ysnim/home/aau_index.jsp
Harlem Globetrotters	http://www.harlemglobetrotters.com
International Association of Approved Basketball Officials	http://www.iaabo.org

Dr Kevin L. Burke's Websites

Dr Burke's Personal Website	http://www.kevinlburke.com
Dr Burke's Sport Psychology Website	http://www.sport-psychology.com

REFERENCES

American Medical Association. (2003). *Current Procedural Terminology (CPT) 2004*. Chicago: American Medical Association Press.
Andersen, M.B. (2000). *Doing Sport Psychology*. Champaign, IL: Human Kinetics Publishers.

Buchanan, G.M. (1995). Explanatory style and coronary heart disease. In G.M. Buchanan & M.E.P. Seligman (eds), *Explanatory Style* (pp. 225–232). Hillsdale, NJ: Erhbaum.

Burke, K.L. (1990). The effect of a tennis-specific meditational training program on concentrational style and tennis service performance. *Applied Research in Coaching and Athletics Annual, 1*, 147–171.

Burke, K.L. (1992). Understanding and enhancing concentration. *Sport Psychology Training Bulletin, 4*, 1–8.

Burke, K.L. (2005). But coach doesn't understand: dealing with team communication quagmires. In M.B. Anderson's (ed), *Sport Psychology in Practice*. Champaign, IL: Human Kinetics Publishers.

Burke, K.L. & Brown, D. (2003). *Sport Psychology Library Series: Basketball*. Morgantown, WV: Fitness Information Technology, Inc.

Burke, K.L., Joyner, A.B., Czech, D.R. & Wilson, M.J. (2000). An investigation of concurrent validity between two optimism/pessimism questionnaires: the life orientation test-revised and the optimism/pessimism scale. *Current Psychology, 19*, 129–136.

Burke, K.L., Peterson, D. & Nix, C. (1995). The influence of humor on athletes' evaluations of their coaches. *Journal of Sport Behavior, 18*, 83–90.

Carboni, J., Burke, K.L., Joyner, A.B., Hardy, C.J. & Blom, L.C. (2002). The effects of brief imagery on free throw shooting performance and concentrational style of intercollegiate basketball players: a single-subject design. *International Sports Journal, 6*, 60–67.

Cohen, G.E. & Kerr, B.A. (1998). Computer-mediated counseling: an empirical study of a new mental health treatment. *Computers in Human Services, 15*, 13–26.

Czech, D.R., Burke, K.L., Joyner, A.B. & Hardy, C.J. (2002). An exploratory investigation of optimism, pessimism and sport orientation among NCAA Division I college athletes. *International Sports Journal, 6*, 136–145.

Filby, W., Maynard, I. & Graydon, J. (1999). The effect of multiple-goal strategies on performance outcomes in training and competition. *Journal of Applied Sport Psychology, 11*, 230–246.

Ghosh, A. & Marks, I.M. (1987). Self-treatment of agoraphobia by exposure. *Behavior Therapy, 18*, 3–16.

Goss, S. & Anthony, K. (eds) (2003). *Technology in Counselling and Psychotherapy: A Practitioner's Guide*. New York: Palgrave McMillan.

Grisaffe, C., Blom, L.C. & Burke, K.L. (2003). The effects of head and assistant coaches' uses of humor on collegiate soccer players' evaluation of their coaches. *Journal of Sport Behavior, 26*, 103–108.

Hatzigeorgiadis, A., Theodorakis, Y. & Zourbanos, N. (2004). Self-talk in the swimming pool: the effects of self-talk on thought content and performance on water-polo tasks. *Journal of Applied Sport Psychology, 16*, 138–150.

Henschen, K.H. & Cook, D. (2003). Working with professional basketball players. In R. Lidor & K.P. Henschen (eds), *The Psychology of Team Sports*. Morgantown, WV: Fitness Information Technology Publishers.

Hsiung, R.C. (ed.) (2002). *e-Therapy: Case Studies, Guiding Principles, and the Clinical Potential of the Internet*. New York: W.W. Norton & Company.

Ievleva, L. & Orlick, T. (1991). Mental links to enhanced healing: an exploratory study. *The Sport Psychologist, 5*, 25–40.

Kingston, K.M. & Hardy, L. (1997). Effects of different types of goals on processes that support performance. *The Sport Psychologist, 11*, 277–293.

Kolt, G.S. (2000). Doing sport psychology with injured athletes. In M.B. Andersen (ed.), *Doing Sport Psychology*. Champaign, IL: Human Kinetics Publishers.

Kottler, J.A. (2000). *Nuts and Bolts of Helping*. Boston: Allyn and Bacon.

Kraus, R., Zack, J. & Stricker, G. (eds) (2004). *Online Counseling: A Handbook for Mental Health Professionals*. Boston: Elsevier Academic Press.

Landin, D. & Herbert, E. (1999). The influence of self-talk on the performance of skilled female tennis players. *Journal of Applied Sport Psychology, 11*, 263–282.

Lehman, K.M., Burke, K.L., Martin, R., Sultan, J. & Czech, D.R. (2001). A reformulation of the moderating effects of productive humor. *Humor: International Journal of Humor Research, 14*, 131–161.

Lewis, L.M., Dember, W.N., Schefft, B.K. & Radenhausen, R.A. (1995). Can experimentally induced mood affect optimism and pessimism score? *Current Psychology, 14*, 29–41.

Mallen, M.J. (2004). Online counseling research. In R. Kraus, J. Zach & G. Stricker (eds), *Online Counseling: A Handbook for Mental Health Professionals*. Boston: Elsevier Academic Press.

Mamassis, G. & Doganis, G. (2004). The effects of a mental training program on juniors pre-competitive anxiety, self-confidence, and tennis performance. *Journal of Applied Sport Psychology, 16*, 118–137.

Murphy, S. & Martin, K. (2002). Athletic imagery. In T. Horn (ed.), *Advances in Sport Psychology* (2nd edn; pp. 405–440). Champaign, IL: Human Kinetics.

Naismith, J. (1941). *Basketball: Its Origin and Development*. New York: Associated Press.

Neuliep, J.W. (1991). An examination of the content of high school teachers' humor in the classroom and the development of an inductively derived taxonomy of classroom humor. *Communication Education, 40*, 343–355.

Peterson, C. (1988). Explanatory style as a risk factor for illness. *Cognitive Therapy and Research, 12*, 117–130.

Peterson, C. (2000). The future of optimism. *American Psychologist, 55*, 44–55.

Rettew, D. & Reivich, K. (1995). Sports and explanatory style. In G.M. Buchanan & M.E.P. Seligman (eds), *Explanatory Style* (pp. 21–48). Hillsdale, NJ: Erlbaum.

Scheier, M.F. & Carver, C.S. (1992). Effects of optimism on psychological and physical well-being: Theoretical overview and empirical update. *Cognitive Therapy and Research, 16*, 201–228.

Schinke, R.J. & Peterson, C. (2002). Enhancing the hopes and performances of elite athletes through optimism skills. *Journal of Excellence, 6*, 36–47. Retrieved from http://www.zoneofexcellence.com/Journal/index.html

Schulman, P. (1995). Explanatory style and achievement in school and work. In G.M. Buchanan & M.E.P. Seligman (eds), *Explanatory Style* (pp. 159–171). Hillsdale, NJ: Erlbaum.

Seligman, M.E.P. & Csikszentmihalyi, M. (2000). Positive psychology: an introduction. *American Psychologist, 55*, 5–14.

Selmi, P.M., Klein, M.H., Greist, J.H. et al. (1990). Computer-administered cognitive-behavioural therapy for depression. *American Journal of Psychiatry, 141*, 51–56.

Singer, R.N. & Burke, K.L. (2002). Sport and exercise psychology: a positive force in the new millennium. In J. Van Raalte & B. Brewer (eds), *Exploring Sport and Exercise psychology* (2nd edn; pp. 525–539). Washington, DC: American Psychological Association.

Smith, D.E. (1999). *Basketball: Multiple Offense and Defense*. San Francisco: Benjamin Cummings.

Taylor, S.E., Kemeny, M.E., Reed, G.M., Bower, J.E. & Gruenewald, T.L. (2000). Psychological resources, positive illusions, and health. *American Psychologist, 55*, 99–109.

Theodorakis, Y., Weinberg, R., Natsis, P., Douma, I. & Kazakas, P. (2000). The effects of motivational versus instructional self-talk on improving motor performance. *The Sport Psychologist, 14*, 253–271.

Thompson, C.L. & Rudolph, L.B. (2000). *Counseling Children* (5th edn). Belmont, CA: Wadsworth.

Watson, J.C. (2004, Summer). Proposed ethical standards for the provision of sport psychology services on the telephone and over the internet. *Association for the Advancement of Applied Sport Psychology Newsletter, 19*, 14–15, 21.

Weaver, R.L. & Cotrell, H.W. (1988). Motivating students: stimulating and sustaining student effort. *College Student Journal, 22*, 22–32.

Weinberg, R.S. & Gould, D. (2003). *Foundations of Sport and Exercise Psychology* (3rd edn). Champaign, IL: Human Kinetics Publishers.

Wilkes, G. (2004). Basketball's best Web site. Retrieved 6 September 2004 from http://www.basketballsbest.com

Wilson, M.J., Hawkins, B., Joyner, A.B., McCullick, B. & Lomax, M. (2004). Optimism and pessimism in coaching techniques in men's Division I intercollegiate golf: a mixed-model design. Manuscript submitted for publication.

Wootten, M. (2003). *Coaching Basketball Successfully* (2nd edn). Champaign, IL: Human Kinetics Publishers.

CHAPTER 7

Psychological Interventions with Football (Soccer) Teams

Joaquín Dosil
University of Vigo, Spain

INTRODUCTION

Historically one of the most traditional sports, football (soccer) is well-known by many people who consider themselves capable of analysing all that occurs within its realms. These circumstances have weighed heavily on the incorporation of sport psychologists in football clubs. The concept of a traditionalist sport in which structural changes are hard to establish has meant an outstanding absence of the sport psychology figure and, in the majority of cases, both coaches and players have been ignorant of its existence.

The presence of sport psychologists in football is still a recent occurrence and has come about thanks to the improved training received by technical staff. Nevertheless, similar to what happened years ago with physical trainers (coaches were originally responsible for physically training players), many coaches remain reluctant to accept the sport psychology figure. Nowadays, physical trainers are regarded as an essential part of football teams and no other professional would be considered for this specialized task. Likewise, psychology finds itself in a similar situation, only that while physical trainers work on a tangible and extremely valued aspect of players' training (physical), psychologists prepare a less objective and more abstract area of their development (mental training). By all accounts, the improved training of coaches, combined with the increased economic capacity of football clubs and, principally, more widespread information on what sport psychology can do, are gradually assisting the incorporation of psychologists into football teams' technical staff.

Although the future prospects of sport psychology in football are optimistic, the current situation forces psychology professionals to adapt to far from favourable circumstances. Therefore, in this chapter it has been deemed necessary to pick out those aspects which may facilitate the work of sport psychologists in this sporting discipline. The text has been divided into four sections. In the first, the psychological peculiarities of football are discussed, in order for readers to discern the keys for intervention with teams. In the second section, two of the most common demands in football are described: working with grass-roots football and working with elite football. The third section of the chapter indicates the

The Sport Psychologist's Handbook: A Guide for Sport-Specific Performance Enhancement.
Edited by Joaquín Dosil. © 2006 John Wiley & Sons, Ltd.

various strategies for guiding the different professionals involved with this sport. Finally, the fourth section represents a possible programme-model which may serve as an outline for sport psychologists working with football teams.

THE PSYCHOLOGICAL PECULIARITIES OF FOOTBALL

Since football is internationally recognized, it is not necessary to explain its basic rules and this text will deal only with those aspects which relate the dynamics of the game with psychology (for basic information on this sporting discipline, the FIFA website may be visited: www.fifa.com). The typical structure of training and competition is usually similar in all professional clubs and teams, independent of the division they play in.

Training is conducted on a daily basis and usually lasts for two hours (sometimes players train twice a day). In the majority of teams, the following routine can be observed: arrival at the football pitch, changing rooms, going out onto the pitch, training, changing rooms and leaving the stadium. This sequence, which remains the most habitual, marks a location that sport psychologists must be aware of and consider in their work, since it is key to conducting quality interventions: the changing rooms. Being a team sport, the coexistence of players in this context is fundamental to understanding what is occurring within the group, as it is here where players talk freely among themselves and make joint decisions in difficult moments. Coaches and technical staff members usually have their own changing rooms, creating clearly marked "distances" between them and the players. Therefore, sport psychologists who enter player changing rooms must be aware that anything said in this environment has an amplified affect.

Training is supervised by the coach and assistant coach, who provide opportune guidance to players and act as team coordinators/directors. The physical trainer, usually someone close to the coach, takes charge of the physical aspects. As will be seen later, varying types of coach can be found, each requiring a different style of psychological intervention. Within this training framework, the work of sport psychologists can be carried out with groups (making the most of the changing rooms, a meeting room or the football pitch itself) or with individuals (in an office or informally, on the football pitch). During training sessions, sport psychologists can make use of the various pauses to increase the overall performance of specific players or to apply specific strategies, adapted to the training being performed. Essentially, it is vital to fulfil the maxim indicated in other texts: psychologists should adapt their strategies to the specific conditions of each sporting discipline.

Competition also displays some very marked characteristics, making it relatively simple to establish a psychological training plan accordingly. Regular league matches are played at weekends, and although some teams are involved in other types of competition which force them to play during the week (implying a certain physical and mental effort), the majority use weekdays for training. Sport psychologists should take into consideration the varying stages of competition, enabling them to establish objectives accordingly: travelling to matches, arrival at the football pitch one or two hours ahead of time, the changing rooms, the warm-up, the first half (45 minutes), the changing rooms, the second half (45 minutes), the changing rooms and the return trip. These routine stages, typical of practically all football teams, enable sport psychologists (through observation) to clearly to establish when to intervene. Likewise, to carry out adequate psychological training with each individual footballer, the different player positions (goalkeepers, defenders, midfielders, strikers) will be considered. Some of the most frequent demands arising in competitions include the following:

- *Achieving the optimum arousal level to commence the match and maintaining it through-out the meeting* Many teams and players fail to "get into the match" for a few minutes, or until a specific situation arises which automatically increases or decreases their arousal to the optimum level (e.g. scoring a goal or a dangerous foul). It is important for players to learn to perform in the best psychological conditions from the first minute, maintaining this level throughout the match. The typical ups and downs of football matches can cause a team to concede a goal or produce counteractive play (e.g. a player being sent off for a foul caused by being over relaxed). These circumstances need to be controlled.
- *Concentrating during the entire match* Given that football matches are long (90 minutes), implying a considerable physical and mental effort, concentration is commonly demanded of players. The strategies players should adopt depend on the position they play in and their personal characteristics. However, the general rule for concentration control training in football is for players to learn how to manage their own attention during matches. Each player must be able to identify when a situation requires increased or decreased concentration, avoiding unnecessary efforts and enabling them to be fully prepared for moments which demand maximum attention (e.g. a goalkeeper shouldn't be concentrating 100 per cent on the position of the ball, rivals and team mates when play is at the opposite end of the pitch. Needless to say, they do require this level of concentration when a free kick is being taken in their area). In a recent study, Moran (2003) presented techniques to improve concentration skills in football.
- *Self-control in the face of adverse situations* (the influence of the score line) During a match, numerous adverse situations arise which require self-control on behalf of players. Those related to the match score and to personal errors are usually the most difficult to control and the most demanding for sport psychologists. Techniques such as thought stoppage and shifting the focus of attention to the next tactic, for example, usually produce effective results when practiced in training and competitions (see Dosil, 2004, or Hardy, Jones & Gould, 1996, for a review).
- *Interaction with referees and rivals* For many players, it is visibly difficult to control their own interactions with referees and rivals. At times, the tension experienced by players escalates to such an extent that great self-control is required if they are to prevent the decisions of referees or the aggressions of their rivals (both verbal and physical) leading to them being booked, sent off or simply losing their concentration.
- *Pressure of coaches, team mates and the public* Football involves a series of stressors which require players to employ psychological strategies to attain peak performance and wellbeing. The coach, just as team mates and even the public, often provokes the sensation of pressure. Holt and Hogg (2002) suggest that coaches are the principal source of pressure in football. Therefore, working with both coaches and players becomes essential to avoid situations which could potentially damage performance. Likewise, personalized attention to specific players helps eradicate the pressure stemming from team mates and the public.
- *Selected players and substitutes* Anxiety to be included in team selections is a source of stress for many players, since it is the only way of being able to show what form they are in and project themselves to the wider public. Coaches are in charge of deciding who will play and who will "rest". Consequently, players who are out on the pitch and feel they are

being evaluated in every move frequently perceive pressure from the coach, preventing them from performing to their full potential. Similarly, in any opportunity given to them by the coach, substitutes are anxious to show how much they have improved and earn their spot in the next match. On many occasions, such haste to create a good impression often provokes poor performances. Sport psychologists should work with substitutes who lack the motivation to train, seeking to optimize their performance on the pitch when they are given the option to play and ensuring they professionally assume the role of substitute.

- *The media* As a sport, football possibly attracts the most media attention. The influence of the media can be both beneficial and damaging to players and teams. Having psychological strategies to control its effects is crucial. From a young age, the sporting development of some players is submerged in continuous media demands, related to which teams are interested in signing them, etc. Once someone has become an elite player, this media following often goes beyond the strictly professional. It is frequent for the "tabloids" to echo the movements of players; which social events they have attended or their personal relationships. Therefore, players are forced to seek harmony between their sporting and private lives. In this respect, sport psychologists should evaluate players, helping them organize their time and offering them psychological strategies for social order.

- *The score-time relationship* On many occasions, the relationship between the score and the time that has passed in a match is a conditioner determining victory or failure, even when the result could still be changed. The psychological effects of scoring a goal are often considered uncontrollable when, in reality, this factor can be trained, establishing a series of routines to control the consequences of the score line. Nevertheless, footballers tend to enter into a playing dynamic they are unable to control, affected by contextual circumstances (e.g. a team is leading 1–0 from the third minute when, with 5 minutes to go, the other side equalizes. The first-mentioned team loses its confidence and the other side goes one goal up). Psychologists should observe the reactions of the team to different results, relating them to the time that has passed in a match. From there, guidelines can be established and transmitted to the group to avoid losing control in certain situations and teaching them how to play with the score line.

These basic aspects related to training and competition should be controlled in order to perform quality psychological interventions. Likewise, sports psychologists are required to adapt to the objectives sought by the clubs they are guiding, focusing on the main reasons for which they have been contracted. The following sections distinguish between the two most common demands.

BASIC RECOMMENDATIONS FOR THE PSYCHOLOGICAL DEMANDS OF FOOTBALL

The focus of sport psychology work varies, depending on whether the intervention is directed towards beginner teams (grass-roots football) or professional teams (the elite). With the first group, it should be determined whether the club's objectives are directed towards training, or creating top-class footballers. Psychological interventions will differ according to these circumstances, as well as the degree of dedication shown by sport psychologists. With the second group, objectives will generally be results-based; that is to say, psychologists will work to achieve better performances. The general aspects to be considered with both types of team are discussed below.

Working with Grass-roots Football

Sport psychologists should not lose sight of the fact that they are working with children, for which their function as educators must remain present in the psychological interventions carried out. Within this category, a distinction can be made between "youth teams", which are affiliated to professional sides (aimed at bringing young players through the ranks), and independent teams, which only participate up to a certain category. Sport psychologists should approach work with all teams in a similar manner, except when faced with teams affiliated to professional sides, or those considered the elite of their category. With the latter, high expectations are generated, meaning psychological interventions must take into account a series of specific contextual elements (e.g. they usually have a following of "talent spotters", the first contract offers begin to appear, an increased media interest, parents believe their child could become the next star, etc).

As will be seen later, parents constitute a significant factor when working with young players. Football is one of the sports where parents have a greater involvement (principally, fathers), meaning psychologists must look for strategies for them to feel integrated within clubs and have a more positive presence. The passion which usually consumes parents means that, at times, their vision of reality becomes somewhat distorted. Therefore, the pressure they exert on their children increases with their desires for them to become professional football players. Sport psychologists must work on this factor so they do not negatively influence the performance and wellbeing of young players.

Participation in football usually begins at a young age, around six years old, frequently in extra-curricular activities or soccer schools. At this initial stage, the objectives of sport psychologists will include the following: identify, select and promote potential talent, and develop and apply specific intervention tools to the situation (García-Más, 2002). Regarding the first aspect, various studies (Llames, 1999; Morris, 2000; Reilly, Williams, Nevill & Franks, 2000; Williams & Reilly, 2000) gather some of the psychological characteristics displayed by talented youngsters in football: control of arousal levels, high self-confidence, high focus on the task and a greater confrontational capacity.

Regarding interventions with youth teams, the tools used will depend on the possibilities offered by each club. The structure of beginner teams usually varies enormously. Therefore, it becomes important to conduct a preliminary study of a club's organizational structure so as to proceed with interventions in the most adequate manner. Frequently, a study can be carried out based on direct psychological interventions with young players, or based on indirect guidance conducted by parents and coaches. In the majority of cases, the second type of action is usually sufficient for a club to function correctly and for children to have an adequate personal sporting development.

The psychological training received by coaches and parents in grass-roots football is fundamental for them to properly apply this knowledge on a day-to-day basis. Coaches are usually respected figures for young players and have an extended importance in their lives, meaning they must employ psychology in training and matches. Some aspects which should be dealt with when working with youth coaches include the following: using fun activities in training (learning through play), the adequate application of rewards and punishments, verbal and non-verbal communication, showing each player how to develop a role in the team, carrying out special training exercises with the less skilled, etc. The work conducted with parents should normally be done through meetings in which psychologists must have their objectives clearly established ahead of time, according to the specific circumstances of the club and the parent profiles they have been able to observe (for a revision of the steps to take, see Anshel, 2003; Dosil, 2004; or Smoll, 2001).

Sport psychologists should work on these two aspects in all areas of a footballer's career. The interventions carried out will be situated within a perfectly marked context, displaying a series of conditions which, once understood, will help the guidance become more accurate (García-Más, 2002): parental pressure/support, physical growth spurts, puberty and adolescence (impact on team mates), changes of coach and training styles, selections for superior teams, the first economic contracts, substitutes/team selections, changes in teams, injuries, and retirement from football.

Working with Professional Sides

The work conducted with high-performance teams is qualitatively different. While not totally ignored, players' training becomes a secondary concern, and results-based objectives are the most sought after. Having reached this high level, players have already "sufficiently" developed their performance facets (technical, tactical, physical and psychological) through an array of phases which have acted as an authentic selection process. Nevertheless, experience in preparing various football teams has confirmed that the psychological aspect is the least-developed area of performance, and the one which elite players most need to improve on.

Psychological training with these teams is usually dependent on their coaches, whose collaboration in this process is fundamental for establishing clubs' psychological objectives. In some cases, while coaches consider psychology as a support to their coaching functions, they do not want direct intervention with players, forcing sport psychologists to conduct psychological studies with coaches alone. In other circumstances, sport psychologists will be granted total freedom, allowing them to consult directly with teams or individual players. In professional football, being able to work directly with teams and players is more important than in the youth game, since coaches at this level require a degree of psychological support they cannot apply alone. The ideal scenario is for clubs to have a resident sport psychologist within their own staff. However, when economic restrictions prevent this, it is most adequate for psychologists to guide youth coaches, leaving direct player interventions for professional sides.

Sport psychologists should be fully aware that, once they reach professional football, their work will become highly specific and they must adapt their interventions to the demands of each club. Along these lines, they will be required to carefully study the various player positions on the pitch, allowing them to better guide and improve the performance of each individual footballer. Regarding this matter, Sharpe (1993) and Sewell and Edmonson (1996) indicate that the psychological work carried out with each player position should be different. Specific tasks must be developed to enhance the performance of goalkeepers, defenders, midfielders and strikers. Therefore, it becomes ideal to conduct personal interviews with players and hold meetings in small groups composed of the different positions (e.g. a meeting with all the strikers), to identify and strengthen the necessary skills.

In elite football, an integrated approach to training is essential, covering all the performance facets. Consequently, apart from working with players, psychologists should also dedicate time to developing strategies so that all members of the technical staff contribute to the team's development. The following section discusses the key issues to consider with the various professionals implicated within the football structure. Likewise, to complement the previously described aspects, the final section of this chapter will describe a possible work system for professional teams.

PSYCHOLOGICAL GUIDANCE WITH INDIVIDUALS INVOLVED IN FOOTBALL

The uniqueness of this sporting discipline means a multitude of people surround football teams and, consequently, influence their performance. Therefore, it is important for sport psychologists to be aware of the various strategies for working with each of these people: coaches, players, physical trainers, parents, directors and referees.

Coaches

While the coaching figure is fundamental in all sports, their collaboration in psychological work is considered essential in football. As previously described, interventions can be directed towards coaches or players, and determining who to focus the interventions on constitutes the first decision to be taken by sport psychologists. Needless to say, it is crucial to identify what type of coach is involved. The strategies described in Chapter 2 are sufficient to conduct an adequate evaluation. Similarly, other studies (Dosil, 2004) have discussed the most common types of coach—democratic, authoritarian and permissive—which may guide sport psychologists in their decisions. Generally speaking, it is usually recommended to work directly with authoritarian coaches, as they frequently prefer having total control over the team situation. Consequently, sport psychologists can provide them with strategies to apply with players to improve their performance. By contrast, with permissive coaches, work can focus more on the players. Coaches can be assisted to gradually dominate the team through learning suitable strategies to employ in the different interactions with their footballers. Finally, with democratic coaches, a bidirectional collaboration can be established, working from a double perspective: that of the coach and that of the players (depending on the requirements, sometimes work will focus more on coaches, and on other occasions, more on players).

Two types of intervention can be distinguished in the psychological guidance of football coaches: direct and indirect (Dosil & González-Oya, 2003). Direct intervention is used when the principal objective is to improve the psychological dexterity of coaches, increasing their personal performance (e.g. to improve their communicational skills so as to feel more comfortable giving team talks prior to and after matches, to help reduce anxiety during matches, etc.). Indirect intervention occurs when coaches act as an intermediary between sport psychologists and players; that is to say, they are provided with strategies to apply with their footballers (e.g. they may be taught how to focus their talks with substitutes in order to keep them motivated; they may be offered more effective reward and punishment strategies, etc.).

The coaching figure bears the weight of the team and constitutes the main reference point for players, directors and other personnel implicated in football (Loughead & Hardy, 2005). All of this implies that their actions and conduct have a direct effect on the various team components. Consequently, the psychological work carried out with coaches is crucial for achieving improved performance and wellbeing among staff. Along these lines, Smoll and Smith (1997) indicate three fundamental strategies for improving the coach–player relationship in football:

1. Changing the concept of results and victory: the majority of football coaches evaluate the performance of players based on match results, a concept which should be changed and transmitted to players, focusing the assessment on the efforts exerted rather than the number of goals scored.
2. Approaching training in a positive manner: the use of positive reinforcement in training favours the learning of skills and the wellbeing of players, as well as establishing a motivating form of understanding activities.
3. Self-evaluation of their own conduct: this is one of the typical errors of football coaches, given that they are accustomed to evaluating players and not themselves. It is recommended that someone from outside helps evaluate the work of coaches, as well as dedicating time to helping them carry out constructive self-criticisms.

These strategies will help coaches improve their functions and learn how psychology can be of use in their daily work. Nevertheless, as indicated by Olmedilla, García and Garcés de Los Fayos (1998), few football coaches fully accept the sport psychology figure, since the majority (98 per cent) stem from the football world and are reluctant to the incorporation of those without experience in this environment, while others (6 per cent) have little experience with sport psychologists and lack information about what psychology can do in their sport. These circumstances reinforce the ideas proposed in Chapter 1, where the need for authentic sport psychology specialists in each sporting discipline was suggested. Likewise, when the possibility to work with football clubs arises, psychologists should meticulously plan strategies for their progressive incorporation into the team (an example will be described in the final part of this chapter).

Players

The objective of all sport psychologists is for players to reach their maximum potential performance, developing as people and as athletes. Consequently, various strategies will be employed, with the aim of achieving the same result: improvement. Consulting with players can be conducted in groups and/or on a personal basis, although the combination of both styles of intervention is considered the most adequate. When working in groups, at regular intervals or as circumstances arise, sport psychologists meet with players to debate issues affecting the team and how each individual member can contribute to solving these problems. Group dynamics are suitable for achieving a greater integration of team members, increased team cohesion and greater understanding between players. On an individual level, psychologists will organize interviews with each player to go deeper into each particular case and help increase personal psychological performance. The fundamental objective of these interviews is to identify both the internal and external factors affecting the performance of each individual footballer. Along these lines, Sewell and Edmonson (1996) identify the psychological needs of each player position. According to these authors, goalkeepers and defenders register the highest levels of anxiety and low self-confidence compared to midfielders and strikers, possibly due to the responsibility involved with their positions.

Logically, the interventions indicated can only be executed with teams whose coach is willing to cooperate and allow players to attend psychological sessions.

Physical Trainers

Since about 1995, the physical trainer figure has been incorporated into the technical staff of football teams. Before, it was the coach who carried out these functions. These professionals pursue a double objective: on the one hand, their activity involves getting players into peak physical form, adequately employing rewards and punishments, verbal and non-verbal communication, etc. On the other hand, they aim to achieve greater self-efficiency in their work, related to variables such as perceiving player competencies, responsibility, motivation and self-esteem (García-Más, 2002).

Sport psychologists should explain to physical trainers what their function is within teams, and how psychology can be used to optimize their work. On occasions, psychologists tend to focus their work on coaches and physical trainers, avoiding other professionals. This approach is incompatible with seeking integral performance.

Parents

The influence of parents in this sport is undeniable. As indicated by Fredericks and Eccles (2004), in the majority of sporting disciplines, the attitude and interest of parents is sufficient for children to participate, determining the degree of their involvement and the focus of their participation. However, this effect has a much greater significance in football. The importance of the parental figure, from grass-roots to peak performance, obliges sport psychologists to introduce training systems for parents, with the aim of achieving the most adequate sporting and personal development for their children.

Smoll (2001) analyses the different ways parents behave on the football pitch, distinguishing between various *types:* the side-line coaches, the excessively critical, those who shout from behind the benches, the overprotective and the uninterested. This description of parental behaviours in training and competition may be observed in any football club. The involvement of their children means parents can frequently be seen at training sessions and competitions, making comments and decisions about the future of their offspring.

Therefore, as indicated by this author, sport psychologists should provide physical trainers with strategies to intervene with each type of parent. Some guidelines may include the following (Dosil, 2004):

- *Sideline coaches, the excessively critical and shouters* With these types of parent, the key is to speak to them individually and choose the correct moment to do so, whether it be at half-time or after a match, seeking a friendly situation in which to exchange opinions. Psychologists should make sure parents understand that their form of behaviour is not beneficial to their child and should offer them alternative ways to act. Likewise, it is important for players to learn to focus exclusively on the instructions of their coach and on the game, avoiding any comments from outside this setting.

• *Overprotective and uninterested parents* These two styles of parent are the extreme opposites of the same typology. In both cases, psychologists should ensure that they move towards a halfway point, providing them information on how to do so. With overprotective parents, this will involve a detailed explanation of how the potential risks of this sport can be reduced through thoroughly planning training, influencing the habits they acquire and showing them how this sporting discipline can have a positive effect on their child. With uninterested parents, the task will focus on informing them of how important their involvement is and how they can help strengthen the positive effects the sport has on their child. (Psychologists and physical trainers must distinguish between uninterested parents and those who are unable to attend as much as they would like due to their professional commitments.)

Although these negative parent typologies may still be found in the football environment and in other sports, an increase in the number of parents displaying positive qualities which complement the sporting activity of their child can be observed. This phenomenon is due to the improved training acquired, often through programmes offered by institutions (clubs, schools, town councils, etc.). Parents who maintain an adequate involvement and who collaborate with coaches in the sporting development of their child may be termed *participators–collaborators* (Dosil, 2004).

Regarding the specific work sport psychologists can conduct directly with parents, various guidelines can be applied before, during and after training sessions or matches. The principal recommendation for training sessions is that parents get fully involved in the development of the activity. Taking an interest in how their child feels in the team, and asking what they think of their coach and their team mates, if they enjoy themselves, if they feel they are improving, etc. are skills parents should approach on a day-to-day basis. Parents should learn to listen, giving relevance to aspects which may be important for their child (e.g. if a coach makes a spectacle of them in public). Learning to motivate them and offer security are other qualities parents must develop. In competition, parents also need to support their children. If the economic situation of the family allows, parents should frequently accompany the team on both home and away fixtures. The role of parents prior to matches is fundamental, given that their comments at such moments will have an affect on the emotional state of the young player. Therefore, they must focus on transmitting certain ideas to the child, ranging from those which develop their efforts, their enjoyment and their respect for others, to those which reduce the fear associated with failure and impose the concept of "doing their best". The conversation should not revolve constantly around the match itself, as this can create pressure for the player. It is recommended to spend a sensible amount of time on this matter, depending on the characteristics of the situation and, principally, depending on the player. With some children it is best not to speak at all, while with others, the more they speak the better, etc. (for this reason it is important for parents to be assessed by sport psychologists). Attending to these details will be of benefit for players, giving them security and enabling them to find a support figure in their parents.

Competition is a process of continuous learning. In the early years, players find it hard to focus totally on the activity at hand, for which other factors (e.g. parental behaviour among spectators), can destabilize them or provide them with security. Given these circumstances, parents should be careful with their behaviour in the stadium, since their conduct will be observed by their children and has repercussions on players' performance and wellbeing. As football players grow, they begin to focus more on the game, and the influence of parents in the stands becomes secondary.

Finally, once a match is over, parents should retake the role assumed prior to the match, spending more time with their child and, often, travelling home with them. At this point, it is important to consider that the emotions the child has experienced are intense and, therefore, it is fundamental to take an interest in what has occurred. The result of matches usually determines a child's mood, making it important to transmit joy when they have won and sorrow when they suffer a defeat, understanding and listening to what the child feels.

Definitively, the principal advice for parents is to focus on aspects related to the development of the physical activity (the process), minimizing excessive interest in the final result of this development (the product), with the aim of the child appreciating, over time, that the effort he or she exerts is the only important factor. Typical questions such as "How did you do?" or "Did you win?" should be replaced with "Did you have a good time?" or "How did you play?".

Directors

Directors occupy a principal role in the decision-making of this sport. Their functions are numerous but can be summarized with the acronym POWER: Planning, Organization, Working with decisions, Education and Representation of entities (Dosil, 2004). The word *power* is neutral, in the sense that it can be related to both positive and negative aspects. Directors should acquire skills which reflect the positive meaning of this word (e.g. the power to improve installations, the power to maintain good communication with parents, the power to sign a sport psychologist, etc.). The decisions made through exerting POWER forge a direct relationship with parents, coaches and players, who act as "fulfillers" of these decisions (Table 7.1).

Depending on the functions carried out by directors, and according to the importance they grant each of these, various management styles can be established, similar to those described for parents and coaches. From a sport psychology perspective, directors have not received the attention they deserve. Psychological guidance in this aspect is infrequent, although a slight, slowly increasing demand can be observed as a result of a growing interest in how psychology can help in the work of these professionals. As with coaches, psychological interventions with managers can be direct or indirect, as follows.

- *Direct* Sport psychologists work with directors as just another member of the sporting context, seeking to increase their capacity to confront the demands of the post. From this perspective, psychologists evaluate how they respond in the varying situations produced in football (through observation or interviews), in order to guide them to improving and optimizing their conduct. Examples of this form of intervention include the following: anxiety reduction, stress control when speaking in public, improving verbal and non-verbal communication, decision-making, organization and establishing objectives.
- *Indirect* Sport psychologists guide directors with the aim of their actions influencing the players, coaches and parents. Having familiarized themselves with the running of the club or team, psychologists advise on how certain actions affect the smooth functioning of the entity, avoiding potential problems and optimizing the available resources. Examples

Table 7.1 Functions of sports directors

Functions	Description
Planning	At the beginning of each season and as required, directors should plan in detail what they consider as suitable for the club. Careful planning can prevent problems and provide information with which to work.
Organisation	Directors should organize the sporting activities, establish regulations, optimize the use of installations, propose reunions with coaches, parents, etc.; that is to say, carry out what has been planned in an orderly manner.
Working with decisions	Directors are required to make decisions on behalf of the club, meaning that strengthening this capacity is fundamental. Knowing how to value the pros and cons of each situation, deciding which philosophy the club or team will follow, the professionals who will collaborate, the destination of economic remunerations, etc. constitute their day-to-day activities.
Education	The management of a club goes far beyond strictly sporting matters, since the way directors behave and focus their activities constitutes potentially educative actions. Therefore, directors should set an example of conduct for club members, who use them as a reference; likewise, they should maintain educative objectives in training, controlling the coaching style and preparation they receive.
Representation	The management is the image of the club, meaning that when directors are representing the entity, they must maintain an adequate position which corresponds to their post. The correct use of psychological strategies is fundamental here.

Source: From Dosil, J. (2004). *Psicología de la actividad física y del deporte.* Madrid: McGraw-Hill.

of this form of intervention may include the following: establishing reward–punishment programmes, identifying the information directors should provide to coaches and parents.

Referees

The study of referees in sport psychology came about relatively late, although in recent years there has been a notable increase in the number of publications dedicated to this population (e.g. Greco, 1996; Grunska, 1999; Weinberg & Richardson, 1990).

The first element to analyse when referring to football referees is their motivation to begin and stay within this profession. In recent years, a decrease in interest for this vocation has been observed as a result of the numerous adversities encountered by referees on the football pitch. This situation has led to the birth of recruitment strategies in various federations/delegations. Creating an adequate environment in delegations could help achieve an increase in the number and quality of referees. A second aspect to be analysed is the training received by referees, and whether it is sufficient to be able to face the various situations experienced in football. Regarding this aspect, some "keys" to psychological training can be observed, providing referees with the resources to approach difficult situations.

The training of football referees focuses on aspects related to regulations, with the idea that the greater the knowledge of these rules, the easier it will be to apply them. While this statement is totally correct, it remains incomplete, avoiding the fact that effectively applying these rules in group situations requires the capacity to interpret behaviours and transmit decisions in an adequate manner. The majority of referees recognize that an important part of umpiring performance depends on psychological aspects (personality, concentration, communication, etc.), indicating that they receive little attention in this area and highlighting it as one of the most important deficiencies in their training (Weinberg and Richardson, 1990).

Taking this into account, Greco (1996) suggests a series of contents which should not be overlooked in the training of football referees, given that their use is essential for correctly carrying out their functions: referee personality, observational capacity, ability to shut out the surrounding environment, decision-making, clarifying and fulfilling their functions, comprehending the value of specific attitudes, knowing how to reduce the "feeling of blame" involved in some decisions, being aware that criticisms are directed towards their conduct and not at them personally, self-control when faced with aggressive behaviours and, more generally, training in pedagogy and education, as well as in-depth knowledge of sporting rules and regulations.

The characteristics referees should posses and, consequently, those which sport psychologists must strengthen are summarized in Table 7.2.

Other Members of the Football Environment and the Technical Staff

From a psychological point of view, other professionals who accompany teams are also considered as important (doctors, masseurs, podiatrists, groundsmen, etc.). For example, masseurs are relevant figures within teams, given that the majority of players use their services for physical recuperation. In many cases, masseurs adopt the role of "psychologist"; that is to say, they assume the task of asking players about their problems and offer their opinions on how best to solve them. While their "counselling" may often be considered adequate (after all, masseurs, just as normal people, may have a capacity for giving appropriate advice), they remain opinions with no scientific backing. Sport psychologists will help create a suitable environment in order for players to feel comfortable with the intervention of their masseurs, clearly defining the roles of each person. Therefore, it is important to hold a meeting with masseurs, with the aim of encompassing them within the integral training system and giving them guidelines to use with players, so their work becomes more effective.

Within the football environment, spectators and the media are two elements to be taken into account when analysing the performance and psychological wellbeing of teams. Journalists are a well integrated part of this sport, accompanying players throughout their football career. As indicated by García-Más (2002), one of the tasks undertaken by sport psychologists involves providing players with psychological tools to control the influence of information depicted about them in the news and other media. Likewise, from a young age, football players must learn to accept journalists as part of their sporting routine, appreciating that to a certain extent the interest their actions provoke is normal.

The influence of spectators has been well studied in the football environment (Nevill, Newell & Gale, 1996). The role of sport psychologists in this aspect involves teaching players to develop the quality of their game in both home and away matches, making the most of spectator support and minimizing the effects of their disapproval at various moments throughout the match or season. Experience dictates that the effect this factor has on each

Table 7.2   Characteristics of referees

Characteristics	Description
Control	It is considered necessary to have both internal and external control; that is to say, control of their own actions, of the game, the teams and the players.
Calmness	Competitive situations are usually potentially stressful, since "pressure" generally exists on behalf of parents (the public), coaches or players, for which the referee must remain both internally and externally calm.
Mutual respect	Referees, despite being the authority on the football pitch, should listen to and respect players and coaches, understanding that they may have a different point of view, which doesn't necessarily mean they are being disrespectful.
Empathy	Appreciating what players and coaches are going through during a competition is fundamental to being able to act correctly in any circumstance.
Verbal and non-verbal communication	Speaking as little as possible and using adequate gestures will benefit the smooth running of matches, increase their credibility and the respect shown towards them.
Physical presence	Looking after their physical aspect helps create a positive first impression, an initial climate which favours the development of the match.
Physical form	Being physically in form is fundamental for football referees as it allows them to move around the pitch at ease, arrive more quickly at players, etc ...
Positioning	Along with the previous aspect, positioning is an essential characteristic for being able to correctly carry out the role of referee, as it is necessary to follow the fast pace of the game without obstructing players.
Confidence	Players should have total confidence in the referee. To achieve this, referees must have total confidence in what they signal and, in the case of committing an error, forget the situation immediately and renew their confidence until the end of the match.
Favouring the game	Referees should almost appear to be invisible during a match, favouring the flow of the game and interrupting only when required.
Attention	This is an extremely important variable to correctly referee a match. Attending to the relevant stimuli and avoiding any distractions during the game helps improve their perception.
Studying the game system	In grass-roots football, strategy does not play such an important role as in the professional game. Therefore, referees need to study the typical characteristics of the game in the category/age group they are working with.
Observing human behaviour	Along with a high concentrational capacity, observational skills are fundamental to refereeing well. Interpreting the behaviour of players and coaches is a skill learned through experience and/or psychological training.
Social skills	Using social skills to obtain greater control is adequate before, during and after matches. Techniques such as dialogue with team captains, approaching coaches at half time to explain a situation that has occurred, etc. allow a better development of the game.

player is relative, since individual perceptions tend to vary (e.g. some players enjoy playing at home because they feel comfortable in front of "their" public, while others prefer to play away matches because there isn't the same spectator "pressure"). It can also be stated that teams, above all those who do not receive any psychological training, allow themselves to be carried along (unconsciously) by the different stages of a match in which the public plays a significant role (e.g. when the crowd cheers on their team for playing well, it has a motivational effect on the players; while when the audience falls silent, players become unable to find the correct arousal levels). These moments need to be prepared for, attaining a solid team who knows how to develop their game, independent of the public's attitude.

A PSYCHOLOGICAL INTERVENTION MODEL FOR FOOTBALL TEAMS

Psychological intervention in football could be set out in a similar way to that of other team sports, such as basketball, handball or ice hockey. Nevertheless, an exhaustive preparation requires sport psychologists to get into the peculiarities of this sporting discipline and, as indicated earlier, adapt their general knowledge to the uniqueness of this sport. This section will discuss some of the aspects to be considered in the psychological intervention with football teams, distinguishing those elements which are unique to this sport.

Psychological Planning and Evaluation of the Season

Psychological training in football should begin with familiarization of the sport (Murphy, 1995). Obviously, psychologists will have a minimum knowledge of the rules of the game, but it remains fundamental to quickly grasp the jargon used in football, as well as the intrinsic aspects of the activity and football clubs (some of these have been described in Chapter 2). Here, the emphasis is on the uniqueness of each sport, meaning that if sport psychologists wish to attain a high professional level, they must become specialists or "experts" in the sport with which they are going to work.

Not forgetting that football is a traditionalist sport, reluctant to change, psychological evaluation within this environment should make the most of establishing collaborative links with coaches. From the beginning, this will constitute one of the personal goals of the sport psychologist. The evaluation stage will be used to ensure that coaches feel comfortable with the sport psychology figure and perceive an improvement in their team's performance thanks to the contributions of this area of knowledge.

The proposed evaluation model to use when commencing work with football teams has three functions: evaluation of the club, evaluation of the coach and evaluation of the players. Firstly, understanding clubs is crucial: their structure, their organization, their economic capacity, their history, the number of members, their investment in new players, etc. Currently, thanks to new technology, detailed information on these aspects can be found on the Internet for the majority of clubs, making accessing this data easier and speeding up the process. The information which becomes relevant for this purpose includes the following: the board of directors (members, whether they change frequently, stability, member profiles, etc.), club grounds and fan base (number of club members, number of fans who usually attend home and away matches, type of stadium, pitch and installations, etc.), sponsors and budget (economic solvency, capacity to sign new players, etc.), the club philosophy (objectives, structure, work with youth players, etc.). This information provides the general context within which to fit psychological interventions, providing the background for the actions taken by sport psychologists. Next, an evaluation of the team itself can be conducted, where it is important to count on the cooperation of coaches. At this stage, the evaluation is fundamental, allowing sport psychologists to identify the coaches' point of view and, at the same time, providing an appropriate way of introducing them to the psychological work. Some aspects which are usually dealt with include: general comments on the team (quality of players, relationships between members, current situation at the point of beginning psychological intervention, etc), members of the technical staff (characteristics of each of them, personal and professional quality, etc.), detailed description of the players (age, position, brief sporting history, personal circumstances, exceptional physical, technical and tactical characteristics, psychological characteristics, etc.), training sessions and competitions (internal team regulations, training timetable, training and match routines, etc.). Finally, it is important to conduct a thorough player evaluation when beginning psychological work in a club. Therefore, tests or questionnaires can be used to measure various psychological variables in training and matches, as well as observation, video recordings or an *ad hoc* gathering of data, adapted to the specific needs of the team (according to the comments made by the coach).

A strategy which usually works well at this stage involves making the most of the evaluation process to give players a simple explanation of what sport psychologists do (doing away with any preconceptions) and how they can help improve their performance as a team and as players. This initial talk is extremely important, as it will be the first time sport psychologists enter the changing rooms (usually the chosen place for this initial contact) and the impression they give in this context will either assist or complicate later interventions. In this sense, the following, simple structure is suggested:

- Firstly, a theoretical explanation, illustrated with examples specific to football so players can identify with them (e.g. situations players frequently experience during matches: lack of concentration and/or lack of confidence some goalkeepers suffer when conceding a goal, the precision of passes required of defenders, a striker losing confidence every time he makes a mistake, the pressure before an important match, etc.).
- Secondly, on a form, players are asked to indicate what percentage of their performance they attribute to physical, tactical, technical and psychological aspects, as well as noting down their positive and negative characteristics related to these factors in a table (at least two or three).

Although many footballers find it difficult to carry out this task, the skills of sport psychologists in this interaction will assist them to complete the form correctly, helping them understand what they need to do and how to convey the information, working on the assumption that the players know themselves best. Through this type of self-evaluation, complete information on players is obtained, combining coaches' and players' perceptions. Likewise, this activity has a positive effect on the team, forcing players to reflect on aspects they were previously aware of, but had not taken into account in their everyday training and matches.

From this point, the psychological work to be conducted is organized; that is to say, the interventions are planned. It is recommended to begin by focusing on the team's priority requirements, thereafter progressing gradually towards the final objective: creating a team with great emotional control and stability in their psychological performance.

Planning will take into account various factors. One of these is at which point of the season the psychological treatment begins and the number of hours the sport psychologist has to perform interventions—according to the contract—(it is not the same beginning interventions halfway through the season as at the beginning, nor is having a contract which allows psychologists to work once a week the same as one allowing them to attend every day). It is fundamental for sport psychologists to plan their interventions correctly, with realistic objectives that cover the basic requirements of the club with which they are working. One common mistake made by psychologists is trying to tackle more aspects than they can manage, forgetting the actual time available to work with teams. Therefore, it becomes crucial to learn how to prioritize and optimize the time spent on interventions.

Psychological Preparation of Training and Competitions

The aforementioned specific circumstances mark the beginning of the psychological work in training and competitions. The characteristics of each team, evaluated in the previous stage, are those which allow sport psychologists to identify which form of psychological intervention is suitable. The two most common models of intervention are: psychological work through the coach, and psychological work with the team itself. As indicated previously, in either case, the coach remains a key figure. In the first model, less direct interaction exists with the players and a greater degree of communication with the coach, while the second model involves more personal contact with the footballers. This is an important factor for sport psychologists, given that the tasks and objectives they set out will depend on the type of coach they come across and their ability to gain their collaboration.

Football training is shaped by competitions which usually take place every weekend, forcing a cyclical training routine. Therefore, sport psychologists will constantly be working with a pre- or post-match situation, one day before and one day after matches. The objective of the remaining four days is to create the physical, technical, tactical and mental base of the team. If sport psychologists begin working with a team early enough, an intervention system can be established with players prior to the beginning of the season (the pre-season). This period of time is generally used for carrying out heavy training workloads so players are able to handle all the matches that take place over the duration of the season. Therefore, during this phase, sport psychologists can make the most of this training to apply strategies which increase players' and coaches' confidence such as: evaluation of the specific intervention needs of each player, strategies to recuperate from the tough physical sessions, team cohesion work, establishing effective communication systems between players and coaches, etc. All of these techniques are applied so that when the first match arrives, players have a solid psychological base, allowing them to overcome any difficult situations which may arise throughout the season. Observation will constitute one of the most frequently used techniques during this time, allowing sport psychologists to understand the relationships between players, the assumption of the physical workload, the way the coach approaches the team and individual players, the roles of the technical staff, etc. Video recordings may also prove important for evaluation, which can be conducted together with the coach or players, to identify different situations which may be positively or negatively affecting the team's progress.

In keeping with the competitive system of football and the training structure between matches, it is relatively simple to establish the psychological interventions to be applied with teams. As indicated by García-Más (2002), sport psychologists will help players manage the typical situations of this sport: travelling to the stadium, warm-up, kick-off, stoppages in matches (injuries, fouls, bookings, etc.), half-time, kick-off for the second half, substitutions, tactics, scoring a goal, conceding a goal, full-time, final score, the closing minutes of the match, extra time, added time, the changing rooms after a match or the return journey. These situations should have been studied previously, since each team/player is unique and may have deficiencies in confronting certain aspects. Having identified any problem areas, a strategic intervention plan can be elaborated, which in the case of football has three parts:

1. *Individual work with players* Individual meetings can be organized to conduct interviews in order to identify both the sporting and non-sporting characteristics of each player. A proportion of this interview will be dedicated to determining the influence of the family and social contexts on players (where they live, with whom they live, members of their family, the relation of their family to football, whether their friends are football players, etc.), while the other half will deal with strictly sporting issues (the position they play in, the position they would most like to play in, their personal evaluation as a footballer, their strengths and weaknesses—the self-evaluation conducted at the beginning of the season may also be used here, etc.).

2. *Group work* The two most frequent methods are working with the entire team, or working in small groups, established according to certain criteria such as: player positions (gathering together all the goalkeepers, defenders, etc.), age (mixing youngsters with the veterans of the team, or just the mature players, etc.), or their level of play (putting the best player together with a reserve player, or a player who headers well with one who doesn't header well, etc.).

3. *Working during training sessions* It is only advisable to introduce psychological aspects to improve training when there is a large involvement on behalf of the technical staff and when the psychologist is contracted by the team to attend training all week. Likewise, if coaches perceive a team as not attaining the adequate psychological level in certain training sessions, or that in matches they are lacking "something psychological", interventions can be designed for use in training, in order to eliminate these errors (e.g. if a team lacks communication in matches, exercises which force players to speak on the pitch can be developed in training sessions, with the aim of transferring these skills into match situations).

The reality of football is often cruel towards sport psychologists. Psychology professionals are frequently contracted only once teams have already covered the majority of their needs. Moreover, in many cases, the agreements between psychologists and clubs often provide them with weekly rather than daily access, meaning the psychological work must adapt to these circumstances. One model based on the competition and training systems of football, and which can be applied in these cases, consists of establishing a communicative routine with coaches, with the aim of conducting psychological analyses of matches and the repercussions they have on players. This model uses a mixed intervention (Dosil, 2004); that is to say, it makes use of email, telephone and face-to-face communication. The steps to be taken with this model are as follows:

- Sending a match "report" (usually by email or telephone), including personalized player comments (coach).
- Response from sport psychologist, where advice is given for confronting the first post-match chat (psychologist).
- Applying the advice given and sending any comments via email or telephone (coach).
- Response from sport psychologist, detailing the work to be conducted during the week in question and explaining what the immediate psychological interventions will consist of—for example, in cases where psychologists attend on a weekly basis (psychologist).

Logically, depending on the number of days psychologists are in the field, some of these steps can be taken out and conducted in person. Nevertheless, it is vital to have alternative resources at hand in case conditions prevent psychologists from attending training or competitions at any time. The quality of the sport psychology service should be guaranteed, regardless of unforeseen circumstances.

CONCLUSIONS

Football is a sport with an intense training and competitive structure, meaning psychological work must adapt to the particular circumstances of each team or club. In recent years, although a timid incorporation of sport psychology has been observed, football teams remain reluctant to allow this professional figure to accompany them as a permanent member of their technical staff. The lack of information and traditionalism are two elements sports psychologists have to confront if they wish to work in this sport.

Throughout this chapter, the basic elements sport psychologists should take into account when approaching the football environment have been discussed. The importance of the coaching figure, interventions in changing rooms, the specific competitive system and the context surrounding this sport are some of the aspects which have been dealt with. The need to profoundly understand this sport and adapt psychology to the specific demands it creates constitute the keys to successful specialist sport psychology in football.

REFERENCES

Anshel, M.H. (2003). *Sport Psychology: From Theory to Practice.* San Francisco: Benjamin Cummings.

Dosil, J. (2004). *Psicología de la actividad física y del deporte.* Madrid: McGraw-Hill.

Dosil, J. & González-Oya, J. (2003). Intervención psicológica en la iniciación deportiva. In E.J. Garcés de Los Fayos (coord.), *Areas de aplicación de la psicología del deporte* (pp. 21–32). Murcia: Región de Murcia.

Fredericks, J.A. and Eccles, J.S. (2004). Parental influences on youth involvement in sports. In M.R. Weiss (ed.), *Developmental Sport Psychology: A Lifespan Perspective* (pp. 145–164). Morgantown, WV: Fitness Information Technology.

García-Más, A. (2002). La psicología del fútbol. In J. Dosil (ed.), *El psicólogo del deporte: asesoramiento e intervención* (pp. 101–132). Madrid: Síntesis.

Greco, P.J. (1996). *Formacao do árbitro: treinamento psicológico.* Belo Horizonte: UFMG.

Grunska, J. (ed). (1999). *Successful Sports Officiating.* Champaign, IL: Human Kinetics.

Hardy, L., Jones, G. & Gould, D. (1996). *Understanding Psychological Preparation for Sport: Theory and Practice of Elite Performers.* Chichester, UK: John Wiley & Sons.

Holt, N. & Hogg, J. (2002). Perceptions of stress and coping during preparations for 1999 women's soccer world cup finals. *The Sport Psychologist, 16,* 251–271.

Llames, R. (1999). Selección de jóvenes deportistas en fútbol. *Revista de Psicología del Deporte, 8*(2), 249–258.

Loughead, T.M. & Hardy, J. (2005). An examination of coach and peer leader behaviors in sport. *Psychology of Sport and Exercise, 6*(3), 303–312.

Moran, A. (2003). Improving concentration skills in team-sport performers: focusing techniques for soccer players. In R. Lidor & K.P. Henschen (eds), *The Psychology of Team Sports.* Morgantown, WV: Fitness Information Technology.

Morris, T. (2000). Psychological characteristics and talent identification in soccer. *Journal of Sports Sciences, 18*(9), 715–726.

Murphy, S.M. (ed.) (1995). *Sport Psychology Interventions.* Champaign, IL: Human Kinetics.

Nevill, A.M., Newell, S.M. & Gale, S. (1996). Factors associated with home advantage in English and Scottish soccer matches. *Journal of Sports Science, 14*(2), 181–186.

Olmedilla, A., García, C. & Garcés de Los Fayos, E.J. (1998). Un análisis del papel profesional del psicólogo del deporte desde la percepción del entrenador de fútbol. *Revista de Psicología del Deporte, 13*(2), 95–111.

Reilly, T., Williams, A.M., Nevill, A. & Franks, A. (2000). A multidisciplinary approach to talent identification in soccer. *Journal of Sports Sciences, 18*(9), 695–702.

Sewell, D.F. & Edmonson, A.M. (1996). Relationships between field position and pre-match competitive state anxiety in soccer and field position and pre-match competitive state anxiety in soccer and field-hockey. *International Journal of Sport Psychology, 27*(2), 159–172.

Sharpe, P. (1993). Elite competitive team participation and personality characteristics: an interaction between personality type and position placed. *VIII World Congress of Sport Psychology,* 959–962. Lisbon, Portugal.

Smoll, F.L. (2001). Coach-parent relationships in youth sports. In J.M. Williams (ed.), *Applied Sport Psychology: Personal Growth to Peak Performance.* Mountain View, CA: Mayfield.

Smoll, F.L. & Smith, R.E. (1997). *Coaches Who Never Lose.* New York: Warde.

Weinberg, R.S. & Richardson, P.A. (1990). *Psychology of Officiating.* Champaign, IL.: Leisure Press.

Williams, A.M. & Reilly, T. (2000). Talent identification and development in soccer. *Journal of Sport Sciences, 18*(9), 657–667.

CHAPTER 8

Focused Baseball: Using Sport Psychology to Improve Baseball Performance

Tom Hanson
Tampa, Florida, USA

INTRODUCTION

Baseball became America's national sport in the 1800s largely because the rapid speed of the game best suited America's fast-paced culture. As the "speed" of American culture has accelerated, basketball and football have surpassed baseball in popularity in the United States. However, baseball will likely always be considered the "national pastime".

Worldwide, baseball is flourishing. Participation is growing in Europe, Asia and Africa, and an ever-increasing percentage of major league players are from Latin America, where the game is a passion. Baseball is a major sport in Australia and it is the number one sport in Japan.

Regardless of where baseball is played, players commonly report that 80 per cent of their baseball performance on a given day is determined by mental game factors such as confidence, focus, attitude and composure (Hanson, 1990). But when asked what percentage of their time they spend working on their mental game, they typically say 0 to 20 per cent. Players and coaches know the mental game is vital, but few know how to develop mental skills. As a result, the players' psychological and emotional development is left largely to chance.

The purpose of this chapter is to provide sport psychology professionals with a foundation to help players and coaches improve their performances and satisfaction in baseball. The chapter addresses the following topics:

1. Objectives of an educational sport psychology approach in baseball.
2. The challenges of baseball.
3. The mental toughness tools.
4. Using the mental toughness tools to build confidence and consistency.
5. Summary.

The Sport Psychologist's Handbook: A Guide for Sport-Specific Performance Enhancement.
Edited by Joaquín Dosil. © 2006 John Wiley & Sons, Ltd.

OBJECTIVES OF AN EDUCATIONAL SPORT PSYCHOLOGY APPROACH IN BASEBALL

Following an "educational" approach, sport psychology professionals (1) provide information, (2) teach skills, and (3) support players and coaches in refining and developing their mental approach to the game (Ravizza, 1990). Three general objectives guide the work.

Long-term Excellent Performance

The perspectives and skills taught are not a quick fix, but rather empower the player to maximize performance throughout his career. It takes consistent practice over a prolonged period of time for a pitcher to learn to throw a curve ball, and it takes consistent practice over a prolonged period of time for a player to learn to control his focus. The objective is for the player, at the end of his career, to know he gave himself his best chance of success.

Self-adjustment

Players cannot rely on coaches to give them feedback. Baseball is a game of adjustments and players need to learn to make adjustments on their own. Therefore, awareness is one of the main goals of mental game consulting. Players must develop the ability to recognize when they are not in control of themselves and have the ability to regain their composure and focus. The skilled batter makes an adjustment during or between at-bats, while the less skilled batter may play poorly for a whole game or week before making an adjustment.

Consistency

Working on the mental game is not about players being in the "zone" all the time. The "zone" happens rarely even for the advanced player. A player with well-developed mental skills is more consistent and plays better on "bad days" than a player with lesser mental skills. Consistency is one of the most desired qualities in baseball.

THE CHALLENGES OF BASEBALL

One of the keys to successful consulting in baseball is understanding the nature of baseball and the unique challenges it presents. Like all sports, the rules of baseball (such as requiring batters to hit a round ball with a round bat, putting nine players out on defense and forcing pitchers to throw the ball over home plate) are intended to make successful performance difficult. Although players often forget this, they play the game because they enjoy attempting to overcome these challenges.

Focus is the most important performance variable in baseball (confidence is second—a player who lacks confidence can perform well if he focuses effectively). To be successful, a player must learn to maintain his focus on the task-relevant cue (the ball for hitters and defenders, the target for pitchers) regardless of distracting circumstances.

For example, the team "at bat" sends one batter to home plate at a time. His objective is to move safely around the three other bases and return to home plate to score a "run". He

To be mentally tough, players must team to generate feelings of confidence and maintain focus, despite many potentially distracting circumstances. Reproduced by permission of Joaquín Dosil.

is allowed to stop at each base and be "safe" while another player from his team attempts to hit the ball in such a way that the "base runner" can run safely home.

The key to success as a batter is focusing on the ball. Great hitters say their main thought when they are at the plate is putting the "fat" part of the bat on the ball when they swing (Hanson, 1992). Since the ball is often traveling over 90 miles per hour, hitters can't control exactly where the ball goes once they hit it.

The key to success in hitting is keeping it simple: more than 90 per cent of the time a batter who is performing poorly ("slumping") is making hitting more complicated than "see the ball, hit the ball". Instead of a simple thought, he is partly focused on his technique or the results he hopes to produce.

Pitchers must throw the ball over home plate between the batter's knees and lower chest. They must get three "strikes" before they throw four "balls" (pitches the batter doesn't swing at that the umpire rules to be outside the strike zone).

The key to success in pitching is keeping it simple. Having practiced their delivery, they need to focus on their target and trust their bodies to execute the desired pitch.

One slang term for losing focus is being "hooked". A hitter or pitcher may be performing well when a circumstance grabs his attention and it pulls him off course. His mind bites on it like a fish on a hook and he becomes upset, frustrated, angry or scared, and his performance suffers. These circumstances can be external or internal.

External Circumstances

External Circumstances that can hook a player include:

- *Statistics* Many players obsess over their statistics. Pitchers have been known to be on the mound calculating their earned run average (ERA) during the middle of an inning ("If this guy scores, that will be three earned runs in five innings so that means my ERA will be . . . "), and hitters often pressure themselves when they are 0 for 3. Instead of being focused on what they need to do to have a great at-bat and help their team, they are selfishly focused on not being 0 for 4.

- *Coaches* Coaches often make unpopular decisions. Even if the player respects his coach, he is apt to disagree with him at some point. Many players not getting the playing time they want focus on how unfair or disappointing that is and lose the positive energy they need to play well when they do get a chance to play.
- *Success* Success is one of the most dangerous and seductive challenges. A pitcher on the mound might think: "I'm really doing great. I'm just five outs away from getting my ERA under 3.00 again." That loss of focus is often enough to cause a major decline in performance. Sometimes hitting a home run is the worst thing that can happen to a hitter if he then starts thinking about hitting more home runs. It may take weeks for him to recover and get back to his optimal focus.
- *Scouts and college coaches* One of the biggest "hooks" can be having scouts and college coaches in the stands. Many players have a hard time staying focused on what is most important (the game) when they want so badly to impress the scouts. It is hard for their body to play well when their heads are in the stands.
- *School* Schoolwork can be a major distraction. If players are behind in school, it drains their energy and hurts their baseball performance because part of their mind is occupied with what needs to be done. They can't be fully 100 per cent focused on the baseball when part of their brain is concerned about school. Often players are not aware of the loss of focus and energy caused by being behind or doing poorly.
- *Relationships* Relationships can be a major distraction, but they can also enhance players' performance. The issue isn't whether players have or don't have a relationship; it is how they are being in the relationship. As with schoolwork, integrity is key. If players are truthful, respectful and do what they say they are going to do, chances are the relationship will help their performance. But if they aren't acting with integrity, the relationship will likely hinder performance.

Other external circumstances that can disrupt focus include:

- bad calls by umpires
- off-the-field issues such as alcohol, drugs, and money
- teammates
- weather
- field conditions
- opponent's ability (good or bad)
- fans
- media
- travel.

Internal Circumstances

Internal circumstances that can hook a player and disrupt his focus include:

- *Fear* Two types of fear come into play in baseball: fear of physical injury (particularly getting hit by the ball), and fear of emotional injury such as embarrassment or disappointment.

Both can "hook" a player's focus and hinder performance. At higher levels of baseball the principal fears are emotional, as players seek to avoid failure, disappointment and embarrassment.

- *Anger* Baseball players must learn to navigate the paradox of having most of the fans' and coaches' focus be on statistics (wins and losses, batting averages, earned run averages, etc.) but having those issues outside of the players' direct control. Players forget this. Anger is caused by a loss or failure of something cared about (e.g. performance) and the assessment that it shouldn't have happened. In other words, in the player's opinion, things went poorly and they shouldn't have. Anger normally creates excessive muscle tension and loss of focus.
- *Frustration* Frustration stems from being blocked from attaining a goal (Hodge, 2004). As noted above, the rules of baseball are designed to make it difficult for players to reach their goals, so frustration is one of the most commonly seen emotions in baseball.
- *Fatigue* The baseball season, particularly in the professional ranks, is very long and each day at the ballpark often requires six to ten hours. Although it is not an aerobic activity, baseball presents the physical challenge of intermittent bouts of intense activity over a prolonged period of time. Pitchers must learn to maintain their focus through fatigue, while hitters must guard against "giving away" at-bats because they were too tired to properly mentally prepare.
- *Negative thoughts/doubt* Players' performance is closely related to their confidence (Vealey, 1986). When players are confident they trust their skills and have access to their full talent. When players have doubts they lose their freedom and normally perform poorly. Rampant failure challenges the best of players to maintain their belief in their abilities.

Ultimately, getting "hooked" is always the result of an internal process. Something happens and the player makes it mean something that upsets him. He thinks something like, "That shouldn't happen", "That's not fair" or "Why does bad stuff always happen to me?" and he's hooked! His body gets tense and he is no longer focused on baseball—he's focused on the circumstance that upset him. As noted in Ravizza and Hanson (1995, p. 5):

> When you strike out, you're just out, that's it. Nowhere in the rulebook does it say you should be upset about it or that the next time up you should swing as hard as you can so you can make up for the strike out! Your emotion about the whole thing results from your thinking, not the event itself.

MENTAL TOUGHNESS TOOLS

A mental toughness program is designed to enable players to overcome the challenges baseball presents. Of all the terms used in the sport psychology literature, "mental toughness" resonates best with baseball players. Coaches and commentators use the term widely and it is well established in the baseball vernacular.

Mental toughness is the ability to consistently play at or near your best regardless of circumstances (Loehr, 1982). Regardless of conditions or past or potential events, the mentally tough player is able to play nearly as well as he is capable of playing.

Any player can play great when they feel great, but players who succeed at the higher levels are able to create good or even great performances when they don't feel 100 per cent.

They might be tired or frustrated, or they might have doubts about their ability to succeed (doubt happens to the best of them, even at the major league level), but somehow mentally tough players are able to focus the energy they do have in a way that produces success.

The mental toughness tools discussed here can be divided into two categories: perspective and mental skills.

Perspective

Perspective is the way a player is looking at his situation. It's the "big picture", the "lens" through which a player looks at the facts surrounding him, and his "attitude". Ironically (and appropriately), there are several ways to look at perspective. A common cognitive-behavioral model holds that a player's cognitive appraisal of a situation creates a physiological response, which then affects the player's performance level (Landers & Boutcher, 1993).

A loose, relaxed physiology generally results in better performance than a tight, tension-filled body, so the perspective a player takes on the game hugely affects his performance (Gould, Hodge, Peterson & Giannini, 1989).

Perhaps *the* primary goal of consulting with a player is to help him view the game and his particular situation in a way that empowers him to consistently perform at or near his best. For example, if a pitcher is able to throw well in the bullpen but performs poorly in a game, have a conversation with him that reveals his current perspective and help him replace it with a more empowering perspective. Address questions such as:

- What does it mean to succeed?
- What does it mean to fail?
- What beliefs are giving rise to your fear?

The goal is to identify the underlying belief the player has about performance, challenge its validity and create a new perspective that frees him to play better. Again, the situation itself isn't causing the stress, the player's perspective is. A solid pre-pitch routine and other mental skills (discussed below) will likely help this player, but a change in perspective will address the cause of his issue rather than just treat the symptoms.

Hear the player's issue, discuss with him how his current perspective is limiting him and, when possible, illustrate the point with a story of another athlete who fell into a similar mental trap.

The vital point of emphasis with perspective is that players have the ability to *choose* their perspective. The range of possible perspective choices is endless, but two warrant particular emphasis: Gamer vs. Victim, and Love vs. Fear.

Gamer vs. Victim

The most important perspective regards personal responsibility. A player must see he has the ability to freely make choices about how and where he directs his attention and what actions he takes. This idea can be expressed by using the terms "Victim" and "Gamer" (Kofman, 2004).

The "Victim" perspective is an "outside–in" approach. A Victim lets external circumstances determine his internal state. A Victim rides the "results roller coaster"—his confidence goes up and down with his most recent statistics. When the hits are falling, he's "The Man"—confident, focused and upbeat. But when he goes a game or two without a hit, his spirits dive.

A Victim focuses on things he can't control. Batters cannot control whether or not they get a hit. They can do everything right and hit a ball directly at a fielder, or they can get called out by the umpire on a pitch that was six inches outside of the strike zone.

Pitchers can't control getting batters out—they can make a great pitch and have it turn into a bloop double or watch a double play ground ball take a bad hop over their shortstop's head.

Since external circumstances are outside of their control, Victims have no chance of being consistent. As long as they take this excuse-making approach to the game, the majority of their talent will remain locked inside them.

A "Gamer", on the other hand, takes an "inside–out" approach. He chooses for himself how he is going to be. Players at the top level such as Derek Jeter, Roger Clemens, Alex Rodriquez and Curt Schilling take what is inside them and pour it out onto the field each day. True professionals determine what qualities they will demonstrate each day—confidence, focus, determination, positive attitude—rather than letting what happens around them determine their mental state.

External circumstances affect the game, but "Gamers" focus their energy on things they can control. They learn to generate from within the focus and feelings they know lead to their best performances, rather than letting random events determine their internal state. Since they see themselves as the source of their own performance, they learn to play consistently at or near their best.

How to Help Players Be "Gamers"

Here are three ways to facilitate someone adopting the Gamer perspective:

1. Listen for "Victimspeak"—excuse-making, blaming external circumstances, and an "I-have-nothing-to-do-with-it" attitude. When you hear it, introduce them to the terms "Victim" and "Gamer". Often just the awareness of the distinction empowers a player to shift his perspective.
2. Ask the player to rate himself from 1 to 10 on his approach this past week, where 1 was being a Victim (what happened to him determined his mental state) and 10 is being a Gamer (where he determined his mental state regardless of his circumstances.) Be sure to ask him to explain his rating.
3. Finally, ask questions that steer him toward taking responsibility for whatever is going on. It can be tempting to console a player when something isn't going well or when something negative happens. Questions such as the following lead the person to take the Victim perspective because they emphasize external circumstances, which renders him powerless:
   - What happened to you?
   - What did they do to upset you?
   - What should they have done instead?

   Instead, ask questions that help him adopt the Gamer perspective such as:
   - What challenge did you face?
   - How did you choose to respond?

- How could you have responded more effectively?
- Could you have prepared better?
- What can you learn from this?

Each of these questions makes his choices the center of the action, empowering him to take responsibility and act powerfully—to be a Gamer.

Love vs. Fear

Once a player sees himself as responsible for his own performance, the second choice of perspectives also creates a major context for performance. Players typically play baseball because they love it, but as the perceived importance of outcomes rises, they often unknowingly shift to fear.

When playing with a love-based perspective, players experience passion, joy, fun and freedom. Their actions are effortless, focused, intense and energetic. They feel a sense of connection with themselves and their performance. When performance is an expression of love for the game players have access to all of their talent (Mack, 2001).

When playing from a fear-based perspective, players experience tension, doubt and pressure. They feel disconnected and mechanical and try too hard. A common form of fear-based play comes from trying to prove themselves. Players try to impress their coach, teammates, parents or themselves.

Similarly, players often base their self-esteem on their performance. If their statistics are good, these players feel they are good and worthy people. But if their statistics are bad they are not worthy. "I gotta ... " is a common way fear-based perspectives begin. For example, "I gotta get a hit", or "I gotta win this game".

The Love vs. Fear issue can be addressed with players in the following way:

> So in the last week of practice or games you played, would you say you were playing from your love of the game or your fear of failure or embarrassment? Put it on a 1 to 10 scale where 1 is lots of fear—and 10 is playing with a passionate love for the game. What would you need to let go of in order to move up two numbers?

Other Common Errors in Perspective

Listed below are some of the common mistakes players make that can be labeled perspective "errors". Players:

- Forget that baseball is difficult and act like it's easy (e.g. hitters get overly upset when they make an out);
- Used to *play* baseball and now they see it as a job;
- Forget that they are playing against the best players in the world;
- Focus on outcomes and statistics instead of the process of playing the game (e.g. trying to get hits instead of connecting with the ball);
- Focus on what others are thinking of them (e.g. front office, manager, family) rather than on being themselves;
- Attempt to play outside of their abilities (e.g. a small player trying to hit home runs or a groundball pitcher trying to strike batters out);

- Don't play one pitch at a time (previous pitches and at-bats are allowed to affect their present performance);
- Focus too much on mechanical/technical aspects of their swing or delivery;
- Believe they need to be perfect.

Occasionally a single conversation can create an "aha" experience, and a significant shift in how the player is performing occurs, but changing a player's perspective more often is a gradual process. Be patient. Allow the player to discover his limiting belief on his own if possible. Telling him to "go out and have fun" is much less powerful than if he comes to that conclusion on his own.

The next step is to devise a plan to put this new approach into action. The Quality Practice Chart at the end of this chapter can be used to help a player adopt and maintain a powerful perspective.

Mental Skills

The second area of emphasis in the mental toughness program is mental skills. These include posture, visualization, self-talk, focusing, breathing and routines. All of these skills are closely related and often used in conjunction with each other. They are considered "ingredients" a player uses to create his personalized "recipe" for success.

Posture: Move Confidently

The fastest and easiest route to becoming more confident is to move confidently. Ask a player:

> When you are playing great, how do you carry yourself between pitches? How do you move when you feel totally unstoppable? Try it right now. Stand up and walk around the room like you feel totally confident. Lift your head up high, let your shoulders roll back, raise your chin and chest and draw full, slow breaths deep into your abdomen. Now get into your batting stance or stand on an imaginary pitching rubber like you're certain you know you are the best, like you are in complete control of the situation.

When a player's body is moving confidently, it sends confident messages to his brain. Moving confidently feels good, so more confident thoughts arise. It is very difficult to think confidently when the body is in a slumped position, and very easy to think confidently when the body is standing tall and broad.

Tell a player: "Pretend you are back in a time when you dominated; when you felt really great. You don't have to make a big show of it, just move confidently." You may also ask him to do an impression of a confident-looking major league player he knows or an impression of *himself* when he is supremely confident. As Flippen (2002) states, "Don't just try to think your way to a new level of moving, move your way to a new level of thinking!"

Visualization

Much has been written about visualization and it is mentioned throughout this chapter and book, so only a few points of emphasis will be given here.

The term "visualization" is something of a misnomer since the most effective form of it includes more than the visual sense. Include as many senses as possible, particularly feeling. Syer and Connolly (1987) use the term "pre-play" which describes the technique more accurately.

It is also important to emphasize that not everyone will see, feel or hear their performance equally well. Some may not get clear pictures or be able to feel their swing or throw. Assure the player that this is normal and that more clarity can be gained through practice. Also, when focusing a pitch or throw, players tend to find it most helpful to only visualize the last few feet of the ball's flight to the target.

Focus

Focus, defined as the concentration of attention or mental energy, is generally agreed to be the most important key to performance (Nideffer, 1985). Performance follows focus. If a person riding a bike looks to the left for a few seconds, the bike will drift to the left. The rider might intend to stay straight and think he's staying straight, but his body (performance) will go where his focus is. If a player focuses away from his task-relevant cue, his performance will drift as well.

A player's success is determined by his ability to have a focused connection with his target regardless of circumstances (Orlick, 2000). In general, for pitchers, the target is the mitt; for hitters and fielders, it's the ball. But each player must determine his best focus.

Focusing effectively allows optimal performance. A professional pitcher who as a rookie won a starting position on a major league team over many other excellent pitchers was asked the key to his success. "I shrunk the game," he said, meaning instead of getting caught up in the many distractions that come with major league baseball, including the media and playing with and against players he had grown up admiring, he chose to focus on a few simple things (anonymous, personal communication, 2001).

Formalized, "shrinking the game" has three components. If a player is struggling in his performance he is probably not doing at least one of them.

1. *Focus on things you can control* Ask a player: "What can you control? Your playing time? The outcome of the game? Getting a base hit? Getting a batter out? Getting a college scholarship?"

   Players can't control any of these things. They care deeply about them, and they can influence them, but they can't control them. Instead of wasting energy or basing their confidence solely on them, players should focus on their thinking, attitude, effort, practice quality and preparation. Focus on the process of playing the game instead of being wrapped up in results.

   Former NCAA Division I Coach of the Year Dave Snow says, "Results thinking is just a big trap. You've got to work on your physical and mental skills and then go out, trust what you've worked on, and accept the results" (Ravizza & Hanson, 1995).

2. *Focus on the present moment* The only time players have any control is right now. They can't change the past, they can't do anything about the future. Regardless of what happened on the last pitch (the circumstances) or what might happen on some later pitch, the only pitch that they can do anything about is this next one. Focus on it.

Play the game *one pitch at a time*. Players hear this phrase often, and they know it is a major issue for them even at the major league level, but they are rarely taught how to do it. It is very difficult to stay fully focused on this one pitch and not be negatively affected by anything that's happened on a previous pitch. Suggestions for how to do this are provided below.

3. *Focus on the most important thing* The final step in shrinking the game is to figure out the most important thing to focus on. During each pitch for pitchers it's the mitt (or whatever they are using for a target). For hitters it's the ball, and for fielders it's the ball and then the target for the throw.

These three elements—focusing on things they can control, in the present moment, that are most important—provide a framework for players to release non-relevant stimuli and fully connect with their performance.

Self-talk: Think Confidently

Self-talk is simply the words an athlete says to themselves (Bunker, Williams & Zinsser, 1993). Thoughts have a significant impact on the performance of motor skills (Weinberg & Gould, 1999). Ask a player: "When you are playing great, what do you spend your time thinking about?"

When players are playing well they spend their time thinking about playing well. Between games they can't wait to get to the park again because their heads are filled with positive self-talk and images of playing great.

Similarly, when slumping, players spend their time thinking about playing poorly. Between games they dread going to the park because their body is filled with thoughts, images and feelings of playing poorly and typically their thoughts become a self-fulfilling prophecies.

Players are surprisingly unaware of their own thoughts. Encourage them to:

> Think in a way that gives you your best chance for success regardless of your circumstances. When you are 0 for 7 or just gave up a 3 run homer to tie the game, you still are able to choose your thinking. You can think: "I'm due! I'm the best man for this situation and I'm going to get the job done right now."

When players choose to think confident thoughts enough it becomes a habit. Great players habitually think in ways that help their performance (Rotella, 1990). Some great players are very hard on themselves mentally, but when it comes time to perform they get their minds out of the way enough to get the job done.

Deep Breath

Many players report deep breathing as the single most helpful mental skills tool they learn. A deep breath (into the belly if possible, into the chest if that is the best the player can do during a game) does several things for a player:

- puts his focus on the present moment
- enables him to "check in" with himself to determine his level of self-control
- helps him gain emotional control

- helps release negative thoughts
- energizes him
- facilitates trust
- helps establish a rhythm to pitching, hitting and fielding.

Here are some basic instructions on how to take a deep breath, also known as "centering".

- Stand with your feet hip-width apart with one foot slightly ahead of the other, with both feet turned out a bit. Let your knees be slightly bent. This is important because if your knees are locked straight you can't feel the weight change that comes with centering and you won't be as aware of your tension level.
- As you inhale deeply into your belly, check the tension in your chest, shoulders and face.
- As you exhale, relax the muscles in your thighs and calves and allow your knees to bend slightly. You should feel yourself sink slightly and an increased connectedness with the ground.

This is simple process, but powerful if practiced. Encourage players to take a deep breath before each pitch. Many players, especially at the higher levels, take a breath as part of their pre-pitch routine (see below).

A skill is a capacity gained through practice. As such, the mental skills discussed above must be practiced in order for them to be maximally beneficial. A daily practice session of at least 10 minutes each day is recommended.

USING THE MENTAL TOUGHNESS TOOLS TO BUILD CONFIDENCE AND CONSISTENCY

The two qualities players desire most are confidence and consistency. In this section, methods of combining the mental skills to build confidence and consistency are discussed.

A Recipe for Confidence

Confidence is a choice. Sometimes it's a choice a player can make in an instant and shift quickly from doubt to belief, but most of the time it is like choosing to add 25 pounds to his maximum bench press: he chooses to take the necessary steps that over time get him there.

The "there" players are trying to get to is being able to generate the feeling or "state" that allows them to play great. Players can play well when they don't feel confident (and in fact they must learn to be able to), but normally best performances come when players feel they are going to be successful.

> What happens to clutch guys in big moments is that everything slows down. You have time to evaluate the situation, and you can clearly see every move you need to make. You're in the moment, in complete control. It's hard to get there; something has to have you thinking you can do no wrong. But once you do get there, you can just come out at the start of a game and generate the feeling.
>
> Michael Jordan (Williams, 2001, p. 1)

One key to a player's success is his ability to learn to *generate the feeling*. It is his ability to create the feeling of confidence, or at least direct his focus and energy in such a way that he is able to let his talent come through. Even at the professional level, players have surprisingly little awareness of the role their thoughts, focus and actions play in their confidence and consistency. They know they can choose to think about whatever they want and they know their thoughts largely determine how confident they feel, but they don't make the link of deliberately and consistently thinking thoughts that build their confidence.

A fundamental way to help a player be more confident and consistent is to help him become more aware of the thoughts, feelings and actions that contribute to his playing great. The goal is to enable him to deliberately choose the actions that help him play great rather than leaving things to chance.

Think of it as creating a "recipe for success". People commonly ask for the recipe for a meal they particularly like. They are given a list of ingredients and a process for combining them in a way that produced the delicious dish. This helps the person repeat the creation of that meal.

Each player has great (delicious) performances in his past and he'd like to play at that level consistently. Have him think back to a time when he was a "10" on a 1-to-10 confidence scale and gave a "gourmet" performance and ask, "How did you do it?"

Specifically, one can say, "Think of a particular time when you played great. Go back there and put yourself right back into that situation."

The more vividly he imagines himself there, the more valuable information he'll get. If the situation allows, have the player actually demonstrate what he looked like—stand up and really pretend he is at that great moment. If needed he can do it sitting down and it can even be done over the phone.

When he gets himself immersed in that past great experience, feeling highly confident, ask questions like:

- What are you thinking?
- What is your attitude?
- How are you moving or carrying your body?
- What are you feeling? Where do you feel confidence?
- What are you focused on?
- How are you breathing?
- What is the look on your face?

Get the "ingredients" and processes he used to create the performance he really liked and write them down. Then identify the things on the list that he can control—things he can choose to do anytime. Chances are his list will include actions like:

- Visualizing hitting his target (the ball or the mitt).
- Imagining himself getting hits or striking batters out.
- Moving his body in a confident way (tall, broad, slow, easy).
- Breathing deeply and calmly.
- Feeling certainty and a sense of dominance.
- Feeling a powerful but effortless swing or delivery.
- Self-talk with an attitude like "This guy has no chance against me" or "I'm going to crush this ball."

Anyone can generate a boost in confidence if they follow the above guidelines. The question becomes: "If you can boost your confidence like this anytime, why wouldn't you do it every time right before you play?"

How to Help Players Be Consistently Confident

Just like doing squats on a regular basis will enhance the strength of his lower body, doing the above exercise on a regular basis will enhance the strength of his confidence. Suggest to players that they do this exercise for at least 5 minutes per day. Put on some favorite music and go back in time to a great performance, immersing themselves in the performance so they generate a feeling of confidence.

All-time career home run leader Hank Aaron said pre-game visualization was the main reason for his incredible focus and consistency. He spent much of each day imagining what he wanted to make happen that night. Making this practice a habit will contribute to a player being consistent (Hanson, 1996).

To summarize, ask each player questions about their best performances. Be like a detective looking for clues—what are the things he does when he is totally confident (that he can choose to do whether he right now feels confident or not)? Then help him determine a way to build those thoughts and actions into routines—pre-game, pre-pitch and post-game—so he can be confident and focused more consistently.

Pre-game Routines: The Key to Consistency

Hank Aaron, the all-time leader in runs batted in, total bases and home runs, was asked about the mental aspects of hitting. His first words were: "Well, it all depends on how a guy prepares himself to do battle" (Hanson, 1996). Aaron attributed his incredible consistency and ability to perform under pressure to his ability to focus. His tremendous focus, he said, resulted from his daily mental preparation.

Hall-of-Fame pitcher Ferguson Jenkins also said pre-game preparation was vital to his success (Jenkins, personal communication, 2001). Jenkins went through the opposing team's line-up in his head not only before the game, but also between innings. He'd prepare while his team was hitting by thinking through the first four hitters of the next inning.

Preparation is one of the most powerful sources of confidence. Like taking an exam at school, the better prepared you are the more confident you feel. In baseball, the better you've done your "homework" studying your opponent and preparing your mind and body to play, the more confident you're likely to be.

To help with this process, a mental preparation strategy called "PREP" was devised that gives players a systematic way to approach this key source of confidence.

P = **P**ick a Quality. Preparation starts with commitment: commit to possessing one quality today.
R = **R**elease Your Circumstances. "Shrink the game" by letting go of anything that won't facilitate great play.
E = **E**nergize Your Body. Get your body "up" or "down" to where it needs to be today to play great.
P = **P**re-Play Your Performance. Imagine the way you want the game to go.

Using the PREP form as a guide (see form below), players can go through each of these four steps before a game or practice. After the game or practice players can deepen their learning by completing the Post-Game PREP form (see below).

P = Pick a Quality

Pick a quality you commit to being today. For example,

- "I will be focused today."
- "I commit to being grateful today."
- "Today I'm passionate about playing."
- "I promise to trust myself fully."
- "I will be positive all day."

The average player takes the Victim perspective and lets his last performance and how he feels at the moment determine how he is being. But the focused, mentally tough Gamer is guided by his commitment. He chooses how he is going to be.

Qualities commonly chosen include being (or having):

- professional
- dedicated
- fun
- a lover of the game
- concentrated
- mentally tough
- trusting
- consistent
- committed
- focused
- composed
- desiring
- having a great work ethic
- passionate
- full of integrity
- having respect for the game
- intense
- honest
- leadership
- pride.

The quality chosen becomes the player's "inner game" for the day (Gallwey, 1974). The "outer game" everyone sees is always baseball, but each player gets to choose the inner game he plays. The rules are simple: see how high a number he can be, from 1 to 10, on the quality he chose.

So, if a player chooses "determination" as his quality, he is playing a determination game. His goal is to be a "10" in that quality today. Often pitchers and hitters say they want to be "effortless" in their deliveries or swings, so they can play an effortless game.

The player is the judge. At the end of the game they rate themselves from 1 to 10, recording their scores on either the PREP form or, when this exercise is used on its own, the Quality Practice Chart.

R = Release Your Circumstances

Now that the player has committed to displaying a quality, he needs to release any circumstances that might get in the way of his being a 10 in that quality. "Releasing" is part of "shrinking the game". Remember, to shrink the game, focus on things

1. you control
2. in the present moment
3. That are most important for your performance.

Let go of anything else.

When asked how he created a masterpiece out of ordinary stone, Michelangelo said, "I just cut away everything that wasn't David." Releasing means cutting away everything that doesn't enhance performance.

The best way to identify what a player needs to release at any moment is to answer some questions. Before a game or practice, invite him to consider:

- What excuses do I already have for not playing well today?
- What beliefs do I have that may keep me from playing well?
- What circumstances might hook me today?
- What am I complaining about today?
- What am I upset about?
- What am I afraid of?
- Am I willing to let go of these things until after the game?

He might need to release any of the internal or external circumstances presented earlier, such as:

- needing to be perfect
- thinking he's not good enough
- wishing something hadn't happened
- complaining that he doesn't feel "right"
- some hassle he's got going off the field.

The anger, frustration, doubt and worry of these thoughts all disrupt his focus and cause unwanted tension in his body.

Releasing distracting thoughts and feelings is easier said than done. Here are some ideas some players find helpful:

- Breathe. Inhale, take a deep breath, exhale let the concern go. Repeat!
- Imagine that when he takes off his street clothes he is taking off all concerns of the "outside" world. Like his clothes, his concerns will be there after the game, so don't worry about them now.

- Body movements. Slumping players often stop moving and stew in how unfair it all is. Ask the player to move, gesture and breathe the way he would if he were totally confident, free from any fear or frustration.
- Write down the circumstances and emotions he wants to release and post the list in his locker or bag, or tear the list up and throw it away.
- Talk through what's upsetting him or getting in his way. He needn't try to solve all his problems, simply speaking them helps release them. He can either find a friend who will simply listen (not tell him what to do) or talk to himself.

E = Energize Your Body

Ask a player, "How do you want your body to feel before a game?"

When playing poorly, players focus *in* on themselves: "Poor me", "Why me?", "It's all about me." As a result, their bodies feel heavy, sad, angry or some other way that interferes with their performance.

When they are playing great they focus *out* on the game. They aren't in their head worrying; they are paying attention to the game, encouraging teammates and moving their bodies.

The player's task before a game or practice is to somehow get his body feeling as close to the way he wants it to as possible. Listed below are some ideas that can help players energize their bodies:

- *Jeter* Stand the way you would stand if you felt great about yourself. Move the way you would if you were totally confident. Not arrogant, just really great. Derek Jeter is one of the mentally toughest players in the game and one reason why is because he carries his body so well. Negative thoughts and energy have a hard time staying in a body that is carried confidently. Suggest to a player that he pretend he is Jeter (or some other role model) throughout his next practice or game. Regardless of how he feels, tell him to be long, broad, free and "up" in his body.
- *Breathe* Long, slow, deep breaths lower energy and help players tune in to what their body most needs. Short, quick breaths through the nose build energy.
- *Jam* Play music that puts you in the mood to play.
- *Be a 24-hour player* Feeling good during games is a 24-hour deal, not some magic players do at the last minute. What they eat, when they eat, the quality of their rest, the quality and timing of their workouts and other choices they make away from the field affect their performance. Whatever they put into their body off the field comes out in their performance on the field.

The key is for the player to study himself. He needs to notice how different foods, workouts and sleep patterns affect him. Getting energized means getting his body ready to go, and no one can tell him exactly how to do that but himself. The PREP sheet provides additional ideas.

P = Pre-Play Your Performance

In the final step to the PREP model, encourage players to use their imagination to see, feel and hear the way they want the game to unfold. As noted earlier, Hank Aaron prepared by visualizing himself facing the pitcher he would see that night. He saw each of the pitchers' pitches coming in, and he put himself in different game situations (Hanson, 1996).

For example,

> Put yourself in different situations, imagine yourself throwing great pitches or hitting the ball on the nose time after time. You can do it throughout the day of your practice or game, or set aside 5 to 10 minutes to really focus in on it. Be sure to feel it and even hear the action, don't just see it. Don't worry if your images aren't perfectly clear, just get into it. You must be focused to pre-play, and doing it will get you mentally and emotionally prepared to play.

The PREP form on page 180 provides specific situations to pre-play.

Pre-pitch Routines: Play One Pitch at a Time

A player's "recipe for success" can also be applied during the game. Much of a consultant's time working with players is spent helping them develop pre-game and pre-pitch routines that help them generate the mindset that leads to their best performances.

A pre-pitch routine is a set series of actions that helps a player create a feeling of confidence and a powerful focus on his target. It "shrinks the game" and helps him connect with the most important thing he can control right now. Instead of being "hooked" by a circumstance, the player is focused on executing his routine.

A well-designed, well-practiced routine is the key to playing one pitch at a time. It is the on-the-field key to being consistent. Players will tell you they have routines, but these are mostly physical routines or superstitions that don't include the mental game elements that make all the difference.

Each of the mental skills listed above (physical posture, visualization, focus, self-talk, breathing) are considered "ingredients" for creating a routine. Explain the skills to players and then let each player experiment to find out what works best for him. Some sample routines are listed below.

Pitcher's Routine

1. Off the rubber
   - Confident body.
   - Check "in"—notice how I feel. If I feel centered, go on. If I'm "hooked" by something and don't feel centered, take extra time behind the mound to center.
   - Check "out"—know the game situation and get an idea of what pitch I want to throw.
2. On the rubber
   - Take a breath.
   - Commit to the pitch I'm going to throw (e.g. fastball, curveball).
   - Connect with my target by pre-playing the pitch: see it, feel it.
   - Cue word as I start my motion: "Free and easy."
3. During the pitch
   - Trust it, let it go.

Hitter's Routine

1. Outside the box
   - Confident body.
   - Check in—notice how I feel. If I feel centered, go on. If I'm "hooked" by something and don't feel centered, take extra time out of the box to center.
   - Check out—know the game situation, get signals from the third base coach.
   - Commit to a plan: "See the ball, hit it up the middle."
2. Inside the box
   - Step into the box the same way each time.
   - Take a breath.
   - Cue words: "See the ball."
3. During the pitch
   - Trust.

Fielder's Routine

Ultimately fielding comes down to having a mindset of "Hit it to me". If you want the ball hit to you, you're ready.

1. Before the pitch
   - Breathe.
   - Pre-play the pitch. See a ball hit to me and imagine myself making the right play.
2. During the pitch
   - Say, "Hit it to me" and trust.

Post-game Routine

After the game is an important time to process the events that transpired and begin preparing for the next game or practice. Reviewing and replaying key moments in the game build awareness and deepen learning. The Post-Game PREP form (on page 181) will guide players through this process.

For more on creating routines, see Ravizza and Hanson (1995).

SUMMARY

The purpose of this chapter is to provide sport psychology professionals with a foundation to help players and coaches improve their performances and satisfaction in baseball. The objectives of an educational approach, the importance of understanding the nature of baseball, tools for developing mental toughness and methods for implementing those tools were provided.

Some effort has been made to explain some of the key elements of the game. For more information on baseball basics, see Glavine (1999). Essentially, players need to understand that baseball is difficult and they will, by design, experience "failure". To be mentally tough, they must learn to generate feelings of confidence and maintain focus on the most important things despite many potentially distracting external and internal circumstances.

One of the main goals of mental toughness training is to shift players' focus from their statistics to their approach to the game. Focusing on the process of playing instead of the results they produce is a difficult challenge. Hopefully the perspectives and tools provided in this chapter will help sport psychology consultants do this more effectively.

APPENDICES

Contact Information

For more information, please contact Tom Hanson, PhD at www.FocusedBaseball.com.

Below are instructions for using the Quality Practice Chart and the chart itself. Here's what to do:

1. *Photocopy the chart*
2. *Write the two qualities* Write two qualities you are committed to being on the lines under where you see the words "Quality" in the middle of the page.
3. *Step 1: Rate yourself* Rate yourself on a 1 to 10 scale on both of these qualities for the past week, 3 days, 24 hours, or however long it's been since you last completed the form. One is low, 10 is high. For example, if one of your qualities is "Focused", a "1" would be very unfocused, a "10" would be highly focused. If you feel you've been a "5", shade in the boxes up to 5 as you see in the example under the date "12 January".

   Be sure to write in the date above the column you shade in. The player in the example completed the form every three days.
4. *Step 2: Coach yourself* Think back to what you did and didn't do that affected your performance since the last time you completed the chart. Ask yourself questions like:
   • What did I do that helped my performance?
   • What did I do that hurt my performance?
   • What didn't I do that I know would have helped?
   • How did I prepare for each performance?
   • How did I carry my body?
   • What did I spend my time thinking about?
   • What did I focus on?
   • What did I eat?
   • Who did I talk with?

In the space provided under the charts, create a list of your coaching advice to yourself of things you want to remember to do (under "Do This") and a list of coaching for yourself about what you want to *not* do (under "Don't Do This"). Add or subtract from the lists each time. Remember to focus on things you can control. Putting "Get four hits each game" on your "Do This" list isn't as helpful as "Be committed to seeing the ball early each pitch."

When you have completed the form seven times you'll need to print yourself a new one. I suggest you keep all your charts organized in a folder or three-ring binder. The forms will be an extremely helpful resource for you as your season and career progress.

Quality Practice Chart

Complete this form daily, every three days or weekly.   NAME _____

STEP 1: RATE YOURSELF. Rate yourself 1 (low) to 10 (high) on the degree to which you've been the Key Qualities you committed to. Color in the number of boxes that correspond to your self-rating. Start a new chart after you've completed this one seven times.

EXAMPLE   Date: **JANUARY**

What Are You Committed To?

Quality: *FOCUS*

Date:

Quality:

Date:

Quality :

STEP 2: COACH YOURSELF. What have you learned? Reflect on what helped and what hurt your performance over this time period and create a list of "Dos" and "Don't" for yourself.

Do This!   Don't Do This!

© Tom Hanson, PhD   Tom@FocusedBaseball.com

Pre-Game PREP

Print this form and complete it before your game or practice.   Name_____

Date _____

Pick a Quality

What one quality do you commit to being today?

Release Your Distractions

Possible Distractions Today (list)   How You Will Release Them
*
*
*
*
*

Energize Your Body

Place an "X" on the number where your body feels now, and circle the number where you want to be at game time.

1	2	3	4	5	6	7	8	9	10	
	Low Energy									**High Energy**

How will you energize your body?

Pre-play Your Performance

See, feel and hear yourself: (check off each when complete)

Making great **Pitches** (wind up and stretch)   **Hitting** great:
    ___Fastball x 5   ___ Fastball x 5
    ___Breaking ball x 5   ___ Breaking ball x 5
    ___Other x 5   ___ Other x 5

Refocusing after: Refocusing after:
    ___ Giving up a hit, home run   ___ Swinging at a bad pitch
    ___ Bad call by umpire   ___ Bad call by umpire
    ___ Error by fielder   ___ Striking out
    ___ Distractions listed in "Release"   ___ Distractions listed in "Release"
___ Finish with seeing yourself being successful

Post-Game PREP

Complete this form as soon as reasonably possible *after* a game or practice.

Name_____ Date _____

P What quality did you "Pick" to be today? _____
Rate yourself on that quality today.

1	2	3	4	5	6	7	8	9	10	
	Low									**High**

R Rate your "Releasing" today. Were you able to let go of distractions?

1	2	3	4	5	6	7	8	9	10
No,									*Yes,*
couldn't let go									*let go great*

E Rate your "Energize" level. Did you get your body ready to perform?

1	2	3	4	5	6	7	8	9	10
No, I									*Yes, I*
was flat									*felt great*

P Rate the quality of your "Pre-Play." Did you see it, feel it, hear it?

1	2	3	4	5	6	7	8	9	10	
	Low									**High**

1. What really helped your performance today?

2. What distractions "hooked" you today? What made you lose focus?
How did you try to Release them?

© Tom Hanson, PhD   Tom@FocusedBaseball.com

REFERENCES

Bunker, L., Williams, J.M. & Zinsser, N. (1993). Cognitive techniques for improving performance and building confidence. In J.M. Williams (ed.) *Applied Sport Psychology: Personal Growth to Peak Performance* (2nd edn; pp. 225–242). Mountainview, CA: Mayfield.

Flippen, M.B. (2002). Executive Leadership Series Program. Presented at IMG Academies, Bradenton, FL by M.B. Flippen and Associates.

Gallwey, W.T. (1974). *The Inner Game of Tennis*. New York: Random House.

Glavine, T. (1999). *Baseball for Everyone—Tom Glavine's Guide to America's Game*. Maddison, WI: Chandler House Press.

Gould, D, Hodge, K., Peterson, K. & Giannini, J. (1989). An exploratory examination of strategies used by elite coaches to enhance self-efficacy in athletes. *Journal of Sport and Exercise Psychology, 11*, 128–140.

Hanson, T. (1990). Self-confidence and collegiate baseball players: an exploratory qualitative analysis. Paper presented at the Southeast Sport and Exercise Symposium, Greensboro, NC.

Hanson, T. (1992). The mental aspects of hitting. Unpublished doctoral dissertation, University of Virginia.

Hanson, T. (1996). The mental aspects of hitting in baseball: a case study of Hank Aaron. *Journal of Performance Education, 1*, 57–76.

Hodge, K.P. (2004). *Sport Motivation: Training Your Mind for Peak Performance* (2nd edn). Auckland, NZ: Reed.

Kofman, F. (2004). Unconditional responsibility: the power of being a player. Paper published on website www.Axialent.com

Landers, D. & Boutcher, S. (1993). Arousal-performance relationships. In J.M. Williams (ed.), *Applied Sport Psychology: Personal Growth to Peak Performance* (2nd edn; pp. 170–184) Mountainview, CA: Mayfield.

Loehr, J.E. (1982). *Mental Toughness Training for Sports*. New York: The Penguin Group.

Mack, G. (2001). *Mind Gym: An Athlete's Guide to Inner Excellence*. New York: McGraw-Hill.

Nideffer, R.M. (1985). *Athletes' Guild to Mental Training*. Champaign, IL: Human Kinetics.

Orlick, T. (2000). *In Pursuit of Excellence*. Champaign, IL: Human Kinetics.

Ravizza, K. (1990). Sportpsych consultation issues in professional baseball. *The Sport Psychologist, 4*, 330–340.

Ravizza, K. & Hanson, T. (1995). *Heads-Up Baseball: Playing the Game One Pitch at a Time*. Indianapolis: Master's Press.

Rotella, R.J. (1990). Providing sport psychology services to professional athletes. *The Sport Psychologist, 4*, 409–417.

Syer, J. & Connolly, C. (1987). *Sporting Body, Sporting Mind: An Athlete's Guide to Mental Training*. Englewood Cliffs, NJ: Prentice Hall.

Vealey, R. (1986). Conceptualization of sport-confidence and competitive orientation: preliminary investigation and instrument development. *Journal of Sport Psychology, 8*, 221–246.

Weinberg, R.S. & Gould, D. (1999). *Foundations of Sport and Exercise Psychology*. Champaign, IL: Human Kinetics.

Williams, P. (2001). *How To Be Like Mike: Life Lessons about Basketball's Best*. Deerfield Beach, FL: Health Communications, Inc.

CHAPTER 9

Thinking Rugby: Using Sport Psychology to Improve Rugby Performance

Ken Hodge and Chris Lonsdale

University of Otago, New Zealand

and

Alex McKenzie

Otago Rugby Union, New Zealand

INTRODUCTION

In this chapter we present the reader with information and ideas about how to use sport psychology to improve performance in the team sport of *rugby*. Rugby is an interactive, continuous, contact/collision, team sport. In an effort to help the reader understand the unique psychological challenges inherent in this sport we outline some of the intricacies of rugby and the importance of "mental toughness" for rugby. Then we briefly outline why rugby is so challenging from a mental perspective and describe the "ideal performance state" in rugby. Following this explanation of the psychological challenges in rugby we provide a simple method for evaluating psychological skills for rugby players (i.e. the peak performance profile). Using an example peak performance profile, we then demonstrate how to determine what psych skills and psych methods to include in a psych skills training (PST) program for a rugby player.

Since rugby is an interactive team sport we also provide some example team-building interventions and explain the role and use of these interventions in a PST program for rugby. Finally, we provide the reader with ideas for integrating PST into training—both at the individual and team level of training. Included within the emphasis on team training is a section on an important but usually neglected aspect of elite sport—training motivation.

KNOWLEDGE OF RUGBY: INTRICACIES OF THE SPORT

Rugby is an interactive, continuous, contact/collision, team sport. The interactive, continuous nature of rugby is characterized by players having to "switch" between attack/offense

The Sport Psychologist's Handbook: A Guide for Sport-Specific Performance Enhancement.
Edited by Joaquín Dosil. © 2006 John Wiley & Sons, Ltd.

and defense many times during a game, as well as having to concentrate on the role(s) required by their playing position. As a team sport, rugby has both individual (e.g. goal-kicking, tackling) and team play components (i.e. playing offense and defense; tactical decision-making). Rugby is a "systems" team game, with each of the 15 playing positions having a role within the team "system" and the team as a whole having a sophisticated game plan with tactics and strategies for both attack and defense—these structural aspects of the game of rugby place considerable demands on each player's *psychological skills*. In addition, rugby has no "time-outs", a short half-time period (5 minutes at club level; 10 minutes at representative level) and coaching from the sidelines is prohibited—consequently players are required to make many tactical decisions "on the move" during the game without support from coaches. The importance of player leadership/captaincy and communication skills thus becomes paramount.

> The whole game is *thought*, gone is the day of brute strength and ignorance. Rugby is a game of thought. Play the game at pace and be a thinker.
> Jack Gleeson (New Zealand All Black coach, 1977–1978)

In 1996 the sport of rugby became professional at the elite level, and rule changes since that time have led to a dramatic increase in the speed and pace of the game. As the pace of the game has increased the time available for thinking and decision-making has decreased accordingly; as a consequence the *psychological challenges* inherent in this interactive, continuous sport have been accentuated. The interactive aspects of the sport off-the-field also include coaches, players, officials and other team personnel; thus the importance of team dynamics is crucial in the sport of rugby.

> Rugby is a game you learn on your feet. Every game throws up a new circumstance, a new challenge. You must work out how best to overcome an awkward opponent, how you may "think" him out of the game because, for all its physical character, rugby is a *thinking game*. The street-smart player, the player who thinks better and longer than his opponent, will overcome and survive.
> Brian Lochore (New Zealand All Black, 1963–1971; New Zealand All Black coach, 1985–1987) commenting on his rugby philosophy.

The Importance of Mental Toughness for Rugby

Coaches often refer to mental strength and mental toughness when attempting to describe that elusive quality that distinguishes the great players from the good ones at any level of rugby. For example, players who consistently handle pressure well are often called "mentally hard" players, while those not so consistent are often told to "get hard" (Hale & Collins, 2002; Hodge & McKenzie, 1999). So what does "mental toughness" mean and what can each player do to develop this quality?

> Toughness to me isn't an aggressive, over-the-top attitude . . . Some people are physically tough, but they might not be emotionally or mentally tough. Some people have it all, but others are mentally babies. They can go and smash someone, but if they get smashed, they back down. I think toughness is really a mindset where you react in game situation without even having to think about it, question it . . . If you're not prepared to believe in yourself and have a go, you may as well pack your bags and go home.
> Zinzan Brooke (New Zealand All Black, 1987–1997)

Reproduced by permission of Chris Sullivan www.seenindunedin.co.nz

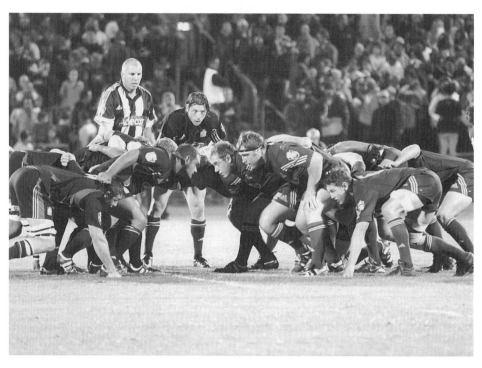

Reproduced by permission of Chris Sullivan www.seenindunedin.co.nz

Typically rugby players and coaches focus on the "horsepower" aspect of rugby performance and thus train hard to improve their fitness, speed and strength to go alongside their rugby skills such as passing and kicking. However, players often neglect the "willpower" aspect of rugby performance; that is, their psych skills and mental toughness (Hale & Collins, 2002; Hodge & McKenzie, 1999).

Rugby performance = Horsepower + Willpower

Some coaches use this basic formula to describe the fundamental aspects of rugby perfor- mance; however, just increasing the training focus on the willpower aspect of this formula will *not* turn a draughthorse player into a thoroughbred—in the first place the player must have the necessary horsepower for that playing position! However, if a player has the neces- sary horsepower, then psych skills will help them to *consistently* perform to the best of their ability; whether that be at the thoroughbred or draughthorse level (Hodge & McKenzie, 1999)! Having mental toughness and willpower is a *skill*; it can be trained and enhanced like the horsepower and technical skill aspects of performance (Hardy, Jones & Gould, 1996).

Hodge and McKenzie (1999) defined mental toughness in terms of achieving high skill level in each of eight psych skills; these are the eight Cs of Commitment, Confidence, Controlling activation, Coping with pressure, Concentration, Team Cohesion, Captaincy, and Communication. These eight Cs of peak performance can be trained to help each player and the team gain what sport psychology consultants often refer to as the "ideal performance state".

Why Work on "Mental Toughness"?

- *Possession* To gain and retain possession of the ball during the game each player needs to have psych skills such as commitment and concentration in order to execute the technical ball-winning skills. Players also need psych skills to make tactical decisions about how to win possession (e.g. lineout throw selection, ruck vs. maul); as well as needing psych skills to make smart tactical decisions about what to do with hard won possession (e.g. run, pass or kick).
- *Position* Each player requires psych skills for smart decision-making in order to gain a tactical advantage and establish field position. Each player also needs psych skills to execute proper body-positioning; and to be disciplined to stick with the jobs/role of their playing position within the team (e.g. flanker, center).
- *Pace* The pace of rugby has increased considerably since the advent of professionalism in 1996 and subsequent law changes in 1996–1997. Consequently, the time available for thinking and decision-making has sharply decreased (Maynard & Howe, 1989; McKenzie, Hodge & Sleivert, 2000). Thus, well-learned psych skills are a must to maintain concentration, cope with pressure and make smart decisions in today's fast-paced rugby.
- *Physical fitness* Rugby is a game typically played at a very fast pace for the full 80 minutes, and the tackles and hits require hard physical conditioning (McKenzie et al., 2000). The physicality of the game increases as players advance to the elite level and this increased demand for fitness, speed and strength highlights the need for the psych skills such as training motivation and commitment.
- *Physical skills* Over recent years rugby has become an interesting paradox of very *specialized* skills for each playing position (e.g. center, lock, wing), as well as the requirement of every player having a set of *all round, multi-skills* for catching, passing, tackling, mauling, and running skills (from "prop" all the way through to "fullback"). Psych skills such as commitment, self-confidence and concentration are required for each player to develop their set of multi-skills.
- *Pressure* At the elite level, rugby creates mental pressure (stress and anxiety) via relentless attack from the opposition and the tactical decision-making required. In combination these stressors make the game a pressure-filled, potentially stressful experience (Jones & Swain, 1992; Lane, Rodger & Karageorghis, 1997). Players must be able to apply pressure to their opponents, but also mentally absorb pressure from the opposition (Hale & Collins, 2002).

Individualized Psych Skills Training

While rugby is an interactive team sport, psych skills training (PST) programs must be separately designed for each *individual* player: "One size does not fit all!" In order to individualize psych skills training, the sport psychology consultant must first identify the mental strengths and weaknesses of each player (i.e. psych skill needs). We have found good success employing a version of performance profiling as a useful means to complete a psych skills assessment (Butler & Hardy, 1992). Typically performance profiling is used in conjunction with the following approach: (1) interview/discussion with the player and their coach, (2) match or video observation by the player, their coach and the sport psychology consultant, and (3) a peak performance profile (filled out by the player and, if possible, their coach). Once the player has completed some form of psych skills assessment, the sport psychology consultant will then need to identify the player's key psych skill strengths and weaknesses—we recommend that these skills be categorized into three types of psych skills. These categories are important for the planning of a structured PST program (see Hodge, 2004a; Vealey, 1988, 1994 for detail). The three categories are: (1) foundation skills (e.g. motivation, self-confidence), (2) performance skills (e.g. pre-game activation/psych-up), and (3) facilitative skills (e.g. team cohesion, communication).

Once the sport psychology consultant has identified each player's psych skill needs and categorized them, they will then be in a position to select psych methods to practice/train for enhancing specific psych skills—the sport psychology consultant needs to match methods with skills. Methods are the "means", not the "end". For instance, to work on the psych skill need of pre-game activation/psych-up, a sport psychology consultant might choose to use the psych methods of mental preparation, imagery, centering and self-talk. It is vital that the sport psychology consultant individualizes psych skills training so that each player practises the most appropriate psych skills and methods required for them to reach their personal ideal performance state.

Ideal Performance State in Rugby

The *ideal performance state* is that mood, feeling or state in which you feel totally focused, both mentally and physically, on your rugby performance and are confident that you will perform to your best; like being on automatic pilot (Hodge, 2004a). The ideal performance state is analogous to "flow" (Jackson & Csikszentmihalyi, 1999). Unfortunately the ideal performance state usually proves to be quite an elusive state for most rugby players—it doesn't happen often enough!

> We played ourselves to exhaustion. The backs ran and ran . . . and ran again. The endless movement as well as the physical contest drained the forwards. The boys who had not played came yahooing down from the grandstand to celebrate another win and were met with a torrent of silence. Heads were between knees or flung back with closed eyes against concrete walls; bodies draped on bodies. Nothing was said for 20 minutes. That's the most peaceful feeling you can ever have in your life—to prepare mentally and physically for a test, to take preparation onto the field, to score tries, to create the positions from which tries are scored, to see a new plan unfold and bewilder the opposition, to win thousands of miles from home in front of a marvellously partisan crowd. And, at the end of it, to be hopelessly, gloriously exhausted. That is perfect peace. That is utter fulfilment. That is why we play rugby. That is why we become hooked on test rugby.
> Brian Lochore (New Zealand All Black, 1963–1971; New Zealand All Black coach, 1985–1987) commenting on the ideal performance state in rugby reached by the 1967 All Blacks vs. France

In a case study of the ideal performance state and peak performance in rugby, New Zealand All Black No. 8 Arran Pene (All Black, 1992–1995; New Zealand Rugby Player of the Year, 1993) identified a number of psychological characteristics that were present before and during his *best* and *worst* performances (Dugdale, 1996). Pene indicated that before his all-time best game he was in an ideal performance state that included a feeling of complete confidence, a peak level of activation and a total focus on the upcoming performance (Dugdale, 1996). During this game he reported a feeling of being totally focused on and immersed in the tasks-at-hand and he also experienced feelings of complete confidence

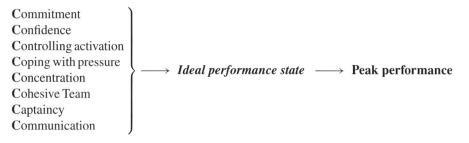

Commitment
Confidence
Controlling activation
Coping with pressure $\longrightarrow$ *Ideal performance state* $\longrightarrow$ **Peak performance**
Concentration
Cohesive Team
Captaincy
Communication

Figure 9.1   Eight Cs of peak performance and the ideal performance state

and control. On the other hand, before and during his worst game Pene commented that he deviated from his normal mental preparation, was not totally focused on his tasks, and experienced a number of negative thoughts and feelings, especially a lack of confidence. During this match he tended to either dwell on past events (e.g. an injury he was carrying) or spend time thinking about future ones, rather than keeping a right now, in-the-present concentration focus (Dugdale, 1996). The psych skill of "focused attention" or peak concentration appeared to be the key aspect of peak performance for Arran Pene. Indeed, Pene reported that the systematic use of psych skills and methods, such as imagery and goal-setting, had played a significant role in helping him achieve his all-time best performance. He also indicated that his worst game was partially a result of him not being able to stick to his PST program. In that game he was carrying an injury and that led him to be preoccupied with a number of distracting thoughts and negative feelings about his confidence to perform on the day (Dugdale, 1996).

Peak performance and the ideal performance state are not about playing perfect rugby; they are about each player playing their best rugby on a consistent basis (Williams & Krane, 2001). In order for a player to achieve their ideal performance state they need to focus on "how to win, not winning itself" (Hodge & Petlichkoff, 2000; Orlick & Partington, 1988). We suggest that the best way to adopt this "how to win" focus is to work on the eight Cs of peak performance (Figure 9.1).

Psychological Skills Training (PST) for Rugby

Psychological skills training (PST) focuses on each rugby player learning practical psych skills and methods so that they can develop their thinking skills (i.e. mental toughness) to the same high level as their physical abilities (Hale & Collins, 2002; Hodge & McKenzie, 1999). Indeed, the *key* difference between a good performance and a poor performance may be the player's psych skill level rather than their physical skill level (Hardy et al., 1996). This does not mean that psych skills are more important than physical, tactical or technical skills. They are all important. Psych skills are just one aspect of performance and, like physical skills, and technical skills, they need to be learnt correctly, fine-tuned by the player and coach, and then *practised* regularly. PST is an integral part of smart training for rugby. To quote an old coaching saying, we are trying to put an old head on young shoulders. PST is designed to ensure that the old head is a "smart" one!

> Experience is something you usually don't get until just after you need it.
>   Anon.

Psychological Skills and Psychological Methods for Rugby

PST skills In the context of PST, a skill is a competency, capability or ability level (e.g. peak concentration). PST skills are developed through the use of a number of PST methods (e.g. goal-setting, self-talk). The key PST skills can be categorized as follows (see Hodge, 2004a; Vealey, 1988, 1994 for detail):

- Foundation skills
  - Motivation
  - Commitment
  - Self-confidence.
- Performance skills
  - Peak physical activation
  - Peak mental activation
  - Peak concentration
  - Coping with pressure.
- Facilitative skills
  - Team cohesion (teamwork, team spirit)
  - Interpersonal skills (e.g. captaincy, communication, media skills)
  - Lifestyle management (e.g. planning for "retirement").

PST methods A method is a technique that is used to help a player develop a particular skill; just like a physical drill is used to develop a particular physical skill (see Hodge, 2004a; Vealey, 1988, 1994). A method in this sense means a procedure, technique or drill (e.g. imagery, centering).

> e.g.   Physical skill = passing, running in "traffic"
>   Physical drill = four corners passing grid

- Foundation methods
  - Physical practice
  - Education (i.e. physical and psych skill requirements)
  - Peak performance profile.
- Specific psych methods
  - Goal-setting
  - Mental preparation (pre-game)
  - Imagery (visualization)
  - Relaxation (centering)
  - Self-talk (thought control)
  - CARS = Critical action response strategies

PST skill match with PST methods The sportpysch consultant needs to select particular psych methods for players to practice/train in order to enhance that player's specific psych skill needs (Hodge, 2004a; Vealey, 1994). Methods are the means, not the end; so PST methods should be chosen as the best means for developing each player's required

PST skills (i.e. the "end"). For example, for the skill need of *activation control* a player might need to use a number of psych methods in combination or separately:

Psych skill need = Pre-game activation/psych-up

Psych methods = Mental preparation, imagery, centering (short-hand relaxation), self-talk . . .

For instance, in the following quote Grant Fox (New Zealand All Black goalkicker, 1984–1993) outlines how he used a combination of three psych methods (i.e. imagery, centering, self-talk) to maintain his concentration skills for goalkicking (a PST skill):

> Relaxation is the mental-physical partnership. How you achieve it is up to you. I use a technique called mental rehearsal [*imagery*]. I have in my mind a picture of the ball going through the posts. The deep breathing, the shaking of the hands, are to rid the body of tension so that all is crystal-clear and unperturbed in the mind [*centering*]—the picture is in focus. I command myself, "Head down. Follow through" [*self-talk*].
>
> Grant Fox (New Zealand All Black goalkicker, 1984–1993: average 15+ points in test matches)

To be able effectively to develop a PST program for each player it is vital that each player's existing PST *skill* levels be assessed, then the skill weaknesses can be attacked via a well-planned program of specific PST *methods*. Too often players and coaches focus totally on the teaching and learning of particular methods (e.g. imagery) and lose sight of the specific PST skill that the method is designed to improve (e.g. peak concentration). It is easy to be seduced by the method as the end itself, rather than as a means to an end (i.e. PST skill development). The methods chosen must have a planned purpose or the desired *skill* development is unlikely to occur (Hardy et al., 1996).

It is important that each player approaches their PST program with the same commitment to planning as they would put into physical training. This requires a simple periodization plan that takes into account all periods of the season (see Hodge, Sleivert & McKenzie, 1996, for details on periodized training). The PST skills and methods must be integrated into their physical training in order to simulate their use during games.

Psych Skills Assessment for Rugby

Assessments

The sport of rugby itself is the first area of assessment required for effective planning of a PST program. Various aspects of each player's playing position should be considered in assessing their rugby requirements—aspects such as physical intensity, type of fitness required, basic physical skills, duration of basic skills, and different critical actions or moments within the game. Assessment of team aspects also need to be accounted for in designing a PST program. This assessment should take account of the coach(es), manager, administrators, leaders, captains and the size of the squad.

The assessment of each player's individual skills is the most important factor in the development of an effective personalized training program. There are a number of ways to assess each player's individual strengths, weaknesses and needs (such as coaching observation, match statistics, video analysis); however, the easiest way to complete a basic assessment of overall PST training needs is to complete a peak performance profile.

Peak performance profile: Self-assessment

The *peak performance profile* procedure is a handy way for each player to put together their own peak performance jigsaw puzzle (Butler & Hardy, 1992; Hodge, 2004a). The profile will help each player to identify the individual pieces of their own jigsaw puzzle, give them direction, and enable them to organize a PST program that puts the "pieces" together to create peak performances for themselves. The peak performance profile helps give each player *direction* by helping them identify the various physical, technical, tactical and psychological requirements for achieving peak performance in rugby.

- *Phase 1. Identifying themes/qualities* Each player is instructed to decide on the important themes, qualities or performance skills that they require to perform well. They should discuss this with their coach or a sport psychology consultant and/or teammates. Qualities or skills can typically be categorized as technical, tactical, physical or psychological. Technical qualities refers to the specific skills required for each playing position (such as passing and tackling, or scrummaging and lineouts). Tactical qualities are the strategies, tactics and game plans used in each playing position. Physical qualities are the endurance, strength, power, speed and flexibility, and nutritional and medical requirements of each playing position; while psychological qualities refers to the mental requirements of each playing position (such as motivation, self-confidence and concentration). These qualities or skills collectively represent the jigsaw pieces of a peak performance in rugby (Hodge, 2004a; Hodge & McKenzie, 1999).

  Each player will have a slightly different set of performance skills/qualities, and a slightly different combination of psychological, technical, tactical and physical skills. Each player must decide for themself how important each skill area or performance quality is to their peak performance jigsaw picture.

  In the first instance, players should use a Peak Performance Skill Worksheet to write out an exhaustive list of all the performance skills/qualities they can identify (see an example completed worksheet, Figure 9.2 on page 193). When the player has finished the Peak Performance Skill Worksheet they then select the top three or four skills in each category of performance (e.g. pick out the top three technical skills/qualities) and transfer these to a Peak Performance Profile form 194 (see an example completed profile in Figure 9.3 on page 194).

- *Phase 2. Assessment of the skills/qualities/themes* The player rates themself on each of the skills/qualities they have identified, using the following instructions:

  Current (right now) performance Using a scale of 0 to 10 (with 0 = poor, 5 = average and 10 = excellent) rate yourself on each of the skills/qualities according to how you currently feel (i.e. right now). You may also want your coach to rate you on these same skills/qualities of peak performance. Your coach's assessment may or may not agree with yours—this can become a basis for greater discussion and understanding between you and your coach.

Connor's example: "No. 8/Flanker"

Peak Performance Skills: Worksheet

Write an exhaustive list of all the performance skills/themes/qualities/characteristics of your playing position.

Technical	Tactical	Physical	Psychological
Passing in "general" play	"Reading" running lines on defence	Aerobic/endurance fitness	Pre-game psych-up—psych-up without psyching-out (activation levels)
Passing from base of scrum (e.g. "8 to 9")	"Reading" running lines on attack	Anaerobic fitness—able to recover *during* the game	
Backrow moves; passing	"Reading" opposition attacking moves		Coping with pressure during the game
"8-ups" from scrum		Speed over 10 to 15 metres	
Backrow moves; body position on the drive	"Reading" holes in opposition defensive pattern	Speed to breakdown or in support	Motivation for skill training
Ball retention in the tackle	Options—lineout jump selection	Upper body strength	Motivation for fitness work
Body position at 2nd phase	Options—choosing the "right time" for a backrow move	Leg strength and lineout jump height	Confidence for each game
Lineout jumping		Flexibility	Commitment to my goals and objectives
Supporting "5" jumper at lineout	Options—choosing correct backrow moves	Recovery from injuries	Team cohesion—follow game plan
Driving on "2" jumper at lineout	Options—"runner" off 2nd phase		Concentration for 80 minutes
Tackling around scrums	Options—"pick and go" off 2nd phase		Ability to shift concentration—focus on the right info at the right time
Tackling around rucks/mauls			
Tackling: cover "D"			

Figure 9.2 Completed peak performance worksheet

Best ever performance Another assessment that you (and your coach) should complete is to rate your best ever performance in relation to these skills/qualities. Most players can recall their best ever performance and, although that performance may not have been ideal, it represents your best so far. Completing a best ever rating profile helps you decide which skills/qualities require and deserve the most work to improve your ability to consistently reach peak performance.

Connor's profile: "No. 8/Flanker"

Peak Performance Profile

List and rate the performance skills/themes/qualities/characteristics of your *best* or *peak* rugby performance. Rate *yourself* on each of the skills/themes/qualities using the following scale:

0	1	2	3	4	5	6	7	8	9	10

Current + Best:	Poor	Average	Excellent
Improvement:	Huge improvement		No improvement needed
Stable:	Unstable, needs control		Very stable, maintain

	Current	*Best*	*Improvement*	*Stability*
Technical				
Body position at breakdown	7	8	5	7
"8-Up" from scrum	8	9	8	9
Tackling around rucks/mauls	6	7	5	7
Tactical				
"Reading" running lines on attack	7	9	7	8
Lineout jump selection	6	8	6	8
Options—choosing backrow moves	4	7	2	5
Physical				
Speed over 10 to 15 metres	8	9	9	8
Upper body strength	10	10	10	10
Aerobic fitness/endurance	9	10	8	8
Leg strength and lineout leaping	8	9	7	8
Psychological				
Pre-game psych-up (activation)	5	9	3	2
Commitment	2	8	2	5
Team cohesion	5	9	5	7
Concentration	4	8	3	5
Confidence	9	9	9	10

Figure 9.3 Completed peak performance profile

Improvement You should also complete ratings on the skills/qualities that need improvement, and determine how much improvement is needed (i.e. 0 = huge improvement needed, 5 = moderate improvement, and 10 = no improvement possible). These ratings are a bit deceptive as the scoring is the opposite of the others; that is, lower scores (e.g. 2 or 3) mean that the player rates themself as having considerable room for improvement, while high scores like 8 or 9 mean virtually no room for improvement.

Stability/consistency The final rating is of the stability or consistency of your performance skills/qualities (e.g. 0 = very unstable, needs control, 5 = moderate stability, and 10 = very stable, maintain). Skills/qualities that are unstable or inconsistent will likely be the most important qualities to improve because their instability works against your ability to consistently produce peak performance. For example, as a hooker you may rate yourself as *currently* having good technical skills for lineout throwing (rating = 8), and in your *best ever* performance you rated yourself highly (rating = 9), but unfortunately your lineout throwing is inconsistent from game to game and sometimes between lineouts in the same game (rating = 4). At this stage your skill at lineout throwing is inconsistent and unstable, possibly due to low levels of psychological skills such as concentration and coping with pressure.

Once each player has identified their PST needs, the sport psychology consultant can begin to design each individual PST program. The sport psychology consultant must choose the appropriate PST methods to develop or improve the psychological skills identified in each player's peak performance profile.

A sample peak performance profile for one player, Connor ('No. 8/Flanker') is provided as an example of this psychological needs assessment process (Figure 9.3). As you can see from the psychological skills section of Connor's profile (see page 194), at the start of this season he needed to commit himself fully to his rugby and his training, take control of his own pre-game psych-up, sharpen up his concentration, and be a more cohesive team player by improving his tactical skills (he had to follow the team's game plan).

Connor was able to follow a Psychological skills training program that allowed him to improve his skill weaknesses. The first step that Connor took was to sort his skill needs into different types of training; he labelled his training as follows: fitness/strength training, technical skills practise and psychological skills training. Among his different skill needs he decided that it was his psychological skills that were most in need of improvement. So his next step was to categorize his psychological skill needs into foundation, performance and facilitative needs; these were (1) commitment (foundation skill), (2) pre-game psych-up = peak activation (performance skill), (3) concentration (performance skill), and (4) team cohesion (facilitative skill). Then, based on this skill categorization, he concluded that he first needed to identify some psychological methods that would help him improve his foundation skill need for greater commitment—he chose to use the methods of goal-setting and self-talk.

Once Connor saw some gains in commitment he was in a position to work on some PST methods to enhance his performance skills of pre-game psych-up and concentration—he chose to combine the use of mental preparation, imagery and self-talk to work on both these two performance skills together. Finally, he decided to use team goal-setting, imagery and self-talk to help him stick with the team's game plan and be a more cohesive team player (i.e. the facilitative skill).

Planning Your PST Program for Mental Toughness in Rugby

PST Program for Each Individual

The key aspect of any effective PST program is that it needs to be personally designed and individually tailored to each individual player's PST skill needs. This personalized program should take into account the need for foundation skills, performance skills and facilitative skills—see the examples above for "Connor".

PST Program for the Team (*Squad*)

The team will have some general or common needs such as cohesion (teamwork, team spirit), awareness of teammate needs, leadership and communication skills. The sport psychology consultant should take these into account before they finalize the plans for each player's PST program (see next section on Team-building).

TEAM-BUILDING INTERVENTIONS FOR RUGBY

A Model of Team Performance

A useful framework for explaining team performance in rugby is expressed in the following equation (Steiner, 1972).

$$\text{Actual performance} = \text{Potential performance}-\text{Losses due to faulty process}$$

Actual performance (or productivity) is what the team actually does (Steiner, 1972). Potential performance is the team's best possible performance given its resources, which are relevant to the task and the demands of that task. Process is everything that the team does while transforming its resources into a performance (Hodge, 2004b).In rugby, process is basically each player's individual skill development combined with teamwork skills developed by the coach, including team tactics and strategies.

Faulty process is the ineffective use of available resources to meet task demands, and can result from two types of loss; that is, coordination losses and motivation losses (Steiner, 1972). Coordination losses include poor timing, teamwork or strategy. Motivation losses occur when all or some members of the team lack effort and desire (Steiner, 1972).

While this model is useful as a general description of team performance, it is the role of team leaders, coaches and the sport psychology consultant to decrease faulty process by developing and practising organizational strategies that reduce coordination losses (i.e. teamwork) and maintain high motivation levels (i.e. team motivation). As you are probably aware, this is nowhere near as easy to achieve as it sounds!

In this section we outline five interventions that we have found to be especially useful with rugby teams. The first three interventions focus on increasing social cohesion (i.e. team spirit) and player identifiability in order to maximize team motivation. The final two interventions focus on promoting optimal team coordination via increased task cohesion (i.e. teamwork).

Building Team Motivation in Rugby

Social Cohesion: Vision and Values

> The culture is bloody important. It's identifying the culture and identifying the values.
> We call them Red and Black values and it's what this team is all about. I think people
> who come into this team really buy into it.
>   Wayne Smith (Coach, Canterbury Crusaders; Super 12 Champions, 1998–2000)

Successful teams have players who work toward common goals (Carron & Hausenblas, 1998; Cartwright & Zander, 1968). The culture of the team will dictate these goals and whether or not they are accepted by all members. Therefore, the team vision and values must be carefully moulded. Many methods can be used; however, any session designed to establish a team's vision and values should include (1) the opportunity for all members of the group to contribute to the process and (2) concrete examples and strategies that ensure the vision and values will manifest themselves in the day-to-day operations of the team. We have developed a number of workshops/exercises that can be used to shape a team's vision and values. An example of one of these workshops/exercises is described below.

Ken Hodge served as the sport psychology consultant for the 2004 New Zealand Colts rugby team during their build-up to the 2004 Under-21s Rugby World Cup in Scotland. Ken used a number of exercises to help the team to define its vision and values.

The first exercise was termed the team legacy speech. The team was divided into groups of five or six players. Each group was pre-selected so that senior players were mixed with newcomers and forwards with backs. Each group was then required to write a "team legacy speech". The players were told that this speech should mimic the one they planned to give at the end of the upcoming tournament. After "writing" and "practice" periods, one member of each group delivered the two-minute speech to the whole team. Each speech included acknowledgement of (only) four important people and focused on "how and why" the team accomplished its ultimate goal of winning the World Cup. The purpose of this exercise was to encourage the group to define success for themselves (vision) and examine the ways in which they could ensure success (values).

The team then participated in an exercise called "team destruction". New groups were formed and each was given the following instructions:

- Imagine you are part of the management team for our main opponents—your mission is to send a saboteur or spy into this rugby team for the season in order to sabotage and destroy our season.
- What would your instructions be? What would you get the spy to sabotage?
- What would you get the spy to do in order to destroy this team and stop us achieving our goal(s)?

The sabotage plans of each group were pooled together and the entire team decided on the most destructive schemes (some were quite innovative and many were humorous!). Each group was then encouraged to devise ways to "spy-proof" the team against the best efforts of the spy/saboteur.

- What plans can be put into place to prevent the spy/saboteur from being successful or cope with problems if they arise?

The final exercise was termed "build the perfect teammate". New groups were formed and instructed to design the "perfect" teammate for the 2004 NZ Colts Rugby Team. Players were asked brainstorm about the behaviors /actions /values that they want this teammate to demonstrate. These "actions/values" were outlined for each of the following team situations:

1. At fitness / individual skill training sessions.
2. At team training sessions.
3. Before the game.
4. During the game.
5. After the game (social activities).
6. When we are "off-duty" as a team (away from rugby).
7. Away from the "team".

The "team legacy speeches", "team destruction" and "perfect teammate" exercises resulted in a variety of ideas concerning the team's vision and values. Overnight, Ken met with the management team to summarize the players' responses on the above exercises, and to write a draft vision and values statement for the team to consider. The next day the team discussed the draft vision and values statement as one large group—suggested revisions were debated and agreed upon. The purpose of this exercise was not only to establish the team's vision and values, but to also encourage the players to identify concrete situations in which the team's values were likely to be most important.

The team's vision was defined as the "why" of the team and questions such as "Why are we together?" and "What sort of team do we want to be?" were used as prompts. The team's values were defined as "how we do things around here" and the players were encouraged to think of their team values as a set of philosophies that could be used to help guide their decision-making.

The draft values statement contained a list of 26 values so the players were then asked to prioritize this extensive list by identifying only four core values as the most important. After some time, a list of the four core values emerged. Groups were formed again and the players were asked to describe concrete examples of behaviors that exemplified each of the four core values (i.e. what does each value actually mean in behavioral terms? what behavior[s] does each value represent?). The seven broad categories from the "perfect teammate" exercise described above were used as cues for identifying potential behavioral examples.

The final version of the team's vision & values statement was signed by each player and a copy was then supplied as part of each player's playbook. In addition these values were referred to at numerous times throughout the tournament by the coaches and management team. Using the three idea-generating exercises and the more formalized vision and values session, the 2004 New Zealand Colts established the foundation for a team with clear goals and strategies to accomplish these goals. The team went on to win the 2004 Rugby World Cup by beating Ireland 47–19 in the championship final.

Social Cohesion in Rugby: Shared Positive Experiences

Brawley (1990) suggested that shared team experiences serve to maintain or develop team cohesion. On-field successes or failures are powerful shared experiences; however, off-field activities can also serve as shared experiences that bind a team together. Unlike actual rugby games, these activities can be structured so that a positive shared experience is ensured.

Any number of activities are possible; however the chosen activities should be enjoyable and require interaction between group members. Bringing players together away from their normal surroundings (i.e. a team camp) can often be an effective method of promoting interaction and cooperation. However, building social cohesion is a not a one-off event and shared experiences should be planned throughout the season (Bloom, Stevens & Wickwire, 2003; Carron & Dennis, 2001). In terms of which activities work well, we have found that rugby players often enjoy physically challenging, outdoor activities such as river rafting and rock climbing. However, as long as the activity is enjoyable and requires interaction among team members, social cohesion is likely to result. Involving senior players in the process of selecting the team activities will also increase the likelihood that the players will look forward to the activity and therefore gain the most benefits in terms of social cohesion (Hodge, 2004b).

Individual Accountability: Performance Tracking

There is an aspect of team dynamics commonly referred to as "social loafing" (Hardy, 1990; Hodge, 2004b). Social loafing means that the average individual performance decreases with increases in team size. Although the number of coordination losses may also increase as the number of people in the team increase, social loafing is usually *not* the result of coordination losses. Coordination losses may be part of the reason, but the key psychological reason seems to be motivation losses, especially social loafing (Hardy, 1990).

Social loafing occurs when the "identifiability" of individual performances is lost in a team performance; performances decrease because of the diffusion of responsibility (Hardy & Latene, 1988; Harkins, 1987). When the identifiability of individual performances is lost in a team performance (i.e. "not my job"; "not my fault"), performances decrease because each player has less apparent responsibility for the overall performance (Harkins & Szymanski, 1987; Williams, Harkins & Latene, 1981).

> We can't just have two or three guys doing all the shit work. We've all got to take our share. It's no bloody good having guys hanging off waiting for a run.
> Todd Blackadder (New Zealand All Black, 1996–1998; Canterbury NPC captain), outlining the need for teamwork to his 1997 Canterbury forward pack; they went on to win the New Zealand NPC first Division in 1997

If players believe that their own performance within the team can be identified (e.g. individual statistics, tackle counts, video analysis), and that they will be held accountable for their contribution, then social loafing typically does not occur (Latene, Williams & Harkins, 1979). Therefore players need to have their individual performances monitored and they need to be made accountable for their personal contribution to the team performance.

Ensuring Team Coordination through Task Cohesion: Non-rugby Activities

Rugby is a technical game that requires coordination of movement without the benefit of planning during long stoppages in play. As mentioned previously, coaching from the sidelines is prohibited, therefore players must learn to think for themselves on the field and to make decisions for the team. While the following activities will not necessarily help players become better leaders or decision-makers, we have found that leaders and decision-makers often emerge as these tasks are completed. We therefore recommend that non-rugby activities that require interaction, cooperation and problem-solving (thinking) are a great way to begin the process of building task cohesion in a team.

Many tasks could be used but all should include:

1. Learning a set of instructions.
2. Planning.
3. Execution of a plan.
4. Review and debrief.
5. Re-execution.

We have found an activity called "tower building" to be particularly effective. Small groups (five or six) are formed and participants are given a simple set of instructions—"Build the tallest free-standing structure/tower using the materials provided." Materials for each group include 50 paper clips, one roll of adhesive tape, and approximately 250 sheets of plain copy paper.

1. Each group is given two minutes to plan how they will build their tower. During this planning period participants are *not* permitted to touch any of the materials.
2. Each group then has ten minutes to build a prototype tower—this tower is only a trial run.
3. Following the trial run each group is allowed another two-minute de-brief and planning period to plan their next tower (scouting the designs and methods employed by other groups is allowed during this period).
4. Each group then has ten minutes to build their final tower.

Groups are usually able to construct a tower two to three metres high. However, some groups have built structures well over five metres! At the end of the session, the entire team gathers to discuss the lessons they can learn from the activity. The sport psychology consultant facilitates this discussion and encourages players to consider how the skills they used building towers may transfer to problem-solving on the rugby training and playing fields. The lessons learned in this process are typically the need for: (a) planning and communication; (b) thinking laterally/being innovative; (c) division of labor, delegation of tasks, (d) accurate evaluation and de-brief; and (e) scouting of opposition ideas/strengths/weaknesses.

Ensuring Team Coordination through Task Cohesion: Team Profiling

Team performance profiling → Goal-setting → Goal-tracking

A second and more rugby-specific way to develop task cohesion is through the use of team performance profiling and team goal-setting. This method is based on the individual peak performance profiles described earlier but has been adapted for use with teams. The overall goal of this exercise is to focus the team's attention on key areas that will enhance overall team performance. We have used this exercise with a number of teams, and players and coaches have been very enthusiastic about the results. Below is a description of a team profile we implemented with a premier club rugby team in New Zealand.

We began by gathering the players together at a regularly scheduled pre-season practice. However, rather than heading out for a physical session we assembled in a meeting room with a large white board. We explained to the players that rather than setting goals concerning number of wins or championships we believed setting goals relating to their actual performance on the field would be a more productive approach. We then asked the players and coaches to brainstorm all the team skills, plays or moves they believed were necessary for success in rugby. We advised the players and coaches that all skills should be specific and measurable. A senior player wrote all these ideas on the white board. Once we had an exhaustive list, players and coaches voiced their opinions concerning which skills they believed would have the most impact on team success. After some debate, a list of six key skills emerged:

1. Percentage of successful two-handed lineout takes.
2. Percentage of stable scrums on our own ball.
3. Percentage of time breaking the advantage line from first phase back moves.
4. Percentage of tackles made.
5. Percentage of successful rucks "cleaned out" three metres past the ball.
6. Percentage of possessions in which we defended successfully for three phases or forced a turnover.

Over the next three games, the manager and injured players tracked each of these statistics, and prior to a training session summary statistics were presented to the players and coaches. As a group, the team decided on three skills that were most important to their performance on the field ("percentage stable scrums", "percentage backs breaking the advantage line", and "percentage tackles made").

With help from the sport psychology consultant, the team then set goals for the next three games for each of these three key skills. Some players suggested that setting any goal of less than 100 per cent success was "defeatist", but the sport psychology consultant used the statistics from the previous three games to show that 100 per cent success was not realistic in the short term. Realistic goals for the next three games were set and coaches planned practice drills that focused on these three skills. After each game, performance on the three critical skills was evaluated and new ideas were put forth about how to improve performance. At the end of the three initial games new goals were set. This process continued for the remainder of the season and players and coaches both felt the use of the team performance profiling, goal-setting and goal-tracking allowed them to focus their attention on key skills that led to better overall performance.

PSYCHOLOGICAL SKILLS TRAINING (PST) FOR INDIVIDUAL AND TEAM TRAINING

Train the way you want to play: with intensity and commitment.

Individual Training for Rugby

Psychological skills are only partially responsible for players achieving peak performance on the field. Psychological skills must be learned, practised and used *in conjunction* with all the other skills that a player needs (Hodge & McKenzie, 1999). Many top players have talked about psychological skills giving them an advantage over their opponents, or as a reason why they have reached the top in rugby. While this may be true, they have been able to gain this advantage only because the psychological skills have been developed *in addition* to the many hours of hard work that they have spent developing their physical and technical skills. Consider the following example:

> Jason was a loose forward who was one of several players competing for a regular place in a top provincial team. Jason went to see a sport psychology consultant because he felt that his confidence was shaky, that he was losing concentration and therefore making mistakes during games. This obviously meant that his on-field anxiety levels were more than they should have been. Consequently, he spent so much energy on the field worrying about losing concentration and making mistakes that he became tired very quickly and felt that he couldn't last the whole game. He began to "coast" through the first half of every game because he felt the need to "save himself" for the last part of the game so that he was better able to contribute to the team effort during this crucial phase of the game. Jason was expecting the sport psychology consultant to perhaps help him with some visualization or self-talk strategies to combat his problem, but was surprised when the first question that the sport psychology consultant asked him was "How fit are you?" Jason admitted that he had not been up to scratch in terms of the fitness standards that had been set for the loose forwards. The consultant then asked him to imagine that he was as fit, as fast, as powerful and as strong as he could possibly be when he went out onto the field to start a game. How would that affect his confidence about lasting the 80 minutes? Would he be anxious about lasting for the whole game? If he wasn't as tired during the game, would he be able to maintain his concentration? If he could maintain his concentration levels, would he make as many mistakes as he had been? If he wasn't making as many mistakes and performing better, what sort of effect would that have on his confidence, concentration and anxiety levels? Jason was forced to admit that although his problem had a psychological effect, it was essentially a problem with his physical fitness, and so Jason and the consultant worked out a goal-setting program that focused on improving his physical fitness (aerobic fitness, strength and power) during the off-season. Using the prescribed fitness standards for loose forwards as the initial goal, they established Jason's current fitness levels, and set goals to work on improving Jason's fitness. After reaching these standards, Jason reset his goals and further developed his fitness. During the following season he reported that his confidence and concentration levels had improved, and that he was no longer as anxious as he had been during the previous season. Jason subsequently established himself as a regular member of the provincial squad.

Jason's case was a good example of how psychological skills can be developed in conjunction with other types of skills. In Jason's case it was in conjunction with physical fitness, but the development of all the different types of skills can occur in this way. This doesn't mean that, by developing physical or technical skills alone, a player will automatically develop all of the psychological skills that they need to be the best they can be, but there is no doubt that improvements in one skill area can have a flow-on effect to other skill areas. It is not a difficult conceptual leap for a player to understand that improving their physical fitness can improve their confidence and concentration levels, and that this can help to improve their ability to perform the technical skills of rugby. For example, if a "No 8" knows that he has worked hard on his strength and power over the off-season, he will be more confident about being able to make the advantage line from the base of the scrum if he decides to run from this position. In addition, he will be more likely to execute the play better from a technical perspective if he has the strength to turn in the tackle, or to stay on his feet and present the ball to his supporting flanker. Furthermore, if all players possess greater strength, power and aerobic fitness, as well as technical ability, then the tactical options for their team become greater because each player will be able to contribute in a greater number of ways. Consequently, the coach will have the luxury of being able to develop tight or expansive game plans to suit the conditions or the opposition, rather than sticking to a particular style because the team is not physically equipped to play an alternative! It will also make it more difficult for other teams to work out how to counter these game plans.

> Fitness comes first, and that means hard work. Do the basics in the off-season, hitting the roads, building up a good aerobic base . . . Remember, without fitness you're nowhere— you won't be in place to make the tackle if you have no aerobic base! . . . Games are so fast, if you have to think, you're too late. Always believe the ball is available, and there's a chance that you'll steal it. This wasn't natural to me, I've worked hard learning it.
>
> Josh Kronfeld (All Black, 1995–2000) describing
> some of the basic requirements of a loose forward

PST for Rugby Training

Although there is no substitute for hard work and effort during off-season physical and technical training, PST training can help to maximize the benefits of this training. For example, setting goals and developing the strategies to achieve these goals can maintain and/or improve a player's motivation and commitment to physical and technical training, and many PST methods such as imagery, relaxation, self-talk and mental preparation strategies can improve the quality of a player's training needs (Hale & Collins, 2002; Hodge & McKenzie, 1999). For example, the various types of physical training in rugby lend themselves well to goal-setting because their performance is easily measured (e.g. runs can be timed, distances can be measured and amounts of weight can be calculated). In addition, the performance of these skills in training can be maximized using PST methods. Players can use imagery or relaxation methods to attain the optimal activation level for lifting heavy weights, and self-talk strategies can be used during hard training sessions to maintain effort, concentration and proper technique while executing the various skills needs (Hale & Collins, 2002; Hodge & McKenzie, 1999).

If players have worked on their physical and technical skills during the off-season, and used a number of PST methods to help them develop these skills to the fullest, then they should begin the season with some confidence. Not only will they be in the best possible physical shape, they will have practised using a number of PST methods that they will now be able to use, refine and further develop during practices and games.

Team Training

Once off-season and pre-season training has been completed, selection trials are over and the team has been selected, players must adjust to a new schedule of team training. There will be certain physical skills and fitness levels that must continue to be developed, or at least maintained, but team practices will become an important focus.

Game Simulation

The basic idea of practices is that the team rehearses what it will be doing during a game. Although it is important to develop and maintain the various rugby skills, techniques and tactics that will be used during games in an initially non-threatening and low-pressure environment at training, once the players' ability to perform these skills improves they will need to perform them in situations that are very similar to what they are likely to experience during a game (e.g. defensive pressure from "opposed" practice, little time for decision-making, making decisions when physically fatigued).

Rugby is a game that requires players to perform under *pressure*. That is, players must react swiftly to developing situations, make quick and accurate decisions, and anticipate where the next play may develop; while their opponents are "pressuring" them physically and mentally (Hodge & McKenzie, 1999). Players will not be able to perform well if the only time that they are exposed to situations that require this ability is during the game itself! Consequently, at some stage during the practices leading up to a game players should experience the pressure of having to perform under these game-like conditions. This is called "game simulation". As Robbie Deans (All Black Assistant Coach, 2001–2003) states in the following quote, the idea is to use game simulation pressure to raise performance levels and to increase mental toughness:

> The emphasis is to put the players under pressure. It's only by putting yourself under pressure that you can raise the threshold of performance. Ideally your training should be more difficult than your match. So when it comes to the game you feel that you've got more time—hopefully. The [training] sessions are not so much for building physical fitness now, that's done as individuals. A team session now is to have the training simulate game conditions as closely as possible.
>
> Robbie Deans (Canterbury NPC Coach, 1997–2004;
> New Zealand All Black Coach, 2001–2003)

Many coaches use the "team run" at the end of practice to simulate some of the pressure situations of a game, but pressure can be simulated in situations other than the team run (e.g. sub-unit training such as opposed second phase, opposed lineouts, live scrummaging). The use of PST methods can be incorporated throughout the practice session to help players *cope* with this pressure needs (Hale & Collins, 2002; Hodge & McKenzie, 1999). The higher the level of rugby that an individual plays, the greater is the pressure to perform. From a playing perspective, there is the pressure to perform not only at a higher level, but at a greater pace. This can be simulated during practices in almost any drill that players are asked to perform. For example, the grids and drills that many teams use as part of their normal warm-up routines can easily be refined to place players under pressure. The coach (or the players) can demand that the grids be performed at full pace for a certain length of time (e.g. 30 seconds), or that a specific number of passes be executed accurately within a specified time. As the players get better at performing under these conditions, they can be altered to better reflect the ability and performance level of the team. The coach or one of the management team can keep a record of the teams' ability to perform that particular grid, and this can be used as the basis for setting goals for the team at subsequent practices where that grid is used.

> The All Blacks work on [game simulation] by making trainings as much like game day as possible. Training under game intensity means when you take the paddock your decision-making should be second nature, without thinking too much.
>   Andrew Mehrtens (New Zealand All Black, 1995–2004)

Other forms of pressure can be created at the same time. For example, in addition to setting a goal for the execution of a particular grid (e.g. to perform a specific number of accurate pop passes within one minute), the coach can place further pressure on the team by setting up a competition between two groups of players (e.g. forwards versus backs) in the performance of that grid or drill, and asking each group to set their own performance goals. Usually these groups have an unrealistic idea of their ability to perform under such pressure, but their performance level is easily determined after the first attempt at the grid. The coach can then ask how they might be able to better perform that grid, and the players themselves will often work out various strategies and techniques to ensure greater accuracy, timing and performance of the grid. This may include various PST methods such as the use of cue-words (i.e. self-talk) during the performance of the grid, imagery of the correct performance of the grid just prior to performance, or refocusing strategies to be implemented if a mistake is made.

Whether the coach uses these techniques or not during practices, the onus should be on players to set their own goals for each portion of the practice, to put themselves under pressure and to implement the PST methods that they may have learned during their off-season training. For example, players should mentally prepare for each team practice session, perhaps setting some personal goals for the session, and/or deciding upon a particular PST method that they may want to incorporate into the session needs (Hodge & McKenzie, 1999). During each particular practice activity, whether it be the warm-up, individual skill work, small group or sub-unit skills, or during the team run, they should decide what it is that they want to accomplish during that activity, perhaps rehearse the image of themselves successfully executing that activity before physically performing it, and use whatever PST method that they find appropriate at that time to get themselves into the ideal mental and physical state for performing that activity. If physical and technical skills are practised at team training so that players can use them automatically during the game, psychological skills should also be practised if players are expected to be able to use them automatically during the game.

If players have already practised these PST techniques during their off-season training, they should not be difficult to perform, will take up very little time, and can perhaps mean that the time taken to successfully learn and perform any skill is decreased. For example, a new type of lineout call and type of jump can be described and discussed by the forwards before being physically practised. The jumper, the thrower, the lifters and the rest of the lineout forwards can use imagery to rehearse the successful execution of the call before being asked to put it into practice. This may only take a few seconds. Similarly, one of the backs may suggest a new attacking move from a midfield scrum. The move can be described, walked through, and then mentally rehearsed by the backs before being physically performed at greater and greater pace. The image of the move will only take a few seconds, and no time will be lost in actual physical performance of the move needs (Hodge & McKenzie, 1999).

Training Motivation for Rugby

While we can outline various strategies for incorporating psychological skills into training, the basic motivation to train in and of itself also needs to be addressed. With the advent of professionalism at the very top echelon of rugby, players have more time to prepare themselves physically, technically, tactically and psychologically for games. However, this has become a double-edged sword for many players. There is no doubt that players have become bigger, faster and more powerful than their predecessors in the amateur era, and that game plans have become more sophisticated with the proliferation of extensive analysis systems, but the amount of time that is spent on rugby-related activities has its downside. Players who spend all their waking hours practising, preparing or playing the game, as well as being involved in all the peripheral responsibilities of being a professional, can become too narrowly focused on rugby to the detriment of other aspects of their lives, and ironically lose their motivation to train for something that used to me more than "just a job"!

> I've never been truly fit, and I realized making the top grade that was something that I just had to do [get fit].
>
> Tana Umaga (New Zealand All Black, 1997) explaining the
> main reason why his performance improved so much
> in 1997 resulting in his selection for the All Blacks

McCarroll and Hodge (2004a, 2004b) conducted a study on the training motivation of a group of professional rugby players in New Zealand and discovered that a number of factors influenced the level of motivation for this group. These included:

1. *Life skills*   Players who had developed a balanced lifestyle, and were involved in meaningful activities (e.g. study or work) outside of rugby, were the players who had higher levels of training motivation, and were regarded as better trainers in contrast to those who had no other commitments in their lives other than playing and training for rugby (McCarroll & Hodge, 2004a, 2004b).
2. *Social support*   Players who received a significant amount of support from team management, especially the team conditioning coach, were more likely to have greater training motivation levels. If the team conditioning coach provided programs that were individualized and varied, and educated the players as to why they were doing the types of training that they were doing, this positively influenced their training motivation. Team coaches also influenced training motivation. The players reported that if they had coaches who were supportive, and whom they respected, they were prepared to train hard so that they didn't let them down. If the coaches also gave them meaningful feedback on the areas that they needed to work on, this gave them some focus and direction for their training, and their motivation increased (McCarroll & Hodge, 2004a, 2004b).
3. *Social environment*   The team environment was a factor that had the potential to influence training motivation. For example, the team's win–loss record had an influence on their training motivation. Being in a team that was consistently losing games influenced some players negatively and others positively in terms of their training motivation. Some trained harder with a view to rectifying the situation, while others reported losing motivation as a result of losing games and not enjoying the environment as a consequence. However,

all players stated that, when the team was winning, training was much more enjoyable and motivation was consequently higher (McCarroll & Hodge, 2004a, 2004b).

> I think I've still got a long way to go to be as good as I can be at rugby. My trainer always gives me grief about the fact that I've never trained before. And I just say, "Well, that just wasn't me." I just tried to get by on natural talent. That was good to a point, but now players are getting bigger and stronger and faster and I'm getting beaten up more.
> Jeff Wilson (New Zealand All Black 1993–2000), talking about his changed attitude to training in 1997

While these factors seemed to influence training motivation in a consistent fashion, numerous other factors were found to influence players' motivation positively or negatively, depending on the individual. McCarroll and Hodge (2004a, 2004b) concluded that players need to be very aware of their personal motivating influences, to know what kind of environment best suits them and to understand why they are sometimes less motivated to train. These influences need to be communicated to the team's conditioning coach in order for that person to be able to structure a training environment that best meets the player's needs.

Summary: PST for Individual and Team Training

The use of psychological skills is an important aspect of individual and team *training*, as well as being an integral part of *playing* the game of rugby (Hale & Collins, 2002; Hodge & McKenzie, 1999). Players must stay motivated, and be able to concentrate on the right cues, control their emotions and develop confidence in their ability to perform under the simulated pressure of an actual game, as well as being able to perform the various physical, technical and tactical skill requirements of the game. As such, they need to be able to implement the appropriate PST methods during training in order to accomplish these things.

Goal-setting, mental preparation, relaxation techniques, mental imagery and self-talk (among other techniques) can all be used to develop, maintain and improve a player's performance during training. No rugby skills exist in isolation, so in order for a player to perform to their potential, they must not only know how to execute a rugby skill *(technical ability)*, and possess the physical resources to perform that skill *(physical ability)*, they must also know when to execute it *(tactical ability)*. However, in order to do all of this effectively they must be motivated to perform the skill, to be able to concentrate on the right cues in order to know when to execute the skill, be confident in their ability to successfully perform the skill, and be able to perform it in a psychological state that will maximize its effectiveness *(psychological ability)*. All of this is a product of training! No single type of training is sufficient by itself. Although there may be flow-on effects from physical training to the development of technical, tactical and psychological skills (and sometimes vice versa), this type of training on its own is not enough. Each of these skill areas needs to be developed and practiced in order for the player to become the best that they can be.

SUMMARY: "THINKING RUGBY"

Rugby is an interactive, continuous team sport that is characterized by players having to switch between attack and defense many times during a game, as well as having to concentrate on the role(s) required by their playing position within a sophisticated team game plan. In 1996 the sport of rugby became professional at the elite level, and rule changes since that time have lead to a dramatic increase in the speed and pace of the game. As the pace of the game has increased the time available for thinking and decision-making has decreased accordingly; as a consequence the psychological challenges inherent in this interactive, continuous sport have been accentuated.

Consequently psychological skills training (PST) or mental toughness training has become a crucial component of peak performance for rugby players. In this chapter we have outlined a PST program to develop what we have labelled the eight Cs of peak performance: Commitment, Confidence, Controlling Activation, Coping with Pressure, Concentration, Cohesive Team, Captaincy, Communication.

> Individuals with a ferocious desire to win and the capacity to think their way to victory are needed. In the final analysis this requirement, a sort of mental athleticism, is the key determinant of who wins and who is second. It's hard to describe but we all know it when we see it . . .
>
> David Kirk (former New Zealand "All Black" Captain—1987 World Cup Champions)

REFERENCES

Bloom, G.A., Stevens, D.E. & Wickwire, T.L. (2003). Expert coaches' perceptions of team building. *Journal of Applied Sport Psychology, 15*, 129–143.

Brawley, L.R. (1990). Group cohesion: status, problems and future Directions. *International Journal of Sport Psychology, 21*, 355–379.

Butler, R. & Hardy, L. (1992). The performance profile: theory and application. *The Sport Psychologist, 6*, 253–264.

Carron, A. & Hausenblas, H. (1998). *Group Dynamics in Sport* (2nd edn). Morgantown, WV: Fitness Information Technology.

Carron, A.V. & Dennis, P. (2001). The sport team as an effective group. In J. Williams (ed.), *Applied Sport Psychology: Personal Growth to Peak Performance*, (4th edn; pp. 120–134). Mountain View, CA: Mayfield.

Cartwright, D. & Zander, A. (1968). *Group Dynamics: Research and Theory.* New York: Harper & Row.

Dugdale, J. (1996). An exploratory investigation into the relationship between focused attention and peak performance. *Unpublished master's thesis.* University of Otago.

Hale, B. & Collins, D. (2002). *Rugby Tough.* Champaign, IL: Human Kinetics.

Hardy, C.J. (1990). Social loafing: motivational losses in collective performance. *International Journal of Sport Psychology, 21*, 305–327.

Hardy, C.J. & Latene, B. (1988). Social loafing in cheerleaders: effects of team membership and competition. *Journal of Sport and Exercise Psychology, 10*, 109–114.

Hardy, L., Jones, G. & Gould, D. (1996). *Understanding Psychological Preparation for Sport: Theory and Practice of Elite Performers.* Chichester, UK: John Wiley & Sons.

Harkins, S.G. (1987). Social loafing and social facilitation. *Journal of Experimental Social Psychology, 23*, 1–18.

Harkins, S.G. & Szymanski, K. (1987). Social loafing and social facilitation: new wine in old bottles. In C. Hendrick (ed.), *Review of Personality and Social Psychology: Vol. 9* (pp. 167–188). Beverly Hills, CA: Sage.

Hodge, K. (2004b). Team dynamics. In T. Morris & J. Summers (eds), *Sport Psychology: Theory, Applications, and Issues* (2nd edn; pp. 210–233). Sydney, Australia: Jacandra Wiley.

Hodge, K.P. (2004a). *Sport Motivation: Training Your Mind for Peak Performance* (2nd edn). Auckland, NZ: Reed.

Hodge, K. & McKenzie, A. (1999). *Thinking Rugby: Training Your Mind for Peak Performance.* Auckland, NZ: Reed.

Hodge, K. & Petlichkoff, L. (2000). Goal profiles in sport motivation: a cluster analysis. *Journal of Sport and Exercise Psychology, 22,* 256–272.

Hodge, K., Sleivert, G. & McKenzie, A. (1996). *Smart Training for Peak Performance: The Complete Sports Training Guide.* Auckland, NZ: Reed.

Jackson, S. & Csikszentmihalyi, M. (1999). *Flow in Sports: The Keys to Optimal Experiences and Performances.* Champaign, IL: Human Kinetics.

Jones, G. & Swain, A. (1992). Intensity and direction as dimensions of competitive anxiety and relationships with competitiveness. *Perceptual and Motor Skills, 74,* 467–472.

Lane, A., Rodger, J. & Karageorghis, C. (1997). Antecedents of state anxiety in rugby. *Perceptual and Motor Skills, 84,* 427–433.

Latene, B., Williams, K. & Harkins, S. (1979). Many hands make light work: the cause and consequences of social loafing. *Journal of Experimental Social Psychology, 37,* 822–832.

Maynard, I. & Howe, B. (1989). Attentional styles in Rugby players. *Perceptual and Motor Skills, 69,* 283–289.

McCarroll, N. & Hodge, K. (2004a). Training motivation in sport: Part I principles and practice. *New Zealand Coach, 12*(1), 19–21.

McCarroll, N. & Hodge, K. (2004b). Training motivation in sport: Part II practical implications. *New Zealand Coach, 12*(2), 16–18.

McKenzie, A., Hodge, K. & Sleivert, G. (2000). *Smart Training for Rugby: A Complete Training Guide for Players and Coaches.* Auckland, NZ: Reed.

Orlick, T. & Partington, J. (1988). Mental links to excellence. *The Sport Psychologist, 2,* 105–130.

Steiner, I. (1972). *Group Processes and Group Productivity.* New York: Academic.

Vealey, R. (1988). Future directions in psychological skills training. *The Sport Psychologist, 2,* 318–336.

Vealey, R. (1994). Current status and prominent issues in sport psychology interventions. *Medicine and Science in Sport and Exercise,* 495–502.

Williams, K., Harkins, S. & Latene, B. (1981). Identifiability as a deterrent to social loafing: two cheering experiments. *Journal of Experimental Social Psychology, 40,* 303–311.

Williams, J. & Krane, V. (2001). Psychological characteristics of peak performance. In J. Williams (ed.), *Applied Sport Psychology: Personal Growth to Peak Performance* (4th edn; pp. 162–178). Palo Alto, CA: Mayfield.

CHAPTER 10

Psychological Aspects in the Training and Performance of Team Handball Athletes

John M. Silva

University of North Carolina, USA

INTRODUCTION

Handball is the second most popular team sport played worldwide. Millions of participants and spectators enjoy the physical, high-scoring, non-stop action of a handball match. The physical and psychological demands necessary to reach an elite level of play in handball are extraordinary. Handball at the highest level of play demands the development and refinement of many fitness, technical, tactical and psychological skills. The purpose of this chapter is to introduce the sport of handball and the nature of the positional, training and competition demands placed upon the athlete playing this sport. From a practical and functional perspective the psychological demands of training and competition will be discussed and enhanced with real-life examples. Drawing from sport psychology research and over 15 years of experience in the sport of handball, psychological aspects important to the coach, the player and the sport psychologist will be reviewed in a manner that can assist each in performing their role in the handball environment at a high level.

TEAM HANDBALL: THE OLYMPIC SPORT YOU MAY HAVE NEVER SEEN

Picture 12 athletically built players running at high speeds on an indoor court measuring 20 meters wide by 40 meters long (a little longer and wider than a regulation basketball court). The six players on offense attempt to advance and shoot an inflated leather ball a little smaller and harder than a volleyball on a defended goal. The ball, 23 inches in circumference weighing 15 to 17 ounces, is advanced primarily by passing. Offensive players work in precision as a group to organize a shot on the goal that can travel upwards of 70 miles per hour. The shot must get past the court defenders who can legally check

The Sport Psychologist's Handbook: A Guide for Sport-Specific Performance Enhancement.
Edited by Joaquín Dosil. © 2006 John Wiley & Sons, Ltd.

the offensive player shooting the ball. If the shot gets through the defenders, a goal keeper stands ready to block the 70-mile-an-hour shot. The goal keeper, dressed in gear similar to what a soccer keeper would wear, carefully measures the expected angle of the forthcoming shot. Upon release of the shot by the advancing offensive player the goal keeper moves to attack the ball with a body part deflecting the shot and thus preventing a goal. At the far end of the court, the goal keeper of the team now on offense prepares to move back to the goal to defend against an impending fast break that may occur when the attacking team's shot is blocked or saved by the opposition's goal keeper.

This high-speed, high-flying action will continue for 2 30-minute halves separated by a 10-minute half-time. There will be contact, collisions, diving shots from the wing players, acrobatic saves by the goal keepers, and a pace of play that is unequalled in most court games. When that 60 minutes has ended the court players will feel like they just completed a 10-kilometer race and a full-scale rugby match. That evening the goal keepers will have badges of honor all over their bodies from direct blocks of blistering shots. During the game the goalies had neither the time nor the inclination to note the bodily sacrifice necessary to make a save in team handball. Hours after the last shower has been turned off the athletes will experience that warm glow of great fatigue. It is that same total body fatigue often experienced after a long cross-country ski in the dead of winter. All the athletes will know they have experienced the great Olympic sport of team handball!

While the athletes take refuge in the recovery process, emotionally fatigued coaches stay up for hours after international competition dissecting the offensive and defensive ebb and flow of the game. There will be much reflection on play selection, defensive strategies and situation substitutions, especially on the crucial penalty shot situation. If the game came down to the last possession, the winning coach will quietly revel in the play selection and the execution of the team. The coach of the losing team will replay those final fatal seconds and think about the "what ifs". The reflection time for both the winning and losing coach will be short since that evening both will be mandated to turn their attention and energy to their next opponent. In international team handball the next match can be less than 24 hours away.

INTRODUCTION TO THE SPORT OF TEAM HANDBALL

Team handball is the second most popular participation team sport worldwide. The sport is governed internationally by the International Handball Federation (IHF) which comprises over 150 member nations representing approximately 800,000 teams and more than 20 million participants worldwide. The origins of the sport trace to ancient Greece and Roman ball games. The modern-day version of the game was popularized by German physical education experts and was introduced to the Olympic Games in 1936 in Berlin as an outdoor event. After a brief hiatus, the sport was reintroduced in the 1972 Munich Olympics as an indoor sport. Women's handball became an Olympic sport during the 1976 Montreal Games.

While the game itself has some similarities to soccer it is a remarkably different game in many aspects. Handball is hand–eye-oriented, high-scoring and very fast paced. Players can be called for "stalling" if they do not attack the goal, and a significant amount of physical contact called "checking" is legally permitted in the sport. The goal keeper rarely catches the shot ball. Instead, in an attempt to stop high-speed and deftly accurate shots they thrust their body into save positions using well-practiced goal keeper techniques. These shots can be placed in any plane from the extended low corners of the goal to the upper body and facial plane. The last line of defense, the goal keeper, is also the first line of the offense, often initiating fast breaks with accurate down-court outlet passes. The goal keepers in handball must be flexible, agile, quick and fearless. They must also have a very high pain tolerance and an ability to play bruised and hurt. Height is an advantage as are long arms and legs as the goal keeper must cover a goal that is 3 meters wide by two meters high (9' 10.5" × 6' 6.75"). Quickness and body length will help the goal keeper particularly when called upon to make a razor-sharp second save off a rebounded shot made by a diving offensive player.

The court players all have positional names but often the court players exchange positions as they move through defensive alignments or weave well-conceived play patterns that attempt to create an "overload" (e.g. three attackers against two defenders) or a wide defensive gap. The offensive court player's positions are the center back, left back, right back, left wing, right wing, and the circle runner, also called the pivot. The center back is like the point guard in basketball and is expected to be a great passer and playmaker. The center back runs the offense and must make micro-second decisions as this player handles the ball with greater frequency than any other court player. The center back is often viewed as an organizer and passer first, a scorer second. Yet the center back must be a threat to score, thus mandating that the defense respect the ball space created by the center back. By drawing defenders into the ball space occupied by the center back, space and gaps are created in the defense that can now be attacked when the center back passes the ball to the right back or the left back. The right and left backcourt players are the shooters on a team. At the international level these players are often over 6' 5" tall, have above-average jumping ability and can throw pure "vapor" when they shoot. The players at the backcourt positions must be good athletes because in addition to their "go to" offensive positions which require one-on-one athletic moves, many backcourt players will be called upon to stay on the court and play defense. The wings are generally the quickest court players and they often have brilliant one-on-one moves. To play this position at a high club or international level the wing must have the ability to dive and lay out horizontally before shooting. This dive shot is common from a good wing player and improves the acute shooting angle from the wing position. Defensively, the wing player must have quick feet and great agility since they will often find themselves one on one against a wing attacker.

At high club and international levels many teams substitute players "on the fly" placing offensive and defensive specialists on the court at the appropriate time. While contact and checking of the shooter is allowed, blatant or unnecessary force is penalized with either a yellow card, a two-minute penalty or a penalty shot. The penalty shot is a dramatic one-on-one confrontation between the shooter who is positioned at a line 7 meters from the goal and the goal keeper. If a violation occurs when a player is attempting a shot and the foul is flagrant, two minutes and a penalty shot can be awarded. Unlike ice hockey, where a penalized player returns to the ice if the short-handed team is scored upon, a penalized team handball player must serve the full two minutes before being released.

The 20 meters wide by 40 meters long playing area easily accommodates the six offensive and six defensive court players and provides enough free space for some athletic, one-on-one, individual offensive tactics. Offensive players commonly use one-on-one techniques such as spin, swim and cross-over moves. While the opportunity for individual offense constantly presents itself, team handball is the model team sport. Offensive players must work with each other to create space and "gaps" in the defense that allow for open shots.

Defensively, players must constantly be communicating since offensive players change positions through cuts, crossing with teammates, sending a wing through the defensive alignment, picks, screens, and tactical repositioning of the circle runner. In addition to a 7-meter penalty line, the court is divided in half by a center line. There is not, however, a back-court violation rule in handball. The goal area line or 6-meter line defines the area where only the goal keeper can stand. This 6-meter line is a curved, half-circle arc that extends 6-meters from the goal, arching goal line to goal line. Offensive players can take this "air space"; however, they must release the ball for a shot or pass before landing in the goal area. Defensive players cannot intentionally go inside the goal area in an attempt to gain a defensive position or advantage. There is a 9-meter "free throw" line which is another half-circle arched line that is used as the point of reference to restart the offense after a minor foul has been committed by the defense between the goal area 6-meter line and the 9-meter line. There is also a clearly marked substitution area at center court extending 4.45 meters in each direction from the center line at the scorer's table. A goalie restriction line 4 meters out from the goal end line defines how far out from the goal line a goal keeper may come toward the shooter when attempting to block a penalty shot.

The sport of handball has been an extremely popular spectator sport in all countries that have hosted the Olympic Games. Handball is played extensively in European countries, Asia and to a lesser extent in Africa and Pan America. Several European countries field professional leagues providing high levels of competition that fuels Olympic hopefuls from many European countries. Countries worldwide who have handball players talented enough to play in the European professional leagues attempt to send their players abroad, fully expecting their players to return to the homeland for World Championships and Olympic competition. The European sports media and club sports system values team handball and understands the global popularity of the sport. Team handball is often televised in many European countries as a professional sport. The European Championship, World Championships and the Olympics receive considerable media and fan attention. In the United States team handball is not widely known nor highly visible in the sports media. It is considered by many sports experts as a sleeping giant and potentially the next high-profile Olympic sport for the USA.

THE PSYCHOLOGICAL DEMANDS OF TEAM HANDBALL

Overall, the demands placed on a team handball player are similar to those of several team sports. The broad similarities to other team sports include the ability to train the physical, technical, tactical and psychological dimensions. From the psychological perspective many team sports vary in the specificity of the psychological demand placed on the individual player and the team. Some team sports—such as basketball, lacrosse and soccer—require the motivation and will to drill individual skills to excellence while concurrently mastering the choreography of precisely timed plays. The interplay between the individual and the team must interface precisely until the individual move and the timed play of the team complement one another as a positive habit. Many team sports require the interaction of several players, the ability to learn quickly in a constantly changing highly interactive environment, and the ability to recover quickly from a mistake or error. The psychological flexibility necessary to learn and play several positions, to adjust to the psychology of offense and to the mentality demanded of a defensive player is a prerequisite in some team sports characterized by athletes playing "both ways". The ability to "think on the fly", to read a changing defense, anticipate correctly and react with the appropriate offensive response is a must in some team sports. The temperament to receive constructive criticism, harsh feedback during practice and competition, and the resilience to bounce back after a bad call by an official are qualities highly valued by coaches in many team sports. What makes handball unique from a psychological perspective is that, due to the hybrid nature of the sport, a handball player needs all of the general psychological qualities described above and some psychological qualities that specifically address the unique demands of the position the player assumes on the court.

PSYCHOLOGICAL CHARACTERISTICS BENEFICIAL TO A TEAM HANDBALL PLAYER

The task demands and game characteristics of team handball require a player to have outstanding individual skills combined with an ability to mesh with teammates using communication and precise timing. This demand is continually placed upon the player on both the offensive and defensive ends of the handball court. A handball player must be a person who is willing to take on opponents one on one and is not fearful of individual failure. The same player must be unselfish enough to make on-court decisions that benefit the team. The team handball player must manage the psychological exposure that comes with high on-court visibility given that there are only six court players on each team playing in an open space. Mistakes by any player are easily visible even to a novice spectator. The handball player must manage the accountability of taking on and defending one-on-one confrontations both on offense and defense. The handball player also must have the discipline and patience not to break off a play too soon before it has fully developed into an overload opportunity. This same player must have the ability to read a moving defense and respond in a creative and productive manner when mismatches, gaps and offensive opportunities appear instantly due to a defensive error. The handball player must have polished individual qualities, yet the player must at the same time be totally unselfish. The handball player must be able to share success that often is a function of team play. This is exemplified when a player instantly helps out a beaten defender by sliding off their mark and taking on the attacking shooter. Team play and unselfishness are also required when a high-scoring back-court player bypasses a decent shot at the goal and makes the last pass to a teammate on the wing for an unabated dive shot. High-scoring, high-profile back-court players are expected to instantaneously slip the ball to the circle on the pick and roll play at the moment the circle becomes open. Perhaps one of the most difficult displays of unselfish play is demonstrated when a player with good offensive skills is asked to substitute out on offense, thus playing only defense because a teammate has superior offensive skills at that position. Substituting out on defense and playing only offense requires the same commitment to team play.

The psychological demand on a team handball player is considerable and complex. How a player psychologically responds to the nature of this sport deserves attention from opponents and is certainly evaluated by both the opposition's coach and the player's own coach. A closer examination of some psychological characteristics that may benefit a team handball player can be instructive to a sport psychology service provider working with a handball team or the coaching staff.

Motivation and Will

Handball can be a little misleading to some athletes. Watching the game many athletes believe, "I can do this"; it looks like an easy game to learn. To be sure, the basics of handball are relatively easy to learn. The sport is dominated by hand–eye coordination and emphasizes basic motor skills such as passing, catching, shooting, running and change of direction. Many players master the basic skill demands of handball fairly quickly. Plus, scoring in team handball is relatively easy compared to soccer, ice hockey or American football. It is common for each team to score 15 to 20 goals in a regulation game. Even inexperienced players move the ball up the court fairly quickly, pass, shoot and score. It is common to hear novice players say, "I like this game"! However, much like a person who mistakenly assumes racketball is "easy" to master because they learn the basic skill demands of racketball faster than they may learn the basic skill demands of tennis, skilled handball requires tremendous drill work in both individual and team formats. In order for a player to advance to the high club level and certainly to the national and international level, a player must have a bevy of offensive moves. They must be able to accurately shoot from various body positions and angles, and they must develop deftly accurate placement of their shots while being hit or checked by an opponent. Defensively, the same player must be physically strong, willing to legally hit or check an offensive player coming full force to the goal, precisely time moving off the 6-meter line to cover an attacking player or a moving circle, and know when and how to time a defensive cover for a teammate.

One of the most distinguishing psychological characteristics that I have observed in talented players in over 15 years of working with team handball at the club, national and international level is the motivation to drill and the will to refine both individual skills and team skills to a high level. Unfortunately, many players are willing to "settle" for the seemingly instant success handball can offer in the form of high-scoring offense. Many talented athletes have failed to develop into talented handball players because they lacked motivation to train and the willfulness needed to refine individual and team techniques. Players must develop autonomous read–react abilities on both offense and defense and this skill takes an understanding of the game that can come only with repetition and good feedback from a coach. It is not that difficult to be an average team handball player and, of course, this is part of the positive attraction to the sport. As the level of play moves up, participants find that the frequency and intensity of body contact permitted by a defensive player while an attacker is shooting increases. At high levels of play, the quickness with which an offensive or defensive mental decision is made is at the speed of lightning. A long court, fast play and multiple games over a period of a few days demands a fitness level and hardness of body that is extreme. The extraordinary level of skill exhibited by elite level goal keepers requires a shooter not only to shoot hard and accurately but also to use ball fakes while in the motion of shooting. A high level of motivated training and the will to train not only in the team setting but also individually is a necessity. This willfulness is important even for players who perceive themselves to be better athletes than their peers. Great players often spend many hours practicing fundamentals with a team manager or alone. Without such motivation and willfulness a player will limit the opportunity for progression to high levels of play. Many players find the early success experienced in team handball due to their athleticism a poor predictor of subsequent success as a handball "player". Ultimately, at the highest levels of competition, team handball is a high-speed sport that demands a high level of technicality, instant strategic "read and react" skills, and the execution of precise skills while being physically contacted by an opponent. The motivation and willfulness to train, drill and blend one's athletic or physical abilities with these demands requires acquisition time. Motivation and will are essential psychological aspects in the development of a team handball player. These qualities should be looked for in any player regardless of their comparative athletic or physical skill level.

Court Sense: Thinking on the Fly

Court sense is a topic often discussed in sport psychology, yet it is seldom systematically studied (Papanikolaou, 2000). Much like intelligence, court sense is widely recognized as a performance factor but it remains difficult to quantify and measure in a reliable and valid manner. The scientific community has struggled with accurately measuring court sense in a general manner and to date has failed to operationalize court sense for specific sports. Yet, any coach, player or sport psychologist will attest to the importance of this ability in many interactive sports. In team handball, court sense or the ability to think on the fly and in the heat of competition is a psychological quality that cannot be underestimated. Handball is a game "on the fly" and, like ice hockey and lacrosse, the action is up and down and virtually non-stop. The referee rarely handles the ball in team handball even when a violation occurs. It is up to the players on both teams to anticipate the call by the referee, read the referee's hand signal as it is being initiated, get the ball and a player to the point of the infraction and restart play. This is especially true on an offensive turnover when the defending team can instantly turn to offense as long as the ball and a player are at the point of the infraction. Court sense is exemplified in many aspects of game play. Team handball is a read-and-react-type sport and, since a majority of the players on offense and defense are moving while the ball is in play, a player must have a high level of "who is where—doing what" at all times. This court sense has to be processed while running, dribbling, passing, catching, making a skilled move or fake, shooting, and reading the goalie. And that is just for a player on offense! On defense, knowing the location of the offensive player in your zone and what that player may do is step one. The defensive player must also know where the offensive player on either side of their mark is located, where the circle is located, and if a wing is coming through the 6-meter area. Players constantly chatter a chorus of "I am out" while a teammate advises, "I have the circle." Losing an offensive player for a flicker of a moment at the point of the offensive attack will result in a high percentage shot when playing against a high-level opponent. While this carousel of defensive activity is transpiring, a defender must be prepared to come off the 6-meter line at the appropriate moment to check (legally hit) the offensive player attacking with the ball. Defensively and offensively the handball player is under a constant mental press to quickly and accurately process information.

Players must learn not only when to pass versus when to shoot, they must learn the precise time to pass or shoot. A moment too soon or a moment too late and the opportunity is missed because so many of the players are in constant movement in team handball on both offense and defense. "Touch" in handball is a type of court sense exhibited on the fly when a player is shooting, passing, cutting and playing defense. There are so many creative passes that can be made in handball purely off reading your teammates and the defense. The speed of the pass in handball is often as crucial as the accuracy of the pass. The proper touch on a pass facilitates the ability of your teammate to catch the ball in traffic, while being hit, or while in a difficult airborne position. The decision-making process and the speed of these decisions is remarkable and this court sense takes time to develop.

Court sense in handball is demonstrated in the many game situations to which a handball player must learn to properly respond. Using court sense regarding shot selection and clock management in player up and player down situations can make the difference between winning and losing. Offensive players are often baited into a relatively quick but low percentage shot from the wing when in a player advantage situation due to a penalty against the opposition. The player misses the wing shot which the goalie and defense may have predetermined would be "the shot to give" in the defensive player down situation. The penalized team takes possession of the ball and may kill off the penalty or may score while a player down. Court intelligence is also crucial during the end of a tight game situation. Players with good court sense do not take the moderately high to high-risk opportunities when ahead by three or four goals and three minutes or less remain in the game. I have witnessed many high-level matches where a player on the team with the lead attempts a high-risk play that if successful may "seal" the game. More often than not the play fails. Equally important, the high-risk play (e.g. a $^3/_4$-court-length fast break pass) often takes very little time off the clock. If the play fails and there is a resulting quick goal scored by the opposition, the differential is closed with little time taken off the clock. If this "hero or zero" play fails it generally produces positive momentum for the trailing team while generating instant pressure for the team whose lead is now quickly cut.

A final example of the important concept of court sense is demonstrated in team handball in the very subjective "stalling" or passive play rule. This call often becomes an issue at the end of closely contested matches. Since there is no shot clock in team handball, referees monitor the speed of play exhibited by the offense. If in the referee's perception the offense is "stalling" or taking too much time to make a realistic attack toward the goal the referee raises the arm closest to the team bench to signify passive play. The team in possession of the ball will be allowed three to four passes (a subjective guideline) and then a shot must be taken. Players with poor court sense often mismanage this crucial time of the game yielding rapid turnovers without a shot. Poor shot selection in the end of game situation can result in a fast break opportunity for the opposition. Court sense is having a "clock in your head". This means a player knows how to burn time with savvy but not get into the passive play situation where offense play is often forced, poorly prepared and may produce a turnover. The "clock in your head" is needed to determine how much time is left in a penalty, how much time is left in player up situation, the end of half or the end of game. In many venues there is not a highly visible clock at both ends of the playing area and the loudness of the crowd makes hearing time left called in from the bench very difficult. Having court sense in these game-determining situations must be practiced and simulated on a regular basis in structured situations created by the coach. In the practice setting, players must be "frozen" when they execute poorly or when they execute very well so the coach can make a teaching point for all team members to see and understand. I use a three-whistle technique in practice. Whenever the whistle sounds three times in practice all players "freeze"; they do not move and only the coaches are permitted to provide feedback. Court sense can be developed through sound coaching techniques that place players in the tactical situations they must manage in the competition. It is important to create psychological stress in these simulations so players get some of the edge or "feel" they will experience in the actual match.

Clearly, players have different aptitudes and learning curves for the development of court sense. My observations as a performance consultant and as a coach have convinced me that all players are capable of developing court sense and improving this ability. Structured repetition of simulated game situations under stress are essential elements that must be realistically created in practice. "Freezing" players in their positions on the court and providing positive as well as corrective feedback are essential to the learning process necessary to develop and improve court sense.

Critical Response Time

Most coaches demand "zero defects" from their players. This demand, however, is unrealistic in all sports, especially highly interactive sports like team handball. Demanding perfection often creates a "fear of failure" mode in many athletes. Coaches are often very upset by players who seem to play with a fear of making a mistake or play "not to lose". What some coaches do not realize is they may be coaching this psychological response into their athletes on a daily basis. Interactive sports like handball will produce many player errors and mistakes. Most coaches work to minimize mistakes and miscues and maximize desired responses in pressure situations. However, there is a fine line between excellence and perfection. Coaches, players, parents and sport psychologists must be aware of this fine line. The fine line is very evident in a sport like handball where mistakes happen to even well-trained and prepared teams. The fine line is the difference between aspiring for excellence and demanding perfection. Coaches who constantly demand perfection often create a fear of failure or a fear of making a mistake in their players. This fear is often magnified when a mistake can put the game on the line. Who needs added pressure of a punitive coach waiting to pounce on your mistake when a player is in that situation? Mistakes more often than not need to be corrected, not punished, in both the practice situation and the game situation. Coaches should expect and command excellence from their players; however, demanding perfection will not achieve this goal. Most outstanding international coaches that I have observed are task masters. Yet, the task to be mastered is not to be feared or hated. The task to be mastered is to be embraced. The challenge of doing the task well and doing it well consistently should be framed to be a "difficult attraction" to players in the training environment and in the actual competition. Players who develop the mentality to do their very best in all situations have consistency in their effort expenditure and in their desire to try and succeed rather than avoid failing. In their quest for success these players have learned that a mistake is something to recover from quickly. This is what I call "critical response time".

A player must mentally respond with quickness and correctness in sports where there are great offensive moves and great defensive stops, turnovers, bad calls, and misjudgments by offensive and defensive players. Handball has all of the elements noted above and more. As mentioned, a great aspect of handball is that the referee rarely touches the ball. There is none of the theatrics of NBA basketball where players argue with referees while keeping the ball in their hands and away from the referee. While the "offended" NBA player defends their bruised ego by projecting the blame on the referee the game is delayed and the truly offended team is placed at a disadvantage since they cannot in bound the ball. While the offending player lags behind to complain to the referee the game is delayed and the team taking possession of the ball is denied the opportunity to fast break. If a handball player does not immediately put the ball down at the point of the infraction, a two-minute delay of game penalty can be expected. The ability to recover quickly from a mistake is essential in the sport of handball. While all coaches should try to minimize errors in team and individual play they should pay equal if not more attention to the "critical response time" of their players. Critical response time is how quickly a player responds to a mistake whether made personally or by a teammate. A player with good critical response time stays in the game mentally. They see and hear the call but rather than respond to the correctness or incorrectness of the call they respond to the game circumstances. A player with good critical response time understands that they turned the ball over, threw the ball away on an easy play, misfired on an open shot on goal, or got beat by a one-on-one move. In handball every player, coach and spectator can easily see "the good, the bad and the ugly". A player with good critical response time does not focus on any of the emotional aspects of the play or the call. Rather, the player with good critical response time gets back on defense after a turnover or after a missed opportunity to score a goal. They transition out of the mistake instantly and into the task demand of the game. In essence, the player with good critical response time does not carry a mistake with them. The time it takes them to respond to a game situation is quick, and they focus clearly on the changing events in the game. I have observed professional and international handball players with levels of critical response time that are seldom observed in many other sports. What is the consequence to soccer players who often walk up-field after misplaying an exquisitely served ball in a close match with time winding down? What is the consequence to the offensive lineman in American football who goes back to the huddle and even comes back to the line of scrimmage for the next play thinking about the blown blocking assignment on the last play? Some players think the nature of their sport "permits" them this long mental recovery time! In the soccer example, the attacker may not be in position to challenge for a free ball that appeared in the midfield as the advancing team's attack was broken up by a good defensive play by one of their teammates. How many potential possessions are lost over the course of a soccer game due to players having poor critical response time? In the American football example, the offensive lineman may be slow off the snap count on the next play, or may badly time the trap block that was his assignment on the next play. How many linemen have had a bad series of downs because they were unable to recover quickly from a mistake they made on first down?

Another interesting characteristic of critical response time that I have observed in top players in many sports is the ability to achieve after a mistake. Critical response time taken to the highest level is exemplified by a quick mental recovery, attention to the task at hand, and an elevation in performance. The athlete with poor critical response time often experiences a drop in effort (the walking soccer player) and a drop in performance. Some players mental recovery is very slow when they make a mistake. Some players never seem to return to their previous level of play, allowing the mistake and perhaps teammates, opponents, or the coach to "get in their head". This response pattern is of course fatal during end-of-game situations. It presents a continuous disadvantage in high-speed, non-stop sports such as handball. The player with good critical response time recovers quickly, gets back to the task at hand and often elevates their level of play. In extensive interviews with handball players who have demonstrated this capacity the common response I have received is that the player with great critical response time does not fear a mistake or the consequences of a mistake. They are motivated and challenged by the mistake. They do not try and overcompensate and perhaps make another mistake. Rather, they attempt get back into the play, make a solid play or go a little harder. I would suggest that these players have learned somewhere in their family socialization and or athletic training that the most important thing is not the fact you made a mistake but rather how well did you respond to the mistake. The very design of the rules and regulations of handball place a premium not on being perfect but rather being self-corrective and challenged by the many difficult adjustments imposed by the game. Handball demands a high level of well-developed critical response ability. Handball is indeed a difficult attraction!

Psychological Flexibility

Psychological flexibility is necessary in many team sports since a dynamic is formed between the coaches and the players and between a player and their teammates. This dynamic is often described as "cohesion" or the ability of a team to stay focused on the same goals and objectives even under the stress of competition or the frustration of a losing season (Carron & Hausenblas, 1998). Psychological flexibility is certainly an asset to the development of team chemistry and team cohesion. In addition to contributing to cohesion, psychological flexibility plays a central role in many other tangible aspects of handball. The handball player often must learn several positions since this sport is characterized by very fluid and constant motion by the court players. Often a center back may move into the circle or pivot position or cross and exchange positions with the left or right back. The wings may "go through" the area just outside of 6 meters and stay in the circle as a second pivot. Left and right backs often cross with wings and temporarily exchange positions. The ability to learn quickly in a constantly changing highly interactive environment is a valuable psychological quality in handball. A player cannot "possess" their position since the technical skills expected of a good court player is for the most part interchangeable with other court positions. While handball players have set positions, players cannot see themselves as fixed to a position. A point guard in basketball, a pitcher in baseball or a quarterback in American football often see themselves as specialists and not needing the techniques and tactics of players who occupy other positions on the team. Handball is very different in this regard and players must be willing to learn and play several court positions. In fact, a handball player often will exchange court positions more than once in a single possession of the ball.

Given the fast pace of the game and the rapid transition from offense to defense and defense to offense, players must also quickly adjust to the psychology demanded at each end of the court. The free form of substituting on the fly allows teams to have offensive and defensive specialists and even penalty shot specialists. On offense the mentality is to be smooth, in rhythm with your teammates and relaxed. The offensive team must be in synch with what is offered by the defense and ready to respond as a unit when a defensive miscue or breakdown occurs. Offensive players must be able to read a changing defense, anticipate correctly and react with an appropriate and instantaneous offensive response. The timing of cuts, crosses, picks and accurate passes defines the difference between an elegant attack and a well-executed shot on goal or a turnover and fast break for the opposition. This offensive "flow" mentality with an emphasis on precision, reading a changing offensive and defensive array, and executing with finesse as a unit is somewhat in opposition to the mentality demanded of a defensive player. Defensive tactics involve extraordinary verbal communication skills since the offense is in constant movement and positional exchange. Defense is intense verbally and physically since defensive players may check the offensive player attempting to shoot the ball on goal. The ability to move "off the line" and hit with controlled force while not abandoning your fundamental defensive zone of coverage requires mental discipline and flexibility. The ability to go from a "dancer" on offense to a "bouncer" on defense requires a type of psychological flexibility few sports demand. This psychological flexibility is a prerequisite in handball since many athletes play offensive and defensive ends of the court. If a player cannot make this adjustment they will either be a weak defender or an offensive player lacking timing and touch.

Another aspect of handball that requires enormous psychological flexibility on the part of the player involves mediating referee calls during the course of the game. Handball is one of the most difficult games to officiate of all team sports. Contact is allowed but only in measured form, only at the appropriate time of a shot and only on the upper body/arm of the shooter. These guidelines are almost impossible to enforce in a consistent manner. The speed of the athletes, the positioning of the referees and the amount of incidental contact that is often allowed results in many perceived inconsistencies in rule enforcement. Since in handball the referee does not touch ball after a call (whether it is a "right" call or not) the offending player or team must immediately place the ball down at the moment of the call. At that very moment the offended team can pick up the ball and put it into play at the point of the infraction. There is no time for arguing with officials. If you were on offense you are now on defense and vice versa—it happens that fast! The ability to "play through" tough calls, goals that are taken away due to a quick whistle and expected calls that were not made becomes an essential aspect of psychological flexibility on the handball court. If a player cannot remain psychologically flexible in these situations they will be completely out of step with the nature and pace of the game.

Lastly, psychological flexibility can be seen in the temperament of the athlete in the heat of competition, in an emotional half-time locker room or while enduring a post-game blasting by a coach. Many coaches provide constructive criticism to their players while others use harsh feedback during practice and competition. Given the nature of handball, emphasizing speed and free-forming plays, many mistakes occur during the course of a game. Handball coaches must coach on the fly much like players must play on the fly. Some coaches are very skilled at this teaching style and can blend tactics and emotion very effectively under the high stress and high speed of competition. Some coaches get swept up in the whirlpool of activity in a handball game and lose the master blend. It can be frustrating to a coach to see the hard work and preparations executed in practice not exhibited on the floor during the actual match. A coach may become less tactical and more emotional as they see a lead slip away due to a performance filled with preventable mistakes and poor execution. I have observed this unraveling at the highest levels of handball in both coaches and players. Emotional outbursts by a coach during or immediately after an intense game can be motivational to some players and amotivational to others. A player with a high level of psychological flexibility will not internalize some of the harsh personal comments that may be made in the heat of battle or shortly thereafter. The player with psychological flexibility will attempt to squeeze out any task-relevant information that may be imbedded in the emotional display. The psychologically flexible player will have the resilience to bounce back and be mentally prepared for the next competition. I have observed highly skilled handball players who lacked this type of psychological flexibility decompose under the stress of several consecutive days of tournament play. Does one important missed shot break a player's confidence, one crucial turnover break a player's intensity and effort, does a comment by a coach or teammate break your spirit? Flexibility off the court is often as important as flexibility on the court. Team sport participants can expect to have their play dissected by the media, fans and friends. Coaches and teammates will have post-game comments and feedback of a positive and negative nature. There will always be "team talk" and the expected "ribbing" or trash talking that is done in jest or done to psychologically disrupt a player's mentality. The player with psychological flexibility will not be overly impacted by these situations and will move past them with less conflict and minimal psychological damage.

Low Anxiety–High Accountability

The fast pace and interactive nature of handball results in spectacular individual and team performance that is easily observable to the spectator, coach and fellow competitors. Handball's combination of team and individual performance demands that players have a unique psychological blend of lower anxiety levels and high accountability. A player who is unselfish, not fearful of individual failure and has the psychological resiliency to come back quickly from failure is well suited for the game. With only six court players occupying an area larger than a basketball court there is plenty of room to operate offensively and plenty of room to be isolated on defense, or overloaded with offensive players in your zone. Just as spectacular plays are readily appreciated, unfulfilled opportunities and individual mistakes are equally observable. The handball player must learn to manage the psychological exposure that comes with an alarming frequency in handball. Every possession presents the opportunity for a one-on-one confrontation. The defender marking the offensive player, the offensive player making a one-on-one move on the defender, and the goalie who stands alone as the final line of defense characterize the high visibility of individual play. There will be several situations in the course of a game where a player makes a great individual move and beats the defender only to have a well-placed shot saved by the goalie. Psychologically, a more difficult situation is presented when an offensive player beats the defender only to shoot the ball off goal, allowing a great scoring opportunity to pass without the goalie having to make a save. Defenders are placed in the same high-visibility encounters. A defender can come off the line and make an outstanding defensive stop or be beaten badly by a great offensive move. This constant offensive–defensive pressure is maintained at a high level throughout the whole game particularly for the athletes who play both offense and defense. One player's great offense may come at the expense of another player's defensive mistake. Since the action in handball is virtually non-stop, players must develop a certain level of immunity to failure or the pace of the game will pass them. The immunity to failure is important since it can prevent anxiety and a loss of confidence. This immunity combined with an instant sense of accountability and team responsibility facilitates in game adjustments. A player with high levels of anxiety, a high fear of failure or a dislike for highly visible on court accountability for success or failure may find handball a psychologically painful experience. Managing anxiety in highly observable, one-on-one game situations allows a player to keep up with the rapid pace of handball. It also decreases the probability of the same mistake repeating itself in the next possession since accountability keeps the athlete on task.

   In some sports such as golf or gymnastics the destructive impact of anxiety is easily observed in a performance. These sports have such a fine margin of error that any cognitive or perceptual distraction or undue physical tension can result in significant performance error. In handball, the effect of anxiety on actual performance is more subtle and not as easily observed. While precision movement plays a role in handball, technique and skill execution is not as fine a motor skill as in golf or gymnastics. In handball, high levels of anxiety are often manifested in players shooting the ball too hard, sacrificing the accuracy of the shot. Players will hit the goal posts or completely miss the goal since their motor program is slightly off due to the anxiety. They will shoot too quickly and not use ball fakes so necessary when shooting on an elite goalie. Players will miss open shots on goal, fumble passes, miss assignments and exhibit poor timing in their playmaking. Manifestations of anxiety in handball are not as obvious as a golfer badly missing a tee shot or a gymnast making several technical mistakes during their routine. Since the technical aspects of handball are not as fine as the demand on the golfer or gymnast a handball player's shot can be off a little and still result in a goal scored. "Anxiety mistakes" can, however, make a several-goal difference in a 60-minute handball match. This is particularly evident at the higher competitive levels where exceptional goal-tending demands a smaller margin of error by the shooter.

The player and team who can come out ready to play and are not overly anxious will be at an advantage. This game readiness could help the team capitalize on the opportunities that often are present at the beginning of a match. Likewise, the end of a close match will present only a limited number of scoring opportunities. Players who can maintain their composure and not allow the stress of the end of game situation create undesirable anxiety will have a greater possibility of executing practiced skills. Overall, an athlete who enjoys a challenge and who enjoys attempting to succeed after failure would seem to be well suited to the psychological demands of handball.

From the group or team perspective, accountability is extremely important on both offense and defense. Many defensive alignments combine zone defense concepts with person-to-person principles. Thus, you may have as your primary defensive responsibility the "2 zone" in a 6–0 or flat defensive alignment. You would protect this "zone" and not follow the player who initially lines up in this zone all over the court. You would "pass" this player on to the defensive player in the zone the offensive player enters as they leaves the 2 zone. However, more than one offensive player often enters into a defensive zone. A high level of communication and accurate accountability of assignment must be enacted as the offensive play is developing or it will be too late to adjust. You must correctly anticipate and be in position to make a defensive stop in handball. Offensive players often catch the ball in a full running stride as they are moving to or "attacking" the goal. The defense will be very late if it is simply reacting to the offense. A late defender is no defender in handball. The offensive player will have caught the ball on the fly, stepped toward the goal, jumped and shot before the defender has moved off the 6-meter line and into a position to make a defensive stop. You cannot react when on defense, you must demonstrate coordinated anticipation. "Who had him?", "She was not mine" are common cries when a team is poorly trained to be accountable on defense. Player accountability is essential to good team defense in a sport where a move to the goal can happen fast off a pass unanticipated by the defense. If players do not take responsibility for defensive mistakes opponents will see this for what it is in handball—a team weakness. The opposition will attack that player or that side of the defense until player and team accountability and coordination is established.

Just as accountability is important in both the individual and team categories, anxiety has an interesting impact on "group think". Anxiety can grip a handball team and spread through the team with amazing speed. A missed shot off a breakaway late in a close game, a goalie making a save off a penalty shot late in a close game, an untimely two-minute penalty on one of the team's top players late in a close game can be taken as a singular event or can create a sense of panic in a team. From the individual and team perspective, the intensity and demands of handball require that players be trained in simulated game conditions in an attempt to facilitate developing the habits of composure and accountability in match play.

Self-discipline

Many talented athletes never make it to the higher levels of competition in the sport they play. Finding participants with athletic ability is not a monumental problem in many major sports. Finding participants with the self-discipline and patience to transform raw athletic ability and hone that athletic ability into the skills of a "team player" is a far more difficult task to accomplish. As Red Auerbach, famous coach of the legendary NBA Boston Celtics, once noted, "Talent alone is not enough. They used to tell me you have to use your five best players, but I have found that you win with the five who fit together best" (Stevens, 2002).

Most team sports require a deceptive amount of self-discipline. The spectator's eye is often trained to the culminating event—the dunk in basketball or the shot that scores the goal in soccer. What the coach or the student of the game sees is the process behind the outcome. The precise timing of a pick set in the play, the great touch and accuracy of the pass, the critical and correct decision made by a teammate earlier in the play that created the culminating event. To become a player is much more difficult than being an athlete because a player has worked to develop the physical, technical, tactical and psychological aspects required in the sport they play. This level of training takes a high level of self-discipline on and off the court or field of play. It takes a significant commitment to develop the physical talents, the physiology and fitness parameters, and to develop the motor abilities and skill aspects of a sport. But these are often fairly tangible elements to develop in a participant. A player knows what specific exercise is necessary to develop endurance, anaerobic fitness, greater agility or more leg strength. What specific exercise develops self-discipline, mental toughness, patience? How do you teach a young athlete to give up immediate rewards, choose a difficult path that holds no guarantee for success, or to do the right thing and not break off a play too soon even though a "decent" scoring opportunity presents itself? How do you help that participant have the self-discipline to make such a determination under the stress of a game on the line?

Self-discipline is a psychological habit that some players have from their childhood rearing practices and early athletic experiences. Some athletes have very little self-discipline and have been provided with everything they have wanted in life. Many have experienced easy and early success in sport and have the impression that their "natural talent" makes them better than other players and thus they do not have to work as hard or as often. Self-discipline is a quality that easily manifests itself in the training environment. It is demonstrated in an athlete's work habits and work rate. Does the athlete show up early for practice, work diligently on fundamentals, spend time working on both strengths and weaknesses? Is the athlete in the habit of structuring their training cycle and then following through on a daily plan? What is the athlete's work rate? How many reps does an athlete complete during a drill? Does a one-hour weight-lifting session take two hours to complete? What is the rate of work completed in a given measure of time? Athletes with high levels of self-discipline do not need to be told to "get to work". When it is work time athletes with high levels of self-discipline are "on". Having good work habits and a good work rate is not easy. It requires effort, dedication and a certain amount of self-reliance. Athletes with self-discipline have an element of tough-mindedness that is demonstrated in their willingness to do repetitive and difficult tasks even though there is no guarantee of success. Their commitment is to the process. They believe that their disciplined training will solidify their performance and they will do the task they have been trained to do under the pressure of competition. Self-discipline is much like self-confidence. These psychological qualities are rarely tested in low-pressure situations. It is easy to appear confident when your team is leading or you are having a great match performance. It is easy to run the offense or play fundamentally sound defense when your team is leading by four or five goals late in a handball match. Self-discipline is tested under pressure. Your offense has not been executing well, you are in a 1-goal game with 40 seconds to play. Do your habits break down under the stress? Can you stay within the context of the offense the coach has called out to be run in the closing moments of the game? Do you have the discipline to manage the clock, avoid a stalling call and take a high-percentage shot on goal? It is easy to panic, take the first good look you get at the goal and shoot the ball. It is also easy to have breaks in self-discipline on defense in late-game situations. I have repeatedly observed high-level club and professional players go for steals late in a game when their team was ahead by a goal or even two. They lose their discipline to stay with team defense and instead they go for the big play. A great coach knows that even if the wrong play works it does not mean that it was the right thing to do. In the long run, breaks in self-disciplined play during crucial situations of a match will result in a negative outcome more often than a positive outcome. Self-discipline does not mean being a robot on the court because handball is a game where information-processing is an essential skill. Self-discipline translated to on-court behaviors means making the right decisions, as you were trained to do in practice, when the pressure and intensity level is immense. Beyond the self-discipline needed for preparation, fitness and skill development, a handball player needs mental self-discipline to facilitate making correct decisions in a changeable and unpredictable competitive environment.

Pain Tolerance

Most contact and collision sports require an athlete to have a fairly high level of pain tolerance (Silva & Hardy, 1991). Handball certainly demands the ability to tolerate pain and to play with pain. Most handball players train and play with minor injuries and the pain associated with injury. It is unlikely that a handball player will perform at 100 per cent of their physical ability level given the frequency and intensity of contact and collisions occurring in handball. Players often play with sore shoulders, tired arms, sprained wrists, dislocated fingers, sprained ankles and sore body muscles. Being able to train and play through a low to moderate level of pain is an essential characteristic for a handball player. Without this psychological capacity a handball player will miss a considerable amount of practice time and competition. Just as court players must manage pain on a daily basis, the goal keeper in handball perhaps more that any fellow player is challenged by pain. Goalies in ice hockey and men's lacrosse as well as handball are in a position to absorb pain every time a shot is taken. While the hockey and lacrosse goalies have some protective padding the impact of many shots penetrates the padding and is absorbed by the body of the goalie. Many shots hit spaces between the pads and are directly absorbed by the goalie's body. A handball goal keeper has no protective padding and must face shots traveling 70 miles per hour. Each save by a handball goalie is made by a body part unprotected by padding or equipment. Handball goalies train and play in constant nagging pain and must endure the daily pain of direct hits to the body during practice sessions. Goalies must also sacrifice their bodies each time a penalty shot is taken in a game since the opposing player stands six meters from the goal in a one-on-one confrontation with the goalie.

When assessing youth and junior level handball goalies, looking for a lack of fear of the ball is essential. The ability to withstand pain or even welcome it is an essential psychological quality for a developing goalie. Goalie techniques can be trained and honed over the years; however, it is extremely difficult to train players to have a mental attitude that makes them fearless of impending pain. Ask court players to voluntarily step in the goal for a few minutes and you will observe that most players immediately refuse your kind invitation! Most handball goalies with low pain tolerance or a fear of pain are eliminated from the competitive pool of goalies prior to the high club level. Some goalies with moderate levels of pain tolerance but exceptional athletic talent may be moved to a court position.

Court players with average levels of pain tolerance but exceptional skills are found on high-level teams. A player with low pain tolerance may seek the trainer more frequently, request or need more time away from practice, and may miss practice for treatment. They may come out of a competitive game when other players would stay and play with the pain. They may delay their return to a contested game until the level of pain is manageable to them. These responses often run counter to the culture and norms found in handball. Teammates may become frustrated with the "prima donna" status of the player who is often out of practice but plays in the games. This situation creates interesting intervention opportunities for a sport psychologist working in the sport of handball. Team cohesion can be impacted, particularly if the "rested" player does not deliver in the competition, or uses pain or an injury as an excuse for their sub-par play in competition. Working with the coach, the player and the team to keep everyone on the same page and maintain team cohesion can be an important function for a sport psychologist especially if the sport psychologist travels with the team. From my experience with US national teams, keeping each player focused on their specific role on the team and their specific contributions to the team is an important task to fulfill. This task is especially relevant when players perceive differential treatment of teammates due to low pain tolerance or reactance to minor injury. As difficult as it may be, players need to remember that the decision to practice and or play a teammate is a decision made by the coach in conjunction with the sports medicine and athletic training staff. Unfortunately, some players, especially on a team that is struggling, become too involved in the management of teammates' health. Players often get too concerned with who is not practicing, and whether a non-practicing player will compete in a forthcoming match.

Another intervention opportunity is working with players interested in enhancing their tolerance to pain. Meichenbaum (1977, 1985) has written extensively on the use of cognitive behavioral techniques to manage pain in various clinical settings as well as athletic settings. It should be noted that any individual intervention with an athlete takes time and the emotional investment of the athlete. This is particularly true in pain management intervention where the symptom being treated is very tangible and identifiable to the athlete. While many athletes, including handball players, learn to manage and tolerate pain they should not be placed at great risk for serious injury. Coaches and sports medicine staff must make careful and well-reflected decisions about the appropriateness of clearing an athlete for practice or play. Most athletes, especially younger players, are highly motivated to play whether hurt, injured or even severely injured. Many young players do not have the playing perspective that comes from years in competition. Their main motivation is to get back in the match as soon as possible. Training and management staff should be cognizant of the likelihood of a younger player wanting to get back to practice and play before they are physically ready. This overeagerness should not be taken advantage of to the detriment of the athlete.

PSYCHOLOGY AND HANDBALL TRAINING

Handball is a year-around sport in most countries. The season varies by continent rather than country; however, most handball players will have at least a 10-month training/competition season. The recommendations provided below are made from over 15 years of consulting with national and Olympic level handball coaches and teams, and from over 15 years of personally coaching handball. The training period is divided into the pre-season, the training environment, the pre-competitive period, the competition and post-competition. During each segment of the season, attention to specific psychological preparations can assist team development and performance.

Psychological Preparation: Pre-season

Communicate the Team Philosophy

Perhaps one of the most important aspects of the pre-season is the opportunity to establish the team philosophy. This should be done as early in the pre-season as possible. During the off-season, the coach should meet with the team captains or team leadership and discuss the team philosophy from the previous year. This should include what aspects of the team philosophy have been successful and have translated into positive player norms and high levels of player performance. This is the time for player input and the open sharing of information with the coach. Players can suggest what they think has worked and what has not facilitated the team's advancement. Ultimately, the captains and the senior leadership need to endorse and support the philosophy of the team, or the coach will find a divided team at the first sign of controversy or adversity. In general terms, the philosophy of the team should include what is expected of all the players and what is expected of all the coaches. It should address what behavior is acceptable on and off the court. More specifically, the philosophy should address how the team will conduct itself in practice, in competition and after competition. It should make tangible and clear the perspective the team has on effort, winning, competing, respecting officials, coaches, teammates and competitors. How player transgressions will be managed and how individual and team decisions will be made should be clearly described to the players. The "chain of command" and the "decision-making tree" for the team should be clear to all coaches and players before the first pre-season practice.

A coach should not underestimate the important role psychological factors play in the development and presentation of a sound team philosophy. The team philosophy establishes a solid foundation for the team from a psychological and procedural perspective. It reduces the likelihood of player ambiguity and players saying, "I didn't know." If a team is a reflection of a coach, the team philosophy will say much about the coach and their approach to competition and team development. Each coach must gather input from captains and team leaders and put together a philosophy that guides players in training and in competition. It is time well invested and can speed the maturity and cohesion of a team.

Establish Team Norms Early

Handball is a team sport that requires players work together and work in a cohesive manner. There is interdependence between the coach, the center back, the court players and the goalie. If team norms are not clear and established early, the precise coordination required for a team to be successful will be compromised. Team norms cover a wide array of behaviors but some of the most important for handball include norms for player behavior in practice and games, player–coach relationships, and player–player relationships. Some practical examples would include: no players speak when the coach is speaking during practice, pre-game talks, half-time talks, or post-game. Commit to the offensive and defensive calls sent in from the coach. Do not prematurely break off plays unless an 80 per cent or higher scoring opportunity presents itself. Support your teammates with corrective and tactical feedback rather than assigning blame when there is a defensive breakdown. Treat all members of the team with respect and as equals. There are many more tangible examples of important team norms that should be established early in the competitive year. It is important for a coach to carefully think about what type of behavior is important to condition in practice and in the games. Once a coach has established these behaviors they should be discussed and refined with the captains and leadership of the team. In order for norms to be effectively established within the fabric of any team, players in leadership positions must actively demonstrate the behavior that establishes the norm. Norms will define appropriate and expected behavior to all team members. This is particularly functional for players who are new to the team and bring their own set of expectations concerning how things are done and what is appropriate behavior on and off the court.

Start Firm with Discipline and Structure

The pre-season should be tough! Tough does not mean being an unfair or punitive coach. Tough means establishing a high standard for individual and team performance right from the start. The pre-season is where self-discipline is tested and developed. The pre-season is where the will and motivation of a player can be developed and honed or can be broken. It is a time of high anxiety for many players since some may not know their likelihood of earning playing time or their ability to secure the starting position held during the last season. The pre-season is stressful for some athletes because the fitness demands are often high in the pre-season as coaches expect players to return in shape ready to build upon their fitness foundation rather than establish it. Pre-season practices should be well developed, structured and have a progression from the teaching–learning perspective and from a fitness perspective. Technical skills, drills and tactical concepts should build upon one another in a logical fashion. The ability to follow instructions and demonstrate discipline in all aspects of practice should be developed in the individual player and in the team fabric. The pre-season shows the team how ready the coach is for the new season. If a coach is not organized or is very loose with the players it can become difficult for the coach to gain the team's respect and recognition as the leader. If a team does poorly in the early season or violates team rules it is difficult for coach who has been loose with the team to implement structure and discipline. This move is often rejected by the team as punitive. If a team is structured during the pre-season and responding well, a coach can give the team an early release from practice or a session off. This action will be greatly appreciated by the hard-working team. It is difficult for a coach to move from lax to firm and disciplined. It is readily accepted, however, when there is a move from discipline and firmness to a rewarded "break" especially during the pre-season.

Reward Desired Behavior Early

The psychological concept of reward is often managed in a very interesting manner by some coaches. It is a common practice in many sports to withhold reward during the pre-season and to maximize punishment. Find out who is tough and who is not right away, who can handle the program and who is not cut out for it. Traditional learning theory suggests that learning can be facilitated by the presentation of reward early and often in the early learning stages (Gleitman, 1992). After the desired behavior has been connected with the reward a shaping of the behavior should follow. Essentially, the athlete exhibits the desired behavior, the action is rewarded and then the standard for reward is made progressively higher and higher. Many players dread the pre-season because it is so physically and mentally punitive. The pre-season can be disciplined and structured to develop desired psychological habits without the use of extreme or constant punishment. The overuse of punishment can result in a player developing anxiety rather than confidence, a fear of failing rather than a will to succeed. Punishment certainly has a role in learning and sometimes it seems like players respond more effectively to punishment. It is important to note, however, player development and morale may suffer in the long run if punishment is used constantly. The effective use of reward in the pre-season combined with appropriate punishments can enhance both the desire to learn and perform and bring some level of enjoyment to the stressful daily grind of pre-season training.

Establish Team and Individual Goals

Many coaches set team and individual goals during the pre-season. Goal-setting has been popularized at every level of sports participation (Gould, 1983; Locke & Latham, 1985; O'Block & Evans, 1984). Many athletes use sound goal-setting techniques and have very favorable experiences with goals and the ability of a goal structure to guide an athlete to successful performance (Johnson, 1996). Unfortunately, for many athletes goals are something set for you by the coach at the start of the season and they may or may not be a source of motivation for the team or for an individual player.

Goals should be motivational, directional and achievable. Perhaps one of the most important aspects of setting goals in a very team-oriented sport such as handball is the involvement of the players in the process. The leadership of the team should be involved in the discussion and rationale for team goals. Too often team goals are set exclusively by the coach and they may or may not be congruent with the goals and aspirations of the players. If a goal is to be motivational it must be committed to by the team. Goals such as "National Championship" and "undefeated season" are often set as team goals but in reality these goals have little motivational value or function for the vast majority of teams. After a team's first loss the undefeated season goal is no longer a motivation. In handball, as in most sports with long season schedules, it is far more important to focus team goals on relatively objective, tangible actions and outcomes. If these team goals are reached they will increase the probability of team success. These team goals may include: keeping turnovers under 15 in a 60-minute game; scoring on 70 to 75 per cent of player advantage situations; allowing a team to score 50 per cent or less when the opposition has a player advantage. Achievement of these team goals requires the effort of all the players. These team goals are not abstract as in "increase scoring percentage per possession". The goals must have an element of tangibility and quantifiability in order for them to be effective.

Being able to quantify team goals and post them after practices and games keeps the team accountable and keeps the goals motivational. The same principles should be followed for individual goals. A coach should not set individual goals for a player without player-involvement in the process. The player should have ownership of the individual goals, should develop them with the coach or an assistant coach, and the player and coach should write the goals down for accountability purposes. Several times during a season a player's progress in achieving individual goals can be monitored and even posted in the locker room (Dorrance & Averbuch, 2002). While some players may bristle at such a public display of their progress, these may well be the same players who are not accountable nor take personal responsibility for their errors in practice or game play.

Psychological Preparation: Training Environment

Habits Are Formed in Practice

The importance of the practice environment in handball cannot be underestimated. The classic work of Hull (1952) and later Fitts & Posner (1967) demonstrated the importance of repetition, and the importance of proper progression through the stages of learning when mastering motor skills. Handball players and many team sport players spend far more time in practice than in actual competition. The precise timing involved in many handball plays demands repetition and over-learning in order to simply learn the basic aspects of the game. The touch of the pass, what a teammate is likely to do in various offensive and defensive situations, goalie technique, individual moves on offense, and one-on-one defense all require endless practice and repetition. The list of technical skills to be learned is virtually endless. Practice is also crucial in the formation of psychological habits such as responding to criticism, recovery from mistakes and missed shots, sprinting back to play defense after a missed shot, playing with a lead, playing when behind, and playing when fatigued. Improper technical, tactical as well as psychological habits can be reinforced or broken in the practice environment. Handball coaches must attend to the details that will promote "good playing habits" and discourage or minimize repetition of techniques and behaviors that will advance "bad playing habits". Technical drills, as well as offensive and defensive executions must be done correctly and must be repeated until they have become virtually automatic for the athlete in various levels of stress. The psychological gravity of a situation cannot be allowed to interfere with or impede the training and habits formed through repetition. When a handball player is unable to allow positive practice habits to carry over to match competition stressful and forced play often results. This is often denoted by inexplicable turnovers, inopportune and frequent hitting of the goal posts by the shooters, and shots which miss the goal entirely.

Given the importance of the practice environment, coaches and players should maximize time on the correct elements of handball and an effort should be made to repeat with a high level of correctness the behaviors, techniques and tactics necessary to play high-level handball. A significant percentage of practice time especially early in the season should be dedicated to positive habit formation through drill work.

Balance Discipline with Novelty and Fun

Drill work and a sound task approach are essential to the development of a good handball team. However, there must be balance in rigorous practice sessions. While hard work and disciplined practice are essential elements for success in handball, the training environment must also have elements of novelty and enjoyment. The aspect of fun should not be removed from the training environment for a number of sound psychological reasons. Constant drill repetition, repetitive low and moderate levels of stress, boredom, and ill-timed physical training impositions can lead to athlete staleness, overtraining and burnout (Silva, 1990). It is essential that a coach provides overload to the athletes but the coach does not want to overtrain the athletes. Overload in the training environment follows the same principles of physiological overload. Gradually, an athlete must be exposed to higher and higher levels of demand until the demand exceeds what will likely be experienced in a competitive game situation. Overloading is presenting just a little more stress, pressure and physical conditioning than the athlete is comfortable with and adapted to. If done properly, the athlete struggles but soon experiences "training gain". If the athlete is presented with too much load and does not make a positive training adaptation the excessive overload results in a negative training response that can spiral from staleness to overstraining to burnout (Silva, 1990).

Removing fun and variety from the training environment can create motivational problems with novice as well as seasoned athletes. Creating this type of training environment with young athletes can lead to withdrawal from the sport (Schmidt & Stein, 1991). Handball is an enjoyable sport to practice and to play. It involves running, jumping, catching and throwing. It is goal-oriented and has the element of high scoring. The combination of these basic motor skills with the frequent opportunity to have court play rewarded with a goal creates a natural environment for personal and team enjoyment. Coaches can capitalize on the atmosphere created in a sport like handball by varying drills in creative ways and by making up mini games that use basic handball skills and rules. Fitness is not compromised and the skills you want to develop are practiced in a fun environment. For example, prior to Carolina team handball practices I often use a warm-up session called "touch down" to get the players' heart rates up and to have them use handball skills in a mini game that uses some American football principles. Players have to pass the ball and use the handball three-step rule to advance the ball inside the handball goal area. If a team passes the ball successfully into the goal area and it is "touched down" before a player is tagged, one point is scored. If a player is tagged with the ball or if a pass is dropped or not completed it is a turnover and the other team gets the ball back immediately, as in handball. The game can be played for time (e.g. five minutes) or it can be played to a score (e.g. first team to five touch downs). The players love this warm-up and often show up to practice and start playing the game before the coaches even arrive for practice! The players learn the value of accurate passing since no dribbling is allowed. They use jukes and dodges to avoid being tagged, and they experience a good cardio-vascular warm-up since the games are always full court and competitive. When drills are creative, fun and varied a coach will know because the team will not resent doing the drills. This positive motivation in many ways permits a coach to have even greater structure and discipline in the training environment because players are engaged and enjoying the "fun of working". Given the rigorous training needed in handball in technical, tactical, psychological and physical areas the culture created in the training environment is crucial to success.

Simulation and Over-simulation Training

The value of simulation training for individual and team sport athletes cannot be under-estimated. Simulation training has been used by basketball coaches for decades as a part of preparing for game competition. During the past 20 years simulation training has been used by coaches and sport psychologists in many sports (Orlick, 2000). Simulation train-ing should include how a team will respond positively in various game situations and how the team should respond when a desired or practiced result does not come about during competition. Simulation training provides many advantages to athletes in preparation for high-level competition. In addition to placing players in the exact situations that are likely to occur during competition, simulation training can also place a high degree of stress on the athlete, much like the stress they may encounter in a competitive match. Handball coaches must be well versed in simulation areas such as the start of a match, a bad start to a match, end of the half close match (up or down), player up and player down situations at various points in the game, passive play warnings (especially late in close matches), penalty shots, end-of-game situations, special defenses, offense against special defenses, and playing through bad officiating calls at various times of the contest. This is but a brief list of common simulated game situations in handball. Coaches can add time pressure to these basic situations by varying how much time is left in a half or match. Coaches should place time on the clock and have assistant coaches or players officiate during simulations. Simulations must be made as real as possible. A very effective simulation in handball is to have the officials intentionally make poor calls at various times during the match. This is most effective when the players do not know that the coach has told the official to make the poor calls intentionally. By providing this type of simulation you will see who can handle the stressful situation and the bad call in the simulated setting. Players unable to "play through" in practice will need some reorienting (coaching) or they will not be effective in the actual competitive situation and may have to be substituted for in a close end of match. This may be particularly true in a match plagued by several questionable officiating calls. As a team gets closer to competition, simulations can play a crucial role in the psychological and tactical preparation of the team.

As valuable as simulations are in the preparation of a team; over-simulation training can be a tremendous asset to the psychological readiness of a team. Over-simulation training involves exposing a team to match situations at a level that exceeds what is likely to occur in competition. Over-simulation training can impact both psychological toughness and readi-ness, and it can impact physiological endurance. A common over-simulation in handball involves making a team compete with a player disadvantage for four minutes rather than the normal two-minute time frame awarded for penalty time. Preventing a team from scoring when you are a player down is difficult to do for two minutes from both a tactical and phys-ical perspective. Training the team occasionally in four-minute segments of player down requires a high level of defensive intensity be demonstrated for twice the normal duration of a penalty. Competing a player down is also physically tiring for the disadvantaged team since their five players must try to cover six opponents who spread out the floor space and move the ball quickly around the perimeter looking for gaps and overloads created by the player down defense not being able to move as fast as the ball or cover the entire defensive area.

Other common handball over-simulations include playing two players down, and playing end of close match player-to-player press defense for four to five minutes rather than the common one- or two-minute time interval. Coaches have also placed two defenders on the circle or pivot player during drill work to emphasize the need to fight through body contact and grabbing by defenders when the ball is passed into the circle player. The use of simulation and over-simulation training is limited only by the creativity of the handball coach. The important aspect of this technique in the training environment is that the events simulated reflect realistic match situations that the team must be able to respond to mentally and physically during competition.

Psychological Preparation: Pre-competition and Match Time

Pre-competition

Athletes spend years training and aspiring to compete at high levels of competition like World Championships and the Olympics. Many athletes are extremely fit, technically and tactically practiced and ready to compete. Ready to compete, that is, until the reality of the pre-competitive period incapacitates some athletes. All that hard work and training can be undermined if an athlete cannot handle the hours before match time. The pre-competitive period is operationally defined as the period of time 24 hours or less prior to competition. Research has demonstrated that successful athletes, especially at the highest levels of competition, demonstrate positive affect or mood during the hours prior to competition (Silva & Hardy, 1984; Silva, Schultz, Haslam, Martin & Murray, 1984; Silva, Schultz, Haslam & Murray, 1981). It is as if these athletes are excited about the opportunity to compete. The match is an opportunity to test against an opponent the training they have dedicated themselves to for months or even years. While this frame of mind showing desire or a "will" to compete may be the case for successful high-level competitors, some very talented athletes literally "blow themselves up" psychologically as they get close to the stress and challenge of competing against another team. Handball is a team sport that is made up of many one-on-one confrontations—player against player and player against goalie. The ability to remain calm and confident especially as the match time approaches is an important aspect of a player's psychological preparation (Manzo, Silva & Mink, 2001). Below are some suggestions and recommendations that may assist a handball player and coach manage the pre-competitive period in a manner that can maximize performance.

Night Before Match

Handball players exert a significant amount of energy during a match. At lower levels of competition, weekend tournaments often require players to participate in three or four matches on a Saturday and two matches on a Sunday. It is extremely important for players to get rest the night before a match and conserve as much energy as possible. During international competition or Olympic competition the night before a match will be well regulated by the coach and the support staff. Players will usually eat together at a specified time, have allocated "free time", an evening meeting and a curfew time. Players at lower levels of competition would be well served if they modeled their night before competition after this schedule. From an individual athlete perspective, the night before competition can be a stressful time since the reality of the competition comes into clear focus. Athletes may become concerned about their shot being off a little in recent practices, a loss of playing time due to an improving teammate, a slight injury that may bother them in the match. If there is anything negative in the back of an athlete's mind it will come to full visual force the night before competition.

To combat a potentially stressful night, one that could be without many hours of sleep, athletes need to structure their time. Excessive time spent alone should be avoided unless the athlete has considerable competitive experience, is very mature and is relaxed about the competition. Group activities that are non-fatiguing are often helpful in filling some of the hours. Athletes should set a routine for themselves the night before that includes listening to music they enjoy, speaking with family, friends and teammates who are positive and optimistic, watching enjoyable events on television, relaxing in a hot tub or jacuzzi, and engaging in some preparatory visual rehearsal. Total body relaxation just before going to sleep accompanied by a brief review of the major objective the athlete has for their play in the match on the following day can be helpful. The athlete may also wish to engage in some confidence-enhancing self-statements and visualize specific shots or brief "clips" of plays or individual moves. The athlete should not try to force information or "dos and don'ts" into their head the night before competition. The night before should be simply an evening for review and psychological reinforcement of the game plan already set in place. By the time the night before competition arrives, the athlete's major preparation in all areas should be complete. Stress should not be added to the athlete's frame of mind by excessive overloading of information by the coach or fellow players. Little or no new information should be provided the night before and the atmosphere transmitted by the coaching staff should be one of calmness and confidence in the team's preparation.

Match Day

Preparation on match day varies a little according to the time of the match. If the match is late in the evening coaches will have to be wise in how they use the many hours that will have to pass before the actual start of the match. The concepts of "off time" and "on time" should be mastered by the coach and the athlete. The handball player cannot spend six hours during the day mentally "on" thinking about the match that evening. Some coaches make a serious mistake when they expect the players to have on their "game face" all day long for a match that is scheduled for 20:00 or 21:00 that evening. This wears out many athletes mentally and they feel flat during warm-ups and exhausted before the ball is put into play. When the match is in the evening, players should be allowed a reasonable wake-up time. Individually, a player may wish to once again relax in bed and go over the personal objectives they have for the match that evening. The mental repetition under a relaxed condition can be confidence-enhancing the day of the match. A fairly structured routine should be in place by the coach. This may include team breakfast, team stretch, an hour of light drill work including goalie warm-up, passing and shooting drills, a brief review of offensive and defensive tactics, team cool down. After the morning session, players should be provided with "off time" until the scheduled team lunch. It is best to allow players to have this time as personal time rather than schedule individual meetings with players. If the coach is going to contact the players at all during this time it should be light and friendly interaction—keep it "off time". After lunch many coaches have team meetings. As a consultant on several international trips, I have found the after-lunch meeting time to be very ineffective. Players have just eaten and are often in a leisurely mood. Since things tend to get serious fast as the match time approaches a brief "nap and pack" afternoon period is often helpful. Players have time to rest after eating (they often fight falling asleep in team meetings right after lunch) and get their equipment packed well before departure time. Many times I have witnessed players late for a team meeting or a team departure time because they were not in the routine of packing early and then making a "final equipment check" at least a half an hour before departure time. A coach does not want problems right before a match such as players late for departure, or finding out on the bus ride to the venue a player does not have needed equipment, jerseys or personal items. A meeting an hour or hour and a half prior to departure is the time it will be most effective. Players are now approaching "game mode" and their arousal level is usually up a little. They are ready to pay attention to the coach's instructions and the players know that match time is near. Shortly after the meeting the team should depart for the venue and the pre-match routine.

Pre-match

The time one to two hours before a match is operationalized as pre-match time. Athletes are usually very focused during this time and may actually be over-aroused or stressed. Two hours pre-match is somewhat of an odd time. It is too early to get an intense focus and hold that focus, yet it is a time interval where players know the match is right around the corner. This time should be very structured since it is important to have the team relaxed yet focused and ready to compete at match time. The more organized the coach and the team, the less stressful the pre-match period. At elite levels of competition everything should be set from where the drop-off point is for the team bus, to the time the team can occupy the locker room, to when players must report back to the team if they are getting taped before the game. If there are disruptions or logistical problems at the venue, the coach and the staff must do their best to keep the players calm and away from such obvious distractions. Players should not be involved in any of the pre-match logistics since this can distract them from their final preparations and can heighten their level of pre-match stress.

From an individual player's perspective this should be a time for a combination of "off time" and "on time". The handball player begins to feel that edge that comes with competition nearing yet the player does not want to be locked in mentally for two hours before a match begins. Each player should engage in the types of activities that help create a relaxed, ready feeling as they move from the two-hour pre-match to the one-hour pre-match mark. Once the one-hour pre-match mark is reached most players begin to get taped by the trainer and final adjustments whether it is equipment adjustments, physical feelings (stretching, arm loose, body warm) or psychological readiness (confident, relaxed, yet intense and ready to get off to a strong start) should be completed as the group readies for the team warm-up. Prior to the team warm-up some players prefer to be physically active playing catch, jogging, moving, while other athletes prefer to be more conservative in their movement patterns. Coaches should allow for these individual differences until it is time for the team warm-up. From a psychological perspective, once inside the one-hour mark, players should be more oriented to "on time" and they should be thinking about their individual objectives for the match and the team objectives for the match. They should be thinking and physically practicing individual moves that they will use in the game both on offense and defense. How much mental rehearsal combined with physical repetition an athlete uses is very individualized during the pre-match time. Players should also interact and communicate with teammates about what they are anticipating or what they are going to try and do in certain situations where they will be involved with that teammate. It has been my observation that coaches should intervene as little as possible with the individual routine the athlete has established during pre-match period. Often a coach will notice that a player does not seem to know how to get prepared during this one-to-two-hour block of time, or the athlete is engaging in behavior that is not helpful to the player or to teammates. When this is observed by a coach or a sport psychologist it should be discussed away from the player and the team the day after the competition. If there is agreement that the player may benefit from a different routine the coach or the sport psychologist (this should be predetermined by the coach) should approach the player, one-on-one, several days before the next competition and discuss the concerns and the potential options that could be used prior to the next match.

Match Time

Perhaps one of the most interesting time frames from a psychological perspective is match time. The weeks and days of preparation are gone. The long, slowly passing hours of the night before and day of the match have vanished. The player is now faced with only moments before all the learning, the practice and preparation becomes translated into performance and outcome. Match time is not a time for rushing a few final shots, or having details of the offensive or defensive assignments rush through your head. Match time provides the final minutes before the throw-in where a handball player can create a state of physical and mental readiness that will increase the opportunity for a solid start in individual and team performance. These final minutes should be structured and practiced by the team well before match day. There should be organization in the team and on the bench in these waning pre-match moments. The impending competition should be a logical extension of the final moments before match time.

Warm-up

Most coaches have a structured warm-up for the team that gets the court players and the goalies ready to play. This is a team function and the time for individual or idiosyncratic warm-up routines is over. In handball, as in other high-speed, high-impact sports, it is extremely important that the players break a good sweat in the warm-up. The heart rate should be very elevated and the shooting arm of the court players should be warm. The goalies should break a sweat also and they should be fully stretched out before the team warm-up. During the team warm-up an emphasis should be placed on making sure the goalie has seen shots from all court positions and from any particular angles or positions they request.

Psychologically, it is best to have a good pace for handball players during warm-up but not a hectic pace. Players should be very "on" during the warm-up and should try to take shots and make moves at game speed. Players should understand that how well or poorly they warm up should not be taken as a predictive barometer of how well or poorly they will play. Unfortunately, many players do this in handball and other sports. They rush at the end of warm-up to make their last shot, even if it is on an open goal! A player's confidence in their ability has to be deeper and based on more reliable information than a ten-minute warm-up prior to a match. The coach should leave two to three minutes after the warm-up before the start of the match to bring the team to the bench and have a few final words for the team. The team should not have a large gap of "dead time" after warm-up and before the start of the match. This "dead time" could serve to cool down the athlete physically, and it could allow the athlete to experience heightened stress as the athlete tries to maintain a "go state" during the excessive time lapse.

A sound and well practiced warm-up routine can help an athlete feel physically comfortable and mentally ready to compete. The routine, however, should not be turned into a ritual by the coach or the players. A warm-up routine is structured yet it has some flexibility. The team should not approach the warm-up routine like a ritual that has to be carried out to exacting detail or the team will not be ready to play well. The player controls a routine. It is a series of actions that helps a player get ready to compete. Rituals control players and players become superstitious. For example, it is "bad luck" if the handball goalie does not make the save on the last shot on net during warm-ups. Providing trivial factors and inanimate objects the power to determine good performance or bad performance can result in high levels of anxiety in players and place in the back of their minds a self-fulfilling prophecy. If the team starts to play badly, the player has an "I knew it" response and a ready explanation for the poor performance based on the superstition. Players should be encouraged to have more of an internal locus of control and take the difficult but necessary responsibility for individual and team performance.

Match Time

The captains have met, the throw-in has been determined, it is match time. When the ball is thrown in, the action in handball is immediate. Players should be physically and mentally ready to go at 100 per cent immediately. Players must come out ready to run, jump, shoot, hit and be hit. Goalies must be sharp at the outset. On the first possession court players will need to hit, and you will be hit. There is very little time in handball for physically or mentally "settling into" the match. A fast break can take place off the first shot on goal. Since handball is such a physical sport, players are often banged and bruised going into a match. When it is match time it is important for a handball player to put those minor injuries out of their mind. A player must learn at match time that "you have to go with what you got". Players should commit to giving 100 per cent of what they have on that match day. It is uncommon for athletes in sports like ice hockey, American football and handball to be fully healthy and fully rested for competition. Often a handball player is at 75 to 80 per cent capacity due to injuries such as a slightly pulled muscle, a broken finger, a sore arm or a sprained ankle. This physical state of affairs cannot be turned into a psychological weakness and be used as an excuse for a poor performance. If a player steps out on the court at match time they must be mentally trained to give 100 per cent of whatever their capacity is at match time. A confident, ready-to-go approach is needed at match time, for a flat team in a handball match can find itself down 4–0 very quickly!

Once in the match, players should do everything possible to "go on automatic" and permit their training and drill work take over. Players should always be mentally in the flow of the game, processing information and making good decisions. These are thinking skills, but the read, recognize and react pattern in handball happens in an instant. Again, this is where the importance of training and proper preparation comes into play. What is occurring on the court should have a high degree of familiarity to the handball player if they have been trained properly in the practice setting. Yet, even the most highly trained handball player will make an individual mistake or be part of a team mistake. Since there is such a high degree of coordination required in the execution of offensive and defensive play, mistakes happen. Thus, a handball player should not expect a perfect match from themself nor from their teammates. It is honorable to strive for zero mistakes in one's game; however, this is highly unlikely to happen in handball. An emphasis on a mental approach geared toward perfection can contribute to player frustration and player anger. This frustration is often directed toward the self, teammates and, in the later stages of a close match, the goalie. The highly interactive nature of handball and the requirements of precise timing, clear and quick communication and rapid recovery make it far more productive for a handball player to play through a mistake and not carry it along as the game progresses. The player who carries mistakes in handball has a very heavy load by the end of the match! This can be unfortunate since many handball matches end up being close encounters. Highly skilled precise play is needed at the end of the match every bit as much as it is needed during the earlier phases of play.

While it is very important that players allow their training to place them in the flow of the game, players must use recycling skills if they become frustrated or they are performing poorly. Recycling skills should be taught and developed in the practice and training environment so they are well conditioned and part of a positive habit in response to mistakes, poor play and frustration. Athletes must learn in practice and transfer to match situations the ability to let go of a mistake, return immediately to the task at hand, and not lose confidence in their ability to perform at their level of capability. Some handball players try to overcompensate for mistakes and take unnecessary risks on defense by trying to make a "big play" after a defensive mistake. This breakdown in fundamental play often results in an unnecessary high-risk play and another defensive breakdown. Since only one time out is awarded to each team per half, handball players must learn to regulate their psychological responses on the court and do so quickly. On offense, a player who can recycle after a mistake gets right back into the team flow on offense and makes good decisions the next time down the court. An offensive player unable to recycle quickly may not only be out of the rhythm of the offense but may turn the ball over or force a low percentage shot on the goal. The center back must have strong recycling skills since this is the position that organizes the offense and makes many calls and adjustments on the floor. The shooters at the left and right back positions benefit greatly from recycling skills since they will often be bumped, hit and fouled while shooting and may not get a call from the official. Wings need recycling skills since they often take diving shots from tough angles that result in a spectacular goal, a block by the goalie or a complete miss. Goalies will be scored upon anywhere from 15 to 30 times in a match. Given the high scoring in handball the goalie must be able to recycle quickly and get ready for the next fast break or offensive thrust by the opposition.

Perhaps one of the most important aspects of player psychology during match play is the ability to play with consistency. Coaches want to know what to expect from a player come match time. Some players are great practice players but they cannot transfer their mentality, skills and overall level of performance to actual match play. The handball player who can go out on the court, match in and match out, and play up to their capabilities places themselves in a position to have a great game. It is easier for a player to elevate their game when they are playing consistently well as opposed to when a player's performance is inconsistent. What distinguishes a "great" player in any sport? Is it the ability to have one great match, or to occasionally have a brilliant performance? Most great players play at a high and consistent level over a long period of time. They become part of the foundation a team can be built around. They can be counted on to be fundamentally sound whether the team is considerably ahead, considerably behind or in a very close match. Players who bring strong recycling skills and who work hard to maintain a high level of consistent play make a contribution that is invaluable to the overall success of a team.

Psychological Preparation: Post-match Considerations

Most coaches and sport psychologists understand the importance of the practice environment, the pre-match setting and of course the actual match. While these aspects of competition attract considerable attention it is very surprising how many coaches and sport psychologists fail to provide guidance to the athlete concerning psychological aspects of the post-match. Post-match is a time when athletes are often most vulnerable to emotional outbursts—positive or negative. The excitement experienced by the winning team or the great frustration and disappointment suffered by the losing team create strong emotional conditions. It is extremely important, especially at higher levels of competition, to prepare athletes for the post-match environment.

Post-match Procedures

Teams should have a post-match procedure just as they have a pre-match procedure. It is easy to lose individual and team discipline after a great victory or a tough loss. Players should be allowed a few minutes of celebration after a win but the celebration should always be kept in perspective and nothing should be done that is at the expense or embarrassment of the losing team. After a loss, players should be instructed to maintain their composure and not antagonize opponents or match officials. Competitive sport is a small world and competitive handball is an even smaller world. It is likely you will compete against this team again and see the game officials again in the not-too-distant future. If there is a norm to shake hands with the opponent after the match, the victorious team should be respectful and not make the losing team wait an excessively long time before lining up for the handshake.

Teams should have a post-game protocol that is followed by all members of the team. The protocol should be established by the coach and should be enforced by the captains and senior members of the team. For example, if there is a handshake tradition, after the handshake the players may gather up their own equipment and players with specific team assignments (such as ball bag duty) should make sure they complete their assignment. The team may be allowed to hydrate briefly before convening in the locker or a designated meeting area for post-match comments by the coach and team. Unless there is a serious injury, players would be permitted to see an athletic trainer after the post-match meeting. Meetings with family and friends would also be arranged for after the post-match meeting or after all players have showered and are departing from the locker room.

Coaches should emphasize to their teams that post-match is a time when it is easy to say something you do not really mean to say. However, once said, many statements cannot be retracted. The post-match is a time when players are overwhelmed by the suddenness with which the end of a handball match can arrive. After nearly 60 minutes of a hard-fought match, characterized by high emotions and high physical intensity, the finality of a close match plays out swiftly in a few passing seconds, and then it is over. You have won or you have lost. There is excitement or there is disappointment. There is a sense of accomplishment or there is reflection on "what could have been". For the losing team, there is often an intense focus on what went wrong, a costly mistake or a great play by the opposition. The outcome is instantly burned into a player's mind—we won or we lost—that is the bottom line. For the losing team, factors like effort and positive aspects of performance are often lost in the psychological intensity surrounding the post-match atmosphere. It is beneficial to the development of the psychological maturity and toughness of a team if a coach emphasizes that each match can be best placed in perspective hours or even the day following the event. The team and each individual player of the winning or losing team need to maintain a degree of stability in the emotionally charged minutes that follow a match. The emotional stability of the athlete will be tested in the post-match period as much as it was tested in the actual match. Both "performances" will be subject to the observation and scrutiny of the media if the match is a high-level or international level match.

Media

There is little doubt that the media play a significant role in the presentation of high-level sport. The media may be local, regional, national or international in scope. Given today's technology, once "online", even a local story can escalate into a national or international media event. Coaches and particularly athletes have to be prepared to work with and speak with the media post-match. Moments after an exciting win or a painful loss a representative of the media may be there to interview an athlete. The sweat may still be dripping off the athlete, and the athlete may still be trying to figure out in their own mind "what just happened" as questions are fired away. With the infusion of the electronic media into all aspects of sport, an athlete's words and images can leave a lasting impression upon the sports world. This is an extremely difficult time for many athletes. Some do not want to speak with media, particularly after a tough loss.

Coaches and sport psychologists can provide a valuable service to athletes involved in high-level sport by preparing them for post-match media interviews. This can be done in either a team or group setting or it can be done individually. When done in a group setting it is often reasonable to follow up with individual meetings as needed to address specific concerns a player may have with the media. Player or coach outbursts after a match often harm the team and sometimes may provide additional motivation to opponents. Some coaches regulate who can and who cannot speak with the media post-match. If a coach institutes this type of restrictive policy the team should be very clear on the policy and the consequences for violating the policy. Obviously, the potential for additional team problems exists when media interaction with players creates or fuels problems that may exist within the team. These problems are always most visible after a difficult loss or after a series of tough matches that resulted in negative outcomes. While some coaches may restrict who speaks with the media in a formal setting, it is difficult to prevent informal or impromptu interactions. Teams may benefit by following a few common-sense guidelines when involved in a media interview:

- Maintain your poise and dignity in any circumstance.
- Be respectful of the person conducting the interview and of your opponent.
- Try to support your teammates' efforts and those of your coaching staff.
- Be natural, yet respond to success and adversity rationally.
- Remain optimistic, and look to the future.
- Try to end the interview with a positive or humorous comment.

These general guidelines can assist an athlete or coach in victory or in the difficult moments following an intense defeat. The recent events surrounding US Olympic gymnast Paul Hamm provide a powerful example of how an athlete on the world stage was forced to manage extremely difficult questions concerning whether he should keep his all-around Gold Medal won in 2004 Summer Olympics (Pells, 2004). Due to a controversy in the scoring, the questioning started within hours of the athlete receiving his medal and continued on for weeks after the Olympics. Hamm was not the only Olympic athlete required to demonstrate poise outside the athletic arena. Athletes representing the host country of Greece even came under the scrutiny of the media after successful medal-winning performances (Lawrence, 2004).

CONCLUSION

Handball is an intense physical game that involves a great deal of emotion and personal expression. Helping players prepare not only for the actual competition but also for difficult situations that may immediately follow the competition is a great service that a well-trained and experienced sport psychologist can offer a team or individual competitor. The player who properly trains physically, technically, tactically and psychologically will increase their opportunity for match success and the team's opportunity for success. Equally important, the athlete will increase the opportunity for managing the stress of competitive sport and thus increase their longevity in the sport and their enjoyment of the sport.

REFERENCES

Carron, A.V. & Hausenblas, H.A. (1998). *Group Dynamics in Sport* (2nd edn). Morgantown, WV: Fitness Information Technology.
Dorrance, A. & Averbuch, G. (2002). *The Vision of a Champion*. Chelsea, MI: Sleeping Bear Press.
Fitts, P.M. & Posner, M.I. (1967). *Human Performance*. Belmont, CA: Brooks/Cole.
Gleitman, H. (1992). *Basic Psychology* (3rd edn). New York: W.W. Norton.

Gould, D. (1983). Developing psychological skills in young athletes. In N.L. Wood (ed.), *Coaching Science Update*. Ottawa, Ontario: Coaching Association of Canada.

Hull, C.L. (1952). *A Behavior System: An Introduction to Behavior Theory Concerning the Individual Organism*. New Haven, CT: Yale University Press.

Johnson, M. (1996). *Slaying the Dragon*. New York: Harper Collins Publishers Inc.

Lawrence, T. (2004). I won fairly, says Flying Fani. Foxsports.com. Retrieved from http://foxsports. news.com.au/olympics/story/ 0,9744,10572982-34055,00.html.

Locke, E.A. & Latham, G.P. (1985). The application of goal setting to sports. *Journal of Sport Psychology, 7*, 205–222.

Manzo, L.G., Silva, J.M. & Mink, R. (2001). The Carolina sport confidence inventory. *Journal of Applied Sport Psychology, 13*, 260–274.

Meichenbaum, D. (1977). *Cognitive-behavior Modification*. New York: Plenum.

Meichenbaum, D. (1985). *Stress Inoculation Training*. New York: Pergamon.

O'Block, F.R. & Evans, F.H. (1984). Goal setting as a motivational technique. In J.M. Silva & R.S. Weinberg (eds), *Psychological Foundations of Sport*. Champaign, IL: Human Kinetics.

Orlick, T. (2000). *In Pursuit of Excellence: How to Win in Sport and Life through Mental Training*. Champaign, IL: Human Kinetics.

Papanikolaou, Z.K. (2000). The athletic intelligence. *International Journal of Physical Education 37*(1) 24–28.

Pells, E. (2004). Hamm: 'I shouldn't be dealing with this'. Washingtonpost.com. Retrieved from http://www.washingtonpost.com/ wp-dyn/articles/A24450-2004Aug22.html.

Schmidt, G.W. & Stein, G.L. (1991) Sport commitment: a model integrating enjoyment, dropout, and burnout. *Journal of Sport and Exercise Psychology, 12*(3), 254–265.

Silva, J.M. (1990). An analysis of the training stress syndrome in competitive athletics. *Journal of Applied Sport Psychology, 2*, 5–20.

Silva, J.M. & Hardy, C.J. (1984). Precompetitive affect and athletic performance. In W.F. Straub & J.H. Williams (eds), *Cognitive Sport Psychology* (pp. 79–88). Lansing, NY: Sport Science Associates.

Silva, J.M. & Hardy C.J. (1991) The sport psychologist: psychological aspects of injury in sport. In F.O. Mueller & A. Ryan (eds), *The Sports Medicine Team and Athletic Injury Prevention*. Philadelphia, PA: Davis.

Silva, J.M., Schultz, B.B., Haslam, R.W., Martin, T.P. & Murray, D.F. (1984). Discriminating characteristics of contestants at the United States Olympic Wrestling Trials. *International Journal of Sport Psychology, 16*, 79–102.

Silva, J.M., Schultz, B.B., Haslam, R.W. & Murray, D. (1981). A psychophysiological assessment of elite wrestlers. *Research Quarterly for Exercise and Sport, 52*, 348–358.

Stevens, D.E. (2002) Building the effective team. In J.M. Silva & D.E. Stevens (eds). *Psychological Foundations of Sport*. Boston, MA: Allyn & Bacon.

CHAPTER 11

Skill Learning from an Expertise Perspective: Issues and Implications for Practice and Coaching in Cricket

Sean Müller
The University of Queensland, Australia
and
Bruce Abernethy
University of Hong Kong/The University of Queensland, Australia

INTRODUCTION

There is perennial interest in all sports in finding new or superior means of improving the performance of players. In this chapter we present an example of an evidence-based approach to the development of enhanced means of learning some of the critical skills needed by players in the sport of cricket. After a brief overview of cricket for readers unfamiliar with the sport, we describe, in turn, the constraints and difficulties associated with the pivotal skill of batting and current understanding of how experts in batting manage to deal so successfully with these task constraints. Determining the nature of expert performance and the locus of expert–novice differences in performance provides a valuable means of both identifying the limiting factors to performance and ascertaining the key factors upon which to focus efforts and resources in practice and coaching. The final section of the chapter then describes some of the traditional approaches to the practice and coaching of batting in cricket. Additionally, the final section highlights issues with, and alternatives to, the current approaches that might be suggested from what is known about batting expertise. Throughout the chapter, the emphasis is upon the valuable role an expertise perspective can play in guiding the development and an evidence-base for the optimizing of practice and coaching efficacy. We believe that the principles we describe are applicable to many, if not all, sports but will obviously be of greatest relevance to the sport psychologist, applied sport scientist, coach or manager seeking an evidence-based approach to prepare amateur and professional cricketers for competition.

The Sport Psychologist's Handbook: A Guide for Sport-Specific Performance Enhancement.
Edited by Joaquín Dosil. © 2006 John Wiley & Sons, Ltd.

ABOUT THE GAME OF CRICKET

In this section we provide only a necessarily brief overview of the objectives of the game and of the batsman within the game. An in-depth description of the rules, fielding positions and terminology of the sport of cricket is beyond the scope of this chapter, but readers seeking more detailed introductions to the sport and its rules should consult Ferguson (1992) or the Marylebone Cricket Club (2003).

A cricket match is played by 2 teams each consisting of 11 players. There are 3 types of cricket match played at the professional level: test matches (played over 5 days at international level), first-class matches (played over 3 or 4 days at state or provincial levels) and limited overs matches (played over 1 day at both international and state or provincial levels). The main difference between these different types of match is that in test/first-class matches each team is permitted 2 opportunities to bat (referred to as an innings). In a limited overs match, each team is permitted only 1 opportunity to bat (1 innings) for a maximum duration typically of 50 overs (each over consists of 6 legal balls delivered by a bowler). The objective of multi-day matches such as test and first-class matches is to score more runs and take more wickets than the opposition. In contrast, the objective of limited overs matches is to simply score more runs than the opposition.

Runs are scored by batsmen who must use the bat (a wooden implement crafted from willow) to strike a ball bowled by a designated member of the opposition team (the bowler). By the rules of the game, the bat can be no more than 96.5 cm in length and 10.8 cm in width. The bat has a circular handle at one end that is covered in re-attachable rubber to provide grip. The ball can be no more than 7.29 cm in diameter (22.9 cm in circumference) meaning that quite precise spatial judgements are necessary for good contact of the bat to be made with the ball. The batsman stands in front of, and protects, a set of wickets (3 vertical wooden stumps of 71.1 cm in height joined at the top by 2 wooden bails of 5.40 cm in length). The bowler delivers the ball with a straight arm action from a second set of wickets located 20.12 m away. The batsman can score runs in 1 of 3 ways: (1) by hitting the ball and then running once or for as many times as possible between the 2 sets of wickets before the ball is fielded and returned next to 1 of the sets of wickets, (2) by hitting the ball so that it bounces in the field of play before reaching the boundary to score 4 runs (the boundary is usually marked by a rope or fence at a distance of approximately 60–70 m from the batsman) and (3) hitting the ball so that it lands over the boundary to score 6 runs.

To make efficient contact the batsman must swing the bat either in a vertical or horizontal plane (resulting in vertical and horizontal bat strokes, respectively), so that maximum bat width is presented for ball contact. It has been reported that ball contact is targeted at the centre of percussion in the lower but towards the medial edge of the bat (the "sweet spot") (Nurick, Balden & Stretch, 2003). Such bat–ball contact can be used to guard against ball contact with the lateral edge (or outside edge) that may result in being caught out (see point 2 below), while it also provides sufficient momentum to steer the ball towards and along the ground, in gaps between the fielders, so that runs can be scored.

There are several ways in which a batsman can be dismissed ("given out") when executing a stroke to score runs. An individual batsman's innings is terminated when they are dismissed and a team's innings terminates when 10 individual batsmen have been dismissed. Common means of dismissal include: (1) bowled (where the ball makes contact with either of 3 wooden wickets causing the bails to be dislodged); (2) caught out by a fielder (after the ball has made contact with the bat or hands and is taken by a fieldsman before it touches the ground); (3) leg before wicket (where the batsman's body prevents a bowled ball from hitting the wickets); and (4) stumped or run out (where one of the wickets is broken with the batsman still outside their safety zone, the crease). Further explanation of these and other methods of how a batsman can be dismissed can be found by consulting the Laws of Cricket (Marylebone Cricket Club, 2003).

Players in a cricket team can also have different roles such as a bowler, wicketkeeper or captain with each comprising of specific duties during a match. All players in the team, however, are required to bat during a match situation to score runs for the team. Therefore, this chapter will focus on the difficulties and constraints associated with this common skill of batting and will compare traditional methods of practice and coaching with alternatives based on evidence available from an expertise perspective. The principles that are discussed can be applied in a similar manner to other roles within a cricket team. Readers seeking explanation on the different roles of players in a cricket team should consult Ferguson (1992) or the Marylebone Cricket Club (2003).

THE ROLE OF THE SPORT PSYCHOLOGIST IN CRICKET

The role of the sport psychologist is to work together with players, the coach and the manager to achieve specific goals. This can involve planning and development with the coach to achieve short-term goals that lead into long-term goals aimed at successful team results (Gordon, 2001). Such strategic goal setting can be achieved by focusing on individual player abilities and needs, as well as distributing responsibilities for goal attainment equally amongst team members (Gordon, 2001). Consequently, mental or psychological skills can provide a means for optimizing performance of individuals and the team as a whole, which can play an integral role in achievement of goals. This chapter, however, presents information that the sport psychologist, as well as the coach and managers, can implement to optimize skill learning. Readers interested in an elaboration on mental skills evaluation or training specific to cricket should consult Gordon (1990, 2001) for a treatment of this topic.

DIFFICULTIES AND CONSTRAINTS IN BATTING

Cricket batting is an extremely difficult skill. The batting task has minimal error tolerance (one performance error can result in dismissal) and time constraints are severe. Accordingly, successful performance requires very high temporal and spatial accuracies in coincidence timing to be achieved under conditions in which there is significant uncertainty about both precisely when and where the ball will arrive. At the highest levels of performance, positional errors of less than 5 cm and temporal errors of less than 2 to 3 ms are consistently maintained in an environment in which the batsman is required to hit a ball that may be travelling at up to 160 km.hr^{-1} (44.8 m.s^{-1}), and may be deviating both vertically and laterally (McLeod & Jenkins, 1991; Regan, 1997). The task must be performed within the inherent constraints imposed by human reaction time and movement time latencies and, like batting in baseball, at the margins of the functional limits of the human visuo-motor system (Bahill & LaRitz, 1984). An elaboration of some of these difficulties and constraints within the batting task follows.

The Time Constraints in Responding

At the highest international level of competition the ball can be bowled at the batsman at velocities exceeding 140 km.hr^{-1} (39.2 m.s^{-1}). At these velocities the ball takes less than 500 ms from when it is released by the bowler to when it reaches the batsman. During this time the batsman must not only determine when and where the ball will arrive (i.e. determine the appropriate time and place for interception) but also organize, initiate and complete the necessary whole body and bat movements necessary for effective contact (Abernethy, 1981). Even for medium pace bowling of around 110 km.hr^{-1}, the ball's travel time is considerably less than the total time, of approximately 900 ms, it takes the batsman to complete their required movements (Gibson & Adams, 1989). A further complicating factor for the batsman is that they must also deal with the constraint of a simple reaction time (SRT) delay of approximately 200 ms—the minimal time it takes to identify and process a visual stimulus prior to initiation of a movement. Consequently, a chronometric analysis of the batting skill would suggest that, when confronted with a ball velocity of 110 km.hr^{-1} and above, the decision to initiate gross body movements (particularly those of the legs) must be made prior to the ball actually being released by the bowler (Abernethy, 1981, 1984; see Figure 11.1). It may be possible to use early-to middle-ball flight information to initiate a decision about the downswing of the bat and allow efficient bat–ball contact (Abernethy, 1981). This analysis suggests that skilled performance in batting may be dependent upon a

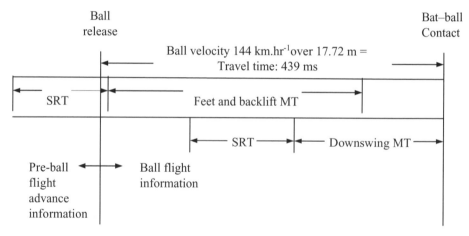

Figure 11.1 A schematic diagram of the time constraints in batting when the bowler delivers a ball at 144 km.hr^{-1} from an effective distance of 17.72 m from the batsman. The movement times (MTs) of the feet and the bat required for successful responding are shown separately, with each preceded by a latency equivalent to simple reaction time (SRT). These analyses suggest that the decision as to which foot movement to select (depicted by the start of the SRT period) must be made well before the ball is released by the bowler while the decision regarding downswing initiation is completed using early to middle sections of ball flight.
Note: Segmented time response sequences for feet, backlift and downswing movements are not to scale.
Source: Figure 11.1 was adapted from Skill in cricket batting: laboratory and applied evidence. In M.L. Howell & B.D. Wilson (eds), *Proceedings of the seventh Commonwealth and International Conference on Sport, Physical Education, Recreation and Dance, 7*, 35–50. Copyright 1984 by B. Abernethy. Adapted with permission.

well-developed capability to use pre-ball flight (advance) information, arising from the bowler's movement pattern and delivery action, as well as later-occurring ball flight information. The time constraints are such that the batsman cannot simply wait until they see the ball in flight in order to make the predictive judgements needed for successful striking of the ball.

Factors Causing Spatial Uncertainty in Batting

Ball Configuration, Ball Flight and Swing

The cricket ball used for senior amateur and professional competition consists of a solid inner sphere of cork encased in an outer leather shell that is dyed red. The leather shell is stitched, first, to join the two halves of the ball (referred to as the "seam" of the ball) and second, to join the two quarters (referred to as the "quarter seams"). The seam is slightly raised above the surface shell of the ball and provides a rough surface for better grip by the bowler and a means of inducing in the ball swing through the air or deviation off the pitch.

A new cricket ball is used at the start of each innings within a match. The new ball is hard, has a pronounced seam and has comparable sheen on both halves (Mehta, 2000). An upright and angled seam, commonly used by faster bowlers, creates pressure asymmetry on either side of the ball, causing the ball to swing while in flight in the direction that the seam is angled (see Barrett & Wood, 1995; Mehta, 2000; for an elaboration). This is referred to as "conventional new ball swing". Once the ball has been used for a number of overs of bowling it becomes softer (more compliant), the seam becomes less pronounced above the surface of the ball, and the two sides of the ball can develop differential levels of shine/smoothness (Mehta, 2000). Together, the characteristics of the seam and the rough side of the old ball can create asymmetrical airflow that generates conventional swing in the old ball (see Barrett & Wood, 1995; Mehta, 2000; for an elaboration). In certain instances when the ball is bowled at high velocity (e.g. above 140 km.hr^{-1}), swing can be generated in the opposite direction to that to which the seam and rough side of the ball is positioned (Mehta, 2000). This is referred to as "old ball reverse swing". Interestingly, a bowler can use the same delivery action (or kinematics) to bowl both conventional and reverse swings, thus deceiving the batsman (Barrett & Wood, 1995; Mehta, 2000).

Slower bowlers, generally referred to as "spin bowlers", can also generate swing during ball flight, in the form of drift and dip. The sidespin imparted by the spin bowler can cause the ball to drift (or swing) either into or away from the batsman (dependent upon what type of spin is applied) and then spin laterally in the opposite direction after bouncing. Additionally, any topspin component applied by the bowler can cause the ball to dip (or drop) earlier than expected towards the pitch. In order to dismiss batsman, bowlers of all types attempt to use their bowling action and the ball configuration to make efficient bat–ball contact difficult. Spin bowlers release the ball at a significantly slower velocity than do faster bowlers (thus reducing the time stresses on the batsman), but compensate for this by generally making the ball deviate more both in flight and after bouncing. Swing, drift and dip all contribute spatial, as well as some temporal, uncertainty to the batting task making difficult the batsmen's task of selecting the appropriate stroke (or hitting action) and then timing it with precision.

Ball Bounce and the Playing Surface

An additional factor in batting that contributes to spatial and temporal uncertainty is how the surface of the pitch (the area between the two sets of wickets) interacts with ball bounce. The most common surface used for the pitch at amateur and professional levels is turf or grass. Being subject to natural elements, the characteristics of turf pitch are quite variable and differ not only from match to match but also across the duration of a match. A turf pitch can be wetter and softer (more compliant) with more grass cover, or dryer and harder (less compliant) with less grass cover. Differences in pitch compliance present difficulty in timing for the batsman. For example, wetter pitches can impede ball travel time, due to greater retarding friction at ball bounce (Carré, Haake, Baker & Newell, 1998). Additionally, grass cover or cracks in the soil can provide an uneven surface for ball bounce. Hence, a new ball with its pronounced seam can swing in the air and deviate right or left when it bounces, depending on which part of the seam makes contact with the pitch surface. The uneven pitch surface can also produce variation in the consistency of bounce height. This can create uncertainty for the batsman in the selection of vertical or horizontal strokes. As it takes some 200 ms to begin to adjust the swing of the bat to any unexpected deviations in ball trajectory (McLeod, 1987), skilled batsmen seek, wherever possible, to nullify the effects of lateral deviation of the ball by hitting the ball as close as possible to when and where it bounces.

Minimal Error Tolerance

Participation as a batsman during match play is constrained by the rules of the game. For instance, in test or first-class cricket, batsmen are provided two opportunities (two innings) to participate in the match by scoring runs. On other occasions (e.g. a limited overs match) a team may have only one innings, or a single opportunity to succeed. Consequently, a single skill error such as an incorrect decision to execute an attacking rather than a defensive stroke, can result in a batsman's dismissal and end their involvement in the match as a batsman. Therefore, a batsman must carefully negotiate the ball's velocity and its movement through the air and off the pitch to ensure that a single skill error is not committed. As we have noted earlier, in many ways batting is an extremely difficult task. Nevertheless, expert batsmen are able frequently to bat for extended periods (sometimes days!) when confronted with these constraints and score many hundreds of runs. Understanding the exceptional skills of expert batsmen may provide a valuable pool of knowledge to help design assessment and intervention programs to assist in the learning and development of batting skills.

EXPERTISE IN BATTING: HOW DO EXPERTS DEAL WITH THE TASK CONSTRAINTS AND DIFFICULTIES?

The analysis of the time constraints in batting suggests that it may be essential for batsmen to predict when and where the ball will arrive for hitting, by making anticipations based largely on information available prior to ball flight. The ability to anticipate i.e. to use advance information (pre-ball flight information from the bowler's delivery action) to predict the trajectory, arrival point and velocity of the forthcoming ball would appear essential for skilled batting for a number of reasons. First, visual anticipation can be used to overcome the inherent reaction time delays. Earlier initiation of useful processing of visual information, from the pre-release action of the bowler rather than from ball flight alone, can provide more time to complete the required response (Abernethy, 1981). Second, visual anticipation can allow earlier initiation and completion of gross body movements (especially those related to stepping movements of the feet), so that a balanced base of support can be established that will allow more efficient and effective bat downswing timing (Abernethy, 1984). Earlier completion of gross movements can also help the batsman achieve the appropriate body positioning to nullify potential lateral movement of the ball. Active pick-up of advance cues from the bowler could help explain the expert batsman's capability to appear to have ". . . all the time in the world".

In order to determine whether expert batsmen are indeed superior in their ability to use advance information, a number of researchers have used video to simulate experimentally the visual display the bowler presents to the batsman. The purpose of such a simulation is twofold: first, to make a faithful replication, in a controllable environment, of the visual demands of the actual performance setting (Abernethy, Wann & Parks, 1998); and second, to provide the platform for an experimental method to help determine expert–novice differences in when, and from where, batsmen pick up advance cues for anticipation. The duration of the information available to batsmen can be examined through the technique of temporal occlusion and the location of the information available through spatial occlusion (Abernethy et al., 1998). It is not uncommon for studies to include a temporal occlusion of all vision at the point of ball release (see Figure 11.2), so as to differentiate

Figure 11.2   Video simulation footage of a swing bowler's delivery action demonstrating temporal occlusion at the point of ball release; additionally, the video simulation has been spatially occluded by removal of the ball and bowling hand. Reproduced by permission of Cricket Australia

players' ability to make predictions of ball type from advance cues compared to ball flight information.

Temporal occlusion studies in cricket have reported that expert batsmen are superior to novices at extracting advance information to anticipate the landing position of the bowled ball (Abernethy & Russell, 1984; Penrose & Roach, 1995, in relation to swing bowling) and predict what type of delivery has been bowled (Renshaw & Fairweather, 2000, in relation to leg-spin bowling). Experts have also been reported to be superior at identifying the point of ball release (Adams & Gibson, 1989, in relation to swing bowling). Some evidence has also been provided from studies in the natural setting to support the findings from video simulation studies demonstrating that expert batsmen, when batting against a live bowler, make earlier and accurate feet movement decisions based on advance information (Abernethy, 1984).

To date, there is little or no evidence of the sources (or visual cues) from which information is gleaned for anticipation of ball length and type in batting, although this type of information is available for some other sports (e.g. see Abernethy & Russell, 1987, for information on advance cue utilization in badminton). The spatial occlusion technique, in which visibility to potential advance cues are selectively masked, has the potential to provide information of this type (see Figure 11.2). The basic premise of the spatial occlusion method is that if occluding a particular region or body segment increases ball prediction error, then that region/s may be an important source of anticipatory information. Experiments are currently progressing in our laboratory to use this and other techniques to further understand the timing and sources of information pick-up in batting against both swing and spin bowling. The approach being used involves combinations of laboratory-based occlusion methods and *in situ* occlusions in which batsmen compete against a live bowler while wearing liquid crystal goggles (Milgram, 1987) that are capable of occlusion of vision during the batting task. As Figure 11.3 illustrates, it is now possible for batsman to wear liquid crystal goggles during the batting task, with the coach or sports psychologist controlling the duration of the bowling action and the ball flight information that the batsman is able to view. The technique provides better prospects for examining the pick-up of information from ball flight than does the film simulation method (in that more realistic ball flight information can be provided).

Additionally, the technique offers an opportunity to understand more about the possibility of expert–novice differences in information pick-up from ball flight. Moreover, if such a technique proves useful in differentiating expert batsmen from less skilled players, then the potential may exist to use the technique to both assess and train anticipation skills for batting.

PRACTICE AND COACHING: INTERVENTION OPPORTUNITIES FOR THE ENHANCEMENT OF SKILL LEARNING

The Traditional Approach to Cricket Practice

Physical practice sessions at amateur and professional levels traditionally focus on "net sessions" of batting and bowling; so-called because batting occurs on a surface surrounded on three sides by netting, eliminating the need for fieldsmen to retrieve the ball after it has been struck by the batsman. Typically, several bowlers will bowl to each batsman,

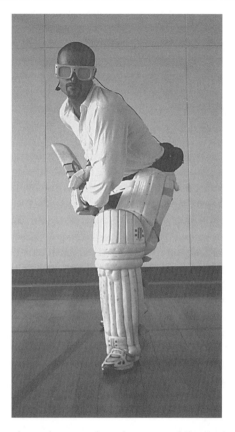

Figure 11.3 Liquid crystal goggles worn by a batsman while playing a stroke. The goggles are connected to a lightweight radio transmitter strapped to the player's waist. Occlusion of vision can be triggered through an infrared controller remote to the batsman. Reproduced by permission of Chérie Harris

with each batsman having an allocated batting time. Batting time in each session can vary from as little as 5 to 6 minutes for amateurs to upwards of 30 minutes for professionals. Many batsmen will also partake in practice against a bowling machine (a mechanical device capable of delivering balls at a pre-determined location and velocity) with the explicit goal of improving batting technique (i.e. the movement execution aspect of the skill). All players will also participate in drills designed to improve their catching and fielding skills. Overall, physical practice time may depend on a number of factors including: (1) the availability of groups of players (to structure a batting session at amateur and professional levels), (2) the availability of adequate daylight (at amateur level as practice is conducted outdoors after work hours to accommodate employment or schooling), (3) the total number of players in attendance (at amateur level depending on whether whole club or individual team practice is planned), and (4) travel, media and sponsorship commitments (for professionals).

The competitive phases for amateur and professional players vary. Amateur players usually compete in matches on weekends during a 5 to 6-month season. Professional players may play up to 5 days per week and, with international seasons and matches, for up to 10 months per year. Amateur players may have the opportunity to practice twice or 3 times per week between weekend competitions, while professionals will typically mix practice and match involvement in a more even manner. At the very top level of international competition the direct playing commitments may be such that it may sometimes be necessary to limit physical practice to prevent burn out and provide time for recovery. Consequently, there are many factors that can constrain the structure of practice, as well as a number of different options that may be possible to strike the critical balance between optimization of practice time and specificity of practice in the form of match play.

The Traditional Approach to Cricket Coaching

The traditional approach to cricket coaching is based around the refinement of batting technique—the emphasis being upon the execution (or biomechanics) of the different batting strokes. Verbal instruction and visual modelling is to the forefront in traditional coaching with each player's batting technique being constantly compared to skill execution as depicted in coaching manuals, as shown by expert batsmen, or as deemed optimal from the particular coach's perception of expert batting technique. Batting skills are frequently taught so as to be modelled on the technique of successful players, with this modelling based solely on perceptions and assumptions that the expert's superior performance levels are directly attributable to their movement mechanics. Therefore, superior technical execution is effectively accepted unequivocally as the principal limiting factor to successful performance in batting, yet there is relatively little evidence to demonstrate this as a key discriminator of expertise (see Bartlett, 2003, for a review). Indeed it is noteworthy that throughout the history of the game expert batsmen have varied quite substantially in the techniques that they have used. Paradoxically, little attention is typically paid in coaching and practice to the learning of expert perception and decision-making skills despite the growing evidence that these skills, rather than movement execution, are critical factors distinguishing the expert player from the less skilled.

Issues with the Traditional Approach to Practice and Coaching

There are a number of issues and assumptions with the traditional approach to practice and coaching that warrant scrutiny. In this section we present some of these issues and assumptions and provide some suggestions for alternative approaches.

Overemphasis on Technique and the Reliance on Expert Opinion

As we noted in the previous section, the traditional method of coaching persists with an overemphasis on technical execution to the neglect of visual anticipation skills. This is commonly fuelled by coaching manuals published by former expert players that focus solely on technique. Reliance on the verbalizations of experts can be fraught with difficulties, however, given the evidence that one of the by-products of expertise is automation of processes and a growing inability to introspect on movement control. As Johnson (1983, p. 79) has noted, 'as individuals master more and more knowledge in order to do a task efficiently as well as accurately, they also lose awareness of what they know'. Experts have difficulty in verbally expressing (explicit knowledge) components of the execution phase of their skills (Beilock, Wierenga & Carr, 2003). For example, Stuelcken (2003) pointed out that in the coaching of batting it has been recommended that the back lift should be taken straight back towards the wickets (see Ferguson, 1992). Such instructions, however, can be misleading as biomechanical studies of international standard batsmen show that these players in fact use a loop during their back lift, with vertical alignment of the bat established at downswing commencement (Stuelcken, 2003). Similarly, players are repeatedly instructed by coaches to watch 'the ball right onto the bat' and experts frequently report seeing the ball hit the bat, yet the evidence from comparable hitting tasks (e.g. Bahill & LaRitz, 1984) is that this is not physically possible given the tracking limitations of the visuo-motor system. Therefore, caution is required when justifying coaching instructions based solely on anecdotal or experiential information.

Although technique is the foundation of the traditional approach, significant variations from even the accepted basics of batting technique are evident even among expert players. For example, Stuelcken (2003) reported that a number of players from among a sample of international batsmen with exceptional performance records did not stabilize their base of support (viz. front foot) prior to bat downswing initiation. The execution of movements in a particular 'textbook' manner does not appear to be a prerequisite for expert performance nor, necessarily, a reliable discriminator of experts from lesser skilled performers. Other factors, such as the capacity to anticipate and use advance cues from the bowler's action, are more reliable discriminators of expertise and more likely to be limiting factors to expert performance. Therefore, practice routines that do not train these limiting factors and instead concentrate on non-limiting factors would seem to warrant re-examination (Abernethy, 1999).

Does the Bowling Machine Provide Useful Task-specific Practice?

As noted earlier, a common tool that is used to assist technique training is the bowling machine. The justification for the use of the bowling machine is that it provides technique practice at ball speeds comparable to a match and allows a quantum of practice, for particular strokes, that is difficult to achieve in either net or match practice against bowlers. The obvious disadvantage of practice of this type is that it creates a task with demands significantly different from that of batting in a match environment. In particular, the task becomes artificial in that (a) the emphasis is placed solely on extraction of ball flight information because no advance information is available and (b) the need to anticipate ball length and type is non-existent because both are completely predictable and predetermined. Attempts to train anticipation by varying ball length and type through respectively altering angle of projection, as well as differential spin speeds of the rotating wheels of the ball-projecting machines are too obvious and easily detected by the batsman.

Rather than using constant practice tasks of the type presented through a bowling machine it would appear to be likely more beneficial to employ more random practice of batting strokes. Random practice is where different skills within a general class of skills (e.g. vertical and horizontal bat strokes) are practiced in a non-fixed sequence in the same session rather than blocked into different practice sessions. It has been reported that while random practice leads to poorer practice performance than blocked conditions it results in learning (as demonstrated by performance at a later instance in time) that is markedly superior (Farrow & Maschette, 1997; Schmidt & Lee, 1999). If bowling machines are to continue to be a major part of batting practice, the challenge for manufacturers is to design a machine that provides simulated advance information, combined with pre-programmed subtle variation of ball length and type.

Training Visual Perceptual Skills as an Alternative to Overemphasis on Technique

Visual perception, and its training, is clearly critical to expert batting yet finding efficacious means of training vision is challenging and for this reason is yet to become a significant part of the practice regime of many players or teams. In the sports vision literature both general and sports-specific approaches have been proposed. The general approach has its foundation in optometry, where the focus is to train visual attributes (e.g. visual acuity) that are involved in the reception of visual information (Abernethy et al., 1998). The premise underpinning this approach is that superior eyesight is the limiting factor to sport performance and, if the visual functioning of the eyes can be improved, sports performance should improve concomitantly.

Control studies of visual training regimes in other sports tasks have failed to demonstrate the translation of any improvements in basic visual functioning through training, to improvements in sports-related motor performance (Abernethy & Wood, 2001; Ward, Williams & Loran, 2000; Wood & Abernethy, 1997). In cricket, West and Bressan (1996) reported that general visual training (based on specific eye exercises) transferred to improved verbal prediction of ball length by batsmen in a field setting. The lack of a placebo group, however, meant that it was not possible to exclude expectancy effects as the cause of the training group's improvement. More recent studies by Golby, Falk and Hollyhead (2000) and Barnard, Nurick and Stretch (2003) were unable to show any positive transfer of a generalized training program to a field-based verbal test of ball length prediction. Therefore, the value of general eye exercises promoted by some optometrists are certainly questionable in terms of their capacity to improve the skills essential for expert batting.

According to what the evidence on expertise in batting reveals, it would appear to be more important to direct time and effort in training to those visual factors that are known to limit performance and to be systematically related to expert performance. It appears that basic visual function attributes (such as acuity, phoria and depth perception) do not reliably differ between expert and novice players (Abernethy, 1987; Helsen & Starkes, 1999). While subnormal levels of basic visual function may have the potential to limit performance (hence the possible need for routine visual screening of players), above normal levels of basic visual function do not appear to characterize expert performance or enhance sport performance. Therefore, it would be more appropriate to expend effort in designing training programs that target perceptual skills, such as superior pick-up of advance information, as a basis for trying to make learners more expert-like. Some examples of training approaches of this type are now appearing in the skill acquisition/expert performance literature.

Video simulation can be used to train anticipation by providing repeated exposure to occlusion tasks similar to those used for the assessment of advance information pick-up. For example, temporal occlusion can be used to progressively invoke earlier anticipation of different ball types. This can be readily achieved by showing players video captured from their normal playing perspective, pausing the video at periods prior to ball release and asking the players to identify the type and landing position of the delivery they are viewing. Release of the pause button to allow the full trial to be viewed can then immediately provide trial-by-trial feedback. Players can then learn, through exposure, the links between early visual information and resultant ball landing position and type. To provide a learning stimulus and progression batsmen could be first shown randomized trials of different ball types occluded two frames after ball release. Once the player's prediction of the ball type becomes consistently above guessing or chance levels, the occlusions can be made earlier (such as at ball release or at the bowler's back foot impact) to force reliance on earlier sources of information as the basis for prediction and anticipation. Groups given this type of visual perceptual training systematically outperform placebo groups, given different types of training with the same expectancy of benefits, and control groups, given no perceptual training, on standard laboratory tests of anticipation (e.g. Abernethy, Wood & Parks, 1999; Farrow, Chivers, Hardingham & Sachse, 1998; Starkes & Lindley, 1994). Moreover, transfer of video simulation training from the laboratory setting to a natural (playing) setting has also recently been demonstrated for similar sports such as tennis (e.g. see Farrow & Abernethy, 2002).

An extension to video simulation training would be to use liquid crystal goggles to progressively occlude vision during physical practice. For example, a soft cricket ball could be used when facing a fast bowler to minimize injury from ball–body contact. Vision could then be occluded close to ball release to invoke earlier anticipation of ball length and to assist earlier stabilization of the base of support. While evidence of the efficacy of this type of perceptual training is needed, at least the potential would appear to exist to develop *in situ* training methods to facilitate improved advance information pick-up by batsmen.

The Abundant Use of Explicit Rules in Coaching

Accompanying the traditional approach to skill learning in cricket is the abundant use of explicit rules to coaching. Rules, such as "Pick the bat up between second slip and wicketkeeper, then swing the bat vertically close to your pad with your elbow up, making contact with the ball near the pad", are commonly used. An abundance of explicit rules is used because it is believed by many in the coaching fraternity that verbal instruction is the sole, or at least the most important, mode of learning enhancement.

Learning through knowledge that is available to consciousness and which can be verbalized is referred to as explicit learning (Liao & Masters, 2001). Another form of learning, implicit learning, is characterized by acquisition of skill without concomitant conscious awareness of the underlying rules (viz. the mechanics) that govern the skill (Maxwell, Masters & Eves, 2000). The advantage of learning skills implicitly is that they can be robust to skill breakdown ("choking") during pressure situations (Masters, 1992). A possible reason for this is that less explicit knowledge can prevent a player from reinvesting in rules during preparation and execution of a skill, hence providing some protection against skill breakdown under conditions of excess conscious processing (Masters, 1992). Given this, it may be beneficial for coaches to minimize the use of explicit rules when coaching complex perceptual-motor skills of the type required in batting.

How Can Practice be Structured to Invoke Implicit Learning?

If implicit learning can indeed result in more enduring learning and greater resistance to stress effects, then finding means of structuring practice to encourage implicit learning is important. Some means by which implicit learning may be invoked include the use of external focus, colour, task-related goals and analogy learning. A number of these (external focus, use of colour and task-related goals) may be potentially used in conjunction with visual perceptual training of the type described in the previous section.

External focus has been defined as direction of attention to the movement effects rather than internal stimuli in the learner's immediate environment (Al-Abood, Bennett, Hernandez, Ashford & Davids, 2002). Accordingly, it has been reported that external focus can be beneficial to skill performance (Al-Abood et al., 2002). Colour may be used to high-light important advance cues (e.g. wrist angle) in a bowler's action. For example, batsmen could be shown footage of a bowler wearing a yellow rubber glove to implicitly attune the batsman to the wrist positions associated with and predictive of different ball types. Simi-larly, task-related instructions such as prediction of ball velocity may be used to implicitly attune visual anticipation skills (see Farrow & Abernethy, 2002). Together, use of colour and task-related goals form external focus interventions that may elicit an implicit mode of learning. Even with such implicit learning aids, it is important that batsmen also be given the opportunity for physical practice in situations where they are exposed to various types of bowlers (e.g. right- and left-arm swing bowlers). This too will provide conditions that are favourable to appropriate links being forged between visual anticipation and positive performance outcomes.

Analogy learning also offers promise as a means of invoking implicit learning of tech-nique. The purpose of an analogy is to act as a biomechanical metaphor for complex rules relating to successful execution of a skill (Masters, 2000; Masters & Maxwell, 2004). For example, when teaching the stance in batting, coaches often recommend that a batsman form a 'figure 9' with their arms, shoulders and bat connections. Complex rules are en-capsulated by the metaphor and do not need to be made explicit (Liao & Masters, 2001; Masters & Maxwell, 2004). Another example is to "rock the cradle", to ensure pivoting of the shoulders (around a horizontal axis) when playing vertical bat strokes. Superior skill learning when using an analogy over explicit instruction has been reported (e.g. Liao & Masters, 2001) but the evidence base for the efficacy of analogy learning, especially for cricket specifically, needs to be expanded.

Can Breakdown of Skills into Individual Components Benefit Learning?

A prominent part of the traditional approach to coaching and skill learning in cricket is to break down the batting skill into individual components. For example, when conducting remedial instruction to correct for assumed technique deficiencies in the downswing path of the bat, a commonly prescribed drill is to execute the downswing to thrown balls that bounce while the feet are stabilized. The premise is that through simplification (and removal of some of the usual degrees of freedom from the task), greater attention can be directed by the player towards each skill component, in turn permitting greater opportunity for feedback to assist learning. Skill breakdown, however, can be detrimental to the learning of the timing of kinematic events within a skill (Davids, Kingsbury, Bennett & Handford, 2001). It may well be that because of their important co-dependence in batting, the backlift and feet movements should always be practised together. Such an approach may assist the batsman to learn the importance of completing the backlift and feet movements early, so that sufficient time is available for downswing completion—important coordination knowledge that may not be acquired under practice or coaching of isolated skill components. Minimizing skill breakdown in coaching and practice will help ensure that the correct temporal coordination of body segments is maintained, while accretion of explicit knowledge that may interfere with performance under stress or fatigue is limited.

CONCLUSION

This chapter has posited that an evidence-based approach to assessment and intervention is necessary for coaching cricketers. Cricket batting has been used as an example to describe some of the key factors that need to be considered in determining how best to structure assessment, practice and coaching. It has been argued that the design of assessment, practice and coaching should be strongly influenced by examination of the constraints and difficulties of the batting skill, as well as an understanding of how these constraints are managed by highly successful (expert) players. Considerations of this type lead to the conclusion that, in relation to the approaches which are currently dominant in cricket, more practice time needs to be devoted to the enhancement of superior anticipation through visual perceptual training and to the use of implicit learning approaches. Alternatives to traditional training and coaching methods need to be systematically assessed in terms of their efficacy and feasibility, such that an evidence-based approach to practice and coaching emerges that can guide the development and nurturing of current and future generations of cricketers. Sport psychologists—both as practitioners and researchers—have an important role to play in advancing the development of superior approaches to skill learning, practice and coaching.

AUTHOR NOTES

The authors would like to sincerely thank Professor Joaquín Dosil for his invitation to write this chapter and disseminate ideas to sport psychologists, applied sports scientists and cricket professionals. Thanks are also expressed to Mr Gary Osmond and Mr Benjamin Williams for feedback on an earlier version of this chapter. Video Vision of Information Technology Services at The University of Queensland supplied the professional video editing of temporal and spatial occlusion footage. This was achieved through a research grant from Cricket Australia and Queensland Academy of Sport. Photography of a batsman wearing liquid crystal goggles was by Chérie Harris and photographic editing by Mona Tiller.

REFERENCES

Abernethy, B. (1981). Mechanisms of skill in cricket batting. *Australian Journal of Sports Medicine, 13*, 3–10.
Abernethy, B. (1984). Skill in cricket batting: Laboratory and applied evidence. In M.L. Howell & B.D. Wilson (eds), *Proceedings of the VII Commonwealth and International Conference on Sport, Physical Education, Recreation and Dance: Vol. 7.* (pp. 35–50). Brisbane: University of Queensland.
Abernethy, B. (1987). Selective attention in fast ball sports II: expert-novice differences. *Australian Journal of Science and Medicine in Sport, 19*(4), 7–16.

Abernethy, B. (1999). The 1997 Coleman Roberts Griffith Address movement expertise: a juncture between psychology theory and practice. *Journal of Applied Sport Psychology, 11*, 126–141.

Abernethy, B. & Russell, D.G. (1984). Advanced cue utilisation by skilled cricket batsmen. *Australian Journal of Science and Medicine in Sport, 16*(2), 2–10.

Abernethy, B. & Russell, D.G. (1987). Expert-novice differences in an applied selective attention task. *Journal of Sport Psychology, 9*, 326–345.

Abernethy, B., Wann, J. & Parks, S. (1998). Training perceptual-motor skills for sport. In B. Elliott (ed.). *Training in Sport: Applying Sport Science* (pp. 1–68). Chichester, United Kingdom: John Wiley & Sons.

Abernethy, B. & Wood, J.M. (2001). Do generalised visual training programs for sport really work? An experimental investigation. *Journal of Sports Sciences, 19*, 203–222.

Abernethy, B., Wood, J. & Parks, S. (1999). Can the anticipatory skills of experts be learned by novices? *Research Quarterly for Exercise and Sport, 70*(3), 313–318.

Adams, R.D. & Gibson, A.P. (1989). Moment-of-ball release identification by cricket batsmen. *Australian Journal of Science and Medicine in Sport, 21*, 10–13.

Al-Abood, S., Bennett, S.J., Hernandez, F.M., Ashford, D. & Davids, K. (2002). Effect of verbal instructions and image size on visual search strategies in basketball free throw shooting. *Journal of Sports Sciences, 20*, 271–278.

Bahill, A.T. & LaRitz, T. (1984). Why can't batters keep their eyes on the ball? *American Scientist, 72*, 249–253.

Barnard, G., Nurick, G.N. & Stretch, R.A. (2003). Improving the accuracy and consistency in cricket batting through a vision training programme [Abstract]. In R.A. Stretch, T.D. Noakes & C.L. Vaughan (eds), *Proceedings of the second World Congress of Science and Medicine in Cricket* (p. 104). Cape Town, South Africa.

Barrett, R. & Wood, D. (1995). The theory and practice of bowling reverse swing. *Sports Coach, 18*(4), 26–30.

Bartlett, R.M. (2003). The science and medicine of cricket: an overview and update. *Journal of Sports Sciences, 21*, 733–752.

Beilock, S.L., Wierenga, S.A. & Carr, T.H. (2003). Memory and expertise: what do experienced athletes remember. In J.L. Starkes & K.A. Ericsson (eds), *Expert Performance in Sports: Recent Advances in Research on Sport Expertise* (pp. 295–320). Champaign, IL: Human Kinetics.

Carré, M.J., Haake, S.J., Baker, S.W. & Newell, A. (1998). The analysis of cricket ball impacts using digital stroboscopic photography. In S.J. Haake (ed.), *The Engineering of Sport: Design and Development* (pp. 295–320). Oxford: Blackwell Science.

Davids, K., Kingsbury, D., Bennett, S. & Handford, C. (2001). Information-movement coupling: implications for the organization of research and practice during acquisition of self-paced extrinsic timing skills. *Journal of Sports Sciences, 19*, 117–127.

Farrow, D. & Abernethy, B. (2002). Can anticipatory skills be learned through video-based perceptual training? *Journal of Sports Sciences, 20*, 1–15.

Farrow, D., Chivers, P., Hardingham, C. & Sachse, S. (1998). The effect of video-based perceptual training on the tennis return of serve. *International Journal of Sport Psychology, 29*, 231–242.

Farrow, D. & Maschette, W. (1997). The effects of contextual interference on children learning tennis forehand ground strokes. *Journal of Human Movement Studies, 33*(2), 47–46.

Ferguson, D. (1992). *Cricket: Technique, Tactics, Training*. Wiltshire: Crowood Press.

Gibson, A.P., & Adams, R.D. (1989). Batting stroke timing with a bowler and a bowling machine: a case study. *Australian Journal of Science and Medicine in Sport, 21*(2), 3–6.

Golby, J., Falk, S. & Hollyhead, S. (2000). The effect of a visual skill training programme on performance in judging the length at which a cricket ball pitches. *International Journal of Sports Vision, 6*(1), 51–64.

Gordon, S. (1990). A mental skills training program for the Western Australian State Cricket Team. *The Sport Psychologist, 4*, 386–399.

Gordon, S. (2001). Reflections on providing sport psychology services in professional cricket. In G. Tenenbaum (ed.), *The Practice of Sport Psychology* (pp. 17–36). Morgantown, WV: FIT.

Helsen, W.F. & Starkes, J.L. (1999). A multidimensional approach to skilled perception and performance in sport. *Applied Cognitive Psychology, 13*, 1–27.

Johnson, P.E. (1983). What kind of expert should a system be? *Journal of Medicine and Philosophy, 8*, 77–97.

Liao, C. & Masters, R.S.W. (2001). Analogy learning: a means of implicit motor learning. *Journal of Sports Sciences, 19*, 307–319.

Marylebone Cricket Club (2003, 8 May). *Laws of Cricket*. Retrieved 8 March 2004, from http://www.lords.org/cricket/laws.asp

Masters, R.S.W. (1992). Knowledge, nerves and know-how: the role of explicit versus implicit knowledge in the breakdown of a complex motor skills under pressure. *British Journal of Psychology, 83*, 343–358.

Masters, R.S.W. (2000). Theoretical aspects of implicit motor learning in sport. *International Journal of Sport Psychology, 31*, 530–541.

Masters, R.S.W. & Maxwell, J.P. (2004). Implicit motor learning, reinvestment and movement disruption: what you don't know wont hurt you? In A.M. Williams and N.J. Hodges (eds), *Skill Acquisition in Sport: Research, Theory and Practice* (pp. 207–228). London: Routledge.

Maxwell, J.P., Masters, R.S.W. & Eves, F.F. (2000). From novice to no know-how: a longitudinal study of implicit motor learning. *Journal of Sports Sciences, 18*, 111–120.

McLeod, P. (1987). Visual reaction time and high-speed ball games. *Perception, 16*, 49–59.

McLeod, P. & Jenkins, S. (1991). Timing accuracy and decision time in high-speed ball games. *International Journal of Sport Psychology, 22*, 279–295.

Mehta, R.D. (2000). Cricket ball aerodynamics: myths versus science. Paper presented at the Third International Conference on the Engineering of Sport, Sydney, Australia.

Milgram, P. (1987). A spectacle-mounted crystal tachistoscope. *Behavior Research Methods, Instruments and Computers, 19*(5), 449–456.

Nurick, G.N., Balden, V. & Stretch, R.A. (2003). Measuring the position of impact on a cricket bat: application for coaches and bat manufacturers [Abstract]. In R.A. Stretch, T.D. Noakes & C.L. Vaughan (eds), *Proceedings of the Second World Congress of Science and Medicine in Cricket* (pp. 37). Cape Town, South Africa.

Pensrose, J.M.T. & Roach, N.K. (1995). Decision making and advanced cue utilisation by cricket batsmen. *Journal of Human Movement Studies, 29*, 199–218.

Regan, D. (1997). Visual factors in hitting and catching. *Journal of Sports Sciences, 15*, 533–558.

Renshaw, I. & Fairweather, M.M. (2000). Cricket bowling deliveries and the discrimination ability of professional and amateur batters. *Journal of Sports Sciences, 18*, 951–957.

Schmidt, R.A. & Lee, T.D. (1999). *Motor Control and Learning: A Behavioral Emphasis*. (3rd edn). Champaign, IL: Human Kinetics.

Starkes, J.L. & Lindley, S. (1994). Can we hasten expertise by video simulations? *Quest, 46*, 211–222.

Stuelcken, M.C. (2003). A kinematic analysis of off-side front foot drives in elite men's cricket batting. Belconen, Australian Capital Territory: Australian Institute of Sport Biomechanics Department.

Ward, P., Williams, A.M. & Loran, D.F.C. (2000). The development of visual function in elite and sub-elite soccer players. *International Journal of Sports Vision, 6*, 1–11.

West, K.L. & Bressen, E. (1996). The effect of a general versus specific visual skills training program on accuracy in judging length-of-ball in cricket. *International Journal of Sports Vision, 3*(1), 41–45.

Wood, J.M. & Abernethy, B. (1997). An assessment of the efficacy of sports vision training programs. *Optometry and Vision Science, 74*, 646–659.

PART III

Individual Sports

The Psychology of Athletics

Joaquín Dosil
University of Vigo, Spain

INTRODUCTION

Athletics is one of the oldest existing sports with the greatest Olympic tradition. Throughout history, its various disciplines have evolved under a conventional structure in which the coach–athlete partnership takes full responsibility for preparing training and competitions, avoiding the presence of any other professionals. Nowadays, elite athletes are usually accompanied by managers, masseurs, physiotherapists, doctors and, in some cases, psychologists.

This chapter presents the basic aspects a sport psychologist should know before working in athletics. We begin by describing the sport's general characteristics, emphasizing the variety of disciplines involved, and go on to define the psychological keys to planning. Finally, we propose some possible models for the psychological preparation of training and competitions.

UNDERSTANDING ATHLETICS AND IMPORTANT ELEMENTS FOR THE SPORT PSYCHOLOGIST

Athletics is a heterogeneous sport which can be performed on four different surfaces: indoor track, outdoor track, cross-country and road. The first two locations encompass all the athletic events (runs, jumps and throws), while the third and fourth settings only allow for running events.

Given the large quantity of disciplines comprising this sport ("mini-sports" in themselves), we limit ourselves to briefly describing the important psychological characteristics of each event (for more information: www.iaaf.org). Needless to say, sport psychologists cannot embark on working with an athletes unless they fully comprehend their chosen speciality. Taking the Olympic Games and the World Championships as a reference, the following disciplines can be described:

- Running events: 100 m, 200 m, 400 m, 800 m, 1,500 m, 5,000 m, 10,000 m, marathon, 100 m hurdles (women), 110 m hurdles (men), 400 m hurdles, 3,000 m steeplechase, 4 × 100 m relay, 4 × 400 m relay.

The Sport Psychologist's Handbook: A Guide for Sport-Specific Performance Enhancement.
Edited by Joaquín Dosil. © 2006 John Wiley & Sons, Ltd.

- Walking events: 20 km walk, 50 km walk (men only).
- Jumping events: High jump, pole vault, triple jump and long jump.
- Throwing events: Shot putt, discus, hammer and javelin.
- Decathlon (men) and heptathlon (women).

Nevertheless, we should highlight that this is by no means a definitive list of what appears in the competition calendar. In indoor track and field championships, just as in meetings or grand prix events, certain variations can be found: 60 m, the mile, 2,000 m, 3,000 m, etc. Likewise, weights (throws) and distances (running events) are often adapted to suit younger age groups.

Every specialty and event has its own characteristics which sport psychologists should consider in their work. Although a detailed analysis is required in each individual case, the most important aspects are summarized below.

Running Events

The psychological characteristics of this type of event vary enormously depending on the distance. However, within this category we can distinguish between conventional running events and running events with hurdles/steeplechase.

Conventional Running Events

Conventional running events are specialties in which there are no obstacles on the track. Distances range from 100 m (60 m on an indoor track) to the marathon (although some ultra-marathon events exist, e.g. 100 km). In between lies a multitude of events progressively increasing in distance: 200 m, 400 m, 800 m, 1,500 m, 5,000 m, 10,000 m. Some recommendations worth remembering for each event are described below.

- *100 m and 200 m* In these events the reaction time is crucial. Therefore, sport psychologists should try to attain extreme levels of concentration to produce a good start and maximum performance during the few seconds the event lasts for. The arousal level required to achieve this should correspond with the characteristics of each athlete. Likewise, sport psychologists should seek the most suitable way of inducing concentration in each individual, ensuring that rivals act as a stimulus rather than a source of intimidation. In the 200 m, athletes start the race on a bend, with the first 100 m being run on a curve and the second 100 m on a straight. Sport psychologists should not disregard this detail, providing adequate psychological strategies such as mental images or key words to make sure the athlete comes off the bend as fast as possible and maintains their speed until the end of the race. Sprinters often have their own series of routines to induce their best performances. Simply observing how they prepare their starts in competition can enable a psychologist to work on maximizing these moments. Similarly, these events require a large amount of weight training and gym work, often proving a tedious chore. In this respect, psychologists can also offer their knowledge, helping athletes make the most of their training time and boosting their self-motivation.
- *400 m* This is the continuous "sprint" event in which an athlete must produce accurate doses of effort (self-regulation). Considering the painstaking difficulty of the last 100 m,

where the legs often seize up totally, psychologists should try to teach athletes techniques to overcome or minimize these moments of extreme physical effort. In this event, as with the 100 m and 200 m, the athlete has a lane to themselves. However, athletes still take references from other competitors, which can prove either motivating or demoralizing, positively or negatively influencing performance. Therefore, psychological work should be directed towards these factors, enabling athletes to set a pace independent to that of their rivals and use their opponents as motivation in moments of extreme physical fatigue.

- *800 m and 1,500 m* These are the so-called "middle-distance" events. Both are run at high speeds with strategy playing a crucial role. They are disciplines in which tactics, and not necessarily physical form, win a race. Athletes should be taught to take quick decisions, concentrate during the event, study their rivals . . . and above all, when victory is often stolen in the closing metres, know how to correctly manage their body's physical limits. Moreover, physical contact is not uncommon, and athletes require both physical and mental strength to defend their position when necessary. In many cases, having the confidence to beat a rival is the "extra" strength an athlete needs to triumph in competition. Times (of repetitions, distances, etc.) are often used as a reference in training for these events (as for distance events) and it is important that a psychologist shows athletes how to evaluate their progress, even when they fail to improve in material terms.

- *5,000 m and 10,000 m* These are typically known as the "distance" events, where many laps of the track are completed, 12.5 and 25 respectively (on an outdoor track). This, of course, involves a lot of time for the athlete to think. The two main psychological objectives of these events are to channel information and achieve an adequate concentration throughout the whole race. Structuring the event into stages may be an appropriate way to focus the attention on specific objectives. Likewise, the weather is an external factor often affecting athletes, and psychologists should train them to put this variable into perspective. Curiously, rivals can actually be of help in these events, forming different groups which enable an athlete to run accompanied at the pace they wish, making the task easier. With around 150–200 km covered on a weekly basis, training is tough and demands the necessary recuperation through rest and an appropriate lifestyle. Having to spend so much time training means team mates also play an important role.

- *Marathon (also half-marathon)* Over a distance of 42,275 m the athlete is submitted to an extreme and prolonged physical effort. Some characteristics of this event include: more than two hours of continuous racing, a lot of thinking time, physical highs and lows which need to be mentally "controlled", km 35 acts as as a psychological barrier, etc. In these disciplines it is fundamental to sustain a constant and relatively comfortable rhythm throughout the event, meaning athletes should be aware of their physical limits beforehand. When athletes fail to pace their race correctly, the repercussions of running this distance at a greater speed than they are physically capable of can be devastating. As with the 5,000 m and 10,000 m, the training involved can be psychologically and physically debilitating, and can be compensated for with the following strategies: training in a group whenever possible, looking for motivating objectives each day, etc. (see Morgan, 1980).

- Finally, within this category are the *4 × 100* m and *4 × 400* m relays. These are the only events where the result does not depend exclusively on the individual athlete, but the sum of four performances. These team disciplines are not practiced very often and competition is principally limited to large championships. The psychological preparation of relays should focus on team cohesion and rapport, the required concentration to pass the baton on correctly, confidence in team mates, etc.

The *hurdles* and *steeplechase races* include 3 disciplines: 110 m hurdles (100 m hurdles for women), 400 m hurdles and 3,000 m steeplechase. The differences between the men's and women's events are reflected in the race distances and hurdle heights Psychologists should consider the following characteristics when working with these disciplines:

- *100 m and 110 m hurdles* As with the sprint events, getting a good start is essential. Therefore, we can apply the characteristics described for the 100 m and 200 m events are applicable here. These disciplines require continuous concentration, since although it is permitted to knock over hurdles, the time and technique lost can affect the result and the athlete's self-confidence.
- *400 m hurdles* Although the characteristics are similar to those of 400 m, the hurdles logically pose an additional obstacle to be considered. Athletes preparing this event should have the number of steps in between each hurdle well-established, being realistic about their physical form and able to recover themselves when confronted with any alteration to their rhythm, caused by tiredness, for example.
- Finally, the *3,000 m steeplechase* Despite traditionally being a men-only event, a female version with lower barriers has emerged in recent years. This discipline has four barrier-style obstacles on the track and an additional "water jump" (as its name suggests, a barrier with a pool of water preceding it). The quantity of participants often poses problems, making it difficult to see clearly where the steeplechase is and causing falls. Moreover, having to negotiate hurdles over the final laps when suffering the effects of fatigue is no easy task. Therefore, psychologists should make sure athletes know how to manage their energy levels correctly, given that any mistake over the final obstacles can mean defeat.

Race Walking Events

Race walking events are battled out over long distances—20 km and 50 km—meaning their characteristics are similar to those of the marathon. An additional problem for competitors is the "three strikes and you're out" rule, which allows walkers just three technical errors before being disqualified for "lifting" (having both feet off the ground at the same time constitutes running). Knowing how to set an adequate pace and make decisions of certain risk are two factors to be taken into account (the greater the rhythm, the more likely they are to commit technical errors).

Jumping Events

Long jump, triple jump, high jump and pole vault are the four jumping events. High jump and pole vault have similar characteristics, where athletes have three attempts to clear a previously chosen height. Decisions regarding the height they choose to jump can prove crucial for taking victory. As with the throwing events, in triple jump and long jump, athletes have four initial attempts, with the best qualifying for a further "final round" of two jumps. Likewise, the decision-making and risk involved in getting as close as possible to the takeoff board without producing a no jump is fundamental. From a psychologist's point of view, the long pauses between attempts constitute a key characteristic of these events. By teaching psychological techniques (visualization, relaxation, thought control, etc.) to use in these moments, athletes may optimize their performance. Coaches, often at trackside, are also influential figures in these pauses, since athletes usually look to them for timely guidance regarding their jumping technique. Working on verbal/non-verbal communication and reinforcement programmes, etc. can prove very beneficial.

Throwing Events

The official throwing events are javelin, shot putt and hammer. They are alike in the sense of having the same number of attempts and the same pauses between throws. Both shot putt and hammer are launched from a circular base which the athlete is not permitted to step out of, as this would constitute an invalid or "no throw". Given the need to produce an efficient throw with this added restriction means the technique is of utmost importance. Therefore, adequate concentration should be attained to avoid committing errors during the throwing process, striving to automate the movements without producing any alterations to the technique as a consequence of external influences (distraction). Moreover, the moments of rest between attempts can be used for correcting technical errors and, of course, for applying psychological strategies to optimize the throw.

Decathlon and Heptathlon

These two disciplines combine running, jumping and throwing events (ten for men and seven for women). The toughness of the event requires athletes to apply a constant effort during two days of competition. A sport psychologist's work will focus on helping athletes rest in between events and minimize the extent to which a good or bad result affects them.

In conclusion, when sport psychologists begin psychologically coaching athletes from a determined athletic discipline, they should spend time studying the event to the point of becoming authentic specialists. If sport psychologists are required to work with a team of athletes, each competing in different events, it is recommended they gather data for each individual, applying the following model:

- Specialty: for example, 1,500 m.
- Physical, technical and tactical characteristics: "This is a tough athlete; they know how to position themselves well in competition, technically they run well, etc."
- Psychological characteristics: "They are strongest when they are leading a race, but become weak when they find themselves at the back of the group, getting very nervous."

Likewise, a study should be conducted of the people surrounding the athletes, both those directly related with the sport, as well as those who may affect them indirectly. Moreover, identifying the athlete's opinion on the previously described characteristics allows a psychologist to better understand them.

SOCIAL INFLUENCES ON THE ATHLETE

Although athletics is considered an individual sport, it is nevertheless characterized by having a technical team supporting the athlete. Within this group, the coach constitutes the fundamental figure, and is usually the one responsible for the athlete's performance. Nonetheless, gradually more and more athletes are forming their own teams in which the coach is not "the only one responsible" and where other professionals play an increasingly important role. Another study (Dosil, 2002) describes the two most common combinations featuring in the current athletics panorama: in the first case, the principal team unit consists of the athlete and his or her coach, with other professionals contributing on a secondary level under the "coach's orders". In the second combination, the athlete is surrounded by a group of professionals, each contributing equally to his or her performance. Although the coach has "more influence", he or she only takes charge of physical preparation: the design, evaluation and supervision of physical training plans. Since both systems have obtained positive results, evaluating which is best can be complicated. Therefore, the sport psychologist should achieve the best performance possible, regardless of which method is employed, ensuring that everyone involved knows their contribution to the process and carries out their functions accordingly.

It is important to clarify the role of sport psychologists within these "teams". Their position will dictate whether they can directly intervene with athletes or whether, as occurs in other sports, they may only do so via the coach. Dosil (2002) suggests that when working with the first training model, where sport psychologists assume an equal "secondary" role to that of other professionals, the athlete usually requests their services on agreement with his or her coach. In these cases, given their influence on the athlete, it is important to establish good communication with the coach. Moreover, it is recommended to hold some sessions with the coach present, including some with the coach only, to establish action guidelines together. In this model, working with the coach is just as important as working with the athlete. In the second model, athletes have "more influence" and decide for themselves to attend a psychologist, considering them as just another specialist who can help improve their performance. Nonetheless, this is the less extended model and experience shows that it is the more "veteran" athletes who tend to opt for this form of collaboration. Perhaps it is their sporting maturity which gives rise to this transfer of responsibilities from coach to athlete.

However, the influence of those surrounding athletes is not limited only to the coaching figure, but also to other people and authorities who may affect their performance. Some of these include the following:

- *Experienced "experts"* This term applies to those athletes who have finished their competitive career and tend to advise other athletes, above all, youngsters. Although the advice of someone with years of experience in the sport can be a positive influence, on some occasions, they end up projecting everything which happened to them personally, imposing their negative experiences on the athlete. Psychologists should train athletes to channel the information they receive, establishing a type of "filter" which allows them to identify when advice applies to them and when it is irrelevant.
- *Parents and family* The support of parents and family is essential at any age. From talented youngsters to "established" athletes, the total backing of their parents is vital. However, their influence is always greater on younger athletes. Parents should be informed of how the psychological training with their child is being directed and why their support at all times is important.

- *The partner* The "girl/boyfriend" or spouse should be taken into consideration when the sport psychologist analyses the athlete's context. The influence of this person is fundamental and may explain the athlete's behaviour at certain times. His or her unconditional support, in the good as well as the bad times, can create a beneficial climate of security for the athlete. On the other hand, the partner may also bring problems: failing to understand such dedication, resenting having less free time, the limitations of training at a high level, having to travel at weekends, etc. Sport psychologists should guide athletes and help them establish good communication and comprehension with their partner.
- *Friends* Peers can also exert an important influence on athletes. Their friends may be team mates or be from outside of the sporting environment. In the first instance, there will be a greater comprehension of their participation in a sport of these characteristics and all that it entails (rest periods, not "going out" as much, athletics taking up a "considerable" amount of their time, etc.). However, psychologists must study whether a situation where "everything" revolves around athletics could become a potential problem (e.g. the athlete having no escape valve). When friends are from outside athletics, they may "not understand" the sacrifices of the sport and "tempt" some potentially counteractive habits. If this is the case, the sport psychologist should try to channel the influence of this peer group.
- *Fans* In recent years, the influence of fans has been widely studied. There is no doubt that without a strong fan base a sport tends to disappear, meaning that fans constitute a fundamental factor in its continuity. The influence of this group can be positive (recognizing the sacrifice involved in training, admiration, urging athletes to carry on, etc.) as well as negative (leaving them when things do not turn out well, excessive pressure if they are injured with continuous questions such as "How are you today?", etc.). The psychologist should monitor this variable.
- *The media* corresponds with the number of fans the sport has; that is to say, the greater the number of fans and spectators attending a sports event, the greater the media coverage will be. From a sport psychology perspective, it should be recognized that the more important a competition, the greater the media coverage will become, which in turn increases the "pressure" placed upon athletes (even more so in a sport like athletics where the athlete will almost certainly not be accustomed to television cameras and camera flashes).

THE ATHLETICS SEASON AND PSYCHOLOGICAL PLANNING

The athletics season contains of a series of divisions and subdivisions which are structured according to the particular objectives of each athlete. García-Verdugo and Dosil (2003) indicate the need to plan the season, taking into account the following concepts:

- Activity: the activity performed in each session.
- Training session: the basic unit of training, including activities and exercises.
- Micro cycle: usually lasting 5 to 10 days, it contains a group of training sessions which maintain a similar structure.
- Monthly cycle: contains various micro cycles, generally lasting 15 to 30 days. The work load may vary in some micro cycles.

- Macro cycle: usually lasts several monthly cycles, coinciding with the season's main objectives (in the winter, the indoor track or cross-country; and in the summer, the outdoor track).
- Season: includes one or more macro cycles and usually lasts approximately a year. Tends to coincide with the athletics federation's calendar.

As a cyclical sport, athletics is divided into macro, monthly and micro cycles (Añó, 1997). Athletes frequently structure their seasons into two macro cycles (the indoor and the outdoor season), with 11 to 12 monthly cycles and 44 to 48 micro cycles (each week of training). Sport psychologists should establish their planning around this physical preparation.

Firstly, along with the coach and/or athlete, sport psychologists should study the main sporting objectives of each cycle. To help achieve these goals, psychological objectives are established accordingly. Secondly, they should define the difficulties most likely to arise in each period, to foresee likely problems. Likewise, they should consider important training and competitive periods. A possible classification may be as follows (Buceta, 1998):

- General preparation phase.
- Basic preparation phase.
- Minor competition phase: 'A' and 'B' competitions.
- Major competition phase: 'A' and 'B' competitions.

To illustrate this, we consult the macro cycle planning of an endurance athlete who is training for the World Indoor Athletics Championships:

- September/October: General preparation phase.
- November: Basic preparation phase, with minor 'B' competitions (cross-country/mile).
- December: Minor 'A' and 'B' competition phase (cross-country and/or road races).
- January: Minor 'A' competition phase (international meetings).
- February: Major 'A' competition phase (Spanish Championships and World Championships).
- March: Major 'B' competition phase (World Cross-country Championships).

As can be observed, each month is labeled according to the objectives set out by the coach–athlete. The psychological objectives in this macro cycle revolve around each physical objective.

Another study (Dosil, 2004) defines each of these periods and their possible psychological implications:

- The *general preparation phase* is a non-competitive stage characterized by light training, focused on "making contact" with the new season following a period of rest.
- The *basic preparation phase* is typically a period of strength-resistance training with heavy work loads (weights sessions, high mileage, etc.). In some cases, advantage is taken to do the odd competition with the aim of "breaking" the monotony of training.
- The *minor competition phase*, including A and B competitions, is a competitive period in which the athlete combines training with competitions. The minor 'B' competitions are those which have a certain social importance (prestige), but which the athlete goes to without resting from training; that is to say, using the competition itself as a heavy training session. They are not considered essential for attaining the more important objectives. The minor 'A' competitions are those which coincide with a micro cycle of rest,

allowing athletes to see what form they are in at a given point in the season. They are ideal competitions for practicing psychological strategies, acting as training for future championships (major competitions). During this stage, the work done in the general and basic preparation phases should be consolidated.

- The *major competition phase*, including A and B competitions, is when athletes focus all of their attention on this competitive period of excellence. The term 'A' corresponds to those championships considered to be the athlete's principal objective (e.g. World Indoor Athletics Championships), as well as any qualifying championships (e.g. Spanish Indoor Athletics Championships). 'B' competitions are considered important, but not the principal objective of the season (secondary objectives): World Cross-country Championships, Spanish Cross-country Championships, etc. The principal psychological objective is for the athlete to put into practice all that has been learned, performing to 100 per cent of his or her ability.

DETECTING POTENTIALLY RISKY SITUATIONS: THE ATHLETE'S TRAINING PLAN

One of the sport psychologist's main functions in athletics, and perhaps in sport generally, is to study the situations that could potentially pose a risk to athletes. With this in mind, it is advisable for sport psychologists to take into account a series of recommendations specific to the athletics context (Dosil, 2002):

- *The athlete's general training plan* The physical training plan of top athletes involves many hours of dedication, both in and outside training. The physical "workload" they submit themselves to should correspond with rest in periods of non-training. In short, considering the athlete's general plan and what he or she does outside of the athletics stadium is fundamental to achieving quality performances.
- *Dedication* Closely related to the previous point is the degree of dedication to the sport. Total dedication is not the same as partial dedication. When athletes are totally dedicated to athletics, as a professional activity, they invest all their time in optimizing their training (they are able to rest after each session, use the most adequate timetable to train, etc.). Semi-dedicated athletes employ a proportion of their time on other daily occupations (work, studies, etc.), which implies less time to assimilate training and produces an "extra" burden. With those who are totally dedicated, the role of psychologists is to make sure that their "personal care" does not become obsessive and, above all, that they learn to disconnect from the athletic world at certain times. With the second group, their function involves trying to make sure that the athlete fulfills the majority of his or her training programme in the conditions available, guiding and directing towards the possibility of total dedication.
- *Financial restrictions* Often the degree of dedication is linked to an athlete's financial possibilities. Although world-class athletes can potentially generate high earnings, many youngsters fail to reach their full potential for lack of funding. While some nations have made a conscious effort to financially guide athletes from youth sport to senior stardom (notably, the USA and Australia), others still fail to provide the necessary support to those whose economic circumstances do not allow them to dedicate all their time to athletics (waiving club fees, paying for physiotherapy, transport and equipment costs, grants, etc.). All too often, talented young athletes are lost in the financial battle.

IMPORTANT PSYCHOLOGICAL VARIABLES IN ATHLETICS

The psychological requirements in each phase will vary from one athlete to another. Therefore, psychologists are recommended to identify the difficulties most likely to arise with each individual and how to handle them. Studying the impact of psychological variables in each period should occupy an important place in the season's planning. Using previous studies (Dosil, 1999, 2002), some observations which may prove interesting for sport psychologists and coaches who wish to delve deeper into the mental training of athletes are described below:

Motivation: The Force Behind Training

Since athletics is a sport in which consistency and repetitive training sessions are fundamental for success, motivation is a key variable which should always figure in psychologists' work (see, for example, Hayashi & Weiss, 1994, and Masters & Ogles, 1995). They should be especially on the look-out for this variable during the preparation phase when athletes confront their toughest training sessions (greater work loads). The importance given to this variable may diminish as the season goes by. As the athlete enters the competitive phase, the competitions themselves have a motivational effect (the higher the level of competition, the greater the motivation). Needless to say, the psychologist should always be prepared for motivational deficits or excesses, stemming from training and competition results. One of the keys to working with this variable is establishing clear and well-structured objectives which allow athletes to remain consistently motivated throughout the season. Likewise, the psychologist should take into account some typical characteristics of this sport which cause motivation to fluctuate: poor training times before a competition, the effort put into training not being reflected in competition, observing how a team mate's progression in training is greater than their own, etc.

Training and "Competitive Stress"

Stressful or potentially stressful situations need to be controlled throughout the season. Circumstances which provoke states of anxiety and stress for athletes can arise in any period (e.g. approaching a major competition and considering they are not in form). Special emphasis should be put on the minor and major competition phases, which are usually the most stressful for athletes. Psychological strategies learned in the preparation stage can be employed to avoid the appearance of "competitive stress". On occasions, training can also be a source of stress. Therefore, observation allows the sport psychologist to determine which day-to-day situations may be having a negative influence on the athlete's sporting progress.

Self-confidence in Athletes

This variable is considered essential for achieving results in athletics (Martin & Gill, 1995). When immersed in major competitions, athletes should have total confidence in their capacity and perform to their full potential. The minor competition and preparation phases should enable an athlete to progressively gain total self-confidence. To avoid forming unrealistic expectations, the sport psychologist must teach them to realistically analyze the form they are in, neither believing they are going to perform better or worse than they really can.

Arousal Level

Periods of competition are suitable for identifying each athlete's optimum arousal level. Athletes must then become aware of their level and learn to adjust it according to the circumstances. When the physical work load is high or when they have been submitted to intense training sessions, athletes' arousal levels will frequently rise above normal.

Attention and Concentration in Athletics

Concentration is an important variable in every period of the athletics season: to achieve established objectives in training; to combine the attentional demands of training and competition in the minor competition phase (concentration and attention control training for major competitions). Major competitions demand total concentration and any slight "lapse" could undermine the athlete's performance.

Group Cohesion

Although athletics is considered an individual sport, club/training team mates are important for achieving high performance. As seen earlier, the tough training in preparative periods becomes more manageable when there is a training squad who share the same objectives and support each other mutually. As the season goes on and with the arrival of competitions, the dynamic of group training is often altered and replaced with more individual work. Athletes begin to focus on their individual competitions, carrying out more specific training sessions to reach their personal best performances.

MENTAL TRAINING AS A COMPLEMENT TO PHYSICAL TRAINING

The need to adapt mental training to physical preparation is another area considered important for psychologists working in athletics. A basic premise to reaching the elite is having certain physical aptitudes for athletics. Without these, however good the psychological work, there will always be certain limits. Regarding this concept and from experience, the following three types of athlete can be distinguished:

1. Those who want to but "can't": athletes whose qualities are limited and for as much as they try, are not capable of reaching the elite.
2. Those who can but "don't want to": those athletes with extraordinary physical conditions (talent), who simply do not put as much as they should into the sport. This may be due to poor guidance or a "passive" attitude.
3. "The others": those who possess certain physical qualities and with the help of well-conducted psychological training could perform at elite level.

From a sport psychologist's point of view, each of these three athlete "types" requires specific treatment. With the first group, it is important to help athletes form realistic expectations and understand to what extent their physical efforts will allow them to improve (Dosil, 2004). With the second category, channelling the external influences which prevent them from "focusing" on athletics, optimizing their performance through psychological techniques, coordinating their sporting activities with academic studies, etc., constitute the psychologist's main tasks. Finally, with the third group, helping athletes appreciate their situation, their limits, the effort that will be required, as well as all the assistance offered to the second group, is needed.

Logically, from a performance perspective, group 2 athletes are like "uncut diamonds" for coaches and psychologists. When an athlete achieves great results without specific psychological training, he or she almost certainly has the potential to improve. Although the work performed with group 1 and 3 athletes is more difficult (not obtaining such important external gratifications) it gives a personal satisfaction which allows one to appreciate the authentic meaning of sport psychology—principally, in its educational aspect—(Dosil, 2001).

All things considered, the predominant existence of these types of athlete brings us to define the two basic functions of the sport psychologist: on the one hand, optimizing athletes' training and competition performance; and on the other, helping them in their overall development as a person.

THE PSYCHOLOGICAL PREPARATION OF TRAINING

On numerous occasions, psychological preparation has focused only on competition, disregarding its importance in daily training.

The sport psychologist should appreciate that if athletes fail to train at the required level, they will be unable to perform at the desired level in competition. With this in mind, some considerations which should figure in the psychological preparation of training are presented.

Generally speaking, when an athlete embarks on work with a sport psychologist there are three possibilities: (1) the athlete has approached the psychologist on his or her own initiative, (2) the athlete attends the psychologist on the initiative of his or her coach, or (3) the athlete goes to the psychologist having made a shared decision with his or her coach.

Logically, depending on who took the initiative, psychologists will proceed in one way or another. If it was the athlete's decision, coaches' opinions of the psychological figure should not be overlooked and, if possible, an interview with them should be held. However, if it was the coach who took the initiative, the initial work will focus on explaining to athletes how sport psychology can help them. If it was a shared decision, full advantage should be taken of the situation to establish good communication, defining the roles and functions of the three figures (athlete, coach and psychologist).

Sport psychology training may be conducted in a clinical setting or in the training field (the athletics track). However, combining treatments in both contexts is ideal. From a psychological point of view, since the initial sessions serve to "establish" the psychologist–athlete–coach relationship, they require a suitable environment and should ideally take place in a clinic (office) or specially adapted classroom (as described in Chapter 1, the online method may also be employed). It is fundamental that athletes explains to the psychologist exactly what they wish to achieve in training/competitions. What is more, certain adherence to mental training should be established, programming regular sessions (just as athletes train physically on a daily basis, mental training requires the same regular dedication).

The Preparation of Training: Important Psychological Aspects

The principal objective of sport psychology is to achieve an adherence to the physical training plan and optimize the time an athlete dedicates to sport. The concept is based on the idea that every day of training is unique and, therefore, produces a series of learning processes which enable an individual to grow as an athlete and as a person. To fulfil the greatest sporting aspirations, all psychological work should function in a similar way.

To begin with, a psychologist can apply motivational strategies to help the athlete overcome the training work load. Athletics demands a whole host of extremely tough training sessions (e.g. a training session for the marathon may involve running 30 km non-stop), sessions the athlete does not like (e.g. 2 hours of gym work for a thrower), some after having competed badly, and some done alone, etc. Therefore, coaches should take into account the motivational factor when designing training plans and athletes should use motivational strategies to help them fulfil them. It is then the sport psychologist's job to act as consultant to them both, guiding them to overcome any difficulties they come across. Observation is fundamental to prevent a lack of motivation towards training (which on occasions, can lead to dropping out of sessions). Logically, every session, every week and every month of training should have fixed, highly motivational objectives (as seen in the planning process).

Establishing objectives should ideally be carried out jointly between the athlete, coach and psychologist. For example, a middle-distance athlete who struggles with continuous runs of over 45 minutes, which are necessary to improve his or her performance, should essentially use strategies to make them easier (e.g. running in a group, listening to music, or other forms of distraction, etc.). In a recent study, Tenenbaum et al. (2004) explain the use of music tapes on running perseverance and coping with effort sensations. Psychologists and coaches should find creative ways to combine physical, technical, tactical and psychological work in training, making it as enjoyable as possible. Many coaches mistakenly believe that when athletes are enjoying themselves they are not focused. This is far from the truth—it is often the best way for an athlete to be motivated and focused on the task; therefore, learning continuously while training. The psychologist will teach athletes strategies such as thought control (Dosil, 2004) so they fully concentrate on their training activities and objectives, escaping any problems in their day-to-day life (e.g. problems at school, family problems, etc.).

For some athletes, training can often become an authentic daily competition, an error which increases the possibility of burnout and evokes stress on a daily basis. The psychologist should bear in mind that training sessions where athletes look for good times (to see what form they are in), as well as those in which they do not perform well, or as well as they think they should compared to their colleagues, may cause anxiety and low self-confidence. In turn, this may lead to "competitive training", where they exert themselves more than is necessary. Likewise, the pressures of the coach and other influencing figures should be considered in the psychological study, as they may cause athletes to feel uncomfortable in their training.

The social factor is relevant in every sport and, in the case of athletics, training sessions are usually carried out in groups. One of the psychologist's and coach's functions is to study (generally through observation) whether there are suitable relationships within the training squad. Working in groups is recommended to obtain greater performances in training and, later on, in competitions. When social relationships within a group are adequate, it acts as an escape valve for athletes, allowing them to feel protected in difficult moments and giving them people to turn to when complicated situations arise throughout the season. Working on empathy, good communication and positive attitudes, both in the face of their own situations as well as those of others, should all form part of athletes' psychological training programme. Just as it is important to look after the athlete–athlete relationship, it is also crucial to maintain the athlete–coach relationship. As indicated earlier, the coach tends to be the fundamental figure in this sport and is usually the one who an athlete turns to and confides in. Therefore, it is essential for the psychologist to work directly with coaches. In fact, such is their influence, it is vital for psychologists to train coaches in how to communicate effectively with their athletes; what to say, how to say it and when to say it.

Finally, in collaboration with the coach, sport psychologists should show athletes the importance of establishing a series of healthy habits which will allow them to better "assimilate" daily training (e.g. stretching 10 to 15 minutes afterwards, resting 9 to 10 hours, making sure they train at the same time every day, separating double sessions sufficiently, looking after their nutrition, etc.).

Controlling Psychological Training

As with physical training, psychological training requires monitoring. The most commonly used methods of evaluation, which have given the best results in the athletic environment, are interviews/questionnaires (clinic) and observation (field). For example, Gaudrean, El Ali and Marivain (2005) used a sample of participants at the 2001 New York marathon to review their Inventory for Competitive Sport.

To control psychological training in the same way as physical training, self-records allow to evaluate to what extent the athlete is complying with the psychological training plan. The majority of athletes are accustomed to filling out their physical training plans; that is to say, recording what training they do each day, what times, etc. Along the same lines, a record of psychological aspects for each athlete can be prepared, recording the following details: the psychological task performed during training, evaluation (e.g. to what degree they met the objective, on a scale of 1 to 10), comments (problems which arose, etc.).

At the end of the season, having gathered all of the athlete's reports, the sport psychologist can produce a final evaluation, presenting it both to the coach as well as to the athlete (not including the specific data provided, as this is confidential, but by demonstrating the general improvement in different aspects through mental training). A progressive study such as this will favour the psychologist continuing in the club and allow objectives to be set for the following season.

THE PSYCHOLOGICAL PREPARATION OF COMPETITIONS

Competition is the moment when athletes have to give their best, where all their training should show and where the result is a product of their efforts over time. However, on many occasions it does not happen like this and athletes find themselves wrapped up in a series of contradictions without explanations ("After all the training I did, what a poor time!", "My training repetitions suggested I was going to do a new personal best time", "My coach said I could run 10 seconds faster", etc.). When these situations arise, athletes usually look for answers in external factors ("It was bad weather", "It was too hot", "My rivals are in better form" . . .) or internal factors ("I didn't feel right", "I didn't give it everything", "I wasn't focused"), avoiding the fact that psychology nearly always determines performance. From this perspective, sport psychology in competition should allow athletes to perform at the same level they have physically achieved in training. In other words, the main objective is to maximize their physical performance.

There are occasions when neither the athlete nor the coach fully appreciate the potential of psychological work. If an athlete is producing reasonably acceptable results it often convinces them to carry on working the physical aspect, neglecting the valuable psychological factor. The majority of sport psychology consultations arise from a specific problem in competitions ("I get really nervous", "I can't get to sleep the night before", "I seize up", etc.), although gradually more athletes include a sport psychologist in their regular team from the start of the season, as just another professional who helps them perform better. Many athletes have been pleasantly surprised by just how favourable a psychological programme has been for them, even if they have not produced personal best performances.

As with training, the sport psychologist should prepare specifically for competitions. Therefore, meeting with the athlete a few days before and after each competition is recommended. Perhaps a useful division, although somewhat generic, is establishing three stages: pre-competition, the competition itself and post-competition. Given the importance of all three, the fundamental aspects for dealing with each one are described (Bloom, Duran-Bush and Salmela, 1997; Dosil, 1999, 2002; Schomer, 1986).

Pre-competition

In the clinic or in a quiet place, the sport psychologist will establish a plan (a form of guide) of what the athlete should do prior to the competition. This session can be structured in the following way:

A Training Plan of the Last Week/Month Prior to Competition

The sport psychologist, along with the athlete (and in some cases, the coach), will carry out an analysis of the final week's/month's training. The objective is to identify the athlete's current physical form, so to establish a series of corresponding competition objectives. However, athletes tend to form narrow perceptions based on their final training sessions. Needless to say, if they happen to train badly on this day for whatever reason, it can knock their confidence prior to a competition and create overly negative expectations. The sport psychologist should prepare for this eventuality, since it is an athlete's perceptions (beliefs) of his or her form which often determine performance in the difficult moments of a competition.

Personalizing Plans

Since psychological characteristics vary from one individual to another, a pre-competition plan should be elaborated for every athlete, each with its own peculiarities. The following aspects may be used as a guide:

- Establishing objectives: the desired result and how the performance will be executed.
- Travelling to the competition: preparing for long journeys (music, magazines, etc.), being aware of possible delays, etc.
- "Planning" the day: planning out the day of the competition so athletes know what they need to do at each moment: "At 10 o'clock I get up and have a shower, at 10:30 I have breakfast, at 11:15 I rest in front of the TV, at 12:30 warm-up and stretching."
- Establishing moments to prepare and study the competition: Two things are intended here: (1) athletes should spend specific moments preparing for the competition (not during rest periods) so as not to spend the whole day "going round in circles", and (2) they should study the tactics of the race, the rivals, etc. which will allow them to carry out a realistic analysis of the competition ahead.
- Including the specific psychological requirements of each athlete in the plan, such as guidelines to improve specific psychological aspects.

The "Competition Card"

This is one method sport psychologists can use, above all during the initial sessions. It involves writing a summary of the most important aspects for an athlete to remember in the competitive environment. More often than not, the psychologist will not be present at trackside when the athlete competes, so having a "psychological support" of this type is very useful to increase the athlete's self-confidence. Experience shows that athletes are extremely grateful for receiving this "reminder" in the form of a traditional letter, in which the guidelines (aspects to go over) are implicit: "You have done some good times in recent training sessions . . . " (self-confidence), ". . . although the competition remains a secondary objective, it should be taken seriously, as it will prepare you for the coming competitions . . . " (arousal and motivation levels).

The Competition

The competition period does not begin when the starting pistol fires, when a throw is launched, or when an athlete sets off down the runway. It begins when the athlete feels that everything revolves around the event. The majority of athletes have a series of routines they perform prior to competing, which a psychologist should study to refine any details which may affect their performance. Some key factors to consider when psychologically preparing a competition are now described.

Travelling to the Stadium and the Moments Prior to Warm-up

The trip to the athletics stadium is a moment which can be prepared for, just as the arrival, the entry and the time which passes before the athlete begins warming up for an event. The comments of many athletes agree on the pressures involved in travelling on a bus or in a car ("It's where you breathe an environment of tension and each person is thinking about what they are going to do"); entering the stadium, where they "confront" a multitude of potentially stressful situations: spectators cheering on other athletes who are already competing, the noise of the loud speaker, the starting pistol, etc. ("It's incredible, you walk into the stadium and your pulse rises, your hands begin to sweat and you think that soon it will be your turn."); or even the time which passes before they begin to warm-up: people who ask what form they are in, they see rivals and friends again, people they race against, etc. ("My rival's comments make me extremely nervous, it's been a while since I saw them and when they start telling me about their training I feel insecure because it's better than what I have done.")

The Physical and Psychological Warm-up

Just as there is a physical warm-up, it is essential to perform a psychological warm-up. Depending on the athlete's personal characteristics, more emphasis will need to be put on one aspect or another: for some it may mean increasing confidence, for others motivation, etc. However, the most important thing is for the athlete to step out onto the track feeling totally prepared, physically and mentally.

Prior to the Start

The immediate moments before a start, a throw or a jump are extremely important from a psychological point of view. Losing concentration at this point can provoke disastrous results in the competition (a false start, a no jump, poor positioning in a middle-distance/distance race, etc.). As suggested in another study (Dosil, 1999), athletes should be totally focused on their race, jump or throw plan, knowing perfectly what they have to do, without allowing doubts to creep in.

The Competition Itself

- *Performance planning* An extremely useful strategy which often goes unnoticed is performance planning. In any discipline (run, throw or jump), athletes should know exactly what they are to do. In jumping and throwing events, learning to relax and psyche themselves up between attempts, maintaining concentration during the event, focusing on technique and improving with each attempt are important factors. In running events, having a clear strategy to follow, where to position themselves, where to change pace, which rivals to keep an eye on, etc. is also essential.
- *"Going beyond the limits"* The ultimate objective in a competition is to "give it everything", perform as well as possible. Therefore, suitable psychological strategies to assist in this labor must be used. On many occasions, the limit lies not in the body but in the mind.
- *Psychological strategies* The strategies used in jumps and throws are not the same as those used in running events. In the first two disciplines, the pauses between attempts mark the competition rhythm, and athletes must adapt to this through using thought control, self-talk, relaxation, visualization and a host of other techniques. However, in running events

there are no pauses and everything happens very quickly. Athletes are at their physical limits (raised heart rate), making it difficult think, so learning to control the mind at "this speed" is an essential skill (in many cases, thoughts appear as "flashes"). Useful strategies include: "key words", which control negative thoughts and convert them into positive reflections, concentrating on external stimuli to minimize suffering, dividing the competition into sections with clear objectives for each stage, etc. (see Goode & Roth, 1993, and Tammen, 1996, for a review of this literature).

Psychological Variables During the Competition

Some important variables are:

- *Confidence* Previous training sessions and competitions should figure in the competitive psychological plan, as they may indicate low confidence, "false confidence" and/or excessive confidence.
- *Concentration on the competition plan* It should be ensured that the athlete is focused on the plan agreed beforehand with the coach and psychologist, although he or she must not disregard the conditions of each competition. The competition plan should be flexible, adapting to unforeseen circumstances. The more focused the athlete is on the plan, the greater the chances of success.
- *Anxiety/stress* In the moment of the competition, athletes should automatically employ techniques to reduce anxiety and stress. If they feel they begin suffering symptoms which could affect their performance, they should employ previously established psychological strategies.
- *Motivation* is important when athletes are not "in form" or when they are competing again following a poor competitive performance or training session. Along these lines, the psychologist should aim to establish motivating objectives for every competition, the athlete learning something new on each outing. Setting out each competition as a new challenge, with new factors to consider (e.g. testing a new psychological strategy in competition), will generate greater motivation and concentration levels.

Post-competition

Once the competition is over, a series of physical and psychological routines can be carried out. Just as it is recommended to stretch and relax the muscles with a gentle warm down jog, etc. psychologically, it is essential to objectively analyze the performance. Some recommendations include:

- The main objective should be regaining control after a competition and composing oneself for any remaining rounds (especially in championships when various events/rounds are contested in a short space of time).
- Design a matrix highlighting the positive and negative aspects and how to improve them (Lorenzo, 1996; Dosil, 1999), being realistic with the performance and clear that "in every competition there is always something positive".
- Carry out a self-report of the competition. It is important for an athlete to record competitions to perform an overall evaluation at the end of a season or cycle. This record

should include: the name of the competition, the date and time/distance/height achieved; evaluation and comments regarding the pre-competition psychological work carried out; evaluation and comments regarding the physical and psychological objectives of the competition (Dosil, 2002).

CONCLUDING REMARKS

In recent years, the psychological demands of a sport such as athletics have led to an increased psychological presence within athlete support teams. The first step towards commencing psychological work with athletes is to understand the sport in depth, the specific events, the professionals who are usually involved, the structure of the season and all its ins and outs. Moreover, planning mental training to correspond with physical preparation is necessary to achieve good results. In this planning process, a distinction has been made between the training and competition phases, each with unique characteristics, which require special treatment.

This chapter has endeavoured to create a guide for sport psychologists embarking on work in athletics, answering all the questions that may arise. Therefore, the previous subjects have been described, aiming to relate theoretical aspects with personal experiences in the applied field.

REFERENCES

Añó, V. (1997). *Planificación y organización del entrenamiento juvenil.* Madrid: Gymnos.
Bloom, G., Duran-Bush, N. and Salmela, J.H. (1997). Pre- and postcompetition routines of expert coaches of team sports. *The Sport Psychologist, 11*(2), 127–141.
Buceta, J.M. (1998). *Psicología del entrenamiento deportivo.* Madrid: Dykinson.
Dosil, J. (1999). *A Formación do Deportista: Preparación psicolóxica do atleta.* Santiago de Compostela: Lea.
Dosil, J. (2001). *Psicología y deporte de iniciación.* Ourense: Gersam.
Dosil, J. (2002). Entrenamiento psicológico en atletismo. In J. Dosil (ed.), *El psicólogo del deporte: asesoramiento e intervención* (pp. 207–238). Madrid: Síntesis.
Dosil, J. (2004). *Psicología de la actividad física y del deporte.* Madrid: McGraw-Hill.
García-Verdugo, M. & Dosil, J. (2003). Bases del entrenamiento deportivo. In J. Dosil (ed.), *Ciencias de la Actividad Física y del Deporte* (pp. 43–90). Madrid: Síntesis.
Gaudrean, P., El Ali, M. & Marivain, T. (2005). Factor structure of the Doping Inventory for Competitive Sport with a sample of participants at the 2001 NY marathon. *Psychology of Sport and Exercise, 6*(3), 271–288.
Goode, K.T. & Roth, D.L. (1993). Factor analysis of cognitions during running: association with mood change. *Journal of Applied Sport Psychology, 15*, 375–389.
Hayashi, C.T. & Weiss, M.R. (1994). A cross-cultural analysis of achievement motivation in Anglo-American and Japanese marathon runners. *International Journal of Sport Psychology, 25*(2), 187–202.
Lorenzo, J. (1996). *El entrenamiento psicológico en los deportes.* Madrid: Biblioteca Nueva.
Martin, J.J. & Gill, D.L. (1995). Competitive orientation, self-efficacy and goal importance in Filipino marathoners. *International Journal of Sport Psychology, 26*(3), 348–358.
Masters, K.S. & Ogles, B.M. (1995). An investigation of the different motivations of marathon runners with varying degrees of experience. *Journal of Sport Behavior, 18*(1), 69–79.
Morgan, W.P. (1980). The mind of the marathoner. *Psychology Today, 11*, 38–49.

Schomer, H.H. (1986). Mental strategy training programme for marathon runners. *International Journal of Sport Psychology, 18*, 133–151.

Tammen, V.V. (1996). Elite middle and long distance runners associatives/dissociatives coping. *Journal of Applied Sport Psychology, 8*, 1–8.

Tenenbaum, G., Lidor, R., Lavyan, N., Morrow, K., Tonnel, S., Gershgoren, A., Meis, J. & Johnson, M. (2004). The effect of music type on running perseverance and coping with effort sensations. *Psychology of Sport and Exercise, 5*(2), 89–109.

CHAPTER 13

Sport Psychology and Tennis

Robert Weinberg
Miami University, USA

INTRODUCTION

Nobody who has played tennis with any intensity or passion would dispute the statement that beyond the purely physical and technical aspects of the game is a mental or emotional component that often overshadows and transcends the physical aspects. For example, most tennis players have probably experienced one or more of the following scenarios: having your mind wander during a match; getting tight (and maybe "choked") at critical points in a match; getting upset and frustrated over what you perceive to be a bad line call; getting frustrated and calling yourself names after missing an easy shot. If you have played tennis competitively, it would be extremely rare not to have suffered through some or all of the above situations. Conversely, most players have probably been "in the zone", where everything seems to be coming easily and winners keep flying off the racquet. The key point is trying to get in that special place where you can play at your best on a consistent basis. Before discussing how players can reach their potential (especially from a mental perspective) it would be important to understand why tennis can be so difficult mentally.

WHY IS TENNIS DIFFICULT FROM A MENTAL PERSPECTIVE?

It is well known that some players are physically talented and have "all the shots". Yet, when they get into matches, they seem to make all sorts of mistakes and often lose to what many would consider inferior players (at least they did not have the strokes of the other player). But good strokes typically do not win tennis matches (unless you happen to be a lot better than your opponent). Rather, a competitive match is usually a mental battle, and the winner of the mental game will usually win the match. So what is it about tennis that makes it so difficult from a mental perspective?

(a) *Thinking time* In a 2-hour match, players are probably playing tennis for about 30 minutes. So what are players doing during the other hour and a half? This "dead time" is where lots of thinking goes on as the stop-and-go nature of tennis puts a lot of pressure on the mind. It is during this time (typically between points and during changeovers) that the mind likes to wander and can get absorbed in many distractions ranging from those related to the match, such as "I can't believe I'm losing to this person", to those unrelated, such as "I have to do several things to get ready for a business meeting I have tomorrow." These thoughts can often cause disruptions in timing and coordination, leading to poor performance. Even during points, players' thinking can be pressured with all the decisions that need to be made (especially on slower surfaces such as clay). It has been found that a player might make between 800 and 1,200 decisions in a match and these can weigh on your mind. Should I come to net or stay back? Should I play conservatively or try to hit out and go for more winners? These are just a couple of decisions that a player may have to make repeatedly as a match progresses. In any case, all this thinking makes tennis difficult from a mental perspective.

(b) *Calling of lines* Unfortunately, most tennis players have to call their own lines (even in tournaments) and this can also weigh on the mind especially when players feel they are not getting fair calls from their opponent. This is a particular problem in the juniors where bad line calls seem to occur too often and this can produce anger, frustration and loss of focus.

(c) *Individual sport* There is nowhere to hide when making mistakes or losing your cool. Players' emotions and execution are out there for everyone to see, which can cause embarrassment, tension and anger.

(d) *Exact nature of tennis* Tennis is a very exacting sport and if a player's racquet face varies by just a couple of inches, this can cause the ball to hit in the bottom of the net or go over the fence. So it can be frustrating trying to consistently hit good shots when very minor variations in racquet angle, positioning and preparation could lead to wide variations in stroke production.

(e) *Scoring system* Players will never lose a match because time ran out. Even though a player might be down 6–0, 5–1, they can still win the match as this has been done even at the professional level. So players never have a match won, nor are players out of a match so they need to keep playing—until the last point is won. This uncertainty adds to the mental strain placed on many matches.

PHYSICAL AND MENTAL TRAINING

From the above discussion, it can be seen that the game of tennis makes unique demands on the mind. As a result, when players practice and prepare for competitive tennis, mental training should be considered as well as physical training. Unfortunately, this is typically not the case as most players do little or no mental training. When I conduct tennis clinics for junior and adult players (most of whom would be considered competitive, playing tournaments, on teams, in clinics or in leagues) I would typically ask how often they played physically per week. Although there is certainly some variation, the more competitive players are playing at least 10 hours a week. When I ask them how often they practice mentally, most players indicate that they do very little in terms of mental training other than maybe getting mentally ready right before a match. Yet when they come off the court after a loss or not playing well, players typically attribute their loss or play to mental factors such as playing tentatively, losing their confidence, making bad decisions or lack of focus. But when they go back out on the practice court, players usually simply try to hit more balls or physically practice rather than working on the mental aspects of their game.

Take the example of a player who hit too many double faults in a match. The typical response in practice is to hit more second serves, maybe working on the ball toss or other mechanics. Although this may be helpful, oftentimes, the reason for too many double faults is more psychological than technical in nature. Specifically, players often double fault due to the pressure in the match either put on by the other player (maybe they are attacking your second serve) or by the closeness of the score. In either case, it is the player or situation that is causing the breakdown in mechanics, making the problem more mental than physical. Therefore, mental skills related to serving second serves would seem more beneficial. This could include relaxation skills, cue words or some other sort of focusing technique (these will be discussed in more detail later) to solve the double fault problem.

Tennis has become a year-round sport (certainly at the professional level) with training and practice occurring throughout the year. In fact, many budding tennis players move to warm weather climates so that they can play year round outside. Although high schools and colleges have specific tennis seasons, players typically play throughout the year to improve their game and refine their stroke production. So there is not one good time to practice mental skills. Rather, it is best to initiate a mental skills training program during whatever would be considered the off-season (when there are no competitive matches) or at least during a time when competition is minimized. At this period, there is more time to learn new mental skills when players are not so pressured with winning. Athletes from a variety of sports (particularly Olympic athletes) have noted that it can take several months to fully understand new psychological skills and integrate them into actual competitions. In essence, mental training is an ongoing process that needs to be integrated with physical practice over time. But let's first take a look at the mental states of successful tennis players.

MENTAL STATES OF SUCCESSFUL TENNIS PLAYERS

Research (see & Jackson & Csikszentmihalyi, 1999 for a review) since about 1980 has revealed that there is a common thread of mental and emotional skills that are related to top performance. For example, when tennis players talk about being in "the zone", they usually are referring to a time when their emotional and mental skills came together to produce peak performance. A composite of the thoughts and feelings that tennis players report during outstanding performance can be summarized by the following quote:

> I felt relaxed but yet I was energized and feeling strong. I enjoyed the tennis competition, and was not afraid to lose. In fact, I felt a sense of calmness and quiet inside, and my strokes just seemed to flow automatically. I really wasn't thinking about my shots and what I needed to do; it just seemed to happen naturally. My shots did not feel rushed, in fact the ball seemed to slow down and I felt as if I could do almost anything. I was totally into the match, but yet I was not consciously trying to concentrate. I was aware of everything but distracted by nothing. I knew no matter how hard I hit my shots they were going in. I felt confident and in total control. (Weinberg, 2002, p. 14).

Of course it is unusual for a tennis player to feel all of these things at one point in time. However, the good news is that research has revealed that players have the ability to control their thoughts and emotions (with consistent practice), which will help create the kind of internal climate that will allow them to reach their potential. So what are these thoughts and feelings that make up this peak performance state (or as Jim Loehr, noted sport psychologist, calls it, the ideal performance state)?

- *Challenge–skill balance* Probably the most fundamental of all the peak performance states is the perceived balance between skills and challenges. It's important to note that the skill–challenge balance is based on the subjective perception of the player, not necessarily the objective nature of the challenge. This naturally occurs when a player plays against another player of equal ability but, unfortunately, this is not always the case. So when players are better, they can "play up" by bringing their level of ability up to meet the challenge or downplay the challenge somewhat (my opponent is good but I can beat him if I play smart). Usually more difficult is playing someone who is weaker in ability. To keep the challenge–skill balance, a player might set some personal goals such as a first serve percentage of 70 per cent (a player usually serves at 60 per cent) or a 2:1 winners to unforced errors ratio (usually 1:1).

- *Merging of action and awareness* This occurs when a player feels at one with the movements they are making. Tennis players have described this feeling as seeing yourself and the racquet as one, as if the racquet is an extension of your arm. As one tennis player described, "Things just happen automatically; I am just hitting the ball, but not really thinking about it." In essence, players report moving effortlessly, with a perception of little effort.

- *Feelings of confidence* Players have a strong belief in their abilities, despite what might be seen as a poor performance. In essence, players' belief in themselves would transcend any particular point, game, set or match as their confidence would not be shaken just because they played poorly or lost a match. Players contend that when they are confident they go for their shots, hit out, and feel that they are never out of a match. There is a supreme belief in self.

- *Focused concentration* Players talk about being totally focused on the present and they do not think of the future or past. In addition, they do not pay attention to or are not even aware of distractions in the immediate environment such as the crowd. As the great champion, Bjorn Borg stated, "Very often in a tennis match you can point to one point or game where for a couple of shots you lost concentration and didn't do the right thing, and the difference in the match will be right there" (Tarshis, 1977, p. 21). Many things such as wind, line calls, sun, noise, and opponent antics can disrupt concentration, which is why staying focused throughout a match is a critical part of playing in the zone.

- *Clear goals* To enter the zone, tennis players need to set goals clearly in advance, so they know exactly what to do. In addition, whether in practice or competition, clear goals help focus a player on what needs to be done and then on doing it. As Brad Gilbert notes in his book *Winning Ugly* (Gilbert & Jamison, 1993), he felt he had to have a specific plan and know what strokes to hit and what areas to attack. In essence, he knew exactly what he needed to do to be successful on the court.

- *Loss of self-consciousness* Many tennis players tend to be especially concerned about what significant others think of them. However, when describing peak performances, tennis players lose their concern for self and do not get caught up with negative self-talk, self-doubt, self-concern and worries. Rather, there is a lack of fear and a kind of quiet and calm inside. When players are not concerned about others and lose their self-consciousness, they tend to feel loose and relaxed on the tennis court. When players' muscles are tight they tend to lose the fluidity in their strokes and start to "push" the ball. So, the key for players is to lose their self-consciousness (not their consciousness) and not be concerned about how others might evaluate how they look or how they play.

In fact, some players, after playing extremely well, will say they were "unconscious out there". But what they are really saying is that they lost their self-consciousness and let their bodies play on automatic pilot with no interference from thoughts or feelings.

- *Enjoyment* A key element to achieving peak performance is enjoying the activity itself. Players might be receiving money or awards for playing or their performance (like most professional players) but the main reason they play is because they enjoy the game itself. People said that Pete Sampras would never win that thirteenth Grand Slam (of course he did win it, winning the US Open) and should quit the game. But during this, Sampras said, "You have to do what makes you happy. If I feel like I am not having fun out there on the court, it is time to do something else." One of the prime reasons for young tennis players burning out is that the game is no longer fun and enjoyable for them. So it is important for sport psychologists to make sure that players keep the fun aspects as part of their tennis experience.

TEACHING MENTAL SKILLS

So now some of the thoughts and feelings typical of high levels of tennis performance or being in the zone have been addressed. But how do sport psychology consultants go about teaching these mental skills to tennis players? The focus will begin by starting with the best time to start a mental skills training program.

When to Implement a Mental Skills Program?

As noted earlier, oftentimes tennis does not really have a season since play, matches and tournaments typically go on year-round. But, as a general rule, it is best for sport psychology consultants to initiate a mental skills training program during the off-season or pre-season (or at least whenever the player is not playing in any tournaments and focusing on practice and training). It is during this time that players can focus on learning new mental skills and integrating these into their physical game, while not feeling the match pressure to win. But it is important to note that athletes have reported it sometimes takes several months to a year to fully understand these new mental skills and integrate them into actual competitions. In essence, mental training is an on-going process that needs to be integrated with physical practice over time and players' first exposure to mental training should last at least three to six months.

As a sport psychology consultant, I am often asked to initiate a mental skills training program in the middle of a competitive season, when tennis players are participating in competitive matches. The start of a mental training program is typically precipitated by some specific situation such as missing a lot of second serves at critical points in a match (the player felt that they "choked"). So players (and sometimes parents/coaches) become desperate to find a solution, but mental training in such a situation is rarely effective. A tennis player wouldn't want to change from a one-handed to two-handed backhand without lots of practice and training. Similarly, if a player wanted to learn some new routines or relaxation skills, then these cannot be integrated into actual competitive matches overnight.

Who Should Administer Mental Training?

Under ideal circumstances, a mental skills training program should be planned, implemented and supervised by a qualified sport psychologist as opposed to a coach. There are several advantages to having a sport psychologist conduct the training. First, the sport psychologist has the expertise, background and training to conduct a mental training program. Second, the sport psychologist represents a neutral individual who does not make decisions regarding playing time or even who stays versus who gets cut from a team. Subsequently, athletes are typically more forthright, open and honest in revealing their true feelings, needs and possible inadequacies. Unfortunately, due to time and financial constraints, it is rare that a sport psychologist can work and travel with a team (or individual in the case of an individual tennis player) throughout a competitive season or to different tournaments. Highly ranked juniors, collegiate or professional tennis players tend to travel a fair amount to different tournaments and thus it is hard for a sport psychologist to travel with them. On the other hand, if a sport psychologist is working with a collegiate team (for example) then it is more likely that they could spend some significant time with the players. Similarly, it is difficult for many coaches to travel with tennis players as the latter are often left to their own devices or may have parents if they are junior players.

So what does this mean for who should conduct the mental training? Since tennis is an individual sport and most sport psychologists agree that best results typically occur at the individual level, it is assumed that the coach/tennis pro or sport psychologist is dealing with individual players, rather than teams. Typically the coach is with the player more frequently but often does not have formal training in sport psychology or the development of a mental skills training program. Thus, one model of service delivery (developed by Smith and Johnson, 1990 in their work with major league baseball) has the sport psychologist training the coach so that the coach could offer mental training to the players in the absence of the sport psychologist (or at least monitor the training). This, of course, would require a great deal of commitment and training from both parties for this to happen in a positive manner. At a minimum, the coach and sport psychologist should communicate on a regular basis and come to an understanding of how and when to integrate mental training into the player's practice schedule.

How Much Time to Spend on Mental Training

Another important question when starting a mental training program is how much time to spend on mental training, Of course this would vary based upon the skills to be learned and the player's experience with mental training. But as a rule of thumb, if a new mental skill is being learned, special 10- to 15-minute training sessions 3 to 5 days a week may be necessary (session content would determine whether it is better held at the beginning or end of practice). As players become more proficient, they may be able to integrate the mental training more with physical training and thus may need fewer special training sessions. Once a skill has been effectively integrated into physical practice, it should be tried in simulated competitions before being used during actual competitions. For example, if a player was learning from a sport psychologist about routines/rituals before playing a point, then some sessions would need to be conducted to just determine what would be the routine, and then practiced using this routine mentally. Then you might try to do this in actual physical practice and then in simulated competitions before finally using this new routine in actual matches.

As noted above, in many circumstances, a sport psychologist is not on site to help players implement their mental training program. More typically, sport psychology consultants are around only sporadically, leaving much of the day-to-day mental training to the players and coaches. Oftentimes the sport psychology consultant starts with a group session (if it is a team) to explain general principles and their philosophy. They then follow up these group sessions with individual sessions with each player. Since, the consultants are not around on a day-to-day basis, it is imperative that they assign training exercises to practice between meetings. If it is a team situation, then tennis coaches can help monitor or provide time so that players could practice their mental skills.

When Should Players' Practice Mental Training?

The rudiments of most mental skills should be taught and systematically practiced during special training sessions. The first or last 15 to 30 minutes of practice is often a good time for mental training, although sport psychologists should be sure not to make mental practice an "add-on" (it should occur during the normal practice time). The content of a particular session would determine if it is better held at the beginning or end of practice. Homework assignments also can be given but, unless the player is self-directed, it is better to have most mental training practice occur under someone's supervision. As soon as possible, the mental skills practice should be integrated with physical skills practice. This integration will be addressed when the actual implementation of a mental skills program is discussed.

IMPLEMENTING A MENTAL SKILLS TRAINING PROGRAM

Thus far the mental states of successful players have been discussed as well as some important questions surrounding the use of mental training programs (who should implement, when to practice mental skills, when to implement the program). Although this information is important in understanding mental training programs, it does not really tell sport psychologists exactly what to do in setting up such a program. Drawing on research and my own consulting expertise/experience, some of the critical elements of implementing a mental skills training program will be discussed.

Initial Meeting(s)

Despite the growth in sport psychology and the use of mental training consultants by athletes, many individuals are still quite naïve or uninformed about what sport psychology is and what sport psychologists do. Therefore this should be carefully spelled out, immediately highlighting the notion that sport psychology has to do with personal growth as well as enhancing performance since many athletes only think in terms of improving performance (related issues of confidentiality and alike should also be spelled out at this time).

In addition, it is also critical to spell out your approach to tennis players. The two major approaches at this time are counseling/clinical and educational. The large majority of athletes require simply an educational approach where psychological skills such as arousal regulation, imagery, goal-setting and concentration are developed. Sport psychologists should emphasize that they are there simply to help athletes improve performance and enhance personal well-being. They should further state that they do not see "head cases" and that they are not "shrinks" (in fact I like to think of myself as a "stretch" rather than a "shrink"). In essence, a sport psychologist is really simply a mental coach trying to help players with the mental part of their game whereas coaches tend to focus on the physical part of their game. Using a "mental coach" should not be seen as a weakness, but rather as simply another way to improve performance and enhance personal growth.

Some (although a lot fewer) athletes require a clinical orientation where the focus might be on more personal and clinical issues such as drug abuse, eating disorders and severe depression, where the focus is more on a more deep-seated severe emotional problem. An individual appropriately trained in clinical psychology should be used in these circumstances. However, the assumption in this chapter is that most sport psychology consultants act as educational sport psychologists designing a mental training program for an athlete.

Assessment of Mental Skills

For most intervention programs, a solid assessment should come first as this will help inform one as to the specific nature of the intervention (or in this case a mental skills training program). Thus, a mental skills training program for tennis players should assess specific mental strengths and weaknesses that appear to have the most direct affect on tennis performance and personal satisfaction. In conducting this initial evaluation, it is important for the sport psychology consultant to understand that there are factors outside of the psychological realm that influence performance (Boutcher & Rotella, 1987) such as conditioning, biomechanics (technique), strategy and equipment. For example, a tennis player may be in a slump and a sport psychology consultant may want to attribute it to lack of confidence, increased anxiety or some other mental state. But the cause might simply be not enough sleep, overtraining or a technique problem. Thus, a sport psychology consultant should be at least aware of these other possibilities (and optimally have some knowledge about them) and integrate them with any psychological issues. There are three different evaluation procedures I utilize to get an in-depth assessment of tennis players. Using these different measures helps in looking for consistencies (and inconsistencies) between oral and written statements.

The first method is a *semi-structured oral interview* where one can probe and elicit detail to the player's responses. This allows for some "richness" in helping to determine the strengths and weaknesses relating to a player's mental skills. Certain questions can form the "backbone" of the interview with various probes to highlight areas the sport psychology consultant feels need to be elaborated upon (Weinberg & Williams, 2001). It is important in the interview to have the player feel comfortable so that they are willing to reveal their true feelings. Being non-judgmental and assuring confidentiality will be helpful in this regard.

A second method is the use of *paper and pencil inventories*. There are many inventories to choose from but sport psychologists should try to employ inventories that are tennis-specific whenever possible (e.g. T-TAIS Van Schoyck & Grasha, 1981) or possibly modify some existing questionnaires to be as specific to tennis as possible. At a minimum, inventories should be specific to sport as opposed to a more general psychological inventory. Some inventories assess a variety of mental skills (e.g. Athletic Coping Skills Inventory-28—Smith, Schultz, Smoll & Ptacek, 1995) while others focus on one skill such as concentration or anxiety management. Sport psychologists want to get as much information as possible but at the same time not overburden the player with too much paperwork.

If these two methods are chosen, then it is recommend that written feedback be provided to each player that highlights their psychological strengths and weaknesses as they relate to tennis performance. Players should be given an opportunity to react to this assessment and thus it provides some sort of consensual validation regarding the accuracy of the combined written and oral evaluation. The assessment should conclude with recommendations for the type of mental skills and intervention program that the sport psychology consultant thinks would best suit the specific player's needs and would thus form the basis of the program to follow.

Although the first two methods can be very successful, the athlete is relatively passive in the process. This can result in the sport psychology consultant having to convince the player that they have to work on a particular mental skill. Thus, a third method was developed by Butler and Hardy (1992), known as *performance profiling*. This method helps identify important mental training skills objectives as well as helping maximize the motivation of players to implement and adhere to a mental skills training program. To use this technique, tennis players would first be asked to identify the qualities or characteristics (specifically mental) of elite tennis players. The tennis player would list all of the qualities on a piece of paper (this could also be done with a team through brainstorming in small groups). After the player(s) stopped the sport psychology consultant (or the coach) might assist in identifying other characteristics noted by other top tennis players. Tennis players would then rate themselves (on a 1 to 10-scale representing the degree to which they felt they had the mental skills of top tennis players) on all the qualities that they identified, and their responses would be translated into a "performance profile", providing a visual representation of the player's strengths and potential areas of improvement. This approach is particularly effective since the player is generating the key mental concepts and also does a self-rating as to which areas most need improvement. Based on the results, a player (and sport psychology consultant) could see the areas in which the player is doing well as opposed to those that need some improvement, forming the basis for a subsequent intervention.

Analyze Demands of the Sport

Every sport has unique physical, technical and logistical demands that require special preparation by players. Some important considerations might include factors such as the degree of precision, strength, explosiveness or endurance required by the sport. In addition, the length of the performance as well as the time between performances and the amount of time within performances would also be important considerations. In looking at tennis in particular, the physical demands of the task require a variety and combination of physical skills since you need fine muscle coordination and precision, strength as well as endurance; a reason why most players now spend a good amount of time in the weight room, running and doing cross-training to increase their physical fitness and flexibility (André Agassi, as he gets older, is a prime example of this philosophy). Thus tennis is a great sport in which to implement mental training, especially due to the 20 to 30 seconds between points, which allow time for players to think (unfortunately they often think about the wrong or negative things). In fact, in a 2-hour tennis match, players are actually playing for only about half an hour. So what are they doing during the hour and a half when they are not actually playing? This is especially where the mental part of tennis comes into play. In addition, most players and coaches would agree that good strokes alone do not win tennis matches. Rather, it's the mental preparation and recovery throughout the match, as well as the mental preparation for the match, that are critical to performing well in the match.

Practicing Mental Skills

As noted earlier, tennis does not have a specific season but there is a seasonal component depending upon who is the specific client. For example, at the professional level, many players focus their training around the four Grand Slam events (which occur in January, May, July and September). College players typically have their major season in the spring with most matches coming in March, April and May. Junior players might play throughout the year with more tournaments over the summer. High-school boys typically have their season late in the spring, whereas high-school girls have their season in early fall. This is to say that there is no one set season, and a mental skills program needs to be developed to fit the specific needs of the individual player/team. Although a sport psychology consultant might work with a tennis team, since tennis is an individual sport and needs are different across players, mental training programs should be individualized whenever possible. If working with a team, a sport psychologist might give group presentations on general topic areas such as goal-setting, imagery, arousal regulation, confidence, concentration, mental preparation, etc. might be desirable (see Weinberg, 2002 for a more complete description of teaching these mental skills in tennis), but these would have to be followed up with individual consultations. Also, as noted earlier, the training program would be most desirable if it were conducted when there is little competitive tennis going on so that the player could learn the mental skills and then integrate them into practice and eventually into match situations over the course of time.

After completing the assessment noted above, it is recommended that the sport psychologist meet with individual players and go over the evaluation and get their input. This "consensual validation" helps to set the stage for the initiation of the mental skills training program and determining what specific skills will be included in the program.

Increasing Awareness

A good way for players to set goals and become more aware of their thoughts and feeling is through writing them down in a journal because, before players can change the way they think or feel, they have to have a clear understanding of their thoughts and feelings. So, in their journal, players can write down their thoughts and feelings before and after (and during) practices and matches as well as how these relate to performance. Once players understand the relationship between thoughts, feelings and performance from a practical perspective, then they will be in a better position to practice these and eventually integrate them into competitive performances.

In some situations, awareness can be increased in other ways. For example, a player might have a lot of negative self-talk. The player could be asked by the sport psychologist to record the frequency of negative self-talk and eventually its impact on performance. In a few cases, I've asked players to carry around a bunch of toothpicks (or paperclips) in one pocket and after every negative self-statement, the player is instructed to move a toothpick from one pocket to another (e.g. left to right pocket). In the course of a practice (or a match) a player will typically move lots of toothpicks due to the frequency of negative self-talk. In fact, on several occasions, players have told me that they were flabbergasted as to the amount of toothpicks they had to move from one pocket to another. In essence, they were simply not aware of how often they had negative self-statements. This served to be the stimulus for making some changes to more positive self-talk.

Learning Mental Skills

Now that players are more aware of their feelings, they can then start to practice learning the skills. The assessment should help target those particular skills that the player might be seen as deficient in, or simply might like to improve. Specific assignments would then be given to practice the different skills. Sport psychologists can start by having players practice their mental skills outside of any formal practice or game situation. For instance, using the self-talk illustration provided above, the player would be instructed to go home and list the situations in which she employed negative self-talk. Then she would replace these negative self-statements with ones that were more positive. After a double fault, for example, instead of saying "You can't serve at all," she could replace this with "Just go through your routine and reach up to the ball." Thus, the player would develop positive statements for all situations in which she previously said negative things.

After perfecting the change from negative to positive self-statements, the player can then move onto the practice court. First of all, the player could practice this using imagery (assuming she had learned the skill of imagery), to see herself reacting to different aversive situations with positive statements, instead of negative statements (this still does not have to be done on-court). This would get her in the habit (mentally) of focusing on the positive self-statements. The next step would be to have the player use this in actual practice situations trying either to replace the negative statement with a positive one or simply just saying a positive statement (this could be done out loud or to oneself—self-talk—depending on the situation). Specific simulated competitive situations could be manipulated in practice by the sport psychologist to increase the importance of the performance, therefore putting more pressure on the player. This might produce more potential negative statements and thus a player can practice replacing these with positive statements (or just saying positive things if the negative statements can be eliminated. The closer the practice situation can be made to the actual game situation, the better the transfer (both for physical and mental skills). For example, tennis coaches sometimes have players (a) practice with the set score tied at 4–4, (b) specifically work on the weaker parts of their game which usually produces more errors and thus more negative self-talk, (c) play each other a tiebreaker with the winner moving up toward the first court (championship court) while the loser moves down. All of these scenarios help increase the pressure and hopefully simulate some aspect of actual match competition.

The assignments for practice might be given one at a time so that the player could practice different aspects of their specific mental skill. They might be asked to record their thoughts and feelings regarding the specific mental practice in a log and then report back to the sport psychology consultant on a regular (possibly weekly or bi-weekly basis). In this way, the success of the mental training (along with any problems or obstacles) can be discussed and modifications can be made for subsequent practice.

After becoming more skilful at changing negative to positive-self talk in practice, it's time to use this skill in game situations. It is recommended that sport psychologists encourage players to employ it in matches that are not that important or pressure-filled, to get used to doing it in competition. Gradually, the player would move to implementing it in more and more critical and important matches. While doing this, the player would also be monitoring the success of this strategy (via logs) to see what is (or what is not) working for her. After practicing the strategy in competition numerous times, the player should start to automate the skill and be able to call upon it as necessary in match situations. As noted earlier, it is optimal if all this practice and training occurs during the off-season or pre-season so that the skill can be developed and integrated into the player's game before important competitions arise. Of course the player would optimally be coming back and reporting in to the sport psychologist, who could then review the player's progress and offer more constructive tips on further practice and integration.

Pre-competition Plans

The ultimate goal of a mental skills training program is for each player to learn how to create consistently at competition time the ideal performance state, typically associated with peak performance. In fact, previous research (Weinberg, Butt, Knight, Burke & Jackson, 2003) has indicated that the most frequent time that athletes employ mental rehearsal is right before a competition. Although this is not the best strategy (unless of course the athlete has been practicing their mental skills on a regular basis), athletes generally don't practice their mental skills and just figure that doing something prior to performance will be beneficial. But as part of a mental training program, pre-competition and competition plans are essential components.

One of the objectives of pre-competition planning is to arrange the external and internal environment in a way that maximizes the tennis player's feeling of control. The external environment consists of the actual things the player does in these physical surroundings, whereas the internal environment consists of the player's thoughts, feelings and mental images. The greater the familiarity, routine, and structure in the external environment, the easier it is for the player to be in control of their internal environment. In working with players, sport psychologists should have them control and stabilize their external environment by doing things such as eating similar meals with the same time lapse before each match, always arriving at the match with a set amount of time for pre-match preparation, establishing a set dressing ritual, and following the same equipment check and warm-up procedures.

Besides being ready for the physical environment, it is also important for players to have a routine regarding their internal environment, often seen as mental preparation. In essence, physical preparations should be supplemented and complemented with emotional and cognitive readying procedures. This entails monitoring and controlling thoughts and emotions so that energy and excitement builds slowly, anxiety levels are managed effectively, thoughts are directed to relevant cues and positive feelings are emphasized. Of course, there are a great many individual differences in devising the most effective pre-competition readying technique for each player. So sport psychologists should first analyze the player's current pre-competition routine and determine if it needs changes or not. Then, with the help of the player, the sport psychologist would devise a pre-competition routine that gets the player physically and mentally ready to play. This routine might include some of the standard mental preparation strategies such as self-talk, relaxation, imagery and focusing, but again it would be individualized based on the needs and interests of each player. Research (Eklund, Gould & Jackson, 1993; Gould, Eklund & Jackson, 1992; Gould, Guinan, Greenleaf, Medberry & Peterson, 1999; Greenleaf, Gould & Dieffenbach, 2001) has demonstrated that Olympic athletes who were medalists had very systematic pre-competition routines that they consistently adhered to throughout the Olympics, whereas non-medalists reported deviating from their pre-competitive routines, especially in events that they considered less challenging or less important (setting the stage for a potential upset or poor performance).

Competition Plans

Just as important as pre-competitive plans are competitive plans. Research cited above also found that medalists had competition plans firmly in their minds and did not second-guess these plans during matches, whereas non-medalists reported that spontaneous deviations from competition plans developed for matches and often had negative consequences (i.e. poorer performance). In tennis, having a specific game plan provides clarity to a player's mission and keeps things simple and straightforward. A game plan gives a player's efforts structure and direction, without which a player is like a rudderless ship. Without a game plan, a player just hits shots back with no structured attack or defense. When a player discards his game plan (not replaced by an alternate plan) this usually results in panic, discouragement and breakdown in resolve and oftentimes signals the beginning of the end.

In essence, when a player has a solid game plan, she does not have to make a lot of decisions and figure out how to play an opponent. Rather, she has already determined what she needs to do to be successful. For example, in the Australian Open, the announcers repeatedly noted that Lisa Raymond had a specific game plan to defeat Venus Williams (who she had never beaten before). That is, she was trying to keep the ball down the middle of the court to reduce some of the speed of Venus who was at her best running wide and finding angles, bringing in to play her athleticism and movement skills. In addition, Lisa Raymond also took pace off the ball to make Venus generate the pace, especially on her forehand side (feeling that she would make more errors this way). She stayed committed to this competition plan and it earned her the most important singles victory of her life. Orlick (1986; 2000) provides some excellent examples of the use of competitive plans with a variety of Canadian Olympic athletes. In tennis, these plans should be carefully developed to maximize the abilities of the player and to highlight any weaknesses in the opponent. Of course a sport psychologist might not develop the specifics of a game plan, but rather make sure there is a game plan that involves consistent routines and ensure that the player is committed to the plan.

Brad Gilbert, in his book *Winning Ugly* (Gilbert & Jamison, 1993), provides a classic example of sticking to a game plan. He describes a quarter-final meeting with Boris Becker at the US Open. Gilbert had scouted Becker and he knew he just could not outhit him since Becker possessed superior physical talent. But maybe he could outthink him with a good game plan. Therefore, he developed a clear game plan based on reviewing Becker's (as well as his own) strengths and weaknesses, which included among other things, the following: (a) increase his first serve percentage, (b) serve to Becker's forehand and look for crosscourt returns, approach down the line, (c) don't give Becker any pace, (d) work hard on every point, (e) don't be impressed by anything Becker does, make him do it again and again, (f) don't try for too much on service returns, just get the ball back. Even though Gilbert lost the first two sets and was down a service break in the third, he stuck to his game plan. His persistence eventually paid off as Becker became frustrated with the lack of pace, humid conditions and staying on court so long which led to rushing, unforced errors and eventually a loss of resolve.

Competition Refocus Plans

Therefore, having a competition (game) plan is critical for success in tennis, and all players should either figure out a game plan prior to a match (if they know the opponent) or figure it out quickly during warm-ups or in the first few games. But even if a player has not seen an opponent, he should still have an initial game plan based on his own strengths and weaknesses. But maybe just as important as a competition plan is a competition refocus plan. Specifically, what will a player do when his original game plan is not going well? In essence, a player has to be prepared with "Plan B" if "Plan A" is not working effectively. But when does a player go to "Plan B?" As noted by Allen Fox in his excellent book, *Think to Win*, "A game plan is a funny animal. It must be taken seriously enough to commit your full mental energy to its execution yet not so seriously that it is rigid and you cannot adjust it" (1993, p. 129). Players know that they should keep a winning game plan and change a losing one but the tricky part is determining when this should occur. For instance, in the above example, should Brad Gilbert have tried a new game plan after losing the first two sets and being down a break in the third to Boris Becker? Most players have a tendency to give up on a game plan too soon, as they blame strategy when things start to go wrong. But oftentimes the game plan is fine, it's just the execution that is poor. So if it's a good game plan, based on multiple observations of the opponent, then a player may want to stick with the plan a little longer to make sure it is not working on that particular day (this is where a sport psychologist might be especially helpful). But if a player has to change a game plan, then it is important to have "Plan B" in mind as a refocusing strategy. This would be part of the mental preparation for a match (developed with the help of a sport psychologist) so that if a competition plan must be changed, then another good plan within your capabilities based on your abilities (and that has a reasonable chance of succeeding) could be implemented. Once again this needs to be practiced so that it can be implemented with confidence in a seamless manner.

SUMMARY

In this chapter, I have attempted to provide some general guidelines along with specific examples of mental skills training for tennis players. Although this chapter focuses on the sport psychology consultant applying principles to tennis players, there are some general principles to keep in mind when implementing a mental skills training program. These include the following: (a) the initial mental skills training program should probably last

3 to 6 months and start in the off-season or pre-season, (b) a sport psychologist should implement a mental skills training program but a coach can work with a sport psychologist to implement a program, (c) mental skills should be systematically employed for about 15 minutes on 3 to 5 days per week, (d) assessments should include both questionnaire and interview (including performance profiling) techniques, (e) the specific nature of the tennis season for the individual player should be considered to determine the course and periodization of the mental training, (f) pre-competition and competition plans should be included, (g) the difficulty of tennis from a mental perspective and mental skills of top performers should be considered when devising a program, and (h) mental skills should be first taught through repetition, then used in increasingly difficult practice situations, and finally incorporated into match situations.

The most important thing is to make sure that the mental skills training program is individualized to each tennis player. Tennis is a sport that has different seasons based on the developmental level and specific goals of the player. Some have a season (like high school and college) but others find this season less important than regional, national and international tournaments. Therefore, mental training (as well as physical training) needs to revolve around the particular schedule of the player. But regardless of the specific schedule, there are guidelines (presented throughout the paper and summarized above) that should be followed to maximize the effectiveness of any mental skills training intervention.

REFERENCES

Boutcher, S. & Rotella, R. (1987). A psychological skills education program for closed-skill performance enhancement. *The Sport Psychologist, 1*, 127–137.

Butler, R. & Hardy, L. (1992) The performance profile: theory and application. *The Sport Psychologist, 6*, 253–264.

Eklund, R., Gould, D. & Jackson, S. (1993). Psychological foundations of Olympic wrestling excellence: reconciling individual differences and nomothetic characterization. *Journal of Applied Sport Psychology*, 35–47.

Fox, A. (1993). *Thinking to Win*. New York, NY: HarperCollins.

Gilbert, B. & Jamison, S. (1993). *Winning Ugly*. New York, NY: Simon & Schuster.

Gould, D., Eklund, R. & Jackson, S. (1992). 1988 US Olympic wrestling excellence: I mental preparation, pre-competition cognition and affect. *The Sport Psychologist, 6*, 358–382.

Gould, D., Guinan, D., Greenleaf, C., Medberry, R. & Peterson, K. (1999). Factors affecting Olympic performance: perceptions of athletes and coaches from more and less successful teams. *The Sport Psychologist, 13*, 371–395.

Greenleaf, C., Gould, D. & Dieffenbach, K. (2001). Factors influencing performance: interviews with Atlanta and Nagano US Olympians. *Journal of Applied Sport Psychology, 13*, 179–209.

Jackson, S., & Csikszentmihalyi, M. (1999). *Flow in Sports: The Key to Optimal Experiences and Performances*. Champaign, IL: Human Kinetics

Orlick, T. (1986) *Psyching for Sport: Mental Training for Athletes*. Champaign, IL: Human Kinetics.

Orlick, T. (2000). *In Pursuit of Excellence*. Champaign, IL: Human Kinetics

Smith, R. & Johnson, J. (1990). An organizational empowerment approach to consultation in professional baseball. *The Sport Psychologist, 4*, 347–357.

Smith, R., Schultz, R., Smoll, F. & Ptacek, J. (1995). Development and validation of a multidimensional measure of sport-specific psychological skills: the Athletic Coping Skills Inventory-28. *Journal of Sport and Exercise Psychology, 17*, 379–387.

Tarshis, B. (1977). *Tennis and the Mind*. New York: Tennis Magazine.

Van Schoyck, S. & Grasha, A. (1981). Attentional style variations and athletic ability: the advantages of a sports-specific test. *Journal of Sport Psychology, 3*, 149–165.

Weinberg, R. (2002). *Tennis: Winning the Mental Game*. Lynn, MA: H.O. Zimman.

Weinberg, R., Butt, J., Knight, B., Burke, K. & Jackson, A. (2003). The relationship between the use and effectiveness of imagery: an exploratory investigation. *Journal of Applied Sport Psychology, 15*, 26–40.

Weinberg, R. & Williams, J. (2001). *Applied Sport Psychology: Personal Growth to Peak Performance*. Mountain View, CA: Mayfield.

CHAPTER 14

Golf: Sport Psychology Challenges

Linda K. Bunker
University of Virginia, USA

INTRODUCTION

The game of golf appears to the layman as a very simple, closed sport. The small round ball sits still, the target (hole on the green) does not move, and there are no competitors to directly interfere with your progress. On the other hand, the player's mind and ability to concentrate, attend to relevant stimuli and focus on the task at hand become enormous challenges. It has been said that golf is a game of mind over muscle and that it is the 6.5 inches between the ears that makes the difference between the very good and the great!

This chapter is designed to introduce the reader to the game of golf and the special psychological challenges that it presents. Topics will include a brief introduction to the game of golf, followed by tips to handling the specific challenges of this sport, including: the origins of golf, a brief summary of the rules and etiquette of golf and, most importantly, the psychological challenges of golf with special emphasis on attention and concentration, arousal control, controlling self-talk (cognitive reconstruction), goal setting and monitoring progress, using imagery for goal attainment.

THE ORIGIN OF GOLF

Golf is one of the oldest sports in the world. Some believe its earliest forms emerged in Greece where ancient shepherds hit stones with their staffs. The game as we know it today probably had its primitive origins in Scotland in the Kingdom of Fife in the fifteenth century, where players would hit a pebble around a natural course of sand dunes, rabbit runs and tracks using a stick or primitive club. However, these early forms of golf lacked the uniqueness of the sport—a target or hole.

Contemporary golf is often ascribed to the original course at St Andrews, Scotland, around 1744 (Owens & Bunker, 1995). Golf had been banished in the mid-fifteenth century because Scotland was being invaded by England and parliament thought too much time was being spent on golf and soccer at the expense of military training. The ban was lifted in

1502 with the Treaty of Glasgow and King James I of England took up the game himself (*A History of Golf*, http://www.golfeurope.com).

Contrary to most popular history, the first golf tournaments were held at Leith near Edinburgh in 1682 when England played Scotland, and the first formal rules of golf emerged from "The Gentlemen Golfers of Leith" and their annual competition which began in 1744 about the same time that St Andrews, Scotland, was founded (Frost, 2002, 2004).

Today there are many forms of competition in the game of golf, the two primary ones being medal or match play. Match play is a type of competition where each hole is won, lost or halved (tied). The winner is whoever won the most holes, and the score is generally recorded in terms such as three and two, which indicates that the winner won by three holes with two left to play. Medal play (stroke play) requires that all shots are recorded and the winner is the one who took the least number of strokes. This is the most common type of play, and there are many forms of individual or team competitions that are generally based on medal play, such as "best ball", and "captain's choice".

THE GAME OF GOLF

Golf appears to be a simple target game, with the objective to hit a small, stationary, hard ball with a stick (*club*) as few times as is necessary for it to travel from the starting point (referred to as the *tee*, or *tee box*) to the target (a 4.5-inch hole cut down in the ground) located on each green. Each player must hit their own ball in the predetermined direction for the desired distance, using one of a variety of clubs of assorted lengths and shapes. The score for a hole is the total number of strokes it takes to hit the ball from the tee into the hole, with rounds containing either 9 or 18 holes, typically varying from 85 to 600 yards.

Almost all golf holes have six components: teeing area, fairway, rough, hazards, putting green, and cup (hole). The central path from tee to green is the fairway, bordered by the rough (or grass cut at a higher level). Hazards are typically either water holes, streams or sand traps (referred to as "bunkers"). The green is the putting surface, which may be smooth or horizontal or undulating and composed of various plateaus or slopes. The grass on the green is usually especially well tended, and when it is cut it is very short and referred to as a "fast green" (resulting in a "fast" surface) or a little longer, resulting in a "slow" surface.

Scoring

Each time the ball is contacted it counts as a stroke and is counted in the total number of strokes for the hole or the round. The fewer the strokes (hence lower score) the better, with totals normally reported in terms of 18 holes or one *round*. A player can measure their skill in comparison to another golfer, though it is more traditional to measure ability against a designated standard of excellence referred to as *par*. Par is the number of strokes thought to be necessary for a very good golfer to complete a hole, and is based on the length of that hole. It is assumed that 2 putts are required for each hole, once the ball has landed on the green. In addition, the total yardage from the tee box to the green adds strokes depending on the distance: Par 3s are short holes (85 to 245 yds) and require only 1 stroke from tee to green; Par 4s are medium-length holes (245 to 445 yds) and require 2 strokes from tee to green; while par 5s are long holes (445 to 600 yds) and require 3 strokes from tee to green.

As is true in most sports, there are special terms which refer to the unique aspects of the sport. In golf, most terms refer to the player's score in relation to par. A *birdie* is one stroke under par for a hole, an *eagle* is two strokes under par, and an *ace* is a hole-in-one, requiring only one stroke. For many players, it is common to take more that the allotted number of strokes on a hole (par), resulting in a *bogey* (one stroke over par) or a *double bogey* (two strokes over par).

The Rules of Golf

The rules of golf can seem quite overwhelming, though there are some wonderful sources for understanding them (*Rules of Golf, 2004–2007*; *USGA Rules of Golf, 2004–2007* for USA and Mexico only) and should be carefully studied by the serious golfer. Golfers should be encouraged to carry a copy of the rules in their golf bag, because the rules are not always easy to interpret or remember. If playing in a tournament and there is a doubt about the rule, always ask for a clarification from a tournament official (Kuhn & Garner, 2004).

In general the rules can be classified in terms of the penalties assessed if a rule is broken. Penalties range from no penalty (*free drop*) to one-stroke penalties, two-stroke penalties and disqualification. Free drops (no penalty) generally involve situations which are beyond your control and for which a player can seek *relief*, with a *free drop* that allows for the relocation of the ball in the fairest way possible. Such situations include ground under repair, sprinkler heads for course watering, casual water from rain, holes made by burrowing animals and staked trees or shrubs.

One-stroke penalties are assessed when the golfer has contributed to the problem by virtue of their previous shot, and include lost balls, out-of-bounds balls, landing in direct water hazards that run across the fairway or a lateral water hazard where the water runs parallel to the fairway. There are generally two options for one-stroke-penalties: go back to the original spot and hit again, or keep on line with the water hazard, and no closer to the hole.

Two-stroke penalties are often related to lapses in attention and can therefore be easily influenced by good mental training. Such situations include grounding a club in a hazard, hitting the wrong ball, requesting assistance, or hitting a ball or flag on the green from a starting position on the green. There are specific rules about where to play the next shot, and golfers should be referred to the official rules of golf for clarification.

Golf Etiquette

Etiquette covers both courtesy and course care, both of which are important parts of the game. One of the most important personal aspects relates to who has the right to tee off first at each hole. This is referred to as *honors*, and goes to the person with the lowest score on the previous hole. In case of a tie, the person with the lower score on the second-to-last hole has the honors.

There are many other socially desirable behaviors that are traditional in golf (see Table 14.1). These not only represent common courtesies, but also contribute to the psychological skills necessary for successful golf. A player is asked not only to take care of their own performance, but to assist accompanying players and care for the course. If there are

Table 14.1   Ten tips to golf etiquette

1. Stand quietly and don't move, talk or stand close to a player making a stroke.
2. Withhold hitting until the group in front of you is safely out of the way.
3. Always play without delay.
4. Leave the putting green as soon as all players in your group have holed out; invite faster groups to play through.
5. Always put an identifying mark on your own golf ball to avoid confusion.
6. Replace divots and smooth footprints by raking sand in bunkers.
7. Don't step on the line of another player's putt.
8. Stand behind and outside of any sun shadow for other players.
9. Be considerate of putting greens; don't drop clubs on the putting green; walk off the green before recording your score.
10. Hold the flagstick for other players at their request, or withdraw it, and replace the flagstick carefully before leaving the green.

local rules or etiquette related to golf carts, water hazards, markers, etc. they are generally found on the back of the course's score card. Following are a few other essential tips to golf etiquette.

SELECTED PSYCHOLOGICAL CHALLENGES IN GOLF

The game of golf requires a great deal of mental control. The fact that the ball sits still, a target can be determined for each stroke and there are no directly opposing or intervening players, makes it seem like it should be a relatively easy sport. However, the truth is that it is perhaps the most challenging of all sports in terms of mental control. During a round of golf, that can take four to five hours to play, it is easy to lose concentration, to have attention distracted, or to become anxious or frustrated by your own play or the play of others. Building and maintaining confidence is another challenge for golfers, as they learn to make appropriate attributions about what they can control and what is outside of their control, and to put themselves in a position to execute and trust what they have practiced.

Golfers sometimes doubt their skills, especially after a poor shot, when they may talk to themselves in non-enhancing ways, and biomechanically over-analyze their skills to the degree that it interferes with the automatic execution of their strokes. Such problems can often be ameliorated through stress management, modifying intra-personal self-talk (cognitive restructuring) and using positive imagery to anticipate and solve problems, and to imagine successful performances. With these skills, coupled with effective planning and goal setting to guide practice, most golfers can greatly improve their performance through the effective development and use of sport psychology skills.

Much recent research has suggested that experts learn psychological skills which distinguish them from others who have good physical talents, but are not successful in a competitive situation. Ericsson and Charness (1994) provided evidence that performance, especially for experts, is mediated by complex psychological skills that have been learned over time. Similarly, Thomas and Fogarty (1997) demonstrated that skills such as mental preparation, automaticity, putting performance, positive emotions and seeking feedback can be learned over as short a time frame as a four training session protocol.

Table 14.2 Elements of excellence for professional
golfers as identified by McCaffrey and Orlick (1989)

1. Total commitment
2. Quality rather than quantity of practice
3. Clearly defined goals
4. Imagery practice on a daily basis
5. Focusing totally on one shot at a time
6. Recognizing, expecting, and preparing to cope
   with pressure situations
7. Practice and tournament plans
8. Tournament focus plan
9. Distraction control strategies
10. Post-tournament evaluations.

Source: McCaffrey, N. & Orlick, T. (1989). Mental factors related
to excellence among top professional golfers. *International Journal of
Sport Psychology, 20,* 256–278.

Many of the skills described in the following sections can be used for multiple purposes in the game of golf. For example, McCaffrey and Orlick (1989) discussed many of the characteristics that are possessed by top professional golfers who had won professional tournaments around the world. They identified 10 elements of excellence, many of which will be discussed in this chapter and are presented in Table 14.2. In addition they focused on a type of self-reflection and personal knowledge which they termed "clear understanding of what helps them play well versus play poorly".

The general findings and implications of this research have been corroborated on many occasions, and provide the skeleton for the outline of this chapter.

Attention and Concentration in Golf

A round of 18 holes of golf can take 4 to 5 hours to play. In the mid-1990s, golfers were instructed to try to completely concentrate throughout those hours, even though at least 50 per cent of the time is spent walking between shots. Today we know that great golfers are able to "focus in and let go" during a round of golf. They concentrate extremely well just before and during the shot, and then "let go" between shots, without losing their ability to take in important information (Zinsser, Bunker & Williams, 2001). As they walk up to the next shot, they once again focus in, look at the important elements, and apply the simple attentional guideline of focusing on *LDT: lie, distance and trajectory*. This LDT guideline is an easy way for players to remember that the most important things to attend to are, in order, the lie of the ball, the distance to the target and the trajectory needed to get the ball to the target (Owens & Bunker, 1992). When players focus on this simple sequence it helps them make better mental decisions and control their anxiety.

The time it takes to complete a round of golf lends itself to diverted attention that might perseverate on the past (the last shot hit out of bounds, or the last bogeyed hole, or the last time a 4-iron was mis-hit, etc.). The research literature would suggest that it is important to focus on the present, and "let go of the past". Golf is a rather unique game in that each hole is a new "mini-game" with the score count starting over each time in match play, and

Focus of attention

	External	Internal
Broad	1	2
Narrow	3	4

Figure 14.1   Utilizing the dimensions of attentional control will allow a golfer to systematically gather information and process decisions

in standard, stroke play, the score accumulates, but there is no real relationship between performance on the last hole, and the potential to perform well on the next hole. That makes it both a challenge and potentially easy to learn to control attention by shutting out the past, and focusing on the present.

One model of attention control suggests that expert athletes must be able to shift from an external to internal focus, and from broad to narrow. This represents a typical problem solving strategy beginning with broad external, then broad internal, then narrow external, then narrow internal (see Figure 14.1). Using this model, golfers learn to start each sequence of shot decisions by analyzing the environmental demands for a shot, with a broad external focus or using the LDT system. Next they analyze their options for shots based on their personal skills, with a broad internal focus. The third step is to consider the specific course management for this shot (e.g. where should the ball land, should it be above or below the pin, what trajectory should be used, etc.) and then lastly matched with the golfer's best option for that particular shot.

When beginners are asked about the purpose of the golf swing, they often say it is to hit the ball, yet if you ask a tour player, the answer is to send the ball to the target. This target awareness is the key to successful golf, and can be enhanced by using a good visualization, committing to a specific focal point.

Another important aspect of attention control deals with staying in the present. Many inexperienced golfers either dwell on a past shot, or think too much about the future, rather than focusing on the present. If you keep berating yourself for the bogey on the last hole, or the bad tee shot, it can only distract your attention. Similarly, if you plan too far ahead and start focusing on playing the next hole with a birdie, you are not focusing on the shot at hand. These problems are often ameliorated through the use of effective self-talk (see the following section).

The attention and concentration of expert players (professionals and top-ranked collegiate players) was extensively researched by Cohn (1991). He found that when players were at their peak, they reported effortless and automatic swings, requiring almost no conscious control. They described a narrow focus of attention and total immersion in the task. They also reported playing without fear of failure or concern for any negative consequences of poor shots.

Another special challenge to attention in golf is the environment in which it is played. For example, the *slow play* of individuals ahead of a player may produce frustration and a tendency to be distracted. It is important to recognize that this slow play can be an opportunity to either "focus in" and mentally rehearse the next shot with plenty of time, or an opportunity to be assertive, and ask to "play through" or, if in a tournament, to ask the official to check on the slow play of others. It is not helpful for a player simply to be frustrated by slow play—do something about it! During tournament play, a golfer might also be faced with the situation when one of their playing partners is playing slow, and an official asks the entire group to speed up. In this case, it is important to focus on getting ready to hit as soon as possible, to read lies, putts and distances as soon as possible, and be ready to hit as soon as possible—this is sometimes referred to as "ready play". If a player allows themself to be distracted by worrying about being penalized by partner's slow play, it can only detract from performance.

Several studies have investigated the relationships between attentional control and performance in golf. Kirschenbaum and Bale (1980) found significant correlations between golf performance and subscales of the test of attentional and interpersonal style (Nideffer, 1976). Other studies have confirmed higher levels of concentration and confidence in low vs high handicapped players. The low handicappers (better golfers) have been found to use greater mental preparation, including pre-shot planning, higher levels of concentration, and were less troubled by negative evaluations of their own performance or self-talk associated with it (Thomas and Over, 1994).

Techniques for Learning to Control Attention in Golf

The wonderful thing about attention and concentration is that they are absolutely under your control. No one can make you be distracted unless you "let it happen". One effective strategy is to record all good or bad shots, including what club was used, and the outcome, focusing on the quality of the shot. Such a technique directs your attention and can give you a chance to review the past hole's shots on the way to the next tee box. Think of your mind as a videotape with which you can "replay the good and replace the bad". Learn from the weaker shots, but then let them go so that they do not occupy too much of your attention. As Owens and Kirschenbaum (1998) suggested, forget problematic shots while you are playing—no one plays perfect golf, and the time to practice is after your round of golf.

During practice there are some creative and fun practice strategies. For example, on the driving range, have players work in partners or trios and attempt to distract each other. They can talk during the swing, or perhaps throw tees or paper down toward the ball as the player is swinging. Partners should have some fun with this practice and see how they can distract each other (Owens & Bunker, 1995).

One of the special challenges of golf is the relatively long wait between shots. It is easy to be distracted, to lose your focus of attention or to let anxiety and arousal get out of control. Many years ago, teachers would tell golfers that they should keep their concentration throughout the round of golf, sometimes for over five hours. Today, the research would suggest that the important thing is to be able to let go after one shot and refocus as you approach the next shot. This refocusing process can be enhanced by using a consistent pre-shot routine to help focus attention, be confident and let the swing occur more automatically.

Arousal Control in Golf

When an individual experiences frustration or a sense that they do not have the ability to meet the demands of a situation, arousal levels may rise quickly. When that happens, the

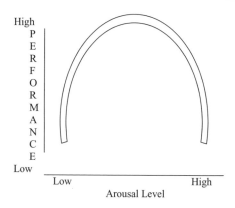

Figure 14.2   The relationship between arousal/anxiety levels and performance suggests that there is an optimal (moderate) level of arousal, when performance is maximal

key to effective performance is two-fold: (a) to monitor and detect changes in arousal; and (b) to manage and control individual arousal. There is a very helpful model that suggests that the relationship between arousal/anxiety and performance is an *inverted-U relationship*. Though there is some controversy over this model, it is a helpful descriptive model, and remains a mainstay in communicating to athletes the importance of controlling their arousal level and maintaining a moderate level in order to maximize performance. If arousal is too low, it produces reduced performance. Similarly, if arousal is too high, performance will be negatively impacted. Therefore it is important for golfers to be able to monitor their own arousal and keep it at a moderate level (see Figure 14.2).

The first step to controlling arousal or anxiety is to be able to detect it. Some golfers experience arousal with a dry mouth, increased sweat, increased respiration or heart rates. Others experience butterflies in their stomachs, tension in the hands, shoulders and neck, or a sense of needing to urinate. Any or all of these are real sensations that each person must interpret. The sensations are the result of the innate *fight or flight mechanism* that automatically adjusts the human physiology to respond to things that are emotionally charged. Humans have the unique "responsibility" to interpret whatever happens in their lives—that is, golfers have the "ability to respond" to any sensation they detect. As Davis Love III, the outstanding professional golfer said in a personal conversation, "When I feel sick to my stomach or have butterflies, I know my body is ready to respond to something important so I reinterpret that feeling to my advantage."

Techniques for controlling anxiety and arousal can take many forms. The use of positive self-talk, relaxation and imagery are three popular, learner-controlled strategies that are discussed later in this chapter. In addition, hypnosis has been shown to be an effective intervention, under the control of a trained therapist. Pates, Oliver and Maynard (2001) showed that hypnosis was effective in increasing confidence, inducing relaxation, enhancing focus and improving golf putting performance. They also emphasized the importance of triggers (sounds, images or natural parts of a routine) to help induce the relaxation response in the absence of the therapist.

Particular moments in a golf round seem to elicit greater arousal. For example, making a clutch putt is often a challenge for golfers. Justin Leonard, the winner of the 1997 British

Open, suggests that his consistent pre-shot routine is the key to effective putting, plus on crucial putts he tries to get his

> mind so wrapped up in making the putt that nothing else enters my thinking. I focus on deciding the line of the putt and the speed of the green. I place my ball on the ground so I can't see anything but white dimples. It helps sharpen my focus (Leonard, 2004, p. 114).

Manipulating arousal is another way to control it. For example, if during a pre-shot routine a golfer senses that there is too much muscle tension in the hands or arms, it is likely the golfer will slice the ball because of a lack of release in the hands. Effective golfers actively monitor their tension and then either relax or add tension as needed. One way to do that is to conceive of a tension monitor (with scores of one to five) with three being the optimal tension and five being too much or one being too little. Practice increasing tension in hands, shoulders, legs, etc. so that as you hit a ball or stroke a putt your tension is at the optimal three level, in the center of the inverted-U model. Intentionally and systematically manipulate tension in all parts of the body is an effective practice strategy.

Building and Maintaining Confidence in Golf

Confidence is one of the most elusive elements in sport. It has been repeatedly found that confidence is a key to success in athletics. For example, Loehr (1984) interviewed hundreds of athletes about their experiences when playing at their best, and found that they consistently linked confidence with optimal performance. Others have emphasized the importance of confidence as reported from athletes. One sample from Garfield and Bennett (1994) captures this relationship for a tennis player: "I felt like I could do almost anything, as if I were in complete control. I really felt confident and positive" (p. 37). In a study on figure skaters, Jackson (1995) investigated factors that influence a "flow state" and found that the most important element was "maintaining confidence and a positive attitude". Zinsser et al. (2001) have provided an extensive review of this literature, plus providing cognitive techniques to build confidence.

Outstanding athletes have developed their self-confidence through experience and have maintained it as a result of effective thinking, evaluations of their performances and their ability to savor successes and learn from (and let go of) failures. There is a wealth of evidence that supports the relationship between situation-specific confidence (self-efficacy) and performance (e.g. Bandura, 1997; Feltz & Chase, 1998). Research indicates that confident athletes think about themselves in different ways, and create more positive mental images of successful performance than less successful athletes. Successful athletes have recognized the importance of controlling their thoughts and images in order to learn from the past and focus on the present, while keeping in mind their long-term goals. They know that their conscious mind is not always an ally, and that it must be disciplined (just as their physical body) in order to maximize performance (Zinsser et al., 2001).

Self-confidence is not a genetic endowment, nor does it develop as an accident. It is the result of early experiences and the way in which individuals learn to interpret and process experiences. Confidence has been shown to be the result of particular thinking habits, rather than innate talent, learned skills, opportunities or previous successes. Confident athletes think about themselves and their skills differently—they *think they can and they do* by focusing on successfully performing skills rather than the *work* or *worry*, or *the fear of failure*. An adjunct to confidence is a sense of optimism and the ability to expect the best outcomes of the next attempt. Robert Rotella, an internationally renowned sport psychologist, emphasized this in his books, *Golf is Not a Game of Perfect* (Rotella & Cullen, 1995) and *The Golfer's Mind: Play to Play Great* (Rotella and Cullen, 2004), in which he tells golfers to expect challenges, and "bad luck", and focus on one's ability to handle them. Let go of the "bad breaks" or less than perfect shots, and focus on learning from them, and doing your best on the next shot—each shot is a new "mini-game".

A variety of research has supported the importance of self-confidence, and strategies for enhancing it. For example, Cohn, Rotella and Lloyd (1990) investigated the use of a cognitive-behavioral intervention that emphasized a total commitment to the club selected and the type of shot to be hit. Results showed an increased adherence to their pre-shot routines and, after four months, improvement was shown in the skills. Similarly, Taylor and Shaw (2002) showed the relationship between positive outcome imagery and confidence and how this effected performance.

There has been a great deal of speculation about the relationship between self-confidence and imagery (see the imagery section later in this chapter). Many authors and many athletes have talked about the importance of imagery in the development and maintenance of self-efficacy. For example, Callow, Hardy and Hall (1998) found a motivational general-mastery imagery intervention improved the confidence of badminton players, while Jones, Mace, Bray, McRae and Stockbridge (2002) showed that receiving imagery training positively affected the confidence of climbers. However, there are a few who have found no relationship between imagery use and self-efficacy (Woolfolk, Parrish & Murphy, 1985b; Martin & Hall, 1995). It may be that these equivocal findings are due to the specific nature of the imagery utilized (see imagery section) or the nature of the skill (golf vs endurance, vs basketball, etc.). Two studies which have found positive relationships between imagery and confidence include Feltz and Reissinger (1990) who used mastery-oriented imagery which encourages images of competence and success, and found a positive relationship between imagery and confidence in a muscular endurance task. For pre-competition, the benefits of imagery related to confidence have been shown in several studies (Hall, Mack, Paivo & Hausenblas, 1998; Moritz, Hall, Martin & Vadocz, 1996; Vadocz, Hall & Moritz, 1997).

Self-confidence is sometimes further differentiated into self-efficacy (situationally specific confidence such as having confidence hitting from a sand bunker or hitting from tall rough, etc.) and in the golf literature has often been investigated in terms of the effect of imagery or self-talk. A theory of self-efficacy (Bandura, 1997) suggested that imagining skillfully executing a skill would raise perceived efficacy and influence the ability to perform the skill. The literature in this area is rather equivocal. Several studies have shown that general motivational imagery is used more often by confident than less confident athletes (Moritz et al., 1996) and that imagery significantly increased participant's belief in their ability to perform a muscular endurance task (Feltz & Reissinger, 1990).

Other studies have shown a correlation between general motivational imagery and self-confidence (e.g. Vadocz et al., 1997) though one must be cautioned not to attribute a causative relationship since these were correlational studies (Short et al., 2002). For example, Woolfolk, Murphy, Gottesfeld and Aiken (1985a) found no relationship between self-efficacy and putting ability in college males.

Techniques for Building and Maintaining Confidence in Golf

Golf is one of the most sensitive sports in which to study the building and maintaining of confidence during the learning process. One effective strategy for practice involves the concept of "personal par" and has been advocated by Owens and Bunker (1992) and Owens and Kirschenbaum (1998) as a strategy for setting expectations during a round of golf. Personal par is the par for the hole, plus the handicap strokes allotted to you on the hole. The player's scorecard for each course identifies par for each hole, and indicates the handicap for each hole. For example, if you have a handicap of eight, you should add one stroke to each of the holes labeled one to eight in terms of the hole's handicap. Hence if hole three is listed as the fifth handicap hole on the course and has a par of four, you should think of your personal par on that hole as five.

Finding your "go-to" shots (Whaley, 2004) is another way to maximize your confidence. Most golfers lose strokes near the green, because they try to do too much with the specific ball location or circumstance (e.g. in the sand trap or 130 yards out). One way to increase confidence in such situations is to have made a decision that there is one shot you can really count on—a "go-to" shot. For highhandicappers, that might be a solid chip shot for use around the green, with firm wrists and the target hand leading. You might utilize your imagery by imaging an extension of your club (like a reflector stick inserted into the hole in the end of the grip), such that the club shaft, stick and your hands stay ahead of the clubhead and ball.

Another "go-to" strategy for high handicappers is to make a commitment either to work through a learning experience (see goal setting section) or, if in competition, to rely on perhaps the most consistent club in your bag, the putter. Neither strategy is "correct"—but not to have a strategy is definitely putting yourself at a disadvantage.

Controlling Self-talk: Cognitive Restructuring in Golf

Every golfer (and for that matter, every human being) talks to themselves. The challenge is to use that self-talk to your advantage rather than letting it be a negative aspect for your performance. Better golfers have consistently been found to be less troubled by negative cognitions or emotions, less upset by mistakes or missed opportunities, and did not generally get anxious or frustrated (Thomas & Over, 1994).

Self talk has been purported to facilitate many elements of performance, including: skill acquisition, to change bad habits, for attentional control, for creating or changing affect or mood, for effort control for building self-efficacy and for increasing persistence (Zinsser et al., 2001). In order to change negative or self-defeating thoughts it is important to (1) recognize the self-defeating or negative thought, (2) interrupt the negative thought with a trigger or physical action, (3) regain control (take a deep breath and exhale the negative thought), and (4) replace the ineffective thought with a self-enhancing thought (see Table 14.3; Zinsser et al., 2001).

Learning to replace a self-defeating thought with a self-enhancing thought is a skill, just like putting. Three good strategies include (1) *countering* the thought with a logical argument or evidence against it; (2) *reframing*, described by Gauron (1984) as creating alternative frames of reference of different ways of looking at the situation; or (3) *dissociation*, or

Table 14.3   Four steps to controlling self-talk and reconstructing cognitions

1. Recognize the self-defeating or negative thought
2. Interrupt the negative thought with a trigger or physical action
3. Regain control (take a deep breath and exhale the negative thought)
4. Replace the ineffective thought with a self-enhancing thought by:
   - Regaining temporal control and getting back to the present tense
   - Reframing the thought and find a different way to look at the situation
   - Countering the thought with logical arguments against it
   - Dissociating from the thought.

Source: Zinsser, N., Bunker, L. & Williams, J.M. (2001). Cognitive techniques for building confidence and enhancing performance. In J.M. Williams (ed.) *Applied Sport Psychology: Personal Growth to Peak Performance* (4th edn; pp. 284–311). Mountain View, CA: Mayfield Publishing Co.

thinking of something that is unrelated to the stressor. The last strategy is perhaps the weakest because it does not allow the learner to actually deal with the stressor.

One technique that works well with golfers is to give them a good way to keep track of their negative thoughts. For example, I was working with an LPGA rookie who was a true "Awfulizer"—everything was terrible. It was awful if it was raining, and terrible if it was sunny. She hated being paired with great veterans on the tour, yet that is the best place from which to learn. She would state things like "I never know what club I should hit, so I stand over the ball and doubt my selection" or "If I don't hit a great shot on the first tee it will be a terrible round". Such statements can do nothing but bring down performance. We began working together by simply monitoring the negative or self-defeating thoughts, and had her fill one pocket with paper clips, and every time she had a negative thought (that was not replaced by a positive thought) she had to move a paper clip to her opposite leg pocket. During the first round we tried this, she shot a 76 but had 78 paperclips in her other pocket— more negative thoughts than contacts with the ball! From there, we agreed to try to replace any negative or self-doubting thought with a positive one. When that was successful, it was a "win" and no paperclip had to be moved. As the number of non-controlled negative thoughts decreased, so did her score, and she went on to be the "rookie of the year"! Figure 14.3 is a good example of reframing and focusing on the possibilities.

The ability to control thoughts and the "chatter in your head" is a crucial determinant of success in motor skills (Bandura, 1997; Zinsser et al., 2001). When internal thoughts are negative or self-doubting, they often correlate with non-optimal performance, while positive thoughts tend to enhance confidence and are linked to better performance.

The effects of negative self-talk have been generally shown to hurt skill performance (Johnson-O'Conner & Kirschenbaum, 1986). Negative self-talk can lead to minimal performance decrements or to the extreme of *choking* when increased pressure leads to a performance breakdown (Leith, 1988). However, there is some research that suggests that trying to suppress negative self-talk may backfire and actually prime or activate the unwanted thoughts (Wegner, Ansfield & Pilloff, 1998; Wegner & Erber, 1992). This process is sometimes referred to as the *ironic process* in self-talk suppression (Wegner, 1994). Another possible outcome of suppressing negative thoughts has been referred to as "thought rebound" in which a participant overcompensates for a negative thoughts. For example, Janelle, Murray, De la Pena and Bouchard (1999) found that when golfers told themselves "not to putt the ball past the hole", they seemed to overcompensate and left the putt significantly short.

Figure 14.3   Reframing a self-defeating thought can help to rebuild confidence and enhance performance
Source: Owens, D.D. & Bunker, L.K. (1995). *Golf: Steps to Success* (p. 127). Champaign, IL: Human Kinetics.

Techniques for Controlling Self-talk and Optimism in Golf

It is important to let go of poor shots. For example, if a golfer continues to focus on the three or four putts just wasted on the last hole, it is impossible to do well on the next hole. The four-F technique advocated by Kirschenbaum (1997) is one strategy to transform a challenging or potentially negative experience into a focus on the next shot. The *four Fs are: Fudge!, Fix, Forget and Focus.* The Fudge! aspect is the acknowledgement that it is OK to be disappointed in a shot (Oh Fudge or Oh S . . .) and to react to it (hopefully silently). "Fix" encourages you to "replace the bad" by taking a new swing either literally, or in your mind, to give yourself confidence that you can "fix it". "Forget" means to let go of the last shot; everyone hits a poor shot and the good players try to forget it after they learn from it. The last F is for Focus, and encourages the golfer to learn from the past, analyze the next shot in terms of course management and to Focus on the present shot.

Using simple swing thoughts is another effective strategy to both control cognitions, and to focus attention. *Golf Digest* in 1997 interviewed five winners of major championships from 1996, including Annika Sorenstam, Mark Brooks, Nick Faldo, Steve Jones and Tom Lehman. Each of them had no more that four swing keys or thoughts that they used before each shot. For example, Tom Lehman, the winner of the British Open, emphasized "getting a good picture, maintaining tempo, finishing the backswing and starting the downswing from the ground up".

Similarly Annika Sorenstam, winner of the 1996 US Women's Open has three thoughts: "Pick your target and trust your aim, maintain a smooth tempo, and commit 100 per cent to the shot and don't worry too much about the result" (*Golf Digest*, January 1997, pp. 72–81).

Many authors have written about the power of taking responsibility for self-talk and about restructuring cognitions if they are not enhancing. For example, if thoughts are about things in the past or future, or doubts about one's ability, they are referred to as "self-defeating". The good news is that each performer has absolute control over their own thoughts, and can change them whenever control is taken. The research suggests that replacing negative (self-defeating) thoughts with positive thoughts will enhance both confidence and performance.

The process of cognitive restructuring begins with identifying a negative thought, and acknowledging the desire to change it, and then changing it *before* taking any physical action. For example if, standing over a putt, you find yourself questioning if you are lined up properly, step back and start your routine over again (Owens & Bunker, 1992).

Setting Goals and Monitoring Progress

Many athletes and coaches talk about the importance of goal setting as a motivational technique to enhance performance. It has been shown to enhance actual performance, and to also produce positive psychological changes in anxiety, confidence and motivation (Gould, 2001).

Setting effective goals directs an athlete's energy and focus during practice and competition. The key is to have effective, specific goals, that are supported by coaches and teammates, and include mechanisms for follow-up and evaluation.

There are generally thought to be three types of effective goals: *outcome goals* that represent standards of performance that focus on the results of a competition (e.g. beating someone), *performance goals* that focus on improving one's past performance (e.g. improving score on 18 holes of golf), or *process goals* that focus attention on movement procedures that will facilitate improvement (e.g. keeping weight equally balanced for a golf drive; Hardy, Jones & Gould, 1996). In addition, there is extensive research about the effects of coach/teacher set, vs performer set goals, and those that are specific vs general in nature (Boyce & King, 1993; Boyce, Wayda, Bunker, Johnston & Eliot, 2001; Weinberg, 1994).

The effectiveness of goal setting seems to be directly related to systematically using them, and to the involvement of both the coach and the athlete. Gould, Tammen, Murphy and May (1989) and Orlick and Partington (1988), have all emphasized the importance of cooperative commitments to goals, and the use of long-term, short-term and daily practice goals. The importance of working with teachers and coaches is that athletes often set unrealistic goals. Burton, Weinberg, Yukelson and Weigand (1998) found that most college athletes set goals but thought they had mixed results, especially if the goals were too hard vs too easy.

Two categories of theories have been proposed to explain the positive effects of goal setting: the mechanistic theory and the cognitively oriented theories. The mechanistic theory proposed by Locke, Shaw, Saari and Latham (1981) suggests that goals affect performance in four ways: directing attention, mobilizing effort, increasing persistence and adapting new learning strategies. The cognitive-oriented theories ((Burton et al., 1998; Garland, 1985) emphasize the link of goals to anxiety, confidence and motivation. This link can be both positive and negative; for example, if an athlete focuses solely on outcome goals, it may result in unrealistic expectations and increased anxiety, while realistic outcome goals can positively effect outcome expectancy.

Table 14.4 Setting SMARTER goals involves focusing on behavior and not dreams

S	Specific
M	Measurable
A	Attractive and desirable
R	Realistic
T	Time-defined
E	Enthusiastically shared with others
R	Recorded and rewarded in imagery and reality.

Make Dreams "Operational"

Some performers think that having a dream is equivalent to setting goals. For example if my "dream" is to win the club championship or qualify for the US Open, I am not creating goals that direct my behavior. Instead, it is essential that goals be specific and measurable in order to focus attention and direct behavior. In fact the acronym of SMARTER goals is a very effective way to help golfers capitalize on the benefits of goal setting (see Table 14.4).

Effective goals must be operationalized so that an individual knows how to make them become reality. For example, if your goal is to lower your handicap by the end of the season, it is not specific enough to direct your behavior. By specifying that your goal is to lower your handicap by 3 strokes, through using 50 per cent of your practice time on your short game, you make the goal both specific and measurable. This is a very smart strategy since more than 65 per cent of the scoring comes from the short game, yet most golfers spend less than 10 per cent of their practice time on their short game (Owens & Kirschenbaum, 1998). If this is something you really want to do, it is attractive, and if you have a handicap of 22, then lowering it to 19 is probably realistic. On the other hand if your handicap is already 4, it is probably unrealistic to think that you can get it to a 1 through this strategy. By sharing your specific goal with someone else, your playing partner can check on you to be sure you are spending 50 per cent of your practice time on your short game, and can reinforce that effort along the way. The last criteria, "rewarded in imagery and reality" suggests that you should visualize or otherwise imagine what it will feel like and look like when you are more effective at hitting short irons, and enjoying your improved golf scores.

The goals that are set should be determined and "owned" by the golfer. If a coach or pro sets goals for a learner they are probably not as meaningful as if the golfer was helped to set goals personally. The most effective goals are moderately difficult and yet realistic (Kyllo & Landers, 1995) and include both long-term and short-term goals. For example, a long-term goal might be to qualify for the championship flight for the city championship next August, while the short-term goal is a realization that your putting must get much better in order to do that. Hence a short-term goal might be to putt at least 50 putts, 3 times a week, starting with sinking 5 3-foot putts in a row and then backing away in 1 foot intervals, and focusing on a parallel pendulum swing with the putter. Notice that these two goals represent examples of an outcome goal and a process goal.

Goals that are related to competition often need to be accompanied by a commitment to "play through" the change. That is, if you are trying to learn to use your sand wedge, but in the past have used a nine-iron in similar situations, make a commitment before the round to work on the change (e.g. use your sand wedge whenever appropriate), even if it may not create the best results.

Imagery in Golf

Imagery is a much discussed and often misunderstood tool for cognitive control in sport. Many of the world's top golfers, including Tiger Woods, Tom Kite, Nancy Lopez, Jack Nicklaus and others, have attributed some of their success to the use of mental imagery. For example, Jack Nicklaus describes the power of imagery as the single most important element in achieving high levels of performance (Nicklaus & Bowden, 1974). Hundreds of research studies have investigated the relationship between imagery and sport performance (Martin, Moritz & Hall, 1999). In particular, Bandura (1997) theorized that athletes who have confident thoughts translate them into positive images of successful performance, that have a positive influence on performance—a luscious cycle. This interactive role of general-mastery imagery and self-efficacy as influences on performance was also recently supported by Beauchamp, Bray and Albinson (2002).

The fundamental concept of imagery suggests that one should positively review the shot about to be performed, using as many sensory systems as possible: visual, auditory, kinesthetic, tactile and olfactory. The major advantage of imagery is its controllability. The golfer can manipulate aspects of the image, use it to both anticipate problems and their solutions (coping imagery) and to imagine perfect performance (mastery imagery) (Goss, Hall, Buckholz & Fishburne, 1986; Janelle, 1999). The perspective of imagery can also vary, with expert performers being shown to prefer an internal perspective (as if looking out from behind your own eyes), while beginners often imagine from a third person perspective (as if watching yourself on a videotape). One good strategy for practicing is to rotate perspectives from internal to external to ball flight. The literature sometimes uses the term "visualization" as if it were synonymous with "imagery", yet the visual system is only one way in which to image the outcome of a performance, and most successful golfers have reported imaging through the kinesthetic and auditory systems as well.

Most sport psychologists suggest that imagery should be about the outcome of the skill, and that it should be positive in nature. Studies that have investigated the differential effects of positive (successful) vs negative (unsuccessful outcomes) have almost unanimously shown the detrimental effects of negative imagery (Beilcock, Afremow, Rabe & Carr, 2001; Martin & Hall, 1995; Taylor & Shaw, 2002).

In recent years some distinctions have been made about the three functions of imagery: to affect skill learning and performance, to modify cognitions or to regulate arousal and anxiety. Hall et al. (1998) identified five functions of imagery in terms of imagery content (see Table 14.5). There is a great deal of evidence supporting the positive effects of imagery (see the meta analyses by Driskell, Cooper & Moran, 1994; and Feltz & Landers, 1983).

In a recent study by Beauchamp et al. (2002), they found that using imagery during pre-competition had several advantages. In particular, pre-competition general-mastery imagery was highly related to higher levels of self-efficacy and better performance. Their research supports not only the importance of self-efficacy but also the value of using imagery to enhance confidence. Like Hall et al. (1998), their research supports the value of using a

Table 14.5 Five functions of imagery

Function of imagery	Explanation
Cognitive:	
Cognitive specific (CS)	Imagining the process of executing specific sport skills
Cognitive general (CG)	Imaging strategies and tactical aspects of the sport
Motivational:	
Motivation specific (MS)	Imaging specific goals or goal oriented behaviors
Motivation general (MG-A)	Imaging feelings of relaxation, stress, arousal or anxiety
Motivation general (MG-M)	Imaging effectively coping and mastering challenging situation, including being confident and focused.

Source: Hall, C.R., Mack, D., Paivio, A. & Hausenblas, H.A. (1998). Imagery use by athletes: development of the Sport Imagery Questionnaire. *International Journal of Sport Psychology, 29,* 73–89.

variety of types of imagery: cognitive specific imagery (to envisage specific elements of a skill); cognitive general imagery (for rehearsal strategies), motivational specific imagery (for goal attainment), motivational general-arousal imagery (to control anxiety and arousal), motivational general-mastery imagery (to reinforce being in control and focused).

Techniques for Developing Imagery in Golf

One of the principal keys to effective imagery is to remember that "Winners see what they want to happen, while losers see what they fear might happen." Good golfers image in every sensory system, and focus on the positive aspects. In order to practice imagery, invite your golfers to imagine a familiar scene from their home golf course. For example, ask them to imagine the first hole and describe what is seen. What does the grass look like? How does the fresh-cut tee box smell? What are the shapes of the hazards and location of trees and bushes? Where are the safe landing areas? What is the general shape or contour of the fairway? Can you see the differences between the grass in the fairway and the rough? What sounds do you hear?

Many golfers are more kinesthetically or "feel"-oriented than visually oriented. As they think about the next shot, they sense the length of their swing, the tension in their muscles, the release of their hands through contact with the ball, etc. One interesting strategy for facilitating kinesthetic imagery was proposed by Gary McCord and Peter Kostis (1996), two extraordinary golf teachers. They were working with a PGA pro who was having major difficulties trusting his swing. They took him to the course at 10 p.m. and had him play four holes. They emphasized just relaxing and "feeling" the ball down the dark fairway, while listening to it. This strategy of "night golf" is a good one to reduce the dependence that some golfers have on their visual system or cognitively controlling their swings.

Another use of imagery may be in facilitating confidence during the golf swing. For example, many players find an intermediate target about two to four feet in front of the ball, directly on the target line, to be very helpful. This intermediate target is generally identified either in reality (a divot, or distinct blade of grass), or as an imaginary tee or target line. The use of this intermediate target is also essential to the most fundamental aspect of each golf shot, the alignment of the body in relation to the target.

Effectiveness of Utilizing Imagery in Golf

Many studies have investigated the use of imagery in multiple sports. Martin et al. (1999) provided a comprehensive review of literature. Research on imagery has often been categorized in terms of the type of imagery—facilitative (imaging positive outcomes) vs debilitative (imaging negative outcomes or failure) (Short et al., 2002). The positive effects of facilitative imagery have been consistently shown initially in research by Powell (1973), and more specifically related to golf by Woolfolk et al. (1985a, 1985b). Short et al. (2002) have defined facilitative imagery as any imagery designed to have a positive effect on learning, cognitions or the regulation of anxiety or arousal.

There is significant research that indicates that elite athletes use mastery-oriented imagery and that it is predictive of their performance (Hall et al., 1998; Hall, 2001; Martin et al., 1999). Some studies have focused exclusively on golf and have incorporated imagery into pre-shot routines and compared its effectiveness with golfers who do not use such routines. For example, Crews and Boutcher (1986) trained beginning golfers in using visualization for putting as part of their pre-shot routines, and found that those who had already developed a good stroke technique benefited most. Other researchers such as Woolfolk et al. (1985b) and Taylor and Shaw (2002) have demonstrated the effects of positive (vs negative) imagery on both confidence and performance, and found that negative imagery has a more powerful, detrimental effect on golf outcome than the enhancing effects of positive imagery (Owens & Bunker, 1995). Therefore it is probably most important to encourage golfers not to create negative images—even no images were found to be better than negative ones.

The research seems rather clear that negative imagery has a debilitating effect on performance while positive imagery has an enhancing effect on motivation and hence performance. Similarly, the consistent use of suppressive imagery (e.g. trying not to make a mistake) has also been found to inhibit performance (Beilock et al., 2001). Callow and Hardy (2001) have provided a theoretical link to Bandura's (1997) work. They suggested that imaging successful outcomes enhances the golfer's confidence and hence the likelihood of future success.

What is not clear is the relationship between the motor equivalence of the imaged action and the actual movement. The psycho-neuromuscular theory of imagery has suggested that the same generalized motor program (GMP) is activated in both imagery and actual performance (Jowdy & Harris, 1990). However, some recent research has suggested that there is a lack of temporal equivalence between imagined and actual movement. For example, Orliaguet and Coello (1998) found that the overall duration of imagined golf putts was longer than for actual putts. This in itself may not mean that they are governed by different GMPs because overall timing is thought to be a parameter which is allowed to change as long as the relative timing within the movement remains consistent (Schmidt, 1991).

SUMMARY OF PSYCHOLOGICAL SKILLS TRAINING IN GOLF

This chapter has integrated golf-related psychological skills training and practice strategies within each sub-section. There is also a body of research about psychological skills training in general. Vealey (1994), Morris and Thomas (1995) and Williams (2001) have provided excellent overviews of such training programs. Morris and Thomas (1995) have also provided a review of many psychological skills training programs and a model proposed by Thomas (1990), based on earlier work by Vealey (1988) and Boutcher and Rotella (1987).

There are many psychological skills inventories available, though some have not been well researched, and the psychodynamics are not available. The advantages of such profiles are for the "conversation" they may facilitate between a coach or mental trainer and the athlete. One example of this is also a "Golf Performance Survey" (GPS; Thomas & Over, 1994) available for junior golfers.

Many publications on mental training for golf performance have supported the importance of attentional and arousal control, building and maintaining confidence, cognitive restructuring and self-talk control, goal setting and performance monitoring, and imagery. Much of this support comes from self-reports of elite golfers, or by the comparison of elite and less skilled performers.

Research on the effects of specific training programs has been less conclusive, with some equivocal or contradictory results in terms of their effects on golf performance. Cohn (1990) has pointed out that the erratic results may be due to several factors, including the homogeneity of participants (ranging from elite to beginner), and the time frames used to determine the effects of the interventions. When studies use primarily elite performers, there may be measurement issues such a ceiling affects that minimize the ability to detect the impact of training on performance.

There are many issues which merit further investigation. One in particular seems to be the balance between individual differences and preferences, and standardized mental training programs. For example, if an individual has a strong preference for processing and storing information visually vs verbally vs kinesthetically, it would be important to know that and to capitalize on their strengths while perhaps building capacity in their less preferred modes.

Pavio (1971) emphasized a "dual code" theory of information processing and suggested two fundamental ways of storing information: verbally or visually. The verbal system was thought to be essentially linear and facilitating to abstract and sequential relationships, while the imaginal (visual) system facilitates memory of non-verbal, concrete and parallel relationships. It seems intuitive that some athletes may prefer verbalization while others may prefer imagery of either kinesthetic or visual modes. One of the few studies to investigate this was conducted by Thomas and Fogarty (1997) who utilized the Golf Performance Survey, which measured five psychological and motor skills: negative emotions and cognitions, mental preparation, automaticity, putting skill, and seeking improvement. They found that club golfers of wide ability levels were very flexible in the cognitive skills they preferred, and did not demonstrate a processing preference.

When attempting to develop good concentration skills, and to rid yourself of self-defeating thoughts, Owens and Bunker (1992) have suggested three phases: (1) focus thoughts and swing cues, (2) utilize thought stoppage; and (3) capitalize on the effects of a consistent pre-shot routine (see Figure 14.4).

SUMMARY

Golf is an amazingly complex and challenging game that can benefit from the variety of psychological skills that have been outlined in this chapter. Recognizing that "attitude is a

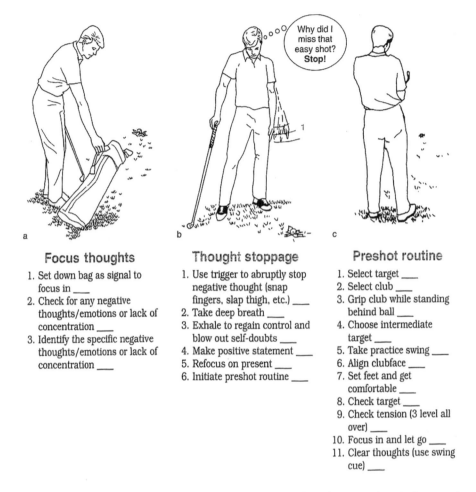

Figure 14.4 An effective strategy for controlling negative thoughts is to identify the negative thoughts, focus in, and use your pre-shot routine to control anxiety
Source: Owens, D.D. & Bunker, L.K. (1995). *Golf: Steps to Success* (p. 119). Champaign, IL: Human Kinetics.

decision" and that each player has complete control over thoughts and anxieties is the first step in becoming a proficient performer. Then practicing the steps outlined in this chapter should enhance the ability to control those thoughts and anxieties in order to optimize golf performance.

APPENDIX

Helpful Internet Sites

[Terminology, History, Rules, Etiquette]   http://www.golfeurope.com
[Rules, Etiquette, Tournaments, Equipment]   http://www.resourcecenter.usga.org/

REFERENCES

A History of Golf. Retrieved 14 June 2004 from http://www.golfeurope.com [Terminology, History, Rules, Etiquette].

Bandura, A. (1997). *Self-Efficacy: The Exercise of Control.* New York: W.H. Freeman.

Beauchamp, M.R., Bray, S.R. & Albinson, J.G. (2002). Pre-competition imagery, self-efficacy and performance in collegiate golfers. *Journal of Sport Sciences, 20,* 697–705.

Beilcock, S.L., Afremow, J.A., Rabe, A.L. & Carr, T. H. (2001). Don't miss: The debilitating effects of suppressive imagery on golf putting performance. *Journal of Sport and Exercise Psychology, 23,* 200–221.

Boutcher, S.H. & Rotella, R.J. (1987). A psychological skills educational program for closed-skill performance enhancement. *The Sport Psychologist, 18,* 30–39.

Boyce, B.A. & King, V. (1993). Goal setting for coaches. *Journal of Physical Education, Recreation, and Dance, 64*(1), 65–68.

Boyce, B.A., Wayda, V., Bunker, L., Johnston, T. & Eliot, J. (2001). The effects of three types of goal setting conditions on tennis performance: A field-based study. *Journal of Teaching in Physical Education, 20,* 188–200.

Burton, D., Weinberg, R., Yukelson, D. & Weigand, D. (1998). The goal effectiveness paradox in sport: examining the goal practices of collegiate athletes. *The Sport Psychologist, 12,* 404–418.

Callow, N. & Hardy, L. (2001). Types of imagery associated with sport confidence in netball players of varying skill levels. *Journal of Applied Sport Psychology, 13,* 1–17.

Callow, N., Hardy, L. & Hall, C. (1998). The effect of a motivational mastery imagery intervention on the sport confidence of three elite badminton players. *Journal of Applied Sport Psychology, 10,* S135.

Cohn, P.J. (1990). Preperformance routines in sport: Theoretical support and practical applications. *The Sport Psychologist, 4,* 301–312.

Cohn, P.J. (1991). An exploratory study on peak performance in golf. *The Sport Psychologist, 5,* 1–14.

Cohn, P.J., Rotella, R.J. & Lloyd, J.W. (1990). Effects of a cognitive-behavioral intervention on the preshot routine and performance in golf. *The Sport Psychologist, 4,* 33–47.

Crews, D.J. & Boutcher, S.H. (1986). The effect of a preshot attentional routine on a well-learned skill. *International Journal of Sport Psychology, 18,* 30–39.

Driskell, J.E., Cooper, C. & Moran, A. (1994). Does mental practice enhance performance? *Journal of Applied Psychology, 79,* 481–491.

Ericsson, K.A. & Charness, N. (1994). Expert performance: its structure and acquisition. *American Psychologist, 49,* 725–747.

Feltz, D.L. & Chase, M.A. (1998). The measurement of self-efficacy and confidence in sport. In J.L. Duda (ed.). *Advances in Sport and Exercise Psychology Measurement* (pp. 65–80). Morgantown, WV: Fitness Information Technology.

Feltz, D.L. & Landers, D.M. (1983). The effects of mental practice on motor skill learning and performance: a meta-analysis. *Journal of Sport Psychology, 5,* 25–57.

Feltz, D.L. & Reissinger, C.A. (1990). Effects of *in vivo* emotive imagery and performance feedback on self-efficacy and muscular endurance. *Journal of Sport and Exercise Psychology, 12,* 132–143.

Frost, M. (2002). *The Greatest Game Ever Played: Harry Varnon, Francis Ouimet, and the Birth of Modern Golf.* New York: Hyperion.

Frost, M. (2004). *Bobby Jones, America and the Story of Golf.* New York: Hyperion.

Garfield, C.A. & Bennett, H.Z. (1994). *Peak Performance: Mental Training Techniques of the World's Greatest Athletes.* Los Angeles: Tarcher.

Garland, H. (1985). A cognitive mediation theory of task goals and human performance. *Motivation and Emotion, 9,* 345–367.

Gauron, E.F. (1984). *Mental Training for Peak Performance.* Lansing, New York: Sport Science Associates.

Goss, S., Hall, C., Buckholz, R. & Fishburne, G. (1986). Imagery ability and the acquisition retention of movements. *Memory and Cognition, 14,* 469–477.

Gould, D. (2001). Goal setting for peak performance. In J.M. Williams (ed.). *Applied Sport Psychology: Personal Growth to Peak Performance* (pp. 190–205). Mountain View, CA: Mayfield Publishing.

Gould, D., Tammen, V., Murphy, S. & May, J. (1989). An examination of US Olympic sport psychology consultants and the services they provide. *The Sport Psychologist, 3*, 300–312.

Hall, C. (2001). Imagery in sport and exercise. In R.N. Singer, H.A. Hausenblas & C.M. Janelle (eds). *Handbook of Sport Psychology* (pp. 529–549). New York: Wiley.

Hall, C.R., Mack, D., Paivio, A. & Hausenblas, H.A. (1998). Imagery use by athletes: Development of the Sport Imagery Questionnaire. *International Journal of Sport Psychology, 29*, 73–89.

Hardy, L., Jones, G. & Gould, D. (1996). *Understanding Psychological Preparation for Sport: Theory and Practice of Elite Performers*. Chichester, UK: Wiley.

Jackson, S.A. (1995). Factors influencing the occurrence of flow states in elite athletes. *Journal of Applied Sport Psychology, 7*, 138–166.

Janelle, C.M. (1999). Ironic mental processes in sport: Implications for sport psychologists. *The Sport Psychologist, 13*, 201–220.

Janelle, C.M., Murray, N.P., De la Pena, D. & Bouchard, L.J. (1999). Overcompensation as a result of faulty mental control processes. Manuscript submitted for publication.

Johnson-O'Conner, E.J. & Kirschenbaum, D.S. (1986). Something succeeds like success–positive self-monitoring for unskilled golfers. *Cognitive Therapy and Research, 10*, 123–136.

Jones, M.V., Mace, R.D., Bray, S.R., McRae, A.W. & Stockbridge, C. (2002). The impact of imagery on the emotional state of novice climbers. *Journal of Sports Behavior, 25*, 57–73.

Jowdy, D.P. & Harris, D.V. (1990). Muscular responses during mental imagery as a function of motor skill level. *Journal of Sport and Exercised Psychology, 12*, 191–201.

Kirschenbaum, D.S. (1997). *Mind matters: Seven Steps to Smarter Sport Performance*. NY: Cooper Publishing Group.

Kirschenbaum, D.S. & Bale, R.M. (1980). Cognitive-behavioral skills in golf: Brain power golf. In R.M. Suinn (ed.), *Psychology in Sports: Methods and Applications* (pp. 334–343). Minneapolis, MN: Burgess.

Kuhn, J.S. & Garner, B.A. (2004). *The Rules of Golf in Plain English*. Chicago: University of Chicago Press.

Kyllo, L.B. & Landers, D.M. (1995). Goal setting in sport and exercise: A research synthesis to resolve the controversy. *Journal of Sport and Exercise Psychology, 17*, 117–137.

Leith, L.M. (1988). Choking in sports. Are we our own worst enemies? *International Journal of Sport Psychology, 19*, 59–64.

Leonard, J. (2004, September). How to make a clutch putt. *Golf Digest*, 113–114.

Locke, E.A., Shaw, K.N., Saari, L.M. & Latham, G.P. (1981). Goal setting and task performance. *Psychological Bulletin, 90*, 125–152.

Loehr, J.E. (1984, March). How to overcome stress and play at our peak all the time. *Tennis*, 66–76.

Martin, K.A. & Hall, C.R. (1995). Using mental imagery to enhance intrinsic motivation. *Journal of Sport and Exercise Psychology, 17*, 54–69.

Martin, K.A., Moritz, S.E. & Hall, C.R. (1999). Imagery use in sport: A literature review and applied model. *The Sport Psychologist, 13*, 245–268.

McCaffrey, N. & Orlick, T. (1989). Mental factors related to excellence among top professional golfers. *International Journal of Sport Psychology, 20*, 256–278.

McCord, G. & Kostis, P. (1996, December) A lesson from the dark side. *Golf Digest*, 40.

Moritz, S.E., Hall, C.R., Martin, K.A. & Vadocz, E.A. (1996). What are confident athletes imaging? An examination of image content. *Sport Psychologist, 10*, 171–179.

Morris, T. & Thomas, P.R. (1995). Approaches to applied sport psychology. In T. Morris and J. Summers (eds). *Sport Psychology: Theory, Applications and Issues* (pp. 215–258). Brisbane, Australia: Wiley.

Nicklaus, J. & Bowden, K. (1974). *Golf My Way*. New York: Simon & Schuster.

Nideffer, R.M. (1976). Test of attentional and interpersonal style. *Journal of Personality and Social Psychology, 34*, 394–404.

Orliaguet, J.-P. & Coello, Y. (1998). Differences between actual and imagined putting movements in golf: A chronometric analysis. *International Journal of Sport Psychology, 29*, 157–169.

Orlick, T. & Partington, J. (1988). Mental links to excellence. *Sport Psychologist, 2*, 105–130.

Owens, D.D. & Bunker, L.K. (1992). *Advanced Golf: Steps to Success*. Champaign, IL: Human Kinetics.

Owens, D.D. & Bunker, L.K. (1995). *Golf: Steps to Success*. Champaign, IL: Human Kinetics.

Owens, D.D. & Kirschenbaum, D. (1998). *Smart Golf: How to Simplify and Score your Mental Game.* San Francisco, CA: Jossey-Bass.

Pates, J., Oliver, R. & Maynard, I. (2001). The effects of hypnosis on flow states and golf-putting performance. *Journal of Applied Sport Psychology, 13*, 341–354.

Pavio, A. (1971). *Imagery and Verbal Processes.* New York: Holt, Rhinehart, & Winston.

Powell, G.E. (1973). Negative and positive mental practice in motor skill acquisition. *Perceptual and Motor Skills, 37*, 312.

Rotella, R.J. and Cullen, R. (1995). *Golf is Not a Game of Perfect.* New York: Simon and Schuster.

Rotella, R.J. and Cullen, R. (2004). *The Golfer's Mind: Play to Play Great.* New York: Simon and Schuster.

Rules of Golf as Approved by the R & A (2004–2007 edn). St Andrews, Scotland: Royal and Ancient Golf Club of St Andrews.

Schmidt, R.A. (1991). *Motor Learning and Performance: From Principles to Practice.* Champaign, IL: Human Kinetics.

Short, S.E., Bruggeman, J.M., Engel, S.G., Marback, T.L., Wang, L.J., Willadsen, A. & Short, M.W. (2002). The effect of imagery function and imagery direction on self-efficacy and performance on a golf-putting task. *The Sport Psychologist, 16*, 48–67.

Swing Keys of the 1996 major champions (1997, January). *Golf Digest*, 71–81.

Taylor, J.A. & Shaw, D.F. (2002). The effects of outcome imagery on golf-putting performance. *Journal of Sports Sciences, 20*, 607–613.

Thomas, P.R. (1990). An overview of the performance enhancement processes in applied sport psychology. Unpublished manuscript, US Olympic Training Center, Colorado Springs, CO.

Thomas, P.R. & Fogarty, G.J. (1997). Psychological skills training in golf: The role of individual differences in cognitive preferences. *The Sport Psychologist, 11*, 86–106.

Thomas, P.R. & Over, R. (1994). Psychological and psychomotor skills associated with performance in golf. *The Sport Psychologist, 8*, 73–86.

USGA Rules of Golf (2004–2007). Colorado Springs, CO: United States Golf Association. Retrieved 13 April 2004 from http://www.resourcecenter.usga.org/ [Rules, Etiquette, Tournaments, Equipment]

Vadocz, E.A., Hall, C.R. & Moritz, S.E. (1997). The relationship between competitive anxiety and imagery use. *Journal of Applied Sport Psychology, 9*, 241–253.

Vealey, R. A. (1988). Future directions in psychological skills training. *The Sport Psychologist, 2*, 318–336.

Vealey, R.A. (1994). Knowledge development and implementation in sporty psychology: A review of *The Sport Psychologist*, 1987–1992. *The Sport Psychologist, 8*, 331–348.

Wegner, D.M. (1994). Ironic processes of mental control. *Psychological Review, 16*, 34–52.

Wegner, D.M., Ansfield, M. & Pilloff, D. (1998). The putt and the pendulum: Ironic effects of the mental control of actions. *Psychological Science, 9*, 196–199.

Wegner, D.M. & Erber, R. (1992). The hyperaccessibility of suppressed thoughts. *Journal of Personality and Social Psychology, 63*, 903–912.

Weinberg, R.S. (1994). Goal setting and performance in sport and exercise settings: A synthesis and critique. *Medicine and Science in Sport and Exercise, 26*, 469–477.

Whaley, S. (2004, September). Find your go-to shots. *Golf Digest*, 209–216.

Williams, J.M. (ed.) (2001). *Applied Sport Psychology: Personal Growth to Peak Performance.* Mountain View, CA: Mayfield Publishing.

Woolfolk, R.L., Murphy, S.M., Gottesfeld, D. & Aiken, D. (1985a). Effects of mental rehearsal of task motor activity and mental depiction of task outcome on motor skill performance. *Journal of Sport Psychology, 7*, 191–197.

Woolfolk, R., Parrish, W. & Murphy, S.M. (1985b). The effects of positive and negative imagery on motor skill performance. *Cognitive Therapy and Research, 9*, 235–241.

Zinsser, N., Bunker, L. & Williams, J.M. (2001). Cognitive techniques for building confidence and enhancing performance. In J.M. Williams (ed.), *Applied Sport Psychology: Personal Growth to Peak Performance* (4th edn; pp. 284–311). Mountain View, CA: Mayfield Publishing Co.

CHAPTER 15

Psychology of Cycling

Jim Taylor

San Francisco, USA

and

Jeff Kress

California State University, Long Beach, USA

INTRODUCTION

Bicycle racing is an endurance sport in which competitors must cope with tremendous physical and psychological demands in training and competition. O'Conner (1992) cites the Tour de France bicycle race as one of the most grueling tests of human athletic endurance. Typical road races for Olympic-level cyclists range between 50 and 250 kilometers and can take from 1 (50 km) to 6 hours or more (250 km) to complete. Weather conditions can vary from hot and humid to wet and rainy to cold and snowy. Cyclists must deal with dehydration, cold, heat, exhaustion and pain while, often, having to assume specified tactical roles within their team (Ryschon, 1994). Attempts at predicting endurance performance in elite athletes solely on the basis of physiological variables have been unsuccessful. Consequently, it has been suggested that psychological factors play an important role in the achievement of outstanding endurance performance (O'Conner, 1992).

This chapter will address the essential role that the mind plays in cycling. It will begin with an overview of cycling in which the demands and complexity of cycling are discussed. You will then learn about the different types of road races in which cyclists compete, providing perspective on the physical, technical, technological, tactical and psychological aspects of cycling. The body of the chapter will explore the impact of four psychological factors on cycling performance: intensity, focus, pain and recovery. We will discuss how these psychological issues influence cyclists, as well as mental training strategies that cyclists can use to develop these areas to maximize their cycling performances.

INTRODUCTION TO CYCLING

Competitive road racing is unique in the realm of sport. Road cycling takes place in an open arena, for example, city streets and country roads, in which, in most cases, nothing

The Sport Psychologist's Handbook: A Guide for Sport-Specific Performance Enhancement.
Edited by Joaquín Dosil. © 2006 John Wiley & Sons, Ltd.

separates the competitors from the spectators. "No other sport dares allow such close contact with the participants. Spectators hear riders breathing as they pass; they smell them; and sometimes—by mistake—they touch" (Roll, 2004, p. 14). Perhaps the most famous example of spectator contact with a cyclist occurred when the five-time Tour de France winner, Eddy Merckx, was racing for a record sixth victory in 1975. While leading the race into the famous climbs of the French Alps, he was punched in the kidney by a spectator. The resulting injury plagued him for the remainder of the race and he eventually finished a distant second.

Racecourse conditions can also vary dramatically. Road racing can take place on surfaces ranging from smooth asphalt streets to brutal cobblestones. In addition, unlike many sports in which their contests are either postponed or canceled due to weather, cycling races are contested through all forms of inclement weather. A memorable stage of the Giro d'Italia (one of the three major road-cycling events along with the Tour de France and the Vuelta a'Espana) occurred in 1988 when the American, Andy Hampsten, persevered through heavy sleet and snow over the 2,621-meter Gavia Pass to take the race lead and eventual victory. Conditions that day were so brutal that many of the support vehicles were unable to drive over the same roads on which the cyclists raced.

The competitive cycling season is also long by most standards of professional sport, lasting more than 9 months. The typical professional road cyclist contests between 90 and 110 races per year. A typical week of training and racing consists of approximately 700 to 1200 kilometers, during which cyclists will log 25 to 30 hours a week of riding time. In addition to training and race time, cyclists also spend many hours traveling to training camps and races all over the world. This level of commitment means considerable time away from home and family.

The races themselves are complex and sometimes chaotic events that place additional demands on cyclists. A typical road race is composed of more than 20 teams of up to 10 riders each, for a total of between 150 and 200 competitors. Each team has differing riding styles, goals and strategies to achieve their goals. In cycling, the best-laid plans can go for naught due to the unpredictable nature of races, including breakaways (when one or more riders try to separate themselves from the peloton or the main pack of riders), crashes, bad weather, poor communication, and equipment malfunctions. The ability of riders to persevere under these conditions and adapt to these capricious and uncontrollable occurrences often determines which cyclists will be successful.

Types of Road Races

Road racing is contested in a variety of formats. It can consist of mass-start single-day events, stage races or solo races against the clock. Each type of road race requires different physical abilities and places unique psychological demands on the riders.

Single-day Races

Single-day races are those that are completed over the course of one day. Perhaps the most traditional form of single-day race is the point-to-point road race, which typically begins at one location and finishes at another. These events often take place between two cities or towns. Examples of well-known professional single-day events include Fleche–Wallonne,

Paris–Roubaix, Ghent–Wevelgem and Het Volk. The courses of single-day races can vary from entirely flat, favoring sprinters, to very mountainous, which benefit climbers.

Circuit racing is another category of single-day racing. These races are contested over courses that begin and end at the same location and consist of multiple laps of which each lap is 25 to 40 kilometers in length. The total distance raced is typically between 200 to 280 kilometers and contests are raced over roads that are flat to moderately hilly. A third type of road racing is the *criterium*, which is similar to circuit racing, but the courses are flatter and shorter, usually 1 to 3 kilometers per lap with races being 70 to 80 kilometers in length. These races tend to be very fast, with the average speed of a criterium being around 42 kilometers per hour while a road race is closer to 34 kilometers per hour.

The psychological demands of these races require that cyclists have a single-minded focus on the coming day. They can learn the specifics of the course (e.g. terrain and road conditions) and develop tactics appropriate for the race. Cyclists must have an intense and focused effort for a relatively short time. They can also give 100 per cent effort in the race because they don't need to conserve their energy for another day of racing.

Time Trials

Time trials have been affectionately called "the race of truth" by cycling aficionados. This event is either contested as a point-to-point race, around a circuit, or out and back on the same road. This style of road racing is unique in that the riders are required to race alone start to finish (they start at 30 second to 2-minute intervals depending upon the race) and must rely on their own fitness and psychological strength, without the aid of teammates or drafting, to reach the finish in the fastest time possible. Cyclists use specialized equipment, including bicycles, helmets and clothing that are designed to maximize aerodynamics and reduce wind drag. Time trials can range in length from a few kilometers to 60 kilometers or more. A sub-discipline of the time trial is the team time trial in which teams compete against each other using the same format. This event typically has 4 to 9 teammates working together to maximize efficiency and speed in an attempt to record a time that is faster than the other teams in the race.

Time trials, perhaps more than any of the other disciplines of bicycle racing, require the utmost amount of focus from cyclists. Because cyclists are racing solo against the clock, there are no team tactics, no one to pace them, they are entirely self-reliant in their own efforts. Cyclists can monitor their efforts in several ways, such as heart rate, speed, cadence and feelings of physical exertion. With an emphasis on all-out speed, cyclists must be acutely aware of the course (e.g. turns, climbs) and road conditions (e.g. wet, rough), and use this information to navigate the course in the fastest and most direct fashion. Because of the focus on absolute speed, time trials are dangerous and extremely physically demanding. They require that cyclists find the line that lies between the fastest route through the course and disaster. Cyclists must maintain focus every moment, calculating how fast they can go around curves and on descents.

They must also effectively apportion their energy throughout the race. Because time trials are usually relatively short in distance (e.g. 8 to 60 kilometers) and the focus is on speed, cyclists must maintain a high level of intensity and sustain a consistent amount of effort throughout the race. If they go out too fast, they may bonk (also known as "hitting the wall") later in the race. If they don't go out fast enough, their early splits will be slow and they won't be able to make up the time late in the race. The winners of time trials are often the cyclists who are able to distribute their energy evenly throughout the race and have nothing left when they cross the finish line.

One method we have found to be successful in getting cyclists to maintain their focus, intensity and effort throughout the duration of the time trial is to have them go through regimented checks of their physical exertion, pace and the course that lies ahead. One prominent cyclist likened the process to having his brain as the central processing unit (CPU) of a computer and it constantly makes checks of the system. Without the required focus, intensity and effort, a time trial can quickly turn into just a long solo ride with no promise of a good placing.

Stage Races

Stage races are multiple-day events that consist of a series of point-to-point, circuit, time-trial and criterium races. Riders must start and finish each stage to continue to race in subsequent stages. The overall winner of a stage race is the rider with the lowest cumulative time of all of the stages. The most famous stage race is the Tour de France, which consists of 20 stages and approximately 3,250 kilometers in distance.

A variety of competitions are held within the stage race itself for which riders compete. Each day's race is contested as a single event and gaining a stage win is a source of great prestige and individual, team and national pride. Awards are also given for the categories of racing that occur within stage races; for example, best climber, best sprinter, best young rider and most consistent rider. The leaders of each of these categories are awarded specially colored race jerseys, which are worn as symbols of status and honor. Points are awarded to the riders in each of these categories and the rider with the most points at the end of the stage race is named the best rider in that category. The most prestigious jersey in road cycling is the Tour de France's Maillot Jaune (Yellow Jersey), awarded to the overall winner of the 20-day stage race. Notes the former professional cyclist, Bob Roll, "Wear yellow even one day and you'll never buy your own drinks in France for the rest of your life" (Roll, 2004, p. 21).

Stage races combine the previously mentioned psychological issues with the need to establish a long-range individual and team tactical plan and awareness of the ongoing physical demands that a stage race places on cyclists. Unlike the single-day events, stage races are not won or lost in a single effort. Cyclists' ability to adhere to their race plan, even when faced with unexpected challenges, allows them to be successful. Patience and the ability to effectively distribute their energy for the duration of the race are also essential qualities of great stage cyclists. Because stage races include the other types of cycling events, they require all of the psychological tools necessary in cycling, which will be described further in this chapter.

PSYCHOLOGY OF CYCLING

Based on the description of road cycling that we just offered, the physical demands and psychological challenges that riders face may be unique in sports. The physical factors of strength, endurance and skill, coupled with the unforgiving weather and course conditions, and cycling being a team as well as an individual sport, present cyclists with rare challenges that test every part of their psychological repertoire. Not only must riders have command over their motivation, confidence, intensity, focus, emotions and pain (Taylor, 2001), but they must maintain their mastery under the most dire physical and environmental conditions with the risk of serious injury or death for extended periods of time.

Though all athletes in every sport must deal with varying degrees of all of the psychological factors described by Taylor (2001), cycling presents particular challenges in a few specific areas. The remainder of this chapter will focus on four psychological areas—intensity, pain, fear, and recovery—which we believe are especially relevant to road cycling. It is worth noting is that these four factors are not exclusively psychological in nature (unlike motivation, confidence and focus). Each is grounded in physical experience, yet the influence of intensity, pain, fear and recovery on cyclists is determined by how they identify, interpret and respond to the physical reactions of the four factors. This process of psychological filtering ultimately determines the impact they have on cyclists' performances.

Intensity

Cycling success involves preserving and apportioning out energy as it is needed during a race. Road racing has ebbs and flows of energy needs that are perhaps like no other sport in the world. During the course of a typical professional road race, which can last five to six hours, there will be extended periods of time during which there is no "racing" taking place—riders are maintaining a comfortable pace in the peloton and saving their energy for difficult parts of the course—and the intensity of the cyclists is low. The riders are simply covering distance on the road prior to a crucial part of the race, which could include a section of cobblestones, a long climb, a breakaway or a sprint finish. Several minutes prior to a key part of the race the tempo will typically pick up as the cyclists position themselves for the upcoming test. The intensity of the riders will rise in preparation for the imminent effort. Their intensity level will be further elevated once they are actively racing and competing with others. If cyclists expend too much energy because of elevated intensity during the slower parts of the race, they will not have enough energy to compete effectively when it matters.

Intensity is a continuum that ranges from sleep (very relaxed) to terror (very anxious) (Sonstroem, 1984; Taylor & Wilson, 2002). Somewhere in between these two extremes is the level of intensity at which cyclists perform their best. One of the confusing aspects of intensity is that there isn't one ideal level of intensity for all riders or all race distances (Landers & Boutcher, 1993; Weinberg & Gould, 2003; Zaichkowsky & Takenaka, 2001). Some cyclists ride best very relaxed, others moderately intense and still others very intense. Shorter distance races, as a rule, require more intensity because more energy and explosiveness is needed. Longer races call for lower intensity because intensity is energy that needs to be conserved for strategic points in a race. Cyclists need to learn what level of intensity they ride best at in the different types of races in which they compete (Raglin & Hanin, 1999).

Awareness of Intensity

One of the first methods for educating cyclists about their intensity is to have them develop an awareness of their intensity while on a bike (Weinberg & Gould, 2003). They must be able to recognize the physical and psychological signs of intensity (Schmidt & Wrisberg, 2000). In a sport in which the environment, race conditions and race strategy are continuously changing, cyclists must have an acute sense of self-awareness to be successful. Riders can use several strategies to increase their awareness of their intensity.

Cyclists can reflect back to recent races in which they rode very well and recall their level of intensity (Hanin, 1999). Were they relaxed, energized or really fired up? Then cyclists can remember the thoughts, emotions and physical feelings they experienced during these races. Were they positive or negative, happy or angry, relaxed or tense? Second, cyclists can reflect back to recent races in which they performed below expectations. They can recall their level of intensity and remember the thoughts, emotions and physical feelings they had in those races. A distinct pattern differentiating between good and poor races emerges for most cyclists. When they performed well, they had a particular level of intensity each time. In contrast, when they rode poorly, there was a very different level of intensity, either higher or lower than their ideal. "Young riders who typically pedal too hard too early, who can't modulate their aggressive instincts, aren't a good bet to compete" (Roll, 2004, p. 101).

Cyclists can also gain insight into how their intensity affects their riding by focusing on their intensity during training rides and races. While riding they can turn their focus inward and pay attention to their physiology (e.g. breathing, heart rate, muscles), body position on the bike, pedal stroke, thoughts and emotions. They can then cross-reference this data with how they are performing at the moment and in the race as a whole.

Pre-race Intensity

Having cyclists become aware of their ideal intensity is a crucial component of cycling success. Some cyclists perform best when they are relaxed before a race. Too much pre-race intensity can hurt performance. Negative effects may include the race feeling faster than they are accustomed to, their thinking may not be clear, and fatigue may set in more quickly because of the unnecessary expenditure of energy before the race (Landers & Boutcher, 1993, Weinberg & Gould, 2003, Zaichkowsky & Takenaka, 2001).

Conversely, some cyclists perform best when they experience higher intensity immediately prior to a race. Their adrenaline is flowing and they feel what they might describe as excitement, jitters or "the edge". Attempting to drastically reduce their pre-race intensity would likely result in a loss of energy, feelings of lethargy and a decline in motivation. The key for these cyclists is to find the balance between keeping their intensity high enough to make them feel comfortable and confident and not allowing their intensity to rise so high that it is uncomfortable and drains energy and wastes fuel that will be needed in the race.

Cyclists can use a variety of common "psych-down" techniques to reduce their intensity when needed before their race. Deep breathing is one of the most powerful, yet neglected, tools for lowering intensity (Taylor & Wilson, 2002). Anxiety can cause a constricted respiratory system, reflected in short and shallow breaths that can limit needed oxygen into their bodies. As cyclists go through their pre-race preparation, they should be keenly aware of their breathing and consciously take slow, deep breaths on a regular basis (Feltz, 1975; Fried, 1987a, 1987b; Weinberg & Gould, 2003; Williams & Harris, 2001). Another valuable, though little used, technique to reduce intensity is to keep cyclists moving prior to the race (Taylor, 2001). If they sit or stand for too long, not only will their muscles tighten, but their anxiety will also rise. Cyclists should warm up on a stationary trainer, walk around, stretch or get a pre-race massage. Another underappreciated tool for staying relaxed is to talk to people, whether it is family, friends, teammates or other competitors. Talking to others takes the focus away from the race and provides support and encouragement that will increase comfort. Other strategies for reducing intensity include progressive relaxation, maintaining a process focus (Jacobson, 1929; Martens, 1987), using positive self-talk, repeating relaxing keywords, using calming imagery and listening to soothing music (Taylor & Wilson, 2002).

Pre-race intensity that is too low, caused by cyclists perceiving that the competition is inferior, a lack of enthusiasm for a particular racecourse, or physical or mental burnout will also hurt race performance (Williams & Harris, 2001). Using "psych-up" techniques can help riders elevate their intensity to a level that will bolster their race efforts. Just as deep breathing can reduce intensity, intense breathing can increase it. If cyclists find their intensity too low pre-race, several hard exhalations can take their bodies and minds to a more intense level. Intense breathing gets more oxygen into their system, increases blood flow and adrenaline, and generally energizes riders. Mentally, intense breathing also creates a more focused attitude and increases feelings of aggressiveness. Increased physical activity—for example, a higher-cadence ride on the stationary trainer—can also elevate heart rate and respiration, and trigger adrenaline (Taylor & Wilson, 2002). Additional techniques for increasing pre-race intensity include high-intensity keywords and self-talk (Raiport, 1988; Zaichkowsky & Takenaka, 2001), motivating music (Rider & Achterberg, 1989; Williams & Harris, 2001), motivating music, and mental imagery that rehearse the race goal (Zaichkowsky & Takenaka, 2001).

Race Intensity

Though cyclists may be at their ideal intensity prior to and in the early stages of a race, intensity can change quickly once the race begins. Intensity can go up in response to frustration and anger of getting cut off or missing a breakaway. It can also rise due to greater effort during a long ascent. This increased intensity, if sustained, will create discomfort and burn unnecessary energy. Cyclists' ability to reduce their intensity when it arises involuntarily or in response to exertion will determine to a large degree whether they have the power and stamina to continue to ride well through the end of the race. Some of the psych-down techniques that cyclists use in their pre-race can also be used during races. Deep breathing, brief progressive relaxation, calming keywords and self-talk, and regaining a process focus can help riders settle down physically and psychologically.

Intensity can decline in reaction to feelings of despair from a flat tire or mechanical failure. It can also drop during periods of races, as we mentioned earlier, where the peloton is not really racing. Intensity that is too low can cause cyclists to be dropped from the peloton, miss a breakaway or lack the energy for a concerted sprint at the end of a race. Pre-race psych-up techniques can also help riders during a race; for example, intense breathing and high-intensity keywords and self-talk.

Pain

Persistent and intense pain is a hallmark of bicycle racing. Pain is an essential part of cycling training and competition and, at the same time, the greatest obstacle cyclists face as they pursue their goals. Cyclist exact a profound physical and psychological toll when they race for hours at a time at the upper end of their lactate thresholds; for example, prolonged effort while ascending long climbs or repeated attempts at breaking away from the main peloton. Asserts three-time Tour de France winner Greg LeMond, "the best climbers are those who can stand the most pain ... in pro cycling everything hurts, but they just ride through it" (Avins, 1986, p. 44). The nature of the sport is such that those athletes who can cope the best with the pain will be more successful.

Pain plays an important role in providing cyclists with information about their cycling, including their level of effort and the intensity of their training program. But pain is also a persistent and powerful physical warning to their body. Cycling pain can be the product of several factors: an elevated heart rate which has exceeded a comfortable level; a build-up of lactate, an end product of glycolysis; a depletion of muscle glycogen from the body's stores; fatigue of the respiratory muscles; and dehydration (Brooks, Fahey & White, 1996). Athletes who have developed effective coping strategies for tolerating higher levels of pain are expected to perform better than those who have not (Egan, 1987; O'Conner, 1992; Scott & Gijsbers, 1981). Bill Koch, the silver medalist in cross-country skiing at the 1976 Olympics, believed that 90 per cent of his success was attributable to his ability to tolerate pain (Iso-Ahola & Hatfield, 1986). Interviews with elite-level cyclists (Kress, 1998) have revealed common methods used for the management of pain while training and racing.

The ability to manage pain nonpharmacologically has improved dramatically (Brena & Chapman, 1983). Developing psychological strategies to deal with pain has become an area of interest since Melzack and Wall (1965) developed the gate-control theory of pain. This model encouraged psychologists to broaden their evaluations to include the assessment of cognitive, affective, psychosocial and behavioral contributors to the perception of pain. One aspect of treatment involves the use of psychological methods to control pain (Gauron & Bowers, 1986). Cognitive-behavioral strategies that alter how people evaluate their pain have been used to reduce pain and help individuals cope with chronic discomfort (Turk, Meichaenbaum & Genest, 1984). Cognitive-behavioral techniques have been shown to be effective in reducing pain; for example, surgical pain (Langer, Janis & Wolf, 1975), and chronic pain in children.

To date, research examining pain among athletes has been limited. Pain-tolerance research has focused on comparing athletes and nonathletes performing a variety of pain-inducing activities (Ryan & Kovacic, 1966; Scott & Gijsbers, 1981). The conclusions of this research were that contact athletes had a higher tolerance for pain than did noncontact athletes and highly trained athletes had a much higher tolerance than did nonathletes. A variety of researchers have examined the use of pain-management strategies among marathon runners and found that they used both associative (focus on the pain) and dissociative (distract from the pain) techniques to manage their pain while competing (Morgan, 1978, 1980; Morgan, O'Conner, Sparling & Pate, 1987; Morgan & Pollock, 1977; Schomer, 1986, 1987; Silva & Appelbaum, 1989). Others have conducted research based on associative and dissociative styles of attention distraction using other activities and have reported similar findings to those just mentioned (O'Conner, 1992; Russell & Weeks, 1994; Weinberg, Jackson & Gould, 1984).

Perspective on Pain

Using pain to cyclists' advantage starts with gaining a realistic perspective on what pain really is (Taylor, 2002). They need to understand the difference between suffering, pain and physical discomfort. Cyclists have a strong tendency to use the term "suffering" when they describe the intense physical feelings they experience when training and racing. What cyclists experience in their training and races is not suffering. People with cancer suffer because their pain is severe, long-lasting, life-threatening and often uncontrollable. What cyclists feel in training and races is not really even pain. Real pain comes from injuries. This pain is similar to suffering, but injury pain—though sometimes severe—is not life-threatening, typically does not last that long and can be controlled much more easily.

What cyclists really feel in training and races and what they call "suffering" or "pain" is discomfort. It hurts and it interferes with their training and competitive efforts, but it is not severe and they have control over it; they can ease the discomfort by slowing down or stopping. For simplicity's sake, though, we will continue to call what cyclists experience "pain", knowing what it really is and that perspective is the first step to mastering pain.

Interpreting Pain

The next step to overcoming cycling pain is to understand that pain is not just a physical experience that cyclists have to tolerate in their training and races (Taylor, 2002). Pain also has a major psychological component to it; how they think about it and the emotions they connect to it affect the pain they feel. How riders interpret their pain either propels them to new and higher levels of performance or it hurts their motivation, reduces their confidence, increases their anxiety and distracts them from their training or competitive focus. If cyclists can interpret their pain in a positive way, their pain will feel less painful (Kress, 1998).

Endurance athletes, such as cyclists, can actually enjoy the pain they experience in training and races. Cyclists can interpret the pain they feel from extreme exertion as rewarding because it affirms their significant efforts. It communicates to them that they are working hard and that their efforts will produce satisfying results. Successful cyclists enjoy the pain because it tells them that they are progressing toward their goals.

The situations in which cyclists find themselves affect their interpretation of pain. If all physical variables, such as heart rate and level of fitness, are kept constant, those competitors who are having a "good day" feel the pain a lot less than those who are having a "bad day". A former Olympian said,

> I don't think the pain actually changes; your perception of it increases and decreases
> ... Suffering really isn't suffering when you are at the top of your form. When you are
> really going for the win and performing the way you ought to and want to, very few
> people would call that suffering even though the pain may be equal. (Kress, 1998).

Cyclists must understand that they have a choice in how they interpret their pain. If they understand that how they interpret their pain affects the pain they feel, then they will come to believe that they have some control over how much pain they experience.

Pain as Enemy

Pain becomes cyclists' enemy when they start to connect negative perceptions such as, "Pain is bad", "Pain means I am weak", and "Pain means I will fail" with the pain they feel. This attitude toward pain puts them in a defeatist mindset in which the first experience of pain in training or competition will set off a vicious cycle of negative thinking and negative emotions. If, for example, while doing hill repeats on their bike during a training session, they start thinking, "I hate this because it hurts so much. Is this really worth it?" this negative self-talk will increase the pain they feel, lessen their desire to fight through the pain and limit the benefits they gain from training (Taylor, 2002).

Some fascinating research has emerged recently that has found that the emotions that athletes connect with their pain have a significant impact on how much pain they feel (Gil, Williams, Keefe & Beckham, 1990; Sullivan et al., 2001; Weisenberg, 1987). All cyclists have had the experience late in a race where they are hurting. They begin to get frustrated that they won't achieve their race goal. They get angry at themselves for not training harder. They may even despair of their ability to finish. When they connect these negative emotions with their pain in training or a race, they will feel more pain. Between the pain they feel, their negative self-talk and the negative emotions, they have little chance of giving their best effort in training or being successful in races (Taylor, 2002).

Pain as Ally

Making pain cyclists' ally is a deliberate process that takes commitment, effort and practice. It starts with accepting that pain is a normal and important part of training and competition (Kress, 1998)—"no pain, no gain", as the saying goes. Staying emotionally detached from training and race pain can also reduce the pain they feel. This can be accomplished by using pain as information during their workouts and races. Pain tells them how hard they are working and whether what they are feeling is due to exertion or injury. With this information, they can adjust their pace, modify their technique, change their body position or shift their tactics. Making these changes will help them reduce the pain and also maximize their performance (Taylor, 2002).

Cyclists can take active physical steps to reduce their pain. When their body begins to struggle, it tries to protect itself from the pain by tightening up. Their bodies do not realize that this only makes it worse, so they need to tell them to relax. Simple techniques during training and races, such as deep breathing, raising and lowering their shoulders every few miles, swinging their arms, shaking out their hands and keeping their face relaxed can make a huge difference in how their body responds to pain. A simple place to start is with the cyclists' grip on their handlebars. Distressed cyclists tend to hold onto the handlebars very tightly with an almost "deathlike" grip. If cyclists release their index or "trigger" finger from the bars, their hands relax and this serves as a starting point for relaxation for the rest of the body.

The experience of pain can be lessened by what cyclists say to themselves (Kress, 1998). Positive self-talk, such "I'm getting stronger with every kilometer I complete", "This is making me tougher" and "This pain is normal and everyone's feeling it" not only reduces their perception of pain, but it has other psychological benefits including increased motivation, greater confidence, better focus and more positive emotions.

As much as negative emotions increase the perception of pain, positive emotions have the opposite effect. Connecting positive emotions, such as excitement, joy and fulfillment, with the pain they feel in training and races reduces the pain and makes it more tolerable. Positive emotions create more positive self-talk and have other psychological advantages, such as greater motivation and confidence. Physiologically, positive emotions release endorphins (neurochemicals that act as our internal painkillers) which not only reduce the perception of pain, but actually lessen the physical pain.

Inspiration may be the most useful positive emotion cyclists can experience when training and racing. They can view pain as part of an epic challenge to achieve their goals. Pain tells them that they are working hard and making progress toward their cycling aspirations. To that end, a two-pronged strategy that combines generating positive self-talk and positive emotions is effective. Smiling also creates positive emotions and releases the pain-killing endorphins. The self-talk tells riders that they are building their fitness that they will be able to rely on in races. Finally, perhaps the greatest lesson cyclists can learn is: the physical pain they feel in training and races in no way compares to the emotional pain they will feel if they do not achieve their goals because they did not master the pain (Taylor, 2002).

Fear

Bicycle racing is one of the most beautiful sports in the world. With all of the different uniforms in a race, a bike race is a colorful tapestry of movement. It takes place over some of the most beautiful scenery in the world, including the Swiss, French and Italian Alps, and through some of the world's most beautiful cities, including Paris, Madrid and San Francisco. It is a graceful sport where a line of 200 cyclists spin their legs almost in unison and flow through the streets as one.

However, along with the beauty comes the beast, which is the speed and dangers that every cyclist is faced with. The close proximity of the riders to each other—physical contact is frequent—allows little margin for error, and crashes and pile-ups are common. Because the only protection riders wear is a helmet (and head protection is not even mandated at the professional level), injuries, ranging from "road rash" to broken bones, are everyday occurrences. For example, a crash during the first stage of the 2003 Tour de France occurred near the finish, in which 2 riders, racing in excess of 55 kilometers per hour, fell, setting off a chain reaction of the almost 200 riders in close pursuit. A mass pileup of riders was the result and race favorites Tyler Hamilton, Jimmy Casper, Fabio Baldato, Marc Lotz, Levi Leipheimer and five-time Tour de France winner Lance Armstrong became just a few of the victims of the crash. While Casper, Baldato, Lotz, Armstrong and several others sustained only minor abrasions, Hamilton sustained a fractured collarbone and Leipheimer a broken coccyx.

Crashes are not always the result of riders contacting each other, but are due to road conditions such as rain, potholes, gravel, or oil on the road. One of the most publicized crashes due to road conditions in recent years also occurred during the 2003 Tour de France. The Spaniard, Joseba Beloki, was in second place during the ninth stage of the race and threatening to take the leader's jersey from Armstrong. Both were descending a narrow, fast and twisting road on a hot day. The intense heat was melting the tar in the road and, as Beloki rounded a corner just ahead of Armstrong, his rear wheel slipped on the soft tar and he flipped violently to the ground. The result of his crash was a broken right femur, wrist, collarbone and elbow, and severe skin abrasions.

In addition to the frequent opportunities for injury, the physical harm is minor compared to the deaths of cyclists that can occur at any time. In recent years, the professional cyclists, Andrei Kivilev and Fabio Casartelli, have lost their lives in crashes. Crashes, whether minor or horrific, are a part of bicycle racing and, as any professional will express, they are simply a part of life in the sport.

Fear of Physical Harm or Death

Cyclists train predominantly on public roads that can be of uncertain quality and filled with automobile traffic. Every time cyclists take to the road for a training ride or race, they put themselves in harm's way. Every cyclist knows or has heard about someone who either crashed or was hit by a car and sustained a serious injury or who died from a cycling accident. What makes this fear so difficult is that cyclists do not always have control over the danger and it often arises unexpectedly; for example, a pothole in the road or a car backing out of a driveway. Additionally, cars and trucks are not always accommodating to bicycles and some drivers are downright hostile.

Despite these dangers, there has been considerable resistance among the professional cycling communities to wearing helmets. In 1991, the Union Cycliste Internationale (UCI), the sport's governing body, attempted to enforce mandatory helmet-use in sanctioned races. The professional riders threatened a strike, after which the UCI backed down. Contributing to the resistance to wearing helmets is a culture of machismo that is entrenched in the European cycling community. It is not uncommon on European roads to see amateur racers and recreational cyclists not wearing helmets.

This fear has taken on greater prominence since the mid-1990s in the world of professional cycling. Italian Tour de France rider, Fabio Casartelli, died from injuries sustained from a crash during a stage of the 1995 Tour de France. In 2003, the Kazakh rider, Andrei Kivilev, crashed during the Paris–Nice stage race while not wearing a helmet and died the next day from a brain hemorrhage. That incident prompted the UCI to make helmets mandatory in all races. Under the new rules, riders are allowed to use their own discretion in the final 5 kilometers of races with summit finishes in Europe, but must otherwise wear helmets or risk being fined. The rules vary slightly between countries but, more often than not, a helmet must be worn at all times during a bike race. Perhaps the most stringent rules are in the United States. For insurance purposes, the United States Cycling Federation has imposed the even more far-reaching rule of requiring all cyclists who are on a bicycle, whether racing or warming-up, to wear a helmet. Some states in the USA make helmets compulsory for any cyclist (whether a racer or not) under the age of 18.

Fear of Overuse Injury

Cycling places significant demands on riders' bodies and these demands increase as the race distances get longer, and frequency, duration and intensity of training builds. It is rare for cyclists not to sustain an injury due to overuse, improper technique or inadequate recovery. The occurrence of injuries, particularly when they are serious—for example, meniscal damage; or recurrent, such as a nagging hamstring pull from hill repeats—can cause riders to fear continuing their training efforts and discourage them from giving their best effort. These fears can also reduce cyclists' motivation to train and limit the intensity they put into their training.

Fear of Failure

In addition to fears of bodily injury, psychological fears can also interfere with cyclists enjoying their sport and achieving their goals. Most common among these fears is the fear of failure that can arise when riders become overly invested in their cycling efforts. Fear of failure is commonly thought of as a belief that failure will result in some type of bad consequence; for example, disappointing others, losing respect, feeling shame and embarrassment and devaluing oneself (Martin & Marsh, 2003). What makes fear of failure so palatable is that people connect their results with whether they will be loved and valued by themselves or others (Conroy, Poczwardowski & Henschen, 2001). Most people are motivated to succeed and to gain affirmation from themselves and praise from others, but those who fear failure are most often driven to avoid failure and the criticism and negative impressions that often come with it. Their self-esteem is based on their ability to avoid failure and gain self-love by achieving success. Fear of failure is a potent and unhealthy influence on people and has been associated with many psychological difficulties including low self-esteem, decreased motivation, physical complaints, eating disorders, drug abuse, anxiety and depression (Conroy, 2001).

Because of the level of commitment that is required for success in cycling, cyclists are particularly vulnerable to fear of failure. The considerable time and energy that cyclists invest in their efforts, and the physical and psychological demands that take their toll, can cause riders to feel the need to justify their investment with success and lead them to believe that failure would render their efforts meaningless. Putting so much on the line whenever they train and race can cause cyclists to put pressure on themselves to succeed and to fear failure if they do not perform up to their expectations.

Psychological Impact of Fear

Fear can be a powerful psychological obstacle to achieving cyclists' goals. Regardless of the source of the fear, it can create a cascade of deficits in psychological areas that are essential for cycling success. Fear reduces riders' motivation to train and race because doing so is unpleasant. Fear also hurts confidence because, inherent in any fear, is the belief that some form of harm—whether physical or mental—will come from their efforts. This loss of motivation and confidence will cause cyclists to become cautious and tentative, and prevent them from fully committing themselves to their efforts. Fear also cripples their ability to focus. Because the emotional and physical experience of fear is so strong, it is very difficult for cyclists to focus on things that will help their performance. Fear also prevents cyclists from gaining enjoyment from their participation.

Physical Impact of Fear

Fear expresses itself most profoundly in the physical symptoms they feel, including anxiety, muscle tension, shallow breathing and loss of coordination. These physical sensations individually and collectively cause cyclists to feel tremendous discomfort. Cyclists often use the term "pedaling in squares" to describe their feelings when they are not physically feeling comfortable on their bike. Fear also creates substantial obstacles to achieving their goals. The physical experience of fear burns unnecessary energy, interferes with effective movement and reduces cardiovascular efficiency, all of which keep cyclists from performing their best.

Mastering Fear

Fear is an essential human emotion that protects people when their physical well-being is threatened (Cannon, 1932). Unfortunately, fear can also arise in situations where it is neither required nor helpful. People often think of courage as the absence of fear; true courage is being able to perform in the face of fear. Cyclists' goal, when they experience fear, is not to banish it thoroughly, but rather to master the fear and not let it interfere with the pursuit of their goals.

Fears come in all shapes and sizes. Some fears are rational—in other words, there is something that is worthy of fear; for example, fear of crashing during a high-speed descent on their bike. Other fears are entirely irrational, such as worry that a bicycle frame or wheel will buckle on a rough road (it can happen, but it is exceedingly unlikely). Some fears have to do with physical injury or death; for example, being hit by a car. Other fears have to do with race performance, such as starting too fast and bonking or having to drop out. Still other fears are related to psychological injury; for example, failing to achieve a race goal will make them a failure in their own view or in the view of others.

However realistic or unlikely their fears are, they are as real as cyclists believe them to be and these fears will keep them from performing their best. Fears also won't just go away. Instead, they tend to continue because they become so persistent that they become ingrained into cyclists' thinking and emotions every time they are faced with the fear-provoking situation. To stop the fears, cyclists must address them, deal with them and put the fears behind them. Only free of fears will cyclists be able to push themselves to their limits and race their strongest and fastest.

The first step for cyclists to master their fear is to *understand what their fear is*. Is the cause of their fear obvious, such as riding on a road with a narrow shoulder with considerable traffic? Or is the source of their fear less clear; for example, feeling fear before the start of the race that they attribute to a tough course, but is actually caused by worry about failing to achieve their goals? Cyclists need to identify the precise cause of the fear so that they can take proactive steps to overcome it.

As part of understanding their fear, cyclists should become familiar with what it is they are afraid of. In what situation does it arise? What thoughts are associated with the fear? How does the fear make their body feel? What helps them lessen their fear? Having a clear understanding of their fear enables riders to directly address its cause and, as a result, relieve it as quickly as possible.

The next step is for cyclists to *gain perspective on their fear*. If cyclists are experiencing fear in some cycling situation, the chances are they are not alone. The fears we just discussed are likely to be felt by many cyclists around them. This should tell them that the fear they are feeling is normal. We have found widespread agreement on the fears we describe in this section. Experiencing the fear does not make cyclists stupid, weird or weak. It just makes them human. Recognizing that their fear is normal will help riders keep it in perspective and prevent them from having the fear consume them. Part of gaining perspective on fear involves cyclists seeing that the fear does not have to cripple them and that they have the power to master it. Talking to others about their fear can help them normalize their fear and give them insights into how others deal with it.

Then they need to *master their fear*. Rational fears are best resolved by finding a solution to the cause of the fear. By gaining relevant information, experience and skills, cyclists can alleviate the source of the fear. Or by changing the situation that causes the fear, they can remove the source of the fear and prevent the fear from arising. For example, a fear of a mass sprint finish is common among cyclists because of the close quarters and frantic pace. This fear can be relieved in several ways. Cyclists can avoid the jostling that causes their fear by being at the front of the peloton and beginning their sprint first. They can also stay on the outside of the peloton, though they will still have to deal with the barriers that may be present that separate the road from the spectators. Finally, riders can choose not to participate in the sprint and finish back in the pack. They can also practice pack sprint finishes by simulating them during training rides with a group of cyclists and working on staying relaxed and focused, and maintaining their sprinting form. They can also reframe the fear as anticipated excitement about the finish of the race.

High-speed descending presents another type of fear some cyclists will encounter and it can be relieved in several ways as well. Cyclists can go down a mountain pass at speeds of up to 100 kilometers per hour on tires that are no more than 23 millimeters in width. Loose gravel, oily roads, tight turns, other cyclists and vehicular traffic are a few of the obstacles that must be safely negotiated at such high speeds. Cyclists can take bike-handling classes that will improve their cycling skills and give them more confidence in descending. They can also gain more experience and comfort by doing a great deal of descending on their training rides. An alternative way to relieve their fear is to simply slow down on the descents, realizing that races are rarely won or lost on the downhills. This last option involves weighing the value of going fast downhill versus their comfort and safety and choosing to follow the adage, "Discretion is the better part of valor".

Mastering irrational fears involves a different approach. Because irrational fears have no objective solutions, cyclists can't solve the fear nor can they readily change the situation that causes it. Instead, they have to counter the irrational beliefs that cause the fear; in other words, be rational with their irrationality. Returning to the bike buckling on a rough road example, cyclists can remind themselves that bikes are tested to withstand such abuse. They can do an Internet search to find any evidence of bikes breaking in half during rides on uneven roads. They can also draw on their own experiences and that of their friends who ride extensively and determine whether anyone has ever had or seen a bike buckle. Even with this rational debunking, irrational fears may linger. When the fear arises, cyclists can accept it as normal, decide to put it out of their mind and focus on things that will help them have a good ride.

Regardless of whether cyclists' fears are rational or irrational, they can use several practical techniques to help them overcome the fears. Positive thinking that focuses on their strengths and their ability to overcome their fears will gird them against the force of those fears. Fears can be overwhelming because they dominate their thinking and cause riders to focus on the things that make the fear worse. They can resist this tendency by focusing on things that will help them deal with the fear; for example, they can focus on using good technique on the bike during high-speed descents. If they are focused on the process of riding and what they need to do to ride well, then they will not be focused on the fear.

Because fears are manifested physically, with muscle tension, increased heart rate and shallow breathing, cyclists can use the psych-down techniques we discussed earlier, including deep breathing and relaxing their body. Creating a physical state that counters the feelings of fear will lessen how much cyclists feel the fear. This strategy has the added benefit of distracting cyclists from the fear, helping them focus on something that actually reduces their fear, and increases their sense of control, the loss of which is a big part of the fear they feel. In cases where the fear is irrational or can cause little real harm, a great way to get over their fear is to just accept it and do the thing they fear. We have found that the most fear-provoking part of cycling is just thinking about it. Once cyclists get into the experience they fear, it is rarely as bad as they think. Finally, riders should not expect their fear to disappear overnight. If they are patient and work on overcoming their fear, as they gain experience, confidence and comfort, they'll often find that the fear fades away.

Recovery and Overtraining

Making rest and recovery a part of cyclists' training program is an indispensable contributor to race preparation and success (Hawley & Schoene, 2003). Taking the time to recover is also, for many riders, a psychological commitment that is difficult to make because many believe that, if they are resting, they are not getting in better condition and may actually be losing fitness.

> One of the biggest challenges for young athletes is realizing how much rest and recovery they need. Their natural tendency is to push themselves extremely hard in an attempt to match the training of their older, more experienced teammates.
>
> (Carmichael, 2001, p. 153)

Building recovery into cyclists' training programs serves several essential purposes (Hawley & Schoene, 2003). Contrary to what many cyclists believe, fitness gains are not made when they are physically training. Their training efforts actually tear down their bodies. It is during periods of recovery that their physical system repairs the damage and gets stronger and more efficient. Rest days should be comprised of extra sleep, rejuvenating activities such as massage or hot baths, and they should be focused on rehydrating and refueling. Recovery also has important psychological benefits. Rest periods give cyclists a break from the mental and emotional demands that training places on them. Rest gives riders time to reinvigorate the motivation, intensity, focus and excitement that was depleted in training and racing. Rest also helps cyclists step back briefly from their training and allows them to maintain perspective on how training fits into their lives.

Scheduled recovery periods enable cyclists to take a mini-vacation from the intensity and monotony of training. These breaks allow them to replenish themselves physically and recharge their psychological and emotional batteries. Recovery should not be optional parts of riders' training program, but rather it is absolutely necessary for them to maximize their training and achieve their cycling goals.

Post-race Recovery

Cyclists allowing themselves to recover adequately following a race is another essential part of a quality-training program. Their willingness to recover fully from a race will affect how readily they are able to return to their season-long training programs and direct their focus and energy into preparation for their next race. Yet post-race recovery can be a source of trepidation for cyclists, raising fears that they will lose their fitness and hinder their preparations for their next race.

Post-race recovery is also necessary psychologically. Cyclists put a great deal of mental and emotional energy into their training and race preparations. Just like with physical effort, they need time to recover from the psychological wear and tear. Additionally, following the excitement of training and the race, some degree of post-race letdown is common in which cyclists may feel some sadness, a loss of motivation and a lack of direction. This reaction is most pronounced when the race is very important and unusually demanding.

How long cyclists should take to recover following a race depends on a variety of factors. The longer the race, the more time they should take off. Criteriums and flat one-day events may require only a few days to recover, while stage races, which can last from two days to three weeks, might require a much longer recovery time. The cyclist's level of fitness also affects the length of their recovery. If riders are in very good condition and their bodies are accustomed to the demands of racing, then a shorter recovery can be expected. However, if they are not in top condition or they are new to cycling, they should allow more time to recover. The effort cyclists expend in the race also influences the amount of recovery needed. It is possible to complete a race, particularly shorter races, at a pace that places few demands on cyclists' bodies, meaning that little damage is done and only a short recovery is required. If, however, cyclists competed aggressively; for example, forced the pace, attacked the climbs or attempted breakaways, they can expect considerable physical damage and an extended recovery will be needed.

Recovery does not mean that cyclists should lie on their couch for an extended period. Exercise physiologists recommend that, after anywhere from two to five days of complete rest, active rest can not only facilitate the recovery, but also begin to prepare them for their return to training. Active rest involves doing light and noninvasive forms of exercise; for example, easy spinning on an indoor trainer. Active rest allows riders to keep their muscles active while placing few real demands on them.

Overtraining

We have found that, as a rule, cyclists are a highly motivated group. Rarely do they come to us because they are not training enough. More often, they are struggling because they are training too much (Keast & Morton, 2002). Overtraining is so common among cyclists because the sport requires so much time, effort and physical exertion. Combine this training load with high motivation and you have a breeding ground for overtraining (Froehlich, 1993). Research has found that 20 to 25 per cent of endurance athletes suffer from overtraining (Taylor & Cusimano, 2003).

Overtraining can be caused by several factors. A poorly planned training program that involves too much volume or intensity with too high frequency can cause the body to break down and lead to overtraining (Foster & Lehmann, 1999). Declines in endurance, strength and flexibility are common indicators of overtraining. Research has shown that overtraining is most often the result of a lack of adequate recovery from training volume and intensity (Taylor & Cusimano, 2003). High volume and intensity are not inherently unhealthy, but become so when cyclists do not provide sufficient time for the body to repair and build on the physical damage that is incurred (Hawley & Schoene, 2003).

Symptoms of Overtraining

The experience of overtraining emerges subtly at first and then blossoms into a full-blown threat to cyclists' training and competitive pursuits. Their goal is to recognize the early signs of overtraining and respond to them appropriately before overtraining sets in and seriously interferes with their cycling efforts (Johnson, 2000). Overtraining presents a number of physical and psychological indicators of which riders can take note (Froehlich, 1993). Physical symptoms related to overtraining include low energy, prolonged muscle fatigue and soreness, difficulty maintaining training intensity, high heart rate and slow recovery from previous workouts. More general physical symptoms consist of lethargy, persistent tiredness, lingering illness or injury due to a breakdown in their immune system (Fry, Morton & Keast, 1992a), and difficulty sleeping (Hawley & Schoene, 2003). Psychological warning signs related to overtraining include a loss of motivation to train and race, decline in confidence, lack of direction, difficulty focusing and reduced pain tolerance. General psychological indicators are depression, irritability, negative thinking and loss of interest in other aspects of their lives (Druckman & Bjork, 1991; Silva, 1990).

Contributors to Overtraining

Underlying the excessive training and insufficient recovery that leads to overtraining, a number of practical, physical and psychological factors contribute to its emergence (Froehlich, 1993; Halson & Jones, 2002). The substance and often times monotonous structure of cyclists' training programs and race schedules can make them vulnerable to overtraining. Elite cyclists compete in anywhere from 90 to 110 races a year and can train up to 1,200 kilometers per week with most of their training intensity occurring at 65 to 70 per cent of maximum heart rate (Halson & Jones, 2002). A training program that schedules too many high-volume or high-intensity workouts each week will place physical demands on riders that can lead to overtraining. For example, more than 2 high-intensity workouts per week is usually discouraged for all but the highest-level cyclist. A training program that does not provide adequate recovery also sets the stage for overtraining. Without sufficient rest after daily workouts, weekly schedules, and high-volume/high-intensity training periods, cyclists' bodies will not have enough time to heal and recover (Hawley & Schoene, 2003). A competitive schedule that has too many races without sufficient time to recover can also result in overtraining.

Physical factors can also contribute to overtraining. Minor illness and lingering injuries, both of which are also symptoms of overtraining, can exacerbate cyclists' vulnerability to overtraining by adding to the already significant demands they place on their bodies in training. Because professional cyclists burn between 6,000 and 10,000 calories a day, poor nutrition before, during and after training and races can cause riders to lack the nutrients necessary to effectively sustain the workload of their training and competitive schedule. Without proper fueling in all phases of training, cyclists will be unable to sustain themselves and overtraining will be the likely result. Inadequate sleep is another physical contributor to overtraining. Because sleep is essential for the body to repair and recharge itself, too few hours or poor quality of sleep can prevent riders from getting the recovery time they need to counter the demands of their training programs. Life stress unrelated to cycling can contribute to overtraining (Budgett, 1994). Stress that cyclists experience at home and at work can place an undue burden above and beyond the demands that come from their training (Kentta & Hassmen, 1998).

Overtraining can also be aggravated by psychological and emotional issues that drive them to train too hard or prevent them from getting adequate rest. An overinvestment in cycling, in which riders' self-identities are predominantly defined by cycling and in which they base their self-esteem on how they perform, can lead them to train excessively. The need for validation of their self-worth by meeting increasingly higher expectations in their training efforts and race results can cause cyclists to ignore reason from coaches and training partners and signals from their own bodies that they are breaking down under the strain. Specific psychological areas that affect this investment include perfectionism, insecurity, fear of failure and self-criticism. Additionally, qualities that are admired—dare we say worshipped—in cycling, such as dedication, hard work, discipline, focus, intensity and pain tolerance, when taken to the extreme, can impel cyclists to overtrain.

Recovery presents its own unique set of mental and emotional issues that contribute to overtraining and that can prevent cyclists from getting the rest they need. If riders train with others, they may feel pressure to keep up with them even when such a pace is harmful. This pressure is particularly compelling during group rides in which everyone is highly motivated to stay with the group for esteem and social-acceptance reasons. In these situations, it is easy for riders to raise their level of exertion and rationalize it as being good for them. Though short periods of this intense effort will do little harm, continued exertion will take its toll and lead to overtraining.

If riders are at all serious about their cycling efforts, they are probably always looking for new ways to improve their fitness. Many cyclists are seduced by the classic mentality that more is better; for example, if a 50-kilometer ride will improve their fitness, then they will gain even more fitness with an 80-kilometer ride. However, a key lesson in cycling is that more is not always better and there are diminishing returns as riders increase their volume and intensity. The more-is-better attitude can lead cyclists to overtraining.

Many cyclists simply do not recognize the warning signs of overtraining. As we just described, overtraining has a clear set of physical and psychological symptoms (Hawley & Schoene, 2003). Unfortunately, these signs are often subtle or less noticeable individually. Cyclists may be so focused on their training that they do not notice them or they rationalize them as temporary states that they will not feel the next morning. Only after the many symptoms have accumulated and overtraining has entrenched itself might cyclists take notice and realize that they are overtrained. Another common reaction is for cyclists to recognize them, but be unwilling to respond to them. Riders might figure that they can just train through the symptoms or they are loath to respond because to do so would be an admission of weakness.

Preventing Overtraining

The best way to deal with overtraining is to prevent it from occurring (Budgett, 1990; Henschen, 2001). Cyclists can take a number of practical, physical and psychological steps to ensure that they strike a balance between training hard enough to achieve their cycling goals and allowing themselves to recover sufficiently so that they can continue their progress toward their training and competitive goals.

Listening to their bodies lies at the heart of preventing overtraining and is at once the most obvious and least followed lesson cyclists need to learn to keep from becoming overtrained. Cyclists' bodies communicate with them constantly about how they are responding to training, with heart rate, respiration, fatigue, pain, illness and injury. These messages are particularly loud when riders are breaking down due to the volume and intensity of their training or a lack of recovery. Cyclists must recognize these warning signs and act responsibly and in their long-term interest by adjusting their training in a way that will alleviate these early symptoms of overtraining.

Prevention of overtraining starts with an understanding of cycling training, the demands it can place on riders and how that knowledge can be translated into a quality-training program (Kuipers & Keizer, 1988). Buying into the notion that cyclists should train smarter, not harder, is the foundation for a sound training program. Effective training involves a periodized program of varying degrees of frequency, volume and intensity in training accompanied by appropriate amounts of rest and recovery that will help them to progressively achieve their cycling goals (Carmichael, 2001; Fry, Morton & Keast, 1992b; Hawley & Schoene, 2003). A quality-training program also includes specific training strategies that are fun, motivating and fresh to help cyclists avoid the monotony and routine that can set in during a long season of training.

Riders must have confidence in and commitment to their training program. One of the biggest causes of overtraining is when cyclists lose faith in their programs and decide to increase the volume and intensity. If riders believe that their programs will give them the results they want, they are more likely to stick with the plan, particularly when they feel a pull to increase their efforts due to slow progress or seeing others improve faster than they do. Cyclists also need to have patience with their programs. Patience is often difficult in the microwave, fast-food, instant-coffee culture in which we live. Like everything of value in life, riders will achieve their cycling goals by being patient and allowing them the time needed to see the results they want.

Cyclists can take several physical steps to prevent overtraining. They can reduce the risk of overtraining by ensuring that they fuel adequately for the demands they are placing on themselves. Riders should be on healthy and balanced diets that provide them with the proper nutrients and sufficient calories to satisfy their training load. Pre-, during and post-workout nutrition, that includes both solid food and hydration, can also protect riders from overtraining by ensuring that their bodies are well fueled for the burden they place them under (Hawley & Schoene, 2003).

Getting enough sleep is also important for preventing overtraining. The more and harder cyclists train, the more time their bodies need to recover and repair themselves. Short-changing their bodies on this essential time of rest increases the chances of overtraining dramatically. Ensuring that riders get plenty of sleep at night and take naps during the day when needed is one of the best preventive measures they can take.

Interestingly, one of the most common causes of overtraining has nothing to do with cyclists' training programs. Unless they are a pro rider whose life is devoted exclusively to the sport, cyclists probably have a career, family and other commitments that place considerable demands on their time and energy. This "real world" can cause life stress that can wear riders' bodies down without even adding cycling to the equation. Cyclists should monitor and respond to life stressors so that their non-cycling stress does not take its toll and interfere with their training and race efforts (Froehlich, 1993).

Psychological and emotional factors are more subtle, yet no less influential, contributors to overtraining. These mental issues are often what drive cyclists to train too often and too intensely, and do not allow them adequate time to recover. As we mentioned earlier, psychological concerns, such as overinvestment in cycling, perfectionism, insecurity, life imbalance, social pressure and unrealistic expectations, can cause riders to make poor decisions in their training that can lead to overtraining. Stepping back from, gaining perspective on and exploring these areas can ensure that cyclists are not driven to overtrain by these unhealthy influences and that their attitude and emotions make a healthy contribution to their cycling participation.

SPECIAL ISSUES IN CYCLING

In addition to the general performance issues that we have discussed, cycling also presents special concerns that have psychological implications. These issues relate to the roles and dynamics that occur within teams and the allure of performance-enhancing drugs whose use is widespread in cycling and a source of concern and embarrassment in the sport.

Team Roles

Cycling is predominantly a team sport in which each team member has a clearly defined role that contributes to the team's goals. In every race, at least one team leader is designated to win the race. The team leader role may change depending on the type of race or the point in the season. For example, during the 2003 professional racing season, the United States Postal Service team (USPS) designated George Hincapie as one of its leaders when the team was competing in the spring single-day "classics" and his teammates, including ostensible team leader, Lance Armstrong, supported his efforts. The leader role then shifted to Armstrong for the Tour de France, his specialty. In the fall of 2003, Roberto Heras, Armstrong's "lieutenant" during the Tour de France, assumed the team leader role on his way to victory in the Vuelta a Espana.

Other members of the team are assigned specific roles as "domestiques", whose job it is to help the team leader achieve the team goal. Their work may include riding at the front to shelter the leader from wind, chasing down breakaways, getting food and water for the leader and other team members, controlling the pace of the peloton and giving up their bicycle to the leader if a flat tire or mechanical problem arises.

Teams face psychological and interpersonal challenges in filling the necessary roles and balancing individual aspirations with team goals. Particularly for stage races and consistent success throughout the race season, successful teams have a balance of riders who can fulfill a variety of roles and compliment and support each other. The most successful teams have members who willingly embrace their roles and offer every team member the opportunity to feel rewarded for their efforts. The domestiques are the most challenged in their roles because they do a disproportionate amount of work supporting their team leader, but receive far less financial reward and attention for their efforts. In some races, such as the one-day events, these riders may not even cross the finish line because their extreme efforts early in the race prevent them from continuing to the end.

Domestiques do, however, have their moments in the sun. For example, at the 2004 Tour de France, the USPS domestique, Floyd Landis, led his team leader, Armstrong, up two major climbs on one stage. On the final descent, Armstrong offered Landis an opportunity to win the stage but, for tactical reasons, he was not able to and Armstrong ended up taking the stage. After the race, Armstrong told the media that Landis was the star of the day. In addition, for each of his six Tour de France victories, Armstrong has given his winnings to his teammates. Domestiques who prove themselves worthy of a more significant team role often move to other teams in need of a team leader; for example, the American Tyler Hamilton and the Spaniard, Roberto Heras, both moved to new teams and became their team leaders a year after being "super domestiques" for Armstrong in the Tour de France.

Teams have other roles that are fulfilled depending on the type of race. Mountainous races are the milieu of the climbers. These cyclists possess immense strength-to-weight ratios, have very high thresholds for pain, and are able to sustain a brutal pace up ascents reaching 15 degrees of inclination. Climbers are usually most successful in stage races because larger gaps of time can be gained in the mountains than on flat stages. The Frenchman, Richard Virenque, is believed to be the best pure climber in the world today.

Flat races often spotlight sprinters. They ride in the main peloton for the entire race conserving their energy and, in the final few kilometers, their teammates work together to position them near the front of the accelerating peloton allowing them to sprint the last 200 meters for the victory. The Italian, Mario Cipollini, has been considered the world's best sprinter in recent years, along with the German, Erik Zabel, and the Australian, Robbie McEwen.

The sprinters are a special breed of competitor. They have the ability to unleash a powerful, perfectly timed sprint after several hundred kilometers of racing. Sprinting at the end of the race is similar to playing an entire chess game in the last few minutes of a race. Sprinters and their teams must make decisions that will allow them to get to the front of the peloton using the least amount of energy, be aware of the positions of the other sprinters who are their biggest threats, negotiate around opposing riders, and then make changes in strategy based on the dynamic situation that is unfolding around them. Sprinters must find their way through a mass of tightly compacted riders in the peloton while traveling at speeds in excess of 50 kilometers an hour and, once near the front of the peloton, begin an all-out sprint reaching speeds of over 70 kilometers an hour or more. Negotiating through the riders, they will often bump each other or be required to swerve and alter their course on a moment's notice, all the while calculating the precise moment when they should launch the sprint to the finish so that their front wheel will be the first to cross the line.

Sprinters are the most fearless and calculating cyclists who put themselves in the most dangerous situations faced in the sport. There have been some horrific crashes in mass-sprint finishes throughout the history of cycling. The crash that occurred during the first stage of the 2003 Tour de France, alluded to earlier in this chapter, is one such incident. Cyclists are exhausted during the final sprint to the finish and occasionally will make mistakes in judgment in their quest to gain the victory. A gap between two riders or a rider and the side barrier might suddenly close as a rider moves over, resulting in a crash. At those speeds and the closeness of the competitors, it doesn't take much for a chain reaction to occur with many cyclists crashing in the process. Because races that end in sprints are routinely determined by inches, sprinters' ability to overcome their fear and to take the necessary risks will often determine who wins the race.

Drugs

Like many endurance sports, cycling has suffered from scandals related to the use of illegal, performance-enhancing drugs. Due to the extreme physical demands of cycling, the rewards for those who achieve success, and its broad acceptance in the cycling community, illegal drug use appears to be more the rule than the exception. Over the last decade the UCI, attempting to clean up the sport, has instituted a rigorous drug-testing program that has resulted in positive tests, suspensions and legal proceedings against some of the most prominent professional cyclists in the world. In 1999, the 1998 Tour de France winner, Marco Pantani, was leading the Giro d'Italia with two stages remaining, when a mandatory post-stage blood test revealed the marker indicative of the illegal performance-enhancing drug, EPO (erythropoietin). He was given what was, at the time, the UCI-mandated 14-day suspension from racing, which effectively ended his pursuit of the Giro title (Wilcockson, 2004). Shortly after, the Frenchman, Richard Virenque, a now 7-time winner of the Tour de France's "best climber" polka-dotted jersey, was implicated in a drug scandal with his team and was later suspended for 2 years. In 2004, 2 current Professional World Champions, the Englishman, David Millar (Individual Time Trial), and the Belgian, Filip Meirhaeghe (Cross-Country Mountain Biking), as well as former Professional World Champion, the Swiss, Oscar Camenzind (Road Race, 1998), tested positive for EPO.

Even more disturbing are the deaths attributed to performance-enhancing drug use in recent years. During a 6-month period beginning in the middle of 2003, 6 European cyclists died from "heart failure" which experts suspect was the result of illegal drug use. In February 2004, Marco Pantani, at age 34, died of a heart attack that was believed to have been caused by a drug overdose.

Cyclists feel significant pressure to use illegal drugs to boost their performances. It is frustrating for cyclists competing at the highest level, whose lives are committed to the sport, to watch competitors beat them because of the unfair advantage they gain by using performance-enhancing drugs. Because of significant amount of money that is invested in cycling teams and the strong national pride that is engendered, particularly in Europe, cyclists may also feel pressure from their teams, sponsors, the media and fans. In 1998, the entire Festina team, one of the oldest and most respected professional teams in Europe, was expelled from the Tour de France after police discovered stocks of prohibited substances. The scandal effectively prompted the creation of the World Anti-doping Agency (WADA). In 2004, the Cofidis professional racing team, another leading European team, was involved in a sweeping drug investigation that eventually led to the arrest of several members of its staff as well as some of the cyclists. The UCI and WADA hope to reduce or eliminate the use of performance-enhancing drugs in professional cycling through a formal system of education, testing and sanctions.

While drug use among professional cyclists gets the attention, competitive cyclists of all levels of ability can be seduced by the benefits of performance-enhancing drugs. Anyone who wants to perform their best and achieve success at the level at which they are competing may be drawn to illegal drug use. While resources for obtaining these drugs may be more limited, amateurs still have access to them. Sport psychologists can play a role in preventing their use by educating cyclists with whom they work about the dangers physically, psychologically and within the legal system. Sport psychologists can also teach cyclists mental-training techniques that cyclists can use in place of performance-enhancing drugs to improve their performance.

CONCLUSION

Competitive cycling is a highly demanding sport that involves long hours, extreme physical exertion, considerable pain, risk of injury or worse, a complex interplay of individual and team goals, and great unpredictability. However, arguably, cycling does not bring anything so psychologically unique that it is that much different from many other sports, particularly other endurance sports. Perhaps what makes cycling unique from other endurance sports, such as running and swimming, is its high-risk nature. This chapter has presented issues we have found to be most distinctive to cycling and with which cyclists are most frequently faced in training and races. In addition to our exploration of the four psychological areas that we deemed most relevant—intensity, pain, fear and recovery—we have offered a variety of practical strategies that have been successful for cyclists with whom we have worked. These tools are valuable to all levels of cyclists and, in fact, to all types of cycling, not just road cycling (e.g. mountain bike racing and track racing).

An obstacle for encouraging the use of psychological information and techniques with cyclists is the dearth of research that specifically examines the relationship of psychology to cycling. Because of the shortage of cycling-specific research, we had to garner scientific support for our views by generalizing the results from investigations that explored the psychology of other sports. With the worldwide popularity of cycling as both a participation and spectator sport, we hope that this chapter will encourage those interested in cycling to explore the psychological contributors to the sport in a more rigorous manner.

REFERENCES

Avins, M. (1986). Interview with Greg LeMond. *The US Interview 3*, 44–47.
Brena, S.F. & Chapman, S.L. (1983). *Management of Patients with Chronic Pain*. New York: SP Medical & Scientific Books.
Brooks, G.A., Fahey, T.D. White, T.P. (1996). *Exercise Physiology: Human Bioenergetics and its Applications*. Mountain View, CA: Mayfield Publishing.
Budgett, R. (1990). Overtraining syndrome. *British Journal of Sports Medicine, 24*, 231–236.
Budgett, R. (1994). The overtraining syndrome. *British Medical Journal, 309*, 465–468.
Cannon, W.B. (1932). *The Wisdom of the Body*. New York: Norton.
Carmichael, C. (2001). *Training Tips for Cyclists and Triathletes*. Boulder, CO: Velo Press.
Conroy, D.E. (2001). Fear of failure: an exemplar for social development research in sport. *Quest, 53*, 165–183.
Conroy, D.E., Poczwardowski, A. & Henschen, K.P. (2001). Evaluative criteria and consequences associated with failure and success for elite athletes and performing artists. *Journal of Applied Sport Psychology, 13*, 300–322.
Druckman, D. & Bjork, R.A. (1991). *In the Mind's Eye: Enhancing Human Performance*. Washington, DC: National Academy Press.
Egan, S. (1987). Acute pain tolerance among athletes. *Canadian Journal of Sport Sciences, 12*, 175–178.
Feltz, D.L. (1975). Coping mechanisms and performance under stress. In D.M. Landers, R.W. Christina & D.V. Harris (eds), *Psychology of Sport and Motor Behavior—II* (pp. 3–24). University, Park, Pennsylvania State University.
Foster, C. & Lehmann, M. (1999). Overtraining syndrome. *Insider, 7*, 1–6.
Fried, R. (1987a). Relaxation with biofeedback-assisted guided imagery: the importance of breathing rate as an index of hypoarousal. *Biofeedback and Self Regulation, 12*, 273–279.
Fried, R. (1987b). *The hyperventilation syndrome—Research and clinical treatment*. Baltimore: Johns Hopkins University Press.

Froehlich, J. (1993). Overtraining syndrome. In J. Heil (ed.) *Psychology of Sport Injury* (pp. 59–70). Champaign, IL: Human Kinetics.

Fry, R.W., Morton, A.R. & Keast, D. (1992a). Overtraining syndrome and the chronic fatigue syndrome Part 1. *New Zealand Journal of Sports Medicine, 19*, 48–52.

Fry, R.W., Morton, A.R. & Keast, D. (1992b). Periodization of training stress—a review. *Canadian Journal of Sports Science, 17*, 234–240.

Gauron, E.F. & Bowers, W.A. (1986). Pain control techniques in college-age athletes. *Psychological Reports, 59*, 1163–1169.

Gil, K.M., Williams, D.A., Keefe, F.J. & Beckham, J.C. (1990). The relationship of negative thoughts to pain and psychological distress. *Behavior Therapy, 21*, 349–362.

Halson, S. & Jones, D. (2002). Detecting and avoiding overtraining. In A.E. Jeukendrup (ed.), *High-performance Cycling.* (pp. 13–24).

Hanin, Y.L. (1999). Individual zones of optimal functioning (IZOF) model: emotions–performance relationships in sport. In Y.L. Hanin (ed.), *Emotions in Sport* (pp. 65–89). Champaign, IL: Human Kinetics.

Hawley, C.J. & Schoene, R.B. (2003). Overtraining: why training too hard, too long, doesn't work. *Physician and Sports Medicine, 31*, 16–33.

Henschen, K.P. (2001). Athletic staleness and burnout: diagnosis, prevention, and treatment. In J.M. Williams (ed.) *Applied Sport Psychology: Personal Growth to Peak Performance* (pp. 445–455). Mountain View, CA: Mayfield.

Iso-Ahola, S.E. & Hatfield, B. (1986). *Psychology of Sports.* Dubuque, IA: L Brown.

Jacobson, E. (1929). *Progressive Relaxation.* Chicago: University of Chicago Press.

Johnson, R.J. (9 June 2000). Overtraining 101: How to overtrain. http://www.letsrun.com/overtrain.html

Kentta, G. & Hassmen, P. (1998). Overtraining and recovery: a conceptual model. *Sports Medicine, 26*, 25–39.

Keast, D. & Morton, A.R. (1 May 2002). Overtraining. http://www.sportsci.org/encyc/drafts/Overtraining.doc.

Kress, J. (1998). A naturalistic investigation of former Olympic cyclists' cognitive strategies for coping with exertion pain during performance. Unpublished doctoral dissertation. Lawrence, Kansas.

Kuipers, H. & Keizer, H.A. (1988). Overtraining in elite athletes: review and directions for the future. *Sports Medicine, 6*, 79–92.

Landers, D. & Boutcher, S. (1993). Arousal–performance relationship. In J.M. Williams (ed.), *Applied Sport Psychology: Personal Growth to Peak Performance* (pp. 170–184). Palo Alto, CA: Mayfield.

Langer, E., Janis, I. & Wolfer, J.A. (1975). Reduction of psychological stress in surgical patients. *Journal of Experimental Social Psychology, 11*, 155–165.

Martens, R. (1987). *Coaches Guide to Sport Psychology.* Champaign, IL: Human Kinetics.

Martin, A.J. & Marsh, H.W. (2003). Fear of failure: friend or foe? *Australian Psychologist, 38*, 31–38.

Melzack, R. & Wall, P.D. (1965). Pain mechanisms: a new theory. *Science 150*, 171–179.

Morgan, W.P. (1978, April). The mind of the marathoner. *Psychology Today,* 38–49.

Morgan, W.P. (1980, July). Test of champions. *Psychology Today,* 92–108.

Morgan, W.P., O'Conner, P.J., Sparling, P.B. & Pate, R.R. (1987). Psychological characterization of the elite female distance runner. *International Journal of Sports Medicine, 8*, 124–131.

Morgan, W.P. & Pollock, M.L. (1977). Psychological characterization of the elite distance runner. *Marathon: Physiological, Medical, Epidemiological, and Psychological Studies,* 382–403.

O'Conner, P.J. (1992). Psychological aspects of endurance performance. In R.J. Shepard & P.O. Astrand, (eds), *Endurance in Sport* (pp. 139–145). Oxford: Blackwell.

Raiport, G. (1988). *Red Gold: Peak Performance Techniques of the Russian and East German Olympic Victors.* Los Angeles: Tarcher.

Raglin, J.S. & Hanin, Y.L. (1999). Competitive anxiety. In Y.L. Hanin (ed.) *Emotions in Sport* (pp. 93–111). Champaign, IL: Human Kinetics.

Rider, M.S. & Achterberg, J. (1989). Effect of music-assisted imagery on neutrophils and lymphocytes. *Biofeedback and Self-regulation, 14*, 247–257.

Roll, B. (2004). *The Tour de France Companion.* Workman Publishing, New York.

Russell, W.D. & Weeks, D.L. (1994). Attentional style in ratings of perceived exertion during physical exercise. *Perceptual and Motor Skills, 78*, 779–783.

Ryan, E.D. & Kovacic, C.R. (1966). Pain tolerance and athletic participation. *Perceptual and Motor Skills, 22,* 383–390.

Ryschon, T.W. (1994). Physiologic aspects of bicycling. *Clinics in Sports Medicine, 13,* 15–38.

Schmidt, R.A. & Wrisberg, C.A. (2000). *Motor Learning and Performance* (2nd edn). Champaign, IL: Human Kinetics.

Schomer, H.H. (1986). Mental strategies and the perception of effort of marathon runners. *International Journal of Sport Psychology, 17,* 41–59.

Schomer, H.H. (1987). Mental strategy training programme for marathon runners. *International Journal of Sport Psychology, 18,* 133–151.

Scott, V. & Gijsbers, K. (1981). Pain perception in competitive swimmers. *British Medical Journal,* 283, 91–93.

Silva, J. (1990). An analysis of the training stress syndrome in competitive athletics. *Journal of Applied Sport Psychology, 2,* 5–20.

Silva, J.M. & Applebaum, M.I. (1989). Association-dissociation patterns of United States Olympic marathon trial contestants. *Cognitive Therapy and Research, 13,* 185–192.

Sonstroem, R.J. (1984). An overview of anxiety in sport. In J.M. Silva III & R.S. Weinberg (eds.), *Psychological Foundations of Sport* (pp. 104–117). Champaign, IL: Human Kinetics.

Sullivan, M.J.L., Thorn, B., Haythornthwaite, J.A., Keefe, F., Martin, M., Bradley, L.A. & Lefebvre, J.C. (2001). Theoretical perspectives on the relation between catastrophizing and pain. *Clinical Journal of Pain, 17,* 52–64.

Taylor, J. (2001). *Prime Sport: Triumph of the Athlete Mind.* New York: iUniverse.

Taylor, J. (2002, November). Pain is your friend. *Inside Triathlon,* pp. 54–55.

Taylor, J. & Cusimano, K. (8 October 2003). Mental training for endurance athletes. Continuing education workshop presented at the annual meetings of the Association for the Advancement of Applied Sport Psychology, Philadelphia, PA.

Taylor, J. & Wilson, G.S. (2002). Intensity regulation and sport performance. In J.L. Van Raalte & B.W. Brewer (eds) *Exploring Sport and Exercise Psychology* (pp. 99–130). Washington, DC: APA.

Turk, D.C., Meichenbaum, D. & Genest, M. (1984). *Pain and Behavioral Medicine: A Cognitive Behavioral Perspective.* New York: Guilford Press

Weinberg, R.S. & Gould, D. (2003). *Foundations of Sport and Exercise Psychology* (3rd edn). Champaign, IL: Human Kinetics.

Weinberg, R.S., Jackson, A. & Gould, D. (1984). Effect of association, dissociation and positive self-talk strategies on endurance performance. *Canadian Journal of Applied Sport Sciences, 9,* 25–32.

Weisenberg, M. (1987). Psychological interventions for the control of pain. *Behavioral Research and Therapy, 25,* 301–312.

Wilcockson, J. (15 February 2004). Marco Pantani: a tragic figure. Velonews.com. http://www.velonews.com/news/fea/5563.0.html.

Williams, J.M. & Harris, D.V. (2001). Relaxation and energizing techniques for regulation of arousal. In J.M. Williams (ed.) *Applied Sport Psychology: Personal Growth to Peak Performance* (pp. 229–246). Mountain View, CA: Mayfield.

Zaichkowsky, L. & Takenaka, K. (2001). Optimizing arousal levels. In R. Singer, M. Murphey and L.K. Tennant (eds) *Handbook of Research on Sport Psychology* (pp. 511–527). New York: Macmillan.

PART IV

Combat Sports

CHAPTER 16

Application of Sport Psychology for Optimal Performance in Martial Arts

Mark H. Anshel and John M. Payne

Middle Tennessee State University, USA

INTRODUCTION

Martial arts refer to various combat systems that originated in Asia (Winkle & Ozmun, 2003), and have become increasingly popular in recent years for a variety of reasons. Most martial arts participants practice this form of combat for physical fitness, sport, law enforcement preparation, and self-defense, particularly in life-threatening conditions. Most communities offer martial arts courses for recreational purposes, and to promote health and well-being. This form of combat has also been used to promote mental health and reduce anxiety (Foster, 1997), build self-concept (Finkenburg, 1990), improve confidence (Chapman, Lane, Brierly and Terry, 1997), treat juvenile delinquency and violent adolescents (Twemlow & Sacco, 1998), and to promote fitness and quality of life for older adults (Birkel, 1998). In recent years, elementary and secondary school physical education programs have included martial arts in their curriculum. This chapter will: (a) provide a definition and historical perspective of martial arts, (b) address the psychological characteristics of successful martial arts competitors, and (c) offer specific cognitive strategies that contribute to successful competitive performance.

MARTIAL ARTS DEFINED

There is no widespread agreement on a clear definition of martial arts. Martial arts is typically defined as empty hand fighting; a form of fighting or defending oneself that uses punches, strikes, kicks, grappling, blocks and throws (Winkle & Ozmun, 2003). Collectively, martial arts are referred to as combat systems that originated in Asia, and have been in existence for thousands of years (see the next section). There are over 30 forms of martial arts,

The Sport Psychologist's Handbook: A Guide for Sport-Specific Performance Enhancement.
Edited by Joaquín Dosil. © 2006 John Wiley & Sons, Ltd.

each consisting of their own philosophy and style. However, all of these styles emphasize the association between mind and body in producing efficient, skilled movement and the promotion of health and well-being. Cunningham (1998) describes martial arts as revolving around the "three culture principle", composed of intellectual, moral and physical culture. Cunningham describes a pyramid with physical culture at the base (i.e. survival; maintaining life), morality at the center (i.e. the moral aspect gives life meaning and value, creating a more fulfilling life), and intellect at the apex (i.e. the mind and spirit which makes possible virtuous conduct). Indeed, character development (e.g. courtesy, confidence, respect for others) is at the core of all martial arts competition.

Brief History of Martial Arts

The most popular forms of martial arts, including karate, judo, taekwondo and aikido, have been in existence for thousands of years. Experts, however, are uncertain about the true origin of martial arts. According to Savage (1995), the Egyptian pyramids contain hieroglyphics demonstrating men engaged in hand-to-hand combat dating back to 4,000 BC. Artwork dating to 3,000 BC. shows men kicking and punching in a style highly similar to the movements of contemporary martial artists.

It is thought that marital arts were first developed by farmers and villagers to defend themselves from repressive governments (Winkle & Ozmun, 2003). Martial arts gained popularity in the USA soon after World War II, as veterans were returning from the Pacific theatre. Many of the soldiers were exposed to various styles of karate that was practiced throughout East Asia. Some of these veterans practiced and studied various styles of karate, becoming proficient enough to teach the movements to others. The US military subsequently included martial arts in their hand-to-hand combat training.

Another source of martial arts popularity was the immigration of many "masters" to the USA from various Asian countries to demonstrate and teach these skills. Heightened US interest in these new techniques resulted in a proliferation of martial arts studios and programs. Hollywood film producers and directors began to include various martial arts movements in film and television. Two forms of martial arts, judo and taekwondo, have become medal sports in the Olympics.

Styles of Primary Forms of Martial Arts

There are over 100 styles of karate, with some more popular than others, yet equally effective. There are only a finite number of techniques for kicking, punching, blocking, grappling or striking an opponent. Different instructors may stress certain movements; however, individuals need to judge technique effectiveness for themselves. A person's size, strength, flexibility, age, physical condition and overall ability may dictate the best style to use. Here are some of the more common and popular forms of martial arts. Each style requires extensive use of mental skills, including psychological readiness, confidence and self-motivation to create and maintain optimal effort.

Karate consists of "point sparring" or "point fighting", the objective of which is to show "control" of the various kicks, punches and strikes. Points may be deducted and the competitor disqualified if the referee assesses a competitor's kick, punch, or strike as too aggressive or lacking control. Points are determined subjectively by an odd number of judges—usually five. Kata competition, part of karate tournaments, consists of a stylized group of movement (e.g. kicks, punches, blocks or strikes) against an imaginary opponent. The performer's use of a weapon ("weapons competition") is also against an imaginary opponent. In both types of competition, the judges observe and assess the performer's movements on a five-point scale. For many martial arts historians, the fundamental concept of "martial arts" is synonymous with karate.

Kendo is another martial art that closely resembles the sport of fencing with the use of bamboo sword and protective armor. Indeed, the word "kendo" literally means "the way of the sword" in Japanese (*Kendo-Jidai Monthly*, 21 October, 2003). The goal of kendo is to attack the body twice within a five-minute time limit, being awarded one point per hit. The first competitor to score two points wins the match. Three referees judge if a point is scored. Tied scores after five minutes result in infinite sudden death overtime until the next point is scored.

Kickboxing is a combination of full contact karate and boxing. Each contact skill—punch, kick or strike—is performed at full speed; the objective is to contact the opponent. Not surprisingly, the risk of injury is higher than in most other martial arts. The movements are designed to render the opponent incapable of inflicting harm. The ethical aspects of this martial art must be explained to the competitors, and only experienced participants should compete in these matches.

Judo probably originated in China and was exported to Japan (Mifune, 2000). The Japanese word *ju* in judo means "mild" and "natural" and *do* means "art" and "way." "Judo", then, means "way to peace" (Mifune, 2000). Judo is a military art for self-defense. The judoist does not attack the enemy without or before being attacked. The judoist who takes the initiative often suffers an injury—or worse.

Judo competitors bow before entering the competition area and, again, after they walk to the outside edge of the contest area on their respective sides. Then they face each other and, after bowing again to each other, take one step forward and stand inside their lines with their hands at their sides and their feet apart. The objective of judo is to score *ippon* (a full point). *Ippon* is scored: (a) if a contestant with control throws the other contestant on their back with considerable force and speed, (b) if a contestant holds the other contestant who is unable to get away for 25 seconds, or (c) if a contestant gives up by tapping twice or more with a hand or foot or says *matte* ("I give up"). Giving up generally occurs as a result of a grappling technique (strangle), *kansetsu-waza* (armlock), or if the referee concludes that a strangle technique or arm lock has immobilized the opponent. An *ippon*, which can be scored standing or on the ground, immediately ends the match, similar to pinning in wrestling or a knock-out in boxing.

Taekwondo, a self-defense sport, originated in Korea over 2,000 years ago (Chung & Lee, 1994). The literal English translation of "taekwondo" means "foot, hand, way". About 70 per cent of taekwondo is comprised of foot techniques, with hand techniques, such as strikes, chops, punches and jabs, comprising the remaining 30 per cent (Chung & Lee, 1994). The concept of *do* in taekwondo includes both physical technique and the performer's mental and spiritual association to these techniques. It is a discipline of both mind and body. The words "respect", "discipline", "self-control" and "honesty" form the spirit of this sport. Martial arts can be considered a competitive sport (with rules) or it can be used as a defensive measure in actual life-threatening situations. Taekwondo depends on short, quick, powerful strikes, as opposed to other types of martial arts, such as aikido, that involve circular movements and much footwork, consisting of explosive muscular effort, to avoid an attack (Park & Seabourne, 1997). These characteristics are important to remember when discussing the application of sport psychology strategies.

From a psychological perspective, the use of mental skills is inherent in taekwondo. Park & Seabourne (1997) contend, "The ultimate ideal of taekwondo practice is to achieve a state of mind in which the performer is acutely aware of the endlessly changing competition environment and can effortlessly react to such changes" (p. 14).

APPLIED SPORT PSYCHOLOGY IN MARTIAL ARTS

Few forms of sports competition include a greater segment of mental skills than martial arts. Psychological aspects of martial arts combat are extensive before, during and even after the event. Concepts such as psychological preparation, concentration, anticipation, flow, emotional control, self-control, confidence and competitiveness are at the heart of this ancient form of combat. A discussion of the application of sport psychology to martial arts includes examining the combatants' desirable psychological dispositions that explain or predict success, and the mental skills and behavioral tendencies before, during and following competition.

Dispositions of Martial Arts Competitors

For many years, sport psychology researchers have attempted to develop personality profiles of athletes to predict future success or to determine the psychological characteristics of high-quality competitors. These attempts have not been met with great success. The ability to predict future success in sport based on personality tests is a very low 8 to 10 per cent (see Anshel, 2003, for a review of this literature). Nevertheless, there are numerous personal characteristics—not necessarily personality characteristics, but rather, psychological dispositions that are more changeable and dependent on the situation than personality traits—that may describe successful martial arts competitors. While very little research exists in this area on martial arts competitors, there are selected characteristics that are commonly associated with success in competitive athletes (Deaner & Silva, 2002; Vealey, 2002).

Desirable Psychological Dispositions

Performance consistency is one of the most difficult objectives in competitive sport, particularly given the extensive mental and physical demands of martial arts. The vast array of personal and environmental factors easily intrude on the martial arts athlete's ability to mentally prepare for the contest, to maintain concentration, to apply previously achieved skills time after time during the event, to deal with environmental factors such as competing in an unfamiliar arena or in front of unfriendly spectators and, of course, confronting opponents and their varying degrees of competence. How does the athlete maintain composure and execute skills at optimal levels consistently? How is it possible to maintain emotional control, and reduce the presence or duration of undesirable thoughts? Successful martial arts athletes are capable of meeting the sport's high mental and physical demands and achieving desirable outcomes by possessing certain psychological dispositions.

Psychological dispositions concern a person's tendency to exhibit patterns of thinking, feeling and performing in particular types of circumstances; for example, prior to sport competition or under certain conditions that occur during the competition (Anshel, 2003). Dispositions (e.g. confidence, coping style, optimism, learned resourcefulness) differ from personality traits (e.g. stability, dominance, neuroticism, self-esteem) that are stable, predictable, cross-situational, developed early in life, and deeply embedded, sometimes inherited, ways of thinking and acting. Unlike personality traits, dispositions may be learned, situationally determined, and susceptible to counseling interventions (Lazarus & Folkman, 1984). They are broad, generalized ways of thinking that may be observed as behavioral tendencies. Thus, the concept of dispositions—which more accurately describe highly skilled, successful competitors than do personality traits—will be addressed in this paper.

While researchers have not been successful in predicting athletic success from personality inventories, measuring the athlete's selected psychological dispositions have proven far more valid (see Anshel, 2003, for a review). This is partly because personality has been misunderstood, inaccurately defined and poorly measured in attempting to predict sport success or to discriminate between successful athletes and their less successful peers as well as among non-athletes.

What are the athlete's thoughts and feelings just prior to the event? While some anxiety is normal, even desirable, over-anxious athletes feel threatened not confident, and tense not relaxed. Low self-confidence heightens pessimistic thinking and reduced effort. Failure is more likely. Spectators, opponents and other stimuli that interfere with attentional focusing and concentration easily distract the high-anxiely, low-confidence athlete. Martial arts competition requires "managed intensity"; that is, brief periods of highly intense concentration and physical energy.

From an information-processing perspective, martial arts competitors must be able to anticipate their opponent's actions and strategies, perceive incoming stimuli quickly, engage in rapid planning and decision-making, and respond automatically, in the virtual absence of thinking. The use of memory, a time-consuming process, should be used in practice settings, where learning and strategy formation occur. Memory processes, such as storage and retrieval, should not occur during the competitive event, where anticipation and unexpected stimuli require rapid, automated responses. Other personal characteristics of successful martial arts competitors include a high degree of *self-motivation, self-awareness*, and *self-control*, all very desirable dispositions for meeting the high physical and mental demands of this sport (Chung & Lee, 1994).

Self-control is necessary to plan and maintain the proper thoughts, emotions and actions over time. The successful performer is required to engage in self-regulation strategies in which they are capable of coping effectively with sudden stressful events and maintaining mastery over the situation. Thoughts of helplessness (i.e. perceptions of low self-control in a present situation) or hopelessness (i.e. perceptions that the situation will not improve) will lead to "giving up" and reduced effort, cognitions that will lead to certain failure in martial arts competition.

Self-motivation refers to the athlete's willingness to train and demonstrate optimal effort over time, usually in the absence of external demands or reminders from others (e.g. coaches, parents, team members). The athlete must demonstrate extreme dedication to their training regimen and mental preparation, often in the absence of recognition, approval and positive feedback. This is the core of self-regulation in sport—the ability to produce and maintain the proper thoughts, emotions and behaviors before and during competition (Anshel, 1995). Self-motivation, however, also includes the self-induced willingness to persist at these thoughts, emotions and actions over time in the absence of external constraints.

Self-awareness pertains to the athlete's ability to monitor and recognize their mental status and to adjust thoughts and emotions in order to reach optimal levels of anxiety (feelings of threat) and arousal (feelings of challenge and heightened somatic responses in preparation for competition). As Jones and Swain (1995) have shown, anxiety may be very desirable for optimal performance if the performer interprets their anxious feelings as facilitative, not debilitative. Some anxiety is necessary to maintain vigilance and the proper attentional focus.

Mental toughness in a sport context is a relatively abstract construct, defined primarily by the actions of athletes who exhibit it. To Loehr (1982), mental toughness refers to: (a) quickly overcoming adversity and meeting challenging situations with greater effort and confidence (i.e. mental toughness); (b) feeling responsible for one's performance level and outcomes (internal locus of control); (c) taking reasonable, yet challenging, risks in addressing an opponent's strengths and weaknesses (risk-taking); (d) overcoming short-term adversity by ignoring (avoidance coping style) or attending to (approach coping style) selected information or experiences that allow the competitor to maintain composure; (e) reducing perceived stress; and (f) performing optimally at all times. Mental toughness is imperative in martial arts competition because the speed of movement and of processing information, and the need to quickly adapt to changing environmental demands require tenacity, extreme concentration, a high degree of self-control and taking responsibility for performance outcomes.

In a rare study of mental toughness, Jones, Hanton and Connaughton (2002) examined components of this construct using a qualitative approach by interviewing 10 international-level sports competitors. They found that mental toughness is:

> having the natural or developed psychological edge that enables you to: (a) generally, cope better than your opponents with the many demands ... that sport places on a performer, and (b) specifically, be more consistent and better than your opponents in remaining determined, focused, confident, and in control under pressure. (p. 213)

According to Loehr (1982), "mental toughness is learned, not inherited" (p. 10). He describes a constellation of mental skills that best describe the mentally tough athlete. They are self-motivated, self-directed, positive but realistic, in control of emotions, calm and relaxed "under fire", highly energetic and psychologically ready for action, determined, mentally alert and focused, self-confident, and fully responsible for their own actions. Each of these characteristics describes the successful martial arts competitor.

Optimism is linked to heightened effort, confidence and performance expectations. Optimism relates to a person's disposition toward feeling that current personal and situational factors will result in favorable outcomes. In general psychology, optimism is associated with reduced stress and lower incidence of heart disease. The optimistic competitor will be encouraged to give 100 per cent effort with the anticipation that success will lead to positive outcomes. The optimistic athlete anticipates success, having positive expectations about the future. The result is high self-expectations, greater effort and higher likelihood of executing skills at one's previous best. Optimism is usually measured as dispositional. It reflects a person's general belief that good things will happen to them whether or not they cause these good things to occur (Scheier & Carver, 1985). Optimism in martial arts is important because it enhances effort, concentration, attentional focusing and positive affect, while inhibiting interfering thoughts and negative emotions (Zinsser, Bunker & Williams, 2001). One area that accompanies an optimistic attitude is confidence.

Sport confidence is defined as "*possessing an optimistic attitude and the belief that one's actions will have an impact on the outcome of a situation*" (Vealey, 1986, p. 222). Similar to the concept of self-efficacy, sport confidence is concerned with optimistic feelings toward success in sport settings. It's a specific state of mind and an attitude that is linked to emotional and physical intensity (Loehr, 1990). Sport confidence is essential in martial arts because it creates anticipated success and changes appraisals of negative situations to positive ones. Confident competitors are less anxious and, therefore, less concerned about negative, intrusive perceptions. The result is improved focusing on relevant cues, strategies and skills during the match (Vealey, 1988). It is important to remember that, similar to arousal level in sport, confidence level can be too high (Vealey, 1986). Athletes who are "overconfident" will lack attentional focus, effort and the necessary vigilance to perform at optimal level, while moderate sport confidence will enhance these psycho-behavioral characteristics. Wann (1997) contends, "Overconfident athletes possess an inaccurate and over inflated belief about their athletic abilities" and, consequently, "may be highly disturbed by a mistake" (p. 232). Overconfidence in martial arts is often the explanation for upsets, in which competitors whose skills and history of success are inferior to their better-skilled opponents, surprisingly, perform better in a given match and are victorious. Self-confidence/self-efficacy reflects an athlete who feels competent and anticipates success.

Self-control consists of learned resourcefulness and hardiness. Rosenbaum (1990) defines learned resourcefulness (LR) "as an acquired repertoire of behavioral and cognitive skills with which the person is able to regulate internal events such as emotions and cognitions that might otherwise interfere with the smooth execution of a target behavior" (p. xiv). In his review of non-sport research, Rosenbaum found that individuals with high LR were superior to their low-LR counterparts on coping with stress, tolerating pain, losing or maintaining body weight, controlling negative habits, reducing the incidence of helplessness, complying with medical treatment and promoting health-engendering behaviors such as exercise and proper nutrition. In the context of the demands of martial arts competition, self-control, LR and hardiness are engaged in self-regulatory behaviors by using personal and social resources for dealing with and overcoming obstacles to success, including temporary setbacks. Perceiving stressful situations as challenging rather than threatening, and then developing proper strategies for reacting to these situations efficiently, characterizes the successful martial arts combatant.

Competitiveness has been defined differently by various authors over the years, yet is an important disposition of successful martial arts competitors. It is formally defined as "achievement orientation toward competitive sport, or a sport-specific form of achievement orientation" (Gill, 1993, p. 314). To Martens (1976), however, "Competitiveness is a disposition to strive for satisfaction when making comparisons with some standard of excellence in the presence of evaluate others in sport" (p. 326). In general, competitiveness is a person's motivation to achieve mastery and success in sport by comparing one's own performance to that of an opponent—in other words: winning. Ironically, not all athletes, even at the elite level, possess this disposition. Perhaps, then, individuals with low competitiveness choose to engage in the type of martial arts that is noncompetitive (e.g. tai chi, hatha yoga, feldenkrais), whereas their highly competitive counterparts are attracted to martial art forms in which competition is inherent (e.g. judo, karate, taekwondo).

The process of feeling stress and anxiety in sport begins with the athlete's perceptions of the situation as unpleasant, or negative (Anshel, Kim, K.-W., Kim, B.-H., Chang & Eom, 2001). These perceptions are usually referred to as "threatening" or "harmful", meaning that the athlete feels anxiety, usually called *state anxiety*. The antecedents of cognitive anxiety include uncertainty and worry about the present situation, and potential harm that might occur, usually in the very near future. While some degree of anxiety is often favorable to the athlete because it raises the level of vigilance and attentional focusing, internal attentional focusing and tightening of muscles accompany too much anxiety. Poor performance usually results. Of main interest here is the source of these thoughts in appraising the situation as threatening. Successful martial arts athletes, instead, use *challenge appraisals* of the competitive situation. This outcome results in positive expectations, heightened vigilance to relevant stimuli in the environment—the athlete is focusing externally instead of being distracted by internal thoughts of worry—and greater arousal and effort. Changing appraisal from threat to challenge is needed prior to any competitive engagement. This cognitive strategy is closely linked to the next process—managing state anxiety.

As discussed in the previous section, successful martial arts participants must feel only moderate and manageable state anxiety—enough to remain aroused, challenged and vigilant when monitoring and reacting to external stimuli. According to their website, the code of Isshin-Ryu karate includes: "The body should be able to change motion at any time", "The time to strike is when the opportunity presents itself", "The ear must listen in all directions" and "The eye must see every way". Some degree of uncertainty—anxiety—is necessary to ensure these processes.

Intrinsic motivation (IM) is an important psychological component of successful martial arts competitors. As an integral part of IM, competitors feel increased satisfaction and enjoyment from their participation due to improved *perceived competence*. In addition, competitors have made self-determined choices to engage in martial arts instruction and competition, and to train at the proper intensity level in order to meet their personal goals. Training and competing are enjoyable and satisfying because martial arts athletes have a sense of achievement and accomplishment.

Perceived competence (PC) is an inherent component of intrinsic motivation. This is because it is human nature to persist at tasks at which we excel and to avoid tasks at which we fail—or perceive ourselves as failing to meet our expectations. Experiencing success and perceiving our efforts as successful engenders PC. Feelings of competence are inherent in successful martial arts competitors and promote self-confidence and other desirable psychological attributes.

It is essential that undesirable thoughts do not accompany the competitor prior to and during the event. Self-destructive feelings that will likely lead to performance failure include pessimism, helplessness (i.e. feeling low self-control in the present situation), hopelessness (i.e. feeling that the perception of low self-control will not improve), low self-efficacy, self-blame, maladaptive coping (e.g. self-destructive thoughts and actions), chronic anxiety and depression. Because there are sources for these unpleasant thoughts, it is important that competitors consult with a counseling or clinical psychologist to resolve the underlying issues.

Morals and Ethical Considerations

Most students of martial arts have to be informed that this form of competition is not about street fighting or hurting another person. In fact, the inappropriate use of martial arts fighting may result in negative consequences in school or from the justice system. Many schools have a zero tolerance policy (i.e. suspension from school) on fighting. It is the instructor's responsibility to remind students that injuring another person while performing martial arts in a non-competitive environment is unethical and carries risks and legal ramifications.

Brief Overview of Health Benefits

Martial arts training meets the exercise recommendations for healthy adults of the American College of Sports Medicine (Toskovic, Blessing & Williford, 2002), and improves flexibility (i.e. enhanced range of motion for a particular joint). These are important outcomes because of the increase of cardiovascular disease and reduced joint flexibility with age. Douris, Chinan, Steffens and Weiss (2004) report that karate performers between ages 40 to 60 years who had practiced for 3 years showed more flexibility and leg strength, less body fat, and superior balance and aerobic conditioning than individuals of a similar age range not involved in karate.

Child Martial Arts Competitors: Special Considerations

Can experiencing martial arts benefit younger age groups? Zivin et al. (2001) found that teaching martial arts in middle school could benefit juveniles who are at high risk for violence and delinquency. They also reported positive changes in various psychological risk factors. Twemlow and Sacco (1998) and Twemlow, Sacco and Williams (1996) found that martial arts instruction prevented or attenuated the incidence of violent behavior and bullying, respectively, among adolescent age groups. Michaelson, Ronnenburg, Walsh and Linden (2000) and Winkle and Ozmun (2003) found that martial arts programs are an exciting addition to various physical education curriculums. Students enjoy this type of physical activity and improve their concentration and fitness. It appears, then, that instruction and competition in martial arts has significant benefits to children and adolescent age groups.

APPLIED SPORT PSYCHOLOGY IN THE PRE-COMPETITION PHASE

The application of sport psychology in martial arts will be addressed in three phases: pre-competition, competition and post-competition.

While psychological and behavioral factors foster successful performance in any sport, certain factors are particularly important prior to martial arts competition. Athletes who have a high need to achieve, have high aspirations to reach their goals and possesses a strong work ethic will more likely be successful in reaching their potential than athletes who do not possess or have reduced levels of these dispositions. Successful martial arts athletes exhibit respect, discipline, self-control and honesty, which forms the spirit of this sport. The pre-competition (preparation) phase concerns the psychological dispositions that are highly desirable for competitors, and use of cognitive and behavioral strategies prior to the competitive event.

Cognitive Strategies

Cognitive strategies consist of *thoughts* that influence the performer's emotions, speed and accuracy of processing information, and subsequent performance quality. They are not observable. Behavioral strategies, on the other hand, are observable. They consist of actions that serve to improve the athlete's preparation for and performance in competition. Cognitive strategies used before the competition include a *mental plan, imagery, association and dissociation* (also used during physical training), alternative use of *approach and avoidance coping, relaxation, scheduling/planning*, and *boxing*.

A *mental plan* (pre-planned thoughts and actions) consists of two segments before, during and after the event: "What will I think and when will I think it?" "What will I do and when will I do it?" (Bull, Albinson & Shambrook, 1996; Orlick, 1986). In addition to preplanned thoughts and actions, the mental game plan also includes a back-up set of thoughts and actions, what Bull et al. refer to as "planning for what ifs" (p. 177), or the refocus plan, in Orlick's (1986) parlance. Thus, if the athlete experiences an unexpected barrier to the original plan, they have a second plan in reserve that can quickly be instituted. In martial arts, mental plans are an integral part of preparing for the match, initiating and maintaining optimal performance during the match, and even following the match.

For example, in kickboxing, the goal is to strike the opponent with maximal force within the rules; no "holding back" or "demonstrating form". This strategy requires a mental plan of psyching up and optimizing arousal level, rather than maintaining a low emotional state. Thus, the mental plan would be to control emotions prior to the match, but to reach a more aggressive demeanor once the match is underway. Kickboxing is very demanding and requires extensive fitness and training.

Imagery consists of thinking through the full competitive event, or a segment of it, even a particular skill, with perfect execution and a desirable outcome. It is usually applied in a quiet setting without being disturbed so that athletes can create their own "videotape" of the desirable performance. Imagery has been carefully researched and proven to benefit sport performance if performed correctly. One way in which imagery can be applied in martial arts is to "think through" the match. Using first-person imagery (i.e. imaging the match "through the mind's eye" as actually experienced rather than viewed as a spectator), the competitor will want to imagine executing actions and reactions against the opponent. The sport of kendo, for example, consists of sword fighting against an imaginary, rather than an actual, opponent. Thus, imagery would be used to execute a series of rapid movements.

The strategy used to connect the athlete's thoughts to their muscular exertion is called *association*, whereas attempts to cognitively ignore bodily sensations are called *dissociation* (Masters & Ogles, 1998). An example of association would be to simultaneously incorporate body and mind to create a calm and tranquil experience for the competitor. The martial arts competitor, however, also needs to *dissociate* thoughts from the body in response to physical discomfort or pain, while concentrating on explosive muscular effort; for example, weight lifting or executing a particular skill requires focusing on the muscle group involved. Martial arts competitors must never show pain to their opponent; clearly a strategy that requires dissociation.

Approach and avoidance coping, also applied during competition, is also useful in practice settings (Anshel et al., 2001). Athletes must *approach cope*, for instance, when planning, analyzing, processing information and using feedback. Examples would include examining an opponent's skills prior to competition, determining the opponent's use of strategies, or quickly regaining control of the situation when temporarily at a disadvantage. Thus, an opponent's skills must be analyzed and reasons for performance failure should not be ignored, especially during rest periods. Competitors have only three three-minute periods, so that the analysis of an opponent must occur quickly.

Avoidance coping, on the other hand, is preferred when there is no time to analyze the cause of performance failure, such as during the three-minute competition period. For example, an unlucky event or call by the official must be ignored, at least temporarily, because examining these sources of stress will not help resolve the situation. Generally, putting stressful events behind you and then focusing on the immediate task at hand is usually the preferred coping style *during* competition. There is little time to process information during rapidly performed actions, and reactions that warrant movements that are virtually automatic. Similar to any skill, the proper use of approach and avoidance coping strategies should be mastered in practice settings before being applied in actual competition.

Relaxation is a strategy that promotes concentration, and the clarity and vividness of mental imagery, and reduces mental and physical fatigue. There are at least eight different types of relaxation techniques, some used more often than others as a function of the athlete's culture, by situational demands and other personal factors. Some athletes prefer not to use relaxation training at all and, instead, prefer to relax through light physical activity. It is important that relaxation not occur too close to the competitive event. Tai chi, for example, is considered a "soft" form of martial arts consisting of slow, flowing movement using all body parts in yoga-like meditation forms. It is a calm and tranquil experience. Relaxation is warranted prior to this form of martial art. In response to martial arts competitors engaged in a more "rapid-fire" performance style, pre-competition relaxation may backfire. If used only minutes before competition, for example, the athlete may experience poor performance due to the lack of proper physiological (e.g. heart rate, respiration rate) and emotional (e.g. enthusiasm, excitement) arousal level.

Planning is a strategy that requires the competitor to know in advance their competition plan—and back-up plan (Plan B)—prior to competing. The sport environment is usually occurring too quickly, and the athlete is exposed to very rapid information, to think through and create a performance strategy. Planning strategy (Plan A) and a back-up strategy (Plan B) in case the initial plan is not effective or impossible to enact allows the athlete to move quickly and efficiently, reducing the chance of being at a disadvantage. The competitor should know the strengths and weaknesses of their opponent prior to the match. This allows for developing "Plan A" that forms the primary set of performance strategies that address the opponent's weaknesses. If, however, certain strategies are not being executed successfully (e.g. the opponent's reaction time is quicker than anticipated or their skills have improved since the last competition), then a pre-planned "Plan B" strategy (e.g. the use of more aggressive tactics) should be executed.

Boxing is a technique developed by Orlick (1986) in which the athlete places negative thoughts and emotions in a "mental box" located away from the sport venue—at home, in the locker room, or on the bench. Instead of letting negative thoughts that reflect self-doubt or anxiety distract the individual, these thoughts are "allowed" to occur when they will do no harm, well before the contest. However, as the contest period nears, these thoughts can be intrusive in developing psychological readiness, managing anxiety and filtering out distractions. To help block out these intrusive, unproductive thoughts, the athlete uses imagery to "put" these thoughts in a mental box, and to place this box in their locker or home, not "opening" the box until they return from competition.

One martial arts athlete, for instance, anticipated an unfriendly reception by spectators. His plan was to filter out extraneous (crowd) noise and to concentrate on covertly rehearsing his performance strategy as he entered the competition area. Another competitor was well aware of the superb talent of his opponent while awaiting competition. Instead of lamenting about the anticipated challenges of overcoming his opponent's talent, he "boxed up" those negative, anxiety-inducing thoughts and remembered his previous successes, then rehearsed his competition plan. Orlick claims that *boxing* is an effective technique to help athletes focus on their immediate thoughts and actions just prior to the competitive event.

A word of caution about the use of cognitive strategies: coaches should be careful not to teach too many cognitive techniques at one time, nor ask the athlete to use them extensively. Cognitive strategies are effective when used automatically. It is usually necessary to teach athletes one strategy at a time and to practice them extensively until they become automated. Athletes may become overwhelmed with the need to use the strategies, which can actually inhibit psychological readiness and performance.

Behavioral Strategies

Behavioral strategies used for psychological preparation in sport consist of observable actions consciously performed by the athlete or coach for the purpose of improving the competitor's thoughts, emotions and performance. Examples of behavioral strategies that may be associated with taekwondo, and have been found in past studies to be effective in the pre-competition phase, include *goal setting, scheduling, self-monitoring (checklist), record keeping, social support, social reinforcement, modeling* and *match simulation*. Goals are needed to direct the competitor's efforts toward achieving specific skills and strategies. Goals also serve to determine achievement and competence; when a goal is met the athlete should feel increasingly motivated and conclude that performance has improved. However, goals must not be unrealistic or too difficult. Setting goals can generate anxiety and a sense of failure in the athlete if the goal is set at a level in which achievement is very difficult and success is unrealistic (Anshel, 2003).

Examples of goals in martial arts include: "I will execute 'x' technique (e.g. blocks, punches, kicks for speed and reflex action) with 100 per cent accuracy", "I will improve my confidence before the match", "I will feel more relaxed before the competition", "I will prevent my opponent from scoring 'x' number of points", "I will improve 'x' number of points on which I am judged on my technique" or "I will improve my performance on 'x' skill (e.g. snap-punch, snap-kick)."

Scheduling is used to ensure the proper frequency and content of training sessions, and that all events leading up to the competition are organized and prepared. Athletes require objectives for training and mental preparation times be scheduled, completed and evaluated on an ongoing basis. What is to be accomplished this week? What is my workout for the week? Which skills, sets of skills or strategies (physical and mental) need more practice and mastery by the end of a certain time period? Scheduling allows athletes to monitor progress and evaluate changes in competence level.

The *self-monitoring checklist* (SMC) is a strategy that requires the athlete and coach to jointly determine the types of thoughts and actions that must be learned and practiced consistently in order to reach optimal performance. Certain training techniques performed on selected days of the week, the use of particular stretching exercises, mental preparation techniques (thoughts and actions), dietary habits, sleep patterns and other related behaviors should be planned and executed according to those plans. The SMC acts as a reminder to athletes to perform these functions during the week and on the day of and immediately prior to competition. The checklist consists of a list of items that is "checked off" as they are completed or are followed by a Likert-type scale, ranging from 1 (*not at all like me*) to 5 (*very much like me*). A similar behavioral strategy is record keeping, in which athletes record, in writing, their thoughts, actions, the quality of performance during practice, the performance outcome and the likely cause(s) of these performance outcomes. Record keeping allows athletes to acknowledge performance changes—better or worse—and to identify areas for further improvement.

The SMC can include thoughts and actions prior to competition, during the competitive event, and after the event. Examples of *pre-competition* items on the checklist could include: "I am focusing on the match", "I feel confident in my preparation", "I have consumed adequate water" or "I am properly stretched." Items that reflect thoughts and actions during competition naturally cannot be completed until after the event, but may be accurately recalled. These include: "I adapted to my opponent's skills with confidence", "I felt in control of my strategy", "I performed according to my plan", "I focused my attention on the most important cues" and "I reacted to unanticipated events with emotional control." *Post-competition* items might include "I consumed an adequate amount of water", "I feel good about the skills I demonstrated", "My competition plan was executed correctly and met my expectations" and "I acknowledge the aspects of my performance that need improvement."

Social support, combined with *social reinforcement*, are very important to maintain motivation, group identity and confidence. Social support consists of providing a warm and positive group climate within which to function through constructive interactions with others. Coaches, teammates and parents form the primary sources of social support. Social support allows athletes to discuss their concerns, to seek information through questions and engage in discussions, to reduce their anxiety and cope with stress, and to maintain confidence, motivation and desirable emotional characteristics. Positive reinforcement is one function of social support. It consists of offering the athlete intermittent and consistent—but not constant—praise that reflects desirable performance. Social reinforcement may be lacking in certain competitive sport situations if the team atmosphere is stressful and cold (e.g. athletes do not relate well to each other or do not support each other's needs), or the team's coach does not provide emotional support through praise and positive feedback. Some coaches believe that only criticism is the best way to motivate the athlete. However, what is incorrect about this assumption is that the rare use of praise and positive feedback results in reduced confidence, lower expectations about future success and heightened anxiety. According to Ginott (1965), compliments must reflect the athlete's behaviors ("That was a well-executed kick, Kim"), not their character or personality ("You are a good competitor"). The application of social support, then, requires the athlete's coaches, teammates and perhaps parents and friends to provide insights (e.g. "You can use your foot speed to better advantage by doing 'such and such'"), information feedback (e.g. "Your opponent can detect when you are about to initiate a kick by the way you raise your eyebrows before execution"), and offering motivational statements without making judgments (e.g. "You are displaying better confidence" or "You are beginning to carry yourself like a champion").

Two behavioral strategies that reflect effective instructional techniques in sport are match simulation and modeling. Match simulation consists of providing practice opportunities that approximate the cognitive and behavioral demands of actual taekwondo competition. Thus, it is important the athletes practice their martial arts skills under conditions that closely approximate the actual competitive event. Modeling is the instructional technique of requiring competitors to observe high-quality competition, while alerting the observers to detect and remember the proper use of particular techniques (e.g. "Kim, watch the performer's foot movement when approaching his opponent").

Developing a Mental Plan

A mental plan is a pre-determined set of psychological and behavioral routines that will be carried out within 24 hours of the competition. Established authors and practitioners in sport psychology such as Loehr (1982), Bull et al. (1996), Orlick (1986) and Weinberg (2002) have espoused the need to develop consistent rituals prior to competition to overcome unexpected problems, maintain consistency in mental preparation from event to event, and to control both positive (e.g. excitement, enthusiasm, confidence) and negative emotions (e.g. fear, anxiety, self-doubt), and retain desirable thought processes (e.g. concentration, focused attention, rehearsal). Mental plans also enhance self-control, the feelings associated with regulating proper habits, what Loehr (1982) calls "positive rituals", rather than allow external events to distract the athlete and impede proper preparation. Mental plans are essential in martial arts competition (Park & Seabourne, 1997).

As discussed earlier in the pre-match section, Bull et al. (1996) and Orlick (1986) have developed their own forms of mental plans. In general, mental plans consist of engaging in pre-planned thoughts and actions prior to the competition, with back-up plans if unanticipated barriers are experienced. The athlete develops these thoughts and actions as part of their training program, and master them to the point where they become automatic on the day of competition. The mental plan's objectives prior to competition are to optimize psychological readiness (e.g. confidence, self-control, concentration) and to regulate emotions (e.g. state anxiety, arousal, aggression). For example, heightened state anxiety is normal—even desirable in moderate amounts—prior to sport competition. However, anxiety can actually improve performance if these feelings are interpreted as facilitative and challenging, rather than as threatening and disabling. The disposition of self-control and making challenge appraisals of the competitive event will greatly promote the desirable interpretations of anxious feelings. The goal of every taekwondo athlete is to ensure that desirable thoughts, feelings and emotions are regulated prior to the event through proper mental preparation and developing a mental plan. In the mental plan, athletes answer these questions: "What will I think and when will I think it?" "What will I do and when will I do it?"

Orlick (1986) suggests that the mental plan should have pre-event, event, and post-event components. *Pre-event* strategies include positive self-suggestions, such as "I have prepared extremely well for this match", "I am capable of adapting to anything my opponent does" and "I am ready; I am at my best; let's do it!" Emotions remain calm and in control.

The night before the match, determine the time to go to sleep and awaken, the time and content of meals, thoughts on the day of the match ("I feel good about my preparation; I'm ready"), and use mental imagery in executing your match performance plan. The *event* focus plan includes the way you will approach your opponent (e.g. "At the start, I will establish my position, determine when and how to initiate movement, and how I will react to the opponent's actions"), what occurs early in the match (e.g. "I will start slowly, then build speed and assertiveness, letting my opponent exert himself and tire early"), middle of the match (e.g. "Keep going; apply pressure; get aggressive"), later in the match (e.g. "I will execute a new strategy that will surprise my opponent", "I feel good; my fatigue is under control"), and at the match's end (e.g. "Push hard, give it 100 per cent, take advantage of my opponent's fatigue").

An effective mental plan also includes "plan B" in which the athlete is capable of responding capably to unanticipated events, such as an opponent's use of a surprising strategy or simply experiencing bad luck (e.g. "My opponent guessed my strategy correctly" or "I slipped").

Finally, the mental plan includes pre-determined thoughts and actions following the event, the *refocusing plan*. Very poor results can be forgotten; however, it is important for the martial arts competitor to reflect on the match's high points and the competitor's strengths, as well as the match's low points and the areas of performance that did not go as anticipated. Issues for post-event analysis might include: "What were the factors that contributed to my *victory/success*?" "To what do I attribute my success? High effort? Great preparation? Good skills? A weak opponent? Good luck?" "To what do I attribute my *loss/failure* to meet performance expectations? Was I too confident? Were my opponent's skills superior to mine? Was I the better competitor but was I just unlucky?"

APPLIED SPORT PSYCHOLOGY DURING COMPETITION

The competitive event possesses unique characteristics and factors that can cause heightened stress, perceived pressure and anxiety. Many athletes with whom I've consulted over the years suffer their greatest psychological discomfort at the competition when their experiences are completely different on the day of competition than on other days. The psychology of competition preparation concerns developing a mental plan—a routine of thoughts and actions—that allows the performer to feel comfortable and secure prior to the event. The performer's psychological characteristics at the event facilitate the pre-competition use of cognitive and behavioral strategies.

Cognitive Strategies

What types of thoughts are best *during* taekwondo competition, that foster desirable thoughts, feelings and emotions? This is a difficult question because the mental and physical demands of this sport are so extreme. Because cognitive strategies take time to implement, sometimes using a mental skill or applying the mental skill incorrectly can slow information processing (e.g. detecting, perceiving, planning, decision-making, reacting and performing), thereby harming rather than helping performance efficiency. However, there are a few mental skills that, if practiced and applied carefully, should help information processing and subsequent performance.

Reduced cognitive (level 1) processing. In general, martial arts combat is performed at a speed that precludes too much information processing. Thoughts usually occur prior to, not during, movement execution. Typically, there is a performance strategy plan prior to beginning the match, usually based on the performer's strengths and/or on the opponent's weaknesses. In addition, however, competitors will react to cues that provide information about the opponent's next move.

Heightened autonomous (level 3) processing. The speed at which martial arts skills are executed mandates actions and reactions in the virtual absence of thinking. Skilled athletes, in general, and advanced martial arts competitors, in particular, react and execute well-learned movements in the virtual absence of thinking. This is called "autonomous information processing", and separates advanced competitors from their less-skilled counterparts.

Pre-cueing is the detection of stimuli in the environment that can be used to anticipate the initiation, arrival or execution of another stimulus or movement. Pre-cueing improves the martial arts competitor's ability to anticipate the next stimulus or event (e.g. observing the placement of an opponent's hands or bend in the knee joint that informs the observer about the next skill or strategy), leading to faster movement speed.

Cognitive appraisals, discussed earlier, consist of perceiving a situation (e.g. challenging vs. threatening; positive vs. negative) prior to and during competition. Successful martial arts competitors tend to interpret competitive situations as challenging.

Psyching up usually consist of thoughts and actions that increase heart rate, feelings of aggression and a positive mood state. While emotion must be regulated during the match, clearly competitors want to intermittently increase arousal level. Psyching up is usually accomplished through self-statements that have arousal value (e.g. "Lets go" or "Come on, come on").

Positive self-talk (PST) is the use of words, expressed internally, that have positive value and serve to increase confidence and effort, and reduce or manage anxiety (e.g. "I am ready", "I have prepared well"). PST should be used prior to, not during, performance execution because any cognitive activity that reduces the competitor's attentional focus on the task at hand will result in slower, less accurate information processing. Detecting environmental cues—such as the opponent's posture, facial expression, or other physical characteristics—will be inhibited. Therefore, PST serves as a vehicle for maintaining emotional control and confidence; however, it should be avoided once the competitors are within striking distance.

Thought-stopping consists of covertly using the word "stop" immediately upon experiencing unpleasant or negative thoughts. Negative thinking is distracting to the athlete's planning, anticipating and other required cognitions during the match. Thought-stopping is a conscious attempt at preventing the negative thought from persisting. For example, if a competitor feels worried about a successful match or is uncertain about their talent as compared to the opponent, the competitor should self-verbalize "stop" as soon as possible, then focus externally on the task at hand.

Effective coping strategies consist of making conscious attempts at managing stress and anxiety, especially when a stimulus or event has been appraised as unpleasant or negative. Skilled athletes adapt to unpleasant experiences during the match by knowing when to approach cope (e.g. analyzing or confronting the situation) or when to use avoidance coping (e.g. filtering out unpleasant stimuli or refusing to think about them). Usually the speed of martial arts matches mandate an avoidance coping style, since approach coping requires time and attentional resources. Neither time nor attention is available to the athlete during most matches. Skilled competitors "let it go" and move on. For instance, the speed of the match does not allow a competitor to reflect on the causes of performance failure or to analyze their own performance. In most cases, avoidance coping is the preferred technique following a stressful event (e.g. discounting, in which the reasons underlying a stressful event is perceived as unimportant, at least temporarily, and filtering out, where the stressful event is ignored and, therefore, not processed). Approach coping (e.g. thinking about the unpleasant situation, then planning a new strategy, or seeking feedback or information to resolve the situation or to reduce the stressor's intensity) is needed if there is adequate time. An example would be to review one's performance during a timeout, between periods or soon after the match.

Attentional focusing (e.g. internal focusing to improve or maintain desirable thoughts and emotions, or external focusing to ignore unpleasant feelings, eliminate negative self-talk or to focus on the opponent as a source of increased arousal) is another cognitive strategy that can either enhance or inhibit performance depending on the situation. Because an opponent may be standing just inches away, attentional focusing is almost always external during the match, unless the athlete has time to plan and analyze. The need to remain externally focused is the reason state anxiety (i.e. thoughts of worry or threat) is so damaging to high-quality performance in martial arts. Anxious athletes are consumed by their thoughts instead of focusing externally on the task at hand (Bull et al., 1996). Instead of negative thinking, competitors need to ask themselves, "What is my opponent doing? What is his posture indicating about his next move or strategy? How will I react to his next, anticipated move?"

Next, we describe a psychological intervention program for taekwondo, consisting of a series of thoughts and actions called the COPE model.

The COPE Model: A Psycho-behavioral Intervention for Coping with Acute Stress

There are numerous interventions published in the sport psychology literature that incorporate the use of selected cognitive and behavioral strategies, sometimes performed in a particular sequence, that facilitate sports performance. One intervention that has particular implications in martial arts competition is the COPE model (Anshel, 1991). The model consists of a series of four psychobehavioral processes in response to stressful events experienced during competition. The rapid and structured nature of this model is compatible with the cognitive and behavioral demands of martial arts. The model consists of four processes after experiencing a sudden stressful event during competition. These are: Controlling emotions (C), Organizing input (O), Planning the next response (P), and then quickly Executing the next task or skill (E).

Controlling emotions consists of regaining composure by taking a deep breath, using positive self-talk ("It's OK; just relax"; "Stay with it"; "settle down"), and regaining control of the situation by taking responsibility for the unpleasant event (mental toughness). Organizing input consists of separating meaningful from non-meaningful information. Sport competition is filled with visual and auditory distractions, much of which is irrelevant to the task at hand. Athletes must learn to filter out input that does not lend itself to meeting performance demands and should be ignored. Other visual and auditory cues and pre-cues, however, should receive the competitor's optimal attention and be quickly incorporated into the decision-making (planning) process. Planning consists of taking available information, then quickly deciding how to meet subsequent task demands. Finally, the competitor is required to execute the skill at optimal effort with minimal thinking. The model has been validated in competitive tennis (Anshel, 1991), in teaching athletes the proper use of selected thoughts and actions in their proper sequence to overcome the unpleasant effects of experiencing stressful events during the contest. Features of the COPE model appear to be compatible with the performance demands of martial arts (Park & Seabourne, 1997).

An example of applying the COPE model in martial arts might be enacted after experiencing a temporary performance failure (e.g. points scored against the competitor or being temporarily disadvantaged). The competitor would take a deep breath and regain composure (C); focus their attention on the most relevant features of the competitive environment (e.g. the opponent's location and gestures, while ignoring stimuli, information, and events deemed unimportant (O); quickly—within seconds—regain composure and plan the next strategy—the plan of attack (P); and finally, execute (E) the plan as soon as the situation warrants. Allowing too much time to accumulate between planning and its execution allows negative thinking (e.g. self-doubt, worry, hesitation) to contaminate the needed rapid, automatic execution of skills.

Martial arts require the rapid collection of information, sorting information into important and unimportant categories, analyzing the information about future events, selecting appropriate action, then executing the chosen action quickly (Chung & Lee, 1994). The series of cognitive and behavioral processes described by Chung and Lee accurately fits the COPE model's components.

POST-COMPETITION APPLIED SPORT PSYCHOLOGY

After the competition, the successful martial arts athlete uses selected cognitive and behavioral techniques that maintain motivation and improve skills and strategies. This section addresses the types of thoughts and actions that martial arts performers should address after the event—post-event cognitions.

Accurate Causal Attributions

Making accurate causal attributions in explaining the reasons for success or failure is a known approach to learn from mistakes, reinforce successes and to maintain long-term intrinsic motivation. The martial arts competitor should have a balanced view of the event, referred to as "accurate causal attributions", to enhance intrinsic motivation and persistence in proper training and future improved performance. Explanations of the causes from performance outcomes have great motivation value—or, conversely, can lead to heightened demotivation, low perceived competence and feelings of helplessness. For example, the competitor will not necessarily accept full responsibility after defeat (i.e. not conclude that defeat was due to low ability or low effort). Instead, a defeat may be due to the opponent's superiority or to bad luck. However, at the elite level, martial arts athletes may also conclude that more vigorous training—including mental training—is necessary to improve the chance of success. Thus, if success is achieved, the competitor should attribute this desirable outcome to high ability, effort and intense training. It is important for all athletes and their coaches to acknowledge achievements with positive social reinforcement. This includes recognizing good effort and superb skills in meeting performance goals.

Post-competition (Skill) Analysis

Elite martial arts competitors examine the positive aspects of the event, what was achieved, what was learned, what factors contributed to success or failure and what must be practiced in the future (Winkle & Ozmun, 2003). Perhaps most important is that, based on the results of the competitive event, the athletes conclude they greatly benefited from the competition—a perception that is confirmed by their coach, a concept called "making accurate causal attributions". In other words, explaining the causes of performance outcomes should have high motivational value. The process of self-examination after the event is similar to a concept called the "complete participant" in which "after the event, the participant becomes the researcher and documents what happened" (Karp, 1989, p. 412). In this case, the competitor becomes the observer and documents what occurred during the event using quantitative data, if possible. The competitor may want to obtain post-competition instructional feedback by dividing the event into time segments, examining performance strengths and weaknesses during the event, or soliciting input from informed observers such as coaches or teammates.

Favorable Social Comparisons

One flaw in post-competitive thought processes is the athlete's propensity to compare his or her performance with unrealistically high standards or superior opponents. Success in martial arts is enhanced when the athlete acknowledges improvement, both on sub-skills as well as overall performance quality. Martial arts competitors do not compare their skills against far superior opponents but rather, make fair judgments against opponents with skills that approximate the competitor's skill level. Competitors also examine the ways in which their own skills have improved over time—*intra*-individual rather than inter-individual comparisons.

Renewed Optimism

Successful competition is not a sprint but rather, a marathon of acknowledging ongoing successes and failures. To maintain intrinsic motivation (enjoyment, pleasure) and to persist at training and learning, it is essential that competitors feel renewed optimism after the match (Durand-Bush & Salmela, 2002). This means making self-judgments about the match's outcomes in a fair and balanced manner, acknowledging the gains and benefits, as well as the difficulties and disappointments from the previous event. Competitors want to continue to set and attempt to meet challenging personal goals and avoid self-defeating thoughts and conclusions (e.g. "I'm not good enough" or "I'll never get better"). Knowing what can be learned from the previous event and how one can improve are characteristics that describe successful martial arts competitors.

Adaptive Coping

Some competitive events will end with physical and mental discomfort. Future success in martial arts depends on adapting to unpleasant experiences, or "storms", in the parlance of Loehr and Schwartz (2003). At times, this will mean moving on and discounting the importance of previous unsuccessful outcomes. At other times, it will be best to analyze the event, acknowledging successes and improvement, as well as failures and areas that require further practice. This process is best accomplished in the presence of the coach or other trained observers (Pensgaard & Duda, 2002).

SUMMARY

Martial arts are a very ancient and honored type of sport from Asia consisting of many styles, each with its own history and set of skills. It is a form of competition that requires extensive use of mental skills—a true mind/body experience. Successful martial arts athletes bring to their match selected dispositions (e.g. optimism, confidence, self-control, assertiveness, high perceived competence) and cognitive strategies (e.g. effective coping skills, manageable anxiety level, optimal arousal, among others), and a mental plan about one's thoughts ("What will I think and when will I think it?") and actions ("What will I do and when will I do it?") prior to and during the event that allow the competitor to focus on the present situation. Perhaps the key general strategy for martial arts performers is to feel mastery over their mental plan prior to the contest, and to be able to execute that plan—or "plan B" (the back-up plan) – with minimal disruption. The other cognitive and behavioral strategies will "kick in" automatically. On the other hand, it is imperative that martial arts athletes are not "paralyzed" by using so many mental skills that they stop acting and reacting automatically. Controlling emotions and speed of movement are essential components of success in this sport. Competitors who use mental skills properly will have a clear advantage over their opponent.

REFERENCES

Anshel, M.H. (1991). Toward validation of the COPE model: strategies for acute stress inoculation in sport. *International Journal of Sport Psychology, 21*, 24–39.

Anshel, M.H. (1995). Examination of self-regulatory characteristics and behavioral tendencies of elite and non-elite male Australian swimmers. *Australian Psychologist, 25*, 78–83.

Anshel, M.H. (2003). *Sport Psychology: From Theory to Practice* (4th edn). San Francisco, CA: Benjamin-Cummings.

Anshel, M.H., Kim, K.-W., Kim, B.-H., Chang, K.-J. & Eom, H.-J. (2001). A model for coping with stressful events in sport: theory, application, and future directions. *International Journal of Sport Psychology, 32*, 43–75.

Birkel, D.A. (1998, Nov./Dec.). Activities for the older adult: integration of the body and the mind. *Journal of Physical Education, Recreation, and Dance*, 69, 23–29.

Bull, S.J., Albinson, J.G. & Shambrook, C.J. (1996). *The Mental Game Plan: Getting Psyched for Sport*. Eastbourne, England: Sports Dynamics.

Chapman, C., Lane, A.M., Brierly, J.H. & Terry, P.C. (1997). Anxiety, self-confidence and performance in Tae Kwondo. *Perceptual and Motor Skills, 85*, 1275–1278.

Chung, K.H. & Lee, K.M. (1994). *Taekwondo Kyorugi: Olympic Style Sparring*. Hartford, CT: Turtle Press.

Cunningham, S.R. (25 September 25 1998). Judo: morality and the physical art. Presentation at the 1998 Coaches Conference, Olympic Training Center, Colorado Springs, CO.

Deaner, H. & Silva, J.M. (2002). Personality and sport performance. In J.M. Silva & D.E. Stevens (eds), *Psychological Foundations of Sport* (pp. 48–65). San Francisco: Benjamin-Cummings.

Douris, P., Chinan, A., Steffens, D. & Weiss, S. (2004). Fitness levels of middle aged martial arts practitioners. *British Journal of Sports Medicine, 38*, 143–147.

Durand-Bush, N. & Salmela, J.H. (2002). The development and maintenance of expert athletic performance: perceptions of world and Olympic champions. *Journal of Applied Sport Psychology, 14*, 154–171.

Finkenburg, M.E. (1990). Effect of participation in Taekwondo on college women's self-concept. *Perceptual and Motor Skills, 71*, 891–894.

Foster, Y.A. (1997). Brief aikido training versus karate and gold training and university students' scores on self-esteem, anxiety, and expression of anger. *Perceptual Motor Skills, 84*, 609–610.

Gill, D.L. (1993). Competitiveness and competitive orientation in sport. In R.N. Singer, M. Murphey & L.K. Tennant (eds), *Handbook of Research on Sport Psychology* (pp. 314–327). New York: Macmillan.

Ginott, H. (1965). *Between Parent and Child*. New York: Avon.

Jones, G., Hanton, S. & Connaughton, D. (2002). What is this thing called mental toughness? An investigation of elite sport performers. *Journal of Applied Sport Psychology, 14*, 205–218.

Jones, G., & Swain, A. (1995). Predispositions to experience debilitative and facilitative anxiety in elite and nonelite performers. *The Sport Psychologist, 9*, 201–211.

Karp, G.G. (1989). Participant observation. In P.W. Darst, D.B. Zakrajsek & V.H. Mancini (eds), *Analyzing Physical Education and Sport Instruction* (pp. 411–422). Champaign, IL: Human Kinetics.

Lazarus, R.S. & Folkman, S. (1984). *Stress, Appraisal, and Coping*. New York: Springer.

Loehr, J.E. (1982). *Mental Toughness Training for Sports: Achieving Athletic Excellence*. New York: Penguin.

Loehr, J.E. (1990). *The Mental Game: Winning at Pressure Tennis*. New York: Penguin.

Loehr, J.E. & Schwartz, T. (2003). *The Power of Full Engagement*. New York: Free Press.

Martens, R. (1976). Competitiveness in sports. In F. Landry & W.A.R. Orban (eds), *Physical Activity and Human Well-being* (pp. 323–342). Miami, FL: Symposia Specialists.

Masters, K.S. & Ogles, B.M. (1998). Associative and dissociative cognitive strategies in exercise and running: 20 years later, what do we know? *The Sport Psychologist, 12*, 253–270.

Michaelson, M.T., Ronnenberg, A., Walsh, D. & Linden, P. (2000, Nov./Dec.). Should martial arts be taught in physical education classes? *Journal of Physical Education, Recreation, and Dance, 71*, 12–14.

Mifune, K. (2000). Judo and its masters. *Journal of Combative Sport*, 14–28.

Orlick, T. (1986). *Psyching for Sport*. Champaign, IL: Human Kinetics.

Park, Y.H., & Seabourne, T. (1997). *Taekwondo techniques and tactics*. Champaign, IL: Human Kinetics.

Pensgaard, A.M. & Duda, J.L. (2002). "If we work hard, we can do it": A tale from an Olympic (gold) medallist. *Journal of Applied Sport Psychology, 14*, 219–236.

Rosenbaum, M. (ed.) (1990). *Learned Resourcefulness on Coping Skills, Self-control, and Adaptive Behavior*. New York: Springer.

Savage, J. (1995). *Karate*. Parsippany, NJ: Silver Burdell Press.

Scheier, M.F. & Carver, C.S. (1985). Optimism, coping, and health: assessment and implications of generalized outcome expectancies. *Health Psychology, 4*, 219–247.

Toskovic, N., Blessing, D. & Williford, H. (2002). The effect of experience and gender on cardiovascular and metabolic response with dynamic tae kwon do exercise. *Journal of Strength and Conditioning Research, 16*, 278–285.

Twemlow, S.W. & Sacco, F.C. (1998). Peacekeeping and peacemaking: the conceptual foundations of a plan to reduce violence and improve the quality of life in a midsized community in Jamaica. *Psychiatry, 59*, 156–174.

Twemlow, S.W., Sacco, F.C. & Williams, P. (1996). A clinical and interactionist perspective on the bully-victim-bystander relationship. *Bulletin of the Menninger Clinic, 60*, 296–313.

Vealey, R. (1986). Conceptualization of sport-confidence and competitive orientation: preliminary investigation and instrument development. *Journal of Sport Psychology, 8*, 221–246.

Vealey, R. (1988). Sport-confidence and competitive orientation: an addendum on scoring procedures and gender differences. *Journal of Sport and Exercise Psychology, 10*, 471–478.

Vealey, R. (2002). Personality and sport behavior. In T. Horn (ed.), *Advances in Sport Psychology* (2nd edn; pp. 43–82). Champaign, IL: Human Kinetics.

Wann, D.L. (1997). *Sport Psychology*. New York: Prentice-Hall.

Weinberg, R. (2002). *Tennis: Winning the Mental Game*. Oxford, OH: H.O. Zimman.

Winkle, J.M. & Ozmun, J.C. (2003, April). Martial arts: an exciting addition to the physical education curriculum. *Journal of Physical Education, Recreation, and Dance, 74*, 29–38.

Zinsser, N., Bunker, L. & Williams, J.M. (2001). Cognitive techniques for building confidence and enhancing performance. In J.M. Williams (ed.), *Applied Sport Psychology: Personal Growth to Peak Performance* (4th edn; pp. 284–311). Mountain View, CA: Mayfield.

Zivin, G., Hassan, N., DePaula, G., Monti, D.A., Harlan, C., Hossain, K.D. & Patterson, K. (2001). An effective approach to violence prevention: traditional martial arts in middle school. *Adolescence, 36*, 443–160.

CHAPTER 17

Psychological Factors and Mental Skills in Wrestling

Brent S. Rushall

San Diego State University, USA

INTRODUCTION

Wrestling is one of the oldest sports having been part of the ancient Olympic Games and recorded in ancient records of many cultures. There are many societal variants of wrestling (e.g. *sumo* in Japan, *sambo* in Russia, *kushti* in Iran) but freestyle and Graeco-Roman are universal (FILA). An endearing quality of the sport is the nature of its conduct: human against human, often regulated for weight, with combat that simulates a fight for dominance, a primal instinct of the animal kingdom. An undeniable winner is declared when one performer is rendered helpless or judged superior. The structure of the sport is basic in human terms and, therefore, evokes fundamental emotions and directions for behavior.

To compete well, wrestlers have to recognize the threat of the opponent and proceed to overcome that challenge by exploiting weaknesses or errors without creating them in their own performance. A critical momentary error often is the difference between winning and losing a wrestling bout for either combatant. While performing, speed, endurance, power and skill are essential, all being performed under intense and unwavering focused attention. Those characteristics suggest the psychological qualities that are necessary for successful competitive performances in wrestling.

The higher the level of performance, the more important is the role of psychology in the sport. This relationship has been recognized for some time. Rushall and Garvie (1977) reported factors (see Table 17.1) that differentiated freestyle wrestlers who were successful at the Canadian Olympic Trials from those who were not. The test used was sport-specific. That was contrary to a study (Kroll, 1967) that tested collegiate wrestlers using a general personality inventory, rather than a test related to sport, and found no distinguishing personality factors. A series of investigations have continued to reinforce the assertion that psychology contributes to wrestling success (Eklund, 1994; Gould, Eklund & Jackson, 1992; Gould, Weiss & Weinberg, 1981; Halvari, 1983; Highlen & Bennett, 1979; Kermanshah, 1986). Silva, Shultz, Haslam, Martin and Murray (1985) quantified the contributions of psychological and physiological measures in wrestling success. At the 1984 USA Freestyle and

The Sport Psychologist's Handbook: A Guide for Sport-Specific Performance Enhancement.
Edited by Joaquín Dosil. © 2006 John Wiley & Sons, Ltd.

Table 17.1   Dominant psychological characteristics in a national olympic wrestling team when compared to non-qualifiers

1. Are upset if criticized in front of other wrestlers.
2. Prefer to be told privately when they have done something wrong.
3. Do not hold back from criticizing coaches and other athletes.
4. Will make sarcastic remarks to other athletes if they think they deserve it.
5. Will come forward on social occasions.
6. Keep quiet in the presence of coaches and senior wrestlers.
7. Admire parents in all they do associated with wrestling.
8. Show their excitement in voice and manner.
9. If an awkward social mistake is made cannot soon forget it.
10. If they feel that something is wrong will voice an opinion.
11. Would prefer to do things their own way if they consider them best no matter what the coach says.
12. Could train without the coach being present if they had directions for what was to be done.
13. Believe they use up more energy in training than other wrestlers.
14. Spirits are generally high no matter what troubles are met.
15. Learn things quickly.
16. Not upset if shouted at or distracted during a contest.
17. Results of competitions are more important for themselves than for the team.
18. Feel sure they can "pull self together" to deal with unusual circumstances during competitions.
19. Small distractions get on their "nerves" before competing.
20. Tremble and feel sick before competing.
21. Do not feel bad if the team loses and they performed well.
22. Wrestling is considered the most important activity they do.
23. Training effort is about equal to competition effort.
24. Are prepared to train no matter how much time is required.
25. In high training fatigue, can persevere and still keep trying their hardest.
26. Do not prefer playing and having fun at practice.
27. Are always free from vague feelings of ill-health, muscle pains, etc.
28. Always have enough energy when difficulties arise at practice and in competitions.

Source: Rushall, B.S. & Garvie, G. (1977). Psychological characteristics of Canadian Olympic and non-Olympic wrestlers. A paper presented at the Ninth Canadian PsychoMotor Learning and Sport Psychology Symposium, Banff.

Graeco-Roman wrestling trials, they evaluated contestants physiologically for wrestling-specific energy systems and psychologically for traits and pre-competitive states. When the two sets of variables were compared for predictive capacity, psychology discriminated qualifiers from non-qualifiers with 78.1 per cent accuracy while physiology was 60.9 per cent accurate. When the 19 total variables were included in a multiple discriminant function, they accounted for 89.06 per cent of the total variance. In the absence of any further research on high-level wrestlers, it is proposed that psychological variables are more important than energy-system physiological factors. For coaching decisions and training program content at the highest level, an emphasis on psychological training and control would be as important as a physiological orientation. The factors determined in the above studies, although "old", suggest the content of psychological training emphases and training programs.

Taking one giant intellectual step, this writer suggests the following framework for developing mental skills that will assist wrestlers in competitions.

- Unwavering focused attention on one's own performance and that of the opponent.
- Attention to preparatory movements, both real and fake, that allow complex skills to be performed with maximized speed and power.
- A preparation that allows all appropriate resources to be mobilized immediately upon the start of a contest.
- A training that produces overlearned skill development and execution.
- Mental skills that allow for coping with defeats, recovery of composure, recapturing a perception of dominance and maximizing assertive behaviors in contests.

While other characteristics could be described, in the context of this book section, the above features will be explored in greater detail and their relevance for wrestling justified.

PLANNING

Most advanced international training programs for wrestlers, as distinct from time-restricted collegiate wrestling in the USA, follow modern training principles for developing skills, fitness and occasionally mental skills. The basic preparatory training phase focuses on foundational fitness that will support significant volumes of intense training and skill development in the specific training and later phases of an annual plan. Once training becomes specific, it is appropriate to begin introducing appropriate mental skills. The initial emphasis should be on the provision of positive feedback and accommodating individual and group motivational needs. The expansion of motivating experiences and an increase in the frequency of perceived positive events serve as an influential factor that drives wrestlers during this most demanding training phase. Once the pre-competition phase is entered, psychological skills training introduces competitive skills that are practiced most frequently through competition simulations and cognitive behavior modification. Steps in building pre-competition and competition strategies should be introduced with an emphasis on individual decision-making. The content of specific preparation outcomes (e.g. new skills, intensity) should be incorporated into competitive strategies to signal developmental progression in a wrestler's career. If a wrestler senses one year of the sport not showing any advancement on previous years, serious motivational problems can occur. In the competition phase, the detailed practice and modification of pre-contest and contest strategies should be an almost daily activity. In that training phase, the monitoring of each wrester's psychological state and well-being should be frequent and used as an indicator of how *coaching adjustments* should be made.

In the training model briefly described above, a psychological emphasis in training gradually replaces a physiological (conditioning) emphasis, justified by the fact that athletes achieve a conditioned state that cannot be improved upon by further training (Rushall & Pyke, 1991). When maintenance training is entered, the reduction in training volume should be replaced by an even greater emphasis on skill development as well as a concentration on mental skills training (Rushall, 2003).

MENTAL SKILLS TRAINING PROGRAMS

The development of beneficial mental skills training programs is a relatively recent innovation for which many coaches are ill-prepared. World-champion athletes display a common set of behaviors irrespective of their sport, gender or culture (Rushall, 1987, 1995, 1997). One part of a mental skills program should include developing behaviors absent from that repertoire. The other part of the program should involve individual features needed by the athlete and, hopefully, located independently of the coach (Rushall, 2004a). Mental skills training for wrestlers would occur at practice and outside of formal training environments as *homework*.

Mental skills training is often compromised by misconceptions that are rife in sport in general and in particular among traditional and long-established wrestling coaches. Some fallacies and a realistic description for each are as follows.

1. *Producing psychological effects is quick and easy.* To improve an athlete's behavior and mental skills, a process that is equally demanding as that appropriated for physical skill and physiological state development is required.
2. *Knowing what to do is the secret of effective psychology.* Simply knowing what to do, usually communicated through single or at most a few instructions, is insufficient for mental skill development or behavior changes. Only when developmental exercises that employ learning principles are followed should one expect specific psychological changes to occur.
3. *Mental skill development does not require the same amount of effort or time as do physical skill development and physiological conditioning.* Mental skill training programs require at least a similar amount of time allocation, effort expenditure and practice in real-life situations as do the other training content and emphases.

The responsibility of and the role played by the athlete are extremely important in mental skills training that employs an exercise approach to learning and development.

1. The athlete must want to perform the exercises.
2. Each exercise must be completed fully.
3. The athlete must be concerned with perfection when completing an exercise.

The content of a mental skills program for athletes depends upon the targeted athletes and each of their existing skills. With young wrestlers, it usually is appropriate to develop a multi-year program that eventually covers all the important areas that directly affect performance and motivation (see Table 17.2). That proceeds even though there might be some duplication (relearning) of existing mental skills. With advanced athletes, personalized programs normally are developed to introduce new or strengthen weak mental skills while periodically reinforcing existing desirable characteristics (see Table 17.3 for an example). The latter feature is considered to be an insurance strategy to prevent good skills disappearing from an athlete's mental skills repertoire.

Table 17.2   A suggested order of exercises for a total mental skills development program in wrestlers

---

Establishing attitudinal and motivational behaviors
   Purpose: to increase the intrinsic positive value of the sporting experience
   • Increasing the intensity of self-reinforcement
   • Positive interactions with others
   • Stopping negative thinking
   • Positive imagery

Table 17.2   *(Continued)*

Purpose: to establish a goal-oriented focus for sporting activity elements
   - Setting and evaluating personal activity goals
   - Setting group training goals

Purpose: to establish a constant orientation to the importance of sport participation
   - Establishment of a daily positive focus
   - Daily positive recall
   - Periodic self-commitment

Important skills

Purpose: to learn imagery that will enhance performance
   - Learning imagery control and vividness
   - Sensory recall training
   - Movement imagery training
   - Performance enhancement imagery

Purpose: to learn relaxation and self-control
   - Learning to relax: stages 1, 2, and 3
   - Relaxation and positive imagery for self-concept
   - Relaxation and positive imagery of an activity
   - Localized relaxation
   - Sleep, rest, and relaxation

Competition psychology

Purpose: to develop a basic competition strategy
   - Segmenting a performance
   - Task-relevant thought content
   - Mood words content
   - Positive self-talk
   - Special considerations
   - Integrating a basic strategy
   - Competition goal-setting

Purpose: to develop competition preparation skills to facilitate the use of strategies.
   - Waking with a positive attitude
   - Trouble free planning
   - Establishing contest site mind-sets
   - Contest build-up routine
   - Learning and using precompetition strategies

Purpose: to refine and embellish competition strategies
   - Coping behaviors for competitions
   - Intensification skill
   - Start segment
   - Debriefing a performance

Long-term orientation

Purpose: to establish a goal structure that will orient performance and participation for a long time
   - Setting sporting career goals
   - Setting relatively long-term goals
   - Setting performance goals
   - Setting performance progress goals

Group orientation

Purpose: to establish a team-spirit atmosphere in the environment
   - Structuring a leadership group
   - Implementing a decision-making procedure
   - Determining rules, punishments, procedures, activities, and actions

Source: Adapted from Rushall, B.S. (2003). *Mental Skills Training for Sports* (3rd edn). Spring Valley, CA: Sport Science Associates.

Table 17.3 A set of mental skills training exercises used for an experienced wrestler who needed to eradicate obsessive negative thinking

Problem	Suggested exercises
Negative thinking/ depression	Stopping negative thinking Increasing the intensity of self-reinforcement Setting and evaluating personal activity goals Daily positive recall

Source: Adapted from Rushall, B.S. (2003). *Mental Skills Training for Sports* (3rd edn). Spring Valley, CA: Sport Science Associates.

The standard of performer and the number of wrestlers will largely determine what elements of a mental skills training program are developed and how it is implemented. It is this writer's opinion that the judgments of even the most competent coaches lack sufficient objectivity to determine a very best program. Familiarity with the athletes, personal involvement in the program and restricted frames of reference of and knowledge about things psychological frequently lead to errors of omission of important factors that should be included for an optimal mental skills program for highly-motivated wrestlers. There are many *psychological tests* available that purport to supply information that will benefit coaching and athletes' performances. It is not within the scope of this chapter to discuss the merits of psychological tests for wrestling despite the author having a proprietary interest in a psychological testing service (Rushall, 2004b).

PSYCHOLOGY AT WRESTLING TRAINING

Psychological elements that should be evident at wrestling training and practices are similar to those required of other sports that have a dominant skill basis and intense work level. Of equal importance are motivational factors to produce full and dedicated participation and performance feedback that produces knowledge of results causing continual skill improvements. The coach at wrestling practice should have little in common with the coach at competitions. The setting elements, coaching skills and athlete-handling techniques are vastly different in the two environments. A coach who fails to recognize these differences will not be very effective.

The elements of a motivated environment are common among many sports and human endeavors. The principles and foci of producing a motivated setting are well-established with only the specific content differentiating the wrestling situation. The structure of a motivated wrestling program involves six elements.

Achievement

Wrestling achievement involves more than competitive results. The social, task and developmental aspects of the practice setting have to be accommodated. Some important achievement areas worthy of emphasis are listed below.

1. *Performance* This is the traditional focus for providing rewards and social recognition. If reinforcements are applied according to sound behavior modification principles, then performance changes can be rapid and reliable. However, the random assignment of modest reinforcements, usually emanating from the coach, has little effect on improving wrestlers' performances. A coach at practice has to be a skilled behavior modifier to be effective. In order to determine skill and mental skill improvements, objective measures need to be provided. For example, for developing skill, a video recording of a wrestler's performance can be analyzed by both the coach and athlete together with the athlete determining the accuracy and quality of the coach's analysis. Feedback from analysis sessions can be used to formulate short-term performance improvement goals. The frequent use of sport-specific psychological tests can provide knowledge of progress toward mental skills development.
2. *Effort level* The demands of competitive wrestling require continual high to maximum levels of exertion. High-intensity physical training produces frequent fatigue and fatigue inhibits skill and psychological learning. The role of judicious beneficial rest for recovery, restoration and overcompensation is critical for producing highly productive training experiences. The conscious efforts of wrestlers to sustain high-intensity work should be reinforced by independent measures and sources of social rewards in the practice setting.
3. *Work volume* Associated with effort is the volume of work performed in a training session and the number of practices attended within each microcycle. While volumes of hard work are often desirable, a coach needs to monitor an athlete's potential for overreaching and reinforce sensible rest and recovery as well as work.
4. *Skill level* Skill is the critical factor in wrestling success. Methods of indicating improvements in skill factors across a full repertoire of wrestling "moves" need to be established. A coach's opinions are insufficient and of low-influence potential to be of great significance. Either self- or peer-evaluations of improvements as achievement have a greater effect on serious athletes (Rushall, 1982, 1991a). A change in the behavior of most wrestling coaches will be the need to emphasize elements of skills that are done well rather than stressing "errors" and "weaknesses" in athletes' skill attempts or level of skill competence.
5. *Task execution* As well as training tasks and compliance, other activities and behaviors are necessary for a practice setting to function well. When athletes facilitate smooth organization and function, such as erecting and dismantling equipment, punctual behaviors and assisting with coaching, those behaviors should be reinforced rather than being taken for granted.
6. *Performer interaction* A strong source of motivation and social influence and facilitation is the positive and constructive interaction between wrestlers. A coach should reinforce inter-athlete behaviors that have desirable qualities.

Observable and measurable criteria need to be established so achievements in these fields can be objectively recognized and rewarded.

Recognition

Social reinforcement from a variety of sources enhances the quality and volume of motivational experiences. Not all individuals in a wrestler's life have the same reinforcing impact.

The strongest source of reinforcement is the wrestler themself. Next strongest source is other wrestlers (Rushall, 1991a). Consequently, the interactions and reactions of other wrestlers to an individual's work will have a significant influence on important wrestling behaviors. The third tier of recognition influence on wrestling motivation is parents and significant others, and usually the coach is a close fourth. Not many wrestling or sport coaches enjoy hearing of their "diminished potential for effect" but reality deems this so.

The more sources of social recognition and the greater the frequency of consequential reactions available in a sporting environment, the greater will be an athlete's motivation. The wrestling coach should engineer situations where:

- The wrestler is encouraged to self-reinforce all aspects of achievement and participation;
- Other wrestlers reinforce skill elements, effort levels, work volume, and participation behaviors;
- Parents and significant others are informed of progress and specific positive behaviors so they can augment practice-setting reinforcement; and
- The coach's own behavior becomes predominantly positive with wrestler's behaviors that need to be changed being disguised as "opportunities to improve".

An environment rich in positive behavioral consequences will motivate an athlete to participate with greater quality and volume.

Responsibility

Athletes need to develop from a coach-dependent relationship, which usually describes the beginner-level association, to a coach-independent relationship at the elite level. As a wrestler matures in experience in the sport, activities and responsibilities should be developed and assigned that publicly imply self-reliance. Some possible activities that promote responsibility are self-monitoring of skill and training activities, coaching assistance, assisting in club organization, program input, self-control over important activities and goal-setting of all types.

Advancement

Advancement is the elevation of status in the activities associated with wrestling over a long period of time. There is a need to define terminal or ultimate status that results from achievement. It is related not only to performance but is also related to other aspects of the sporting experience as listed above under "Achievement". Advancement is long-term, very gradual, should not be particularly easy and above all should be challenging.

Growth

Growth concerns the expansion of a wrestler's participation. It leads to the concept of a career in the sport. Growth is bi-dimensional. If implemented correctly, the scope of involvements and activities broadens the longer the athlete stays in the sport. Leadership roles, assisting the coaching staff and mentoring younger wrestlers are examples of widening responsibilities. Growth can also occur vertically with the attainment of performance statuses (e.g. senior, senior national, national team) and responsibilities outside of the home club (e.g. national team vice-captain). Within the home environment, growth experiences might be extending and increasing knowledge and involvement in coaching, particularly of younger performers, attaining officials' qualifications and participating in more and varied events (e.g. different styles, and possible sports—judo and wrestling often go together). From a training viewpoint, growth is manifested in the elevation of training standards and formats so they become more complex, individualized and academic.

The Activity Itself

The final element of a full-scope motivational program for wrestling involves the activity itself. The physical tasks of practices must have features that are conducive to continued participation. Some features that enrich physical elements of training are:

- A self-set goal for every training unit.
- A method of evaluation to provide feedback for every training unit.
- The activities undertaken must be purposeful and have obvious relevance (specificity) for wrestling.
- Most activity outcomes should be positive.
- Variety in training content should produce novelty and prevent boredom.
- Practice should be in tolerable amounts.
- Tasks and practice elements need to be acceptable to the wrestler.

Wrestlers have to want to and accept the need to do physical tasks. There should be some intrinsic or extrinsic assessments or reasons for repeating and/or intensifying personal application to the work of training.

The six features of motivation discussed above produce a wide and rich source of experiences in the activities of wrestling and in the practice setting. It is a "full-picture" concept of motivation and relies heavily on variety in activities and experiences, the frequent occurrence of positive reinforcement, purposeful or goal-directed behaviors, and an adaptation to maximize the experience for each individual. Anything less than a total motivational environment will reduce participants' application to the sport as well as diminish the total (intrinsic and extrinsic) motivation of the experience.

The above discussion covered elements that should be involved in the conduct of a wrestling program. Of further importance is the effectiveness of the coach. It is worthwhile to consider the important activities that could be performed by a coach at training sessions. Descriptions of effective behaviors were supplied by Rushall (1994). The Practice Session Coaching Performance Assessment Form (PSCPAF) contains definitions of 20 behaviors that coaches should endeavor to perform at a practice session (see Table 17.4 for definitions). Rather than repeat the definitions here, the reader is encouraged to study the definitions and attempt to implement as many of the described behaviors as possible at every wrestling practice.

Table 17.4 Definitions of effective coaching behaviors that should be performed at a wrestling practice

Definitions of desirable behaviors evaluated on the Practice Session Coaching Performance Assessment Form (PSCPAF).

1. **The majority of coaching time was spent on technique/tactics instruction.** The most important factor in sports from an athlete's viewpoint is improvement in technical features. It is necessary for coaches to concentrate on providing this type of information. This contrasts with the more usual coaching emphasis on effort. To accomplish this behavior, the coaching focus should be on skill (technical) features of performance and/or tactical factors for competitive situations. For a "yes" to be recorded, this must have been the most frequently exhibited category of behavior in the coaching session.
2. **Individual interactions occurred more often than group instruction.** The coach interacted with athletes on an individual basis more frequently than they performed group instructional behaviors.
3. **More time was spent coaching than in watching/managing.** The major activity of the coach was instructing. Long periods of observation or engagement in organizational/management tasks should not have been evident. Coach participation in the activity (e.g. playing a game, participating as a team member in a scrimmage) for any extended length of time should not have occurred.
4. **Positive reinforcement occurred much more frequently than correction/direction.** The coach reacted to athlete behaviors in a positive and encouraging manner. Where possible, the reactions should have occurred immediately after activity-related behaviors rather than being delayed. Few instances of negative feedback (e.g. an emphasis on erroneous technical features) should be evident.
5. **All areas of the practice environment were supervised satisfactorily.** The coach moved around the training area and provided responsible supervision.
6. **Demonstrations/models were used appropriately.** Verbal instruction was supplemented with demonstrations by the coach or team participants, and/or teaching aids were used to provide added information.
7. **Commented to every athlete about the quality of and performances in the practice session.** The coach communicated to each athlete a general assessment of their performance quality for the total session.
8. **Interacted individually with every athlete during the session.** The coach interacted in a meaningful way with every athlete on an individual basis.
9. **Monitored and ensured that no athlete experienced excessive fatigue.** The level of fatigue that was exhibited by athletes was monitored. No athlete was expected to continue to perform when both technique and performance levels had deteriorated. Continued participation when technique and performance are both poor provides no beneficial training experience.
10. **Provided variety in the training stimuli in the program.** There was sufficient variety in the training program to maintain the interest of all athletes for the total practice session.
11. **Athletes established goals for each important training item.** Before each important training item, athletes were encouraged/instructed to set performance goals for that item so that they could evaluate whether they did or did not perform to a self-set level of accomplishment.
12. **Athletes were asked or were given an opportunity to evaluate whether they achieved or did not achieve their self-set goals for each important training item.** After important training items, the athletes were given an opportunity to self-evaluate if they achieved their self-set goals.
13. **Asked each athlete's opinion of how they felt.** The coach asked each athlete for a general indication of how they felt during the practice session. This behavior is normally exhibited at the end of or after the session.
14. **Asked each athlete's perception of their performance quality.** The coach asked each athlete for a general indication of the quality of their performance in the practice session. This behavior is normally exhibited after the last important training segment.

Table 17.4   *(Continued)*

15. **The training session content was in accord with a sound training plan.** The activities and goals of the training session were appropriate for a particular stage of a periodized training plan and were determined well before the practice session. The coach did not devise the content as the session started or progressed.
16. **Training session content was made known to the athletes prior to the start of practice.** Before the practice started, athletes were told what would occur in the session. This information allowed the athletes to allocate their resources and efforts appropriately.
17. **Athletes were kept busy all the time.** No period occurred where athletes wasted time by being idle or doing activities that were not related to the sport.
18. **Athletes were shown videos of themselves for technique analysis.** Athletes were able to view videos of their performances and engage in some form of self-analysis which may or may not have been complemented by the coach's input.
19. **Directions and communications were based on sound reasoning and were well thought-out.** The coach only offered appraisals and directions that were based on careful consideration. No communications were made impulsively or were based on unfounded beliefs.
20. **Each athlete left practice with a positive feeling.** As the athletes left the practice arena, they gave the impression of positive feelings indicating that they willingly wanted to return for the next practice session.

Source: Adapted from Rushall, B.S. (1994). *The Assessment of Coaching Effectiveness.* Spring Valley, CA: Sports Science Associates.

PSYCHOLOGY AT MAJOR WRESTLING COMPETITIONS

The mental activities of wrestlers in competition settings have been reported as a differentiating factor between successful and unsuccessful performers, the difference being more important the higher the level of competition (Eklund, 1994; Horton & Shelton, 1978). Rushall (1975) described the basic factors involved in a "mind training" program of mental skills for the Canadian Freestyle Wrestling Team. Over the years, the important elements of competition thinking have been refined into mental skills training exercises (originally Rushall, 1976, and now Rushall, 2003).

The time to begin preparations for an important competition varies with the individual. Serious competitions should be a measure of the effectiveness of training that has occurred since the previous seasonal unloading phase of the annual plan. Not only should wise physical, skill and mental training have advanced the performance potential of an athlete, but the physical and mental activities preceding a major competition should be different from those that preceded in-season competitions.

In-season competitions are mostly used to evaluate and experiment with skill and mental strategies, physical conditioned state and overall competition-setting management. Most frequently, participation is unaccompanied by any reduction in workload or training frequency. No discussion of in-season competition conduct will be entertained here.

The Competition Phase

The competition phase of a training plan recognizes the need for an altered practice plan. It involves at least a microcycle of physical unloading (*tapering*), cautious programming that diminishes the possibility of injury, an increased emphasis on the continued development and practice of pre-competition and competition strategy elements, and a change in wrestling-environment atmosphere that promotes positiveness, a heightened feeling of well-being and confidence, and a perception of exceptional wrestling competence. The duration of this first part of the competition phase will be particularly individual and modified by the trained and skill state of the athlete when entering it. It is beyond the scope of this discussion to discuss this very variable phase of competition-phase programming.

Pre-competition Strategies

Pre-competition strategies concern all the behaviors and thoughts that occur away from and at the competition site before a wrestling tournament. The usual duration that is considered is one day, that being the day of the competition. However, some athletes start their final preparations and approach to competing as much as two days before a very important contest. In that case, the contents of the following sections should be extended and repeated to consume the total period between an individual's first instance of contest-awareness and the contest start.

Pre-competition strategies are needed to prepare a wrestler to start a contest with the best form of competition readiness. The main concerns of these preparations are to:

- minimize the effects of distractions on an athlete's appraisal of the preparations for the contest;
- focus attention on the contest;
- eliminate negative thinking and uncertainty;
- attain the best form of control so that readiness will peak at the start of the contest; and
- produce a feeling of controlled assertiveness that will energize the initiation of the contest.

The development and refinement of pre-competition strategies should produce a relatively standardized form of pre-competition activities. A desirable state should be attained whereby maximum skill precision and effort allocation occurs at the start of each match. By knowing what has to be done to produce the best form of competition readiness, an athlete should expect to perform consistently well in important tournaments. Pre-competition strategies need to be individualized so a performer can follow a preparation that is appropriate and designed to produce the best possible "starting state".

The coach has a vital role in the pre-competition stage. No new information should be introduced, activities should facilitate each wrestler's preparations, and negative or emotional outbursts should not occur. As athletes increase their readiness states to compete, their ability to assimilate, understand or even attend to coaching instructions diminishes greatly. The only effect that pep talks or team meetings can have on performers when they are conducted immediately before a competition start is distraction or disruption. The higher the caliber of an athlete, the earlier the preparatory procedure should begin.

A wrestler's pre-competition preparation should conclude with a directed and determined set of activities which allows an entry into the competitive arena in the best possible readiness state. This requirement will have to be contemplated against sporting traditions and rituals which were established before there was a clear understanding of what is required to prepare for a contest in the best manner possible. The essence of the final stages of a pre-competition procedure is that the athlete develops a feeling of total control in a positive atmosphere.

What is described in this section will require some drastic alterations in pre-competition procedures and emphases for many athletes. It is this writer's contention that what happens before a contest is as important as that which occurs during a contest. Competitions can be won or lost by what occurs before they start. It is necessary to structure thoughts and participate in activities that will reduce the likelihood of disruptive events. The production of predictable and effective activities that will produce the best state of readiness in an athlete should be maximized.

The development of pre-competition strategies requires time and practice. They have to be constructed, experimented with and learned. Their practice should be part of the wrestling training program.

Pre-competition strategies contain all the thoughts and actions that need to take place to prepare a wrestler to enter a bout with the best form of mental and physical readiness. The main outcomes of these preparations are to:

- Minimize the effects of distractions on the athlete's appraisal of preparations for competing.
- Focus the wrestler's attention on the overall competition.
- Control the development of contest readiness so that it will peak at the start of each bout.

The content of this discussion is limited to actions on the day of a tournament. It recognizes that some athletes start their preparations before then. Pre-competition readiness is best formulated by developing formal detailed strategies (Rushall, 2003). The pre-competition strategy is divided into the phase of being away from the competition venue (e.g. at the hotel, on the team bus, traveling to the tournament site), and what occurs at the actual venue.

Away from the Tournament Site

Wake-up procedures How one feels when waking in the morning markedly affects a person's perceptions, mood and attributes of that day's events. When waking on the morning of a tournament day, initial perceptions should be positive and enjoyable. If perceptions were negative, the rest of the day's events would be biased towards a negative appraisal. That negative "attitude" would have detrimental effects on match preparations and subsequent performances.

Individuals can learn to wake positively after a night's sleep or long rest. The aim of a wake-up procedure is to establish a positive mood in the athlete so that ensuing events are likely to be interpreted positively. Some features of a positive wake-up procedure are:

- *Wake slowly* Sudden changes in posture and activity levels have shock potential. Slow waking, where one lies in bed and controls the sensations that are experienced, can be the basis for producing a positive mood.
- *Engage in positive self-talk* The first thoughts that are recognized are important for mood. The wrestler should self-talk with positive statements, such as "I feel great", "It's going to be a great day", "The sleep felt good" and "Now I am fully rested". A repertoire of positive statements aimed at producing a positive attitude for use in the waking procedure should be developed.

- *Stretch slowly* While still in bed, a slow stretching routine that exercises as many muscles as possible should be performed. The intensity of such activities should not be great. It should be at a level that produces pleasurable feelings.
- *Smile* The act of smiling is conditioned to pleasant feelings and associations. Thus, simply smiling while waking will add to the development of a positive attitude.
- *Feel good* The aim of the process is to feel good. The above activities should be continued until a positive attitude is achieved.

Waking and deliberately developing a positive attitude can be learned. Normally, this is achieved in five to eight days. To develop this control, the following actions should be performed.

- Place some unusual object next to the bed to serve as a signal to start the wake-up procedure as soon as it is noticed upon waking. It should be positioned so that it is likely to be the first object recognized.
- Practice the procedure. The first interaction of the day between the athlete and another significant person should be for them to inquire about the adequacy of the wake-up procedure and what mood eventuated. Throughout the unloading phase, positive waking should be an expected behavior.
- Use the wake-up procedure for both night sleep and extended rest periods.

This simple procedure influences a wrestler's attitudes for the day by producing a positive approach to daily events. Although it may seem trivial, no event is too small to be considered and/or used if it will assist in producing the best performance of which a wrestler is capable.

Normal planned routine Most of the time between waking and competing should be devoted to following activities that avoid upsets. The most influential events are psychological in nature. Activities during this time should be planned and monitored. Some of the major events of this period are mentioned below.

- *What and when to eat* Before competition day and when away from home, food service availability should be determined. Features such as rush times, length of lines waiting for service, service speed and extent of menu should be investigated. As a coping response, alternative eating places should be found. For very important tournaments, it probably is wisest to take one's own food. This would place this potentially upsetting event under the athlete's complete control.
- *Rest or mild activities* A large proportion of the pre-tournament events is devoted to consuming time. Planned activities should be enjoyable and non-stressful. Minor diversionary activities should be tolerated. No matter what is done, the athlete should always have the upcoming bouts in the back of their mind. Impulsive or silly actions could produce distractions and possibly injury.
- *Equipment preparation and list* The wrestler should ritually attend to their equipment before leaving for the tournament venue. This serves as a way of focusing the athlete's attention on the importance of the competition.
- *When and how to travel to the competition site* This should be scheduled and adequate time planned for it to be achieved. It is also necessary for an alternative route and mode of transport to be determined. If a problem was to arise with the "normal" transport, a coping response would be to use alternative arrangements.

- *When to do performance-enhancement imagery* This assists the athlete to keep the principal purpose of the day in mind. If it is done periodically, it will focus the athlete on pre-match preparations and the assessment of their goals.
- *Group activities* Stress reactions are reduced in groups. If some wrestlers wish to participate in group activities they should be encouraged to do so. Group activities should be monitored particularly if there is a potential for personality conflicts. The group atmosphere must be positive, light and active.

Two psychological problems often arise during this time.

- *Loss of confidence* This causes a change in an athlete's appraisal of achieving tournament goals. Symptoms may be any or some of the following: reduced activity, lethargic movements, unhappy appearance, isolation from others, answers to questions do not contain much information, a reluctance to talk to the coach or others, does as told without enthusiasm, and a lack of attention to equipment. As an attempt to overcome this problem, several actions can be followed.
  - Use performance-enhancement imagery (Rushall, 1991b, 2003) to rehearse sections of competition strategies.
  - Describe to others or mutter to oneself what will be done in various scenarios that could occur in the match.
  - Say out loud the positive self-statements that will be repeated during the preparation.
  - Simulate parts of an imagined bout by using a longer than usual warm-up. Once confidence is regained the planned pre-competition strategy should be recommenced at an appropriate stage.
  - Perform assertive and/or aggressive activities such as mild forms of wrestling and pushing. Fast movement contests produce sensations that are incompatible with reduced enthusiasm.

  Some or all of the above activities should be repeated until confidence is restored. It is helpful to include some of these actions in pre-competition strategies to serve as "insurance" against a loss of confidence.
- *Increase in tension* This problem usually is a precursor to anxiety. It results from becoming too aroused without appropriate mental control. Tension needs to be dissipated through diversionary activities that have some energy cost. Activities such as walking, easy running, table tennis and playing cards or games in groups are useful. Activities such as reading, writing letters and watching television may be too passive to be of value. The level of activity has to moderate the level of tension in the wrestler.

The main challenge for pre-competition preparation away from the tournament site is biding one's time so that no detrimental events occur. Little can be done at this time to enhance performance, but much could happen to detract from performance. Events should be planned so that activities are purposeful and beneficial.

At the Tournament Site

Everything undertaken at the tournament venue should be planned. This is where performances can be affected dramatically by seemingly insignificant events. Initial activities after arrival will "set the stage" for the activities that follow. Undertaking deliberate activities immediately upon arrival will set the pattern for the remainder of the pre-competition strategy.

Initial mental activity A major task for achieving control over competition readiness is to produce a constant reference point for preparations to commence irrespective of the venue. One way of doing this is to perform enhancement imagery while moving around in an open space as the first activity. This produces a focus of attention on the impending first match in the environment in which it will occur. The scope of imagery in this early stage of preparation should encompass the whole bout. This contrasts with what will be imagined later because as the match approaches the scope of imagery should narrow to the early segments of the competition strategy.

Some individuals prefer to start the real preparation for a match by completing a relaxation session with mental imagery immediately before leaving for the competition site. Others prefer to engage in relaxation as the first activity when they arrive at the venue. The purpose behind those activities is to develop a consistent starting point for the planned routines that lead to the start of a match. It is good practice to have a consistent comfortable activity as the first at the tournament site. From that consistent reference point, all planned activities should start on a predictable path.

Warm-up Warm-up should be as close as possible to the first bout. If it occurs too early it is possible that benefits may dissipate before the contest starts.

There are three major effects to be achieved through a warm-up. First, the core temperature of the body should rise to the point where the skin is moist with a light sweat. Second, the neuromuscular patterns of the skill activities that will occur in the match should have been practiced through some match-intensity specific activity. This second feature means that the skill patterns exhibited in the warm-up should match those that are likely to occur in the contest. Third, it is the first opportunity to focus on features of the physical and mental dimensions of the match.

When deciding on warm-up activities, the athlete must:

- justify the purpose behind each activity;
- have the content, quality and intensity of the activities eventually be the same as those of the match;
- perform some activities at an intensity that matches the highest effort levels that will occur in the contest; and
- have a warm-up that is open-ended; that is, it is not completed until the wrestler is "ready".

Once a warm-up is completed, the effects developed should not be allowed to wear off. Layers of clothing to preserve the elevated body temperature should be worn and repeated precise-skill activities should occur in the period between the finish of the warm-up and the match. There is no need to worry about expending energy that otherwise might be used in the contest. During this time, fluid levels should be maintained. Drinks should be permitted although some individuals should not take those with sugar in the last two hours before the start. Coaches and advisers should offer no new information or instructions, but should elicit responses from the athlete by questioning them about some part of the intended competition strategy, and only focus on the early segments of the match.

At this time, it is also advisable for athletes to start to isolate themselves from others (e.g. well wishers, competitors, media, advisers). That facilitates focusing on the upcoming event and reduces distractions.

Stretching is an activity that should be used in moderation. Recent research has shown that excessive stretching diminishes strength, something that would be harmful for a wrestler. Exercises should involve all joints. However, each exercise should have a purpose to achieve some feeling of warmth and/or looseness. Stretching exercises should be performed alone so that there is no reliance upon another being. At this late stage of preparation, unnecessary second-party dependent activities (e.g. rubdowns, massages) should be avoided.

As the bout approaches, the content of the pre-competition strategy should be such that the wrestler relies more and more on events and actions over which they have total control. By keeping active and warm and focusing on deliberate and practiced activities, a state can be developed that is incompatible with psychological problem states, such as anxiety, loss of confidence and increased tension. The warm-up signals that the "match" has begun and that final preparations for competing have started.

Match build-up routine At some designated time prior to the match start, the wrestler should enter a phase of pre-competition preparations that serve to heighten their responses and readiness to perform. This concerns a physical and mental build-up that is to peak and coincide with the start of the contest. A variety of activities are possible in this build-up routine.

- The routine should start with the athlete isolating themselves from all personal interactions, even with a coach. The role of a coach or adviser at this time should be one of purely monitoring what the athlete is doing and being a resource if required. This isolation allows the wrestler to concentrate on planned physical and mental activities.
- Physical activities should increase in their intensity as the bout approaches. Bursts of activity should become faster and more intense. The amount of physical activity also increases at this time so that just before the bout, the wrestler is in constant motion. That motion will facilitate the control of physical arousal, which needs to be high if the wrestler is to start well.
- The athlete should engage in positive self-talk. If it is difficult to concentrate on covert self-talk, then the positive statements should be muttered aloud. Muttering requires more concentration than thinking and may have better potential for self-control effects.
- Task concentration should change as the match approaches. The closer the start, the greater the concentration on the start and the early match segments. The last thoughts before the start should be of how to do the best start possible. Thus, as the bout approaches, distant and final segments of a competition strategy drop out of the athlete's sphere of concentration.
- A procedure used by some of the greatest athletes in the world is called "emotional build-up". It consists of selecting some aggressive or assertive emotion (e.g. being furious or angry, hating some object, being wild or mad, wanting to attack). This emotion is deliberately imagined. It usually should occur quite close to the match start, possibly in the last five to ten minutes. As the start approaches, the intensity of the emotion is increased so that, at the referee's whistle, the wrestler controls optimum emotional and physical arousal through concentration on perfection of the initiation of the match. That state constitutes the development of a maximum match-readiness state.
- Performance-enhancement imagery should be used frequently as a procedure for maintaining focus on the contest. As the start approaches, segments rehearsed should increasingly be those of the early part of the match. Distant segments will lose their effect as the start becomes imminent. The last imagery should be of the starting segment.

A pre-competition strategy requires an athlete to achieve certain outcomes.

1. Minimize the chances of distractions or problems occurring that might interfere with the production of a perfect match.
2. Emotional control and intensity should peak in the seconds before the start.
3. Never lose deliberate control over the emotional states that are created.
4. Control thinking so that it is on the task of wrestling and proper preparations.
5. Thought control should narrow to focus on the bout as it approaches.
6. Time the highest physical arousal (developed through physical and emotional activities) with the narrowest focus of attention (the start) just as the match begins.

The above features require an athlete to perform a pre-competition strategy that will produce the desired outcome of maximum competition-readiness. The match build-up routine is the most appropriate preparatory strategy to be used between bouts as the wrestler progresses through the competition. Between matches, it is the quality of the preparation, not the volume, that will produce the best readiness state.

Preparation of Pre-competition Strategies

Pre-competition strategies should be developed on strategy planning sheets. Each item should be justified on the basis of its producing a desirable outcome. Phases of the strategy should achieve predetermined goals.

Pre-competition strategies should be learned. Some training sessions should be devoted to the total practice of at least the venue-specific activities. The first pre-competition strategy should serve as the basis for future strategies. It should be altered with each successive competition as new elements are included and tried and others discarded. In time, precision and competence for developing the ideal match-readiness state will improve. Too much detail in a pre-competition strategy is better than too little.

Written strategies should always be taken to competition venues. Should there be difficulty in concentrating on what should be done or thought, then the strategies should be read. That will serve to focus the athlete's attention on the task at hand.

Much learning is involved in the development and deployment of strategies. Practice at training and experience in matches will contribute to the development of their desirable effects. They need to be worked on with the same intensity and importance as is given to any activity surrounding wrestling.

Competition Strategies

Competition strategies contain all the behaviors and thoughts to be performed in a wrestling match. The preparation of a competition strategy should develop sufficient information and mental activities to totally consume the duration of the bout. Pre-planning competitive performances in this way reduces stress in the wrestler and directs behavior to reduce uncertainty. A competition strategy is a script of what to do and think in a match.

Segmenting the Match

Segmenting a match is the best way to approach a complicated event such as a wrestling match. A match should be divided into wrestler-determined units of concentration, each with its own challenges and content, goals, and evaluation criteria. The actual dissection of a bout is a particularly individual process and almost invariably does not follow the official two three-minute periods. Segments are much shorter than periods. The purpose of segmenting is to make the concept of a match be one of sequentially concentrating on and achieving short-term goals that are intermediate to achieving final-bout goals.

Segments constitute the basic units for the mental rehearsal of matches. In a pre-competition strategy, any mental rehearsal should attempt to focus on an entire segment rather than isolated features taken out of context.

Whether segment goals were or were not achieved should be evaluated quickly at the end of each segment within the contest. If they were not achieved, then a goal-recovery routine should be immediately implemented to recapture the features that should have been achieved. This means two things could happen at the transition stage from one segment to the next. First, if segment goals were achieved the athlete would proceed with the entire next segment. Second, if segment goals were not achieved a goal-recovery routine would be implemented. After a recovery routine, the wrestler would enter the scheduled segment at the most appropriate place for the stage of the match.

Segmenting a performance produces sustained elevated performances. An athlete should not think of the next segment until the current one is completed. Strategies should be developed around a segmented match plan.

Task-relevant Thinking

At least two-thirds of the thought content of a competition/match strategy should involve task-relevant thinking. Task-relevant thinking is essential for maintaining form and purpose. The technical aspects of wrestling—for example, positioning, intensity, movement initiation, holds, continuity, and body positions, adapting to changing conditions, etc.—contribute to the major improvements in performance that result from using strategies. Task-relevant thinking is stressed when increased speed is required. An improvement in action speed should be attained through a technique change, not increased effort.

What types of task-relevant thoughts are used depends upon the stage of the bout. When an athlete is not fatigued, such as in the first segment, specific technique factors should not be considered. Form that has been developed by training and is unhindered by fatigue will naturally emerge. If technique items were thought of early in a match, the phenomenon of "cognitive interference" would occur. Thinking about doing automatic neuromuscular patterns while not fatigued usually reduces efficiency of function. It is only when fatigue is first recognized that thoughts should turn to specific technique features. Thus, in early stages of a bout, task-relevant thinking should be general focusing on strategy, positioning, the clarity of thinking of the strategy, speed of movement, etc.

If a wrestler "runs out" of things to think of, or suddenly goes "blank" while using a competition strategy, that is called the "dead-spot" phenomenon. It indicates lost control of focus and is a serious problem. This problem usually arises when too little strategy content was planned. Dead-spots degrade performances. To avoid prolonged detrimental effects from this phenomenon, a wrestler should plan a dead-spot recovery routine. A popular approach is to prepare some task-relevant action with which the athlete feels very safe and competent, and use that as the thought focus-point to recover and return to the strategy. That re-entry point will prompt concentration once again on task-relevant actions and thoughts.

To avoid dead-spots or distractions, the manner in which task-relevant thoughts are used is important. Planned content should be cycled through a number of times. Constantly changing content keeps the information being considered fresh and vibrant. Developing different ways of thinking about each technical aspect is beneficial as it avoids monotony. This variety assists in keeping thoughts vital. Through variety and a constant change in control emphasis, the probability of dead-spots occurring is reduced.

The actual task-relevant content considered in a match strategy depends upon the individual athlete. It should focus on producing the most efficient form of energy application and effective form of skill. Because of the complexity of combative matches, one should never have difficulty in developing sufficient task-relevant content for a complete strategy. Task-relevant thoughts sustain form, retard loss of efficiency, and block the recognition of fatigue for extended periods.

Mood Words

Generally, two-thirds of a competition strategy is consumed by thinking of task-relevant features. The other third is partly consumed by thinking of "mood" words. Mood words set the mood of a performance. Language has certain basic or primitive words that, when said or thought, have some movement or emotional component. They cause a physical reaction in the body. The word "crunch" conveys the feeling of strength more than does a sterile statement such as "create force". When one thinks of words that produce a physical and/or emotional component, performance is increased.

It is an advantage to think mood words that fit the mood of a performance. When an athlete wants to be strong; they should think mood words that generate strength; when they want to be quick, they should think speed words. *How one thinks determines how one acts; therefore, words that have an appropriate and direct action meaning should be used in strategies.*

Mood words are differentiated from other words because of the physical/emotional reaction component. If a word or phrase does not produce that component, then it is not a mood word. Table 17.5 lists some synonyms for various wrestling match capacities. From this list individuals may select words that "work for them" or add words from their own experience. The words should be interspersed throughout the strategy to match the variations

Table 17.5   Mood words—suggested synonyms for wrestling match capacities

Strength	crush, squash, violent, solid, crunch, intense, muscle, haul, bear-hug, might, force, drive, grind, drag, press, push, lean
Power	might, force, heave, impel, smash, snap, rip, blast, boom, bang, thump, thrust, explode, hoist, crumble
Speed	fast, explode, alert, lunge, thrust, jab, rap, smack, brief, flick, whip, fling, pop, dash, quick
Agility	nimble, move, dance, prance, brisk, alert, quick, shuffle, agile
Balance	rock-hard, block, dead, solid, firm, rooted, anchored, set, rigid, hard
Endurance	bold, great, on-plan, comfortable, control, continue, relentless, press, hustle, push, drag.

Source: Adapted from Rushall, B.S. (2003). *Mental Skills Training for Sports* (3rd edn). Spring Valley, CA: Sports Science Associates.

in performance capacity demands. When power is needed, the words ("pump", "thump", "rip", "blast", etc.) should be spread throughout the segment. When tiring, endurance might be enhanced by concentrating on words such as "control", "press", etc. Mood words are used to embellish task-relevant thoughts. They are used to control actions and the mood (capacity) of a bout.

The mood word content will comprise a "sport language" as opposed to being a technical language. Thinking of pure technical statements, such as "extend the leg" or "elevate the hand", may interfere with performance. The processing of the sterile language components can be distracting, which causes performance to suffer. On the other hand, if the technical statement is translated into mood and primitive words that require no translation and are understood easily, performance will be enhanced. *The expression of a strategy must consider the language used. The language should be that of the wrestler and phrased in simple terms that do not require translation.*

Mood words should also be spread throughout a segment and said purely by themselves. The high-intensity utterance of "blast, blast, blast" can produce an increase in performance quality if power is required. A similar phenomenon occurs with other mood components depending upon the capacity required at any particular stage of the bout. Mood word utterances need to be added to a strategy. They can be used to break up sections of task-relevant thinking and will consume some of the remaining one-third of the competition thought-content that is not used by task-relevant thoughts.

The role of mood words is twofold. First, they are used to enhance performance capacities used in a match if they are uttered in concert with the appropriate capacity. Second, they make the language of a strategy more meaningful. They are more expressive and effective than most of the bland technical statements used by coaches. *Mood words enhance performance. They are an important feature of the content and expression of competition strategies.*

Positive Self-statements

A critical feature of good match preparation and performance is positive thinking. The remaining competition-strategy content, after task-relevant thinking and mood words have been developed, comprises positive self-statements. These three emphases of thought content constitute the total strategy. The statement of meaningful positive phrases helps sustain effort. Athletes should be encouraged to talk positively to themselves mentally or aloud, as if they were coaching themselves in a match.

Positive self-statements should not be meaningless, cheerleader-type expressions, for example, "Go, go, go", and "Let's do it now". Rather, they should be meaningful phrases. Table 17.6 lists some examples of positive statements for four different situations in a match, (1) encouraging oneself, (2) handling effort, (3) evaluating segment goals, and (4) general positive self-talk. Positive self-talk should be spread completely throughout the strategy. Its inclusion should prevent any tendency to develop negative appraisals of performance. As with task-relevant content and mood words, positive self-talk in endurance activities has been shown to enhance performance.

The expression of positive self-statements and mood words is best if second-person phrasing is used. If that does not work, then first-person expressions might be tried. The use of the second person appears to produce a perception of control over oneself. This is a consistent feature of the strategies that are formed by champions in many sports.

Table 17.6   Examples of positive self-statements that may be used in a wrestling match strategy

---

Self-encouragement
"You are doing great"
"Keep achieving those goals"
"This is the opportunity to dominate"

Effort control
"It may hurt but concentrate on upper body twists"
"You have prepared for this so execute your strategy"
"He is hurting just as much but he doesn't have a strategy"

Segment goals
"The intensity and single-leg attacks have him defending. Now look for an upper body attack"
"Your counters are just what you wanted"
"That segment has slowed him down"

Positive Self-talk
"Great work"
"This will be even better than planned"
"This feels great. You really are getting on top"

Source: Adapted from Rushall, B.S. (2003). *Mental Skills Training for Sports* (3rd edn). Spring Valley, CA: Sports Science Associates.

Coping Behaviors

Coping behaviors are important for match strategies because they reduce the level of disruption when problems occur. For every preferred action an alternative action for achieving the same outcome should be planned. This allows the wrestler to cope with any problems that arise in a match.

A number of general problems can occur in wrestling bouts. These general problems are different from when a deliberate planned activity does not work. Strategies should be developed for handling these general difficulties although they do not appear in the body of a match strategy. Rather, they are included as a general problem-solving capacity that should be developed, learned and taken to every tournament and match.

1. *A feeling of loss of control* If a wrestler develops a general appraisal or feeling of losing self-control with regard to a match strategy, a number of coping behaviors that might assist in regaining self-control are possible. For example:
   • Return to basic fundamental moves with which the wrestler feels very comfortable;
   • Engage in emotional positive self-talk; and/or
   • Concentrate on mood words that are appropriate for the segment being executed.
2. *Dead-spots* The reactions to a loss of control also are appropriate for this problem. A re-entry point to the strategy should be at a very well-learned and comfortable phase of the segment being executed.
3. *Distractions* Dead-spot recovery routines are useful for regaining a focus of attention on the planned strategy. Another alternative is to analyze the situation and determine exactly where the strategy should be re-entered and execute from there.
4. *Errors* Execute planned coping behaviors.

The major feature of coping behaviors and general coping strategies *i* should never become rattled. The capacity to develop problem-solving difficulty should be an aim of training and strategy development. With wrestler should be able to fight with confidence and certainty. The mat be appraised as being a potentially positive happening.

The Match Start

The start of a wrestling match warrants particular attention because it initiates strategy execution. It is important that bouts commence in the best possible manner because the first impression of the contest will influence ensuing appraisals during the performance.

The start segment is the final focus of the pre-competition strategy in the match build-up routine. When facing the opponent on the mat, the only goals considered should be those of the start segment. At that stage, to all intents and purposes, the wrestler should perceive the match as being a challenge to do the planned start. Once the start is initiated, the athlete focuses only on strategy content. If it has been learned well, it will unfold in sequence much the same way as does a script in a play.

The execution of the start segment should not require any settling-in phase. All actions need to be self-controlled and aimed at producing the best start possible. The intensity and ferocity of the very first movements should be equal to those of the highest intensity of any other segment. The principal reason behind a start strategy is to introduce strategy concentration and performance intensity with the utmost precision and effect.

De-briefing

One of the most significant features for learning to occur is the provision of immediate feedback. After a match, this rarely is considered. It is advocated that de-briefing should become a part of match conduct. Before a wrestler dresses, celebrates or warms down, they should de-brief the match performance and preparations. Some de-briefing topics are:

- Evaluate the goal achievements for each segment and the match.
- What can be improved in the strategy?
- How can concentration be improved?
- What content changes are required for task-relevant mood words, and positive thinking?
- What was done but was not planned for?
- What was not done but had been planned?
- Are there any preparation improvements needed?
- Does anything need to be added to either the competition or pre-competition strategies?

De-briefing is a necessary feature of strategy development and learning. The effects of competing will be more influential on subsequent performances. The institution of this process will alter the nature of contests. It will focus the evaluation of competing on strategy execution. This in turn will likely produce a perception that *the goal of competing is to execute a total planned strategy.*

Learning Competition Strategies

Learning competition strategies is very similar to learning pre-competition strategies. Some features that should be followed in the learning process are listed below.

1. Practice competition strategies and segments as the mental content of physical activities at training.
2. Competition strategy segments should be the content of mental rehearsals for preparations.
3. One-fifth of strategy learning and rehearsals should be devoted to coping alternatives as well as recovery routines.
4. The first attempt at strategies will likely be very detailed and lengthy. With time, practice and the requirement to refine only previous strategies, development will become less time-consuming. After considerable practice, strategies will become a series of key words that trigger chains of thoughts. For very experienced wrestlers, it may not be necessary to write strategies for every match. However, it always remains necessary to prepare a strategy for serious tournaments.
5. The detail, sequencing, and alternatives of the competition-strategy must be learned. A coach should ask a wrestler what they will be thinking at a particular stage of a bout and the athlete should respond with a conscious stream without hesitation. That is the test of whether the wrestler is prepared to execute a strategy in an acceptable manner.
6. No matches will have the same strategy. Adjustments to every opponent, previous learning experiences and competition conditions produce the need for a continual refinement in strategy development and execution competence. This should result in continual improvements at tournaments.

CLOSURE

Attention to the details of appropriate mental activities before, during and after wrestling tournaments should be a central part of a wrestling program. Without total control, performances will vary in standard, oscillate in intensity and offer no hope from any psychological problems associated with competing. A pre-competition strategy offers the development of self-control on the day of a tournament. That perception of control will directly influence confidence and certainty. Having a complete competition strategy will virtually eliminate uncertainty, the single most influential factor that reduces performance abilities and standards. Without a full-picture appreciation of the need for mental content at wrestling practices and tournaments, a coach should not expect performance excellence from most wrestlers.

REFERENCES

Eklund, R.C. (1994). A season-long investigation of competitive cognition in collegiate wrestlers. *Research Quarterly for Exercise and Sport, 65*, 169–183.

FILA. http://www.fila-wrestling.com/home/index.php3

Gould, D., Eklund, R.C. & Jackson, S.A. (1992). 1988 US Olympic wrestling excellence: II Thoughts and affect occurring during competition. *The Sport Psychologist, 6*, 383–402.

Gould, D., Weiss, M. & Weinberg, R. (1981). Psychological characteristics of successful and non-successful Big Ten wrestlers. *Journal of Sport Psychology, 3*, 69–81.

Halvari, H. (1983). Relationships between motive to achieve success, motive to avoid failure, physical performance, and sport performance in wrestling. *Scandinavian Journal of Sports Science, 5*, 64–72.

Highlen, P.S. & Bennett, B.B. (1979). Psychological characteristics of successful and nonsuccessful elite wrestlers: an exploratory study. *Journal of Sport Psychology, 1*, 123–137.

Horton, A.M., Jr. & Shelton, J.K. (1978). The rational wrestler: a pilot study. *Perceptual and Motor Skills, 46*, 882.

Kermanshah, A. (1986, March). An exploratory study of locus of control, self-confidence, and success in wrestling. *Dissertation Abstracts International—A, 46(09)*, 2618.

Kroll, W. (1967). Sixteen personality factor profiles of collegiate wrestlers. *Research Quarterly, 38*, 49–57.

Rushall, B.S. (1975). The psychological preparation of Canadian Olympic performers. An invited major address for the Canada Week Program at St Lawrence University, New York.

Rushall, B.S. (1976). The scope of psychological support services for Canadian Olympic athletes. A paper presented at the Annual Conference of the Australian Sports Medicine Federation, Surfers Paradise, Australia.

Rushall, B.S. (1982). What coaches do—behavioral evidence on coaching effectiveness. In L. Wankel & R.B. Wilberg (eds), *Psychology of Sport and Motor Behavior: Research and Practice*. Edmonton: University of Alberta.

Rushall, B.S. (1987). Caracteristicas conductuales de los campeones. In G. Perez (ed.), *Proceedings of the Jornades Internacionals de Medicina I Esport*, INEF, Barcelona, Spain.

Rushall, B.S. (1991a). Motivation and goal-setting. In F.S. Pyke (ed.), *Better Coaching*. Canberra, Australia: Australian Coaching Council.

Rushall, B.S. (1991b). *Imagery Training in Sports*. Spring Valley, CA: Sports Science Associates.

Rushall, B.S. (1994). The self-appraisal of practice session coaching performance. In B.S. Rushall, *The Assessment of Coaching Effectiveness*. Spring Valley, CA: Sports Science Associates (pp. 1.1–1.8).

Rushall, B.S. (1995). *Think and Act Like a Champion*. Spring Valley, CA: Sports Science Associates [http://members.cox.net/brushall/#books].

Rushall, B.S. (1997). Champion characteristics. *Coaching Science Abstracts*, 3(3) [http://www-rohan.sdsu.edu/dept/coachsci/csa/vol33/rushall5.htm].

Rushall, B.S. (2003). *Mental Skills Training for Sports* (3rd edn). Spring Valley, CA: Sports Science Associates [http://members.cox.net/brushall/#books].

Rushall, B.S. (2004a). *Exclusive Elite Athlete Psychological Testing*. Spring Valley, CA: Sports Science Associates [http://members.cox.net/brushall/#testing].

Rushall, B.S. (2004b). *The Sport Psychology Consultation System*. Spring Valley, CA: Sports Science Associates [http://members.cox.net/brushall/spcsinfo.htm].

Rushall, B.S. & Garvie, G. (1977). Psychological characteristics of Canadian Olympic and non-Olympic wrestlers. A paper presented at the Ninth Canadian Psychomotor Learning and Sport Psychology Symposium, Banff.

Rushall, B.S. & Pyke, F.S. (1991). *Training for Sports and Fitness*. Melbourne, Australia: Macmillan of Australia.

Silva, J.M., Shultz, B.B., Haslam, R.W., Martin, T.P. & Murray, D.F. (1985). Discriminating characteristics of contestants at the United States Olympic Wrestling Trials. *International Journal of Sport Psychology, 16*, 79–102.

PART V

Winter Sports

CHAPTER 18

Sport Psychological Consulting in Ice Hockey

Wayne Halliwell
University of Montreal, Canada
Len Zaichkowsky
Boston University, USA
and
Cal Botterill
University of Winnipeg, Canada

INTRODUCTION

Ice hockey has truly become an international game. The dressing rooms of many teams to-day are a virtual United Nations of subcultures. It is not unusual to find players from Russia, the Czech Republic, Sweden, Finland, the United States and Canada playing together on professional, college and junior hockey teams. Switzerland, Austria and Germany are also passionate ice hockey countries in the heart of Europe with extensive programs. International exchange and competition in ice hockey is thriving with youth teams, women's teams, old-timer teams, college teams and junior teams playing against each other throughout Europe and North America. Under-18 and World Junior Championships have become extremely popular events for hockey fans and provided excellent development experiences for participants and coaches. The Olympics have been the stage over the last few years for the best male and female ice hockey players in the world. As well, ice hockey has a strong following in countries as far away as China, Japan and Australia.

The exchange and competition between ice hockey subcultures seems to bring out the best in the game and the people in it. Every subculture and country brings its unique contribution to the game. Canada and Russia have perhaps the greatest rivalry in ice hockey with competitions like the 1972 Summit Series immortalized in the minds and hearts of fans. The upsets in the 1960 and 1980 Olympics by USA also constitute pivotal emotional accomplishments and they are sterling examples of how teamwork, belief and hard work can win ice hockey championships. It is safe to say that the sport of ice hockey is one of the most emotional and complex team sport environments. Its participants bring tremendous

The Sport Psychologist's Handbook: A Guide for Sport-Specific Performance Enhancement.
Edited by Joaquín Dosil. © 2006 John Wiley & Sons, Ltd.

skill and speed, but they also bring tremendous passion. The roots of ice hockey originated in North American "pond hockey". In particular, it became part of Canada's culture and heritage (Dryden & MacGregor, 1989). Canada's passion for the game is often hard for others to understand or appreciate.

Ice hockey may initially have been played recreationally, but it soon came to epitomize the "pioneering spirit" of a New World. The passion, the toughness and the competitiveness that was deemed necessary to explore and develop the Canadian frontier and its rugged climate became part of the "the game".

To this day, passion, toughness and competitiveness are considered fundamental requirements of the game of ice hockey. Add elements like ferocious fore-checking and bodychecking, increasing speed, bigger, stronger and fitter players, better equipment, huge competitive salaries, passionate public and media interest, the oldest most cherished team sport trophy—the Stanley Cup, and the mix is "dynamic" to say the least. Certainly the dynamics have changed in many ways since Botterill (1990) and Halliwell (1990) wrote about their consulting experiences in professional hockey 15 years ago. In the next section we will examine some of the unique features of the ice hockey culture.

ICE HOCKEY CULTURE

Appreciating and understanding the world of ice hockey is not an easy task. It is certainly a "culture" that is different from any other sport. With its roots tied to the early Canadian pioneering spirit—where being tough, persistent, extremely competitive and able to defend oneself were seen as personal qualities necessary to survive—these cornerstones provided a foundation for the acceptance by players of a "win-despite-costs" and "eye-for-an-eye" value system in ice hockey.

In the hierarchy of moral functioning, "win-despite-cost" and "eye-for-an-eye" are not considered very mature advanced values and behaviors (Weinberg & Gould, 2003). When passionately exaggerated, these outlooks can be very destructive to the game and its participants. The cost can certainly outweigh the benefits and in the National Hockey League (NHL) these attitudes have led to violent on-ice incidents resulting in serious injuries and legal repercussions. The inability to officiate this passionate, dynamic game in a consistent, just way has resulted in "enforcers" on professional hockey teams being called upon to enforce the "olde code" and to ensure justice and the protection of their team's skill players at any cost.

Built into this culture is a fierce player allegiance to their teammates and their team. Players are expected to support one another in all circumstances and are also expected to play through pain and "play hurt" if necessary to help the team. As a result, injury dynamics can often be complex with players sometimes risking long-term health and capability for the team's short-term ambition.

Having briefly described this history and culture, it is important to point out that many of ice hockey's better players and "character" people have demonstrated higher levels of values and functioning. Certainly Wayne Gretzky, the greatest player to ever play the game, seemed to epitomize a positive rivalry approach throughout his career. His humility, respect and love of a challenge provided a refreshing improvement in ice hockey perspective and moral functioning (Gretzky, 2001). Also, Steve Yzerman, captain of the Detroit Red Wings and three-time Stanley Cup winner, is highly respected by both his teammates and his opponents for a 20-year NHL career in which he has demonstrated fierce competitive desire, passion for the game, resiliency, leadership by example, selflessness, humility and modesty (Hunter, 2004).

Even some players who excelled at the "olde code" brought character and growth to the game of ice hockey. The Sutter brothers grew up on a pioneering prairie farm in Western Canada, so they knew the code (Spiros, 1990). They also were part of a strong, caring family and they knew the value of humility, respect, hard work and teamwork. These six brothers from the same family, who all played in the NHL, were impressive "transition" players who knew and lived the olde code but had the attributes to bring positive rivalries, teamwork and emotional preparation to the game (Botterill, 1990).

Today, Jarome Iginla, captain of the Calgary Flames in the NHL, may be the best-known example of an ice hockey player whose perspective and attributes reflect the full spectrum of the olde and developing codes. Is there progress? Hopefully a higher-level moral and functioning code is developing. More severe penalties for violent on-ice acts and the emergence of high-quality female ice hockey have probably both helped the development of the game. However, it should be pointed out that even female hockey, which does not allow bodychecking, at times regresses toward the olde code with instances of overly aggressive play at the higher levels of competition. Hopefully strong monitoring and a desire for a better product will enable female hockey to become a leader in highlighting the beauty of the game with its appealing combination of speed, skill, emotion and teamwork. We must remember though that cultural effects can be pervasive in both men's and women's ice hockey. Any sport psychology consultant working in ice hockey needs to understand these cultural effects, the passion of the participants, and the uniqueness of the sport.

Following this brief discussion of the historical and cultural underpinnings of the sport of ice hockey, we will now examine the mental and emotional skills required to play ice hockey and strategies which sport psychology consultants can use to teach these psychological skills to ice hockey players. Then we will discuss the role of planning and psychological preparation during various phases of the hockey season and specific techniques which hockey players can use to get ready for competitions. This section will also provide suggestions for getting teams mentally and emotionally ready for regular season games and playoff competition. In the final section of the chapter we will share certain consulting experiences which require specific training and specialized intervention to deal with "critical incidents" during ice hockey games.

MENTAL AND EMOTIONAL SKILLS IN ICE HOCKEY

As mentioned in the introduction section, ice hockey is a game played with great passion and emotion and it is one of the fastest, most exciting sports in the world. It requires players to have a highly developed set of physical, technical, tactical, mental and emotional skills. To help sport psychology consultants be effective in working with ice hockey teams, it is useful to identify these skills and discuss how they interact with the players' knowledge base and attitude. Pat Quinn, head coach of the Toronto Maple Leafs in the National Hockey League, has developed a useful model with *skill, knowledge* and *attitude* forming the three corners of a triangle and linked together to determine a player's performance (see Figure 18.1). This

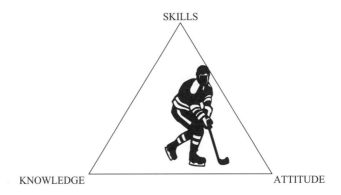

SKILLS

KNOWLEDGE   ATTITUDE

Figure 18.1   An interactionist model for teaching mental and emotional skills to ice hockey players

interactionist model enables us to examine—in a systematic manner—the skills, the knowledge and the attitude which hockey players must possess if they hope to realize their potential.

Skills

Physical Skills

Hockey players require speed, strength, agility, flexibility and endurance as well as fine and gross motor skills. Elite teams have strength and conditioning coaches to help players develop these physical skills in hockey-specific conditioning programs. An excellent source of information is the book *Complete Conditioning for Ice Hockey* written by Peter Twist, former strength and conditioning coach with the Vancouver Canucks in the NHL (Twist, 1997).

Technical Skills

Ice hockey is a game which requires players to skate with speed and agility, to stickhandle the puck, to pass the puck to and receive passes from teammates, to shoot the puck with speed and accuracy, to bodycheck opposing players, to use stick skills to win battles for the puck and to win face-offs. Coaches are constantly working with their players to improve these skills during practices.

Tactical Skills

Understanding the team's offensive and defensive systems is fundamental to each player's success. This skill set consists of being able to read and react to what is happening on the ice and to anticipate what the opposing team is trying to do within their offensive or defensive game plan. Coaches of elite players show them game videos to help improve their "read and react" skills and to improve their ability to play without the puck. The sport psychology consultant can help players improve their tactical skills by teaching them to visualize game situations and thereby improve their ability to anticipate offensive and defensive situations during the game.

Mental Skills

These skills are cognitive in nature and they include concentration, self-talk and imagery. For a hockey player, the mental skill of concentration consists of being able to get focused for the game, stay focused during the game and refocus if distracted by things such as bad plays (e.g. bad passes, bad decisions, missed scoring opportunities or missed checking assignments), bad luck (e.g. shots hitting the goalpost or pucks taking bad bounces) or questionable calls by the officials. Self-talk enables players to not only create the proper perspective ("Enjoy the moment", "Enjoy the challenge") it also helps them bolster their confidence through self-affirmations such as "I'm ready" and "I feel strong". In addition, self-talk also helps players perform to their potential by focusing on hockey-specific action words such as "Move your feet", "Drive the net", "Win the battles", "Close the gap", "Stay on rebounds", "Get pucks deep", etc.

These key words help players improve performance by directing their attention to the process of playing and by keeping their focus in the present instead of thinking about the consequences of the outcome of the game. By using these key word reminders, players can also control their anxiety level by getting totally immersed "in the moment" and fully engaged in performing their on-ice role with technical and tactical proficiency.

Self-talk also facilitates the use of imagery by enhancing the control and clarity of images related to on-ice performance and by creating the kinesthetic feelings associated with the technical and tactical facets of the game. For example, key words such as "crisp, hard and quick" can help create positive images of good passes, and words like "loose hands" and "quick hands" can help players see and feel themselves stickhandling and shooting the puck with great speed and dexterity. From a tactical perspective, by using key words such as "head on a swivel", players can create images in which they see themselves reading the play and making good decisions and good passes as they see the whole ice in front of them. Of course, all of these key words can be used not only to enhance pre-game imagery, but they can also serve as self-talk reminders during the game to facilitate performance.

In a recent study by Rogerson and Hrycaiko (2002), the researchers found that ice hockey goaltenders who used two mental skills, self-talk and relaxation, in the form of centering, improved their performance over the course of a hockey season. These 16- to 19-year-old junior goaltenders not only demonstrated improved performance through higher save percentages, but also social validation results showed that they enjoyed the mental skills and were satisfied with the results obtained from the mental training. A nice feature of this study was the simplicity and non-intrusive nature of the mental training intervention. The relaxation component consisted of taking a single deep breath (centering) and there were three types of self-talk: positioning/focus, self-affirming and mood words. The goaltenders were instructed to use the mental skills after each whistle and they could choose to use the relaxation or self-talk alone, as well as choose the type of self-talk.

Unfortunately there has been very little mental skills training research in the sport of ice hockey and this study is the only one that examines the effects of a mental training program on the performance of a specific position player for an entire hockey season.

Emotional Skills

Whereas the aforementioned mental skills are cognitive in nature, there are a number of emotional skills which have an affective component and they interact with the mental skills to determine each player's psychological state. Before describing some of these emotional skills, it should be mentioned that words like "cognitive" and "affective" should *never* be used when making a team presentation to a group of hockey players or when meeting with an individual player. These athletes understand terms such as "thoughts", "focus", "nervousness", "fears" and "pressure". Using simple terminology and providing hockey-specific examples of the use of mental and emotional skills in both pre-game preparation and game situations enhances the consultant's ability to communicate effectively with players and coaches (Halliwell, Orlick, Ravizza & Rotella, 1999).

Two of the more important emotional skills that hockey players need to master are anxiety/stress management and activation/energizing. Ice hockey players want to be able to play with lots of energy and sustained effort for 60 minutes each game. However, if players are tight because of heightened anxiety and nervousness, they will not have the fluidity in their skating stride which allows them to skate at top speed and rapidly change direction to accelerate past opponents.

Likewise, feeling tight and nervous prevents players from having "loose hands" which enable them to make hard, crisp passes and quick, accurate shots on goal. High levels of anxiety can also lead to early fatigue due to tension in the player's neck, shoulder and chest muscles leading to ineffective, shallow breathing. Learning to breathe properly, especially when sitting on the bench between shifts, is a simple but important skill to teach young players. Muscles need oxygen and they get oxygen only through proper breathing techniques. Many NHL players can be seen taking slow, deep breaths on the bench between shifts on the ice and young players should be encouraged to imitate them. Raymond Bourque, Hall of Fame defenseman with the Boston Bruins, could be seen during games taking slow deep breaths on the bench and this recovery skill combined with his high level of fitness enabled him to play over 30 minutes per game during his stellar 20-year NHL career.

Getting energized before games and finding the optimal level of arousal is another important emotional skill which hockey players must learn. Hockey is a sport which has three different positions; namely, forward, defense and goal, and each position has different task demands requiring specific physical, technical, tactical, mental and emotional skills. Thus, the challenge for sport psychology consultants working with ice hockey teams is to gain an understanding of the task demands of each position and thereby be able to help each player attain an "ideal performance state" (Loehr, 1995). Goalies, for example, must remain calm and focused and ready to stop shots which can reach speeds up to 100 mph. On the other hand, defence players need high levels of activation and aggressiveness to win physical battles in front of the net and in the corners, but they must also remain calm and have "soft hands" to make accurate, crisp passes.

In a later section we will discuss techniques for teaching mental and emotional skills to hockey players while taking into consideration the unique task demands of playing the positions of forward, defense and goal. We will also discuss in a later section some of the strategies that the sport psychology consultant can use to get both ice hockey players and ice hockey teams mentally and emotionally ready to play with intensity, focus, emotion, confidence and consistency.

Knowledge

In the same manner that the skills part of the interactionist model presented in Figure 18.1 is made up of a number of specific skills, the knowledge part of this conceptual model can also be divided into specific components. An ice hockey player's knowledge base can be viewed as consisting of knowledge of oneself, knowledge of the game of hockey and knowledge of situations. We will now examine each of these types of knowledge.

Self-knowledge

This form of knowledge can also be referred to as "self-awareness". It consists of knowing what pre-game routines are most effective in getting oneself ready for games, knowing what key words and thoughts to focus on during pre-game preparation, and knowing how to get focused, stay focused and refocus. Self-knowledge also consists of knowing why one gets nervous and how to channel nervous energy and adrenaline to enable oneself to play with more energy and alertness. Another important part of self-knowledge for athletes is their awareness of why they play the game of hockey and what are the greatest sources of enjoyment that they derive from playing ice hockey. Being aware of these sources of enjoyment is a great way for hockey players to maintain their passion for the game, stay motivated, and deal with pressure by keeping things in perspective.

From a goal-setting perspective, it is important for hockey players to be aware of both their strengths and their areas of improvement. Notice the use of the words "areas of improvement" instead of the word "weaknesses". It is always better to refer to a player's and a team's "areas of improvement" instead of their "weaknesses" because improvement has a positive connotation while weakness has a negative ring to it. We like to tell our players that each of them has aspects of their game which they can improve and the opposition has certain "weaknesses" which they can try to exploit. Thus, the combination of a comprehensive self-assessment and increased self-knowledge leads to the development of meaningful personal improvement plans for each player, with attention directed to the continued improvement of physical, technical, tactical, mental and emotional skills.

Knowledge of the Game

Coaches can often be heard saying that certain players really "understand the game" because they know what to do on the ice when they don't have the puck and they are able to anticipate plays made by their teammates or the opposition. These players have highly developed awareness and anticipation skills, and researchers in the area of decision-making (Klein, 1998) would say that they possess "rapid cognition" skills. They are able to instinctively make the right plays at the right time as they have figured out how to "read and react" during the game with quick decision-making abilities.

Players with a good knowledge of how to play the game of ice hockey are also able to do many "little things" during the game such as being patient with the puck, knowing when to commit themselves to block shots, knowing what to do after a face-off win or loss, knowing how to play with a lead late in a game, etc. Experience can help players acquire this type of knowledge, but good coaching and proper pre-game mental preparation (e.g. visualizing game situations) can also enhance a player's ability to understand the game and make quick, intelligent decisions in a variety of game situations.

Knowledge of Situations

Hockey players are required to adjust to many different situational factors. For example, North American players must adapt to larger international ice surfaces when playing in Europe, and European players must conversely make the adjustment to playing on smaller ice surfaces when they play in North America. Also, the quality of the ice conditions can vary from one arena to another and even during the course of a game, especially if a game goes into overtime. Playing at altitude and playing in hot arenas also require certain adjustments such as shorter shifts and even the use of oxygen between shifts. The Tampa Bay Lightning players could be seen taking oxygen from oxygen bottles at the bench between shifts during the Stanley Cup final against the Calgary Flames in June 2004 in Calgary, Alberta, which has an elevation of 1,140 metres.

From a psychological perspective, situational factors such as ice dimensions, quality of the ice, temperature in the arena and altitude can be distractions for certain players. The sport psychology consultant can play an important role in helping the coaching staff, support staff and players develop a thorough distraction control plan which will help players feel that they are well-prepared and ready to deal with these different playing conditions.

In addition to the aforementioned situational factors, players must also learn to cope with scheduling situations which may see them playing three games in three nights or playing afternoon games as opposed to evening games. When players are used to playing evening games, the afternoon games will require them to alter their pre-game routines as they will be eating their pre-game meal at a different time and they will not be able to have their pre-game nap.

Playing in different conditions and adapting to scheduling demands are only some of the situational factors that players must learn to cope with. On the social side of things, players are required to adjust to new coaches with different personalities, different coaching styles and new systems. Also, at times coaches may ask players to play out of position (e.g. a center being asked to play as a winger, an offensive player being assigned to a checking role, or a left-hand shot defence player playing as a right defence player). The consultant can help players view these situations as "challenges" which are part of the process of becoming a more complete and a more mature ice hockey player. Sharing examples and stories of other players who have successfully dealt with these challenging situations is a good way to help players adopt the proper perspective.

Sometimes it helps to sit down with a player and make a list of things that they can control and things that they can't control. By doing this, players feel more prepared in dealing with these situations and they learn to adopt a "stay in the solution" approach to new challenges.

Attitude

This final component of the *skills–knowledge–attitude* interactionist model is arguably the most important determinant of a player's performance potential.

Coaches, management and scouts in the sport of ice hockey refer to attitudinal factors as "character", and personality researchers might refer to them as "traits"; but whatever terminology is used, there would be agreement that the following list of personal attributes are major contributors to a player's success:

- Commitment
- Work ethic
- Passion for the game
- Drive and determination
- Perseverance
- Competitiveness
- Modesty
- Humility
- "Team first" attitude
- Selflessness

- Respectfulness
- Honesty
- Optimism
- Mental toughness
- Resiliency
- Responsibility
- Accountability
- Maturity
- Pride

A number of these intrapersonal factors are included in the "big five" model of personality (Gill, 2000) and from a trait theory perspective they are deemed to be relatively stable and enduring over time. However, even if personal attributes such as traits, character and attitude are relatively stable, the influence of situational factors such as a strong team environment and a team-oriented culture can have a significant influence on each player's attitude and subsequent behaviour. The sport psychology consultant can help the coaching staff establish a "team first" culture and help individual players develop the aforementioned attitudinal attributes. This form of consulting intervention has the goal of helping each athlete *grow* as a player and *grow* as a person within the overall goal of aiding the team to *grow* to its potential. In a later section we will discuss the use of role models, reinforcement and other intervention techniques to create a positive team environment and positive player attitudes.

TEACHING MENTAL AND EMOTIONAL SKILLS TO ICE HOCKEY PLAYERS

In this section we will discuss various strategies, techniques and modalities which sport psychology consultants can use to teach mental and emotional skills to ice hockey players. These skills overlap many of the mental and emotional skills required in other team sports; however, there are some skills which are unique due to the nature of the game, and the task demands of the three positions in hockey—goaltender, defence player or forward—which are similar to the positions in the sport of soccer. As mentioned in the previous section, it is important for the sport psychology consultant to be aware of the physical, technical, tactical, mental and emotional demands of each position and to let the coaching staff know what mental and emotional skills the players are working on. In this way the coaches can reinforce what is being taught when they interact with players during practices and games and at team meetings. It is strongly suggested that coaches attend the sport psychology consultant's team mental training meetings so that they become aware of the mental and emotional skills that are being taught. Likewise, strength and conditioning coaches and sports medicine personnel should be aware of what psychological skills are being developed so they can incorporate these skills into their intervention with the players. The key is to have a coherent approach with the coaching staff and support staff all using the same mental training terminology and constantly reinforcing players' efforts to stay focused, stay calm and stay relaxed while playing with lots of energy and competitive drive.

When teaching mental and emotional skills to ice hockey players, a useful model for helping players and coaches understand the link between these psychological skills and performance is the following:

Thoughts influence **Emotions** which influence **Actions/Performance**

Performance in turn provides the athlete with feedback that influences thoughts that again influence emotions. In essence a feedback loop is formed and by being conscious of their own thoughts and emotions, the players can take steps to control their self-talk/key words and feelings (Zaichkowsky & Naylor, 2004).

Since mental and emotional skills are intricately linked, it is valuable to identify a list of "psychological" skills that hockey players should master. They include but are not limited to self-awareness, self-regulation, managing stressors, arousal control, attention control, thought control, motivation, self-esteem, self-efficacy/confidence, handling injuries, resiliency, interpersonal skills, communication and leadership skills. A variety of *techniques* can be used to teach these skills to players and they include: goal-setting plans, diaphragmatic breathing, muscle relaxation, imagery, self-talk, simulation and biofeedback. In some cases the skills can be taught using a group/team approach but much of the time it requires one-on-one training because each player has unique individual needs for improvement.

For the consultant it is extremely useful to assess each player's knowledge of their mental and emotional skills so that a personalized plan can be established for teaching the most essential or foundational psychological skills. Assessment can take place in a number of ways, but it usually involves one or more of the following approaches: (1) an interview, (2) brief questionnaire, (3) observation or videotape of the athlete in practices and in games, (4) information provided by the coaching staff, (5) objective performance analysis such as statistics on retaliatory penalty minutes, (6) standardized mental skills instruments such as the OMSAT (Durand-Bush, Salmela & Green-Demers, 2001).

Improving Self-awareness and Knowledge

As discussed earlier, knowledge of oneself, knowledge of the game of hockey, and knowledge of situations are all important parts of the mental side of the game. By using the aforementioned assessment techniques, the consultant can help the athletes gain a greater awareness of their knowledge in these three domains. From this information, plans can be developed to improve specific mental skills. For example, if over-thinking and over-analyzing during games is identified as an area for improvement, the player should set, as a mental skill goal, the ability to make quick, accurate decisions during games. The player should then sit down with the coach to discuss the most frequently occurring challenges for that specific position during a game and review videotapes showing other players demonstrating proper execution because of rapid, accurate decision-making. The player then models this desired behavior covertly numerous times over the course of a day. What is important here is that the imagery events occur in "real time", or perhaps slightly faster than game speed, and the decision is always the correct one. This method is analogous to "over-speed" training of skating skills.

In addition to using imagery and thinking about specific game situations in advance (competition planning), the ability to focus and refocus are also important mental skills. Focusing is the ability to direct and maintain attention to important on-ice tasks and being able to stay in the moment. However, many athletes after making mistakes will begin to analyze the situation, dwell on it and lose focus. This is where the mental skill of refocusing comes into play as it enables the player to quickly regain effective focus after they have been distracted. The best way to intervene with loss of focus is to have hockey players identify potential distractions and develop a refocusing plan. An expanded version of the three Rs model, which Ken Ravizza used to help the Nebraska football team adopt a one-play-at-a-time approach to each game (Ravizza & Osborne, 1991), can be used to help ice hockey players stay in the present and play one-shift-at-a-time. This hockey-specific refocusing plan consists of seven Rs (see Figure 18.2).

The first R in this model is the player's ability to *Recognize* that he has made a mistake or a bad play and he needs to stay in control of his thoughts and emotions. At this point, while skating back to the bench after the stoppage in play, the player should *Relax* and take a quick deep breath to rid himself of any tension build-up which might occur because of the negative emotional response to the bad play or mistake. Then, while sitting on the bench awaiting his next shift, the player should take specific steps to *Release* the negative thoughts and the negative image of the mistake from his mind. This can be done by having the player first take another deep cleansing breath (note the word "cleansing"), then tap the shaft of his stick on the boards in front of him to symbolically send the negative thought and image elsewhere. At the same time he can tell himself to "park it" or "forget about it". Some players also find that it helps to do a quick *Review* of the mistake that they have just made, and to change the negative picture in their mind to a positive one by visualizing themselves making the right play. Other players prefer to wait until between periods or after the game to review the bad play on video with one of their coaches. This is just a personal preference

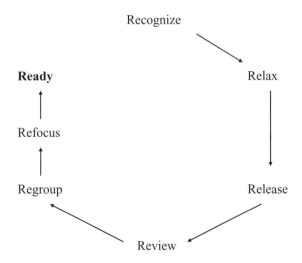

Figure 18.2 Using the Rs to regroup and refocus in ice hockey

and each athlete has to "figure out" what works best for them. Since many players tend to hang their heads and drop their shoulders when sitting on the bench after a difficult shift on the ice, the next step is important as the athletes learn to take control of their body language and *Regroup* by getting their head and shoulders up and their eyes back on the play, instead of looking down. These steps help the athlete get their attention out of the past and into the present, and prevent them from dwelling on the mistake. The player is now focused on the action on the ice in front of them and they are getting *Ready* for the next shift.

The nice thing about using the Rs in the sport of ice hockey is that players return to the bench after a 40- to 60-second shift on the ice and they have time to regroup and refocus before going back on the ice for their next shift. Eventually, by using the Rs repeatedly over time, players will learn to get from Recognition to Ready very quickly and this refocusing mental skill becomes a learned response which they utilize automatically.

Ice hockey players should also be encouraged to use the Rs during practices and to include them in their imagery sessions. This will enable them to practice and train with greater quality and consistency as they have more control of their thoughts, their emotions and their focus. Coaches can help players master the Rs and refocus by telling them when they return to the bench after a bad play or mistake, to "park it" and focus on the next shift.

When teaching focusing and refocusing skills to hockey players, it helps to point out that hockey is a simple game and so are the concepts of focusing and refocusing. Focusing comes down to doing three basic things—getting focused for the game, staying focused for 60 minutes, and refocusing if the athlete gets distracted. Also, in terms of an athlete's focus it can be in one of three places—in the past, in the present or in the future. The key for players is to have their focus in the present (here and now) and to play "one shift at a time". It is nice to have some fun with the players and tell them that this focus and refocus stuff isn't exactly "rocket science"!

Stephen Covey in his new book *The 8th Habit* (Covey, 2004) summarizes the mental skill of attention control very nicely when he states: "You should no longer waste your energy on something that you can do nothing about" and that people "should not let their past hold their future hostage" (p. 135). This is simple but "timeless wisdom".

On a similar note, in a recent article based on Doug Newburg's resonance performance model (Newburg, Kimiciek, Durand-Bush & Doell, 2002), the authors present research findings which show that peak performers in the fields of sports, music, surgery and business have learned to: "manage their feelings when faced with obstacles. Rather than focusing on their initial response, which may often be negative, they quickly change their reaction to a more positive and appropriate one" (p. 257). This is similar to Deci's (1996) notion of people controlling their emotions in difficult situations and learning to have power over their emotions instead of being "pawns" to them.

In teaching hockey players mental skills such as refocusing and the use of the Rs, it really helps if you can provide hockey-specific examples with professional players discussing their use of these skills. The following quote from a highly respected NHL player, Steve Yzerman, is a perfect example of a credible role model using the aforementioned refocusing technique to keep his focus in the present and not dwell on mistakes.

> I don't dwell on mistakes. I see the mistake only once to learn what I did wrong. Then
> I review the same situation in my mind and change what I did to eliminate the mistake.
> Steve Yzerman (Detroit Red Wings Captain, three-time Stanley Cup Champion)

In addition to sharing quotes from professional athletes, the consultant can communicate mental skills information to hockey players by showing them video clips with high-profile players discussing their use of mental skills both in pre-game preparation and during games. These video clips can be obtained by videotaping interviews with professional athletes before, during and after games. The interviews do not have to be limited only to professional hockey players as athletes have respect for high-profile figures in other sports, and a good example of this is Tiger Woods discussing the strategy that he uses to refocus after a bad shot in golf. In a recent interview on the television program *60 Minutes*, Tiger Woods said that after a bad shot he does three things—first he *analyzes* what went wrong, then he *learns* from it, and finally he tells himself to *move on*. Tiger Woods is one of the mentally toughest athletes in the world and, like Steve Yzerman, he has "figured out" how to control his thoughts and his focus and "stay in the moment".

Developing a library of pertinent video clips and showing them at team meetings is a great way for the sport psychology consultant to demystify the use of psychological skills and motivate hockey players of all ages to work on improving their mental and emotional skills. It helps if the video clips are from current sporting events including professional sports, college sports, Olympic Games and World Championships.

Controlling Emotions

As previously mentioned, ice hockey is a sport which is played with great emotion and it is important to understand the interesting history related to the construct of "emotion" and its relationship to other related terms such as "anxiety", "stress" and "arousal". For a review of this history we refer you to Hanin (2000) and Zaichkowsky and Baltzell (2000).

After more than 50 years of research on stress and emotions, Lazarus (2000) has isolated 15 emotions and placed them into several categories. The emotions include: anger, fright, guilt, shame, sadness, envy, jealousy, happiness, pride, relief, hope, love, gratitude and compassion. After working with hockey players for many years it is clear that the most important emotions are: anger, anxiety, happiness, pride and gratitude. Anger and anxiety are typically negative emotions that constantly have to be controlled. Being happy (a positive emotion), in contrast to being sad, allows a player to be in the proper mood when going into training and competition. Coaches want hockey players to "have fun" while training and competing and this would not be possible if a player constantly displayed the emotion of sadness. Pride is another positive emotion which players feel in pulling on the hockey jersey with the logo of their country, their city or their school. This emotion is especially strong when players represent their country at the Olympic Games and other international competitions. Coaches often refer to pride in their team or in their country when motivating players. Also, players feel a lot of pride when their gritty, competitive efforts are recognized by their coach after the game in front of their teammates. Every player wants to feel that they have contributed to the team success and it is important for coaches to recognize and reinforce the many ways in which players fulfill their roles during the game and "make a difference" in the outcome of the competition.

Gratitude is a seemingly unimportant emotion in sport but it warrants discussion when dealing with hockey players. Lazarus (2000) defines gratitude as an "appreciation for an altruistic gift that provides personal benefit". In the world of professional and Olympic sport, many athletes are criticized by the media for being selfish and egocentric. However, hockey players in general have not been branded with this label. Most hockey players show the emotion of gratitude and it may be due to the earlier mentioned historical and cultural heritage which many players came from, grew up in, and were socialized into.

A number of techniques are used by sport psychology consultants to teach hockey players and other athletes strategies for controlling their emotions (Zaichkowsky & Baltzell, 2000). In some instances players need to decrease arousal or emotional intensity and in other cases they need to increase their emotional intensity. It is important that players learn to "self-regulate" their emotions, although it is well known that certain psychologically minded coaches are capable of brilliantly influencing the emotions of their players.

Following is a brief discussion of commonly used techniques to regulate emotions:

1. Breathing is a powerful physiological technique that regulates emotion. Slow diaphragmatic breaths allow a player to decrease anxiety, nervousness or arousal.
2. Progressive muscle relaxation is used to teach athletes to "relax" muscles that have become tense because of perceived stress or pressure of the competition.
3. Stretching and exercising muscles can serve to reduce tension.
4. Emotions can be intensified by having players do rapid muscle tensing or physically "hit" each other under controlled conditions.
5. Meditation and yoga are techniques that are typically used to teach "calmness" and lower arousal.
6. Biofeedback is another technique that can be used effectively to both reduce and increase arousal (Zaichkowsky & Naylor, 2004).
7. Music is another powerful method of both reducing arousal and increasing it. Players enjoy listening to their favourite music to relax their body and their mind; however, they should know that that there are certain pieces of music that can energize them. Gifted coaches will use music to help regulate the emotions of their players in creative ways as they prepare for competition. For example, soft relaxing music can be played in the dressing room as players dress and prepare for the pre-game warm-up. Then, prior to going on the ice for warm-up, more up-tempo music is played to "energize" the player. Some players enjoy listening to CDs on their personal headsets that contain relaxing music and subliminal messages such as "You are strong", "You are quick", "You are ready".

As mentioned earlier, imagery is a favourite technique for teaching effective decision-making and mastering certain technical and tactical skills; however, it can also be very valuable for teaching the control of emotions. Players simply identify their most positive emotions and they mentally rehearse playing with these emotions activated. The consultant can help the athlete identify those moments in games when they were playing with lots of confidence and were really happy and enjoying the challenge of a hard-fought contest.

If anger and subsequent frustration for being high-sticked, or cross-checked by an opponent is part of a player's emotional response and behavior, then imagery can be used effectively to help eliminate this undesirable behaviour. Cautela and Samdperil (1989) have developed an excellent method called the "self-control triad" for teaching anger self-regulation and controlling other negative behaviors. The procedure has the athlete say "Stop!" to himself (self-talk), take a deep breath through the mouth, slowly exhale through the nose thus relaxing the body, and then quickly visualize a positive outcome.

As mentioned earlier, the use of video is also a powerful method for teaching mental and emotional skills. Technology today permits rapid digital editing of "success" frames from game tapes. Video clips can be obtained showing teammates, top players or Hall of Fame players from the past demonstrating mental and emotional parts of the game such as "mental toughness", "emotional control", "intensity" and "selflessness" (Haberl & Zaichkowsky, 2003; Halliwell, 1990). Players enjoy watching and modeling from game videos and also videos from other body contact sports such as football and soccer. Video clips from Hollywood films can also serve a useful purpose when excerpts are used to demonstrate people using mental and emotional skills in a variety of situations.

Finally, the use of bulletin boards and pep-talks from the coach can usually serve to increase players' emotions. It is common for coaches to capitalize on disrespectful quotes made by an opposing coach or player that belittle a player or the team. The belief is that posting these quotes and giving an inspirational pre-game pep-talk will energize the emotional system of each player to the point where they will play with increased passion and intensity.

In concluding this section on teaching mental and emotional skills, we have found that many players enjoy reading newspaper articles, short essays and in some cases books that teach lessons about the mental and emotional keys to success. A good example of this type of intervention occurred when John Tortorella, head coach of the Tampa Bay Lightning in the NHL, placed a copy of the book *Good to Great* (Collins, 2001) in each player's locker at the team's training camp in 2004. The players were asked to read about how a number of companies went from being "good" to "great" by adhering to mental and emotional principles such as a "culture of discipline", vision, passion and a "team first" attitude. It is hard to extrapolate a cause–effect relationship, but the Tampa Bay Lightning ended up winning the Stanley Cup championship nine months later.

It should be noted that the reading materials distributed to hockey players do not have to be hockey-specific, as most players like to learn from athletes and coaches in other sports. There is a great mutual respect among world-class athletes and they are genuinely interested in knowing more about other elite performers' mental training techniques.

PLANNING AND PSYCHOLOGICAL PREPARATION

An ice hockey season consists of a number of distinct parts and, as opposed to individual sports, the athlete is very dependent on the team to provide a training plan and to take care of all logistics related to training, pre-game meals and travel to competitions. The sport psychology consultant can play an important role in helping a hockey player look at the 12 months in a year and do some effective planning to optimize their training and ensure that they have a comprehensive plan to improve not only their physical, technical and tactical skills, but also their mental and emotional skills.

The hockey season can be viewed as having six parts. The first part is often called the "off-season" and in years past hockey players would have four to five months "off" where they would play other sports and do very little hockey-specific off-ice training. However, today most ice hockey players from a very young age participate in summer training at summer hockey schools or play in elite summer hockey tournaments. Professional hockey players work with their personal trainers during the summer months to gain explosive strength and improve their aerobic capacity and flexibility. The summer months are no longer an "off-season" for elite or even youth hockey players and this is a good time to construct an annual plan and to read and learn more about the mental and emotional side of ice hockey.

Following the summer months "off-season" period there are essentially five other phases of a hockey season and they are: pre-season, early season, mid-season, late season, and post-season or playoff time. There are a number of times during these six periods when the sport psychology consultant can work with both individual players and with hockey teams. The summer is a good time for individual meetings to discuss a player's dreams and goals. A personal improvement plan with specific goals and strategies to improve physical, technical, tactical, mental and emotional areas of the athlete's game can be developed. On elite teams the consultant can work closely with the team's conditioning coach and the coaching staff to construct an overall plan to help the athlete maximize their potential as a hockey player.

The pre-season is a time when the consultant can schedule team meetings to present the major components of a mental training program and get to know new players on the team. The first team meeting is a great opportunity for the consultant to share their knowledge, experience and passion for teaching mental and emotional skills. This is an ideal time to show videos with testimonials from elite hockey players and other elite athletes discussing the strategies that they use to get mentally and emotionally ready for practices and games. Also, the skills–knowledge–attitude model presented earlier (Figure 18.1) can be used to show athletes the many ways that they can improve specific areas of their game by having a plan and working hard every day. Using expressions like "Success is a choice", "Training hard is not a sacrifice—training hard is a choice!" and "Success happens by choice—not by chance!" is a good way to help players realize that commitment, work ethic and discipline are fundamental to all athletic success.

In a recent television interview at the World Junior Hockey Championships, when Wayne Gretzky was asked to explain how he became the greatest hockey player in the world, he paused and then stated that there were three reasons for his success—*consistency, work ethic and pride.* We could also add passion to this list as Wayne Gretzky exudes passion when he talks about his playing career, and his present managerial work with the Olympic Hockey Teams and World Cup teams in Hockey Canada's successful Program of Excellence.

Another concept that can be discussed at a team pre-season meeting is the analogy that the team is about to embark on a great "journey" which will end sometime in the spring with the team having an "opportunity" to win a championship together. The key is for the team to focus on the process of "getting better every day". Words like "opportunity" and "choices" should be front and center in the players' thoughts, and it helps to post banners or have words on the dressing-room wall which use these words. A great banner to help players focus on commitment, consistency and choices is the expression: "Daily decisions determine destiny". The alliteration with the four Ds helps these words "stick" in players' minds.

The pre-season is also a good time for the consultant to discuss with the coaching staff and the players the development of a team theme or slogan for the upcoming season. These team themes help establish the team's identity as they capture the way that the team trains on and off the ice and their style of play. Examples of these team themes are the following:

- "It's all about commitment".
- "Whatever it takes".
- "Win the battles".
- "Ever excel".

- "Win from within".
- "Get better every day".
- "No regrets".
- "No excuses".

In the hallowed Montreal Canadiens dressing room, head coach Claude Julien has posted a sign above the door that the players pass through each day as they go onto the ice. The message which the players see each day is: "Work together—Grow together—Win together".

Brent Sutter, the coach of Canada's gold medal winning National Junior Team at the recent World Junior Hockey Championships is also the head coach of the Red Deer Rebels junior team in Western Canada, and he has only one word on the wall in his team's dressing room; that word is: "Work".

The Montreal Canadiens and the Red Deer Rebels teams both play hard for 60 minutes every game and a strong work ethic is an integral part of their team identity. By having these work-oriented team themes on the dressing-room walls, the players have daily visual reminders of a value that is at the foundation of everything that they do. As discussed in the introduction section of this chapter, the work ethic was an integral part of Canada's historical and cultural heritage and the influence of this strong value system is still evident in modern-day hockey.

As the team moves through the season, the consultant should try to see a number of games in person to get a "feel" for how the team plays and to watch players' actions and reactions both during play and between shifts when they are sitting on the bench. Likewise, attending the team's games is a great opportunity for the consultant to observe the coach's behavior, body language and comments to the players during the game. If possible, it helps if the sport psychology consultant can make a road trip with the team and get a chance to know the players a bit better while observing how they interact with each other off the ice and how they play in away games.

The final part of the season and the post-season with playoffs are the most fun for everyone. In the final weeks of the season the teams are competing for playoff positions and home ice advantage, and then during the playoffs all games are "must-win" situations. This gives the consultant an opportunity to see how the players and coaches deal with pressure situations and different forms of adversity such as injuries, questionable officiating and bad breaks.

In preparation for the playoffs the sport psychology consultant can play an important role in helping the team get "emotionally" ready for the intensity of playoff hockey. To this end, the consultant can help facilitate the development of a specific team theme which serves as an emotional mantra of how the team wants to play in the playoffs. These themes and slogans evolve from discussions with the coaching staff and input from the players. The key is that the players have to feel "ownership" of the playoff theme. For a more in-depth discussion of the dynamics of developing team playoff themes, the reader is referred to an article by Halliwell (2004) entitled, "Preparing professional hockey players for playoff performance". Examples of playoff themes include:

- "Pay the price".
- "Empty the tank".
- "Make it happen".
- "Get it done".
- "Focus and enjoy".

- "Team first".
- "Walk away".
- "Discipline over emotion".

The last two playoff themes are extremely effective because they focus the players' attention on the need to play with discipline and control their emotions. It is very important for players to play hard in the playoffs but they must also be able to control their emotions and not retaliate when infractions are committed against them. In playoff games the teams with the greatest discipline get more power-play opportunities and this gives them a tremendous advantage for creating scoring chances. The other playoff themes in this list capture the importance of emotional preparation, selflessness, competing with intensity, and enjoying the challenge of playoff hockey. Being able to keep things in perspective and approaching the playoffs with excitement instead of fear are key to creating a mindset which enables players to "free up" and "let their talent come out" (Botterill & Patrick, 2003). When Wayne Gretzky talked to the Canadian National Junior Team before the gold medal game at the recent World Junior Hockey Championships, he told the players to pretend that they were kids playing "pond hockey" and to be "excited" about this great "opportunity" to play for their country. These words of wisdom from a Hall of Fame player, who has won a number of Stanley Cup finals and World Championship gold medals, were well received by the 17- to 19-year-old members of Team Canada and they went out and played a great game and defeated the Russian team to win the gold medal.

The aforementioned playoff themes can also be printed onto T-shirts which the players, coaches and support staff wear throughout the playoffs. These theme T-shirts have a team-building effect as everyone makes a commitment to the words on their back and plays hard for "each other" as the team pursues its mission of winning a championship. Also, creating highlight videotapes with music chosen by the players is another way to emotionally energize the players and help them play with confidence and consistency during the playoffs. For more details on preparing motivational videos for hockey teams please refer to the articles by Halliwell (1990, 2004).

Psychological Preparation for Competitions

Most ice hockey players have pre-game routines and rituals which they follow when they arrive at the arena. In the hallway outside a hockey team's dressing room, players can be seen working on their hockey sticks with a saw, a torch or a file to get the shaft of their sticks cut to the proper length, and the blade of their stick shaped and bent until it "feels" just right. Also, players will tape the blades of their sticks and make a knob at the top of the shaft of their stick so that the stick feels comfortable in their hands. They will also check their skate blades to make sure that they are sharpened perfectly and don't have any nicks on them.

In addition to making sure that their sticks and skates are ready, players usually do some form of off-ice physical warm-up prior to the game to ensure that the muscles in their body core are warm and their leg and shoulder muscles have been stretched. As a follow-up to this off-ice physical warm-up, the players also have a 10- to 15-minute skate about 30 minutes prior to the game to further warm up their muscles while participating in a programmed series of passing, shooting and skating exercises.

Before going on the ice for their pre-game skate, the players also attend a short team meeting in which the coaches discuss the offensive and defensive game plan and specific assignments for line combinations and defence pairings. From this brief description of an ice-hockey player's pre-game routine, it is clear that players engage in specific steps to ensure that they are physically, technically and tactically prepared to start the game. This leads to the question, "What are players doing to get themselves mentally and emotionally ready for the game?" Unfortunately, the answer is probably, "Not much!" To help underscore the importance of each player's pre-game mental preparation, it can be helpful if the sport psychology consultant writes the following words on a blackboard or whiteboard during a team meeting:

Skates ✓
Sticks ✓
Body   ✓
Mind   ?

This simple visual, with check marks beside the words "skates", "sticks" and "body", and a question mark beside the word "mind", is a simple but effective way to remind players that the mental part of their pre-game preparation has not been attended to. The consultant can then begin to discuss how players can use mental skills such as visualization, relaxation, activation and self-talk in their pre-game preparation routines.

For example, after the pre-game meeting players can take a moment to visualize their role in the offensive system or defensive system and they can see and feel themselves playing in each of the three zones on the ice. Mark Recchi, an experienced NHL player who plays with a lot of intensity from the first minute until the last minute of every game, attributes his consistency to his pre-game preparation and the imagery that he does before every game. His imagery consists of seeing himself playing his role in each of the three zones on the ice. First of all, he sees himself playing his role in the defensive zone, and then when his team has possession of the puck he feels himself moving through the neutral zone in synch with his teammates. The third component of his imagery consists of seeing and feeling himself entering the offensive zone and "driving to the net", "staying on rebounds", "winning battles" for loose pucks in the corners and playing "short shift hockey"—i.e. playing hard, short shifts of 40 to 45 seconds. This type of pre-game imagery has helped Mark Recchi become a more complete and responsible hockey player as he has learned how to contribute to his team's performance in both a defensive and offensive role.

To enable players to understand the concept of pre-game mental preparation and getting their minds ready for the game, it helps to compare the player's mind to a computer which needs to be programmed with good thoughts and good pictures. The thoughts are the key words in the athlete's self-talk and the pictures are the images that they visualize. The use of self-talk in combination with imagery serves a dual purpose as it helps players to get focused prior to the game and control their pre-game anxiety by becoming totally immersed in thinking about things that they can control such as their effort and the execution of their role on the team. By thinking about and focusing on the process of playing the game, instead of worrying about the outcome of the game, players feel less anxiety as they get totally absorbed in performing and contributing to the team. Jackson and Csikszentmihalyi (1999) in their excellent book, *Flow in Sports*, refer to total absorption and immersion in performing the task at hand as being one of the keys to "getting into the groove", "getting in the zone", and into a state of flow where the athlete performs with effortless efficiency. By using self-talk, imagery, relaxation and focusing techniques in their pre-game prep, ice hockey players can create an ideal performance state and enhance their ability to perform with confidence and at times get into a state of flow.

Specific Psychological Interventions in Ice Hockey

Having described the culture of ice hockey and the planning, teaching and use of mental skills in pre-game and game settings, we will now examine specific situations in which the sport psychology consultant's knowledge and experience can benefit ice hockey teams when they face unexpected adversity. In this regard, from time to time the consultant may be called upon to assist a team following "traumatic" events and assist with team bereavement and critical incident intervention. At Boston University, in the last decade, at least three hockey-related incidents could be classified as traumatic. The first incident involved a Boston University goaltender who had potential for a promising professional career. While returning from work one evening on his bicycle, he was struck by a car and received massive head injuries. He was rushed to a hospital and remained in a coma for several days. Medical prognosis moved from probable death to recovery, but with permanent motor and psychological damage. The hockey player, however, began a "miraculous" recovery over a two-year period with the assistance of physical therapy and psychological support to the point where he was able to play one more season of college hockey and one year at the professional level. The sport psychology team at Boston University provided both "grief" assistance to the hockey team following the accident and psychological support for the hockey player during his recovery.

A second case occurred several years later and has become an international story (Roy & Swift, 1998). Travis Roy was a promising 20-year-old hockey player participating in his first collegiate game. Eleven seconds into the game, Roy fell head first into the boards, cracked his fourth cervical vertebrae and injured his spinal cord. He was paralyzed from the neck down. The coaching staff, sports medicine staff and team sport psychology consultant learned by the end of the first period that Roy's injury was serious and that in all likelihood he would have permanent paralysis. However, his teammates were not informed of the severity of the injury until the conclusion of the game. Extensive debriefing and critical incident counselling was provided to the team as they attempted to cope with the loss of a teammate. During recovery, the paralyzed player received counseling to help him adjust to a life that went from being an elite athlete to that of an individual confined to a wheel chair.

The third and most traumatic incident involved a Boston-area high school hockey team that had a player tragically die during a game. The 16-year-old player was hit squarely in the chest by an opponent during a routine bodycheck. The player fell to the ice but died instantly from what was considered "concussion of the heart" (Curfman, 1998). The sport psychology team at Boston University, along with the broader professional and amateur hockey community, assisted the high school team with the trauma of coping with tragedy.

The lessons learned from these traumatic or catastrophic injuries is that sport psychology consultants need to be prepared for these situations even though they are relatively rare. Athletes typically do not want to have outside clinical psychologists help them with this emotional trauma. Rather, they prefer to work with individuals who have an understanding of their "sport" culture and this is usually a sport psychology consultant who knows the players and the team dynamics. In 1992, when we first encountered "traumatic events", there were no textbooks or manuals to assist consultants in helping athletes during catastrophic incidents. Not much has changed; however, there are guidelines that have been published (Neal, 2003) as well as an article that describes "critical incident stress debriefing" (CISD) (Vernaccia, Reardon & Templin, 1997). We have learned that every sport organization should have their own "catastrophic incident plan" so that they may provide information and support to family members, teammates, coaches and staff following a catastrophe. By having a systematic plan in place that includes a management team, an action plan, chain of command and critical phone numbers, then uncertainty, chaos and confusion can be avoided.

Further, sport psychology consultants should learn about interventions beyond "performance-enhancing" interventions. Critical incident stress debriefing (Mitchell & Everly, 1993) is a skill that all members of the sports medicine support team should learn. They can be involved in pre-incident education, understand how to advise and support at the scene of the trauma, and play an important role in the debriefing process.

Debriefing typically includes seven phases and they include:

1. An introduction phase where ground rules and confidentiality are established with participants such as the members of a hockey team,
2. Fact phase where specific details of the trauma are communicated,
3. Thought phase where athletes are asked to think seriously about the injury and what impact they believe that it has on them,
4. Reaction phase where teammates are asked to communicate their reactions to the event even though many athletes feel uncomfortable talking about the traumatic event,
5. Symptom phase where teammates share their reactions,
6. Teaching phase where the sport psychology consultant provides post-incident education in order to decrease stress, and finally,
7. Re-entry phase where the sport psychology team expands on points that are important for the specific situation and help the athletes deal with emotions so that they are still not "raw".

This description of the "psychological effect" of a traumatic incident on the team leads us to consider other personal and situational factors that can have a significant "psychological effect" on the team environment. In fact, the perceptive sport psychology consultant might quickly notice that trying to improve the "psychological effects" in the environment, and the reaction to them, may often be the first intervention priority. Even though teaching psychological skills to the players is the main reason that sport psychology professionals are invited to work with ice hockey teams, being aware of and attending to the psychological impact of the hockey culture and the emotional strain of competition may need attention first.

For example, supporting the trainer, who may be tired, overloaded and stressed, can be the sport psychology consultant's best initial investment. The trainer has extensive contact with players, coaches and staff and it is often critical to help them cope and set a positive, fun, emotional tone in the team's dressing room. Similarly, assistant coaches, equipment managers, massage therapists and strength coaches all periodically need reinforcement and feedback on the important role they play in optimizing the psychological effects in the team environment. Head coaches, management, scouts and travel assistants can also benefit from feedback on their roles in establishing a positive climate. Perhaps the most important people affecting psychological effects with professional players are spouses, partners and family. Efforts to make members of the players' immediate families feel informed, supported and made aware of their important support role for the players can dramatically improve psychological effects.

For players, good team discussion of shared priorities (e.g. family first), commitments and clarified roles on the team can have positive psychological effects on both the individuals and the team. Players wrestling with injury dynamics and their role and contribution to the team may need work on "perspective", and the use of relaxation techniques and imagery to optimize recovery. The player getting limited ice time might need reminders from the sport psychology consultant on how to optimize preparation and maintain a high level of readiness if called upon to play. For example, if the player is sitting on the bench for long periods, or watching the game from the stands, he can use imagery to "play his position in the skates of the person on the ice" and be mentally ready to contribute when his chance to play occurs. In the playoffs it is especially important to stay "ready" to step into or "up" the lineup because injuries are almost inevitable due to the increased physical and emotional intensity of the games.

SUMMARY

In this chapter we have taken a look at the role of the sport psychology consultant in working with athletes, coaches and support people in a sport which is played with passion and emotion and is often referred to as the "fastest game in the world". Ice hockey is played amidst a unique combination of physical, social and cultural forces, and hopefully the topics discussed have shed informative light on both the psychological dynamics of this fascinating sport, and the various ways that sport psychology consultants can help the participants optimize their performance and enjoyment of the game.

REFERENCES

Botterill, C. (1990). Sport psychology and professional hockey. *Sport Psychologist, 4*, 358–368.
Botterill, C. & Patrick, T. (2003). *Perspective : The Key to life.* Winnipeg: Lifeskills Inc.
Cautela, J.R. & Samdperil, L. (1989). Imalgetics: the application of covert conditioning to athletic performance. *Journal of Applied Sport Psychology, 1*, 82–97.
Collins, J. (2001). *Good to Great.* New York: Harper Collins.
Covey, S. (2004). *The 8th Habit: From Effectiveness to Greatness.* New York: Free Press.
Curfman, G.D. (1998). Fatal impact-concussion of the heart. *New England Journal of Medicine, 338*(25), 1841–1843.
Deci, E.L. (1996). *Why We Do What We Do: The Dynamics of Personal Autonomy.* New York: Putnam.
Dryden, K. & MacGregor, R. (1989). *Home Game.* Toronto: McClelland & Stewart.
Durand-Bush, N., Salmela, J.H. & Green-Demers, N. (2001). The Ottawa Mental Skills Assessment Tool (OMSAT-3*). *Sport Psychologist, 15*, 1–15.
Gill, D. (2000). *Psychological Dynamics of Sport and Exercise.* Champaign, IL: Human Kinetics.
Gretzky, W. (2001). *On Family, Hockey and Healing.* Toronto: Random House.
Haberl, P. & Zaichkowsky, L. (2003). The US Olympic women's Olympic gold medal ice hockey team: optimal use of sport psychology for developing confidence. In R. Lidor & K.P. Henschen (eds) *The Psychology of Team Sports* (pp. 217–233). Morgantown, WV: Fitness Information Technology Publishers.

Halliwell, W. (1990). Delivering sport psychology services in professional hockey. *Sport Psychologist,* *4,* 369–377.

Halliwell, W. (2004). Preparing professional hockey players for playoff performance. *Athletic Insight,* 6(2), September.

Halliwell, W., Orlick, T., Ravizza, K. & Rotella, R. (1999). *Consultant's Guide to Excellence.* Chelsea, CAN: Baird, O'Keefe.

Hanin, Y.L. (2000). *Emotions in Sport.* Champaign, IL: Human Kinetics.

Hunter, D. (2004). *Yzerman: The Making of a Champion.* Toronto: Doubleday Canada.

Jackson, S. & Csikszentmihalyi, M. (1999) *Flow in Sports.* Champaign, IL: Human Kinetics.

Klein, G. (1998). *Sources of Power.* Cambridge, Mass: MIT Press.

Lazarus, R. (2000). How emotions influence performance in competitive sports. *Sport Psychologist,* *14,* 229–252.

Loehr, J. (1995). *The New Toughness Training for Sports.* New York: Plume.

Mitchell, J.T. & Everly, G.S. (1993). *Critical Incident Stress Debriefing: (CSID).* Ellicott City, MD: Chevron Publishing Company.

Neal, T.L. (2003). Catastrophic incident guideline plan. *NATA News, 12.*

Newburg, D., Kimiciek, J., Durand-Bush, N. & Doell, K. (2002). The role of resonance in performance excellence and life engagement. *Journal of Applied Sport Psychology, 14,* 249–267.

Ravizza, K. & Osborne, T. (1991). Nebraska's 3 R's: One-play-at-a-time preperformance routine for collegiate football. *Sport Psychologist, 5,* 256–265.

Rogerson, L.J. & Hrycaiko, D.W. (2002). Enhancing competitive performance of ice-hockey goal-tenders using centering and self-talk. *Journal of Applied Sport Psychology, 14,* 14–26.

Roy, T. & Swift, E.M. (1998). *Eleven Seconds: A Story of Tragedy, Courage and Triumph.* New York: Warner Books.

Spiros, D. (1990). *Six Shooters: Hockey's Sutter Brothers.* Scarborough, Ont: Prentice-Hall.

Twist, P. (1997). *Complete Conditioning for Ice Hockey.* Champaign, IL: Human Kinetics.

Vernaccia, R.A., Reardon, J.P. & Templin, T.J. (1997). Sudden death in sport: Managing the aftermath. *Sport Psychologist, 11,* 223–235.

Weinberg, R. & Gould, D. (2003). *Foundations of Sport and Exercise psychology.* Champaign, IL: Human Kinetics.

Zaichkowsky, L. (1994). Biofeedback and imagery assisted self-regulation training in sports: research evidence and practical application. In S. Tsutsui & M. Kodama (eds) *Biobehavioral Self-regulation in the East and West.* Tokyo: Springer-Verlag Inc.

Zaichkowsky, L. & Baltzell, A. (2000). Arousal and performance. In R.N. Singer, H.A. Hausenblas & C.M. Janelle (eds) *Handbook of Sport Psychology.* (2nd edn; pp. 319–339). New York: John Wiley & Sons.

Zaichkowsky, L. & Naylor, A. (2004). Arousal in sport. In C. Spielberger (ed.) *Encyclopedia of Applied Sport Psychology.* New York: John Wiley & Sons.

CHAPTER 19

A Mental Preparation Guide for Figure Skaters: A Developmental Approach

Eva V. Monsma

University of South Carolina, USA

and

Deborah L. Feltz

Michigan State University, USA

INTRODUCTION

A unique combination of artistry and athleticism define the sport of figure skating, which has seen an increase in worldwide popularity over the past decade. This interest has stimulated a variety of recreational learn-to-skate programs and expanded competitive skating opportunities including those for adult (even Senior Olympics participants), intercollegiate and Special Olympic athletes. Such extensions have increased ice-time demands, specialized training and injuries, and thereby opportunities for working with figure skaters, especially in Canada and the United States. Considering the costs of ice-time, multiple coaches, skates and costumes, nowadays skaters and parents are certainly interested in efficient development as well as in achieving a competitive edge.

Competitive figure skating is divided into four disciplines: singles free skating (men or women), ice dancing, pair skating and, the most recent addition, the team event of synchronized skating. Because each discipline has its own idiosyncrasies, we have focused each section to highlight discipline-specific issues. We begin with acquainting practitioners with testing and competition structures and related judging criteria. Next, we summarize research on the experiences of elite competitors followed by an overview of potential issues that professionals face when working with this population. Because figure skaters are predominantly young female participants, we have given special attention to developmental or age-related physical and psychological differences. We also address planning for the season. The chapter concludes with age-appropriate intervention solutions beneficial for dealing with the stresses within this sport.

The Sport Psychologist's Handbook: A Guide for Sport-Specific Performance Enhancement.
Edited by Joaquín Dosil. © 2006 John Wiley & Sons, Ltd.

AN OVERVIEW OF TESTING AND
COMPETITION STRUCTURES

Eligibility to compete in any skating discipline requires the mastery of basic introductory skating skills which are generally taught in cost-effective group lesson environments. This initial phase of once-a-week participation lasts approximately three years (Scanlan, Ravizza & Stein, 1989a). Competitive structures emulate the testing ladder with skating programs consisting of choreographed sequences of movements including required elements that increase in technical difficulty as skaters move up the testing and competition structures. The rules governing figure skating in Canada and the USA, and in most other countries worldwide, are directed by the International Skating Union (ISU) which also directs the sport of speed skating. National skating federations such as Skate Canada and the United States Figure Skating Association (USFSA) ultimately follow guidelines put forth by the ISU, although there are some minor variations. Rulebooks presenting details of elements required for technical programs, among other attributes of testing and competition, are modified annually and are available in September of each year for a nominal fee from respective national organizations.

Rulebooks in North America can be ordered on respective websites http://www.skatecanada.ca/en/skate_for_life/programs and http://www.usfsa.org/Programs.asp?id=120. These websites host a wealth of current information useful for understanding skating elements, judging criteria, the basic structure of various tests including age specifications and the current required elements for various programs in singles, ice dancing, pair skating and synchronized skating.

Although figure skating in both Canada and the USA are governed by the ISU and have a similar approach for teaching fundamental movements and basics skating skills, offering hockey-specific programs and programs for developing artistry (interpretive and artistry in motion, respectively), there are marked differences in program titles, competitive levels and geographical divisions for national qualifying competitions. The details of basic instructional programs and competitive titles are explicitly outlined on respective websites. In sum, from a geographic standpoint, skaters eligible for qualifying competitions in the USA compete in regional and sectional competitions towards qualifying for nationals; whereas, Canadian skaters compete in sectionals and divisionals to gain eligibility for nationals. Perhaps the most important differences relevant to professionals interested in psychologically preparing figure skaters for testing and competing are approaches towards discipline-specific talent development and the nature of recognizing achievement.

Discipline specialization is an early feature of the US basic skills structure offering programs for free skating, dance, synchronized skating and pairs. In contrast, figure skating in Canada does not emphasize basic pair skating skills in developmental programs, but follows a more holistic approach in their athlete development model. Here, general skating skills, physical development, spinning, jumping, life skills and psychological development are written into the frameworks of their programs. The Canadian Starskate testing structure is followed by both recreational and competitive track skaters and is designed to develop figure skating skills in four different areas: skills, test, achievement and recognition. At the highest levels of competition (junior and senior), both countries' competitive structures follow similar tracks geared at qualifying skaters for national level competition.

Testing Structures

After learning basic elements, skaters join skating clubs and continue to develop their skills in recreational or competitive tracks with private professional coaches called "Pros". Tests function to provide a sequential structure for learning skills and the development of performance artistry, enabling skaters to challenge their abilities. Skaters develop their skills within the testing structure and train for "trying" tests (i.e. attempting a test in front of judges) on specific test dates regularly offered at local skating clubs. Tests are generally marked on a pass or retry basis with each test specifying the standards for passing. Like competitions, taking tests are high-stakes, anxiety-provoking assessment situations requiring significant amounts of physical and mental preparation. Competitive and recreational skaters take the same tests enduring identical scrutiny from judges and, thus, both recreational and competitive skaters stand to benefit from psychological skills preparation. They are also similar in the frequency and type (e.g. off-ice conditioning, choreography) of training. For example, Vadocz, Siegel & Malina (2002) found that recreational skaters spend 4 to 12 hours a week practicing on-ice and an additional 1 to 7 hours in off-ice practice; whereas, novice, junior and senior level skaters practice an average of 5.5 hours a day, 6 days a week, and 50 weeks per year (Scanlan, Stein & Ravizza, 1991).

Moving through the testing structure can be just as stressful as, if not more than, competitive contexts. The relative novelty of skating alone on the ice can contribute to performance anxiety in both test and competitive contexts. Tests are done in isolation, with coaches at the side of the boards and skating performances under the scrutiny of one judge, or a panel of three judges where the decision of the majority dictates a pass or a 'fail'.

Modifying this frequently used term, "fail", for needing to *retry* a test is one area where practitioners can begin to restructure skaters' perceptions of achievement. Test dates occur throughout the year with test date frequency based on available judges in the area. Belonging to a large club, particularly in urban areas, increases the likelihood of trying tests at a home club and, thus, is less anxiety-provoking. As in competitive contexts, it is not uncommon for skaters to try tests at unfamiliar rinks. Special attention should be given to helping skaters anticipate attributes of the novel environment in preparation for such performances. The USFSA website offers a link to regional test schedules and can be valuable when planning for the season.

There are seven different kinds of tests: moves in the field, free skating, pairs, compulsory dance, free dance, synchronized, and figures.[1] Tests in all disciplines are mutually exclusive, increase in difficulty and must be taken in order; skaters are not eligible to take the next test within a discipline until they have passed all previous levels in that discipline. The dance structure of figure skating includes testing compulsory dances involving three to nine dances per level, and free dance tests involving lifts, dance spins, twizzles, and step sequences done holding the partner or in separation. Compulsory dance tests are tried with qualified partners (i.e. partners who have already passed the test being tried), usually of the

---

[1] Moves in the field replaced 'figures' in the testing structure because of the radical 1996 ISU decision to remove figures from competition. This change was designed to improve the authenticity of testing elements relevant to skating movements which are predominately gross motor skills, rather than the fine motor skills such as those involved in figures. Although it is still possible to test figures, this practice is rare because of low demand and limited judging availability. The effects of this change are about to be realized at the time of authorship; skaters who have never practiced figures are currently appearing in national-level competition and moving into coaching positions. The full effects of the removal of figures will be fully realized when the skaters of post-figures coaches move up through the testing structure.

opposite sex who are often awarded an honorarium for attending practices and test dates. Qualified partners may not always be locally available, especially male partners for female test takers and those who are competent to partner senior dance tests. Accordingly, practice time with partners can be limited and a significant source of anxiety in preparing for trying dance tests. Partners (i.e. a male and female set of skaters who train and compete together) specializing in the discipline of dance try free-dance tests together, where programs consist of a sequence of choreographed steps, dance-specific elements, holds and lifts to a specific genre of music (e.g. tango). Traditionally the male skater assists the female skater through lifts, which are restricted to keeping the female's waist below the head of the male.

Skaters are evaluated as a unit for pair skating tests. Like other disciplines, required elements are specified according to the specific developmental level. The difficulty of elements and the music time increase with each test passed. Because figure skating is stereotypically not a popular sport for men, there are significantly more female skaters than male skaters. Together with the challenging technical criteria and physical characteristics necessary for matching a pair, pair skating is the least common discipline, but many would agree the most exciting to watch. It is not surprising that acute head injuries are most common in this discipline (Dubravcic-Simunjak, Pecina, Kuipers, Moran & Haspl, 2003). Male skaters lift and throw female partners who complete multiple rotations in throw jumps and elements involving twists. Mandatory elements also include side-by-side jumps and spins and the elusive death spiral where the male skater pivots, holding the arm of the female skater whose head is inches away from the ice while on a single edge of her skate.

Synchronized skating began in 1954 (USFSA, 2004) and is the fastest-growing competitive discipline in the United States with over 500 figure teams and 14 different levels, 8 of which are competitive. The synchronized skaters tend to be older than skaters in other disciplines because skaters often transition into this discipline after terminating solo or partner careers. A highly technical form of team skating—synchronized skating—also has test requirements. Although competition eligibility is contingent on moves-in-the-field tests (see below), there are 5 levels of synchronized skating tests. These optional tests comprise 2 parts: required elements, and a program to music (with the exception of the fifth level).

Competition Structures

Typically, competitive figure skating begins around 8 years of age, with elite level skaters competing on average about 2 years earlier than recreational level skaters (Vadocz et al., 2002). The competitive careers of skaters spans up to 12 years, with training time increasing with level of competition (Scanlan et al., 1989a; Starkes, Deakin, Allard, Hodges & Hayes, 1996; Vadocz et al., 2002). As previously noted, even recreational skaters spend 4 to 12 hours per week training on-ice while elite skaters practice as much as 25 hours and dance and free skaters practice significantly more than free skaters (Vadocz et al., 2002). Clearly, developing skating talent requires immense dedication, time and financial commitment. It is not surprising that former figure skaters attribute their success, in part, to various sources of support including parents, coaches and significant others (Gould, Jackson & Finch, 1993b).

Although skaters at junior and senior level competitions receive the most national media attention, the possibilities of offering services to other developmental levels are ample. The possibility of securing endorsements has heightened the stakes for success, creating an intertwined network of pressures involving athletes, coaches and skating clubs who all stand to benefit financially from fame. Contrary to the earlier amateur–professional dichotomy restricting payment to only the latter, skaters can now earn money while maintaining amateur status provided they are eligible for competitions sanctioned by a country's skating federation such as Skate Canada and the USFSA.

There are two tiers of competitions: non-qualifying and qualifying. Non-qualifying competitions, such as club competitions and invitationals, cater to a broad range of skaters from young children experiencing their first competitive experiences to elite level skaters experimenting with new programs. These are frequently held throughout the year and do not preclude eligibility for any subsequent competitions. Strategically planning to attend invitational competitions throughout the year can help build competition efficacy and modify a variety of test and competitive goals. Qualifying competitions, such as regionals and sectionals, channel top-place finishers towards national or European championships. Elite level skaters are exempt from qualifying competitions and spend the fall season competing in Grand Prix competitions (USFSA, 2004).

While the scandals of the 1994 Olympics led to a proliferation of ice skating popularity, particularly in North America, the recent recognition of synchronized skating has also extended competitive opportunities to masses of figure skaters. This team-oriented discipline accommodates skaters with world-class competitive opportunities otherwise unattainable by those who may not be suited for the demands of the more specialized and technical disciplines that heavily rely on aerial rotation and/or skating with male partners. The team aspect of this discipline along with those involving partners lend themselves to various team-building strategies.

Singles, Pairs and Synchronized Skating

Skaters at the highest competitive levels (e.g. junior and senior) in free, pairs and synchronized skating disciplines perform two programs for qualifying competitions: short and long programs. Although the short program is shorter in music length (usually about 2.5 minutes) and worth only one-third of the overall score in a competition, skaters find it more stressful than the long program. It consists of a group of required elements, specified annually by the ISU and skating federations, that can be performed in any order. However, failure to execute any one of these elements precludes a skater from attempting the element again and results in a mandatory deduction. It is not unusual to drop out of medal contention if an element is missed. Judges award two sets of marks, one for the required elements and another for presentation.

The long program comprises the remaining two-thirds of the overall score. Although no specific requirements are specified, skaters strive to complete as many difficult jumps and spins as they can to take the competitive edge. Mastering skating elements, on an individual level and for the sport as a whole, occurs with skaters taking the chance of performing challenging elements, usually in terms of multiple rotation (e.g. quadruple jumps in singles competition) and combinations of jumps (e.g. quadruple–triple–triple combinations). Mastery of these difficult elements is not a necessary condition for inclusion in a program but successful performance can lead to a medal standing. Coaches frequently take chances of including nearly mastered elements to gain a competitive edge but this practice undoubtedly heightens the stakes for competing skaters and calls for strategic mental preparation. The long program component of singles, pairs, and synchronized skating is awarded scores for technical merit and presentation.

The ISU recognized competitive synchronized skating in 1994 and, like other disciplines, teams compete internationally including World Championships which began in 2000. Competitive synchronized skating in the USA is elaborate, consisting of 14 different levels representing juvenile, intermediate, novice, junior, senior, collegiate, masters and adult levels. The number of skaters, age, program types and lengths, and type and difficulty of maneuvers define competition at each level. Teams consist of 12 to 20 skaters performing programs involving complex formations and intricate transitions. Circle, block, spin, intersections and moves in the field are categories of the complex formations. Eligibility to compete requires specific moves in the field tests, 3 levels or higher than the level of competition. For example, a skater wishing to compete at the senior level must pass the intermediate moves in the field test.

Ice Dancing

Ice dancing is the newest Olympic figure skating event which began in 1976, emphasizing rhythm, music interpretation and precise steps (USFSA, 2004). Dance competition can be done solo, or in pairs. National and international competitions and their qualifiers restrict competitions to a pair comprised of a male and a female skater. However, in domains of recreational skating including club, invitational and varsity competitions, skaters may compete solo or in similar pairs (traditionally, a pair of two female skaters).

National and international level competitions involve three components: (1) performance of one or two compulsory dances, depending on the level; (2) the original set pattern; and (3) free dance. These components are worth 20 per cent, 30 per cent and 50 per cent, respectively. Compulsory dances are prescribed pattern dances set to a specific rhythm and tempo (e.g. tango, waltz). For each level of competition in a given year the ISU and/or skating federation specifies dances from respective test levels to be performed for the competitive year. In recreational-level dance competitions (solo and pairs), skating officials draw dances from the skating organization's pre-established set of dances for each level. Two marks are given for each dance: one for technique involving accuracy, placement and unison and one for timing and expression which reflect style as well as unison.

The original set pattern component involves translating a ballroom dance onto the ice through the use of edges, flow and positions. The specified tempo and rhythm aspect of the original set pattern is similar to the compulsory dance portion of competition, but this component differs in that the steps are (or originally were) choreographed to a 2.5-minute chosen piece of music that may include vocals. In general, skaters are judged on creativity, music and rhythm interpretation, and utilization of the ice surface. Composition, involving originality and step difficulty and presentation reflecting interpretation and artistic impression, are the two marks given by judges for this component. Upcoming rule modifications may be in place to remove this component from competition.

The free dance also involves novel choreography and music choice as long as the music is danceable and lasts a specified time (e.g. 4 minutes for senior competitors). Technical skills, interpretation and inventiveness using changes of position, intricate and varied dance holds, small lifts and jumps and difficult footwork are displayed in this heavily weighted component. Choreography specifications include a maximum number of lifts, separations, separation durations, and remaining on the ice except during jumps and lifts. One body part of the skater being lifted must remain below waist level of the one assisting and pair skating lifts and positions must be avoided. Judges award technical merit and presentation scores.

PLANNING FOR THE SEASON: TRAINING FOR TRYOUTS, TEST AND COMPETITIONS

Although the competitive season is generally from September through March, year-round training is common for both recreational and competitive figure skaters with specific training-related events such as tryouts, seminars and qualifying competitions occurring annually. Tests can be tried throughout the year but some research may be required to find clubs that are providing judges for specific levels. Parents, coaches and skaters should be involved in planning for the season. Because it often takes longer than a year to learn required elements for specific skating tests, planning a skater's career in two-year increments is advised. Despite having abilities to try higher-level tests, coaches will frequently hold eligible skaters back from trying the next test level to help develop the competitive edge necessary for competing at a lower level. The practice of 'holding back' skaters has several anxiety-management and goal-setting implications for practitioners. Elite-level competition certainly requires significant planning and is indicated as a stressor among elite-level skaters (Scanlan et al., 1991).

The following season-specific calendar of events should be considered by sport psychologists when planning a skater's training timeline for mental training. The competitive season begins in the fall with regional-level qualifying competitions that lead to sectionals, divisionals and nationals and extends through March with World Competition. Finishing in the top four at a respective sectional competition qualifies skaters or teams for national-level competition. The synchronized season ends just after the regular skating season. Several invitational competitions are held throughout the year but do not provide competitive opportunities for all disciplines. Helping skaters prioritize disciplines is important for multi-discipline competitors. The culmination of the competitive season is followed by club ice shows, which tend to be less stressful than competitions.

May and June are considered the off-season but have become a popular time for selecting synchronized skating teams and conducting pair or dance seminars. Discipline-specific tryouts are also considered high-stakes assessment situations where skaters would benefit from anxiety-management strategies. Finding a partner is highly contingent on physical characteristics and skating abilities matching that of the male partner (Monsma & Malina, 2004), among several other issues such as willingness to relocate and transferring coaches. Practitioners should be aware of the stresses associated with partner searches and not being selected to have one (Scanlan et al., 1991). The male-to-female ratio at dance or pair skating seminars can be exorbitantly uneven, but partner searches are now facilitated by the Internet. A link for skaters searching for dance and pair skating partners as well as synchronized skating team tryouts can be found on the USFSA website (USFSA, 2004).

POTENTIAL PSYCHOLOGICAL ISSUES

Figure skating is an early-entry sport (Malina, 1998) where children begin participation as young as four years of age and often specialize (participate exclusively) prior to eight years of age (Monsma & Malina, in press; Scanlan et al., 1989a). Although sport scientists have increased their focus on figure skaters recently, psychological and physical domains rarely follow an interdisciplinary perspective advocated by contextual (Lerner, 1985) and ecological theorists (Newell & Molenaar, 1998) and by practitioners (Burwitz, Moore & Wilkinson, 1994; Sabatini, 2001). Theoretically, positive affect and performance emerge as a function of individual factors (i.e. physical and behavioral) interacting with environmental characteristics (e.g. subjective evaluation, training schedules) and specific task demands (e.g. throws and lifts). From a practical standpoint, practitioners should consider the interacting physical and psychological issues of the skater, especially given the tumultuous periods of developmental change faced by the predominantly young participants. Many emerging psychological issues involve physical development and handling environmental pressures tied to aesthetic achievement and maintenance. Practitioners also need to consider the changing self-perceptions relative to physical maturation and their link with disordered eating (Brooks-Gunn, 1988; Monsma & Malina, 2004). The constant subjective evaluation inherent in the skating environment can exasperate stresses associated with normal physical and psychological changes.

To better understand the sources of stress and enjoyment in the skating context, the results of two separate qualitative studies conducted by Gould and colleagues and Scanlan colleagues are summarized. With the goal of helping skaters adjust to growing up under the scrutiny of the subjective evaluation as the means to defining success in this sport, we discuss age-, maturational status- and timing-related changes in physical and psychological development. Given that disordered eating risk is well documented in this population (Hausenblas & Mack, 1999; Monsma & Malina, in press; Taylor & Ste. Marie, 2000), it is discussed next, followed by the psychological impact of frequently occurring injuries.

Sources of Stress and Enjoyment

To address the increasing performance demands placed on figure skaters striving towards elite status, Scanlan and her colleagues and Gould and his colleagues interviewed two separate samples of national-level competitors. The following is a summary of these qualitative reports describing the sources of stress (Gould, Jackson & Finch, 1993a; Scanlan, Stein & Ravizza, 1991) and enjoyment (Gould et al., 1993b). Gould's work compares experiences prior to and after securing a national title while Scanlan's work shows variation across competitive level and highlights coaching as a final stage of talent development.

Descriptions of the journey towards elite status are rich in sources of enjoyment and it is encouraging that elite skaters view their experiences, partially, in mastery- as opposed to ego-related terms. General themes represent mastery experiences such as striving for a sense of accomplishment, achieving perfection and mastery goals, and perceived competence represented by demonstrating abilities, mastery processes and goals. Skaters also enjoyed the fame of being a skater in terms of social recognition and gifts. Social and life opportunities were represented by traveling, international friendships, touring, experiencing different cultures and getting out of school (Gould et al., 1993b; Scanlan, Stein & Ravizza, 1989b).

Several double-edged swords were apparent when comparing sources of enjoyment and stress. Skaters who felt the *need* to skate flawlessly perceived perfectionism as a stressor (Gould et al., 1993a; Scanlan et al., 1991), whereas skaters who strived to skate flawlessly experienced *enjoyment* (Gould et al., 1993a; Scanlan et al., 1989b). Psyching skaters out with one's talent was cited as a source of enjoyment while, in part, was also cited as psychological warfare contributing to stress in other skaters. While some skaters found "showing up" (i.e. skating better than) others at practice enjoyable, skaters not performing well were highly sensitive to these superiorities and experienced heightened stress levels. The research findings suggest that performing in front of an audience, when there is positive energy exchange as a result of spirited performance, can be enjoyable, but if accompanied by falling can catastrophically turn into a source of stress and anxiety. It is not unusual for skaters to have a spectacular performance until a fall with subsequent falls on even otherwise simple elements. Finally, the research also showed that social recognition, while seen as initially enjoyable and desired, demands increasing amounts of time and becomes stressful when it diminishes.

Common themes across samples that were associated with competition included self-doubts, lack of confidence, fear of falling in front of others, social comparison anxiety, and anxiety about what others would say about performance. It is important to note that these themes were also apparent after securing the national title (Gould et al., 1993a). Significant others were salient sources of stress, especially mothers whose criticism and generated guilt were associated with poor performances and financial costs. In addition to poor relationships, with coaches, partners were also implicated in poor communication, injuries, secret romantic relationships and withholding praise. Financial and time demands were major themes in the environmental demands of skating. Skaters reported not being able to afford lessons and costs associated with prime-time ice resulting in practicing during the night. They also indicated missing academic, social and work opportunities as stressful. Performance expectations of oneself, parents, partners and the media were also consistently reported as stressors in both samples, and these stressors increased after securing a title. Winning a title amplified skating politics, media attention and undesirable training situations (Gould et al., 1993a). Parental performance expectations were cited as significant sources of stress and, surprisingly, this was especially true among senior competitors.

Physical demands and psychological struggles coinciding with key periods of maturation were frequently cited stressors. Depression from not meeting expectations, lack of individuality and independence were implicated. Developing skills in an accelerated time frame, pressures to maintain a certain weight, maturity fears, loss of self-worth and identity, illness and injury, overtraining and dealing with homosexuality point towards the importance of an interdisciplinary focus for professional consultants. Clearly, these issues emphasize the need for merging disciplines for integrating typical physical and psychological transitions in development for performance enhancement and wellness interventions.

Physical Development Issues

During adolescence, females increase from an average height of 144 cm and average weight of 37 kg to 158 cm and 48 kg, respectively, from 11 to approximately 16 years of age (Hamill,

Drizd, Johnson, Reed & Roche, 1977) and begin to worry about their weight as young as 5 years of age (Davison, Earnest & Birch, 2002). In addition to broadening skeletal breadths, increases in muscle mass and limb circumferences, females also progress from an estimated 8 per cent body fat at the beginning of puberty to about 22 per cent at the end of puberty (Killen et al., 1992). These changes reflect modifications in physique and body composition. Cross-sectional evidence indicates that competitive figure skaters at recreational, pre-elite (novice) and elite levels (junior and senior) are shorter and lighter (Monsma & Malina, in press) than age-specific normative data (NCHS, 2004). The overall physique (somatotype) of competitive figure skaters is characteristic of meso-ectomorphy (muscular but linear). Variations across level and discipline indicate that elite competitive skaters are more muscular compared to pre-elite skaters. As a group, free skaters are taller, heavier, have greater BMI and sum of 6 skinfolds compared to pair and dance competitors who also have longer legs than free skaters but there is no apparent variation in physique across discipline (Monsma & Malina, in press).

Girls generally begin skating around 6 years of age, while boys begin around 10 (Scanlan et al., 1989a) and it is common for figure skaters to achieve elite status prior to 16 years of age (Vadocz et al., 2002). Tracey Wainman and Sasha Cohn are examples of child champions. Physical demands on the body, pressure to attain and maintain low body weight and lack of improvement due to body maturation are confirmed sources of stress that coincide with critical training periods (Gould et al., 1993a; Scanlan et al., 1991). An imbalanced energy intake–expenditure ratio is documented among figure skaters (Rucinski, 1989; Ziegler et al., 1998b), and dietary restrictions associated with environmental pressures are likely contributors. In contrast, the imbalance may also be due to energy expenditures required for growth and hours of program repetitions, replete with multi-rotational jumps, spins and lifts. Such imbalances can influence performance and injury risk, and compromise bone and reproductive health which have prompted the American College of Sports Medicine (ACSM) to recognize that pubertal female athletes may be at special risk for a triad of related health issues: eating disorders, amenorrhea and osteoporosis (Sabatini, 2001; Yeager, Agostini, Nattiv & Drinkwater, 1993). Furthermore, researchers have suggested that the onset of puberty and variation in pubertal timing themselves may be risk factors for disordered eating (Attie & Brooks-Gunn, 1989; Killen et al., 1992; Monsma & Malina, 2004).

Puberty, or maturational timing, is assessed relative to somatic maturity (peak height velocity: PHV) in both boys and girls and age at menarche in girls. PHV is the age at maximum rate of growth in stature during the adolescent growth spurt. On average, girls attain PHV about 2 years earlier (11.5 years) than boys (13.5 years) and can expect to gain 8 cm and 9.25 cm, respectively. This growth in height is also accompanied by growth in muscle and fat mass, which has implications for motor performance (see Malina, Bouchard & Bar-Or, 2004, for a review). Notably, such growth spurts occur during critical periods of figure-skating skill development. Late-maturing skaters appear to be at an advantage because they are able to maintain a petite physique conducive for the greater moment of inertia required in rotation (Harris, 1986; Niinimaa, 1982; Ross, Brown, Yu & Faulkner, 1977) for a longer period of time. Essentially this enables them to have a smaller body for a longer period of time accommodating the learning time needed for difficult multi-rotational jumps (e.g. doubles, triples and quadruples). It is common for skaters to 'lose their jumps' and endure frequent unexpected falling during growth spurts. Consistent with the literature (Gould et al., 1993a), skaters seem to anticipate lack of improvement due to body maturation.

Age at menarche (age at first menstrual period) is an alternative to longitudinal growth assessments (i.e. PHV). The population average for girls with European ancestry is 12.8 +1.0 (Eveleth & Tanner, 1990), but overall, competitive figure skaters are late maturing (Brooks-Gunn, Burrow & Warren, 1988; Ross et al., 1977; Ziegler et al., 1998a). This trend is even more apparent among elite competitors, especially pair skating and ice dancing specialists (Monsma, Feltz & Malina, 2004). The importance of considering maturational timing variability lies in the associated physical characteristics that accompany early (<11 years), average (11.8–13.8 years) and late (>16 years) maturation. Practitioners may find these systematic variations intriguing because specific physical characteristics direct selection into, and away from, the sport (Malina, 1998). To illustrate, from normative data, we know that later maturation is associated with leanness, linearity and longer leg length relative to the torso (i.e. sitting height/stature ratio) (Malina et al., 2004). Now, we ask the reader to consider the empirical evidence showing the prevalence of leanness and linearity in most aesthetic sports including figure skaters (for a review see Malina, 1998) and anecdotally, the characteristics of known elite skaters such as Oksana Baiul, Ekaterina Gordieva, Michelle Quan and Tara Lapinski whose talent peaked prior to puberty. Each one of these skaters had pre-pubescent physiques during the height of their careers. Descriptive data showing variation across competency level support this argument; not only is late maturation prominent (Vadocz et al., 2002), skaters' anthropometric profiles (Brooks-Gunn et al., 1988; Comper, 1991; Gledhill & Jamnick, 1992; Monsma & Malina, in press) reflect physical characteristics of late maturation (Malina et al., 2004). Furthermore, it is rare to find an endomorphic (i.e. relatively fat) skater able to execute triple jumps and appease the artistic favor of judges. The finding that early maturing skaters were under-represented (n = 2) in a study of 161 competitive female figure skaters (Vadocz et al., 2002) bolsters the idea that skaters who do not possess some of these characteristics may not reach elite status. While the physical activity benefits of figure skating certainly contribute to cardiovascular, muscular strength and bone density benefits, successful experiences are not guaranteed and may influence attrition.

While several studies have focused on elite skaters, little attention has been given to the psychological well-being of skaters who do not reach elite status, the contributing factors towards self-selection away from the sport and the associated wellness implications. Clearly, skaters considering, or faced with, transition would benefit from professional attention. Ultimately, heightening awareness and educating skaters and their support network about the implications of growth acceleration and its implications can help skaters and their networks mentally prepare for associated physical and psychological changes.

Psychological Development Issues

The research on sources of stress indicates individual variability in sources and their impact. That is, while for some skaters performing in front of others is stressful (Scanlan et al., 1991), others find the experience to be thoroughly enjoyable. These differences are proposed to be connected to interactions among the individual, the environment and the task (Lerner, 1985). For example, despite typically being below the population norm in height and weight (Comper, 1991; Gledhill & Jamnick, 1992; Monsma & Malina, in press; Ziegler et al., 1998b) skaters frequently face pressures to lose weight from agents in their training environment (i.e. coaches, judges, parents and partners). It is not uncommon for coaches to publicly post skaters' weights and/or individual body mass index (BMI) values. A noteworthy observation is the common misinterpretation of BMI scores as indicators of fatness. As evident from the equation [BMI: weight (kg)/height (m^2)], the BMI does not separate fat mass from fat-free mass. Thus, muscular skaters who are less fat than the general population may have an elevated BMI because they are heavier and leaner. The practice of using the BMI to gauge physique changes as a remedy for performance improvements (Ryan, 1995) further compromises wellness.

Understanding developmental changes in physical self-perceptions is worthy of consideration because the controlling aspect of the skating environment (Gould et al., 1993a) has the potential to restrict psychological development during childhood and adolescence. To illustrate, significant structural and content changes in physical self-perceptions occur during late childhood (8 to 11 years) and adolescence (12 to 18 years). In the general population, childhood sub-domains include scholastic and athletic competence, physical appearance, peer acceptance behavioral conduct and global self-worth domains (Harter, 1990). Subsequently, self-perceptions that emerge during adolescence include job competence, close friendships, romantic relationships and morality domains. Stressors associated with an accelerated timetable for skating progression, expectation of others and time demands (Gould et al., 1993a), can potentially restrict adolescent proliferation of self-perception sub-domains. Scanlan et al. (1991) reported loss of self-esteem and feeling inadequate because a partner quit as sources of stress. Skaters who attach too much importance to their skating and have limited internal and external resources may find it difficult to cope with poor performances. Restricted internal and external resources can also lead to over-identification as a figure skater, amplifying the negative effects of poor performances. The narrow range of social resources and the social interaction centering on the skating environment may lead to over-identifying with the sport. The findings of Gould et al. (1993a) that living up to family, coach and peer expectations are significant sources of stress among skaters indicate a need for intervention; skaters should be encouraged to keep their reasons for skating separate from those of their social agents.

Since self-perceptions mediate life stress and depression (Deal & Williams, 1988), increasing self-perceptions should be a focus of interventions. Over-identification is unlikely to emerge until later adolescence because younger adolescents (12 to 14 years) do not integrate their sub-domains (Fischer, 1980). During mid-adolescence (14 to 16 years), reconciling individuality across different domains creates confusion in identities across environments (Horn, 2004) and thus may be a period of emerging over-identification. Although older adolescents (17 to college years) can integrate self-evaluations across sub-domains (Horn, 2004), in the restrictive skating environment, skaters may be left placing too much emphasis on self-evaluations stemming from the skating domain.

Helping skaters lead a balanced life in academic, social and sport domains can be one of the greatest challenges faced by practitioners, especially when the bulk of training is supported by parents' financial resources or sponsors. Balancing skating with school or work and having a reduced social life due to training demands are confirmed sources of stress (Scanlan et al., 1991). Practitioners should beware of unhealthy coping skills such as drug and alcohol use, reported especially among pair skaters and ice dancers (Gould et al., 1993a). Although the skating environment challenges skaters' coping skills, it is also apparent that skating serves as a form of coping. The majority of 29 skating coaches, who were former national champion skaters, used skating as a means of coping with life pressures and perceived their talent development continuing past retirement from competition and into their coaching careers (Scanlan et al., 1989a).

Another important change in self-perceptions is the emergence of global self-esteem—individual's assessment of the worth of self which has multiple sub-domains. Children younger than eight years old have limited awareness of global self-esteem because they think in concrete, observable and behavioral terms (Harter, 1999) and are unable to adequately articulate their self-assessments. Nevertheless, practitioners can capitalize on these characteristics by using augmented video feedback for introducing artistic self-awareness of skating. In conjunction with terms such as "stretching", "standing tall" and "flow" and emotive terms to help develop facial expression important for interpreting program music, artistic impression can begin at an early age. Artistry was often overlooked by coaches working with younger skaters because of the time demands required by figures and the importance placed on learning skills.

At approximately eight years of age, children are ready to differentiate between the real self and the ideal self (Harter, 1999). The degree of importance individuals attach to each sub-domain influences higher orders of self-perceptions (see Fox & Corbin, 1989) and social agents are significant contributors to self-worth (Harter, 1999). Accordingly, introductions to goal-setting and self-monitoring are developmentally appropriate because these two skills enable control over personal potential. Given the interacting effects of task demands, environmental pressures and restricted social support, practitioners are encouraged to focus on helping skaters expand their social network but learn how to filter information transmitted within the skating context.

Understanding gender differences in self-esteem and self-worth are noteworthy when dealing with pair and ice dancing teams. Adolescent girls generally exhibit lower self-esteem than boys of similar age and this gender-gap widens between 14 and 23 years of age (Block & Robbins, 1993). No known information exists on male figure skaters, but cross-sectional data indicates an inverse relationship between age and self-esteem along with its physical domains, among competitive female figure skaters across free, dance and pair skating disciplines (Monsma et al., 2004). Maturational rate is implicated in influencing gender variation in self-perceptions (Brooks-Gunn, 1988) where early and late maturing children may experience more negative affect associated with development.

> Because girls, on average, tend to experience pubertal changes earlier than do boys, such gender differences in the timing of the physical maturation may be one of the causes of observed gender differences in overall self-esteem at the beginning of the adolescent period. (Horn, 2004, p. 122)

Despite the intuitive appeal of this general relationship applied to figure skaters, Monsma et al. (2004) did not find variation in self-esteem or its contributing factors across average- and late-maturing figure skaters. However, consistent with hypothesized variation in the biology literature, late-maturing girls had a lower sum of 6 skinfold thicknesses and were lower in endomorphy compared to average-maturing skaters in the sample. It is also interesting to note that despite being highly specialized and lean relative to free skaters, skaters with partners (ice dancers and pair skaters) reported lower sport competence and satisfaction with health as measured by Marsh's (1996) Physical Self Description Questionnaire (PSDQ). Emphasizing the dance and pair skaters' highly specialized achievements and genetic predisposition to physical characteristics are advocated for improving self-competence perceptions.

Gender-orientation is tested during adolescence (Horn, 2004). Some skaters struggle with fears of becoming gay, or endure turmoil in the process of accepting their gender identity (Scanlan et al., 1991). This finding together with anecdotal evidence indicates especially male figure skaters must deal "with established stereotypes depicting males skaters as gay or about to become gay during their careers" (p. 116). Parents and schoolmates reinforce these views.

The final psychological developmental changes to consider are cognitive processes used to evaluate competence in terms of sources of competence information and the way youth conceptualize ability (see Horn, 2004). Success in skating is contingent on social comparison of technical difficulty, artistry and related factors contributing to subjective decisions made by coaches and judges who direct competency levels and competitive outcomes. Given the decreasing age of competitive skating, it is important to note the age-related changes in sources of competence information. Critical periods for facilitating high self-perceptions are highlighted next.

Early to middle childhood (four to seven years) may be the most vulnerable to change because children can not yet verbalize their self-worth, do not have the abilities to differentiate between the real and ideal self nor to differentiate between effort and ability. Although self-perceptions may be generally high at this time, competitive skating environments may compromise positive attributes of participation. Children do not use peer comparisons as information about their competence beyond learning how to improve their own performances. Rather, during this age range, competence source information that children use include (1) simple task accomplishment (e.g. completing a one-foot spin) and the effect of their performance (e.g. spinning really fast makes small circles on the ice); (2) evaluative feedback from adults; and (3) personal effort. Mastery experiences and the provision of contingent, clear and consistent feedback from significant others tied to the mastery experiences are suggested to develop high self-perceptions.

From 8 to 12 years of age, sources of competence are primarily environmental. Children are capable of differentiating the number of sources used, are very concrete in the self-evaluation process and place increasing importance on peer comparisons. Integrating adult feedback with other sources of information is also a salient feature. Accordingly, this age range may be a critical period for helping skaters redefine success and integrate actual performance quality and performance outcome with other sources of information such as peer comparisons and feedback from significant others. The competition to practice time ratio is highly disproportionate in this sport and, thus, defining competence in terms of competitive success can be a liability to self-competence potentially leading to competitive anxiety and its consequences.

Early to middle adolescence (12 to 15 years) is noteworthy as a critical period for facilitating high self-perceptions because of the myriad of maturational and socio-contextual changes experienced by youth (Horn, 2004). Pubertal changes in physical characteristics, cognitive-maturational changes including sensitivity to others' evaluations and increasing expectations in performance standards and peer comparisons are inherent in the aesthetic sport context and as sources of stress among figure skaters (Gould et al., 1993a).

Disordered Eating and the Controlling Aspects of Figure Skating

Participation in aesthetic sport such as figure skating may heighten weight and body shape concerns among very young children (Davison et al., 2002). Standardized assessment data (e.g. Eating Disorder Inventory (EDI): Garner, Olmstead & Polivy, 1983) do not indicate that eating disorders (i.e. anorexia nervosa and bulimia nervosa) are prevalent among figure skaters (Monsma & Malina, in press; Taylor & Ste. Marie, 2000; Ziegler et al., 1998a).

However, because of the secretive nature of these disorders, social desirability and the intrusiveness of conducting this kind of research, the incidence is more than likely under-reported (Swoap & Murphy, 1995). The findings of Taylor and Ste. Marie (2000) corroborate this notion. In a sample of 41 pair skaters and ice dancers, 92.7 per cent reported that they perceived weight loss pressures to be associated with the sport and 100 per cent of sample reported engaging in weight control measures at some point in their lives. In addition to environmental variables, skaters' physical self-perceptions are also risk factors. Social physique anxiety—anxiety experienced when presenting oneself in front of others—was the most salient predictor of 6 of the 8 EDI subscales accounting for from 4 to 13 per cent of the variance (Monsma & Malina, 2004). Other self-perception predictors included PSDQ (Marsh, 1996) subscales of satisfaction with body fat, appearance, self-esteem and global physical self-concept.

Anorexia nervosa is characterized by refusal to maintain body weight over a minimal normal weight for age and height or inability to make expected gains during period of growth leading to body weight 15 per cent below that expected weight; intense fear of gaining weight or becoming fat even though underweight; disturbance in which one's body weight size or shape is perceived (e.g. feeling fat while emaciated); and, in females, an absence of three consecutive menstrual cycles when otherwise expected to occur. In contrast, the characteristics of bulimia nervosa are recurrent episodes of binge eating, feeling lack of control over eating behaviors during the eating binges; regular engaging in self-induced vomiting, use of laxatives, diuretics, strict dieting or fasting or vigorous exercise to prevent weight gain; a minimum average of two binge-eating episodes a week for at least three months and persistent concern with body shape and weight (DSM-IV, APA, 1994).

Early detection and intervention have been associated with recovery success (Rocco, Ciano & Balestrieri, 2001; Thompson, 1987). Sport psychology practitioners, while not qualified to diagnose or treat eating disorders, can consider administering a standardized assessment or assessing behavior and personality (e.g. weight loss, eating alone, preoc-cupation with food, mood changes and body distortion statements) in making referral de-cisions. It is important to note that athletes, especially those with eating disorders, have perfectionist tendencies and will have difficulties admitting a problem exists. Approach-ing an athlete with a non-confrontational demeanor and an emphasis on feelings may help the athlete confide in the referring person. To increase the likelihood of compliance, re-ferrals should be made immediately to specific persons or clinics (Swoap & Murphy, 1995).

Many of the environmental risk factors such as weigh-ins, postings of weight, and pres-sures to lose weight including communications concerning weight between judges, coaches and athletes are surmountable requiring education and perhaps policy change. More implicit factors involve incongruence between physical characteristics and task demands, perfec-tionist tendencies, and the controlling aspect of the skating environment. That is, restricted eating among aesthetic sport athletes may in part be a response to a lack of control over performance pressures and outcomes primarily controlled by judges (Monsma & Malina, in press).

Risk Factors and Common Figure Skating Injuries

Similar to the prevalence of disordered eating, a myriad of converging environmental, per-sonal and task demands are injury risk factors. In addition to the aforementioned physical development and environmental stressors, Lipetz & Kruse (2000) cite poor communication skills, performance anxiety and stress as injury risk factors. Anecdotally, task demands of jumping, lifts, skating in unison and close proximity contribute to performance anxiety.

Acute injuries, overuse syndromes and, to a lesser extent, lower back pain, are common among male and female figure skaters, with dancers and pair skaters experiencing more acute injuries as a function of lifting and throwing task demands (Smith & Ludington, 1989). Ankle sprain is the most common acute injury among female skaters followed by patella tendonitis (jumper's knee) which is the most common among male skaters. Stress fractures and Osgood-Schlatter disease are most common overuse syndromes for females and males, respectively (Dubravcic-Simunjak et al., 2003).

Stress fractures occur more often in the take-off foot than in the landing foot (Dubravicic-Simunjak et al., 2003; Oleson, Busconi & Baran, 2002) but whether this overuse injury occurs as a function of low bone density or excessive force to the normal skeleton remains unclear. Although skating is a weight-bearing and/or high-impact activity, and is considered one of the best sports for increasing bone mineral density and perhaps for preventing osteoporosis, these benefits are often diminished by overuse injuries and energy intake–expenditure imbalances that may lead to a host of complications involved in the female athlete triad (Ziegler et al., 1998a; Ziegler et al., 2002). This disorder is difficult to treat and requires intense clinical counseling (Sabatini, 2001).

Regarding the psychological impact of overuse injuries, some skaters do not feel or remember when their injuries occurred. Acute injuries such as head injuries happen more frequently among ice dance and pair skaters and could be subsequently associated with fears of falling or injuring a partner (Dubravcic-Simunjak et al., 2003). As such, interventions geared at injury prevention, recovery, practice return and controlling subsequent injury-related anxieties are warranted when working with figure skaters.

SPECIFIC INTERVENTIONS

Figure skating with its various disciplines can be an expensive sport, especially with increasing levels of competencies and specialized disciplines. The reasons for choosing the interventions described in the following sections include relevance for maximizing expensive ice-time, facilitating learning and enhancing performance in high-stakes testing, tryout and competitive contexts. Moreover, the actual use of these interventions with figure skaters are well documented. The interventions presented are certainly not exhaustive; other interventions such as goal-setting, relaxation and other arousal-regulating techniques would certainly benefit this clientele. However, those techniques are covered in other chapters.

Modeling Applications for Developing Figure Skating Talent

Modeling can benefit a multitude of skating skills including the mechanics of elements (e.g. body-positioning, timing, principles of plyometrics, coordination), choreography and artistic impression, coping with adversity and developing and maintaining positive self-perceptions. Modeling is defined as a learning strategy involving cognitive, affective and behavioral changes occurring after observing a performance where the model uses verbalizations and non-verbal expressions that ultimately serve as cues for subsequent trials (McCullagh & Weiss, 2001). Observed task characteristics are encoded and translated into meaningful coordinated patterns that can be subsequently performed to begin the calibration between encoded information and mechanically accurate physical performance (Shea, Wright, Wulf & Whitacre, 2000). Further, these covert rehearsal attempts establish symbolic codes, or internal representations that act as internal standards for subsequent performance (McCullagh & Weiss, 2001). There are several key attributes to consider when utilizing this technique such as model type (coping or mastery models), model similarity or self-modeling, and demonstration characteristics.

Coping with competition fears, learning difficult lifts or aerial rotation skills and injury recovery are common situations requiring effective coping skills that may be challenging, especially for younger participants. In contexts where tasks are perceived as difficult or fearful, mastery models demonstrate effortless, mastered performance. In contrast, coping models show progression of low ability to cope with the demands of the task to ideal performance through repeated trials in conjunction with verbalized thoughts, affect and correct performance. Research indicates coping models are superior to mastery models, especially when the model and learner are similar (Weiss, McCullagh, Smith & Berlant, 1998).

While evidence suggests that choosing a model of the same gender, age and slightly higher ability can increase confidence and motivation to attempt new skills that can be intimidating (McCullagh & Weiss, 2001), no known research has been conducted on figure skaters. However, age variations in encoding processes are evident among dancers. Cadopi, Chatillon & Baldy (1995) found 8-year-old dancers reported using imagery more to encode a modeled ballet sequence compared to 11-year-olds who used more verbal cues to encode sequences, suggesting that it may be developmentally appropriate to augment modeling with imagery in aesthetic activity contexts.

Self-modeling, or viewing oneself in a variety of possible mediums, could be particularly effective for figure skaters. The basis of self-modeling lies in self-efficacy enhancements that lead to improved performance. While highlights of successful performances can be used for motivation, when the goal is to enhance efficacy in learning situations, eliminating performance errors by viewing oneself on edited video tape is recommended. Although video tape is the most common source of self-modeling, strategies involving audiotapes, imagery, role-playing or still photographs are possible intervention alternatives (Dowrick, 1999). A plausible explanation for the effectiveness of self-modeling is the perceived similarity between the learner and the model. Thus, consideration of the use of models with similar status (ability level), age, gender and perhaps physical size is warranted.

Demonstration characteristics are also important to consider. Contextual interference literature indicates that blocked practice—all trials of one task are performed before moving to another—is effective for learning but random practice conditions lead to higher retention. However, evidence suggests that when modeling is used with blocked and random practice, performance variation diminishes (Lee & White, 1990). The reverse information required in viewing mirror images of the model as opposed to viewing the model from the rear leads to greater performance effects (Ishikura & Inomata, 1995). The importance of augmented information also appears to be important for modeling effectiveness in figure skating. For example, auditory information or verbal cues appear to enhance rhythmical and ballistic movements and those highly contingent on timing (see McCullagh & Weiss, 2001).

Mental Practice Techniques

Mental practice, in its broadest definition, involves rehearsing athletic skills or sequences in the mind's eye. While imagery is often used synonymously with mental practice, imagery is one feature of mental practice, which can also include other overt skills such as self-talk, floor walkouts and paper drawing of programs. Each of these techniques can be used alone or in combination with one another. Mental practice can be considered the most valuable intervention technique for figure skaters because of its advantages for learning and high-stakes assessment contexts. Skaters strive to perfect the most difficult elements for their competitive level including exuding artistry to every beat of music in their programs. Even with the mastery of elements, skaters may spend several hours learning new programs to gain a competitive edge against competitors in a context where the contents of their peers' programs are often unknown. Figure skaters tend to perform better in home environments (i.e. home club competitions) (Balmer, Nevill & Williams, 2001) compared to unfamiliar settings (i.e. other skating rinks). Accordingly, using mental practice to familiarize oneself with a novel environment may help skaters focus on performance attributes rather than attending to unfamiliar surroundings.

Skating programs across all disciplines involve sequenced elements and/or connecting steps performed to music. With each test passed, it is common for skaters to change their music and choreography that will showcase the required elements to pass the subsequent test or maintain competitiveness at the next level. Mental practice is one of the most valuable tools for learning new elements and programs. Skaters as young as six years of age become responsible for memorizing the sequence of elements and connecting steps while learning increasingly difficult moves. Thus, strategies are geared toward helping young skaters memorize not only critical elements of their new skating skills, but also their program sequences. We find program blueprinting and floor walkouts (detailed below) particularly facilitative for memorizing critical elements of skating skills and program sequences, especially among young skaters.

Several mental practice studies have devised interventions for figure skaters testing their effectiveness on performance (Mumford & Hall, 1985; Palmer, 1992; Rodgers, Hall & Buckoltz, 1991). With the exception of Mumford and Hall (1985), these studies have shown positive effects on performance and/or were perceived as beneficial by skaters and their coaches bolstering anecdotal observations with our own clients. Aligned with Martin (1993), three important features of mental practice should be conveyed to skaters using this valuable technique. First, mental practice of elements or sequences of elements should last the same length of time as the actual physical performance. While there are some exceptions to this feature described in the imagery section below, mentally practicing in real time can be crucial for skaters learning the correct timing of jumps and other elements involving potentially dangerous aerial rotation. Second, skaters should imagine themselves in the actual competitive or test settings in which the skills are to be performed especially because testing and competition times are significantly out-weighed by practice time. By frequently focusing on the attributes of high-stakes assessment (e.g. being alone on the ice, wearing competition clothes, being in an unfamiliar rink etc.), skaters can potentially become desensitized to the anxiety associated with these contexts that would be otherwise unfamiliar. Finally, employing the kinesthetic sense during mental practice can prime the neuromuscular pathways involved in physical performance. Because figure skating involves precisely timed fine and gross motor movements, efforts to enhance kinesthetic awareness may benefit successful physical execution of elements. This can be done by focusing on the force produced by muscles to achieve varying degrees of rotational pull. For example, a coach could have skaters complete a one-foot spin with arms and legs pulling in slowly and remaining slightly open versus pulling in fast and tight. Focusing on the timing of movement in slow motion, real time and fast motion can also help train the kinesthetic sense.

The following is a presentation of various mental practice techniques we use that are adaptations of those described in the intervention-based literature. They include self-talk, program blueprinting, floor walkouts, and imagery for figure skating.

Self-talk

In general, self-talk involves mentally rehearsing a skill by identifying cue words associated with critical elements of the particular skill and repeating the cues in the order in which they appear in the physical performance of the skill. This technique helps keep athletes focused on task and can help energize the athlete during difficult physical performances. A self-talk technique for figure skaters was originally developed for practicing figures (Ming & Martin, 1996), but can be easily adapted for young skaters in any discipline including young children.

Skaters, with the help of their coaches, select words to help them concentrate on and correct specific sections of a single skating element (e.g. a twizzle in dance; a jump take-off) or program. Cue words are repeated aloud or mentally while physically practicing the skill. This technique can be used during on-ice practices, or used in conjunction with other mental practice vehicles (Martin, 1993) such as paper drawings of programs and floor walkouts described below.

When working with young children, we often use metaphors that help skaters relate an inanimate object to the desired movement characteristic (Overby, 1991). For example, to help skaters elongate their arms and free leg during a spiral, we use the cue words 'soar with pride' or 'eagle's wings'. Devising cue words for specific skating elements can be facilitated with focus groups where a coach and all of her students meet to brainstorm cue words for specific elements. Skaters can then choose a personally meaningful and effective cue word.

Skating Program Blueprinting

Skaters across all disciplines can benefit from program blueprinting—drawing diagrams of elements and connecting steps as they appear in programs while using cue words and visualizing their program as its music plays. We've coined the term "program blueprinting" as a collective for Palmer's (1992) paper patch and Garza & Feltz's (1998) paper freestyle drawing, an adaptation of paper patch. Program blueprinting encompasses all disciplines and gives coaches and/or choreographers a role in helping skaters mentally practice their programs. Program blueprinting facilitates concentration on critical elements of specific skills, timing of elements, connecting steps and artistry, memorization of element sequences and key features of artistry choreographed to specific beats of music. It can also be used by skaters while they are alone away from the ice or as a final ritual to preparation just prior to taking the ice in high-stakes situations.

The following are features of paper drawing techniques from the literature (Garza & Feltz, 1998; Palmer, 1992) with asterisks to indicate our own adaptations.

1. In a workbook designated for skating, skaters list all of the elements of their program, writing them on a sheet of paper (Garza & Feltz, 1998). Coaches and choreographers can be involved in initial trials of this technique helping skaters develop their program blueprints.*
2. Skaters develop cue words designed to help increase concentration and avoid distraction (Palmer, 1992).
3. Skaters visualize themselves in a high-stakes setting to make the simulation as real as possible. This includes seeing their coach at the boards, seeing themselves in their skating costumes and the judging panel before them (Garza & Feltz, 1998).
4. Skaters 'feel' themselves skating their program from beginning to end.
5. Next, skaters draw their programs on paper while their program music is played, placing each element in the correct location on the paper, as they would be on the ice and saying their cue words aloud. The music helps skaters keep the timing of elements congruent with the time or speed it takes to skate the program on the ice (Garza & Feltz, 1998).
6. Skaters then go back through their program focusing on key features of presentation, or artistic impression. These program features on the program blueprint should be reviewed prior to subsequent mental practice sessions.
7. This strategy can be practiced daily at home in a quiet place and one final time just prior to a high-stakes performance to help relax and improve concentration (Palmer, 1993).

Floor Walkouts

Although floor walkouts can be practiced anywhere, skaters are frequently observed at competition and test sites engaging in this technique just before they take the ice. It involves moving through an element or program on the floor while listening to the music using headphones. As with program blueprints done to music, listening to music helps skaters keep time with their program as if they were performing it on-ice. Other commonalities between the two mental practice techniques include the use of cue words as skaters move through their program, use of visual imagery pertaining to the test or competition context, and kinesthetic imagery pertaining to the elements.

Figure skaters and their coaches have long used variations of paper program and floor walkout techniques. Two studies compared the efficacy of these techniques with adolescent figure skaters ages 10 to 18 years (Garza & Feltz, 1998, Palmer, 1992). While Palmer (1992) found her paper patch technique superior to Martin's (1992) floor walkout technique for improving figures, Garza & Feltz (1998) later compared paper drawing to imagery used while physically moving through the program (i.e. walkouts) and found both mental practice techniques equally effective for coach-rated jump and spin performance improvements as well as skaters' competition confidence. None of these studies included imagery ability as an individual difference variable, which is proposed to mediate the effectiveness of mental practice interventions and performance outcomes according to the applied models of mental imagery (Martin, Moritz & Hall, 1999). Moreover, taken with results from the modeling literature that physical practice used in conjunction with modeling is effective for performance enhancement (Shea et al., 2000), practitioners should consider augmenting floor walkouts and program blueprinting with peer models to maximize learning effects.

Imagery

Imagery, often referred to as "mental practice", involves evoking physical characteristics of an object or a performance that has taken place in the past or is anticipated to take place in the future (Hall, 1998). Imagery can be one of the most useful psychological skills for figure skating because it enables skaters, their coaches and choreographers to mentally construct, rehearse or anticipate technical and aesthetic performance attributes which almost always involve sequenced elements performed to music. Accordingly, visual, kinesthetic and auditory imagery abilities are most relevant in figure skating contexts. Imagery can also be a significant part of mentally preparing for high-stakes contexts including discipline-specific tryouts and performing in front of judges in testing and competitive contexts. Figure skaters are frequently subjects in imagery studies, which have shown that experienced coaches are more open to using imagery and skaters benefit from learning how to use imagery effectively (Hall & Rodgers, 1989).

Imagery ability is thought to be a function of genetic variability interacting with experience (Paivio, 1985) suggesting imagery skills can be enhanced with training. Rodgers et al. (1991) found support for this contention among a sample of adolescent figure skaters (mean age: 13.7) who underwent a 16-week imagery training program and showed significant improvements in movement visual imagery ability. They also showed several changes in imagery use including: using more imagery in practice, engaging in more structured imagery practice, and reporting seeing and feeling their programs more easily than a verbal instruction experimental group. Demonstrating that imagery is also related to performance, skaters in the imagery group (and in the verbal instruction group) attempted and passed more tests than the control group.

In accordance with the Kantian notion that thinking in pictures precedes thinking in words, we contend that young children can learn to modify their active imaginations towards structured deliberate mental practice of sport-related skills and strategies. Coaches can direct young figure skaters even as young as five years of age to mentally practice, or image, in conjunction with teaching basic skating skills using metaphorical imagery. This technique involves introducing an inanimate object having similar properties with a critical element of a sport skill, discussion about the similarities, practicing the movement associated with the skill and using the metaphor as a cue word to reinforce the skill (Overby, 1991).

The following example of metaphorical imagery draws upon visual and kinesthetic senses. When teaching skaters how to execute the mechanics of a one-foot spin, the coach could introduce a magnet demonstrating its ability to attract metal. The coach can then ask the skater to hold the magnet while holding a paper clip in each hand an equal distance from the magnet. As the coach lets both paper clips go at the same time, demonstrating the force of a magnet attracting metal (e.g. paper clip), skaters are asked to imagine their body is the magnet and their arms and free leg are paper clips being slowly drawn towards the body. Once children can generate simple visual and kinesthetic images, a variety of imagery strategies can be employed to enhance players' imagery abilities. These strategies include varying internal and external imagery perspective, focusing on the properties of imagery, matching image content to desired learning or motivational objectives, and generating imagery scripts.

Educating skaters and their coaches about the structure of imagery including its variability along sensory domains, perspectives, its properties and functions can enable skaters towards developing contextually sensitive, individualized imagery scripts. Athletes can use imagery from two different perspectives, or viewpoints: externally—imagining themselves performing a skill as if they are watching a video tape of their performance; and internally—seeing their performance as if they were looking through their own eyes, capturing peripheral movement in space. According to White & Hardy (1998), athletes use both perspectives as they rehearse their roles in the action and anticipate the role of teammates and opponents. Applied to skating internal imagery enhances the feeling of movements involved in athletic skills; it allows the skater to be aware of the distance and timing involved in various movements. These researchers also contend that external imagery is similar to modeling because they both can serve as an internal standard for reproducing desired outcomes.

There is, however, much more to imagery than just perspective. Denis (1985) contends that for imagery to have beneficial effects, the content of the imagery must accurately reflect the intended outcome. Incorporating key properties of imagery during imaging sessions can help to improve imagery ability. These properties include vividness (clarity), controllability, and exactness of reference (Denis, 1985). The following application of Denis's properties can assist young skaters in developing their imagery skills:

- *Vividness* Better imagers learn skills quicker. Teaching skaters how to develop high levels of vividness would be an essential step in developing the skill. For example, a coach or consultant could have skaters visually image a performance of a double Lutz jump from the external perspective, focusing on the angle of their body as they jump into the air and complete each of the two revolutions. Or, using auditory imagery, the professional could direct skaters to hear the tempo and beat of their music feeling their body hold the positions to the music.
- *Controllability* Learning how to manipulate images so they correspond to objectives enables skaters to recover from mistakes.
  - Controlling performance example: a professional directs skaters to image working through a skill that has yet to be mastered, pointing out critical elements involved in the errors. The professional encourages skaters to successfully perform the skill while seeing and feeling the movements. For example, a skater who drops their skating shoulder on the entry of a double axel may see and feel themselves stopping the movement upon making the drop, image stopping the action, reversing the image as if rewinding a videotape, and continuing from the beginning focusing on correcting the error by keeping the skating arm stretched up.
  - Controlling emotions: a professional poses a stressful context for skaters such as experiencing a fall in a synchronized skating competition, or a partner falling during a free dance performance, or a fall on a required short program element where the skater would be required to regain and maintain emotional control in the face of losing concentration and confidence. The professional encourages the skater to recreate the situation especially focusing on the associated negative feelings. Then they ask the skater(s) to image dealing with the emotions in a positive way such as imaging the anger, tension or anxiety lift away from their bodies.

- *Exactness of reference* The exact replication of successful performances is required. Research has shown that practicing errors or wrong images produces a tendency to perform those errors (Woolfok, Parrish & Murphy, 1985). Exactness of reference includes imaging detailed force production and timing attributes of skating skills.
  - Example: the professional encourages skaters to image, kinesthetically, the difference in force associated with doing a single/double jump versus a double/triple jump. The exactness of reference can also apply to the speed of imagery. Guiding skaters to image their skills in slow motion enables them to attend to correct body positions and critical elements involved in a specific skill.

The following key points are recommended for incorporating imagery as intervention. Although it is beneficial to individualize imagery programs, introducing imagery in a group format is advised for skaters of 11 to 14 years of age. Once the basic imagery characteristics such as sensory imagery, imagery perspective, its properties and content have been introduced, children can develop their own imagery scripts. Coaches can help athletes write scripts to read and rehearse in their "mind's eye" and even tape-record their voice as they perform their imagery exercises. While players can formally practice their imagery during explicit imagery session, they should also be encouraged to use imagery in training periods between competitive events, immediately prior to and during a competitive event, and when they are rehabilitating an injury (Martin et al., 1999). It is important to note that physical practice is superior to imagery practice (Hird, Landers, Thomas & Horan, 1991); imagery should be a supplement to physical practice, never a replacement. There are many appropriate times to use imagery including before, during and after practice, during breaks in daily activity and at night just before bed. Systematic daily imagery practice can motivate skaters for physical practices. A coach may also want to build in time for imagery during a practice because it is especially helpful in strengthening the relationship between kinesthetic imagery ability and the mechanical form of skills. Finally, using imagery after a practice session while taking off skates or on the drive home from the rink can help reaffirm lessons.

Self-Monitoring during Skating Practice

Considering the cost of ice-time and the developmental readiness of young participants, maximizing young skaters' practice time is a central concern of parents and coaches. A typical free skating session lasts approximately one hour with a five to ten minute warm-up session, a portion of practice often devoted to dance practice and a subsequent cool-down period called 'stroking'. It is important that skaters focus intensely on maximizing skating element repetitions and program run-throughs while enduring distractions that occur in a relatively short time frame. Talking with friends, standing by the boards observing peers and getting on and off the ice are frequent off-task behaviors that can be expected from young participants (Hume, Martin, Gonzalez, Cracklen & Genthon, 1986).

In response to these concerns, Hume and her colleagues (1986) devised a behavioral modification system called a 'self-monitoring feedback package' consisting of a frequency and quality checklist of program elements and instructions. The effectiveness of this system was compared to regular coaching practices. Six skaters aged 14 to 16 years were assigned to either the behavioral modification group or a control group. The checklist consisted of a list of practice elements organized by jumps and spins, a list of program elements in order of appearance and two graphs: one of typical off-task behavior and another of total elements attempted during a regular practice period. These checklist items and the instructions were contained on the skater's display board, which was kept on the side of the boards. The instructions were as follows:

1. Practice the first three elements twice each, and then come and record them on the chart (frequency and quality).
2. Now practice the next 3 elements listed and record them. Continue until all elements have been practiced (approximately 15 minutes).
3. After all elements have been checked twice, do your program without the music.
4. Record elements tried in program and assess quality.
5. Immediately do program again.
6. Record as in #4.
7. Go and work on those elements you have rated as bad in the program, and those you did not attempt in your program. Record frequency and quality after every sixth element (approximately 10 minutes).
8. Go and do your program again.
9. Rate program quality as before.
10. For the remainder of the session, practice elements rated as bad. Continue to record after every sixth element.

When compared to normal coaching practices, the frequency of elements performed increased by 90 per cent compared to baseline practice off-task behaviors decreased and successful skating outcomes were in part, attributed to use of the package by coaches and two out of three skaters. Consistent with Hume et al. (1986) are observations in our own work with skaters: data sheets designed to track the frequency and quality of skating elements, regardless of discipline and program run-throughs, help keep skaters on task by providing specific goals, processing specific feedback and conditioned reinforcement, and serve to prompt other skaters that skaters are working and should not be approached unnecessarily. The system can be easily customized for skaters of any level and discipline. Coaches can be encouraged to adapt the self-monitoring system for skaters at lower reading and writing levels by involving parents or placing colored stickers beside a list of elements indicating varying degrees of performance.

Augmented Sensory Feedback during Skating Practice

Sensory feedback is also known as task-intrinsic feedback "available during or after a person performs a skill in its naturally occurring part of the skill performance situation" (Magill, 1998, p. 186). In contrast, augmented feedback involves sources external to the skater such as the coach who provides technical feedback associated with the sensory feedback, thus enhancing the intrinsic features of the sensory aspect. There are two common forms of augmented sensory feedback used in figure skating: the use of harnesses and video. Harnesses support the skater's weight by suspending the skater in the air during a jump. Coaches pull the harness to assist the skater with additional height required to make the necessary revolutions in double, triple or quadruple jumps. Video feedback, or self-modeling, involves recording trials of elements, sections of programs or entire programs and having the skater watch the recorded performances immediately after the trial. Both of these techniques assist the skater with important kinesthetic feedback involving timing, force and proper mechanics involved in the preparation, execution and follow-through phases of jumps.

CONCLUDING COMMENTS

Young skaters are typically well disciplined, work hard and are capable of setting and self-monitoring mastery-related goals. They can certainly be resilient. Interactions among individual, environmental and task demands present unique challenges for practitioners. Considering factors related to growth and development is imperative for working with this population. Occasionally clinical referrals will be required, especially where eating disorders and substance abuse coping are concerned. Ironically, the frequency of landing and falling in a given practice session, season and throughout the course of a career mimic the psychological triumphs and tribulations of figure skating. Helping figure skaters achieve their potential, albeit challenging at times, can be the most gratifying aspect of professional practice.

REFERENCES

Attie, I. & Brooks-Gunn, J. (1989). Development of eating problems in adolescent girls: a longitudinal study. *Developmental Psychology, 25*, 70–79.

Balmer, N.J., Nevill, A.M. & Williams, A.M. (2001). Home advantage in the Winter Olympics (1908–1998). *Journal of Sport Sciences, 19*, 129–139.

Block, J.H. & Robbins, R.W. (1993). A longitudinal study of consistency and change in self-esteem from early adolescence to early adulthood. *Child Development, 64*, 909–923.

Brooks-Gunn, J. (1988) Antecedents and consequences of variations in girls' maturational timing. *Journal of Adolescent Health Care, 9*, 365–373.

Brooks-Gunn, J., Burrow, C. & Warren, M.P. (1988) Attitudes toward eating and body weight in different groups of female adolescent athletes. *International Journal of Eating Disorders, 7*, 749–757.

Burwitz L., Moore, P.M. & Wilkinson, D.M. (1994). Future directions for performance-related sports science research: an interdisciplinary approach. *Journal of Sport Sciences, 12*, 93–109.

Cadopi, M., Chatillon, J.F. & Baldy, R. (1995). Representations and performance: reproduction of form and quality of movement in dance by eight- and 11-year-old novices. *British Journal of Psychology, 86*, 217–225.

Comper, P. (1991). Predicting athletic success: talent identification among Canadian amateur figure skaters. Unpublished doctoral dissertation, York University, Toronto, Ontario, Canada.

Davison, K., Earnest, M.B. & Birch, L.L. (2002). Participation in aesthetic sports and girls' weight concerns at ages 5 and 7. *International Journal of Eating Disorders, 31*, 312–317.

Deal, S.L. & Williams, J.E. (1988). Cognitive distortions as mediators between life stress and depression in adolescents. *Adolescents, 90*, 477–490.

Denis, M. (1985). Visual imagery and the use of mental practice in the development of motor skills. *Canadian Journal of Applied Sport Science, 10*, 4S–16S.

Diagnostic and Statistical Manual of Mental Disorders—Fourth Edition (DSM-IV) (1994). Washington, DC: American Psychiatric Association.

Dowrick, P.W. (1999). A review of self-modeling and related interventions. *Applied and Preventative Psychology, 8*, 23–39.

Dubravcic-Simunjak, S., Pecina, M., Kuipers, H., Moran, J. & Haspl, M. (2003). The incidence of injuries in elite junior figure skaters. *American Journal of Sports Medicine, 31*, 511–517.

Eveleth, P.B. & Tanner, J.N. (1990). *Worldwide Variation in Human Growth* (2nd edn) Cambridge: Cambridge University Press.

Fischer, K.W. (1980). A theory of cognitive development: the control and construction of hierarchies of skills. *Psychological Review, 87*, 477–531.

Fox, K.R. & Corbin, C.B. (1989). The Physical Self-Perception Profile: development and preliminary validation. *Journal of Sport and Exercise Psychology, 11*, 408–430.

Garner, D.M., Olmstead, M.P. & Polivy, J. (1983). Development and validation of a multidimensional eating disorder inventory for anorexia nervosa and bulimia. *International Journal of Eating Disorders, 2*, 15–34.

Garza, D.L. & Feltz, D.L. (1998). Effects of selected mental practice on performance, self-efficacy and competition confidence of figure skaters. *The Sport Psychologist, 12*, 1–15.

Gledhill, N. & Jamnick, V. (1992). Fitness test result comparisons: world versus national team members and 1975 versus 1992 national team members. *Coach to Coach, 9*, 6–9.

Gould, D., Jackson, S.A. & Finch, L.M. (1993a). Sources of stress in national champion figure skaters. *Journal of Sport and Exercise Psychology, 15*, 135–159.

Gould, D., Jackson, S.A. & Finch, L.M. (1993b). Life at the top: the experiences of US national champion figure skaters. *The Sport Psychologist, 7*, 354–374.

Hall, C.R. (1998). Imagery in sport and exercise. In R.N. Singer, H.A. Hausenblas & C.M. Janelle (eds), *Handbook of Sport Psychology* (2nd edn; pp. 529–549). New York, NY: John Wiley & Sons, Inc.

Hall, C.R. & Rodgers, W.M. (1989). Enhancing coaching effectiveness in figure skating through a mental skills training program. *Sport Psychologist, 3*, 142–154.

Hamill, P.V.V., Drizd, T.A., Johnson, C.L., Reed, R.B. & Roche, A.F. (1977). NCHS growth curves for children, birth to 18 years, United States. *Vital and Health Statistics, Series 11, No. 165.*

Harris, R. (1986). On aspects of jumping. *Skating, 63*, 10–13.

Harter, S. (1990). Causes, correlates, and the functional role of global self worth: a lifespan perspective. In, R. Sternber & J. Kolligan (eds), *Competence Considered* (pp. 67–98). New Haven, CT: Yale University Press.

Harter, S. (1999). *The Construction of the Self: A Developmental Perspective.* New York: Gilford Press.

Hausenblas, H.A. & Mack, D.E. (1999). Social physique anxiety and eating disorder correlates among female athletic and non-athletic populations. *Journal of Sport Behavior, 22*, 502–513.

Hird, J.S., Landers, D.M., Thomas, J.R. & Horan, J.J. (1991). Physical practice is superior to mental practice in enhancing cognitive and motor task performance. *Journal of Sport and Exercise Psychology, 8*, 281–293.

Horn, T.S. (2004). Developmental perspectives on self-perceptions in children and adolescents. In M.R. Weiss (ed.). *Developmental Sport and Exercise Psychology: A Lifespan Perspective* (pp. 101–144). Morgantown, WV: Fitness Information Technology, Inc.

Hume, K.M., Martin, G.L., Gonzalez, P., Cracklen, C.C. & Genthon, S. (1986). A self-monitoring feedback package for improving freestyle figure skating practice. *Journal of Sport Psychology, 8*, 333–343.

Ishikura, T. & Inomata, K. (1995). Effects of angle of model demonstration on learning of a motor skill. *Perceptual and Motor Skill, 80*, 651–658.

Killen, J.D., Haywar, C., Litt, I., Hammer, L.D., Wilson, D.M., Taylor, C.B., Varaday A. & Shisslack, C. (1992). Is puberty a risk factor for eating disorders? *American Journal of Diseases in Children, 146*, 323–325.

Lee, T.D. & White, M.A. (1990). Influence of an unskilled model's practice schedule on observational motor learning. *Human Movement Science, 9*, 349–367.

Lerner, R.M. (1985). Adolescent maturational changes and psycho-social development: a dynamic interactional perspective. *Journal of Youth and Adolescence, 14*, 355–372.

Lipetz, J. & Kruse, R.J. (2000). Injuries and special concerns of female figure skaters. *Clinician and Sports Medicine, 19*, 369–380.

Magill, R.A. (1998). *Motor learning: Concepts and Applications* (5th edn). Boston, MA: McGraw-Hill.

Malina, R.M. (1998). Growth and maturation of young athletes: is training for sports a factor. In K.M. Chan & L.J. Micheli (eds), *Sports and Children*, 133–161. Hong Kong: Williams & Wilkins.

Malina, R.M., Bouchard, C. & Bar-Or, O. (2004).*Growth, Maturation, and Physical Activity* (2nd edn). Champaign, IL: Human Kinetics.

Marsh, H.W. (1996). Construct validity of Physical Self Description Questionnaire responses: relations to external criteria. *Journal of Sport and Exercise Psychology, 18*, 111–131.

Martin, G.L. (1993). Research on mental practice techniques: Comment on Palmer's study. *The Sport Psychologist, 7,* 339–341.

Martin, K., Moritz, S.E. & Hall, C.R. (1999). Imagery uses in sport: a literature review and applied model. *The Sport Psychologist, 13*, 245–268.

McCullagh, P. & Weiss, M. (2001). Modeling: considerations for motor skill performance and psychological responses. In R.N. Singer, H.A. Hausenblas & C.M. Janelle (eds), *Handbook of Sport Psychology* (2nd edn; pp. 205–238). New York, NY: John Wiley & Sons, Inc.

Ming, S. & Martin, G.L. (1996). Single-subject evaluation of a self-talk package for improving figure skating performance. *The Sport Psychologist, 10*, 227–238.

Monsma, E.V., Feltz, D.L. & Malina, R.M. (2004). Puberty and physical self-perceptions of competitive female figure skaters: an interdisciplinary approach. Manuscript submitted for publication.

Monsma, E.V. & Malina, R.M. (2004). Correlates of eating disorder risk among competitive female figure skaters. *Psychology of Sport and Exercise, 5*, 447–460.

Monsma, E.V. & Malina, R.M. (in press). Anthropometric characteristics and somatotype in competitive female figure skaters: variation across competitive level and skating discipline. *Journal of Sports Medicine and Physical Fitness*.

Mumford, B. & Hall, C.R. (1985). The effects of internal and external imagery on performing figures in figure skating. *Canadian Journal of Applied Sport Sciences, 10*, 171–177.

National Council of Health Statistics (NCHS) (2004). http://www.cdc.gov/growthcharts/. Accessed 29 September 2004.

Newell, K.M. & Molenaar, P.C.M. (1998). *Applications of Nonlinear Dynamics to Developmental Process Modeling*. Mahwah, NJ: Lawrence Erlbaum Associates.

Niinimaa, V. (1982). Figure skating: what do we know about it? *Physician and Sports Medicine, 10*, 51–56.

Oleson, C.V., Busconi, B.D. & Baran, D.T. (2002). Bone density in competitive figure skaters. *Archives of Physical Medicine and Rehabilitation, 83*, 122–128.

Overby, L.Y (1991). Imagery use in children's dance. In L. Overby (ed.). *Early Childhood Creative Arts* (pp. 160–166). Reston, VA.

Paivio, A. (1985). Cognitive and motivational functions of imagery in human performance. *Canadian Journal of Applied Sport Science, 10*, 22–28.

Palmer, S. (1992). A comparison of mental practice techniques as applied to the development of competitive figure skaters. *The Sport Psychologist, 6*, 148–155.

Palmer, S. (1993). Mental practice with figure skaters: a rebuttal to Martin. *The Sport Psychologist, 7*, 342–343.

Rocco, P.L., Ciano R.P. & Balestrieri, M. (2001) Psychoeducation in the prevention of eating disorders: an experimental approach in adolescent school girls. *British Journal of Medical Psychology, 74*, 351–358.

Rodgers, W.M., Hall, C.R. & Buckolz, E. (1991). The effect of an imagery training program on imagery ability, imagery use and figure skating performance. *Journal of Applied Sport Psychology, 3*, 109–125.

Ross, W., Brown, S., Yu, J. & Faulkner, R. (1977). Somatotype of Canadian figure skaters. *Journal of Sports Medicine, 17*, 195–205.

Rucinski, A. (1989). Relationship of body image and dietary intake of competitive ice skaters. *Journal of the American Dietetic Association, 89*, 98–99.

Ryan, J. (1995). *Little Girls in Pretty Boxes*. New York, NY: Warner Books.

Sabatini, S. (2001). The female athlete triad. *American Journal of Medical Science, 322*, 193–195.

Scanlan, T.K., Ravizza, K. & Stein, G.L. (1989a). An in-depth study of former elite figure skaters: I. Introduction to the project. *Journal of Sport and Exercise Psychology, 11*, 54–64.

Scanlan, T.K., Stein, G.L. & Ravizza, K. (1989b). An in-depth study of former elite figure skaters: II. Sources of enjoyment. *Journal of Sport and Exercise Psychology, 11*, 65–83.

Scanlan, T.K., Stein, G.L. & Ravizza, K. (1991). An in-depth study of former figure skaters: III. Sources of stress. *Journal of Sport and Exercise Psychology, 13*, 103–120.

Shea, C.H., Wright, D.L., Wulf, G. & Whitacre, C. (2000). Physical and observational practice afford unique learning opportunities. *Journal of Motor Behavior, 32*, 27–36.

Skate Canada (2004). http://www.usfsa.org/Programs.asp?id=120. Accessed 29 September 2004.

Smith, A.D. & Ludington, R. (1989). Injuries in elite pair skaters and ice dancers. *American Journal of Sports Medicine, 17*, 482–488.

Starkes, J.L., Deakin, J.M., Allard, F., Hodges, N.J. & Hayes, A. (1996). Deliberate practice in sports: what is it anyway? In K.A. Ericsson (ed.) *The Road to Excellence: The Acquisition of Expert Performance in the Arts and Sciences, Sports and Games* (pp. 81–106). Mahwah NJ: Lawrence Earlbaum Associates.

Swoap, R.A. & Murphy, M.M. (1995). Eating disorders and weight management in athletes. In S.M. Murphy (ed.) *Sport Psychology Interventions* (pp. 307–330). Champaign IL: Human Kinetics.

Taylor, G. & Ste. Marie, D. (2000) Eating disorders symptoms in Canadian female pair and dance figure skaters. *International Journal of Psychology, 31*, 1–8.

Thompson, R.A. (1987). Management of the athlete with an eating disorder: Implications for the sport management team. *The Sport Psychologist, 1*, 114–126.

United States Figure Skating Association (USFSA) (2004). http://www.skatecanada.ca/en/skate_for_life/programs. Accessed 29 September 2004.

Vadocz, E.A., Siegel, S.R. & Malina, R.M. (2002). Age at menarche in competitive figure skaters: variation by competency and discipline. *Journal of Sport Sciences, 20, 2*, 93–100.

Weiss, M., McCullagh, P., Smith, A.L. & Berlant, A.R. (1998). Observational learning and the fearful child: influences of peer models on swimming skill performance and psychological responses. *Research Quarterly for Exercise and Sport, 69*, 380–394.

White, A. & Hardy, L. (1998). An in-depth analysis of the uses of imagery by high-level slalom canoeists and artistic gymnasts. *The Sport Psychologist, 12*, 387–403.

Woolfolk, R.L., Parrish, M.W. & Murphy, S.M. (1985). The effects of positive and negative imagery on motor skill performance. *Cognitive Therapy and Research, 9*, 335–341.

Yeager, K.K., Agostini, R., Nattiv, A. & Drinkwater, B. (1993) The female athlete triad: disordered eating, amenorrhea, and osteoporosis. *Medicine and Science in Sports and Exercise, 25*, 775–777.

Ziegler, P., Hensley, S., Roepke, J.B., Witaker, S.H., Craig, B.W. & Drewnowski, A. (1998a). Eating attitudes and energy intakes of female skaters. *Medicine and Science in Sports and Exercise, 3*, 583–587.

Ziegler, P.J., Jonnalagadda, S.S., Nelson, J.A., Lawrence, C. & Baciak, B. (2002). Contribution of meals and snacks to nutrient intake of male and female elite figure skaters during peak competitive season. *Journal of the American College of Nutrition*, 21 (2), 114–119.

Ziegler, P.J., Khoo, C.S., Sherr, B., Nelson, J.A., Larson, W.M. & Drewnowski, A. (1998b). Body image and dieting behaviors among elite figure skaters. *International Journal of Eating Disorders, 24*, 421–427.

PART VI

Water Sports

CHAPTER 20

The Sport Psychology of Olympic Sailing and Windsurfing

Ian Maynard
Sheffield Hallam University, United Kingdom

INTRODUCTION

Sailing is an astonishingly broad sport, with appeal for every age, athletic ability or disability. From cruising yachts on holiday, through weekend dinghy racing in clubs, to Olympic competition it can accommodate most aspirations and all shapes and sizes.

Every 4 years the Olympic regatta attracts small boat racers of the very highest calibre. As in most dinghy racing, medals are decided on minimum points scored over a series of races (usually 11), with all racers competing in all races. The winner of each race scores the least points and the last to finish, the most points. The specific classes of boats are reviewed after each Olympiad but currently there are 11 classes that vary from a women's keelboat, the Yngling, which has 3 sailors on board to a men's lightweight single-hander the Laser. Also included are the men's and women's windsurfing classes which both require immense endurance, combined with power and technical ability (to learn more about sailing and windsurfing see Sleight, 2002).

The Royal Yachting Association (RYA) is the national governing body of sport for sailing and windsurfing in the United Kingdom. As part of this remit the RYA is responsible for the development and preparation of Olympic sailors for the Great Britain (GB) team. In both the Sydney Olympics (2000) and the Athens Olympics (2004) the GB were from the most successful sailing nation, winning five medals on each occasion, and this is the basic justification why this chapter will focus on the approach, methods and much of the content developed by the RYA Sport Psychologists.

The RYA has coordinated an integrated sport science and sport medicine support service for its Olympic sailors since 1988. The service covers the disciplines of physiology, meteorology and psychology with access to nutrition, strength and conditioning, performance analysis and sports engineering as desired within sports science, and physicians and physiotherapists with access to surgeons and radiologists within sport medicine. The programme

The Sport Psychologist's Handbook: A Guide for Sport-Specific Performance Enhancement.
Edited by Joaquín Dosil. © 2006 John Wiley & Sons, Ltd.

Reproduced by permission of Peter Bentley © Peter Bentley

Reproduced by permission of Peter Bentley © Peter Bentley

is primarily funded by the National Lottery, is elitist in nature and philosophy and is based on a 3-tier developmental structure. At the base of the pyramid is "World Class Start" which caters for junior and youth sailors. At this stage the primary aims are talent identification and talent development. Currently between 600 and 800 sailors have been placed on the programme, mostly between the ages of 8 and 14 years. The second tier is "World Class Potential". These sailors are mostly between 14 and 25 years of age and are thought to be potential future Olympians. Between 60 and 100 athletes form this group with their main focus being the 2008 and 2012 Olympiads. The third and most elite tier is termed "World Class Performance" and is comprised of those sailors and windsurfers who are thought to have the talent, ability and experience to represent Great Britain in the current or next Olympic cycle. Depending on the stage of the Olympic cycle anywhere between 30 and 45 sailors may be funded to complete a full-time sailing campaign.

This chapter will outline the basic sport psychology programme that underpins the three tiers of the RYA "World Class" programme. A network of seven British Association of Sport and Exercise Science-accredited sport psychologists deliver the programme, with four practitioners servicing "Start", two "Potential" and one the "Performance" elements. An eighth psychologist with a clinical qualification and experience has been identified should the primary network consultant discover athletes with problems or issues that demand referral.

The psychologists have identified a backbone of mental skills and strategies that are increasingly developed at each tier of the RYA programme. The core mental skills are professional attitude development, performance-profiling and goal-setting, concentration, anxiety management and activation, mental rehearsal, teamwork and performance planning (developing regatta focus). Each area is underpinned by a modular pack that has been written and formatted in a structure that can if appropriate be delivered by the class coach. Hence, the content can be made sport-specific, class-specific and, as is warranted, even sailor-specific. This chapter will outline the basic content of each of these modules. Each section will, as appropriate, describe the theoretical principles governing practice and will explain some of the exercises that sailors and coaches complete in the development of the various mental skills.

PROFESSIONAL ATTITUDE DEVELOPMENT IN SAILING AND WINDSURFING

In every situation in sailing, as in life, there will be things that are outside of the control of the athlete. One characteristic of many people who have achieved a high level of personal success is their ability to sort out those things which they can control and to work at these, rather than concerning themselves with the things which are out of their control. This may seem a very simplistic principle but it is fundamental to all aspects of sport psychology as well as all aspects of sailing (Bull, Albinson, & Shambrook, 1996).

The RYA defines a professional attitude as the "identification and control of as many of the controllable variables in your preparation and performance as possible". Hence, each sailor's aims are to try to cover every angle in terms of their preparation and that each angle should be covered to the best of their ability. They should score ten out of ten on all controllable factors and not worry about those factors that they cannot control because these will induce anxiety which may be detrimental to their performance.

In learning to "control the controllable" the first step is for sailors to identify what they can control and what they cannot control in their preparation and performance. These exercises

Table 20.1   Controllables and uncontrollables for performance sailors

Controllables for performance sailors	Uncontrollables for performance sailors
You can control...	*You cannot control...*
• Rig settings • Not worrying about other UK sailors' performance • Ferry bookings • Determination • Dedication • Discipline • Thoughts—positive and negative • Technique • How much you eat and drink during racing • Decisions • Reactions to "hassling" situations • Routines (warm-up and starting procedures) • Time management • Fitness (injury prevention and strength/flexibility) • Your PR/sponsorship campaign • Getting time away from sailing • Your attitude to your crew/helm if they make a mistake • Communication in the boat • Concentration • Equipment preparation—i.e. spares • Your training programme (time on water) • What you say to yourself • Process orientation—focusing on technique rather than winning or losing	• Winning • Losing • Wind • Waves • Protest jury decisions • Mistakes by the race officer/race officials • Conditions • The performance of *all* the other sailors • Equipment breakages • Luck • Illness • Location of event • Tide/weather • Other sailors' speed breakthroughs "Technological availability" • The press/media • Accidents • Venues
NB This is not the "definitive" list—it will be different from sailor to sailor and, even with each sailor, it will change over time.	

are usually performed in a brain-storming type session and are delivered individually to a specific Olympic class. As variables are agreed by the group, they are classified as either controllable or uncontrollable and are recorded for subsequent inclusion on individual specific lists tailored to the needs of each sailor. Typical lists as compiled by performance' sailors are shown in Table 20.1.

Three factors that the RYA is particularly keen to ensure that all sailors classify correctly are performance, winning and losing. The RYA feels that sailors can control their performance but cannot control winning and losing. If sailors prepare consistently and correctly (by scoring ten out of ten on those factors in the controllable list), they are much more likely to perform to their potential and that is all that the RYA desire. However, because of things like "how well the opposition perform on the day, a poor decision by the race committee or perhaps just bad luck", even the best sailor cannot control the outcome/results of a race/regatta. Hence, if each sailor can maximize their potential they are much more likely to win the race and to maximize their potential each sailor should only focus on the controllable factors.

The psychologists also endeavour to ensure that sailors are aware that factors in the controllable list are task-relevant. In other words, as sailors encounter the pressure of competition it will help to focus on "communication" or "boat speed" whereas all the factors in the uncontrollable list tend to be task-irrelevant and will not enhance performance. Finally, we ask sailors to identify which factors within the controllable list are not thought to be currently under their control. Each factor that fits these criteria is eventually incorporated into the athlete's goal-setting programme. Therefore, every three months or so as the sailors re-evaluate their goals they may be asked to devise strategies that bring one further factor within their control. Hence, over time, they work to gain a consistent, high level of control over all the factors within the controllable list.

PERFORMANCE-PROFILING AND GOAL-SETTING IN SAILING AND WINDSURFING

Understanding about goals and being able to set goals effectively is possibly the most important of the mental skills (Kingston & Hardy, 1997). Likewise, while it is quite easy to comprehend the concept it is often difficult to implement with young sailors. A process that overcomes most of the problems associated with goal setting is called "performance-profiling" (Butler & Hardy, 1992). Performance-profiling allows the coach to understand the sailors' perspective, so not only do we improve both the sailors' and coaches' awareness of each other but also the sailors' ownership of the situation and hence their motivation. The process allows goals to be mutually agreed and also provides a good benchmark of current ability against which future progress can be measured.

The process has been found to have a variety of uses:

1. To highlight perceived strengths and weaknesses so training can meet the individual or teams'/boats' needs. This will enhance the sailors' commitment and adherence to training (Bull, 1991).
2. To monitor change, i.e. to assess the effectiveness of training.
3. To identify any mismatch between the perceptions of the coach and the sailor/boat.
4. To analyse performance following competition. (Butler, 1996)

The process should begin with the development of an appropriate performance profile. Ultimately the profile will need to be class-specific and even individual-/boat-specific. With young sailors the RYA go no further than a 16 to 20 segment 'dartboard', yet with older and more experienced sailors we may go to 2 pages that include technical, tactical, physical, mental and lifestyle factors at both the individual and boat level (see Table 20.2). A profile can be generated via a brain-storming session when sailors and coaches are asked to identify all the qualities required for performance excellence in their class of sailing, in each of the areas previously highlighted. Once the class profile has been developed it tends to remain fairly constant; however, each sailor or boat is always given the opportunity to modify the content each time that goals are established or re-evaluated.

At this stage both the sailor/boat and the coach complete the profile independently, rating the sailor/boat on each one of the constructs. Younger sailors fill in the dartboard and shade in their scores to get a visual display of their perceptions of their current ability and performance. A comparison of the sailor/boat rating and coach rating is then undertaken.

Table 20.2   Olympic 470 performance profile

Self-evaluation

	Importance for next training period	Current performance	Best/ideal performance
Equipment Hull (including fairness, gaskets, etc.)			
Foils			
Mainsail			
Jib			
Spinnaker			
Tuning numbers/settings			
Technique Starting			
Acceleration from start			
Mark rounding			
Pressure boat-handling			
Spinnaker hoist			
Tacking			
Gybing—reach to reach —run to run			
Waves upwind—long swell —short chop			
Waves downwind			
Running			
Kinetics			
Strategic / tactical Percentage sailing			
Covering			
Boat on boat			
Reaching options			
Running options			
Rules			
Compass/shift work			
Currents/tides			
General skills Meteorology			
Great escapes			
Protest technique			
Extreme options (win)			
Target areas Weight			
Diet/dehydration			
Event preparation			
Event analysis			
Fitness—targets			
Enough sleep			
Regatta lifestyle			

Table 20.2 (*Continued*)

Self-evaluation

	Importance for next training period	Current performance	Best/ideal performance
Mental aspects Arousal control—racing —training			
Confidence			
Positive thinking			
Concentration			
Goal-setting			
Race evaluation			
Professional areas Boat preparation			
Effective communication (sailor/coach)			
Dealing with outside factors—press —officials —sponsors —outside coaches			
Other areas Logistics			
Home affairs			
Finance			

Note: For evaluation below, use the following scoring scheme:
1 = Very poor/unimportant   10 = Excellent/very important.

If scores are similar or differ by two or less, then the average is agreed for that quality. However, if scores differ by more than two points, we have a mismatch. Mismatches have to be negotiated. The discussion usually involves the sailor(s) and the coach explaining how they reached their evaluation (usually via examples of recent performance) and one side tends to move up or down, or an agreement in the middle is struck. Hence, agreement on all scores is reached. Obviously agreed higher scores are the sailors' strengths and agreed lower scores are the sailors' weaknesses. Finally, the sailor(s) and the coach are required to agree the constructs where goals are to be set. For younger sailors, we tend to identify three qualities where they believe that improvement would have the greatest impact on their overall performance. For older and more experienced sailors the number of goals could increase to eight or ten, but will be a function of what both sailor and coach agree that sailors will be able to cope with. Older and more experienced sailors also use the formula developed by Jones (1993) to prioritize the areas for goal setting.

The process should be repeated at regular intervals using the same profile. This procedure provides a measure of progress. Within the RYA the process is usually completed three to four times per year for all sailors and at the "performance level" the procedure is used to drive the funding system.

As areas of concern are identified and agreed it is then important to establish SMART goals (specific, measurable, adjustable, realistic and time-based) (Bull et al., 1996). SMART goals are motivational whereas vague goals tend to be demotivational. Hence profiling identifies

Table 20.3   Strong and weak examples of goal behaviour

Setting goals

Phrased positively	*Not negatively*
Develop my boat-handling	Don't capsize
Be aggressive on the start-line	Don't be in the second tier at starts
Improve my kinetics in the boat	Reduce slow body positions
Process/performance tasks	*Not outcome (for the short-term)*
Focus on boat speed	Win the start
100% effort at all times	Win the race
Communicate with my crew and coach	Win the regatta
Controllable	*Not outside your control*
Boat preparation	Force my opponent into errors
Develop my technical knowledge	Win all protests
Better understanding of the weather	I never win at this venue
Specific	*Not global*
Dominate my part of the start-line	Become more aggressive
Understand the rules at mark roundings	Be a better sailor
Briefings/debriefings for all sessions on the water	Get fitter
Achievable	*Not unrealistic*
Develop key-words for my speed cues	Aim for 100% good starts
Get rig-settings sorted for light winds	Top 10 at the first mark
2 OBLA runs and 2 weights sessions per week	Win all regattas

Source: Adapted from Butler, R.J. (1996). *Sports Psychology in Action*. Butterworth-Heinemann: Boston, USA.

the qualities that the sailor is striving to improve and goal-setting provides a framework for achievement. The best goals are self-determined (Filby, Maynard & Graydon, 1999) and the RYA is keen to encourage sailors to take control of their own goals and goal setting.

Table 20.3 outlines examples of strong and weak descriptions of goal behaviour and is adapted from Butler (1996). The RYA also encourages a combination of different types of goals (Filby et al., 1999). Sailors are asked to establish process, performance and outcome goals and learn when to focus on the different types of goal. For example, outcome goals (e.g. winning an Olympic gold medal) can be very motivational, but would not be an appropriate focus during competition.

Having identified positive, controllable and SMART goals the final process involves the generation of strategies to achieve the goals (see Table 20.4). An important by-product of asking sailors and coaches to play a role in the procedure allows the coach to have a good working knowledge of the sailor's short-, medium- and long-term plans. This ensures not only that the coach can structure training sessions and the training programme around the specific needs of sailors or the class, but also that drills within the sessions can be progressive (this is illustrated within Table 20.4 where boat-handling techniques are gradually turned into skills by gradually applying more and more pressure).

CONCENTRATION IN SAILING AND WINDSURFING

Concentration is a skill that is central to performance. It is also a skill that can be trained and developed with practice and dedication (Nideffer, 1976). Poor performance is often decided by a small margin which in many cases can be traced back to a lapse in concentration, usually

Table 20.4   Defining strategies to reach the goal

Goal	Strategies for reaching goal
To improve boat-handling at starts	1. Establish and agree the relevant coaching points for the techniques. 2. Practise the techniques (without pressure). 3. Use 'time and space' to put the techniques under more and more pressure, i.e. 4 tacks between two marks 50 yds apart / 4 tacks in 45 seconds (can use a combination of time and space to increase pressure). 4. Use short start-lines to force good close boat-handling practices/ask sailors to "battle" for a certain position on the start-line. 5. Gradually increase the nature of opposition (opposition can start off as relatively friendly but ultimately you can demand match-racing type situations at the start). 6. Use full-on competition regularly in training.

NB   Note how the technique is gradually put under more and more pressure, until it becomes a skill.

near the end of the race when sailors are under greatest pressure and at their most fatigued (Maynard, 1997, 1998).

A common definition of concentration is "the ability to focus on the relevant cues in your environment and to maintain that focus for the duration of the competition" (Nideffer, 1976, p. 394). In practice this means directing attention to the most important factors for good performance. For example "boat-speed" or "head out of the boat" may be useful cues at different times of a race, rather than focusing on irrelevant factors or uncontrollables such as worrying about losing the race or the opposition.

Every sport has unique cues that need to be attended to for optimal performance and it is helpful to apply Nideffer's (1976) model to analyse the attentional demands of sailing. This model identifies two dimensions to help in this assessment. These dimensions are width of attention—whether attention is narrowly focused or more broadly focused—and the direction of attention—whether attention is directed toward the external environment or internally to the self. The width dimension refers to how many stimuli the athlete should attend to. At certain times in the race a very broad focus of attention is desirable, such as a busy start-line; at other times a very narrow focus is required for example, looking for the first mark. The direction dimension refers to external events such as wind shifts or tidal fluctuations or may involve an internal focus to analyse strategy for the first beat.

Typically, sailors tend to favour one of these four quadrants and this is termed their "attentional strength". The quadrant in which sailors are least effective or feel most uncomfortable is termed their "attentional weakness". Under relaxed conditions sailors are capable of shifting among these different attentional styles, as the situation requires (Maynard, 1997).

Figure 20.1 outlines the strengths and weaknesses of each style in sailing. Common attentional problems in sailing include attending to too many cues, attending to past or future events, and paralysis by analysis, fatigue or the effect of excess anxiety. Sailing takes place in an open environment and therefore tends to have many distractions as well as key cues. Hence, the skill is to identify and maintain focus on those cues that are task-relevant, rather than attend to too many cues. By attending to past events such as a mistake or future events such as the implication of winning or losing the race, sailors are no longer

External

Strength	*Strength*
Reading a complex environment well (e.g. "busy start line")	Good concentration on one thing.
Weakness	*Weakness*
May react too quickly without thinking (e.g. keep selecting the wrong option)	May stick to the same response even though it is not working (e.g. going left up the beat, when the right is consistently paying).
Broad	Narrow
Strength	*Strength*
Good analytical ability, organizes and makes long-range plans (e.g. through post-race analysis)	Good concentration on one thought or idea (e.g. knowing what you have to achieve in the last race).
Weakness	*Weakness*
Can become overly analytical. Have trouble sticking to one thing. May not react quickly enough (e.g. thinking when you should be doing)	Fails to attend to and incorporate new information. Not sensitive to what is going on around ("miss the wood for the trees" i.e. so intent on winning the right side that sailors fail to notice early that the left side of the beat is paying).

Internal

Figure 20.1 Strengths and weaknesses of each attentional style
Source: (Adapted from Nideffer, R.M. (1976). The test of attentional and interpersonal style. *Journal of personality and Social Pshychology, 34,* 394–404.

in the here and now, where the task-relevant cues can be found. A further inappropriate, attentional focus involves focusing internally for too long. Getting "stuck inside your head" or "paralysis by analysis" can mean that sailors are no longer attending to the important cues in the environment. Most sailors identify the end of a race or the end of a regatta as the most common time for concentration lapses due to fatigue. Concentration requires effort and as sailors become fatigued that effort declines and concentration can wander. Improving all aspects of physical and mental fitness can improve concentration and hence it is essential that sailors practise under conditions of fatigue so they are able to cope in competition. Finally, excess anxiety can inhibit attentional flexibility and therefore anxiety management strategies will also play a role in improved concentration.

Being aware of the problems associated with concentration is an important first step. The next is to identify some techniques and strategies to help improve concentration and focus on appropriate attentional cues. The RYA advocates that these strategies and techniques are perfected in training and low-pressure situations before they are used in important regattas.

One of the biggest obstacles to maintaining concentration during a race is when sailors become distracted by sights and sounds in the environment irrelevant to their performance. They do not have a cue or "fundamental focus" to return to; that is, an important task-relevant performance cue, to "look-at" or "attend-to" that will get them back in control. These cues can be verbal, visual or physical (Maynard, 1998) and can be used for instructional, motivational or psychological purposes. A verbal instructional cue may be "head out of the boat", a verbal motivational cue could be "work every wave" or a verbal psychological cue could be "think broad" or "focus", a visual motivational cue could be the crew's signal to "up our work-rate" and the visual psychological cue may be the "smile" from the helm that says we are in control. The physical or action cue with an instructional bias may involve our "kinetics" in the boat and a physical psychological cue may be taking a deep breath when things are getting a little frantic. These cues can be instigated by the sailor for themselves or

Table 20.5 Pre-race routine (last 30 minutes)

Time to go to start	Activity
30 minutes to go:	Sail upwind on the first beat. Split tacks with a partner. Check rig. Find the numbers (compass). Consider first beat tactics. Practise boat-handling. Find the first mark (if laid).
20 minutes to go:	Sail downwind back towards the start-line. Practise boat-handling. Check wave patterns.
15 minutes to go:	Back at start area. Tides (time on distance). Last chat with coach. Food and water.
10 minutes to go:	Transits and line-bias. Check the boat over. Keep an eye on the line. Check the wind.
5 minutes to go:	Set the watch and check at 4 minutes. Think about starting position on the line. Check transits. Bearing for first mark.
1 minute to go:	Line-up. Holding position.
0:	"B" of the bang.

may come from their partner in the boat. Of course the cues should be agreed and practised in training and kept as simple as possible.

Another way to minimize distractions and focus concentration is to develop consistent routines. An obvious example of when a routine may enhance concentration is prior to the start of a race (see Table 20.5).

By doing things in a consistent order in the last 30 minutes before the race starts, the mind learns to "switch on" and become focused. Consistent preparation leads to consistent performance. Likewise, during training or a race when sailors have lost their concentration a "breath–talk–sail" refocusing strategy can help. The breath will be part of the somatic anxiety management technique and will take the focus away from the distraction and onto the movement of the chest; the talk would be a relevant cue word or action that takes the sailor back to the "here and now" and an appropriate performance-related cue, and the "sail" refers to the need to "do" rather than "think about it". Some sailors use the word "Nike" (Just do it) in exactly this context.

RELAXATION AND ACTIVATION IN SAILING AND WINDSURFING

Most sailors and coaches of sailing agree that to perform your best you need to be in the "right frame of mind and physically feel good". Arousal control and anxiety management have a central role to play in reaching this optimal performance state (Maynard & Cotton, 1993). Although recognized as over-simplistic and possibly theoretically flawed the RYA use the inverted-U model (Yerkes & Dodson, 1908) to initially explain the arousal/performance relationship. We have found that sailors can grasp the concept and that this understanding of the topic increases motivation and ownership if intervention is required. The inverted-U model suggests that performance will increase as arousal increases up to some optimal level, whereupon further increases in arousal will produce a decrease in performance. This explanation indicates that sailors may require activation strategies if suffering from under-arousal or relaxation strategies if over-arousal is a problem.

Although some sailors have reported issues of under-arousal (usually in training or low-pressure regattas) the vast majority of interventions performed in sailing are due to problems of over-arousal. When over-arousal is labelled as "unpleasant" or "dysfunctional" the emotion tends to be identified as anxiety. Short-term anxiety or state anxiety (Spielberger, 1966) tends to take two forms: either somatic anxiety (bodily manifestations of anxiety such as rapid heart-rate, sweaty palms, tight muscles, etc.) or cognitive anxiety (the worry and negative thoughts that many experience just prior to performance). In short, sailors of the RYA are taught both activation strategies and/or relaxation strategies which include elements or components that can deal with either cognitive or somatic issues. The RYA philosophy is underpinned by the matching hypothesis (Maynard, Hemmings & Warwick-Evans, 1995a; Maynard, Smith & Warwick-Evans, 1995b). If the main source of the problem is cognitively based then a cognitive technique is instigated, while if the problem is fundamentally somatic a somatic intervention is applied.

Initially sailors are taught to become more aware of their thoughts, feelings and behaviours during practice and competition. This involves self-monitoring via diaries or the occasional use of state anxiety measures such as the Competition State Anxiety Inventory-2 (CSAI-2) modified to measure both the intensity and directional perception of anxiety (Swain & Jones, 1993). The aim of the self-monitoring is to get the sailors to recognize how their feelings are associated with performance outcomes; that is, to understand the relationship between how they feel on the inside and how they perform on the outside (Maynard, MacDonald & Warwick-Evans, 1997).

A final consideration that the RYA sport psychologists are asked to monitor prior to any intervention is whether the sailor will benefit most from a unimodal or a multimodal intervention (Maynard, Hemmings, Greenlees, Warwick-Evans & Stanton, 1998). The unimodal somatic intervention used is applied relaxation (AR) (Ost, Jerremalm & Johanson, 1988), the cognitive unimodal is positive thought control (PTC) (Suinn, 1987) and the multimodal intervention is stress management training (SMT) (Smith, 1980). All three interventions are modified to be both sailing-specific and sailor-specific. The unimodal/multimodal decision is based on the sailor's perceptions of the problem, which is the balance between intensity and direction of both cognitive and somatic anxiety and the time available to complete the intervention. If either cognitive or somatic anxiety alone is perceived to be a problem a unimodal matched intervention is usually advocated, whereas if both cognitive and somatic state anxiety are seen as issues, and sufficient time is available, then a multimodal solution is usually investigated. Because the multimodal intervention usually takes three to four months for the sailor to master sometimes both the unimodal packages (which can usually become effective within two months) are used.

AR is a six-stage process. The initial stages involve improving the sailor's awareness of physical tension and physical relaxation. Based on progressive muscle relaxation (Jacobson,

1938) the sailors are taught the difference between tension and relaxation. At the third stage the focus becomes the breathing. At this stage inhalation is conditioned to tension and activation and the exhalation is conditioned to relaxation. This exercise involves breathing in to a count of four and breathing out to a count of eight (for twice as long) a one to two ratio, to help relaxation. Alternatively, breathe in to a count of eight (creating tension in the stomach and chest) and breath out to a count of four (two to one ratio) to help activation or the generation of a more energized state. In the later stages of AR the breathing technique is made quick and portable. The technique is then built into a skill by gradually putting it under more and more pressure, hence it is initially used in practice and training, then low-level competition until ultimately the sailor feels happy using the procedure in high-level regattas.

PTC is a three-stage process. Initially the sailor must become aware that they are thinking negatively; second they must learn to stop the negative thoughts; and third they must replace the negative thoughts with a positive thought. Again, the rationalization and re-framing procedure usually takes about two months to master and must be gradually developed into a skill. SMT has also been adapted into a six-stage process (see Maynard et al., 1998). The procedure involves the integration of somatic and cognitive components and is made both sport- and individual-specific but it usually takes much longer for the sailors to hone the skill.

In dealing with under-arousal the RYA again advocate a self-monitoring procedure to the sailors as a means of increasing awareness of the potential problem. This education phase emphasizes that lethargy, feeling heavy-legged and, under-energized with no bounce or power are somatic signs of under-activation. Likewise, a lack of concern about the performance, mind constantly wandering, feeling bored or lacking enthusiasm are highlighted as signs of a lack of cognitive activation. Sailors are made aware that they do not need to experience all of these signs to be under-aroused, but the more indications they notice, the more likely it is that they will require some form of activation training.

Somatic techniques for activation tend to be the opposite of those practised for relaxation. Sailors are taught to increase the breathing rate and focus on the inhalation rather then the exhalation for their ratio breathing. Breathing from the chest (rather than the stomach) tends to activate and speed up the nervous system and forceful movements are also found to be useful. Sailors may do short, sharp press-ups or tuck jumps (when on land) or practise contracting and relaxing the major muscle groups, clench the fists (perhaps squeeze the tiller) or grit their teeth (if in the boat). Acting energized even though they feel lethargic may also help the sailors recapture their energy levels.

Similarly for cognitive techniques the sailors are asked to use energized cue words like "strong", "tough", "aggressive" or "quick" and positive self-statements like "get going", "hang in there" and "keep working". They also often use goals to overcome the lethargy. A goal of "getting-up" for all their performances can be used as an appropriate challenge with personal pride and determination in always giving 100 per cent effort being used as their trademark.

Finally, the RYA sport psychologists work closely with class coaches to ensure that stressful situations become the norm in practice and training. A very successful way to prepare for stressful or pressure situations in sport is to occasionally practice under pressure. Hence, as the sailors become more accustomed to performing under these conditions, they become less affected and desensitized in important regattas. These pressure drills and practices involve the manipulation of time, space, fatigue and level of opposition.

MENTAL REHEARSAL IN SAILING AND WINDSURFING

> Mental rehearsal allows me to practice my boat-handling when I am off the water. I find
> if I do the physical (move my hands or body in time with the manoeuvre) while I am
> imaging, the picture becomes that much clearer.
>
> Ian Walker (Olympic Silver Medallist, Atlanta 1996 and Sydney 2000)

Within the RYA, "mental rehearsal" has become the preferred term, over "imagery" and "visualization", because it doesn't limit the activity to the use of a single sense. With practice sailors can develop pictures in their head that involve most (if not all) of the senses of seeing, hearing, feeling, smelling and even tasking. In short the RYA advocate total "functional equivalence" as the Ian Walker quote suggests (Holmes & Collins, 2001), which also includes physical movements to complement the mental component of the experience. In addition to using the different senses and functionally equivalent physical movements during mental rehearsal, sailors are taught that the integration of emotions and feelings will also add to the value of the experience. Recreating emotions such as anxiety, anger or pain through mental rehearsal can help in the control of these states, just as the creation of pride, joy and self-confidence can add important meaning to positive experiences (Lang, 1979). Mental rehearsal works on the pretext that the mind–body connection occurs whether one actually executes a task or just thinks about executing the task. Your body does not know whether the controlling nervous impulses that move the muscles are generated through imagination or the unconscious brain, for purposeful movement (Hale, 1998). Hence, the effects of mental rehearsal of a skill or the actual physical execution of that skill are very similar. However, mental rehearsal is not a substitute for physical practice; it should be used to augment practice. It is most likely that sailors who train and perform mental rehearsal consistently will achieve greater performance levels than sailors who only train.

Although most sailors understand that mental rehearsal can be used to improve the learning of new skills, few are totally aware of the many and varied uses of the skill. As well as learning new skills or refining previously learnt skills the RYA advocate the use of mental rehearsal to practise strategy, control emotional responses, improve concentration, recover from injury and to help build and maintain self-confidence.

Before sailors embark on the specific use of mental rehearsal they are taken through a series of exercises designed to enhance the vividness and controllability of their images. The more senses the sailors can stimulate through mental rehearsal, the more vivid and intense the images tend to be. Likewise, while vividness is important, it is essential that sailors have the ability to control their mental rehearsal. The productive imager manipulates shapes and moves their images towards a desired goal. Vivid but uncontrollable mental rehearsal can be counter-productive to performance. Research also suggests (Hale, 1998) sailors should learn to use both internal and external perspectives and that by using relaxation to precede the mental rehearsal more productive imagery usually results. Hence, sailors usually do a few minutes of relaxation, possibly one of the breathing exercises outlined previously, prior to the start of each mental rehearsal session.

Most sailors find the production of a "mental rehearsal script" to be very useful. Hale (1998) suggests there are three stages or steps to producing the script; first tell the basic story, second add the detail and finally, refine the script so that it can be read easily and clearly (see Table 20.6 for details of a start). The script will help the sailor remember the image or it could be read out by a fellow sailor, coach or parent, if the sailor prefers.

Table 20.6   Imagery script for a start

I can *see* the committee boat, the start-line and the other boats around me. I *hear* the one-minute gun, and *feel* a sense of excitement. I pull in the main sheet, *hear* the sail fill and *feel* the boat begin to pick up speed. The waves catch the boat and I can *taste* the salty water. I *hear* calls of "portside" as the other boats jostle for position. I call "my water" as I *see* a space and *feel* me move the boat into position. My heart is racing, and I *feel* determined to hold my space. I can *see* the line and know I'm going to make a good start. I *feel* the anticipation as I wait for the gun. I *see* five seconds on the watch and pull in the main sheet; I feel the boat start to accelerate. I *hear* the gun and hike harder, feeling the acceleration and the water on my face. I *see* I'm first across the line and *feel* excited and happy to have made such a good start.

TEAMWORK IN SAILING AND WINDSURFING

Effective teamwork is often the difference between success and failure. Within sailing even the single-handers need to possess basic team skills. Personal preparation, boat preparation, coaching, sport science and sport medicine support when combined with the logistics of an all-year-round Olympic sailing programme, require good planning, coordination and communication, the basic elements of teamwork. With double-handers and three-person boats the need for teamwork becomes even more obvious and necessary. To build an effective team its members must learn to interact, to work towards shared goals, adapt to environmental demands and balance their individual needs with the needs of the other team members and/or the team itself (Hardy & Crace, 1997)

There are many factors that when combined help to influence the way in which a team performs. A comparison of successful teams and non-successful teams indicated that successful teams share a similar set of characteristics. The members of successful teams are happy in their roles and responsibilities within the team, they are committed to the team effort, they are happy to talk to one another in an open and honest way (either to resolve issues or conflicts or simply to try to move forwards) and successful team members all share the same hopes and aspirations, that is they are working towards the same shared goals. These factors are summarized by the terms "goals", "roles" and "communications" and these are the core elements of team-building within the RYA programme (Bull, et. al., 1996).

Improving teamwork requires an intervention that enhances team performance by positively effecting team processes and/or team synergy. Teamwork can be improved by the sailors agreeing on goals and/or priorities (via performance-profiling and team goal-setting), by analysing each other's roles and responsibilities (team processes), by examining the relationships among team members and by improving the way that sailors and/or support staff talk to one another (communication channels).

The RYA are very keen that its sailors are aware that their team isn't just restricted to their own boat and support staff; that is the team extends to training partners and other squad members. By being professional and by creating an environment when information is shared within a positive and supportive atmosphere, several things are likely to happen. The overall standard of sailing will improve as success is attributed to skills and learning, rather than being dependent on secrets, which in turn builds confidence and team spirit.

The RYA also has three corner-stones to improving teamwork:

1. Improving teamwork is hard work. All helms and crews must be committed to the team effort and be willing to take responsibility to make it work.
2. All helms and crews must be committed to monitoring the team processes and routines, must be prepared to be self-critical, and must be prepared to be open and honest.
3. All helms and crews must understand that team-building is a continuous process that requires thought and effort, action planning, implementation and evaluation.

Team goals are established via profiling in a similar fashion to individual goals. Appropriate constructs are elicited from the group to establish the profile, crews and helms work together to complete the profile and then scores are compared and contrasted to an independent evaluation completed by the coach. Again, using Jones's formula (Jones, 1993) priorities are established, goals are identified and strategies developed in order that goals may be reached.

When establishing roles "in and out" of the boat the following exercise is advocated. Sailors are asked to establish a list of all the different roles and responsibilities that are involved in Olympic-class racing (see Table 20.7 for an example of the type of content that such a list contains).

Independently from their sailing partner(s), the sailors are then asked to record who is responsible for each of the items on the list, for their boat. The results are then compared and discussed. The sailors are asked to ensure that they agreed on who is responsible for what and that the balance of roles and responsibilities is in the best interest of the boat. If this is not found to be the case, then amendments are made as necessary. It is important

Table 20.7   Roles "in" and "out" of the boat

- travel arrangements
- accommodation
- information on the venue
- reading the sailing instructions
- gathering weather information
- tidal information (if appropriate)
- boat set up for the day/race
- strategy
- timing the start
- line bias
- where to start
- upwind tactics
- downwind tactics
- information regarding other boats
- when to hoist/drop the chute
- calling laylines
- calling crosses
- roles at mark roundings
- boat preparation
- preparing protests
- signing off
- goal-setting
- regatta lifestyle
- planning (time management, use of diary, when to sail, etc.)

Table 20.8 Examples of good and poor communication in the boat

- We might get lifted in a minute.
- If only the breeze would knock another 10 degrees we would cross the fleet.
- I think there is more pressure on the left.
- Hurry up!
- This is useless, concentrate will you!
- We might cross and we might not.
- We can probably lay it from here.

- There is a starboard lift in 30 seconds.
- There is definitely more pressure on the left.
- We will cross by 1 boat length, but don't give any height away.
- We are 10 boat lengths from a clear lane on the starboard layline.

(Be aware that different people will prefer different types of information. The above examples are not necessarily right or wrong though the second set of examples are clearly more positive and to the point).

that each person's roles are clear and unambiguous and that sailors appreciate the fact that compromise and flexibility may be required.

A similar simple exercise is often used to improve the sailor's awareness of communication, both "in" and "out" of the boat. For example, the sailors may be asked to record a list of comments that their helm/crew makes that annoy them or that they feel are inappropriate. Similarly, sailors are then asked to record a list of comments that sailing partner(s) make that are helpful and constructive. (See Table 20.8).

Finally, sailors are asked to compare the lists and discuss in more detail the ways in which they communicate with each other. For example, do the comments support the agreed roles in the boat? What sort of information do you each prefer to receive? Why do you need this information and when do you want to receive it?

This exercise helps to improve communication by ensuring that sailors receive only the type of information that they "want" or "need" to hear (i.e. information that is task-relevant). The exercise also facilitates open and honest interaction which in turn tends to underpin mutual trust.

PERFORMANCE PLANS AND COMPETITION STRATEGIES IN SAILING AND WINDSURFING

If you have ever had the opportunity to watch elite sailors, or for that matter elite performers across most sports, it becomes clear that they have some well-learned and consistent routines which they execute each and every time they perform (Thelwell & Maynard, 2003). They seem to do the same things, in the same order and with the same timing. In contrast, less-experienced sailors tend to show many inconsistencies in preparation and performance. By the same token well-prepared sailors will have well-learned race plans and a systematic approach after the race or regatta has finished. As has been noted, consistent preparation underpins consistent performance. Obviously the detail in the performance plan may vary as a function of individual sailors, the class or the format of the regatta, but in all cases there should be themes that are common to the various contexts.

The following exercise is designed to break down performance into meaningful and important segments that follow a logical progression from pre-performance to post-performance evaluation. Whereas some sailors will have plans that stretch from the week before a regatta others will be happy with a short, 10-minute, pre-race routine and little else. The art is for sailors or boats to identify what is right for them.

Step 1 Determine the start and finish point for your plan. Remember that you can plan for some eventualities during the performance and you can certainly plan for most eventualities before and after the performance. Therefore, most plans should have the before, during and after elements defined.
Step 2 List or name the parts or segments in the plan (for example, night before routine, pre-race routine, pre-start routine, between-race routine, post-race evaluation, etc.). The number of segments will depend on how detailed individuals decide the plan should be.
Step 3 Record the details in each segment; that is, the activities that have to be completed. Ensure the activities are adaptable as sailors often want to add or amend segments.
Step 4 Learn the plan. Pin a copy of the segments somewhere prominent so that they will serve as a constant reminder. Practise the various parts of the plan in training and in minor competitions before trying them in major regattas. Practise the plan as often as possible; if it doesn't work in training it won't work when it matters.
Step 5 Fine-tune the plan. Amend the plan as you or the boat develops. As the plan becomes more automatic it may be possible to simplify elements.
Step 6 Take the plan to competitions. (See Table 20.9 for an example of part of a completed performance plan). (For two or three-handed boats the plan should also identify who does "what", "when" and "how".)

RYA sailors are encouraged to develop a series of competition strategies that will help them cope with the pressure of a big regatta. These strategies may be technical, tactical, physical, professional or mental. One mental strategy that many of the sailors have found useful involved the use of reminder sheets. Reminder sheets are fundamentally tools that may help with concentration and confidence.
This reminder sheet is to:

1. Remind sailors of good performances and remember when they sailed well.
2. Remind sailors of what they are good at—their strengths—so that they can focus on positive factors rather than anything else.
3. Remind sailors of their focus during the race and during the regatta. (See Table 20.10 for a completed reminder sheet).

SUMMARY

This chapter has outlined the basic foundation mental skills programme that the RYA delivers to their elite Olympic-class sailors. In most cases sailors will be confronted by the various topics at least twice during their development from "start" to "performance" athletes. On each occasion the subject is taken to a new level in terms of its theoretical underpinning and its practical utility, via a spiral-curriculum type process. The process is educational in

Table 20.9 An example of segmenting and performance-planning

Segment 1 The night before competition	1. Prepare and check equipment 2. Relaxation—music, read, TV, etc. 3. Review tactics 4. Check for sailing instruction amendments 5. Go-to-sleep strategy
Segment 2 From waking until departing for the venue	1. Check the notice board 2. Check weather forecast 3. Get food and drink organized for the day 4. Meet coach and discuss options
Segment 3 From arrival until setting sail	1. Arrive at pre-determined time 2. Tactical check 3. Technical check 4. Rig boat 5. Get changed 6. Relaxation and best performance imagery 7. Warm up, stretch, key words 8. Set sail
Segment 4 Pre-race routine *Segment 5* Between races *Segment 6* Post-performance	

Table 20.10 A sailor reminder sheet

My best performances	*What was good about them*
1. Beating a highly ranked opponent at match racing	1. Aggressive tactics and focused performance
2. Last race at the 420 nationals	2. Brilliant start and good boat-handling
3. Southern areas	3. Stayed confident and focused in spite of setbacks

Replay these performances in your head as often as possible.

My strengths are:

1. Tactics
2. Fitness
3. Mental toughness

I need to be:	*Therefore I need to:*
1. Positive	1. Use positive self-talk
2. Focused	2. Use reminder sheet and process goals
3. Well-prepared	3. Warm up, think through tactics, have a game plan

Before each race I will: take a few deep breaths—imagine myself racing well—positive thought—action.

PHRASE OF THE DAY

Never give up

its conception, can be delivered by sports psychologists or coaches and tends to grow out of basic cognitive-behavioural techniques.

Readers should note that integration has become a key tool in the "plan of action" of the RYA programme. The sport psychology programme is designed to build on itself. For example, sailors are made aware of the connections between the "controllables" and the elements underpinning a process-orientation in profiling and goal-setting. They are taught how process goals should be the central focus during competition, but that performance and outcomes goals have an important role in long-term motivation (Filby et al., 1999). They learn how process goals and "controlling the controllable" can reduce anxiety, but also how arousal and anxiety management techniques can play an important role in concentration and mental rehearsal and vice versa. The teamwork and performance planning/competition strategies modules are used to pull the whole programme together and sailors will often have elements of all the individual mental skills integrated to form a comprehensive competition-coping mechanism.

Integration also occurs across the various disciplines within the programme. For example, a psychologist may help with adherence to the physiology programme or perhaps a physiotherapy rehabilitation programme, and the physiologist will often work closely with the strength and conditioning expert. Likewise, the sports scientist and sports medics will be involved in coach education, with coaches having the responsibility to drive the whole of the sailor-centred programme.

ACKNOWLEDGEMENTS

The author would like to thank the Royal Yachting Association for permission and their support in the production of this manuscript. Likewise I would like to thank my fellow sport psychologists working on the RYA programme for their help in the development of the education modules and the ongoing delivery of the mental skills programme; Ian Brown, Jeanette Wardrop, Neal Bowes and Ben Chell.

REFERENCES

Bull, S.J. (1991). Personal and situational influences on adherence to mental skills training. *Journal of Sport and Exercise Psychology, 13*, 121–132.

Bull, S,J., Albinson, J.G. & Shambrook, C.J. (1996). *The Mental Game Plan: Getting Psyched for Sport*. Sports Dynamics.

Butler, R.J. (1996). *Sports Psychology in Action*. Butterworth-Heinemann Boston, USA.

Butler, R.J. & Hardy, L. (1992). The performance profile: theory and application. *The Sport Psychologist, 6*, 253–264.

Filby, W.C.D., Maynard, I.W. & Graydon, J.K. (1999). The effect of multiple goal-setting styles on performance outcomes in training and competition. *Journal of Applied Sport Psychology. 11*(2), 230–246.

Hale, B.D. (1998). *Imagery Training: A Guide for Sports Coaches and Performers*. Leeds: National Coaching Foundation.

Hardy, C.J. & Crace, R.K. (1997). Foundations of team building: introduction to the team building primer. *Journal of Applied Sport Psychology, 9*, 1–10.

Holmes, P. & Collins, D. (2001). The PETTLEP approach to motor imagery: a functional equivalence model for sport psychologists. *Journal of Applied Sport Psychology, 13*, 60–83.

Jacobson, E. (1938). *Progressive Relaxation*. Chicago: University of Chicago Press.

Jones, G. (1993). The role of performance profiling in cognitive behavioural interventions in sport. *The Sport Psychologist, 7*, 160–172.

Kingston, K.M. & Hardy, L. (1997). Effects of different types of goals on the processes that support performance. *The Sport Psychologist, 11*, 277–293.

Lang, P.J. (1979). A bio-informational theory of emotional imagery. *Psychophysiology, 17*, 495–512.

Maynard, I.W. (1997). The Test of Attentional and Interpersonal Style (TAIS) and its practical application. In R. Butler (ed.), *Psychology in Sports Performance*. Oxford: Butterworth Heinemann.

Maynard, I.W. (1998). *Improving Concentration*. The National Coaching Foundation.

Maynard, I.W. & Cotton, P.C.J. (1993). An investigation of two stress management techniques in a field setting. *The Sport Psychologist, 7*(4), 375–387.

Maynard, I.W., Hemmings, B., Greenlees, I.A., Warwick-Evans, L. & Stanton, N. (1998). Stress management in sport: a comparison of unimodal and multimodal interventions. *Anxiety, Stress and Coping: An International Journal, 11*, 225–246.

Maynard, I.W., Hemmings, B. & Warwick-Evans, L. (1995a). The effect of a somatic stress management intervention strategy on semi-professional soccer players. *Sport Psychologist, 9*(1), 51–64.

Maynard, I.W., MacDonald, A.L. & Warwick-Evans, L. (1997). Anxiety in novice rock climbers: a further test of the matching hypothesis in a field setting. *International Journal of Sport Psychology, 28*, 67–78.

Maynard, I.W., Smith, M.J. & Warwick-Evans, L. (1995b). The effects of a cognitive intervention strategy on competitive state anxiety and performance in semi-professional soccer players. *Journal of Sport and Exercise Psychology, 17*(4), 428–446.

Nideffer, R.M. (1976). The test of attentional and interpersonal style. *Journal of Personality and Social Psychology, 34*, 394–404.

Ost, L., Jerremalm, A. & Johanson, J. (1988). Individual response patterns and the effects of different behavioural methods in the treatment of social phobia. *Scandinavian Journal of Behavioural Research and Therapy, 19*, 1–16.

Sleight, S. (2002). *The KISS guide to Sailing*. UK: Dorling & Kindersley.

Smith, R.E. (1980). A cognitive affective approach to stress management for athletes. In C.A. Nedeau, W.R. Halliwell, K.M. Newell and G.C. Roberts (eds), *Psychology of Motor Behaviour and Sport* (pp. 141–167). Champaign, IL: Human Kinetics.

Spielberger, C.D. (1966). Theory and research in anxiety. In C.D. Spielberger (ed.). *Anxiety and Behaviour*. New York: Academic.

Suinn, R.M. (1987). Behavioural approaches to stress management in sports. In J.R. May & M.J. Asken (eds). *Sport Psychology*. New York: PMA.

Swain, A.B.J. & Jones, J.G. (1993). Intensity and frequency dimensions of competitive state anxiety. *Journal of Sport Sciences, 11*, 533–542.

Thelwell, R.C. & Maynard, I.W. (2003). The effects of a mental skills package on "repeatable good performance" in cricketers. *Psychology of Sport and Exercise, 4*, 377–396.

Yerkes, R.M. & Dodson, J.D. (1908). The relation of strength stimulus to rapidity of habit formation. *Journal of Comparative Neurology and Psychology, 18*, 459–482.

CHAPTER 21

Psychological Aspects of Rowing

Michael Kellmann
University of Bochum, Germany
Gaby Bußmann
Olympiastützpunkt Westfalen, Germany
Dorothee Anders
University of Hamburg, Germany
and
Sebastian Schulte
University of Bochum, Germany

INTRODUCTION

Rowing requires of athletes an extremely complex sports motor performance, which covers various, partly contrasting aspects. More often than not, the crucial factor limiting improvement in overall performance of highly trained rowers competing in top-level, international races with the best possible material is mental strength. That is why in sports with a tough and extensive training schedule, such as rowing, the relevant knowledge of performance-related physiology, sports medicine and training science has to be combined with the psychological consulting of athletes. Only a training regime that takes into account the latest findings of all the above-mentioned scientific disciplines ensures that athletes can enhance their level of performance in the long run.

Using arithmetical terms, the following statement applies in addition to the big boats, such as the eight. Accumulating eight strong rowers in a boat is a necessary but not necessarily sufficient condition for sporting success. To give an example, even eight Marcel Hackers, who is the world champion, current record holder and one of the fastest scullers in the world, would not guarantee a world-class eight—in this case, only the necessary condition would have been met undoubtedly.

It is the aim of the chapter to provide an overview of the sport of rowing including basic information of the structure as well as on technical and physiological issues. The focus is on the psychological aspects of rowing which will be illustrated by the men's eight.

The Sport Psychologist's Handbook: A Guide for Sport-Specific Performance Enhancement.
Edited by Joaquín Dosil. © 2006 John Wiley & Sons, Ltd.

However, to a certain extent the smaller boat types follow the same rules. Three approaches such as (1) *coach the coach*, (2) *team consulting*, and (3) *individual consulting* can be used in psychological consulting in rowing. Based on these concepts, specific psychological techniques will be introduced which have been used with the German men's eight during the preparation for the Olympic Games.

BASICS OF ROWING

Rowing is a cyclic sport with the motions being repeated many times, which requires of athletes characteristic prerequisites in terms of physical condition and motor skills. The pattern of motions is determined by the sports apparatus provided and can be described by means of physical attributes relevant to the motions. With an intermediate rowing time between 5'20" and 8 minutes depending on the boat type, rowing belongs to those sports requiring an intermediate endurance capacity and is marked by loads of high intensity and physiological diversity. Of particular concern are the flexibility, strength and endurance components, which all depend on each other and are interrelated in a mostly complex way (e.g. Adam, 1982; Hill, 1995).

According to Hill (1995), particularly demanding and partly diametral requirements in terms of physical conditions have to be met by rowing athletes. While the rower is required to generate maximum power in order to propel his boat to the greatest extent per stroke, he will also have to pull on his oar(s) 200 to 250 times to cover a distance of 2,000m. This requires an optimum compromise between maximal strength, endurance and coordination. Compared to athletes competing in other sports, successful rowers are characterized not only by a highly developed aerobic capacity but also by an anaerobic capacity that allows them to produce peak rowing power; for instance, at a racing start. Only if the conditional prerequisites are evenly balanced will the athlete perform to his full potential.

Apart from the aerobic and anaerobic capacities, other crucial factors in rowing are, above all, technique, strength and motion velocity. Technique refers to the athlete's ability to balance the boat and pull the oars or sculls in an efficient and effective manner. As a reaction to the rower's movements, a refined technique is to result in a minimal rotation of the boat about its three axes. The motion velocity depends on the strength and the reaction velocity of the motor system of muscle and nerve and relates to the time frame in which a movement can be induced. A high velocity enables an athlete, for instance, to get off to an explosive start (Adam, 1982). Finally, strength means the absolute amount of power that a rower has to generate when pulling on his oars to achieve the best possible result. As the speed a rowing boat can gather primarily depends on the absolute performance of the athlete and, at the same time, water resistance opposing higher weights rises only less than proportionately, height and weight matter in rowing. In addition, the muscle mass turns out to be a discriminating variable, as about 70 per cent of the all muscle fibres in the human body are involved when a rower pulls on his oars (Steinacker et al., 2000b).

On the whole, rowing is one of the most intensive sports when it comes to training. It needs an enormously complex training program, which has to be planned and monitored very closely. As all relevant components affecting the overall performance have to be considered, apart from the actual on-water sessions, rowing training incorporates specific gymnastic exercises, strength and power endurance work-outs, endurance training as well as exercises to improve the athletes' velocity and agility (Fritsch, 1990; Steinacker et al.,

2000b). Elite level rowers train between 10 and 14 times (about 20 to 28 hours) a week; in training camps the number of training sessions increases considerably.

There is hardly any other sport in which athletes depend on and affect each other to such an extent as they do in rowing. Contesting successfully in an eight-person boat needs considerably more than a random combination of eight strong guys, who row across the sea like galley slaves; a lightweight coxswain, who steers the boat and does the thinking for their strong men; plus a coach, who selects the team and makes them give it their all in every single race. That is why abilities such as the intuitive understanding of one's team mates as well as a feeling for boat and motion are of paramount importance to make the boat float. As an optimum prescriptive structure of stroke technique has not been clearly defined allowing the athletes ample scope to adapt the fundamental elements to their individual prerequisites, it is considered most important to get into a rowing rhythm (Hill, 1995).

Although it is difficult to improve a steady rhythm within a crew through training, it nearly always decides whether a team does well in the race. This rowing rhythm has to be kept reasonably constant in changing external (e.g. wind, rain) and internal conditions (e.g. fatigue), which can be achieved only through a complete harmony within the crew (Reiß & Pfeiffer, 1991). In this context, in 2003 and 2004 the men's oar national team of Canada had a distinct, rather unorthodox manner of rowing compared to their competitors. However, this technique was employed by the entire team in such a harmonious way that it resulted in a remarkable racing speed.

Competitions

On international level, rowing competitions are held in 14 different boat types. Ranging from singles to eights, the boats are between 8m and 17.50m long and have a weight of 14kg to 90kg. Depending on the boat type, rowers use 2 sculls of a length of about 3m or a oar, which is about 3.85m long.

The race calendar of elite-level rowers includes 4 to 7 regattas from April to October peaking in the Olympic Games or the World Championships respectively. Competitions can be divided into preparation, test and qualifying races, nomination regattas and major competitions, which also differ in terms of objectives and importance. Whereas preparation and test regattas aim at building up the specific endurance capacity and assessing the level of performance, the German rowers and crews have to meet specified criteria at the nomination regattas in order to qualify for the major competitions, at which they are supposed to achieve their best results (Fritsch, 1990).

For the athletes in the German A-Team, the season is divided into several periods of internal nomination for the boat types. Speaking in soccer terms, these phases can be described as "after the match is before the match". As soon as the athletes return from their three-week vacation after the World Championships (WCh) or the Olympic Games (OG), the process of internal qualification kicks off—the qualifying rounds. The athletes can make a first good impression on the coaches not only by competing in various forms of ergometer tests (ET, see Figure 21.1), but also by demonstrating the ability to harmonize technically with other crew members in the boat (B). The athletes are presented with the opportunity to amplify this first impression in late November and late March when they compete in long-distance regattas (LD) or—if they failed to get their names into the coaches' books—to

Figure 21.1   Schematic order of phases in the process of preparing for the season's peak event, i.e. the World Championships (WCh) or the Olympic Games (OG)

show their true potential. The spring test in April (ST) marks the temporary end of the qualifying rounds.

Assessing all the figures at hand and evaluating the results of all test contests, the coaches finally put together the crews for the different boat types, who are to compete in the first World Cup (WC). Obviously, in the process of evaluating the data the coaches may set different priorities in certain areas tested. During the following competition phase, coaches watch the athletes' performances in the three WCs very closely to find out how well the crews in the respective boat classes compete against international opposition. If necessary, changes are made and the newly formed crews have to prove in further WCs that their nominations have been justified. After the third WC (which, as a rule, is the WC in Luzern) the rowers, who are to compete in the various boat classes, are named and the crews enter the final preparation phase (FPP), i.e. the immediate build-up for the season's peak event.

In rowing, the FPP usually starts five to six weeks before the season's peak event (WCh or OG). What is to be achieved in athletes in this phase is improving endurance, specific strength and power endurance capacities, stabilizing the rowing technique to be used in the competition, adopting and applying tactical skills as well as improving stress and competition stability. When preparing for the FPP, these targets have to be set and specified, taking training methods and total amount of training into account. As the above-mentioned training dimensions cannot be targeted simultaneously, the FPP is divided into several slots, with priorities set on one specific methodical training area at a time. According to the principle of super-compensation, in the first phase of the FPP the total work load is first increased, then cut back again when the competition draws nearer. In this context, the work loads in this first part of the FPP are mostly half-specific with a rather low share of specific workouts, whereas in the second part shorter, high-intensity and highly specific work loads prevail (Steinacker et al., 2000a).

Relevance of Sport Psychology in Rowing

In addition to the physical prerequisites of rowing athletes already mentioned above, in a highly complex sport, such as rowing, there are mental factors that have a crucial impact on the performance being delivered and established. Provided that the best material available is given, psychological and communicative aspects often turn out to be the limiting factor between top-level athletes. That is why it is both important and necessary that athletes are looked after by professional sports psychologists in order to mobilize all resources available and make sure of optimum training and a positive attitude towards performance. In this case, the way the psychological training is applied is based upon a strategy of systematically optimizing the psychological capacity to act by means of psychological methods (Seiler & Stock, 1994). Psychological training is always used with a purpose (i.e. always focused on a clearly defined objective), systematic (specified and planned in terms of time), repeated (is not applied only once) and monitored (have the desired effects

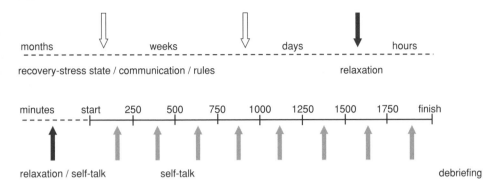

Figure 21.2   Order of phases within the preparation period, during which psychological techniques may be applied

been produced?). Psychological training aims at synchronizing internal processes (thoughts, emotions, self-talk) and improving the motions. Ultimately, the internal processes are to work as a guideline for athletes how to act and also to support the technique in which they produce a specific movement (Eberspächer, 2001; Seiler, 1992).

As part of the long-term preparation for the season's peak event (WCh/OG), every single regatta requires a medium-term, a short-term and an immediate preparation for the race, during which athletes not only work out physically but also prepare mentally for the competition to come by further developing their skills in certain areas (Figure 21.2).

The skills acquired in the preparatory period will then have to be tested and stabilized in competitive races. However, they will have to be modified, if necessary. In this chapter selected techniques of psychological training are presented that can be applied in the different stages of the preparatory periods. In this context, the recovery-stress state and the communication between coaches and athletes as well as the team talk within the crew in the long- and medium-term preparation are crucial elements when it comes to monitoring the training process. Although developing relaxation skills should be high on the list in the long-term preparation, in most cases these skills are utilized only in the immediate build-up to a competitive contest (during the evening before race day or on the day itself). Regulating self-talk is also relevant in training sessions; however, it unfolds its true potential only when the athlete applies self-talk in a contest situation. Starting with the first tests and competitions, debriefing on a regular basis becomes an integral part of the athletes' psychological counselling and care. The above-mentioned skills are to be acquired and trained in the pre-season already. Consequently, it is highly recommended to make sure of a medium- and long-term psychological care of athletes, as only under these circumstances can the developed skills be tested and optimized in a competitive race.

When selecting a certain psychological method to be applied in rowing training, sport psychologists will always have to consider the boat type, i.e. the number of rowers involved and the amount of interaction expected. Generally speaking, three approaches can be differentiated in psychological counselling. These concepts can be applied one after the other, in parallel, or even in an interactive manner. They are as mentioned before (1) *coach the coach*, (2) *team consulting*, and (3) *individual consulting*. The German eight will be taken as an example to discuss important aspects that illustrate the high complexity of interactive psychological counselling.

THE MEN'S EIGHT

The biggest boat in competitive rowing, the men's eight, is the flagship of every rowing nation. There is no other boat type and hardly any other sport in which perfect teamwork is as decisive as in the eight. Similar to a soccer team, every single member of the crew has his specific tasks to fulfil. The coxswain steers the boat, cheers on the crew and decides on the tactical approach to the race. The stroke sets the rhythm for the boat, which is passed on to starboard by the rower right behind the stroke ("co-stroke"). Moreover, the athletes seated in the front part of the boat (the bow) row in a manner differing from those sitting in the middle (often labelled as "the engine")—that is why every single athlete takes his share of responsibility for the rhythm. If a rift occurs anywhere in the boat, even a perfect stroke stands no chance of turning around a 700-kilogram body working against him behind his back (cf. Schulte, 2004).

But simply characterizing the single positions in a boat, even in the most objective way, does not suffice to account for the specific phenomenon of the eight. Every crew has developed a complicated hierarchical order, which becomes most obvious from the outside when a crew has competed together for a long time. Every athlete is not only aware of his own strengths and weak spots, but also of those of his team mates.

Only rarely is the coaches' wish for physically capable athletes who have developed both a refined rowing technique as well as a perfect feeling for rhythm met as only few rowers bring in the perfect mix of all these skills. It is often the physically weaker athletes who manage to compensate for their physical deficits through technique and rhythm, whereas the strong guys need their strength and endurance to make up for their technical shortcomings. Apart from individual physical differences, the athlete's experience has a significant impact on performance. Experienced rowers, who have raced on top level for years winning big trophies, are regarded as highly respected authorities in the boat. Advice as well as criticism voiced by those athletes is generally accepted by less-experienced rowers. Critical remarks are usually made in the boat and are mostly centred on improving the motions. What is more, criticism is also expressed 'on shore'; for instance, when the crew members work out in the gym or do cross-country skiing. In these cases, criticism is not to be understood primarily as merely pointing out other athletes' mistakes and weak spots, but identifying a team mate's potential that has not been fully reached but could contribute to the entire team's success.

An eight plus coach and coxswain is a reasonably sized group, in which none of the rowers can hide. However, not all athletes have the same standing within the group. The idiosyncrasies of rowing, compared to a sport such as professional soccer, become obvious when we take a closer look at the positions of coach and coxswain. The coach can be seen as a constant factor, who is not in immediate danger of being sacked when his crew has fallen short of expectations in a regatta. A hurried substitution of the coxswain would not have any positive short-term effects either, as they bring a wealth of experience into the boat as well. That is why there is no genuine competition for this position in the eight. Apart from these two constant factors, the crew consists of eight variable values that have to prove their quality in every single race. If they fail to deliver, they are in danger of being replaced with highly motivated rowers, who come off the subs bench and strive for a position in the prestigious eight. Athletes succeed in making the German eight only when they have gone all the way through the tough qualifying rounds prior to the team selection. However, there may be exceptions to the rule 'everybody can be replaced', which have to be applied in

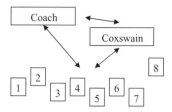

Figure 21.3   Hierarchical structure within an eight team

certain cases. The best rowers are well aware of their qualities knowing that they cannot be axed easily. On the other hand, those who are on the brink of losing their place in the eight do realize that they are not in a strong position.

To sum up what has been pointed out so far, every eight establishes a hierarchical order in which every single rower has his place. This structure is called 'horizontal hierarchy' and describes the order among the rowers within the crew, which is determined by such factors as skill and experience.

Besides the athletes, the coach who is in charge of the eight plays a vital part. Despite the extensive qualifying process, in which the most capable rowers are selected, it is up to the coach to come to the ultimate decision who makes the final eight. This decision is even tougher as not all important criteria that contribute to the boat's success or failure can be measured in an objective manner. Whereas strength data and the level of performance in ergometer tests can be assessed easily, it requires an undoubtedly more complex expertise to evaluate rowing technique and rhythm.[1] When it comes to judging such partly subjective areas, more often than not different coaches disagree in their opinions. The selection process of the 'perfect eight' is followed by a tuning phase which aims at finding the right position for every single athlete in the boat. This process often turns out to be lengthy and more demanding than the actual selection and requires of coaching staff a sensitive nose for the moods and mental state within the team. Once the athletes have found their final places in the boat, the coach starts with the fine-tuning of the eight rowers. He accompanies his crew in long on-water sessions in order to correct individual mistakes and, finally, to make the motions of his eight rowers work together to perfection. If the team selected fails to reach a certain standard, the coach can either rearrange the seating order within the boat or go even further and substitute one or several athletes. The decisions made by the coach are crucial for the athletes. Similar to the relations among the athletes, there is also a hierarchical structure between the coach and the team, which is called 'vertical hierarchy'.

As the extended arm of the coach, the stroke has a special status in the eight. His specific responsibilities are to make the crew put the coach's instructions into action as the stroke usually is in closer contact with the athletes than the coach himself. When incorporating the coxswain in the hierarchical structure, a horizontal and a vertical hierarchy are created. Considering all the people involved, an eight team forms a highly complex network of interrelations that is determined by hierarchical structures to a great extent.

Figure 21.3 illustrates this hierarchical network. The numbers 1 to 8 represent the 8 rowers. Due to the specific responsibilities required of him, the stroke (No. 8) occupies a consciously exposed position. The positions of rowers no. 1 to no. 7 in relation to a virtual

---

[1] On a standard rowing ergometer, athletes row a virtual 2,000-meter distance. The time reached, i.e. the performance in absolute terms, is then related to the rowers' weight, which provides the data needed for a clear ranking (cf. Grabow, 2003).

horizontal axis have been chosen arbitrarily. What is to be illustrated is the differing stand-ings of the 8 athletes within the horizontal hierarchy. Strictly speaking, arrows would have had to be drawn connecting the single athletes. For reasons of clarity, these arrows have been left out. Moreover, coach and coxswain develop distinguished (hierarchical) relations to rowers 1 to 8, which would also have to be demonstrated through additional double arrows.

Adding up all constellations between rowers, coxswain and coach, 45 different combina-tions are possible, which, in the worst case, would constitute 45 potential sources of conflicts and frictions. What is more, this figure would even multiply if relations between various groups were considered as well (such as bow rowers and strokes, strokes and coxswain). Two typical problems, which may result in a significant drop in the level of performance of an eight, are the loss of stroke rhythm in the boat and frictions within the team's spirit.

Case 1: Loss of Stroke Rhythm

Every team member—the rowers, the coxswain and the coach—try (in their minds, at least) to identify the reasons why the stroke rhythm has been lost. Coach and coxswain can look at this issue from a relatively neutral perspective. However, both have developed their personal views on the single athletes, which may prevent them from assessing the problem in an entirely objective way. What remains to be clarified is: what actually happens in the boat? In a previous section the different types of rowers have already been described ranging from technically versatile athletes to power-oriented engines. Every rower has developed his personal view on his every single team mate, whom he considers to belong to either the former or the latter category. When the rhythm is lost in an eight, usually the first group to be blamed is the technically weaker, strong guys. If further limiting factors already mentioned above (little race experience, recent inclusion in the crew) apply to one particular suspect, a powerful but technically ordinary rower is often spontaneously identified as the weak spot in a team. Ideally, it turns out that this is the case and the team succeeds in overcoming the problem and finding back the rhythm as either the accused manages to correct his mistakes or is replaced by another athlete.

Unfortunately, in reality it is hardly as simple to solve this problem. The rower identified as the source of the loss of rhythm may not be the decisive factor. Or he is not able to solve the problem himself, but at the same time there is no appropriate replacement available who could take his place in the boat. This may result in a tense atmosphere in the team—not only does the central dilemma remain but it could even intensify and, in the worst case, have a negative impact on the entire team. As a result, the problems described below in case 2 can arise, which could ultimately prevent the team from working as a unit.

Case 2: Frictions within the Team's Spirit

Interpersonal conflicts occur between rowers A and B, who, to make it worse, sit one behind the other in the eight. Even in the boat, in training sessions and/or in competitions, they are unwilling to contain their resentment and ignore their discrepancies. What could possible consequences be? Rower A discovers a mistake made by rower B and confronts him with his findings. Although rower B is willing to accept criticism in principle, he does not put up with anything rower A has to tell him. As a result, rower B does not regard the remark as constructive criticism, but considers it generally destructive and personally insulting. His reaction is not positive by any means. He rather waits for a suitable opportunity to open up to criticize rower A as an act of retaliation. Obviously, rower A notices that rower B does not respond to his criticism at all and rejects any critical suggestions brought forward by rower B. The situation exacerbates with rowers A and B building up more and more aggression, which may have a negative impact on the entire team. The worst-case scenario sees half of the team side with rower A, the opposite half with rower B. As a matter of fact, a personal dispute between two rowers only can result in the entire eight losing its stroke rhythm.

These examples are to illustrate that social, atmospheric frictions and the level of team spirit are closely interrelated. Ultimately, the latter factor is a necessary precondition for the crew's success.

PSYCHOLOGICAL COUNSELLING IN ROWING

After a longstanding and successful cooperation between the first-named author and the German National Junior Rowing Team of the *Deutscher Ruderverband* (German Rowing Association, Kellmann, Kallus, Günther, Lormes & Steinacker, 1997; Kellmann, Altenburg, Lormes & Steinacker, 2001), in 2003 the *Team Deutschlandachter* (Team German-Eight) from the rowing training center in Dortmund (Germany) consulted the first- and second-named authors for the first time asking for psychological advice. Apart from central measures implemented at the rowing training center and external training camps with the team (*team consulting*), the counselling also comprised personal talks with the athletes (*individual consulting*). Although the central measures were not made compulsory and athletes could take part in the program on a voluntary basis, in general, the turnout was very high. Central measures the program started off with included a general, comprehensive introduction into the field of sports psychology, a survey of the athletes' current recovery-stress state (Kellmann & Kallus, 2001) followed by individual evaluations of single athletes and several sessions on relaxation strategies. About half the team's active rowers seized the opportunity for *individual consulting*. Those athletes who accepted the offer turned up regularly and unanimously reported back in a positive way. In addition, coaches received regular feedbacks on areas in need of improvement, which were later discussed with the athletes in team meetings. This direct cooperation is called the *coach the coach*-approach.

Coach the Coach

Coaching and supporting coaches with regard to their psychological skills is the central target of this strategy. In the process, not only those issues are raised that coaches suggest themselves but also subjects are brought up in team meetings in the absence of the coach. Before those matters can be discussed with the coach, the team has to give its full approval. Traditional topics that also apply to many other sports are competition-related aspects of the training regime as well as communication. Which is the most suitable time before and after a race to hold a team meeting? What does an appropriate setting look like? How

Table 21.1   Eleven coaching rules

1. In training and race situations, rowers have to remain receptive for counselling. A sufficient level of relaxation and concentration is a must.
2. Activate as many senses as possible.
3. Do your coaching both rationally and (!) emotionally.
4. Limit the amount of information. Restrict yourself to two or three specific issues.
5. Sum up several pieces of information and repeat central aspects.
6. Choose simple diction as athletes can work more easily with clear instructions under stress.
7. Agree with athletes on a specific sign that is to indicate that your instructions have been understood.
8. Improve the level of attention by keeping eye-contact and by addressing athletes with their names.
9. Only use positive statements! Give your rowers a clear indication of what you expect them to do.
10. Give clear and specific orders and tell athletes how to carry them out. Deliver practically oriented instructions.
11. Avoid overdoing matters (otherwise your rowers become bored, thinking "Not again..." and drift off).

much information is to be provided? Does the coach address the athletes on the water and on shore in a manner specific for rowing? Does the coach give permanent advice or only specific pieces of information? Do coach and coxswain coordinate their instructions? to name just a few questions that come up. Consequently, Bußmann and Kellmann (2004) have put together a catalogue of 11 rules adapted from Linz (2004, see Table 21.1).

In particular, phrasing your statements in a positive manner that focus on the action itself (rules 8 and 9) makes the athletes become more relaxed. As coaches tend to give feedback on what has been done wrong instead of pointing out positive areas, the athletes' attention is drawn to stimuli irrelevant to the task, which, unfortunately, may result in self-fulfilling prophecies come true. The reason why this happens is that negations do not enter our subconscious. When athletes are told explicitly what they are not to do, there is a high risk that they do exactly that—namely what they are *not* supposed to do. In a race situation in particular, coaches and coaching staff tend to bombard athletes with an abundance of information, which may prevent athletes from recovering fully. That is why the amount of information given should be limited categorically to two to three specific items (rule 4), which the coach makes available in an easy-to-understand diction to make sure that all athletes can benefit from the coach's advice even under acute stress (rule 6).

Rowing is an outdoor sport subject to external conditions (rain, wind, sun) that can have considerable effects on the outcome of rowing competitions. As has been the case after many races, athletes name external factors when accounting for their respective performance. What is even more striking is the mental attitude of some athletes who are convinced that they are unable to do well under certain weather conditions. The basics of psychological intervention suggest pointing out to those athletes that they are to focus on those areas only that they can work upon themselves; in this case, their own performance and the preparation for the race, but not external factors such as the weather or the opponents. Generally speaking, a good result in a race reflects only the athlete's optimum level of performance. If the athlete succeeds in focusing on himself and his own performance instead of being distracted by external factors, he has taken the first step to realizing his true potential.

The situation is different when it comes to regatta courses renowned for their extreme weather conditions. That wind, for instance, may have an irregular impact on the outcome of races was shown at the World Junior Rowing Championships 2003 in Schinias (Greece) as well as the canoeing competitions at the previous Olympics in Sydney 2000 (Australia). In the aftermath of the World Junior Rowing Championships 2003 the international rowing federation (FISA) has worked out entirely novel terms for competitions staged at the Olympics under extreme weather conditions. The changes range from starting races in quicker succession to modifying the race schedule at short notice and even cutting race distances from 2,000m to 1,000m. The decision which scenario to play out depends on the current weather conditions and the race schedule. The changes in the regulations provide for the possibility to reassess the weather conditions at 5.45 a.m. on race day, which can result in the original schedule being rearranged. In this case, races in the respective boat types will be held with roughly a 2-hour notice prior to the start. This means a sequence of events is possible that has not occurred at any previous regatta, leaving organizers and athletes alike without any past experience. That is why preparing mentally for the Olympics also includes maintaining sufficient flexibility to mentally cope with any kind of sudden changes and to accept them in a relaxed manner. One possible scenario could see the repechages being cancelled with the rowers having to qualify for the final in the preliminary heats already held.

Therefore, in the final preparation phase (FPP) athletes are faced with situations that simulate possible competition schedules at the Olympics. Following the concept of self-efficacy (Bandura, 1977), these measures aim at enhancing the athletes' mental flexibility to make them be convinced that they are able to perform well under any possible circumstances. If certain weather conditions are given, getting up at 5.45 a.m. to receive the latest report from the course may be too late, for example. In this case, athletes had better get up as early as 4 a.m. to make sure of the necessary physical mobilization of their bodies. The current regulations especially put those lightweight rowers at a disadvantage who have to lose weight before the race, which may even become worse when the wind conditions remain adverse for several days. When it comes to playing out these competition-related scenarios, in a training camp for instance, both coach and coxswain have to be consulted to discuss details and time frame. The rowers will obviously not be involved directly in the planning process.

Team Consulting

The strategy *team consulting* has the team in the centre of attention. One important issue is actively working on the interpersonal relations within the entire group consisting of rowers, coxswain and coach.

Communication, Rules and Agreements

In a previous passage, the authors made the attempt to illustrate the structure of relations in an eight on an abstract level in a model. In numerous talks between rowers, coach and the external—and therefore neutral—sport psychologists, the above-presented conceptual diagram could now be based on hard facts gathered in a partly almost playful manner by watching the team closely in training and contest situations. Sources of conflict that had either broken out or were latently simmering could be identified and possible solutions were worked out. By simply putting these into practice in the team, a potential conflict situation involving two of the athletes could be avoided. Another key aspect: the communication between coach and team was optimized. Problems that may arise even in the best of relations between coach and athletes obviously existed in the Team German-Eight as well, but these were identified, faced and settled as far as possible. The routes to the various solutions developed together with the team were put down in writing. By doing so, the team itself has laid down strict regulations that not only every team member has to comply with but that also provides a guideline for how to deal with similar problems in future. One necessary step to be taken in the process was to increase the athletes' awareness of potential sources of conflicts, which would enable them to avert conflict situations as far as possible. Therefore, the team's energy will not be unnecessarily wasted on such matters. The motto in this context is noticing frictions and intervening in good time.

Often, conflicts arise because a team is made up of ambivalent characters. Without a set of strict rules, conflicts between, for instance, introvert and extrovert athletes are almost bound to occur. Even though a code of conduct does exist in professional sport, no guidelines have been set out for athletes on how to behave in certain areas. Especially tense situations, such as the immediate build-up before an important race, could then give rise to a tense atmosphere in the team (having an immediate impact upon the team spirit), which puts the team's unity at risk. Considering the expected weather conditions at the 2004 Olympics in particular—the renowned Meltemia winds might have made the outcome of rowing competitions totally unpredictable—it was essential that various behavioural strategies were designed to cope with different worst-case scenarios. What is more, all team members had to agree on these measures, which guaranteed a widespread acceptance and, ultimately, was a precondition for these strategies to be implemented successfully. For this purpose, the eight rowers together with the coach, the coxswain and the substitutes drew up a detailed time schedule for the last 24 hours before the targeted competition. In the process of working out the timetable, it became clear that those involved had similar ideas of what the basic structure had to look like. However, opinions differed to some extent when it came to working out the details, which then had to be discussed with the team to frame a concept that all team members were willing to support. Apart from a schedule designed for the different possible scenarios, the entire team also agreed on a general code of conduct. What can be seen here is that although the individual needs of all team members have to be considered to some extent, a successful crew has to develop a collective attitude that puts the team's success first.

Debriefing

"Debriefing" refers to the process-oriented review of competitions and tests, during which athletes and coach make their personal evaluations to analyse the performance given. This aims at providing those involved with a sense of satisfaction with both their performance and themselves and also at making the athlete enjoy his sport on a higher level (Hogg, 1998). Debriefing helps athletes to divert their attention from past events and also to build up a fundamental knowledge of understanding themselves better and of how to acquire strategies that make them enhance their level of performance. Provided that an action can be considered complete only when the action's result has been evaluated, a conclusion is reached by debriefing athletes. As a result, athletes can enter the following competition or

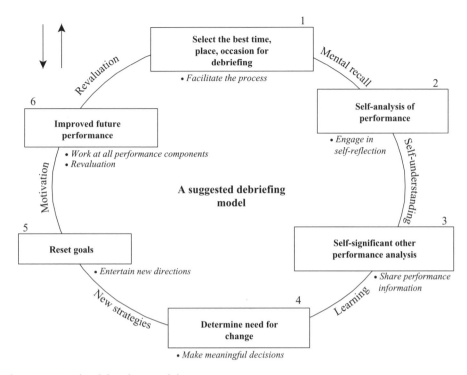

Figure 21.4 The debriefing model

test without any burdens of the past and a clear head. Debriefing and the accompanying reflection processes enable athletes to actively part with any negative thoughts. If athletes fail to come to terms with what happened in previous events, they are highly likely to drag this unfinished business with them into competitions/tests to come, which, on top of that, may also disturb the necessary recovery process (Hogg, 2002; Kellmann, 2002a). As an optimized standard procedure, debriefing supports the mental and emotional recovery in athletes and, consequently, helps them perform on a higher level.

Hogg and Kellmann (2002) describe the six stages of the systematic and interactive debriefing model (see Figure 21.4).

- *Stage 1: selecting the most suitable time, place and occasion for debriefing*
  Basically, what has to be taken into account is that the debriefing process is influenced by the preceding performance, i.e. whether it has been (very) good or poorer than expected. If the performance has been below standard, negative moods prevail and athletes are opposed to an appropriate reflection at first. If the performance has been (very) good, athletes are mostly in high spirits, which can also result in a reluctance to analyse what has happened, as a reflection is basically regarded as unnecessary. As for the descriptive feedback, Hogg and Kellmann (2002) recommend that it is to be given ideally in private, right after the action and in a constructive way to make sure of a continuous development. The *normative evaluating feedback* is to be employed in an emotionally stable setting considering the current situation. It is even more important when the subsequent level of performance may have far-reaching repercussions on the athlete (such as losing the

right to train in specific squad or with regard to the rowers and the current situation not being nominated for the boat and, as a result, not being nominated for the Olympics). It is sensible to have coach and athletes together choose the appropriate time, place and setting for a quick and immediate or, if necessary, longer feedback.

- *Stage 2: self-analysis and self-evaluation of the performance*
After having digested emotionally what has happened in a race/test, athletes should be enabled step by step to reflect on their performance in an objective and responsible manner. Apart from compiling check lists and performing video analyses, athletes can profit considerably from practising self-reflection and/or keeping a 'mental training log'. In addition, the authors suggest carrying out self-evaluation as immediately after the race/test as reasonably possible. Recognizing the necessity to make changes should be seen as an opportunity to further enhance the level of performance and not considered a sign of weakness by the athlete. Adapted from Hogg (2002), Hogg, Bußmann, Kellmann, Dobmeier and Hense (2003) have compiled a list of questions for athletes to practise self-reflection. Here, questions on the previous race/test are listed. It is up to the athletes to decide which of those questions are relevant to their personal situation. The questions refer to a retrograde (past-oriented), reflexive and anterograde (future-oriented) evaluation (Table 21.2). The

Table 21.2   Exemplary questions taken from the questionnaire concerning debriefing

Key Questions
- What has exactly happened? . . . to myself? . . . to the team?
- What effects does my performance in the competition/test/regatta bring about for myself and the team respectively?
- How did I feel during the competition/test/regatta (while doing my sport)?
- What am I going to do exactly the same way in the competition/test/regatta to come? What am I going to change in the competition/test/regatta to come?

Specific Questions
- Which targets did I set myself before the competition/test/regatta?
- What have I achieved so far with regard to the targets set? In which areas have I moved closer to reaching my targets?
- Where am I going from here? Which targets will I aim for?
- How do I rate my performance compared to my team mates and to other athletes?
- What can I change? What am I willing to change?
- Have I used all opportunities to perform to my full potential in the competition/test/regatta?
- Does the performance shown in the competition/test/regatta correspond with the level of performance developed in training? May there be any discrepancies in this area?

Important Questions with Regard to My Performance
- Did I primarily aim at avoiding defeat or did I strive for success in the first place?
- Do I apply self-protection mechanisms (e.g. the judges cannot stand me, everybody is against me, I am not able to do well at this place) as an excuse for a poor performance?
- Am I asking enough of myself or do I simply produce the movements required?
- Am I scared of or do I have bad feelings about competitions/tests/regattas to come?
- Do I really believe in myself even at a time when I am not doing well?
- Do I let other people influence my thoughts?
- Do I react effectively upon any elements of interference so that I am still able to pursue my aims independently?
- Do I rather suffer from building up my personal expectations or do I look forward to the challenge?
- Do I really use all the means available to give the optimum performance? Does my training program take the latest and most effective training methods into account?

questions aimed at going over results from a retrograde or reflexive perspective may help athletes to examine their behaviour in the past and the way athletes see themselves and others, the anterograde approach gives useful hints about possible changes that may have an impact on the level of performance and about future objectives (Kleinert & Mickler, 2003).

- *Stage 3: exchanging my views with other people's feedback on my performance*
  Coach and coaching staff are also to go through a process of self-reflection after a race/test, which is to ensure that they are in the position to give an appropriate feedback on the athletes' performance. This exchange of internal and external feedbacks seeks to create a feeling of safety, confidence and conscientiousness. What has to be borne in mind is that this exchange is not to be delayed unduly, otherwise the athlete(s) will be left alone to contemplate past events for too long. At this stage, two important questions are to be faced: (a) Have the targets been reached and, as a matter of fact, why or why not? and (b) How much effort have we put in to perform at a certain level—was the amount of effort moderate or disproportionately enormous?

- *Stage 4: determining the benefits that changes may produce*
  After going through stage 3, a sufficiently detailed picture should have emerged to help athletes detect what priorities to set in future training sessions (focusing on tactical, technical, physical, mental or emotional areas respectively). The appropriate measures should then be introduced, but also become clear and transparent for all those involved. It has often turned out to be helpful to record in writing which measures have exactly been taken. In the field of sports psychological intervention, we have always kept records for internal purposes and also to provide athletes with useful information. What has to be considered is that athletes will be reluctant to accept changes if they do not understand how those measures will be implemented or if they cannot see why certain changes have to be made in the first place. Ideally, experts from relevant sports scientific fields can be consulted (forming a multi-disciplinary team) when taking appropriate measures.

- *Stage 5: defining new challenges and targets*
  After completing the race analysis, it is essential to quickly shift back the focus to enhancing the level of performance, taking on new challenges and summoning up all the strength to face future tasks and achieve the targets set.

- *Stage 6: self-monitoring of the enhanced performance*
  Self-monitoring is a cognitive skill that helps to identify what exactly happened before, during and after the performance. Athletes have to analyse in retrospect how they prepared for a particular race and make out noticeable discrepancies between conception and reality. At first, this skill is closely linked to constantly making athletes aware of its necessity in training, but it can be developed further by using check lists and practising self-reflection. After a while and continuous practice, monitoring will be automatized.

The sport psychologist could offer debriefing sessions on a regular basis to the team as well as single rowers on request after important competitions or tests. In the process, we used the above-mentioned list of questions to train and improve the self-reflection skills in athletes. An important aspect in this context was to ensure the exchange within the team, i.e. not only among the rowers but also between rowers and coxswain. Measures that brought about changes in the field of sports psychology were talked over with both team and coach and the effects of those measures were monitored.

Individual Consulting

The individual face-to-face talks are attended by about half of the team members, some of whom even insist that sessions be held as scheduled. Compared to technique, strength or endurance training, psychological training must aim at meeting the individual needs of athletes to a greater extent. Whereas one particular exercise in weight training, for instance, fulfils the same purpose for all athletes, a specific psychological measure can cause completely different reactions in different athletes. That is why psychological counselling has to be planned carefully and worked into the individual training program. On top of that, *individual consulting* was offered to those rowers who were considered potential candidates to make it into the eight but were eventually left out. For these athletes in particular, it was essential to go over this disappointing experience, i.e. not being selected for a team that stands a decent chance of winning a medal at the Olympics. From our point of view, this is also an important part of our sports psychological work.

Mental training means optimizing specific cognitive processes by undergoing various training schemes. Cognitive processes refer to operations carried out by the brain during which items of information are dealt with that control human movement as well as help to synchronize objective physical appearance and subjective perception. As a motor-oriented training focusing on refining the motions only has the desired effects when cognitive processes are stimulated, it makes sense to further develop these processes through a mental training plan. Similar to a motor-oriented training, mental training has to be done regularly and intensively in order to enable rowers to benefit from their cognitive skills in a specific situation at any time (Eberspächer, 2001). These skills include relaxation techniques, which may also be of great help for a number of rowers.

Using Relaxation with Rowers

According to Kellmann and Beckmann (2004), relaxation techniques have five main objectives in the sporting context:

1. In the long run, athletes are to develop a higher degree of calmness with regard to stressful situations in training and competitions including a growing expectation of being able to effectively deal with tricky situations themselves.
2. With regard to the immediate preparation for a competition, athletes are to block out any distracting thoughts that could prevent them from fully focusing on the event. However, the necessary tension typical of competitive situations must not be reduced.
3. Relaxation enables athletes to forget about everything for a while or regenerate during breaks or delays without completely losing the necessary tension.
4. Relaxation speeds up the recovery process after training sessions or when athletes are injured.
5. Finally, relaxation lays the foundation for acquiring further self-regulation skills, such as imagination, which is similar to the systematic desensitization applied in behaviour therapy.

In the short-term and immediate race preparation in rowing, relaxation has two important functions, which athletes can actively control themselves. First, numerous, even experienced, athletes report that two to three nights before the competition they start to find it difficult to get to sleep and also drift in and out of sleep at night. This restricted quantity and quality of sleep can lead to direct and indirect negative effects on the level of performance because of the athletes' lack of relaxation or emerging doubts about their abilities after a restless night. In this situation, the deliberate transition into a state of relaxation can facilitate athletes to fade out any disturbing and distracting thoughts, which may help them fall asleep more quickly and benefit from a restful sleep. Using relaxation as a key to sleep is a directive and functional way for most athletes to react to unwelcome cognitions.

On race day, athletes experience different levels of activation depending on their experience and their competence in self-regulation. As mentioned above, a certain level of tension is imperative in competitive sport to exploit the full potential and perform at the highest level possible. That is why an extensive relaxation session could turn out to be counterproductive and should not be held on race day. Only if athletes have developed strategies to refocus physically and mentally on the following competition (mobilization, e.g. through rhythmic movement of body parts, cf. Eberspächer, 2001), can implement relaxation measures (e.g. progressive muscle relaxation, autogenic training) be considered reasonable even on race day. For some athletes, relaxation is both a strategy and a prerequisite to build up the concentration needed for the competition to come.

If athletes have not acquired sufficient skills to use relaxation and mobilization to their full extent, the relaxation reaction should be triggered off by constructing a mental image. In general, it is possible to promote relaxation by focusing on breathing. Basically, in the build-up to the race athletes should relax at an early stage and in intervals for a short while to prevent uncontrollable activation peaks from happening. The same principle applies to the immediate race preparation. As is the case in rowing, official rules stipulate, for instance, that up to 10 minutes before a particular race is started, boats have to be in close proximity of the starting area. Athletes use this time to go through a ritualized routine doing specific, simple exercises to direct their full concentration on the race and also prevent cognitions springing to their mind that are irrelevant to the task ahead. If they fail to eliminate these thoughts, athletes should try to create a relaxing mental image that is to set off a relaxation reaction that helps them focus on the competition.

The structure of relaxation techniques in sport corresponds with the structure of relaxation techniques in general consisting of an introductory phase (revision of ill-judged expectations and fears), the relaxation induction (diverting attention to a [passively] receptive inward direction; reduction of the sensory input) and the establishment of a relaxation state (resting in an intermediate state between being awake and falling asleep; pre-sleep state). Additionally, the completion of stage 3 is followed by an imagination phase. At this stage, the athlete is to place himself into a relaxing and positive situation and, subsequently, create a link between relaxation state and a mental image he can choose himself. What is to be achieved by going through this exercise repeatedly is to establish a strong connection between relaxation and mental image. As a result, by thinking of that particular image, the athlete relaxes (cf. Martin, Moritz & Hall, 1999; Petermann & Kusch, 2004). The relaxation process concludes with the taking-back phase. After the first few sessions, a critical evaluation is to show whether the different phases of the relaxation state have worked out, which difficulties have been encountered in the process or whether and which possible modifications are advisable. One possibility to find out when a mental image for relaxation purposes is to be triggered off is the conscious perception and the monitoring of self-talk.

Using Self-talk in Rowing

Be it in sport or in daily life, information is always processed via thoughts, which form the basis of real actions—seen from a rowing perspective, especially before and during a race. These thoughts are often expressed in self-talk, a process that people go through consciously or instinctively. Self-talk helps people to sort out their thoughts, to plan their actions using instructions and, finally, to comment on them (Eberspächer, 2001; Hatzigeorgiadis, Theodorakis & Zourbanos, 2004). Taking into account that actively managing self-talk can contribute to lifting the level of performance to new heights, it becomes clear that positive self-talk can be the decisive factor for athletes in certain situations. Basically, internal and external self-talk are distinguished. Internal self-talk remain unnoticed by the outside world; it cannot be identified from the outside. External self-talk, however, is held aloud by athletes and occurs more often when athletes are faced with an awkward situation.

The intensity of self-talk strongly depends on the level of stress felt by athletes. Whenever athletes find themselves in a tense situation, which they feel extremely uncomfortable with, their self-talk is more passionate and often external. That is why in endurance sports, such as rowing, self-talk becomes even more intense, the greater the physical stress experienced by the athlete, such as approaching the last 250 meters in the race. In these situations, the question whether to hang in or give up is answered by the brain as it is only when the self-talk switches completely that the level of performance drops. In principle, this sequence can always be observed in competitive situations. When striving for performing a certain action, positive and constructive self-talk can help athletes, provided that the strategy of self-talk is practised systematically. Most importantly, however, the action has to correspond with what the athlete can realistically achieve, as in rowing a joint and realistic target is the necessary precondition for acting appropriately with regard to situation and requirement (cf. Eberspächer, 2001).

Depending on structure and contents, two main functions of self-talk are generally distinguished. The motivational function refers to building up self-confidence and controlling the mental commitment, regulating relaxation and mobilization, and monitoring motivation and stress. In comparison, the cognitive function primarily relates to working out and optimizing general race strategies and tactics as well as preserving and refining a specific technique or movement (Immenroth, Eberspächer & Hermann, in press).

The men's eight serves as an example to illustrate how action plans as part of a race strategy can be verbally codified in self-talk in a way that makes them easily accessible to athletes whenever needed. The strategic game plan of an eight is similar in any race and, consequently, known to the opposition. At a 2000-meter race distance, the boat sets the first sprint at the 750-meter mark and the second after 1,250 meters. Even before the boats approach these marks, the opposition can adapt to this strategy and attempt to thwart the plan by taking their own tactical measures. This continuously repeated basic strategy is the master plan of the eight. If unexpected tactical measures implemented by the opposition cause problems in the boat, the rowers must be in the position to launch alternative plans, which are also verbally codified and given out by the coxswain or the stroke. In training, rowers have to be made thoroughly familiar with both master plan and alternative plans designed to react to unanticipated race situations.

In numerous athletes, self-talk pursues various strategies, which are followed systematically depending on the specific situation. In this context, psychology differentiates between four techniques: these techniques aim at self-motivation, rationalization, diverting attention and solving problems (Eberspächer, 2001). Generating and implementing self-talk requires four successive steps. In a first step, the athlete is advised to monitor his motion- and process-related self-talk. In a second step, he is then to identify those areas within his self-talk that he considers disturbing in the process of rowing and, in a third step, is asked to rephrase the contents initiating task-related and positive self-talk, which will then support him in his rowing motions. In a fourth and final step, the athlete is to habituate himself with the generated self-talk through intensive exercises in training (Immenroth et al., in press).

One part of psychological consulting is leading athletes through the four steps of generating and implementing self-talk and systematically teaching them how they are to be applied in practice. First, athletes are to become actively aware of their self-talk and figure out which type of self-talk they hold in both good and bad races as well as in various phases in training and also what effects this talk has on their performance. Building on this, in a further step, athletes have to develop the skills to verbalize positive self-talk that will support their motions. Rower C, for example, recalled in one meeting how a bad performance in the morning warming-up session on race day led to a loss of concentration and resulted in a dispute in the boat. He suggested describing aloud the sequence of a satisfactory training session. By focusing on a positive performance in training, the athlete builds up a tension and reaches the right level of activation for the race. In order to even amplify the effect and to make sure of an alternation between tension and relaxation, which is essential for the performance, rower C should draw his personal mental image that he linked with a state of relaxation in the previous relaxation exercises, which should provoke a state of feeling relaxed.

When reflecting on the race, which suddenly did not run smoothly, a number of rowers remember having held negative self-talks before the level of performance dropped. Rower C tries to describe in which situations the self-talk changes abruptly:

> When I get the feeling that the boat does not run smoothly but I feel unable to turn things round, I am getting impatient. I know then that we could do a lot better, and that irritates me. On top of that, I get annoyed by the external circumstances and I let those distract me away from the race. I get annoyed fairly quickly anyway and I start to think that now there is no way that I will reach my aim.

Rower D told us that he often started to panic when something did not go according to the plan. He said that then his thoughts circled around the mistakes he had made, which led to more mistakes. If attempts were made at correcting his mistakes, the crew lost the feel for boat and rhythm completely as then every single rower paid attention only to what he was doing.

These statements illustrate that self-talk frequently has a negative effect upon the performed action when it is not actively controlled. Particularly in sports such as rowing, in which athletes influence and depend on each other to the greatest extent, the negative self-talk of one single rower can crush the rhythm of an entire boat. That is why in this case, for instance, an intervention by applying the thought-stop strategy is the adequate measure. As soon as athletes notice that thoughts emerge which are considered disturbing or irrelevant to the task, they are to say 'Stop!' to themselves and/or draw a mental stop sign in their mind. By actively intervening, they break the negative chain of thoughts. They are to repeat the word 'Stop!' as long as the chain is completely interrupted. Afterwards, a short relaxation phase is to follow (either by breathing deeply or getting into an image-induced relaxation state) in order to redirect the full attention back to the action. Some athletes find it easier to make an intervention when, at an early stage, they can look at a physical stop sign, which can be easily produced for this purpose.

Monitoring the Individual Recovery-stress State with Rowers

Especially during the training camps in the FPP (see above), the objective is to improve endurance, specific strength and power endurance capacities, to stabilize the rowing technique to be used in the competition, to adopt and apply tactical skills as well as to improve stress and competition stability. All peripheral and central signals having an impact on the human brain are integrated in the hypothalamus. That is why an accumulation of stress originating from different areas without a sufficient recovery leads to a change in the central regulation and the psycho-physical state. If the initial situation changes, the individual abilities in terms of action and performance, the current mood and the potential to adapt to further work loads also alter (Steinacker et al., 2000a). In rowing, scientific evidence has been found that a connection between stress accumulated through training workouts and recovery exists (Kellmann, 2002a; Kellmann & Günther, 2000; Kellmann et al., 1997, 2001), which depends on the respective activity. High-intensity training has an enormous impact upon the athletes' mood, which athletes can only get through, though, when they have the necessary mental prerequisites. If they lack mental stability, high-intensity training workouts can result in an undesirable physical overload instead of an enhancement of performance. What is essential for the performance is not primarily the objectively measured work load but the subjective stress felt by the athlete. This stress state interacts with relaxation processes and, depending on the athlete, identical work loads can cause different levels. As a matter of fact, the stress state depends on stress factors that are situated outside the realms of training and competition. Private stressors, such as disputes with partners or parents as well as stress at school/college/in the job, have an impact on the stress state. That is why it is to be recorded and reported back to athletes during high-intensity training periods on a regular basis. Particularly in training phases during which the amount of training is increased, it is important to monitor the recovery-stress state in athletes in order to detect any negative training effects as early as possible and, accordingly, take countermeasures. In rowing, especially at the juniors level (age 16 to 18 years), training camp differs greatly from 'home training'; for example, the total training time is often increased by approximately 2.5 times (Kellmann & Altenburg, 2000). This training increase is taken differently by the athletes, some of them can deal with it; others cannot. The impact of the increased training load on the individual accumulates if recovery cannot take place sufficiently; for example, due to a lack of sleep (Kellmann & Kallus, 1999). If the stress felt by an athlete is too high for a long time and cannot be adequately compensated through sufficient recovery periods, it finally leads to a state of overtraining (Kellmann, 2002a, 2002b).

Measuring and monitoring the recovery-stress state on the basis of objective parameters is often difficult in practice because many physiological parameters vary when the training intensity is enhanced. In order to be able to differentiate changes that are normal reactions in training from those changes typical of an overtraining syndrome, it is vital not only to record medical but also psychological data. For years now, in psychological research the link between overtraining and mood has been assessed on the basis of a Profile of Mood States (McNair, Lorr & Droppelmann, 1971, 1992). It has turned out that emotional ups and downs are connected with changes in the training amount and that a change of mood for the better correlates directly with a reduction in the training amount. In recent years, in many cases the Recovery-stress Questionnaire for Athletes has successfully been used (RESTQ-Sport, Kellmann & Kallus, 2000, 2001). This questionnaire is designed to reveal the interaction between recovery and stress states in a more differentiated manner. The RESTQ-Sport is a procedure for collecting quantitative data of a person's current degree of stress. It comprises a structured questionnaire with scales referring to general aspects and sports-specific stress- and recovery-related issues and, thus, systematically records the recovery-stress state in an athlete (Kellmann & Kallus, 2001). In the last few years, the RESTQ-Sport has been used on a regular basis when consulting the German National Junior Rowing Team and has proven a neutral instrument that facilitates athletes to express their needs and moods. It has turned out that the RESTQ-Sport is not only sensitive for hidden problems, e.g. with regard to sleep or injuries, but that it can also reveal important aspects at a very early stage, such as a dwindling self-efficacy or the reduced application of self-regulation techniques (e.g. relaxation, self-talk).

CONCLUSION

The chapter in hand illustrates in which areas psychology can have a positive effect upon rowing in a team in general, and in the eights in particular, especially when it comes to optimizing interpersonal relations. The *Team Deutschlandachter* (Team German-Eight) has discovered that psychology can play a vital part in the build-up to the Olympics and, for this purpose, has consulted sports psychologists, who, apart from offering individual consulting in the above-mentioned areas, are primarily to help eradicate atmospheric frictions, optimize the team spirit and define ideal routines and performance principles. It remains to be seen whether the desired success can be achieved at the Olympic Games in Athens. However, one thing has become obvious: incorporating sports psychology into the process of preparing for the Olympics has, from a subjective perspective at least, already had a positive impact upon the team. In addition to optimizing the physical level of performance, the rowing technique, the team spirit and the boat material, sports psychology is an important element on the road to success.

REFERENCES

Adam, K. (1982). *Kleine Schriften zum Rudertraining*. (Schriftenreihe des Bundesausschusses Leistungssport. Trainerbibliothek, 22). Berlin: Bartels und Wernitz.

Bandura, A. (1977). Self-efficacy: toward a unifying theory of behavioral change. *Psychological Review*, 84, 191–215.

Bußmann, G. & Kellmann, M. (2004). *11 Regeln des Coachings*. Dortmund: Selbstverlag.

Eberspächer, H. (2001). *Mentales Training*. München: Compress-Verlag.

Fritsch, W. (1990). *Handbuch für das Rennrudern: Planung—Training—Leistung*. Aachen: Meyer & Meyer.

Grabow, V. (2003). Der Einfluss des Faktors Körpergewichts auf die ruderspezifische Leistungsfähigkeit. In W. Fritsch (ed.), *Rudern—erfahren, erkunden, erforschen* (pp. 197–203). Gießen: Wirth, Sport Media Verlag.

Hatzigeorgiadis, A., Theodorakis, Y. & Zourbanos, N. (2004). Self-talk in the swimming pool: the effects of self-talk on thought content and performance on water polo tasks. *Journal of Applied Sport Psychology*, 16, 138–150.

Hill, H. (1995). *Inter- und intraindividuelle Veränderungen von Koordinationsmustern im Rudern.* Regensburg: S. Roderer.

Hogg, J. & Kellmann, M. (2002). Debriefing im Leistungssport [Debriefing in elite sports]. *Psychologie und Sport, 9*, 90–96.

Hogg, J.M. (1998). The post performance debriefing process: getting your capable track and field athletes to the next level of performance. *New Studies in Athletics*, 3, 49–56.

Hogg, J.M. (2002). Debriefing: a means to increasing recovery and subsequent performance. In M. Kellmann (ed.), *Enhancing Recovery: Preventing Underperformance in Athletes* (pp. 181–198). Champaign, IL: Human Kinetics.

Hogg, J.M., Bußmann, G., Kellmann, M., Dobmeier, H. & Hense, T. (2003). *Debriefing (prozessuale Nachbereitung): Stellen Sie sich/Stelle Dir die richtigen Fragen.* Dortmund: Selbstverlag.

Immenroth, M., Eberspächer, H. & Hermann, H.-D. (in press). Training kognitiver Fertigkeiten. In J. Beckmann & M. Kellmann (eds.), *Enzyklopädie der Psychologie: Anwendungen der Sportpsychologie*. Göttingen: Hogrefe.

Kellmann, M. (ed.). (2002a). *Enhancing Recovery: Preventing Underperformance in Athletes*. Champaign, IL: Human Kinetics.

Kellmann, M. (2002b). Underrecovery and overtraining: different concepts—similar impact? In M. Kellmann (ed.), *Enhancing Recovery: Preventing Underperformance in Athletes* (pp. 3–24). Champaign, IL: Human Kinetics.

Kellmann, M. & Altenburg, D. (2000). Betreuung der Junioren-Nationalmannschaft des Deutschen Ruderverbandes [Consultation of the German Junior National Rowing Team]. In H. Allmer, W. Hartmann & D. Kayser (eds), *Sportpsychologie in Bewegung–Forschung für die Praxis* [Movement within sport psychology—applied research] (pp. 67–80). Köln: Sport & Buch Strauss.

Kellmann, M., Altenburg, D., Lormes, W. & Steinacker, J.M. (2001). Assessing stress and recovery during preparation for the World Championships in rowing. *The Sport Psychologist, 15*, 151–167.

Kellmann, M. & Beckmann, J. (2004). Sport und Entspannungsverfahren [Sport and relaxation]. In D. Vaitel & F. Petermann (eds), *Handbuch der Entspannungsverfahren* (pp. 320–331). Weinheim: Beltz.

Kellmann, M. & Günther, K.-D. (2000). Changes in stress and recovery in elite rowers during preparation for the Olympic Games. *Medicine and Science in Sports and Exercise, 32*, 676–683.

Kellmann, M. & Kallus, K.W. (1999). Mood, recovery-stress state, and regeneration. In M. Lehmann, C. Foster, U. Gastmann, H. Keizer & J.M. Steinacker (eds), *Overload, Fatigue, Performance Incompetence, and Regeneration in Sport* (pp. 101–118). New York: Plenum.

Kellmann, M. & Kallus, K.W. (2000). *Der Erholungs-Belastungs-Fragebogen für Sportler; Manual.* [The Recovery-stress Questionnaire for Athletes; Manual]. Frankfurt: Swets Test Services.

Kellmann, M. & Kallus, K.W. (2001). *The Recovery-stress Questionnaire for Athletes; Manual.* Champaign, IL: Human Kinetics.

Kellmann, M., Kallus, K.W., Günther, K.-D., Lormes, W. & Steinacker, J.M. (1997). Psychologische Betreuung der Junioren-Nationalmannschaft des Deutschen Ruderverbandes [Psychological consultation of the German Junior National Rowing Team]. *Psychologie und Sport*, 4, 123–134.

Kleinert, J. & W. Mickler (2003). Erfolgsdruck. In J. Kleinert (ed.), *Erfolgreich aus der sportlichen Krise. Mentales Bewältigen von Formtiefs, Erfolgsdruck, Teamkonflikten und Verletzungen* (pp. 93–124). München: BLV.

Linz, L. (2004). *Erfolgreiches Teamcoaching.* Aachen: Meyer & Meyer.

Martin, K.A., Moritz, S.E. & Hall, C.R. (1999). Imagery use in sport: a literature review and applied model. *The Sport Psychologist, 13*, 245–268.

McNair, D., Lorr, M. & Droppelmann, L.F. (1971, 1992). *Profile of Mood States Manual.* San Diego: Educational and Industrial Testing Service.

Petermann, F. & Kusch, M. (2004). Imagination. In D. Vaitel & F. Petermann (eds), *Handbuch der Entspannungsverfahren* (pp. 159–176). Weinheim: Beltz.

Reiß, M. & Pfeiffer, U. (1991). *Leistungsreserven im Ausdauertraining: Erfolgreiche Trainingsstrategien mit Beispiellösungen im Sportschwimmen, Rudern, Radsport, leichtathlet. Lauf/Gehen und Eisschnelllauf.* Berlin: Sportverlag.

Schulte, S. (2004). Psychologie im Ruderachter [Psychology in the rowing eight]. *Leistungssport, 34* (4), 67–70.

Seiler, R. (1992). Performance enhancement—a psychological approach. *Sport Science Review, 1*(2), 29–45.

Seiler, R. & Stock, A. (1994). *Handbuch Psychotraining im Sport: Verfahren im Überblick.* Reinbek: Rowohlt.

Steinacker, J.M., Lormes, W., Kellmann, M., Liu, Y., Reißnecker, S., Opitz-Gress, A., Baller, B., Günther, K., Petersen, K.G., Kallus, K.W., Lehmann, M. & Altenburg, D. (2000a). Training of junior rowers before World Championships. Effects on performance, mood state and selected hormonal and metabolic responses. *Journal of Sports Medicine and Physical Fitness, 40*, 327–335.

Steinacker, J.M., Lormes, W., Liu, Y., Lehmann, M., Kellmann, M. & Altenburg, D. (2000b). Die unmittelbare Wettkampfvorbereitung (UWV) im Rudern am Beispiel der Junioren-Nationalmannschaft des Deutschen Ruderverbandes: Leistungsphysiologische, psychologische und sportmedizinische Aspekte [The training camp in rowing described at the example of the German Junior National Rowing Team—performance, physiological, psychological, and sportmedical aspects. *Leistungssport, 30*(4), 29–34.

CHAPTER 22

High Performance Thinking for Professional Surfers

Michael Martin

Australian Institute of Sport, Australia

INTRODUCTION

Surfing is cool! Let us face it, when most people see surfing they cannot help but feel a sense of freedom. Surf clothing manufacturers have tapped into this feeling and have created a US$4.1 billion per annum industry in North America alone (Surfing Industry Manufacturing Association, 2004).

The International Surfing Association says there are as many as 18 million surfers world-wide including men, women and children of all ages. There are surfers in over 100 countries on all 5 continents (International Surfing Association, 2004). Surfing takes many forms including short board riding, long board surfing, body boarding, knee boarding, skim boarding, and bodysurfing.

As with any recreational activity, when you get enough people participating, it does not take too long before a competition takes place. Surfing is no different. However, surfing competitions are ancient and have their roots back in Polynesian history and, even then, the competition surfers were under enormous pressure.

THE ANCIENT SURFING COMPETITION ARENA

Pressure in competition surfing is thousands of years old. In early Hawaii, gambling on contest winners was integral to the surfing culture of the time. The Hawaiians staked canoes, nets, fishing lines, *kapas* (cloth), swine, poultry and all other property and, in some instances, life itself was put as a wager (Gault-Williams, 2004).

Competing surfers would paddle out to a predetermined position to wait for a wave. As soon as a large wave rose up behind them they would paddle, catch it together and ride until they reached a *pua* (buoy) anchored inshore. The first man to the buoy won the heat and probably several such rides determined the winner of the contest. The winners carried off their riches, and the losers and their families passed into a life of poverty or servitude (Gault-Williams, 2004; Young & McGregor, 1983).

The Sport Psychologist's Handbook: A Guide for Sport-Specific Performance Enhancement.
Edited by Joaquín Dosil. © 2006 John Wiley & Sons, Ltd.

THE MODERN SURFING COMPETITION ARENA

The pressure on the ancient surfers was enormous and things are not that different for competitive professional surfers of today. Personal pride is still on the line along with prize money and million-dollar sponsorship endorsements available to those who best cope and perform under the pressure of competition.

Today, there are a number of professional tours for body boarders and long boarders. However, this chapter will focus on the World Championship Tour (WCT), which is the elite level of professional short board surfing. It is the men's and woman's WCTs that every year decide both the Men's and Women's Association of Surfing Professionals (ASP) World Champions.

Events take place in Australia, Fiji, Tahiti, Japan, South Africa, USA, France, Spain, England, Portugal, Brazil and Hawaii and have minimum prize money of US$260,000 for men and US$62,500 for women. The top 45 men and top 17 women from the previous year's rankings make up the pro circuit touring entourage. At each competition, there are event wild cards, which bring the fields up to 48 for the men and 18 for the women.

Typically in both the men's and women's event the first round comprises heats of three competitors, with first place (and second in the women's) advancing to Round 3. Second and third are re-seeded into Round 2, which then goes to the one-on-one format. Surfers continue in this one-on-one format through the rest of the quarters, semis and finals.

Six judges score each wave that the surfers ride during the heats (normally 20 minutes) and allocate points according to the ASP judging criterion which states:

> The surfer must perform committed radical manoeuvres in the most critical sections of a wave with style, power and speed to maximize scoring potential. Innovative progressive surfing will be taken into account when awarding points for committed surfing. The surfer who executes these criteria with the highest degrees of difficulty and control on the better waves shall be rewarded with the highest scores. (Association of Surfing Professionals, 2004).

Regardless of how many waves surfers ride during their heat, only their two highest-scoring rides count in the final wave tally that decides the eventual heat winner. It is no use if a surfer has ridden the highest-scoring wave in the heat unless they have a second scoring wave to back up the first. In fact, many surfers have won heats with two mediocre waves, despite the fact that neither of their two highest-scoring rides topped the heat. The bottom line for competitive surfers is that they have 20 minutes to surf the two highest-scoring waves of their heat. This is one of the sources of pressure for the competitive professional surfer.

As with the elite tour in any professional sport, there is relatively little difference in the skill level of the top competitors. On any given wave, while free surfing outside the competition arena, all these WCT surfers can perform all the manoeuvres with high degrees of style, power and speed. However, this can quickly change when these surfers are in a competition situation, where there are equally talented and focused competitors jockeying for their waves. Add to this the time limits, minimum wave counts and an often inconsistent and unpredictable ocean and this is where the psychology of surfing becomes a critical factor in competition success.

SPORT PSYCHOLOGIST OR SURF PSYCHOLOGIST?

A sport psychologist working with elite surfers can certainly provide a range of performance enhancement and support services without needing to have any specialist surfing knowledge. However, if the sport psychologist wishes to become a surf psychologist, then they need to have a good understanding of the physical, technical and tactical aspects of competition surfing.

Surfing's technical intricacies are actually the building blocks for the mental side of a surfer's performance. Therefore, the surf psychologist needs to make sure that they can address the surfer's understanding of these technical cornerstones. If the surfing client has a strong technical understanding of what they need to focus on while riding the wave, then it is relatively easy to add core mental skills and performance strategies. However, if the surfer is unclear about their technical wave-riding focus, then trying to add mental skills and strategies will prove fruitless.

Consequently, it is essential that the surf psychologist and the surfing clients have good working relationships with knowledgeable surf coaches who can assist with the discovery and refinement of the key technical thoughts that the surfer uses when riding waves. This process of discovery is both psychological and technical, and this chapter covers the process at length. In a best-case scenario, the coach, with some input and guidance by the surf psychologist, will undertake much of what the technical thinking sections in this chapter describe.

Technical information is at the heart of what a surf psychologist needs to understand if they are to work effectively with surfers and their coaches in developing the intricacies of quality technical thinking. The chapter also covers a range of additional mental skills strategies that the surfer can use before, during and after competition to maximize their performance.

THE CONTENT OF COMPETITION THINKING

For the surf psychologist it is critical to understand that there are four key thought strategies used by the surfer prior to and during competition to maintain focus and maximize their scoring potential. The four thought strategies are (1) technical thinking, (2) tactical thinking, (3) positive self-talk, and (4) mental rehearsal.

Technical thoughts are cues that focus the surfer's attention to a particular aspect of their surfing technique. Surfers need to think technical or "tech" thoughts when riding waves so that they can perform committed radical manoeuvres in the most critical sections.

Tactical thoughts refer to a structured internal dialogue that guides the surfer to get into the position to catch the best waves available in the time remaining for the heat. Tactical thoughts are used during the paddle back out to the take-off area and while waiting in the take-off area for waves to come through.

The surfer also uses positive self-talk during the paddle out and waiting periods. Positive self-talk allows the surfer to maintain or build confidence during the heat. A superior level of self-belief is necessary to execute the high-risk innovative surfing that scores highly with the judges.

Finally, the competitive surfer can also use mental rehearsal during the heat to review waves that have already been ridden. This mental rehearsal review occurs during the paddle out or in the take-off zone during the waiting periods and promotes technique reinforcement as well as building self-belief. Mental rehearsal is also used by the surfer to "preview" what they are about to do on the next wave.

Much of the content of these four thought strategies is prepared and rehearsed while training before the competition. The surfer can gather additional strategic information throughout the competition period, particularly during the observation of the surfing in the competition area in the prior heats.

Rather than explain each of these thought strategies in isolation, this chapter puts them into a performance context, so the surf psychologist can see how they can work with surfers and coaches. The chapter starts with one of the key aspects of the surfer's pre-competition preparation—developing technical thinking. Next, the pre-heat planning process is considered. Here, technical thinking interplays with tactical strategizing, positive self-talk and mental rehearsal. Then the chapter goes into the physical and psychological strategies of the competition build-up. Finally, it moves to the actual competition performance where all the skills and strategies interplay. All the essentials are here for the surf psychologist to assist the coach and surfer with preparation and performance.

PRE-COMPETITION PREPARATION

Segmenting Manoeuvres to Provide a Focal Point

For most elite surfers, identifying that they are in a critical part of the wave and responding with the "right" manoeuvre for the conditions is an intuitive, implicit act. The challenge comes in the effective execution of that "right" manoeuvre. Many surfers falter at this stage by producing a technically and mechanically poor version of the manoeuvre that they intended to perform (Etnier & Sibley, 2002). There is a breakdown between what the surfer intended to do and what actually happens.

Unlike sports with a long tradition of performance problem-solving through coaching, many surfers are unaware that they can make changes to their thinking, which in turn lead to changes in their physical performance. For that reason, the first step in effectively structuring the surfer's competition thinking is to get the surfer to start to think of their major point-scoring manoeuvres as having a number of phases. For example, instead of thinking of a backhand cutback as just one action, it is better for the surfer to think of this manoeuvre as having three distinct phases.

When performing backhand cutbacks, the surfer should perform a quality top turn to generate speed and direction. This is the entry phase. Impacting with the white water and turning back around on the wave face follows next. This is the action phase. Finally, the surfer has to re-centre over the surfboard to complete the successful manoeuvre. This is the recovery phase (Dunn, 2004).

When the surfer starts to segment their thinking about their manoeuvres down into smaller chunks then this allows them to narrow their focus of attention to effectively executing the most critical phase of the manoeuvre. This basic selective attentional strategy supports the surfer to focus on a few specific cues, which assist performance (Ming, 1993; Sherwood & Rios, 2001). The narrow focus of attention also works to screen out a mass of irrelevant internal and external information that detracts from the performance.

Figure 22.1 Backhand cutback—showing the three main phases: the entry, action, and recovery phase
Reproduced by permission of Surfcoach.com

Potential Sources of Poor Performance

Narrowing attention down into smaller chunks is a critical skill that the surfer must develop; however, it is critical that the surf psychologist understand some of the reasons or potential sources for a surfer's poor attentional control. For most surfers the breakdown between intention and action is attributable to three potential origins:

1. the surfer simply does not have any structured thinking around their manoeuvre completion,
2. the surfer has problems with preceding or linking manoeuvres as well as no structured thinking, or
3. the surfer is distracted by the pressure of competition, is "rushing" and has no structured thinking to use to regain control.

1. No Structured Technical Thinking for Manoeuvre Completion

Biomechanical analysis of the surfing of the top professionals clearly indicates that they approach and execute each manoeuvre in a similar way. There are common body movement patterns, or biomechanical techniques, which surfers can copy so that they can successfully complete their manoeuvres. Even the advanced moves like aerials (where the surfer's board leaves the wave face) and reverses (where the surfer lands an aerial tail first) all have a common recognizable biomechanical thread, which surfers can study and incorporate into their surfing performances (Dunn, 2004).

When the surfer routinely works with a coach who uses video analysis for breaking problematic surfing moves into their segmented phases, then the surfer can diagnose where the manoeuvres fail. This makes it easier to identify the specific technical cue to use to fix the problem permanently. These technical cues provide relevant focal points for the surfer to attend to during critical manoeuvres in competition.

For example, a surfer may identify that they have been unable to perform aerials effectively. The forehand aerial is one of the ultimate attacking manoeuvres of the competitive surfer. This is where the surfer launches off the wave's surface into the air before landing back on the wave to complete the manoeuvre successfully. Aerials are the type of innovative committed surfing that judges like to see, and are scored highly.

After watching video with their coach, the surfer identifies that, during aerial attempts, they typically launch into the air and lose contact with the surfboard. In addition, the surfer is unable to re-centre over the surfboard on landing. The coach is able to point out to the surfer that the major key to success when attempting aerials is in the entry phase. The surfer needs to have good speed before launching off the wave. This allows the surfer to stay connected (action phase) and centred over the board (recovery phase).

The coach should also point out that it is essential for the surfer to "pump" both arms in the entry phase to create the speed needed for the aerial. The throwing or "pumping" of the arms unweights the surfboard, allowing it to accelerate faster than if the arms were not used. The surfer now needs effortful, directed thinking about "pumping the arms" if they are to refine their skills in this particular manoeuvre phase.

This explicit, effortful, surfer-directed thinking is at the heart of what the coach and surfer are trying to achieve so they can take surfing to the next level. Ultimately, with regular practice of this effortful focusing on task-relevant cues, the surfer can change their thinking from a burdensome, conscious, extrinsic process to an effortless, intrinsic process (Boutcher, 2002; Magill, 1997).

2. Problems with Linking Manoeuvres and Unstructured Technical Thinking

If an elite level surfer has difficulty with a particular manoeuvre, usually it is only one phase of the manoeuvre that is completed poorly. However, the educated and experienced coach will not simply focus their "fix", and consequently the surfer's attentional focus, on just the faulty phase. Naturally, the surfer's manoeuvre phases link together and interact with each other. Often by backward tracking through this linking (following the surfer's manoeuvres in reverse on video), the coach can highlight where the real problem lies.

A surfer who is not performing a quality bottom turn, because they are not compressing low enough (entry phase), may end up running out of speed just ahead of the top of the wave, catching a rail (side edge of the surfboard) before the re-entry (action phase) thus causing the surfer to fall. This makes the vertical moves (action phase) inconsistent, yet attempts to fix this problem alone will prove fruitless. However, when the bottom turns (entry phase), which are the preceding link to the vertical moves are fixed, by the surfer using some clear self-instructional cues, then the vertical moves improve dramatically.

3. Problems with "Rushing" and Unstructured Technical Thinking

If a surfer has no structured technical thinking, they will not only have weak technical performance and deficient linking, but also usually end up "rushing" one or more manoeuvre phases. Even if a surfer is technically sound, without any structured technical thinking, under the pressure of competition, the surfer will miss performing fully completed manoeuvres and may even wipe out because they are "rushing".

"Rushing" is particularly precarious when the surfer attempts high-risk manoeuvres, such as floating a pitching section (surfing along the top of a breaking wave), where the recovery phase is critical. If the surfer "rushes" and does not get into a compressed, centred body position at the end of this manoeuvre, they will slide out of control or grab a rail on landing. The surfer needs structured thoughts that focus on making a low and centred recovery before looking at what future opportunities the wave might offer.

Typically, "rushing" surfers are considering possible future moves, heat outcomes and the consequences of winning and losing. They do not focus on finishing the moves they are attempting. The irrelevant cues attract the surfer's attention and the quality of the technical performance suffers. The "rushing" surfer cannot selectively attend to task-relevant biomechanical cues because task-irrelevant information has taken over (Boutcher, 2002).

The Range of Biomechanical Cues

In the earlier example, "pump the arms" is a clear, unambiguous focal point for the surfer to concentrate on while executing the entry phase of the aerial manoeuvre. However, the biomechanical focal points for some manoeuvre phases are not so clear or unambiguous to the surfer. This is where the surfer, coach and surf psychologist can work together to optimize the surfer's selective attention through experiential learning.

Take, for example, the forehand bottom turn, which is the most important manoeuvre in a surfer's forehand repertoire. Quality bottom turns set up fast, vertical explosive manoeuvres off the top of the wave that score highly. Poor bottom turns mean that the surfer runs out of speed halfway through the manoeuvre, or if they do manage to hit the lip they will nosedive on their way back down the wave face.

The coach and surfer may identify that the poor forehand bottom turn is due to the surfer not "leaning in" enough at the bottom of the wave. Leaning is where the surfer must essentially squat down and lean in towards the wave face during the bottom turn to be able to maximize their use of the accumulated kinetic forces as they start to head vertically up the wave face.

While "pump the arms" provides an unambiguous focusing cue for the surfer working on building up speed for an aerial, "lean in" during a bottom turn is not a specific cue, because it can be achieved by the surfer attending to a range of possible focal cues. A surfer can "lean in" effectively by getting their chest close to the wave face, by trailing their backhand in the water or by getting their stomach down onto the thighs. These are all legitimate biomechanical cues, but on which cue should the surfer focus?

The large majority of surfing manoeuvres have multi-cue technical solutions, just like the bottom turn example given above. The forehand cutback is another case in point. When a wave fattens out, the forehand cutback allows a surfer to link between the outside shoulder and the inside section of the wave. The performance of the classic cutback brings the surfer back to the wave's power source, allowing time for the next section of the wave to build up. This then allows the surfer to perform a more critical manoeuvre in the following section.

Looking back up to the wave's pocket (the breaking section of the wave), rotating the upper body and touching the outside hand onto the wave face are all legitimate cues to prompt the biomechanical movements of the action phase of the forehand cutback. Common sense and a simple information-processing perspective clearly indicate that the surfer would have difficulty focusing on all these cues simultaneously. The surfer's attentional capacity is limited, so determining what cue the surfer should focus on is the challenge.

Even though every phase of each surfing manoeuvre has its own biomechanical theme, identifying the faulty phase and recognizing the appropriate range of technical solutions is only the first component in refining the surfer's wave-riding thought content. At this stage of the process the surfer is aware of the range of solutions that may be focused on to create the required technical change, but the real challenge still lies in determining how these cues should be thought about to optimize attentional capacity and maximize performance.

There is no sophisticated way to determine which of the range of technical thoughts is most appropriate for the surfer to focus on in each problematic phase. The best results come through a structured trial-and-error approach, which the surfer needs to set up with the assistance of the coach and the surf psychologist.

Determining Which Cues to Use

Once the surfer has worked with the coach to identify a faulty phase in one of their problematic major manoeuvres, and the coach has then presented to the surfer the technical cue solution range for this problematic phase, the surfer can start to experiment with that range of cues to determine the most relevant cues to focus on. For example, in the situation where the surfer and coach have identified a problem with the action phase of the forehand cutback, then the surfer now needs to start experimenting with the technical cue range for this phase. As indicated earlier, there are three different technical focusing cues in the range—looking back up into the pocket (the breaking section of the wave), rotating the upper body and touching the outside hand onto the wave face. A focus on any of these cues will produce the torqueing rotation necessary to get the surfer whipping their body and board around the 180-plus degrees to set up a high hit on the white-water, which initiates the recovery phase.

Initially the surfer may use a Carveboard (specialized skateboard that rides like a surfboard; http://www.carveboard.com/) to experiment with the cue range on dry land. This assists with experience on how to use the cues. It can also narrow the cue range, with cues that "don't feel right" immediately rejected. Then, assuming that surf conditions allow, a structured trial-and-error process with the remaining cues can take place. It may run along these lines.

At first, the surfer would catch a wave where, during the action phase of the cutback, the surfer would focus only on the first cue, "look back" up into the wave's pocket. The surfer may execute three or four cutbacks on that one wave using only this attentional cue. The surfer may then catch three to four more waves, again, using only this cue during the cutback's action phase. This forces the surfer's attentional capacity to be limited to one attentional cue, ensuring that the self-cueing capacity is not exceeded. The surfer is not trying to focus on using all three technical cues simultaneously. Typically, attempting to focus on multiple tasks will overload the surfer's attentional capacity and degrade rather than improve performance (Hardy, Jones & Gould, 1996).

Next, the surfer can then switch the focus of attention onto the second technical cue. On the subsequent waves, the action phase focus for the cutback is "rotate" the body. Again, the surfer should ride several waves, executing a number of cutbacks using this focus. Finally, the surfer should repeat the process but this time focusing on the third cue, using the outside hand to "touch" the wave face.

The surfer should undergo this process with all their faulty phases over several days, weeks or months in a range of surf conditions, systematically working through the cue range for each manoeuvre phase until the surfer is confident that they have identified what cues do and do not "feel" right. Coach and video feedback can provide additional input to the surfers' subjective feelings about what works. The surfer should document in a training diary their responses to the range of technical cues for each of their problematic phases. This process will assist the surfer to identify confidently the appropriate focusing cues for training and competing in any conditions (Zimmerman & Kitsantas, 1996).

Because the acquisition of skill knowledge requires many practice trials (Magill, 1997) the surfer can supplement this achievement process with dry land trials. Surfing simulations using the Carveboard provide an opportunity for the surfer to increase the number of learning trials undertaken for each appropriate cue.

Determining How to Use Each Cue

Finding the right technical cue is essential if the surfer wishes to generate a clear and unambiguous instructional self-coaching command to assist in the performance of their most challenging major manoeuvres. However, in addition to identifying the correct cue from the technical range for that manoeuvre phase, the specifics of "how" the surfer self-instructs to achieve the correct technical outcome is another critical aspect of the surfer's thinking.

Assume the coach and surfer identified a problem in the action phase of a forehand cutback. Through a trial-and-error process, the surfer has nominated "rotating the upper body" as the most beneficial of the three possible technical cues to develop a fast, powerful forehand gouge. The next challenge is for the coach to assist the surfer actually to think about the "rotate" cue to maximize performance.

The surfer could use either a visual, kinaesthetic or an auditory cue to self-instruct. This is the next component of developing clear, unambiguous self-instructional cueing that needs to be refined through a structured trial-and-error process. The challenge is not only to find the right cue, but also to find the best way for the surfer to self-cue or self-instruct.

The surfer may use an internal, auditory, self-instructional cue like "jam" or "now" or even "oomph" to initiate the upper body rotation. Alternatively, the surfer may focus on creating a kinaesthetic feel through the movement of the arms or shoulders. The surfer may even focus on generating a visual cue such as seeing the hand of the inside arm moving into the peripheral vision at chest height. Any of these styles of cueing may become the attentional cue for initiating the rotation during the cutback.

After working with the coach, using video analysis, and taking a structured trial-and-error approach to self-instruction discovery, the competitive surfer should be able to articulate quickly and clearly a number of concentration cues for the major manoeuvres in both their forehand and backhand surfing (Theodorakis, Chroni, Laparidis, Bebetos & Douma, 2001).

The process that the surfer has gone through with the coach and surf psychologist to get to this point includes being able to identify:

1. the most problematic manoeuvres
2. the most problematic phase of each of those manoeuvres
3. the correct range of technical solutions for that phase
4. the preferred technical solution and
5. the preferred self-cueing strategy for the chosen technical solution.

How Much Cueing Should the Surfer Use?

While it is important that the competitive surfer have a clear "road map" of thoughts for major manoeuvres while surfing, it is also important for those assisting the surfer with the development of the competition thinking content to understand the need to establish a balance between too much and too little technical thought content. Theoretically, there are multiple concentration cues for every phase of every manoeuvre; however, it would be impossible for the surfer to ride a wave and to concentrate on a cue for every phase of every manoeuvre for every wave ridden. This would simply overload the attentional capacity of the surfer and disregard their already developed automatic processing skills.

Skilled surfers have the ability to execute a large range of manoeuvres without having actually to focus their attention on performing these moves (Magill, 1997). For many surfers this instinctual, automatic functioning is generated through years of trial-and-error experience. They can surf automatically. However, too few attentional cues can "leave the door open" for outcome thoughts to enter into the surfers' minds. Likewise, too many attentional focusing cues lead to over-thinking or "analysis paralysis".

The challenge is not to overload the surfer with these manoeuvre-relevant cues to the point that there are far too many cues to focus on in the short amount of time that it takes to ride a wave. The surfer cannot be charging down the line trying to analyse the wave terrain and then matching that analysis to a large collection of cues. It is far better for the surfer to work to identify a few key "cutting-edge" major manoeuvre cues that can then be clearly focused on in order for the brain to send an unambiguous message to the body to perform.

Surfers need to feel confident that they are able to execute fully the manoeuvre opportunities that each wave presents during the heat. Therefore, they need to have in their mind a limited menu of concentration cues to draw on as soon as they see the prospect of a manoeuvre occurring. With just a matter of seconds between manoeuvres, surfers need to read the wave situation and then quickly respond with a technical solution that will generate the required move.

If the surfer does some pre-heat manoeuvre planning, then typically there will be little doubt in the surfer's mind about what manoeuvre to do and where it is likely to occur during the wave. This will assist the surfer to make sure that they are able to find the right balance between too few and too many concentration cues while surfing.

While each move has an entry, action and recovery phase, the speed at which the surfing move takes place means that it is virtually impossible to concentrate on all but one "tech" cue per move and typically only a few cues per wave. Whether that cue is in the entry, action or recovery phase of the major manoeuvres is irrelevant from a thought-content perspective. What is relevant is that the surfer has a pre-planned, well-rehearsed cue for each of the major manoeuvres that the waves of the heat will present. Essentially the surfer is pre-planning a number of key thoughts to focus on at critical times throughout their performance.

The Use of Technique Thoughts Under Pressure

When surfers can clearly identify what they need to concentrate on when riding waves during a heat, they can maximize their technical performance. However, too often a competitive surfer's mind is distracted away from the process of high-performance surfing at critical moments because they are concerned about and focused on a range of possible outcomes of the heat. "Will this wave be enough to get me through the heat?" "Don't blow this one, don't fall off here", "I hope I can nail this ride, I really need it" are some typical thoughts that can go through the mind of the competitive surfer while riding a wave.

While many of these thoughts may be legitimate as far as the outcome of the heat is concerned, these thoughts are irrelevant to the process of performance surfing. These thoughts are actually "off task" and interfere with the perception–action coupling necessary to read and respond to the wave. Social psychologists would say that this supports their distraction theory. That is, focusing attention on irrelevant cues equates to a loss of attention on what matters, and consequently it disrupts performance. This means that if surfers enter a critical manoeuvre phase and their thoughts are not focused on the appropriate task- relevant cue, because they are thinking about a future outcome, then they are less likely to succeed. They decrease their chances of successfully making this critical manoeuvre because they are not focused on the task (Boutcher, 2002; Magill, 1997).

That is why it is so important that surfers identify the key focusing cues for their major manoeuvres. These cues provide a mental "road map" while surfing. They provide an alternative set of thoughts that are performance-focused, not outcome-focused. Providing these cues have been learned and rehearsed, they will provide a positive and productive focal point.

The surfer's thoughts are pre-planned and not left to chance, decreasing the likelihood that outcome thoughts will surface. The competitive surfer can "hold out" the unproductive, non-performance-focused outcome thoughts by providing a set of alternative process-oriented, performance-focused thoughts by using technical cueing.

However, even the best-prepared surfer will find that outcome thoughts appear in the midst of some quality process thinking. It appears the surfer, coach, or surf psychologist can do little to stop this happening. For the professional surfer the outcome of the heat may contain a lot of meaning. Personal pride and big dollars in prize money and sponsorship become potent and attractive outcomes. However, although the surfer may become outcome-distracted while surfing, it is much easier for the process surfer, with a clear performance "road map", to quickly get back on track, even during a wave. A well-drilled set of performance-focused thoughts is critical for those times when outcome thoughts jump into the surfer's head while surfing.

The use of mental rehearsal or "virtual surfing" is a powerful tool to assist surfers in training their technical thinking and holding out distracting outcome thoughts. This is discussed later in the chapter.

An additional and equally powerful benefit for surfers having clear, proven and controllable technical goals is that it engenders confidence. Perception of control is one of the primary keys in enhancing self-belief. Surfers with clear "tech" cues know exactly what to do to get results in critical situations. They know what cues to focus on and they know that by focusing on those cues they will succeed on a regular basis. Their training and past competitive experience with the use of "tech" cues give them legitimate reasons to feel in control and confident while surfing.

Part of the reason that clearly identified technical goals positively impact self-belief is that surfers now have a tool that will not only assist in getting results, but it will also assist them in staying focused under pressure. After going through the process of experimenting with a range of cues and cueing strategies, determining appropriate cues and then practising those cues during free surfing, then competitive surfers can quickly identify if their thoughts during the competition heat are or are not performance-focused. The "tech road map" allows the surfer to get back on track quickly and confidently.

Technical cueing impacts attentional focus and confidence. The major role for the coach and surf psychologist is to assist in the cue-refinement process. This ensures surfers ride waves to their utmost capacity. This maximizes scoring and the potential for a winning performance. Having optimized the thought content for wave-riding, the next step is to fine-tune the thought strategies that lead to catching the best waves in the heat.

PRE-HEAT PLANNING

Obviously, the identification of "tech" cues and refining their use takes place long before the surfer arrives at the competition arena. The expectation is that the surfer will arrive at the competition with a refined "tool kit" of technical self-coaching cues that can be accessed heat by heat depending on the wave size and type. Matching technical cues to the conditions by pre-planning what types of manoeuvres will be done on various parts of the wave is the next psychological challenge the competitive surfer must face.

The underwater terrain and swell conditions at the contest location will, to a large degree, determine the type of technical cues used by the surfer. For example, the typically small and weak, sand-bottom beach waves of Japan's contest circuit require completely different mechanics and "tech" cueing to the big, powerful reef waves of Hawaii and Tahiti. Similarly, the type of manoeuvres required to score highly in the long walling point breaks of South Africa's Jeffery's Bay or Australia's Snapper Rocks are different from the manoeuvres required to succeed in the shorter, flatter waves of California's Huntington Beach. Therefore, the surfer must be able to identify the type of wave condition and match the manoeuvre type accordingly.

Even at the contest venue, changing swell, wind and tide conditions mean that a variety of wave types will occur during the contest; in turn surfers may need to change their thought content for each heat. Most importantly, surfers must be looking at the specific type of wave they will be riding in the heat and pre-planning the types of manoeuvres they will be performing.

The wind, tide and swell conditions can influence the nature of waves, even on an hourly basis, so an observation of wave conditions from the beach is an essential part of a competition strategy. Planning for wave types, probable manoeuvres, and the "tech" thoughts that will be required while surfing the heat helps a competitor feel confident about the challenge ahead.

BEACH OBSERVATIONS

One of the primary keys that determines winners and losers in each heat is the ability of surfers to select waves that will allow them to execute their most radical high-scoring manoeuvres. Therefore, surfers must spend time before each heat observing the ocean conditions. Structured beach observation not only allows surfers to plan manoeuvres and "tech" thoughts that match the wave conditions, but it also fosters the development of a tactical plan that incorporates potential winning wave (primary) and back-up wave (secondary) locations. These observations are the basis for a heat strategy. A structured approach to the assessment of the waves in the competition arena, along with manoeuvre planning, is critical for the psychological preparation of surfers (Hanton & Jones 1999).

A surfer should identify wave locations through a systematic beach observation process. The surfer could illustrate clearly observable landmarks on a hand-drawn beach map. Trees, access tracks, signs, rock formations, as well as wind and tidal conditions, should be noted.

The tide constantly changes and affects wave features; therefore surfers need to ensure that their beach observation, to determine winning wave locations, is undertaken as close as possible to their upcoming heat. After watching the performances of the surfers in the two heats before their own heat, the surfer can then mark on the beach map where the winning waves break in relation to the identified landmarks.

After indicating on the beach observation map where winning waves are breaking, the surfer then needs to indicate the path of the wave by drawing a line from the starting point of the wave towards the beach. At the end of the line, the surfer should record a number to indicate how many major manoeuvres should be performed on that particular wave. For example, a three at the end of the line would indicate a three-manoeuvre wave.

The surfer must then go back and plan what major manoeuvres need to be undertaken according to the observations. For example, the wave may require a forehand re-entry, followed by a cutback, with a floater to finish off the ride. Depending on the demands of the major manoeuvres, the thought strategy should then be planned accordingly. Some of the major manoeuvres may already be automated and require no thought by the surfer while riding the wave. Other manoeuvres may require intensive self-cueing.

Surfers are encouraged to isolate themselves from others during the beach observation phase. This helps maximize their focus of attention and assists in avoiding those who may unintentionally distract their preparations. Surfers may use their coach, surf psychologist or fellow surfer to assist them with the beach observation process.

Once the beach observation is complete, surfers then have to plan where heat-winning waves can be caught. They should also have a back-up wave location mapped in case conditions change during the heat. A clear plan of what manoeuvre sequences are possible at each of these locations is also essential. Finally, they should have a thought strategy for performing the required manoeuvres at each of the locations. This type of preparation provides a strong basis for feeling legitimately confident because as much preparation as possible for the heat has been accomplished. After planning is completed, surfers may choose to write their key "tech" points on the nose of their boards to assist them to remain focused, and to serve as cues for "preview" mental rehearsal during the heat. This type of preparation also provides a perfect script for using "virtual surfing" before the heat.

Virtual Surfing

"Virtual surfing" refers to a process where surfers rehearse, on land, the movements and thoughts of surfing. When virtual surfing, surfers should look at the type of waves in the competition area and then "see" and "feel" themselves surfing those waves. Within the limitations of the physical surrounding, the surfer should physically imitate the same motions, movements and timing that they would enact in water (Weinberg, Seabourne & Jackson, 1981). Virtual surfing can be performed on a Carveboard (skateboard) for maximum simulation or the surfer can simply move their arms and legs in an appropriate manner.

The physical impact of using mental rehearsal is well documented, as is all the "how to do it" information (Hecker & Kaczor, 1988; Rushall & Lippman, 1997). That does not need to be repeated in this chapter. What is important is the content of the virtual surfing scenarios. This is what is precisely planned through the beach observation process. Surfers are encouraged to virtual surf any time and anywhere. However, virtual surfing is particularly relevant to the competition build-up process. The amount of virtual surfing performed is very individual, but seems to be performed more by better surfers.

COMPETITION BUILD-UP

The Pre-heat Surf

As part of the physiological warm-up before commencing the heat, the surfer needs to have a warm-up surf. However, the pre-heat surf can also be used to a psychological advantage. The pre-heat surf should be addressed in a strategic way to build momentum, self-belief and technical focus leading into the competition heat. The surfer should take the opportunity to practice manoeuvres that are appropriate for the wave conditions in which they are about to compete.

The competition arena is secured for the entire duration of a contest. The surfer needs to head up or down the beach away from the contest site to find similar conditions that allow them to simulate manoeuvres that will be appropriate for their upcoming heat. While physiological warm-up could happen in any wave conditions, the psychological advantage is dependent on the pre-heat surf practice of self-cueing for the manoeuvre sequences in the upcoming heat.

For that reason, a surfer preparing to surf on a right-hand bank (waves breaking from right to left as seen from the beach) for the competition, should head down the beach to warm up on a right-hand bank and not a left-hand bank (waves breaking from left to right as seen from the beach). Sometimes the nature of the contest site prevents a pre-heat surf. Surfers can still simulate the manoeuvres and thoughts on the beach or on their Carveboard in the car park.

Rehearsing manoeuvre sequences and associated thought strategies in the pre-heat surf promotes a strong "top of the mind" awareness of what to focus on and when to focus. It promotes the competing surfer to focus on the right technical aspects at the right moment.

The pre-heat surf also allows the surfer to rehearse some of the tactical thinking and positive self-talk that will be used in the upcoming heat (Rotella, Gansneder, Ojala & Billing, 1980).

The Pre-heat Checklist

The surfer should have a time-sequenced checklist that covers all logistical preparations to be followed in the 20 minutes before the competition. This allows the surfer to continue virtual surfing what will be done in the upcoming heat (Minas, 1978), while at the same time feeling confident that everything has been done in preparation to allow an optimal performance.

Typical pre-heat preparations include: allowing time to prepare the surfboard (e.g. apply wax, change fins, check leg rope), stretching, energizing, hydrating, checking-in with the competition director to get the contest singlet, maintaining periodic beach observations, monitoring the timing of the heat that is currently running, doing some virtual surfing, performing positive self-talk, setting the watch, and paddling to the competition area. Pre-heat planning is essential if surfers wish to maximize their performances. The theme of complete preparation runs through the all the components of pre-heat planning. The beach observations allow planning to catch the best waves the heat has to offer, and to prepare clear mental "road maps" of what needs to be focused on during rides to maximize scores. The pre-heat surf provides further preparation opportunities to rehearse the key elements of performance before a heat. Finally, the pre-heat checklist ensures that the surfer is prepared in the most practical ways for the challenge ahead. All this preparation provides a legitimate basis to feel a growing sense of confidence and self-belief as the competition approaches.

COMPETITION THINKING

Once a heat has started, the key challenge when not riding waves is to get to and hold the primary wave location. This places the surfer in the best position for when the set waves come through. Therefore, surfers need to follow a brief tactical analysis after each wave to guarantee they are at the best wave location at that time in the heat. Surfers need to consider the primary determinants of the heat outcome and adjust their strategies accordingly.

Tactical Thinking

Asking the Right Questions

Three key determinants affect a heat outcome. They are the basis for the tactical review that should occur after each wave. The tactical review should consist of an internal dialogue where three specific questions are asked.

1. *What have I got?* This question relates to the wave scores that the surfer has achieved up until that point during the heat. The scores will subsequently affect the strategy for the next wave. For example, if the surfer only has one high-scoring wave and two are

needed to go through to the next round, it is important to return to the primary wave location as soon as possible.

If the surfer already has two high-scoring waves then the surfer might paddle back to the take-off zone and put pressure on the other competitors in the heat, possibly limiting their ability to catch further high-scoring waves. Alternatively, if the surfer has only two low-scoring waves then an alternative might be paddling to the secondary wave location to get a high scoring wave. Each of these scenarios is influenced by the pressure exerted by the amount of time remaining in the heat.

2. *How long is there to go?* With only 20 minutes to get the two highest-scoring waves, it is essential that surfers use their time wisely. Checking the amount of time remaining throughout the heat allows a surfer to change locations, pressure or shut down other surfers accordingly.

3. *What do I need to do now?* This is the final assessment and action-planning phase based on the responses to the first two questions. For example, with only one high-scoring wave and two minutes left in the heat, it is important for the surfer to reposition quickly for any type of scoring wave to ensure that there are at least two scoring waves in the surfer's final tally. Results are calculated using the competitor's best two wave scores. A quick last wave at least provides the possibility of beating another surfer in the heat.

The process of reviewing the score and the time remaining, and then determining the subsequent strategy should happen while the surfer is paddling back out to the take-off zone. It should also happen while waiting in the take-off zone for waves. The inconsistent nature of the ocean and relentless time pressure means a surfer must be constantly reassessing the strategic approach to the heat to maximize wave-catching potential. This simple tactical review process allows the surfer to make confident decisions as the heat progresses.

If the surfer is surfing well, using technical self-coaching, and catching great waves because of effective tactical positioning, then the use of positive self-talk will also assist in maximizing confidence and performance.

Positive Self-talk

In the pressure of a competition situation, human nature seems to focus attention on all the things going wrong with a performance. Typically, surfers focus on the poor aspects of performance and the impact of the poor performance on their careers, even while they are still in a heat.

A surfer who has just missed a wave may start to focus on the fact that, with more than half the heat time elapsed, an opponent now has two high-scoring waves while they only have one. This could lead to doubts as to whether they will advance from the heat. A situation like this often leads to questions in the surfer's mind that are not immediately answerable. "Will I still be able to maintain my position in the rankings?" "Will I be able to stay on the tour or will I be relegated?" "Will I lose my sponsors?" "Will I lose my income?" Self-doubt questions could occur while the surfer should be focusing on position within the line-up and what is to be done on the next wave. However, while these are legitimate concerns for the surfer, focusing on these concerns during the competition is inappropriate (Psychountaki & Zervas, 2000). Moreover, if the surfer continues to entertain these thoughts then their performance and self-belief will suffer. It is possible to prevent negative and doubting thoughts through mental skills training and, in particular, negative thought-stopping. However, the most powerful strategy is to have the surfer focus on positive evidence.

Evidence: The Basis of Self-belief

The use of positive evidence provides an alternative set of thoughts for the surfer to focus on when concerns about performance outcomes and subsequent consequences start in the surfer's mind. If the surfer generates an alternative set of thoughts through a review of positive evidence, the negative spiral of outcome- and consequence-related thoughts can be broken, allowing a refocusing on the performance (Hanton & Connaughton, 2002).

Having a high degree of self-belief during the heat is critical to optimizing the technical and tactical performance of the surfer (Rushall, Hall, Roux, Sasseville & Rushall, 1988). Good self-belief while competing is an important discriminating factor between more and less successful competitors in a wide range of sports (Hardy et al., 1996). Without strong self-belief, a surfer will not be as aggressive or technically competent as possible. Similarly, from a tactical point of view, if surfers do not believe in their ability to decide which waves to take and where to take them from, they will open the window for forceful competitors to steal waves and earn higher scores. Therefore, in order for surfers to create strong feelings of self-belief, they must use legitimate strategies. The use of self-aggrandizing statements such as "I'm the greatest surfer in the world" and "No one can beat me" does little to build legitimate self-belief (Rushall & Potgieter, 1987). Beliefs must be accurate and realistic.

In order to create legitimate feelings of self-belief, surfers need to use an evidence-based approach that allows them to create strong, believable, positive self-statements, which they can use during various stages of the heat. If the surfer can consider legitimate evidence of quality past performances that support the notion that a personal best performance is possible, that increases the likelihood the surfer will have strong self-belief while competing (Bandura, 1977; Hoigaard & Johansen, 2004).

A key is to identify evidence that supports the notion of having a legitimate claim to perform to the best of one's ability during the heat. This evidence may come from quality experiences during dry-land or in-water training, or current or past competition performances (Rushall, 1979).

A surfer might focus on the evidence of past failures; this too will negatively impact the surfer's performance and self-belief (Weinberg, Gould & Jackson 1980). Some examples of negative evidence are: the surfer keeps focusing on issues such as a fall on the first wave, scores being worse than those of the other competitors, and the board not feeling right. These types of negative evidence will generate feelings of self-doubt that will influence detrimentally both wave-catching and surfing ability.

On the other hand, when surfers focus on performance positives during a heat, strong positive self-belief usually results. There is a structured approach to how the surfer should review evidence during a heat to build self-belief. However, it is important for the surf psychologist to understand the competitive environment so they can effectively support surfers to use positive self-talk to develop self-belief.

The nature of competitive surfing is that there are large periods of time when the surfer is not involved in the actual process of riding waves. Anywhere from 80 per cent to 90 per cent of a surfer's time during a heat is spent either paddling back out to the take-off zone to get into position to catch the next wave or waiting for waves in the take-off zone. While some of this paddling and waiting time is spent in tactical thinking and planning, there is still a large amount of time left where the surfer can generate strong self-belief mainly by using positive evidence review.

The evidence review during the heat is typically undertaken using various combinations of both mental rehearsal and positive self-talk. For example, the surfer may choose to positively self-talk about their ride and then review-visualize it again multiple times, before again talking positively about the ride. The role of the surf psychologist is to assist the surfer to identify a simple and effective approach to using these two mental skills in their evidence review.

What Evidence is Reviewed?

The evidence that is reviewed during the heat falls into two categories. One category of evidence has to do with what happened up to that point in the heat and the other category is about what happened before the heat.

1. Positives that Have Happened During the Heat

During the heat, the best time for the surfer to start the positive evidence review is at the start of the paddle back to the take-off zone after each ride. Because the strongest impact on self-belief can be made when the surfer reviews the most recent positive evidence, the surfer initially should go over the wave that has just been ridden and identify the positives from that ride. For example, a surfer may wish to review-visualize quality manoeuvres which were just executed and to self-talk positively about those manoeuvres. They may also choose to review-visualize and positively self-talk about performance quality in specific phases of individual manoeuvres or they may review-visualize a sequence of manoeuvres that were put together. After some review mental rehearsal on the paddle back out, some examples of self-talk are "That was an awesome wave! I really smacked those two reos [re-entries] out there! I felt the fins bust out on both of them! What a wave!"

As a heat progresses and more waves are ridden, the surfer should continue with positive evidence review. With an emphasis on reviewing the positives of the most recent wave, a higher degree of self-belief is likely to be generated. Additionally, the surfer should continue to review all the positives of earlier waves ridden during that heat. As the heat progresses, continuous reviewing of all the positives provides a real depth of positive evidence for the surfer to focus on; consequently, creating stronger self-belief as the heat progresses.

Generally, surfers should avoid focusing on the judges' scores. Scores received are not something over which the surfer has specific control and focusing on those scores may lead to an undermining of self-belief. While some surfers like to incorporate their wave scores into their positive evidence review, this may also become a negative for a surfer who does not score well on a particular wave. For example, a surfer may do two major manoeuvres at the start of a wave and then fall off. Evidence-based self-belief clearly indicates that the surfer needs to focus on successfully completed radical manoeuvres rather than a fall that resulted in an incomplete ride and a low and potentially unusable score.

By focusing on the score, the surfer thinks how poor was the ride that resulted in an unusable score for that wave and undermines self-belief. However, when a surfer focuses on the precision and degree of radicalness of the manoeuvres preceding the fall, that evidence allows the surfer to maintain or build self-belief during the heat.

2. Positives that Have Happened Before the Heat

The other source of evidence that the surfer can review during the heat has to do with what has happened before the start of the heat. Here, the surfer can find an extremely wide range of evidence to visualize and talk about that will promote self-belief while competing. Within the menu of evidence that a surfer can review, some of the following evidence sources should be considered.

In-water Training Evidence

Before the heat, the surfer should identify a number of specific occasions from the training diary where surfing well in similar conditions has occurred. For example, a surfer who has been training well in the long right-hand points of South Eastern Queensland in Australia can find legitimate reasons why performance should be equally as good when surfing right-hand point waves at South Africa's Jeffery's Bay. This surfer can legitimately generate self-belief bolstering self-talk which says, "I've been belting waves just like this at Snapper (in Australia) for the last few months, so I know what to do here." Having this piece of evidence organized and highlighted before the heat provides the surfer with legitimate reasons to believe a good performance should occur in similar conditions.

Another piece of in-water training evidence may relate to a manoeuvre specific situation in the upcoming heat. Competitors facing the hollow left-hand barrel of Tahiti's Teahupoo may be able to draw on some evidence and say, "I really refined my tube riding skill at Pipe (Hawaii's Pipeline), this is big and hollow just like that, so I'm ready for this." In addition to repeating this positive self-talk the surfer may also review visualize the waves that were ridden at the Pipeline (Kendall, Hrycaiko, Martin & Kendall, 1990). Through this process the surfer can then produce legitimate evidence to believe that a successful heat is possible. The surfer can self-talk about this evidence in the lead up to the heat as well as during the heat.

Dry-land Training Evidence

Competitors can also generate positive review mental rehearsal scripts and self-belief statements that relate to the work and training that they have been doing away from the water. Strength and conditioning, core stability, yoga, equipment-testing, diet and mental skills are just some of the pieces of evidence that a surfer could use to build self-belief in a competition setting.

Bell's Beach in Australia has long rides and subsequently requires the surfer to paddle a considerable distance back to the take-off zone after each wave. If the surfer has improved their upper body and paddling strength through a rigorous off-season training program, then a legitimate self-belief statement could be developed by the surfer to use later in the heat when it is difficult to sprint paddle back towards the peak (Weinberg, Smith, Jackson &

Gould, 1984; Taylor, 1979). When surfers find paddling challenging, they could rightfully say to themselves, "C'mon, you can keep going, you've worked hard over the last few months on your fitness, and you're a lot stronger now. C'mon, let's go."

Past Competitions' Evidence

Surfers can also use surfing well in similar wave conditions at other competitions as evidence for the self-belief to perform well. Past competitions provide a great opportunity for "mining" evidence. Competitions in similar wave locations provide genuine evidence for building self-belief. For instance, a surfer may have travelled from Europe to Japan after a successful contest campaign surfing small beach breaks in Europe. The surfer would be better prepared to surf a contest in similar conditions in Japan. A successful European contest leg would provide valid self-belief building evidence for the surfer to consider during a heat in Japan. In addition to review-visualizing the successful waves of Europe during the heat, the surfer could use positive self-talk such as, "I went off in waves just like this in France so here we go again."

It is essential to plan and prepare all of these evidence strategies, which relate to in-water training, dry-land training, and past competitions, for use in competitions. Under the pressure of competition the surfer does not want to be spending time trying to drill back into the evidence in their own mind to come up with something positive to say or review-visualize. It is an essential role of the coach and the surf psychologist to assist the surfer before the heat to identify clear and specifically related self-belief building evidence.

With evidence identified, the next challenge is for the surfer to be able to remember this evidence during the heat. The simple strategy of pencilling some key reminder words or symbols on the nose of the board can assist during the paddle out and while waiting. These reminders have meaning for the surfer and trigger them to remember the prepared evidence.

Evidence preparation is particularly useful for surfers who may find it difficult to catch a high-scoring wave during the early part of heat. Surfers are always keen to initiate the competition by catching a good wave early; however, the nature of ocean swells is such that waves are not always available when the surfer would like. Subsequently, the surfer may spend anywhere between five to ten minutes waiting for their first scoring ride. This situation has the potential to undermine self-belief. A surfer who has observed this inconsistency can plan to refer back to evidence of previous successes in similar situations. A surfer who can review-visualize and positively self-talk about a previous contest when two winning waves were scored within the last ten minutes, should feel confident despite the doubt that comes while waiting for extended periods to get a scoring wave.

COMPETITION DEBRIEF

After each heat, the surfer should review, in a strategic and logical way, what occurred during the heat. The performance "blueprint" which was developed before the heat becomes the guideline for the debrief. Did the pre-planned thoughts and strategies work? What went wrong? What improvements need to be made?

The surf psychologist should specifically challenge the surfer to identify at least five positives that went well during each competition heat. This trains the surfer to start to identify positives on a regular basis and allows the surfer to develop a list of evidence that can be used in pre-heat evidence development for future competitions.

The surfer should also identify what it is that needs to be improved from the heat that was just completed. The debrief may indicate that a simple, short-term fix is needed. It may be something that the surfer can deal with during the next heat, such as sticking closer to the landmark or paddling hard at the peak. Sometimes the debrief will reveal things that need to be improved and are longer-term projects; for example, increasing leg strength to improve the ability to pump the board while arm surfing between flat sections of the wave. Debriefing leads to action plans for training before the next competition or heat.

CONCLUSION

The psychology of high- performance surfing is particularly specialized and any sport psychologist wishing to become a surf psychologist needs to understand the terminology and the challenge that surfers face. Learning to surf is a good way to start to understand the sport; reading surfing magazines, watching surf movies and talking to local surfers will begin to put you in the picture. Another Australian surf psychologist, Richard Bennett, has written *The Surfers Mind*, available through http://www.thesurfersmind.com/, which is a comprehensive book full of practical information and strategies to help surfers of all abilities reach their potential in surfing and life. Like any sport, it takes time and passion to refine surf psychologist skills, but what an amazing sport and sporting environment to work in. Go for it!

ACKNOWLEDGEMENTS

The author wishes to acknowledge the support and advice received on earlier drafts of this chapter by two surfing academics; Professor Brent Rushall, Sport Science Associates at http://members.cox.net/brushall/ and Martin Dunn, Head Coach at http://www.surfcoach. com/.

REFERENCES

Association of Surfing Professionals (2004). http://www.aspworldtour.com/.
Bandura, A. (1977). Self-efficacy: toward a unifying theory of behavioral change. *Psychological Review, 84*, 191–215.
Bennett, R. (2004). *The Surfers Mind*. http://www.thesurfersmind.com/.
Boutcher, S. (2002). Attentional processes and sport performance. In T. Horn (ed.) *Advances in Sport Psychology*, (pp. 441–454). Champaign, IL: Human Kinetics.
Dunn, M. (2004). http://www.surfcoach.com/.
Etnier, J.L. & Sibley, B.A. (2002). Attention demands during the performance of a volleyball setting task. *Medicine and Science in Sports and Exercise,* 34 (5), Supplement abstract 1200.
Gault-Williams, M. (2004). Legendary surfers: a definitive history of surfing's culture and heroes. http://www.legendarysurfers.com/.
Hanton, S. & Connaughton, D. (2002). Perceived control of anxiety and its relationship to self-confidence and performance. *Research Quarterly for Exercise and Sport, 73*, 87–97.

Hanton, S. & Jones, G. (1999). The acquisition and development of cognitive skills and strategies: I. Making the butterflies fly in formation. *The Sport Psychologist, 12*, 1–21.

Hardy, L., Jones, L. & Gould, D. (1996). *Understanding Psychological Preparation in Sport.* Chichester, West Sussex: John Wiley & Sons.

Hecker, J.E. & Kaczor, L.M. (1988). Application of imagery theory to sport psychology. *Journal of Sport and Exercise Psychology, 10*, 363–373.

Hoigaard, R. & Johansen, B.T. (2004). The solution-focused approach to sport psychology. *The Sport Psychologist, 18*, 218–228.

International Surfing Association (2004). http://www.isasurf.org/.

Kendall, G., Hrycaiko, D., Martin, G.L. & Kendall, T. (1990). The effects of an imagery rehearsal, relaxation, and self-talk package on basketball game performance. *Journal of Sport and Exercise Psychology, 12*, 157–166.

Magill, R. (1997). Knowledge is more than we can talk about: implicit learning in motor skill acquisition. *Research Quarterly for Exercise and Sport, 69*, 104–110.

Minas, S.C. (1978). Mental practice of a complex perceptual-motor skill. *Journal of Human Movement Studies, 4*, 102–107.

Ming, S. (1993). A self-talk package for improving figure skating performance by young competitive figure skaters. *Masters Abstracts International, 31*(4), 1929.

Psychountaki, M. & Zervas, Y. (2000). Competitive worries, sport confidence, and performance ratings for young swimmers. *Perceptual and Motor Skills, 91*, 87–94.

Rotella, R.J., Gansneder, B., Ojala, D. & Billing, J. (1980). Cognitions and coping strategies of elite skiers: an exploratory study of young developing athletes. *Journal of Sport Psychology, 2*, 350–354.

Rushall, B.S. (1979). *Psyching in Sports.* London: Pelham Books.

Rushall, B.S., Hall, M., Roux, L., Sasseville, J. & Rushall, A.C. (1988). Effects of three types of thought content instructions on skiing performance. *The Sport Psychologist, 2*, 283–297.

Rushall, B.S. & Lippman, L.G. (1997). The role of imagery in physical performance. *International Journal for Sport Psychology, 29*, 57–72.

Rushall, B.S., & Potgieter, J.R. (1987). *The Psychology of Successful Competing in Endurance Events.* Pretoria: The South African Association for Sport Science, Physical Education, and Recreation.

Sherwood, D.E., & Rios, V. (2001). Divided attention in bimanual aiming events: effects on movement accuracy. *Research Quarterly for Exercise and Sport, 72*, 210–218.

Surfing Industry Manufacturing Association (2004). http://www.sima.com/.

Taylor, D.E.M. (1979). Human endurance—mind or muscle? *British Journal of Sports Medicine, 12*, 179–184.

Theodorakis, Y., Chroni, S., Laparidis, K., Bebetos, V. & Douma, I. (2001). Self-talk in a basketball shooting task. *Perceptual and Motor Skills, 92*, 309–315.

Weinberg, R., Gould, D. & Jackson, A. (1980). Relationship between self-efficacy and performance in a competitive setting. A paper presented at the Annual Meeting of the Canadian Association of Sport Sciences, Vancouver, British Columbia, Canada.

Weinberg, R.S., Seabourne, T.G. & Jackson, A. (1981). Effects of visuo-motor behavior rehearsal, relaxation, and imagery on karate performance. *Journal of Sport Psychology, 3*, 228–238.

Weinberg, R.S., Smith, J., Jackson, A. & Gould, D. (1984). Effects of association, disassociation, and positive self-talk strategies on endurance performance. *Canadian Journal of Applied Sport Science, 9*, 25–32.

Young, N. & McGregor, C (1983). *The History of Surfing.* Palm Beach, NSW, Australia: Palm Beach Press.

Zimmerman, B.J., & Kitsantas, A. (1996). Self-regulated learning of a motoric skill: the role of goal setting and self-monitoring. *Journal of Applied Sport Psychology, 8*, 60–75.

PART VII

Motor Sports

CHAPTER 23

Psychological Training in Motorcycling

Joaquín Dosil
University of Vigo, Spain
and
Enrique J. Garcés de Los Fayos
University of Murcia, Spain

INTRODUCTION

Motorcycling is an exciting sport which appeals greatly to both riders and fans. As a motor sport, it displays some unique characteristics which distinguish it from other pastimes. Such is the mechanical dependency (having a good engine), that the chances riders or motorcycling teams have of taking victory are often dictated by this factor. This statement is as extreme as it is real, implying a series of peculiarities sport psychologists must be aware of before working in this sport. Nevertheless, motorcycling history is riddled with numerous cases of riders failing to produce good performances despite having excellently designed motorbikes and adequate physical, technical and tactical training, while others manage to reach the top on relatively inferior machines. On many occasions, the explanations given are related to psychological aspects (e.g. "I lost my concentration and went down", "I was forced into the lead", "I couldn't handle the psychological burden of so many laps", etc.). Despite this, few riders work with sport psychologists to improve or optimize their concentration, motivation and anxiety control skills, amongst others. This chapter, guided by these factors, is structured to first focus on the general, then the specific aspects of this sport. That is to say, the basic elements of motorcycling are discussed before separating those of special relevance to the work of sport psychologists. Initially, the keys to understanding the motorcycling world are described, followed by a brief introduction to the sport itself and a definition of the various world championship categories. Moreover, the factors conditioning the rider–motorbike relationship, such as economic investment and the family and team structure, are also detailed. The text goes on to analyse the distinctive psychological demands placed upon riders, describing variables such as anxiety, concentration, self-confidence and decision-making. The following section reflects upon the importance sport psychology can have in the overall training of professional motorcyclists; analysing aspects such as

The Sport Psychologist's Handbook: A Guide for Sport-Specific Performance Enhancement.
Edited by Joaquín Dosil. © 2006 John Wiley & Sons, Ltd.

adherence to gym work or the planning of technical and physical preparation. Finally, the chapter concludes with a detailed description of the elements conditioning competitions (free training, classification training, the grid, the warm-up lap, the start, etc.), and their psychological implications.

UNDERSTANDING MOTORCYCLING: FIVE ASPECTS

Motorcycling has a number of specific elements, some of which are important to know before beginning work in this sport. From a psychological perspective, these keys can explain certain behaviours which may be observed in training and competition, as well as determining the uniqueness of the sport.

- *Understanding the technical jargon to fit in with rider teams*   One of the essential characteristics of every sport is its jargon. In the case of motorcycling, the quantity of technical words, as well as implicit forms of communication, make following conversations between riders and their teams, or even between riders and their psychologists, a complicated task. Therefore, it becomes necessary for sport psychologists to study the typical language used beforehand.
- *If the motorbike fails, the competition is lost*   During training and competitions, the ultimate objective of riders and all team members is to ensure the motorbike is fully prepared. Among other aspects, this may mean ensuring that the suspension or chassis setup is optimum for producing a good race. This "obsessive" concern for the bike to be in perfect condition ("the setup") is due to the fact that any slight problem has its consequences. At best, it may mean riders not placing highly, but in the worst of cases, it may cause them to abandon races or suffer falls (with obvious physical risks).
- *The risks taken by riders*   The current speed record of a GP motorbike (the most powerful on the circuit) is around 340 kilometres per hour (on any track, reaching 250 kilometres per hour is normal in world championship categories). At these speeds the possibility of suffering serious accidents is evident. Despite riders wearing suits, boots, gloves and helmets made from increasingly more resistant materials, and the ever-improving safety measures of race tracks, fatalities and injuries (or even deaths) may be considered an inherent characteristic of this sport.
- *Technical training is related to driving motorbikes*   All the technical preparation or the "technical attitude", as it is known, is orientated towards optimizing driving the motorbikes. The true technical training of this sport is characterized by aspects such as adopting the most aerodynamic position on straights, inclining the bike as much as possible and picking the best line on bends, calculating with greater precision the moment and intensity of breaking to overtake and accelerating to come out of the manoeuvre, and picking the best positions in breaking to enter and come off turns. Likewise, especially during pre-season training, but also prior to competitions, seeking the best position in relation to the motorbike's chassis, or the best posture in relation to its bodywork, are other examples occupying the technical training of riders.
- *Everything revolves around the motorbike and the rider, but feeling isolated is frequent*   In the three days that pass from the initial free training sessions to the definitive race, everything revolves around the bike and achieving maximum unity with the rider. Teams focus on what their riders tell them; while riders take care to see that the mechanics prepare

the bikes to their "demands". Nevertheless, riders frequently feel alone. The total lack of interaction with their components and the psychological toughness of completing such an enormous amount of laps (the overall quantity involved in training and competition), are factors to be taken into account.

Related to these aspects is the media importance generated by this sport. For example, the 2003 World Championships held in Valencia (Spain) attracted the most public ever, with 200,000 spectators over 3 days of Grand Prix competition. What is more, after football and Formula One, motorcycling receives the most media coverage in Europe. Along these lines, it is likely that the Grand Prix will return to the United States, where even their own national championships create a media storm.

Large telecommunications, petrol and tobacco companies invest enormous quantities of money in sponsoring riders and their teams. Finally, to demonstrate the significance this sport is achieving worldwide, 2004 was the first time a motorcycling Grand Prix was held in Qatar, on a track built in under a year with the sole purpose of it becoming a permanent world championship circuit and hosting an annual Grand Prix. Similarly, other countries such as China will soon figure in the world motorcycling calendar with a Grand Prix in 2005.

DESCRIPTION OF THIS SPORT AND ITS PSYCHOLOGICAL DEMANDS

Firstly, in order to sufficiently understand the psychological demands of motorcycling, it is important to appreciate the main keys to competition. Therefore, the following factors will be examined along with their psychological implications for riders.

The Competitive Structure

From a young age, those entering the motorcycling world appreciate that competition involves accepting certain characteristics such as a very long competitive season (between 7 and 9 months of racing); a minimum of 12 to 16 races a year, covering many thousands of kilometres as fast as their bikes will allow; 3 intensive days battling out official training, free training and, finally, the race itself, not to mention all the physical preparation required to remain in-form throughout the season. Obviously, a situation with these characteristics is physically and mentally debilitating for riders. As described earlier, various psychological factors come into play (e.g. anxiety prior to competitions, lack of self-confidence or lack of confidence in the motorbike, distorted self-defeating thoughts, tolerating the boredom involved when time is not managed efficiently, etc.), as well as concerns for bikes not being "setup" correctly (e.g. among other aspects, that they don't provide the expected power, that they fail to accelerate as predicted, that they produce undesired movements when breaking sharply coming into bends). This form of "living for the bike" shapes riders from the beginning, in such a way that their psychological profile is linked to their experiences in this sport. Nor should it be forgotten that, together with the previously described factors, the actual psychological and physical workload of managing the motorbikes becomes relevant at various moments in competition: breaking, accelerating, skidding, etc. (weights range from 72 kilos with the smaller 125cc bikes to 150 to 160 kilos with the GP super bikes).

The Main Sporting Categories

From the smallest motorbikes (mini-motorbikes designed for children beginning in the sport) to the GP super bikes, more than 30 categories can be counted. Nonetheless, in this chapter, five of the most relevant and well-known categories in the international scene will be described. The first three are organized by the Spanish company Dorna, under the auspices of the World Motorcycling Federation; while the remaining two are organized directly by the International Federation, with support from specific sponsors in each race. These five categories are detailed below:

- *125*   This category is formed by special motorbikes, designed and constructed for competition. Although they bear some similarities to the standard 125cc bikes built for the general population, in reality, the internal modifications (motor, chassis, exhaust pipe) and external changes (bodywork, swing arm, tyres, etc.) set them apart. It is a category designed for the youngest riders. The last two world champions have been no older than twenty and are usually riders originating from the various national as well as European championships. Often described as a "pool" for future champions on the larger bikes, the psychological intensity stems from there being many candidates hoping to participate in the Grand Prix, and few who are able to do so (on the starting grid there is room for only thirty six motorbikes). The "pressure" of parents and sponsors should also be taken into account by sport psychologists, since the capacity of youngsters to dominate these pressures while performing optimally may not be compatible, leading to them abandoning the sport.
- *250*   In this category, riders compete on 250cc motorbikes. Although they possess certain external similarities to mainstream bikes of the same cubic capacity, practically all the internal and external parts are modified, adapted to the characteristics of each rider (weight and/or stature). Although a predominant proportion of young riders also compete in this category, it is perhaps much tougher psychologically, since only the best riders from the previous category qualify (125cc), as well as those coming from the super sport categories (inferior) described below. Likewise, serving as an "intermediate" category between the smaller and the larger bikes, many riders end their sporting career at this cubic capacity. Therefore, riders must be able to tolerate the frustration of not being able to "move up" a category or seeing how other younger riders pass them by. A typical exit for some riders who fail to triumph in this category is to dispute races in other disciplines, such as super bikes or super sport. However, it is important for riders to assess the situation before taking this step, given that depleted motivational levels and emotional exhaustion from competing in an undesirable category may prove counterproductive to their performance.
- *GP* The so-called GP motorbikes (Grand Prix motorbikes) are the stars of this sport. They are prototypes which cannot be acquired outside of the sporting context of world-class motorcycling. With a cubic capacity of 1,000 centimetres, they reach 250 horse power and maximum speeds of 350 kilometres/hour (a similar speed to a Formula one car). Being the supreme category, only the best riders get this far, whether they come from the 125cc or 250cc categories (normally world champions and those who placed highly in

inferior competitions), or from the minor super sport and super bike categories (also world championships and those riders who placed highly). Therefore, it is extremely difficult for riders to access this category and even more difficult for them to stay within the competitive structure. Moreover, GP motorbike teams require a budget so high that only multinationals are able to sponsor these sporting structures. The influence of psychological factors must be managed not only by recently promoted riders, but also by those fighting against relegation and fundamentally, those battling to become GP motorcycling world champions. All in all, it should be highlighted that the majority of GP riders have been world champions in at least one of the other categories and, therefore, display a great "emotional toughness" as a product of their years of training and competition.

- *Super bikes*   These bikes reach a capacity of 1,000 cubic centimetres. As with the 125 and 250 categories, they are significantly modified from the standard models, but to a lesser extent. Although future GP riders often come from super bikes, those failing to triumph in GP also "end up" in this category, along with world and European super sport champions and a large number of North American riders who treat it as a springboard to GP motorcycling. It is worth mentioning that while media attention does not reach the same scale as in GP motorcycling, it remains a significant factor, since these are the largest and most powerful bikes after the supreme GP category. Perhaps the two categories are distinguished only by the fact that all super bikes are required to use the same brand of tyre and therefore cannot be considered prototypes.

- *Super sport*   Finally, the super sport category is composed of 600cc bikes. Being the closest to the larger bikes, it is considered a "special" category which allows riders to progress in a more logical manner. Therefore, two interesting aspects can be seen here. On the one hand, riders are often young and have stepped up to this division in the hope of reaching the maximum categories. On the other hand, the majority of super sport champions have previously triumphed in the super bike category and, in some cases, also in GP motorcycling. The psychological factors to consider with these riders are similar to those observed in 125cc or in super bikes. Notably, the pressures to "go up" a category and reach the maximum ranks of motorcycling constitute the predominant aspects.

The Development of Competitions

Perhaps one of the most noticeable characteristics of motorcycling competitions is their duration, approximately three days. On the first day there is usually free training (where the motorbike setup is established) and official training (where riders clock times which allow them to access certain positions on the starting grid). The second day involves more official training, where riders take more risks to improve their position on the grid. Finally, the third day is occupied by a final free training session (riders aim to make contact with the track and give the final touches to the bikes' setup) and the race itself. All of these factors require riders to be capable of performing an array of functions: maintain adequate tension levels at each moment, focus on the different aspects of conditioning training and competition, concentrate during boring waiting times and develop activities which allow them to remain emotionally "stable", etc. Without a doubt, one of the fundamental tasks of sport psychologists is to prepare for these three days of competition through psychological training.

The Track, the Boxes and the Paddock

During competitions, riders spend most of their time in the track, the boxes and the paddock. To plan psychological training adequately, psychologists must familiarize themselves with the contexts within which riders operate, adapting to the environmental circumstances and personal characteristics of each individual. Training sessions and races are disputed on race tracks, each displaying its own characteristics and peculiarities. Therefore, to better adapt psychological training (just as technical, tactical and physical training are modified according to this factor), the following characteristics should be taken into account: the road-holding, the distance of each lap, the layout of bends, the distance of the finishing straight or the incline of the circuit. On the other hand, it is in the boxes that riders and technical teams set up the bikes, solving any problems which arise during training or races. Generally speaking, it is here that all aspects of competition are dealt with and where, from a psychological perspective, the various emotions riders may endure must to be tackled. These emotions may range from the euphoric (when things go better than expected), to satisfaction (when things go as planned), to the most dramatic (when confronted with poor times, a defeat or a fall). Overall, riders best develop their psychological skills (the rider setup) in the boxes. Finally, the paddock is the area adjacent to the boxes where team vehicles are parked, including the "motor home" where riders live during competitions, another relevant area where sport psychologists should work.

The Rider–motorbike Interaction

Despite all that has been previously described, the key to adequate competitive development is achieved through a maximum interaction between riders and their motorbikes. A large number of variables have a bearing on this relationship. Whether a motorbike is official (total development and support from the factory where it was built) or private (partial development and support from its makers) influences the level of interaction; and the capacity of riders to adapt to bikes is a direct result of their psychological state, meaning suitable mental training can assist in this process. Sport psychologists should work with riders in both aspects.

The Rider–team Interaction

Just as it is important to maintain the rider–motorbike interaction, it is also fundamental to achieve an optimum interaction between riders and their teams. These teams vary in size, ranging from no more than eight to ten members in the small, private or "manufacturer client teams", to up to fifty people in the largest "manufacturer teams". A team does not necessarily adapt better the larger it is, but it does influence the way in which psychological work should be established during competitions, the channels of communication and, above all, choosing the people of support for riders when they need to solve technical or even personal problems. In these teams, it is essential for sport psychologists to appropriately situate themselves within the structure to attain the objectives of mental optimization in the clearest manner.

Once these principle indicators have been revised, the three remaining key factors to the sporting development of riders need to be analysed. Here, reference is made to the economic component, the influence and importance of family, and the definition of what is understood in motorcycling as the "sports team".

The Economic Factor

After motor racing, motorcycling is probably the most expensive sport there is. From the moment a child decides to begin in an inferior category, the expenditure on all the necessary equipment for them to train and compete begins, spending which rapidly spirals to enormous amounts when they are promoted to higher categories. The following expenses can be observed: travel to race tracks to train and compete, food during competitions, use of race tracks, race fees, technical team salaries, tyres, parts, maintenance, hiring of boxes, suits, boots, helmets . . . among others. Regarding the main earnings of riders, the only two possibilities are prize money (the highest amounts for victory and bonuses for starting the race in each competition—according to the finishing position, prizes get smaller in relation to the points score) and sponsorship. Without detailing the specific sources of remuneration, the variability of earnings is large (according to journalistic sources, in 2003 the GP World Champion received a salary of 12 million dollars, while the runner-up in the same category earned just 1.5 million dollars). Logically, this unstable form of earning money gives rise to a "vicious circle", provoking strong psychological tensions in riders who, on many occasions, do not know until the last minute whether they will be able to compete in the coming season. Moreover, good results do not always enable pilots to move up a category or gain sponsorship. On the contrary, this often depends on more complicated factors such as a rider's "selling capacity", an aspect defined by the marketing specialists in sponsorship companies.

Family

In the beginning, the family constitutes the main support for riders. Not only do they accompany them, as in the majority of other sports, but they are also involved on two levels. Firstly, they are with riders during competitions, which creates a strong bond between the family members as a result of the demands of this sport. Secondly, fathers usually acquire a special role as manager, collaborator in the technical team or evaluator/coach, depending on their knowledge. However, without a doubt, families assume the high economic investments involved in competitions. Normally, with time and as riders achieve good results, sponsors and teams start to appear, and families assume a secondary role in all of the aforementioned aspects. As riders approach world championship competitions, the role of their families diminishes to practical nonexistence, with the exception of a few fathers who still accompany them. Logically, going from being "protected" by a family unit to forming part of a large group of totally professional people is very different, and riders need to adapt to the psychological demands created through these changing circumstances. Lorenzo (2003) offers a personal example of this process (describing his own son's progress in reaching the world championships), defining the key elements to consider in the sporting development of riders and illustrating the correct steps to "creating a champion", a process he considers many more parents could participate in.

Team Structure

It is of interest to briefly describe how team structures are formed. The analysis will be based on an average team competing in the world championships. Although many variations exist, essentially, the following members are found: 2 riders (around which the structure of the maintenance team organizes itself); a team manager (in charge of organizing everything concerned with the competition, strategy, media and even marketing, both internally and externally); a mechanical manager (in charge of structuring all the work done by the mechanics, with the aim of it working as an authentic task team); 3 mechanics (one is an assistant, who is in charge of minor jobs, and the other two are much more experienced, assuming the most responsible and demanding tasks); and engineers (the telecommunications experts who accompany riders, usually only in large manufacturer teams). In an average-sized or small team, members work directly at trackside, carrying out the required tasks so competition unfolds adequately. However, in larger teams, auxiliary personnel may be added to this list, including chefs, media and PR assistants, vehicle fleet drivers, and personal assessors, creating structures of over 30 people in some cases. Nor should the various technical personnel, required by riders between races, be forgotten, ranging from sport psychologists, physical trainers, to doctors, nutritionists or physiotherapists, to mention but a few specialists. Riders should optimally develop determined social skills, which allow them to emotionally adapt to the situations arising from this conglomerate of people. Such situations may involve leading the team, communicating adequately with team members, being even-tempered in situations where a person's professional responsibility is in play or knowing how to delegate tasks, optimizing the team's performance.

THE MOST COMMON PSYCHOLOGICAL DEMANDS ON RIDERS

In discovering this sport, it becomes evident that psychological aspects can distinguish one rider from another. It is no wonder that authors take particular interest in the existence of certain psychological rider "profiles", which could prove crucial to understanding why some manage to reach the top, while others get lost along the way. For example, Carzedda and Massara (1990) studied variables such as extroversion–introversion, emotional stability, paranoia, anxiety, depression and hostility; Battista (1995) conducted a broad study into various aspects conditioning the psychological characteristics of motorcycle riders and, more recently, Fuller and Myerscough (2001) investigated the different indicators which help understand a rider's assumption of physical risks, referring to the psychological characteristics associated with perception.

Nevertheless, despite the aforementioned bibliographical references, studies into the psychological aspects of motor sports in general have been scarce, and even more so in motorcycling. Therefore, when reviewing these aspects, the tendency is to refer to classical studies, which focus on aviation in the majority of cases. Henry (1941) studied the personality differences between athletes from non-motor sports and aviation students; Delucchi (1943) noted the psychological factors to be considered in the training of aeroplane pilots: attention span, speed perception, judgement, psychomotor reactions, calculating distance skills, memory or emotional response.

Turning to more recent studies, Ifrán (2001), Suay (2002), Lorenzo (2003) and Cohen (2003), and based on experience in the mental training of motorcycling riders, the main psychological demands and the principal psychological strategies to be employed with each will be discussed. In this analysis, only those psychological aspects related to the specific demands of competition are detailed, not entering into other aspects where psychological work may also have an influence, in physical and technical training, for example. Although not exhausting all of the possibilities, the most frequent and significant psychological demands on motorcyclists are described below.

Pre-competition Anxiety

Spending three days preparing each race makes it is easy for riders to feel violently anxious prior to competitions. Carrying out training sessions to test whether motorbikes respond to the predicted demands and fighting for positions on the starting grid provoke differing emotions. Therefore, riders not only feel anxiety, but feel it at varying intensities according to each moment of competition: when they are training with two days to go, when they are training to qualify for a good position on the final day, when they are on the starting grid with five minutes remaining, etc. Riders' personalities, combined with these environmental conditioners makes them more or less inclined to suffer anxiety, and from a psychological perspective, create a complex situation which needs to be confronted. Certain psychological strategies, which help motorcyclists maintain equilibrium in their shows of anxiety, may be applied. Firstly, various forms of relaxation, together with good breathing management, controlling muscular tension-distension and relaxing thoughts can be conducted. Moreover, these relaxation techniques should be combined with continuous cognitive reasoning work on the different situations that will be faced during competitions. With these behavioural measures, riders can optimize the most positive moments for relaxation and diminish the risks of anxiety in potentially unnerving situations, assisting a greater adaptation through diminishing the thoughts which release anxiety. An appropriate place to conduct anxiety control exercises should be established in previous meetings between sport psychologists and riders. While a number of possibilities exist, the "time-outs" could be used for this (i.e. while riders wait for mechanics to make adjustments to the bike's setup or when they are fixing a small breakdown). Studying the riders' routines is usually sufficient to detect critical moments, where their arousal levels are high and anxiety is likely (some of these moments are described in the second part of the chapter).

Concentration

Two aspects of concentration usually concern riders. On the one hand, they want to remain highly focused during the race itself; and on the other hand, they want to be capable of maintaining this concentration during the three days of competition, not losing their focus in activities which do not provide them with any psychological benefit. With respect to the race itself, typical concentration training is required, based on three basic pillars which vary between riders according to their specific demands and personality traits:

1. Achieving an optimum arousal level which can be maintained throughout the race. In preliminary training sessions, and depending on the characteristics of the track, riders should detect their optimum arousal level, which will allow them to reach their maximum performance during the race. Therefore, riders should be trained to use subjective

evaluation scales (from a very low 0 arousal level, to a 10 for highly aroused), to produce the most adequate arousal level for each race (for example, one competition may require an arousal level 8 while others will only demand a level 6).

2. Breathing and "blank mind" exercises. These tasks enable riders to adequately prepare the mind to be "programmed" for the race, erasing any other thoughts and creating a state of total concentration.
3. Thoughts which assist concentration. This involves concentrating the mind on certain thoughts, normally orientated towards victory, the physical demands of races and specific technical factors related to driving, to ensure the cognitive process is focused only on the competition. Riders frequently establish objectives with their psychologist, with the aim of focusing the attention on what they need to do at each and every moment of the race, not leaving space for any other thoughts.

Regarding concentration during the three days of competition, two psychological strategies may be adopted:

1. Creating a plan of action. Planning the three days of competition ensures no idle moments exist, and riders have a sense of control through having something to do in each and every moment of the day.
2. Planning activities which are either of a sporting nature (increases energy levels) or fun for the rider. This technique optimizes time and puts riders in the best possible condition to compete.

Focusing Attention

When referring to the focusing of attention, riders usually demand to be attentive at all times to specific stimuli which they consider to have a positive influence on their performance throughout the race. Faced with a number of specific competitive circumstances, psychological work should endeavour to be equally specific in responding to these demands. Despite there being several possibilities, the most common option is to search for stimuli related to the race, with which riders feel most comfortable (e.g. technically: the noise of the engine, the inclination of the bike on bends, or the position they adopt on the different sections of the track). Riders may also be shown alternative stimuli related to the competition which they rarely work on (e.g. physically: sensations of effort, different pressures of the hands on the varying sections of the track or physical reactions in the legs when entering and coming out of bends). Finally, they may be taught to use stimuli of a psychological nature, a novelty for the majority of riders (e.g. increased concentration when entering a turn, increased emotional reaction when skidding off a bend, or improved motivation when overtaking a rival). The variations between the stimuli used will depend on the characteristics of each rider. To improve concentration, general work with physical and technical stimuli can be conducted, while more specific psychological stimuli can be established for each section of the race track.

Assuming Risks

To name but a few scenarios, motorcycling involves disputing races at high speeds, overtaking on the inside, "touching" bikes, skidding out of control, breaking recklessly to enter bends and speeding up to come off turns or even continuing a race with worn-down tyres. Therefore, one of the psychological characteristics displayed by the majority of riders is a capacity to take risks, which in some cases can cost them their lives. Therefore, riders do not want us to show them how to take risks, but rather show them how to do so in a more rational way. In other words, they need to learn how to objectify risks, measure them whenever possible, know where the limits of each situation lie and appreciate where imprudence could cause a fall. Classical psychological techniques, such as establishing objectives or decision-making, assist risk assumption, converting it into an almost "mathematical" process. Likewise, a "perception of risk scale" may be used, employing a subjective evaluation from 0 (no risk) to 10 (maximum risk) to allow riders to dominate risk-taking. This scale is elaborated on the premise that the riders themselves are the best authority on which risks they *can* and *should* assume. Hence, riders regulate the making of risky decisions, applying the aforementioned scale on the different sections of the track and varying situations in the race. The maximum risk (10 points) should be assumed only in those circumstances where it is favourable to do so, and where a fall has less importance than the benefits they could receive if they take the risk and it turns out well.

Capacity to Reproduce Images

One of the psychological techniques that motorcyclists should use is visualization or imagery, which allows them to experience the different emotions and feelings produced during training and competitions. This involves teaching riders, throughout various training sessions, how to visualize scenes. To begin with, neutral training and competition scenes will be used, later adding various combinations of light, colour, sound and touch. The objective of this technique is to enable riders to train technical and psychological aspects without having to get on the motorbike: mentally rehearsing the race tracks they will most likely compete on during the season and, fundamentally, the various physical, technical and psychological stimuli which should form part of their concentration, attention, arousal level and emotional state during the race. This provides riders with greater security when it comes to competing and allows them to focus more easily on the key aspects which determine their performance.

Emotional Self-control

In a high-risk sport such as motorcycling, the emotional state of riders becomes essential, not only for attaining determined performances and results, but also for their physical safety. Losing control emotionally during training or racing can lead to errors which could cause an immediate fall. Therefore, well-designed psychological training plans will always include strategies to maintain emotional self-control, fundamentally, in the most decisive or risky moments. Here, two types of psychological strategies may be used. Firstly, cognitive-behavioural strategies, based on what is known as "thought stoppage" (Dosil, 2004) seek to block thoughts on a key word (e.g. "stop"), image (e.g. the stop sign) or movement (slightly lowering the head when they are on the bike). Secondly, studying the rational and emotional components of riders allows them to contextualize races, confronting them with sufficient emotional toughness to "deaden" any situation which could potentially create emotional instability (in this case, the principles used in rational-emotive-based cognitive work are valid).

Establishing Objectives

In top-level motorcycling, the majority of riders already know exactly what they want to achieve (become World Champion). Nevertheless, and somewhat surprisingly, the essential principles of establishing objectives are rarely worked on. Therefore, while riders often propose broad objectives, sport psychologists can explain how breaking these down into manageable goals can help accomplish them. This psychological strategy involves a number of phases. Firstly, a series of technical, physical and psychological objectives for the season are established with the rider. These objectives are then defined in terms of specific results (titles, positions, races), refining them as much as possible to make focusing easier. Next, the season is divided into identical time periods (e.g. weeks) with corresponding sub-objectives. Time periods with no sub-objective are included, giving flexibility in case objectives take longer than planned to achieve. Once completed, personnel and team resource needs are established for each sub-objective, and the training required to achieve each goal is examined. Moreover, in parallel to this planning, evaluation systems are designed to identify whether the predicted objectives have been achieved. Finally, each established time period is evaluated with the aim of correcting potential deviations. Throughout the season, a rider's training should be covered by this objectives framework. Above all, these objectives should be attainable but sufficiently challenging, and always related to victory, the most important term in motorcycling.

Communication Skills

Riders should establish a multitude of communicative interactions with their team members. The most important interactions are those in which riders give information to their mechanics regarding any adjustments required to the motorbike. On the other hand, a large number of people living together during three days in clearly insufficient space can give rise to conflicts which could be resolved through adequate communication. Among this tangle of crossed communicative interactions is where the work of sport psychologists comes into play, endowing riders with specific strategies and working on aspects such as: active listening, the transmission of simple information, precise and free of unnecessary contributions, the analysis of communicational blockages and how to solve them, and applying empathetic attitudes in the entire communicational process. Moreover, all aspects included in the cognitive parameters of psychological behavioural programmes may be included, such as improving social skills, with a special emphasis on communication.

Decision-making

As already seen, riders are constantly making decisions, some allowing for certain reflection (e.g. choosing tyres for a race), while others are immediate (e.g. deciding whether to overtake on the inside or outside). The latter are the more complicated and riskiest decisions, but are also the most important for the development of any race. The work sport psychologists carry out with riders aims to automate the phases involved in opportune decision-making and enable them to accurately analyse situations in tenths of a second, which is often all the time they have. Therefore, sport psychologists contribute in two ways. Firstly, they teach riders to analyse the five decision-making phases. While the average person performs this process without realizing, riders must be made aware of it to attain the speeds required in race situations:

- identifying when a situation requires an immediate decision;
- analysing which aspects are related to the situation;
- eliminating irrelevant variables;
- strengthening the analysis with a few key variables; and finally,
- making an optimum decision according to the entire process.

This process must be practiced in simulated and real situations (where possible), working on the systematic repetition of racing scenarios, where riders are required to make precise and quick decisions. The aim is not only to mechanize what is learned at the first phase, but also to significantly speed up the development of the decision-making process.

Self-confidence

In this sport, it is fundamental for riders to be self-confident. Two types of self-confidence can be distinguished: confidence related to driving the motorbike and assuming risks without fear of suffering an accident; and confidence related to achieving results. The first type was analysed in the section '*Assuming Risks*'. The sport psychology work to be conducted with the second type is similar, and involves including the following aspects within riders' plans: analysis of achieved results, highlighting potentially positive aspects; analysis of errors committed in previous races and how to solve them with rational approaches; analysis of the risks riders must overcome to avoid losing self-confidence, and ensuring they are not suffering irrational feelings of insecurity. Moreover, riders must appreciate why irrational ideas exist, searching for key psychological points on which to base a greater "mental strength". They should discuss the different factors which impede their motivational development in competition and, above all, endeavour to be effective in establishing self-confidence, learning to avoid any emotionally unproductive components in the competitive development process.

Global Performance Evaluation

Few riders develop a global performance evaluation, but such a system, once learned, allows them to optimize their training and competitions. Having such a system becomes necessary when faced with unexpectedly poor performances, where riders have no logical explanation for what occurred. Specifically, the fundamental objective of this psychological strategy is to detect what is happening in each and every moment, with the aim of performing precise analysis to make it simpler to identify solutions. Along these lines, sport psychologists teach riders the following aspects: establishing general parameters which allow them to analyse race situations, including the three race dimensions (technical, physical and psychological); identifying formulas to score achieved results with time splits; distinguishing subsections in each of the established dimensions with the aim of increasing the precision of the achieved performance analysis; contemplating the overall scores and those of specific sections according to the situation under analysis; obtaining conclusions to carry out a pertinent and thorough analysis, leaving no alternative overlooked; and concluding with a proposal of options for improving future performances.

It must be stressed that the aforementioned psychological strategies will not be effective if applied only in specific moments and without predetermined objectives. Their effectiveness is achieved through forming part of a continuous and overall training process (as with any other area of training).

HOW PSYCHOLOGY CONTRIBUTES TO THE TRAINING OF RIDERS

The previous section aimed to demonstrate how psychological training can provide solutions to the various demands placed upon riders. The aspects in which sport psychology can positively influence their technical and physical training will now be discussed. The most relevant variables, which help to adequately contextualize how combined training systems (technical, physical and psychological) can benefit a rider's development, will be explained.

Planning Psychological Training Around the Overall Training Plan

First of all, it should be taken into account that psychological training aims to approach riders' preparation as a unified process (technical, physical and psychological), the only way of achieving peak performance. The entire planning sequence revolves around the principal results and performance objectives pursued by riders, and physical and psychological objectives are established accordingly to help achieve their principal aspirations, without disregarding the technical possibilities of their motorbikes. Therefore, any psychological training conducted in these areas should always be closely related to riders' overall aims.

Adherence to Physical Training

Generally speaking, physical training represents the most boring activity for sportspeople. Nevertheless, associating each training session with the attainment of physical and psychological objectives not only diminishes the possibility of them becoming monotonous, but may even transform them into enjoyable activities. More importantly, it assists riders to adhere to training sessions, positively influencing their performance and results. An example of uniting proposed objectives to physical training may involve asking a rider to run for 30 minutes at a determined rhythm, while visualizing various laps of the circuit they are going to race on, at a determined speed and with a precise competition rhythm.

Improving Global Planning

As described in the previous section, one of the psychological possibilities taught to riders is the planning of objectives, a technique which directly influences the planning of physical and technical training. In turn, this strategy improves the process of establishing objectives, which may be of a general or more specific nature—for a particular race, for example. Similarly, riders experience an increased sensation of security when shown how each facet of their training, whether it be physical, technical or psychological, forms part of a global effort to improve performance, in the quest for better results.

Strengthening Environmental Variables

At any given moment, independent of the aspect riders are working on, the people around them (team members, family and friends), the climate or the media presence constitute environmental conditioners which may affect their training development. Once again, the varying psychological strategies (e.g. concentration, planning or emotional self-control) can help manage these environmental variables, reinforcing performance and results in future competitions.

Planning Training on the Race Track

As seen previously, correctly distributing the time riders spend on the race track, from the initial preliminary training sessions to the moment of the race itself (some three days), is extremely important. In the case of failing to distribute this time adequately, feelings of anxiety, frustration, boredom and despair are likely to emerge. Various tasks can be prepared to control these emotions. Combining physical training exercises with psychological training activities allows riders to achieve an optimum technical state, improving performances and, consequently, the results attained.

Continuous Strategic Training

Finally, when riders first begin psychological training, strategic approaches are taught. All the work carried out in training (physical, technical and psychological) must be orientated towards attaining determined objectives which form part of the overall performance plan. Therefore, riders should plan and execute all of their training in a strategic manner.

THE COMPETITION: THE MIND–BODY–MOTORBIKE INTERACTION

Motorcycling races are the ultimate expression of the mind–body–machine interaction (psychology, physiology and technology). Although previous sections indicated the main characteristics of this relationship, as well as the psychological strategies to be employed, it is necessary to discuss some of the basic factors involved in specific aspects of competition.

Travelling to the Race Track

However accustomed riders become, transporting all the people and technical equipment which accompany motorcycling teams over long distances constantly generates stress and anxiety. During these journeys, the time riders spend thinking about what is at stake in the coming race, what times they need to produce in preliminary training, what form their rivals are in, or what strategy to use during the competition, are all aspects they need to manage with great self-control. Knowing how to confront these trips and make the most of their time can create a competitive advantage over rivals. For example, riders could psychologically train some preparative aspects of the race.

Three Days to Go, Making Contact with the Race Track

While team technicians prepare to begin training the following day, riders should familiarize themselves with the race track. Therefore, walking around the circuit, alone or accompanied by someone close to them, often proves a useful tactic. While passing through all the accessible areas, the boxes, the paddocks (even doing some physical exercise in these places), riders can identify the different demands these places are likely to pose the next day. The idea is to "make the track their own" and begin to generate the first positive sensations.

Two Days of Training Sessions

These sessions are key to achieving the required times for occupying a good position on the starting grid. Anything but treating these sessions as if they were the race itself is unacceptable, especially given that good performances at this stage normally have a positive influence on the final race performance. During these two days, riders endure free training in the morning (lasting 45 minutes in 125cc and 1 hour in 250cc and GP motorbike races) and official training or classification in the afternoon (with time limited to 30 minutes in 125cc, 45 minutes in 250cc and 1 hour in GP motorbikes). Riders should apply the psychological strategies they have been taught and which they have systematically trained, with the aim of quickly adapting to the various situations arising in training: racing several laps at a previously established speed, racing with qualifying tyres, analysing a new part being tried out on the bike, improving on a time towards the end of training sessions, evaluating why the bike presents a specific problem at a certain point on the track, etc.

Race Day: The Warm-up

Any professional rider knows that warming-up is a brief confirmatory training session prior to the race. In this session, the aim is for riders to confirm the bike's setup, check that the tyres have been selected correctly (among other aspects), "psychologically get into" the competition and "make the track their own" again (the warm-up lasts for 20 minutes). In the case of previous training sessions having not gone well, emotional control training should ensure riders do not try and make amends for everything at the last minute. This control allows them to perform systematic analysis to make the final opportune decisions for the race.

Emotional Intensity in the Box

The box is a physically miniscule place where various emotions bloom; these may be positive when riders observe that the bike is working well, when they feel comfortable and above all, when they achieve times which will guarantee a good classification. However, these emotions may be negative when the bike produces problems, if riders fail to produce the times required for a good classification, or if they consider the bike is not working as it should be and are unable to explain what is wrong. Regardless of the outcome, up until the moment the race begins and during the days that training lasts for, the emotional intensity of riders and their team members fluctuates. Therefore, riders must know how to control these emotional highs and lows, avoiding situations they know make them anxious, and increasing their self-confidence in delicate moments. The time between the warm-up and going out onto the track to race (almost 2 hours in 125cc and up to nearly 4 hours in GP motorbikes) is spent in the box, and constitutes an ideal moment to employ psychological strategies and commence the rider's "setup".

The Familiarization Lap and the Warm-up Lap

During the two laps prior to the start, riders should achieve two objectives. Firstly, they must discharge a large amount of the energy accumulated during the previous days of competition, regulating their arousal levels and adjusting them as required for the start of the race. Secondly, they need to familiarize themselves with the tarmac, the various twists and turns of the track and think about the potential breaking strategies they will use, how they will exit bends or where they will overtake. Following this familiarization lap, time is spent on the starting grid. This is a key moment in which many riders lose control, their anxiety levels suddenly shooting up. Once again, applying the previously described psychological strategies allows them to arrive at the start of the race in an ideal psychological state. During the warm-up lap, performing a final mental recap of the specific keys to each race enables riders to gain the sensation of control.

The Grid and the Start

The final moments prior to a race involve the formation on the grid and the start. These are considered as two crucial moments in pre-competition development (a good start can guarantee winning a race). One important factor not to be overlooked in psychological training is that riders are aware of their position on the starting grid the day before, enabling them to carry out the required mental training and visualization techniques ahead of time. Likewise, the importance of regulating arousal levels, without allowing irrational thoughts or ideas to enter the mind, should be stressed. In short, such is the precision required that psychological factors can make the difference between getting a good or bad start.

The Race Itself

Finally, after all the physical and psychological effort and exertion riders have undergone in the previous days, the race itself gets underway. At this moment, two issues come into play. Firstly, if all the psychological training has been developed adequately, good performances and even improved results can logically be expected. However, on the other hand, riders must know how to manage their own minds when they are in the race alone. Previously mentioned aspects such as continuous strategic actions, focusing attention on selected stimuli, maintaining concentration over all the laps and not losing self-confidence, acquire all their value during this time.

A summary of the competitive factors affecting riders is described below, including all the aspects analysed in the psychological training framework.

CONCLUDING REMARKS

This chapter has tackled a sport which is rarely dealt with by psychology, whether it be for its complexity, its uniqueness, or simply the fact that other sports are more socially accessible. This text has been written from an applied perspective, developing four keys to this sporting discipline:

- *The uniqueness of motorcycling* Firstly, the reality of this sport has been briefly described, including the characteristics of competition and the motorbikes themselves. Along these lines, three basic moments have been distinguished: free training, official training and the race itself. Together with the aforementioned point, various concepts and characteristics have been introduced to assist readers in better understanding this sporting discipline.
- *The general psychological demands placed on riders* The principal psychological demands most commonly described by motorcyclists have been discussed. Therefore, not only has each of these demands been defined and described, but also a series of basic guidelines for the psychological work with each one has been proposed. This chapter has endeavoured to offer a global image of the psychological training required in this sport, preparing for every eventuality.
- *The integration of psychology in physical and technical training* Throughout the text, a broad proposal of training has been offered (combining physical, technical and psychological aspects), based on the idea that these three facets, when united, enormously strengthen the performance of riders.
- *The specific psychological demands of competition* Finally, in keeping with the second point, a brief analysis of the specific psychological demands placed upon riders in competitions has been developed. To some extent, those demands directly related to competition constitute the most crucial psychological work to be carried out with motorbike riders.

In conclusion, sport psychology professionals approaching motorcycling should attend to the aforementioned sections with the aim of designing adequate psychological training programmes, which adapt optimally to the needs of each rider.

REFERENCES

Battista, I. (1995). *Istinto e ragione nella psicologia del motocilista*. Roma: Pieraldo.

Carzedda, G. & Massara, G. (1990). Caratteristiche personologiche in rapporto al fattore rischio negli sport motoristici. *Movimento, 6*(1), 14–20.

Cohen, R. (2003). El entrenamiento para el piloto de automovilismo y practicante de deportes de motor. Planificación y organización del entrenamiento psicofísico. *Revista Digital Efdeportes.com, 9*(63).

Delucchi, J.R. (1943). Psychological factors in the training of airplane pilots. *Journal of Aviation Medicine, 14*, 84–87.

Dosil, J. (2004). *Psicología de la actividad física y del deporte*. Madrid: McGraw-Hill.

Fuller, C.W. & Myerscough, F.E. (2001). Stakeholder perceptions of risk in motor sport. *Journal of Safety Research, 32*(3), 345–358.

Henry, F. (1941). Personality differences in athletes and physical education and aviation students. *Psychological Bulletin, 38*, 745.

Ifrán, H. (2001). Capacidades condicionales en el automovilismo. *Revista Digital Efdeportes.com, 7*(34).

Lorenzo, C. (2003). *Iniciación al motociclismo deportivo*. Barcelona: Hispano Europea.

Suay, F. (2002). Preparación psicológica para el motociclismo de velocidad. In J. Dosil (ed.), *El psicólogo del deporte*. Madrid: Síntesis.

PART VIII

Shooting Sports

CHAPTER 24

Psychological Aspects of Archery

Kathleen M. Haywood
University of Missouri-St Louis, USA

INTRODUCTION

Of all the sport skills, the shooting skills generally require the smallest and finest movements. Archers need only relax their fingers to shoot an arrow, once the bow is drawn and aimed. Rifle and pistol marksmen need only flex a finger. It is no wonder that, with such a minimal physical component, most attribute much of one's success in the shooting sports to psychological preparation.

There is another reason the mental aspects of performance are considered so important in the shooting sports. When competing in most sports, athletes who are anxious about the competition can run, throw or strike to dissipate some of their nervousness. The shooting sports are a stark contrast. One must be calm and steady! The typical responses to nervousness, such as increased heart rate and sweating, work against accurate performance.

The goal of this chapter is to review what is known about mental control of the archery shot and to explore the various mental skills that can be used to improve shooting performance. This process begins with a brief description of what is involved in shooting archery. Then, managing nervousness or anxiety while shooting is addressed, followed by the topics of focusing attention, building confidence, rehearsing mentally, and using aids to performance. Finally, suggestions for managing training schedules are made, including an example of retraining when archers find themselves anticipating release of the bowstring.

THE SPORT OF ARCHERY

Unlike most sports archery has only one action. Archers raise their bows, draw their bowstrings back, aim at the target, and release their bowstrings. Yet, to shoot accurately, archers must perform this single action with great care and precision. They must also be able to repeat their movements as exactly as humanly possible when archery events consist of an

The Sport Psychologist's Handbook: A Guide for Sport-Specific Performance Enhancement.
Edited by Joaquín Dosil. © 2006 John Wiley & Sons, Ltd.

accumulated score. Success in archery, then, is related to the degree archers can repetitiously make very fine and precise movements.

Generally, the archery shot proceeds this way. The archer assumes a stable stance, weight evenly distributed, with the bow-arm side toward the target. The bow is held in front of the body until the arrow is *nocked* onto the bowstring and the fingers of the string hand or the mechanical release are placed on the bowstring. The bow arm is then extended toward the target and the string hand draws the bowstring back toward the face. The string hand is *anchored* in contact with the face, jaw or neck. The archer aims, the bow arm gradually settling to a near-stationary position. The archer releases the bowstring so that it travels forward, projecting the arrow to the target. The follow-through is a maintenance of position so not to affect the arrow before it clears the bow.

Archers strive for "good form" in shooting, good form generally consisting of a position that aligns limbs and trunk in balanced or neutral positions (not flexed and not hyper-extended). For example, archers want to stand erect without bending at the waist. They want to extend the bow arm straight from the shoulder. Hunching the shoulder is problematic. They want the wrist of the string hand to be straight and aligned with the forearm. As the bowstring is drawn back, archers strive to keep the string arm in line with the shoulders, even while the elbow is flexed and shoulder horizontally extended.

A "T" is often used as a descriptor of desired shooting form (see Figure 24.1). Positions that are not aligned directly or at right angles are more difficult to replicate precisely. Holding a flexed or extended rather than a neutral, balanced position against resistance over a long time tends to fatigue the muscle group on one side of the joint relative to the group on the other side. For example, if an archer hunches the front shoulder during the draw and anchor (in effect, bending the crossbar of the "T" in Figure 24.1) the muscles that elevate the shoulder are tensed. Over hours of shooting these muscles can fatigue, causing alignment to vary from shot to shot. If "T" alignment is used, the muscles elevating and depressing the shoulder remain balanced. One group does not fatigue before the other.

The release of the bowstring and follow-through of the shot also are unique compared to most sport skills. For archers who draw the bow and hold the bowstring with their fingers, the "release" is simply a relaxation of the fingers so that the bowstring can move forward on its own and project the arrow. For those archers who use mechanical releases, the release might be a trigger squeeze. In either case, the movement is small and subtle. Follow-through is maintenance of form until the arrow has cleared the bow.

Interestingly, archers can have great success in the short term by exactly repeating their movements, even if some aspects of their form are poor. Achieving the same positions and repeating the same movements, shot-to-shot, are relatively more important than having classic form. The difficulty is that poor form is more difficult to maintain over the long-term and in the pressure of competition. Ultimately, archers strive to attain classic form as the one that will bring more long-term success.

The ideal situation for archers is to learn classic form and then to strive to repeat the associated movements and positions as exactly as possible. Electromyographs (EMGs) record the electrical activity of neuromuscular innervation of the underlying muscles by the nervous system via electrodes placed on the surface of the skin. A number of studies using EMGs have shown that consistency of movement is more strongly associated with good performance than the specific pattern or intensity of muscle use. Reproducing identical executions of the shot and constancy of neuromuscular control of the muscles are associated with higher performance levels (Clarys et al., 1990; Leroyer, van Hoecke & Helal, 1993; Martin, Siler

Figure 24.1 Classic archery form is sometimes characterized as "T" form because archers strive for right-angle and straight-line alignments of the body and limbs

& Hoffman, 1990). Coaches and teachers must motivate archers to work for classic form and reproducibility despite any short-term performance success with form flaws.

Most archers are taught early on to establish a mental checklist of steps to execute a shot. This is a natural outcome of the sequential nature of the archery shot and the need for exact duplication of positions and movements. An example of the cues representing these sequential steps for a beginning archer might be: stance; nock arrow onto string; place fingers on string; raise bow; draw string back; anchor the string hand; aim; relax to release string; maintain position. Such mental checklists change as archers become more experienced. Fundamental steps that become second nature with practice drop off the list. Finer points are added. Cues to offset individual bad habits during the draw are added, too. This is necessarily a brief description of archery technique. Detailed information is available elsewhere (Haywood & Lewis, 1997; Pellerite, 2001).

With the movements of archery being small and subtle, archery equipment takes on a relatively bigger role in excellent performance. It is good to understand what equipment has to do with performance and how archers regard their equipment. Archers develop a level of confidence in their equipment and naturally, for peak performance to occur, the level of confidence needs to be high. Also, archers are placed into classifications for competition based on their equipment, as well as individual factors, such as gender, age and physical disability.

The bow, the bow sight and the type of bowstring release are typically the pieces of equipment considered in forming competitive divisions. Archery bows generally fall into one of two categories: traditional bows consisting of a handle, limbs and a bowstring; and compound bows incorporating pulleys or cams and cables into the design of the bow. The reason for dividing archers based on the type of bow has to do with the number of pounds/kilograms of force archers overcome to draw the bow and hold the string at anchor. With traditional bows, archers meet increasing resistance as they draw the bowstring farther and farther back toward their anchor point. The resistance at the anchor point must continue to be met while the bow is aimed. With compound bows, resistance increases as the archer begins to draw the string, but soon reaches a peak and then decreases as the archer continues to draw the bowstring back, thanks to the off-center pulleys or cams to which the bowstring is attached through a cabling system. At the anchor point the archer must meet a level of resistance that is only a fraction of the pounds/kilograms of thrust the bow will impart to the arrow. This makes it possible for archers to shoot compound bows of many more pounds of thrust than they would be able to shoot with a traditional bow. The more pounds of thrust used to project the arrow, the flatter the arrow's trajectory can be to reach a distant target, minimizing the effect of any flaw in the archer's form or degree of misaim.

Archers can shoot with or without a bow sight. Obviously, more accurate shooting can be expected with a bow sight. Bow sights also can be of different types. Some have fixed sighting pins representing settings for selected distances. These are generally used for equipment classifications that mimic hunting conditions. Other bow sights have only one sighting pin but it can be adjusted before any shot, up, down, left or right. Finally, some bow sights incorporate magnifying lens, or "scopes", to facilitate precise aiming. All of these factors can be used as criteria for competition classifications.

Traditionally, archers curl two or three fingers around the bowstring and draw it back to their anchor point. Releasing the string ideally is a subtle extension of the fingers to achieve a smooth release. No matter how smooth the release, though, the bowstring tends to roll off the fingers, deflecting it slightly from a path directly forward. In reaction, the string travels back across that imaginary straight line, alternately crossing this line back and forth until it stops. This introduces some variation from shot to shot and also necessitates equipment adjustments and arrow-size selections to minimize the effects. To offset this variation, mechanical releases were invented. They permit the bowstring to travel more directly forward and allow for the most accurate shooting. Archers using their fingers to release and archers using mechanical releases are almost always placed in different divisions for competition.

While the rules of archery dictate some other equipment limitations, these are the major equipment factors in forming the competitive divisions in archery. Once an archer selects an equipment set-up appropriate for a particular competitive division, there are a host of adjustments that can be made to maximize the accuracy of shooting. These adjustments are collectively referred to as "tuning" one's equipment. With the need for such precision in archery comes a great need for archers to have equipment set-ups that are as precisely matched to their shooting form and physical attributes as possible. It is extremely important to archers to approach any event with equipment they feel maximizes their accuracy. It is tempting to blame a poor outcome on one's equipment being "out of tune". In archery, the temptation to externalize failure to equipment is greater than in some other sports, again, because the actions are so subtle and the complexity of the equipment so great. With this brief description of archery shooting and archery equipment in mind, consider the various mental skills that can be used to maximize shooting accuracy.

PSYCHOLOGICAL CONSIDERATIONS

As mentioned earlier, most shooters feel that psychological skills play a relatively bigger role in the shooting sports than in most sports. The movements of archery are very small and precise and the same movements are made on every shot. Many people can learn to shoot well, but not as many can compete well and the mental aspects of competing often make the difference. Sport psychologists need to consider a range of psychological aspects of physical performance and how they impact archery in particular. Among these are anxiety/arousal, attention, confidence, mental rehearsal and dependence on performance aids.

Nervousness is a common experience for all athletes. Recall that it is a particular challenge for archers because good shooting requires precise positions and movements as well as a steady hand for aiming. The physiological markers of nervousness are often increased heart rate and breathing, shaking, sweating and digestive system discomfort. Archers must learn effective interventions for dealing with their natural tendency to be nervous while competing or hunting. Given this, the next section begins with a discussion of managing anxiety and arousal level.

Managing Anxiety and Arousal Level in Archery

While being overly anxious about competing is undesirable, being completely calm is not necessarily ideal. Nervousness is a natural response to participating in an event that is important to an athlete and in which the athlete desires to do well. Anecdotally, many athletes report that if they ever stopped being nervous before competition, they would know it is time to retire because competing was no longer important to them! So, some level of anxiety is optimal for good performance and it is not surprising that this topic has been of interest to sport psychologists for some time. Many of the theories about anxiety and arousal in sport address performance aspects relevant to archery. These theories or models are briefly outlined below and then investigations of their application to archery or shooting are reviewed.

Before taking up the selected theories, realize that a barrier to discussions of anxiety and arousal in sport performance has been an interchange of terms. At times, "stress", "anxiety", and "arousal" have been equated when they actually represent slightly different concepts, both by definition and in practice. For example, competitors can report not *feeling* anxious while, in fact, markers of their physiological arousal (heart rate, respiration rate, perspiration rate) are elevated. In this discussion, arousal is considered to be physiological arousal, reflected by the aforementioned physiological markers. Two dimensions of anxiety are discussed: somatic anxiety, reflected in arousal; and cognitive anxiety, reflected in worry. Stress is a state of physical or psychological strain.

The Inverted-U Hypothesis

The predominant model for predicting performance level from arousal level has been the inverted-U hypothesis. This hypothesis predicts that best performance coincides with a moderate level of arousal while poorer performances come at arousal levels that are either too low or too high (Yerkes & Dodson, 1908). Hence, if graphed against arousal level, the curve representing performance takes on an inverted-U shape. The optimal level of arousal, though, is thought to shift, depending on whether the task requires large, vigorous or strength movements or it requires fine, small and precise movements. The optimal level would be higher in absolute terms for the former and lower for the latter. The ideal arousal level for a shooter, then, would be relatively low compared to other sports (Landers & Boutcher, 1993).

There have been challenges to the inverted-U hypothesis and other proposed hypotheses that some consider to be refinements of the inverted-U notion. Among the alternatives are: the individual zones of optimal functioning (IZOF) model (Hanin, 1980); the reversal theory (Kerr, 1985); the catastrophe theory (Hardy, 1990); and the multidimensional anxiety theory (Martens, Burton, Vealy, Bump & Smith, 1990). Some of these models have been tested with archers. Let's consider what tests of these models tell us about anxiety and arousal levels in archery competition.

The IZOF Model

The individual zones of optimal functioning (IZOF) model of anxiety and performance rejects the notion that optimal levels of anxiety can be described at the group level. Rather, every individual has an optimal range or zone of pre-competition anxiety for performing at their best. So, optimal anxiety can be low, moderate or high depending on the individual athlete. When pre-competition anxiety is outside this personal zone, poorer performance can be expected (Hanin, 1986, 1989; Salminen, Liukkonen, Hanin & Hyvonen, 1995). The IZOF model has been expanded to include positive and negative emotions other than anxiety (Hanin, 1997).

Robazza, Bortoli & Nougier (2000) applied the IZOF model in a case study of an elite archer. This female archer was a 6-year member of the Italian national archery team with international competitive experience. The investigators used measures of: pre-competitive somatic anxiety, cognitive anxiety and self-confidence; facilitating and inhibiting emotions; and heart rate. On one day, the archer identified up to 3 emotions associated with optimal performance and 3 emotions associated with past poor performances. She then rated the intensity of these 6 emotions plus pre-start tension, worry and self-confidence. This process was repeated over the next several days before practice sessions to allow for modifications. Her emotions then were measured 15 minutes before 2 practice and 5 competitive shooting rounds at a world archery championship. An interview was conducted after the event.

The investigators found that the archer's psychological condition worsened from practice to competition. In competition the "emotion" scores were similar to those for recalled events with poor outcomes and in fact the archer performed poorly at this event. The heart rate patterns recorded did not follow what is considered to be an optimal pattern and the archer confirmed her worsening trend in the post-event interview. Robazza et al. felt that this case study was consistent with the IZOF model: the archer fell outside her optimal zone and performed poorly.

Catastrophe Theory

Hardy's catastrophe theory maintains that the inverted-U relationship only holds when cognitive anxiety, or worry, is low (Hardy, 1990, 1996). When cognitive anxiety levels are high, increased physiological arousal is thought to quickly pass the optimal point and catastrophic deterioration of performance occurs with increasing physiological arousal. Robazza et al.'s case study (2000) also supports the catastrophe theory. The archer reported high tension and worry scores before competition and the outcome was one of the poorest experienced by the archer in major competitions.

The Reversal Model

The reversal model proposes that athletes alternate between metamotivational states, of which four separate pairs are described (Apter, 1982). They are: telic-paratelic; negativistic-conformist; mastery-sympathy; and autic-alloic. Kerr, Yoshida, Hirata, Takai & Yamazaki, (1997) explored the relationship between the telic-paratelic pair and felt arousal during archery performance. In the telic state individuals are serious, planned, goal-oriented, and prefer to experience low felt arousal. In the paratelic state, they are spontaneous, impulsive, not goal-oriented, and prefer to experience high felt arousal. Everyone reverses between these states, but individuals have a tendency to spend more time in one or the other, making them telic-dominant or paratelic-dominant.

Kerr et al. (1997) proposed that top archers prefer a telic state before performance and that a combination of telic state and low arousal would be conducive to optimal performance. They placed 28 members of a university archery club into combinations of telic-paratelic state and felt arousal. Half shot under both telic/low arousal conditions and paratelic/low arousal conditions, with the order counterbalanced. The other half shot under telic/high arousal and paratelic/high arousal conditions, again with order counterbalanced. States were manipulated through verbal instructions but confirmed with metamotivational state and arousal measures. Heart rate also was recorded. Although the manipulations were successful, archery performance did not follow the hypothesized pattern. Superior performance did occur, though, when the felt arousal level matched the level preferred in the telic or paratelic state, low felt arousal in the telic state and high felt arousal in the paratelic state.

It is interesting to contrast these notions to those of Herrigel (1953) in the well-known text, *Zen in the Art of Archery*. The principles of Zen Buddhism that Herrigel applied to archery hold that the "Zen" state is achieved when scoring well is of little concern. Rather, the archer strives to have bow, arrow and target come together as one with the archer (concentrated attention). This would be similar to the paratelic state of reversal theory in regard to goal orientation. On the other hand, the Zen state would be one of low arousal, consistent with the telic state (Kerr et al., 1997). Herrigel's principles, then, do not match those of the reversal model in regard to optimal archery performance.

Heart Rate Patterns

Heart rate is commonly recorded as a measure of physiological arousal. The heart beat pattern associated with good shooting performance has been determined through studies of these patterns during shooting. In experienced archers performing well, the heart rate decelerates in the seconds prior to release of the arrow (Landers et al., 1994). This pattern also has been observed in shooting (Hatfield, Landers, & Ray, 1987) and golf (Boutcher & Zinsser, 1990).

Why would heart rate decelerate before release? Several explanations have been offered. Lacey (1967; Lacey & Lacey, 1970, 1974) proposed the intake-rejection hypothesis, saying that heart rate decreases when attention is externally focused (intake task, as opposed to an internally oriented, rejection task). In the few seconds before arrow release experienced archers focus externally, on aiming. Another view is the cardiac coupling hypothesis, that deceleration comes with motor quieting so that stimuli can be detected. In archery, motor quieting would reduce disturbance from heart pumping. Another suggestion, that heart rate deceleration results from respiratory sinus arrhythmia, has not been well supported by observations, since shooters demonstrate a variety of breathing patterns during the shot.

While heart rate deceleration in experienced shooters performing well is an established pattern, it is not clear that archers can be taught the pattern. Robazza, Bortoli & Nougier (1997) successfully taught young experienced archers to modify their physiological arousal level before shooting. It wasn't clear, though, that these modifications impacted the heart deceleration pattern (although the pattern was observed in individuals) or performance outcomes among the group of archers.

In a subsequent study, Robazza, Bortoli & Nougier (1998) taught relaxation and energizing procedures to 10 women archers on the Italian national team. The archers then shot under a variety of conditions: an optimal condition to achieve the best score possible; a delaying condition in which archers waited an extra 5 seconds before releasing their arrows; a blind shooting condition at a short distance; mimicked shooting without equipment; high-arousal shooting in which the energizing procedures were used; and low-arousal shooting in which the relaxing procedures were used. The arousal manipulations were achieved by: changes in breathing; changes in muscular tension; and changes in activity level (performing movements vs. quietly blocking external cues with visual attention on the ground).

Heart rate deceleration was found in the optimal, blind and simulated (mimicked) conditions. This might reflect the realism that can be achieved in mental rehearsal and simulated shooting conditions. Archers scored best in the optimal condition and worst in the delayed condition. Performance also was poor in the high-arousal condition. There was no difference in performance between optimal and low-arousal conditions. Perhaps the optimal condition was characterized by low arousal, particularly because the optimal condition was not an actual competitive setting. Modifying arousal level is likely to be most helpful when archers realize they are not at an optimal level for competition.

Taken together, examinations of anxiety and arousal seem to indicate that a relatively low level of arousal is ideal for shooting, but that individual archers might have their own zone of optimal arousal level. Psychologists can help archers monitor their arousal levels and develop an awareness of the level that an archer associates with their own optimal performance. Archers can be taught to modify arousal levels and, for competitors who approach competition with anxiety or worry about their level of preparedness, such modifications might help them achieve success. Psychologists also can teach archers to use mental rehearsal or mimicking so that they can practice these modifications to arousal level. Mental rehearsal or mimicking can be used to practice these modifications. It is likely that the relatively low level of arousal seemingly ideal for archery goes hand-in-hand with a facilitation of ideal attentional focus. This additional important psychological consideration is reviewed next.

Attentional Focus while Shooting

Another important mental aspect of shooting is attentional focus. Most theories of skill-learning address attentional focus. Generally, such theories include a transition from an early cognitive stage to a final automatic stage. Beginners must focus intentionally on perceptual cues and consciously control their movements. With practice, skilled performers come to execute their movements relatively automatically. They can focus on the goal of their task and attend less to the conscious regulation of their movements. While theorists have differed in the number of learning stages proposed and their specific characteristics, automaticity at the most advanced and experienced stage of skill performance has remained a common theme over decades of research (Abernethy & Russell, 1987; Fitts & Posner, 1967; Starkes, 1987; Wrisberg, 1993).

EMG recordings during the archery shot confirm the automaticity of skilled shooting. Hennessy and Parker (1990) positioned electrodes over 7 upper extremity muscles in 2 experienced archers and examined their electrical activity from 120msec before release of the bowstring to 60msec after release. They observed a complex pattern of neuromuscular coordination that revealed anticipation of changes in forces at the various joints at release of the bowstring. Likely, these changes in muscle tension 60msec before the release stabilize and protect the joints. They are carried out at subconscious level.

An automatic stage of performance has several implications for shooting sports. One obvious implication is that sufficient practice should lead shooters to a stage requiring less conscious thought about the specific movements needed to execute a shot. Perhaps a more significant implication is that, once shooters have achieved this automatic stage, conscious thought and analysis during the execution of a shot might be a detriment to good performance.

These notions have been examined empirically through the tool of the electroencephalo-gram (EEG). The EEG measures changes in the electrical voltage in the brain's cortex through electrodes placed on the scalp (Hatfield & Hillman, 2001; Lawton, Hunt, Saarela & Hatfield, 1998). Archery, pistol shooting and rifle marksmanship often are the sports chosen in EEG studies, since performers are stationary and make small, subtle movements.

Generally, empirical studies have confirmed that expert shooters perform with little conscious regulation or thinking about the actions involved in shooting. Early EEG studies focused on fluctuations of electrical voltage in the left temporal region of the cortex since that region is active during cognitive analysis but quieter during visual-spatial task performance (Smith, McEvoy & Gevins, 1999).

EEG studies examine component frequencies of the fluctuating voltages, in particular the alpha band (8 to 13 Hz) and low-beta band (13 to 22 Hz). Increasing alpha power in the left temporal region leading up to the release or trigger has been associated with expertise, superior performance and with increased practice/improved performance (Hatfield et al., 1984; Haufler, Spalding, Santa Maria & Hatfield, 2000; Kerick et al., 2001; Landers et al., 1994). On the other hand, excessively high alpha power has been associated with poorer performance and rejected shots stopped by the shooter (Hillman, Apparies, Janelle & Hatfield, 2000; Salazar, Landers, Petruzello & Han, 1990a; Salazar, Landers, Petruzello, Crews and Kubitz, 1990b). So, low levels of alpha power in the left temporal region might reflect ongoing cognitive analysis of skill being executed; moderate levels a reduction of cognitive analysis; and high levels a less-than-optimal engagement in the task (Deeny, Hillman, Janelle & Hatfield, 2003).

Of course, regions of the brain other than the left temporal region are involved in executing a shot. EEG coherence analysis recently has been used to measure functional communication between different brain areas. High EEG coherence indicates that different areas of the cortex are communicating while low coherence implies autonomy or independent activity of the regions. The expectation is that as a skill is learned coherence would *decrease* as various areas of the cortex specialize and functional communication between those areas decreases. In the shooting sports, decreased EEG coherence would be expected during the aiming period. Motor areas of the brain execute the task with little verbal or analytical processing to interfere with the execution.

Deeny et al. (2003) recently studied EEG coherence in expert vs. skilled rifle marksmen. Low-alpha, high-alpha and low-beta coherence between premotor regions and the left temporal region of their brains were recorded during a four-second aiming period prior to the shot. Generally, the experts demonstrated lower coherence between the left temporal region and motor control regions. The implication is that in expert marksmen there is a lower level of cognitive activity during execution of movement.

Studies of changing electrical voltage in the cortical areas of the brain during shooting generally agree with reports of superior shooters. Robazza and Bortoli (1998) used qualitative research techniques to identify the mental factors and strategies used by members of the 1996 Italian Olympic team. Expert shooters report the absence of thinking or conscious regulation of their movements during performance at a high level.

In working with archers, then, sport psychologists can expect that with developing skill will come "automatic" performance. Once full draw is reached little conscious regulation of the release is needed, freeing the archer to focus on aiming. For an archer who has advanced to the automatic stage through repetitious practice, analysis of how a shot is set up once an archer is at full draw is counterproductive, detracting from a concentrated focus on aiming. A poor performance result might be due to the archer attempting to analyze their shooting during execution of the shot. Sport psychologists can work with archers to better shift their attention to aiming and to maintain their attention on that single concern.

This research also tells us that any "retooling" of an archer's technique needs to come during a period of preparation for competition, with sufficient practice time to allow new positions or movements (technique refinements) to become automatic before the competition. An archer must accept, at the time of competition, that their technique and equipment are what they are and that attentional focus should be on aiming alone, once full draw is achieved. Competition is not the time to make technique refinements. Sport psychologists can assist archers in "centering" their concentration before competition. For archers who tend to analyze their form during competition, psychologists can suggest the centering include a "release" from worry or thoughts about form, technique and equipment. Thought should shift to a readiness for total focus on aiming. Certainly confidence is related to a trust that needed movements will be executed automatically. This mental factor is considered next.

Building Confidence in Archers

Self-confidence often has been identified as a discriminating factor between successful and unsuccessful performers (Jones, Hanton & Swain, 1994). It is not surprising, then, that the Italian Olympic archers interviewed by Robazza and Bortoli (1998) frequently named components of "positive expectation" as an important pre-competitive psychological factor in good performance. This general dimension consisted of confidence, competitiveness, being determined, feeling able and being motivated. An outstanding American archer interviewed by Vealey and Walter (1994) named self-confidence as *the* most critical mental factor to success. Likely, a confident archer is less likely to second-guess their technique and equipment during shooting, is less worried about the outcome of competition and is free to focus on aiming.

How do archers build confidence? The Olympic archers interviewed by Robazza and Bortoli (1998) believed that their repetitive practice built a high level of technical preparation and was a prerequisite to sustaining confidence. One reported building confidence by "shooting a lot". The American archer interviewed by Vealey and Walter (1994) believed his high ability was attributable in part to his extensive physical practice regimen. Scoring well in practice probably gives archers the confidence to enter competition with a positive expectation.

D-Arripe-Longueville, Saury, Fournier and Durand (2001) studied the interactions between male archers on the French national team and their coach at two important competitions. An interesting finding was the importance given to autonomous functioning by both archers and the coach. While the coach was helpful in overcoming difficulties, aid from the coach never precluded the archer's own analysis. The coach's help was viewed as an instrumental tool when it allowed for archers to arrive at solutions themselves. Since even in elite competition it was not possible for the coach to watch each and every shot of every archer, archers must be capable of analyzing their shooting and arriving at the necessary adaptations on their own initiative when adjustments are necessary. This autonomous functioning is probably an additional aspect of building confidence. Archers who rely on a teacher or coach to supply direct solutions cannot build the confidence to shoot well, especially when the teacher or coach is not immediately available with a solution.

Sport psychologists can apply confidence-building exercises to assist archers. Stopping negative thoughts and verbalizing or thinking them as positive expectations can build confidence. Goal-setting can build confidence when the goals are realistic and attainable. Goals for archery do not always have to involve scoring. When archers are working on aspects of their technique, for example, goals can be set for length of practice with a particular technique.

Mental rehearsal, especially of successful shooting, also can build confidence and a positive expectation for shooting success. Use of mental rehearsal and imagery in archery are reviewed next.

Mental Rehearsal and Imagery of the Shot

Mental rehearsal and imaging, especially of successful performance, is a common intervention for athletes. Archery and the shooting sports probably are among the sport contexts easiest for athletes to image. Obviously, the setting for target shooting changes very little. The shooting sports are what is often called a "closed" environment: nothing an archer does in executing a shot is influenced by an opponent and the target is not moving. Wind or rain can change the environment, but few other external factors impact shooting. So, it is relatively easy to construct a mental image of shooting conditions that are very close to those in competition. Recall, too, that Robazza et al. (1998) observed the classic heart rate deceleration pattern, found during *actual* shooting, in *simulated* shooting, too.

The value of mental rehearsal and imaging might depend on the individual archer. When Robazza and Bortoli (1998) interviewed their eight Olympic archers, three reported visualizing themselves from an internal perspective, two also saying they "saw" the arrow traveling to the bull's eye, and one reported visualizing from an external perspective. One archer, though, avoided imagery, reporting that trying to visualize shooting "makes me feel uncertain". It is unknown whether this archer ever undertook a systematic program of imagery or whether this comment represents a lack of success with spontaneous imagery.

Given the successful use of mental rehearsal and imagery by many athletes, including archers, it is likely that a systematic program of imaging performance, practiced in ideal conditions, could help archers. Those most likely to benefit would be archers who need to build confidence by imaging successful performance; those who want to practice switching their attentional focus away from distracting thoughts and to aiming; and those tending to approach competition at too high an arousal level, who can apply relaxation techniques and then mentally rehearse shooting.

Aids to Archery Performance

All athletes are tempted to use aids to performance. In many sports, the difference between first place and second place is very small. This is particularly true in archery, where that difference can be one point, determined by whether one arrow lands in a higher scoring zone on the target or misses it by a millimeter. In the shooting sports, too, the contribution of physical training is not as great as in many sports, so shooters dedicated to sound physical training cannot separate themselves from others by as wide a margin. It is important to consider the use of aids to archery performance, at least briefly, because their use interacts with a shooter's mental approach to competition.

Perhaps the aid most frequently tried by archers over the years is alcohol. Archers know that steadiness is needed to shoot well. Facing the nervousness associated with archery competition, some archers believe alcohol can steady the hands in shooting. Reilly and Halliday (1985) studied the effect of ingesting alcohol on a series of tasks related to archery shooting: reaction time; extended arm steadiness; isometric arm strength; muscle endurance; and an electromyogram (EMG) profile during release of a bowstring. The tasks were performed by nine male participants in each of four conditions: sober, placebo, 0.02 per cent blood alcohol concentration (BAC), and 0.05 per cent BAC. Arm steadiness and reaction time both deteriorated in the alcohol conditions. There were no differences in performance on the strength and endurance tasks across the four conditions. Greater muscle relaxation was recorded on the EMG in the BAC conditions, but there were notable individual differences among the participants. Overall, and considering these were not actual shooting conditions, a strong case cannot be made for improving performance by ingesting alcohol.

Norland, Bergman and Archer (1999) investigated the use of a pre-training sensory isolation session, or restricted environmental stimulation technique (REST). In this particular version the archer lay in a tank filled with saltwater of a very high salt concentration. Light and noise were reduced to enhance relaxation. Twenty men and women archers either relaxed in an armchair or reclined in the REST tank for 45 minutes before shooting. There were no performance differences between the two pre-training sessions, but with REST archers perceived less exertion during shooting, the better archers were more consistent, and some archers had lower arm muscle tension.

Hypnosis is another aid archers sometimes use. Traditional hypnosis can lower arousal level and induce relaxation so that other mental skills, such as imagery, can be applied more effectively. Reducing arousal below the optimal level before performance, though, might work against good performance. Robazza and Bortoli (1995) combined the use of traditional hypnosis after practice with the use of active-alert hypnosis after and during practice. Active-alert hypnosis replaces suggestions of relaxation and drowsiness with suggestions of alertness and readiness for activity. They worked with a male archer who had 17 years of archery experience. The archer improved his shooting performance after 20 weeks of mental training.

Leroyer et al. (1993) suggested, based on their EMG study, that archers could benefit from biofeedback during training. They fed an auditory signal back to archers to help them attain regularity and consistency in increasing muscle tension through to the release. For five of six archers, motor control regularity improved with biofeedback. Such training requires the necessary equipment and more information is needed on how well the training transfers to improved performance.

It is common to find variability among athletes with the use of performance aids. Some seem to benefit while others do not. This might reflect the initial need of an archer for the particular type of assistance the aid provides. Also, short-term gain from a performance aid often does not translate to sustained success for an archer. A consideration in the use of performance aids must be the dependence on an aid the archer could potentially develop. An archer who comes to believe they cannot perform well without the performance aid is not likely to perform well if the aid is withdrawn or unavailable. Particularly problematic would be a dependence on substances, use of which is banned for competition. Over time, archers likely can be more successful by developing strong mental skills that they control than by depending on performance aids that might not be consistently available. Sport psychologists should play a role in leading archers away from an overdependence on performance aids and toward the development of strong mental skills.

TRAINING AND COMPETITIVE SCHEDULES FOR ARCHERY

In many sports athletes perform a variety of skills. For example, they might execute a serve, a forehand, a backhand, a volley, an overhead, and so on. Each stroke can be practiced and practice settings can be created for each. The practice drill might not be specifically like competition. For example, a tennis player can practice hitting forehands crosscourt, then "down the line", then deep into the opponent's court, and so on. In the shooting sports, the practice setting and the competitive setting all tend to be the very same and, of course, the goal is to execute each shot the very same! So, while archers identify particularly important competitions and work toward them, their practice tends to be identical to competition.

At the same time, it is clear that research on shooting emphasizes the importance of reaching an automatic stage, especially of the release, through repetitious shooting. Once at this stage, conscious attention to aiming alone is associated with excellent performance. Archers must trust that their technique and their equipment are what they are when they enter a competition. Engaging in conscious analysis at a time they should be aiming detracts from good performance. Obviously, then, archers who find it necessary to adjust a part of their technique, to change equipment or to adjust their existing equipment should do so well before a competition. Repetitive practice is needed to make the new technique automatic so that it can be executed in competition with little conscious monitoring. Sport psychologists can work with archers as a competitive event nears, to ensure that they are shifting their attention to aiming once at full draw, maintaining that attention on aiming and not shifting to an analysis of "executing" the release.

Since "practice" in archery is so much like "competing" in archery, it is easy for archers to overemphasize scoring. If practice is always on a scoring target, archers tend to "keep score" and desire to *make* good scores happen. They often overlook the value of practicing an aspect of technique or a smooth release without scoring. The constant desire to score well and to score almost every time one participates often leads many archers to develop shooting flaws. These are collectively known as "target panic". The next section reviews target panic as an example of a common problem faced by most archers and the role of sport psychologists in helping them overcome the problem.

The Example of Target Panic

Many, if not most, archers experience one of many symptoms of "target panic" some time during their careers. Target panic is an anticipation of the release that results in a disruption of a smooth and accurate shot. When archers anticipate release, they gradually begin to move before the arrow has cleared the bow, influencing the arrow's flight. Target panic can range in severity and frequency of occurrence. Consider some of the symptoms of target panic, keeping in mind that archers can have one or more symptoms:

- *Flinching* is sudden movement immediately prior to or during the release, often of the bow arm, resulting in a errant shot.
- *Snap shooting* is releasing immediately when the bow sight first crosses the bull's eye and before the archer has settled the sight on the bull's eye; this symptom may advance to the archer releasing even before the sight gets to the bull's eye.
- *Freezing* is inability to move the sight from a spot off the bull's eye to the bull's eye (or, in hunting to the "kill" zone); inability to release even when the sight is settled in the bull's eye; or, with archers who use a device called a "clicker" that promotes increasing back tension, inability to move the arrow through the clicker.
- *Punching* is jerking a mechanical release in an effort to release immediately, or for archers who hold the bow string with their fingers, plucking the bowstring or moving the release hand *forward* (toward the target) upon release.

Obviously, these are all actions that detract from accuracy. When the symptom becomes severe and frequent an archer can struggle, first to shoot well, but eventually to enjoy shooting at all. Again, these problems result from an archer anticipating the release of the bowstring. This is somewhat to be expected in a shooting sport. After all, there is only one "skill" in archery and it is repeated over and over!

Pellerite (2001) believes that this anticipation comes from archers trying to consciously do two things at once: aim and cause the release to happen. Recall from our earlier discussion of attentional focus that expert shooters, when performing well, exhibit little cognitive activity. That is, they trust their movements to occur automatically so that they are free to aim. Pellerite suggests that once archers reach full draw, they begin aiming. When the sight moves to the center of the target, they are anxious to release. They try to *cause* the release, meaning of course that they have brought the release action back to a conscious level. They are now trying to regulate two things consciously and simultaneously when, in fact, the conscious mind can attend to only one thing at a time. When a bad shot results, the belief that the release must be better controlled is reinforced. A fear of missing can develop and archers then no longer trust the release to happen subconsciously.

The release of the bowstring must be relegated to the subconscious mind. Archers need to focus their attention on aiming and trust the subconscious to execute the release, programmed through thousands and thousands of repetitions. Once archers commit to a shot, they must consciously aim and trust their subconscious minds to control release of the bowstring.

Pellerite (2001, 2003) suggests that once target panic has become a problem for an archer, the remedy is to "reprogram" a subconscious control of the release, by hundreds of shot repetitions over weeks, in front of a backstop without a target. After this, a "bridge" program of hundreds of shots over additional weeks is needed to move from large targets and close distances to regulation targets and competition distances. If any step in the transition tends to bring back the target panic symptom, the archer must go back to previous step and spend more time in repetitious practice. In terms of the skill-learning theories reviewed earlier, archers must begin again at a cognitive stage and, through thousands of repetitions, arrive again at the automatic stage. Scoring during this rebuilding program would only set archers back in their efforts to develop trust in an automatic release.

Sport psychologists can play an important role in helping archers with target panic. First, psychologists can help archers identify whether a short-term solution during the competitive season is possible or whether a longer-term reprogramming without scoring is needed. If a short-term solution is possible, psychologists can help archers determine their optimal arousal level and practice modifying their level to reach the optimum. They can work with archers on concentration and focus, moving from exercises in shifting and maintaining attention to shooting with the attention solely on aiming.

If a long-term reprogramming intervention is needed, psychologists must first help archers establish long-term goals. It is natural for archers to want to score, even if just to "see how they are progressing". Scoring, though, sets back the reprogramming, so archers must commit to a length of time without participation in leagues, hunts or competitions. As archers move to the end of the reprogramming and begin to shoot at targets again, psychologists can again help with the arousal level and concentration exercises. An advantage should be that archers reprogramming their automatic release without shooting at a target should find it easy to approach their practice with little anxiety. After all, it is the scoring that typically causes anxiety! This should be an ideal time to reinforce a level of arousal that is relatively low.

SUMMARY

Archery and other shooting sports are different from many sports. The movement skills executed are small, fine movements and these movements are repeated as identically as possible on each and every execution. The approach to shooting associated with excellent archery performance is characterized by: a relatively low level of arousal, although the level itself might be individualistic; a facility for shifting attention, once full draw is reached, to aiming alone; and the avoidance of any analysis of the movement necessary to release the bowstring. To avoid a cognitive analysis of how to make the release happen, archers must be confident and trust that thousands of repetitions allows their subconscious minds to control the release.

Sport psychologists can play an important role in supporting archers. They can help archers acquire the skills of regulating arousal level, shifting and maintaining attention, mentally rehearsing or imaging to build confidence, setting realistic goals, and learning to trust their preparation for competition. Strong mental skills are a vital component of archery. At the highest levels of competition it is likely that mental skills determine the outcome of a competition as much as, if not more, than any other single factor.

REFERENCES

Abernethy, B. & Russell, D.G. (1987). Expert-novice differences in an applied selective attention task. *Journal of Sport Psychology, 9*, 326–345.

Apter, M.J. (1982). *The Experience of Motivation: The Theory of Psychological Reversals.* London: Academic Press.

Boutcher, S.H. & Zinsser, N.W. (1990). Cardiac deceleration of elite and beginning golfers during putting. *Journal of Sport and Exercise Psychology, 12*, 37–47.

Clarys, J.P., Cabri, J., Bollens, E., Sleeckx, R., Taeymans, J., Vermeiren, M., van Reeth, G. & Voss, G. (1990). Muscular activity of different shooting distances, different release techniques, and different performance levels, with and without stabilizers, in target archery. *Journal of Sport Sciences, 8*, 235–257.

D-Arripe-Longueville, F., Saury, J., Fournier, J. & Durand, M. (2001). Coach-athlete interaction during elite archery competitions: an application of methodological frameworks used in ergonomics research to sport psychology. *Journal of Applied Sport Psychology, 13*, 275–299.

Deeny, S.P., Hillman, C.H., Janelle, C.M. & Hatfield, B.D. (2003). Cortico-cortical communication and superior performance in skilled marksmen: an EEG coherence analysis. *Journal of Sport and Exercise Psychology, 25*, 188–204.

Fitts, P.M. & Posner, M.I. (1967). *Human Performance.* Belmont CA: Brooks/Cole.

Hanin, Y.L. (1980). A study of anxiety in sports. In W.F. Straub (ed.), *Sport Psychology: An Analysis of Athlete Behavior* (pp. 236–249). Ithaca, NY: Mouvement.

Hanin, Y.L. (1986). State-trait anxiety research on sports in the USSR. In C.D. Spielberger & R. Diaz-Guerrero (eds), *Cross Cultural Anxiety* (vol. 3, pp. 45–64). Washington, DC: Hemisphere.

Hanin, Y.L. (1989). Interpersonal and intragroup anxiety in sports. In D. Hackfort & C.D. Spielberg (eds), *Anxiety in Sports: An International Perspective* (pp. 19–28). New York: Hemisphere.

Hanin, Y.L. (1997). Emotions and athletic performance: Individual Zones of Optimal Functioning model. *European Yearbook of Sport Psychology, 1*, 29–72.

Hardy, L. (1990). A catastrophe model of performance in sport. In J.G. Jones & L. Hardy (eds), *Stress and Performance in Sport* (pp. 81–106). New York: Wiley.

Hardy, L. (1996). Testing the predictions of the cusp catastrophe model of anxiety and performance. *Sport Psychologist, 10*, 140–156.

Hatfield, B.D. & Hillman, C.H. (2001). The psychophysiology of sport: a mechanistic understanding of the psychology of superior performance. In R. Singer, H. Hausenblas & C. Janelle (eds), *Handbook of Sport Psychology* (pp. 362–386). New York: John Wiley & Sons.

Hatfield, B.D., Landers, D.M. & Ray, W.J. (1984). Cognitive processes during self-paced motor performance: an electroencephalographic profile of skilled marksmen. *Journal of Sport Psychology, 6*, 42–59.

Hatfield, B.D., Landers, D.M. & Ray, W.J. (1987). Cardiovascular-CNS interactions during a self-paced, intentional state: elite marksmanship performance. *Psychophysiology, 24*, 542–549.

Haufler, A.J., Spalding, T.W., Santa Maria, D.L. & Hatfield, B.D. (2000). Neuro-cognitive activity during a self-paced visuospatial task: comparative EEG profiles in marksmen and novice shooters. *Biological Psychology, 53*, 131–160.

Haywood, K.M. & Lewis, C.F. (1997). *Archery: Steps to Success* (2nd edn). Champaign, IL: Human Kinetics.

Hennessy, M.P. & Parker, A.W. (1990). Electromyography of arrow release in archery. *Electromyography and Clinical Neurophysiology, 30*, 7–17.

Herrigel, E. (1953). *Zen in the Art of Archery*. London: Routledge & Kegan Paul.

Hillman, C.H., Apparies, R.J., Janelle, C.M. & Hatfield, B.D. (2000). An electrocortical comparison of executed and rejected shots in skills marksmen. *Biological Psychology, 52*, 71–83.

Kerick, S.E., McDowell, K., Hung, T., Santa Maria, D.L., Spalding, T.W. & Hatfield, B.D. (2001). The role of the left temporal region under the cognitive motor demands of shooting in skilled marksmen. *Biological Psychology, 58*, 263–277.

Kerr, J.H. (1985). The experience of arousal: a new basis for studying arousal effects in sport. *Journal of Sport Sciences, 3*, 169–179.

Kerr, J.H., Yoshida, H., Hirata, C., Takai, K. & Yamazaki, F. (1997). Effects on archery performance of manipulating metamotivational state and felt arousal. *Perceptual and Motor Skills, 84*, 819–828.

Jones, G., Hanton, S. & Swain, A. (1994). Intensity and interpretations of anxiety symptoms in elite and non-elite sports performers. *Personality and Individual Differences, 17*, 657–663.

Lacey, J.I. (1967). Somatic response patterning and stress: some revision of activation theory. In M.H. Appley & R. Trumbull (eds), *Psychological Stress: Issues in Research* (pp. 170–197). New York: Appleton-Century-Crofts.

Lacey, B.C. & Lacey, J.I. (1970). Some autonomic-central nervous system interrelationships. In P. Black (ed.), *Physiological Correlates of Emotion* (pp. 205–261). New York: Academic Press.

Lacey, B.C. & Lacey, J.I. (1974). Studies of heart rate and other bodily processes in sensorimotor behavior. In P.A. Obrist, A.H. Black, J. Brener & L.V. Dicara (eds), *Cardiovascular Psychophysiology*. Chicago: Aldine.

Landers, D.M. & Boutcher, S.H. (1993). Arousal-performance relationships. In J.M. Williams (ed.), *Applied Sport Psychology: Personal Growth to Peak Performance* (2nd edn; pp. 170–184). Mountain View, CA: Mayfield.

Landers, D.M., Han, M., Salazar, W., Petruzzello, S.J., Kubitz, K.A. & Gannon, T.L. (1994). Effects of learning on electroencephalographic and electrocardiographic patterns in novice archers. *International Journal of Sport Psychology, 25*, 313–330.

Lawton, G.W., Hunt, T.M., Saarela, P. & Hatfield, B.D. (1998). Electroencephalography and mental states associated with elite performance. *Journal of Sport and Exercise Psychology, 20*, 35–53.

Leroyer, P., van Hoecke, J. & Helal, J.N. (1993). Biomechanical study of the final push–pull in archery. *Journal of Sports Sciences, 11*, 63–69.

Martens, R., Burton, D., Vealy, R.S., Bump, L.A. & Smith, D.E. (1990). Development and validation of the Competitive State Anxiety Inventory-2. In R. Martens, R.S. Vealey & D. Burton (eds), *Competitive Anxiety in Sport* (Part III). Champaign, IL: Human Kinetics.

Martin, P.E., Siler, W.L. & Hoffman, D. (1990). Electromyographic analysis of bow string release in highly skilled archers. *Journal of Sports Sciences, 8*, 215–221.

Norland, T., Bergman, H. & Archer, T. (1999). Primary process in competitive archery performance: Effects of flotation REST. *Journal of Applied Sport Psychology, 11*, 194–209.

Pellerite, B. (2001). *Idiot Proof Archery*. Gahanna, OH: Robinhood Video Productions.

Pellerite, B. (2003). When the empty bale fails and your target panic returns! *The US and International Archer, 22*, 164–166.

Reilly, T. & Halliday, F. (1985). Influence of alcohol ingestion on tasks related to archery. *Journal of Human Ergology, 14*, 99–104.

Robazza, C. & Bortoli, L. (1995). A case study of improved performance in archery using hypnosis. *Perceptual and Motor Skills, 81*, 1364–1366.

Robazza, C. & Bortoli, L. (1998). Mental preparation strategies of Olympic archers during competition: an exploratory investigation. *High Ability Studies, 9*, 219–235.

Robazza, C., Bortoli, L. & Nougier, V. (1997). Physiological arousal and performance in archery: a preliminary investigation. In R. Lidor & M. Bar-Eli (eds), *Innovations in Sport Psychology: Linking Theory and Practice. Proceedings of the IX World Congress of Sport Psychology (ISSP)*, Part II (pp. 573–575). Israel: International Society of Sport Psychology.

Robazza, C., Bortoli, L. & Nougier, V. (1998). Physiological arousal and performance in elite archers: a field study. *European Psychologist, 3*, 263–270.

Robazza, C., Bortoli, L. & Nougier, V. (2000). Performance emotions in an elite archer: a case study. *Journal of Sport Behavior, 23*, 144–163.

Salazar, W., Landers, D.M., Petruzzello, S.J. & Han, M. (1990a). The hemispheric asymmetry, cardiac response, and performance in elite archers. *Research Quarterly in Exercise and Sport, 61*, 351–359.

Salazar, W., Landers, D.M., Petruzzello, S.J., Crews, D.J. & Kubitz, K.A. (1990b). The effects of physical/cognitive load on electrocortical responses preceding response execution in archery. *Psychophysiology, 25*, 478–479.

Salminen, S., Liukkonen, J., Hanin, Y.L. & Hyvonen, A. (1995). Anxiety and athletic performance of Finnish athletes: application of the Zone of Optimal Functioning model. *Personality and Individual Differences, 19*, 725–729.

Smith, M.E., McEvoy, L.K. & Gevins, A. (1999). Neurophysiological indices of strategy development and skill acquisition. *Cognitive Brain Research, 7*, 389–404.

Starkes, J.L. (1987). Skills in field hockey: the nature of the cognitive advantage. *Journal of Sport Psychology, 9*, 146–160.

Vealey, R.S. & Walter, S.M. (1994). On target with mental skills: an interview with Darrell Pace. *Sport Psychologist, 8*, 427–441.

Wrisberg, C.A. (1993). Levels of performance skill. In R.N. Singer, M. Murphy & L.K. Tennant (eds), *Handbook of Research on Sport Psychology* (pp. 61–72). New York: Macmillan.

Yerkes, R.M. & Dodson, J.D. (1908). The relation of strength of stimulus to rapidity of habit formation. *Journal of Comparative and Neurological Psychology, 18*, 459–482.

PART IX

Equestrian Sports

Of Two Minds: Consulting with the Horse-and-Rider Team in Dressage, Showjumping and Polo

Grace Pretty and Don Bridgeman
University of Southern Queensland, Australia

INTRODUCTION

The sport psychologist who has had little experience of horses, and how they challenge human competition ambitions, can be disadvantaged in grasping the complexities inherent in the equestrian client's quest for better performance. For, while many of the performance enhancement approaches used with other kinds of athletes are applicable to the rider, there can be issues related to the rider's partner, the horse, that can compromise the effectiveness of traditional sport psychology approaches. The principal aim of this chapter is to increase the psychologist's knowledge of the psychology of horse-and-rider dynamics, and thereby improve skills in adapting traditional strategies to performance enhancement in equestrian teams. The reader will be informed regarding some of the typical issues faced by equestrians in dressage, showjumping and polo. These illustrations will then be followed by examples of assessment and intervention approaches that address the psychological horse-and-rider dynamics often embedded in an equestrian's request for assistance.

Because the primary focus of most riders is the horse's well-being and performance, rather than their own (Pretty, 2000), the discussion here considers both equine and human psychologies. That is not to say that riders see themselves as passengers only. They recognize the paramount importance of their technical skills, and most recognize the role of mental preparation. However, equestrians' engagement in sport psychology consultation will be better sustained if riders see direct relevance between the psychologist's human intervention and the horse's behaviour. Some fundamental information regarding horse behaviour is therefore presented at the start of this chapter. It will help the consultant formulate a strategy in a way that demonstrates the relationship between the rider's mindful preparation and the horse's mindful performance.

The Sport Psychologist's Handbook: A Guide to Sport-Specific Performance Enhancement.
Edited by Joaquín Dosil. © 2006 John Wiley & Sons, Ltd.

Extraordinary Psychological Dimensions of the Horse–rider Relationship

Equestrian sport is unique in the partnership between human and another animal species. Thus, the training process and subsequent performance outcomes are dependent on the cooperative interaction of two species to achieve a goal. One of the earliest Greek masters, Xenophon, in approximately 400 BC maintained that an understanding of horse behaviour is vital in becoming a successful equestrian. In modern-day competitive equestrian sports, the rider's success still demands comprehension of the horse's behaviour, social and hierarchical system to establish submission, trust and communication.

The sport media lead many people to take horse–human cooperation for granted. This overlooks the extraordinary nature of equine sporting events. The horse, a prey animal, gives up its physical power to the human, a predator, to perform tasks that are of no intrinsic interest to the horse and, indeed, are sometimes intrinsically threatening to the horse's self-preservation.

The equestrian partnership is challenged by differences in motivations of self-preservation versus personal achievement, as well as differences in modes of thinking. It is not natural within the animal world for a predator to be a partner or companion with the prey. Predators hunt their prey, and the horse behaves consistently with these innate survival instincts to avoid or defend against their predators. While humans may perceive most novel stimuli as non-threatening until proven dangerous, horses perceive everything as dangerous until proven otherwise (Rees, 1984). Hence what a human member of the equestrian team may perceive as a lack of submission or cooperation by the horse is actually a logical act of self preservation by the equine member of the team. To truly understand the mental challenges faced by equestrians, the sport psychologist must understand the mental challenges faced by the horse. Such comprehension will cause even the most avid proponent of relaxation and cognitive restructuring techniques to carefully consider their approach.

When the Rider is "Able" but the Horse is "Unwilling"

Frustration, anger and disappointment are common threats to any rider's successes, and to the survival of any promising horse-and-rider combination. While these feelings are inherent in any sport, they are inescapable in equestrian sport. This is because of the nature of the horse and his senses that operate contrary to the demands of a competitive sport. The following demonstrates what the human athlete has to grapple with upon taking the equine athlete to any competition. It sets the context for an empathic understanding of the mental distress of horse and rider.

The Unnatural Competition Lifestyle

The horse, when left to his own devices, will have a time budget of 60% eating, 20% standing, 10% lying down and 10% engaging in other behaviours (Duncan, 1979). When placed under human management this changes significantly. If stabled the time spent eating is reduced to 15% and the time spent standing is increased to 65%, and lying down to 15%

(Kiley-Worthington, 1990). Sleeping can be an issue for the competition horse. Horses are unique as they are able to drowse and gain short-wave sleep standing up, but it is very important for the horse to experience REM sleep for which they must become laterally recumbent. When they are being transported, stabled in an unfamiliar location or with unfamiliar horses, or subjected to crowding, their sleeping patterns are disrupted and may cease for days or weeks (Fraser, 1992). These changes in the horse's normal routines are responsible for many health and stereotypic behaviour problems in the competition horse. The rider makes demands when the horse is least able to meet them. As the horse is unable to put his case to the rider or the coach, he is often mistakenly labelled as "unwilling" rather than "unable". The emotional response to one who is perceived to be "unable" to meet another's demands is usually not fraught with the same depths of frustration and anger as the reactions to one who is perceived to be "unwilling" to meet one's demands. Hence the sport psychologist frequently hears accounts of how a horse "deliberately" refused to gallop as fast or jump as high as required in a competition. In these instances the psychologist begins to see opportunities for restructuring the motives and attitudes attributed to the horse.

The Influence of Horse Sense

The attention and focus demanded of any performance horse is counter-intuitive to its needs and abilities as a prey animal to remain hyper-vigilant regarding all aspects of its environment. Whether it is the triple combination in the showjumping arena, or the rider's request for a pirouette in the dressage arena, there are always other stimuli competing for the horse's attention. The challenge to the rider is to keep the horse's concentration while executing the task at hand. The challenge to the horse is to ignore his senses and to trust and submit to his rider. The following describes why this is so difficult.

Horses have a well-developed hearing at frequencies from 60 Hz to 33.5 Khz, and there-fore can hear even ultrasonic sounds. Horses are most sensitive to sound around 2 Hz and communicate their most frequent calls between 2 and 5 Hz, which is the range for human speech. It is also suggested that horses can hear very low frequencies such as geophysical vibrations. Horses are able to protect their ears by laying them flat in order block loud noise (Mills & Nanketrvis, 1999). This becomes unfortunate in the dressage arena where a judge may attribute flattened ears to evidence of a lack of submission or harmony, which will be discussed later.

The ability to detect and interpret airborne chemicals is very strong in horses. This is very important, as smell is one of the main ways that horses identify each other and their human handlers, their predators and their food. As the wind carries a number of scents and chemicals it makes it possible, for example, for a stallion to identify a mare in season upwind of him to distances of six kilometres or more (Jones, 1996). If a scent triggers a competing instinct the horse and rider are again confronted with threats to the team's performance.

The horse's eyes are 5 to 6.5 cm in size, the largest of any mammal, indicating that sight is a very important component of information gathering. Horses have a panoramic view of nearly 290 degrees and a binocular vision directly in front of the head of 60 to 70 degrees. There is a blind spot directly in front of the head for 0.50 m and below their nose and directly behind them. The eyes contain rods allowing for night vision, and cones, which respond to different wavelengths allowing horses to distinguish between different colours. Horses are long-sighted and the peripheral vision in the horse is very sensitive to movement (Mills & Nanketrvis, 1999). These components are important for consideration in showjumping where a horse is jumping obstacles that he cannot see until he gets within one or two strides out from the fence. He may even tilt his head at the last moment to see the fence if he is unsure. In team sport, such as polo, vision also complicates performance. Objects, such as a mallet or ball, which appear out of the blind spot, can startle the horse. It is therefore imperative that the rider is confident, and this confidence must be felt by the horse. Otherwise the horse will avoid the obstacles assuming they are not safe, and will not attend confidently to the task at hand.

Finally, horses are very sensitive to touch; they are able to twitch the skin when a fly lands. However, there are areas of the horse that are more sensitive around the face, in particular the eyes and mouth. Areas that are well supplied with nerves are the neck, withers, shoulders and parts of the lower leg. Horses mainly touch each other while grooming and only on the top section of the body and rarely on lower neck and shoulders. The lower part of the body and hind legs are usually off limits to other horses and humans (Budiansky, 1997). However, the horse must be desensitized to these innate reactions to touch for competition purposes. The equipment on which equestrians depend to ride and control their horses, and the grooming practices for appearance-conscious sports such as dressage, require the horse's submission. At the same time the rider demands the horse remain sensitive to the subtle pressure of the leg, hand and seat to respond instantly to the rider's cues. When the rider describes the stress they feel working with the noncompliant horse, the sport psychologist must appreciate the reactivity of the horse to the physical interactions between horse and rider—quite unlike that between the team mates of other athletes. This aspect of the physical relationship between horse and rider can be further understood within the social context of horse's psychology and how communication is constructed.

Being Part of the Herd: Dilemmas of Dominance, Submission and Trust

Horses are very social animals and live in stable, structured society groups with clearly identifiable hierarchies. The advantage of this society is that there are more eyes to watch for predators resulting in a better chance of survival. Horses have clear dominance boundaries, which maintain stability in the herd. However, a horse's position in the herd is always up for a renegotiation depending on the bonds made or broken when horses move in and out of the group (Fraser, 1992).

This becomes an issue for the rider as the human is naturally positioned by the equine partner into its "herd". The rider who does not establish a dominant position in the equine team will experience further frustration and negative consequences. Equality is not desirable in the equestrian team; the rider must always claim at least 51 per cent.

As social animals, horses need effective communication methods. Horses' communication methods are similar to humans in that they send and receive specific signals. These signals are vocal, chemical, visual and tactile. The auditory system is very important to receiving vocal information in the form of squeals, snorts, screams, roars, grunts, groans and nose-blowing. Through these sounds the horse interprets warnings, challenges, introductions, excitement and relaxation. The olfactory system is important in identifying airborne chemicals from various sources, including people and other horses. These chemicals allow the horse to determine the dominance rank of the other horses, whether they are friend or foe, as well as information about people (Kiley-Worthington, 1987). Horses are very tuned to body language such as the twitch of an ear, the curl of a lip or the swish of the tail, all of which indicate the intentions of the other horse. Horses commonly threaten to bite, kick and strike at another herd member of lesser rank. If the other horse does not respond it will complete the activity of the bite, kick or strike in order confirm the position of dominance in the herd or protect itself from a threat.

Again, as the rider is considered a member of the herd, all of the above sensitivities and communication behaviours are inclusive of the rider. The horse "reads" and responds to the rider's body language, tone of voice, etc. The information the horse obtains determines whether he will acknowledge the rider's dominance on the day and submit to the rider's requests out of respect, or take a chance re-negotiating a herd position higher than the rider. A rider therefore cannot become complacent about their own mental state and the behaviour toward the horse that results from it, especially during training and competition. A rider cannot be seen to be unfair in behaviour toward the horse because of temper or frustration. Riders cannot use the energy emanating from these emotions to exert dominant punitive behaviour toward the horse. As in human relationships, uncontrolled anger is very damaging. Maintaining a calm and authoritative attitude is essential to competition preparation, so that the horse and rider will trust each other on approach to a three-metre fence or in full gallop down a polo field. The sport psychologist must appreciate the influence of the rider's anger, anxiety and frustration on the horse as well as on the rider's performance because of the horse's reactive nature.

Who is Training Who?

Individual horses vary in intellect. The length of time a horse can remember a signal or command in training is the most common measure of intelligence (Fraser, 1992). Horses are strongly motivated to explore and investigate all aspects of their living environment. Similarly they are adept at controlling their environment through habitual behaviour and conditioning responses to other horses and people that make their environment comfortable and predictable. Horses establish reinforcement paradigms with their riders. These become evident to the sport psychologist when riders justify their behaviours and feelings on the basis of how the horse reacts, what the horse does and does not like, and will and will not do. Instruction in basic learning paradigms has humbled many riders who come to understand how their performance anxieties and fears have been cleverly reinforced by the horse. For example, by ducking out from jumping the water obstacle most dreaded by the rider, or resisting riding down an aggressive polo player that the rider fears, the horse avoids work, and further conditions the rider's fear. A significant challenge for the horse and rider is establishing productive behaviour patterns that resolve the tension between the need to be safe on the one hand and the risks necessary for success on the other. This can result in the sport psychologist sometimes challenging the equestrian whether avoidant behaviour and resistance is really about the horse or about themselves.

To summarize, when an equestrian trains and competes some of the psychological demands reside within their psyche, while other demands are inherent in the nature of their team mate, and still others arise from the relationship between the two.

To Ride a Horse

Before discussing psychological aspects of specific equestrian disciplines, it is helpful to note the basic physical skills necessary to ride a performance horse in any sport. To the observer an elite horse–rider combination appears as if the horse implicitly understands what is required of him. In fact, the rider is constantly communicating with the horse using a language involving riding "aids". There are "natural" aids consisting of leg, seat and hands, and "artificial" aids consisting of whip, spurs, etc. The natural aids communicate different messages to the horse depending on emphasis and timing: slight individual hand movements adjust the pressure and direction on each rein, subtle individual leg movements adjust position and pressure against the horse's side in relation to the girth, and adjustments in the saddle position the seat bones to put pressure on different points of the horse's back. Further description of the basic training of horse and rider across various equestrian disciplines can be found in manuals of national equestrian federations found in each country, for example, the British Horse Society's Manual of Equitation (1990).

To ride a horse well requires the control and coordination of these aids; to compete a horse successfully requires the addition of mental focus to use these aids precisely and consistently. For many riders mastery of the technical skills only will not assure progress in competition performance. The rider must master what Pretty (2001) has called the "fourth riding aid", the mental connection between the rider's mind and the horse's mind. The impact of this fourth aid on the execution of the other three is significant. The development of this aid is within the domain of the equestrian sport psychologist who is cognisant of the challenges of working with the two minds of horse and rider.

A particularly demanding aspect of competition riding is that many riders will compete on more than one horse at any tournament. Each of these horses may be trained to a different level. In other words, it is not the rider who is deemed to be ready to compete at a particular level as much as it is the horse. Hence the rider is required to adjust their mental preparation and attitude to that of the particular horse for a particular event. The rider may find that while some techniques work well for one horse, these need adjustment for another horse. It is not unusual for a rider to seek assistance in managing performance on a particular horse because of temperament or traumatic events experienced with that horse, such as an accident.

It is also important to understand the degree of time and commitment required to be an equestrian. Unless a person has the means to employ an assistant, the time spent actually riding the horse is relatively short compared to grooming, feeding and stable maintenance. Hence the financial and personal investment in a horse is to be considered when trying to understand the extent to which a rider is depressed or angry about a lack of success.

One final note about the equestrian competitor is that there is often "down-time" when the horse is unfit for competition due to injury or needing to recover from an illness. In addition there are times when the horse is given a rest in the paddock to restore its mental and physical stamina. Some riders do not cope well with these lapses in their training schedule, especially if they are unplanned. Unlike other sport it is not a simple matter to find another horse on which to train or compete. It is during these times when a rider might be most responsive to engaging in mental training activities which will be discussed below.

There is very little empirical work in the field of equestrian sport psychology on which to base claims of evidence-based interventions. It is necessary therefore to consider techniques and methods from other sports that parallel the human performance of the particular equestrian discipline. However Edgette (1996) addresses general aspects of equestrian sport psychology.

Three sports will be used to illustrate how the sport psychologist might assess and assist the equestrian with specific performance issues in light of the above discussion.

DRESSAGE—A MATTER OF ATHLETICISM AND ART

Performance Criteria

Dressage is often described as "horse and rider dancing together". Dressage requires training of the horse in the execution of gymnastic movements, which demonstrate the trainability, suppleness and athleticism in the use of the horse's power, and training of the rider in the skill of directing the horse in these movements, making the most of his natural ability but not interfering with it. Dressage riders perform in a 60 × 20 metre arena, doing tests that require specific movements in walk, trot and canter at specific positions around the arena. These movements range in difficulty from circles and loops at the preliminary training level to the more advanced movements of passage and pirouettes at the elite Grand Prix level. A rider will perform one to three tests on any one horse in a competition, and may compete more than one horse in any one competition. These horses may vary in their training level, such that a rider may compete a young horse at novice level and another horse at Grand Prix level.

Penalties are incurred for errors of course (3 errors = elimination). The performance is evaluated by 1 to 5 qualified judges depending on the test level. Each movement is scored on a scale from 0 (not executed) to 10 (excellent). In dressage even Olympic-level riders do well to get more than an overall 70+ per cent. The score is determined by several factors: the quality of the rhythm and freedom of the horse's paces, the degree to which horse and rider look as if the movements flow without effort, the impulsion or energetic forward activity of the horse, and the skill and precision of the rider. The overall impression that judges look for and riders strive for is one of harmony, that horse and rider are in rhythm with each other being relaxed, energetic and confident. As with gymnastics and figure skating, it is not enough to execute technically correct movements. The athlete has to make it look effortless.

The Challenge of Harmony between Horse and Rider

It is important for the sport psychologist to appreciate the nature of how dressage performance is judged as it can be an aspect of the competitor's frustration and, sometimes, despair. Harmony between horse and rider is evaluated subjectively and hence carries many of the same frustrations in competition evaluation as figure skating, for example. While there is usually inter-judge agreement on the technical aspect of a performance, scores related to artistic impression are less consistent between judges. Peham, Licka, Kapaun & Scheidl (2001) compare dressage with other sports where there is a debate over judging visual impressions.

Recent research (Bridgeman, 2004) has demonstrated a relationship between judge's evaluation of harmony and the physiological representation of harmony between horse

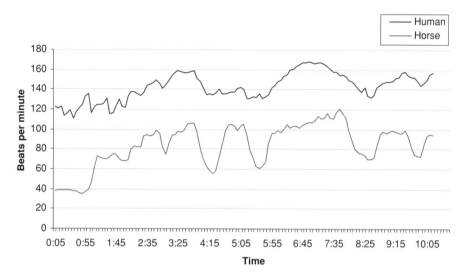

Figure 25.1 Heart rate of horse and rider during a novice dressage test

and rider through the use of heart rate monitors. Heart rate has been used as a measure of emotionality in horses (Visser, Van Reenen, Schilder, Barneveld & Blokhuis, 2003) and as a measure of activity in human athletes such as sailboarding (Guevel, Maisetti, Prou, Dubois & Marini, 1999) and long-distance running (Lambert, Mbambo & St Clair Gibson, 1998). This research is the first to synchronize and compare heart rate indicators in horse and rider. To emphasize just how closely horse and rider can be linked physically, Figure 25.1 and Figure 25.2 illustrate a pair competing in a dressage test where the heart rate displayed is for the same rider on two horses of different training levels.

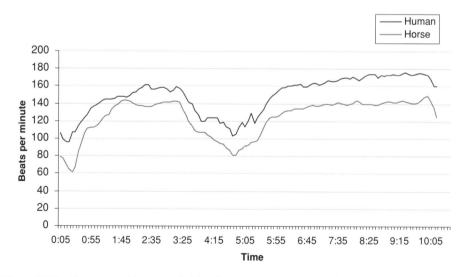

Figure 25.2 Heart rate of horse and rider during a Prix St George dressage test

The figures reveal the rise and fall of rhythm, and effort of the horse and rider, are parallel. However, the relationship between the novice horse and rider (Figure 25.1) is not as strong as the relationship between Prix St George horse (Figure 25.2) with correlations of 81% and 94% respectively between the horse and rider. The judge's score for harmony for the rider and each of these horses mirrors these physiological differences. The novice horse–rider pair was scored 5 for harmony whereas the Grand Prix horse–rider pair was scored 6.

As more emphasis is put on harmony as the ultimate performance criteria, the rider is challenged to achieve it, despite the conditions described above that may interfere. Clear communication and cooperation between horse and rider is essential. There is no place for anxiety, unresolved anger, frustration or depressed resignation. Hence the management of these emotions within the horse-and-rider relationship frequently becomes the objective of the sport psychologist.

Helping the Team Achieve Harmony

This performance problem usually presents itself as follows. A dressage rider is unable to get higher than seven on most movements despite the technical training going well and expert opinion that the horse is physically capable of producing a better performance (a common complaint that threatens the motivation of even the most dedicated riders). Riders will likely have been told that what is missing is the harmony and energy required for higher marks. Judges' comments will suggest that they need to develop a better feel for the horse; to keep him more relaxed; to allow him to work more freely but still focused; to generate more power from the hindquarters but keep it contained and directed. These are skills that cultivate the art of dressage. While technical behavioural specifications of hand, leg and seat aids produce part of the desired result, the rider has to "feel" the horse's response to these aids. This requires a conversation between horse and rider that continues throughout the test—it is the basis of harmony.

Most riders know this, but often report that the conversation gets disrupted in the test (indeed judges will often write that the rider and horse appear blocked in their movement). It is somewhat like two people who have an argument before going on the dance-floor— they are together physically but the energy and flow of the dance is blocked by resistance stemming from their unresolved anger, frustration and disappointment in the other person. The psychologist's job then is to teach the rider how to manage the development of these feelings, how to either resolve them or set them aside before the competition.

Most psychologists will be skilled at helping a client uncover the sources of negative mental states, and with some knowledge of the equine psyche presented above, this can be accomplished with appropriate empathy for the rider's difficulties. After reviewing the history of dynamics between horse and rider, or between the rider and other horses, the psychologist will uncover the feeling that is blocking the conversation between horse and rider and preventing harmonious execution of the test. Things to look for are: fear that the horse can't be trusted to be allowed to move freely, or to be energized for bolder paces; anger that the horse is not giving his best or deliberately making it difficult; frustration and resentment that despite all the training at home it is not working well in the competition arena; disappointment and resignation in one's self. Many of these feelings will have been accumulating over past competitions, and the rider has not learned to be forgiving of self or horse.

What blocks the communication on competition day are those feelings rising from unfinished business between the horse and the self. Such negative mental states disturb the rider's focus, as well as the sensitive communication with the horse through the aids. While there is little research regarding the relationship between mood states and equestrian performance (Meyers, Bourgeois, LeUnes & Murray, 1999), elite riders in the field have documented how destructive the confrontation between the rider's negative mental state and the horse's negative mental state can be (Williams et al., 1999). Effective solution strategies include teaching riders the basics of cognitive behaviour therapy and how to become more problem-focused than emotion-focused. Riders concerned about harmony need to:

- Recognize the early beginnings of these feelings in training and competition, not to wait until tempers are lost and horses become even more reactive and threatened by the tone of voice or aggressive posturing. Any rider who is asked to visualize a flowing performance with their horse while feeling angry or frustrated will be quickly convinced of the need to get these emotions out of the arena.
- Understand the sources of the horse's behaviour, and react reasonably to these sources. This requires problem-solving rather than making anthropomorphic attributions. The horse is not deliberately sabotaging the rider's success; there are technical problems to be solved rather than arguments to be won. It can be during such times that a rider is presented with the need for new skill acquisition or a revision of their competition goals. A horse's "attitude" can always be analysed in terms of obtainable strategic behavioural change if the rider can overcome emotional blocks to motivation.
- Ride without past fears, disappointments, anger and resentments toward the horse. Physical tension due to anger, and conversely lack of energy due to depressed resignation, need to be worked through before getting in the saddle. The rider cannot continue yesterday's argument today. Chances are the horse has not been holding a grudge since the last training session and is willing to begin his work on the day without reference to unresolved disagreements. However, with attentiveness to the rider's verbal and nonverbal communication, the horse will quickly sense if his team mate is holding grudges.

Research has shown that dressage riders do not recall aspects of their own competition performance as well as they recall that of the horse (Tenenbaum, Lloyd, Pretty & Hanin, 2002). It would seem that psychologists should not rely only on rider's recall to identify emotional or cognitive events associated with unsuccessful performance. As with so many aspects of equestrian consultation, the psychologist gets a more accurate account of events if the focus is on the horse's behaviour, whereby the rider's behaviour is assessed indirectly.

There are many helpful references to assist the sport psychologist in understanding the complexities of dressage training. A psychological perspective has been discussed by Marshall (1998), or to understand further the principles of dressage itself see Von Ziegner (2002).

SHOWJUMPING—A MATTER OF POWER AND CONTROL

Performance Criteria

Though they are driving only a one-horse-power engine, showjumpers report experiences indicative of what are called "extreme sports". Showjumpers ride their horses around a course of approximately ten fences or obstacles set at varying distances and angles from each other. The showjumping course has individual fences and combinations of fences designed by a trained course builder. The levels of difficulty are defined in terms of the height, combinations of types of obstacles, position of obstacles in relation to each other, and the amount of time allocated to complete the course. Showjumping competitions are described in terms of height classes or the more conventual Grand Prix, A, B, C and D grade classes The number of rounds may vary and there may be time restrictions. Penalties are incurred for knocking a rail from the fence, for refusing to jump a fence (two refusals = elimination), and for not completing the course within the time allowed. When a rider falls from the horse they are eliminated from the competition. Thus the winner of a showjumping class is the horse and rider who finish all rounds with the least number of penalties and, in some cases, with the fastest time around the course. Riders may enter a single horse in three classes per day and enter a maximum of three horses in each class. Some riders enter only one horse per class and others will ride several horses in different classes over a number of grade levels in a single day. Riders are given a period of time to walk the course before competing. It should be noted that the first time the horse sees the obstacles is when it is on course. Riders are given an area to warm up over a few practice fences before entering the showjumping course. The overall objective for the rider is to get maximum power from the horse while also having absolute control over the use of this power.

The Challenge of Power and Control

Showjumping requires a great deal of mutual trust between the horse and the rider. As a horse gets its last view of the fence a few strides out it must trust the rider to have placed it in a spot to safely jump the fence. The horse does not know on all occasions what is on the other side of the fence. Thus, for a horse to successfully complete a showjumping course it will rely on the rider's judgement for line of approach to each fence, the speed that they need to travel, the placement of the horse to take off and jump the fence, and where they will land in relationship to the next fence. It is important that the rider not confuse the horse with indecision in use of the aids, or over-face the horse with obstacles and positions that are too difficult. Once the horse is placed in the correct position at a fence the horse must exercise a great deal of concentration, power and athleticism to jump the fence. Ignoring all other stimuli present to its many senses and all impulses to react to these stimuli, the horse relinquishes his power to the rider. The rider then must have the concentration, courage and conviction to direct this power. When a rider senses the powerful and excited horse is not under their control, concentration and confidence can be quickly lost.

Helping the Rider Maintain Control

Unlike dressage riders, showjumpers are more likely to have concerns regarding the physical risks of their sport, although few would admit on first interview that their performance issues were related to fear or anxiety. However, considering the need for critical momentary judgement in the face of power and speed, the threat of injury to self and horse as a consequence of error, and the fact that horses do not see what they are jumping, nor do they have an natural inclination to jump an obstacle in front of them, this anxiety response is understandable. Indeed one of the mental challenges to the showjumper is to avoid getting caught in the horse's anxiety about a jump as well as their own anxiety.

Figure 25.3 Power and control: Australian Asia Pacific World Cup champion Chris Chugg competing Carbine
Reproduced by permission of Bev Edwards

Showjumpers often present with concerns about accuracy and focus in getting the horse to the best spot for take-off over the jump. Timing, rhythm and length of stride, all controlled by the rider, will determine this. In considering the best psychological tools to use when consulting with showjumpers, psychologists do well to work with an important component of a showjumper's own mental skill repertoire—imagery. Before riding a course, a showjumper walks the course, considering the best approach to fences, the number of strides to put between fences and the most appropriate speed at which to approach the jump. They rehearse the course in their minds to remember their strategies for approach.

While imagery is used to strategize the course as a whole, riders do not necessarily mentally experience the intricacies of their preparation between fences. They are often unaware of how their anxieties regarding particular obstacles may interfere and how they might improve. Imagery can be a good diagnostic tool to assess the focus of a rider's concentration. Showjumpers wanting to improve their skill at putting the horse in the best spot need to:

• Be aware of the progression of mental preparation, as well as riding skill and horse power, that is required to compete at higher grades. While the horse may be capable and ready to manage more demanding obstacles, the rider may not.

- Improve their concentration and focus when under pressure, such that critical decisions can be made when there is an alteration in the planned course strategy.
- Improve the confidence with which they ride the horse through critical decisions. Horses do not respond well to ambivalence or uncertainty in terms of competition goals. In such instances they will usually revert to innate impulses or "please themselves". Through use of imagery recalling past successes, the psychologist may help the rider find evidence to dispute a lack of competence in course strategies. However, such imagery can also help the rider become aware of new goals by identifying a particular skill that has yet to be learned but will improve competence and confidence on course.
- Be attuned to their own thoughts and behaviours between fences as well as the horse. Thoughts, feelings and use of riding aids must be consistent with a forward, flowing and relaxed rhythm, visually locking on to the next fence, and committed to the "leap of faith" as Schinke and Schinke (1997) so aptly describe it.
- Consider how well the horse's nature is suited to the rider's disposition toward competition; are they both cautious and careful, or bold and risk-taking. The rider may have to reconcile the horse's disposition with their own in order to resolve ongoing conflicts at fences.

While some equestrians may compete on horses they know well, or have even bred and trained themselves, other professional riders may not have such a history with their mounts. However, professionals carry with them into the saddle the histories of all the horses they have ridden before, as well as the expectations of owners with considerable investment in their horse's performance. Knowing the rider's history with the competition horse can be helpful in uncovering sources of confidence, unrealistic expectations, pessimism and sometimes financial pressure.

There are several helpful references for the psychologist who seeks to understand more about the anxiety and performance factors in showjumping, including Williams et al. (1999) and international equestrian and sport psychologist Robert Schinke (Schinke & Schinke, 1997).

POLO—A MATTER OF ASSERTIVENESS IN THE "HERD"

Performance Criteria

Polo has been described as a "hectic equestrian ballet" (Watson, 1989); from a more athletic perspective it looks like golf on horseback with the speed and physical contact of ice hockey. The sport requires the coordination of a good ball-game athlete along with the balance, calm authority and sensitivity of a competent horseperson. The objective of the game is to drive a small ball down the polo pitch, which is 300 yards long and 200 yards wide, and through the opposition's goal posts at the other end using a long mallet. This involves riding a pony at a full gallop while defending against the offensive tactics of opposition players and their ponies. The frenzy of whirling mallets amidst trampling horse hooves at stampede speed produces an exhilarating experience on and off the field. There are rules of play, and skilled umpires, to ensure the safety of riders and horses.

Each team usually has 4 horse-and-rider combinations to play a match which is divided into 6, 7-minute chukkas. At the end of each chukka there is a 3-minute break to change horses; the halftime break is approximately 5 minutes. Each rider requires a team of well-trained horses as each horse is competed for only 2 chukkas, which are not continuous. Polo players ride particular positions in each chukka. Each player has a handicap between −2 and +10. The handicap does not indicate the number of goals they are expected to score. It reflects "value" to the team in terms of their position as a high to low goal scorer. It is the individual ambition of each player to increase their handicap, while contributing to the collective ambition of the team to win the match. Polo ponies are attributed similar human characteristics as good offensive or defensive players. Polo players must therefore be attentive not only to the human players they mark, but also to the equine players. Human players must know their team of horses well to choose the right mount for each chukka; that is, one capable of riding off the mount of the marked opponent.

The challenges of Individual, Horse–rider and Team Performance

The polo player has to consider skill and focus across three levels of performance: as an individual, to strike the ball accurately with the right velocity and length; as an equine team mate, to communicate to the horse the desired position and speed to either strike the ball or ride off an opponent; as a team member, to play strategically, being mindful of the rest of the team.

In any tournament, polo teams are likely to have players with varying handicaps, and horses with notable reputations. Hence a talented player may become less confident when playing against a team with a high goaler and a horse reputed to be indomitable in his riding-off ability. If this player has a performance objective of increasing his handicap, it may be necessary to address the anxiety associated with the opposition, as well as the technical skills of hitting the ball. As many players are not forthcoming about such anxiety, it may take the psychologist some time in building rapport to get to the source of, for example, the lack of focus or inaccurate strokes. If the sport psychologist is able to watch the player, it may become evident that the player is often not in a good position to strike the ball. While this may suggest deficits in the player's riding skill—for example, the rider pulls back on the reins to reduce the horse's speed too soon—it may also be a diagnostic of anxiety. A further consequence of this anxiety is that any hesitancy on the part of the rider will be felt by the horse. This creates confusion for the well-trained pony on the exact line of the ball, or focused on his mark. Performance anxiety of the individual therefore becomes an issue for the horse–rider combination.

Polo ponies require considerable training, depending on the aptitude they show naturally towards the demands of the game. In addition to the other competition venue challenges noted earlier in this chapter, polo ponies must perform counter-intuitive behaviours of calmly accepting objects being swung around their heads and invading the space of another horse at full gallop. The effectiveness of each horse–rider combination is increased by sensitivity toward the characteristics of each horse. However, many players do not have their own stable of horses. They play on horses they have not ridden prior to the game. Nevertheless, the polo player must show confident authority in directing the horse, while being sympathetic not to put the horse in harm's way or to harm the horse's mouth by pulling or balancing on the reins. Clear communication through the aids results in precise stopping, turning and change of speed to put the rider in the desired position in relation to the ball and opponents. While tempers may flare if the game is not progressing as hoped, or anxious minds may be distracted from the play at hand, these must be contained if riders are to get the best effort from their equine partners, not to mention their human team mates.

It takes little time for a horse to gallop from one end of the pitch to another and hence the team has little time to change tactics in play. The speed of polo requires players to have extraordinary reaction times. The swiftness with which a horse can turn itself 180 degrees and resume a gallop requires the individual player to have active peripheral vision at the same time as immediate focused vision. These dimensions add to the challenge of good strategic team play. Polo requires an attitude of flexibility, a high level of awareness on the field, and knowledge and consideration of team mates' skills. These enable interchange between players in an instant.

Helping the Rider with Multiple Demands

It can take time to uncover the source of a polo player's performance problems as the interactive nature of individual, horse–rider and team skills is difficult to untangle. The sport psychologist might consider working with some of the following strategies:

- Review the player's perceptions of each level of performance before targeting specific objectives. While many clients present with goal-scoring issues, consideration of their riding experiences—such as quality and training of their horses and injuries during riding off—and of their attitude toward the team may suggest how these contexts of the individual player require attention.
- Deconstruct the player's experiences of each of these components and address separately each component with basic problem-solving processes coupled with goal-setting strategies. This can significantly reduce the feeling of despair that comes from a long season without improving.
- Assess how the player identifies and manages anxiety, anger and frustration prior to and during competition. Ridden onto the polo pitch such emotions can devastate the player's mental and physical game, which is further compromised by undesirable reactions from the horse.
- Use imagery to improve the synchronicity of horse and rider. As with other stick-and-ball sports, imagery can be very effective in improving the stroke. Rhythm and timing constructed in terms of an image or piece of music can help the player find a coordinated rhythmical pattern of movement that can be consistently practised mentally and physically. When using such strategies with a polo player it is important to integrate the rhythm and movement of the horse into the imagery, as if horse and rider were one.

For further information on the sport of polo and the training of players, the sport psychologist is referred to Watson (1989) for a readable description.

SUMMARY AND CONCLUSION

There are many psychological assessments and interventions related to the performance of, for example, figure skating, ski jumping and hockey, that are applicable to dressage, showjumping and polo, respectively. This chapter attempted to help the sport psychologist appreciate the added challenges of the equestrian that are inherent in the nature of the horse. The discussion has been directed at the interactive nature of humans and horses, and the reactive nature of humans and horses. Assessment of an equestrian's lack of focus, motivation, anxiety and control, for example, need to be considered in the context of the horses they are riding. Similarly, strategies to assist in these areas need to consider the applicability to equestrian training and competition arenas.

The sport psychologist would be advised to watch the client with their mount if possible, as much can be revealed through the observation of this interaction. If this is not possible, the least the psychologist should do to "interview" the rider's "other half" is to ask the client to share a photo of the horse and to invite stories of the best and worst of times in the relationship. It is expected that with such an invitation most clients will instil in the psychologist empathy for the relationship that exemplifies the principles included in this chapter. It is difficult for even the most non-animal-oriented psychologist not to be impressed with the ability of horses to incite the deepest of emotions and hence the greatest of mental challenges.

REFERENCES

Bridgeman, D.J. (2004). Behavioural, physiological and psychological aspects of the equestrian team at training and competition, Unpublished doctoral manuscript. University of Southern Queensland, Toowoomba.

British Horse Society (1990). *Manual of Equitation: The Complete Training of Horse and Rider.* London: Threshold Books.

Budiansky, S. (1997). *The Nature of Horses: Their Evolution, Intelligence and Behaviour.* London: Phoenix.

Duncan, P. (1979). Time-budgets of Camargue horses II. Time-budgets of adult horses and weaned sub-adults. *Animal Behaviour, 72*(1–2), 26–49.

Edgette, J.S. (1996). *Heads Up: Practical Sports Psychology for Riders, their Families and Their Trainers.* New York: Doubleday.

Fraser, A.F. (1992). *The Behaviour of the Horse.* Oxon, UK: CAB International.

Guevel, A., Maisetti, O., Prou, E., Dubois, J.J. & Marini, J.F. (1999). Heart rate and blood lactate responses during competitive Olympic sailboarding. *Journal of Sports Sciences, 17,* 135–141.

Jones, A.R. (1996). From your horse's point of view. *Hoofbeats, 18*(4), 10–13.

Kiley-Worthington, M. (1987). *The Behaviour of Horses: In Relation to Management and Training.* London: J.A. Allan & Co. Ltd.

Kiley-Worthington, M. (1990). The behaviour of horses in relation to management and training—towards ethologically sound environments. *Equine Veterinary Science, 10*(1), 62–71.

Lambert, M.I., Mbambo, Z.H. & St Clair Gibson, A. (1998). Heart rate during training and competition for long-distance running. *Journal of Sports Sciences, 16,* S85–S90.

Marshall, L. M. (1998). *A Mental Attitude toward Dressage.* London: J.A. Allen.

Meyers, M.C., Bourgeois, A.E., LeUnes, A. & Murray, N.G. (1999). Mood and psychological skills of elite and sub-elite equestrian athletes. *Journal of Sport Behaviour, 22,* 399–409.

Mills, D.S. & Nanketrvis, K. (1999). *Equine Behaviour: Principles and Practice.* Oxford: Blackwell Science Ltd.

Peham, C., Licka, T., Kapaun, M. & Scheidl, M. (2001). A new method to quantify harmony of the horse–rider system in dressage. *Sports Engineering, 4,* 95–101.

Pretty, G. H. (2000). Understanding the enmeshment in equine and human relationships: how riders think about the horse in their attributions of performance success. *Australian Journal of Psychology Supplement, 107.*

Pretty, G. (2001). Consulting with the horse and rider team: challenges for the sport psychologist. In G. Tenenbaum (ed.), *The Practice of Sport and Exercise Psychology: International Perspectives.* Fitness Information Technology, Inc

Rees, L. (1984). *The Horses Mind*. London: Stanley Paul & Co.

Schinke, R. & Schinke, B. (1997). *Focused Riding*. London: Compass Equestrian.

Tenenbaum, G., Lloyd, M., Pretty, G. & Hanin, Y. (2002). Congruence of actual and retrospective reports of pre-competition emotions in equestrians. *Journal of Sport and Exercise Psychology, 24*, 271–288.

Visser, E.K., Van Reenen, C.G., Schilder, M.B.H., Barneveld, A. & Blokhuis, H.J. (2003). Learning performances in young horses using two different learning tests. *Applied Animal Behaviour Science, 80*, 311–326.

Von Ziegner, K.A. (2002). *Elements of Dressage: A Guide to Training the Young Horse*. London: Lyons Press.

Watson, J.N.P. (1989). *A Concise Guide to Polo*. London: Sportsman's Press.

Williams, M., Young, L., Jones-Sparrow, M., Marshall, L., Breisner, Y. & Diggle, M. (1999). *Understanding Nervousness in Horse and Rider*. London: J. A. Allen.

PART X

Fitness Sports

CHAPTER 26

Sport Psychology and Fitness Activities

Diane L. Gill
University of North Carolina at Greensboro, USA

INTRODUCTION

Sport psychology and fitness activities appear to be an unlikely combination. Fitness activities are seldom considered "sport", and indeed fitness activities differ from the sports covered in the other chapters in this volume in important ways. First, fitness activities do not involve the distinct training and competition periods of other sports. Fitness activities are lifestyle activities; maintenance of physical activity, rather than peak performance is the overriding goal. Second, fitness participants engage in varied activities rather than focusing on one sport or one specific event. Indeed, that variation often is intentional and desirable to achieve overall fitness goals. Just as fitness activities are varied, participants are much more diverse than the typical athletes in other sports. In this chapter, we will focus on typical adult fitness participants, a diverse population itself, but fitness participants also include children, older adults and clients in a variety of medical and health programs. Just as the other chapters focus on performance skills and competition, most applied sport psychology research and practice focuses on competitive sports and related skills. Sport psychology is just as relevant for participants focusing on fitness activities as for athletes focusing on sport skills and competitive performance. However, as this chapter will suggest, the guiding psychological models and specific psychological skills and strategies fit in different ways.

FITNESS ACTIVITIES

Fitness activities are those that promote *physical fitness*. Physical fitness is the body's ability to function efficiently and effectively or, as Nieman (1998) states, "Physical fitness is a condition in which an individual has sufficient energy and vitality to accomplish daily tasks and active recreational pursuits without undue fatigue." (p. 4). Most authorities, including researchers and authors of major fitness texts (e.g. Corbin, Welk, Lindsey & Corbin, 2003), as well as professional organizations and agencies (e.g. American College of Sports Medicine, ACSM, website: www.acsm.org), describe physical fitness as consisting of skill-related

The Sport Psychologist's Handbook: A Guide for Sport-Specific Performance Enhancement.
Edited by Joaquín Dosil. © 2006 John Wiley & Sons, Ltd.

fitness and health-related fitness. Skill-related fitness (e.g. agility, speed, power) is relevant to most sports, but skill-related fitness has little relationship to health and wellness. The focus here is *health-related fitness*. Corbin et al. (2003) and Nieman (1998) refer to the World Health Organization (WHO) constitution preamble of over 50 years ago, and define health as more than the absence of disease and illness. Health is optimal well-being that contributes to quality of life; optimal health includes mental, social, emotional, spiritual and physical wellness. Fitness activities discussed in this chapter are those physical activities that promote optimal health.

Physical Fitness and Health

In the United States, physical fitness is a prominent public health issue, and information on fitness activities is increasingly found in the popular media, as well as in sport and exercise science resources. The US Department of Health and Human Services published the Surgeon General's report on physical activity and health in 1996, and the *Healthy People 2010* objectives in 2000, and both are widely circulated and available as publications and through Internet sites. For example, the Centers for Disease Prevention and Control (CDC) website (www.cdc.gov) includes a section on physical activity that offers resources and information on fitness activities.

Physical inactivity has been linked to nearly all the major health problems including heart disease, diabetes, osteoporosis and negative psychological conditions such as depression and anxiety (USDHHS, 1996). A recent consensus statement (Kesaniemi et al., 2001) concluded that regular physical activity is associated with a reduction in all-cause mortality, fatal and nonfatal total cardiovascular disease, coronary heart disease, obesity and type-2 diabetes. Further benefits include improved physical function and independent living in the elderly, and less likelihood of depressive illness. Although the major consequences of inactivity may not appear until later in life, even youth are experiencing an increased risk of health problems. Physical activity (or inactivity) patterns of childhood and adolescence begin the lifetime patterns that promote health or health risks in adulthood, but unfortunately the evidence indicates that activity declines in adolescence, particularly for girls. The Youth Behavior Risk Survey (Heath, Pratt, Warren & Kann, 1994) indicated that between grades 9 and 12, the percentage of boys participating in vigorous physical activity declined from 81% to 67% while for girls, participation rates declined from 61% to 41%, and the Surgeon General's report on physical activity and health (USDHHS, 1996) noted the consistent epidemiological reports of lesser activity of female adolescents. In particular, obesity and obesity-related health problems, including diabetes, have increased dramatically in youth and young adults in recent years, and the increase appears to be accelerating (Booth, 2002).

The interest in physical activity and health promotion is not limited to North America. The World Health Organization (WHO) includes physical activity as a public health priority and has developed a Global Strategy on Diet, Physical Activity and Health, which was endorsed by the May 2004 World Health Assembly. The WHO website (www.who.int.org) contains information on physical activity and health paralleling US reports. Physical inactivity was estimated to cause 1.9 million deaths worldwide annually, according to World Health Report 2002. Physical inactivity is a major health problem around the world, and WHO reports that currently 60 per cent of the world's population is estimated to not get enough physical activity to achieve even the modest recommendation of 30 minutes per day, with adults in developed countries most likely to be inactive. Like CDC, ACSM and many governmental and professional organizations in North America, WHO promotes physical activity, and includes recommendations for individuals and public policies.

Components of Physical Fitness

These many popular and professional resources emphasize health-related fitness, and related physical activities. All cite the five key components of fitness and emphasize the inclusion of activities related to all components for overall physical fitness. Corbin et al. (2003) describe health and wellness as integrated states, and overall physical fitness as a multidimensional state made up of five main components:

- *Cardiovascular fitness* is the ability of the body's circulatory and respiratory systems to supply fuel during sustained physical activity. Activities that keep the heart rate elevated at a safe level for a sustained length of time such as walking, swimming or cycling, improve cardiovascular endurance. The activity does not have to be strenuous, and most fitness programs involve starting slowly and gradually working up to a more intense pace. However, any fitness program must include aerobic activities that are more strenuous than lifetime activities for optimal gains in cardiovascular fitness.
- *Muscular strength* is the ability of the muscle to exert force or lift a heavy weight during an activity. The key to making muscles stronger is working them against resistance from weights or gravity. Exercises such as lifting weights or rapidly taking the stairs increase muscle strength.
- *Muscular endurance* is the ability of the muscle to repeatedly perform without fatigue. Cardiovascular fitness activities such as walking, jogging or dancing can improve muscle endurance, but muscular endurance and cardiovascular endurance are not exactly the same. Muscular endurance depends on skeletal muscles, and activities such as progressive resistance exercise focus on developing muscle fitness (both strength and endurance).
- *Body composition* refers to the relative amount of muscle, fat, bone, and other tissues of the body. Although low body fat (under 5 % for men, 10% for women) is a health issue, the primary health-related issue is excessive body fat, or obesity (over 25% for men, 35% for women). Many factors affect body composition, including heredity, and of course diet. Physical activity is a component of most effective programs for controlling body fat and maintaining a healthy body composition. Most activities in the physical activity pyramid, including aerobic activity and active sports, can promote healthy body composition, but lifestyle activities are especially effective.
- *Flexibility* is the range of motion around a joint. Activities that lengthen the muscles such as swimming or a basic stretching program improve flexibility.

Fitness Activity Pyramid

Corbin et al. (2003) present an activity pyramid to describe recommended fitness activities. Activities at the lower or base levels require more frequent participation, while those at the upper levels require less frequency. The base of the pyramid is lifetime physical activity. Lifetime activities are physical activities such as walking, play and light-to moderate-intensity sports. Lifetime activities can be performed by nearly everyone, and they form the base and foundation for other fitness activities. Recommendations for lifetime activities typically follow the Surgeon General's report and suggest an accumulation of 30 minutes per day of moderate physical activity on most, if not all, days of the week.

More vigorous aerobic activity and active sports form the next level, and those activities are particularly important for building cardiovascular fitness. Sports such as tennis or basketball, as well as hiking or skiing, fit at this level. Exercises for flexibility and exercises for muscle fitness are at the third level. Both flexibility and muscle fitness are necessary for overall fitness, and activities at the lower level seldom contribute. Fitness activities should include both stretching for flexibility and weight training or calisthenics for muscle fitness. The top of the pyramid is inactivity. Some rest is necessary for fitness, but inactivity times, other than sleep, should be short and infrequent.

Case Examples

To illustrate typical fitness activities, and to set up examples that we can reference throughout this chapter, we will consider two cases. First, Marie is a 25-year-old woman working with a personal trainer for her fitness activities. Marie is a former soccer player who is physically active, and has been doing regular endurance activities (running) and weight training on her own. She is now working with a personal trainer to develop a more comprehensive program to stay in shape and maintain her fitness level. Our second case is George, a 60-year-old man, who has not been engaged in any regular physical activity. His physician and family have encouraged him to become active for health reasons, and he has just joined an exercise program for middle-to older-age adults.

Both George and Marie will need to build a base of lifetime activities. For George, lifetime activities are the primary focus and the first step toward fitness. For Marie, who is already active, lifetime activities are important as she moves from her status as an athlete in training who focuses on performance, to an active adult who incorporates exercise into her overall lifestyle. Both Marie and George will include activities that develop cardiovascular endurance in their fitness programs. George will start slowly, and his group program includes walking, which is the most common activity for previously inactive adults. Marie will be encouraged to continue her running activity but, like many runners, she over-emphasizes running to the exclusion of other activities, and will be advised to expand her options. Specifically, her trainer will suggest that she try alternative endurance activities such as cycling or swimming on her own, and will provide instruction in aerobic routines during training sessions.

For Marie, it is particularly important for her to move up the pyramid and include activities that enhance other fitness components for a more balanced overall program that she can continue through life. She is doing some weight training, and the trainer will introduce more variation and options for strength training including free weights as well as machines. Marie will also include more stretching and flexibility exercises in her training sessions.

Strength training and flexibility are even more important for George, and the group sessions will include several more varied activities. Instruction on resistance training with weights will be included in the group sessions, with an emphasis on choice and staying within physical limits (no pain for these exercises). Stretching, flexibility and balance exercises will be included in all group sessions, with allowance for individual limits (again—no pain).

Specific exercises will be varied during the group sessions, including activities with stretch bands, exercise balls and partner exercises.

Both Marie and George will be encouraged to exercise outside of their training sessions, and to discuss the overall balance of fitness activities with their instructor. Marie will be developing a balance of varied fitness activities, maintaining her current fitness level, but also developing more options and alternatives that will allow her to maintain fitness activities through life changes and transitions. George will be taking small steps toward major lifestyle changes. For George, just doing any activity is a step. He will focus on taking small steps, including walking, strength training and flexibility/balance exercises. Both George and Marie are working toward lifestyle fitness activities that include all components of the fitness pyramid.

A FRAMEWORK FOR FITNESS PSYCHOLOGY

Psychology Issues for Fitness Participants and Professionals

Although most of the background research on physical activity and health, which is the base for the public policy and health promotion recommendations, is based in exercise physiology and public health research, sport psychology can play a central role in fitness activities. Indeed, "fitness psychology" may be the most important discipline for professionals and participants in fitness activity programs.

Much of the interest in fitness psychology stems from the increasing public recognition of the health benefits of exercise coupled with the fact that most people do not act on that recognition. The US Centers for Disease Control and Prevention (CDC) and the American College of Sports Medicine (ACSM) (Pate et al., 1995) recommend at least 30 minutes of moderate physical activity most, if not all, days of the week. Yet, data from population-based surveys consistently show that over 50 per cent of the US population is sedentary. Sedentary behavior is related to the demographic characteristics of being older, African-American, female, poorly educated, overweight and having a history of being physically inactive. After adolescence and early adulthood, participation decreases, and progressively larger proportions of older adults report no leisure physical activity. In a recent text, Lox, Martin and Petruzzello (2003) summarize the epidemiological data on physical activity patterns around the world as follows:

• The number of people worldwide who exercise at even the minimal level to achieve physical benefits is very low, conservatively 50 per cent, and at least 25 per cent do not exercise at all.
• Physical activity declines linearly through childhood, and continues to decline throughout the lifespan.
• Males are more likely to engage in vigorous activity, although women engage in as much moderate physical activity.
• Differences are small, but low-income groups and ethnic minority groups tend to partic-ipate in less physical activity than the overall population.
• The higher the education level, the greater the participation in physical activity.

Moreover, 50 per cent of the adults who start to exercise in fitness programs drop out within 6 months and, as Buckworth and Dishman (2002) note, this high drop-out rate has not changed over the past 20 years. Clearly, we are dealing with human behavior; sport psychology, which involves research and practice related to behavior in sport settings, can contribute to the development of effective exercise programs that promote health-related fitness. The issue is behavior and, more specifically, the overriding issue for fitness activities is behavior change. Sport psychology research and guidelines related to motivation and behavior following a health promotion and prevention approach is particularly relevant for getting started and maintaining fitness activities. Before moving to specific behavioral and cognitive strategies for fitness activities, the next section presents an overall model for fitness psychology.

Overall Model of Fitness Behavior

Elsewhere (Gill, 2000) I have used Lewin's classic formula for explaining behavior to provide a framework for sport and exercise psychology. Sport psychologists want to understand behavior in the real world and use that knowledge in practice to help sport participants, including participants in fitness activities. Human behavior is complex. One underlying theme that helps us understand sport and exercise behavior was set forth in a formal but simple way by Kurt Lewin (1935) as:

$$B = f(P, E).$$

That is, behavior is a function of the person and the environment.

As Lewin emphasized, individual and environmental factors interact. Personal characteristics influence behavior in some situations and not others; situational factors (e.g. spectators, instructor's comments) affect different people different ways; and the person affects the situation just as the situation affects the person. Any behavior takes place within the context of many interacting personal and environmental factors, and all those factors change over time. We may not predict how one person will react to a certain instructor's comments, but we may help the instructor, coach, fitness director or consultant relate to different individuals within sport and fitness activity settings, and enhance the experience for all participants.

Within that framework, we can consider individual differences (P), environmental factors (E) and their multiple interactions in relation to fitness behaviors. Individual differences typically include personality factors, such as introversion–extraversion and emotional stability, but those global personality factors have not been very useful in applied work. Dishman incorporated the personality construct of self-motivation in his psychobiological model of exercise adherence, and developed the Self-Motivation Inventory (Dishman & Ickes, 1981). Dishman and colleagues have continued to investigate exercise adherence, and the SMI was recently revised (Motl, Dishman, Felton & Pate, 2003), but most exercise behavior research has incorporated more social and cognitive components into a *biopsychosocial* model.

Our fitness psychology framework is a dynamic, interactive model with individual characteristics and the environment influencing behavior. Behavioral strategies are particularly relevant in maintaining fitness activities, but perceptions and cognitions are key links in the model. Indeed, as the next section suggests, social cognitive models dominate research and practice in fitness and exercise behavior.

FITNESS PSYCHOLOGY THEORIES AND RESEARCH

This section includes psychological models and theories that may guide sport psychologists focusing on fitness activities. Because behavior change and maintaining activity are the main issues, the models draw heavily upon behavioral and social cognitive models that have been applied with health behaviors. The section also includes information on behavioral approaches and social support that have been applied with exercise and health-related fitness activities, as well as strategies from typical psychological skills training (PST) that might be applied with fitness activities.

Self-Perceptions

Self-perceptions, including self-esteem and specific perceptions of ability in specific settings, are particularly relevant when considering individual differences in relation to fitness activities. Multidimensional, hierarchical models of self-esteem, such as Shavelson, Hubner and Stanton's (1976) model and Marsh's (1990, 1996) more recent and considerable work on multidimensional self-concept, serve as the basis for sport-specific measures.

Physical Self-concept

Sonstroem (1978) was one of the first scholars to develop sport-specific constructs and measures with his Physical Estimation and Attraction Scales. Ken Fox (1990; Fox & Corbin, 1989) followed the Shavelson et al. model to develop his hierarchical model with global self-esteem at the top level. Physical self-worth, at the next level, is based on the four subdomains of sports competence, attractive body, physical strength and physical condition. Fox's Physical Self-Perception Profile (PSPP) matches this model and includes subscales for:

- *Sports competence*: Perceptions of sport and athletic ability, ability to learn sport skills, and confidence in the sports environment.
- *Physical condition*: Perceptions of level of physical condition, stamina and fitness, ability to maintain exercise, and confidence in the exercise and fitness setting.
- *Body attractiveness*: Perceived attractiveness of figure or physique, ability to maintain an attractive body and confidence in appearance.
- *Physical strength*: Perceived strength, muscle development, and confidence in situations requiring strength.
- *Physical self-Worth*: General feelings of happiness, satisfaction, pride, respect and confidence in the physical self.

Fox and Corbin (1989) provided initial validity support. Sonstroem, Speliotis and Fava (1992) subsequently found that the PSPP separated exercisers from nonexercisers and predicted degree of exercise involvement among adults, and they recommended its continued use.

Sonstroem and Morgan (1989) proposed a similar model with three associated hypotheses:

- Physical fitness is more highly related to physical self-efficacy than to physical competence, physical acceptance and global self-esteem.
- Physical self-efficacy is more highly related to physical competence than to physical acceptance or global self-esteem.
- Physical competence is more highly related to global self-esteem than is physical self-efficacy or physical fitness.

More recently, Herbert Marsh (Marsh, Richards, Johnson, Roche & Tremayne, 1994; Marsh, 1996) developed the Physical Self-Description Questionnaire (PSDQ), a multidimensional physical self-concept measure with 11 scales: strength, body fat, activity, endurance/fitness, sports competence, coordination, health, appearance, flexibility, global physical and global esteem. These specific physical self-perception measures, developed within conceptual frameworks, give sport and exercise psychologists valuable instruments for research.

Body Image

Perceptions of the physical body are part of self-concept, and particularly relevant to physical self-concept. Moreover, body image is particularly relevant to sport psychology work on eating disorders and related issues, as well as to participation in fitness activities. Body perceptions and body image measures have been associated with self-concept for some time. In 1953, Secord and Jourard found body satisfaction was related to self-concept, particularly for women. Body image is related to psychological well-being and self-esteem, and poor body image is consistently associated with depression and anxiety, as well as with eating disorders (Polivy & Herman, 2002; Rodin, Silverstein & Streigel-Moore, 1985).

Hart, Leary and Rejeski (1989), drawing on self-presentation and self-esteem literature, developed the Social Physique Anxiety Scale (SPAS) to assess anxiety associated with having one's physique evaluated by others. They provided reliability and validity evidence, and also found that women scoring high on SPAS reported being less comfortable and having more negative thoughts during physical evaluations than did women scoring low on SPAS. SPAS has been widely used for research on exercise settings and participants, and with body image and eating disorders.

Fitness Activities and Self-Perceptions

Overall, sport, exercise and physical activity programs do not have strong effects on global self-worth, and we would not expect such effects. However, activity programs may well influence specific perceptions of physical competence or body-concept. More specific perceptions of self-efficacy for specific tasks are even more amenable to change. Over the last 10 years, several studies used these multidimensional models to investigate the psychological outcomes of fitness activities. McAuley, Mihalko and Bane (1997), examined self-perceptions with adults in a walking program, and found improvements in perceptions of physical condition as well as physical and global self-esteem. Others have reported similar improvements in self-perceptions, particularly in physical self-perceptions, with exercise and fitness, but relationships are not entirely consistent and underlying processes continue to be debated.

In their review, Martin and Lichtenberger (2002) concluded that exercise training can improve body image. Both aerobic activity and strength training have been shown to improve body image, with weight training having the stronger effects. Several studies have examined the relationship of improved physical fitness to body image, and generally find benefits, particularly for changes in body composition (McAuley, Bane, Rudolph & Lox, 1995; Tucker & Maxwell, 1992). Improvements are seldom dramatic, and several scholars suggest that perceived improvements are the key predictor of enhanced body image and psychological well-being.

Case Examples and Self-perceptions

Physical self-perceptions influence exercise behavior, and are important considerations in fitness psychology. Many previously inactive adults, like George, have low confidence in their physical capabilities, and even active exercisers, like Marie, can have body-image issues that affect exercise behavior. Developing fitness programs and activities that allow accomplishment and the development of positive physical self-perceptions are key components of effective programs. Fitness participants are even more diverse than most sport groups, and allowing for individual preferences is important to enhancing self-perceptions. Participants are likely to be particularly concerned about body image. By encouraging participants to dress for comfort and movement, by avoiding activities and formats that make individuals self-conscious, and by emphasizing activity rather than specific outcomes, we can help make the fitness setting more inviting and thus more effective for participants.

Theories and Models of Exercise Behavior

When focusing on behavior change, and participation in fitness activities, we have considerable theory-based work to draw upon. Bess Marcus, a major contributor to that work, and her colleagues (Marcus, Bock, Pinto, Napolitano & Clark, 2002) have reviewed theoretical models that have been applied to exercise behavior. The following section provides a summary of the main theoretical models, followed by applications for our cases.

Health Belief Model

The health belief model, developed by Rosenstrock (1974) consists of four major components: (a) perceived susceptibility, or the assessment of risk for the particular health threat, (b) perceived severity of the health threat, (c) perceived benefits of taking action to reduce the threat, and (d) perceived barriers or costs to the action. An individual first assesses perceived severity and susceptibility to the illness, then weighs the costs and benefits of taking action, such as beginning a fitness program. The health belief model has considerable support in relation to health behaviors and medical compliance, but limited application to exercise and fitness activities. Support has been found for selected components with investigations following other models. Specifically, perceived barriers, has stronger support than other components.

Theories of Reasoned Action and Planned Behavior

The attitude-based theories of reasoned action and planned behavior have received more attention in sport and exercise psychology. Both the theory of reasoned action (Fishbein & Ajzen, 1974), and its extension, the theory of planned behavior (Ajzen, 1985) propose that *intentions* are the main determinants of behavior. Behavioral intentions, in turn, are determined by *attitudes*, along with *social norms*. The theory of planned behavior adds the notion of *perceived behavioral control*. Perceived behavioral control is similar to self-efficacy in that it involves perceptions of ability to carry out the behavior. Several sport and exercise psychologists have applied reasoned action or planned behavior to understand and predict exercise behavior (Godin, 1993; McAuley & Courneya, 1993).

Decision Theory

Decision theory (Janis & Mann, 1977) involves the individual's perception and evaluation of the relative costs and benefits of exercise. In applied settings, individuals might generate lists of short- and long-term consequences of an exercise program, and then evaluate the balance of those lists. Decision theory was applied successfully with smoking behavior, and these decision-balancing procedures have been adopted and applied for exercise behavior (Marcus, Rakowski & Rossi, 1992; Wankel, 1984).

Self-determination Theory

Self-determination theory (Ryan & Deci, 2000) focuses on self-motivation and ways the social environment can optimize performance and well-being. Deci and Ryan's (1985) extensive research on cognitive evaluation theory and intrinsic motivation has often been applied in sport psychology. Oman and McAuley (1993) found intrinsic motivation related to attendance in an eight-week fitness program, and others are investigating strategies to increase intrinsic motivation as participants move to maintenance stages of fitness programs.

Social Cognitive Theories

Bandura's (1977, 1986) elegant model of self-efficacy and behavior has been applied often and successfully in sport and exercise settings, and that model is highlighted as a framework for fitness psychology. *Self-efficacy* is situation-specific self-confidence, or the belief that one is competent and can do what needs to be done in a specific situation. Bandura asserts that self-efficacy predicts behavior when necessary skills and appropriate incentives are present, and that efficacy expectations are the primary determinants of choice of activity, level of effort and degree of persistence. Self-efficacy theory implies that various techniques and strategies used by instructors, consultants and participants affect behavior because they affect self-efficacy, the critical mediating variable. Efficacy expectations develop and change through four major types of information: performance accomplishments (the strongest source), vicarious experiences, verbal persuasion and emotional arousal. Changes in self-efficacy, in turn, influence actual behavior.

Subsequently Bandura (1986) progressed to *social cognitive theory*, which posits recipro-
cal interrelationships among cognitions (self-efficacy), the environment and behavior. That
model encompasses self-efficacy, but offers a more dynamic and social model. Self-efficacy
and social cognitive theory have been applied widely in exercise activities, as well as in
sport settings, often adopting approaches from behavioral medicine and health psychology.
Ewart, Taylor, Reese and DeBusk (1983) reported that postmyocardial infarction patients
who were more efficacious about their physical capabilities exerted more effort, recovered
faster and returned to normal activities more quickly. Taylor, Bandura, Ewart, Miller and
DeBusk (1985) reported that not only patients' efficacy, but also their spouses' efficacy
predicted cardiac function.

Several studies support strong links between self-efficacy and fitness activities. For
example, Dzewaltowski (1989) and colleagues (Dzewaltowski, Noble & Shaw, 1990)
found self-efficacy predicted exercise behavior in college undergraduates; McAuley (1992)
demonstrated that self-efficacy predicted exercise adherence for middle-age adults; and
Sallis et al. (1986) reported relationships between efficacy and physical activity in a community sample.

Social cognitive approaches dominate in the theoretical and research literature related
to exercise and fitness behavior. Clearly people's thoughts and perceptions are critical
determinants of physical activity and behavior change. However, those fitness programs
that also incorporate behavioral approaches and active social influence strategies are more
comprehensive and may be tailored to the wide range of fitness participants. In the following
sections, behavioral approaches and social influence are considered in relation to fitness
programs.

Case Examples and Theoretical Applications

Although the theoretical models have differing constructs and relationships, we can find
some common themes that fit with several models to guide applications. The primary behavior of concern in fitness activities is adherence, or maintaining exercise behavior. Several
models suggest that adherence is enhanced when participants develop perceived control,
confidence and efficacy for fitness activities, and when they see benefits that outweigh
drawbacks or barriers. Helping participants see the overall health and fitness benefits and
overcome perceived barriers is a major task for fitness instructors and consultants. Many
benefits are long-term and not immediately evident to participants. On the other hand,
barriers—including time, boring exercises and environmental issues—are quite evident.
Fitness instructors are a primary source of health and fitness information for participants
like George, and can provide resources such as current health and fitness publications,
hand-outs, brochures, websites and information on community programs. Instructors can
continually emphasize health and fitness outcomes rather than appearance and weight. Participants may begin programs because of concerns about weight or appearance, or because
of pressure from others, but those reasons will not keep them in a fitness program. Long-
term exercisers stay with fitness activities because of the fitness benefits and the overall
positive health gains (emotional and social wellness as well as physical health). Instructors
and consultants who emphasize overall fitness and health benefits, and help participants
recognize their fitness and wellness gains, will help George and Marie adhere and gain
those benefits.

Nearly all theories suggest that giving participants control or choice, as well as ensuring that they can experience accomplishments, will enhance motivation and adherence. Focusing on slow progressions and small steps with George, and recognizing those accomplishments in the group sessions will enhance his efficacy and perceived control to help overcome barriers to exercise. Marie can keep a journal to record her exercise activities, as well as her feelings (affect) with exercise sessions to help her see her accomplishments as well to make the psychological wellness gains evident to here.

Behavioral Approaches

Although social cognitive models dominate the literature, behavioral approaches are also effective and desirable in fitness activities. In contrast to cognitive approaches that focus on the individual as an active perceiver and interpreter of information, behavioral approaches assume that behavior is determined by past reinforcements and contingencies in the present environment. Today, few psychologists take a radical behaviorism approach and suggest reinforcement is the *only* determinant of behavior. Instead, many applied psychologists, particularly those working with clients on health-related behaviors, incorporate behavioral strategies within a multifaceted program. Behavioral strategies, whether included in an organized program, or an individual's self-regulation program, can be effective in helping a person start and continue fitness activities.

Most fitness activities involve interactions with personal trainers, instructors and sport psychology consultants all aiming to influence behavior and enrich the experience for participants. We will focus on behavioral approaches that instructors or consultants might use to work effectively with individuals to develop skills, strategies and desired behavior patterns.

Behavioral Basics

Behavioral theories and reinforcement constructs are among the most widely researched and accepted principles of modern psychology. Behavioral approaches emphasize the environment, and are based on the fundamental assumption that behavior is determined by its consequences. That is, behaviors are strengthened when they are rewarded, and weakened when they are punished or ignored. Most instructors keep records, evaluate performance, provide feedback, and generally use reinforcing behaviors, but most instructors are not very systematic, and consequently not very effective, at using reinforcement techniques.

The two basic behavioral operations are reinforcement and punishment. *Reinforcement* strengthens a behavior, and *punishment* weakens a behavior. Reinforcement may occur by presenting something positive (positive reinforcement) or by taking away something negative (negative reinforcement). Similarly, punishment may occur by presenting something negative, or by taking away something positive. Reinforcement is effective only when it is applied immediately and consistently, and only when both the instructor and client know what specific behaviors are being reinforced. For fitness activities, the following guidelines adapted from Kauss (1980) are relevant.

- Respond to effort and behavior, not to performance outcome alone. Reinforce efforts and behaviors that move toward the desired outcomes. Fitness is not an immediately observable outcome, and responding to behavior is critical. Instructors can help participants move toward physical fitness by reinforcing desired steps even when fitness seems a distant goal.
- Remember that learning has ups and downs. Clearly the path to fitness has ups and downs and detours. Instructors can continue to reinforce desirable fitness behaviors without putting pressure on the individual. Extra pressure may increase anxiety and prompt withdrawal from the activity. Participation is the goal.
- Use reinforcement to maintain desired behaviors. Maintaining behavior, or developing the *habit*, is the key to fitness activities. Occasional or intermittent reinforcement helps to maintain desired behaviors.

Of course, behaviors that do not occur cannot be reinforced. If you wait for a beginning fitness participant to run the 10K before giving reinforcement, you will wait a long time. *Shaping* refers to the reinforcement of successive approximations of the final desired performance. To shape behavior, reinforce small changes toward the desired behavior. Shaping is a key technique for fitness activities because physical fitness develops gradually through progressive steps.

Behavioral Approaches to Exercise Adherence

Exercise adherence is a problem in fitness programs, and behavioral approaches may help. Martin and Dubbert (1984) provide a useful framework. First, they separate exercise behavior into the two stages of: *acquisition* of the exercise habit, and exercise *maintenance*. Like Marcus, they suggest that different strategies are more effective at different stages. Specifically, during the acquisition phase, Martin and Dubbert suggest the following behavioral strategies:

- *Shaping* is an important strategy for establishing a long-term exercise habit. With previously sedentary adults, establishing the exercise habit is more important than building training effects, and gradual progression with reinforcement for small steps is more effective than exercise goals that cannot be reached within a reasonable time.
- *Reinforcement control* Frequent reinforcement is advocated during the acquisition phase. Social support and praise during sessions is effective, and specific reinforcers, such as tokens, as well as attention and specific feedback, may also be used.
- *Stimulus control* Stimulus control, involving the use of cues is helpful in acquisition of the exercise habit. Many morning exercisers put their gym bags out the night before as a prompt, and organized programs typically use cues in both their advertising and ongoing programs.
- *Behavioral contracts* Specific contracts, often in writing, may be effective for some beginning exercisers. Contracts are a form of goal-setting that can provide direction and incentive for exercise behavior.
- *Cognitive strategies* Martin and Dubbert suggest several cognitive strategies such as goal-setting, positive self-talk and association–dissociation (distraction) as part of a cognitive-behavioral approach during the acquisition phase.

After an exerciser has developed the habit, behavioral strategies should change to match the needs of the exerciser in the maintenance phase. Specifically, behavioral strategies should help the person move from a structured, organized program to individual, continuing exercise maintenance.

- *Generalization training* Generalization training involves the gradual fading of the program as the person makes the difficult transition from a structured to an unstructured setting. Generalization refers to generalizing the exercise behavior to other settings or circumstances. Organized programs might incorporate home exercise during the program to aid the transition, and generalization training might include family or friends.
- *Reinforcement fading* Gradually reinforcement fades in frequency and intensity as the person transfers to "natural" reinforcers such as increased feelings of control, and increased energy.
- *Self-control procedures* As discussed earlier, a sense of control leads to intrinsic motivation, which is essential for exercise maintenance. Self-monitoring is the most common procedure, and actually should begin in the earlier phase. Self-evaluation and reward may also be included, often in a contracting procedure.
- *Relapse prevention training* Most exercisers, even the most faithful program adherents, eventually relapse. Thus, most professionals advocate some type of relapse prevention training. Exercisers are taught to view exercise as a continuum, to recognize and avoid risk situations, and sometimes to try a planned relapse.

Many exercise programs and personal trainers adopt some of these behavioral strategies, and most practitioners use a variety of strategies incorporating cognitive approaches as well as behavioral techniques. Given the diversity of fitness participants, multifaceted programs with varied strategies and approaches are most likely to meet participants' needs and preferences.

Case Examples and Behavioral Approaches

Both Marie and George can benefit from the use of behavioral approaches in their training programs, and on their own. George is at earlier stages, and shaping, reinforcement control, contracts and cognitive strategies may be especially helpful. The group instructor can and should provide considerable reinforcement and support for George's activities, including acknowledging his attendance with a welcome. The instructor can also help George progress through activities at a pace that allows accomplishments and shaping of the exercise habit. Behavioral contracts and goal-setting strategies, particularly focused on the behaviors of participating and doing exercises, can be effective with George and his fellow group participants. Maintaining charts or records for each group member where they can record their daily activities can act as reinforcement. Many programs use such incentives as water bottles and T-shirts, and those may provide support for George. However, such tangible reinforcers are most effective if they are tied to activity (water bottles are useful during activities), and are used sparingly with more emphasis on shifting to positive feelings and enhanced fitness as reinforcers.

Marie is less likely to benefit from such tangible reinforcers, but encouragement and reinforcement for desired activities are important for all participants. Marie can benefit from an effective self-regulation program, and a trainer can help her develop some effective strategies for maintaining her fitness activities outside of her training sessions. Most people benefit from using behavioral techniques to make exercise a priority, such as scheduling in a daily planner, or keeping exercise equipment in a visible location. Relapse prevention training and planning for breaks in her exercise routine will also be helpful for Marie.

Social Support

Even though we often assume exercise is an individual activity, most fitness activities take place in social settings, and social interaction has a great influence on fitness participants' behaviors. Social support logically refers to the support of others, and researchers have often operationally defined social support as the number of friends, relatives or social involvements. In current research, social support is a multidimensional construct, and consensus suggests that quality of support is more important than quantity of social contacts. Shumaker and Brownell (1984, p. 13) define social support as, "an exchange of resources between at least two individuals perceived by the provider or the recipient to be intended to enhance the well-being of the recipient".

Shumaker and Brownell's definition, which is consistent with current research, suggests that social support is a process. Rosenfeld and Richman's (1997) model depicts that process and includes the commonly accepted dimensions of social support as: *tangible* (e.g. assisting someone with a task), *informational* (e.g. telling a client about community resources), and *emotional* (e.g. comforting someone). Rosenfeld and Richman note that behaviors are social support when the recipient perceives those behaviors as enhancing well-being. The perceived communicated behaviors take eight forms in the Rosenfeld and Richman model:

- *Listening support* Others listen to you without being judgmental.
- *Emotional support* Others comfort and care for you.
- *Emotional challenge* Others challenge you.
- *Task appreciation* Others acknowledge your efforts and express appreciation.
- *Task challenge* Others challenge your way of thinking.
- *Reality confirmation* Others help you confirm your perception of the world.
- *Tangible assistance* Others provide you with financial assistance, products or gifts.
- *Personal assistance* Others provide services or help, such as running errands or providing expertise.

Others have listed different specific forms of social support, but most authors agree that social support benefits are based on direct assistance (tangible support), advice (informational support) or encouragement (emotional support). Social support measures have been developed in conjunction with models, and reflect similar dimensions, and these measures have been used to investigate social support in sport and exercise settings. Duncan and McAuley (1993) found that social support did not directly influence exercise behavior with sedentary, middle-aged men and women, but had an indirect effect through self-efficacy, suggesting social support may help promote self-efficacy for exercise, and thus health-related fitness. They cautioned that, in practice, exercise leaders may have difficulty matching support to needs, and that monitoring perceived support in relation to intentions and program goals is important. Also, with the mediating role of self-efficacy, supportive interventions should be designed to foster self-reliance and avoid dependency.

Spanier and Allison (2001) found number of friends or family members and frequency of social contact were positively associated with higher physical activity levels, but familial structure (being married and having children) was associated with lower levels of physical activity. Eyler and colleagues (1999) found that women with higher perceived support were less likely to be sedentary and more likely to accumulate greater total physical activity per week, but social support had no influence on regular exercise. They suggest that exercise-specific social support may provide the initial motivation and may be more important for moderate than regularly sustained physical activity.

Physical activity intervention studies have revealed inconsistent results on the relationship between social support and physical activity behavior. Baseline perceptions of both general and exercise-specific social support have been found to predict exercise behavior at three months into an exercise program (Courneya & McAuley, 1995; Litt, Kleppinger & Judge, 2002). However, in an intervention study with older adults, neither baseline levels nor changes in exercise-related social support were related to exercise adherence (Brassington, Atienza, Percek, DiLorenzo & King, 2002). Turner, Rejeski and Brawley (1997) found that when exercise leaders followed a positive approach, provided frequent individual attention and engaged in general conversation, participants were more positive and increased more in self-efficacy.

Carron, Hausenblas and Mack's (1996) meta-analysis found social influence to be positively associated with exercise behavior, exercise intentions and attitudes associated with the exercise experience. In addition, support from non-familial important others (e.g. physicians, work colleagues) had a stronger influence on exercise behavior than support from family members. Although this meta-analysis and related research supports a relationship between social influence, exercise motivation and exercise behavior, we are far from understanding all the interrelationships of social influence with exercise motivation and fitness behavior.

Case Examples and Social Support

Social support is an element of most effective fitness programs, and both George and Marie can benefit. An instructor is a source of informational support for any fitness participant, and instructors must provide accurate information and feedback on techniques, training effects and health outcomes for fitness activities. For George, the group, as well as the instructor, provides social support. Being in a group of others who are similar in their fitness levels and experiences provides considerable support, and emotional support and encouragement is important to help George stay with fitness activities.

An Integrated Approach: Transtheoretical Model

Several researchers have advocated integration of the many available theoretical approaches. At this time, the most useful approach for practicing professionals is the transtheoretical model (Prochaska & DiClemente, 1983) applied to exercise behavior by Marcus and her colleagues. According to the model, individuals progress through a series of stages of change:

- precontemplation
- contemplation
- preparation
- action
- maintenance.

Precontemplators do not exercise and do not intend to do so within the next 6 months. Contemplators do not exercise, but intend to start within six months. Preparers are exercising, but not regularly (3 or more times per week for 20 minutes or longer, or accumulating 30 minutes or more per day 5 or more days per week, as recommended by ACSM; Pate et al., 1995). Individuals at the action stage exercise regularly, but have done so less than 6 months, whereas those at the maintenance stage have been exercising regularly for over 6 months (Marcus, Rossi, Selby, Niaura & Abrams, 1992). The main point for professionals is that intervention programs should match the stage of change. The work of Marcus and colleagues has been especially useful in promoting physical activity. At the end of this chapter we will return to more specific applications using the stages of change as a framework for effective physical activity promotion.

Relapse Prevention Model

Regardless of how one starts exercising, relapse is a problem, as it is for most health behaviors (Brownell, Marlatt, Lichtenstein & Wilson, 1986). As noted earlier, about 50 per cent of exercise program participants typically drop out within six months. The principles of relapse prevention include: (a) identifying high-risk situations (e.g. change in work hours), and (b) problem-solving solutions for those high-risk situations (e.g. when it starts to snow, move inside the mall to walk).

When individuals experience a relapse they must deal with the *abstinence violation effect* (AVE). AVE is the belief that one slip means doom (one cookie ruins the diet, one missed exercise class and you're a couch potato). Brownell (1989) differentiates a lapse (slip), relapse (string of lapses) and collapse (giving up and returning to past behaviors), and advocates helping individuals become aware of AVE and the differences among lapse, relapse and collapse to reduce recidivism. Marcus, Dubbert and colleagues (2000) suggest the relapse prevention model can be a useful framework for understanding the lapse to relapse process in exercise behavior.

PSYCHOLOGICAL SKILLS AND STRATEGIES FOR FITNESS ACTIVITIES

Psychological skill training (PST), which is discussed in more detail in other chapters in this text, implies the application of sport psychology theories and research to enhance the performance and the overall experience of participants. Most PST focuses on competition and elite athletes, but psychological skills are for everyone, including younger or inexperienced athletes. Moreover, psychological skills can be used by fitness activity participants, including Marie and George. Effective goal-setting, as discussed in earlier sections can help participants stay with the program and get optimal benefits, and effective emotional control strategies are especially helpful to fitness participants as part of an overall health and wellness program. In this chapter, we will focus on the aspects of PST that are particularly relevant for fitness activities.

Educational Sport Psychology Approach

Psychological skills training (PST) complements physical training, and follows an educational approach. The educational approach highlights *individualization* and emphasizes *self-control*. Most programs combine *cognitive control skills*, such as goal-setting and concentration, with *emotional control skills*, such as relaxation techniques.

These cognitive and emotional control skills are components of more elaborate psychological skills training programs that many sport psychology consultants use in working with athletes. Individualized programs are tailored to match changing situations, individual skills and preferences, and balanced with other physical training demands and lifestyle concerns. The aim is to educate and develop skills so that the participant can control their behavior and achieve their goals. To gain confidence and control, participants use PST to develop cognitive control skills (to control their thoughts) and emotional control skills (to control anxiety and other emotions). These same general goals and guidelines apply to PST for fitness activities. PST can help the fitness participant gain confidence and control, which are important to behavior change and maintenance. PST must be individualized, and fit the person's preferences and characteristics (such as stage of change), and the specific skills should be targeted to the participant's overall physical fitness goals and lifetime activity.

Cognitive Control Skills

Cognition or thoughts are key components of the fitness psychology framework, and psychological interventions aimed at controlling thoughts are often effective. The most common cognitive control skills in PST are goal-setting, attention and thought control, and imagery. Cognitive control skills are useful in fitness programs, and goal-setting is particularly appropriate. Consultants working with fitness participants need to keep in mind that fitness goals are quite different from typical competitive sport goals. Fitness participants are not focused on a peak performance, but on lifetime activity. Also, participants typically have goals that are achieved *through* fitness, such as maintaining independence, rather than focused performance achievement goals.

Goal-setting

Participants usually hold multiple goals, and exercise instructors, physicians, family or friends may hold goals for them. Goal-setting has been a popular research topic since the 1960s, and research continues to confirm the benefits of goal-setting. Common as goals are, though, goals are not automatically effective. The research on goal-setting and the reports of sport psychology consultants suggest guidelines for using goal-setting effectively. The following suggestions are adapted from Weinberg (2002) and Gould (2001) and seem particularly relevant for fitness activities:

- *Set specific goals* One of the most consistent research findings is that specific goals enhance performance more than "do-your-best" or no goals. "To get stronger" is not a specific or effective goal. Marie might set goals to increase the weight and number of repetitions in her weight-training routine over a 6-week program. George, an older participant with a lower fitness level, might start with goals related to his life situation, such as walking up a long flight of stairs.
- *Set realistic but challenging goals* Goals should be attainable, but when participants are aiming for improved fitness, challenge is essential. Strength training and aerobic training are accomplished only with challenge to the cardiovascular and muscular systems. However, it is important to note that fitness participants are not solely focused on improving fitness. Even Marie, who likely has some specific fitness goals, is not continually striving to attain higher levels. Maintaining fitness, balance of fitness components, and attention to non-fitness health and wellness outcomes are even more important for Marie. For both Marie and George, goals are best focused on activity behaviors such as attending group sessions, engaging in endurance activity for a certain time (running or cycling for 30 minutes on 3 days per week; walking for 20 minutes each day).
- *"Ink it, don't think it"* Write down and record goals. Many fitness participants keep logs, and many organized exercise programs maintain records of individual goals and accomplishments. Participants might keep individual goals for weight training in a log, or walking programs may keep charts for participants to mark off miles as they "walk across the state". Such records often add variety and give some purpose to what might otherwise seem a rather monotonous activity. For George and Marie, recording goals or activities in a session chart or journal can help them recognize accomplishments, and serve as a reinforcement for their activities.
- *Set performance/process goals* Goals should focus on performance or the process rather than outcomes. Physical fitness is a process, and goals should reflect fitness activities and behaviors. Although improved fitness is clearly a goal, fitness improvements are not easily observed and may seem unreachable to participants. George will not immediately see that he has more cardiovascular endurance, but he can see that he can walk several laps each session, and may walk more laps after two months in the program. An instructor can also help George see the fitness gains by pointing out that he can lift more weight, and asking about outside activities (playing with grandchildren, doing yardwork), as well as by using periodic fitness evaluations during the program.
- *Provide support for goals* Support is particularly important for fitness participants. Physical fitness is a process and outcomes are not readily apparent. As noted earlier, social support and expectations have been shown to enhance exercise adherence. Many fitness instructors now routinely include activities to promote social support among participants, such as exercise "buddies", as well as providing support themselves.
- *Evaluate goals* Goals must be evaluated and revised throughout the fitness program. Fitness is a process, and both the individual and the situation will continually change, calling for revisions in goals and strategies. Many fitness participants start with unrealistic goals, or a focus on weight and appearance. Effective instructors can help participants focus on activity itself as a goal, and recognize positive changes in emotional and psychological wellness through activity.

Attentional Control/concentration, Self-talk, Imagery

Attentional control and concentration, self-talk and imagery are all key components of PST programs. For fitness participants, these skills can be useful, but are not as common as goal-setting, and we will not devote as much space to them here.

Many athletes use verbal or kinesthetic cues to focus or regain concentration. For fitness participants, cues can be especially useful in keeping up regular exercise activity. Setting your exercise bag by the door, or setting a watch alarm for the noon exercise hour, can be effective prompts for exercisers like Marie.

Zinsser, Bunker and Williams (2001) argue that self-talk is the key to cognitive control. Self-talk may help correct bad habits, focus attention, modify emotional state and, especially, build self-confidence. Many beginning fitness participants, like George, have poor physical self-perceptions and lack confidence in their ability to be physically active. Some of the common techniques that Zinsser et al. (2001) suggest for athletes may be useful for fitness participants, including thought-stopping, which involves the use of a cue to interrupt unwanted thoughts, and then substituting a positive, constructive thought. For example, "I will never be able to walk one mile"—*Stop*! "But I can walk to the end of the block today, and next week I will walk two blocks." When we are faced with physical limitations or barriers, as many participants are, we cannot always think of those positive substitute thoughts. Consultants might help George or Marie make a list of barriers and typical negative thoughts and then write a positive substitute next to each one.

Imagery involves using all the senses to create or re-create an experience in the mind. Imagery can be an effective strategy for practicing other psychological skills, such as stress management, as well as for developing and maintaining physical skills and strategies for fitness activities. Gould, Damarjian and Greenleaf (2002) reviewed the literature and provided guidelines and specific exercises for imagery training that may be useful for some fitness settings. For example, an instructor might suggest that participants use imagery to practice a new aerobic exercise routine, or to prepare for lifting weights. Generally, fitness participants are less likely to use imagery for skill development than are competitive sport participants. Fitness participants may well find imagery useful for relaxation and stress management, or for developing coping strategies to deal with barriers or relapses.

Emotional Control Skills

Stress management and emotional control are particularly relevant, and have an important role in fitness activity programs. Emotional control skills are critical for overall fitness, and stress is a major barrier to health and fitness. Stress management not only enhances fitness activity, but has direct benefits for overall wellness, and is a key component of any health-related fitness program. Physical activity can act as a stress management tactic, particularly for relieving muscle tension. Participants may also benefit from additional coping strategies that help them manage the range of stresses in their lives. Active (to directly solve the problem or minimize stress) and passive (to minimize emotional or physical effects of the stressful situation) coping strategies may help in coping with a wide range of stressors, and help move toward health-related fitness.

Stress or anxiety is common in sport, and stress management techniques are key psychological skills. Sport psychology work suggests that the ability to *control* anxiety is the key. While competitive anxiety is not typically a problem for fitness participants, anxiety, stress or depression are often issues, whether they arise within the program or from outside sources. Some people easily control their emotions with simple techniques and have few problems. Others have considerable difficulty and may even seek professional help. Because stress and anxiety have cognitive and physiological components, stress management includes both cognitive and physical relaxation techniques.

Simple cognitive techniques, such as thought-stopping, can be applied to control anxiety, and imagery also may be used as a relaxation technique. Simply imaging a calm, peaceful scene may allow an individual to transcend a stressful situation mentally and gain control. The most widely recognized stress management techniques work directly on physiological arousal. Relaxation techniques include simple breathing exercises, meditation, progressive relaxation and many variations on those techniques.

- *Breathing exercises* One of the simplest but most effective relaxation techniques is slow, deep breathing. Increased respiration rate is part of the autonomic stress response, and respiration is one of the physiological responses that is easily controlled.

  One simple technique is to breathe in slowly and deeply while counting ("1 – 2 – 3 – 4"), then hold the breath for 4 counts, and then exhale slowly ("1 – 2 – 3 – 4"). A consultant might help by starting the exercise and counting aloud for the individual. Many other relaxation techniques incorporate similar deep breathing. Both progressive relaxation and mediation—two popular techniques—include attention to slow, deep breathing.
- *Progressive relaxation* Progressive relaxation, which involves the progressive tensing and relaxing of various muscle groups, is a popular relaxation technique in sport psychology. Progressive relaxation is relatively simple, but practice is needed to become proficient and effective. Typically a consultant will conduct several sessions, giving cues to tense and then relax specific muscle groups. As individuals become more proficient, sessions become shorter as specific muscle groups are combined and the tension phase is gradually reduced. The goal is for the individual to recognize subtle levels of muscle tension and to relax those muscles at will. For example, a person might notice tightness in the neck and shoulders, and then focus attention on those muscles, relax them, and re-focus on the fitness activity.
- *Meditation* As a stress management technique, progressive relaxation involves relaxing the muscles and letting the mind follow. Meditation techniques work in the reverse direction: relax the mind and let the body follow. Meditation generally involves a relaxed, passive focusing of attention; tension and strain are avoided. Often the person simply focuses on breathing with no analytic thought or special effort.

  Benson's relaxation response is one of the easiest and most popular meditation techniques. To use the Benson method, the person finds a quiet setting without distractions, and then attends to breathing. Meditation involves *passive* attention—simply attending to breathing without straining or worrying about it.

Case examples and stress management

Both Marie and George, and all fitness participants, can benefit from stress management and relaxation exercises. Simple relaxation techniques can be incorporated in the fitness session. George's activity group might start with slow deep breathing, followed with periodic reminders to attend to breathing during the exercise activity. As well as including simple techniques during exercise sessions, fitness instructors can include stress management sessions for clients. For example, Marie's trainer might introduce a progressive relaxation exercise, Benson's technique and an imagery exercise with instructions, practice in a session, and tapes or guidelines for home practice. Marie could then try different techniques and find ones that would be useful to deal with stressors in her daily life.

Comprehensive Psychological Skills Programs

The cognitive and relaxation techniques just covered are relatively simple techniques that participants can use without special training. More elaborate and comprehensive stress management combining relaxation exercises with cognitive interventions may be appropriate, especially when working with a client over a longer time period. Just as sport psychology consultants often combine psychological skills in a comprehensive training program for athletes, consultants working with participants in fitness activities can combine psychological skills and cognitive-behavioral strategies in a comprehensive program. Moreover, the program must be tailored to the individual to be effective. Marcus has provided an effective program using the transtheoretical model as a framework, with cognitive-behavioral strategies matched to the individual. The following section presents that model as a practical guide for fitness activities.

THE TRANSTHEORETICAL MODEL: A PRACTICAL GUIDE

The transtheoretical model incorporates aspects of other theories, with the underlying theme that people are at different readiness levels, and different interventions or strategies are needed to change exercise behavior. Marcus and her colleagues have gone beyond proposals to carry out interventions based on the transtheoretical model. In the Imagine Action campaign, 610 adults who enrolled through worksites, in response to community announcements, received a six-week intervention consisting of stage-matched self-help materials, resource manual, weekly fun walks and activity nights. The manual for contemplators was called *What's in it for You?* as this is the critical question at that stage. Similarly, the preparation manual was *Ready for Action*, and the manual for those in action called, *Keeping it Going*. Following the intervention, 30% of those in contemplation and 61% of those in preparation progressed to action, and an additional 31% of those in contemplation progressed to preparation, whereas only 4% of those in preparation and 9% in action regressed. A subsequent controlled, randomized design investigation of a stage-matched intervention at the workplace (Marcus et al., 1994) was successful with more subjects in the stage-matched group demonstrating stage progression at the 3-month follow-up; in contrast, more subjects in the standard care group displayed stage stability or regression.

More recently, Marcus and Forsyth (2003) have compiled related research and theoretical work into a practical guide titled, *Motivating People to be Physically Active*. That guide emphasizes stages of change as an individual difference variable, and then suggests behavioral and cognitive strategies, as well as social support and environmental approaches, to promote physical activity. Sources of information and guidelines for the general public, such as Corbin et al.'s (2003) fitness manual and the CDC website, reference Marcus and recommend a similar approach. Project Active (Dunn et al., 1999) has successfully applied the model in a community-based physical activity program.

Marcus and Forsyth (2003) use the stages-of-change model as framework for individualizing intervention strategies. As noted in the earlier section, individuals are at different stages depending on their current level of physical activity. Precontemplators do not exercise and do not intend to do so. Contemplators do not exercise, but intend to start within six months. Preparers are exercising, but not regularly. Individuals at the action stage exercise regularly, but have done so less than six months, whereas those at the maintenance stage have been exercising regularly for over six months. The main point for professionals is that intervention programs should match the stage of change.

Processes of behavior change are strategies and techniques individuals use to modify behaviors (*how* people change). Processes fall into two categories: cognitive (increasing knowledge, being aware of risks, caring about consequences to others, comprehending benefits and healthy opportunities), and behavioral (substituting alternatives, enlisting social support, rewarding yourself, committing yourself and reminding yourself).

Programs based on the model match interventions to the individual's stage of readiness. People in the early stages (precontemplation, contemplation) might use more cognitive strategies, whereas those at later stages (preparation, action, maintenance) use mostly behavioral strategies. Within that general framework, Marcus and Forsyth provide more specific examples and suggestions that consultants or fitness psychologists might use to help clients use these strategies in the process of behavior change. Many of the specific strategies draw upon the behavioral and cognitive strategies and psychological skills discussed in the previous sections. Strategies that are appropriate for the individual's current stage are used to help the person take positive steps toward fitness, while overcoming barriers and building confidence. The Marcus and Forsyth book is readable and practical, but based on current theory and empirical evidence. I recommend that book as a guide for sport psychologists working with clients in fitness activities.

CONCLUSIONS

Although fitness activities differ from the sports covered in other chapters in many ways, sport psychology can be applied to enhance fitness activities. Indeed, effective application of behavioral and cognitive strategies, within a theoretical framework, is essential for effective fitness programs. Fitness activities are lifestyle activities, with the overriding goal of maintaining activity rather than continually striving to achieve performance standards. Applied sport psychology interventions that help participants focus on lifestyle activity are likely to be effective. Behavioral strategies and social cognitive approaches that focus on recognizing health and fitness benefits, overcoming barriers and developing self-control and perceived competence in a supportive environment are particularly appropriate. Specific behavioral and cognitive strategies used within an integrative model that matches strategies to the individual can help George, Marie and other fitness participants overcome barriers, develop confidence and gain greater health and wellness through fitness activities.

REFERENCES

Ajzen, I. (1985). From intentions to actions: a theory of focus on these important subgroups. In J. Kuhl & J. Reckman (eds), *Action-control: From Cognition to Behavior* (pp. 11–39). Heidelberg: Springer.

Bandura, A. (1977). Self-efficacy: toward a unifying theory of behavioral change. *Psychological Review, 84*, 191–215.

Bandura, A. (1986). *Social Foundations of Thought and Action: A Social Cognitive Theory*. Englewood Cliffs, NJ: Prentice-Hall.

Booth, F.W. (2002). Cost and consequences of sedentary living: new battleground for an old enemy. *President's Council on Physical Fitness and Sports Research Digest*, Series 3, No. 16.

Brassington, G.S., Atienza, A., Percek, R.E., DiLorenzo, T.M. & King, A.C. (2002). Intervention related cognitive versus social mediators of exercise adherence in the elderly. *American Journal of Preventive Medicine, 23*, 80–86.

Brownell, K.D. (1989). *The LEARN Program for Weight Control*. Dallas, TX: Brownell & Hager.

Brownell, K.D., Marlatt, G.A., Lichtenstein, E. & Wilson, G.T. (1986). Understanding and preventing relapse. *American Psychologist, 41*, 765–782.

Buckworth, J. & Dishman, R.K. (2002). *Exercise Psychology*. Champaign, IL: Human Kinetics.

Carron, A.V., Hausenblas, H.A., & Mack, D. (1996). Social influence and exercise: a meta-analysis. *Journal of Sport and Exercise Psychology, 18*, 1–16.

Corbin, C.B., Welk, G.J., Lindsey, R. & Corbin, W.R. (2003). *Concepts of Physical Fitness* (11th edn). Boston, MA: McGraw-Hill.

Courneya, K. & McAuley, E. (1995). Cognitive mediators of the social influence-exercise adherence relationship: a test of the theory of planned behavior. *Journal of Behavioral Medicine, 18*, 499–515.

Deci, E.L. & Ryan, R.M. (1985). *Intrinsic Motivation and Self-determination in Human Behavior*. New York: Plenum Press.

Dishman, R.K. & Ickes, W. (1981). Self-motivation and adherence to therapeutic exercise. *Journal of Behavioral Medicine, 4*, 421–438.

Duncan, T.E. & McAuley, E. (1993). Social support and efficacy cognitions in exercise adherence: a latent growth curve analysis. *Journal of Behavioral Medicine, 16*(2), 199–218.

Dunn, A.L., Marcus, B.H., Kampert, J.B., Garcia, M.E., Kohl, H.W. & Blair, S.N. (1999). Reduction in cardiovascular disease risk factors: 6-month results from Project Active. *Preventive Medicine, 26*, 883–892.

Dzewaltowski, D.A. (1989). Toward a model of exercise motivation. *Journal of Sport and Exercise Psychology, 11*, 251–269.

Dzewaltowski, D.A., Noble, J.M. & Shaw, J.M. (1990). Physical activity participation: social cognitive theory versus the theories of reasoned action and planned behavior. *Journal of Sport and Exercise Psychology, 12*, 388–405.

Ewart, C.K., Taylor, C.B., Reese, L.B. & DeBusk, R.F. (1983). Effects of early post myocardial infarction exercise testing on self-perception and subsequent physical activity. *American Journal of Cardiology, 51*, 1076–1080.

Eyler, A.A., Brownson, R.C., Donatelle, R.J., King, A.C., Brown, D. & Sallis, J.F. (1999). Physical activity social support and middle- and older-aged minority women: results from a US survey. *Social Science and Medicine, 49*, 781–789.

Fishbein, M. & Ajzen, I. (1974). Attitudes toward objects as predictors of single and multiple behavioral criteria. *Psychological Review, 81*, 59–74.

Fox, K.R. (1990). *The Physical Self-Perception Profile manual*. DeKalb, IL: Office for Health Promotion, Northern Illinois University.

Fox, K.R. & Corbin, C.B. (1989). The Physical Self-Perception Profile: development and preliminary validation. *Journal of Sport and Exercise Psychology, 11*, 408–430.

Gill, D.L. (2000). *Psychological Dynamics of Sport and Exercise* (2nd edn). Champaign, IL: Human Kinetics.

Godin, G. (1993). The theories of reasoned action and planned behavior: overview of findings, emerging research problems, and usefulness for exercise promotion. *Journal of Applied Sport Psychology, 5*, 141–157.

Gould, D. (2001). Goal setting for peak performance. In Williams, J.M. (ed.). *Applied Sport Psychology* (4th edn; pp. 190–205). Mountain View, CA: Mayfield.

Gould, D., Damarjian, N. & Greenleaf, C. (2002). Imagery training for peak performance. In J.L. Van Raalte & B.W. Brewer (eds), *Exploring Sport and Exercise Psychology* (2nd edn; pp. 49–76). Washington, D.C.: APA.

Hart, E.A., Leary, M.R. & Rejeski, W.J. (1989). The measurement of social physique anxiety. *Journal of Sport and Exercise Psychology, 11*, 94–104.

Heath, G.W., Pratt, M., Warren, C.W. & Kann, L. (1994). Physical activity patterns in American high school students: results from the 1990 Youth Risk Behavior Survey. *Archives of Pediatric and Adolescent Medicine, 148*, 1131–1136.

Janis, I.L. & Mann, L. (1977). *Decision Making: A Psychological Analysis of Conflict, Choice and Commitment*. New York: Free Press.

Kauss, D.R. (1980). *Peak Performance*. Englewood Cliffs, NJ: Prentice-Hall.

Kesaniemi, Y.K., Danforth, E. Jr., Jensen, M.D., Kopelman, P.G., Lefebre, P. & Reeder, B.A. (2001). Dose-response issues concerning physical activity and health: an evidence-based symposium. *Medicine and Science in Sports and Exercise, 33*(6 Supplement), S351–S358.

Litt, M.D., Kleppinger, A. & Judge, J.O. (2002). Initiation and maintenance of exercise behavior in older women: predictors from the social learning model. *Journal of Behavioral Medicine, 25*, 83–97.

Lewin, K. (1935). *A Dynamic Theory of Personality*. New York: McGraw-Hill.

Lox, C.L., Martin, K.A. & Petruzzello, S.J. (2003). *The Psychology of Exercise*. Scottsdale, AZ: Holcomb Hathaway.

Marcus, B.H., Bock, B.C., Pinto, B.M., Napolitano, M.A. & Clark, M.M. (2002). Exercise initiation, adoption and maintenance in adults: theoretical models and empirical support. In J.L. Van Raalte & B.W. Brewer (eds), *Exploring Sport and Exercise Psychology* (2nd edn; pp. 185–208). Washington, DC: APA.

Marcus, B.H., Dubbert, P.M., Forsyth, L.H., McKenzie, T.L., Stone, E.J., Dunn, A.L. & Blair, S.N. (2000). Physical activity behavior change: issues in adoption and maintenance. *Health Psychology, 19*(Suppl. 1), 32–41.

Marcus, B.H., Emmons, K.M., Simkin, L.R., Taylor, E.R., Linnan, L., Rossi, J.S. & Abrams, D.B. (1994). Comparison of stage-matched versus standard care physical activity interventions at the workplace. *Annals of Behavioral Medicine, 16*, S035.

Marcus, B.H. & Forsyth, L.H. (2003). *Motivating People to be Physically Active*. Champaign, IL: Human Kinetics.

Marcus, B.H., Rakowski, W. & Rossi, J.S. (1992). Assessing motivational readiness and decision-making for exercise. *Health Psychology, 11*, 257–261.

Marcus, B.H., Rossi, J.S., Selby, V.C., Niaura, R.S. & Abrams, D.B. (1992). The stages and processes of exercise adoption and maintenance in a worksite sample. *Health Psychology, 11*, 386–395.

Marcus, B.H., Selby, V.C., Niaura, R.S. & Rossi, J.S. (1992). Self-efficacy and the stages of exercise behavior change. *Research Quarterly for Exercise and Sport, 63*, 60–66.

Marsh, H.W. (1990). A multidimensional, hierarchical self-concept: theoretical and empirical justification. *Educational Psychology Review, 2*, 77–172.

Marsh, H.W. (1996). Construct validity of physical self-description questionnaire responses: relation to external criteria. *Journal of Sport and Exercise Psychology, 18*, 111–113.

Marsh, H.W., Richards, G.E., Johnson, S., Roche, L. & Tremayne, P. (1994). Physical self-description questionnaire: psychometric properties and multitrait-multimethod analysis of relations to existing instruments. *Journal of Sport and Exercise Psychology, 16*, 270–305.

Martin, J.E. & Dubbert, P.M. (1984). Behavioral management strategies for improving health and fitness. *Journal of Cardiac Rehabilitation, 4*, 200–208.

Martin, K.A. & Lichtenberger, C.M. (2002), Fitness enhancement and body image change. In T.F. Cash & T. Pruzinsky (eds), *Body Images: A Handbook of Theory, Research, and Clinical Practice*. New York: Guilford Press.

McAuley, E. (1992). Understanding exercise behavior: a self-efficacy perspective. In G.C. Roberts (ed.), *Motivation in Sport and Exercise* (pp. 107–127). Champaign, IL: Human Kinetics.

McAuley, E., Bane, S.M., Rudolph, D. & Lox, C. (1995). Exercise and self-esteem in middle-aged adults: multidimensional relationships and physical fitness and self-efficacy influences. *Journal of Behavioral Medicine, 20*, 67–83.

McAuley, E. & Courneya, K.S. (1993). Adherence to exercise and physical activity as health-promoting behaviors: attitudinal and self-efficacy influences. *Applied and Preventive Psychology, 2*, 65–77.

McAuley, E., Mihalko, S.L. & Bane, S.M. (1997). Physique anxiety and exercise in middle-aged adults. *Journal of Gerontology, 50B*, 229–235.

Motl, R.W., Dishman, R.K., Felton, G. & Pate, R.R. (2003). Self-motivation and physical activity among black and white adolescent girls. *Medicine and Science in Sports and Exercise, 53*, 128–136.

Nieman, D.C. (1998). *The Exercise-health Connection*. Champaign, IL: Human Kinetics.

Oman, R.F. & McAuley, E. (1993). Intrinsic motivation and exercise behavior. *Journal of Health Education, 24*, 232–238.

Pate, R.R., Pratt, M., Blair, S.N., et al. (1995). Physical activity and public health: a recommendation from the Centers for Disease Control and Prevention and the American College of Sports Medicine. *Journal of the American Medical Association, 273*(5), 402–407.

Polivy, J. & Herman, C.P. (2002). Causes of eating disorders. *Annual Review of Psychology, 53*, 187–213.

Prochaska, J.O. & DiClemente, C.C. (1983). Stages and processes of self-change of smoking: towards an integrative model of change. *Journal of Consulting and Clinical Psychology, 51*, 390–395.

Rodin, J., Silberstein, L.R. & Streigel-Moore, R.H. (1985). Women and weight: a normative discontent. In T.B. Sonderegger (ed.), *Nebraska Symposium on Motivation, Vol. 32* (pp. 267–307, Psychology and gender). Lincoln: University of Nebraska.

Rosenfeld, L.B. & Richman, J.R. (1997). Developing effective social support: team building and the social support process. *Journal of Applied Sport Psychology, 9*, 133–153.

Rosenstrock, I.M. (1974). Historical origins of the health belief model. *Health Education Monographs, 2*, 328–335.

Ryan, R.M. & Deci, E.L. (2000). Self-determination theory and the facilitation of intrinsic motivation, development, and well-being. *American Psychologist, 55*, 68–78.

Sallis, J.F., Haskell, W.L., Fortmann, S.P., Vranizan, K.M., Taylor, C.B. & Solomon, D.S. (1986). Predictors of adoption and maintenance of physical activity in a community sample. *Preventive Medicine, 15*, 331–341.

Secord, P.F. & Jourard, S.M. (1953). The appraisal of body cathexis: body cathexis and the self. *Journal of Consulting Psychology, 17*, 343–347.

Shavelson, R.J., Hubner, J.J. & Stanton, G.C. (1976). Self-concept: validation of construct interpretations. *Review of Educational Research, 46*, 407–441.

Shumaker, S.A. & Brownell, A. (1984). Toward a theory of social support: closing conceptual gaps. *Journal of Social Issues, 40*, 11–36.

Sonstroem, R.J. (1978). Physical estimation and attraction scales: rationale and research. *Medicine and Science in Sports and Exercise, 10*, 97–102.

Sonstroem, R.J. & Morgan, W.P. (1989). Exercise and self-esteem: rationale and model. *Medicine and Science in Sports and Exercise, 21*, 329–337.

Sonstroem, R.J., Speliotis, E.D. & Fava, J.L. (1992). Perceived physical competence in adults: an examination of the Physical Self-Perception Scale. *Journal of Sport and Exercise Psychology, 10*, 207–221.

Spanier, P.A. & Allison, K.R. (2001). General social support and physical activity: an analysis of the Ontario Health Survey. *Canadian Journal of Public Health, 92*, 210–213.

Taylor, C.B., Bandura, A., Ewart, C.K., Miller, N.H. & DeBusk, R.T. (1985). Exercise testing to enhance wives' confidence in their husbands' cardiac capabilities soon after clinically uncomplicated acute myocardial infarction. *American Journal of Cardiology, 55*, 6335–6638.

Tucker, L.A. & Maxwell, K. (1992). Effects of weight training on the emotional well-being and body image of females: predictors of greatest benefit. *American Journal of Health Promotion, 6*, 338–344, 371.

Turner, E.E., Rejeski, W.J. & Brawley, L.R. (1997). Psychological benefits of physical activity are influenced by the social environment. *Journal of Sport and Exercise Psychology, 19*, 119–130.

US Department of Health and Human Services (1996). *Physical activity and health: A report of the Surgeon General*. Atlanta, GA: U.S. Department of Health and Human Services, Centers for Disease Control and Prevention.

US Department of Health and Human Services (2000). *Healthy People 2010*. Washington, D.C.: DHHS.

Wankel, L.M. (1984). Decision-making and social support strategies for increasing exercise involvement. *Journal of Cardiac Rehabilitation, 4*, 124–135.

Weinberg, R.S. (2002). Goal setting in sport and exercise psychology. In J.L. Van Raalte & B.W. Brewer (eds), *Exploring Sport and Exercise Psychology* (2nd edn; pp. 25–48). Washington, DC: APA.

Zinsser, N., Bunker, L. & Williams, J.M. (2001). Cognitive techniques for building confidence and enhancing performance. In J.M Williams (ed), *Applied Sport Psychology* (4th edn; pp. 284–311). Mountain View, CA: Mayfield.

CHAPTER 27

Psychology and Bodybuilding

Dave Smith

University of Chester, United Kingdom

INTRODUCTION

Bodybuilding is a very popular activity. Many millions of people worldwide lift weights for the purpose of reshaping their physique. However, only a very small percentage of bodybuilders actually take part in bodybuilding competitions, and it is this population with which sport psychologists are likely to be working. Competitive bodybuilding is a truly unique sport that offers many interesting challenges to the sport psychologist. This chapter will discuss key issues that sport psychologists need to consider when working with bodybuilders, and also give advice on some of the key psychological skills from which bodybuilders are likely to benefit.

First, however, a brief overview of the sport of bodybuilding will be provided, together with a short bibliography of bodybuilding for sport psychologists who would like to work in this sport. It is often said that one of the keys to successful psychology consulting in any sport is to have a good understanding and experience of that particular sport. Nowhere is this more true than in bodybuilding; it is such an unusual sport in many respects that the training and competitive arenas may well feel like a totally alien environment to many sport psychologists, even those with experience in a wide variety of different sports. Being able to empathize with the client is clearly crucial, and therefore a good understanding of the bodybuilding scene and of the psychological makeup of bodybuilders are absolute requirements to even begin working in this area. The following section will deal with the former issue.

BODYBUILDING COMPETITION AND TRAINING

Competitive bodybuilding in the UK is very much a minority sport, with a small but dedicated following and little media coverage or recognition from the general public. There are no bodybuilding competitions shown on any major television channels in the UK, and when English bodybuilder Dorian Yates won professional bodybuilding's premier competition, the Mr Olympia, six years running this feat gained almost no nationwide media coverage. The sport has a rather higher profile in the USA, but is still a minority activity. However,

The Sport Psychologist's Handbook: A Guide for Sport-Specific Performance Enhancement.
Edited by Joaquín Dosil. © 2006 John Wiley & Sons, Ltd.

the sport does have a professional circuit, though very few bodybuilders are able to make a living purely from competing. Many others work as personal trainers, own gymnasia or sell bodybuilding clothing or supplements to make ends meet. Except for a few bodybuilders at the elite level, it is not a very lucrative occupation.

There are various bodybuilding organizations that organize competitions around the world. The dominant professional league is that of the International Federation of Body Builders, which organizes the Mr Olympia and a number of other professional competitions as well as regional, national and international amateur championships. Other prominent organizations include the National Amateur Body Building Association and the Association of Natural Bodybuilders, which organizes competitions for drug-free bodybuilders. Whoever the governing body, the format of bodybuilding competitions tends to be as follows. There are a number of rounds (usually three), the first of which usually requires each bodybuilder to strike a number of compulsory poses. These usually include the front double-biceps, back double-biceps, lat spread (front), lat spread (back, showing one calf) and the "most muscular". The next round then allows the bodybuilder to perform a freestyle posing routine to music of their choice. On the basis of their scores in these two rounds, a number of competitors are then chosen for the final round, the posedown, in which the competitors pose off against each other. This usually lasts several minutes and then the final placings are decided. In many competitions, the compulsory poses are performed in a morning session (called the "prejudging") where most of the decisions will be made by the judges, and the individual posing routines and the posedown are performed in an evening session called the "show", which the spectators will come to watch. The evening show will often involve a guest appearance from a top bodybuilder, including either guest posing or a seminar, a demonstration from a top-strength athlete or some other novelty event. For amateur competitions, competitors are divided into weight classes and often the winners of each weight class will enter a final posedown to decide an overall winner. Competitors are judged on muscular size, definition (a low percentage of body fat, enabling the muscles to stand out in sharp relief) and symmetry. It is important to stress the great physical demands of posing. It may appear that standing around showing off one's muscles is a pretty undemanding task, but in fact it is extremely important for the competitors to tense each muscle as hard as possible both during and in between poses to optimize the appearance of their physiques. This can be extremely tiring and can lead to muscle tremors and cramp (Kennedy, 1988). Thus, bodybuilding contests are very physically demanding. However, such demands are relatively minor compared to those involved in actually preparing for competition.

Preparing for a bodybuilding competition is extremely hard work. In fact, the arduous training and stringent dieting make this one of the most physically demanding sports. Although bodybuilders' training routines and contest preparation vary a great deal, they all have several things in common. First, competitive bodybuilders divide their training periods into the "off-season" and "pre-contest" training. In the off-season, bodybuilders perform heavy weight training and consume very high-calorie diets to increase muscle mass as much as possible. A mixture of "free weights" (barbells and dumbbells) and resistance machines is used by most bodybuilders, the proportion of each depending on personal preference. The vast majority of competitive bodybuilders perform a "split" routine, working different muscle groups on different days. Currently, most professionals appear to prefer working each muscle group about once per week (Dobbins, 2002). However, the total volume and frequency of training varies widely between athletes. For example, current Mr Olympia Ronnie Coleman's biceps training routine consists of 22 sets per workout (Coleman, 2004).

In contrast, Dorian Yates, dominant in professional bodybuilding in the 1990s, performed just 2 or 3 sets per muscle group (Yates & Wolff, 1993). The issue of training volume and related psychological considerations will be examined in the section below on overtraining and burnout. Unlike athletes in many other sports, most bodybuilders do not have a "coach" as such. Instead, they tend to seek advice from a wide variety of sources including other competitors, gym owners and bodybuilding literature.

In the "pre-contest" training phase, bodybuilders try to reduce body fat levels as low as possible so that the muscles show through the skin as clearly defined as possible. This defined, or "ripped" look, is achieved through aerobic exercise and severe dieting, a combination that can be exhausting. For example, in his autobiography, former bodybuilding champion Sam Fussell noted that, on the morning of an important competition, due to his severe dieting his energy levels were so low he was unable to walk to the car in his driveway and had to be carried (Fussell, 1991). In 1991, professional bodybuilder Mohammed Benaziza died from dehydration shortly after a competition. It emerged that he had been severely restricting his water intake during contest preparation in an effort to minimize water retention. A similar story, which has since passed into bodybuilding folklore, occurred with another pro, Renel Janvier. He collapsed due to dehydration during the morning prejudging of a bodybuilding show, and was taken to a hospital. He spent the afternoon hooked up to an intravenous drip, returned to the show in the evening and won it!

Therefore, bodybuilding competition is not without health risks. Another issue that needs to be addressed in this regard is that of drugs. The use of anabolic steroids has been commonplace in bodybuilding, and almost ubiquitous in competition, since the 1960s. Human growth hormone (HGH) has also become popular in the last decade. It is now widely accepted not only that steroids can significantly increase muscle mass, but also that the effects that can be achieved through a combination of steroid use and weight training are impossible to duplicate without the drugs (Lombardo, 1993). Drug testing is not conducted by most of the major bodybuilding governing bodies, and it has become widely accepted in bodybuilding that, to compete, steroid use is a necessity. The Association of Natural Bodybuilders carries out drug testing but this is a relatively small organization. Anyone considering working with bodybuilders should be under no illusions that steroid use is the rule rather than the exception in the sport.

As is probably clear already, there are many fascinating issues for the sport psychologist to deal with in the world of bodybuilding. The following section will deal explicitly with some of the key issues that need to be considered by the consultant when working in this sport. However, prior to examining such issues, a short bibliography will be presented to aid those seeking more information regarding this sport. Over one thousand books have been published on the topic of bodybuilding, mostly providing advice on training and nutrition, but also including biographies of bodybuilding champions and analyses of the social and cultural aspects of bodybuilding. The following books provide useful information on the lifestyles, training, nutrition, drug use, competition and psychological strategies of bodybuilders:

- Fussell (1991): the candid autobiography of a self-confessed "98-pound weakling" who became a bodybuilding champion;
- Hotten (2004): a writer explores the world of professional bodybuilding;
- Kennedy (1988): discusses the art of bodybuilding posing;
- Klein (1993): explores the social aspects of the bodybuilding world;

- Paris (1998): former professional bodybuilder Bob Paris discusses his experiences in the sport;
- Whitmarsh and Paa (2001): psychological strategies for bodybuilders;
- Yates and McGough (1998): six-time Mr Olympia Dorian Yates discusses his life and his approach to bodybuilding training.

There are, of course, many other books the sport psychologist will find useful in this regard, but the books listed above will provide a useful grounding in many of the key issues the sport psychologist will need to understand to be able to work effectively in the sport.

KEY PSYCHOLOGICAL ISSUES IN BODYBUILDING

It is immediately apparent to any outsider entering the world of bodybuilding that the lifestyle of many bodybuilders is very different not only from that of the general population, but also from that of most other athletes. There are some psychological issues relating to this lifestyle that are very important for the sport psychologist, and therefore this issue will be examined first in this section. The closely related issues of overtraining and burnout, which have been identified as key issues for sport psychologists to consider (Gould, Tuffey, Udry & Loehr, 1996; Schmidt & Stein, 1991) and which appear commonplace in bodybuilding, will then be considered. Given that a small but dedicated group of competitive female bodybuilders is an important part of the bodybuilding scene, issues specific to women will then be examined. Finally, given the extreme physical and psychological challenges presented by the competition itself, it would seem appropriate to discuss the psychological issues relating specifically to bodybuilding competition.

The "Bodybuilding Lifestyle"

Some of the most important issues the consultant will face in working with bodybuilders are related to lifestyle. Indeed, peruse almost any bodybuilding magazine and you will find references to the "bodybuilding lifestyle". The magazines seem at pains to challenge the image of the bodybuilder as a one-dimensional person, and of being all brawn and no brains. In fact, as Fussell (1991) points out, if the magazines are to be believed most bodybuilding champions, when not lifting weights, spend their time composing violin concertos and reading advanced physics manuals. However, for most bodybuilders the reality of the bodybuilding lifestyle is very far removed from this "bodybuilder as polymath" ideal. In fact, among serious bodybuilders a Stakhanovite work ethic and slavish devotion to the sport seems much more common. For a classic case study of such behaviour, see Fussell's (1991) autobiography. This book chronicles a lifestyle which was entirely geared around the world of bodybuilding. After losing his job (indirectly due to his obsession with bodybuilding), he devoted his every waking hour of the day to the gym. Time which was not spent lifting was spent preparing for it. This obsession was clearly detrimental to his health. For example, he noted that when preparing for an important competition:

> Thanks to the rigors of my training, my hands were more ragged, callused and cut than any long-shoreman's. Thanks to the drugs and my diet, I couldn't run more than twenty yards without pulling up and gasping for air. My ass cheeks ached from innumerable

steroid injections, my stomach whined for sustenance, my whole body throbbed from gym activities and enforced weight loss. Thanks to the competition tan, my skin was breaking out everywhere. (p. 197)

Fussell states that the lifestyle he describes was relatively common among the US bodybuilding community, a claim supported by the observations of Klein (1993) and, more recently, Hotten (2004). Such behaviour also appears common among British bodybuilders. In the radio documentary *Iron Maidens* (Thompson & Mares, 1993), several top British female bodybuilders discussed their lifestyles. A former British champion stated that bodybuilding was her whole life; her commitment to her training even led to the breaking off of her engagement to her fiancé. Another woman's daily training programme involved such long weight training and aerobics workouts that it left virtually no time for her to do anything else. When faced with injuries that forced her to withdraw from an important competition, she said:

I was dead depressed and really down about the whole thing. All this year I've been training for this competition and now I'm not doing it everything has just totally stopped. My life has just fell apart really because I have been training non-stop and I just don't know what to do with myself now. I'm lost.

In a study of professional female bodybuilders, Fisher (1995) found that, on average. the women spent five to six hours per day in bodybuilding-related activities, and another six hours thinking about bodybuilding. As one woman put it: "The great majority of women I know that are involved with it are obsessed with their weight . . . just compulsive about it".

Of course, it could be argued that these may just be isolated examples, and that my personal experiences may also not be representative. However, empirical research (Hurst, Hale, Smith & Collins, 2000; Smith & Hale, in press; Smith, Hale & Collins, 1998) has found that this is unlikely to be the case. Incidence of exercise-dependence in most exercise activities tends to be fairly low, with only a few per cent of most exercising populations exhibiting symptoms. However, in bodybuilding this figure appears to be much higher, with such behaviours fairly commonplace in the sport. Given the sorts of problems that can arise from taking such an obsessive approach to training, it would appear that this is a serious problem in the sport. Bodybuilding journalist T.C. Luama summed up the obsessive attitudes of many bodybuilders well by noting: "Many bodybuilders do nothing else. They spend every living hour, every minute of the day, building their muscles, to the exclusion of any kind of life" (Luama & Mentzer, 1995).

So why do so many bodybuilders appear to develop obsessive attitudes to their training? An understanding of this is very important for the practitioner who wishes to work in the bodybuilding environment. The attraction of bodybuilding is easy to see; the possibility of bodily transformation through proper training and attention to diet is clearly attractive, given that, for males, the mesomorphic (muscular) body type is the most preferred and socially desired in Western culture (Tucker, 1982). The mesomorphic male is generally viewed as possessing more favourable skills and personality traits, and to be more physically adept and athletically capable, than his less mesomorphic counterparts (Berscheid & Walster, 1972). It is not surprising, therefore, that many studies have shown that weight training can significantly enhance self-esteem (see, for example, Tucker, 1982, 1983, 1987). It seems that as an individual increases his muscular strength through weight training, he will often begin to view himself more favourably.

Of course, the fact that individuals can use weight training to improve self-esteem is a very positive thing. The problem is that some individuals begin to rely exclusively on their training to feel good about themselves. Such individuals often appear to have low self-esteem in most or all of the areas of their life that they feel are important to them, and thus the time they spend in the gym may be the only time they feel a high degree of self-efficacy (Smith, et al., 1998). Because of this, they can become compulsive about their training, prioritizing it above even very important activities, and neglecting other responsibilities in order to train. Thus, such an obsessive approach can lead to work problems, relationship problems and lack of a social life. In addition, and somewhat ironically, this can also hamper the individual's bodybuilding efforts—a point that will be explored in the following paragraph.

Overtraining and Burnout

A number of bodybuilding coaches and writers have pointed out that the compulsive attitude of many bodybuilders has led to gross overtraining and burnout becoming very common in the sport. For example, Ellington Darden, former Director of Research for Nautilus Sports/Medical Industries, points out that "If it's worth doing it's worth overdoing seems to be the mindset of numerous bodybuilders" (Darden, 1990, p. 207). Mr Universe and bodybuilding trainer Mike Mentzer argued that "The vast majority of bodybuilders are chronically, grossly overtrained" (Luama & Mentzer, 1995). Arthur Jones, the inventor of Nautilus and MedX exercise machines, argued in a recent article that the training routines typically used by bodybuilders, and espoused in the bodybuilding magazines, are almost certain to lead to overtraining and burnout for the vast majority:

> Almost every one of the training schedules published in the muscle magazines during the last twenty years has been outright hogwash. The writer always urges you to train as hard as possible and then lists a workout schedule that makes hard training impossible. So the poor kids read this garbage, look at the pictures of their hero—the supposed author—try to follow a similar routine, and end up with a case of nervous exhaustion, and no muscles. So most of them quit in disgust—wrongly convinced that exercise is of no value, for them at least. And a few stick it out, with little or nothing to show for their efforts apart from a constantly dragged-out feeling and no energy for a normal life. (Jones, 2000, pp. 22–23).

Clearly, therefore, the obsessive mindset of many bodybuilders can be very counter-productive, often leading to overtraining, and eventual burnout actually making it less likely that they will achieve their bodybuilding goals. It is hardly surprising that longevity in the sport seems a rarity, with many top bodybuilders appearing on the scene suddenly and then disappearing again just as quickly. This should be a primary concern of the sport psychologist, as overtraining and burnout will obviously prevent the individual reaching their potential in the sport. Therefore, one of the sport psychologist's key roles may be encouraging and facilitating the integration of bodybuilding training, diet and sufficient rest into a well-balanced lifestyle in such a way that the bodybuilder can lead a well-balanced, fully rewarding life without compromising their bodybuilding progress.

The extent to which these goals can be achieved are of course largely dependent upon the athlete's willingness to change. The consultant should emphasize that there is nothing wrong with wanting to develop a muscular physique, but if it becomes an obsession, and interferes significantly with work and family commitments and intellectual and other leisure pursuits, then is the time to take stock of the role bodybuilding plays in one's life. One possibility, suggested by Darden (1989) may be to encourage the bodybuilder to take up another, physically non-strenuous hobby. This may help them realize that other interests and pursuits can also be very rewarding, and help them to place bodybuilding in its proper perspective, i.e. an important but not all-consuming part of life. It doesn't really matter what that hobby is; anything that the bodybuilder finds interesting—reading more, learning to play a musical instrument, learning a foreign language, going to the movies or theatre more often. Anything that helps the bodybuilder realize that there is more to life than slaving away for hours every day in the gym.

Role models may be useful to emphasize here. For example, Dorian Yates has often stated the importance of having a balanced lifestyle and keeping bodybuilding in its proper perspective (for example, Yates & Wolff, 1993). Yates also has a very strong family life, as does eight-time Mr Olympia Lee Haney. Therefore, it is perfectly possible to juggle optimal bodybuilding progress with a balanced and psychologically healthy lifestyle, and the sport psychologist can be instrumental in encouraging this. It must be emphasized that this is necessary not just for optimal psychological health but also for optimal bodybuilding progress, a point that is explored in the following paragraph.

Obviously, overtraining and burnout are very detrimental to a bodybuilder's progress, yet as we have seen they appear to be common phenomena within the sport. It is supremely ironic that, in a sense, the immense enthusiasm of some bodybuilders can be the greatest enemy to their bodybuilding progress. The amount of training these individuals perform may lead to overuse injuries in the muscles and joints, a weakened immune system, chronic fatigue and even muscle atrophy (DeBenedette, 1990; Wichmann & Martin, 1992). However, the widespread belief that a very high volume of training is necessary to produce optimal progress is not supported by scientific evidence. In fact, many scientific studies have shown that relatively brief but intense training, with one set per exercise performed to muscular failure no more than three times per week, produces optimal gains in size and strength (see, for example, Carpenter et al., 1991; Carpinelli & Otto, 1998; Peterson, 1975; Pollock et al., 1993; Starkey et al., 1996; Tucci, Carpenter, Pollock, Graves & Leggett, 1992). This approach, which contrasts sharply with the traditional six-day-per-week and even twice-per-day approaches advocated in the bodybuilding magazines, may have a double benefit of avoiding overtraining while allowing the bodybuilder more time for family and social life and other interests. A number of top bodybuilders, including Dorian Yates, IFBB professional Aaron Baker, Mr Olympia Sergio Oliva, Mr America Casey Viator and Mr Universe Mike Mentzer have advocated and successfully used this training method.

Therefore, for the very common problems of bodybuilders showing signs of overtraining and burnout, the "high-intensity" training method could be suggested. Of course, the psychologist must be careful not to stray into areas outside their competence, and therefore consultation with a properly qualified strength and conditioning coach or an exercise physiologist with specialist knowledge of bodybuilding is recommended before making such suggestions.

Female Bodybuilders

Although I am not aware of any published statistics, it is quite clear that the vast majority of bodybuilders, both competitive and non-competitive, are male. Walk into any mixed bodybuilding gym and the number of male clients will almost certainly outnumber the number of female clients by a factor of at least ten to one. This is perhaps not surprising: after all, on average, the potential for females to develop muscle bulk is much less than for males, due to the much lower testosterone levels in women. Also, there are strong social pressures that women may perceive as off-putting. Although muscular males are usually regarded quite positively, researchers have found that the great majority of both males and females regard female bodybuilders as unattractive (see Pope, Phillips & Olivardia, 2000). In addition to their greater-than-normal muscularity, another physical characteristic that many individuals appear to find unattractive in competitive female bodybuilders is the breast shrinkage that occurs due to their severe dieting and, often, steroid use (Pope et al., 2000).

Thus, female bodybuilders often find themselves subject to negative reactions from the general public, even being labelled as "freaky" and "weird" (Thompson & Mares, 1993). This is unfortunate, given that the health benefits of weight training are probably even greater for women than they are for men, helping to increase bone mineral density and thus making osteoporosis less likely, and also making the debilitating muscle weaknesses that cause many women to lose their independence in later life less likely to occur (Peterson, Bryant & Peterson, 1995). However, given the negative perceptions of the general public, it is perhaps surprising that women's bodybuilding attracts enough adherents to make it a viable and lively amateur and professional sport. The fact that female bodybuilders have to overcome the psychological effects of the negative perceptions of the public to enter the sport suggests that they are a highly-motivated group of athletes. Indeed, the determination these women exhibit in their quest to achieve their dream physique appears even more remarkable than that of the male bodybuilding fraternity. However, as noted previously, this determination can easily become an obsession, and therefore the consultant should take care to ensure that this determination is channelled appropriately and does not become all-consuming.

Studies (Freedson, Mihevic, Loucks & Girandola, 1983; Fuchs & Zaichkowsky, 1983) have found that women bodybuilders appeared to have very positive mental health, exhibiting the classic "iceberg profile" on the Profile of Mood States (POMS; McNair, Lorr & Dropplemann, 1971). That is, they score significantly lower than the general population average on tension, depression, anger, fatigue and confusion, and significantly higher on vigour. However, even the most positive, upbeat, resolute female bodybuilder can be upset by the negative stereotyping that surrounds the sport. For example, in *Iron Maidens*, former British champion Loretta Lomax noted that she had been hurt by the rude and insensitive comments made regarding her body by some of the general public, particularly by men. Therefore, the sport psychologist may wish to emphasize to the client the reasons why men sometimes make such remarks. That is, males may feel that their masculinity is threatened by women who are stronger and more muscular than they are, and this may make them feel insecure. For this reason, it should be emphasized that, in a sense, this is really a back-handed compliment. After all, if the woman had not achieved a significant level of muscular development (i.e. achieved her bodybuilding goals) she would not attract such comments.

Bodybuilding Competition

Bodybuilding contest preparation must be one of the most arduous challenges in all of sport. During the "off-season", when bodybuilders are not competing, they will try to add as much muscle bulk as possible. However, it is much easier to add muscle when consuming a high-calorie diet that may also add some fat. During contest preparation, bodybuilders try to remove this fat through severe dieting and aerobic exercise, while attempting to maintain as much muscle mass as possible. It is not unknown for bodybuilders to lose as much as 40 pounds during the contest preparation phase. The pre-contest trials and tribulations of Sam Fussell, who reduced his calorie intake to 500 calories per day prior to competition, have been noted above, and this appears fairly representative. British bodybuilder Gaynor Jones existed for several months on an 800-calorie-a-day diet while preparing for the British championships, and former British champion and IFBB professional Loretta Lomax regularly performed several hours of aerobic training per day to aid fat loss (Thompson & Mares, 1993). Gaynor noted that during her contest preparation she was unable to drive as she constantly felt faint due to lack of energy. Sam Fussell spent days prior to competition lying on a sofa unable to move, again due to a lack of energy from his extreme low-calorie diet. Such diets can have health dangers: the case of Mohammed Benaziza has been noted above, and a recent case study (Too, Wakayama, Locati & Landwer, 1998) found a bodybuilder to be suffering from hypoglycaemia due to his low carbohydrate intake on his pre-contest diet. Another case study (Sturmi & Rutecki, 1995) found that a bodybuilder's severely restricted pre-contest diet had led to life-threatening cardiac problems, and a study by Kleiner, Bazzarre & Ainsworth (1994) found the diets of elite female bodybuilders to be deficient in various vitamins and minerals.

Of course, all this is not just physically challenging, but psychologically challenging as well. Mood swings, tears, feelings of irritability and depression are common as competition nears. For example, Wilson-Fearon and Parrott (1999) found that the multiple drug use and severe dietary restraint in a Mr Universe competitor led to marked increases in negative mood states. Therefore, pre-competition is a time when the sport psychologist can make a significant contribution to the bodybuilder's training programme. Various psychological skills, such as goal-setting, imagery and anxiety management techniques, will be very useful at this time and will be covered later in this chapter. The sport psychologist can also emphasize the crucial importance of social support. Many bodybuilding champions have emphasized the importance of social support in their bodybuilding success (e.g. Yates & Wolff, 1993), and research suggests that this is crucial to bodybuilding progress (Hurst et al., 2000). Therefore, it is important that the bodybuilder should educate non-bodybuilding family members and friends as to the physical and mental challenges of bodybuilding competition, and emphasize the fact that they will need a lot of emotional support at this time. In addition, social support from other gym members can be very important. Usually, when a bodybuilder is training for competition, they will automatically gain attention and support from other gym members. When the competitor is finding the going tough, they should be encouraged to confide in and discuss the difficulties with other gym members, who will usually be very sympathetic and supportive. Therefore, although training for bodybuilding competition can be an arduous and difficult experience, there is really no need for the competitor to feel on their own.

Monitoring of mood states prior to competition is also important. As noted above, on the POMS women bodybuilders tend to exhibit the classic "iceberg profile" indicative of positive mental health, and this is also true of men (Fuchs & Zaichkowsky, 1983). However, as competition approaches this is likely to change, for the reasons noted above (Wilson-Fearon & Parrott, 1999). The bodybuilder who scored high in vigour, but low in tension, depression, anger, fatigue and confusion the day before a bodybuilding competition would be a rare creature indeed! Therefore, using the POMS or another mood-measuring instrument, in conjunction with discussions with the athlete, will enable the psychologist to gain an in-depth view of how the athlete feels, thus enabling the consultant to make suggestions and tailor interventions to the athlete's psychological state on a daily basis.

This may also be of use to the athlete in enabling close monitoring of the psychological effects of their exercising and diet. For example, it may be that a dietary restriction or increase in aerobic exercising makes the athlete feel so fatigued that their motivation to train hard is affected. Therefore, although such a move may in theory be beneficial to the individual's physical condition, the psychological ramifications may be such that they have undesirable medium- or long-term physical effects. For example, reducing calories almost to starvation levels may improve the competitor's muscular definition. However, an additional result may be to make the bodybuilder so physically weak and psychologically fragile that they lack the motivation and/or physical capacity to train intensely and therefore loses significant muscle mass. Thus, the overall effect of such a dietary adjustment on the physique may actually be negative. This has been noted by Walberg-Rankin (1995), who recommended a more moderate reduction in calories pre-contest to minimize reduction in lean body mass. However, the bodybuilder may not be so self-aware as to realize this without the feedback the psychologist can provide based upon quantitative and qualitative data. In this way, by monitoring the bodybuilder appropriately, the sport psychologist can play a valuable role in helping them to make adjustments to diet and training to optimize performance. Of course, where dietary manipulation is concerned, the bodybuilder should also always be encouraged to consult a qualified dietician.

PSYCHOLOGICAL SKILLS TRAINING

When many people think of the work of the sport psychologist, the first thing that springs to mind is psychological skills training. Athletes are always searching for techniques that will give them a mental edge, and bodybuilders are no exception. In fact, bodybuilders are generally very open to the idea that mental factors are very important to bodybuilding success, and are usually keen to make use of suggested psychological performance-enhancement techniques. Many bodybuilding champions, in training and instructional texts, emphasize the importance of psychology. According to Dorian Yates: "The most important part of my approach is the mental. The training, diet, nutrition and supplementation don't mean anything unless the right mental approach is there. It's like the glue that holds everything together". (Yates & Wolff, 1993, p. 73).

Similar comments are made by Mr Universe Tom Platz, who even claims in his book (Platz, 1982) that the bodybuilding process is more psychological than physical. In my experience, I think it unlikely that the sport psychologist working with bodybuilders will find the same scepticism and resistance that has been noted by sport psychologists working in some other sports. This is fortunate, as there are some psychological skills that, if practised by the bodybuilder, can significantly enhance their progress. The aim of this section is to discuss some of these techniques and how they can be used to best effect in bodybuilding. This is not, however, meant to be a set of "off-the-shelf" psychological strategies to be applied blindly with all bodybuilders. Instead, it is imperative that these techniques are applied in an individualized manner, in accordance with the athlete's needs and preferences. Rather than providing sketchy details of many different psychological skills the sport psychologist can work on with bodybuilders, this section provides a more detailed account of three skills that are particularly important and useful when working with bodybuilders. Of course, there are many issues that may arise requiring other skills and techniques to be used.

Imagery

Imagery is arguably the most effective of all psychological tools that the bodybuilder can use. There is a great deal of anecdotal evidence suggesting that imagery can improve muscle strength, and many bodybuilders do believe in, and use, this technique. For example, Tom Platz attributes much of his bodybuilding success to this technique. Arthur Jones is also an advocate of imagery, once claiming, "I can add a quarter of an inch on my arms by just *thinking* about training my biceps and triceps" (Darden, 1986, p. 112). I have used this technique myself with individuals I have trained in the gym, with considerable success.

One might reasonably ask the question here, are these anecdotes backed up by scientific evidence from controlled studies? In fact, some studies have found imagery to be ineffective in enhancing muscular performance. For example, in a meta-analysis by Feltz and Landers (1983), the effect of imagery on the performance of strength tasks averaged an effect size of only 0.2. More recently, Tenenbaum et al. (1995) found that a control group, who had not received any intervention, performed significantly better on an isokinetic knee extension machine than an imagery group. Such findings have led some to question the usefulness of imagery for strength athletes and bodybuilders, but other studies (Smith, Collins & Holmes, 2003; Smith & Collins, in press; Yue & Cole, 1992; Yue, Wilson, Cole, Darling & Yuh, 1996) have contradicted these earlier findings. In fact, in these latter studies imagery has been found to produce strength gains of at least 50 per cent of those obtained from actual training. So why these apparently contradictory findings? Why is imagery sometimes effective and sometimes not? This is not only an academic argument, but has important implications for the practising sport psychologist. If we know how imagery interventions produce their performance-enhancing effects then we are in a much better position to know how to perform imagery interventions for best results. Without this knowledge our interventions are more likely to be based on guesswork, and are thus less likely to be effective.

The answers as to why imagery can enhance motor performance, and why different studies have produced widely differing results regarding the effectiveness of imagery, may well be found in the world of cognitive neuroscience. Studies using electroencephalography (EEG) and positron emission tomography (PET) scans have shown similarities in brain activity prior to and during imagery and the physical performance of motor tasks (Fox, Pardo, Petersen & Raichle, 1987; Naito and Matsumura, 1994; Stephan et al., 1995; Cunnington, Iansek & Bradshaw, 1996). Put simply, it appears that the same areas of the brain, such as the primary motor cortex and supplementary motor area, are active during both imagery and actual performance. Thus, from such studies, cognitive neuroscientists have concluded that there exists a "functional equivalence" between motor imagery and motor performance, and that this explains the effect of imagery on performance. As Jeannerod (1995, p. 1425) notes,

> If one considers the strong relationships of motor imagery to the neural substrate, it is logical to expect that the central changes produced during imagery will affect subsequent motor performance. Conversely, the observed changes might represent an explanation for those effects known to arise as a result of mental training.

However, functional equivalence, and the consequent improvements in performance, are not inevitable consequences of imagery. In fact, recent research (Smith & Collins, in press) has shown that functional equivalence is most likely to occur when the imagery involves all the physiological and behavioural responses (i.e. response propositions; Lang, 1979, 1985) that would occur in response to the imagined scenario. For example, when imagining lifting weights, the individual should attempt to make the imagery as realistic as possible by imagining the feelings of tension in the muscles, the rapid heartbeat and breathing, the friction of the knurled bar against the hands, the music being played on the gym sound system, the smell of the gym, and so on. Everything that the individual experiences when actually weight training should be included in the imagery, making the experience meaningful, vivid and realistic.

Of particular importance are the physiological reactions that accompany the training: these appear to be important in enabling imagery to be functionally equivalent to actual training. In two recent studies (Smith & Collins, in press) we examined movement-related EEG activity, studying the late contingent negative variation (CNV; Walter, Cooper, Aldridge, McCallum & Winter, 1964), an electrical brain potential related to movement preparation. This EEG wave takes the form of a negative shift from the EEG baseline, and is believed largely to reflect the nerve signals being sent from the cortex to the muscles to enable contraction (Brunia, 1993; Rohrbaugh & Gaillard, 1983). We found similar late CNV waves occurring prior to imagery and actual movement. This always occurred when the imagery emphasized the bodily feelings experienced during the movement (i.e. muscle tension and so on). However, when the imagery was primarily visual in nature (i.e. seeing oneself move but not feeling oneself move), the late CNV was less likely to occur. These findings strongly suggest that multi-sensory involvement in imagery helps to achieve optimal functional equivalence.

Unfortunately, the imagery advice given in bodybuilding books and magazines, by coaches and even by many sport psychologists, fails to take this issue into account. For example, imagery is often referred to as "visualization", and trainees are often advised to "see themselves" lifting weights. Articles containing such advice have appeared in magazines such as *Muscle and Fitness*, *Flex* and *Men's Fitness* in the last couple of years. In such articles scant attention is paid to the importance of multi-sensory involvement in imagery. Such techniques, however, may be less effective than the multi-sensory approach for the reasons given in the above paragraph. This may explain the lack of positive results from some imagery and strength studies. For example, in the Tenenbaum et al. (1995) study, imagery was referred to as "visualization", with participants encouraged to visualize themselves doing the leg extension.

In addition, it is often said that it is important to be relaxed during imagery, and techniques such as progressive muscle relaxation, which involves the tensing and relaxing of muscle groups to reduce overall levels of tension, are often included as part of imagery training (for example, see Cabral & Crisfield, 1996). Also, many psychologists advise that it should be performed lying down in a quiet environment such as in your bedroom prior to falling asleep. These ideas really defy common sense, as well as the neuroscience research findings noted above. If it is important to make imagery as realistic as possible, why should you be relaxed? After all, you do not feel relaxed when performing a heavy set in the gym. Also, you do not lift weights lying on your bed, so why should you perform imagery in this position? When seen from a functional equivalence perspective, such advice appears questionable.

So if the traditional, relaxation-based "visualization" approach to imagery is unlikely to be optimally effective in enhancing weight training performance, are there better guidelines available for trainees to use to enhance the effectiveness of their imagery? An approach that may prove useful has been developed by Holmes and Collins (2001). This approach, known by the acronym PETTLEP, is based on the functional equivalence research findings and some of the sport psychology research noted above. The PETTLEP model comprises the following elements: physical, environment, task, timing, learning, emotion and perspective. Each element relates to important practical guidelines that those seeking to perform imagery interventions with bodybuilders will find useful. Each element, and its practical implications, is described below.

Physical

As noted above, it is important that imagery is as physically similar to actual weight training as possible. Therefore, the bodybuilder should be encouraged to imagine the muscle fatigue and discomfort they feel when actually training. They should also adopt the same posture as when actually performing the exercise. For example, if imaging leg extensions the bodybuilder should sit down, whereas if imaging standing calf raises they should stand upright. The bodybuilder should be encouraged to make movements that approximate the actual exercise; many people find that makes the experience more vivid. Individuals should even wear their gym clothes and chalk their hands if that is what they do normally.

Environment

It is important for the person to imagine performing their workout where they would actually perform it, to make the imagery realistic. To help, bodybuilders could use video or audiotapes recorded at the gymnasia where they train, and perform their imagery while listening to the same music played at the gym. Particular features of the gym should be incorporated into the image.

Task

During the imagery, attention should be focused on the same things as during the actual workout. So, if a bodybuilder really focuses in on the discomfort in the muscle when performing a set, and keeps attention on the muscle being worked, they should do this during their imagery. However, if they focus more on the rising and falling of the bar, this should be done during imagery instead.

Timing

Preparation for and execution of weight training exercises should be imaged in real time rather than slow motion. The whole of each set should be imaged, not just a couple of reps. The bodybuilder should imagine taking the set from the first rep all the way through to failure. The same rest periods should be used as during the actual workout.

Learning

Changes in how movements feel will occur over time. If you ask a bodybuilder to think back to the first time he performed the bench press, he will probably note that he felt really awkward and struggled to balance the bar evenly. However, within a short time he could perform the movement much more smoothly, and it felt totally different. Such learning effects occur with all movements, and therefore the bodily sensations that accompany movements will change over time. Imagery should reflect this by involving the sensations that the individual actually feels when performing the movement, and as these change over time so should the imagery.

Emotion

Imagery should also involve the emotions felt when performing the workout. Most bodybuilders, prior to and during a workout, feel physiologically and psychologically aroused, ready to give their all. This is also how they should feel prior to and during imagery. Contrary to the advice of some psychologists, the athlete should *not* feel relaxed during movement imagery.

Perspective

Imagery can be performed in either the first person (internal imagery) or the third person (external imagery). In internal imagery, one imagines being inside one's own body and seeing what one would see when in the imagined situation. In external imagery, one sees oneself performing the task, like in a home movie. There is no simple answer as to which is best, with people often reporting preferences for one or the other. Performing internal imagery will produce a more realistic imagery experience, and therefore should be generally preferred for imaging weight training, but external imagery (i.e. seeing oneself lift really heavy weights) will be effective in improving confidence. Therefore, it may be best to use both, with internal imagery to rehearse the movement and external imagery to increase confidence. External imagery may be particularly useful when attempting to learn a posing routine, as it may help enhance the form of the movement (cf. Hardy & Callow, 1999).

The above model provides a useful framework to help guide imagery interventions. However, it is important to emphasize to the athlete that imagery is not a shortcut to building great muscle mass. As with actual weight training, optimal improvements will occur only through hard work, dedication and the use of sound training techniques.

Goal-setting

Bodybuilding lends itself extremely well to goal-setting. For example, amount of weight lifted, number of repetitions, muscle girth, percentage body fat, etc. can all be measured accurately and easily, and therefore it is relatively easy to evaluate the bodybuilder's progress. Many top bodybuilders have advocated goal-setting as a useful, or even essential, tool in maximizing bodybuilding progress. For example, Dorian Yates states that "Setting goals and then achieving them has been very important to my success" (Yates & Wolff, 1993, p. 73).

It may be somewhat surprising, therefore, that few bodybuilders appear to keep detailed training journals (Darden, 1989). Without detailed training records, it is impossible to monitor progress and therefore the process of goal-setting and monitoring becomes extremely difficult. Therefore, one of the most valuable things the sport psychologist can do is to encourage the bodybuilder to keep an accurate record of their progress. This should include comprehensive details of each workout, including the amount of weight lifted on each exercise, the number of sets and repetitions performed, notes on cadence and form, and any information regarding motivation, fatigue, concentration or anything else that may be of relevance to the bodybuilder's performance during the workout. In addition, records should be kept of their bodyweight (preferably with weekly weighings), percentage fat (obtained usually through skinfold measurements), and muscular size (e.g. through measurements of chest, neck, upper arms, forearms, thighs and calves). In addition, regular photographs should be taken of the bodybuilder from various positions in various poses, to keep a visual record of progress. After all, in competition the bodybuilders are judged on how they look, not on their measurements, and therefore this is the most important way to monitor the bodybuilder's progress. For detailed instructions on before- and after- measurements and photos, see Darden (1988, 1992).

When the bodybuilder records progress in the ways outlined above, proper goal-setting and evaluation of progress becomes much easier. Goal-setting can be a very useful motivational tool, as it can serve to focus the individual on what they need to do to achieve their goal(s). As well as acting on a conscious level, goal-setting can also programme our behaviour subconsciously, as Locke and Latham (1990, p. 5) point out: "Usually a goal, once accepted and understood, will remain in the background or periphery of consciousness, as a reference point for guiding and giving meaning to subsequent mental and physical actions leading to the goal."

However, as with any sport psychology intervention, goal-setting should not be performed as an automatic, off-the-shelf prescription for every bodybuilder the sport psychologist works with. Research suggests that it would be a mistake to presume that formal goal-setting will always enhance performance, a point that is explored in the following paragraph.

A great deal of research in the field of industrial psychology suggests that the setting of specific, measurable goals can considerably increase output (see Locke & Latham, 1990). These findings, of course, have not gone unnoticed in sport psychology, where goal-setting has become a very widely used technique. As with relaxation and imagery, virtually all sport psychology self-help books and general textbooks include a section on goal-setting. A number of research studies have been carried out to determine the effects of goal-setting on athletic performance, but the results have proved disappointing (see Hardy, Jones & Gould, 1996; Locke, 1991). In fact, there has largely been little support for the industrial psychology findings in a sport setting. Goal-setting doesn't seem to always be the sure-fire performance-enhancer that some sport psychologists suggest. One of the goal-setting pioneers from industrial psychology has blamed a lack of methodological rigour in some of the studies that have examined goal-setting in sports settings (Locke, 1991). However, although this may be a contributory factor, it may also be that goal-setting simply isn't as effective with some sport performers as it is in many industrial settings. In many of the workplace-based studies, researchers have used tasks that are presumably pretty boring for those who perform them every day for a living, such as working on a factory production line. In such cases, setting goals may well serve to make the task more interesting, thereby serving as a useful motivational tool. However, as Hardy et al. (1996) noted, serious athletes are already highly motivated, and therefore setting goals may have less of a motivational effect.

This is not to suggest that goal-setting serves no purpose in sport and should be avoided. Quite the contrary: as noted above, with some individuals in some circumstances, goal-setting may well enhance performance. The point is that, like all sport psychology interventions, it should not be applied blindly with everybody in the belief that it will always work. Rather, a more useful approach would be for the sport psychologist to use it selectively, in specific cases; for example, where it appears that motivation is lacking in an athlete, and where there is also reason to believe that, in this particular individual, goal-setting will help to improve motivation.

So, if the sport psychologist decides to undertake a goal-setting intervention with a bodybuilder, how should it be conducted? There are many excellent general resources offering guidelines for goal setting (see for example Locke & Latham, 1990), and even some specifically related to bodybuilding (Bass, 1999; Vost, 2002). The guidelines below are based on the guidelines provided by Locke and Latham (1990).

Guidelines for effective goal setting in bodybuilding :

1. Goals should be both specific and measurable. Research shows that specific goals are much more effective than vague, "do your best" goals. Therefore, a goal of "perform at least 10 repetitions on the bench press with 250 lbs" would be much better than "increase my weight on the bench press". A goal of "increase the circumference of my biceps by half an inch" would be much better than "increase the size of my biceps".
2. Goals should be challenging. Goals that are easy to achieve will not motivate the body-builder to work hard. Difficult goals, on the other hand, will stretch the athlete and motivate them to work as hard as possible to achieve them. Of course, it is impossible to give specific guidelines here on what constitutes a difficult goal, as that depends very much on the individual. The general rule, however, is that the goal should be hard enough that it cannot be achieved without great effort.
3. At the same time, it is important that goals are realistic. Goals that are completely over-ambitious may achieve the opposite of the desired effect, leading to frustration and reduced motivation. It is important that goals are set to challenge the individual with a realistic view of the individual's capabilities and potential. Therefore, setting goals relating to other bodybuilders, such as "having forearms as thick as Dorian Yates", is inappropriate. That is not to say that other bodybuilders cannot serve a useful motivational purpose; they can and should, but the bodybuilder should always be encouraged to make comparisons with themself rather than with others. There are simply too many inter-individual differences to make such comparisons meaningful. Therefore, a goal such as "increasing the circumference of my thighs by one inch" would be more appropriate than "having thighs as big as Tom Platz", but to help motivate a bodybuilder toward achieving this goal he could use pictures of Platz's thighs, and of Platz performing leg training, to inspire him towards achieving his goal.
4. Progress towards goals should be closely monitored. As noted above, progress towards bodybuilding goals can be easily measured, and therefore it should not be too difficult to ensure that the bodybuilder tracks their progress toward goals very closely. Charts can

be used to track weights used and repetitions performed, body weight and level of body fat. If a goal is not met, encourage the bodybuilder to reflect on why this could have been the case and to make the necessary adjustments to training and/or diet.

5. Goals should be time-orientated. A large, long-term goal can, on its own, often seem unrealistic as it is too large a leap from the present situation. However, breaking the large goal down into smaller, more manageable goals will make the goal much more achievable and less intimidating. Slowly but surely, the achievement of lots of smaller goals will eventually lead to the achievement of the bigger one. For example, if at the outset of their competitive career a bodybuilder was to focus on the goal of becoming the national champion, this goal would probably seem overwhelming and the bodybuilder would become discouraged. However, if the bodybuilder was to break this into smaller steps, such as first competing in a local competition, then winning a local competition, then winning a regional competition, then winning the nationals, they would be continually motivated by striving for these smaller, but more achievable goals. Realistic deadlines should be set for both short- and long-term goals. However, goals should also be reasonably flexible. After all, many unexpected events such as changes in personal circumstances and injury can affect progress towards goals. Therefore, it is important to emphasize to the client that revising goals in the light of changes in circumstances is OK.

Concentration

An event that has entered bodybuilding folklore is the 1980 Mr Olympia. This marked Arnold Schwarzenegger's return to competition after a five-year absence, and one of his main rivals in the competition was Mr Universe Mike Mentzer. According to many observers Mentzer was in fantastic shape that day, and appeared to have a great chance of winning. However, in the end Arnold Schwarzenegger triumphed. According to Schwarzenegger, one of the reasons for this was that disparaging comments made by himself to Mike Mentzer about Mentzer's physique caused Mike to become angry and lose concentration. Schwarzenegger claims that when Mentzer was near him he (Mentzer) became so angry that he forgot to tense his muscles properly, possibly costing him the Mr Olympia title (Kennedy, 1983; Leigh, 1990).

The above anecdote illustrates the importance of concentration in bodybuilding. Indeed, few psychological factors are as important to performance in the weight room or on the posing dais. It may be rather surprising to learn, therefore, that the lack of concentration displayed by most of the trainees is quite startling. As Darden (1992, p. 186) notes, "Walk into almost any bodybuilding gym and what you're likely to witness is a romper room. Jokes, small talk, loud music and goofing-off proliferate." In bodybuilding gyms it is even common to see people carrying on conversations while performing their set. This sort of behaviour is simply incompatible with high-level athletic performance of any kind. Clearly, a bodybuilder cannot expect to be goofing around one minute and be 100 per cent focused on giving an all-out effort the next. If a bodybuilder seems not to be entirely focused on the workout, it may be worth asking if they think Tiger Woods would play a great round of golf if he was messing around sharing jokes with his buddies prior to each shot. The bodybuilder will invariably reply something to the effect of "obviously not", in reply to which you can point out that, for the same reason, they shouldn't expect to be messing around one minute and then performing a set with 100 per cent intensity the next. As Darden (1992, p. 186) says, "To get the best workout you possibly can, you must concentrate. You must put your mind into it."

Given the importance of concentration, then, why do so many bodybuilders seem to find it so difficult? One important reason is that they seem to view concentration purely as an innate ability, rather than as a skill that can be trained and improved. Some individuals clearly find it easier to concentrate than others, but even those who find it very difficult to focus on anything for even a short period of time can help themselves to improve. Provided below are some simple strategies that can be effective in improving the concentration skills of bodybuilders. Of course, they will not turn someone who has trouble concentrating into a highly focused individual overnight, but if persevered with they can help improve attention in a relatively short period of time.

One of the simplest, but most effective, ways of ensuring effective concentration in the gym is to encourage the bodybuilder to reflect on the reason they are there in the first place. If a bodybuilder goes to the gym primarily to socialize and have fun, it is very unlikely that they will be able to focus effectively on achieving high-intensity muscular contractions. This is because, as every bodybuilder is well aware, to set the muscle growth machinery into motion takes brutally hard work, which can hardly be considered fun. It needs to be emphasized that, as a bodybuilder, the main aim of going to the gym should be to get bigger. If that is the case, and the bodybuilder understands that to achieve this they will have to focus very hard, they will be unlikely to have a problem achieving this high level of concentration.

Of course, this is not to say that even some highly motivated individuals may not have difficulty concentrating from time to time. The gym is an environment where many potential distractions exist: the guy screaming at the top of his lungs while doing squats, someone cracking jokes, someone posing in the mirror right in front of an individual in the middle of a set. Even those with generally good concentration may find their focus disrupted occasionally.

As well as there being environmental distractions in the gym, there are other factors that mean the bodybuilder may occasionally have difficulty focusing on the workout, such as having work or relationship problems. So how can the individual block out such distractions? One of the most useful techniques is to develop a systematic pre-workout routine. This might involve, for example, a bodybuilder always packing his gym bag at the same time and in the same way, then reading his training diary to check exactly what he's going to be doing that workout, then always driving the same route to the gym, then once he's at the gym always warming up in the same way. Once such a definite routine is developed, the bodybuilder should be encouraged to practise it consistently. They can then develop the ability to focus on training by associating concentration with the pre-performance routine. Over time, these behaviours will automatically trigger the high level of concentration needed to have an effective workout. Research has shown such pre-performance routines to aid concentration and performance in many sports (Boutcher & Crews, 1987; Marlow, 1998; Salmela, 1976), and over time they will aid the bodybuilder's concentration in the gym.

Attentional cues and triggers can be used both to focus concentration and to regain it once it is lost. These can be verbal, i.e. self-talk, or behavioural. Like pre-performance routines, self-talk is effective in enhancing concentration and sports performance (Rogerson & Hrycaiko, 2002). Cue words can be used to trigger concentration prior to or during the workout. In this context, forceful-sounding words or phrases will probably be best, helping the client to focus on the necessity of giving an all-out effort during each set.

It is crucial that cue words are individualized, as what is effective for one person may not be for another. Cues used by bodybuilders I have worked with include "Give it everything", "Blow it out", "Fire", "Attack", "100 per cent", "All the way", etc. The point is to use whatever verbal cues are meaningful to the individual. It is important that the cue words are always positive, as negative self-talk can reduce confidence and disrupt attention (Kubistant, 1988).

Behavioural cues could include, for example, changing into gym clothes, or walking through the front entrance to the gym. Such events can be used as a trigger to focus attention on training. In this way, such tasks can serve the important function of telling the individual that it's now training time, and to leave all their non-training problems and concerns at the gym door. Some individuals find it difficult to change their focus instantly, and such people may find it useful to use their warm-up as a sort of attentional focus changer, using that time to let go of any outside stresses they may be feeling, focusing progressively more singularly on their training until that is all that is on their mind. Then, and only then, should they proceed to the intense portion of the workout, fully focused on the task in hand.

In addition, it is important to explain to the bodybuilder how to eliminate negative or task-irrelevant thoughts. This technique, known as "thought-stopping" (Ziegler, 1987), is commonly used by elite athletes (for example, Jackson & Baker, 2001), is very useful for those who have thoughts in the gym that are not relevant to their training, and like most of the best psychological interventions is very simple. Bodybuilders should be encouraged to monitor their self-talk and to remove task-irrelevant thoughts and replace them with task-relevant ones. For example, the athlete could be given the example that they are just about to perform a set of bicep curls, and someone nearby cracks a joke, moving the athlete's attention to that person rather than their own biceps. Rather than proceeding with the set, they should take as long as needed to refocus. They should empty the mind of all thoughts regarding the interruption, and then bring the focus back to the set. The use of cue words or phrases could again be suggested here, such as, in this case, "Think biceps". Again, it doesn't matter what the cue words are as long as they are meaningful to the individual. It should be emphasized that the bodybuilder should only begin a set when they are again 100 per cent focused on the muscle group they are about to train.

If followed correctly and persevered with, these simple guidelines will enable the bodybuilder to focus more effectively in the gym, and thus to achieve better results. Of course, no psychological technique (or physical training method, for that matter) can guarantee a Herculean physique, but by unleashing their mental energies effectively in the gym, bodybuilders will be much more likely to reach their full physical potential.

CONCLUSION

Bodybuilding is a very challenging, but interesting and rewarding, sport in which to work. Many bodybuilders are of the opinion that psychological factors can have a considerable impact upon their bodybuilding progress, and therefore they tend to be open and receptive to psychological interventions, and their adherence to psychological skills training is usually good. However, overtraining, burnout and drug use are commonplace within the sport, and the motives of bodybuilders in engaging in the activity can sometimes appear psychologically dysfunctional. Therefore, the sport psychologist needs to be aware of this and prepared for the possibility that, in extreme cases, bodybuilders may need referral to a clinical psychologist. Possibly the best piece of advice for any psychologist contemplating involvement in the sport would be to spend a considerable amount of time getting to know the sport and its participants before performing any applied work. This is obviously true with all sports, but given the radically *different* nature of bodybuilding and bodybuilders compared to any other sports and clients the practitioner may be involved with, this is essential to gain the background knowledge and understanding necessary to work effectively in the sport.

At present, there appear to be few sport psychologists working in the sport. However, given the clear importance of psychological factors in bodybuilding success, the potential for the provision of sport psychology services in bodybuilding, particularly at an elite level, is considerable. Given the extreme physical and mental demands the sport makes upon its competitors, sport psychologists can make a considerable contribution towards the optimizing of bodybuilding performance.

REFERENCES

Bass, C. (1999). *Challenge Yourself: Leanness, Fitness and Health at Any Age*. Albuquerque, NM: Ripped Enterprises.

Berscheid, E. & Walster, E. (1972). Beauty and the best. *Psychology Today, 5*, 42–46.

Boutcher, S.H. & Crews, D.J. (1987). The effect of a preshot attentional routine on a well-learned skill. *International Journal of Sport Psychology, 18*, 30–39.

Brunia, C.H.M. (1993). Stimulus preceding negativity: arguments in favour of non motoric slow waves. In W.C. McCallum and S.H. Curry (eds), *Slow Potential Changes in the Human Brain* (pp. 147–161). New York: Plenum Press.

Cabral, P. & Crisfield, P. (1996). *Psychology and Performance*. Leeds, UK: National Coaching Foundation.

Carpenter, D.M., Graves, J.E., Pollock, M.L., Leggett, S.H., Foster, D., Holmes, B. & Fulton, M. N. (1991). Effect of 12 and 20 weeks of resistance training on lumbar extension torque production. *Physical Therapy, 71*, 580–588.

Carpinelli, R. N. & Otto, R.M. (1998). Strength training: single versus multiple sets. *Sports Medicine, 26*, 73–84.

Coleman, R. (2004). *Training*. http://www.ronniecoleman.com/training.htm.

Cunnington, R., Iansek, R. & Bradshaw, J.L. (1996). Movement-related potentials associated with movement preparation and imagery. *Experimental Brain Research, 111*, 429–436.

Darden, E. (1986). *Super High-intensity Bodybuilding*. New York: Perigree.

Darden, E. (1988). *Big Arms in Six Weeks*. New York: Perigree.

Darden, E. (1989). *100 High-intensity Ways to Improve your Bodybuilding*. New York: Perigree.

Darden, E. (1990). *New High-intensity Bodybuilding*. New York: Perigree.

Darden, E. (1992). *Bigger Muscles in 42 Days*. New York: Perigree.

DeBenedette, V. (1990). Are your patients exercising too much? *Physician and Sports Medicine, 18*(8), 119, 122.

Dobbins, B. (2002, November). Ten ways to grow faster. *Muscle and Fitness*, 31–34.

Feltz, D.L. & Landers, D.M. (1983). The effects of mental practice on motor skill learning and performance: a meta analysis. *Journal of Sport Psychology, 5*, 25–27.

Fisher L.A. (1995). Building one's self up: bodybuilding and the construction of identity among professional female bodybuilders. Proceedings of the annual meeting of the Association for the Advancement of Applied Sport Psychology, New Orleans, LA, October 1995. Lawrence KS: Allen Press.

Fox, P.T., Pardo, J.V., Petersen, S.E. & Raichle, M.E. (1987). Supplementary motor and premotor responses to actual and imagined hand movements with positron emission tomography. *Society for Neuroscience Abstracts, 13*, 1433.

Freedson, P.S., Mihevic, P.M., Loucks, A.B. & Girandola, R.N. (1983). Physique, body composition and psychological characteristics of competitive female body builders. *Physician and Sports Medicine, 11*(1), 85–93.

Fuchs, C.V. & Zaichkowsky, L.D. (1983). Psychological characteristics of male and female bodybuilders: the iceberg profile. *Journal of Sport Behavior, 6*, 136–145.

Fussell, S. (1991). *Muscle: Confessions of an Unlikely Bodybuilder*. London: Abacus.

Gould, D., Tuffey, S., Udry, E. & Loehr, J. (1996). Burnout in competitive junior tennis players: II. Qualitative analysis. *The Sport Psychologist, 10*, 341–365.

Hardy, L. & Callow, N. (1999). Efficacy of external and internal visual imagery perspectives for the enhancement of performance on tasks in which form is important. *Journal of Sport and Exercise Psychology, 21*, 95–112.

Hardy, L., Jones, G. & Gould, D. (1996). *Understanding Psychological Preparation for Sport: Theory and Practice of Elite Performers*. Chichester, UK: John Wiley & Sons.

Holmes, P.S. & Collins, D.J. (2001). The PETTLEP approach to motor imagery: a functional equivalence model for sport psychologists. *Journal of Applied Sport Psychology, 13*, 60–83.

Hotten, J. (2004). *Muscle: A Writer's Trip through a Sport with No Boundaries*. London: Jonathan Cape.

Hurst, R., Hale, B., Smith, D. & Collins, D. (2000) Exercise dependence, social physique anxiety, and social support in experienced and inexperienced bodybuilders and weightlifters. *British Journal of Sports Medicine, 34*, 431–435.

Jackson, R.H. & Baker, J.S. (2001). Routines, rituals and rugby: case study of a world class goal kicker. *The Sport Psychologist, 15*, 48–65.

Jeannerod, M. (1995). Mental imagery in the motor context. *Neuropsychologia, 33*, 1419–1432.

Jones, A. (2000). My view on muscle magazines and their training routines. In B. Johnston (ed.), *Fitness Fraud: Exposing the Exercise and Nutrition Industries* (pp. 22–23). North Bay, Ontario: BODYworx Publishing.

Kennedy, R. (1983). *Hardcore Bodybuilding*. New York: Sterling.

Kennedy, R. (1988). *Posing! The Art of Hardcore Physique Display*. New York: Sterling.

Klein, A.M. (1993). *Little Big Men*. Albany: State University of New York Press.

Kleiner, S.M., Bazzarre, T.L. & Ainsworth, B.E. (1994). Nutritional status of nationally ranked elite bodybuilders. *International Journal of Sports Nutrition, 4*, 54–69.

Kubistant, T. (1988). *Mind Pump: The Psychology of Bodybuilding*. Champaign, IL: Leisure Press.

Lang, P.J. (1979). A bio-informational theory of emotional imagery. *Psychophysiology, 16*, 495–512.

Lang, P.J. (1985). The cognitive psychophysiology of emotion: fear and anxiety. In A.H. Tuma and J.D. Maser (eds). *Anxiety and the Anxiety Disorders* (pp. 131–170). Hillsdale, NJ: Lawrence Erlbaum Associates.

Leigh, W. (1990). *Arnold: An Unauthorised Biography*. London: Sphere Books.

Locke, E. (1991). Problems with goal-setting research in sports—and their solutions. *Journal of Sport and Exercise Psychology, 8*, 311–316.

Locke, E. & Latham, G.P. (1990). *A Theory of Goal Setting and Task Performance*. Englewood Cliffs, NJ: Prentice Hall.

Lombardo, J. (1993). The efficacy and mechanisms of action of anabolic steroids. In C.E. Yesalis (ed.), *Anabolic Steroids in Sport and Exercise* (pp. 89–106). Champaign, IL: Human Kinetics.

Luama, T.C. (interviewer) & Mentzer, M. (interviewee). (1995). *Muscle Media 2000 Audio Tape Interview Series: Mike Mentzer Part 3*. Golden, CO: Muscle Media 2000.

Marlow, C. (1998). The use of a single case design to investigate the effect of a pre-performance routine on the water polo penalty shot. *Journal of Science and Medicine in Sport, 1*, 143–155.

McNair, D.M., Lorr, M. & Dropplemann, L.F. (1971). *Profile of Mood States Manual*. San Diego: Educational and Industrial Testing Service.

Naito, E. & Matsumura, M. (1994). Movement-related slow potentials during motor imagery and motor suppression in humans. *Cognitive Brain Research, 2*, 131–137.

Paris, B. (1998). *Gorilla Suit: My adventures in Bodybuilding*. New York: St Martin's Press.

Peterson, J.A. (1975). Total conditioning: a case study. *Athletic Journal, 56*, 40–55.

Peterson, J.A., Bryant, C.X. & Peterson, S. (1995). *Strength Training for Women*. Champaign, IL: Human Kinetics.

Platz, T. (1982). *Pro-style Bodybuilding*. New York: Sterling.

Pollock, M., Graves, J.E., Bamman, M.M., Leggett, S.H., Carpenter, D.M., Carr, C., Cirulli, J., Matkozich, J. & Fulton, M. (1993). Frequency and volume of resistance training: effect on cervical extension strength. *Archives of Physical Medicine and Rehabilitation, 74*, 1080–1086.

Pope, H.G., Phillips, K.A. & Olivardia, R. (2000). *The Adonis Complex.* New York: Free Press.

Rogerson, L.J. & Hrycaiko, D.W. (2002). Enhancing competitive performance of ice hockey goaltenders using centering and self-talk. *Journal of Applied Sport Psychology, 14*, 14–26.

Rohrbaugh, J.W. & Gaillard, A.W.K. (1983). Sensory and motor aspects of the contingent negative variation. In A.W.K. Gaillard and T.W. Ritter (eds), *Tutorials in ERP Research: Endogenous Components* (pp. 269–310). Amsterdam: North-Holland.

Salmela, J.H. (1976). *Competitive Behaviors of Olympic Gymnasts.* Springfield, IL: Thomas.

Schmidt, G.W. & Stein, G.L. (1991). Sport commitment: a model integrating enjoyment, dropout and burnout. *Journal of Sport and Exercise Psychology, 13*, 254–265.

Smith, D. & Collins, D. (in press). Mental practice, motor performance and the late CNV. *Journal of Sport and Exercise Psychology.*

Smith, D., Collins, D. & Holmes, P. (2003). Impact and mechanism of mental practice effects on strength. *International Journal of Sport and Exercise Psychology, 1*, 293–306.

Smith, D. & Hale, B. (in press). Validity and factor structure of the Bodybuilding Dependence Scale. *British Journal of Sports Medicine.*

Smith D., Hale B.D. & Collins, D.J. (1998). Measurement of exercise dependence in bodybuilders. *Journal of Sports Medicine and Physical Fitness, 38*, 1–9.

Starkey, D.B., Pollock, M.L., Ishida, Y., Welsch, M.A., Breche, W.F., Graves, J.E. & Feigenbaum, M.S. (1996). Effect of resistance training volume on strength and muscle thickness. *Medicine and Science in Sports and Exercise, 28*, 1311–1320.

Stephan, K.M., Fink, G.R., Passingham, R.E., Silbersweig, D., Ceballos-Baumann, A.O., Frith, C.D. & Frackowiak, R.S.J. (1995). Functional anatomy of the mental representation of upper extremity movements in healthy subjects. *Journal of Neurophysiology, 73*, 373–386.

Sturmi, J.E. & Rutecki, G.W. (1995). When competitive bodybuilders collapse: a result of hyperkalemia? *Physician and Sports Medicine, 23*(11), 49–53.

Tenenbaum, G., Bar-Eli, M., Hoffman, J.R., Jablonovski, R., Sade, S. & Shitrit, D. (1995). The effect of cognitive and somatic psyching-up techniques on isokinetic leg strength performance. *Journal of Strength and Conditioning Research, 9*, 3–7.

Thompson, H. (writer and presenter) & Mares A. (producer). (1993). *Iron Maidens.* Manchester, UK: BBC Radio 4.

Too, D., Wakayama, E.T., Locati, L.L. & Landwer, G.E. (1998). Effect of precompetition bodybuilding diet and training regime on body composition and blood chemistry. *Journal of Sports Medicine and Physical Fitness, 38*, 245–252.

Tucci, J.T., Carpenter, D.M., Pollock, M.L., Graves, J.E. & Leggett, S.H. (1992). Effect of reduced frequency of training and detraining on lumbar extension strength. *SPINE, 17*, 1497–1501.

Tucker, L.A. (1982). Effects of a weight-training program on the self-concepts of college males. *Perceptual and Motor Skills, 54*, 1055–1061.

Tucker L.A. (1983). Weight training: a tool for the improvement of self and body concept of males. *Journal of Human Movement Studies, 9*, 31–37.

Tucker L.A. (1987). Effect of weight training on body attitudes: who benefits most? *Journal of Sports Medicine and Physical Fitness, 27*, 70–78.

Vost, K. (2002). Goal setting for the A+ physique. http://www.exercisecertification.com/articles/goalssettingA+.html.

Walberg-Rankin, J. (1995). A review of nutritional practices and needs of bodybuilders. *Journal of Strength and Conditioning Research, 9*, 116–124.

Walter, W.G., Cooper, R., Aldridge, V.J., McCallum, W.C. & Winter, A.L. (1964). Contingent negative variation: an electric sign of sensori-motor association and expectancy in the human brain. *Nature, 203*, 380–384.

Whitmarsh, B. & Paa, H. (2001). *Mind and Muscle.* Champaign, IL: Human Kinetics.

Wichmann, S. & Martin, D.R. (1992). Exercise excess: treating patients addicted to fitness. *Physician and Sports Medicine, 20*(5), 193–196, 199–200.

Wilson-Fearon, C. & Parrott, A.C. (1999). Multiple drug use and dietary restraint in a Mr Universe competitor: psychobiological effects. *Perceptual and Motor Skills, 88*, 579–580.

Yates, D. & McGough, P. (1998). *Portrait of Dorian Yates: The Life and Training Philosophy of the World's Best Bodybuilder.* Birmingham, UK: D. Yates.

Yates, D. & Wolff, B. (1993). *Blood and Guts.* Woodland Hills, CA: YB Small Books.

Yue, G.H. & Cole, K.J. (1992). Strength increases from the motor program: comparison of training with maximal voluntary and imagined muscle contractions. *Journal of Neurophysiology, 67,* 1114–1123.

Yue, G.H., Wilson, S.L., Cole, K.J., Darling, W.G. & Yuh, W.T.C. (1996). Imagined muscle contraction training increases voluntary neural drive to muscle. *Journal of Psychophysiology, 10,* 198–208.

Ziegler, S.G. (1987). Negative thought stopping: a key to performance enhancement. *Journal of Physical Education, Recreation and Dance, 58,* 66–69.

CHAPTER 28

Sport Psychology in Gymnastics

Karen D. Cogan
University of North Texas, USA

INTRODUCTION

Gymnastics is a wonderful, all-around fitness sport in which athletes develop strength, grace, endurance, and persistence. Almost anyone who has trained, coached or seriously observed gymnastics will agree that psychological skills play a significant role in gymnastics success, and provide an added edge. This chapter focuses on the psychology of gymnastics, but before examining the psychological factors, it is useful to outline some general knowledge about the sport.

GYMNASTICS BASICS

Women's gymnastics is composed of four events: vault, uneven parallel bars (bars), balance beam (beam) and floor exercise (floor). Men's gymnastics is composed of six events: floor exercise (floor), parallel bars, high bar, pommel horse, rings and vault. Gymnasts who compete on all events in a single meet are considered all-around competitors. When gymnasts perform routines in a meet, their performance is evaluated by judges. Each judge assigns a score that ranges from 0.00 to 10.00, with 10.00 being a perfect performance, and then judges' scores are averaged. Each routine is assigned a start value, which is the highest possible score attainable given the overall difficulty of the routine, and many routines start lower than a 10.00. Every gymnast dreams of achieving that perfect 10.00, but only a few of the best in the world ever achieve that perfection.

For girls, training usually begins at a young age, often as young as 5 years old. Some gymnasts train for fun and others train for competition. Each country has its own system that allows competitors to progress from beginning competition levels up to the national or Olympic level. Because girls reach their gymnastics peak at a young age, intensive preparation and training in the early years become important if a gymnast is to achieve her goals. If the gymnast chooses to be a serious competitor and devotes herself to the sport, by the age of 12 or 13, she may be spending 20 to 30 hours per week in the gym. A gymnast

The Sport Psychologist's Handbook: A Guide for Sport-Specific Performance Enhancement.
Edited by Joaquín Dosil. © 2006 John Wiley & Sons, Ltd.

who trains for the Olympics can spend up to 40 hours a week in the gym. With this training intensity, most of her social activities will likely center on the sport and her teammates, and she has probably given up other activities to train.

For boys, the same type of environment exists though intensive training may begin at a slightly older age. To be successful, boys need physical strength that they generally do not develop until they reach adolescence. The top junior boys, though, still may be training 20 hours a week by age 14. College is when many of the top male gymnasts are just reaching their prime and are training for international and Olympic as well as college competitions. They all work for team success, but some also must diligently focus on their personal goals. In the right environment the gymnast can accomplish both goals without sacrificing either. Men also may experience the additional pressures of what seems like two competitive seasons superimposed on top of each other. They compete in collegiate meets and are also participating in additional national or international meets outside of the college season. Sometimes they must peak more than once throughout the year.

Some gymnasts who have Olympic or world-class aspirations even move from home to train in high-level gyms with well-known coaches in hopes of reaching their goals. Parents and families often sacrifice to finance this training or relocate with the gymnast to train at the best gyms. Other gymnasts may train just as intensely, but are able to stay close to home. Even training close to home can require sacrifices of a family, such as training costs, driving to the gym and giving up family activities (Cogan & Vidmar, 2000).

Some gymnasts may work toward competing in college. Many college teams recruit former Olympians or world-class athletes, but lesser-known gymnasts also are recruited by universities and successfully reach their prime in their college years. Even making a college team, however, is becoming more and more competitive.

When gymnasts first begin competing, they usually train in a team environment where others at a variety of different skill levels train together for competition. Unlike sports such as basketball or soccer, gymnasts are not required to work in unison to reach a team goal. One athlete's performance does not affect a teammate's score. Despite the team training atmosphere, gymnastics is generally considered an individual sport in which gymnasts compete for individual honors. Although there are some selected team competitions, such as the Olympic Team Finals and other invitational meets, gymnasts are usually recognized for what they individually accomplish. This type of environment can create competition between teammates, but spending three to six hours or more a day in the gym requires teammates to get along and support each other, and often results in life-long friends.

A team focus is especially important if the gymnast plans to compete in college. At the college level, the primary focus becomes the team achievements. Although individual achievements are recognized, these achievements are secondary to those of the team. In addition, because there are only six competitors on each apparatus, not all the gymnasts can compete on every event in each meet. Some members of a team may specialize in only one or two events or may not compete at all. All athletes are vying for the top six spots on each event, while simultaneously the coaches are encouraging them to be team-oriented and supportive of each other. Gymnasts often experience mixed feelings in that they want what is best for the team, but also wish to achieve their own personal goals. Collegiate coaches emphasize team support and encourage the gymnasts to "do what is best for the team" rather than strive only for personal goals. Gymnasts often have difficulty rapidly adjusting their attitudes to accept this new team-centered approach after many years as individual competitors. The changes in competition procedures and the new focus on the team can contribute to a lack of cohesiveness in the environment. If gymnasts begin training with a "team attitude" early in their careers, the transition to college can be made more smoothly (Cogan & Vidmar, 2000).

Although sport psychology consultants may work on more individual mental skills with gymnasts, team-building interventions are needed in the gymnastics arena as well. Sport psychology consultants can encourage athletes to develop a team-oriented atmosphere, and to be gracious in accepting their own and teammates achievements as well as disappointments.

The gymnastics environment shapes how gymnasts learn and cope with challenges. Understanding the environment allows a sport psychology consultant to better appreciate the important mental abilities necessary for training and competing in gymnastics. The next section outlines psychological issues that gymnasts face.

COMMON PSYCHOLOGICAL ISSUES FACED BY GYMNASTS

Many gymnasts and sport psychology consultants alike believe that gymnastics is one of the most mental of all sports. There are countless psychological issues gymnasts face daily that can interfere with training. The following section will highlight some primary issues including anxiety, low confidence, focus, negative thinking, fear, eating disorders, clinical issues and parental involvement. It is useful for gymnasts to begin learning skills to cope with these issues at a young age just as they would any other physical skill, and sport psychology consultants can be instrumental in introducing these topics so that they become a standard part of training. In addition, this chapter will pay special attention to eating disorders because so many gymnasts struggle with eating and body image and because of the potentially life-threatening nature of those issues.

Anxiety

Anxiety can be experienced by athletes in any sport, and gymnastics is no exception. In fact, anxiety is a common presenting complaint among young gymnasts who seek sport psychology consulting services. Anxiety can have a positive function as it can serve to increase effort and preparation; however, too much anxiety can result in performance decrements (Balague, 2004). There are many sources of anxiety including, but not limited to, intensive training for several hours a day at a young age, competition anxiety, parental pressures, coach pressures, questions about whether to remain involved in the sport, and injury.

Focus

Gymnasts need to maintain focus. There is a high risk of injury if the athlete takes a wrong step or is slightly out of position in the air. A gymnast cannot afford to lose focus, but there are many demands competing for their attention. There is activity on all four or six events at the same time in the gym or in meets, and gymnasts have to shift focus from one to the next as they rotate among them. During training or warm-ups many gymnasts may be training on the apparatus at the same time (e.g. multiple tumblers on floor). Gymnasts must be focused on what they are doing yet also be aware of what is going on around them to be sure there are no injuries or crashes.

Confidence

Many young gymnasts struggle with building and maintaining confidence in this sport where minor errors and fractions of a point may make the difference between an Olympic gold and no medal. Gymnasts face constant pressures to learn new and harder skills that involve risking injury. Gymnasts often perfect a skill only to lose it later because of fear or incorrect timing in doing the movement. Also, if gymnasts repeatedly make the same error on a skill, a series of skills or in competition, their confidence can be eroded and is extremely difficult to rebuild at that point.

Negative Thinking

Sport in general is an ideal environment for fostering irrational thinking (Williams & Leffingwell, 2002), and gymnasts in particular struggle with negative attitudes, especially when learning new skills or if learned skills are not going well. Poor performance at a competition also can lead to a negative spiral of thinking. In addition, gymnasts are very aware of the changes that occur in their bodies during adolescence, which can affect their gymnastics ability and timing as well as body image. Often these physical changes lead to negative thinking.

SPECIFIC PSYCHOLOGICAL ISSUES

There are some psychological issues that are more relevant to gymnastics than other sports, and the next portion of this chapter will offer a more detailed explanation of these issues.

Fear

Fear is a major psychological barrier in gymnastics. Many gymnasts try to eliminate fear, but fear is a natural reaction to the risky skills gymnasts perform and is actually a necessary component for advancement in gymnastics. Fear helps a gymnast maintain enough adrenalin and focus to perform difficult skills safely. Therefore, a gymnast's goal should be to learn to work with fear rather than to eliminate it (Cogan & Vidmar, 2000).

Fear comes in different forms. One is a mental block in which gymnasts are just learning a skill and the coaches step away to allow them to do it alone, but the gymnast is unable to "go for it". Something stops them from throwing it even though the ability is clearly there. For example, a gymnast pulls out in the middle of a vault (does not complete the flip on the second half) or can do a double back into the pit (soft foam landing) but not on regular mats. Most gymnasts have experienced one or more of these blocks as they try to learn new skills, and mental blocks can be one of the most frustrating aspects of training.

Often mental blocks occur because a gymnast thinks too much. The mind actually gets in the way of the body's ability to do what it knows how to do. Instead of just throwing a skill, the gymnast starts thinking about all the possible ways for injury to occur. For instance, a gymnast may be trying a standing back tuck on the beam and begins thinking about how she can miss the beam on the landing. Once she has that picture in her mind, she is immobilized, as if there were steel bolts attaching her feet to the beam.

Another type of mental block is losing a skill that a gymnast has previously performed alone or even in competition without difficulty. Most gymnasts have experienced this type of block too. One day the gymnast feels a little disoriented and does not throw the double full on floor quite right, or her timing is off. She starts twisting too early off the ground and does not know where she is in the air. From there, her performance deteriorates until she cannot do the skill at all. Coming into the gym the next day, all she can think about is how hard it was to get the double full right. She says to herself, "I hope I don't mess it up today", but she struggles again. The next day she has psyched herself out before she even tries the double full. Often gymnasts become fearful of back tumbling in general, and the fear can even generalize to other events (e.g. fear of back tumbling series on beam, or flipping backward on vault). She has the physical skills because she has done it countless times before, but now the mental component is preventing her from doing what was previously mastered.

Disordered Eating

A second issue that is prominent with gymnastics is disordered eating. With the emphasis on thinness and appearance in gymnastics, it has been suggested that these athletes are at greater risk for the development of disordered eating patterns and diagnosable eating disorders than the general population or other "non-aesthetic" sports (Burckes-Miller & Black, 1991; Petrie 1993). Aesthetic sports generally involve scoring systems that are subjective, and grace and body appearance can affect the scoring on some level. Therefore, awareness and knowledge of eating disorders is important for any sport psychology consultant working with gymnasts. As mentioned earlier in the chapter, special attention will be paid to eating disorders because of the serious, potentially life-threatening nature of these disorders.

Much of the literature on eating disorders has focused on females because historically females have been more at risk for the development of eating disorders. Though generally males appear to be less at risk for eating disorders than women, males can develop eating disordered behaviors as well, especially in gymnastics where the ratio of body weight to strength is vital to performance. Discussions in this chapter related to eating apply to both men and women, but because of eating disorders' prominence in girls and women, most references in this section will be to female gymnasts.

In any population, general or athletic, it is useful to view disordered eating on a continuum (Mintz & Betz, 1988). On one end of the continuum are severe, diagnosed eating disorders including anorexia, bulimia, and compulsive overeating. To be diagnosed with an eating disorder, an individual must meet certain criteria, which are outlined in the DSM–IV, TR (American Psychiatric Association, 2000), and only a small percentage of the population meets these specific criteria. On the other end of the continuum are individuals with no symptoms of eating disorders. In between these two end points is "disordered eating" behavior in which individuals demonstrate some characteristics of eating disorders but not enough to warrant a diagnosis. These behaviors cause a variety of problems even if they do not meet the specific eating disorder criteria, and should not be ignored. It is unclear how many individuals fall into this middle category, but some studies report more than 60 per cent of the general population demonstrate some type of disordered eating behavior (Mintz & Betz, 1988).

In a study of gymnasts specifically, Petrie (1993) found that, consistent with the general population, over 60 per cent of gymnasts fell in the middle of the continuum and could be classified as having disordered eating behaviors. Comparisons among different types of sports have found that female aesthetic sport athletes (e.g. gymnasts, divers) have a greater tendency toward anorexia than ball game athletes or endurance athletes (Sungot-Borgen, 1994). For male athletes, both aesthetic and weight-dependent (e.g. wrestling) athletes had greater bulimic symptomatology than endurance athletes.

Some gymnasts will hide disordered eating behavior behind a "healthy eating" façade. For instance, gymnasts will talk about eating healthy (cutting out virtually all the fat content in their diet, eating only foods where the calorie content is clear, cutting out *all* junk food to the point that there is very little they are "allowed" to eat) but they are really undereating and severely restricting their food intake. Because coaches encourage healthy diets, they may not see this pattern as a problem until it is too late. Sport psychology consultants can assist by being aware of even subtle types of eating issues and monitoring the possibility of the development of more severe eating symptoms.

The American College of Sports Medicine (1997) and Yeager, Agostini & Nattiv (1993) have identified another type of disordered eating condition called "female athlete triad". Women athletes can be at risk for female athlete triad, which consists of three interrelated components: disordered eating, amenorrhea (cessation of menstrual periods for 3 or more months or no menstrual periods by age 16) and osteoporosis (bone loss). Disordered eating leads to a negative energy balance, which occurs when the amount of energy consumed is less than the amount of energy expended. Eventually the body interprets a negative energy balance as starvation and may shut down the body's reproductive capability by shutting down the menstrual cycle. The result is a decrease in estrogen and, consequently, amenorrhea. Decreases in estrogen and in dietary intake of calcium (which occurs with restricting food intake and lack of nutritional knowledge) signal the bones to release calcium to replace low calcium levels in the bloodstream, resulting in bone loss or formation of unhealthy bone (osteoporosis). There is some evidence that high-impact sports such as gymnastics provide protection against low bone density, but it is still important to prevent disordered eating and amenorrhea in gymnastics because the long-term effects are uncertain (Kirchner, Lewis & O'Connor, 1996; Nichols, Sanborn & Bonnick, 1994).

Clinical Issues

In addition to eating disorders, other clinical issues such as depression and anxiety disorders can develop. A gymnast is not operating in a vacuum, and often these outside issues interfere with a gymnast's training and performance. Those sport psychology consultants who are clinically trained are aware of interventions to address these issues. Those consultants who are not clinically trained will want to have referral sources in case a clinical issue with which they are uncomfortable arises.

Parents

Because gymnasts begin intensive training at young ages, parents are often very involved. Parental support is a key factor in gymnastics success, and parents are often instrumental in the success of their child. Most parents want what is best for their children, but because parents can have such a strong influence, they sometimes exert unnecessary pressure, which reduces young gymnasts' sport satisfaction. Parents can exert too much pressure if they become overly invested in their child's sport. Sometimes parents can get so absorbed in their own goals and desires for their child that they are not aware that the child is losing interest in the sport. Parents can try to live vicariously through their child if they never achieved their sport goals and the child shows potential to excell. In this instance, the children may feel pressure to perform well and keep training when they would rather be doing something else. The challenge for any gymnastics family is to find a balance between minimal involvement and over-involvement. Sport psychology consultants can assist here in educating gymnastics parents about appropriate and inappropriate involvement in their child's sport experience.

PSYCHOLOGICAL SKILLS TRAINING FOR GYMNASTICS

Based on the environment and issues identified above, the next section offers some interventions. Many of these are standard sport psychology techniques that most sport psychology consultants will know and thus examples specific to gymnastics are provided to add to the sport psychology consultant's repertoire.

Anxiety Control

Anxiety in gymnastics it to be expected, especially in high-pressure situations, and a goal to eliminate anxiety entirely would be unrealistic. Rather, anxiety has to be accepted and managed. There are strategies gymnasts can learn to help cope with anxiety. First, determine if there is any way to eliminate the source(s) of anxiety. This strategy works only if the source of anxiety is not a priority. For instance, a gymnast might decide to eliminate an extracurricular activity at school that they have little interest in continuing, to free up some time.

It is also helpful to assist athletes in examining what they can and cannot control in their lives. For instance, gymnasts cannot control their coach's or teammate's behaviors, the judges' subjective impressions, or their placement in the competition order lineup, but often gymnasts become anxious about these types of things and spend energy worrying about them. Unfortunately, this worry only distracts them from putting energy into their performances. Instead, a sport psychology consultant can help them focus on the things they can control and change (primarily their personal performance) so that they have more opportunities to control their success.

Gymnasts also can control how they prepare to cope with stress. A sport psychology consultant can guide the athlete in learning relaxation exercises. Relaxation exercises work best when the athlete consistently trains them much as they train physical skills. There are many relaxation strategies, but the following are some that work well with gymnastics.

If the gymnast experiences high physical anxiety (e.g. sweaty palms, butterflies in the stomach), physical relaxation strategies are the most useful. Deep breathing, progressive muscle relaxation, and cue-controlled relaxation are some popular strategies to control physical anxiety.

1. *Deep breathing* The simplest and quickest exercise for managing physical anxiety is deep breathing (Williams & Harris, 1998). Taking a few deep breaths can quickly bring anxiety levels down. Each time the gymnast exhales, they release tension. Deep breathing

is particularly useful for gymnasts in the few moments before they compete on an event such as beam where they need to be steady and calm. Deep breathing is just the first step and, to really master relaxation, a gymnast must practice more involved relaxation techniques.

2. *Progressive muscle relaxation (PMR)* PMR involves systematically tensing and relaxing groups of muscles throughout the body (Jacobson, 1930). Typically, a gymnast begins with the hands and arms, moves to the head and body, and then legs and feet. In this way, the gymnast can begin to feel the difference between tension and relaxation and can more easily choose the "relax" option when needed. Athletes can use PMR in two ways:

   a. A sport psychology consultant can take gymnasts through the exercise and tape-record it at the same time. Then gymnasts can practice with it once a day on their own. Remember to leave pauses in between muscle groups so that there is enough time to tense and relax.

   b. Gymnasts can memorize the exercise after reading through it a few times and use it on their own anytime.

   PMR is useful for athletes who have ongoing challenges with anxiety. It encourages consistent and detailed learning about how the body feels when anxious and gives the athlete practice in countering anxiety. It is most effective when practiced regularly in the pre-season so that it can be easily implemented in a competitive situation where anxiety is elevated.

3. *Cue-controlled relaxation (CCR)* CCR (Russell, Miller & June, 1974) is an extension of PMR. After gymnasts learn PMR, they choose a cue word that is relaxing in nature. Many athletes choose "calm" or "relax" or some other similar word. The session begins by progressing through the tense/relax phase for each muscle group. Once gymnasts have become completely relaxed, they focus on breathing. Gymnasts then sub-vocalize the cue word on every exhale for approximately one minute. Gymnasts stop saying the cue word for approximately two minutes and maintain the relaxed state. Then they begin repeating the cue word on each exhale for another minute. It is best to practice this exercise every day for several weeks for maximum benefit. In the future, if gymnasts feel tense, they simply repeat the cue word with each exhale and can more automatically let go of the tension.

Mental Relaxation

Sometimes the gymnast's mind is the source of the anxiety. If this is the case, then mental relaxation is an appropriate intervention. The following are some examples of mental relaxation strategies. These strategies also help to replace negative thinking with more positive thoughts.

1. *Thought stopping* Thought stopping is used in general psychological treatment (Burns, 1980) as well as for athletes (Meyers & Schleser, 1980). Gymnasts often say things to themselves such as "I can't do my series on beam or my double back on floor", "I'm going to fall", "I might hurt myself." These self-statements can contribute to and increase anxiety. If a gymnast is saying these types of statements, the next statement should be the word "*Stop!*" Then the gymnast can take a deep breath and begin doing some thought replacement as outlined next.

2. *Thought replacement* Gymnasts can tell themselves to stop thinking negative, unproductive thoughts, but keeping those thoughts out of their minds may be more difficult. Unfortunately, when gymnasts say, "Don't think about falling", falling is all they think about. It is necessary to put something in place of that thought. Instead try: "My beam series is difficult, but it has been improving; the more I do it, the better it will get." A replacement thought for, "I'm afraid I'll get hurt on my double back", would be: "Just focus on a good take-off. I know what to do, and I've done it hundreds of times into the pit." Instead of, "I'm too tired to make it through this floor exercise routine", encourage gymnasts to think: "Go hard, stay energized, push through to the end." They can also use energized breathing (see below). These replacement thoughts are much more productive and calming than negative ones and help the gymnast focus on their goals.

Many gymnasts experience anxiety both physically and mentally. When that is the case, they benefit from using a combination of strategies to relax both the mind and body. One relaxation strategy that does both is meditation. See Benson's (1975) *The Relaxation Response* for guidelines on using meditation strategies.

Sometimes gymnasts face the opposite problem: they need to energize. Possibly the gymnast is exhausted prior to a workout or has been sitting for a while waiting to vault during a meet. All of a sudden he realizes he is next up and feels cold and stiff. In these types of situations, the gymnast needs to increase energy rather than relax.

One way to energize is through breathing. A gymnast can energize by taking deep, pumped-up breaths. The sport psychology consultant can suggest the following:

1. Begin breathing deeply with a regular, relaxed rhythm.
2. Increase breathing rhythm and, with each exhale, imagine producing more and more energy.
3. With each inhale, think "energy in", and with each exhale think "fatigue out".

Gymnasts also can add energizing imagery by imagining an "energy bolt" coursing through their body, or imagining their muscles becoming stronger and putting forth power.

In addition, gymnasts can benefit from using energy-inducing cue words for situations in which they need to psych up quickly. A sport psychology consultant can assist gymnasts in choosing a word or two that help to quickly achieve an energized state. For instance, gymnasts might choose words like "fast", "explode", "go", or "push".

Focusing through Imagery

Mental practice or imagery facilitates the development of attentional focus in athletes. With imagery, athletes are better able to focus on relevant aspects of performance thus reducing the potential for distraction (Feltz & Landers, 1983). Imagery is a top-priority mental skill in gymnastics where so much of the sport's movement is technical and precise. Many gymnasts believe if they cannot imagine doing a skill then they cannot do it physically. Imagery assists gymnasts in mastering their ability to focus. The following are guidelines for effective use of imagery (Gould, Damarjian & Greenleaf, 2002) that should be familiar to most sport psychology consultants. Examples specific to gymnastics have been added.

1. *Use all senses when imaging* Encourage gymnasts to see in vivid color, hear the sounds in the gym, smell the smells in the gym (chalk, mats), and feel the equipment as they touch it or how their bodies feel when training a skill.

2. *Develop control of imagery skills and visualize positive outcomes* Gymnasts will want to master control of imagery skills. Rather than visualizing over- or under-rotating a tumbling pass or vault, missed landings or falls, they are encouraged to picture nailing every skill and sticking the landing and work toward visualizing the desired body positions for every skill.

3. *Use internal and external imagery* Some gymnasts use external imagery (watching themselves in their minds as if they were watching a DVD) while others use internal imagery (visualize as if they were looking out of their eyes). Some gymnasts use a combination of internal and external imagery. Both types of imagery can be effective, and each gymnast will want to determine what type or combination works best.

4. *Practice imagery regularly* For imagery to work, it must become part of each gymnast's practice routine so that it is as natural every day as warm-ups. In fact, it can be used every day when a gymnast warms up to prepare for the workout.

5. *Practice imagery in a relaxed state* Research shows that imagery practiced in combination with a relaxed state is more effective than imagery alone. Relaxation can clear gymnasts' minds of distractions so that they can concentrate on imagery skills. There is one caveat, though: most competitions and often training are not relaxed, so in order to practice for the realities of competition, gymnasts will also want to include imagery practice under conditions other than a relaxed state.

6. *Develop coping strategies through imagery* Although it is most helpful to see positive outcomes when using imagery, sometimes it helps to visualize an unexpected event and then determine how to cope with it. This way, the gymnast is prepared if it happens and can use a pre-determined plan rather than having to think on the spot. For instance, a gymnast might envision her floor music stopping three-quarters of the way through her routine and then finishing the routine without missing a beat. A gymnast might envision preparing to begin a high bar routine and then being delayed because the judges are conferencing about the previous competitor's score. In this case, the gymnast can mentally practice going back to the waiting area and refocusing as he would if there was still another competitor to go.

7. *Use cues or triggers to help with imagery rehearsal* Some athletes find certain words or phrases serve as cues or triggers that help them focus on imagery strategies. For instance, on vault, a cue might be "power" or "push", but each individual will want to experiment with words that make imagery more powerful for them.

8. *Practice kinesthetic imagery* Imagery is most useful when a gymnast can practice feeling the sensations in her body as she performs on each event. She can focus on feeling her muscles working, hands sweating and moving in the air. Sometimes prior to competition on pommel horse, a gymnast might close his eyes and slightly move his shoulders as he mentally practices his routine. Before a twisting tumbling pass, some gymnasts might stand at the corner of the mat, close their eyes, and quickly raise their arms above their head with a twisting motion. In this way, they practice what they will feel as they tumble.

9. *Image in "real time"* Sometimes it is tempting to image in slow motion to really understand how to do a skill. Alternatively, a gymnast might be rushed and run through imagery practice quickly. Because routines are not performed in slow or fast motion, it

Table 28.1 Imagery log

Date	Time	Describe Imagery	Practice time	Success
4/28	1.30 p.m.	Practiced 10 double backs on floor; used internal and kinesthetic imagery	5 minutes	A little trouble feeling landings; landed 3 in gym
4/30	9.00 p.m.	practiced 3 beam (or high bar) routines in prep for meet tomorrow	10 minutes	Able to image layout pass (or release moves) solidly!

is most useful to visualize at the true pace of a performance. This makes imagery more realistic. The only exception is when gymnasts are having difficulty seeing a desired outcome; for example, they cannot envision the correct positioning in the air on a vault and then cannot stick the landing. In this case, it is helpful to use slow-motion imagery so that gymnasts move frame by frame through the vault, checking that each position is correct. Then they can eventually speed up the image into real time.

10. *Use imagery logs* New gymnastics skills can best be monitored with a written record. The same can be done with imagery so that the gymnast can keep track of what, when and how much imagery is practiced. A chart can be set up, as shown in Table 28.1. Table 28.2 suggests some imagery exercises specific to gymnastics.

Confidence-building

Attaining and maintaining confidence involves a complex set of interactions including messages from parents, peers and coaches, history of success in sport and general personality characteristics. Therefore a variety of interventions can be effective depending on the needs of the particular gymnast. It is beyond the scope of this chapter to present all possible interventions for building confidence, especially those on a family systems level. The basis for building confidence, though, is positive self talk and imagery. Most sport psychology consultants are familiar with positive self talk and the reader is referred to page 648–649 for ideas on thought stopping and replacement. Likewise, imagery (visualizing positive outcomes and qualities about oneself) is a good method for building confidence, and again the reader is referred to page 650 for ideas on using imagery.

Negative Thinking

Thought stopping and thought replacement as well as positive imagery can also be used to counter the negative thinking that gymnasts often experience. Again the reader is referred to the previous discussions in this chapter.

General Mental Skills Training

Two other general strategies that can assist gymnasts in achieving peak performances are to develop pre-performance plans and to institute competition simulations into practice.

Table 28.2   Imagery exercises specific to gymnastics

Vivid Imagery
Close your eyes and take a few deep breaths. Picture yourself walking into the gym when no
one is there. Look at the layout of the equipment. Notice the colors of the mats and other
equipment. Listen to the sounds in the gym, such as the buzz of the lights, the "squish" of
the mats as you walk across them, your own breathing. Take a deep breath and notice the
smell of the metal on the equipment, plastic on the mats, or chalk in the chalk bins. Touch
the bars and feel how your hands grip them. Then put your hand on the beam and feel the
leather beneath your fingers. Step onto the floor exercise area and feel the slight spring as
you walk on the floor. Now open your eyes.

Controlling imagery
Close your eyes and take a few deep breaths. Imagine yourself doing a simple move such as a
cartwheel. Stand with your arms raised. Shift your weight to your first leg; place your first
hand on the floor. Allow your legs to begin moving over your body. Place your second
hand. Feel your straight legs and pointed toes. Bring your legs down on the other side and
hands up. Make sure your cartwheel is exactly as you want it to be. Open your eyes.

Energizing imagery
When a gymnast is experiencing a mental block (e.g. cannot do a standing back tuck on the
beam), positive imagery is helpful. Instead of focusing on her legs being bolted to the
beam, she could imagine her legs feeling like pistons that could propel her off the beam
and through the air.

Doing a routine with imagery
Pick an event. Close your eyes. Breath deeply as you begin to relax. Do a routine mentally in
real time. You can do this by timing your imagery and confining it to the real length of a
routine. Be sure to use the guidelines that have been discussed for enhancing imagery.
Open your eyes. You can try this example with all other events too.

Practicing imagery in the gym
Next time you are on beam or parallel bars, mentally rehearse how you want your most
difficult skills to feel before you get up and actually do them. If your coach gives you a
correction, imagine doing the skill with the correction before you actually do it again. If
you make a mistake, stop. Imagine doing the skill the right way. You don't want to
remember the mistakes; you want to focus on doing the skill correctly. These "in the gym"
imagery exercises can be used for all events.

Competition Imagery
Imagine walking into the competition arena for an important meet. There is the buzz of
excitement in the air and bright lights. Look at the spectators and other competitors in their
uniforms. Walk to the equipment, touch it, get a feel for it. Walk over to the floor, stretch,
and watch as more people enter the arena. Envision warming up on each event, feeling the
movements for each skill.

Note: As the gymnast masters control over the imagery of easier moves, they can progress to visualizing more difficult
moves with control. For example, they can work up to a round off, back handspring, double back tuck on floor.

1. *Pre-performance plans* A pre-performance plan is a consistent set of planned behaviors,
   thoughts, words and/or feelings that a gymnast has developed to prepare for competition.
   Each component of the plan helps athletes reach their ideal mindsets that will enable
   a high-level performance, and the plan helps build their self-confidence to meet the
   challenges of competition. Pre-performance plans work best if they become habit, and
   are practiced before every competition. Many gymnasts use pre-performance strategies
   before even arriving at the competition site. They can choose specific activities to use
   during warm-up, just prior to competition, throughout competition, and directly after
   competition. In short, the plan is a script of what they will do, be and think on the day of

the meet. This mental pre-performance plan can be incorporated into physical preparation during warm-up for competition. Consistently performing the plan will assist gymnasts in achieving an ideal performance because it helps them to focus and deal effectively with distractions. A pre-performance plan can consist of any combination of the following:

- *Self-talk* Encourage the gymnast to define positive, motivating and instructive self-talk that can be used during training and before competition.
- *Cue words* Gymnasts can benefit from choosing cue words such as "go", "fast", "focus" and "be aggressive" to eliminate distractions and stay focused.
- *Imagery* Imagery can be practiced anywhere and can be incorporated into a pre-performance plan. Gymnasts can use it to practice coping with potential difficulties that could arise in a meet.
- *Attentional focus* Gymnasts are encouraged to use visual reminders and/or cue words to direct their attention appropriately to the chosen task Mentally tough gymnasts can shift attentional focus as needed and are not distracted by other activities in their environment.
- *Competition goals* Goal-setting can be an important part of the pre-competition plan and should be included to assist the gymnast in focusing on what they are trying to accomplish.
- *Activation/energy regulation* Every gymnast on every event has his or her own optimal level of activation. On the beam, a gymnast will need less activation, and on the vault she will need more. The consultant can help the gymnast determine what is an appropriate level for each event and then design relaxation strategies to bring down an activation level that is too high, and psyching or energizing strategies to increase an activation level that is too low.

2. *Competition simulations* In addition to pre-performance plans, gymnasts can set up practices similarly to competition in order to be prepared for meets. There are a variety of ways to simulate meet situations. Some of these include:

- Make practice into a meet. Asking gymnasts to pretend they are in an important competition can create a meet environment. The consultant can intentionally set up a hypothetical meet situation, with the expected distractions and procedures that would exist in a real meet.
- Ask everyone in the gym to stop and watch as each gymnast performs a routine.
- Videotape routines or take photographs as each gymnast performs a routine.
- Ask coaches or teammates to "judge" routines by adding up deductions and giving a final score estimate.
- Have an intersquad meet with real judges, scores and awards.
- Hold a dress rehearsal in which athletes dress in competition uniforms and perform.
- Conduct warm-ups in the gym as if practice were a meet. For example, take 20 minutes (or some pre-determined amount of time) on each event to do a full warm-up; then do one routine on each event. Make sure gymnasts take a one-touch (three-minute) warm-up before each routine.
- Practice going first or last. In a meet, a gymnast may compete immediately after warm-ups or may need to wait, sometimes for an extended time. A gymnast can practice for these lineup placements by warming up and then performing a routine immediately or waiting and taking time to focus.
- Mentally rehearse competition routines. This can be done any time and any place without an elaborate set-up.

FEAR

As discussed in the beginning of the chapter, it is not uncommon for gymnasts to have difficulty with a skill once it is learned, often due to fear and mental blocks. Sometimes if gymnasts leave the skill alone for a time, they can come back renewed. The challenge occurs when gymnasts feel pressure to continue doing it, and begin practicing it in this new, incorrect way. They lose confidence in the ability to do it correctly and become continually frustrated, having a negative association with any practice of that skill (Cogan & Vidmar, 2000).

The way in which fear or a mental block is handled from the start can make a huge difference in how the gymnast gets past it. If the gymnast or coaches over-focus on it, chances are it will be harder to manage. If, however, everyone can recognize that blocks occur, relax, and work toward gradually overcoming it, then success is more likely. In addition, sport psychology consultants can instruct gymnasts in the following strategies to overcome fear and blocks as outlined in Cogan & Vidmar (2000):

1. First, get off the equipment and walk away to the side. Take a few deep breaths and relax. Then think about what is getting in the way of performing the skill.
2. If fear of injury is the block, think about how unrealistic the possibility of injury is. Of course, any time aerial movements are performed, injury is a possibility, but gymnasts do hundreds of gymnastics moves a day and do not get injured. The consultant can help gymnasts understand that given their skills and the coach's confidence that they can perform the skill alone, injury is unlikely. If the gymnast is ready for a skill, injury is unlikely as long as there is no holding back. In addition, encourage the use of positive self-talk to replace the negative thinking.
3. If athletes think too much, it may be easiest to get off the equipment, do relaxation skills, and get back on without thinking. Then they can allow their body to do what comes naturally. Instruct gymnasts to practice imagery and feel their body doing the skill perfectly.
4. Use distraction. Encourage the gymnast to think about something else before attempting the skill (though not to the degree that they are not paying attention and then risking injury). For instance, try listening to motivating music or doing mental math (count backward from 100 by 7s) to distract the mind from thinking about difficulties with the skill. Another strategy is to ask a teammate to call out a question to answer just before the gymnast turns around to do the skill, and then go without thinking.
5. Another form of distraction is to count and go. Gymnasts can walk to their ready position and, without waiting, say "1, 2, 3, Go." Then they can do the skill immediately.
6. Encourage the gymnast to talk to coaches, teammates or the sport psychology consultant. Others in the gym may be able to offer some encouraging suggestions that they have found helpful, or they may be able to provide a distraction. Encourage the gymnast not to blindly accept every suggestion but rather to evaluate the personal relevance of each comment. Just because advice is given does not mean it will fit for every individual. Gymnasts are encouraged to be selective.
7. Use rewards for overcoming a mental block. Gymnasts may be tempted to punish themselves when frustrated with the inability to perform a skill that was previously mastered, but punishment is not as effective as reward. Punishment only reduces self-esteem and increases frustration further. Positive incentives, on the other hand, will

push the gymnast in the right direction. The sport psychology consultant can assist the gymnast in making a list of treats. Treats could include a bubble bath, a massage, a CD, a film, time to read a good book, or a meal out at a favorite restaurant, to name just a few. Monetary incentives from parents are discouraged. When gymnasts succeed and work through a block, or even reach small goals in working toward getting past the block, they can choose a reward from the list.

8. Start over with small steps. Good coaches will take the athlete through progressions as new skills are learned. They do not encourage work on a double back tuck before a single back tuck is mastered. When working toward a skill, gymnasts do drills and develop the skills over time. If gymnasts develop a mental blocks, they might have to go back to some of the basics before working back up to more difficult skills.

9. If gymnasts have tried many of these suggestions and still feel blocked, they may need to leave the skill for a while. It helps to come back to it later that day, the next day or even the next week.

10. Use imagery. Imagery is extremely useful for overcoming mental blocks. Encourage the gymnast to imagine doing the skill perfectly and fearlessly over and over until it becomes second nature. The gymnast can continue to imagine this skill in and out of the gym.

11. Fears may be the result of deeper, more psychological issues. For instance, the gymnast wants to quit but does not know how to say it or is coming back from a serious injury and fears reinjury. If the above strategies do not work, then the sport psychology consultant will want to consider these other more involved factors and spend time exploring those issues. There are no simple intervention strategies and no quick solutions, and therefore the consultant will need to be patient and creative in addressing the cause of the block or fear.

EATING DISORDER INTERVENTIONS

The ideal approach is to eating disorder intervention is prevention, although the literature focuses more on how to treat eating disorders after they have developed. Education and risk reduction are primary components of eating disorder intervention and should be directed toward both athletes and sport management personnel (e.g. coaches and trainers; Cogan, 2004).

Education

It may seem that education about eating disordered behaviors is a good starting point for gymnasts, but some educational efforts have been counterproductive. Instead of avoiding disordered eating behaviors, gymnasts learn unhealthy strategies and experiment with them for weight loss they are trying to achieve. Gymnasts may be more likely than the general population to use this information inappropriately because of the tendency to try anything to get that extra performance edge. The most helpful approach in educating gymnasts is to focus on health and performance rather than dieting or purging behaviors or symptoms. A gymnast is more likely to pay attention to information about how eating correctly if they realize that it can improve sport performance (Cogan, 2004).

Gymnasts can benefit from nutritional information from a registered dietician or nutritionist so that their food choices are not based on myth or misinformation. Gymnasts are more likely to listen to a dietician who has experience working with gymnasts and who is aware of specific nutritional needs of the sport to redirect their efforts to healthy eating patterns. A sport psychology consultant can be instrumental in making referrals to a sport nutritionist or arranging for a nutritionist to talk to the athletes.

Gymnasts often want to diet but, in general, diets are not effective. It is most useful to have a discussion about how dieting can negatively affect training and competition. The focus should be on healthy eating that fits the energy output of gymnastics. It should be suggested that performance can be enhanced by increasing physical fitness, strength, speed and quickness. Athletes should also be informed that decreases in these physical attributes may occur as a result of too much weight loss that is done too quickly or by unhealthy weight loss methods. Again, education from a nutritionist or exercise physiologist can be useful.

Education of sport management personnel is critical in the prevention and treatment of eating disorders because of their strong influence on gymnasts. Generally, sport management personnel need the same type of information about nutrition, dieting and weight, and factors affecting performance as athletes. They also need information about eating disorders, warning signs, and female athletes' menstrual functioning. Most sport management personnel do not ask about menstrual functioning, probably due to discomfort discussing such a personal thing or because of lack of knowledge. Tracking menstrual functioning can be a good indicator of health because as a woman's body fat decreases too much, her periods stop (Thompson & Sherman, 1999).

Risk Reduction Strategies

Education is the first step, but coaches and sport management personnel need to translate that into actions. The following are strategies for risk reduction (Thompson & Sherman, 1999).

- *De-emphasize weight* Refrain from weighing athletes. Weight monitoring by coaches is unnecessary and may even be detrimental in terms of gymnasts achieving their ideal weight or fitness level. Keep the focus on physical conditioning and strength development as well as increasing mental toughness for performance.
- *Eliminate group weigh-ins* Group weigh-ins are potentially the most destructive form of monitoring. Many gymnasts are already self-conscious about their weight, and this type of public exposure can be degrading and embarrassing. If there is a legitimate reason for weigh-ins, the gymnast should be weighed privately by a sport professional other than the coach and should be made aware of the rationale for the weigh-ins.
- *Eliminate unhealthy subcultural aspects* Sometimes disordered eating and weight loss patterns become accepted and even valued in gymnastics. There are anecdotal examples of coaches encouraging gymnasts to purge in order to control their weight. Coaches and sport psychology consultants can play an important role in providing athletes with correct information about unhealthy weight management strategies and communicating the seriousness consequences that can result from these strategies.
- *Treat each athlete individually* Individual differences must be taken into account especially when dealing with weight. Weight is determined by a complex interaction of

genetics and biological processes and not just will power. Some athletes may be trying to achieve a shape and size that cannot occur in a healthy manner.

- *Offer guidelines for appropriate weight loss* Thompson and Sherman (1993) recommend that athletes not be asked to diet. In reality, though, athletes will diet. So if they are going to diet, athletes need guidelines for healthy dieting. See Thompson and Sherman (1993) for specific ideas.
- *Control the contagion effect* Gymnastics teams develop norms about eating, dieting and losing weight that can become "contagious" or spread from one athlete to another through communication or observation. Unfortunately, we know more about how the contagion effect operates than how to prevent it. If sport personnel de-emphasize weight and thinness, perhaps gymnasts can adopt these attitudes, beliefs and behaviors as well.

Even with prevention, eating disorders still develop. Sport psychology consultants with clinical training and expertise in eating disorders will likely feel comfortable treating a gymnast for this issue, but those trained in sport sciences may want to consult and refer. If an athlete seems to be practicing eating disordered behaviors, then the following ideas and recommendations are suggested by Swoap & Murphy (1995) as well as Rosen, McKeag, Hough & Curley (1986).

1. The coach or staff person (e.g. sport psychology consultant or trainer) who has the best rapport with the athlete should arrange a private meeting with her. The sport psychology consultant can be an advisor if not the one to conduct the meeting.
2. The tone of the meeting should be entirely positive and supportive. The staff member will want to express concern for the best interest of the individual (not just as a gymnast).
3. Start by expressing concern about how the gymnast might be feeling rather than focusing on the eating itself. For example, "It seems like you have been struggling lately. Is there something I can do to help?" If they will confide in you, let gymnasts know that outside help is often required to heal from disordered eating. Then you can offer to help arrange treatment, and refer to a specific person, preferably someone who has experience with athletes and with eating disorders. A clinical sport psychologist is a good option, or alternatively a counselor in a college counseling center if the gymnast is at a university. There may be referral resources in the community or through insurance companies as well.
4. If the gymnast does not acknowledge difficulty with eating, the concerns may need to be addressed more directly. Indicate what signs led to the belief that there is a pattern of disordered eating. Be as non-punitive as possible when outlining these concerns, and then allow the gymnast to respond.
5. Affirm that the gymnast's role on the team will not be jeopardized by the admission of eating-disordered behavior. Participation would only be affected if the eating behavior were to compromise the gymnast's health or possibly lead to injury.
6. Try to determine if the gymnast feels the behavior is no longer under his or her control. Realize, though, that most believe they are in control and can stop at will unless they have seriously tried to curtail it and failed.
7. If the athlete denies any disordered eating and the behaviors do not seem severe, you may choose to observe the athlete without requiring any treatment. It is best to avoid any power struggles as this will only exacerbate the eating difficulties.

8. If the behaviors become more severe, then another meeting may be needed to suggest treatment again. When eating patterns reach a high level of seriousness, the health of the athlete takes precedence over anything else, and treatment may be required even it if is not the gymnast's choice.

9. Gymnasts are more likely to benefit from treatment if they choose it themselves, but in many cases they refuse to seek it. If a gymnast's health is severely compromised, treatment may become mandatory as a condition of continued team membership. Also, you can institute a "no-train" option in which the gymnast's training or competing time is restricted if eating behaviors become dangerous. You will want to rely on the advice of an eating disorders professional in such cases.

10. Arrange for follow-up meetings outside of practice time with the gymnast to determine progress. Realize that the gymnast may show some resistance to talking about these issues, and the focus should not be on food anyhow, but instead on how she is feeling and how she is managing any pressures she feels. If the gymnast is seeing an eating disorder specialist, you may also wish to contact that person to see if they can offer you any guidance.

Parent Notification

The issue of notifying parents about disordered eating can be complex. If an athlete is under 18, parents have a right to know about eating disorder behaviors, and they will be primarily responsible for arranging treatment. If an athlete is 18 or older, then legally parents do not need to be informed, but it may be in the athlete's best interest for parents to understand what their son or daughter is facing. Initially, it is best to allow the athlete to choose with whom to share information about the eating disorder. However, if an eating disorder becomes serious, it may be necessary for the coach or sport psychology consultant to notify the athlete's parents. It is important that the sport psychology consultant is honest and informs the athlete of plans to have a conversation with their parents. Recognize that most parents will want to help and support, but they can also be a part of the problem, and athletes may be resistant to involving them. Again, seek the guidance of an eating disorders specialist if there are any potential conflicts with informing the parents.

Treatment Options

Eating disorders are psychological disorders and have complex causes including biological factors, self-esteem, emotional issues and societal pressures. Sport rarely causes eating disorders but being involved in sport can exacerbate a disorder. If it is determined that an athlete needs treatment, several modalities can be considered. In general, the treatment modalities used for the general population are also used for gymnasts. It is beyond the scope of this chapter to discuss treatment options in detail, but in general treatment options include: individual counseling, medication, group therapy, family therapy and inpatient treatment. Gymnasts also can benefit from a team-based approach utilizing a variety of professionals in the athletic environment.

TEAM-BUILDING

Although gymnastics is an individual sport, gymnasts train in teams. At the college level, team takes on an additional importance. Most psychological interventions focus on individual skills such as relaxation and imagery, but team-building can be a useful intervention component as well. Again, it is beyond the scope of this chapter to discuss specific examples, but sport psychology consultants will find it useful to include team-building activities with a gymnastics team. See Cogan & Petrie (1995) for team-building suggestions.

PARENTS

Parents are an important support system for young gymnasts, but also can become over-involved. Sport psychology consultants may hear about pressures from parents through the gymnasts and coaches or observe these types of pressured behaviors. If gymnasts feel too much pressure, they are encouraged to talk to their parents, but these conversations do not always produce a desired change in behavior. If the sport psychology consultant has good rapport with the gymnast, the consultant may serve as a facilitator for a conversation about how to balance parental involvement. These conversations should be approached in a positive manner, encouraging everyone to work together for the best interest of the gymnast.

A final general topic is the role of gymnastics in the child's life. Gymnastics has many positive qualities. It teaches young participants discipline and persistence, how to work hard to achieve goals, how to work with coaches, teammates and parents, and how to overcome challenges. It also places pressure on young athletes to perform to perfection, or to maintain a physique that may not be realistic for many body types. In addition, gymnasts find they may miss out on other activities if they put many hours in at the gym. I am often asked if gymnastics is good for young children. My response is that there are no right or wrong answers to that question, only answers that each individual gymnast and their family determine. Many young gymnasts thrive on the competition, training and pursuit of excellence. As long as they are enjoying the overall gymnastics experience, then maintaining involvement is a good decision. Unfortunately, for many, the enjoyment of the sport eludes them after intensive training, and then a decision about discontinuing the sport must be made. If all the complexities of each individual's circumstances and goals are considered, then a decision can be made that is in the best interest of the gymnast.

CONCLUSION

The mental side of gymnastics has a huge impact on the athlete's performance and enjoyment of the sport. In order to be successful, gymnasts must master a variety of general psychological skills that are helpful to any athlete in addition to facing issues more specific to gymnastics such as fear and the potential for disordered eating behaviors. This chapter outlines general and specific mental skills as applied to gymnastics. Sample exercises to use with gymnasts are provided to assist the sport psychology consultant in translating their mental skills training knowledge into more specific gymnastics interventions. The ultimate goal is for the gymnast to participate safely and to enjoy the gymnastics experience. Too many gymnasts walk away from the sport with a negative experience. A sport psychology consultant can be instrumental in setting the stage for a positive sport experience and effectively working through the numerous challenges a gymnast may face.

REFERENCES

American College of Sports Medicine Position Stand on the Female Athlete Triad (1997). *Medicine and Science in Sports and Exercise, 29*, i–ix.

American Psychiatric Association (2000). *Diagnostic and Statistical Manual –IV, TR*. Washington, DC: American Psychiatric Association.

Balague, G. (2004). Anxiety: From pumped to panicked. In S. Murphy (ed.) *The Sport Psych Handbook*. Champaign IL: Human Kinetics.

Benson, H. (1975). *The Relaxation Response*. New York: Avon Books.

Burckes-Miller, M. & Black, D.R. (1991). College athletes and eating disorders: a theoretical context. In D.R. Black (ed.), *Eating Disorders among Athletes: Theory, Issues and Research* (pp. 11–26). Reston, VA: American Alliance for Health, Physical Education, Recreation and Dance.

Burns, D.D. (1980). *Feeling Good: The New Mood Therapy*. New York, NY: William Morrow & Company, Inc.

Cogan, K.D. (2004). Eating disorders. In S. Murphy (ed.), *The Sport Psych Handbook*. Champaign IL: Human Kinetics.

Cogan, K.D. & Petrie, T.A. (1995). Sport consultation: an evaluation of a season-long intervention with female collegiate gymnasts. *The Sport Psychologist, 9*, 282–296.

Cogan, K.D. & Vidmar, P. (2000). *Sport Psychology Library*: Gymnastics. Morgantown, West Virginia: Fitness Information Technology.

Feltz, D.L. & Landers, D.M. (1983). The effects of mental practice on motor skill learning and performance: a meta-analysis. *Journal of Sport Psychology, 5*, 25–57.

Gould, D., Damarjian, N. & Greenleaf, C. (2002). Imagery training for peak performance. In J.L. Van Raalte & B.W. Brewer (eds) *Exploring Sport and Exercise Psychology*. Washington, DC: American Psychological Association.

Jacobson, E. (1930). *Progressive Relaxation*. Chicago, IL: University of Chicago Press.

Kirchner, E.M., Lewis, R.D. & O'Connor, P.J. (1996). Effect of past gymnastics participation on adult bone mass. *Journal of Applied Physiology, 80*, 226–232.

Meyers, A.W. & Schleser, R.A. (1980). A cognitive behavioral intervention for improving basketball performance. *Journal of Sport Psychology, 3*, 69–73.

Mintz, L. & Betz, N. (1988). Prevalence and correlates of eating disordered behaviors among undergraduate women. *Journal of Counseling Psychology, 35*, 463–471.

Nichols, D.L., Sanborn, C.F. & Bonnick, S.L. (1994). The effects of gymnastics training on bone mineral density. *Medicine and Science in Sport and Exercise, 26*, 1220–1225.

Petrie, T.A. (1993). Disordered eating in female collegiate gymnasts: Prevalence and personality/attitudinal correlates. *Journal of Exercise and Sport Psychology, 15*, 424–436.

Rosen, L.W., McKeag, D.B., Hough, D.O. & Curley, V. (1986). Pathogenic weight-control behavior in female athletes. *Physician and Sports Medicine, 14*, 79–86.

Russell, R., Miller, E. & June, L. (1974). Group cue-controlled relaxation in the treatment of test anxiety. *Behavior Therapy, 5*, 572–573.

Sungot-Borgen, J. (1994). Risk and trigger factors for the development of eating disorders in female elite athletes. *Medicine and Science in Sports and Exercise, 26*, 414–419.

Swoap, R.A. & Murphy, S.M. (1995). Eating disorders and weight management in athletes. In. S.M. Murphy (ed.). *Sport Psychology Interventions*. Champaign, IL: Human Kinetics.

Thompson, R.A. & Sherman, R.T. (1993). Reducing the risk of eating disorders in athletics. *Eating Disorders, 1*, 65–78.

Thompson, R.A. & Sherman, R.T. (1999). Athletes, athletic performance and eating disorders: healthier alternatives. *Journal of Social Issues, 55,* 317–337.

Williams, J.M. & Harris, D.V. (1998). Relaxation and energizing techniques of regulation of arousal. In J.M. Williams (ed.). *Applied Sport Psychology: Personal Growth to Peak Performance* (3rd edn; pp. 219–236). Mountain View, CA: Mayfield.

Williams, J.M. & Leffingwell, T.R. (2002). Cognitive strategies in sport and exercise psychology. In J.L. Van Raalte & B.W. Brewer (eds) *Exploring Sport and Exercise Psychology* (2nd edn; pp. 75–98). Washington, DC: American Psychological Association.

Yeager, K.K., Agostini, R. & Nattiv, A. (1993). The female athlete triad: disordered eating, amenorrhea, osteoporosis (commentary). *Medicine and Science in Sports and Exercise, 25,* 775–777.

PART XI

Sports For Athletes
with Disabilities

CHAPTER 29

Providing Sport Psychology Support for Athletes with Disabilities

Mark Bawden
Sheffield Hallam University, United Kingdom

INTRODUCTION

The purpose of this chapter is to outline some of the issues that the sport psychologist needs to consider when working with athletes who have a disability. In many respects a chapter is not long enough to go into all the intricacies of disabled sport. There are many different sports to consider, many different types of disability and many different classifications within each disability, all of which have their own characteristics and specific psychological demands. Therefore, many of the recommendations in this chapter are generalized and sport psychologists should simply see this chapter as an initial guide to working with athletes who have a disability. In many respects working with an athlete with a disability is very similar to working with an able-bodied athlete. It is right to assume that a mental skills training programme that is designed for the able-bodied athlete should be just as applicable to the athlete who has a disability. However, there are a number of similarities and differences that are worthy of discussion and explanation in order for the sport psychologist to work most effectively with the disabled performer. Many of the observations that are included in this chapter are related to experiences with athletes who represent Great Britain and therefore readers should be aware that some of the issues that are discussed could be specific to this population.

This chapter will include the following sections: a brief description of classification of disabilities; a section on psychological skills for athletes with disabilities; factors to consider when working with a disabled athlete; principles of consultancy with athletes who have disabilities.

The modern-day Paralympic Games were created through the vision of Sir Ludwig Guttman. Sir Ludwig Guttman who was a neurosurgeon at Stoke Mandeville Hospital in Aylesbury, England. Sir Ludwig introduced sports activities as part of the rehabilitation process for individuals who experienced spinal injuries. Through his vision the first Stoke Mandeville Games were held on 28 July 1948, with the first official Paralympic Games

The Sport Psychologist's Handbook: A Guide for Sport-Specific Performance Enhancement.
Edited by Joaquín Dosil. © 2006 John Wiley & Sons, Ltd.

being held in Rome in 1960. This Paralympics has been held in "parallel" with the Olympic Games ever since. The first series of Paralympic Games included only wheelchair athletes, but as the Games grew in strength many other classes were added. These included events for amputees and visually impaired athletes, athletes with cerebral palsy, athletes with learning difficulties and *les autres* (athletes with polio sequela and muscular dystrophy, etc). The Paralympics are now the pinnacle of competition for athletes who have a disability. Those that compete at the Games have to qualify under the strictest and toughest selection procedures in order to represent their country and compete with the best disabled athletes in the world.

Over the last decade the perception of disability sport has changed dramatically. The Sydney Paralympic Games demonstrated that disability sport was a very serious pursuit and that the athletes who competed there were under considerable pressure to achieve excellence in the same way as their able-bodied counterparts. Many athletes with a disability now receive World Class Performance funding and are therefore highly professional in their approach to training and competition. As one Paralympic coach put it,

> The days of shaking cans in the streets to get funding to go to competitions is over, we now have funding to attend competitions. With the funding also comes the pressure to perform and the need for professionalism, this is a cultural change in perception for many disabled athletes.

This quote highlights the change in professionalism that has occurred in elite disabled sport over recent years and also some of the pressures that are associated with this cultural change.

Paralympic athletes within Great Britain, such as Tanni Grey-Thompson and the judo player Simon Jackson, are now household names and are recognized as elite performers in a similar fashion to their able-bodied counterparts. This new professional approach has meant that many disabled athletes have started to receive a comprehensive sport science support package. This support includes receiving guidance from a wide range of sport science services including: physiologists, physiotherapists, nutritionists, biomechanists, performance analysts and sport psychologists. Therefore, these athletes have experienced a considerable change in their lifestyle and their general approach to both training and competition.

Asken (1989) conducted a highly informative, descriptive research project in which he interviewed a Paralympic archer. In this interview the athlete emphasized the need for more access to sport science in disabled sport and stressed the importance of sport psychology for the disabled athlete. The athlete stated, "We need access to sport scientists and sports training professionals—especially in the area of sport psychology" (p. 169). Now it is apparent that sport psychology is more accessible to athletes with disabilities and for many it is a regular part of their daily training routine. Thus, sport psychologists need to be aware of the specialist issues of working with disabled performers and some of the challenges that they are likely to face.

The professionalisation of disability sport has led more sport psychologists to come into contact with athletes with disabilities and therefore has brought with it many challenges in being able to deliver psychological skills effectively to this specialist population. However, Porretta & Moore (1996/1997) suggest there is still a very limited amount of research that has investigated: how mental skills training should be adapted for athletes with disabilities, the principles of best practice for sport psychologists working with athletes who have a disability, and specialist knowledge about the implications of working with the disabled athlete.

In their research Porretta and Moore (1996/1997) provided a comprehensive review of the research that has been conducted in the field of sport psychology for athletes with disabilities. Within their review the authors highlighted the lack of research that exists in the area of applied sport psychology and reinforced the need to develop more research that investigates techniques to enhance performance in highly competitive settings. Therefore, the aim of this chapter is to discuss some practical issues to help the sport psychologist work most effectively with athletes who have a disability in an applied setting.

CLASSIFICATION

Classification in able-bodied sport is apparent in sports such boxing and judo in terms of weight divisions. However, classification in disabled sport is far more complex. In disabled sport, classification considers the condition of the disability as well as the functional ability of each athlete. Traditionally athletes belong to one of six different disability groups within Paralympic sport. These are: spinal cord injuries, amputees, cerebral palsy, visual impairment, intellectual disability and *les autres* (a group of athletes who do not fit into any of the other groups). Each of these groups employs its own classification system. For example, visually impaired athletes are classified into: B1 for totally blind athletes; B2 for those with minimal vision; and B3 for those with minimal but functional vision. When you consider that within this, each sport has its own classification system then the complexities of classification should be obvious. The basis of classification is to ensure that all athletes compete on an equal playing field. In addition there is also a wide range of Paralympic sports. These are: archery, athletics, boccia, cycling, equestrian, fencing, football, goalball, judo, powerlifting, sailing, shooting, standing volleyball, swimming, table tennis, tennis, wheelchair basketball, wheelchair rugby, biathlon, cross country and sledge hockey. Many of these sports such as boccia, goalball and wheelchair rugby are specialist sports for disabled athletes and have their own specific rules and psychological demands.

Based on the fact that there are many different groups of disabled athletes, many different classifications within each group and many different sports, it would be impossible to address all of these issues throughout this chapter. Therefore, the primary aim of this chapter will be to focus on athletes with spinal cord injuries as this is where the author has had the most applied experience and also tends to be the group that has received the most attention in the research. However, references will be made to other disability groups at the appropriate juncture throughout the chapter.

For a more detailed sport specific description of classification please see the International Paralympic Committee web site: http://www.paralympic.org/release/Main_Sections_Menu/Sports/Classification/

PSYCHOLOGICAL SKILLS FOR ATHLETES WITH DISABILITIES

The need for greater research in sport psychology for athletes with disabilities has been well documented within the literature (DePauw, 1988; Page, Martin & Wayda, 2001; Sachs, 1988; Sherrill, 1998). Sherrill (1999) stated that there is a lack of theory-based research in sport psychology for athletes with disabilities and that this has limited progress in the area. Porretta and Moore (1996/1997) have also suggested that research and knowledge in applied sport psychology is limited for athletes with disabilities. These authors also highlighted that sport psychology research that directly influences performance outcomes was behind many of the other sport science disciplines. This point was also made by White and Zientek (1990) who suggested that more research should be conducted that has a direct impact on the competitor and coach. Thus, Porretta and Moore (1996/1997) proposed a number of applied areas of research that they considered would be beneficial to the disabled athlete; these included: goal-setting, self-regulation, visual rehearsal, relaxation training and identification of motivators.

Cox and Davis (1992) conducted a research study in which they investigated the differences in psychological skill between elite wheelchair track and field athletes and able-bodied collegiate athletes. The psychological skills inventory for sports was administered to the athletes to identify their level of skill in relation to anxiety control, concentration, confidence, mental preparation, motivation and team emphasis. The results suggested that elite wheelchair athletes had a superior psychological skills profile to that of collegiate athletes. There were significant differences, with wheelchair athletes scoring higher on the items of anxiety control, confidence and motivation. An explanation for these results provided by Cox and Davis (1992) was related to the experience of being disabled and the mental toughness that naturally develops as a result of having had to cope with a disability. Cox and Davis (1992) suggested that disabled athletes have a great deal to cope with both physically and mentally and that overcoming the psychological effects of disability could result in enhanced psychological skills.

The need for the disabled athlete to work on psychological skills in order to be mentally tough is now paramount in order to be successful at an elite level. This point was emphasized by the judo player Simon Jackson before the Sydney Paralympics.

> I haven't just been out here training for the last month on the gold coast, I've been training hard for four years; it's the mentally toughest athlete that will win gold, and I know I'm the mentally toughest.
> Simon Jackson—three times Paralympic Gold Medallist

Many disabled athletes are very mentally strong in their sporting performance because they need to be mentally tough to cope with their disability in life itself. This is an issue that needs to be considered by the sport psychologist when developing any mental skills programme.

Pensgaard, Roberts and Ursin (1999) conducted a study on the Norwegian Paralympic and Olympic winter sport athletes. The focus of the study was to determine whether Olympic and Paralympic athletes perceive different motivational climates. The authors hypothesized that, because there is more focus on the Olympic Games, that Olympic athletes would use coping strategies more often than Paralympians. The actual results demonstrated that Olympic and Paralympic athletes had very similar motivational profiles and that both used similar coping strategies to a similar extent.

Research studies that have investigated the psychological profiles of both able-bodied and elite disabled athletes have found that their psychological profiles are very similar (Henschen, Horvat & French, 1984; Horvat, French & Henschen, 1986). However, the characteristic that tends to separate disabled athletes from the able-bodied athlete is the fact that many disabled athletes have experienced a traumatic event that has resulted in their disability. The impact of this experience has to be considered throughout the work with the disabled athlete. Many able-bodied athletes will have experienced a temporary injury in their sporting careers and will understand some of the responses they experience at this time, but these responses to a temporary injury are not comparable with the intensity of the experience following a situation that has resulted in a permanent loss of function.

A number of research studies have found that athletes with disabilities cope better than able-bodied athletes (Cox & Davis, 1992). The typical profile of the disabled athlete is one who is very resilient, copes well with adversity and is highly determined to achieve their goals. However, through the use of mental skills, mental toughness can be developed and improved (Jones, Hanton & Connaughton, 2002). When working with athletes with disabilities many mental skills and psychological tools need to be refined or considered in different ways. Crocker (1993) highlighted that it would be wrong to assume that performance enhancement techniques that are successful for non-disabled athletes will work with athletes who have a disability and that practitioners should be cautious of this. The purpose of the following section is not to explain how the core mental skills are delivered; it is more to identify special considerations when using these skills with athletes with disabilities.

Controlling the Controllables

Focusing on factors that an athlete can control and understanding those that they can't is a fundamental component of sport psychology and of an athlete being a successful performer (Bull, Albinson & Shambrook, 1996). However, for the disabled athlete there are far more uncontrollable factors that they have to cope with. Some factors that may be outside of the disabled athlete's control include:

- leg spasms
- the need to go to the toilet
- help from others to gain access to venues, etc.
- pressure sores
- disabled access
- transport issues
- accommodation issues.

A good example of the frustration of uncontrollable factors significantly influencing performance is highlighted by the experience of a Paralympic shooter. The shooter was practising her finals technique and found herself somewhat "in the zone" and was on course for a personal best score. For the first 9 shots out of 10 the shooter scored 10.5, then with the final shot experienced an involuntary leg spasm which resulted in a 7.5. The fact that such a factor can happen completely involuntary and therefore is completely beyond the control of the shooter can become a great source of unnecessary and unwanted stress. The "what if I spasm?" could become a significant negative thought that could be hard to deal with. One way in which this shooter has coped with the problem is by making herself train when she is experiencing involuntary spasms, so that she can get used to the feeling and adopt coping strategies such as re-focusing routines to stay calm and focused until the spasm has deteriorated.

A practical example of factors outside the athlete's control effecting stress levels was evident for one disabled performer who almost missed his flight before a major competition. The problem that the athlete faced was that the bus that transferred the athlete from the airport car park to the terminal building was not disability-friendly and subsequently he needed to wait for a bus to be specially delivered from another terminal. This issue was made worse considering that the athlete had phoned ahead and specifically pre-warned the airport about this issue. This kind of delay is not considered by able-bodied athletes yet can become a major obstacle for the disabled athlete before they get anywhere near the competitive environment.

Goal-setting for Disabled Athletes

Porretta and Moore (1996/1997) highlighted goal-setting as a major area that could enhance the performance of the disabled athlete. In their review the authors stated that athletes with disabilities could have problems setting realistic goals. This issue would be particularly evident for individuals who had recently become physically disabled.

- A consideration when setting goals is to ensure that the disabled athlete does not limit what they think they are capable of based on their physical problems (e.g. physically I am limited so therefore mentally I am limited too).
- When helping the athlete set goals related to physical exercise it is important to have a good understanding of the level of ability, so that unrealistic goals are not set.
- It is also important to understand if the athlete has a degenerative condition in which they could be physically more disabled in the future; this could have implications for the long-term goals they need to set.

An example of understanding an athlete's degenerative condition was emphasized by an athlete who completed a performance profile (Butler & Hardy, 1992) as part of their pre-intervention assessment with the sport psychologist. The function of the profile was to assess the athlete's current strengths and weaknesses mentally, physically, technically and tactically and establish her process goals for the season, from the profile. Based on this profile the athlete worked with the sport psychologist to establish where she perceived she currently was and where she would like to be at the end of the season. The athlete then established the process goal that she would need to obtain in order to achieve the desired outcome across the various dimensions. Upon inspection of the profile it was apparent that the athlete had rated herself to be lower in standard at the end of the season than she currently was at the beginning. This was due to her degenerative disability and the fact that in a year's time she perceived that she would be physically less able. This decrease in physical ability could possibly result in her disability being re-classified and therefore competing in a different class division. Due to this change in physical ability the athlete also perceived that her technical and tactical ability would also decrease accordingly. Through this the athlete worked with the coach and sport psychologist to learn ways to exploit her strengths more effectively and established that any physical changes to her physical ability would not significantly affect her technique.

Some Keys to Relaxation for Disabled Athletes

When using any kind of relaxation technique it is important for the strategy to reflect the disability of the athlete that the sport psychologist is working with. An obvious example here is that if the athlete does not have feeling in their lower limbs then any progressive muscular relaxation (Jacobson, 1938) exercise/script or tape should reflect this. If limbs are included in this process that the athlete does not have control over, then this can be a great source of frustration and can end up having the opposite effect to relaxing the athlete. A further way to counteract this problem was proposed by Goodling and Asken (1987). They suggested that groups of muscles can be visualized as tensing and relaxing in order to complete the technique.

A further issue related to relaxation strategies that require specific breathing techniques was suggested by Hanrahan (1995). Hanrahan (1995) who stated that athletes who have limited use of abdominal muscles find the physical mechanics of abdominal breathing very difficult. This is a factor that needs to be considered if the sport psychologist is working through the applied relaxation technique with disabled athletes.

An example of the need to develop relaxation scripts that are specific to the athlete was highlighted by a tetraplegic athlete who has limited control in their hands. The first instruction on the progressive muscular relaxation tape that they attempted to use began with the instruction: "Make a tight fist, and feel the tension." This was not possible for the athlete to do and subsequently resulted in the athlete being frustrated from the start of the relaxation process. In this case the athlete and the sport psychologist discussed which instructions would be most beneficial to them and developed a relaxation tape that was completely specific to the needs of the individual.

Pre-performance Preparation

> The key is being able to get over certain difficulties with your disability, while concentrating on the event. When you get on the line you have to be fully focused for every shot and not let any outside distractions in.
> Di Coates, SH1 Air rifle—three times Paralympic gold medalist

This quote reflects a key issue in the psychological preparation for disabled sport. Keeping focused in the build-up to a major competition is highly important and being able to keep outside distractions away is paramount. However, for the disabled athlete many practical issues can become distracting and become a greater focus than the performance itself. This is often evident at major competitions where athletes can have issues relating to transport and accessibility. Such issues can become a source of great frustration to the athletes. Most experienced athletes plan a series of practical "what ifs" to ensure that they have a game plan for a number of eventualities. An example of a typical "What if" would be "what if I am unable to access the bathroom in the hotel?" A practical solution to this has often been to take the bathroom door off or to call ahead and establish the measurements of the doorways. It is often important to do this as even when hotels have disabled access, this does not always accommodate the various different shapes and sizes of wheelchair. A further consideration with accessibility involves transfer issues, such as whether the athlete can transfer from the chair onto the toilet or into and out of the bath. These practical issues can become major distractions for the athlete if they are not considered in advance.

A good exercise for the sport psychologist to do with a disabled athlete is to identify any potential practical issues that the athlete is concerned about and identify practical solutions to each of these issues. This can be linked to a "what if" session in which the sport psychologist and the coach can identify a game plan for the many different eventualities of competing in a disabled competition.

Having a pre-performance routine that the athlete knows and trusts is a key part of any athlete's pre-performance preparation. The disabled athlete has far less control of their routine as they are usually dependant on other individuals for help during the process. This can sometimes lead to athletes feeling "out of control" before they perform.

The goal of the sport psychologist should be to help the athlete develop a routine in which they are as independent as possible while understanding that there may be aspects of the routine that will require assistance (e.g. physiotherapy or massage support). This routine needs to be highly flexible due to organizational issues related to disability sport. Because of the nature and complexity of competition structures at disabled competitions, time scales are often not adhered to as efficiently as in some able-bodied competitions and therefore the pre-performance routines of the athletes need to reflect this variable. For many disabled athletes the need to develop "hanging around" strategies is paramount. With the many complexities of transporting the athletes on and off transport from the accommodation to the sports venue, time scales are often not adhered to and therefore the athlete may have a significant amount of redundant time. Many disabled athletes attempt to use this time productively either by having appropriate "distractions" with them such as a book or game, or using performance enhancement strategies. These strategies could include best performance mental rehearsal, relaxation strategies and tapes or reading through pre-performance reminder sheets.

Concentration Techniques for Disabled Athletes

Having techniques to be able to focus and re-focus during performance are very important for the disabled performer. Athletes will experience the same psychological distractions in performance as able-bodied athletes. However, as we have already discussed they also have to contend with other distractions that are even less inside the athlete's control, such as experiencing involuntary leg spasms. Therefore, having a re-focusing routine is key. The majority of these routines will involve the athlete taking their time, using deep relaxing breaths, using positive self-talk and then performing. However, due to some practical differences between able-bodied and disabled sports performance there can be differences that make re-focusing more problematic.

This problem was made apparent by one Paralympic table tennis player who had problems focusing and re-focusing between points. It became apparent that this player found himself rushing between points and was unable to get himself into the right mindset when under pressure. The key factor for the player was that he needed time in order to develop a clear tactical focus between points. However, in disabled table tennis there are usually two ball boys or girls who collect the ball for the players between points. This results in the players having very little time to re-focus, as the ball is brought back to the table almost immediately after the point is won or lost. This is very different from able-bodied table tennis where the player uses this crucial time between points to calm their mind, relax themselves and get tactically focused for the next point. In this case the disabled player requested to play without ball boys or girls so that he could use this time to gather his thoughts and use his breathe–talk–play routine more effectively. This is a good example of why the sport psychologist needs to have a sound understanding of the potential differences between able-bodied and disabled sports and the possible influences that these differences can have on the athlete psychologically.

Anxiety Control

> About 50 per cent of my anxiety before a major competition is concerned with my performance, and the other 50 per cent is related to organizational issues, such as transport, accommodation and disabled access.
>
> David Heaton, Fencer—three times Paralympian

Cox and Davis (1992) found that elite wheelchair athletes were significantly better at controlling anxiety than a group of able-bodied collegiate athletes. The authors suggested that having the ability to deal with anxiety and frustration associated with a disability could transfer into an ability to cope more effectively with anxiety in sporting performance.

Campbell and Jones (2002) examined the sources of stress in an international squad of elite wheelchair basketball players. The results produced ten distinct sources of stress: pre-event concerns, negative match preparation, on-court concerns, post-match performance concerns, negative aspects of a major event, poor group interaction and communication, negative coaching style/behaviour, relationship issues, demands or costs of wheelchair basketball, and a lack of disability awareness. The one source of stress that was very disability-specific was the lack of disability awareness. This particular source of stress was characterized by issues such as poor access to competition venues, hotel accommodation and toilets, and lack of understanding of the needs relating to an individual's disability. The authors suggested that these stressors are not necessarily caused by an individual's disability, but by physical and attitudinal barriers created by society.

Campbell and Jones (1997) investigated the competitive anxiety and self-confidence responses of wheelchair participants in the build-up to a competition. The findings suggested that the athletes demonstrated a similar pre-competitive anxiety response to able-bodied athletes. However, there were differences in the intensity of somatic symptoms and the reduction in self-confidence prior to performance. The authors concluded that the findings supported adopting a process orientation in the build-up to competitions for athletes with disabilities.

Many disabled athletes experience as much anxiety related to their disability as they do related to their sporting performance. Often many of these worries are associated with medical issues related to their disability. It is imperative for the sport psychologist to establish the source of an athlete's anxiety and not to presume that all of the athletes stressors will be performance-related.

An example of such a misconception involved an athlete in their preparation for the Sydney Paralympics. During the preparation the sport psychologist discussed possible stressors at the Games and worked with the athlete to identify coping mechanisms and strategies to prepare for these. These factors included living in a Paralympic village, coping with the media, being away from family for over four weeks and issues related to performance anxiety. At the end of the consultation it became apparent that the athlete was still concerned about the various plans that had been established. Upon further enquiry it became obvious that the number one source of anxiety for the athlete was in fact the 26-hour journey that they were going to have cope with. Within this journey there were several key stressors such as whether they would be transported on and off the plane safely, who they would be sitting next to and whether their seat would be situated close to the toilet. The biggest source of anxiety was whether they would need assistance with personal care issues during the flight.

After these stressors had been clarified, plans could be put in place to control for some of these factors and thus the athlete felt that they were more in control and better prepared for their flight to Australia.

Mental Rehearsal

Many disabled athletes with spinal injuries and amputees appear to be excellent at using visualization. Many of these athletes have used visualization skills to see themselves moving in order to reduce phantom limb pains. Therefore, they find that they are excellent at converting this skill into their sports performance. One concern here is that athletes may see themselves performing in their sport as an able-bodied athlete, which can be upsetting for the individual and actually have a negative effect on performance. Therefore, the need to develop highly controlled imagery skills are essential. The sport psychologist should ensure that they evaluate the athlete's imagery skills in order to ensure that the athlete is not using imagery in a detrimental fashion. This point was emphasized by a disabled athlete who used imagery very effectively which gave them a great deal of confidence. However, whenever they would dream they would always "dream on their feet" and see themselves as an able-bodied competitor, which could be distressing for the athlete.

It is important to try and teach the athletes about the different modalities of imagery and to establish each athlete's dominant imagery style (internal, external, kinaesthetic). If the athlete is dominant in kinaesthetic imagery then it is important to remember that some disabled athletes will not have feeling in all of their limbs and thus imagery scripts should be tailored accordingly.

Visually impaired athletes are able to use visual imagery (Eddy & Mellalieu, 2003). A study that tested the Great British Goalball team concluded that athletes used visual imagery from an internal perspective and that they used both cognitive and motivational forms of mental imagery in order to achieve psychological outcomes in both training and competition. Therefore, this is a skill that the sport psychologist should not presume that visually impaired athletes are unable to use.

Hanrahan (1995) stated that, for some amputee athletes, using an imagery programme made the athletes more concerned about muscle imbalances, which could have a negative effect on their confidence and ultimately their performance.

An example of how it is important to check how athletes are using mental rehearsal was highlighted by an amputee athlete who was working on a visualization programme to help reinforce their best performance and subsequently develop positive reminders and triggers for best performances. The athlete worked with the sport psychologist to develop an imagery script that they could listen to in order to re-create some of their most prolific accomplishments. After the athlete had been working on the programme for some time the sport psychologist conducted a full evaluation of the effectiveness of the imagery. During this evaluation it became apparent that the athlete could use both internal (through their own eyes) and external imagery (as if watching themselves as a spectator) perspectives and in fact would change these perspectives throughout the visualization task. Both perspectives they found to be useful. However, when they saw themselves from the external perspective they saw themselves with their disability. When they used the internal perspective they also were aware of an increased sense of kinaesthetic feel during the task; this resulted in them perceiving that they were fully able-bodied and in fact caused them a great deal of stress.

This was due to the fact that they would visualize how they used to be able to perform before they had their road traffic accident. Upon establishing this fact, the athlete worked with the sport psychologist to develop control of the imagery perspective and focused on using the external perspective whenever they wanted to re-create best performances.

FACTORS TO CONSIDER WHEN WORKING WITH A DISABLED ATHLETE

To be an effective sport psychology consultant working with a disabled athlete there are a number of unique factors that need to be considered. Page et al. (2001) investigated attitudes towards sport psychology among wheelchair athletes. The findings suggested that wheelchair athletes were open towards sport psychology and recognized a need for the discipline in their preparations. Asken (1991) suggested that any sport psychologist wanting to work in disabled sport should have a very clear understanding of their own personal thoughts and motivators. Such personal attitudes should begin with their own attitude about disability and the disabled in general. The author highlighted that working with a disabled athlete means working with a disabled person which will involve experiencing some areas of potential sensitivity such as the appearance of prosthetics, amputated stumps and adapted self-care related to bowel and bladder incontinence. Clearly, these are factors that the consultant needs to be prepared for and to be comfortable with. The author also stated that sport psychology consultants require some further specialist skills and knowledge in the psychology of disability to be effective in their work with disabled athletes.

Asken (1991) identified five areas of specialist knowledge that the sport psychologist should have in order to work effectively with an athlete who has a disability. The first area of specialist knowledge is having an understanding of the background of psychological trauma associated with disability. The second unique factor is the need to have a greater understanding of physical responses and medical problems that the disabled athlete faces. An example of such a medical condition is autonomic dysreflexia, which is a life-threatening condition which occurs in disabled people with lesions above the sixth thoracic vertebra. This syndrome occurs as a result of uncontrolled reflex sympathetic activity which results in a significant rise in blood pressure. The most common cause of the problem is bladder dysfunction; however, there are other causes such as pressure sores and bowel distention (Karlsson, 1999). As a sport psychologist it is not important to be an expert in these medical issues; however, it is important to be aware of such conditions. This is especially evident when you consider that the major symptoms of the problem are pounding headaches coupled with heightened feelings of anxiety and apprehension. This is one of the major benefits of working in an interdisciplinary team where the sport psychologist will work closely with other sport science support staff.

The third factor is the complexity in motivation for a disabled athlete to compete. Research has shown that disabled athletes see sport as a means of affirming competence, a way of focusing on their ability rather than their disability (Goodling & Asken, 1987; Montelione & Davis, 1986). Thus, sport can be used as a mask to avoid dealing with their disability. Therefore, the sport psychologist needs to be aware of the athlete's motivation to compete and understand how well they are adapting to their disability (Asken, 1991). Further unique issues proposed were those related to physical responses and performance. Athletes may experience physical responses linked to their disability, which can cause psychological problems. Asken (1991) cites the example of a swimmer with cerebral palsy who developed anxiety attacks during training due to her condition. Through the introduction of a thorough mental skills program the athlete was able to overcome her anxiety.

The final area of specialist knowledge outlined was that of an understanding of the organization of disabled sports. Asken (1991) suggests that disabled sport competition might be a very different working environment to that which most sport psychologists have experienced. This environment might involve working with athletes within the same squad who differ greatly in terms of their age, ability, motivation and professionalism. A further issue would be that coaches might not be as educated as those that are generally encountered in elite able-bodied sport. Since the publication of this paper in 1991 the professionalism of disabled sport at an elite level has changed dramatically and, while these issues are still evident in disabled sport, the gap between the disabled and able-bodied support experience has closed significantly.

The following section will attempt to address some further issues that are unique to working with disabled athletes based on applied experiences.

Establish Whether the Athlete Knows about Sport Psychology

Many disabled athletes are beginning to have the opportunity to work with a wide range of different sport science support disciplines. However, some disabled athletes may have had contact with a psychologist through their rehabilitation phase. It is therefore important to educate the athlete about the boundaries of a sports psychologist. Hence, it is imperative that the sport psychologist makes the athlete aware of their skills, limitations and code of conduct before developing any intervention strategies (British Association of Sport and Exercise Sciences, 2000).

As has been mentioned already, Cox and Davis (1992) highlighted a particularly positive factor that disabled athletes may have derived from working with a psychologist. The authors suggested that wheelchair athletes may enjoy a high level of psychological skill in sport because of the years of therapy that they will have had. This therapy may have resulted in the athlete acquiring coping skills that can be readily transferred to the sporting environment.

An important factor for the sport psychologist is to make the athlete aware that they need to have an understanding of their disability, yet their main focus will be on performance issues. Thus, the need to reinforce the role of performance enhancer rather than the "shrink" mentality is important.

The Nature of the Athlete's Disability

A sport psychologist needs to be aware of the elements of the athlete's disability which have a bearing on the way they perform. Sometimes an athlete will use a physical factor as a smoke screen when the real problem is mental, and the sport psychologist should be sufficiently aware of a disability's implications to be able to spot this type of occurrence.
Source: Isabel Newstead, Gold Medalist SH1 Air Pistol Sydney 2000/Athens 2004

One of the first factors to consider when working with an athlete is the nature of their disability. Does the athlete compete in a wheelchair? Are they able to walk? If they are visually impaired, establish to what extent they can see. If the athlete has cerebral palsy establish to what extent they have control over their movements and also the extent to which their speech is impaired. It is also important to understand whether the athlete has been disabled since birth or whether they have experienced some form of trauma which has resulted in them being in a wheelchair. This information could have important implications for the way in which you work with the athlete, as some athletes will have had experiences as an able-bodied person and others will not have. This information is important, yet will often be discussed when the athlete is ready to do so.

Whether the Athlete Requires Assistance to Perform Their Sport

In many disability sports, the athlete will require assistance to be able to perform, e.g. a visually impaired athlete will have a guide runner and a boccia player with cerebral palsy may require an assistant. In cases such as these it is important to also work on the mental skills and understanding of the assistant. Factors such as effective communication are obviously going to be key in developing the most positive environment for the athlete. There is no point in working closely on the mental skills development of the athlete if their guide or assistant does not share the same mental approach. An example of this would be if a shooter needed assistance in loading their rifle due to uncontrollable shaking, strength or coordination issues associated with their disability, and their assistant suffered from performance anxiety that could have a negative effect on performance. It is important to understand that the assistant is also performing in a highly pressurized environment and to ensure that they are mentally prepared for this. Some athletes will also require the assistance of carers away from their performance, therefore it is important for the sport psychologist to understand the role of the carer and ensure that they are also mentally prepared for their role at a major championship.

Different Rules in Comparison to Able-bodied Equivalent Sports

There are many common sports between able-bodied and disability sports; however, often the rules are very different. Therefore, it is important for the sport psychologist to have a full understanding of the sport and any differences in the rules. For example, in disability table tennis the player is not allowed to serve off the side of the table, whereas in able-bodied table tennis this is allowed. It is very important to get a full appreciation of the rules and not to presume knowledge based on equivalent able-bodied sports.

Disability-specific Sports

When first working with a disabled athlete, the sport psychologist may come into contact with sports that they have not previously experienced before. Sports such as boccia, goalball and wheelchair rugby are sports that have been designed specifically for athletes with disabilities. Hence, the sport psychologist needs to develop a good understanding of these sports before working with athletes who play such disability-specific sports.

Disabled Athletes and Career Termination or Retirement

Asken (1989) highlighted an issue for disabled athletes and the way in which they deal with the end of their sporting career. The author suggested that in some circumstances sport can act as a way for disabled athletes to avoid dealing with their disability. Therefore, when the athlete comes to the end of their sporting career they may have many issues to contend with—not only with career termination but also having to cope more overtly with their disability. The author suggests that while the pursuit of competitive sport can be an indication that an athlete is adapting to their disability it may also be symptomatic of a failure to adequately adjust. A further issue is that if the athlete has used sport as a way of psychologically adjusting to their disability then it may delay working through and accepting the physical, psychological and emotional consequences of their disability.

Disabled Athletes May Have to Compete with Athletes More Able-bodied than Themselves

Sport psychologists should be aware that some disabled athletes may have to compete against athletes who are physically more able than themselves. Thus, psychologically this can become a barrier that needs to be tackled. In some sports where the range of movement of the athlete is crucial this can become an issue for athletes. The sport psychologist should work closely with the athlete to rationalize any concerns that they have, and get them focused on their own strengths and performance strategies, regardless of the physical ability of their opponents.

Travelling with the Disabled Athlete

Many sport psychologists will have experience of travelling with able-bodied sports teams. However, when going to foreign competitions or training there are a number of further issues that need to be considered when travelling with the disabled athlete or team. The logistics of travel are often complicated for disabled athletes. Transport on and off planes can sometimes cause problems as the athlete may need to be carried on and off the plane by airport staff. Other issues here are often that wheelchair athletes will have a competition wheelchair and a day chair. A cause for concern is always ensuring that both chairs make it onto the plane.

Being a member of support staff with a disabled team requires the individual to go "the extra mile" with support and help. Thus, the "gopher role" of the sport psychologist becomes essential such as helping athletes with transport baggage, etc.

PRINCIPLES OF CONSULTANCY WITH ATHLETES WHO HAVE DISABILITIES

All of the key principles of being an effective sport psychology consultant are just as applicable when working with a disabled athlete as they are when working with an able-bodied athlete. However, there are a number of issues that warrant further attention when considering being an effective consultant to an athlete with a disability (Page, et al., 2001). The challenge of providing effective sport psychology to an athlete with a disability was highlighted by Asken (1991) very succinctly:

> Although many counterparts to the issues described for disabled athletes may be found in various areas of able bodied sport, it may be that consultation to the physically disabled athlete brings together in one focus more of these diverse issues and professional requirements than any other area of sport psychology. (p. 373)

Create an Appropriate Environment

- Ensure that the room or consultation area is accessible.
- Make sure that the environment in which you have your consultation is appropriate for the nature of the disability of the athlete (e.g. if the athlete is in a wheelchair then make sure that you are on the same level as them). Make sure that there is room for a wheelchair in the room.

Set out the Ground Rules from the Start of the Consultation Process

- Be very clear from the outset about issues related to confidentiality, as the disabled athlete may share details about themselves and their disability that they need to kept confidential (British Association of Sport and Exercise Sciences, 2000).
- Be very clear about the boundaries and limitations of your work as a sport psychologist. Some athletes will use you as a counsellor and therefore your professional boundaries need to be established at the start of any consultation process.
- If the sport psychologist finds themselves in a situation where the athlete is not coping with their disability then they should be prepared to refer the athlete on to an expert in this field. This is particularly evident with individuals who have recently become disabled and have taken up sport as part of their rehabilitation, or athletes who have come to the end of their sporting careers and are having to cope with that transition. Another group of disabled athletes that this can be an issue for are those that have been elite able-bodied athletes, and have experienced a life trauma and then go on to continue in the same sport as a disabled athlete. For many athletes, this transition can be a difficult one as they can discover that they are not able to perform to the same standard that they were previously used to.

Communicate in an Appropriate Style

- If more than one person is in the consultancy make sure that room is set out appropriately. If you have a consultancy with an athlete who has cerebral palsy and has speech which is hard to understand, then they might want to have another person in the session to help you to understand what they are saying. If this is the case then it is important that you face the athlete and direct the questions at them and not the person who is interpreting the conversation for you. When you start getting into dialogue with someone it is easy to forget that it is the athlete who you are working with.

- You might need to adjust the style of communication that you use to the nature of the athlete's disability. An example of this would be if you are having a consultation with a visually impaired athlete when non-verbal forms of communication such as "nodding" to demonstrate "active listening" is clearly not going to be appropriate.
- Politically correct terminology can become an issue, if you make it one. Most athletes are not preoccupied by ensuring that support staff are politically correct in their communication. Athletes want you to talk to them honestly, openly and effectively. If you become too concerned with references to "wheeling" rather than "walking" or going for a "push" rather than going for a "run" then often you will be unable to communicate naturally with the athlete, and beyond anything else that is what they want. This is the author's experience of working with athletes with disabilities; each consultant will have to judge the situation they are in order to develop the most effective communication strategy.

Build Trust, Develop Rapport and Show Empathy

- As with any athlete it is important to build trust and rapport in order to have a successful working relationship (Hales & Hales, 1995). This is no different with the disabled athlete, as they will need to trust you implicitly in order to share information about the nature of their disability. Most athletes choose to discuss this with their sport psychologist when they feel it is necessary.
- It is important to show empathy for the athlete and not to be sympathetic. The athletes will not want sympathy from their sport psychologist; they will want to be treated in the same way in which an able-bodied athlete is treated, with genuineness (Raskin & Rogers, 1995). Asken (1991) reinforced this point by stating that sport psychology consultants should not get involved in disabled sport because of pity or sympathy. The author stated,

> Just as a given sport is required for successful consultation with an able bodied athlete in that sport, there must be a true appreciation of the value and beauty of disabled sport competition. Involvement motivated by pity is not only inappropriate and condescending but underscores a misunderstanding of the dignity and pride of the physically disabled athlete and physically disabled sport in general. (p. 380)

See Beyond the Wheelchair

- It is important for the sport psychologist to first and foremost recognize that they are working with a person, rather than working with a disability (Martin, 1996). This point was emphasized by the Great British fencer David Heaton who stated, "I see myself as a fencer who competes in a wheelchair and not a wheelchair fencer; this distinction is important to me." This distinction puts the emphasis onto the sport rather than the wheelchair and focuses on the ability of the performer rather than the disability. Many athletes will have different perspectives on such issues; however, the sport psychologist should remember that they are working with an athlete. Martin (1996) emphasized the need for sport psychology consultants to be aware of the "whole person" and not to simply focus on the athlete's disability.

Provide Summary Feedback in an Appropriate Format

• Ensure that any feedback information that you need to give to the athlete is in the most appropriate format (e.g. visually impaired athletes might prefer to have an audio cassette or email communication).

Self-reflect and Don't Be Afraid to Ask

• As with any consultancy experience, self-reflection is vital (Anderson, Knowles & Gilbourne, 2004). Learning from each consultation and finding innovative ways to improve the delivery of sport psychology to athletes with disabilities is key to developing the area. Honest self-reflection and appraisal is important to progress the learning experience and to improve service delivery. It is also important to have a comprehensive evaluation of the sport psychology service from the athlete's perspective (Anderson, Miles, Mahoney & Robinson, 2002). This will provide a sound basis for future work and should identify the consultant's strengths and weaknesses and the needs of the athlete.
• If you are in doubt about an issue with a disabled athlete, then don't be afraid to ask them. The best way to learn is by exploring the issues with each individual athlete and establishing how they respond to issues related to their disability. A good example of this on a practical level is. "Do they need help coming in the door as they struggle through"; the answer more often than not is: "They will tell you when they need help."

SUMMARY

This chapter has outlined some of the issues that sport psychologists face when working with athletes who have disabilities. This chapter has aimed to identify some applied issues in disabled sport that need to be considered when working with disabled athletes and also some basic principles for consultation. These issues are based on applied experiences of working with athletes who have a disability. As has been stated throughout this chapter, it is important that further research is conducted in disability sport to improve our understanding of the psychological demands of the disabled athlete. It is recognized that many of the performance enhancement strategies that are used with able-bodied competitors are transferable to disabled athletes. However, a greater understanding of the psychological demands of disabled sport is needed to fully appreciate the most effective way to work with the disabled performer.

Working with athletes who have disabilities has many challenges associated with it and sport psychologists will have to be innovative in their delivery of psychological skills in order to provide an effective service. The face of disabled sport is rapidly changing and sport science support is now commonplace for elite Paralympic athletes. Hence, sport psychologists are increasingly likely to have access to athletes who have disabilities. With this change in culture it is hoped that a greater knowledge base evolves about applied issues specifically related to disabled sport, and that consultants have a greater understanding of the techniques that are most effective. It is also hoped that, with the increasing popularity of the Paralympics, the awareness of disability issues will increase. With this increase in awareness some of the physical and attitudinal barriers that disabled people experience can be eliminated and, as with the Olympic Games, that will enable spectators to focus on the ability of the athlete.

ACKNOWLEDGEMENTS

The author would like to thank the many athletes that helped with the development of this chapter. I would also like to thank the current British Paralympic Association Consultant Sport Psychologist, Jonathan Katz for his contribution.

REFERENCES

Anderson, A.G., Knowles, Z. & Gilbourne, D. (2004). Reflective practice for sport psychologists: Concepts, models, practical implications, and thoughts on dissemination. *The Sport Psychologist, 18*, 188–203.

Anderson, A.G., Miles, A., Mahoney, C. & Robinson, P. (2002). Evaluating the effectiveness of sport psychology practice: making the case for a case study approach. *The Sport Psychologist, 16*, 432–453.

Asken, M.J. (1989). Sport psychology and the physically disabled athlete: interview with Michael D. Goodling, OTR/L. *The Sport Psychologist, 3*, 167–176.

Asken, M.J. (1991). The challenge of the physically challenged: delivering sport psychology services to physically disabled athletes. *The Sport Psychologist, 5*, 370–381.

British Association of Sport and Exercise Sciences (2000). *Code of Conduct*. Leeds: British Association of Sport and Exercise Science.

Bull, S.J., Albinson, J.G. & Shambrook, C.J. (1996). *The Mental Game Plan: Getting Psyched for Sport*. Sports Dynamics.

Butler, R.J. & Hardy, L. (1992). The performance profile: theory and application. *Sport Psychologist, 6*, 253–264.

Campbell, E. & Jones, G. (1997). Pre-competition anxiety and self-confidence in wheelchair sport participants. *Physical Activity Quarterly, 14*, 96–107.

Campbell, E. & Jones, G. (2002). Sources of stress experienced by elite male wheelchair basketball players. *Physical Activity Quarterly, 19*(1), 82–92.

Cox, R. & Davis, R. (1992). Psychological skills of elite wheelchair athletes. *Palestra, 8*(3), 16–21.

Crocker, P.R.E. (1993). Sport and exercise psychology and research with individuals with physical disabilities: using theory to advance knowledge. *Physical Activity Quarterly, 10*, 324–335.

DePauw, K. (1988). Sport for individuals with disabilities: research opportunities. *Adapted Physical Activity Quarterly, 5*, 80–89.

Eddy, K.A.T. & Mellalieu, S.D. (2003). Mental imagery in athletes with visual impairments. *Physical Activity Quarterly, 20*(4), 347–369.

Goodling, M. & Asken, M. (1987). Sport psychology and the physically disabled athlete. In J. May & M. Asken (eds), *Sport Psychology: The Psychological Health of the Athlete* (pp. 117–133). New York: PMA Publishing.

Hanrahan, S.J. (1995). Sport psychology for athletes with disabilities. In T. Morris & J. Summers (eds), *Sport Psychology: Theory Applications and Issues* (pp. 502–515). Chichester, UK: John Wiley & Sons.

Hales, D. & Hales, R. (1995). *Caring for the Mind*. New York: Bantam Books.

Henschen, K.P., Horvat, M. & French, R. (1984). A visual comparison of psychological profiles between able bodied and wheelchair athletes. *Physical Activity Quarterly, 1*(2), 118–124.

Horvat, M., French, R. & Henschen, K. (1986). A comparison of the psychological characteristics of male and female able bodied and wheelchair athletes. *Physical Activity Quarterly, 1*, 118–124.

International Paralympic Committee. (2004). http://www.paralympic.org/release/Main_Sections_Menu/Sports/Classification/, updated 12 November 2004.

Jacobson, E. (1938). *Progressive Relaxation*. Chicago: University of Chicago Press.

Jones, G., Hanton, S. & Connaughton, D. (2002). What is this thing called mental toughness? An investigation of elite sports performers. *Journal of Applied Sport Psychology*, *14*, 205–218.

Karlsson A.K. (1999). Autonomic dysreflexia. *Spinal Cord, 37*(6), 383–391.

Martin, J.J. (1996). Transitions out of competitive sport for athletes with disabilities. *Therapeutic Recreation Journal, 30*, 128–136.

Montelione, T. & Davis, R. (1986). Physically disabled athletes successfully compete. In C. Sherrill (ed.), *Sport and Disabled Athletes* (pp. 225–230). Champaign, IL: Human Kinetics.

Page, S.J., Martin, S.B. & Wayda, V.K. (2001). Attitudes toward seeking sport psychology consultation among wheelchair basketball athletes. *Adapted Physical Activity Quarterly, 18*, 183–192.

Pensgaard, A.M., Roberts, G.C. & Ursin, H. (1999). Motivational factors and coping strategies of Norwegian Paralympic and Olympic winter sport athletes. *Physical Activity Quarterly, 16*, 238–250.

Porretta, D.L. & Moore, W. (1996/97). A review of sport psychology research for individuals with disabilities: implications for future inquiry. *Clinical Kinesiology, 50*(4), 83–93.

Raskin, N. & Rogers, C. (1995). Person-centered therapy. In R. Corsini & D. Wedding (eds). *Current Psychotherapies* (pp. 128–161). Itasca, IL: F.E. Peacock Publishers.

Sachs, M.L. (1988). Sport psychology's neglected population: persons with disabilities. *AAASP Newsletter*, 8–9.

Sherrill, C. (1998). *Adapted Physical Activity, Recreation and Sport: Crossdisciplinary and Lifespan* (5th edn). Madison, WI: WCB/McGraw-Hill.

Sherrill, C. (1999). Disability sport classification theory: a new era. *Adapted Physical Activity Quarterly, 16*, 206–215.

White, S.A. & Zientek, C. (1990). Role conflict in a sport psychologist: working with athletes or special needs populations. In G. Doll-Tepper, C. Dahms, B. Doll and H. von Selzam (eds), *Physical Activity Quarterly—An Interdisciplinary Approach* (pp. 131–134). Berlin: Springer-Verlag.

PART XII

Afterword

CHAPTER 30

It's All About Sport Performance . . . and Something Else

Mark B. Andersen
Victoria University, Australia

INTRODUCTION

This book is directed at sport psychologists who will be working hands-on with athletes. The charge given to the authors was to write about their sports, explaining the characteristic features and the special sport psychology interventions that might be applicable. This approach was designed to help recently qualified sport psychologists, who may not be too familiar with some sporting disciplines, get up to speed on their knowledge in order to work more effectively with specific groups of athletes. This focus is a laudable and important one, and the authors in this book have done an admirable job of meeting the challenge set forth.

Although this publication serves as an adequate guide to the unique psychological demands of each sport, sport psychologists are advised to follow two basic steps before commencing work:

1. *Doing one's homework* For example, in all the major water-based sports (swimming, diving, waterpolo, synchronized swimming, open-water swimming), sport psychologists should visit www.fina.org. On the FINA (La Fédération Internationale de Natation; the world's governing body) website one can find a wealth of information about the rules, regulations, and competition procedures for all international water-based sports.
2. *Consulting with coaches* When starting with a new sport, a sport psychologist would also be wise to ask the coach, "I need to get up to speed on your sport, what books would you suggest I read?" Often a coach will lend a book or two. The advantage of this approach, rather than reading a sport summary, is that then one is reading what the coach, and usually the athletes, think is valuable. Through getting a hold of what the people in the sport value as informational resources, one begins to establish common ground. One also defers to the experts (the coach and athletes), and that may help further rapport.

The Sport Psychologist's Handbook: A Guide for Sport-Specific Performance Enhancement.
Edited by Joaquín Dosil. © 2006 John Wiley & Sons, Ltd.

What this Afterword explores are some major issues not discussed enough in sport psychology: What does it really mean to be effective as a sport psychologist? What is the role of the relationship between the sport psychologist and the athlete? Moreover, it approaches the related concern and discomfort at tackling complex issues such as sport psychologist personal investment, and the quality of relatively long-term, close relationships between athletes and their sport psychologists, along with other issues such as sexuality, homophobia, and other "isms" (racism, sexism, weightism, ageism). These concerns affect all segments of the population, and athletes are no exception.

THE QUESTION OF EFFECTIVENESS

Sport psychologists would like to think that their interventions to enhance performance will help athletes get better in their sports. There is no doubt that some sport psychologists work effectively with their athletes. Nevertheless, explaining exactly why the interventions sport psychologists employ are effective is not easy. Literally tonnes of research articles have examined interventions such as imagery and relaxation, and their influences on competition anxiety, motivation and, in some studies, actual performance. Although many research articles are attempts to discover if techniques are effective, when they *are* effective, and *why* they are is not explained. Many of these studies, however, are missing the point, and are not really helpful for sport psychologists out in the applied field. This judgment may seem harsh, but will be justified in due course.

In general, when speaking about service delivery, sport psychologists are usually talking about, at least, two people engaged in some sort of relationship, usually to their mutual benefit (e.g. monetary reward and job satisfaction for the provider of service, solving personal problems or gaining insight for the receiver of service). This idea may be illustrated with a non-sport psychology example.

In terms of someone's trusted auto mechanic, the direct recipient of service is the person's car, but that individual still has a personal relationship with the mechanic based on history, trust, rapport and often other shared interests, such as sport, that they chat about during service encounters. It is the quality of that relationship that keeps people going back to their mechanics for service. In sport psychology service, it is probably not the relaxation exercises, or even the changes in performance, that keep the athlete coming back to the psychologist. Most likely, it is the relationship that drives and sustains the service.

From a historical point of view on the process of psychological service, George Kelly wrote, in the middle of the twentieth century, about the "client as scientist". He was focusing on psychotherapy clients, but what he said fits well with the work of providing service to athletes and coaches. In updating Kelly, one might say that athletes are somewhat like scientists. They are on various personal quests for knowledge. They observe themselves, and others, in the arenas of sport and competition. They formulate hypotheses about what works well in training and competition (mentally and physically). They try out all sorts of behaviours to test those hypotheses (e.g. new training regimens, pre-competition routines, new diets, superstitious acts). They reformulate their hypotheses, and test them again, trying to change for the better. Unfortunately, many of the personal "experiments" athletes perform on themselves meet with repeated failure and frustration due to long-established patterns of maladaptive behaviours and rigid modes of thinking that block the ability to change. One of the many reasons athletes' attempts to change what happens to them in sport do not meet with success is that they are trying to effect a difference on their own. A few gifted people can pull themselves up by their own bootstraps and reconstruct their lives. Most people cannot; they need help. One needs a psychotherapist, or one needs a sport psychologist to assist in the change process. In Kelly's formulation of psychotherapy, the client learns, through the relationship with the practitioner, to become a better scientist and, one hopes, a happier person. The same might apply to sport psychology service.

Aaron Beck, author of the *Beck's Depression Inventory*, built on Kelly's ideas of the client as scientist and described what happens in psychotherapy as a process of "collaborative empiricism". That descriptor fits well and addresses the essence of psychotherapy and sport psychology service. As Andersen (2005a) stated:

> Here we have two people, engaged in collaboration, trying to figure out the experiential world of one of them, a world often filled with terrors, hopes, frustrations, joys, anxieties, and failures to change. It is amazing how many students come to graduate school and think that empirical evidence is the same as experimental evidence. In psychotherapy and sport psychology, the empirical data are the data of a life. And the two scientists are on a journey together to understand those data. Telling the tales of that collaborative empiricism, of that journey, is one of the best ways to understand the dynamics of sport psychology service, and ultimately effectiveness.

In a related anecdote on professional service relationships, an *exercise physiologist* at the Australian Institute of Sport in Canberra, Dr David Martin, believes that the reason some exercise physiologists seem to have more success with helping athletes is that they are able to form strong, caring bonds with them, and that the "bells and whistles" and $VO_{2\,max}$ tests are really just window dressing. At a meeting of exercise physiologists at the Institute, where they were trying to decide their purpose and mission to justify their work (e.g. get more gold medals, and all those features connected to Olympic ideals of *citius*, *altius* and *fortius*), Martin stood up and said, "I think our goal should be the happiness of the coaches and athletes. Do they like what we do? Are they happy with us? And do they want to come back for more?" That suggestion was received with blank looks. An improved time in the 200 metres backstroke is multi-determined. There is no possible way one can tease out the contribution of the exercise physiologist's or the sport psychologist's interventions. Improved times are not necessarily adequate measures of effectiveness. Athlete happiness, or improved communication with the coach, or more solid self-esteem, however, may be better barometers by which to determine whether what sport psychologists are doing is helpful.

Improved performance, however, is often the goal of athletes, coaches, exercise physiologists and sport psychologists, but is it the only collaborative empiricists' goal? Is "curing" competition anxiety in service of faster times the focus of the work with one particular athlete? It may very well be, but is that the case with all athletes? This point is where performance enhancement sport psychology service begins to look myopic and even naïve. Improved sport performance is not just a faster time or a greater distance. Performance is only one part of the performer, and success or failure on the playing field is intimately tied to feelings of self-worth (and a host of other "self" issues such as self-concept, identity, self-esteem, and self-efficacy), family dynamics, ontogenetic histories, relationships between coaches and athletes and, ultimately, happiness and misery. It is quite surprising that sport psychologists still make the distinction between *performance* and *personal* issues. This distinction has been present and argued loudly in sport psychology circles for a considerable time. It is about time it was seen for the false dichotomy it is. Performance is a deeply personal issue, and counseling athletes on performance touches areas of their lives that go to the core of their being. Improving performance may be the manifest goal of sport psychology work, but the health, welfare and happiness of athletes are the foundations of why sport psychologists do what they do. Martin's talk to the exercise physiologists at the Australian Institute of Sport echoes one of the giants in psychology, Sigmund Freud. Freud is mentioned here because his discoveries form the basis of some of the arguments below, and because happiness was also his barometer of successful treatment. As the distressed mother of a gay son once asked Freud, "Can you cure my son's homosexuality?" Freud replied something like, "No, Madam, but I can probably help him become a happier homosexual." If sport psychologists believe that improved performance is the measure of their work, then they have a lot of disappointments ahead of them. If they focus on the happiness of their athletes, then they may have considerably more "success" connected to their endeavors.

Case Study

Looking in the Wrong Place
There is the story of a man who, passing a friend's house late at night, comes upon his intoxicated friend on his hands and knees under a street lamp in front of his home, obviously looking for something. The man asks his drunken friend, "What are you doing down there?" His friend's slurred reply is, "I've lost my keys, and I can't find them." The man, suspecting that the keys could be anywhere, given the state his friend is in, asks, "Do you have any idea where you might have lost them?" The friend replies, "Oh yes, I lost them over there by the door." Completely confused, the man asks, "Then why are you looking for them here?" As if it was quite self-evident, the ethanolized friend answers, "Because over there by the door it's very dark, and here there is more light."

That story has relevance for research in sport psychology intervention efficacy and effectiveness (two quite different concepts). A great deal of research in sport psychology, especially in the quantitative realm, has been focused on answering questions as to whether interventions, such as relaxation or imagery, help performance. There is substantial evidence, in both practice (effectiveness) and research (efficacy), that many interventions do help, but the process by which they help is not really investigated and seems missing from the literature. In psychotherapy research it has been established that the one variable always associated with outcome is the relationship between the therapist and the client (Sexton & Whiston, 1994). It really does not matter if one uses psychodynamic, cognitive-behavioural, gestalt or drum-beating approaches for that matter (maybe an exaggeration there). If the relationship is solid, then people tend to get better but, like the intoxicated friend in the story, researchers are looking in the wrong places. Times, distances and other such improvements are measurable and "in the light" for everyone to see, as are visible interventions such as relaxation and goal-setting. Relationships and individual misery and happiness are darker, murkier (even scarier), so researchers do not look in those directions, but fumble around in the "light".

As a summation, one might say that the effectiveness, or what works in the real world of practice, of sport psychology interventions is dependent on the quality of the interpersonal relationships athletes and sport psychologists establish. That connection between effectiveness and relationships is why one needs to think and act and interact with athletes on a field of interpersonal respect, trust, and care in order for the "play" of the interventions to become effective.

But how much time do teachers spend training their students to be mindful of the developing relationships they are forming with athletes? Do sport psychology professors and supervisors instruct their students to develop therapeutic, caring, human approaches to their work? In some ways they do; in many ways they do not. This focus on relationships brings up the psychodynamic concepts of transference and countertransference and the legacy of Freud.

The Phenomena of Transferring and Countertransferring

The terms *transference* and *countertransference* (Lane, 1986; Meyers, 1986; Racker, 1968) stem from the work of Freud (Freud 1912, 1915). In the simplest terms, transference describes a process whereby the client begins to respond, on a variety of levels (e.g. emotionally, behaviorally), to the therapist in patterns that have roots in past relationships with significant others.

> For example, if a young man had a turbulent time dealing with an authoritarian father, and rebelled and resisted his father, he may in therapy (especially with an older man) begin to see the therapist as an authority figure and start resisting the therapist's help. The therapist may not be acting in any objective authoritarian way, but the major pattern for relationships with older males for a client like this is one of authority and rebellion. That pattern then gets projected on to the therapist, and in this case, makes for a block in therapy.
>
> (Andersen, 2004, p. 75)

Countertransference is the name for the similar process when practitioners begin to act and respond to clients in similar patterns as they had with past important people in their lives (Epstein & Feiner, 1983; Gabbard, 1995; Greenson, 1992; Stein, 1986; Strean, 1994).

> As an example, say a male sport psychologist was raised in a household surrounded by females: two sisters, a working mother, and a grandmother who took over a lot of the child rearing. He and his father would have been outnumbered. He may have fantasised often of having a little brother whom he could tease, beat up, and who would look up to him like the little brothers so many of his friends had. That fantasy brother may come back to him sometimes when working with younger male athletes where he might get powerful protective take-care-of-little-brother feelings, even though he never had a brother.
>
> (Andersen, 2004, p. 75)

Many in counseling and clinical psychology have misinterpreted these dynamic phenomena as counterproductive. Transference and countertransference are universal phenomena and probably form a core of most human interactions. Learning how to use them to positive effect is the task of sport psychologists, teachers, coaches, supervisors, athletic trainers and medical practitioners (see Henschen, 1991; Mann, 1986; Ogilvie, 1993; Petitpas, Giges & Danish, 1999; Yambor & Connelly, 1991). Sport provides numerous stories of transference and countertransference. Coaches fall in love with athletes; athletes have conflicts with coaches that mirror the dynamics in the family of origin. Athletes with abusive parents find the fantasized "good mother" or "good father" they have dreamed about. As Andersen (2004) stated:

> If one reflects on one's athletes, and how one feels about each of them, that may help to get a feel for transference and countertransference. In an ideal world, we should treat and respond to all clients in the same manner, with respect, unconditional positive regard, empathy, and genuineness. But we don't, and why don't we? The answer to that question lies at the heart of transference and countertransference. (p. 74)

Case Study

Here is an example of a sport psychologist and two of her clients that illustrates the power of transference and countertransference. Melissa in these examples is not a bad sport psychologist; she is a human one, and her different responses to her clients are deeply human responses.

Melissa is a sport psychologist in the USA. She has an older brother and a younger sister. Her mother is an accountant, and her father is an alcoholic who abandoned the family and disappeared when she was 14 years old. All during her childhood and early adolescence, Melissa never felt safe. It was a toss-up which father would be home, the mean drunk physically abusing her mother, or the regretful sober father. When her father finally left, Melissa's constant background anxiety began to abate. Melissa is heterosexual, but her older brother, who physically defended her mother against her abusive father, is gay. Her older brother remains her hero to this day. Melissa has a client, Freddy, a diver, whom she looks forward to working with every week. They have a great time during their sport psychology sessions. They laugh a lot and tell stories. Freddy is gay, and part of why Melissa and Freddy work so well together is that Freddy knows Melissa has a gay brother and is sensitive to the gay community and the difficulties gay and lesbian people face, especially in sport. So Freddy can be himself and be frank and talk about anything on his mind. For Melissa, talking with Freddy is like being with her older brother, so she has many good sibling feelings towards him. Also, Freddy flirts shamelessly with Melissa in a teasing but jovial manner. Many straight women enjoy the flirtations of gay men because they are playful, safe and fun. So, these two people get along well with each other. What is happening is a dance of positive transference and countertransference that is helping the sport psychology service process.

Melissa's other client, William, a swimmer, is uncommunicative, surly and sometimes comes to sessions with bloodshot eyes and smelling of marijuana (some sport psychologists may be surprised how many swimmers, even elite ones, smoke marijuana). He comes to Melissa primarily because the coach mandated his attendance. Melissa dislikes working with him, is also relatively uncommunicative, goes about the relaxation exercises methodically, and gets the job done as quickly as possible. So why does Melissa have empathy and unconditional positive regard for Freddy, yet for William she is almost a robot and hardly human? Many children of alcoholics develop strong aversions to anything that smacks of substance abuse, and often have little tolerance of those who abuse substances. William evokes countertransferential responses in Melissa that are tied to both her father's alcoholism, the physical abuse of her mother and, oddly enough, her being abandoned by her father. There is a jumble of emotions that William evokes in Melissa, and in order to handle them Melissa shuts down and goes cold, getting rid of William as fast as possible. Freddy is like someone Melissa loves; William is like someone who has seriously hurt her.

There are few better lessons learned in sport psychology than the ones that start with the questions: "Which athletes do I really like?", "Which athletes do I dislike?", "Why do I interact with athletes differently?", and "What am I bringing to my interactions with those athletes that influences my responses?" Sport psychologists have two powerful instruments that they bring to treatment and interactions with clients. They have their knowledge and their cognitive-behavioral interventions skills, and they have their personalities. Unfortunately, the number of hours sport psychologists spend during their training and practice examining their *second instrument* (their personalities) and the quality of their interactions with clients is unknown, but it is most assuredly low. The emphasis on self-reflective practice and examining the self in service does not have the tradition in sport psychology that it does in clinical and counseling psychology.

Case Study

Transference and countertransference bring out a variety of responses—love, hate, desire, identification, projection, regression, and really the whole gamut of human reactions. Here is a story about an applied sport psychology student the author supervised. The student gave his permission to tell this tale.

Trevor had begun to develop a close relationship with a young Australian Rules football player. Substantial good big brother–little brother transference and countertransference was happening. They had worked some on performance enhancement training together, and they really liked each other. One day they were sitting in the bleachers on the practice field having a chat, and the athlete leaned over to Trevor and said what was really troubling him: "You know, there has been a lot of death in my life recently." It happens more often than not that once the gears of transference and countertransference start rolling, sport issues and performance enhancement work take a back seat, and the concerns of central importance begin to emerge.

Trevor helped him tell his story of four deaths in the last few months of parents of a good friend, of a horrible death in a car accident, and of the suicide of a friend's brother. Needless to say, the athlete was confused, hurt, angry, sad—a jumble of mixed-up emotions. These stories brought up in Trevor his unresolved reactions to a death in his life of a fellow friend and athlete, a cyclist who was killed on a road in Vancouver, a place where Trevor still trains when he goes home to Canada. He knows the spot well and the heartache it evokes every time he cycles by. Trevor then related that story and all his confusion and sadness to the athlete. Then it began to rain, and they moved into a small shelter on the field. Trevor sat down first, and then the football player sat next to him. They both, without thinking, drew their knees up to their chests and pulled their arms around their knees, like two 10-year-old boys, looking out at a dark and rainy world in sad wonder and confusion. They both needed a hug, but guys don't do that in Aussie Rules, so they hugged themselves, and by proxy hugged each other. They had both regressed to that earlier childhood time, and they stayed there in shared silence for quite a while.

Their sibling transference and countertransference, and their shared hurt, sadness and confusion helped them truly "be" with each other, separate on the bench by a centimetre, but together in being human. There is not a better picture of a therapeutic encounter than that one. To *be* is to *be related*. The athlete, a bit later, said to Trevor, "Girls have it easy, they can just have a hug and a good cry." It is heart-breaking, but in such a sweet way. This beautiful transference and countertransference is only one example. These processes can move beyond shared confusion and pain into the realm of the erotic.

Erotic Transference and Countertransference

Case Study

Here is a story one can use with sport psychology students to illustrate erotic transference and countertransference. Sport psychologists work with a great-looking population, usually dedicated, fit people, often very physically attractive. To deny the erotic is to deny being human. If any readers have ever worked on pool deck with swimmers and divers, the erotic atmosphere is obvious. What does one do with those erotic responses? Well, here is a tale of Jake and Johanna that is summarized from a previous in-depth case study (Andersen, 2005b).

Jake was being supervised in an applied sport psychology practicum. He was a former wrestler, short, with an asymmetrical, sort of goofy-cute face, with evidence of his wrestling career left on his ears. He was intelligent, enthusiastic, hard-working, and seriously wanted to become a good sport psychologist. His supervisor knew Jake had not had many positive experiences in the romantic area with women, and he had hopes that Jake would find a nice young woman and be able to offer her all the caring and love the supervisor could see inside him.

Jake was helping with a women's volleyball team. The supervisor had worked with the team doing group psychoeducational sessions, and he knew the members well. Jake had been assisting in those sessions and was attending all the practices to get to know the squad. Johanna was a player who showed great potential in practice, but in competition she had problems with anxiety that interfered with her performance. She was tall, beautiful in body, and with a lovely spirit. One day the supervisor was at practice, and she asked him if she could get some one-on-one sessions, and he suggested working with Jake. She agreed and they arranged for them to meet. In retrospect, unconscious processes were in operation. The supervisor had a substantial parental countertransference to Jake, wanting the goofy guy to beat out all the other handsome male jocks and run away with the homecoming queen. There was also a regressive identification with Jake in that the supervisor had been a goofy semi-jock swimmer himself, 30-plus years previously, and had resented the big handsome swimmers who got all the attention. For Jake, his supervisor had turned into a matchmaker.

Jake and Johanna did some great work together, and her competition performance was improving. About four weeks after they started working together the supervisor was at practice and Johanna came up to him and said, "Thanks so much for giving me Jake, he's wonderful." That phrase, "giving me Jake", is a worrisome one. Red flags should have been flying, but denial is a wonderful thing. The supervisor was basking in his narcissistic interpretation that he was such a good supervisor, producing effective young sport psychologists. He should have seen the erotic rearing its affectionate head, but self-delusion was one of his strong suits. As stated, Johanna was gorgeous in body and soul and had probably been approached by men constantly. Then there was Jake, a very proper young man, paying much attention to her, wanting the best for her, helping her in her sport with good results, and not even a trace of masculine swagger or hints of wanting seduce her. What's not to love? A good question to ask students is, "If you wanted to do a really intelligent job of seducing someone, how would you behave?" Many of the answers they come up with (e.g. pay a lot of attention, communicate your interest and care, let the person know their happiness is your only agenda, have unconditional positive regard) sound suspiciously like what good psychologists do. Psychological service is designed, albeit not intentionally, for seduction.

A few weeks later, Johanna had a tremendous competition where her skills in play matched her practice performances. The next day in supervision Jake said, "Did you see Johanna last night? She was awesome!" The supervisor directed the session to the issue of being in "awe" of clients and all that implies and how it might affect the quality of service delivery. He ignored the erotic flavour of Jake's awe. Jake was smitten, and the supervisor stayed in denial.

About two days later, the supervisor received a phone call from Jake. He sounded distressed and asked if they could have an extra supervision session immediately. The supervisor was free, so he told Jake to come over at once. Jake arrived, slumped in the comfortable supervisee chair, sighed hugely and said, "She kissed me." Then, for the supervisor, all the pieces of the puzzle fell together. Jake had been helping put away equipment after practice, and everyone had left the gym except Johanna. She had walked up to him and said, "Thanks so much for everything. You're the best" and planted a kiss right on his lips, and then turned back to the locker room saying, "I'll see you tomorrow." The event was only about 20 minutes old, and Jake was still shaking.

Jake and his supervisor explored his responses to the kiss, and he was quite frank and honest when the supervisor asked about his first response. He said, "I just wanted to rip our clothes off and do it right there on the gym floor." He was ashamed of that response. The supervisor tried to help him move from shame to fascination. "Of course you wanted to make love right there. You are working with a wonderful young woman who thinks the world of you, and if I hadn't been so blind, I should have seen this all coming, so your supervisor screwed up on this one." The supervisor explained to Jake his countertranferential responses to him and his unconscious regressed fantasies about Jake getting the girl and how that blinded him to what was going on and all the signs he had missed. The supervisor modelling his own fallibility with humour and self-acceptance helped Jake take a step back and see how complex, scary and fascinating this world of helping athletes is.

Now, what to do about Johanna? No one gets out of this sort of situation without being hurt. How was Jake going to talk to Johanna the next time he saw her, minimize the hurt and keep the working alliance viable? Jake and the supervisor spent a long time discussing how to go about his next encounter with Johanna. They role-played several scenarios of the possible ways the meeting could go. The story of how all that went is a long one, with a happy ending, and the details can be found in Andersen (2005b).

The erotic is everywhere. It is just that many sport psychologists, when talking with athlete-clients, have these lacunae in their vision. "How awful, how awkward, if the athlete becomes attracted to the sport psychologist, or, God forbid, how unethical if the professional become attracted to them." One could counter those negative responses with "How perfect! How much does that tell us about the person? How much about ourselves? And how much about the dynamics of the therapeutic sport psychology encounter?" The erotic opens up huge windows into the lives of sport psychologists and others, but when eyes are closed tightly, it is difficult to see anything.

Connected to the story of Jake and Johanna is an issue that does not get addressed much in sport psychology, and that is the question of self-disclosure. In some schools of psychotherapy, students are warned self-disclosure is a slippery slope that has the potential to feed therapist narcissistic needs and evoke unhealthy fantasies in the client and, thus, is to be avoided. The classic rigid response to a client who asks about the therapist's personal life is to turn the focus back on the client's need to know things about the therapist and what that means. When the client asks, "What did you get up to over the weekend?" the therapist may respond with, "Well, let's examine why you want to know those things." The assumption is that a neurotic transference is behind the question. If a sport psychologist said that to his athletes, they might respond, "Oh, piss off" and go find a more human therapist. Admittedly, self-disclosure can have negative countertransferential sources and serve the pathological narcissistic needs of the therapist or sport psychologist, but many requests for information are attempts to balance relationships, get closer to the sport psychologist, and help enhance the feeling that *we are in this thing together* (and promote the building of positive transference and countertransference). In working with students who are in training to become sport psychologists one should encourage them to keep building the relationship with their clients by answering their personal questions, and also self-disclose to their clients how their stories are affecting them. That is what humans do with each other; they transfer and countertransfer all the time. Supervisors should do the same with their students, modeling self-disclosure by letting them know what is going on with them in their interactions. It is all about open, honest, and caring relationships.

A FINAL METAPHOR

A useful metaphor in teaching future sport psychologists is that of a "gift". An athlete comes to a sport psychologist with a gift wrapped in a box. In that box there are hopes, fears, dreams, desires, frustrations, secrets, joys and unhappiness. The athlete can do a lot of things with that gift. He can keep it hidden in his pocket. She can place it on her knee and talk about it, but never put it out on the table. It is an odd package, this gift; it does not adhere to the laws of physics. If the gift is opened, it can suddenly become quite large and scary, almost filling the room with threat and pain (e.g. a history of sexual abuse). Or, it can, once it is opened, become quite small and manageable (e.g. a misinterpretation of coach communication that can be easily resolved). Even so, the gift, and the giving of the gift to another usually involves some level of risk, and often the gift is set on the table but never opened fully and only talked about in a superficial (and safe) manner. Sometime the gift has a card on it that says "performance", but the contents say much more. Too often sport psychologists only read the card or look at the colourful wrapping. For example, the athlete may say, "I get so nervous before each match that I throw up every time." Metaphorically, the athlete has made a small tear in the gift's wrapping paper. The sport psychologist then brings forth a bit of sticky tape (e.g. relaxation exercises) and proceeds to repair the rip in the wrapping without actually taking the paper off and looking into the box to find what is behind the anxiety (e.g. the horrible equation that *good performance = good person*, fears of losing parental love). When the rip in the wrapping is made by the athlete, the sport psychologist could also say, "OK, let's slowly start to take the paper off this gift and see what there is here. I'll be with you all the way."

The sport psychologist also has a gift (cf. Yalom, 2003). And that gift contains her expert knowledge, her personality, her genuineness, care, empathy, appreciation for beauty, compassion for human frailty, the ability to handle the athlete's gift with unconditional positive regard and, yes, even love. The handling of both gifts between these two people can be a model for the finest there is in human relationships. The core of the working alliance, the collaborative empiricism between athlete and sport psychologist, is how both these gifts are presented, examined and accepted. This final point seems to be a good stopping place for this Afterword.

The editor and the contributors to this book deserve a great deal of thanks. They are excellent practitioners who have been out there in the real world doing good work. They have brought their experiences back from the locker rooms, pool decks and playing fields and have reported on what works and doesn't work in applied service. It takes some measure of courage to put oneself and one's work out in the public domain for scrutiny. Their efforts are much appreciated, and I believe this book will be used for years to come by students and practitioners alike.

REFERENCES

Andersen, M.B. (2004). Transference and countertransference. In G.S. Kolt & M.B. Andersen (eds), *Psychology in the Physical and Manual Therapies* (pp. 71–80). Edinburgh, Scotland: Churchill Livingstone.

Andersen, M.B. (2005a). Coming full circle: from practice to research. In M. B. Andersen (ed.), *Sport Psychology in Practice* (pp. 287–298). Champaign, IL: Human Kinetics.

Andersen, M.B. (2005b). Touching taboos: sex and the sport psychologist. In M.B. Andersen (ed.), *Sport Psychology in Practice* (pp. 171–191). Champaign, IL: Human Kinetics.

Epstein L. & Feiner A.H. (1983). *Countertransference: The Therapist's Contribution to the Therapeutic Situation.* Northvale, NJ: Jason Aronson.

Freud, S. (1912). The dynamics of transference. In: J. Strachey (ed. and trans.), *The Standard Edition of the Complete Psychological Works of Sigmund Freud, Vol 12* (pp. 97–108). London: Hogarth Press.

Freud, S. (1915). Observations on transference-love: further recommendations on the technique of psycho-analysis III. In J. Strachey (ed. & trans.), *The Standard Edition of the Complete Psychological Works of Sigmund Freud, Vol 12* (pp. 157–173). London: Hogarth Press.

Gabbard, G.O. (1995). Countertransference: The emerging common ground. *International Journal of Psychoanalysis, 76*, 475–485.

Greenson, R.R. (1992). Countertransference In A. Sugarman, R.A. Nemiroff & R.R. Greenson (eds), *The Technique and Practice of Psychoanalysis, Volume II: A Memorial to Ralph R. Greenson.* Madison, CT: International Universities Press.

Henschen, K. (1991). Critical issues involving male consultants and female athletes. *The Sport Psychologist, 5*, 313–321.

Lane, F.M. (1986). Transference and countertransference: definition of terms. In H.C. Meyers (ed.), *Between Analyst and Patient: New Dimensions in Countertransference and Transference* (pp. 237–256). Hillsdale, NJ: Analytic Press.

Mann, J. (1986). Transference and countertransference in brief psychotherapy In H.C. Meyers (ed.), *Between Analyst and Patient: New Dimensions in Countertransference and Transference* (pp. 119–129). Hillsdale, NJ: Analytic Press.

Meyers, H.C. (ed.). (1986). *Between Analyst and Patient: New Dimensions in Countertransference and Transference.* Hillsdale, NJ: Analytic Press.

Murphy, S.M. (2000). Afterword. In M.B. Andersen (ed.), *Doing Sport Psychology* (pp. 275–279). Champaign, IL: Human Kinetics.

Ogilvie, B.C. (1993). Transference phenomena in coaching and teaching. In S. Serpa, J. Alves, V. Ferreira & A. Paulo-Brito (eds), *Proceedings of the VIII World Congress of the International Society of Sport Psychology* (pp. 262–266). Lisbon, Portugal: International Society of Sport Psychology.

Petitpas, A.J., Giges, B. & Danish, S.J. (1999). The sport psychologist-athlete relationship: implications for training. *The Sport Psychologist, 13*, 344–357.

Racker, H. (1968). *Transference and Countertransference*. London: Karnac.

Sexton, T.S. & Whiston, S.C. (1994). The status of the counseling relationship: an empirical review, theoretical implications, and research directions. *Counseling Psychologist, 22*, 6–78.

Stein, M.H. (1986). Acting out—transference and countertransference: technical considerations. In H.C. Meyers (ed.), *Between Analyst and Patient: New Dimensions in Countertransference and Transference* (pp. 63–75). Hillsdale, NJ: Analytic Press.

Strean, H. (1994). *Countertransference*. New York: Hawthorn Press.

Yalom, I.D. (2003). *The Gift of Therapy: Reflections on Being a Therapist*. London: Piatkus.

Yambor, J. & Connelly, D. (1991). Issues confronting female sport psychology consultants working with male student-athletes. *The Sport Psychologist, 5*, 304–312.

Index